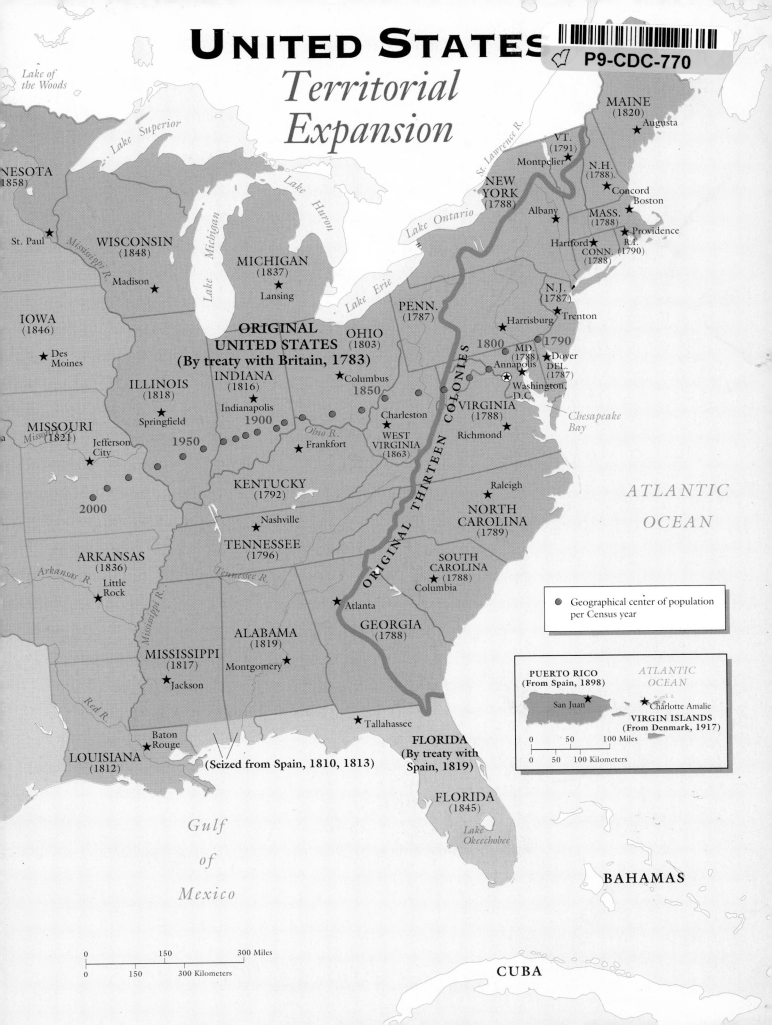

UNITED STATES
Territorial Expansion

Lake of the Woods

Lake Superior

MINNESOTA (1858)

St. Paul

WISCONSIN (1848)

Madison

Lake Michigan

MICHIGAN (1837)
Lansing

Lake Huron

Lake Erie

Lake Ontario

St. Lawrence R.

MAINE (1820)
Augusta

VT. (1791)
Montpelier

N.H. (1788)
Concord
Boston

NEW YORK (1788)
Albany

MASS. (1788)
Hartford
Providence
R.I. (1790)
CONN. (1788)

IOWA (1846)

Des Moines

ILLINOIS (1818)
Springfield

ORIGINAL UNITED STATES
(By treaty with Britain, 1783)

OHIO (1803)

Columbus
1850

INDIANA (1816)
Indianapolis
1900

PENN. (1787)

Harrisburg
Trenton

N.J. (1787)

1800
1790

MD. (1788)
Annapolis

Dover
DEL. (1787)

Washington, D.C.

MISSOURI (1821)

Jefferson City
1950

Missouri

Frankfort

Ohio R.

Charleston

WEST VIRGINIA (1863)

VIRGINIA (1788)
Richmond

Chesapeake Bay

ORIGINAL THIRTEEN COLONIES

KENTUCKY (1792)

2000

Nashville

TENNESSEE (1796)

Raleigh

NORTH CAROLINA (1789)

ATLANTIC OCEAN

ARKANSAS (1836)

Arkansas R.

Little Rock

Tennessee R.

SOUTH CAROLINA (1788)
Columbia

Mississippi R.

ALABAMA (1819)
Montgomery

MISSISSIPPI (1817)
Jackson

Atlanta

GEORGIA (1788)

● Geographical center of population per Census year

Red R.

Baton Rouge

LOUISIANA (1812)

(Seized from Spain, 1810, 1813)

Tallahassee

FLORIDA (By treaty with Spain, 1819)

PUERTO RICO (From Spain, 1898)
San Juan

ATLANTIC OCEAN

Charlotte Amalie
VIRGIN ISLANDS (From Denmark, 1917)

0   50   100 Miles

0   50   100 Kilometers

FLORIDA (1845)

Lake Okeechobee

Gulf of Mexico

BAHAMAS

0   150   300 Miles

0   150   300 Kilometers

CUBA

www.wadsworth.com

www.wadsworth.com is the World Wide Web site for Thomson Wadsworth and is your direct source to dozens of online resources.

At *www.wadsworth.com* you can find out about supplements, demonstration software, and student resources. You can also send email to many of our authors and preview new publications and exciting new technologies.

www.wadsworth.com
Changing the way the world learns®

VOLUME II: SINCE 1863

AMERICAN PASSAGES
A History of the United States

Edward L. Ayers
University of Virginia

Lewis L. Gould
University of Texas at Austin, Emeritus

David M. Oshinsky
University of Texas at Austin

Jean R. Soderlund
Lehigh University

Third Edition

THOMSON
✦
WADSWORTH

Australia • Brazil • Canada • Mexico • Singapore
Spain • United Kingdom • United States

THOMSON

WADSWORTH

American Passages: A History of the United States
VOLUME II: SINCE 1863
Third Edition
Edward L. Ayers, *University of Virginia*
Lewis L. Gould, *University of Texas at Austin, Emeritus*
David M. Oshinsky, *University of Texas at Austin*
Jean R. Soderlund, *Lehigh University*

Publisher: *Clark Baxter*
Acquisitions Editor: *Ashley Dodge*
Senior Development Editor: *Margaret McAndrew Beasley*
Assistant Editor: *Jessica Kim*
Editorial Assistant: *Kristen Judy*
Technology Project Manager: *David Lionetti*
Marketing Manager: *Lori Grebe Cook*
Marketing Assistant: *Teresa Jessen*
Project Manager, Editorial Production: *Katy German*
Creative Director: *Rob Hugel*
Art Director: *Maria Epes*

Print Buyer: *Barbara Britton*
Permissions Editor: *Joohee Lee*
Production Service: *Graphic World Publishing Services*
Text and Cover Designer: *Kathleen Cunningham Design*
Photo Researcher: *ImageQuest*
Copy Editor: *Graphic World Publishing Services*
Cover Image: *A Horse Comes to the Assistance of a Car.* © *Reg Speller/Fox Photos/Getty Images*
Compositor: *International Typesetting and Composition*
Printer: *Quebecor World/Versailles*

Thomson Higher Education
10 Davis Drive
Belmont, CA 94002-3098
USA

For more information about our products, contact us at:
Thomson Learning Academic Resource Center
1-800-423-0563

For permission to use material from this text or product, submit a request online at
http://www.thomsonrights.com.
Any additional questions about permissions can be submitted by e-mail to
thomsonrights@thomson.com.

Printed in the United States of America
1 2 3 4 5 6 7 09 08 07 06

Library of Congress Control Number: 2005938040

ISBN 0-495-05063-6

About the Authors

EDWARD L. AYERS is the Hugh P. Kelly Professor of History and Dean of the College and Graduate School of Arts and Sciences at the University of Virginia. He was educated at the University of Tennessee and Yale University, where he received his Ph.D. in American Studies. Ayers was named National Professor of the Year by the Carnegie Foundation and the Council for the Support of Education in 2003. His book, *In the Presence of Mine Enemies: War in the Heart of America, 1859–1863* (2003), won the Bancroft Prize for distinguished work on the history of the United States. *The Promise of the New South: Life After Reconstruction* (1992) won prizes for the best book on the history of American race relations and on the history of the American South. It was a finalist for both the National Book Award and the Pulitzer Prize. He is the co-editor of *The Oxford Book of the American South* (1997) and *All Over the Map: Rethinking American Regions* (1996). The World Wide Web version of "The Valley of the Shadow: Two Communities in the American Civil War," was recognized by the American Historical Association as the best aid to the teaching of history. His latest book is *What Caused the Civil War? Reflections on the South and Southern History* (2005).

LEWIS L. GOULD is Eugene C. Barker Centennial Professor Emeritus in American History at the University of Texas at Austin. After receiving his Ph.D. from Yale University, he taught at Texas for 31 years before his retirement in 1998. He was honored for outstanding undergraduate and graduate teaching during his career. His most recent books include *The Modern American Presidency* (2003), *Grand Old Party: A History of the Republicans* (2003), and *The Most Exclusive Club: A History of the Modern United States Senate* (2005). He has written op-ed essays for the *Washington Post,* the *Austin American-Statesman,* and the *Dallas Morning News,* and has been a frequent commentator on radio and television about modern politics, First Ladies, and Congress.

DAVID M. OSHINSKY received his undergraduate degree from Cornell University and his doctorate from Brandeis. He is currently Littlefield Professor of History

The *American Passages* Author Team (left to right) Ed Ayers, David Oshinsky, Jean Soderlund, Lewis Gould

at the University of Texas at Austin. Prior to that he taught for 26 years at Rutgers University, where he held the Board of Governors Chair as well as chairman of the History Department. Oshinsky is the author of five books, including *A Conspiracy So Immense: The World of Joe McCarthy* (1983), which was voted one of the year's "best books" by the *New York Sunday Times Book Review,* and won the Hardeman Prize for the best work about the U.S. Congress. His book, *Worse than Slavery: Parchman Farm and the Ordeal of Jim Crow Justice* (1996), won both the Robert Kennedy Book Award for the year's most distinguished contribution to the field of human rights and the American Bar Association's Scribes Award for distinguished legal writing. Oshinsky's latest book is *Polio: An American Story* (2005).

Oshinsky is a regular contributor to scholarly journals, the *Washington Post Book World, New York Sunday Times Book Review, New York Times* op-ed page, and *New York Times Sunday Magazine.* He was awarded a senior fellowship by the National Endowment for the Humanities and spent 1999–2000 as a Phi Beta Kappa Visiting Scholar.

JEAN R. SODERLUND is Professor of History and Deputy Provost for Faculty Affairs at Lehigh University. She received her Ph.D. from Temple University and was a post-doctoral fellow at the McNeil Center for Early American Studies at the University of Pennsylvania. Her book *Quakers and Slavery: A Divided Spirit* won the Alfred E. Driscoll Publication Prize of the New Jersey Historical Commission. Soderlund was an editor of three volumes of the Papers of William Penn (1981–1983) and co-authored *Freedom by Degrees: Emancipation in Pennsylvania and Its Aftermath* (1991).

She has written articles and chapters in books on the history of women, African Americans, Native Americans, Quakers, and the development of abolition in the British North American colonies and early United States. She is currently working on a study of the Lenape people within colonial New Jersey society. She is a council member of the McNeil Center for Early American Studies, and she served as a committee chair for the American Historical Association and the Organization of American Historians.

VOLUME II: SINCE 1863

AMERICAN PASSAGES
A History of the United States

Edward L. Ayers
University of Virginia

Lewis L. Gould
University of Texas at Austin, Emeritus

David M. Oshinsky
University of Texas at Austin

Jean R. Soderlund
Lehigh University

Third Edition

THOMSON

WADSWORTH

Australia • Brazil • Canada • Mexico • Singapore
Spain • United Kingdom • United States

THOMSON
★
™
WADSWORTH

American Passages: A History of the United States
VOLUME II: SINCE 1863
Third Edition
Edward L. Ayers, *University of Virginia*
Lewis L. Gould, *University of Texas at Austin, Emeritus*
David M. Oshinsky, *University of Texas at Austin*
Jean R. Soderlund, *Lehigh University*

Publisher: *Clark Baxter*
Acquisitions Editor: *Ashley Dodge*
Senior Development Editor: *Margaret McAndrew Beasley*
Assistant Editor: *Jessica Kim*
Editorial Assistant: *Kristen Judy*
Technology Project Manager: *David Lionetti*
Marketing Manager: *Lori Grebe Cook*
Marketing Assistant: *Teresa Jessen*
Project Manager, Editorial Production: *Katy German*
Creative Director: *Rob Hugel*
Art Director: *Maria Epes*

Print Buyer: *Barbara Britton*
Permissions Editor: *Joohee Lee*
Production Service: *Graphic World Publishing Services*
Text and Cover Designer: *Kathleen Cunningham Design*
Photo Researcher: *ImageQuest*
Copy Editor: *Graphic World Publishing Services*
Cover Image: *A Horse Comes to the Assistance of a Car.* © *Reg Speller/Fox Photos/Getty Images*
Compositor: *International Typesetting and Composition*
Printer: *Quebecor World/Versailles*

Printed in the United States of America
1 2 3 4 5 6 7 09 08 07 06

Library of Congress Control Number: 2005938040

ISBN 0-495-05063-6

Thomson Higher Education
10 Davis Drive
Belmont, CA 94002-3098
USA

For more information about our products, contact us at:
Thomson Learning Academic Resource Center
1-800-423-0563

For permission to use material from this text or product, submit a request online at
http://www.thomsonrights.com.
Any additional questions about permissions can be submitted by e-mail to
thomsonrights@thomson.com.

Brief Contents

Detailed Contents

Passages 1960 to 2005   836

Doing History Features

List of Maps

For animated versions of selected *American Passages* maps, please visit the companion website at http://history.wadsworth.com/passages3e.

Preface

American Passages: Context and Narrative Create a More *Historical* Approach...

There are plenty of U.S. history textbooks. Why did we feel a need to write another one? The textbooks on the market when we first considered writing a book of our own were written by leading historians. They were accurate and they were fair. What made us think we could improve on books that had long been in use, often through many editions?

We thought we could write a new kind of text, one that applied the lessons we have learned in our own classrooms. All four of us had seen that students could be engaged in history if that history was conveyed in ways that tap its inherent interest. We had seen the attraction of surprise, of unexpected outcomes. We had seen students intrigued by discovering hidden connections. We had seen the power of simple narrative, of one thing triggering another, showing cause and effect.

In short, we thought we could write a more *historical* history text. Textbooks often bear little resemblance to our favorite works of history. Texts tend to replace the concrete with the general, the individual with the aggregate, the story with the summary. Most dulling, we thought, was the tendency for texts to rip things out of context, to present history as processes and trends unfolding in a timeless abstraction. We had watched students bored by chapters on "industrialization" and "urbanization." We had seen regions, especially the South and the West, often torn from the flow of American history and deposited in separate chapters. We had seen ethnic and racial groups isolated and frozen in ahistorical "communities." We had seen the end of the story given away too easily, drama squandered.

"Time is what makes history History...."

We believed that we could write a book that captured what we love most about history and, just as important, what explains the most about history. We decided to write the first U.S. history text in which time stood front and center. Time is what makes history History rather than sociology, anthropology, or economics. And time is what most textbooks sacrificed in the name of convenience and false clarity.

While many history texts claim to be "chronological," *American Passages* is unique in its insistence, in every part of every chapter, that time, with the characteristics of sequence, simultaneity, and contingency, is the *defining nature* of history. Sequence shows how events grow from other events, personalities, and broad changes. Simultaneity shows how apparently disconnected events were situated in larger shared contexts. Contingency shows how history suddenly pivots, how it often changes course in a moment.

No other text has this focus on time. The differences are easily apparent in our table of contents, in the Passages sections, in the Flashpoints, in the timelines, and in the Enduring Issues sections—and in the narrative analytical history that is the core of this book.

Now, more than 10 years after we began work on *American Passages,* we feel more strongly than ever that students and teachers should have such a book. We insist, with some passion, that our textbooks should embody and express the essential attributes that can make, in the right hands, our discipline exciting.

Framework and Features
of *American Passages*

American Passages is written to convey the excitement and uncertainty of this nation's past—to see it whole. Eight **"Passages"** sections, appearing regularly throughout the text, provide broad overviews that connect ideas and themes across chapters. In addition to a textual outline, the "Passages" sections weave in photographs, posters, graphs, and maps illustrative of the period. **"America and the World" maps** help set the American story in global context. The maps identify specific locations in the world and briefly explain why those places were particularly important to the United States in the years covered in each Passage section. Two-page **Passages Chronologies** help students place smaller stories into context and to understand interrelationships of people, ideas, movements, and events.

American Passages, Third Edition, incorporates two new features to help students see how individual events and people fit into the broad picture of our past. Remember the feelings you had when you heard about the terrorist attacks of September 11, or the fall of the Berlin Wall, or the assassination of President John F. Kennedy? Each of these events caused the course of history to shift suddenly—and we felt the impact on a personal, national, and global level. Pivotal events or **Flashpoints** in our nation's history—such as Haymarket Affair, the Boston Tea Party, or the 1936 Berlin Olympics—emphasize contingency. These brief essays, appearing one per chapter, show students how key events and personal decisions have turned the story and influenced historical outcomes over time.

The second new feature, **Enduring Issues,** traces and links broad themes and issues that are touched on in multiple chapters. Essay topics include the evolution of women's roles in war, the relationship of religious reform in the democratic development of the United States, how the concept of Manifest Destiny shaped our nation's boundaries, perceptions about the place of Native Americans as allies or outsiders, and views on medical breakthroughs and military drafts. Looking both back and forward in time, these essays synthesize the various perspectives or evolution of the topic across time to highlight recurring patterns in various contexts. Enduring Issues appear approximately every other chapter. Both Flashpoints and Enduring Issues include assignable "Questions for Reflection" to encourage critical thinking.

American Passages has always incorporated primary source materials, allowing students an opportunity to see the evidence on which historians base their interpretations. In the Third Edition, the sources are presented in **Doing History** modules, which include a collection of two to four brief excerpts from primary sources on related topics, to show varying perspectives. Exposure to multiple sources and different types of historical evidence provides students with manageable opportunities to "do history." Brief commentary by the authors guides students, and assignable "Questions for Reflection" encourage critical thinking or provide framework for class discussion. In addition, **Doing History Online** boxes highlight assignable exercises from the *American Passages* **HistoryNow** website, offering students another easy way to explore documents, maps, and images specifically related to material in the text.

At the beginning of each chapter, **outlines** provide an overview of the stories they are about to read. Chapter chronologies have been adapted to graphic **timelines** to portray the duration and overlap of crucial historical processes and occurrences.

"Identification" terms appear in boldface in the chapter, are listed at the end of the chapter for easy review, and are explained in a **Glossary** to ensure that students know the significance of important people, events, organizations, and movements. At the end of each chapter, new review questions entitled **Making Connections Across Chapters** guide students in their study, helping them to locate crucial issues in the stories they have just read and to anticipate the future implications of the events and changes they have just encountered.

Because photos, cartoons, maps, and other visual materials are so important in our understanding of the past, we have paused a little longer over a few images in each chapter to call students' attention to the detail and meaning those images convey. These **Picturing the Past** features consist of extended captions that are labeled corresponding to the three major organizing principles of the Passages chronologies—Politics and Diplomacy, Social and Cultural Events, and Economics and Technology—and are color-coordinated to those categories as well. This visual and thematic association will help students understand how people and events connect across time. And the exercise of looking at images through a historian's eye will also help them develop skills to evaluate images on their own.

Content Revisions

The authors have carefully reviewed each chapter and incorporated minor revisions, clarifications, and updates throughout. Following are selected notes about specific content revisions, many resulting from reviewer suggestions:

Chapters 9–15: new emphasis on the role of the post office and communication in general, the importance of international abolitionism to the United States, the international significance of the U.S. federal plan of government, the story of Mexico in its early dealings with Texas, and the evolution of the two-party system in the face of slavery.

Chapter 16: enhanced emphasis on the role of African Americans in the narrative of Reconstruction.

Chapter 17: a more nuanced discussion of the origins of industrialism that students will find easier to understand.

Chapter 18: more attention to the roots of urbanism and a more compact narrative about Populism.

Chapter 19: now incorporates the latest information about the debate over imperialism.

Chapter 20: greater emphasis on social history and a less political focus on Progressivism.

Chapter 21: a closer look at the cultural impact of the Taft and Wilson years.

Chapter 22: integrates more successfully the social and political effects of World War I.

Chapter 23: provides a more focused examination of the 1920s, especially for such episodes as the Sacco-Vanzetti case.

Chapter 24: places the Great Depression and its causes in better perspective.

Chapter 31: more attention to the origins of the problem of international terrorism.

Chapter 32: now provides a better overview of the continuities and differences between Bill Clinton and George W. Bush.

ACKNOWLEDGMENTS

I would like to thank my students and colleagues at the University of Virginia who have helped me struggle with the tough questions of American history. I am grateful, too, to Katherine Pierce and Margaret Beasley for their imagination, hard work, and good advice in the creation of this book. Finally, I am very appreciative of my co-authors, who have been engaged scholars, thoughtful critics, devoted teachers, and good friends throughout the years it took us to write American Passages.

Edward L. Ayers

I would like to acknowledge the help of the following former students who contributed in constructive ways to the completion of the textbook: Martin Ansell, Christie Bourgeois, Thomas Clarkin, Stacy Cordery, Debbie Cottrell, Patrick Cox, Scott Harris, Byron Hulsey, Jonathan Lee, John Leffler, Mark Young, and Nancy Beck Young. Karen Gould gave indispensable support and encouragement throughout the process of writing the text. Margaret Beasley supplied patient, informed, and thorough editorial guidance for the third edition, and the authors are all in her debt for that significant contribution. I am grateful as well to the readers of my chapters who made so many useful and timely criticisms.

Lewis L. Gould

I would like to thank my colleagues and students at Rutgers for allowing me to test out an endless stream of ideas and issues relating to modern American history, and also for their thoughts on how a good college textbook should "read" and what it should contain. As always, the support and love of my family—Matt, Efrem, Ari, and Jane—was unshakable. Above all, I must commend my co-authors and my editors for their remarkable patience and professionalism during this long collaborative process.

David M. Oshinsky

I am grateful to my husband, Rudolf Soderlund, and my family for their support throughout this project. Many scholars in the colonial and early national periods shared their ideas orally and through publications. For this edition, I would particularly like to thank Holly Kent for her capable assistance in revising the text and Margaret Beasley for her unfailing enthusiasm and expertise. As always, I am indebted to my co-authors for their collegiality and commitment to making this a great book.

Jean R. Soderlund

Reviewers

The authors wish to thank the following professors who provided useful feedback and suggestions for the third edition:

Ginette Aley, *Drake University*

Rebecca Bailey, *State University of West Georgia*

Abel Bartley, *Clemson University*

Troy Bickham, *Texas A&M University*

Jerome D. Bowers II, *Northern Illinois University*

Thomas A. Britten, *University of Texas at Brownsville*

Roger Bromert, *Southwestern Oklahoma State University*

Stacy A. Cordery, *Monmouth College*

Yvonne Cornelius-Thompson, *Nashville State Community College*

Lisa Lindquist Dorr, *University of Alabama*

Laura A. Dunn, *Brevard Community College*

Michael H. Ebner, *Lake Forest College*

Keith Edgerton, *Montana State University, Billings*

Michael Garcia, *Arapahoe Community College*

Paul J. L. Hughes, *Sussex County Community College*

Charles F. Irons, *Elon University*

Stephen Patrick Kirkpatrick, *Blinn College*

David Marcus Lauderback, *Austin Community College*

Alan Lehmann, *Blinn College*

Michael Light, *Grand Rapids Community College*

Mary K. McGuire, *Southern Illinois University, Carbondale*

Gregg L. Michel, *University of Texas at San Antonio*

Mark A. Panuthos, *Saint Petersburg College*

Melvin H. Pritchard, *West Valley College*

Stephen L. Recken, *University of Arkansas at Little Rock*

Lewie Reece, *Anderson College*

Amy K. Rieger, *Brevard Community College*

Thomas J. Rowland, *University of Wisconsin, Oshkosh*

Robert D. Sawrey, *Marshall University*

E. Timothy Smith, *Barry University*

Don A. Whatley, *Blinn College*

Ralph Young, *Temple University*

And these professors who served as reviewers in earlier stages of the writing and revising of *American Passages:*

Joseph Adams, *St. Louis Community College at Meramec*

Dawn Alexander, *Abilene Christian University*

Charles Allbee, *Burlington Community College*

Julius Amin, *University of Dayton*

Melodie Andrews, *Mankato State University*

Richard Baquera, *El Paso Community College-Valle Verde*

Robert Becker, *Louisiana State University*

Peter Bergstrom, *Illinois State University*

Blanche Brick, *Blinn College*

John Brooke, *Tufts University*

Neil Brooks, *Essex Community College*

Linda D. Brown, *Odessa College*

Colin Calloway, *Dartmouth University*

Milton Cantor, *University of Massachusetts*

Kay Carr, *Southern Illinois University*

Paul Chardoul, *Grand Rapids Junior College*

Thomas Clarkin, *University of Texas, Austin*

Myles Clowers, *San Diego City College*

William Cobb, *Utah Valley State College*

David Coon, *Washington State University*

Stacy Cordery, *Monmouth College*

Debbie Cottrell, *Smith College*

A. Glenn Crothers, *Indiana University Southeast*

David Cullen, *Collin County Community College*

Christine Daniels, *Michigan State University*

Amy E. Davis, *University of California, Los Angeles*

Ronnie Day, *East Tennessee State University*

Matthew Dennis, *University of Oregon*

Robert Downtain, *Tarrant County Junior College, Northeast Campus*

Robert Elam, *Modesto Junior College*

Rob Fink, *Texas Tech University*

Monte S. Finkelstein, *Tallahassee Community College*

Linda Foutch, *Walter State Community College*

Robert G. Fricke, *West Valley College*

Michael P. Gabriel, *Kutztown University*

David Hamilton, *University of Kentucky*

Beatriz Hardy, *Coastal Carolina University*

Peter M. G. Harris, *Temple University*

Thomas Hartshorne, *Cleveland State University*

Gordon E. Harvey, *University of Louisiana at Monroe*

Ron Hatzenbuehler, *Idaho State University*

Robert Hawkes, *George Mason University*

William L. Hewitt, *West Chester University*

James Houston, *Oklahoma State University*

Raymond Hyser, *James Madison University*

Lillian Jones, *Santa Monica College*

Jim Kluger, *Pima Community College*

Timothy Koerner, *Oakland Community College*

James Lacy, *Contra Costa College*

Alton Lee, *University of South Dakota*

Liston Leyendecker, *Colorado State University*

Robert Marcom, *San Antonio College*

Greg Massey, *Freed-Hardeman*

Michael Mayer, *University of Montana*

Randy McBee, *Texas Tech University*

Loyce B. Miles, *Hinds Community College*

Kimberly Morse, *University of Texas, Austin*

Augustine Nigro, *Kutztown University*

Elsa Nystrom, *Kennesaw State*

David O'Neill, *Rutgers University*

Elizabeth R. Osborn, *Indiana University—Purdue University Indianapolis*

Betty Owens, *Greenville Technical College*

Mark Parillo, *Kansas State University*

J'Nell Pate, *Tarrant County Junior College, Northeast Campus*

Louis Potts, *University of Missouri at Kansas City*

Noel Pugach, *University of New Mexico*

Alice Reagan, *Northern Virginia Community College*

Marlette Rebhorn, *Austin Community College, Rio Grande Campus*

David Reimers, *New York University*

Hal Rothman, *Wichita State University*

Erik S. Schmeller, *Tennessee State University*

John G. Selby, *Roanoke College*

Ralph Shaffer, *California Polytechnic University*

Kenneth Smemo, *Moorhead State University*

Jack Smith, *Great Basin College*

Thaddeus Smith, *Middle Tennessee State University*

Phillip E. Stebbins, *Pennsylvania State University*

Marshall Stevenson, *Ohio State University*

William Stockton, *Johnson County Community College*

Suzanne Summers, *Austin Community College*

Frank Towers, *Clarion University*

Daniel Usner, *Cornell University*

Daniel Vogt, *Jackson State University*

Stephen Webre, *Louisiana Technical College*

John C. Willis, *University of the South*

Harold Wilson, *Old Dominion University*

Nan Woodruff, *Pennsylvania State University*

Bertram Wyatt-Brown, *University of Florida*

Sherri Yeager, *Chabot College*

Robert Zeidel, *University of Wisconsin.*

AMERICAN PASSAGES

15 Blood and Freedom, 1863–1867

Ill and injured men filled the ground around the surgical and hospital tents where horrifying surgery often awaited them.

© Bettmann/CORBIS

The Civil War enveloped the entire nation, home front and battlefield alike. The outcome of a battle could win an election or trigger a riot, while events at home affected the leaders' decisions of when and where to fight. In the North, the strong political opposition to Abraham Lincoln and his policies exerted a constant pressure on his conduct of the war. In the South, slaves abandoned plantations and white families' hardships led soldiers to rethink their loyalties.

The outcome of the Civil War was not predetermined by the North's advantages of population and resources. Deep into the war, events could have taken radically different turns. Slavery might have survived the conflict had the Confederacy won at particular junctions or, what would have been more likely, had the United States lost the will to push the devastating war to the South's full surrender and the immediate abolition of slavery. Even with the war's end the future course of the nation remained in doubt as Americans confronted the greatest rupture in their history.

People at War: Spring 1863

Both Northerners and Southerners expected the spring of 1863 to bring the climax of the Civil War. Yet while generals and armies determined the result of battles, the women, slaves, workers, bureaucrats, draft dodgers, and politicians behind the lines would determine the outcome of the war.

Life in the Field

Soldiers eventually adjusted to the miseries of sleeping on the ground, poorly cooked food, driving rain, and endless mud. They learned to adapt to gambling, drinking, cursing, and prostitution, either by succumbing to the temptations or by steeling their resolve against them. They could toughen themselves to the intermittent mails and the arrival of bad news from home. Men recalled their initial mortification and humiliation of discovering the entire company infested with lice, a shame that turned to indifference when the sharper horror of wounds descended.

Even the most stalwart of soldiers could not adapt to the constant threat of diseases such as diarrhea, dysentery, typhoid, malaria, measles, diphtheria, and scarlet fever. As bloody as the battles were, disease killed twice as many men as died from the guns of the enemy. Many doctors of the Civil War era used the same instruments of surgery on soldier after soldier, unwittingly spreading

Timeline

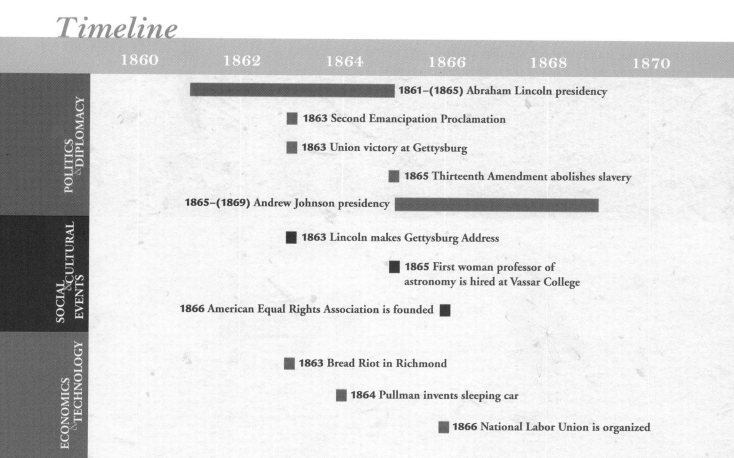

	1860	1862	1864	1866	1868	1870

POLITICS & DIPLOMACY
- 1861–(1865) Abraham Lincoln presidency
- 1863 Second Emancipation Proclamation
- 1863 Union victory at Gettysburg
- 1865 Thirteenth Amendment abolishes slavery
- 1865–(1869) Andrew Johnson presidency

SOCIAL & CULTURAL EVENTS
- 1863 Lincoln makes Gettysburg Address
- 1865 First woman professor of astronomy is hired at Vassar College
- 1866 American Equal Rights Association is founded

ECONOMICS & TECHNOLOGY
- 1863 Bread Riot in Richmond
- 1864 Pullman invents sleeping car
- 1866 National Labor Union is organized

disease and infection. After every battle, screams filled the night as surgeons sawed off legs and arms, feet and hands, in often vain hopes of stopping gangrene.

Purposes

The North fought for ideals of union and democracy; the South fought for ideals of self-determination. Yet soldiers acted courageously not only because they believed in the official political purposes for which they were fighting, but also because they wanted to be admired by the people at home, because they wanted to do their part for their comrades, because they wanted to bring the war to a quicker end, and because they grew to hate the enemy.

Many men fought alongside their brothers, uncles, cousins. A steady stream of letters flowed back and forth between the units and the families and neighbors back home. Gossip, praise, and condemnation flourished. Any soldier who planned to return home knew that his deeds in the war would live with him the rest of his life. As a result, even fearful or halfhearted soldiers might throw themselves into battle to demonstrate their courage.

Whereas about three-fifths of Civil War soldiers were over 21 at the age of enlistment, the largest single group of soldiers was 18. For those who passed the birthdays of their late teens or early twenties on the battlefields, the transition to manhood became inseparable from the war. A soldier from Illinois proudly wrote his family that "this war has made a man of your son." To be manly meant more than the simple ability to inflict violence on the enemy. It meant pride, responsibility, loyalty, and obedience. Every battle became a test of manhood, which had to be proven every time it was challenged under fire.

Courage developed, too, out of hatred. People on both sides spread the worst stories and rumors about one another. Newspapers printed exaggerated or fabricated atrocity reports about the enemy. While many were repelled by battlefield carnage, others took satisfaction. One Confederate artillery officer admired the "severed limbs, decapitated bodies, and mutilated remains" at Fredericksburg and declared that it did "my soul good" to ride over the bodies of the Federal dead. Union troops also hardened their attitudes. A Wisconsin soldier informed his fiancée that his unit wanted to fight until "we kill them all off and cleanse the country." The longer the war went on, the more people felt they had to hate one another to justify so much bloodshed.

The sermons men heard in the camps told them they were fighting on the side of the right. The Old Testament afforded rich imagery and compelling stories of violence inflicted for good causes. Many Americans believed that God's will was enacted directly in human affairs. As the war ground on, the leaders, the soldiers, and the civilians of both sides came to feel that events were more than the product of human decision or even courage. Surely, they told themselves, so much suffering and sacrifice had to be for a larger purpose.

The Problems of the Confederate Government

Convinced that greedy merchants were holding supplies of flour until prices rose even higher in the spring of 1863, poor women in Richmond broke open the stores of merchants accused of hoarding the precious staple, taking what they needed. After President Davis climbed on a wagon and threw coins at the crowd, he ordered a militia unit to prepare to fire on them. The threat of violence and of arrest, as well as the promise of free supplies, broke up the riot, but similar events occurred in several other Southern cities such as Atlanta, Columbus, and Augusta. No one could tell when even larger riots might erupt again. Fearing the consequences for morale, military officers in Richmond ordered the press and

This Northern portrayal of the Richmond bread riots imagined the rioters as fearsome, gaunt amazons; other accounts emphasized their respectability. In either case, they behaved in ways quite remarkable for any women in nineteenth-century America.

The Library of Virginia

Once the United States instituted conscription men rushed to enlist in units that offered, as this poster put it, their "last chance to avoid the draft!"

telegraph office to suppress news of the riot, but word of the riot soon spread.

The rioters were not the only ones who took what they needed. Confederate officers in the field forced reluctant farmers to accept whatever prices the army offered, in an increasingly worthless currency. In the spring of 1863, the Confederate government attempted to curb the worst abuses of this practice in the Impressment Act. If a farmer did not think the prices he or she received were fair, the case could be appealed before local authorities. In practice, however, this cumbersome system failed. Farmers hid their produce from officers and resented it when they were forced to sell. North Carolina's governor denounced impressments to the

War Department in Richmond: "If God Almighty had yet in store another plague . . . I am sure it must have been a regiment or so of half-disciplined Confederate cavalry."

The Southern government could not afford to lose civilian support. Although the absence of political parties originally appeared to be a sign of the South's consensus, that absence eventually undermined what original consensus the Confederacy had enjoyed. Jefferson Davis, without a party mechanism to discipline those who spoke out against him, could not remove enemies from office. Davis's own vice president, Alexander Stephens, became a persistent and outspoken critic of the Confederate president's "tyrannical" policies, actively undermining support for Davis and even allying with avowed enemies of Davis and his policies.

The Confederate government faced a fundamental dilemma. The whole point of secession had been to move political power closer to localities, protecting slavery in particular and self-determination in general. The government of the Confederacy, however, had to centralize power. If the armies were to be fed and clothed, if diplomats were to make a plausible case for the Confederacy's nationhood, if soldiers were to be mobilized, then the Confederate government had to exercise greater power than its creators had expected or intended. Jefferson Davis continually struggled with this tension. For every Southerner who considered Davis too weak, another considered the president dangerously powerful.

The Northern Home Front

In the North, the war heightened the strong differences between the Democrats and the Republicans. The Democrats won significant victories in congressional elections in the fall and winter of 1862, testifying to the depth and breadth of the opposition to Lincoln and his conduct of the war. Wealthy businessmen were eager to reestablish trade with their former Southern partners, whereas Irish immigrants wanted to end the risk of the draft and competition from freed slaves. Many citizens of Ohio, Indiana, and Illinois, whose families had come from the South, wanted to renew the Southern connections that had been broken by the war.

The Union passed its Conscription Act in March of 1863 because disease, wounds, and desertion had depleted the ranks of soldiers faster than they could be replaced. When drafted, a man could appear for duty, hire a substitute to fight in his place, or simply pay a fee

© Kean Collection/Hulton Archive/Getty Images

Black men had called for their inclusion in the U.S. Army from the beginning of the war. In the spring of 1863, the U.S. Colored Troops were formed and more than 180,000 African American men fought for the Union over the next 2 years.

THE SOLDIER IN OUR CIVIL WAR.

THE NEGRO IN THE WAR—VARIOUS EMPLOYMENTS OF THE COLORED MEN IN THE FEDERAL ARMY.

FROM SKETCHES BY C. E. F. HILLEN.

206-207

© The Stock Montage

This magazine illustration detailed the many tasks and great deeds performed by the U.S. Colored Troops in one of their earliest challenges, at the Battle of Milliken's Bend in Louisiana.

of $300 directly to the government. Poorer communities resented the wealthy who could avoid service. Demonstrations broke out in Chicago, Pennsylvania mining towns, Ohio, rural Vermont, and Boston. State and federal governments often paid bounties—signing bonuses—to those who volunteered. More than a few men took the bounties and then promptly deserted and moved to another locality to claim another bounty.

The opposition to the Lincoln government raised crucial issues. With the North claiming to fight for liberty, what limitations on freedom of speech and protest could it enforce? A Democratic congressman from Ohio, Clement Vallandigham, tested those limits in the spring of 1863. Hating both secessionists and abolitionists, Vallandigham refused to obey a general's orders to stop criticizing the Lincoln administration. He was arrested, tried before a military court, and sentenced to imprisonment for the rest of the war. Lincoln was dismayed by these events. He commuted Vallandigham's sentence, sending him to the Confederates in Tennessee, hoping to make

Vallandigham appear a Southern sympathizer rather than a martyr to the cause of free speech. Vallandigham quickly escaped to Canada, however, where he continued his criticisms. Ohio Democrats defiantly nominated Vallandigham for governor in the elections to be held in the fall of 1863. If things continued to go badly for the Union, who knew what kind of success a critic of Lincoln might find?

African American Soldiers

Though Northern civilian and military leaders remained deeply divided and ambivalent about black freedom, it became clear to everyone that black men could be of great value to the Union. In May 1863, the War Department created the Bureau of Colored Troops.

African American men from across the North rushed to enlist as soon as they heard of the new black regiments.

At first, black recruits found themselves restricted to noncombat roles and a lower rate of pay: $10 a month versus the $13 a month and $3.50 clothing allowance given to white soldiers. Black men, though eager to serve, protested that they could not support their families on such amounts. African Americans knew, and coveted, the rights and privileges of other Americans. They wrote petitions and appealed to higher authorities, often in the language of the Declaration of Independence and the Constitution.

Confederate officials who expected black soldiers to make reluctant or cowed fighters soon discovered otherwise. In May of 1863, two black regiments stormed, seven times, a heavily fortified Confederate installation at Port Hudson, Louisiana. Soon thereafter, black soldiers found themselves on the other side of the barricades. At Milliken's Bend, Louisiana, they fought Confederates hand-to-hand. Northern newspapers echoed the words of praise from generals in the field: "No troops could be more determined or more daring."

Encouraged and frequently supported financially by their communities, African American men in the North went to the recruiting tables in great numbers. Frederick Douglass, the leading spokesman for black Americans, celebrated the enlistments: "Once let the black man get upon his person the brass letters, *U.S.;* let him get an eagle on his button, and a musket on his shoulder, and bullets in his pocket, and there is no power on earth which can deny that he has earned the right to citizenship in the United States." From Rhode Island to Ohio, black troops prepared to head south.

The Battlefields of Summer: 1863

Everything seemed in place for a climactic culmination of the war in the summer of 1863. The Union had almost severed the western half of the Confederacy from the eastern; the Federal army had penetrated deep into Tennessee and stood on the threshold of Georgia. On the other hand, Confederate armies maintained their morale and learned to make the most of their advantages.

Vicksburg and Chancellorsville

Union leaders needed all the help they could get in early 1863. Grant and Sherman remained frustrated in their goal of seizing Vicksburg; Rosecrans faced Bragg in Tennessee; Lee's army had yet to be decisively defeated despite the men, resources, and determination thrown into battle against him. Lee would face General Joseph Hooker, whom Lincoln had chosen to replace Ambrose Burnside. Throughout the spring, "Fighting Joe" Hooker energized his men and repaired some of the damage to morale and readiness inflicted at Fredericksburg. But no one knew if he would be able to handle Lee.

The Northern public was especially impatient with Grant and Sherman. Grant knew the delays threatened his command. Vicksburg, heavily fortified by both geography and the Confederates, seemed most vulnerable to attack from the southeast, but to get there Grant would have to find a way to move his men across the Mississippi River without landing them in swamps. Throughout the long wet winter, Grant had tried one experiment after another, including digging canals. Nothing worked.

Grant finally decided on a bold move: he would run a flotilla of gunboats and barges past Vicksburg under the cover of night to ferry his men across the Mississippi south of the city, where the land was better (see Map 15.1). The guns of Vicksburg stood 200 feet above the river, ready to fire down on any passing craft, but the Union men covered their ships' boilers with sacks of grain and bales of cotton to protect them from the shelling. Most of the boats made it through. Grant had Sherman create a diversion, confusing the Confederates, and then ferried his entire army across the Mississippi. Grant's army remained vulnerable, cut off from his allies and his major supply base, but by mid-May, Grant had fought four battles, cost the South 8,000 dead and wounded, marched 200 miles, and pinned 30,000 Confederates within Vicksburg's fortifications.

In the same week Grant made his landing near Vicksburg, Hooker began his attack on Lee, still based in Fredericksburg (see Map 15.2). Hooker commanded 130,000 men. Unlike Burnside, however, Hooker intended to outsmart Lee rather than try to overwhelm him with numbers. A large Union force would sweep around Lee and attack him from behind, even as another force attacked from the front. To keep from being bottled up in Fredericksburg, Lee would have to emerge from his well-entrenched defensive position. Lee met this bold move with an even bolder one. He would divide his forces and send Stonewall Jackson to attack Hooker's

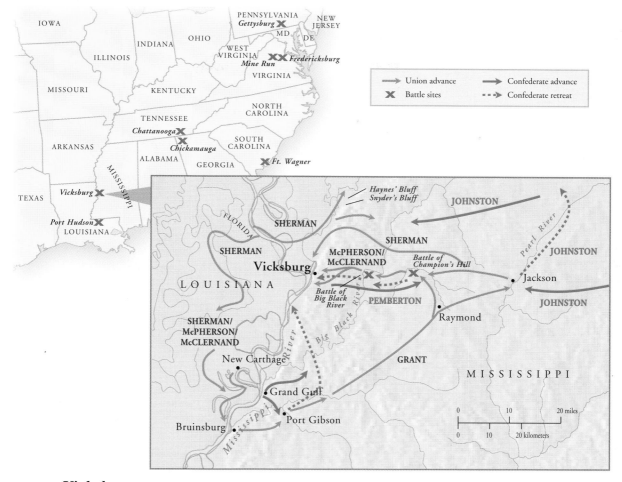

MAP 15.1 Vicksburg
After months of frustration, Ulysses S. Grant and William T. Sherman found a way to attack Vicksburg from the south and east. Following great struggle, the Union generals were able to take the city on July 4, 1863. View an animated version of this map or related maps at http://history.wadsworth.com/passages3e.

men from the rear, outflanking Hooker's own flanking maneuver.

On May 2, Jackson assaulted Hooker's troops near Chancellorsville. The outnumbered Confederates defeated the surprised and indecisive Hooker, achieving a major victory. Southern jubilation, though, ended the very night of this triumph, for nervous Confederate soldiers accidentally shot Stonewall Jackson while he surveyed the scene near the front lines. The surgeons removed his arm that evening and hoped that he might live.

While Jackson lay in his tent, fading in and out of consciousness, Lee managed to contain another assault on Fredericksburg and to push the Union troops away from their positions. The losses had once again been staggering—13,000 casualties, roughly 22 percent of the army—but Lee had overcome a larger opponent. After the last battles quieted, however, Jackson died. His death took with it Lee's most skillful general.

Gettysburg

Despite his victory at Chancellorsville, Lee recognized that the Confederacy was in trouble. Rosecrans still threatened to break through Tennessee into Georgia, Grant clawed his way closer to Vicksburg, and the Union blockade drew an ever tighter net around the

---

DOING HISTORY ONLINE

The Civil War and the Mississippi River
Access the module, locate the Mississippi River, and then "play" the interactive map. According to the map, how did the river affect the course of the war?

History Now™   Visit HistoryNOW to access primary sources and exercises related to this topic: http://now.ilrn.com/ayers_etal3e

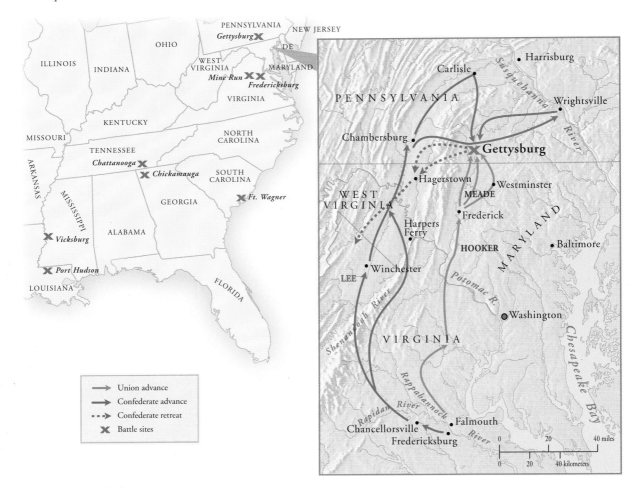

MAP 15.2 Virginia, 1863

The battle of Chancellorsville, not far from Fredericksburg, was a great victory for the Confederates. But it marked just the opening stage of a long summer of fighting that would culminate at Gettysburg two months later. In that battle, the Confederates sorely missed General Stonewall Jackson, accidentally killed by his own troops at Chancellorsville. View an animated version of this map or related maps at http://history.wadsworth.com/passages3e.

coast. Some of his generals urged Lee to rush with his troops to Tennessee to defend the center of the Confederacy and pull Grant away from Vicksburg. But Lee decided that his most effective move would be to invade the North again, taking the pressure off Virginia and disheartening the Union. A successful strike into the North might even yet persuade Britain and France to recognize the Confederacy and give heart to Peace Democrats in the North.

In early June, Lee began to move up through the Shenandoah Valley into southern Pennsylvania with 75,000 men. Hooker seemed confused. When, after a minor dispute, Hooker offered his resignation to Lincoln, the president quickly accepted and put General George Meade in charge. Meade had to decide how best to stop the greatest threat the Confederate army had yet posed to the North. Washington and Baltimore lay in danger, along with the cities, towns, and farms of Pennsylvania.

There, the Confederate troops enjoyed taking food and livestock from the rich land. Free blacks and fugitive slaves were also seized and forced south into slavery.

Although Lee and his men moved unchecked across the Potomac and deep into Pennsylvania, they found themselves in a dangerous situation. Lee had permitted Jeb Stuart's cavalry, his "eyes," to range widely from the main army; as a result, the Confederates had little idea where the Union army was or what moves it was making. For their part, Meade and his fellow officers decided to pursue Lee, but not too aggressively, looking for a likely time and place to confront the enemy.

On June 30, units from the Confederacy and the Union stumbled over one another at a small town neither side knew or cared much about: Gettysburg. On July 1, they began to struggle for the best defensive position near the town, fighting over the highest and most protected land. It appeared at first that the Southerners had

The battle at Gettysburg, in an obscure town in southern Pennsylvania, provided some of the most memorable struggles of the entire war, especially the Confederate charge up an unprotected slope to Cemetery Ridge, where massed Union troops awaited.

the better of the first day's battle, but as the smoke cleared both sides could see that late in the day the Union army had consolidated itself on the most advantageous ground. Meade's men, after fierce fighting at the ends of their line, occupied a fishhook-shaped series of ridges and hills that permitted them to protect their flanks. The second day saw the Confederates slowly mobilize their forces for assaults on those positions and launch attacks late in the afternoon. The resulting battles in the peach orchard, the wheat field, Little Round Top, and the boulder-strewn area known as the Devil's Den proved horrific—with 35,000 men dead or wounded—but left the Union in control of the high ground.

Despite the Union's superior position, Lee decided on a frontal attack the next day. The Confederates hoped their artillery would soften the middle of the Union lines. The Confederates did not realize how little damage their guns had done until well-entrenched Union troops decimated waves of an attack led by George E. Pickett. Only a few Southern men made it to the stone wall that protected the Northerners, and even those Confederates quickly fell. It proved a disastrous three days for the Army of Northern Virginia, which lost 23,000 men through death or wounds, about a third of its entire force. While the Union lost similar numbers of men, it had more to lose. The Northerners and their new general had fought a defensive battle; the Southern side, short of supplies and men, had gambled on an aggressive assault. Elation swept the North. "The glorious success of the Army of the Potomac has electrified all," a Northerner exulted. In the wake of Chancellorsville

and Lee's apparently effortless invasion of Pennsylvania, he admitted, many Northerners "did not believe the enemy could be whipped."

The next morning, a thousand miles away, Vicksburg surrendered to Ulysses S. Grant. Unlike Gettysburg, where the battle had been fought in a place no one considered strategically crucial, Vicksburg held enormous tactical and psychological importance. It had been the symbol of Confederate doggedness and Union frustration. After six weeks of siege, after six weeks of near starvation behind the Confederate defenses, Vicksburg fell. The Mississippi River now divided the Confederacy while it tied the Union to the Gulf of Mexico.

Some Southerners, including Jefferson Davis, did not perceive Gettysburg as a defeat. In their eyes, Lee and his men had pushed deep into the Union, inflicted heavy losses, and damaged Northern morale without being trapped there. Northerners at the time often agreed that Gettysburg had not been a decisive Union victory, pronouncing themselves more frustrated than satisfied with Meade, who had not destroyed Lee's army despite his greater numbers. During the Confederate retreat to Virginia, the Southerners found themselves caught between a swollen Potomac River and pursuing federal troops. Meade, his army exhausted and weakened, chose not to fight against the defenses Lee's men hurriedly put up against their pursuers. Meade could not know that the condition of the Southern troops was even worse than his own. Fortunately for the Confederates, the river soon calmed enough that they were able to escape back into Virginia.

The New York City Draft Riots

On the very day that Lee struggled across the Potomac to safety, riots broke out in New York City. Northern working people had complicated feelings about the war. Many of those who labored in the North's factories, mines, farms, and railroads had come to the United States during the previous 15 years. These people, mostly Irish and Germans, volunteered in large numbers to fight for the Union cause. Between 20 and 25 percent of the Union Army consisted of immigrants, the great majority of them volunteers.

Despite their patriotism for their adopted country, many of the immigrants viewed black Americans with dread and contempt. Urban labor organizations divided over Lincoln's election and over the response to secession. Many Catholic Irishmen, almost all of them Democrats, proclaimed that they had no quarrel with white Southerners and that they resented the federal

Flashpoints | The New York City Draft Riots

In March 1863 the government enacted a conscription law, making all men between 20 and 45 years of age liable for military service. Unlike today's Selective Service, this federal draft used crude encouragements to get men to "volunteer."

Quotas were assigned to each community, quotas that could be filled by voluntary enlistments, sparing the town further call-ups. While communities worked to fill their allotments with volunteers, many, particularly larger urban areas, fell short. Northern farmers and workers bitterly resented that the law permitted wealthier citizens the chance to hire a substitute to serve in his place for a fee of $300. The monies collected would be paid as enlistment bonuses to volunteers, particularly experienced veterans whose enlistments were expiring. Some towns and employers paid the commutation fee for poorer residents.

Roughly 133,000 men were drafted, but 60 percent paid the fee to escape service. Peace Democrats across the North took up the cry, "a rich man's war, but a poor man's fight!" to rally opposition to the draft, to Lincoln, and the continuation of the war. Military provosts attempted to enforce conscription across the North. Men resisted or fled; some sold themselves as substitutes several times and promptly deserted.

The attempt to enforce the draft in New York City on July 13 ignited the most destructive civil disturbance in the city's history. Rioters torched government buildings, and, on July 15, fought pitched battles with troops rushed from their recent victory at Gettysburg. Conservative contemporary commentators, concerned

about an anti-Union plot, claimed that 1,155 people were killed. In fact, about 300, over half of them policemen and soldiers, were injured, and there were no more than 119 fatalities, mostly free blacks and rioters.

A majority of the rioters were Irish who lived in poverty and were likely candidates for the draft. They linked the draft to Lincoln's call for slave emancipation and they turned their anger at the draft against New York's black population. Many innocent blacks were slain and their homes sacked. A Colored Orphan Asylum was razed to the ground. White workers in New York City destroyed the central recruiting station, rail lines, small factories and homes of wealthy citizens. Similar protests erupted in Boston, Toledo, Newark, and Troy, New York.

Following the riots and resistance to the draft across the North, Lincoln repealed the draft in 1864 and expanded the enlistment bounty system. Immigrants and black men became the targets of recruitment efforts. By 1865, 25 percent of the recruits were immigrants and 10 percent were black. Conscripts never amounted to more that 2 percent of total army strength out of a 2.1 million man armed force.

Questions for Reflection

1. Should we be surprised by the draft riots?

2. Was the Civil War a war that fell especially hard on the poor?

3. Why did the Confederacy not have riots of similar size and effect?

government's draft. The obvious effect of inflation on the wages of workers created strong resentments as well. Working people sneered at those men who had enough money to hire substitutes to fight in their place. Three hundred dollars, after all, constituted half a year's wage for a workingman.

Irish immigrants despaired at the losses among Irish-American units in the field. When their regiments were decimated at Fredericksburg, Gettysburg, and elsewhere, Irish people began to wonder if commanders valued their

lives as highly as those of the native-born. When word came—just as the draft lottery was to take place in New York City on July 11, 1863—of the 23,000 men lost at Gettysburg, the fury of working people rose. On July 13, it exploded. Mobs began by assaulting draft officials, then turned their anger on any man who looked rich enough to have hired a substitute, then on pro-Lincoln newspapers and abolitionists' homes. They assaulted any African Americans they encountered on the streets, burning an orphanage, whipping men and women, and hanging

Riots in New York City were triggered by an impending draft lottery and by news from Gettysburg that told of heavy Union losses there. Black Americans suffered the most from the riots.

victims from city lampposts. Lincoln was sickened by accounts of the riot and a city editor despaired, "Great God! What is this nation coming to?"

The police struggled for three days to control the riot. Eventually, troops (including all-Irish units) rushed from the battlefields of Pennsylvania to aid the police. The troops fired into the rioters; more than a hundred people died and another 300 were injured. The working people got some of what they wanted: more welfare relief, exemptions from the draft for those whose families would have no other means of support, and an exodus of black people who feared for their lives.

Ironically, a few days after the New York **draft riots,** scores of black troops died during a bold nighttime assault on Fort Wagner near Charleston, South Carolina. Despite the bravery of the African Americans, the assault failed. The Confederates made a point of burying the African American soldiers in a mass grave along with their white officer, Robert Gould Shaw, intending to insult him and his memory. Instead, they elevated him to a Northern martyr. The *Atlantic Monthly* marked a change in Northern attitudes toward black soldiers: "Through the cannon smoke of that dark night, the manhood of the colored race shines before many eyes that would not see."

Chickamauga

After Gettysburg, Vicksburg, and the New York riots in July, events slowed until September, when Union General William Rosecrans left Chattanooga, near the Georgia border, and began moving toward Atlanta. His opponent, Braxton Bragg, hoped to entice Rosecrans into dividing his forces so that they could be cut off. The armies confronted one another at Chickamauga Creek—a Cherokee name meaning "river of death." The Confederates took advantage of Union mistakes on the heavily wooded battlefield, inflicting harrowing damage and driving Rosecrans back into Chattanooga. The Union troops were trapped there, the Confederates looming over them on Lookout Mountain and Missionary Ridge, with few routes of escape and limited supplies. The Northerners had gone from a position of apparent advantage to one of desperation.

Lincoln, judging Rosecrans "confused and stunned" by the battle at Chickamauga, used this opportunity to put Grant in charge of all Union armies between the Appalachian Mountains and the Mississippi River. In the fall of 1863, Grant traveled to Chattanooga, where Sherman joined him from Mississippi and Hooker came from Virginia.

The Gettysburg Address

The North's victories in the summer of 1863 aided Lincoln's popularity. The draft riots in New York City damaged the reputations of Democrats, whereas the bravery of black soldiers on the battlefields of Louisiana and South Carolina led white Northerners, particularly Union soldiers, to rethink some of their prejudices. In the fall of 1863, the Republicans won major victories in Pennsylvania and Ohio. Lincoln determined to make the most of these heartening events.

When Lincoln received an invitation to speak at the dedication of the cemetery at Gettysburg on November 19, he saw it as a chance to impart a sense of direction and purpose to the Union cause. The event had not been planned with him in mind and the president was not even the featured speaker. But Lincoln recognized

---

DOING HISTORY ONLINE

Chickamauga and the Civil War

Study the map for the years 1864 and 1865 and read the sections in the text from "Chickamauga" through "Union Resolve." Explain why the Union victory at Chickamauga was so significant.

History⧖Now™   Visit HistoryNOW to access primary sources and exercises related to this topic: http://now.ilrn.com/ayers_etal3e

DOING HISTORY

Freedom's Promise

PERHAPS THE MOST influential and memorable brief passage in American history, Lincoln's "remarks" at the opening of the Gettysburg battlefield in November 1863 articulated the highest ideals with which the war could be associated. The letter to the Union Convention in Nashville documents the insistence by black Americans that the "new birth of freedom" embrace those who had been formerly held in slavery. They received no response.

Abraham Lincoln, "The Gettysburg Address"

Four score and seven years ago our fathers brought forth on this continent, a new nation, conceived in Liberty, and dedicated to the proposition that all men are created equal.

Now we are engaged in a great civil war, testing whether that nation, or any nation so conceived and so dedicated, can long endure. We are met on a great battle-field of that war. We have come to dedicate a portion of that field, as a final resting place for those who here gave lives that that nation might live. It is altogether fitting and proper that we should do this.

But, in a larger sense, we can not dedicate—we can not consecrate—we can not hallow—this ground. The brave men, living and dead, who struggled here, have consecrated it, far above our poor power to add or detract. The world will little note, nor long remember what we say here, but it can never forget what they did here. It is for us the living, rather, to be dedicated here to the unfinished work which they who fought here have thus far so nobly advanced. It is rather for us to be here dedicated to the great task remaining before us—that from these honored dead we take increased devotion to that cause for which they have the last full measure of devotion—that we here highly resolve that these dead shall not have died in vain—that this nation, under God, shall have a new birth of freedom—and that government of the people, by the people, for the people, shall not perish from the earth.

Black Citizens of Tennessee, "Letter to the Union Convention 1865"

To the Union Convention of Tennessee Assembled in the Capitol at Nashville, January 9, 1865:

We claim to be men belonging to the great human family, descended from one great God, who is the common Father of all, and who bestowed on all races and tribes the priceless right of freedom. . . . We know the burdens of citizenship, and are ready to bear them. We know the duties of the good citizen, and are ready to perform them cheerfully, and would ask to be put in a position in which we can discharge them more effectually. . . . This is a democracy—a government of the people. It should aim to make every man, without regard to the color of his skin, the amount of his wealth, or the character of his religious faith, feel personally interested in its welfare.

Source: Roy P. Basler, ed., *Collected Works of Abraham Lincoln,* Vol. VII (New Brunswick, NJ: Rutgers University Press, 1953), p. 23; Ira Berlin et al., eds., *Free At Last: A Documentary History of Slavery, Freedom, and the Civil War* (New York: New Press, 1992), pp. 497–505.

Questions for Reflection

1. Why did Abraham Lincoln not mention slavery directly in his remarks?

2. What other themes might Lincoln have evoked that he did not? What is the general tone of his brief speech? How was that tone shaped by the setting?

3. What unified the Gettysburg Address and the letter to the Union Convention? Did anything divide them?

4. Why would the white Unionists to whom the black petitioners wrote this letter not be receptive to this eloquent plea?

5. How did Republicans renounce Lincoln's goals in 1877?

Explore additional primary sources related to this chapter on the Wadsworth American History Resource Center or HistoryNOW websites:

http://history.wadsworth.com/rc/us
http://now.ilrn.com/ayers_etal3e

that a battlefield offered the most effective backdrop for the things he wanted to say.

Burial crews had been laboring for weeks on the Gettysburg battlefield. Thousands of horse carcasses had been burned; thousands of human bodies had been hastily covered with a thin layer of soil. Pennsylvania purchased 17 acres and hired a specialist in rural cemetery design to lay out the burial plots so that no state would be offended by the location or amount of space devoted to its fallen men. Only about a third of the reburials had taken place when Lincoln arrived; caskets remained stacked at the station.

Lincoln, contrary to legend, did not dash off his speech on the back of an envelope. He had reworked and polished it for several days. The "remarks," as the program put it, lasted three minutes. Lincoln used those minutes to maximum effect. He said virtually nothing about the details of the scene surrounding the 20,000 people at the ceremony. Neither did he mention slavery directly. Instead, he spoke of equality as the fundamental purpose of the war. He called for a "new birth of freedom."

Lincoln was attempting to shift the purpose of the war from Union for Union's sake to Union for freedom's sake. He sought to salvage something from the deaths of the 50,000 men at Gettysburg. Democratic newspapers rebuked Lincoln for his claim, arguing that white soldiers had "too much self-respect to declare that negroes were their equals." But other Northerners accepted Lincoln's exhortation as the definition of their purpose. They might not believe that blacks deserved to be included as full participants in a government of, by, and for "the people," but they did believe that the Union fought for liberty broadly conceived. As battles and years went by, the words of the **Gettysburg Address** would gain force and resonance.

Just 4 days after Lincoln's speech, Grant gave the North new reason to believe its ideals might triumph. On November 23, Grant's men overwhelmed the Confederates on Lookout Mountain outside Chattanooga; 2 days later, Union soldiers shocked the Confederates by fighting their way up the steep Missionary Ridge because Confederate artillery could not reach opponents coming up directly from below. The Union, now in control of the cities and rail junctions of Kentucky and Tennessee, had a wide and direct route into Georgia.

England and France finally determined in late 1863 that they would not try to intervene in the American war. First Britain, then France detained or sold to foreign powers warships intended for the Confederacy. The Northern public, encouraged by events on the battlefield, supported Republican candidates in the congressional elections of 1863 more vigorously than had seemed possible just a few months before.

The Winter of Discontent: 1863–1864

The battles of the summer had been horrific. Both sides held their victories close to their hearts and brooded over their losses. The resolve and fury of summertime faded into the bitterness and bickering of winter. As the cycle rolled around again, people steeled themselves for another bloody year of war.

Politics North and South

Lincoln hoped to end the war as soon as possible, using persuasion as well as fighting to entice white Southerners back into the national fold. In early December 1863, Lincoln issued his proclamation of amnesty and reconstruction. To those who would take an oath of loyalty to the Union, Lincoln promised a full pardon and the return of all property other than slaves. Though he excluded Confederate leaders and high officers from this offer, Lincoln tried to include as many white Southern men as possible. As soon as 10 percent of the number of voters in 1860 had sworn their loyalty to the Union, he decreed, those Southerners could begin forming new state governments. Education and apprenticeship programs would aid former slaves in the transition to full freedom. He did not provide for African American participation in these new governments of the South.

Two factors worked against acceptance of Lincoln's policy. First, Northern Republicans and much of the public overestimated the extent and depth of Southern Unionist sentiment after years of war and occupation. Second, even in areas under federal control such as Tennessee and Kentucky, guerrilla bands and raiders terrorized the local population. Elections in parts of Tennessee were blocked by irregulars. "The people are warned . . . not to hold such an Election under pain of being Arrested and Carried South for trial," one observer reported. Civilians were often caught between threats. Those who failed to aid Union forces were perceived as "enemies of mankind" with "the rights due to pirates and robbers," whereas those who actively aided the Federals were liable to find crops trampled, barns burned, and vigilante justice enacted by neighbors and guerrillas. Politics frequently offered an excuse for acting on old rivalries, for murder and pillaging.

Abolitionists and their allies attacked Lincoln's reconstruction plan as far too lenient to the Rebel masters and not helpful enough for the former slaves. In the Wade-Davis bill of February 1864, Republican congressmen attempted to inflict more stringent conditions on former Confederates and offer more help to former slaves. They wanted to use the power of the national government to enforce a standard set of laws across the South and to require 50 percent, rather than 10 percent, of the population to swear the loyalty oath, an oath of past as well as future loyalty. They feared that too weak a plan of reconstruction would permit former slaveowners and Confederates to negate much of what the war might win. Congressmen and Secretary of the Treasury Salmon P. Chase worked behind the scenes in opposition to Lincoln's plan. With an eye toward the upcoming election and the need to entice Arkansas and Louisiana to rejoin the Union, Lincoln refused to sign the Wade-Davis bill.

Although Jefferson Davis did not have to worry about his own reelection in late 1863—the Confederacy had established the presidential term at six years—he did have to worry about congressional elections. They did not go well: 41 of the new 106 representatives expressly opposed Davis and his policies, and he held only a slight majority in the Senate. Just as Northern Democrats called for compromise and peace, so did some Southerners. When Davis took a hands-off policy, he was criticized for doing too little. When he tried to assert more control, he found himself called "despotic" by his own vice president. Editors savaged Davis as responsible for the South's worsening fortunes: "Had the people dreamed that Mr. Davis would carry all his chronic antipathies, his bitter prejudices, his puerile partialities, and his doting favoritisms into the Presidential chair, they would never have allowed him to fill it." The Confederacy stumbled through the winter and into the spring of 1864, desperately watching for signs that the North might be losing heart.

Prisons

Early in the Civil War, both sides had exchanged prisoners of war rather than spending men and resources to maintain prisons. Such arrangements worked well enough into 1863, but then things began to break down. The Confederates decreed that any former slave captured would be executed or re-enslaved, not taken prisoner. The Union, as a matter of principle, refused to participate in any exchanges so long as this policy remained in effect. Prisoners began piling up on both sides, and stories of mistreatment became more frequent and more horrifying.

Northerners became livid when they heard about conditions at the Confederate camp at Andersonville, Georgia. The camp was built early in 1864 when the Confederates decided to move prisoners from Richmond. Not only would prisoners be less likely to be rescued by Northern troops moving south, but supplies could more easily be transported by railroad away from the heavy fighting in Virginia. The camp, built for 10,000 men in an open, partly swampy field, soon became overcrowded; it held 33,000 by August. Gangs of Northern soldiers controlled daily life within the prison, routinely beating and robbing new arrivals. Of the 45,000 men eventually held at Andersonville, 13,000 died from exposure, starvation, and brutality. The camp's commander, Colonel Henry Wirz, was the only Confederate official executed for war crimes after the war.

Even higher proportions died at smaller camps in North Carolina. Although Confederates held in Northern prisons were better supplied, even there, death rates reached as high as 24 percent with rations often short and men reduced to eating rats. Overall, about 16 percent of Northern soldiers and 12 percent of Southerners died in prison. Many in the North criticized Lincoln for refusing to reinstitute exchanges, but Lincoln would not sacrifice the former slaves. Moreover, he knew that exchanges helped the soldier-starved Confederacy more than they did the North.

Union Resolve

In March 1864, Lincoln gave new direction and purpose to the Union effort by putting Ulysses S. Grant in charge of all Northern forces. Grant and Lincoln agreed that the Union had to use its superiority in materiel, manpower, and navy to attack the Confederacy on every front at once, forcing the South to decide what territory it would sacrifice. While Grant would fight in Virginia (see Map 15.3), Lincoln left **William T. Sherman** in charge in Chattanooga. Sherman would attack the railroad center of Atlanta, cutting the Gulf South off from the Upper South. The loss of Atlanta would chop the Confederacy into pieces too small to resist the Northern army.

In retrospect, the events of 1864 may appear anticlimactic. The Confederates seemed to face

This Confederate prisoner of war camp in Andersonville, Georgia, witnessed great brutality and appalling death rates from disease and hunger.

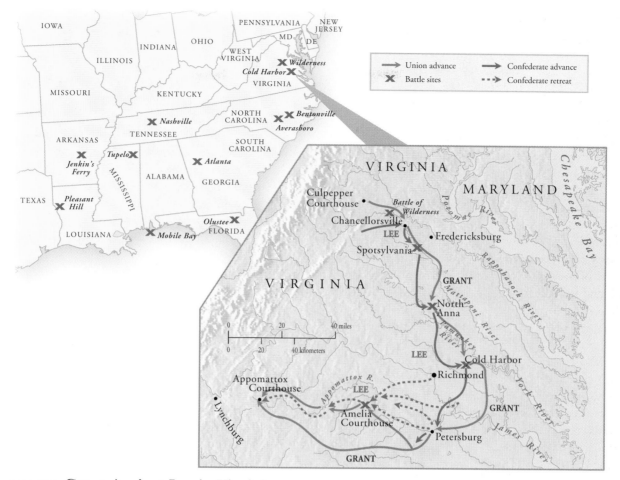

MAP 15.3 Grant Against Lee in Virginia

The two most important generals of the war confronted one another at one brutal battle after another between May 1864 and April 1865. View an animated version of this map or related maps at http://history.wadsworth.com/passages3e.

overwhelming odds. Yet Southerners recognized that everything turned around holding the Northerners off until the presidential election in the North. If the Southerners could inflict enough damage on the Union army, Northerners might elect someone willing to bring the war to an end through compromise. The Confederates knew, too, that the three-year terms of the most experienced veterans in the Union army expired in 1864. More than half of those veterans chose to leave the army, even though the war was not over. They would be replaced with younger, less seasoned soldiers. The Confederates also realized that Grant, new to his command, would be confronting Robert E. Lee, who was fighting with an experienced army. All things considered, it was by no means clear in 1864 that the Union would win in Virginia or win the war.

African Americans played an increasingly large role in Union plans, for more than 180,000 black soldiers enlisted just when the North needed them most. By the

spring of 1864, the means of recruitment, training, and pay for these soldiers had become well established (see Map 15.4). The Confederates, however, refused to recognize the same rules of warfare for black soldiers that they acknowledged for whites. In April of 1864, at Fort Pillow in western Tennessee, Confederate cavalry under the command of Nathan Bedford Forrest shot down black Union soldiers and their white commander who attempted to surrender.

With the election clock running, Grant set out in May 1864 to destroy Lee's army. The Battle of the Wilderness near Chancellorsville saw brutal fighting and horrible losses. Fire in the tangled woods trapped wounded men, burning them alive. Grant lost more men than Hooker had in the battle of the previous year, but whereas Hooker treated such losses as a decisive defeat and retreated, Grant pushed on.

The two armies fought again and again over the next two months in the fields of Virginia. The Confederates

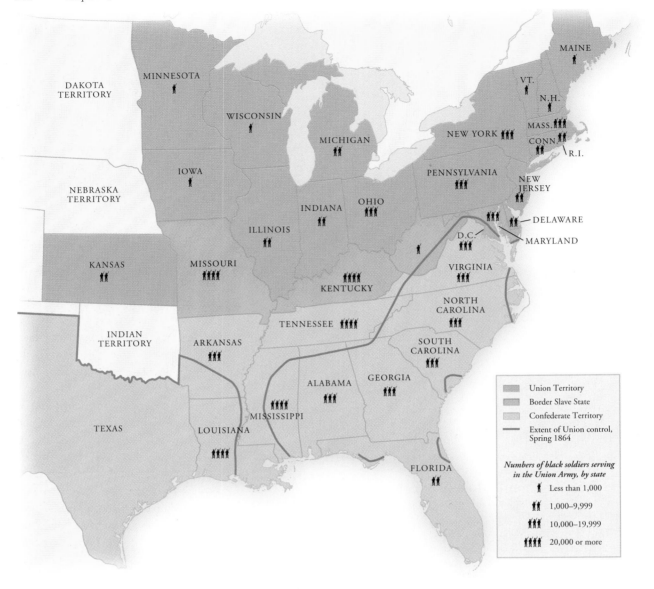

MAP15.4 **Black Soldiers in the Union Army**
African American men streamed into the U.S. Army from all across the country, but they were especially prominent in the occupied South where they had been enslaved.

turned the Union army back to the east of Richmond and rushed up the Shenandoah Valley to threaten Washington itself. Although they failed to take the capital, Confederate raiders "taxed" Maryland towns for thousands of dollars of greenbacks and burned the town of Chambersburg, Pennsylvania, when it refused to pay $500,000. The North repulsed the invasion and dispatched Philip Sheridan to the valley to make sure the Confederates did not regroup. With the Confederates pinned down in Petersburg, near Richmond, Pennsylvania coal miners volunteered to tunnel under the fortifications and plant explosives. Throughout July, they dug; finally, at the end of the month, they detonated a charge and blew an enormous crater in the Confederate lines.

DOING HISTORY ONLINE

Confederate Hopes

Read the document on the Aftermath of the Destruction of a Town Near Washington, D.C., 1864 and "play" the interactive map. Why could Confederates hold out hope of victory as late as 1864?

History Now™　Visit HistoryNOW to access primary sources and exercises related to this topic: http://now.ilrn.com/ayers_etal3e

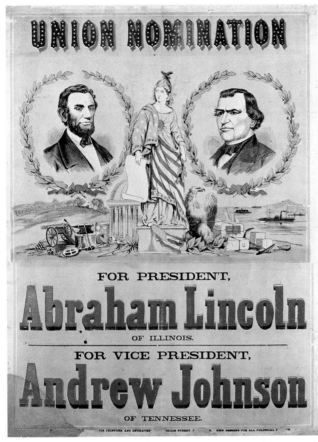

With the war driving to a culmination, the Republicans called themselves the "Union Party," nominated a Unionist from Tennessee alongside Lincoln, and painted pictures of peace and prosperity in their campaign poster.

The attack that followed the explosion, however, failed. Union soldiers piled into the crater, where the rallying Confederates trapped them.

Fortunately for Lincoln, things were going better farther south. Throughout June and July, Sherman pushed relentlessly through north Georgia toward Atlanta. By the end of July, the Southern army had fallen back into Atlanta, preparing to defend it from siege. It seemed only a matter of time before the Union triumphed. But how much time? After rapidly advancing, federal troops slowed as they closed on Atlanta and many feared Sherman was "on the eve of disaster."

The Northern Election of 1864

The president had to fight off challenges even within his own party. Some Republicans considered Lincoln too radical; others considered him too cautious. Through adroit use of patronage, however, Lincoln managed to win renomination in June. The Republican party tried to broaden its appeal to Democrats by nominating **Andrew Johnson,** a former Democrat from Tennessee, to the vice presidency.

In the meantime, the Democrats confidently moved forward. They knew that in the eyes of his critics, Lincoln had caused the war, trampled on constitutional rights, consolidated too much power, and refused to end the war when he had a chance. The Democrats intended to take full advantage of such criticisms by nominating General George McClellan as their candidate. McClellan demonstrated that a person could oppose Lincoln's political purposes of the war without being a coward or traitor. McClellan and the Democrats portrayed themselves as the truly national party, for they were determined to restore the United States to its prewar unity and grandeur. McClellan said he would end the war if the South would reenter the Union—bringing slavery with it. It was a bargain that appealed to many in the North.

Just when it appeared that the Democrats would unseat Lincoln, however, news from the battlefield changed everything. Sherman swung around Atlanta and began destroying the railroads that made the

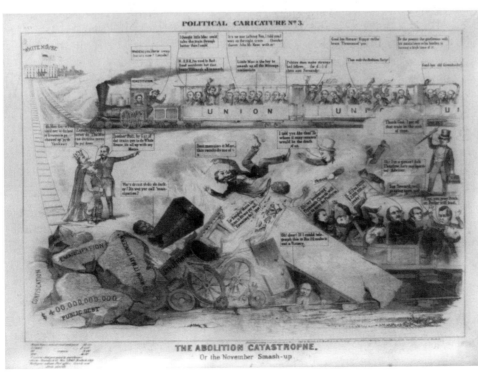

This elaborate cartoon from New York City contrasts George McClellan's supposedly smooth ride to the White House on the "Union" train with President Lincoln's predicted "November Smash-up" caused by emancipation.

The Election of 1864

To attract Democrats who supported the war, Lincoln and the Republican leadership renamed their party the National Union party and chose a Southern Unionist, Senator Andrew Johnson of Tennessee, as vice president. Though Lincoln won easily in the electoral college vote, he faced strong opposition throughout much of the North from George McClellan, who claimed 45 percent of the popular vote.

With the popular vote so close, in many states the outcome hinged on the votes of soldiers. In earlier wars, when soldiers departed home for service, they no longer voted, so no provision existed in law or practice for military personnel to vote away from their home polling site. By 1864, thirteen states permitted soldiers to vote in the field, while five continued to

disenfranchise soldiers. Democrats had opposed absentee voting because they suspected soldiers would vote Republican, but hoped that General McClellan still enjoyed the favor of soldiers. Democrats lobbied senior generals while crying fraud. After three years of war, soldiers in the field, even those who considered themselves loyal to McClellan, would not support the Democratic peace platform. A Union colonel, a staunch Democrat, wrote his wife, "I have not come across an officer or a man that will vote for McClellan." This had always been considered a Democratic corps, but these formerly loyal Democrats voted for Lincoln by a factor of 10 to 1. Compare the distribution of votes for Lincoln in 1864 and 1860 (page 395) and note the areas where Lincoln gained and lost support.

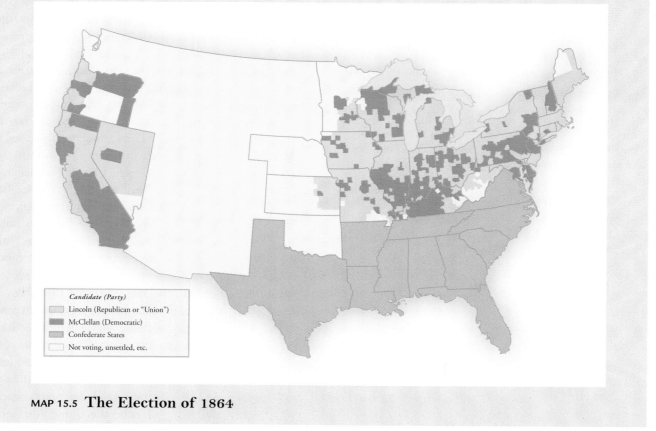

MAP 15.5 The Election of 1864

small city an important junction. The Confederates, afraid they would be encircled and trapped within the city, set much of Atlanta on fire and abandoned it. Sherman and his army marched into the city on September 2. Two weeks later, Sheridan attacked the Confederates in the Shenandoah Valley, systematically destroying the valley's ability to support the Southern army again.

Even with these military victories, Lincoln won only 55 percent of the popular vote (see Map 15.5). Contrary to expectations, Lincoln carried the large majority of the armies' votes. In their letters, soldiers who identified themselves as Democrats rejected McClellan. A Vermont soldier who described himself as "a McClellan man clear to the bone" would not accept "peace by surrendering to the rebels"; instead "he would let his bones manure the soil of Virginia." Lincoln did much better in the electoral college, sweeping every state except three. The Republicans also elected heavy majorities to both houses of Congress and elected the governor and legislative majorities in all states except New Jersey, Delaware, and Kentucky. Lincoln believed the election validated the strength of republican government: "We can not have a free government without elections; and if the rebellion could force us to forego, or postpone a national election, it might fairly claim to have already conquered and ruined us."

The March to the Sea

Jefferson Davis traveled through the Lower South after the fall of Atlanta, exhorting citizens to remain defiant. A week after Lincoln's election, Sherman set out across Georgia, provisioning his army along the way, taking the war to the Southern people themselves. Such a march would be as much a demonstration of Northern power as a military maneuver: "If we can march a well-appointed army right through [Confederate] territory," Sherman argued, "it is a demonstration to the world, foreign and domestic, that we have a power which Davis cannot resist." The triumphant army of 60,000 made its way across the state throughout the fall of 1864. Large numbers of deserters from both sides, fugitive slaves, and outlaws took advantage of the situation to inflict widespread destruction and panic. Sherman arrived at Savannah on December 21. "I beg to present to you, as a Christmas gift, the city of Savannah," Sherman buoyantly telegraphed Lincoln. Contrasting with the devastation of the South, the president's annual message to Congress outlined a portrait of a North gaining strength with "more men now than we had when the war began . . . We are gaining strength, and may, if need be, maintain the contest indefinitely."

From War to Reconstruction: 1865–1867

As the war ground to a halt in early 1865, Americans had to wonder if they remembered how to share a country with their former enemies. They had to wonder, too, how different the country would be with African Americans no longer as slaves. Of all the changes the United States had ever seen, **emancipation** stood as the most profound.

War's Climax

Events moved quickly at the beginning of 1865. In January, Sherman issued **Special Field Order 15,** which reserved land in coastal South Carolina, Georgia, and Florida for former slaves. Those who settled on the land would receive 40-acre plots. Four days later, the Republicans in Congress passed the **Thirteenth Amendment,** abolishing slavery forever. Antislavery activists, black and white, packed the galleries and the House floor. Observers embraced, wept, and cheered. A Congressman wrote his wife that "we can now look other nations in the face without shame."

At the beginning of February, Sherman's troops began to march north into the Carolinas (see Map 15.6). Columbia, South Carolina, burned to the ground. Growing numbers of Confederate soldiers deserted from their armies. Lincoln met with Confederate officials at Hampton Roads on board the steamship *River Queen* to try to bring the war to an end, offering slaveowners compensation for their freed slaves if the Southerners would immediately cease the war. Jefferson Davis refused to submit to the "disgrace of surrender."

At the beginning of March, Lincoln was inaugurated for his second term. Rather than gloating at the impending victory on the battlefield, Lincoln called for his fellow citizens to "bind up the nation's wounds." That same month, Congress created the Bureau of Refugees, Freedmen, and Abandoned Lands to ease the transition from slavery to freedom. Nine days later, the Confederate government, after hotly debating whether to recruit slaves to fight as soldiers if their owners agreed, finally decided to do so after Lee, desperate for men, supported the measure.

Appomattox and Assassination

The Confederates' slave recruitment law did not have time to convert slaves to soldiers, for Grant soon began his final assault on Confederate troops in Virginia. Petersburg fell on April 2, Richmond the next day. Lee hoped to lead his army to the train station at **Appomattox** Court House to resupply them, but on April 9 Grant intercepted Lee's men just short of their destination. Lee, with nowhere else to go and no other armies to come to his aid, surrendered.

A number of Confederate armies had yet to surrender, and Jefferson Davis remained at large, but it was clear that the war had ended. Cities and towns across the North erupted in celebration and relief as crowds filled the streets to sing, embrace, fire salutes, and wave the flag. Southerners began to straggle home. Two days later, Lincoln addressed a Washington audience about what would come next for the freedmen. He admitted that Northerners differed "as to the mode, manner, and means of Reconstruction" and that the white South was "disorganized and discordant."

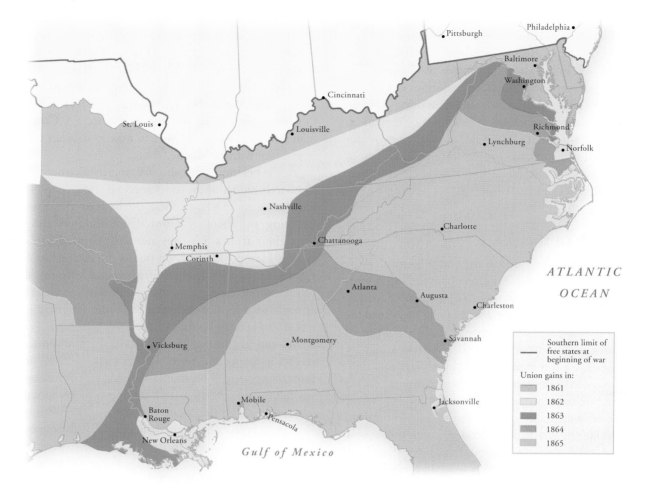

MAP 15.6 The Territory of War

The Confederacy managed to protect large parts of its interior throughout the war, but the Union increasingly controlled the crucial rivers, rail lines, and ports. View an animated version of this map or related maps at http://history.wadsworth.com/passages3e.

Lincoln did not live to take part in the planning, for he was assassinated on April 14 by **John Wilkes Booth,** a failed actor and Southern sympathizer. Booth attacked Lincoln while the president sat with Mrs. Lincoln at Ford's Theater in Washington, shooting him in the back of the head and then leaping to the stage. Lincoln never recovered consciousness; he died early the next morning. After a long and frantic search, Booth was captured and killed in a burning barn.

The Costs and Consequences of the War

The North lost almost 365,000 men to death and disease in the Civil War, and the South lost 260,000. Another 277,000 Northerners were wounded, along with 195,000 Southerners. Black Americans lost 37,000 men in the Union army and at least another 10,000 men, women, and children in the contraband camps.

Widows and orphans, black and white, Northern and Southern, faced decades of struggling without a male breadwinner. Many people found their emotional lives shattered by the war. Alcohol, drug abuse, crime, and violence became widespread problems.

The Southern slave-based economy collapsed. Major Southern cities had been reduced to ash. Railroads had been ripped from the ground, engines and cars burned. Fields had grown up weeds and brush. Farm values fell by half. Livestock, tools, barns, and fences had been stolen or destroyed by the armies of both sides. Recovery was slow. In Georgia, for example, as late as 1870 the state recorded 1 million fewer pigs, 200,000 fewer cattle, and 3 million fewer acres under cultivation than in 1860. Just as damaging in the long run, lines of credit had been severed. Before emancipation, planters had used their slaves as collateral for loans. Now, with the destruction of that form of "collateral," few people outside

This picture of Lincoln, taken 4 days before his assassination, shows the toll four years of war had taken on the 56-year-old president.

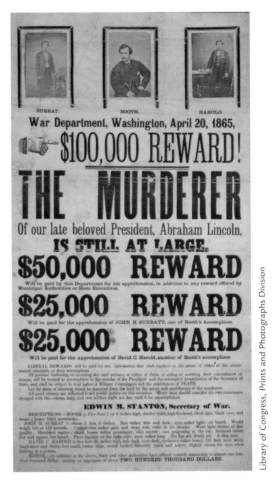

The United States put out this reward for John Wilkes Booth and his conspirators who had killed "our late beloved President."

the South were willing to loan money to planters or other investors.

The Civil War did not mark a sudden turn in the Northern economy, but it did accelerate processes already well under way. The nationalization of markets, the accumulation of wealth, and the consolidation of manufacturing firms became more marked after 1865. Greenbacks, bonds, and a national banking system regularized the flow of capital and spurred the growth of business. The Republicans passed the Department of Agriculture Act, the Morrill College Land Grant Act, the Homestead Act, and the Union Pacific Railroad Act, all using the power of the federal government to encourage settlement of the West, strengthen public education, and spur economic development.

Emancipation and the South

As the battles ground to a halt, slaves became former slaves. Some, especially the young, greeted freedom confidently,

whereas others, especially the elderly, could not help but be wary of anything so strange, no matter how long and how much they had prayed for it. Some seized their freedom at the first opportunity, taking their families to

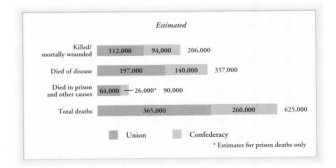

CHART 15.1 The Causes and Numbers of Civil War Deaths

Disease killed even more men than did the bullets of the enemy.

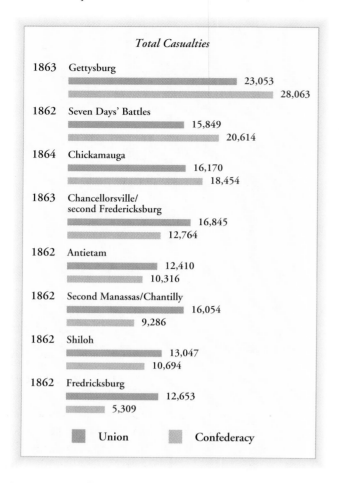

Total Casualties

1863 Gettysburg
23,053
28,063

1862 Seven Days' Battles
15,849
20,614

1864 Chickamauga
16,170
18,454

**1863 Chancellorsville/
second Fredericksburg**
16,845
12,764

1862 Antietam
12,410
10,316

1862 Second Manassas/Chantilly
16,054
9,286

1862 Shiloh
13,047
10,694

1862 Fredricksburg
12,653
5,309

■ Union   ■ Confederacy

CHART 15.2 The Most Costly Battles

Battles exacted horrible costs from early in the war until near its very end.

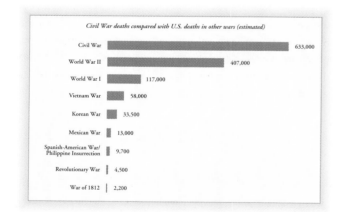

Civil War deaths compared with U.S. deaths in other wars (estimated)

Civil War — 633,000
World War II — 407,000
World War I — 117,000
Vietnam War — 58,000
Korean War — 33,500
Mexican War — 13,000
Spanish-American War/
Philippine Insurrection — 9,700
Revolutionary War — 4,500
War of 1812 — 2,200

CHART 15.3 Civil War Losses

The Civil War exacted a horrible cost, far outstripping every other conflict in which the United States has fought.

Union camps or joining the army. Others celebrated when the Yankees came to their plantations, only to find that their owners and white neighbors retaliated when the soldiers left. Others bided their time. Some refused to believe the stories of freedom at all until their master

Desolation of the South

After four years of war, little remained in many cities of the Confederacy. Atlanta, Columbia, and Richmond had been ravaged by fire; Vicksburg, Petersburg, and Fredericksburg had been pummeled by siege and battle. Union troops had destroyed railways, rivers were blocked by the refuse of war, and fields and farms had been stripped by the marauding troops of both sides or simply overrun by weeds. Roads, wagons, and riverboats were choked with civilian refugees, returning soldiers, and prisoners of war. In the countryside, even on farms and plantations

© Bettmann/CORBIS

untouched by combat, former slaves abandoned masters to seek family members and new opportunities.

Thousands of refugees from the countryside relied on federal aid and rations to survive. White women, particularly those from slaveholding families, found adjusting to defeat and emancipation trying. One woman from North Carolina bitterly lamented her transformation from "social queen" to "domestic drudge." African American women looked forward to working for the benefit of their own families.

or mistress called them together to announce that they were indeed no longer slaves.

Upon hearing the news, the freed people gathered to discuss their options. For many, the highest priority was to reunite their families. Such people set off on journeys

North Wind Picture Archives

Black Southerners took advantage of the presence of Union troops to leave the farms and plantations on which they had been held. Many set out to find family members.

DOING HISTORY ONLINE

Emancipation

Read the excerpts in this module and consider the following questions:
According to the articles, how has life changed for freedmen?
How would you describe Southern white reaction to emancipation?

History ⊗ Now™   Visit HistoryNOW to access primary sources and exercises related to this http://now.ilrn.com/ayers_etal3e

in desperate efforts to find a husband, wife, child, or parent sold away in earlier years. For others, sheer survival was the highest priority. Freedom came in the late spring, barely in time to get crops in the ground. Some former slaves argued that their best bet was to stay where they were for the time being. They had heard rumors that the government would award them land. Between July and September of 1865, however, those dreams died. Union officers promised land to former slaves in Virginia, Louisiana, Mississippi, and South Carolina, but then Washington revoked the promises. The land would be returned to its former owners.

Former slaveowners also responded in many different ways. Some fled to Latin America. Others tried to keep as much of slavery as they could by whipping and chaining workers to keep them from leaving. Still others offered to let former slaves stay in their cabins and work for wages. The presence of black soldiers triggered resentment and fear among former slaveowners who marked the increased independence among blacks that was encouraged by "Negro troops." One slaveowner believed "the people of the South are in very great danger . . . I tell you most seriously that the whole south is resting upon a volcano."

African Americans had no choice but to compromise with white landowners. At first, in the spring of 1865, planters insisted that the former slaves work as they had worked before emancipation, in "gangs." In return for their work, they would receive a portion of the crop, shared among all the workers. Many black people chafed at this arrangement, preferring to work as individuals or families. In such places, landowners found that they had little choice but to permit black families to take primary responsibility for a portion of land.

The former slaves provided the labor and received part of the crop as a result. Planters, though reluctant to give up any control over the day-to-day work on their land, realized they had few choices. They possessed little cash to pay wage workers and no alternative labor.

The Bureau of Refugees, Freedmen, and Abandoned Lands—the **Freedmen's Bureau**—oversaw the transition from a slave economy to a wage economy. Its agents, approximately 900 for the entire South, dispensed medicine, food, and clothing from the vast stores of the federal government to displaced white and black Southerners. The Bureau created courts to adjudicate conflicts and to draw up labor contracts between landholders and laborers. It established schools and coordinated female volunteers who came from the North to teach in them. Although many white Southerners resented and resisted the Freedmen's Bureau, it helped smooth the transition from slavery to freedom, from war to peace.

© The Granger Collection, New York

The Freedmen's Bureau, created in the spring of 1865, adjudicated conflicts between white landowners and black workers.

Enduring Issues   Legacy of Civil War

When the final Confederate armies laid down their arms, the military phase of one of history's bloodiest civil wars ended. The vision of a short but heroic conflict was erased by the human cost of the war. Battle deaths and wounds were far from glorious. Many families, sundered by distance and the uncertainties of war, never recovered. Over 600,000 men died in battle, 4 million slaves gained their liberty, and tens of thousands of men, women, and children were displaced, injured, or died of disease and complications induced by hunger and want.

Both the political system and economy were fundamentally altered by the war. Politics became dominated by sharp-eyed career politicians who reigned over spoils and served the interests of the rising industrial barons. Railroad scandals, Tammany Hall, and graft in every state house seemed to mark a new, tawdry era in politics—Twain's Gilded Age, a bright and false covering masking a base low metal. Post-war Republicans waved the bloody shirt and dubbed their opponents, the Democrats, the party of "Rum, Romanism, and Rebellion," marking them as drunken, Catholic, and at fault for the Civil War. Democrats focused on the destruction of the Republican Party in the South. For much of the last half of the nineteenth century, the North and West dominated the federal government and the patronage and subsidies it controlled. For more than the next 50 years no Southerner would serve as President and a minority would be appointed to the Supreme Court.

Another outcome of the war was the departure from the federal government of representatives of the southern states and the defeat of many Democrats perceived as pro-southern. The Republican party enjoyed nearly 5 years of control of the American state. This dominance extended until the 1870s, with periodic Democratic successes in Congressional elections. From this near single-party control of the government came a series of policy decisions that served the party's core constituents and interest groups: western homesteads, Pacific and western rail construction, tariff protection for selected industries, pensions for Union veterans, and easy expansion of commercial and financial markets. The system of national currency made the federal government a tangible part of each economic transaction among its citizens. The scope and scale of the Civil War revealed the importance of finance, organization, industrialization, and efficiency. Andrew Carnegie learned lessons from his time at the Pennsylvania Railroad that would assist his creation of the world's largest integrated coal, iron, and steel empire after the war.

Although Jefferson Davis was imprisoned for 2 years, no Confederate general or senior official ever suffered more than temporary bars to voting and holding office. No treason trials or committees investigated the causes of the war or sought to punish leading rebels. There are no comparisons in world history to such bloody, hard-fought civil war ending in such a gentle peace for the defeated. Only the commandant of Andersonville prison, Col. Henry Wirz, charged with the deaths of 13,000 prisoners, was hanged for war crimes in 1865. Unlike most defeated rebels, southerners mounted no guerilla campaigns or seriously contemplated a second attempt at secession. Southerners reserved violence and midnight raids for crushing black demands for a just labor system.

Demobilization was swift after the war. The citizen-soldier had completed his duty and over 80 percent of the 1-million-man Union Army was discharged by summer of 1865. By the fall of 1866, the army had shrunk almost to its pre-war level. The integrated Union military, with 180,000 black soldiers and sailors, persisted in a few western cavalry regiments, but soon faded from public memory.

Each section had its caretakers of war's memory. In the South, women and veterans created organizations to celebrate the memory of military valor and dedication to community. Like Jefferson Davis' multi-thousand page "history" of the war, they made the war about defending states' rights and southern culture without mentioning slavery. Memorial parades, children's education, and a flood of memoirs combined to create the myth of the Lost Cause that influenced both popular and historical thinking about the Civil War for the hundred years after Appomattox. Northern veterans created the Grand Army of the Republic to keep the memory of Union victory alive, mobilize veterans for

Black Mobilization

Black Southerners mourned the loss of Abraham Lincoln. Without his leadership, former slaves rightly worried, the forces of reaction might overwhelm their freedom. Southerners of both races watched to see what Andrew Johnson might do.

Throughout the South, former slaves and former free blacks gathered in mass meetings, Union Leagues, and conventions to announce their vision of the new order. They wanted, above all else, equality before the law and the opportunity to vote. Their spokesmen did not demand confiscation of land, nor did they speak

political rallies, pursue federal pensions, and instruct children in patriotic values. The flagpoles that stand outside public schools were the result of GAR activity to increase patriotic values in young children.

After the Civil War, the language and goals of reform spoke less to preparing for the millennium and saving souls and more to the interests of increasingly focused groups: women, blacks, immigrants, labor, skilled workers, temperance, suffrage, settlement houses. Reform became more secular, more targeted on issues of justice on earth: votes, wages, healthy and safe cities and food. The Fifteenth Amendment, granting suffrage to black men, split women's support for racial justice. Elizabeth Cady Stanton and Susan B. Anthony demanded the same rights for women recently granted to black men. Many Republicans who had aggressively supported legalized racial equality refused to risk their political future on a challenge to traditional roles for women. Women such as Mary Livermore recalled in her memoirs that she delivered over 8,000 suffrage lectures from coast to coast. Conservative women such a Lucy Stone advocated a more cautious change to women's public role. They supported suffrage, but rejected changes to the divorce laws that might put women at risk.

The federal pension program for Union veterans, which consumed an accelerating portion of the federal budget, brought little or no cash into the South. Southern states received little direct federal aid for rebuilding. Tariffs, treasury and monetary policy, transportation subsidies for the West, and federal patronage favored the North and West. Even cotton exports were subject to an excise tax that further withdrew scarce cash from the economy. Both Native Americans and former slavers found themselves subject to federal and state policies designed to uplift and civilize them, usually without soliciting their opinion of the policies. Where millions of dollars and hundreds of thousands of acres of western lands were granted to railroads and mining interests, no lands were set aside for former slaves, and native peoples were driven from desirable lands with water and gold to marginal territories stripped of buffalo, timber, and resources.

The Civil War settled the question of chattel slavery and secession forever. While the Thirteenth, Fourteenth, and Fifteenth Amendments and the Civil Rights Act of 1870 set a precedent for racial justice, little progress was made in eradicating racism. During the years of Reconstruction in the South, many black men served in state legislatures of southern states. Equality before the law, in the market, in education, and political participation were denied and fettered by law and custom across the country. Racism fused with popular ideas that social mobility was a function of hard work and character to make a vicious circle for black Americans. Many Americans saw only the absence of blacks in their schools, neighborhoods, and professions and believed that this proved black inferiority and lack of ambition.

The latter part of the nineteenth century witnessed the gradual construction of a system of racial segregation enforced by law and local violence. By 1915, millions of white Americans would applaud the era's first film blockbuster, *Birth of a Nation*. Endorsed by President Woodrow Wilson, the film inverted the war's results, celebrating the Ku Klux Klan and demonizing blacks, mulattoes, and Yankee carpetbaggers.

Many Americans looked back over the abyss of the war years and perceived a country and way of life permanently altered. Much of the rhetoric of free labor and independence grounded in an agricultural republic endured, but the realities of Americans' relationship to their government, freedom for 4 million slaves, the rapidly changing nature of the economy, and imminent explosive growth of the cities and immigrant populations signaled a very different nation than that men had marched to war to create or defend in 1861.

Questions for Reflection

1. Has there been any other event in American history that exerted an impact of the scale of the Civil War's impact?

2. What might the United States have looked like in, say, 1900, had there not been a Civil War?

3. What might we have expected the Civil War to change that it did not?

extensively of economic concerns in general. Let us have our basic rights before the courts and at the ballot box, they said, and we will take care of ourselves. Such concerns and confidence reflected the perspective of the conventions' leadership: former free blacks, skilled artisans, ministers, and teachers. The great mass of

Southern blacks, former slaves, found their concerns neglected.

Black Southerners agreed on the centrality of two institutions, however: the church and the school. At the very moment of freedom, they began to form their own churches. For generations, African Americans had

A Black School

As growing numbers of African Americans gained literacy after emancipation, they increasingly taught in their own schools. To gain access to schools for their children and themselves, former slaves migrated to cities and towns and frequently demanded construction of a schoolhouse as a condition for signing a labor contract. Less than a month after the fall of Richmond, more than 1,000 black children and adults attended schools begun by the city's black churches.

© CORBIS

Across the South, blacks organized and collected money to buy land, constructed schools with their own labor, and funded teacher salaries from self-imposed taxes and tuition. Teachers often advocated racial equality before the law and suffrage, as well as encouraging black political mobilization. Many Northern blacks, including a large number of women, helped found the first black colleges in the South, such as Fiske, Hampton, and Tougaloo. By 1869, black teachers outnumbered whites among the 3,000 teachers in the South.

been forced to worship alongside whites. For many ex-slaves, one of their first acts of freedom was to form their own churches. Before the war, 42,000 black Methodists in South Carolina attended biracial churches. By 1870, only 600 mostly elderly blacks remained. People who owned virtually nothing somehow built churches across the South. A black church in Charleston was the first building raised from the ruins of the city in 1865. Those churches often served as schools as well.

Andrew Johnson

In the meantime, events in Washington undermined the efforts of black Southerners to build a new world for themselves. Andrew Johnson wanted to attract moderates from both the North and the South to a political party that would change the nation as little as possible. Johnson had been selected to run for the vice presidency because he was a Southerner who had remained true to the Union. As a result, both Northerners and Southerners distrusted Johnson. A longtime Democrat before the crisis of the Union, Johnson maintained a limited view of government. The new president's well-known disdain for the wealthy planters of the South appealed to equally disdainful Republicans in Washington. His public statements suggested a harsh peace for former slaveowners and Confederate leaders: "*Treason* is a crime, and *crime* must be punished." Unlike some Republicans, however, Johnson held little sympathy for black people or for expansion of the powers of the federal government. Johnson saw himself pursuing Lincoln's highest goal: reuniting the Union. He believed that reunification should start by winning the support of white Southerners.

Johnson enjoyed a brief period to enact his vision of how to return the South to the Union. Congress was not

© CORBIS

Andrew Johnson attempted to forge a new alliance between white Northerners and white Southerners, callously abandoning black Southerners in the process.

in session at the time of Lincoln's death and would not be for seven months, so Johnson used the opportunity to implement his vision of reunion. In what became known as "Presidential Reconstruction," Johnson offered amnesty to former Confederates who would take an oath of loyalty to the Union, restoring their political and civil rights and immunizing them against the seizure of their property or prosecution for treason. By 1866, Johnson granted more than 7,000 pardons to wealthy Southerners and Confederate senior officers who applied individually for amnesty.

Johnson's plans for political reunion made no provisions at all for black voting. Indeed, his plan threatened to return the South to even greater national power than it had held before because the entire African American population would now be considered individually when the number of representatives was calculated, not merely as three-fifths of a person as before the war.

White Southerners could hardly believe their good fortune. The state conventions elected in 1865 flaunted their opinions of the North. Some refused to fly the American flag, some refused to ratify the Thirteenth Amendment, some even refused to admit that secession had been illegal. Former Confederates filled important posts in state governments. Georgia elected Alexander H. Stephens, the ex-vice president of the aborted nation, to Congress. Even Johnson recognized that far from inaugurating new regimes led by Unionist yeomen, "there seems, in many of the elections something like defiance."

The North erupted in outrage when the new state governments enacted the so-called "**black codes**," laws for controlling the former slaves. The Southern white legislatures granted only the barest minimum of rights to black people: the right to marry, to hold property, to sue and be sued. Most of the laws decreed what African Americans could not do: move from one job to another, own or rent land, testify in court, practice certain occupations. When the members of Congress convened in December of 1865, they reacted as many of their constituents did—with fury. To Northerners, even those inclined to deal leniently with the South, the former Confederates seemed to deny all the war had decided with this blatant attempt to retain racially based laws. And many Northerners blamed Johnson.

Johnson and the Radicals

It was not that most Northerners, even most Republicans, wanted the kind of policies promoted by Radicals such as Thaddeus Stevens, who called for land to be seized from wealthy planters and given to the former slaves, or of Charles Sumner, who wanted immediate and universal suffrage for blacks. But neither did they

Thaddeus Stevens, a congressman from Pennsylvania, was among the leaders of the Radical Republicans.

North Wind Picture Archives

want the sort of capitulation that Johnson had tolerated. A Chicago editor spoke for his readers: "As for Negro suffrage, the mass of Union men in the Northwest do not care a great deal. What scares them is the idea that the rebels are all to be let back . . . and made a power in the government again." Moderates tried to devise plans that would be acceptable to both sides.

The moderates sought to continue the Freedmen's Bureau. The Bureau was understaffed and underfunded, but it offered some measure of hope for former slaves. The Bureau saw itself as a mediator between blacks and whites. Its commissioner, General Oliver Howard, advocated education as the foundation for improving living conditions and prospects for blacks. By 1869, approximately 3,000 schools, serving more than 150,000 students, reported to the Bureau, and these numbers do not include the many private and church-funded schools throughout the South.

The Bureau insisted on the innovation of formal contracts between laborer and landlord. Although these contracts infuriated Southern white men, the Bureau ended up supporting landowners as often as black laborers. The moderates also attempted to institute a Civil Rights bill to define American citizenship for all those born in the United States, thereby including blacks. Citizenship would bring with it equal protection under the laws, though the bill said nothing about black voting. The Bureau struggled against strongly held prejudice. Its Mississippi commissioner despaired of a public that failed to "conceive of the Negro having any rights at all."

In this riot of July 1866, Southern whites killed 34 blacks and 3 white supporters after a Republican meeting in New Orleans.

The Ku Klux Klan emerged in 1866, devoting itself to the maintenance of white supremacy in all its forms.

Republicans supported the Freedmen's Bureau and Civil Rights bills as the starting place for rebuilding the nation. But Johnson vetoed both bills, claiming that they violated the rights of the states and of white Southerners who had been excluded from the decision making. Republicans closed ranks to override Johnson's veto, the first major legislation ever enacted over a presidential veto.

To prevent any future erosion of black rights, the Republicans proposed the Fourteenth Amendment, which, as eventually ratified, guaranteed citizenship to all American-born people and equal protection under the law for those citizens. The amendment decreed that any state that abridged the voting rights of any male inhabitants who were over 21 and citizens would suffer a proportionate reduction in its congressional representation. This clause offered white Southerners the choice of acceptance of black suffrage or reduced congressional representation. It also was the first Constitutional amendment to use the word "male," angering feminist abolitionists who challenged the Republicans' denial of suffrage based on sex. Johnson urged the Southern states to refuse to ratify the amendment, advice they promptly followed.

Throughout the second half of 1866 the North watched, appalled, as much that the Civil War had been fought for seemed to be brushed aside in the South. Not only did the Southern men who met in the state conventions refuse to accept the relatively mild Fourteenth Amendment, but they made clear their determination to fight back in every way they could against further attempts to remake the South. The spring of that year saw riots in Memphis and New Orleans in which policemen and other whites brutally assaulted and killed black people and burned their homes with little or no provocation.

It was in 1866, too, that the **Ku Klux Klan** appeared. Founded by Nathan Bedford Forrest in Tennessee, the Ku Klux Klan dedicated itself to maintaining white supremacy. The Klan dressed in costumes designed to overawe the former slaves, hiding behind their anonymity to avoid retaliation. The Klan became in effect a military wing of the Democratic party, devoting much of its energy to warning and killing white and black men who dared associate with the Republicans or supported black rights.

Johnson toured the country in the fall of 1866 to denounce the Republicans and their policies. Even his supporters saw the tour as a "thoroughly reprehensible" disaster. The voters rejected both Johnson and the Democrats, as the governorship and legislature of every Northern state came under the control of the Republicans. In the next Congress, Republicans would outnumber Democrats sufficiently to override any presidential veto. The Republicans felt they held a mandate to push harder than they had before. They had only a few months, however, until the congressional term ended in March, to decide what to do. They bitterly disagreed over the vote, land distribution, the courts, and education. Some wanted to put the South under military control for the indefinite future, whereas others sought to return things to civilian control as soon as possible. Finally, on March 2, 1867, as time was running out on the session, they passed the Reconstruction Act.

The Reconstruction Act

The **Reconstruction Act** placed the South under military rule. All the Southern states except Tennessee, which had been readmitted to the Union after it ratified the Fourteenth Amendment, were put in five military districts. Once order had been instituted, then the states would proceed to elect conventions to draw up new constitutions. The constitutions written by those conventions had to accept the Fourteenth Amendment and provide for universal manhood suffrage. Once a majority of the state's citizens and both houses of the national Congress had approved the new constitution, the state could be readmitted to the Union.

To ensure that Andrew Johnson did not undermine this plan—which soon became known as "Radical Reconstruction"—Congress sought to curb the president's power. With no threat of his veto after the 1866 elections, the Republicans could do much as they wanted. Congress decreed that it could call itself into special session. There, it limited the president's authority as commander-in-chief of the army and, in the Tenure of Office Act, prevented him from removing officials who had been confirmed by the Senate.

Johnson, characteristically, did not quietly accept such restrictions of his power. When he intentionally violated the Tenure of Office Act by removing Secretary of War Edwin Stanton in the summer of 1867, many in Congress decided that Johnson warranted **impeachment.** Matters stewed throughout the fall, while the first elections under the Reconstruction Act took place in the South.

Reconstruction Begins

After word of the Reconstruction Act circulated in the spring and summer, both black and white men claimed leadership roles within the Republican party. Black Northerners came to the South, looking for appointive and elective office. Ambitious black Southerners, many of whom had been free and relatively prosperous before the Civil War, put themselves forward as the natural leaders of the race. Such men became the backbone of the Republican party in black-belt districts.

White Southerners sneered at white Northerners who supported the Republican cause. They called them "carpetbaggers." These men, according to the insulting name, were supposedly so devoid of connections and property in their Northern homes that they could throw everything they had into a carpetbag—a cheap suitcase—and head south as soon as they read of the opportunities created by Radical Reconstruction. The majority of white Northerners who became Republican leaders in the South, however, had in fact moved to the region months or years before Reconstruction began. Many had been well educated in the North before the war and many held property in the South. Like white Southerners, however, the Northern-born Republicans found the postwar South a difficult place in which to prosper. Black people were no more inclined to work for low wages for white Northerners than for anyone else, and Southern whites often went out of their way to avoid doing business with the Yankees. As a result, when Reconstruction began, a considerable number of Northerners took up the Republican cause as a way to build a political career in the South.

White Southern Republicans, labeled "scalawags" by their enemies, risked being called traitors to their race and region. Few white Republicans emerged in the plantation districts, because they endured ostracism, resistance, and violence. In the upcountry districts, however, former Whigs and Unionists asserted themselves against the planters and Confederates. The Republican party became strong in the mountains of eastern Tennessee, western North Carolina, eastern Kentucky, northern Alabama, and northern Georgia. Many whites in these

African American men could vote in the South during Reconstruction, but often risked their livelihoods or their lives to do so.

districts, though unwilling to join with low-country African Americans or their white leaders, struck alliances of convenience with them. Black voters and white voters generally wanted and needed different things. Blacks, largely propertyless, called for an activist government to raise taxes to provide schools, orphanages, and hospitals. Many whites, on the other hand, owned land and called mainly for lower taxes.

Throughout the South, most whites watched, livid, as local black leaders, ministers, and Republicans mobilized black voters in enormous numbers in the fall of 1867. Membership in Union Leagues swept the region, with local leagues assisting with labor contracts and school construction as well as political activity. An Alabama league demanded recognition of black citizenship: "We claim exactly the same rights, privileges and immunities as are enjoyed by white men—we seek nothing more and will be content with nothing less." While many white Democrats boycotted the elections, the Republicans swept into the constitutional delegate positions. Although many black men voted, African American delegates made up only a relatively small part of the convention's delegates. They held the majority in South Carolina and Louisiana, but much smaller proportions elsewhere. About half of the 265 African Americans elected as delegates to the state conventions had been free before the war, and most were ministers, artisans, farmers, and teachers. Over the next two years, these delegates would meet to write new, much more democratic, constitutions for their states.

At the very moment of the success of the Southern Republicans, however, ominous signs came from the North. Republicans were dismayed at the election returns in the North in 1867, for the Democrats' power surged from coast to coast. Many white voters thought that the Radicals had gone too far in their concern with black rights and wanted officeholders to devote their energies to problems closer to home. Racism linked Democratic appeals against blacks in the Midwest with western diatribes against the Chinese. Integrated public schools and confiscation of plantation lands for former slaves were soundly defeated. The Republicans in Washington heard the message. They began scaling back their support for any further advances in Reconstruction.

Conclusion

The Civil War changed the United States more deeply than any other event in the nineteenth century—indeed, perhaps in all of American history. The conflict brought the deaths of more than 625,000 soldiers, the equivalent of 5 million people today and nearly as many as have died in all other American wars combined. Men who had been seriously wounded and disfigured would haunt the United States for generations to come, reminders of a horrific war. Children would grow up without fathers and many young women would never find husbands.

The war, despite the blessings of Union and freedom it brought, also brought a steep price in social disorder. The Civil War saw bitter rioting in the streets in both the North and the South. It saw political parties arguing over the very future of the nation. And it saw the first assassination of a president.

The Civil War triggered a major expansion of the federal government. The demands of wartime created greenbacks, the draft, and government involvement in transportation and business. It also brought a profound shift in the balance of power among the regions. Since the founding of the nation, the South had wielded influence out of proportion to its population. One president after another owned slaves and others did the bidding of slaveholders. After Appomattox, however, the South's political domination was broken. It would be half a century before a Southern-born man was elected president.

Most important, the war brought what few Americans could have imagined at the end of 1860: the immediate emancipation of 4 million enslaved people. Nowhere else in the world had so many people become free so quickly. Yet freedom emerged from the war through a circuitous route. The war began as a war for Union, but as the deaths mounted and African Americans seized freedom at every opportunity, abolitionists and Republicans increasingly demanded that the war become a war to end slavery. Many white Northerners supported emancipation because it seemed the best

The Democrats exploited, successfully, Republican support for black voting. In this image, caricatured black men press into the polls while white men are pushed aside.

way to end the war. Abraham Lincoln worked desperately to keep the support of both the advocates and foes of emancipation, knowing that moving too quickly would shatter the fragile support that kept him in office. The New York City draft riots and the close elections of 1863 demonstrated that many Northerners resisted the continuation of the war and its embrace of black freedom. Only Union success on the battlefield in late 1864 permitted Lincoln's reelection. His assassination made an already confused situation far more so, ending slavery and restoring the Union without a blueprint and without leadership.

The end of the fighting saw the conflict shift in the South, as people struggled to determine what freedom would mean. For black Southerners, the goal was autonomy and respect. For white Northerners, the goal was to reconstruct the South in an idealized image of the North. For white Southerners, the goal was the reassertion of the power they had held before the war, especially power over the black people in their midst. Such goals could not be reconciled. The era of Reconstruction would be devoted to the struggle among people determined that their vision of freedom would predominate.

The Chapter in Review

In the years between 1863 and 1867:

- African American soldiers began to enlist in great numbers.
- The Union won decisive victories at Gettysburg and Vicksburg.
- Southerners rioted in Richmond; Northerners rioted in New York City.
- The Union drove to victory in the Shenandoah Valley, in Tennessee, in Georgia, and in the Carolinas, but struggled in Virginia until the spring of 1865.
- Robert E. Lee surrendered his troops in April 1865.
- Abraham Lincoln, reelected in the winter of 1864, was assassinated in the spring of 1865.
- Andrew Johnson and the Radicals fought over the nature of Reconstruction.
- White Southerners resisted emancipation and Reconstruction through riots, through the Ku Klux Klan, and at the polls.
- The Republicans created the Reconstruction Act.

Making Connections Across Chapters

LOOKING BACK

Chapter 15 shows that at every point in the war both Northerners and Southerners thought it might end with one more key victory by their side. Instead, each battle seemed merely to bring another one, even bloodier than the one that came before.

1. Did the Civil War have a turning point, a point beyond which it became clear that the United States would defeat the Confederacy?

2. How did emancipation become a central war aim for the Union?

3. To what extent did the Confederacy collapse from within or was it overwhelmed from without?

LOOKING AHEAD

Chapter 16 will show that the most profound change in American history—the end of slavery—came to a nation exhausted by war and to a region unprepared for freedom. Black and white, Northern and Southern, struggled over the shape of the American future.

1. Could white Southerners have minimized the extent of freedom enjoyed by black Southerners if whites had behaved differently in 1865 and 1866?

2. What did black Southerners most want and need from emancipation? Did they receive that?

Recommended Readings

Berlin, Ira, Barbara J. Fields, Steven F. Miller, Joseph P. Reidy, and Leslie S. Rowland, eds. *Freedom* (1985) is a rich and fascinating multivolume documentary collection.

Blight, David W. *Race and Reunion: The Civil War in American Memory* (2001) documents the roles of politics, myth, and race in shaping how the Civil War is remembered.

Cashin, Joan E., ed., *The War Was You and Me: Civilians in the American Civil War* (2002) offers a series of interesting case studies.

Donald, David. *Lincoln* (1995) stands as the most elegant biography.

Faust, Drew Gilpin. *Mothers of Invention: Women of the Slaveholding South in the American Civil War* (1995) offers a challenging and interesting interpretation.

Fellman, Michael. *Inside War: The Guerilla Conflict in Missouri During the American Civil War* (1989) makes palpable the internal struggles in the border areas.

Foner, Eric. *Reconstruction: America's Unfinished Revolution, 1863–1877* (1988) is a magisterial interpretation of the struggle over black freedom.

Gallagher, Gary W. *The Confederate War: How Popular Will, Nationalism, and Military Strategy Could Not Stave Off Defeat* (1997) explores why the Confederacy could fight as long as it did.

Grant, Susan-Mary, and Peter J. Parish, eds. *Legacy of Disunion: The Enduring Significance of the American Civil War* (2003), puts the war in its largest contexts.

Harris, William C. *With Charity for All: Lincoln and the Restoration of the Union* (1997) offers a fresh assessment of Lincoln's attitudes toward the white South.

Hattaway, Herman, and Archer Jones. *How the North Won: A Military History of the Civil War* (1983) authoritatively describes strategy and tactics.

Litwack, Leon. *Been in the Storm So Long: The Aftermath of Slavery* (1979) beautifully evokes the conflicting emotions and motives surrounding freedom.

Neely, Mark E., Jr. *The Union Divided: Party Conflict in the Civil War North* (2002) examines impact of political dissension in North on war effort.

Roark, James L. *Masters Without Slaves: Southern Planters in the Civil War and Reconstruction* (1978) describes the war from the perspective of those who lost the most in southern defeat.

Rose, Willie Lee. *Rehearsal for Reconstruction: The Port Royal Experiment* (1964) is a classic account of the first efforts to create northern policy toward the freed people.

Silber, Nina. *Daughters of the Union: Northern Women Fight the Civil War* (2005) gives a fine overview of women's experiences in the North.

Identifications

Review your understanding of the following key terms, people, events, and dates for this chapter (these terms also appear in the Glossary at the end of the book):

African American soldiers
draft riots
Gettysburg Address
William T. Sherman
Andrew Johnson
emancipation
Special Field Order 15

Thirteenth Amendment
Appomattox
John Wilkes Booth
Freedmen's Bureau
black codes
Radical Republicans
Ku Klux Klan
Reconstruction Act
impeachment

Online Sources Guide

Use this listing to find online documents, images, interactive maps, simulations, and other resources related to this chapter:

American History Resource Center

http://history.wadsworth.com/rc/us

Documents

The Emancipation Proclamation (1863)
The Gettysburg Address (1863)
Resolutions from the 1864 Republican National Convention

Selected Images

Dead at Chancellorsville, Va., May 1863
Pickett's Charge at the Battle of Gettysburg, July 1863
African American recruiting poster
4th U.S. Colored Infantry E Company
Ulysses S. Grant at Cold Harbor Virginia, June 1864
Andersonville Prison, August 1864
Major General Philip Sheridan and his staff, 1864
Freed slave children in Charleston, South Carolina, 1865
Lincoln assassination
The Lincoln conspirators on the gallows
Union troops parade in Washington, 1865
Burning of a Freedmen's school, 1866

Simulation

Reconstruction (Choose to be a Southerner, former slave, carpetbagger, or Native American and make choices based on the circumstances and opportunities afforded.)

Document Exercises

400 Women, 1866

HistoryNOW

http://now.ilrn.com/ayers_etal3e

Primary Source Exercises

The Civil War and the Mississippi River
Confederate Hopes
Chickamauga and the Civil War
Illustrations of Black Soldiers in Northern Journals, 1863–1865
Emancipation

16 Reconstruction Abandoned, 1867–1877

The effort to create a more just society for African Americans after the Civil War was caught in such images as this one showing liberty looking for assistance for the black veterans who had been wounded in the conflict. That spirit of mutual sacrifice between blacks and whites proved difficult to sustain.

© Stock Montage, Inc.

Republicans in 1867 believed that they had taken important steps toward a newer and more just society with their Reconstruction legislation. "We have cut loose from the whole dead past," said Timothy Howe of Wisconsin, "and have cast our anchor out a hundred years." But the struggle over black rights that had begun during the Civil War was far from over. The battle shifted from the halls of Congress back to the South. There, in the decade that followed the war, blacks pursued their dreams of political equality and economic opportunity. Whites sought to preserve as many of the features of slavery as they could. Violence, brutality, election fraud, and raw economic intimidation ended the experiment in multiracial politics known as Reconstruction.

While racial prejudices were the main cause, other forces hastened the abandonment of Reconstruction. In the mid-1870s, a severe economic depression made African American rights seem a less urgent issue. White Americans feared that the national government was becoming too powerful; a renewed commitment to localism and states rights helped southern whites repress black aspirations. For many in the North, the hum of industry, the spread of railroads, and the rise of cities seemed more in tune with national progress than preserving the rights of former slaves.

With a western frontier to open and Native Americans to subdue, the nation retreated from the principles for which the Civil War had been fought. In the case of women's rights, for example, an initial surge of hope that women might join in the political process receded as male institutions reacted against this new movement. By the disputed presidential election of 1876, it was evident that white Americans no longer wished to be involved with the fate of blacks in the South. After a decade of slow, painful withdrawal from a commitment to equality, an informal sectional compromise sealed the return of white rule to the South in 1877. That political adjustment helped structure American responses to race questions down to modern times.

From Johnson to Grant

The struggle between the executive and legislative branches over the fate of the South continued into the second half of 1867. Because President Andrew Johnson sought to impede the Radical Reconstruction program, Republicans in Congress argued that he should be impeached and removed from office. When the president tried to oust Secretary of War Edwin M. Stanton in

Timeline

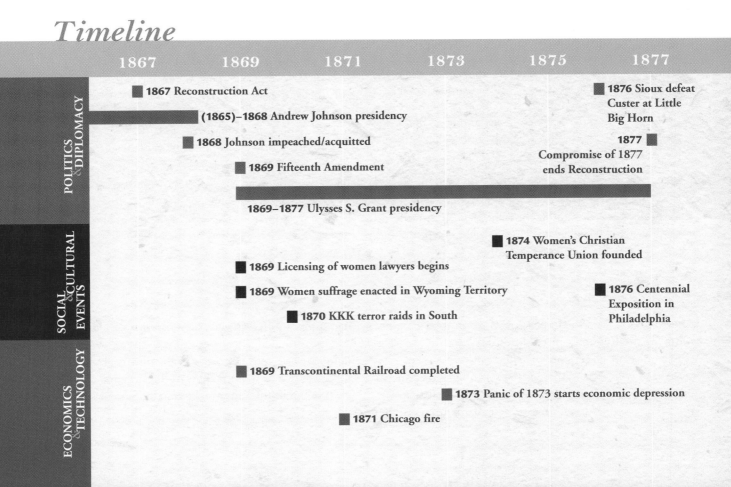

	1867	1869	1871	1873	1875	1877
POLITICS & DIPLOMACY	1867 Reconstruction Act					1876 Sioux defeat Custer at Little Big Horn
	(1865)–1868 Andrew Johnson presidency					
	1868 Johnson impeached/acquitted					1877
	1869 Fifteenth Amendment					Compromise of 1877 ends Reconstruction
	1869–1877 Ulysses S. Grant presidency					
SOCIAL & CULTURAL EVENTS				1874 Women's Christian Temperance Union founded		
	1869 Licensing of women lawyers begins					
	1869 Women suffrage enacted in Wyoming Territory					1876 Centennial Exposition in Philadelphia
	1870 KKK terror raids in South					
ECONOMICS & TECHNOLOGY	1869 Transcontinental Railroad completed					
			1873 Panic of 1873 starts economic depression			
	1871 Chicago fire					

Flashpoints | The Impeachment of Andrew Johnson

The trial of the president had been going on for six weeks. Republicans in the House of Representatives, angry at Andrew Johnson's efforts to block Reconstruction, had impeached him for his opposition to laws they had passed to restrain the powers of the chief executive. The Senate had met as a court to hear the allegations against the president. Now it was May 16, 1868, and the decisive moment for voting had come. The Republicans thought they had the votes, but no one was really sure of the outcome. If the Senate voted to convict Johnson and remove him from office, a permanent shift in power within the government could occur. Yet the president had often acted in ways that frustrated the attempts to bring justice and political equality to African Americans in the South.

© CORBIS SYGMA

Johnson's enemies needed a two-thirds vote to oust the president. As the roll call began, it was apparent that the vote would be very close. The key number to achieve was 36 in favor of conviction. Most of the Republicans were expected to vote to remove Johnson whereas all the Democrats would be recorded for acquittal. As the votes came in, 7 Republicans joined 12 Democrats to make 19 votes for allowing Johnson to remain in office. Thus, the effort to find the president guilty and force him from his post fell one vote short when the finally tally came in as 35 for conviction and 19 against.

Andrew Johnson had been a racist, stubborn, and obstructive president. The case for impeachment and conviction was a strong one on political grounds. Yet in the end it was probably the right result to leave him in office. He had only a little more than nine months remaining in his presidency, with no chance of being elected for a full term in 1868. Some of his most ardent foes wondered about the wisdom of removing a president for anything less than a criminal act committed while in office.

The acquittal of Andrew Johnson discredited impeachment as a political weapon against a president. No serious attempt to impeach a president would be made again until the Watergate scandal of Richard Nixon in 1973–1974 and the impeachment trial of Bill Clinton in 1999. Congress in 1868 had decided to let the political process determine who served in the office of president. That judgment allowed the presidency to become a powerful institution during the twentieth century. What happened on May 16, 1868, thus had a constitutional significance that endured long after Andrew Johnson, with his unfortunate political career, had left the national stage.

Questions for Reflection

1. How had Andrew Johnson convinced the Republicans that impeachment was their only recourse against him in 1868?

2. Why was it possible to conclude that removing Johnson from office was not a desirable result?

3. How much did the nearness of the 1868 presidential election figure in the calculations of the enemies and friends of Andrew Johnson in the Senate?

4. If you had been a member of the Senate in 1868, how would you have voted on the issue of finding Johnson guilty and why?

August 1867, cries for impeachment mounted. For the moment the Republicans could do little until Congress reassembled in December.

After lawmakers gathered, the sentiment for removing the president had lessened, and it appeared that the president would survive for the rest of his term. As he had done so often in the past, Johnson defied Congress and precipitated a confrontation. After the Senate in January 1868 refused to accept his dismissal of Stanton, Johnson replaced him anyway. Presidential stubbornness, Republicans said, was a clear violation of the Tenure of Office Act.

Emboldened by Johnson's defiance, the solidly Republican House voted for his impeachment and leveled eleven charges against him. None of the specifications in the articles of impeachment alleged violations of criminal laws; they dealt instead with Johnson's Reconstruction policies and his obstruction of Congress. The trial came in March. Two months later the Senate failed to achieve the necessary two-thirds vote to convict Johnson. The impeachment attempt lost because moderate Republicans feared that if Johnson were convicted on political grounds it would set a bad precedent. Moreover, Johnson himself eased up on his obstructive tactics. With the 1868 presidential election looming, it seemed less urgent to oust a man who would soon leave office. True to his nature, Johnson did not become more conciliatory. He encouraged southern whites to resist Reconstruction and contributed to the denial of rights to African Americans that marked the 1870s. Few presidents have done less with their historical opportunities than Andrew Johnson.

During the months of Johnson's impeachment and trial, Congress concluded a major territorial acquisition that completed expansion on the North American continent with the purchase of Alaska from Russia. The Alaska purchase was a major strategic and geographic victory for the United States. Amid the controversy over the impeachment of Johnson and the upcoming presidential election, the acquisition of this northern territory did not attract great attention.

The Election of 1868

Both parties looked ahead to the first postwar presidential contest, but the issues of the Civil War defined the contest. The Republicans nominated the great hero of the conflict, Ulysses S. Grant. As the architect of Union victory, his popularity transcended partisanship. Republicans believed that they had selected a candidate "so independent of party politics as to be a guarantee of peace and quiet." In his official letter of acceptance, Grant said "let us have peace" and that phrase became the theme of the Republican campaign. The Republicans were not campaigning on any promise to expand Reconstruction or to do more for the rights of black Americans.

The Democrats turned to the former governor of New York, Horatio Seymour. Along with his running mate, Frank Blair of Missouri, Seymour relied on racial bigotry and white supremacy as the keynotes of his appeal. To win, the Democrats agreed, they had to arouse "the aversion with which the masses contemplate the equality of the negro." Seymour went out to campaign; Grant stayed home. The Republicans won, but not by a

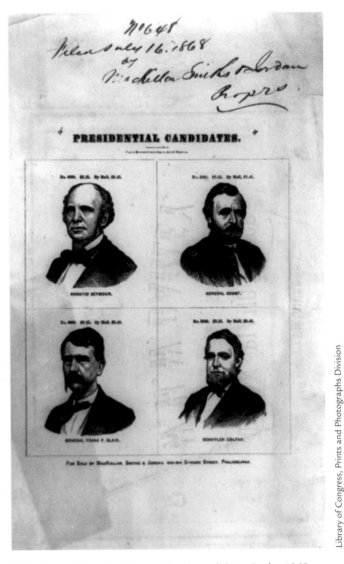

This picture shows the four national candidates in the 1868 presidential election, Horatio Seymour (Democrat), Ulysses S. Grant (Republican), Frank P. Blair (Democrat) and Schuyler Colfax (Republican).

landslide. Grant garnered 53 percent of the vote; Seymour totaled 47 percent. Although Grant carried the electoral college by a margin of 214 to 80, the signs were not good for a continuation of Reconstruction. White voters were less willing to help African Americans; whatever goals African Americans sought, they would have to achieve them on their own. The high point of post–Civil War racial reform was in the past.

The Fifteenth Amendment

After the 1868 election, Republicans pushed for the adoption of the Fifteenth Amendment to the Constitution to finish the political reforms that Reconstruction brought. Under its terms, the federal and state governments could not restrict the right to vote because of race, color, or previous condition of servitude. Congress approved the amendment in February 1869 over Democratic opposition. The purpose of the change was to limit the legal right of the southern states to exclude African Americans from the political process, and Democrats assailed it as a step toward black equality and a social revolution. In fact, the new amendment did not assure African Americans the right to hold office, and it left untouched the restrictions that northern states imposed on the right of males to vote. Literacy tests and property qualifications remained in place in some states outside of the South. State legislatures endorsed the amendment promptly and it was added to the Constitution in 1870. The adoption of the three Civil War amendments had changed the nature of the government as the administration of President Grant got under way, but American politics responded slowly to the impact of these new additions to the nation's fundamental law.

The Grant Era

Ulysses S. Grant came to the White House with almost no political experience. He believed that he should administer the government rather than promote new programs. "I shall on all subjects have a policy to recommend," he said in his inaugural address, "but none to enforce against the will of the people." He promised, unlike Andrew Johnson, to carry out the laws that Congress passed. Nineteenth-century Americans did not expect a president to be an activist and neither did Grant himself. However, those who hoped for a period of calm after the storms of Johnson's presidency were soon disappointed.

Grant's passive view of the presidency allowed Congress to play a dominant role in his administration. As a result, the executive office itself lost some of the authority Lincoln had given it during the Civil War. A generation passed before power shifted back toward the White House. Because Republicans were suspicious of strong presidents, that development aroused little protest from the governing party.

Hard choices confronted the new president. Southern Republicans begged for help from Washington to fight off resurgent Democrats. Yet, many party members in the North believed Reconstruction was no longer wise or practical. Support for black aspirations seemed an electoral loser. As a result, African Americans in the South had to rely more and more on their own resources and personal courage. They made valiant efforts to involve themselves in regional politics, often at the risk of their lives.

Grant tried to stay away from partisan battles. Without a clear objective of a war before him in which victory was the goal, the president seemed confused. As a result, he followed a shifting policy in selecting his cabinet and making appointments. The president did not accept the advice of influential Republicans but depended instead on men who shared his cautious governing style. The president gave cabinet officers wide discretion to pick subordinates without worrying about their political connections. His cabinet mixed some strong appointments such as Secretary of State Hamilton Fish with some other individuals whose qualifications for high office were questionable.

The South posed the most immediate problem for Grant as he learned the presidency. Playing down their dislike of blacks in public statements, the Democrats argued that former Confederates should now be allowed to participate in public life. The strategy produced mixed results in 1869. Republicans did well in Mississippi and won a close race for governor in Texas. Democrats triumphed in Virginia and Tennessee. Overall, the results suggested that Republican strength was eroding as the Democrats got back into politics. Southern white Republicans and their black allies found that Washington often left them on their own to confront the resurgent Democrats. The white South waged a constant struggle to overturn Reconstruction and the Republicans struggled to find an answer for this strategy.

A Troubled Administration

Making matters worse were allegations of scandal against the new administration. In the summer of 1869, two speculators, Jay Gould and Jim Fisk, manipulated the gold market to achieve huge profits for themselves. The price of gold rose until financial turmoil erupted on September 24, 1869. Investors who had promised to sell gold at lower prices faced ruin. Then the government sold its own gold supplies, the price of gold broke, and the market returned to its normal level. In the resulting inquiries about what had happened, the public learned that some members of Grant's family had helped Gould and Fisk carry out their plan. Whispers had it that Julia Grant, the president's wife, might have been involved. The story was not true, but doubts spread about the ethical standards of Grant's presidency.

To the odor of corruption was soon added a sense of White House disarray and incompetence. The administration talked of forcing Spain to give up Cuba and then backed away from the idea. The president wanted to annex the Dominican Republic (Santo Domingo). An agent of the president worked out a treaty of annexation with Santo Domingo's rulers, and the pact was sent to the Senate. Grant pushed hard for approval of the treaty, but the Senate, fearful of the influence of speculators and lobbyists, was suspicious of the president's goals. As a result, the treaty was defeated and the president embarrassed.

Grant's administration had more success in the resolution of American claims for maritime losses against Great Britain. The claims were related to the *Alabama,* one of several Confederate raiders that had been constructed in British shipyards during the Civil War. The *Alabama* had sunk numerous Union vessels. Charles Sumner, chair of the Senate Foreign Relations Committee, wanted to use the claims as leverage in an effort to acquire Canada. In 1871, the State Department worked out an amicable settlement of the issue that left Canada alone.

Grant and Congress

The president deferred too much to Congress. In the process, congressional Republicans split on issues such as the protective tariff and the currency. The mainstream of the party believed that a tariff policy to "protect" American industries against foreign competition was in the best interest of business, workers, and the party itself. A minority of Republicans called the protective policy wrong economically and a potential source of corrupt influence from the affected industries. On the currency, eastern Republicans favored the gold standard and what was known as "hard money," where every dollar was backed by an equal amount of gold. Western Republicans advocated an expansion of the money supply through paper money, or "greenbacks," and, when necessary, even the issuance of dollars backed by silver as an alternative to gold. In the Grant years, these issues loomed as large as debates about the size of the federal budget do in modern times.

Since government was still small, who served in these coveted jobs became a question for public dispute. Some Republicans argued that the government should follow a merit system of appointing its officials. This idea became known as "civil service reform." Reformers maintained that competence and nonpartisanship were better ways to staff these positions. Republicans who wanted to reduce the tariff, rely on the civil service, and treat the South with more leniency defected from the Grant administration. They formed "Liberal Republican" alliances with Democrats in such states as West Virginia and Missouri. In the 1870s, "liberal" meant someone who favored smaller government, lower tariffs, civil service, and most important, an end to Reconstruction. If African Americans were the victims of southern violence, the liberal Republicans were willing to tolerate that result.

Grant and His Party

With his presidency under attack, Grant turned to the Republican leaders in Congress for support. These politicians disliked the Liberal Republican program and its leaders. Angry Liberals threatened to bolt the party. Grant knew that he could never satisfy the demands of the Liberals on Reconstruction or the civil service. Following that logic, Grant conciliated mainstream Republicans. He dismissed cabinet officers who disagreed with him and aligned himself with party members willing to defend Congress and the White House. Officeholders who supported Liberal Republican candidates or Democrats were fired. Despite these actions, the 1870 elections went to Grant's opponents. Liberal Republicans won races in West Virginia and Missouri. The Democrats added 41 seats to their total in the House and picked up another 6 seats in the Senate in the 1870 voting. The Republicans retained control of both houses, but their position was weakening. Grant's enemies even thought he might be defeated in 1872.

The Rise of the Klan

Mounting racial violence in the South added to the president's problems. By the summer of 1870, reports reached Washington of violence against blacks and white Republicans across the South. Roving bands of whites organized since 1866 as the Ku Klux Klan (see Chapter 15) made the attacks. Throughout the South, the Klan asserted white dominance. One Republican in Louisiana pleaded that "murder and intimidation are the order of the day in this state."

The Klan and its offshoots, such as the Knights of the White Camelia, White Leagues, and the White Brotherhood, acted as the paramilitary arm of the Democratic party to crush Republicanism through any means. In Tennessee a black Republican was beaten after he won an election for justice of the peace. His assailants told him "that they didn't dispute I was a very good fellow . . . but they did not intend any nigger to hold office in the United States." Violence then as now often supported racism in the United States.

The Klan stopped at nothing to eliminate its opponents. Leaders of the Republican party were hunted and killed. Four blacks died when the Klan attacked an election meeting in Alabama in October 1870. A "negro chase" in South Carolina left 13 blacks dead. The Klansmen rode in white robes and hoods; their aim, they said, was to frighten their racial foes. The disguises also hid their identity from law enforcement. A wave of shootings and brutality undermined the chances of the Republican party to survive and grow below the Mason-Dixon line.

Picturing the Past   POLITICS & DIPLOMACY

A Cartoonist Attacks the Ku Klux Klan

The use of political cartoons to convey ideas about contemporary issues became more sophisticated after the Civil War. One of the great popular artists of the day was Thomas Nast. In the 1870s, his images attacked the refusal of southerners to grant real freedom to African Americans and the increasing reliance in the South on such terror organizations as the Ku Klux Klan and the White Leagues. Nash dramatized for his audience that southern whites, in or out of a hood, had the same goal—"a white man's government." These

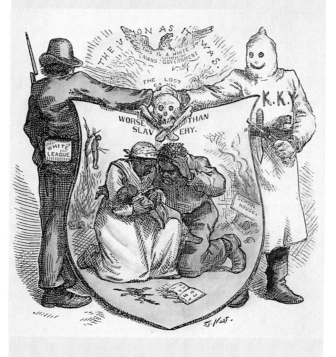

striking pictures helped sustain the Republican party during the presidency of Ulysses S. Grant. Unfortunately for blacks in the South, neither Nast nor the white political leadership in the North persisted in their commitment to equal rights. By the end of the decade, other cartoons depicted blacks in a degrading manner that justified white dominance and paved the way in time for racial segregation.

The Government and the Klan

Viewing the wreckage of their southern parties after the 1870 elections, Republicans recognized that the Klan's terror tactics had worked to intimidate voters and demoralize their leaders. Yet the party was divided about the right answer to terror in the South. As 1871 began,

the Republicans had less stomach for sending troops to the South to affect politics. As an Illinois newspaper observed, "the negro is now a voter and a citizen. Let him hereafter take his chances in the battle of life." This view represented insensitive advice to the blacks in the South who were pushing to get into politics under desperate conditions. Yet, Republican leaders asked themselves whether the cost of maintaining party organizations in the South in the face of such resolute Democratic opposition justified the effort.

The violence of the Klan presented a challenge that could not be ignored. Without firm action, the Republican party in the South might disappear. Congress adopted legislation to curb election fraud, bribery, and coercion in elections. When these measures proved inadequate, the lawmakers passed the Ku Klux Klan Act of 1871. This law outlawed conspiracies to deprive voters of their civil rights and banned efforts to bar any citizen from holding public office. The government also received broader powers to fight the Klan through the use of federal district attorneys to override state laws. As a last resort, military force could also be employed.

The Democrats labeled these laws an unconstitutional interference with the rights of the states. Their passage was "the crowning act of centralization and consolidation," said one critic. A Republican countered by saying: "Tell me nothing of a constitution which fails to shelter beneath its rightful power the people of a country." As long as that commitment existed, southern Republicans, black and white, had a chance to establish themselves as an alternative to the Democrats.

Breaking the Power of the Klan

Republicans determined to end the lawbreaking and violence that the Klan embodied. The Justice Department, which had been established in 1870, argued that the threat the Klan posed to democratic government amounted to war. Officials in Washington mobilized federal district attorneys and United States marshals to institute prosecutions against the Klan. The legal offensive in 1871 brought results; in state after state Klan leaders were indicted. Federal troops assisted the work of the Justice Department in South Carolina. The Klan was discredited as a public presence in southern politics; its violence became more covert and less visible. Even though the prosecutions of the Klan showed that effective federal action could compel southern states to comply with the rule of law, sentiment in the North for such stern measures was receding. Reconstruction did not seem to be a noble crusade for human rights but part of a troubling pattern of corruption and excessive government power. With new economic issues on the political agenda, the problems of the South had to compete with the problems arising from the spread of the railroad network after the Civil War.

Farmers and Railroads

The expansion of railroads after the Civil War posed new challenges for farmers in the South and West. Throughout the 1860s, two transcontinental railroads had put down tracks across the country. The Union Pacific built westward while the Central Pacific started eastward from the West Coast. The two lines faced difficult obstacles of money and geography. The Central Pacific crossed the Sierra Nevada Mountains through rocky gorges and across treacherous rivers. Several thousand Chinese laborers did the most dangerous work. They tunneled into snowdrifts to reach their work sites and then toiled on sheer cliffs with picks and dynamite. On the Union Pacific side, more than 10,000 construction workers, many of them Irish immigrants, laid tracks across Nebraska and Wyoming.

When the two lines met at Promontory, Utah, on May 10, 1869, it was a major news event. Railroad executives drove a golden spike into the ground with a silver sledgehammer. The transcontinental lines were a reality. Loans and subsidies from the federal government to the railroads had enabled the lines to be built quickly. The way the railroads were paid for would become a subject of scandal within a few years.

Following this accomplishment, railroad construction accelerated. In 1869, railroad mileage stood at about 47,000 miles; 4 years later the total had risen to 70,268 miles. The new railroad lines employed tens of thousands of workers and extended across a far larger geographical area than any previous manufacturing enterprise. American business was starting to become much larger than any previous endeavor in the nation; that development would have important consequences. For the moment, as long as business expanded, the railroads seemed a boon to the economy.

Farmers too enjoyed postwar prosperity because of higher prices for wheat and other commodities. Beneath the surface, however, tensions between agrarians and the new industries grew. In late 1867, the Patrons of Husbandry, also known as the Grange, was formed to press the case for the farmers. In its political goals, the Grange focused on complaints about the high mortgages the farmers owed, the prices they paid to middlemen such as the operators of grain elevators, and the discrimination they faced at the hands of railroads in moving their goods to market. These grievances would persist throughout the remainder of the nineteenth century

In the work of building the transcontinental railroad, the grueling labor of Chinese workers was indispensable. They toiled for low pay in difficult conditions in a society that scorned them and often subjected them to harsh discrimination.

California History Section, California State Library

and contribute to the turbulence of politics in the 1880s and 1890s.

To balance the power of the railroads, some states created railroad commissions to oversee how the companies operated. One such state was Illinois, where a new constitution in 1870 instructed the legislature to pass laws establishing maximum rates for the movement of passengers and freight. The legislature set up the Illinois Railroad Commission and gave the new agency wide powers. Neighboring states such as Iowa, Minnesota, and Wisconsin followed the Illinois example during the next several years. Railroad companies challenged some of these laws in court, and a case testing the constitutionality of the Illinois statute worked its way toward the U.S. Supreme Court as *Munn v. Illinois*. The justices handed down their decision in 1877, as the railroad industry faced a nationwide strike. (See Chapter 17.)

Indian Policies

The opening of the West to railroads and the spread of farmers onto the Great Plains meant that Native Americans once again had to resist an encroaching white presence as had happened in the 1830s and 1850s. What had once been called "The Great American Desert" before the Civil War now beckoned as the home for countless farmers. The tribes who were living in the West and the Indians who had been displaced there in the 1830s and 1840s found their hunting grounds and tribal domains under siege as white settlers appeared.

The Peace Policy

Treatment of the Indians after the Civil War mixed benevolence and cruelty. Grant brought more insight and respect to the issue of Native Americans than most previous presidents. His administration pursued what became known as the "peace policy." While a majority of western settlers advocated the removal or outright extermination of the Indian tribes, Grant's conciliatory approach won applause in the East.

The policy issues took shape in the years before Grant became president. Advocates of the Indians contended that the hostile tribes should be located in Dakota Territory and the Indian Territory (now Oklahoma). The government would stop treating the entire West as a giant Indian reservation. Instead, specific areas would be set aside for the Native Americans. On these "reservations" the inhabitants would learn the cultural values of white society, be taught to grow crops, and be paid a small income until they could support themselves.

Grant took up the ideas of the Indian reformers. He appointed Ely Parker, a Seneca, as commissioner of Indian affairs. Congress appropriated $2 million for Indian problems and set up a Board of Indian Commissioners to distribute the funds. Indian agents would be chosen from nominees that Christian churches provided. The peace policy blended kindness and force. If the Indians accepted the presence of church officials on the reservations, the government would leave them alone. Resistance would bring the army to see that Indians stayed on the reservations. To whites, the peace policy was humane. For the Indians it was another in the long series of white efforts to undermine their way of life.

Pressures on the Indians

The 1870s brought increasing tensions between white settlers and the Indians. The 1870 census reported more than 2,660,000 farms; that number rose to more than 4 million within 10 years. A competition for space and resources intensified. With millions of acres under cultivation and the spread of cattle drives across Indian lands, the tribes found themselves squeezed from their traditional nomadic hunting grounds.

The systematic destruction of the buffalo herds dealt another devastating blow to the Indians. In the societies of the Plains tribes, the meat of the bison supplied food, while the hides provided shelter and clothes. Removal of

Library of Congress, Prints and Photographs Division

President Grant's peace policy with the Indians attracted national attention. This drawing illustrates a meeting of the president, his commissioner of Indian Affairs, Ely Parker, and the Indian chiefs Red Cloud, Spotted Tail, and Swift Bear, as published in *Harper's Weekly*, June 18, 1870.

these resources hurt the Indians economically, but the cultural impact was even greater. Buffalo represented the continuity of nature and the renewal of life cycles.

The decline of the herds began during the 1860s as drought, disease, and erosion shrank the habitat of the buffalo. Then the demand for buffalo robes and pemmican (dried buffalo meat, berries, and fat) among whites spurred more intensive hunting. As railroads penetrated the West, hunters could send their products to customers with relative ease. More than 5 million buffalo were slaughtered during the early 1870s, and by the end of the century only a few of these animals were alive. Conservation eventually saved the buffalo from the near extinction that this animal had faced because of the ruthless exploitation during the late nineteenth century.

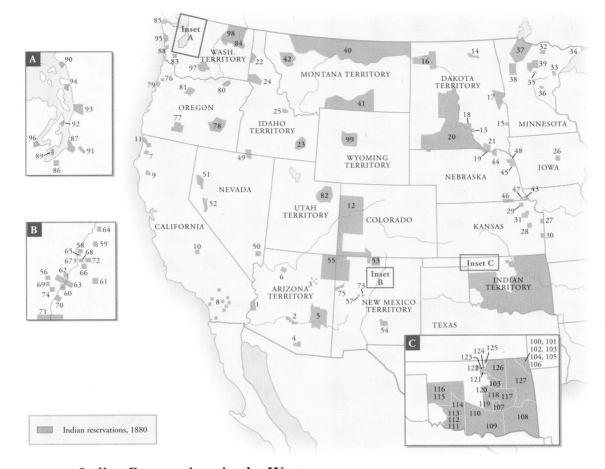

MAP 16.1 Indian Reservations in the West
Following the end of the Civil War and with the adoption of the peace policy of President Ulysses S. Grant, a network of Indian reservations spread across the West. This map shows how extensive the reservation system was.

During the mid-1870s, Native Americans tried a last effort to block the social and economic tides overwhelming their way of life. By that time, Grant's peace policy had faltered. Corruption and politics replaced the original desire to treat the Indians in a more humane manner. The tribes that continued to hunt and pursue their nomadic culture found unhappy whites and a hostile military in their way. The Red River War, led by Cheyenne, Kiowas, and Comanches, erupted on the southern plains. Indian resistance ultimately collapsed when food and supplies ran out.

The discovery of gold in the Black Hills of Dakota brought white settlers into an area where the Sioux had dominated. The Indians refused to leave, and the government sent troops to protect the gold seekers. The Indian leaders, **Crazy Horse** and **Sitting Bull,** rallied their followers to stop the army. Near what the Indians called the Greasy Grass (whites called it the Little Bighorn), Colonel **George Armstrong Custer** led a force of 600 men. With a third of his detachment, he attacked more than 2,000 Sioux warriors. Custer and his soldiers perished. The whites called it "Custer's Last

Stand." The Indian victory, shocking to whites, was only a temporary success. The army pursued the Indians during the ensuing months. By the end of the Grant administration, the Sioux had been conquered. Only in the Southwest did the Apaches successfully resist the power of the military. Indians now faced cruelty, exploitation, and oppression that extended through the rest of the nineteenth century and then beyond 1900. In the face of these relentless pressures from white society, Indians struggled just to survive as a people.

Women in the 1870s

White women during this time did not have anything that approached social or political equality with men. Amid the male-dominated public life, women struggled for some political rights, a foothold in the new industrial economy, and a way to make their voices heard about social issues. Indeed, they faced significant barriers to any kind of meaningful participation in public affairs, a condition that continued into the early twentieth century.

Slaughter of the Buffalo

The manner in which the opening of the West after the Civil War is depicted in textbooks has changed in dramatic ways during the last two decades. More attention is now given to the impact on the environment and on the nomadic lifestyle of the Native American residents of the Great Plains arising from the disappearance of the buffalo herds. The critical role that these animals played in sustaining the Indian way of life meant that the task of white settlers became much less dangerous when the buffalo were

Kansas State Historical Society

gone. Pictures such as this one of 40,000 hides piled up outside Dodge City, Kansas, convey a dramatic sense of the extermination of these animals. Of course, no text can impart the odor of that many hides.

The individuals in the image are small compared to the mass of hides, but their presence reveals how the trade in buffalo had become a key aspect of the western economy. When the buffalo were gone, as happened within a few years, residents moved on to another boom and bust cycle, whether it was in cattle ranching or farming. The picture serves as an evocation of a vanished time and place, but also says something permanent about the nature of the West.

The debates over the adoption of the Fifteenth Amendment underscored the importance of this problem. Women had hoped that they might share in the expansion of political rights. In fact, several major advocates of woman **suffrage,** including **Susan B. Anthony,** opposed the amendment because it left women out. In Anthony's mind, black and Asian men should be barred from voting unless women had the right of suffrage as well. That put her at odds with champions of black suffrage such as Frederick Douglass.

The Fifteenth Amendment Debate

How did women's suffrage become entangled in the debate over the issue of black voting rights and the Fifteenth Amendment?

History ⧗ Now™   Visit HistoryNOW to access primary sources and exercises related to this topic: http://now.ilrn.com/ayers_etal3e

At a meeting of the Equal Rights Association in May 1869, such differences about how to achieve suffrage produced an open break. Two distinct groups of suffragists emerged. The National Woman Suffrage Association reflected the views of Susan B. Anthony and Elizabeth Cady Stanton that the Fifteenth Amendment should be shunned until women were included. The American Woman Suffrage Association, led by Lucy Stone and Alice Stone Blackwell, endorsed the amendment and focused its work on gaining suffrage in the states. Amid this dissension, the new territory of Wyoming granted women the right of suffrage in 1869. The Wyoming legislature wanted Americans to notice their underpopulated territory; woman suffrage was a means to that end. Nonetheless, their action represented a small step forward while the major suffrage groups feuded. A united front among suffrage advocates probably would not have made a great deal of difference in the 1870s, but the lack of cohesion was a weakness in this cause.

Another champion of women's rights was Victoria Claflin Woodhull. A faith healer and spiritualist from Ohio, she and her sister Tennessee Claflin came to New York, where in 1870 Victoria announced her candidacy for president of the United States. She published a weekly newspaper that endorsed the right of women to practice free love outside the subordinate role of marriage. In 1873, she denounced one of the nation's leading ministers, Henry Ward Beecher, for having had an alleged affair with a member of his congregation. The revelation led to one of the most sensational public trials of that century. The proceedings ended in a hung jury and the Claflin sisters had to flee to England to escape public outrage. Woodhull's experience and social disgrace demonstrated the perils that faced women who defied the strict cultural conventions of the post–Civil War era.

For women who did not become celebrities as Woodhull did, the decade of the 1870s offered some opportunities and more reminders of their status as second-class citizens. On the positive side, educational opportunities expanded during this decade. The number of women graduating from high school stood at

DOING HISTORY

Women's Rights and Black Suffrage During Reconstruction

Elizabeth Cady Stanton

"WE DO NOT demand the right step for this hour in demanding suffrage for any class; as a matter of principle I claim it for all. But in a narrow view of the question as a feeling between classes, when Mr. Downing puts the question to me, are you willing to have the colored man enfranchised before the woman, I say no; I would not trust him with all my rights, degraded, oppressed himself, he would be more despotic with the governing power than even our Saxon rulers are."

Elizabeth Cady Stanton

The Granger Collection, New York

Frederick Douglass

"I champion the right of the Negro to vote. It is with us a matter of life and death, and therefore cannot be postponed. I have always championed woman's right to vote; but it will be seen that the present claim for the Negro is one of the most urgent necessity. The assertion of the right of women to vote meets nothing but ridicule; there is no deep seated malignity in the hearts of the people against her; but name the right of the Negro to vote, all hell is turned loose and the Ku-Klux and the Regulators hunt and slay the unoffending black man. The government of this country loves women. They are sisters, mothers, wives and daughters of our rulers; but the Negro is loathed."

One of the unexpected aspects of Reconstruction occurred during debates about the wisdom of extending the vote to black makes but not to women in general. Out of these discussions in time would come the Fifteenth Amendment to the Constitution. That document affirmed the right of citizens to vote without regard to their race, color, or status as former slaves. The amendment, however, said nothing about gender and the assumption was that it applied only to black men. Advocates of woman suffrage believed that women should be accorded the right to vote as well as

Frederick Douglass

© Bettmann/CORBIS

men. The dispute divided African American men such as Frederick Douglass from champions of woman suffrage such as Elizabeth Cady Stanton. In the process, fault lines over race and the status of women in society emerged. As the quotation from Stanton indicates, she believed that black and Asian men should not get the vote if women were denied the franchise. Douglass and his supporters argued that it was more important to get the vote for black men as a further step toward Reconstruction. Their view prevailed when the Fifteenth Amendment was adopted in 1869–1870. The divisions between Stanton and Douglass shed light on the interplay between race and gender that cut across American society in the nineteenth century.

The exchange of views between Stanton and Douglass came at a meeting of the American Equal Rights Association in New York City during May 1867. George Downing was a black man who had asked Stanton about views on male suffrage for blacks and suffrage for all Americans.

Source: Both quotations are from Elizabeth Cady Stanton et al., *History of Woman Suffrage* (6 vols.,

New York: Flower and Wells, 1881–1922), 2: 214 (Stanton), 310–311 (Douglass), as cited in Rosalyn M. Terborg-Penn, "Afro Americans in the Struggle for Woman Suffrage," (Ph.D. dissertation: Howard University, 1977), p. 77 (Stanton), p. 79 (Douglass).

Questions for Reflection

1. What was Stanton's opinion of the capacity of black men to use the vote wisely?

2. To what extent did she share the attitudes of Democrats about the policies of Reconstruction?

3. How did Douglass see the issue as between black suffrage and votes for women?

4. How much did political expediency influence Douglass's argument?

5. In what ways did racial ideas and gender biases shape the debate about the Fifteenth Amendment?

Explore additional primary sources related to this chapter on the Wadsworth American History Resource Center or HistoryNOW websites:
http://history.wadsworth.com/rc/us
http://now.ilrn.com/ayers_etal3e

---

nearly 9,000 in 1870, compared with 7,000 men. Aware of these statistics, state universities and private colleges opened their doors to women students in growing numbers. By 1872, nearly 100 institutions of higher learning admitted women. This trend continued despite the overwrought fears of male academics. Edward Clarke, a retired Harvard medical professor, warned in 1873 that when women expended their "limited energy" on higher education, they put their "female apparatus" at risk.

Cornell University began accepting female applicants in 1875, and one of its first woman graduates was M. Carey Thomas, who received her B.A. in 1877. Five years later, she earned a Ph.D. at a German university. By the 1890s, she had become the president of Bryn Mawr, a woman's college outside Philadelphia. Like other women in male-dominated professions, she encountered rudeness and indifference from her masculine colleagues. She later recalled that "it is a fiery ordeal to educate a lady by coeducation."

Obtaining a degree was not a guarantee of access to professions that males controlled. Myra Bradwell tried to become a lawyer in Illinois, but the state bar association rejected her application. She sued in federal court, and in 1873 the U.S. Supreme Court decided that the law did not grant her the right to be admitted to the bar. One justice wrote that "the paramount destiny and mis-

sion of woman are to fulfill the noble and benign offices of wife and mother." That restrictive decision allowed the Illinois legislature to deny women the chance to practice law. In 1870, there were only five female lawyers in the nation.

The Supreme Court also rebuffed efforts to secure woman suffrage through the courts. Virginia Minor, president of the Woman Suffrage Association of Missouri, tried to vote during the 1872 election, but the registrar of voters turned her away. She sued on the grounds that the action denied her rights as a citizen. In the case of *Minor v. Happersett* (1875), the Supreme Court unanimously concluded that suffrage was not one of the rights of citizenship because "sex has never been made one of the elements of citizenship in the United States." To gain the right to vote, women would have to amend the Constitution or obtain the right of suffrage from the states, a process that took another four decades to complete.

The Rise of Voluntary Associations

Blocked off from politics, women carved out a public space of their own through voluntary associations. Black churchwomen established missionary societies to work both in the United States and abroad. Clubs and literary societies sprang up among white women as well. In New

"GET THEE BEHIND ME, (MRS.) SATAN!"—[SEE PAGE 145.]

WIFE (with heavy burden). "I'D RATHER TRAVEL THE HARDEST PATH OF MATRIMONY THAN FOLLOW YOUR FOOTSTEPS."

Victoria Woodhull came under scathing popular attack for her views on women's issues. This cartoon, published in 1872, by Thomas Nast depicts her as a Satanic enemy of marriage and shows a wife, with children and an alcoholic husband, saying, "I'd rather travel the hardest path of matrimony than follow your footsteps."

York City, women created Sorosis, a club for women only, after the New York Press Club barred females from membership. In 1873, delegates from local Sorosis clubs formed the Association for the Advancement of Women. The New England's Women's Club, located in Boston, had local laws changed during the early 1870s to allow women to serve on the city's School Committee. Later the club founded the Women's Education Association to expand opportunities for their sex in schools and colleges. During the two decades that followed, the women's club movement put down strong roots in all parts of the nation. Soon they also found ways to exert an influence on political and cultural issues.

Despite being turned away at the polls, women made their presence felt. Women in New York, Ohio, and Michigan protested against the sale and use of alcohol, marching in the streets to demand that saloons and liquor dealers close down. They urged drunkards to reform. Middle-class women prayed in front of bars and smashed barrels of liquor to emphasize their determination. Men joined the **temperance** movement, too, but it was the fervor of women that gave the antialcohol crusade new energy. "The women are in desperate earnest," said a Missouri resident who witnessed one of these campaigns.

As their protest successes grew, women sought to make their antidrink campaign more than a momentary event. In August 1874, a group of women active in the temperance cause met at Lake Chautauqua, New York. They set a national meeting that evolved into the Woman's Christian Temperance Union (WCTU). Over the next five years, temperance leagues and local branches of the WCTU worked against intoxicating drink. By the end of the 1870s, a thousand unions had been formed, with an estimated 26,000 members. In 1879, Frances Willard became president of the WCTU, and she took the organization beyond its original goal of temperance and into broader areas of social reform such as woman suffrage and the treatment of children. As it had before the Civil War, the campaign against alcohol revealed some of the underlying social and cultural strains of society.

Women at Work

The 1870s brought greater economic opportunities for women in sales and clerical positions in the workplace. The typewriter appeared in the early part of the decade. E. Remington and Sons, which produced the typewriter, said in 1875 that "no invention has opened for women so broad and easy an avenue to profitable and suitable employment as the 'Type-Writer.'" By 1880, women accounted for 40 percent of the stenographers and typists in the country. These developments laid the foundation for growth in the number of female office workers during the rest of the nineteenth century.

The most typical experience of American women, however, remained toil in the fields and at home. Black women in the South labored in the open alongside their husbands who were tenant farmers or sharecroppers. They did "double duty, a man's share in the field and a woman's part at home." In the expanding cities, women worked in textile factories or became domestic servants. Many urban women also took in boarders. As a result, their intensified routine equaled that of operating a small hotel. In the daily rhythms of American society in this period, as in earlier times, the often unpaid and unrecognized labor of women was indispensable to the nation's advancement.

Middle-class women with domestic servants had some assistance, but they still did a daunting amount of work. Preparing food, washing laundry by hand, keeping

Picturing the Past SOCIAL & CULTURAL EVENTS

The War Against Drink

The temperance crusades of the 1870s against alcohol and its evils brought women into politics in an era when they could not even vote in most of the nation. This cartoon links the campaign of the Women's Christian Temperance Union (WCTU) to the chivalry of the Middle Ages as the mounted women, armored in a righteous cause, destroy whisky, gin, brandy, and rum. The connection of reform with religion and patriotism gave the antialcohol crusade a powerful claim on middle-class sentiments. For those groups whose

© The Granger Collection, New York

religious creed did not bar the use of liquor, the WCTU was an intrusive force seeking to interfere with personal rights. This cartoon thus reveals how long what are now called "social issues" have affected the nation's politics and how they grow out of cultural and economic divisions within American society. In fact, controlling the use of alcohol has been one of the most persistent sources of social contention in the nation's history.

the house warm before electricity, and disposing of waste all demanded hard labor. Mary Mathews, a widowed teacher in the 1870s, "got up early every Monday morning and got my clothes all washed and boiled and in the rising water; and then commenced my school at nine." Other days of the week passed in the same fashion for her and other women.

To assist women in performing these tasks, manuals about housework became popular, along with cooking schools and college courses in home economics. Catherine Beecher collaborated with her famous sister, Harriet Beecher Stowe, author of *Uncle Tom's Cabin,* in writing *The American Woman's Home* (1869). In this volume, they argued that "family labor and care tend, not only to good health, but to the *highest culture of the mind.*" Women, they continued, were "ministers of the family state."

In the new coeducational colleges and universities, home economics programs offered instructions in operating kitchens and dining rooms efficiently. Cooking schools appeared in large cities with separate instruction for "plain cooks" and a "Ladies Class" for affluent women who sought to link "the elegancies of artistic cookery with those economic interests which it is the duty of every woman to study." Assumptions about the secondary role of women pervaded these institutions.

Not all families experienced domestic harmony. Divorce became an option in many states, and defenders of marriage moved to tighten the conditions under which marriages could be dissolved. Laws to limit the sale of birth control devices and restrict abortions reflected the same trend. The New York Society for the Suppression of Vice was formed in 1872 under the leadership of Anthony Comstock. It lobbied successfully for a national law barring information deemed obscene about birth control and abortion from being sent through the mails. Modern debate about these issues has precedents that reach back a century or more and reveal the persistence of such concerns in American history.

Although women had made some gains after the Civil War, they remained second-class citizens within the masculine political order of the period. However, that brand of politics was also coming into question as voters prepared to decide whether President Grant deserved a second term.

Grant and the 1872 Election

By 1872, many commentators and voters in the North were dismayed at the spectacle of national politics. "We are in danger of the way of all Republics," said one critic of the existing system. "First freedom, then glory; when that is past, wealth, vice and corruption." Restoring ethical standards was the goal of the **Liberal Republicans** who wanted to field a candidate against President Grant in 1872. They believed that only in that way could Reconstruction be ended and civil service reform achieved. Leading the campaign were Senator Carl Schurz, a Missouri Republican; Edwin L. Godkin, editor of *The Nation;* and Charles Francis Adams, the son of former president John Quincy Adams.

Liberals argued for smaller government and an end to the protective tariff. "The Government," wrote E. L. Godkin, "must get out of the 'protective' business and the 'subsidy' business and the 'improvement' business and 'development' business . . . It cannot touch them without breeding corruption." But Reconstruction was their main target. They saw what happened in the South as an unwise experiment in racial democracy. Jacob D. Cox, who had been secretary of the interior under Grant, maintained that "the South can only be governed through the part of the community that embodies the intelligence and the capital." In effect, black Americans in the South would have to look to whites in that region for protection of their rights and privileges.

The problem was that the Liberal Republicans did not have a good national candidate to run against Grant. Few party leaders were men with real stature. Schurz was a native of Germany and therefore ineligible to run under the Constitution. The race came down to Charles Francis Adams, Lyman Trumbull of Illinois, and **Horace Greeley,** editor of the New York *Tribune.* After six ballots, Greeley became the nominee. At the age of 61, Greeley was an odd choice. He favored the protective tariff, unlike most reformers, and he was indifferent about the civil service. His main passion was ending Reconstruction. Once a harsh critic of the South, he had now mellowed. His personal opinions, which included vegetarianism and the use of human manure in farming, made him an eccentric to most Americans. "That Grant is an Ass no man can deny," said one Liberal in private, "but better an Ass than a mischievous idiot."

The 1872 Election

Grant was renominated on a platform that stressed the need to preserve Reconstruction: Voters in the North must safeguard what they had won during the Civil War. The Democrats were in a box. If they rejected Greeley, they had no chance to win. Picking him, however, would alienate southern voters who remembered Greeley's passion against the Confederacy. In the end, the Democrats accepted Greeley as their only alternative. The Liberal Republican–Democratic nominee made a vigorous public campaign, while Grant observed the tradition that the incumbent did not take part in the race personally.

The Republicans made their appeal on the issues of the war. One speaker told his audience that they could either "Go vote to burn school houses, desecrate churches and violate women or vote for Horace Greeley, which means the same thing." The black leader Frederick Douglass said of the impending contest: "If the Republican party goes down, freedom goes down with it." When the voters went to the polls, the outcome was a decisive victory for Grant and his party. The president swamped Greeley in the popular vote and in the electoral tally. There were still enough Republicans in the South to enable Grant to carry all but five of the southern states in one of the last honest elections the region would see for many years. The Democrats had reached a low point behind Greeley. Worn out by the rigors of the campaign, he died in late November. The triumph was a mixed one for Grant. He remained in the White House, but scandals would soon plague his second term.

A Surge of Scandals

As the excitement of the 1872 election faded, allegations of corruption in Congress surfaced. The first controversy turned on the efforts of the Crédit Mobilier Company (named after a French company) to purchase influence with lawmakers during the 1860s. The directors of the Union Pacific had established Crédit Mobilier to build the transcontinental line. By paying themselves to construct the railroad, the participants in the venture sold bonds that were marketed at a large profit to investors and insiders. The only problem was that much of the money in effect came from the federal government through loans and guarantees.

To avoid a congressional probe into the company, Crédit Mobilier's managers offered leading Republicans a chance to buy shares in the company at prices well below their market value. When the lawmakers sold their shares, they pocketed the difference, the equivalent of a bribe. A newspaper broke the story in late 1872 and an investigation ensued. The probe produced a few scapegoats but cleared most of the individuals involved. Nevertheless, the episode damaged the credibility of public officials.

Another embarrassing scandal occurred in February 1873. At the end of a congressional session, a last-minute deal gave senators and representatives a retroactive pay increase. The public denounced the action as the "Salary Grab." The *Chicago Tribune* said that it was

DOING HISTORY ONLINE

Grant and the Union Pacific Railroad

How do you think the scandals of the Grant era affected Reconstruction policy?

History ⧗ Now™   Visit HistoryNOW to access primary sources and exercises related to this topic: http://now.ilrn.com/ayers_etal3e

"nothing more nor less than an act of robbery." When Congress reconvened in December 1873, repeal of the salary increase sailed through both houses as politicians backtracked. These two incidents produced widespread calls for reducing government expenditures and rooting out corruption. As the humorist Mark Twain said, "It could probably be shown by facts and figures that there is no distinctly native American criminal class except Congress."

The scandals persisted throughout the remainder of Grant's presidency. Within the Treasury Department, the Whiskey Ring was exposed. Officials involved took kickbacks from liquor interests in return for not collecting federal excise taxes on whiskey. President Grant appointed a new secretary of the treasury, Benjamin H. Bristow, and told him, "Let no guilty man escape if it can be avoided." The administration also faced queries concerning the secretary of war, W. W. Belknap. For some time, Belknap's wife had been receiving cash gifts from a man who sold supplies to the army. When these ties were revealed, a congressional committee sought to start impeachment proceedings. Belknap resigned and Grant accepted his hasty departure. Critics of the president argued that the trail of scandal reached close to the White House. Few doubted Grant's personal honesty, but his cabinet selections often seemed inadequate and sometimes corrupt.

Mark Twain himself captured the spirit of the times in his novel *The Gilded Age,* published in 1873. The main character, Colonel Beriah Sellers, was an engaging confidence man who embodied the faith in progress and economic growth of the postwar years, along with a healthy amount of fraud and deceit that accompanied the rapid expansion of business. In time, the title of Twain's book came to be used for the entire era between the end of Reconstruction and the start of the twentieth century. Beneath its appealing surface, this period grappled with issues of political corruption, social disorder, and economic inequities in ways that challenged older assumptions about the role of government in society.

The Panic of 1873 and Its Consequences

The sense of national crisis deepened in September 1873 when the banking house of Jay Cooke and Company failed. The bank could not pay its debts or return money to its depositors; it had to close. The

THE PANIC.—INSIDE THE STOCK EXCHANGE, READING THE LIST OF FAILURES.

The Panic of 1873 shook Americans's confidence in their economic system. This contemporary drawing of the New York Stock Exchange shows the names of the business failures being read.

Library of Congress, Prints and Photographs Division

disaster came because the bank could not market the bonds of the Northern Pacific Railroad in which it had invested heavily. As this important bank collapsed, others followed suit, businesses cut back on employment, and a downturn began. The problems rivaled similar panics that had occurred in 1819, 1837, and 1857; however, the Panic of 1873 was the worst of them all.

The immediate effects of the problem lasted until 1879. In fact, an extended period of economic hard times had begun that extended through the 1890s. A hallmark of the "Great Depression," as it was then called, was declining prices for agricultural products and manufactured goods. Americans faced an economy in which falling prices placed the heaviest burdens on people who were in debt or who earned their living by selling their labor. An abundance of cheap unskilled labor proved a boon for capitalists who wanted to keep costs down. For the poor, however, it meant that they had little job security and could easily be replaced if they protested against harsh working conditions. Industrialization went forward at a substantial human cost.

The Panic of 1873 occurred because of a speculative post–Civil War boom in railroad building. In 1869, railroad mileage stood at about 47,000 miles; 4 years later it had risen to 70,268 miles. The new railroad lines employed tens of thousands of workers and extended across a far wider geographical area than any previous manufacturing enterprise. When large railroads such as the Northern Pacific failed because of their overexpansion and inability to pay debts, the resulting damage rippled through society. Economic activities that were dependent on the rail lines, such as car making, steel rail production, and passenger services, also fell off. Layoffs of employees and bankruptcies for businesses followed. More than 10,000 companies failed in 1878, the worst year of the depression.

The Plight of the Unemployed

Americans who were thrown out of work during the 1870s had no system of unemployment insurance to cushion the shock of their plight. In some cities, up to a quarter of the workforce looked for jobs without success. Tramps roamed the countryside. The conventional wisdom held that natural forces had to restore prosperity; any form of political intervention would be useless and dangerous. When President Grant proposed that the national government generate jobs through public works, the secretary of the treasury responded: "It is not part of the business of government to find employment for people."

People out of a job during the mid-1870s became desperate. Laborers in the Northeast mounted a campaign called "Work for Bread" that produced large demonstrations in major cities. The marchers asked city and state governments to pay for projects creating parks and constructing streets so jobs would be provided. In January 1874, a demonstration at Tompkins Square in New York City pitted a crowd of 7,000 unemployed laborers against police. Many marchers were arrested; others were injured in the melee.

Labor unrest crackled through the first half of the decade. Strikes marked 1874 and 1875. In Pennsylvania the railroads used their control of police and strikebreakers to put down the "Long Strike" of coal miners and their supporters. Twenty alleged members of a secret society called the Molly Maguires were hanged. Conservatives feared that the nation was on the verge of revolution.

Distress and Protest among the Farmers

Discontent also flared in the farm belt. The price of wheat stood at $1.16 a bushel in 1873; it dropped to 95 cents a bushel a year later. The price of corn stood at 64 cents a bushel in 1874 but went down to 42 cents in 1875. These changes meant substantial drops in farm income. As a result, farmers' land- and equipment-related debts posed an even greater burden. Faced with the economic power of the railroads and grain merchants, the farmer, said one newspaper, was alone, "confronting organized and well-equipped enemies."

The Patrons of Husbandry, also known as the Grange, led the farm protests. Created in 1867, the nonpartisan Grange focused on complaints about the high mortgages that farmers owed, the prices they paid to middlemen such as the operators of grain elevators, and the discrimination they faced at the hands of the railroads in moving their goods to market. The pressure for regulatory legislation reached Congress in 1873–1874 but little was accomplished for the next 15 years.

Inflationary Solutions

The decline in consumer prices and the growing burden of debt on farmers and businessmen in the South and West created pressure for laws to put more money into circulation. That would make debts easier to pay. The Treasury Department's decision to end the coinage of silver aroused particular anger among southern and western advocates of inflation; they called it the "Crime of 1873." Proponents of the move argued that an overabundance of silver in the marketplace required the move to a gold standard. By coining silver into money at a price above its market levels, the government was subsidizing American silver production and cheapening the currency. Opponents of the change responded that eastern bankers were setting financial policy to the detriment of farmers and debtors.

An effort to inject a modest amount of inflation into the economy came in 1875. A currency bill cleared both houses of Congress; it provided some $64 million in additional money for the financial system. President Grant decided, after getting conservative advice to do so, to veto the bill in April 1875. Congress sustained his action. The government would not intervene in the deepening

The hard times that arose from the Panic of 1873 produced labor unrest in many cities. Here an artist recreates the riot in Tompkins Square in New York in 1874.

economic crisis. A similar reluctance to use government authority would contribute to the decline of the northern involvement with Reconstruction in the South.

The Failure of Reconstruction

After the presidential election of 1872, the North's already weakened commitment to Reconstruction ebbed still more. The Panic of 1873 distracted attention from the rights of black Americans. The Grant administration backed away from southern politics, and the Justice Department prosecuted fewer individuals for violations of the Enforcement Act against the Klan and pardoned some of those who had earlier been convicted of terrorist activity.

Northern support for Reconstruction eroded because of charges that the experiment in multiracial government was a failure. Liberal Republicans and northern Democrats spread racist propaganda to block the aspirations of southern blacks. The editor of *The Nation* said that black residents of South Carolina had an "average of intelligence but slightly above the level of animals." Northerners found it easier to believe that the South would be better off when whites were dominant. Black Americans should be left "to the kind feeling of the white race of the South."

A damaging setback to the economic hopes of African Americans came in 1874 with the failure of the Freedmen's Savings and Trust Company in Washington, D.C. Since its founding in 1865, the bank had managed the deposits of thousands of former slaves. It was supposed to provide lessons in thrift for its depositors. However, its manager sought larger returns by investing in speculative railroad projects. The Panic of 1873 caused huge losses, and the bank failed a year later. A few customers received a portion of their savings; most lost all their money.

The Stigma of Corruption

Corruption among southern Republican governments became a favorite theme of critics of Reconstruction. There were some genuine instances of wrongdoing, but these actions were far from widespread or typical. Moreover, the white governments that took over after Reconstruction also displayed lax political ethics and committed more serious misdeeds than their predecessors had. Nevertheless, the corruption issue gave the opponents of black political participation a perfect weapon, which they used to the full. Of course, it would not have mattered if Reconstruction governments had lacked any moral flaws

at all. Any government that represented a biracial community was unacceptable to white southerners.

Although participation of African Americans in southern politics increased dramatically during Reconstruction, their role in the region's public life never approached that of whites. Sixteen blacks served in Congress during the period, most only briefly, and several were unseated by white opponents. Many more held offices in the state legislatures, but even there, their numbers were comparatively modest. In 1868, for example, the Georgia legislature had 216 members, of whom only 32 were black. In only one state, South Carolina, did blacks ever hold a majority in the legislature, and they did so in only one house. One black man, P. B. S. Pinchback, served as governor of Louisiana for a little more than a month. Six African Americans held the office of lieutenant governor in the states of Louisiana, Mississippi, and South Carolina.

Two blacks served in the U.S. Senate. Hiram Revels became the first African American to enter the Senate. Elected to fill out an unexpired term, he served only one year. From 1875 to 1881, Blanche K. Bruce represented

Hiram Revels, senator from Mississippi, was one of the African American politicians whose national career, though brief, was one of the fruits of Reconstruction.

Mississippi for a full term. Thus, by the 1870s, blacks had made their presence felt in politics, but the decline of Reconstruction made that trend a short-lived one.

The Resurgence of the Democrats

The return of the Democrats as a political force further weakened support for Reconstruction. Hard economic times arising from the Panic of 1873 worked against the Republicans. Discontented farmers wanted the government to inflate the currency and raise prices on their crops. Factory workers clamored for more jobs to become available. In this setting, the fate of African Americans in the South became a secondary concern. Angry voters turned to the Democrats in the 1874 congressional races. The party used the issue of Republican corruption to regain control of the House of Representatives for the first time in 16 years. The Democrats added 77 seats in the House and also added 10 seats in the Senate in what one happy party member called a "Tidal Wave."

In the South, the revitalized Democrats "redeemed," as they called it, several states from Republican dominance. They began with Texas in 1873, then won back Arkansas the next year, and elected most of the South's members in the U.S. House of Representatives. Louisiana saw the emergence of the White League, which was determined that "the niggers shall not rule over us." In September 1874, open fighting erupted in New Orleans between armed Republicans and more than 3,000 White League partisans. President Grant sent in federal troops to restore calm. In Alabama, the Democrats also relied on violence and murder to oust the Republicans. Some blacks who attempted to vote in that state's Barbour County election were shot; 7 were killed and nearly 70 wounded. In view of the wide support for the Democratic party among southern whites, honest elections would probably have produced similar results for that party at the polls; but intimidation and violence were key elements in the victories that the Democrats secured in the South in 1874.

The Democrats intended to use their control of the House of Representatives to roll back Reconstruction and also prevent any further expansion of black rights. During the lame-duck congressional session of 1874–1875, Republicans, who were soon to lose power, enacted a path-breaking civil rights law that gave black citizens the right to sue in federal courts when they confronted discrimination in public accommodations such as a hotel or restaurant. The law involved a further expansion of national power; it remained to be seen how federal courts would rule when black plaintiffs sued to enforce their rights under the new civil rights statute.

Early in 1875, the Grant administration used troops to prevent occupation of the Louisiana state capital and illegal seizure of the state government by the Democrats in the midst of an election dispute. The action drew widespread protests from many northern Democrats and a growing number of Republicans who said that the white South should handle its own affairs. Meanwhile, the Democrats used more violence to overturn Republican rule in Mississippi. The state's governor, Adelbert Ames, stated that he was "fighting for the Negro, and to the whole country a white man is better than a 'Nigger.'" Without a national consensus behind civil rights and Reconstruction, the fate of black Americans lay in the hands of white southerners who were determined to keep African Americans in economic, political, and cultural subjugation.

Why Reconstruction Failed

Reconstruction failed to change American race relations because it challenged long-standing racist arrangements in both the North and South. The Civil War had called these traditions into question. In the years after the fighting ended, African Americans had acted to expand their political role and take charge of their own destiny. They sought and to some degree succeeded in becoming more than passive recipients of white oppression or largesse. Then the Panic of 1873, the scandals of the Grant presidency, and waning interest in black rights led white Americans to back away from an expansion of racial justice.

To help the freed slaves overcome the effects of slavery and racial bias would have involved an expansion of national governmental power to an extent far beyond what Americans believed was justified during the nineteenth century. Better to keep government small, argued whites, than to improve the lot of the former slaves in the South. As a result, black Americans experienced segregation and deepening oppression. The political gains of the Reconstruction era, especially the Fourteenth and Fifteenth Amendments, remained unfulfilled promises. That failure would be one of the most bitter legacies of this period of American history.

The Centennial Year

Several themes of late-nineteenth-century life intersected as the 1876 presidential election neared. The centennial of the Declaration of Independence offered citizens an opportunity to reflect on the nation's progress and the social issues that remained unresolved. The race question confronted leaders and citizens even as the

MAP 16.2 **Reconstruction in the South**
This map shows the times at which the states of the former Confederacy reentered the Union and then saw the Democrats regain political control. Note how quickly this process occurred for most of the southern states. The relative brevity of Reconstruction is one of the keys to why more sweeping racial change did not take place.

passions and commitments of Reconstruction faded. The contest for the White House seemed unusually important because it would shape the direction of the country for several decades.

Marking the Centennial

As the nation's 100th birthday neared, the Centennial International Exhibition to be held in Philadelphia attracted public fascination. In May of 1876, some 285 acres of fairgrounds held several hundred buildings crammed with exhibits, specimens, and artifacts from thirty-seven nations. The doors opened on May 10 for 200,000 spectators, including both houses of Congress, who heard a welcoming address by President Grant. The throng poured into the building to see what had been assembled as evidence of the advance of civilization in the United States. One of the stellar attractions was the huge Corliss steam engine. Standing 40 feet tall, it weighed 700 tons. Equally alluring was the "harmonic telegraph" of **Alexander Graham Bell,** as the telephone was then called.

The complexity of American life in the 1870s was not depicted at the exhibit. African Americans had almost no representation. Native American cultures were displayed as "curiosities" consisting of totem poles,

tepees, and trinkets. The Women's Pavilion stressed the joys of homemaking. That exhibit evoked a protest from Elizabeth Cady Stanton and Susan B. Anthony. On July 4, 1876, they read a "Women's Declaration of Independence" that contrasted their aspirations with the traditional attitudes toward women expressed at the fair. Their protest had little effect on public opinion.

Nearly 10 million Americans came to the fair during its run, which ended on November 10. They learned to eat bananas, and hot popcorn became a fad among city dwellers. The fair lost money, but at the same time contributed to a growing sense of national pride and confidence. Those emotions would be tested during the bitter presidential election that dominated the second half of 1876.

The Race for the White House

A key test of the nation's institutions occurred during the disputed presidential election of 1876. The closest electoral result up to that time produced a quarrel that threatened to renew hostilities between North and South. As the election process commenced, the Democrats felt optimism about their chances to regain power for the first time since 1860. Most of the southern

The Centennial Exposition in 1876 summed a century of the nation's progress. The opening ceremonies were recorded in this painting.

states would vote for the Democratic nominee; difficult economic times in the East and Middle West made voters sympathetic to the party out of power.

For its candidate, the party selected **Samuel J. Tilden,** the governor of New York. An opponent of corruption in his home state, he was regarded as a reformer even though smaller government was about all he stood for. A corporate lawyer, he believed in the gold standard, limited federal action, and restraints on spending. The Democratic platform spoke of a "revival of Jeffersonian democracy" and called for "high standards of official morality." Because Tilden was not in good health, the custom that presidential candidates did not campaign during that era worked to his advantage.

Among Republicans, there was some talk of a third term for President Grant, but the scandals of his presidency made him a liability. The front-runner for the nomination was James G. Blaine, a former Speaker of the House of Representatives. With the nomination seemingly in his grasp, Blaine came under fire for financial dealings with an Arkansas railroad while he was in the House. Despite his vigorous response to the charges, Republicans were wary of selecting him to run against Tilden.

At the national convention, Blaine took an early lead. As the balloting continued, his candidacy lost momentum. Instead, the Republicans selected Governor **Rutherford B. Hayes** of Ohio. Hayes had the virtues of a good military record in the Civil War and a spotless record in public office. In the campaign, the Democrats stressed Republican corruption and Tilden's honesty. In response, the Republicans relied on Reconstruction and war memories, as they had in 1868 and 1872. This rhetoric became known as "waving the bloody shirt," in memory of a Republican speaker who had held up a bloodstained Union tunic and urged voters to remember

the sacrifices of the Men in Blue. As one Republican put it, "Soldiers, every scar you have on your heroic bodies was given to you by a Democrat." Hayes saw the wisdom of this strategy: "It leads people away from hard times, which is our deadliest foe."

When the election results rolled in, it seemed at first that Tilden had won. With most of the South in his column, the Democrat had carried New York, Connecticut, and New Jersey. The electoral vote totals indicated that Tilden had won 184 votes, one short of the 185 he needed to become president. Hayes, on the other hand, had 165 electoral votes. Three southern states, Louisiana, Florida, and South Carolina, plus a disputed elector in Oregon, were still in doubt. If they all went for Hayes, he might be in the White House.

Republican operatives moved to contest the outcome in the three undecided states. Telegrams to party members asked for evidence that African American voters had been intimidated. Honest returns from these states, Republicans argued, would show that Hayes had carried each one. The Republicans believed,

In the dramatic 1876 election, the Democrats put forward "Honest Sam Tilden," who lost to Rutherford B. Hayes in the disputed contest.

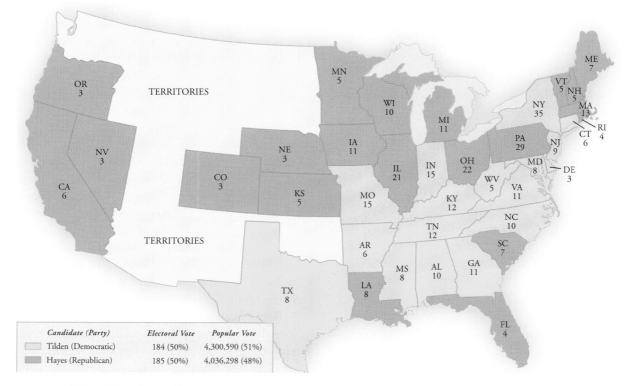

MAP 16.3 The Election of 1876

The presidential election of 1876 between Samuel J. Tilden for the Democrats and Rutherford B. Hayes for the Republicans turned on the votes of Florida, Louisiana, and South Carolina to produce the narrow one-vote victory in the electoral college for Hayes.

View an animated version of this map or related maps at http://history.wadsworth.com/passages3e

moreover, that they had the advantage. In the three states they were contesting, the Republicans could rely on federal troops to safeguard state governments that were loyal to their cause. Otherwise, Democrats could simply occupy the state capitals and count the election returns their way.

The Constitution did not specify how a contested presidential election was to be resolved. Each of the states in question was submitting two sets of election returns that claimed to be official and to reflect the will of the people. The House of Representatives had the responsibility for electing a president if no one won a majority in the electoral college. At the same time, the Senate had the constitutional duty to tabulate the electoral vote. With Republicans in control of the Senate and with Democrats in control of the House, neither party could proceed without the support of the other.

To resolve the crisis, Congress created an electoral commission of 15 members, 10 from the Supreme Court. As originally conceived, the panel was to have 7 Republicans, 7 Democrats, and a politically independent Supreme Court justice named David Davis. Then Davis was elected to the U.S. Senate by the Illinois legislature with Democratic votes in a move to defeat a Republican

incumbent. That tactic won a Senate place for the Democrats but injured Tilden's chances of prevailing in the election controversy. Davis resigned from the commission, and another member of the Supreme Court, this time a Republican, took his place. In a series of 8–7 votes along straight party lines, the electoral commission accepted the Republican returns from Louisiana, Florida, and South Carolina, and allocated the single disputed Oregon electoral vote to Hayes as well. The ruling declared that Hayes had received 185 electoral votes and Tilden 184.

Who had really been elected president in 1876? Tilden had a margin of 250,000 popular votes over Hayes and had carried 16 states. Hayes had won 18 states in addition to the 3 contested southern states. In Louisiana, Florida, and South Carolina, Tilden had received a majority of the white vote, but black Republican voters had been intimidated and terrorized to such an extent that an honest count was in doubt. Essentially the election had ended in a tie. Resolving the issue of which man would be president became an issue for the two political parties to decide.

Despite the decision of the electoral commission, the Democratic House still had to declare Hayes the winner. With the March 4, 1877, inauguration date approaching, the Democrats postponed tallying the electoral vote in an effort either to make Tilden president after March 4 or to extract concessions from the Republicans. To prevent a crisis, negotiations began among leaders from both sides to put Hayes in the White House in return for Republican agreement to end Reconstruction. The discussions were complex, involving a variety of issues such as railroad subsidies for the South, but the underlying issue was Reconstruction. If Hayes became president, the South wanted assurances that Republican rule would not be maintained through federal military intervention. After much discussion, an unwritten understanding along these lines led Congress to decide on March 2, 1877, that Rutherford B. Hayes had been elected as president of the United States.

Conclusion

The events that led to Hayes becoming president had great historical significance. Although the new president did not withdraw federal troops from the South, neither did he use them to keep Republican governments in power. Nor did Hayes attempt to enforce Reconstruction in the courts. Whites regained control of the South's political institutions, and black southerners remained second-class citizens with limited political and economic rights.

Several powerful historical forces produced that sad result. Pervasive racism in both the North and the South labeled African Americans as unfit for self-government. Pursuing Reconstruction into the 1880s would have involved giving to the national government more power over the lives of individual Americans than would have been tolerated in that era. Weary of Reconstruction and its moral claims, the generation of white Americans who had fought the Civil War turned their attention to other national problems. In so doing, they condemned black citizens to continued segregation and oppression.

The era of the Civil War and Reconstruction did have a positive legacy. Slavery was abolished and the Union

preserved. Black Americans had demonstrated that they could fight and die for their country, help make its laws, and function as full citizens when given an honest chance to do so. The Fourteenth and Fifteenth Amendments at least contained the promise of the further expansion of the rights of black Americans in the future. But for the moment the nation had missed a historical opportunity to create a more equitable, multiracial society.

As with any postwar period, the decade between 1867 and 1877 mixed constructive changes and lamentable results. The end of the fighting released energies that produced the construction of the transcontinental railroad, a surge of industrialization, and a renewal of white settlement in the West. At the same time, Native Americans saw their way of life threatened with extinction. Political corruption infected public life, and observers lamented a general slackening of the moral tone of the nation. After economic prosperity following the war, the Panic of 1873 and the hard times that ensued tested the endurance of average Americans.

Society found that women also wanted to share some of the fruits of emancipation. Campaigns for woman suffrage got under way, only to encounter adamant male resistance. Women turned to campaigns against alcohol as another means of making a political difference. In cultural realms, these were the years of Mark Twain, William Dean Howells, Henry James, and Bret Harte—American prose stylists who looked toward the creation of a national literature. Amid the discord and clamor of a society bent on economic expansion and a return to peacetime endeavors, Americans engaged problems that would carry on to the end of the century and beyond: racial justice, industrial growth, urbanization, and the proper balance between business and government. That citizens of that generation failed to solve all their difficulties is not surprising. What this chapter reveals is that they poured their energies and imagination into the task of creating a better nation in the wake of a destructive war that had shaped their lives in such a distinctive way.

The Chapter in Review

In the years between 1867 and 1877:

- The country embarked on an experiment in a multiracial democracy.
- African Americans in the South made a brave effort to participate in politics and economic life.
- Currents of racism and the opposition of white southerners doomed Reconstruction.

- Settlement of the West accelerated with the end of the Civil War and put pressure on Native American culture.
- Transcontinental railroads brought the nation together as a more cohesive economic unit.
- The Panic of 1873 began a decade-long slump that brought protests from unhappy farmers and workers.

- Although they were excluded from voting, women played a significant part in public life through voluntary associations.
- By the nation's centennial in 1876, the disputed election between Hayes and Tilden marked the ebbing away of the issues of the Civil War and the eventual abandonment of Reconstruction.

Making Connections Across Chapters

LOOKING BACK

The working out of Reconstruction and its ultimate failure forms the key theme of Chapter 16. Because the decision not to pursue racial justice had such long-range consequences for the United States, the substance of this chapter is central to an understanding of subsequent history.

1. How did the Republicans intend to reconstruct the South after the Civil War? What obstacles did they encounter?

2. How did the election of Ulysses S. Grant help or hinder the Reconstruction effort?

3. Why did Reconstruction not succeed in the South? What obstacles did white southerners place in the way of black participation in politics?

4. What defects in the national political system between 1865 and 1877 helped derail the chances of Reconstruction?

5. Which groups fully participated in making decisions about the direction of society? Which groups were either not represented or ignored?

LOOKING AHEAD

The next chapter takes up the process of industrialization and its effects on the economy and society. Elements in this chapter explain the rise of industrialism and set up the treatment of this issue in Chapter 17. Let's examine a few of them now.

1. What economic changes in the 1870s undercut Reconstruction and made industrialism seem more important?

2. How did the political system respond to the economic downturn of the 1870s, and how did these attitudes carry forward during the rest of the nineteenth century?

3. How did the political system then resemble modern alignments between Republicans and Democrats, and in what important ways were there differences?

Recommended Readings

Edwards, Laura F. *Gendered Strife and Confusion: The Political Culture of Reconstruction* (1997). Looks at the role of women after the Civil War.

Foner, Eric. *Reconstruction: America's Unfinished Revolution, 1863–1877* (1988). An excellent treatment of the whole period, especially the decline of Reconstruction.

Perman, Michael. *Emancipation and Reconstruction, 1862–1879,* 2d ed. (2003). A good brief account of the issues and problems of Reconstruction.

Richardson, Heather Cox. *The Death of Reconstruction: Race, Labor, and Politics in the Post-Civil War North, 1865–1901* (2001). Considers how changing attitudes toward African Americans and labor undercut Reconstruction.

Simpson, Brooks D. *The Reconstruction Presidents* (1998). A treatment of Reconstruction from the perspective of the chief executives.

Smith, Jean Edward. *Grant* (2001). A full-scale, sympathetic biography of the general and president.

Summers, Mark Wahlgren. *The Era of Good Stealings* (1993). Uses the corruption issue of the 1870s to produce a political history of the decade.

Wang, Xi. *The Trial of Democracy: Black Suffrage and Northern Republicans, 1860–1910* (1997). Discusses how voting issues shaped the adoption and then the abandonment of Reconstruction.

Identifications

Review your understanding of the following key terms, people, events, and dates for this chapter (these terms also appear in the Glossary at the end of the book):

Crazy Horse
Sitting Bull
George Armstrong Custer
suffrage

Susan B. Anthony
temperance
Liberal Republicans
Horace Greeley
Alexander Graham Bell
Samuel J. Tilden
Rutherford B. Hayes

Online Sources Guide

Use this listing to find online documents, images, interactive maps, simulations, and other resources related to this chapter:

American History Resource Center

http://history.wadsworth.com/rc/us

Documents

Fort Laramie Treaty

Interactive Maps

Presidential Elections by State, 1824–1876
Territorial Possessions of the United States, 1775–1870

Selected Images

Charles Sumner
Andrew Johnson
Depiction of Andrew Johnson as unsympathetic to South (cartoon)
Black schoolhouse during Reconstruction
Edwin Stanton
Ticket to Andrew Johnson's impeachment proceedings
Hiram Revel and Blanche K. Bruce, U.S. Congressmen from Mississippi

Driving the golden spike to form the first transcontinental railroad
Destroyed buffalo herds
George Armstrong Custer
Sitting Bull

Simulation

Reconstruction (Choose to be a southerner, former slave, carpetbagger, or Native American and make choices based on the circumstances and opportunities afforded.)

Document Exercises

1866 Emigration to Washington Territory of Four Hundred Women on the Steamer "Continental"

HistoryNOW

http://now.ilrn.com/ayers_etal3e

Primary Source Exercises

Support for Black Suffrage 1867 & 1869
Northern Whites and Black Rights
The Fifteenth Amendment Debate
Grant and the Union Pacific Railroad

Passages 1877 to 1909

To white Americans during the late 1870s, the Civil War and Reconstruction seemed to be receding into history. That was a comforting illusion for them, but a misleading one. African Americans knew that the problem of race remained alive and painful for the entire society. At the same time, important forces were transforming the country. The national journey was leaving an agricultural, rural, underdeveloped economy and culture. An industrialized society was in the making. Out of these changes would come the modern United States.

Industry shaped the lives of more and more Americans during the years from the presidency of Rutherford B. Hayes (1877–1881) through the end of Theodore Roosevelt's administration in March 1909. The railroads appeared first and then in rapid succession steel, oil, machinery, telephones, and, after 1900, the automobile.

Families left the country to move to the city. The look and the population of major urban centers were altered. Society kept pace to the rhythm of the machine and the factory.

Business leaders dominated the popular mind with the innovations and their faults. Reporters chronicled the doings of Andrew Carnegie, John D. Rockefeller, and J. P. Morgan in the way that they had written about politicians. Average Americans wondered and worried about their in the face of such concentrated economic power.

Industrialism brought material abundance for some and great want for many others. The ability of factories to provide cheaper, standardized goods such as canned foods, sewing machines, tools, and clothes pleased those who could afford to buy them. For those left behind or shut out from society's bounty, the riches of the new system seemed a mockery. Industry knit the country

The spread of technology during the late nineteenth century opened up new opportunities for women, as this picture of female operators at a telephone exchange reveals.

One of the driving forces of American economic growth between 1877 and 1909 was the flow of immigrants into the United States. Their travels from Europe were often harsh and uncomfortable. These immigrants had to sleep on deck as their ship made its way across the North Atlantic.

together in a shared experience as consumers in a national market; it alienated others who saw their hard work bringing no fair reward for themselves.

Immigration into the United States changed the shape of the nation's population and instilled an even richer diversity in the society. Older residents reacted with suspicion and hostility to the influx of newcomers from southern and eastern Europe, and ethnic tensions underlay voting decisions, residence patterns, and social conflict. The immigrants filled the nation's cities, tilled and settled the western plains, and did much of the work of the industrial sector. By the first decade of the twentieth century, pressures mounted for immigration restriction.

Politics hardly kept pace with accelerating change in the business sector. An even balance between Republicans and Democrats from 1877 to 1894 kept the national government passive and slow to react. An expansion of governmental power took place on the state level despite claims that the era favored noninvolvement in social policy. An economic depression during the 1890s destroyed the national stalemate, wounded the Democrats, and gave the Republicans a majority of the electorate. A third party, the Populists, failed meanwhile to halt the erosion of the once powerful agricultural sector.

By the end of the 1890s, the United States stepped into the arena of international politics when it acquired an empire from Spain after a war over Cuba. The heyday of imperialism did not last; the consequences of

The demand for labor swept up even young children. Here boys work in a shop in unsafe conditions with faces dulled by the toil they endured. Efforts to regulate child labor largely came to nothing before 1909.

overseas expansion endured. New responsibilities in the Atlantic and Pacific meant a growth in the power of the federal government to fulfill the world role. Currents of isolationism persisted to limit foreign adventures, but the movement toward world power continued.

The nation mixed confidence and doubt as the twentieth century opened. From the small nation of 1800 had emerged a continental giant, the world's largest internal free market, and a functioning experiment in political democracy. All that bred optimism by 1900. Social critics, however, pointed out the other side of the ledger. Too many in the United States—African

Urbanization, 1860–1910

Class and population size	1860	1870	1880	1890	1900	1910
URBAN TERRITORY	392	663	939	1,348	1,737	2,262
Places of 1,000,000 or more	– – –	– – –	1	3	3	3
Places of 500,000–999,999	2	2	3	1	3	5
Places of 250,000–499,999	1	5	4	7	9	11
Places of 100,000–249,999	6	7	12	17	23	31
Places of 50,000–99,999	7	11	15	30	40	59
Places of 25,000–49,999	19	27	42	66	82	119
Places of 10,000–24,999	58	116	146	230	280	369
Places of 5,000–9,999	136	186	249	340	465	605
Places of 2,500–4,999	163	309	467	654	832	1060
RURAL TERRITORY				6,490	8,931	11,830
places of 1,000–2,499				1,603	2,128	2,717
places under 1,000				4,887		9,113

– – – Represents zero.

Americans, Hispanics, Indians, immigrants, and women—did not share in all that the country offered. In retrospect, the verdict would be that the late nineteenth century fell short of its historic duties. To Americans who lived through these times, who saw Hayes enter the White House and Roosevelt give way to William Howard Taft, it appeared that they had left the country better than they found it when they first addressed its problems during the 1870s. Their part in the American journey will be the underlying theme of the four chapters that follow.

America and the World: 1877–1909

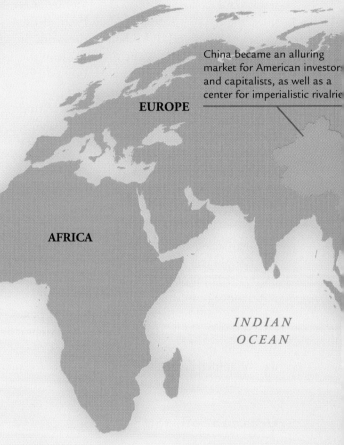

EUROPE

China became an alluring market for American investors and capitalists, as well as a center for imperialistic rivalries

AFRICA

INDIAN OCEAN

ASIA

NORTH AMERICA

ATLANTIC OCEAN

The acquisitions of the Philippines involved the United States in a protracted war against the resistance of the inhabitants of these islands.

PACIFIC OCEAN

In Latin America, the United States pursued a canal across Central America and asserted its dominance in the region.

SOUTH AMERICA

AUSTRALIA

ANTARCTICA

Chronology

	1877	1882	1888
POLITICS & DIPLOMACY	**1877:** Rutherford B. Hayes elected president after disputed election Nationwide railroad strike Supreme Court decides case of *Munn v. Illinois* **1878:** Bland-Allison Act for silver passed over Hayes's veto Congress passes Timber and Stone Act **1879:** Exoduster movement of blacks to Kansas **1880:** James A. Garfield defeats Winfield Scott Hancock in presidential election **1881:** Garfield assassinated in July; dies in September Chester A. Arthur becomes president	**1882:** Chinese Exclusion Act passed **1883:** Supreme Court rules in *Civil Rights Cases* that Civil Rights Act of 1875 does not apply in southern states Mongrel Tariff law enacted Pendleton Civil Service Law passed **1884:** Grover Cleveland defeats James G. Blaine in presidential election **1886:** Haymarket Riot in Chicago Great Southwestern Strike occurs **1887:** President Cleveland calls for reform of tariff in annual message **1888:** Benjamin Harrison defeats Cleveland in presidential election	**1889:** Opening of Oklahoma Territory to non-Native American settlement Jane Addams starts Hull House settlement house program **1890:** Passage of Sherman Silver Purchase Act, McKinley Tariff, and Sherman Antitrust Act Battle of Wounded Knee Candidates identified with the Farmers Alliance make electoral gains in South and West Republicans suffer major losses in congressional elections **1891:** Federal Elections Bill to regulate elections in South blocked in the Senate **1892:** Cleveland defeats Harrison in 1892 presidential election
SOCIAL & CULTURAL EVENTS	**1877:** New York YMCA offers first typing course for women **1880:** Metropolitan Museum of Art opens in New York City **1881:** Helen Hunt Jackson publishes *A Century of Dishonor* about treatment of Native Americans Boston Symphony Orchestra established	**1882:** American Association of University Women founded **1883:** Lester Frank Ward publishes *Dynamic Sociology* **1884:** Mark Twain's *The Adventures of Huckleberry Finn* is published **1885:** William Dean Howell's book *The Rise of Silas Lapham* appears **1886:** Death of poet Emily Dickinson Coca-Cola goes on sale in Atlanta Statue of Liberty dedicated **1888:** Edward Bellamy's *Looking Backward* becomes best-seller	**1889:** Singer electric sewing machine introduced Safety bicycle enjoys wide popularity **1890:** Daughters of the American Revolution founded Poems by Emily Dickinson published **1891:** James Naismith invents basketball University of Chicago opens **1892:** *Ida Wells-Barnett* begins anti-lynching campaign Ellis Island in New York opens to receive immigrants
ECONOMICS & TECHNOLOGY	**1877:** Bell Telephone Company organized Thomas Edison invents the phonograph **1878:** General Assembly of Knights of Labor founded **1879:** Thomas Edison invents incandescent lamp Henry George publishes *Progress and Poverty* **1880:** George Eastman patents first successful roll film camera **1881:** American Federation of Labor (AFL) formed	**1882:** Standard Oil becomes first trust Observance of Labor Day begins **1883:** Railroads create national time zones **1884:** Bureau of Labor established in federal government **1885:** American Telephone and Telegraph Company organized **1886:** Southern railroad tracks moved closer together to comply with national standards **1887:** Interstate Commerce Act passed to regulate railroads First electrical streetcar service in Richmond, Virginia	**1888:** George Eastman perfects Kodak hand camera **1889:** Electric sewing machine developed **1891:** Thomas Edison receives first radio patent in United States **1892:** Homestead strike is broken in Carnegie Steel

1893

1892: (*continued*) Democrats gain control of both houses of Congress
1893: Sherman Silver Purchase Act repealed amid economic hard times
1894: Coxey's Army makes protest march to Washington
Republicans make large gains in congressional elections
1895: Venezuelan crisis with Great Britain
1896: McKinley defeats Bryan in presidential election
Supreme Court upholds segregation in *Plessy v. Ferguson*
1897: Dingley Tariff enacted
1898: Hawaiian Islands annexed
Spanish-American War begins;

1893: Columbian Exposition offers "Great White City" in Chicago
1894: Radcliffe College for Women opens in Cambridge, Massachusetts
1895: Stephen Crane publishes *The Red Badge of Courage* about Civil War
Booker T. Washington proposes "Atlanta Compromise"
Anti-Saloon League established
1896: Trading stamps offered by stores in the United States
First commercial movie showing occurs
1897: Jell-O is introduced
1898: Condensed soups are offered to consumers

1893: Panic of 1893 begins four-year depression
1894: Pullman Strike occurs in midst of economic hard times
1895: Supreme Court ruling in *U.S. v. E. C. Knight* case weakens Sherman Antitrust Act
1896: Gold discovered in Klondike in Canada and helps ease deflation
1897: Depression of 1890s eases
1898: Burst of industrial consolidation as mergers accelerate

1899

1898: (*continued*) United States defeats Spain and acquires Philippine Islands
Philippine Insurrection begins
1899: Open Door policy in Far East announced by John Hay
1900: McKinley defeats Bryan again in presidential race
Theodore Roosevelt is McKinley's running mate
1901: McKinley assassinated
Theodore Roosevelt becomes president
1902: Northern Securities case filed by Justice Department
Anthracite coal strike settled
1903: Panama Canal Zone acquired
Canadian boundary dispute settled

1899: Scott Joplin publishes "Maple Leaf Rag"
Edward Kennedy "Duke" Ellington born in Washington, D.C.
1900: Olds Motor Works begins mass-producing cars
1901: Dorothy Dix advice column begins in New York *Evening Journal*
Jazz trumpeter Louis Armstrong born in New Orleans
1902: Teddy Bear toy developed
Muckraking journalism begins in *McClure's Magazine*
1903: National Women's Trade Union League formed
Great Train Robbery, first western movie, premieres

1899: Founding of National Consumers League
1900: Gold Standard Act passed
1901: United States Steel created as first billion dollar corporation
1902: Newlands Act passed to promote irrigation in the West
U.S. files suit against Northern Securities Company
1903: Department of Commerce and Labor created
Wright brothers make first airplane flight

1904

1904: Theodore Roosevelt elected president over Alton B. Parker
1905: Roosevelt mediates Russo-Japanese War
1906: Hepburn Act passed to regulate railroads
Pure Food and Drugs Act and Meat Inspection Act passed
1907: Gentleman's Agreement with Japan over immigration policy
1908: William Howard Taft defeats Bryan for presidency
1909: Theodore Roosevelt leaves office; Taft inaugurated president

1904: Ice cream cone marketed
1905: Edith Wharton publishes *The House of Mirth* about New York upper class
1906: Theodore Roosevelt attacks muckrakers
1907: Self-contained electric clothes washer developed
1908: Henry Ford introduces Model T automobile
First Mother's Day observed
Jack Johnson becomes heavyweight boxing champion
1909: National Association for the Advancement of Colored People founded

1904: In *Northern Securities Co. v. U.S.,* Supreme Court upholds government position against railroad holding company and strengthens Sherman Antitrust Act
1905: In *Lochner v. New York,* Supreme Court rules that maximum hours law for bakers is not constitutional
1906: Bureau of Immigration established
1907: Panic of 1907 results in calls for banking reform
1908: In *Muller v. Oregon,* U.S. Supreme Court upholds law specifying maximum hours that women can work
1909: Payne-Aldrich Tariff enacted

17

An Economy Transformed: The Rise of Big Business, 1877–1887

Industrialism was a major theme of American life in these years. This image of men working in the steel mill under intense heat and dangerous conditions captured the spirit of the decade.

Once Rutherford B. Hayes took office on March 4, 1877, national interest turned away from Reconstruction and toward scientific inventions, the rise of cities, and the explosion of industrial growth. Politicians struggled with the new issues that this economic upheaval produced. The agenda of social and economic problems that the nation faced was formidable. For the next 25 years, the American people had to come to terms with industrial growth as a constant in their lives. These changes affected all regions, the way people spent their time, and the political decisions of their leaders.

Railroads and A "Locomotive People"

The belching, noisy, indispensable railroad stood as the symbol of industrialization. One British writer noted that "The Americans are an eminently locomotive people." The completion of the transcontinental railroads underscored the energetic pace of rail development. During the 1880s, the amount of tracks rose steadily, reaching 185,000 miles in 1890. By that time, the United States had a more extensive railroad network than all the European countries combined, even with Russia included.

Creating the Railroad Network

Railroads crafted from iron and steel drew the nation together as bridges and tunnels swept away the obstacles that rivers and mountains posed. Another step toward unification was the establishment of a standard gauge, or width, for all tracks. Some railroads used the standard gauge of 4 feet 8.5 inches; others relied on tracks as much as 6 feet apart. Inconsistencies translated into extra equipment, higher costs, and lost time. By 1880, the standard gauge dominated, with the South the principal holdout. Then, on a single day in 1886, all the southern lines moved their rails to the standard gauge. To put all railroads on the same set of working times, in 1883 the railroads agreed to establish four time zones across the country. Railroads could not operate effectively when times varied from state to state, as had been the case before. Having standardized time zones promoted national cohesion.

Timeline

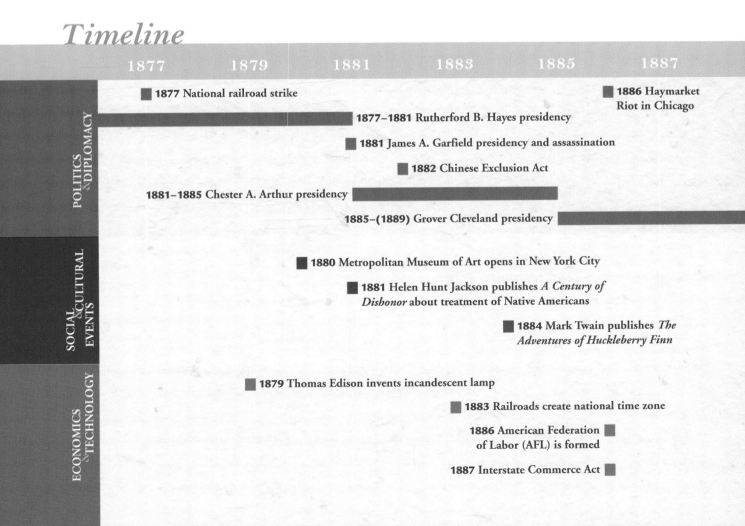

| | 1877 | 1879 | 1881 | 1883 | 1885 | 1887 |

POLITICS & DIPLOMACY

1877 National railroad strike

1886 Haymarket Riot in Chicago

1877–1881 Rutherford B. Hayes presidency

1881 James A. Garfield presidency and assassination

1882 Chinese Exclusion Act

1881–1885 Chester A. Arthur presidency

1885–(1889) Grover Cleveland presidency

SOCIAL & CULTURAL EVENTS

1880 Metropolitan Museum of Art opens in New York City

1881 Helen Hunt Jackson publishes *A Century of Dishonor* about treatment of Native Americans

1884 Mark Twain publishes *The Adventures of Huckleberry Finn*

ECONOMICS & TECHNOLOGY

1879 Thomas Edison invents incandescent lamp

1883 Railroads create national time zone

1886 American Federation of Labor (AFL) is formed

1887 Interstate Commerce Act

Consistency streamlined the operation of the railroads. Freight moved with greater ease through bills of lading (a statement of what was being shipped), which all lines accepted. Standard freight classifications appeared and passenger schedules became more rational and predictable, especially after the establishment of standard time zones. After the enactment of the **Interstate Commerce Act** (1887) and the passage of other relevant legislation during the 1890s, all railroads adopted automatic couplers, air brakes, and other safety devices.

Railroad travel also became more comfortable for passengers and more accommodating to food and other perishables. The refrigerator car preserved food for transport to distant consumers. George Pullman pioneered the sleeping car. The railroads built huge terminals through which millions of passengers and countless tons of freight moved each day. These structures, symbolic of industrialism, underlined the effect of the railroad on everyday life.

More than $4 billion was invested in the railroad system by 1877. The entire national debt was just over $2.1 billion. To finance this huge commitment of money, the railroads drew upon the funds of private investors both in the United States and Europe. An impressive amount, however, came from government. To aid in the construction of the western transcontinental railroads, for example, the federal government made direct loans of almost $65 million to the rail lines along with millions of acres of land grants. Total federal land grants to railroads exceeded 130 million acres, and state and local governments added another 49 million acres. Other examples of state aid included loans, tax reductions, and issuing of bonds. The total amount of all such assistance approached $500 million.

By 1880 the railroad network had assumed a well-defined shape. East of the Mississippi River to the Atlantic seaboard ran four *trunk* (main line) railroads that carried goods and passengers from smaller towns connected by *feeder* (subsidiary) lines. The trunk lines were the Pennsylvania Railroad, the Erie Railroad, the New York Central Railroad, and the Baltimore and Ohio Railroad. The transcontinental lines included the Union Pacific/Central Pacific, Northern Pacific, and Southern Pacific. In the South the trunk lines emerged more slowly. During the 1880s and 1890s, southern railroads built five trunk lines, including the Southern Railway and the Louisville and Nashville Railroad. These lines, interconnected and interdependent, provided Americans with cheaper, more efficient transportation to accelerate industrial expansion.

Organizing the Railroad Business

Since they conducted their affairs on a grand scale, railroads became the first big business. Factories in a single location had fewer than a thousand workers; the railroads extended over thousands of miles and employed tens of thousands of workers. The railroads required an immense amount of equipment and facilities; no single individual could supervise it all directly.

New management systems arose to address these problems. Executives set up clear lines of authority. Separate operating divisions purchased supplies, maintained track and equipment, handled freight, dealt with passengers, and transmitted information. Local superintendents took care of day-to-day matters; general superintendents resolved larger policy issues; and railroad executives made the overall decisions. By the 1870s, the organizational structure of the railroads included elaborate mechanisms for cost accounting.

Railroads stimulated the national economy. From the late 1860s through the early 1890s, the railroads consumed more than half the nation's output of steel. Railroads also used about 20 percent of coal production. Their repair shops created a market for industrial workers in Middle Western cities such as Chicago and Cleveland.

The United States was becoming a national economic market in which similar goods and services were available to people throughout the nation. The development of a national market also encouraged the growth of big business to meet consumer demand for canned goods, ready-made clothes, and industrial machinery. Thus, the expansion of the railroads was a key element in the dramatic changes that industrialization produced.

The Railroad as a Social and Political Issue

Because they shaped the economy in so many ways, railroads also raised concerns about their effect on government and society. Land grants affected numerous communities, and railroad executives provoked controversy. Cornelius Vanderbilt of the New York Central, Collis P. Huntington of the Southern Pacific, and Jay Gould of the Union Pacific, among others, were renowned for the ruthless methods they employed against their competitors. Their critics called them "**robber barons,**" a name that came to be applied to entrepreneurs from this period in general.

Railroad leaders believed that too much competition caused their economic and political problems. Because a railroad ran constantly and had to maintain its equipment, facilities, and labor force on a continuing basis, its operating costs were inescapable, or "fixed." To survive, a railroad needed a reliable and constant flow of freight and passengers and the revenue they

The Railroad Network

A key economic development of the late nineteenth century was the spread of the railroad network and the national market that it helped to create for goods and services. This map shows the extent of progress by 1880 as well as the emergence of the system of time zones that facilitated the smooth operation of the railroad timetables. Note the more developed state of rail lines in the Northeast and Middle West where industrialism had taken hold.

The map also makes clear why the railroads were such a significant political issue in so many states and why those who used the rail lines often resented business practices that adversely affected their interests. Within a few years, in 1887, Congress created the Interstate Commerce Commission to provide some degree of regulatory supervision for the railroads. Real control of the railroads did not come until the early twentieth century, and by then, the automobile and truck had challenged the railroad's dominance of transportation.

MAP 17.1 The Railroad Network

supplied. One strategy was to build tracks and add lines in order to gain more business. Each new line required more business to pay off the cost of building it. Railroads therefore waged a constant economic struggle for the available traffic.

One obvious solution was to lure customers, either openly or secretly, with reduced prices. From 1865 to 1900, railroad rates declined. Some of the reduction in rates stemmed from the general deflation in prices that marked this period. Other price declines came about because the railroads and their workers found efficient ways to move freight and passengers.

To maintain their share of the total available business, railroads relied on secret procedures. The rebate was a discount on published rates given to a favored shipper in the form of cash payments. Other customers had to pay the listed rate or were charged more. When faced with potentially destructive competition, the railroads engaged in price wars or tried to acquire their rivals. Railroads (and other industries) also used the pool, a private agreement to divide the available business in an industry or locality. Working together, the railroads hoped to maintain rates at a level that ensured profits for all members of the pool.

Attractive as a means of restraining competition, pools were impossible to enforce because their secrecy violated state laws against economic conspiracies. Weaker railroads were willing to cheat on the pool if it would bring in more business. Railroad men wanted the federal government to legalize pooling through legislation, an approach that was politically unpopular because it meant price-fixing and monopolies. By the middle of the 1880s, therefore, the larger railroads moved toward consolidation as the answer to too many railroads and too much competition.

Regulating the Railroads

While rebates, pools, and consolidation made sense to the railroads, they angered those who traveled or shipped their goods by rail. Shippers who did not receive rebates regarded the tactic as unfair. Railroads often charged more for a short haul than for a longer one because fewer exchanges and stops made the long haul cheaper. Because of the advantage they gave to some shippers over others, railroad rates also served the interest of cities such as Chicago or Kansas City but hurt others in the Middle West. Railroads also posed dangers to the traveling public. In 1888 alone, some 5,200 Americans were killed while traveling or working on the railroad. Another 26,000 were injured.

Americans debated how society should respond to the railroads. Few advocated government ownership that would compete with private corporations. Using legislatures or courts to oversee the railroads was not popular either. Instead, Americans developed a middle way between those apparent extremes that became a hallmark of the emerging industrial society.

The answer to the railroad problem during this period was the regulatory commission. Ideally, such a body, created by the state legislature, was composed of experts who decided issues of rates, finance, and service in a neutral, nonpartisan way. The first railroad commission had been created in New Hampshire in 1844; there were four in existence in 1861. After the war, the commission concept spread; there were 28 such agencies by 1896.

Railroad commissions came in two kinds. One variety advised railroads of possible violations and publicized information about railroad operations. The most notable example of this form of commission was the one in Massachusetts. Critics claimed that the Massachusetts commission was weak; it lacked the power to set rates. The second kind of railroad commission was established

Table 17.1 Railroad Mileage, 1869–1887

1869	46,844
1870	52,922
1871	60,301
1872	66,171
1873	70,268
1874	72,385
1875	74,096
1876	76,808
1877	97,308
1878	103,649
1879	104,756
1880	115,647
1881	130,455
1882	140,878
1883	149,101
1884	156,414
1885	160,506
1886	167,952
1887	184,935

Source: *The Statistical History of the United States*, p. 427.

in Illinois in 1871. It had the power to set rates and put them into effect in 1873. Because of this authority, which other Midwestern states adopted, the Illinois model became known as the strong form of the railroad commission.

During the 1870s railroads challenged the authority of these state commissions. The most important case involved Illinois, and it reached the U.S. Supreme Court in 1876. The decision of *Munn v. Illinois* (1877) declared that the state could establish a commission to regulate railroad rates. Railroads, the Court said, were "engaged in a public employment affecting the public interest." Because Congress had not yet acted to regulate interstate commerce in railroad matters, a state could make "such rules and regulations as may be necessary for the protection of the general welfare of the people within its own jurisdiction."

Despite such successes, reservations about the effectiveness of state commissions grew. Critics complained that the railroads had too much influence over the state commissions. There was some corruption, and the process of regulation was often cumbersome. Most important, however, the state commissions could not deal effectively with interstate railroads. In 1886, in the case of *Wabash, St. Louis, and Pacific Railway Company v. Illinois*, the Supreme Court ruled that enforcement of the Illinois law infringed on interstate commerce. Congress needed to establish a national policy for regulating the railroads.

The Interstate Commerce Act

Political and economic forces combined to stimulate the demand for railroad regulation in the mid-1880s. Western and southern farmers lobbied for such a policy. However, their influence was less significant than that of merchants and shippers on the East Coast, who wanted a government agency to ensure that they received fair treatment from the rail companies. Some railroads preferred federal regulation to the confusion of competing state commissions. Congress responded to these pressures by passing the Interstate Commerce Act in 1887. This law set up an Interstate Commerce Commission (ICC), composed of five members, that could investigate complaints of railroad misconduct or file suit against the companies. The law forbade rebates and pooling. The new regulatory agency was the first of its kind on the federal level. Despite a shaky start for the ICC in its first decade, commissions became a favored means of dealing with the problems of managing an industrial society. By the mid-1880s, it was apparent that the rise of big business was posing even greater challenges for government and society.

Big Business Arrives

Although the growth of the railroads laid the basis for further industrial expansion, the overall success of big business came during difficult economic times. The depression of the 1870s ebbed by 1879, but the prosperity that followed was brief. From 1881 to 1885, there was another slowdown, with numerous business failures. Two years of good times preceded another recession during 1887 and 1888. In the late nineteenth century, businesses grew larger even though prosperity was elusive.

Deflation brought about by increased productivity, a tight money supply, and an abundant labor force set the tone for business. Companies with high fixed costs, such as railroads, oil, and steel, experienced intense, constant pressure to reduce competition and avoid its impact through arrangements such as pools. In a few industries it even seemed possible to escape competition and achieve monopoly.

John D. Rockefeller and the Emergence of Trusts

The oil industry, especially, was being shaped by competitive forces, and **John D. Rockefeller** of Standard Oil became the leading example of monopoly power and economic concentration. Starting in the mid-1860s, he expanded from his base in Ohio and founded the Standard Oil Company in 1870. Despite his success in

A young-looking John D. Rockefeller was on his way during this period to a dominance of the American oil industry.

Courtesy of the Rockefeller Archive Center

obtaining rebates from the railroads when he assured them of a dependable supply of oil to haul, Rockefeller still faced an industry with too many producers. He set up Standard Oil to impose control on a chaotic business. Through rebates, other secret payments from railroads, and price-cutting, he sought to dominate his business. By the end of the 1870s, he controlled about 90 percent of the nation's oil-refining capacity and had achieved a **horizontal integration** of the oil business.

As a virtual monopoly in oil appeared, a political response followed. Under state law, Standard Oil of Ohio could not legally own stock in other oil companies or conduct its business in other states. Yet registering to do business in other states could reveal aspects of the company's business to competitors and expose it to legal challenges in the courts. In 1882, a lawyer for Rockefeller, S. T. C. Dodd, formulated a new use for an old legal device. Standard Oil became the first example of the trust in American business. In the common law, trustees for a widow, orphan, or an estate had wider powers than a corporation, a point that Dodd and Rockefeller exploited.

The 41 stockholders of Standard Oil created a board of 9 trustees. In return the board held the company's stock in trust and exercised "general supervision over the affairs of said Standard Oil Companies." The trustees could select the board of directors and set policy for all Standard Oil subsidiaries in other states. In this way the trust escaped the restrictions of state laws everywhere. The term *trust* soon lost its legal connotation and became a general label for the rise of big business.

The trust device was used only for a brief period. In the late 1870s, several states passed laws that allowed corporations to own branches in other states, to hold the stock of other corporations, and to pursue a policy of consolidation to the extent that their industry and its conditions permitted. The "holding company" law, first enacted in New Jersey and later in Delaware, was more efficient than the trust approach. A large company simply held the stock of its subsidiaries. The spectacle of the trust swallowing up its rivals became ingrained in the popular imagination and produced calls on government for remedial action.

Andrew Carnegie and Steel

Almost as famous as Rockefeller was **Andrew Carnegie.** He was one of the few prominent businessmen of the era who rose "from rags to riches." An immigrant from Scotland, he moved from telegraph clerk to private secretary of the president of the Pennsylvania Railroad. During the 1860s, he played the stock market through investments in railroading, oil, and telegraph company securities. By 1873, however, he focused on steel. He summed up his philosophy: "Put all your good eggs in one basket, and then watch that basket."

In the 1870s, the technology of steelmaking relied on the Bessemer process of steel production in which molten

Table 17.2 Steel Production (in tons), 1877–1887

1877	569,618
1878	731,977
1879	935,273
1880	1,247,335
1881	1,588,314
1882	1,736,692
1883	1,673,535
1884	1,550,879
1885	1,711,920
1886	2,562,503
1887	3,339,071

Source: *The Statistical History of the United States*, p. 416.

pig iron was placed in a receptacle or converter and air was blown across it to remove impurities through oxidization. The result was a flow of steel in about 15 or 20 minutes, much faster than the earlier process in which an individual "puddler" had worked the molten iron. Eventually the open-hearth method of steelmaking supplanted the Bessemer technique. In this method the iron ore was heated and scrap metal was then added to the mixture. The Bessemer process dominated the construction of steel rails; the open-hearth method proved better for heavy machinery, skyscraper beams, and other uses. By 1890, steel production had risen to 4,277,000 tons annually; it would climb still more, to 10,188,000 tons by 1900.

Carnegie became the dominant figure in steelmaking. "Watch the costs," he preached, "and the profits will take care of themselves." Between 1873 and 1889, Carnegie cut the cost of steel rail from $58 a ton to $25 a ton. He poured money into new equipment and plowed profits back into the business. During the 1880s, steel production at Carnegie's works rose, costs went down, and his profits grew by over a million dollars annually. Carnegie sought to achieve the **vertical integration** of his steel interests; this meant controlling all the steps in the process of making steel. Carnegie acquired mines to ensure that he had raw materials, boats to move ore on rivers, railroads to carry it to his mills, and a sales force to market his many products.

Carnegie's innovations in steelmaking shaped the economy. The lower cost of steel spurred the mechanization of industry. As machines became more complex and more productive, machine tools were needed to turn out these laborsaving and cost-cutting devices in sufficient amounts. In such industries as firearms, bicycles, and sewing

The massive Carnegie steel works attested to the dramatic changes that Andrew Carnegie's methods had made in how steel was produced.

machines, the use of machine tools spread technological innovations throughout the economy. Carnegie's and Rockefeller's managers broke work down into specific, well-defined tasks for each employee. They made everyone in the workplace follow standardized procedures. Mass production and a continuous flow of resources into factories and of goods to the consumers were part of the larger process of industrialization that reshaped the American economy.

The Pace of Invention

Inventive Americans poured out a flood of new ideas; an average of 13,000 patents were issued each year during the 1870s. In the next 20 years, the annual total climbed to about 21,000. Among the new devices were the phonograph (1877), the cash register (1879), and the linotype in newspaper publishing (1886). The Kodak camera went on the market in 1888. The process of innovation led to such constructive changes as the twine binder, which made harvesting straw more efficient; time locks for bank vaults; and the fountain pen. As one writer put it, "Our greatest thinkers are not in the library, nor the capitol, but in the machine shop."

Alexander Graham Bell and **Thomas Alva Edison** were major figures among the thousands of inventors. A Scottish immigrant from Canada, Bell wanted to transmit the human voice by electrical means. In 1876, he and his assistant, Thomas A. Watson, created a practical device for doing so: the telephone. By 1877, it was possible to make telephone calls between New York and Boston; New Haven, Connecticut, established the first telephone exchange. Soon President Hayes had a telephone installed at the White House. Long-distance service between some cities arrived in 1884.

An even more famous inventor was Thomas Alva Edison, the "Wizard of Menlo Park." Born in 1847, Edison was a telegrapher during the Civil War with a knack for making machines and devices. By the end of the 1860s, he had already patented some of his nearly 1,100 inventions. In 1876, he established the first industrial research laboratory at Menlo Park, New Jersey. His goals, he said, were to produce "a minor invention every ten days and a big thing every six months or so." In 1877, he devised the first phonograph, although it would be another decade before he perfected it commercially. More immediately rewarding was the invention of the carbon filament incandescent lamp in 1879. Edison decided to use carbonized thread in the lamp, and it glowed for more than 45 hours.

For the electric light to be profitable, it had to be installed in a system outside the laboratory. In 1882, Edison put his invention into operation in New York City.

Thomas A. Edison's many inventions enabled Americans to light their homes, listen to music, and in time to go to the movies.

Library of Congress, Prints and Photographs Division

The area covered was about a square mile, and after a year in service there were 500 customers with more than 10,000 lamps. Electric power caught on rapidly. Edison's system, however, relied on direct electric current for power. As the distance traveled by the current increased, the amount of usable electric power decreased. One of Edison's business rivals, George Westinghouse, discovered how to use a transformer to render electricity safe at the point where the consumer needed it. This device made possible alternating current, which could transmit higher amounts of electricity. Soon the United States was on the way to using more and more electricity in its homes and factories.

Inventions, trusts, and cost-cutting were reshaping the economy, but what of the workers who lived in this new world of industry?

Americans in the Workplace

Amid industrialization, individual Americans struggled to improve their lives within a society that at first resisted efforts to lessen the harmful effects of industrial growth. In 1877, there were 15 million nondomestic workers, more than half in agriculture and another 4 million in manufacturing. The economy was in the fourth year of a depression, stemming from the Panic of 1873, and almost 2 million people were unemployed.

The labor force grew by more than 29 percent during the 1870s. One-fifth of the increase came from immigrants. Four out of every ten of these working immigrants were unskilled; their sweat helped the new industries

Enduring Issues   Industrialism

The wave of industrial growth that appeared in the United States after the Civil War transformed American society away from the older, agrarian past. These developments drew on economic and political trends that had been gathering strength during the nineteenth century. Once the process of industrial growth accelerated during the 1870s and 1880s, issues and problems emerged that would dominate American life for the next century. Few issues have influenced the nation's history in more profound ways than did the spread of industry and the rise of big business in this period.

Economic growth was a key to national development, and how to promote the expansion of the economy was a major concern of government officials and private citizens from the early days of the Republic. Whether through protective tariffs, subsidies to business enterprise, or the construction of roads and canals, government sought to release the productive energies of capitalists. Differences over how large a role government should play in stimulating enterprise shaped the destinies of the Whig and Democratic parties during the era of Andrew Jackson. The interplay of the two parties prevented clear policies from emerging, but the overall effect was to lay the foundation for spreading industry once capitalists moved in that direction.

By the 1850s, industry had taken hold in the North with the spread of railroads and the development of smaller businesses and factories. Railroads would set the pattern for bigger firms since rail lines employed thousands of people and spread across thousands of miles. The South emulated these trends, although on a much smaller scale and with less enthusiasm. The dependence on agriculture held back the South from a fuller commitment to industrialism. That disparity helped the North prevail in the Civil War because of its ability to mobilize economic resources for the protracted civil conflict that ensued.

Following the end of the fighting, industrialism and big business accelerated as railroads, petroleum, steel, and other enterprises reshaped the economy. Workers found themselves in large firms with managerial bureaucracies that expected high productivity from their employees. Railroads helped shape a national market for consumer goods. Cities grew because companies concentrated where workers and resources could be brought together. Though the extent of industrialism was spotty by the end of the nineteenth century, the overall trend toward a capitalistic economy dominated by large, integrated corporations was clear.

The social problems that accompanied these developments emerged with great speed. Economic change proved advantageous to some sectors of the population and very unsettling and traumatic to others. Complaints from southern and western farmers led, for example to the rise of Populism in the 1880s and 1890s. The adverse impact of the Panic of 1893 and the ensuing depression caused urban residents in the Middle West to ask government to become more active to relieve the resulting social distress from hard times.

The dilemmas of industrialism brought calls for government to take action to readjust social inequities.

---

expand and the cities to rise. Most of the immigrants left from northern Europe as they had before the Civil War. Irish, Germans, British, and Scandinavians made up the bulk of the newcomers. The expansion of the transatlantic steamship business and the aggressive work of emigration agents in Europe helped persuade many to come to the United States; hard times in Europe impelled others to make the trip. Western states and territories hoped that the new arrivals would become farmers, but the majority found work in the cities of the Northeast and Midwest. Soon distinctive ethnic communities grew up in New York, Boston, and Philadelphia.

The New Workforce

Whether a worker had a skill or not, these were challenging times. Technology replaced craft skills with machines, and market pressures led businesses to limit their dependence on trained artisans. Management became more of a hierarchy. Supervisors frowned on skilled workers who sought autonomy in doing their jobs. These new policies reduced the control artisans had once exerted in the workplace. The use of apprenticeship as a way of rising in industry receded, and the workforce was divided into unskilled and semiskilled employees.

Workers resisted these changes through mutual support in times of crisis, often with disappointing results. In 1882, the Amalgamated Association of Iron and Steel Workers struck for higher pay from the owners of steel rolling mills in Pennsylvania. For five months the union held together against unified management, but finally the workers were forced to go back on the job.

Women represented another new element in the labor force. They appeared in greater numbers as teachers and office workers, and as sales clerks in the expanding department stores. Eight thousand women worked

Unbridled capitalism, many social critics believed, brought grave injustices to the nation. But what was to be done in response? The view that government should simply stay out of the process and let the invisible hand of the economy work for the common good went against American instincts for prompt solutions. On the other hand, the idea of government ownership and control of the means of production never seemed palatable to more than a minority of the population. So the nation decided to attempt government regulation of the economy through commissions and agencies that would oversee specific industries to insure that they conformed to law, ethical practices, and fair competition. Framed in the early twentieth century, this approach to managing the economy has continued in modified forms down to the present time. In that sense, the response to industrialism has remained within the intellectual framework established more than a century ago.

As industry evolved and the economy became more complex during the past 100 years, new issues and concerns have emerged to drive the debate about the price of living in a technologically advanced society. Environmental concerns, which were only dimly seen in the Progressive Era, now affect the ways in which industrialism is practiced. In recent decades, computers and the Internet have revolutionized how individuals work and how productive the society is. More advances are certain to occur as the dizzying pace of industrial change persists into the future.

But the terms in which Americans think about the economy and their place in it still owe much to the pioneering work done in the late nineteenth century when the older, agrarian lifestyle began to disappear. The fresh economic ideas that Thomas A. Edison, John D. Rockefeller, and Andrew Carnegie, among others, first explored in those turbulent decades after the Civil War set the nation on a new path. An acceptance of rapid change, an embrace of technology, and a dependence on industry would be key characteristics of the United States, as with other industrial democracies, once the twentieth century began. The days of farm and field, of working by the sun and moving to the rhythm of the seasons, yielded instead to a faster-paced, more hectic existence in which construction and destruction became the dominant social process. The men and women who lived in that birth of the industrial era knew that something important was happening to their nation and their world. The issues they left for other Americans to engage still influence how citizens earn their living, find a place in society, and evaluate the role of government. The age of industry began in the Gilded Age. It has yet to end.

Questions for Reflection

1. In what ways have the problems of industrialism in the late nineteenth century defined the political and policy agenda for the United States down to the present time?

2. How has industrialism shaped the way Americans define the role of government at all levels?

in sales in 1880; a decade later the total was more than 58,000. Many stores preferred women, especially native-born white women. Many immigrant women toiled as domestic servants, but they also found work in the sweatshops of the textile trades. For the most part, the jobs open to women were lower paid, required fewer skills, and offered less opportunity than those open to men.

Real wages for workers increased as the prices of farm products and manufactured goods fell during the deflation that lasted until the late 1890s. The hours that employees worked declined from more than 65 hours a week in 1860 to under 60 by 1900. Gradual though they were, these changes represented real gains.

Although workers were making progress, the industrial economy presented serious dangers to many employees. Steelworkers put in 12 hours a day 7 days a week amid the noise, heat, and hazards of the mills. In the coal mines, in the factories, and on the railroads, work was hazardous and sometimes fatal. From 1880 to 1900, some 35,000 of the 4 million workers in manufacturing died in accidents each year and another 500,000 were injured.

Workers had almost no protection against sickness, injury, or arbitrary dismissal. If an injury occurred, the courts had decided that the liability often belonged to another worker or "fellow servant" rather than to the company that owned the factory. For a worker who was fired during an economic downturn, there were no unemployment benefits, no government programs for retraining, and little private help. Old-age pensions did not exist, and there were no private medical or retirement insurance plans. Child labor reached a peak during this period. Almost 182,000 children under the age of 16 were at work in 1880 with no health and safety restrictions to protect them.

Workers had few ways to insulate themselves from the impact of harsh working conditions and often-cruel employers. There were sporadic attempts at labor organization and strikes throughout the nineteenth century, but unions faced legal and political obstacles. The law said that a worker and his employer were equal players in the marketplace, one buying labor for the lowest price possible, the other selling labor for as much as could be obtained. Real equality in bargaining power rarely existed. The worker had to take what was offered; the boss set the conditions of employment.

The Rise of Unions

During the 1860s and 1870s, skilled workers in cigar making, shoemaking, and coal mining formed unions. The National Labor Union (NLU), a coalition of trade unions, was established in 1866. In 1868, its leader was William Sylvis, the head of the union of craftsmen in the steel industry known as iron-puddlers. Under his direction, the NLU pursued the eight-hour day and other improvements for labor. Sylvis's death in 1869 and the dominance of middle-class social reformers in the organization eroded the influence of the National Labor Union by the early 1870s. Other union organizers would soon try again to form a national labor organization.

Because of the number of workers they employed, railroads were the first business to confront large-scale labor issues. The professional skills that engineers, firemen, brakemen, and others possessed made it more difficult for railroads to find replacements during a strike. Railroad workers joined unions based around these crafts such as the Brotherhood of Locomotive Firemen

and the Brotherhood of Locomotive Engineers. "Unless labor combines," said one engineer, "it cannot be heard at all." The issue, according to one railroad executive, was, "who shall manage the road?" From this difference of opinion flowed the labor disputes that marked the decade from 1877 to 1887 and beyond.

A bitter railroad strike erupted during the summer of 1877. On July 1, in the middle of an economic depression, the major eastern railroads announced a 10 percent wage cut. Facing their second pay reduction in a year, railroad employees launched an unplanned protest. Strikers disrupted train traffic across Pennsylvania, West Virginia, Maryland, and Ohio. In Baltimore and Pittsburgh, strikers battled state militia. A general strike spread to Chicago, St. Louis, and other large cities. Railroad unions played a relatively small part in these walkouts, however; during the depression their membership had declined as had their economic impact on the roads.

The governors of the states with riots called out the militia. Some militia units refused to fire on their fellow citizens. As violence spread, the Hayes administration sent in the army. Deaths ran into the hundreds; many more were injured. Newspapers sympathetic to the strike said that "never before has the cause of justice been so thoroughly on the working-man's side." Faced with the overwhelming force of the government, the unrest died away. Nevertheless, the strike had touched most of the nation.

The Knights of Labor

The strike increased support for a new national labor organization: the Noble and Bold Order of the **Knights of Labor**. The Knights combined fraternal ritual, the language of Christianity, and belief in the social equality of all citizens. While advancing the cause of labor through unions and strikes where necessary, the Knights wanted government to play a larger role in protecting working people who produced goods and services for the economy. The order spoke about the "Commonwealth of Toil" and deplored "the recent alarming development of aggregated wealth." Instead it wanted "a system adopted which will secure to the laborer the fruits of his toil." By the mid-1870s, the Knights was established among coal miners in Pennsylvania. After the railroad strike, the Knights saw membership grow to 9,000 in 1879 and 42,000 by 1882.

The leader of the Knights was known as the grand master workman. Terence V. Powderly was elected to that post in 1879 and became the first

The Great Railroad Strike of 1877 left many railroads in ruins as vandals ripped up property along the tracks. The walkout became a symbol of the social disorder of the decade and its hard times.

Library of Congress, Prints and Photographs Division

The Knights of Labor had women as full members of its organization, and this picture shows eight delegates to the order's 1886 convention. The woman holding her 2-month-old baby in the front is Elizabeth Rodgers. Although men dominated public life in this period, the role of women was expanding in ways that foreshadowed their greater participation after 1900.

national labor figure. The Knights grew because it had few membership requirements, and its ideology reached out to the entire working population. Its ranks embraced workers from skilled craft unions, agricultural laborers in the South, and women who were new entrants into the workforce. The willingness of the Knights to include women and blacks set it apart from other unions. By 1885, the union claimed more than 100,000 members. Its message of working-class solidarity and mutual assistance among all producers appealed to many laborers.

Success brought problems of internal strain and union discipline. In 1885, the Knights conducted a strike against a railroad owned by Jay Gould, one of the most hated of the rail executives. The Knights struck his Wabash, Missouri Pacific, and other lines, and achieved a form of official recognition that allowed the order to represent the company's employees in relations with management. Because it appeared that the Knights had beaten Gould, the order's popularity exploded among workers. By 1886, there were more than 700,000 members. A second walkout was called against Gould in February 1886, but this time the strike was broken through the use of police and violence against those who had walked out.

The **Haymarket affair** in Chicago on May 4, 1886, in which anarchists were accused of throwing a bomb and sparking a deadly riot, shocked the nation. As a result, the public support for labor's demands for an eight-hour workday and other concessions dried up. In fact, widespread antiradical hysteria spread. The Knights felt the shift in public attitudes the most. Even though the leadership of the Knights had questioned the wisdom of strikes, business leaders and conservatives blamed them for the violence and unrest. The union went into a permanent decline. To some workers, the failure of the Knights demonstrated the need for more violent action. Some labor leaders questioned whether the strategy of a broad, inclusive appeal and an avoidance of strikes had been wrong from the start. The shift in emphasis that followed had important long-term consequences for the history of American labor.

The American Federation of Labor

One vigorous critic of the Knights of Labor was Samuel Gompers. Because a philosophy of "pure and simple unionism" had worked for his own Cigar Makers International Union, he believed that only such an approach could help labor. The son of a British cigar maker, Gompers had come to the United States in 1863. During his years of employment in the cigar trade, he decided that labor should accept corporations as a fact of life, seek concrete and limited improvements in living and working conditions, and avoid political involvements.

Late in 1886, Gompers and others organized the American Federation of Labor (AFL) whose participating unions had 150,000 members. An alliance of craft unions and skilled workers, the AFL did not try to organize the masses of industrial workers. The union opposed immigrant labor, especially of the Chinese on the West Coast, and was cool toward the idea of black members. Nevertheless, the AFL's membership rose to more than 300,000 during its first 10 years, and it achieved considerable benefits for its members through judicious use of strikes and negotiations with employers. Most of the men and women who worked as unskilled labor in the nation's factories and shops, however, derived little benefit from the AFL's policies. In the minds of many middle-class Americans that was as it should be. Unions and government involvement in the economy were, according to this way of thinking, wrong in themselves.

Social Darwinism

The political doctrine that took this stance was known as **Social Darwinism.** Charles Darwin's famous work *On the Origin of Species,* published in 1859, offered an explanation

Flashpoints | The Haymarket Affair (May 4, 1886)

Chicago was on edge. A strike against the factory where Cyrus McCormick's company made reapers for farmers had turned violent. In the first days of May, police and union members clashed in the streets. To protest, the International Working People's Association called a rally to meet in the city's Haymarket Square. The gathering on May 4 went off peacefully. As it proceeded, only about 300 people remained in attendance. As the police moved in to disperse the crowd, a bomb was tossed at the officers. Eight of the police died from the effects of the blast. The police shot into the crowd and bystanders ran. In the melee, police wounded protestors and each other. Eight more people died in the confusion, and numerous others were wounded.

Among those present at the gathering were anarchists who believed that all governments should be abolished. The police put the blame on these individuals and their unpopular political views. Newspaper headlines asked for swift vengeance against those believed to be responsible. Chicago officials charged eight anarchists on the grounds that they had encouraged whoever threw the bomb to act. The case was thin and the evidence weak. But the prosecution used perjured testimony and guilt by association to convict the accused men. Seven defendants received death sentences, four of which were carried out; the other man on trial was sentenced to life in prison.

Six years later, Governor John Peter Altgeld, a Democrat who was sympathetic to the grievances of labor, pardoned three surviving defendants on the grounds that their trial had been unfair. Altgeld was depicted in the conservative press as an ally of anarchism.

Haymarket came at a time when organized labor seemed to be gaining momentum through the Knights of Labor. Fears abounded among middle-class Americans about the imminent breakdown of social order. Calls for repressive measures were in the air even before the Haymarket incident occurred. The May 4, 1886, bombing gave new impetus to conservatives who believed that labor was securing too many concessions. In the wake of the violence, labor found itself on the defensive as respectable newspapers lumped anarchism, the Knights, and unhappy workers into one group. Editors charged that this alleged alliance wanted to undermine the accepted arrangements that held society together. The linking of organized labor with social violence and European ideologies such as anarchism became a favored tactic of conservative opponents of unions over the next century. In that respect, the unhappy events of May 4, 1886, set the tone for how labor and management interacted and made their cases to the public long after the immediate effects of the Haymarket incident had died away.

Questions for Reflection

1. What successes had organized labor achieved nationally in 1885–1886 that helped set the context in which the Haymarket riot took place?

2. How did middle-class opinion react to what had happened in Chicago and why did the case arouse such fears?

3. What were the long-range consequences of this controversy and how did it shape the future of organized labor in the United States?

---

for why some species survived and others became extinct. Darwin contended that a process of "natural selection" occurred in nature that enables the "fittest" animals and plants to evolve and develop. Darwin did not attach any moral virtue to the ability of one species to survive and reproduce as a result of the process of natural selection. He was simply analyzing the workings of the world. Advocates of Darwin's ideas, such as the English writer Herbert Spencer, applied them to human existence. If the doctrine of "survival of the fittest" operated in the natural world, Spencer argued, it governed human affairs as well. Since capitalists and the wealthy represented the "fittest" individuals, it was folly to interfere with the "natural" process that produced them. "The law of the survival of the fittest was not made by man and cannot be abrogated by man," said William Graham Sumner, a

leading exponent of this doctrine. "We can only by interfering with it produce the survival of the unfittest." A professor at Yale University, Sumner won a wide audience for his ideas among middle- and upper-class Americans. On the other hand, few businessmen looked to Sumner or Spencer for advice about how to succeed in the marketplace when they sought government help through tariffs and subsidies.

Social Darwinism popped up in popular culture. The "rags to riches" novels of Horatio Alger, a popular writer of the day, spread these ideas. Alger argued that men of energy and determination (i.e., the "fittest") could triumph in the competitive system even against great odds. He wrote 106 books with such titles as *Brave and Bold* and *Paddle Your Own Canoe*. The central characters were impoverished young boys who used their

Horatio Alger's books, like this one in the "Luck and Pluck" series, won millions of readers with their tales of bright young boys rising through the economic system to achieve wealth and happiness.

natural talents to gain the support of wealthy benefactors and go on to achieve riches and success. The public consumed millions of copies of Alger's books despite repetitive plots. They taught the lessons of self-reliance and personal commitment, though few corporate leaders started at the bottom as Alger's characters did. Despite the popularity of Social Darwinism, the impact of these ideas was limited. While many Americans applauded Social Darwinism in theory, they also tolerated considerable government intervention in the economy and social relations.

Social Darwinism attracted credible critics. One of the most famous social critics of the day was Henry George. A California newspaperman, George said that the gap between the wealthy and the poor was caused by the monopoly of land by the rich and the rents that landowners charged. He expressed his ideas in a book titled *Progress and Poverty* (1879), which sold more than 2 million copies in the United States and more abroad. Rent, he wrote, was "a toll levied upon labor constantly and continuously," and the solution for this social ill was a "single tax" on rising land values. With such a tax, all other forms of taxation would be unnecessary. George's writings enjoyed worldwide influence. Single-tax leagues

flourished in the United States, and his ideas promoted social reform among clergymen in the 1890s and early 1900s. What gave *Progress and Poverty* its major impact was the moral intensity of George's analysis of the ills of capitalist society. The single-tax crusade was evidence that not all Americans favored an inactive and passive government.

Another challenge to Social Darwinism came in 1883 when a government geologist, Lester Frank Ward, published *Dynamic Sociology* in which he assailed Social Darwinism's view of evolution as applying to human society and not just to the natural world. The process of evolution did not work, he wrote, because of "the unconscious forces of nature, but also through the conscious and deliberate control by man." The idea that government should not interfere with the workings of society did not apply to its advocates: "Those who dismiss state interference are the ones who most frequently and successfully invoke it." Ward had a good point. From protective tariffs to land grants, from railroad subsidies to strike breakers, the well-off in America constantly asked government at all levels to help them with positive action. After all, the government had been a major force in promoting the development of the West at this time.

The Changing West

The vast spaces beyond the Mississippi Valley were still not fully part of the United States during the 1880s. The end of Indian resistance to white incursions and the economic development of the frontier brought the West into the political and social mainstream of the country. In so doing, they also contributed an enduring saga of the range cattle business and the cowboy to American folklore.

The defeat of Custer at the Battle of the Little Big Horn in June 1876 was one of the final flurries of combat on the Great Plains. Some sporadic resistance continued. During 1877, the Nez Perce tribe in Oregon, led by Chief Joseph, resisted attempts to move them to a reservation. Through four months of running battles, Joseph led his band of 650 people toward Canada, but they were beaten before they could reach safety. "From where the sun now stands," said Joseph, "I will fight no more forever." The Nez Perces were sent to the Indian Territory in Oklahoma, where they fell victim to disease.

Another famous example of Native American resistance was **Geronimo,** the Apache chief in New Mexico. With a small band of followers, he left the Arizona reservation where he had been living in 1881 and raided across the Southwest for two years. After brief periods of surrender he resumed his military forays. Finally, in

September 1886, confronted with the power of the army, he was persuaded to surrender once again and was exiled to Florida.

As Native American resistance ebbed, the national government shaped policy for the western tribes. Many white westerners believed that the "Indian question" could be solved only when the tribes were gone. Easterners contended that Native Americans should be assimilated into white society. Organizations such as the Indian Rights Association lobbied for these policies, and a book by Helen Hunt Jackson, *A Century of Dishonor* (1881), publicized the plight of the Native Americans. Although the eastern policies were more benevolent than the westerners' destructive motives toward the Indians, their combined efforts devastated Indian culture.

Congress passed the **Dawes Severalty Act** in 1887. Named after Senator Henry L. Dawes of Massachusetts, the law authorized the president to survey Native American reservations and divide them into 160-acre farms. After receiving their allotment, Native Americans could not lease or sell the land for 25 years. Any Indian who adopted "habits of civilized life" became a U.S. citizen, but most Indians did not achieve citizenship. Any surplus land after this process was finished could be sold to white settlers. For the reformers, this law pushed Indians toward white civilization; for the western settlers it made Indian land available. During the next 50 years, the total land holdings of Native Americans declined from 138 million to 47 million acres. By dividing up tribal land holdings and putting Indians at the mercy of white speculators, the Dawes Act undermined the tribal structure and culture of the Native Americans. These tactics also helped allow whites to start mining and cattle ranching.

The Mining and Cattle Frontier

Mining "booms" drew settlers to seek riches in a series of bonanzas, first of gold, later of silver, and eventually of copper in territories and states such as Colorado, Montana, and the Dakotas. The mining camps became notorious for their violence and frenzied atmosphere. More than 90 percent of their inhabitants were men; most of the women were prostitutes. During the 1870s, the western mining industry came to resemble other businesses. Individual miners gradually gave way to corporations that used industrial techniques such as jets of water under high pressure to extract the metal from the ground. The ravaged land left farmers with fouled rivers and polluted fields.

White settlement on the Great Plains during the 1880s started with the cattle ranchers, who dominated the open range in Wyoming, Colorado, and Montana. After the Civil War, ranchers in Texas found that their steers had multiplied during their absence. Enterprising cattlemen drove herds north to market at rail lines in Kansas and Nebraska. Up the Chisum and Goodnight-Loving Trails came Texas longhorns to the cattle towns of Ellsworth, Dodge City, and Abilene. Unlike the mining towns, these communities were not violent; respectable citizens quickly imposed law and order on their temporary guests.

During the late 1870s and early 1880s, cattle raising shifted from Texas to areas nearer the railroads and the Chicago stockyards. The growth of the railroad network gave ranchers access to eastern and foreign markets. Improved breeding and slaughtering practices produced beef for consumers both in the United States and in Europe, and the demand grew. With cattle easy to raise in the open spaces of the West and with an efficient transportation system, entrepreneurs in New York, London, and Scotland wanted to buy cattle cheaply in the West and resell them to eastern buyers at a profit. Money poured into the West and increased the number of cattle on the ranges of Montana and Wyoming.

Being a cowboy was not glamorous. Drudgery and routine marked ranch life. Cowboys worked 14-hour days, with death near if the cattle stampeded. Much of what they did—riding the line, tending sick cattle, and mending fences—consisted of grinding physical labor in a harsh environment. One of every seven was African American. Former slaves from ranches in Texas or fugitives from the oppression in the South, these black cowboys gained a living but were not granted social equality. Other cowboys included Hispanics and Native Americans, and they also faced discrimination. From the Hispanic *vaqueros* and the Native Americans, other cowboys learned the techniques of breaking horses and the complex skills of managing cattle. Western development involved a subtle interaction of cultures that few whites understood.

The boom years did not last. As the ranges became overstocked in 1885 and 1886, prices for western cattle fell from 30 dollars to less than 10 dollars. Then came the "hard winter" of 1886–1887. Thousands of cattle died in the blizzards. Before prices rose, investors from the East and Great Britain lost all they had. There were 9 million cows in Wyoming Territory in 1886; 9 years later, that number had fallen to 3 million. The cattle industry became a more rational, routine business.

Ranchers in the West faced other challenges. Sheep raisers moved onto the range and discovered that sheep could graze more economically than cattle. Range wars between cattle and sheep growers broke out in Arizona and Wyoming. In the long run, however, sheep raising

The actual routine of work in the range cattle business was more arduous than glamorous. Here a group of cowboys makes camp after a long day of herding steers. Low pay and difficult conditions stimulated cowboy strikes on more than one occasion.

proved to be a viable business, and by 1900, there were some 30 million sheep on western ranges. Both sheep raisers and ranchers now faced competition from farmers who were moving westward.

Farming on the Great Plains

During the 1880s, hundreds of thousands of farmers swept onto the Great Plains. Advertising by the railroad companies drew them from Midwestern states and from northern Europe. Advertising said that land, water, and opportunity abounded. The Homestead Act of 1862 gave farmers public land, which they could use and eventually own. In practice, the 160-acre unit of the Homestead Act was too small for successful farming; a serious settler had to purchase two or three times that acreage. The Homestead Act did not provide the money to go west, file a claim, and acquire the machinery

DOING HISTORY ONLINE

Westward Expansion

Study the photos in this module. What do they suggest about the process of moving west?

History Now™ Visit HistoryNOW to access primary sources and exercises related to this topic: http://now.ilrn.com/ayers_etal3e

required for profitable farming. Few laborers in the East became homesteaders and most of the settlers had some farming experience.

Congress complicated the land system. Cattle ranchers pushed for the Desert Land Act (1877), which allowed individuals to obtain provisional title to 640 acres in the West at 25 cents an acre. Before securing a title, they had to irrigate the land within 3 years and pay a dollar an acre more. Cowboys filed claims for their employer, threw a bucket of water onto the property, and swore that irrigation had occurred. A year later, lumber interests in the West obtained the Timber and Stone Act (1878). Directed at lands that were "unfit for cultivation" in Washington, Oregon, California, and Nevada, it permitted settlers to acquire up to 160 acres at $2.50 per acre. Lumber companies used false entries to gain title to valuable timber holdings

Most settlers obtained their land from the railroads or land companies. Congress had granted the railroads every other 160-acre section of land along their rights of way. Large tracts were closed to settlement until the railroads sold the land to farmers. From 1862 to 1900, land companies acquired almost 100 million acres from railroads or the government. Other lands had been granted to eastern states to support their agricultural colleges under the Morrill Land-Grant Act of 1862. These western holdings went into the hands of speculators who purchased the lands, as did the land of Native Americans that had been sold off to white buyers.

Farmers had to purchase their land at prices that often ranged between 5 and 10 dollars per acre. To buy the land, the farmers borrowed from loan companies in the East and Midwest. Interest rates on the resulting mortgages were as high as 25 percent annually. As long as land values rose and crop prices remained profitable, the farmers made the needed payments. When prices fell, however, they faced economic ruin.

Industrial growth and technological advances made farming possible in the West. Joseph Glidden of Illinois devised the practical form of barbed wire in 1873. Soon Glidden's invention came to the attention of the Washburn and Moen Company of Massachusetts, which developed a machine to produce barbed wire. By 1880, some 80 million pounds had been produced and the price of fencing stood at 10 dollars per pound. Improved plows, the cord binder for baling hay, and grain silos also aided western farming. During the 1880s, steam-powered threshers for wheat and corn-husking machines were developed.

Machines alone could not provide enough water for farming. West of the 98th meridian, which ran through the

MAP 17.2 Railroad Land Grants

To encourage the building of railroads across the West and to a lesser degree in the South, Congress and the states made sizable land grants in alternate sections to the rail lines. This map indicates how large these grants were and how they influenced patterns of settlement.

Dakotas, Nebraska, Kansas, Oklahoma, and Texas, fewer than 20 inches of rain fell annually. Efforts to irrigate the land with the waters that ran from the Rocky Mountains worked in certain areas, but the region lacked adequate rivers. Ordinary wells did not reach the waters far below the surface. Windmills offered a possible solution, but the high cost of drilling and installing a windmill made it too expensive. The most practical technique was "dry farming," cultivation using water that the land retained after rainfall.

For the farm families, life on the western farms was a grind. With little wood available, shelter often consisted of a sod house made of bricks of dirt or dried sod. When it rained, the house became a mixture of mud and straw. To keep warm in the winter, the farmers burned buffalo chips (droppings) or dried sunflower plants. Grasshoppers ruined crops, animals trampled fields, and the weather was always uncertain.

The burdens of farmwork fell hardest on women. "I never knew Mama to be idle," the daughter of one farm woman recalled. The child of another farm woman remembered, "Bake day, mending day. A certain day for a certain thing. That is what I remember, those special days that my ma had." Amid the endless spaces, women labored on small plots of land, sustained by a network of friends and neighbors. Some women achieved a degree of independence in the male-dominated West. They operated farms, taught school, ran boardinghouses, and participated in politics and cultural life.

By the late 1880s, some of the western territories were ready for statehood. The territorial system had transferred eastern political ideas and values to the West and integrated settlers into the national political structure. In 1889 and 1890, Congress admitted the Dakotas, Montana, Washington, Idaho, and Wyoming into the Union.

Ranchers and settlers had overcome natural obstacles, political difficulties, and economic problems to build new societies on the Great Plains. Their efforts had created an elaborate economic and environmental system that linked the city and the country in mutually interdependent ways. By the end of the 1880s, however,

The Harshness of Farm Life

This picture of a farm woman and her daughter collecting Buffalo chips in Kansas conveys a striking image of the emptiness of the Great Plains at the end of the nineteenth century and the ways in which settlers had to adapt to a harsh, new environment. Given the photographic equipment of this time, the two figures were posed for maximum effect—the hardworking mother with her wheelbarrow full of buffalo and cattle chips, and the small daughter with her white doll. Behind them, the plains stretch endlessly away. Nonetheless, whatever its arranged qualities, the photo evokes a moment when traditional rural life met the immensity of a semiarid landscape. The crops that this woman and her husband produced then had to compete in a world market of falling prices. So the farm families who experienced these challenges would be the constituency for the farm protest movement called Populism that emerged in the late part of the 1880s.

Kansas State Historical Society

the process of development stalled as farmers failed to achieve the anticipated prosperity. Crop prices fell, and the debts that settlers owed became an ever greater burden. Farm protest stirred in the West even as the same sentiments were building in the southern states.

The New South?

Reconstruction ended after the 1876 election. Democrats took over state governments in South Carolina, Louisiana, and Florida. In both the North and the South, the Democrats believed that white supremacy and limited government were the basic principles of political life. The bitter memories of Radical Reconstruction and the need to maintain the South as "a white man's country" made the Democrats dominant among white southerners.

Not all southerners became Democrats, however. Blacks voted Republican, as did whites in the southern mountain regions. Independents and others cooperated with Republicans against the Democrats.

The individuals who now led the state governments in the South believed that they had "redeemed" the region from the mistaken Republican experiment in multiracial politics. Their policies, they claimed, lacked the corruption and waste of their Republican predecessors. In reality, the record of these politicians was worse as scandals and frauds marred the Redeemer administrations.

The Redeemers were a diverse lot. They included plantation owners, a generous assortment of one-time Confederate officers, and aspiring capitalists who sought a more urban and developed South. This coalition dominated the politics of many southern states throughout the 1880s, though they could agree on only the most general (and vague) principles. Slavery had vanished, never to return, but white supremacy remained entrenched.

A key theme in the South during these years was embodied in the phrase "the New South." Proponents of the New South argued that the region should welcome industrialization and economic expansion. An Atlanta newspaper editor named Henry Grady became the biggest backer of the idea. He thrilled northern audiences, anxious for markets and cheap labor, when he said, in 1886, that the South would soon have "a hundred farms for every plantation, fifty homes for every palace, and a diversified industry that meets the complex needs of this complex age." All over the region, steel mills, textile factories, and railroads arose.

The Industrial South

Manufacturing capacity in the South grew between 1870 and 1900. In the major cotton producing states of South Carolina, Georgia, Alabama, Mississippi, and Louisiana, capital invested in manufacturing increased about 10-fold between 1869 and 1889. Southern railroads expanded during the postwar period; by 1880, there were 19,430 miles of track, double the total in 1860. Other key industries grew during this decade as well. Southern forests fell to satisfy the growing national demand for lumber. Almost 3 million board feet of yellow pine were produced in 1879 by crews working under dangerous conditions for less than a dollar per day. The region's ample deposits of iron ore stimulated the expansion of the iron and coal industries. Production of iron ore rose from 397,000 tons in 1880 to almost 2 million tons 20 years later. Birmingham, Alabama, became a center of the burgeoning southern iron industry.

Before the Civil War, tobacco had been popular as something to chew, smoke in a pipe, or use as a cigar. During the war, northern soldiers tried the variety of bright leaf tobacco grown in North Carolina, and demand for Bull Durham and other products of the area increased. During the 1880s, James Buchanan Duke developed a practical cigarette-making machine.

Production costs fell rapidly, and cigarette use skyrocketed. By the end of the 1880, Duke's company made more than 800 million cigarettes annually. Americans adopted smoking as an addictive habit.

New cities and towns sprang up as the South's economy expanded. Although industrialism led to greater prosperity for the region, not all southerners benefited. Those who worked in the factories and mills bore the burden of progress. Wages were often low and conditions crude. Tobacco workers in North Carolina earned around a hundred dollars a year. In the cotton mills an average workweek might be more than 60 hours for wages that could be as low as 15 cents a day. Influential southerners resisted arguments against child labor, even as others tried to end the practice.

Problems of Southern Agriculture

Cotton was the money crop of the South, with 5,709,000 bales produced in 1880. Growing cotton made economic sense. The crop rarely failed, caused less depletion of the soil, and brought a higher price per acre than any other alternative.

World production of cotton was increasing, however, and prices fell accordingly. Unable to increase their productivity to make money despite lower prices, cotton farmers were debt ridden and dependent.

Cheap labor thus became essential. Whites held most of the land while blacks were forced to sell their labor. The result was a system that combined **sharecropping,** tenant farming, and the "furnish merchant" who provided the farmers with the "furnish" (whatever was needed) to get them through the year.

Sharecroppers received as their wage a designated proportion of the crops they produced. The landlord or

The South became more mechanized in the 1880s. One of the key industries where that occurred was in tobacco and the production of cigarettes. In this image from *Harper's Weekly,* a Richmond cigarette factory is shown in various stages of production. Note the presence of women engaged in rolling cigarettes. Soon machines would take over that task.

© CORBIS

Table 17.3 Wholesale Prices of Wheat and Cotton, 1877–1887

Year	Wheat (per bushel)	Cotton (pound)
1877	1.69	0.117
1878	1.252	0.113
1879	1.223	0.104
1880	1.057	0.120
1881	1.154	0.113
1882	1.198	0.122
1883	1.038	0.106
1884	0.913	0.106
1885	0.864	0.105
1886	0.797	0.094
1887	0.769	0.103

Source: *The Statistical History of the United States from Colonial Times to the Present* (Stamford: Fairfield Publishers, 1965), p. 123.

owner controlled the crop until some of it was allocated to the sharecropper. Tenant farmers, on the other hand, owned the crop until it was sold. They then paid to the owner of the property either cash or a fixed amount of the crop. Both tenants and "croppers" depended on a local merchant for food, clothing, farm equipment, and crop supplies until their harvests were completed. To safeguard the merchant's investment, southern states passed crop lien laws that gave the merchant a claim on the crop if a farmer could not pay off his debt. Thus, the farmers in the South, both black and white, were in a cycle of debt first to the landlord and then to the "furnish" merchant. In bad years the farmers did not make enough to get out of debt. With interest rates as high as 50 percent, croppers and tenants were often in a situation that resembled slavery.

The South had long lacked adequate capital, and losing the war made the situation worse. The region lacked sufficient banks to extend credit, and the national government followed policies that kept the money supply down. The South's absence of capital worsened during the 1880s.

Southern farmers believed that they faced an economic conspiracy. The furnish merchant represented the power of northern bankers, international cotton marketing companies, and industrialism. The cotton farmers tolerated these conditions because there appeared to be no other way to participate in the South's burgeoning economy. By the end of the decade, however, the problems of perpetual debt were becoming acute and political discontent mounted. White southerners relied on one continuing advantage. They lived in a segregated society where blacks had been returned to a condition as close to slavery as the law would permit.

Segregation

Racial segregation evolved slowly but steadily across the South despite the national Civil Rights Act in 1875, which prohibited racial discrimination in public accommodations. In the *Civil Rights Cases* (1883), the Supreme Court ruled that under the Fourteenth Amendment Congress could prohibit only *state* actions that violated civil rights. For individual acts of racial discrimination in restaurants, hotels, and other public places, it was up to the states to ban discrimination. Southern states chose instead to allow and encourage racial segregation as a preferred policy.

During this period, segregation lacked the rigidity and legal power that it acquired later. In some southern states, black citizens used railroads and streetcars on a roughly equal basis with whites. Elsewhere in the region travel facilities were segregated. Under the regimes of the Redeemers, black men voted in some numbers before 1890, retained the right to hold office, could be members of a jury, and were permitted to own weapons.

These minimal rights existed alongside an overall system of racial discrimination and bigotry. Black men often found their choices at the polls limited to approved white candidates, and if too many African Americans sought to cast ballots, white violence erupted. By the end of the 1880s, growing numbers of white politicians believed that blacks should be barred from the electoral process altogether.

Thus, for African Americans in the South, the 15 years after the end of Reconstruction began with hopeful signs but had a bleak outcome. Black families wanted to rent farms and work land for themselves rather than return to the plantation system. They believed that growing cotton in the delta of Mississippi gave them a chance to participate in that region's expanding economy. The area saw

---

DOING HISTORY ONLINE

Description of Sharecropping Tenants on a Georgia Plantation, 1881

Read the document in this module and the section on "Problems of Southern Agriculture" in the textbook. Why did sharecropping develop as the most common form of labor relations between white planters and freedmen in the post–Civil War South?

History Now™   Visit HistoryNOW to access primary sources and exercises related to this topic: http://now.ilrn.com/ayers_etal3e

an influx of blacks at the end of the 1880s as African American men competed for new jobs and the opportunity to acquire land. Sharecropping and tenant farming were also present, but in this part of the South for a brief period there was a chance for black economic advancement. African Americans created networks of black churches and sought to educate their children.

Booker T. Washington's leadership of the Tuskegee Institute in Alabama, which began in 1881, symbolized what education and training could do. Growing up with no direct experience of slavery, a new generation of southern blacks demanded their legal rights. When older blacks warned of the possible consequences of such behavior, the younger generation answered that "we are now qualified, and being the equal of whites, should be treated as such."

Some African Americans preferred to get out of the South if they could. At the end of the 1870s, rumors spread that Kansas offered a safer haven. During 1879, some 20,000 blacks—known as Exodusters because they were coming out of bondage as the children of Israel had in the Exodus—arrived in Kansas. More settled in the cities than actually farmed on the prairie. Hundreds of thousands of other blacks left the South in these years.

At the end of the 1880s, white spokesmen for the South boasted of the region's progress. The South produced more cotton than ever before; towns were growing throughout the region; industries had developed; and tens of thousands of black southerners had accumulated property. Yet there were danger signs. State legislatures wrote new laws to segregate first-class railroad passengers by race. Farmers who grew more cotton each year without getting ahead organized to oppose the power of merchants and railroads. Tenants and laborers of both races seemed restless and in constant motion. Racial violence reached unprecedented levels. Southerners asked whether industrialism had brought all that much in the way of real benefits. Would the New South be any better than the Old?

Life and Culture During the 1880s

Although important regional differences still affected the nation, some experiences were common to all Americans during this decade. The daily rhythms of life were those of the country and the small town where most people, more than 70 percent in 1880, still resided. Of the nearly 10 million households in the nation, the most common family consisted of a husband, a wife, and their three children. The father worked the family farm or at a job in an office or at the factory. The mother stayed at home and did the endless round of cleaning, cooking, sewing, and shopping. The children attended schools near their home or, in less prosperous families, labored to bring home income.

Prosperous Americans ate large meals. For those fortunate ones, breakfast often included fried eggs, biscuits, wheatcakes, potatoes, and steak. The afternoon and evening meals were also substantial. Among the upper classes a fancy dinner might provide 10 or 11 courses of meats, fish, salads, and starchy foods. The poor found whatever they could scrape together. These stark divisions between rich and poor were one of the enduring features of this period.

Industrialism changed the way Americans ate. Millions of tin cans made vegetables and fruits available at the twist of a can opener. In large cities, fresh meats became more accessible as the Armour meat company moved beef in iced railroad cars. Brand names told Americans that "Uneeda" biscuit and a portly Quaker figure appeared on containers of Quaker Oats. In 1886, an Atlanta druggist, **John Pemberton,** mixed syrup extracted from the cola nut with carbonated water and called it "Coca Cola." A year later he sold out to Asa Candler, who made Coca-Cola a household word.

In the homes of city dwellers, gas and electricity provided new sources of power. No longer did people have to chop and gather wood, clean fireplaces, and maintain a multitude of candles and lamps, if they had the money to afford the newer utilities. Running water replaced water drawn by hand. Refrigeration reduced the need for daily shopping; ready-made clothing relieved housewives of constant sewing chores. Although machines reduced the burdens of the husband and children, the duties of the wife were still time-consuming. However fuel was supplied, she had to prepare the meals. Despite the availability of canned fruits and vegetables, many women canned and preserved. Sewing, cleaning, and household maintenance were done without the assistance of the male members of the family. To a large extent, the wife and mother found herself alone in the house each day as the husband went to work and the children went to school.

The children were educated in schools that were locally controlled and designed to instill patriotism and moral values. "We went to school to work," remembered one student, "our playing was done elsewhere." City children attended school for some 180 to 200 days a year. In rural areas, however, the demands of farm work often limited school attendance to fewer than 100 days a year. Courses included arithmetic, the history of the United States, geography, reading, grammar, and spelling. Many students read the famous series of *McGuffey's Readers,* which stressed religion, obedience, and family. In the better school systems, students received instruction in

A Refreshing Pause

The continuities of American life are often best revealed in the routines of everyday existence. This advertisement for Coca-Cola attests to the enduring appeal of carbonated soft drinks to thirsty Americans and the devices advertisers have used to pitch their products. The well-dressed, respectable young woman quaffing the last drop of her Coke in the 1880s, while watching the viewer outside the ad, would become 120 years later a gyrating teenage heartthrob hawking the same brand of sugar-laden refreshment. Only the price of

© Bettmann/CORBIS

the drink now seems historic. In their own bubbly way, soft drinks sparkled into one of the shared experiences of Americans in an industrialized, homogenized culture. Past advertisements from the pages of newspapers and magazines are thus one of the best windows into how Americans lived generations ago in ways that we still recognize.

Latin and at least one other foreign language; less attention was given to the sciences. For new immigrants, the school system taught the values of the dominant culture and prepared their children for citizenship.

Although only a small percentage of students attended high schools and even fewer pursued a college degree, the late nineteenth century brought rapid growth for institutions of higher learning. Wealthy businessmen created private universities such as Johns Hopkins in

Economic Change and Workers' Reactions, and New Ideas in American Life

Read the sources in both modules. How do these modules relate to one another? What is the connection between them?

History Now™   Visit HistoryNOW to access primary sources and exercises related to this topic: http://now.ilrn.com/ayers_etal3e

Baltimore (1876), the University of Chicago (1890), and Stanford in California (1891). State universities expanded in the Midwest and were created in the South. Modeled on the German educational system, these universities established academic departments and stressed research and graduate training. Higher education in the United States became increasingly professionalized.

Arts and Leisure in the 1880s

Americans of all classes found an abundance of ways to entertain themselves. Appealing to a wider audience were the circuses and Wild West shows. The first three-ring circus debuted in Manhattan in 1883, and P. T. Barnum, with his "greatest show on earth," became the entertainment equivalent to the giants of industry. During the same year, William "Buffalo Bill" Cody assembled a troupe of former Pony Express riders, stagecoach robbers, and riding artists that toured the United States and Europe. Vaudeville, a form of entertainment consisting of a series of singers, comedians, and specialty acts, was a favorite of urban audiences.

Baseball dominated the sporting scene. The National League, founded in 1876, entered an era of prosperity after 1880. Baseball fans, known as "kranks," delighted in baiting the umpire. In the 1880s, many new rules were adopted, including the three strikes, four-balls format; overhand pitching; and substitutions of players. Attendance figures rose, with as many as 30,000 people turning out for games on Memorial Day. Sunday contests were banned, as was the sale of beer at ballparks. It was a golden age for baseball.

Literate citizens found an abundance of reading for varied tastes. The magazines of the day, some 3,300 in all, carried articles on every possible subject. Americans also read popular novels such as Lew Wallace's *Ben Hur* (1880), an engrossing blend of religion, ancient history, and a good story. Probably the most important literary work of the 1880s was *The Adventures of Huckleberry*

Finn, written by Samuel L. Clemens ("Mark Twain") in 1884. In it, Clemens uses an adventure in which a boy helps a runaway slave to create a chronicle of the nation's experience with slavery, freedom, the wonders of childhood, and the ambiguities of adult life. The most popular writer of his era, Twain captured the images of a vanishing America of Mississippi riverboats, small towns, and the social tensions that lay beneath the tranquil surface.

Visual arts also fascinated Americans. Private acquisitions of paintings grew; about 150 such collections were in existence in 1880. Museums were founded in St. Louis, Detroit, and Cincinnati between 1879 and 1885, continuing a trend that had begun earlier in Boston, Philadelphia, and New York. Notable artists included Frederic Remington, who had gone west in 1880 to improve his health and arranged to accompany the army on campaigns against the Indians. His evocations of frontier life, published in *Harper's Weekly,* made him famous. Two of the most important figures of the decade were Thomas Eakins and John Singer Sargent. Eakins lived and worked in Philadelphia where he was forced to resign from the Pennsylvania Academy for using a naked male model in a class of female students. His most notable works included *The Swimming Hole* and *The Agnew Clinic.* Sargent became famous for portraits such as *The Daughters of Edward Boit* and *Mrs. Edward Burkhardt and Daughter Louise.*

Two symbols of the era were the Brooklyn Bridge in New York and the Statue of Liberty in New York City. Completed in 1883, the bridge allowed 11 million people to cross the East River from Brooklyn to Manhattan in its first year of operation. It took John A. Roebling and his son Washington Roebling 12 years to construct the longest suspension bridge in the world, but the resulting structure demonstrated what the new processes of industrialism could accomplish. The Statue of Liberty was dedicated three years later on October 28, 1886. The work of a French sculptor, Frédéric-Auguste Bartholdi, it was sponsored by a public fund-raising effort in the United States; the statue was placed on Bedloe's Island, now called Liberty Island, at the entrance to New York Harbor. Out of the campaign to raise money came the celebrated poem by Emma Lazarus that promised the "golden door" of opportunity to Europe's "huddled masses yearning to breathe free."

Political America, 1877–1887

The world of politics reacted slowly to the new issues of the industrial era. In politics, both of the major parties sought to overcome an electoral stalemate. The Republicans won the presidency in 1876, 1880, and 1888; the Democrats triumphed in 1884 and 1892. Neither party controlled both houses of Congress on a regular basis. The Republicans had control twice, from 1881 to 1883 and 1889 to 1891; the Democrats only once, from 1893 to 1895. Outside the South, elections often were close and hard fought.

Americans lavished time on their politics. Only men took part in elections, and most of them were whites. (A few black men voted in the South.) Those who did vote turned out at a record rate. About 8 out of every 10 eligible voters went to the polls. Women could vote only in Wyoming and Utah. When they were not voting, Americans listened to long speeches by candidates and read about politics in the extended stories that partisan newspapers printed.

Moral and religious values shaped the way that people voted and helped define which party won their support. The prohibition of alcohol, the role of religious and sectarian education in the public schools, and the observance of the Sabbath were hotly contested questions. Republicans favored government intervention to support Protestant values; Democrats thought the government should keep out of such subjects.

The most prominent national issues involved the kind of money Americans used, how the government raised revenue, and who served in the government itself. Some Americans believed that for every dollar in circulation an equal amount of gold should be stored in the Treasury or in banks. Others contended that the government should issue more money by coining silver into currency on an equal basis with gold. Debtors favored inflation, which made their loans easier to pay; creditors liked the deflation that raised the value of their dollars. The South and West wanted inflation; the Northeast and developed portions of the Midwest preferred the existing financial system.

Other major concerns were taxation and the protective tariff. There was no federal income tax; the government raised money from excise taxes on alcohol and tobacco, and customs duties (taxes) on imported goods. The protective tariff became a hot political issue. Those who favored it believed that high customs duties protected American industry, helped workers, and developed the economy. Republicans championed the protective system; Democrats countered that tariffs raised prices, hurt the consumer, and made government too expensive. The South liked the Democratic position, but Republicans found support from business and labor.

At bottom the argument was over the size and role of the national government. Should the government stimulate the economy, as the Republicans wanted, or allow natural forces to operate, as the Democrats advocated? Finally, there was the question of who should serve in

DOING HISTORY

Debating the Protective Tariff

William McKinley

"WE DO NOT appeal to passions; we do not appeal to baser instincts; we do not appeal to race or war prejudices. We do appeal to our own best interests, to stand by a party that stands by the people. Vote the Republican ticket, stand by the protective policy, stand by American industry, stand by that policy which believes in American work for American workmen, that believes in American wages for American laborers, that believes in American homes for American citizens. Vote to maintain that system by which you can earn enough not only to give you the comforts of life but the refinements of life, enough to educate and equip your children, who may not have been fortunate by birth, who may not have been born with a silver spoon in their mouths, enough to enable them to educate and prepare their children for the great possibilities of life. I am for America because America is for the common people."

D. H. Chamberlain

"A protective tariff is intended to shut out importations and keep the market for home productions. Keeping out foreign goods does not enrich but impoverishes a nation. If I am a farmer and want European goods which I can pay for with my farm products, if a tariff shuts them out, it likewise destroys the market for my products. I am just so much poorer for the tariff. My surplus farm products are worthless when what I desire to buy with them is shut out of my reach. My surplus crops go to waste, and I am so far impoverished and the country through me, and with me, and an impoverished many or country must pay lower wages than if rich and prosperous.

But a tariff which shuts out or hinders or reduces imports, so far deprives the community or nation on which it operates, of many opportunities and forms of labor. See how many laborers are employed in the strict work of importing foreign goods now. Whatever forbids, prevents or hinders such employments, obviously and necessarily deprives men of labor and reduces the demand for laborers and the wages of labor."

The protective tariff became a major dividing line between the two major parties in the 1880s. In these two addresses from a proponent of the tariff in William McKinley and an opponent in D. H. Chamberlain, the main points of contention are laid out. The two men differ about the impact of the protective policy on the economy and the average wage worker. Consider how each speaker sees society and the relationship of one part to another. The use of patriotism in McKinley's remarks was one key to the Republican appeal. Critics of the tariff such as Chamberlain stressed the economic arguments for free trade and international interdependence.

Source: William McKinley, "What Protection Means to Virginia," Petersburg, Virginia, October 29, 1885, in *Speeches and Addresses of William McKinley* (New York: D. Appleton, 1893), p. 194; D. H. Chamberlain, *Tariff Aspects With Some Special Reference to Wage: Speech of D. H. Chamberlain of New York City Before the Reform Club of New York*, August 24, 1888 (New York: Albert King, 1888), pp. 27–28.

Questions for Reflection

1. To what American values did each of the speakers appeal?

2. How does each speaker see the role of the worker in the economy and society?

3. How did the two political parties see the role of government in shaping economic policy and how are those views reflected in each of these statements?

4. Do you hear any echoes of modern political debates in these speeches?

Explore additional primary sources related to this chapter on the Wadsworth American History Resource Center or HistoryNOW websites:

http://history.wadsworth.com/rc/us
http://now.ilrn.com/ayers_etal3e

government. Politicians preferred the "spoils," or patronage, system. Allocating government jobs to partisan supporters enabled them to strengthen their party. Critics of the patronage system called it a corrupt and inefficient way to choose government officials. They favored a civil service, in which individuals, chosen through competitive examinations, would administer government without being subject to partisan pressure. Civil service reformers urged Congress to write laws to reduce the power of patronage during the 1870s, but incumbents of both parties liked the existing system.

The Republicans began the period with Rutherford B. Hayes in the White House. He pushed for civil service reform and resisted pressure from Congress to base his appointments on candidates that lawmakers favored. Hayes had promised to serve only one term. To succeed him, the Republicans nominated James A. Garfield of Ohio, and Chester Alan Arthur of New York as his running mate. The Democratic candidate was a former Civil War general named Winfield Scott Hancock. After an intense campaign that focused on the tariff issue, Garfield won by a narrow plurality in the popular vote and a larger margin in the electoral college.

Garfield's presidency lasted only four months. On July 2, 1881, he went to the Washington railroad station to leave for a vacation. Presidents were not well guarded at this time, and a crazed assassin shot Garfield. He died on September 19, and Chester Alan Arthur became president. Much to everyone's surprise, Arthur, who was widely regarded as a mediocrity, proved a competent chief executive. During his single term, Congress passed the Pendleton Act (1883), which created a civil service system and limited the practice of assessing campaign contributions from federal employees. The act also established rules about where and how government officials could raise campaign funds.

Arthur was a caretaker president. In 1884, the party selected its most popular figure, James G. Blaine of Maine, to run for the presidency. An advocate of the protective tariff, Blaine had been a potential presidential candidate in 1876 and 1880. Questions had been raised about his political honesty, though, which hurt his chances in the general election. His enemies said that Blaine had helped railroads while he was Speaker of the House in return for money (see Chapter 16).

To run against Blaine, the Democrats selected the governor of New York, Grover Cleveland. Cleveland had risen from political obscurity. He was a lawyer in

The first Democratic president since the start of the Civil War, Grover Cleveland, despite claims that he had fathered an illegitimate child as a younger man, won a close victory over James G. Blaine in 1884. He then demonstrated that his party could govern at a time of intense partisanship and even balance between the two major parties. This cartoon shows Cleveland reacting to the revelations about his personal difficulties.

Buffalo, New York, when he was chosen to be its mayor in 1881. A year later he was the Democratic nominee for governor. Elected because of Republican disunity, Cleveland proved to be a popular state executive. The national Democrats wanted a fresh face, and the stocky Cleveland (relatives called him "Uncle Jumbo") was an attractive blend of honesty, conservatism, and independence. His campaign suffered a setback when it was revealed that some years earlier he had accepted responsibility for an illegitimate child in Buffalo. Cleveland acknowledged his part in the episode, however, and his candor defused the issue. Meanwhile, the issue of Blaine's public morality worked against the Republicans.

Cleveland was helped by the defection of upper-class Republicans in the Northeast. These voters, calling themselves "Mugwumps" (an Indian word meaning "Big Chief"), threw their support to the Democrats. The outcome of the election was very close, reflecting the even balance of the major parties. Cleveland carried the South, New York, New Jersey, Connecticut, and Indiana, receiving 219 electoral votes to Blaine's 182. After 24 years in power, the Republicans had been defeated and the Democrats had their chance to direct national policy.

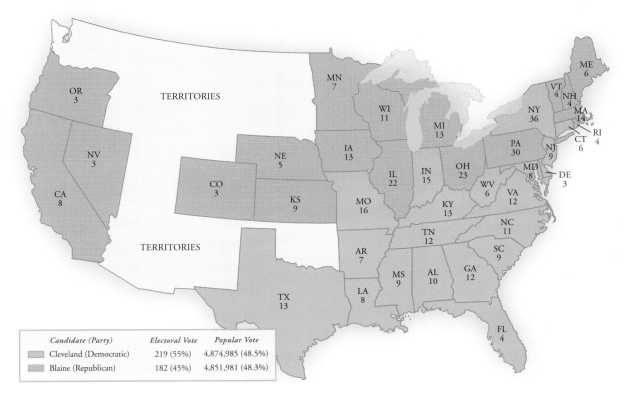

MAP 17.3 The Election of 1884

This map illustrates the tight presidential race between Grover Cleveland for the Democrats and James G. Blaine for the Republicans in 1884. Amid talk of scandal and corruption, the two parties battled to a virtual dead heat. Cleveland carried New York and eked out a narrow victory.

View an animated version of this map or related maps at http://history.wadsworth.com/passages3e

Cleveland took office on March 4, 1885. During his first term, he established that his party could govern, and his political opponents gave him grudging respect. For the Democrats, however, Cleveland proved to be a mixed blessing. He was slow to turn Republican office-holders out of office, and he alienated many Democrats with his patronage policies. Still, Republicans made few gains in the congressional elections of 1886, and Cleveland seemed to have good prospects for a second term in 1888.

In December 1887, hoping to establish an issue for his reelection campaign, the president devoted his annual message to Congress (known as the State of the Union message) to tariff reform. With a surplus in the Treasury, Cleveland believed that the tariff could be reduced, leading to lower prices for consumers. The Republican reaction to Cleveland's move was one of delight. Now the 1888 election could be fought on the issue that united the Republicans and divided the Democrats.

With the stage set for the election, the stalemated politics of the 1880s slowly broke up. For the next 12 years, American politics would experience a turbulent and decisive period of change and partisan realignment.

Conclusion

The 1880s were lived out in the shadow of the recently concluded Civil War. As one veteran, Oliver Wendell Holmes, Jr., said in 1884, "Through our great good fortunes, in our youth our hearts were touched with fire." Having experienced so much as young people, between 1877 and 1887 they sought harmony, prosperity, and stability. They pursued industrialism and its benefits with intense energy. Their achievements—in terms of railroads and factories built, inventions developed, and society transformed—were striking.

Yet the transformation of the American economy came at a cost. In 1887, deep social divisions and economic inequality characterized the United States. Regional differences remained unresolved. Industrialism had produced serious changes in the environment that would imperil the natural resources available to future generations. The animosity between capitalists and workers smoldered behind a facade of calm. The nation had yet to work out the tensions that had accompanied industrial growth. That task would be addressed in the succeeding decade in a setting in which the rise of the American city would grow to be as important a force for change as industrialism had been in the years after 1877.

The Chapter in Review

In the years between 1877 and 1887:

- Railroads emerged as the first big business.
- Initial efforts were made to regulate railroads through state railroad commissions.
- Standard Oil became a monopoly in the oil business and the new form of business called the trust was formed.
- Andrew Carnegie turned the steel industry into a major force for economic growth.

- The merits of Social Darwinism as an ideology were debated.
- The West was opened to mining and the range cattle industry.
- Industrialization spread through the South.
- The evenly divided party system produced few policies to address the issues of industrialism effectively.

Making Connections Across Chapters

LOOKING BACK

The focus of Chapter 17 is on the ways that industrialism affected the United States between 1877 and 1887. The ramifications of the industrializing process would have large consequences for the subsequent course of American history. Pay particular attention to how various groups in society, and specific regions of the country, responded to these new developments.

1. What conditions in the previous decade made it possible for industrialism to take hold?

2. How did cost-cutting and reducing labor expenses become a central effect of industrial growth?

3. How did the United States respond to the political problems arising from the spread of railroads?

4. In what ways was the country becoming more of a national market and economy?

5. What regions were left behind as industrialism grew?

LOOKING AHEAD

Chapter 18 will consider how cities developed in response to industrialism and look at the ways in which the South and West reacted to the changes agriculture was experiencing. Some of these shifts in thinking are anticipated in this chapter.

1. What pressures did industrialism place on farmers in the South and West?

2. How did the even balance of the political system prevent solutions to the economic changes of industrialism from being developed?

3. How did minorities fare during industrial growth?

Recommended Readings

Ayers, Edward. *The Promise of the New South* (1992). A fine modern treatment of the South in the years after Reconstruction ended.

Calhoun, Charles W. *The Gilded Age: Essays on the Origins of Modern America* (1996). A valuable assortment of excellent essays about this period.

Cherny, Robert. *American Politics in the Gilded Age, 1868–1900* (1997). A good, brief introduction to the public life of the period.

Edwards, Rebecca. *Angels in the Machinery: Gender in American Party Politics from the Civil War to the Progressive Era* (1997). Shows that women played a much larger part in political affairs than earlier historians had realized.

Porter, Glenn. *The Rise of Big Business, 1860–1920* (1992). An excellent short introduction to the economic trends of the Gilded Age.

Saum, Lewis O. *The Popular Mood of America, 1860–1890* (1990). Considers how the nation responded to social change.

Schlereth, Thomas J. *Victorian America: Transformations in Everyday Life, 1876–1915* (1991). A good survey of the impact of the changes brought by industrialism on the lives of Americans.

Summers, Mark Wahlgren. *The Gilded Age, or The Hazard of New Functions* (1997). A lively romp through the politics and leaders of the late nineteenth century.

Identifications

Review your understanding of the following key terms, people, events, and dates for this chapter (these terms also appear in the Glossary at the end of the book):

Interstate Commerce Act
robber barons
John D. Rockefeller
horizontal integration
Andrew Carnegie
vertical integration

Alexander Graham Bell
Thomas Alva Edison
Knights of Labor
Haymarket affair
Social Darwinism
Geronimo
Dawes Severalty Act
sharecropping
John Pemberton

Online Sources Guide

Use this listing to find online documents, images, interactive maps, simulations, and other resources related to this chapter:

American History Resource Center

http://history.wadsworth.com/rc/us

Documents

Chester Anders Fee, "Biography of Chief Joseph"
Helen Hunt Jackson, "A Century of Dishonor"
Henry W. Grady, "The New South" (1886)

Interactive Maps

Presidential Election Results, 1876–1896

Selected Images

1887 land promotion poster enticing settlers to Dakota Territory
Nebraska family in front of sod house
Mechanization on the farm
Cattle drive

40,000 buffalo hides, Dodge City, Kansas, 1878
Chief Joseph of the Nez Perce
Geronimo and his followers after surrender, 1886
Sharecroppers' cabin in North Carolina
Advertisement for the Missouri Pacific Railroad
Women delegates, Knights of Labor convention, 1886

Document Exercises

1877 Ku Klux Klan
1877 Sahara
1883 Elizabeth Knap of Groton

HistoryNOW

http://now.ilrn.com/ayers_etal3e

Primary Source Exercises

Westward Expansion
The Albuquerque Indian School in 1885
Description of Sharecropping Tenants on a Georgia Plantation, 1881
Economic Change and Workers' Reactions
New Ideas in American Life

18 Urban Growth and Farm Protest, 1887–1893

When the Oklahoma territory was opened to white homesteaders in April 1889, a wild land rush ensued. This photograph conveys the frenzy with which prospective settlers hurried to establish their claims to the best holdings.

As the United States approached its 100th birthday in 1889, its burgeoning urban population posed growing social problems. Huge gaps between rich and poor marked the new cities. Americans sought to reconcile traditional rural values with the diversity and turbulence of the metropolis. The political system struggled to adjust to the new demands that the people of the cities posed.

The farm problems that had simmered during the early 1880s reached a crisis. In the South and West, angry farmers formed a new political organization, the People's party, to make their grievances heard. For Indians, African Americans, and Hispanics, the new decade brought more painful reminders of their marginal status. The end of the nineteenth century saw renewed questions about the future of a nation of cities on its way to becoming a world power.

The New Urban Society

After **Grover Cleveland** made tariffs the central issue in the 1888 election, the united Republicans rallied behind their candidate, **Benjamin Harrison,** and the doctrine of tariff protection for American industries. Cleveland won the popular vote, but Harrison gained a majority in the electoral tally. The Republicans also secured control of both houses of Congress. With this hold on the executive and legislative branches, the Republicans intended to move ahead with an ambitious agenda of legislation. The stalemated system that had existed since the end of Reconstruction was about to break down.

During 1889 two events reflected the contrasting directions of the United States. Since the 1820s, the Five Civilized Tribes of Native Americans had lived in what is now Oklahoma. By the 1880s, however, pressure from white settlers to be given access to the territory proved irresistible in Congress. The Dawes Severalty Act of 1887 completed the process of stripping Indians of their rights. President Harrison announced that unoccupied land could be settled beginning April 22, 1889. One hundred thousand people rushed to acquire the newly available land. Within a few hours, the "Sooners," who entered the territory early, and the "Boomers" (a general

Timeline

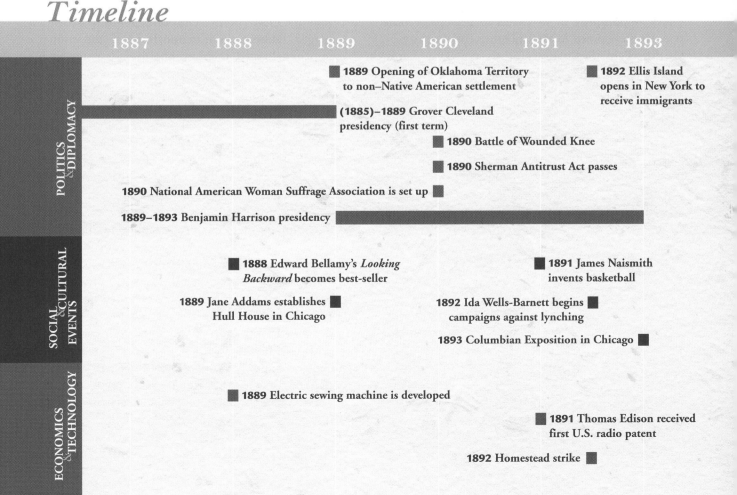

	1887	1888	1889	1890	1891	1893
POLITICS & DIPLOMACY			1889 Opening of Oklahoma Territory to non–Native American settlement			1892 Ellis Island opens in New York to receive immigrants
		(1885)–1889 Grover Cleveland presidency (first term)				
				1890 Battle of Wounded Knee		
				1890 Sherman Antitrust Act passes		
	1890 National American Woman Suffrage Association is set up					
	1889–1893 Benjamin Harrison presidency					
SOCIAL & CULTURAL EVENTS		1888 Edward Bellamy's *Looking Backward* becomes best-seller			1891 James Naismith invents basketball	
		1889 Jane Addams establishes Hull House in Chicago		1892 Ida Wells-Barnett begins campaigns against lynching		
				1893 Columbian Exposition in Chicago		
ECONOMICS & TECHNOLOGY			1889 Electric sewing machine is developed			
					1891 Thomas Edison received first U.S. radio patent	
				1892 Homestead strike		

name for eager settlers) had created towns and staked out farms. The Indians had to make do with land that whites did not occupy.

A few months later, in August 1889, **Jane Addams** and Ellen Gates Starr founded **Hull House**, a settlement home in a Chicago neighborhood. They hoped that solutions to the problems of poverty, disease, and political corruption could be found in their new residence. Hull House and Addams became famous. Her experiment reflected the views of many Americans that "the concentration of population in cities was "the most remarkable social phenomenon" of the nineteenth century. Jane Addams and like-minded Americans wanted to be part of making the new cities work.

The place that Addams and Starr had chosen for the social experiment symbolized what had happened in urban American since the Civil War. In 1860, Chicago had been the nation's ninth-largest city, with a population of just under 109,000. Thirty years later, Chicago held second place, with 1,099,850 people. The major east-west railroads ran through the city. To the stockyards came beef cattle from the West, to its elevators grain from the prairie, and to its lumberyards wood from the forests of Wisconsin and Minnesota. After the great fire of 1871, Chicago had built the skyscrapers that gave it a distinct skyline and created the ethnic neighborhoods whose residents Hull House served. With so much economic opportunity in its streets and shops, Chicago's population boomed in the late nineteenth century.

Elsewhere, the nation's urban population growth accelerated. In 1879, only nine cities had more than 100,000 inhabitants; in 1890 there were 28 with populations of that size. Most of this population surge happened in the Northeast and Middle West. Americans moved to the cities to escape the routine of "hard work and no holidays" that dominated rural life. Immigrants from Europe, many of them from cities in central and eastern Europe, remained in the large cities after they arrived. Newcomers came to Chicago and New York,

worked there for months and years, and then moved on to other cities, returned to the rural areas, or, in the case of some immigrants, went back to their home country.

The Structure of the City

After 1880 American cities grew in dramatic ways. The horsecar gave way to electric-power cable cars in San Francisco and other hilly cities. Relying on heavy cables running on the street, these devices were clumsy, inefficient, and expensive. Electric streetcars or trolleys, powered by overhead cables and moving at 10 miles an hour, soon replaced the cable system. Across the nation, urban transit soon electrified. To avoid traffic jams, some cities ran the streetcars on elevated tracks; others went underground to create subways. The older "walking city" soon disappeared.

As their populations shifted away from their core areas, the cities annexed their suburbs. Within the center of the city, race and ethnicity determined where people lived. The more affluent residents moved as far from the center as they could to get away from the lower classes and what they deemed their social inferiors. Social and cultural ties among the city's residents loosened. Each class, racial, and ethnic group had fewer encounters with people in other sections of the city than had been the case before the city expanded out to the suburbs.

In the heart of the city, central business districts emerged. Railroads built terminals, banks and insurance companies located their main offices downtown, and department stores anchored shopping districts. Streetcars brought customers from the suburbs to Macy's in New York, Marshall Field's in Chicago, and Filene's in Boston. In these "palaces of consumption," middle-class women spent their time in leisurely shopping for an array of attractive products. Museums, theaters, and opera houses added to the cultural resources of the industrial city.

Two new types of structures marked the new metropolis. Architects created the *skyscraper* as a practical solution for the need to conduct business in an often-compressed central business district. Louis Sullivan of Chicago developed techniques that made it possible for buildings to rise higher than the 5 to 10 stories that had been the upper limits of tall structures in the past. Passenger elevators, lighter walls reinforced with iron piers, and a framework of structural steel made it feasible to erect buildings with 20 to 40 stories or more. The skyscrapers allowed the business district to accommodate thousands of office workers each day.

The sheer numbers of people who crowded into the expanding cities strained the available living space. For the middle and upper classes, apartments were a practical answer and apartment buildings replaced the

---

DOING HISTORY ONLINE

Jane Addams, "First Days at Hull House"
In what ways were social reformers like Jane Addams different from the urban poor they sought to help? How aware were they of these differences? Did such an awareness affect their attitudes toward the poor or the ways in which they sought to help them?

History ⏳ Now™   Visit HistoryNOW to access primary sources and exercises related to this topic: http://now.ilrn.com/ayers_etal3e

© The Granger Collection, New York

The clutter and congestion of the city was one of the hallmarks of the urbanizing of the United States. This scene of Dearborn Street in Chicago illustrates the bustle and energy of the city as the 1890s began. Transportation by carriages and trolleys was common in the decade before the arrival of the automobile.

single-family home. Poorer city residents lived in the *tenement houses*, six- or seven-story houses built on narrow lots. New York City had 20,000 such structures, most of them 25 feet wide and 100 feet deep, with windows only at the front and back. During the late 1870s, after legislation mandated that at least some ventilation be provided, "dumbbell tenements" appeared. These had tiny indented windows along the sides. In these edifices, dozens of people lived in small, dark rooms. From the outside, the buildings looked decent, but as the novelist William Dean Howells noted, "To be in it, and not have the distance, is to inhale the stenches of the neglected street and to catch the yet fouler and dreadfuller poverty-smell which breathes from the open doorways."

Inside the tenement or on the teeming sidewalks, the crush of people strained the city's water and sanitation systems. The stench of manure, open sewers, and piled-up garbage filled their nostrils. Smoke from the factories and grime from machinery were everywhere. Chicago's water system struggled to work during the 1880s. Residents of Philadelphia described their water as "not only distasteful and unwholesome for drinking, but offensive for bathing purposes."

The cities expanded their facilities to meet the needs for better services. New York City created a system of reservoirs that brought water to the residents from surrounding lakes and rivers. Chicago faced immense

difficulties in transporting water from Lake Michigan for drinking needs and providing adequate sanitation. Park building became a priority of urban political machines and reformers alike. Although most of the new parks appeared on the outskirts of the city, away from the poorer sections, the amount of parkland in the larger cities doubled during the decade after 1888.

The New Immigration

The cities grew because people flocked to them from the countryside and foreign nations. For the 20 years after 1870, net immigration totaled more than 7.5 million people. Unlike the immigrants from northern and western Europe who had come during the first 75 years of the nineteenth century, these "New Immigrants" were mainly from southern and eastern Europe. These Italians, Poles, Hungarians, Russian Jews, and Czechs brought with them languages, lifestyles, and customs that often clashed with those of native-born Americans or earlier immigrants. Marrying within their own ethnic group, speaking their own language, and reading their own newspapers, they created distinctive, vibrant communities within the cities.

Many newcomers first saw the United States when they entered New York Harbor. They were processed at Castle Garden at the Battery in lower Manhattan. By the end of the 1880s, these immigration facilities had become inadequate. They were closed in 1890 and a new, more extensive immigrant station was opened in 1892 on **Ellis Island** in the harbor.

On Ellis Island the new arrivals were given a medical examination and questioned about their economic prospects. Sometimes even the names were changed. One often-told story was that of a German Jew confronted by an inspector who fired numerous questions at him. When finally asked his name, the man replied in Yiddish: "Schoyn vergessen" (I forget). The inspector heard what the words sounded like and said that "Sean Ferguson" was eligible to enter the United States.

The new arrivals made their living any way they could. They provided the labor for city construction gangs that built New York City's subways, the steel mills of Pittsburgh, and the skyscrapers of Chicago. Some men sold fruits and vegetables from pushcarts, others worked as day laborers, and increasing numbers built their own small businesses. Italian immigrant women "finished" garments for the clothing industry or made artificial flowers.

The cultural values and Old World experiences often dictated the jobs that men and women took. Italians preferred steady jobs with a dependable salary that left time for family life. Greeks joined railroad gangs where

Tenement Life in the Growing Cities

Documentary photographs became a favored way of depicting social problems at the end of the nineteenth century, and Lewis Hine was one of the most famous practitioners of the technique. His camera went inside the tenements of the growing cities to show the crowded conditions that confronted urban families. In this nicely wallpapered room, a mother minds six small children, most of them under the age of 10. The photograph cannot convey the noise or the smells of the scene, nor the fate that awaits the children in a few years.

© Bettmann/CORBIS

The older girl on the right will soon have to earn a living to assist the harried mother with the family's upkeep. Yet this family is also a little better off than the more desperate urban poor who do not have metal beds, chairs to make cradles, or this much space for six children.

they could work in the open. Jews became shopkeepers, merchants, and peddlers, the trades that had been open to them in the anti-Semitic world of eastern Europe. Some nationalities, Bohemians and Slovaks for example, allowed women to work as domestic servants; others, such as Jews, Italians, and Greeks, barred women from domestic work outside the home.

Ethnic neighborhoods appeared. In New York City, immigrants from Naples lived on Mott Street; Sicilians resided on Prince Street. Churches and synagogues shaped community life. Newcomers formed self-help societies to ease the transition for those who came after them—the Polish National Alliance, the Bohemian-American

National Council, and the Hebrew Immigrant Aid Society. They built theaters and concert halls, and created schools to educate their children. Some of the new arrivals moved away from their ethnic roots as they prospered; other immigrants soon replaced them. In the Tenth Ward of New York, the Jewish immigrant population in 1900 had a density of 900 people per acre, one of the highest in the world.

As the communities of immigrants grew, older residents expressed fears about the impact of the newcomers on traditional values and customs. Prejudice and religious intolerance flared. Editors of urban newspapers, speaking to the prejudices of their upper-class readers, called immigrants "the very scum and offal of the earth." During the 1880s, the anti-Catholic American Protective Association recruited those for whom the immigrants were a threat to Protestant religious values or a source of economic competition. Its members resolved to limit the role of Catholics in politics. These sentiments that favored "native" Americans (hence "nativist") led to calls for legislation to restrict immigration through literacy tests for entrance into the United States or quotas based on national origin.

Anti-Semitism permeated American society during these years. In addition to the long-standing religious roots of prejudice among Christians against Jews, the struggle over inflation and deflation in monetary policy drove notions that Jewish financiers dominated world banking. Among academics, social scientists, and historians, quasi-scientific arguments arose to justify exclusion of Jews from universities and businesses.

The Urban Political Machine

Politicians in the large cities grappled with a volatile mix of ethnicity, race, and economic class divisions. Most cities had a mayor–council form of government in which the entire population elected the mayor. Council members represented individual districts or wards. Divided, ineffective government resulted as council members traded favors and blocked legislation that hurt their districts.

The urban "political machine" led by the "**political boss**" developed. The word *machine* masked a more complex reality. The organization that dominated city politics consisted of an interlocking system of operations in each ward that delivered votes for their party at city and county conventions. The machine relied for its existence on the votes of the large inner-city population. They turned out faithfully on election day to support the candidates that the machine had designated.

The organization of the machine began in the ward. The leader of the ward got the vote out because he supplied his constituents with employment, help in an economic crisis or brush with the law, and regularly attended the weddings, funerals, and wakes of the neighborhood. A ward leader like George Washington Plunkitt in New York or John F. "Honey Fitz" Fitzgerald in Boston was the man to see when disaster threatened an urban family. "I think that there's got to be in every ward somebody that any bloke can come to—no matter what he's done—and get help," said a Boston ward leader. "Help, you understand, none of your law and justice, but help!"

The most notorious political machine of the era was the one connected to William Magear Tweed and the "Tweed Ring" of the late 1860s in New York City. Associated with the Democratic organization known as Tammany Hall (after the name of the clubhouse where its members met), Tweed used his influence to gain lucrative city contracts for his associates and supporters.

Democratic voters in New York applauded the ring as a source of jobs and patronage. Yet, Tweed's heyday was brief. He came under assault from major newspapers for corruption, but his most effective adversary was the cartoonist, Thomas Nast. Nast's drawings depicted Tweed as the leader of a band of criminals. Revelations about tainted contracts and crooked deals brought Tweed down in the early 1870s. The conditions that assisted his rise to power still existed, and machines flourished in New York and other major cities.

As the big cities grew, contracts were awarded to businesses to build the streets, install the sewers, lay the gas

DOING HISTORY ONLINE

Servicing the Urban Poor

Examine items two and three in this module, and consider the following questions. Political machines and political bosses were a source of controversy in the 1880s and 1890s. On what grounds does Baker attack them? How does Croker defend them? Who's argument do you find more persuasive?

History Now™   Visit HistoryNOW to access primary sources and exercises related to this topic: http://now.ilrn.com/ayers_etal3e

lines, and erect the elevated trains. These projects presented abundant chances for politicians to decide how money was spent. Judgments about who built streets, parks, and sewer connections depended on payoffs and graft to the boss and his associates. The flow of money, much of it based on corruption, enabled the machine to provide the social services that people wanted.

In the public's mind, the political boss stood at the top of the machine. Careful to keep their influence out of the spotlight, these men rarely held office and managed affairs from behind the scenes through their control of the local Democratic party. "Honest John" Kelly and Richard Croker of Tammany Hall were among the more celebrated of such leaders, but almost every major city had one. Their enemies depicted the bosses as unchallenged dictators of the city's destiny. In most cases, however, the bosses were shrewd politicians who balanced factions and interest groups in a constantly shifting political scene. The coming of industrialism had overwhelmed the old forms of city government that were based on a relatively small number of residents and a geographically limited urban area. The boss and the machine provided central direction for the city and represented an important innovation.

Reformers saw the machine as evil and graft-ridden. The president of Cornell University charged that the cities of the United States were "the most corrupt in Christendom." Members of the middle and upper classes, disturbed by the new power of the immigrants, attacked the boss and the machine as inefficient and wasteful. The boss and his allies often defeated the campaigns of the reformers because inner-city residents appreciated what the machine did for them. Reformers came and went; the machine was always there. As George Washington Plunkitt said, reformers "were mornin' glories—looked lovely in the mornin' and withered up in a short time, while the regular machines went on flourishin' forever, like fine old oaks."

"GROSS IRREGULARITY NOT 'FRAUDULENT.'"

Boss SWEED. "To make this *look straight* is the hardest job I ever had. What made WATSON go sleigh-riding?"

© CORBIS

Thomas Nast used his cartoons to attack the Tweed Ring in New York City. Here Nast shows the boss talking with cronies in his head quarters about one of their corrupt plans.

The rank-and-file residents also knew that reformers wanted to shift power away from the lower classes. The reform program often involved cutbacks in even the already minimal services that the poorer areas of the city received. On balance, the machines and bosses supplied reasonably good city government. Services were provided and economic opportunity expanded. City residents endorsed the results with their voters. Most cities had water, fire, and health services of a quality that compared with those found in the industrial nations of western Europe. In the city parks—Central Park in New York, the Boston park system, and the sprawling green spaces of St. Louis and Kansas City—the generation of the 1880s left a positive legacy to future urban residents.

The settlement houses that Jane Addams and others launched at the end of the decade proved a strong force for improving city life. There were citizenship classes, training in cultural issues, and sports programs for local youth. Often settlement workers approached the ethnic neighborhood with arrogance and insensitivity. In time, some of these individuals gained a better understanding of the obstacles that the immigrants faced. The experience in the ghettos and the streets of the cities prepared future reformers for work in subsequent campaigns. At the same time, Addams and her colleagues conveyed a strong sense of moralistic paternalism to the people they sought to serve. Their goal was to "build a bridge between European and American experiences" over which the immigrants could pass toward integration into the dominant culture. Despite this condescending attitude, the settlement house movement did soften the impact of the urban experience on some new immigrants. Still, the urbanizing process of the late nineteenth century had left the nation with accumulating social problems that would tax leaders and institutions for decades.

Dawes Severalty Act of 1887 was already taking away their lands. Bowed down by despair and hopelessness, the Plains Indians were receptive to any leaders who offered them a chance to regain their lost cultural values.

The appearance of a religious movement, called the Ghost Dance, promised Plains Indians the return of their buffalo herds and an end to white domination. If the Indians performed the rituals of the dance, said a Paiute messiah named Wovoka, the Indian dead would be reborn and the whites would vanish for all time. Apprehensive whites saw the Ghost Dance as a portent of another Indian uprising.

When the army moved against the Sioux in December 1890, fighting occurred on Wounded Knee Creek on the Pine Ridge Reservation in South Dakota. Despite bitter hand-to-hand combat, the "battle" was no contest. The army's machine guns cut down the Indians; they suffered 146 dead and 51 wounded. Army losses were 25 killed and 39 wounded. The **Battle of Wounded Knee** was the last chapter in the Indian wars.

While the Indian conflicts were ebbing, social conflict involving Mexican Americans erupted in the territory of New Mexico. A major political issue was the land grants that the Spanish crown had made. Anglo lawyers acquired title to these properties in order to assemble large landholdings of their own. Hispanic residents had grazed their cattle on communal lands that all ranchers shared. Now Anglo ranchers and settlers divided up the land with fences and sold it among themselves.

Spanish Americans tried to resist this trend by forming a secret vigilante organization, *Las Gorra Blancas* (The White Caps). In 1889, they cut fences and burned Anglo property such as railroads and lumberyards. Thus, ethnic and economic tensions led to social violence in the territory as part of the resistance to the dominant power of white settlers.

The Diminishing Rights of Minority Groups

The United States was not a very tolerant nation at the end of the 1880s. For Native Americans, Mexican Americans, Chinese, and African Americans, these were years when their rights were at risk from repressive forces within white society. As a result, the period saw a narrowing of the possibilities for Americans who belonged to one of these distinct racial or ethnic minorities. In the case of the Indians, the disastrous effects of the attitudes of whites played themselves out in tragic ways.

The end of large-scale Indian resistance to white expansion left them with few viable ways to protest policies that destroyed their traditions and confined them to reservations or government schools. The

The Battle of Wounded Knee provided this cartoonist with an opportunity to contrast how the United States denounced the imperialism of other nations with its own harsh treatment of Native Americans.

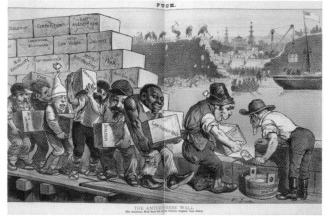

Cartoonists in the 1880s depicted minorities in racial and ethnic stereotypes. In this antitariff drawing, the artist portrays African Americans, Chinese, and Jews creating a wall to keep Chinese goods out of the United States while the Chinese remove barriers to American goods in their country.

Chinese immigrants came to the United States during the 1840s and 1850s to work the gold mines. They then constructed the transcontinental railroads in the 1860s. Energetic and thrifty, the Chinese soon engaged in manufacturing enterprises and farming. White Californians reacted. Laws barred the Chinese from professions in which they competed with whites. A movement to ban Chinese immigration grew. An 1868 treaty had guaranteed free access to Chinese immigrants to the United States. Twelve years later Washington pressured the Chinese to change the treaty to allow for the regulation of Chinese immigrants. As a result, the Chinese Exclusion Act of 1882 barred Chinese entry into the United States for 10 years.

Prejudice against the 104,000 Chinese in the West became more intense in these years. Congress moved to tighten further restrictions on immigration. In 1889, the Supreme Court upheld the constitutionality of such laws and stated that such measures would help in "the preservation of our civilization there." Congress extended the Chinese Exclusion Act in 1892 for another 10 years. By 1900, the number of Chinese living in the United States fell to 85,000. Most of the Chinese Americans resided in cities where they established laundries, restaurants, and other small business that served members of their own community. The Chinese Benevolent Association or "Six Companies" offered support for a Chinese culture that existed in a rich and complex setting of its own.

The Spread of Segregation

The most elaborate and sustained policy of racial separation was aimed at African Americans in the South. As blacks tried to take part in politics and seek wealth and

happiness, white southerners responded with a caste structure to ensure their continued dominance.

An important national trend allowed the South to pursue these policies. White Americans in all parts of the nation believed that blacks were their inferiors. Reconstruction had been, in the minds of whites, a failure. Accordingly, white southerners, it was argued, should deal with the black population as they deemed best. Northern willingness to abandon the aims of the Civil War and Reconstruction was a key element in the rise of segregation.

With the tacit approval of the North, the white politicians of the South devised segregation laws to cover most spheres of human activity. Blacks were barred from white railroad cars and had to use the inferior and often shabby cars assigned to their race. Whites had their own hotels, parks, hospitals, and schools. Blacks had either to make do with lesser facilities or do without them entirely.

Informal restrictions also shaped the everyday life of blacks. African Americans were expected to step out of the way of whites, be respectful and deferential, and never, by manner or glance, to display resentment or anger. A young black man was a "boy" until he became old enough to be labeled "uncle." To call an African American person either "Mr." or "Mrs." would have implied a degree of individuality that the culture of segregation in the South could not tolerate.

Laws removed blacks from the political process. They could not serve on juries in judgment of whites. They experienced harsher penalties when convicted of a crime than white offenders did. Although some blacks had voted during the 1880s, in the next decade laws were passed to make it impossible for African Americans to vote. The South took its cue from Mississippi; that state's constitutional convention, held in 1890, required that voters demonstrate their literacy and pay a poll tax before they could cast a ballot. An illiterate man had to qualify to vote by demonstrating that he could "understand" a provision of the state constitution when it was read to him. Election judges were lenient in allowing illiterate whites to vote;

Serving in the military, where they were known as Buffalo Soldiers, was one occupation that offered black males some degree of opportunity.

black voters were asked questions about the state constitution that a trained lawyer would have found difficult to answer. A poll tax had to be paid in advance and a receipt presented at the polls. These laws worked against poor whites and most blacks, who found it easier not to vote. In states like Mississippi and Louisiana, the number of registered black voters fell during the early 1890s; the number of white voters declined as well.

If legal restrictions were not sufficient to maintain white supremacy, blacks faced the constant possibility of extralegal violence. In the 1890s, an average of 187 black Americans were lynched annually. Blacks convicted of crimes were imprisoned in brutal circumstances in overcrowded penitentiaries or made to work on gangs that the state leased out to private contractors. The convict-lease system produced inmate death rates as high as 25 percent in some states.

Blacks resisted the rising tide of segregation in the courts. In Louisiana, African Americans tested an 1890 law specifying that they must ride in separate railroad cars. On June 7, 1892, **Homer A. Plessy,** who was one-eighth black, boarded a train bound from New Orleans to Covington, Louisiana. He sat in the car reserved for whites, and the conductor instructed him to move to the car for blacks. He refused and was arrested. When his case came before Judge Thomas H. Ferguson, Plessy's claim that the law violated his constitutional rights was denied. The case, now known as *Plessy v. Ferguson,* was appealed to the U.S. Supreme Court. A decision was not expected for several years.

Black leaders resisted to the extent they could. The remaining African American members of southern legislatures argued against discriminatory legislation, but they were easily outvoted. A Richmond Virginia Democrat boasted of the tactics used to exclude blacks from elections. "It was well understood that the blacks had to be beaten by hook or by crook—they knew what to expect and they knew who was putting the thing on them but they could not prevent it." By the mid-1890s, the South was as segregated as white leaders could make it. For most blacks the constitutional guarantees of the Fourteenth and Fifteenth Amendments existed only on paper. The fate of minorities had a low priority in a society where racial stereotypes infused the mind-set of a Victorian society.

A Victorian Society

In the late nineteenth century, the social customs embodied in the term "Victorian" provided the context in which most white Americans lived. Like their counterparts in Great Britain, where Queen Victoria ruled between 1837 and 1901, these Americans professed a public code of personal behavior that demanded restraint, sexual modesty,

temperate habits, and hard work. They failed to see how much the minorities in the United States also exemplified these precepts, and in their own lives white Americans often fell well short of these ideals.

The Rules of Life

The precepts of Victorian morality applied to every aspect of daily life. Relations between the sexes followed precise rules. Unmarried men and women were supposed to be chaperoned when they were together before marriage. A suitor asked a woman whether he might write to her before presuming to do so. A kiss resulted in an engagement or social disgrace. Premarital sex was taboo. People married for life, mourned a dead spouse for at least a year, and showed fidelity by not remarrying. Some people flouted these guides, of course, but many followed them and the social conventions that they represented.

Once married, a couple was expected to engage in sexual intercourse only for the purpose of having children. The wife was to tame the husband's baser instincts. She was considered to be naturally pure; the husband was prey to the animalistic drives in his masculine nature. "The full force of sexual desire is seldom known to a virtuous woman," said one male writer, with the implication that women did not achieve the same pleasure in sex that men did.

In reality, of course, women's desires did not conform to these stereotypes. One mother of four in her thirties remarked that sexual relations "makes more normal people." A survey of 45 married women, done by Professor Clelia Mosher in 1892, found that almost three-quarters of them experienced pleasure during lovemaking. Limits on the frequency of sex may have been to reduce unwanted pregnancies in a time before birth control devices became widespread.

Middle-class and upper-class men in Victorian society pursued careers out of the house, doing what a leading magazine took for its title—"The World's Work." They spent their days at the factory or office, and the children saw them in the evening and on Sundays. Males displayed the right virtues in what was called their "character." In these classes, men might sow their "wild oats" before marriage, but after that were expected to adhere to their wedding vows. The rising number of divorces (56,000 by 1900) indicated that many did not do so. People looked the other way when men patronized prostitutes or had discreet sexual adventures outside wedlock. When it became know than a woman had followed such a course, she was disgraced.

A strict moral code governed the raising of Victorian children. Parents instilled character in their children, often by spanking or more intense physical abuse. Children were to be seen and not heard, and were required to show respect to their elders. Discussion of sex was rare. Many women knew nothing about it until they were married.

Despite the constraints placed on children's behavior, youthful high spirits found an outlet in games and play. Entertainment was centered in the home, where families assembled to play board and card games, sing around a parlor organ or piano, and for the wealthier Americans, play croquet and lawn tennis.

On Sundays, the middle-class family went to church. Religion permeated the nation of 63 million people. In 1890, there were 145 different Christian denominations with nearly 22 million members. More than 8 million people were Roman Catholics; Presbyterians, Methodists, and Southern Baptists were the major Protestant denominations. Despite fears that religious convictions were waning in the face of growing secularism, thousands responded enthusiastically to the religious revivals that Dwight L. Moody and other celebrated evangelist conducted. Yet at the same time, Victorian ideas were under attack. Though some mainline Protestant churches assimilated the teachings of Charles Darwin without protest, other denominations contended that evolution and religion could not coexist. "The human soul shrinks from the thought that it is without kith or kin in all this wide universe," concluded an observer of the intellectual currents of the decade. The struggle about Darwinism continued over the course of the next century.

A Sporting Nation

While thinkers debated the impact of modern ideas on old-time religious verities, Americans sought relaxation and recreation in popular spectator sports. Among the upper and middle classes, football had emerged as second only to baseball in its appeal. The first intercollegiate football game occurred between Princeton and Rutgers in 1869; the modern game evolved as rules for scoring became established. Walter Camp, the unofficial coach at Yale University and the founder of the "All-American" teams, devised the line of scrimmage and the requirement that a team gain 5 yards in three attempts in order to retain possession of the ball. Dividing the field into 5-yard squares produced the "gridiron." With regular rules came recruitment of talented athletes, charges of professionalism, and obsession with the sport among alumni. Football appealed most to those who believed that young men should demonstrate commitment to a strenuous existence in a violent game that tested their masculine courage.

Boxing had a wider appeal to all classes of society, especially because it gave ethnic groups and immigrants a chance to advance in life. Irish American boxers dominated the sport, with **John L. Sullivan** the most famous

By the end of the 1880s, college football was becoming a major spectator sport. Here a photographer records the crowd watching Cornell University and the University of Rochester in an 1889 game. The players performed without the equipment and padding of the modern game.

© The Granger Collection, New York

champion. Some matches were held in secret and continued for as many as 75 bloody rounds. The contestants did not use gloves. Gloves and formal rules appeared during the 1880s. Sullivan lost his heavyweight crown in 1892 to James J. "Gentleman Jim" Corbett in the first gloved title fight. African American fighters appeared in interracial bouts in some divisions, but before 1900 white heavyweight champions observed the "color line."

Another popular diversion was bicycling, which became a craze after 1890. At first, cycling was a sport for those who could master the brakeless "ordinary" bikes with their oversize front wheels. Then in the 1880s the "safety" bicycle, so called because of its brakes and inflated pneumatic tires, appeared. Technology had now produced a bicycle that the average person could ride in relative comfort, and the fad was on. Some 10 million bikes were in use by 1900. Cycling led women to adopt looser garments and, according to some enthusiasts, eased childbirth. After the automobile appeared at the beginning of the twentieth century, the passion for bicycling receded, and memories of the craze that had marked the early 1890s faded away.

Voices of Protest and Reform

Bicycles were not the only craze that swept the nation at the end of the 1880s. **Edward Bellamy,** a former reporter turned novelist, published a tale called *Looking Backward: 2000–1887* in 1888. Its main character, Julian West, had gone to sleep in 1887 and woke in 2000. In the future he met Doctor Leete, who told him how the world had

Bicycling became a popular fad during the 1890s. Its low cost and convenience made it an attractive recreation for millions of Americans. This race attracted a large crowd of spectators.

changed during the 113 years he had been asleep. In the new industrial order of "Nationalism," efficiency and discipline had replaced the chaos of the late nineteenth century. Citizens had purpose in their lives. Members of an industrial army, they served the state that in turn provided them with material rewards. Bellamy's argument offered the promise of a nation organized for a common purpose in pursuit of abundance without the coercion of the government.

Bellamy became an overnight celebrity. *Looking Backward* sold hundreds of thousands of copies. "Nationalist" clubs sprang up to spread his doctrine. The fad ebbed quickly, but Bellamy had hit a nerve in a society that was restive about industrialism. His evocation of community and cooperative action resonated in a competitive, capitalist society. Troubled individuals turned to their faith, to organization, and to political action to deal with their unease about the direction of the nation.

Religion offered one answer to the social ills of industrialism. Many clergymen had defended the inequalities of wealth and status in society. This harsh response offended younger members of the ministry who sought to improve society rather than to save individual souls. They rebelled against the tenets of Social Darwinism and the idea that the ills of society were the results of natural selection. Walter Rauschenbusch, a Baptist clergyman in Rochester, New York, had seen firsthand the hardship and despair that slum dwellers experienced. He believed that it was necessary to "Christianize" the social order to bring it "into harmony with the ethical convictions which we identify with Christ." The church, he wrote, must "demand protection for the moral safety of the people."

Rauschenbusch's ideas came to be known as the Social Gospel. He and other ministers went into the city to preach the Gospel to poor slum dwellers. Washington Gladden spoke out from the First Congregational Church

in Columbus, Ohio, and wrote a book entitled *Applied Christianity,* which was published in 1886. "The Christian moralist," he wrote, had to tell "the Christian employer" that the wage system "when it rests on competition as its sole basis is anti-social and anti-Christian." Similar doctrines were promoted within Judaism and Catholicism. The Social Gospel contributed to the reform impulses that extended through the 1890s.

Middle-class women were leaders in the reform efforts of the 1890s. The Woman's Christian Temperance Union (WCTU) expanded its role under Frances Willard, its president from 1879 to 1899. It pursued missions to the urban poor, constructive changes in the situation of prison inmates, and protests against male-dominated politics. Prohibition thus became more than just the restriction of alcohol; for the WCTU it included a spectrum of ideas to improve society.

Women who had gained leisure time during the 1880s transformed their literary and discussion clubs into campaigns with a more ambitious agenda. A leading feminist, Charlotte Perkins Gilman, saw clubs as "the first timid steps toward social organization of these so long unsocialized members of our race." In 1890 the General Federation of Women's Clubs was founded, with a core membership of 200 clubs and some 20,000 women on its rolls. It sponsored cultural and educational activities for working women and homemakers. In Chicago, women's clubs supported the Legal Aid Society and other "child-saving" endeavors to help mothers raise their children in healthier settings.

The campaign to achieve woman suffrage had remained divided after the National Woman Suffrage Association and the American Woman Suffrage Association split over the Fifteenth Amendment and African American voting rights. The rift was healed through the efforts of Lucy Stone Blackwell. In 1890, the **National American Woman Suffrage Association** (NAWSA) appeared. The president was Elizabeth Cady Stanton; Susan B. Anthony succeeded her in 1892. Progress toward suffrage was slow at first. Elections to secure suffrage usually failed and by the middle of the 1890s only four states (Wyoming, Utah, Colorado, and Idaho) allowed women to vote. Nonetheless, NAWSA provided an important organizational foundation for future growth.

Other reform goals attracted the support of committed women. Josephine Shaw Lowell animated the Charity Organization Society which sent "friendly visitors" into urban slums to instruct residents and "in great measure prevent the growth of pauperism." Homes were established for the impoverished mother and prostitute where she could obtain "Friends, Food, Shelter and a HELPING HAND by coming just as she is." Florence Kelley of Hull House carried the ideas of the settlement movement into the more ambitious Illinois Women's

Alliance in 1892. The New York City Working Women's Society protested harsh working conditions in that city in 1890; its activities led to the formation of consumers' leagues in other cities. These diverse examples of social criticism and constructive action taught lessons about the effects of industrialism that would shape the experience of the coming generation.

Looking Outward: Foreign Policy in the Early 1890s

Interest in the world beyond the United States was also growing. After several decades of internal development, the nation sought a larger role in world affairs. The campaign for an expansionist foreign policy moved slowly at first in the face of persistent isolationism. Between 1887 and 1893, the country adopted the first policies that would help it move toward becoming a world power.

In 1889, the United States was a weak military and diplomatic force. The army was small, with fewer than 25,000 men who served in isolated posts in the West. The navy was equally insignificant. One congressman called the fleet "an alphabet of floating washtubs." Sails and wooden vessels were the rule until the 1880s when four steel ships were built. National attitudes would have to change for the nation to become a world force.

One apparent source of support for expansion was the interest in overseas markets that surfaced during these years. In 1890, the Census Bureau announced the official closing of the frontier with the disappearance of a clear line of unsettled territory. Further expansion would have to be international. Noting the size of the nation's industrial output, business leaders and farmers worried about whether the home market could consume everything that factories and farms produced. Perhaps it would become necessary to secure overseas markets to relieve the pressure. The United States still imported more than it exported; in 1887, exports stood at $810 million; imports at $967 millions. Exports fluctuated during the last quarter of the nineteenth century, but the overall trend was gradually upward. By the middle of the 1890s, the nation would export more than it imported.

The zeal for overseas markets helped feed a general enthusiasm for expansion, but the direct impact on policy was less certain. The percentage of the gross national product devoted to exports remained low. The official economic policy toward foreign trade was protectionist. Proponents of tariffs resisted efforts to lower trade barriers in order to expand overseas commerce. As a result, the sentiment for imperialism in the United States had an economic component, but the real drive for an international role had different causes.

The Roots of Imperialism

The example set by European powers scrambling to expand their empires had a powerful impact on Americans' attitudes toward world affairs. As Africa and Asia became colonies and protectorates of Great Britain, Germany, France, and other countries, Americans worried about being left behind. Applying the doctrines of Social Darwinism to foreign nations, advocates of empire said that a nation that did not expand would find itself unfit to survive.

A leader in the campaign for expansion was Captain Alfred T. Mahan of the U.S. Navy. Mahan's research into naval history led to his most important work, *The Influence of Seapower on History, 1660–1783*, published in 1890. Mahan wanted his country to embark on the path to global greatness, and he believed that sea power was the way to achieve it. Only through naval bases, a powerful battleship fleet, and an aggressive foreign policy could the United States compete in a world of empires. He told policymakers that the United States should expand its foreign commerce, construct a strong navy, and acquire overseas bases. Of particular concern was a canal across Central America. Secretaries of the navy from 1889 onward listened to Mahan, as did such future leaders as Henry Cabot Lodge and Theodore Roosevelt.

The notion of Anglo-Saxon supremacy fed the new interest in foreign affairs. The Protestant minister Josiah Strong contended in *Our Country: Its Possible Future and Its Present Crisis* (1885) that "God, with infinite wisdom and skill, is training the Anglo-Saxon race for an hour sure to come in the world's future." The popular author John Fiske gave lectures on "Manifest Destiny." In them he predicted that "every land on the earth's surface" that was not already civilized would become "English in its language, in its religion, in political habits and traditions, and a predominant extent in the blood of its people." These statements helped make expansionism seem aligned with the nation's future.

New Departures in Foreign Policy

During the brief administration of James A. Garfield, Secretary of State James G. Blaine tried to renegotiate the Clayton-Bulwer Treaty (1850) to give the United States control over any canal across Central America. Blaine hoped to create a Pan-American system that would promote stability and security in the Caribbean and South America. The end of the Garfield administration took Blaine out of office and postponed any further action on Pan-Americanism for almost a decade.

The gradual movement toward a greater international role continued under Presidents Chester Arthur and Grover Cleveland. Secretary of State Frederick T. Frelinghuysen pursued treaties for trade reciprocity with

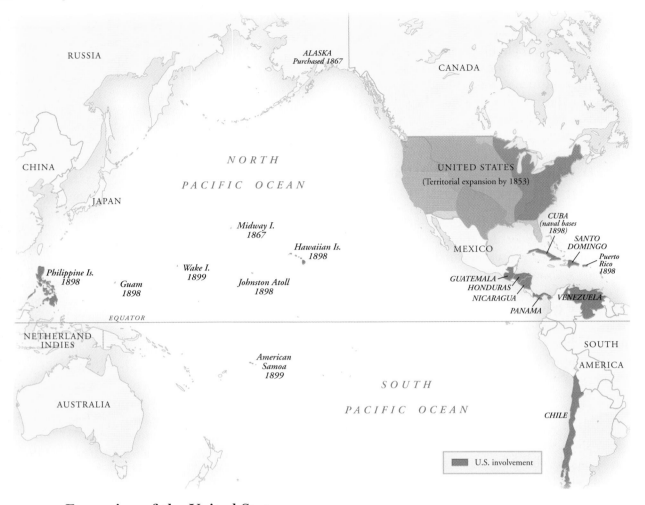

MAP 18.1 **Expansion of the United States**

In the late nineteenth century, the United States established a military and economic presence in the Pacific and Latin America. This map shows the areas in which the nation became involved and where new possessions in the Pacific were acquired.

nations such as Mexico, Santo Domingo, and Colombia. Much as Blaine had done with South American, Frelinghuysen believed that these treaties would unite the interests of those countries with those of the United States. Congress, however, declined to act on the pacts.

Under Cleveland, the process slowed as the administration showed less enthusiasm for a canal across Nicaragua or a greater American presence worldwide. Still, the size of the navy grew during the Cleveland years. When Blaine returned to the State Department under Benjamin Harrison in 1889, the drive for an expansionist policy resumed.

Blaine sent out invitations for a conference to Latin American countries, and delegates from 19 nations assembled in Washington on October 2, 1889, for the first International American Conference. Blaine urged the delegates to set up mechanisms for freer trade among themselves and to work out procedures for settling their regional conflicts. Unwilling to accept what seemed to be the dominance of the United States, the conference declined to pursue these initiatives. Instead, it established

the International Bureau of the American Republics, which became the Pan-American Union in 1910.

Blaine persuaded his Republican colleagues in Congress to include language allowing for reciprocity treaties in the McKinley Tariff Act of 1890. A number of products were placed on the free list, including sugar, molasses, coffee, and tea; the president could impose tariffs on such items if Latin American countries did not grant the United States similar concessions on its exports. Blaine used the reciprocity clause of the McKinley Tariff to negotiate treaties with such South American countries as Argentina. U.S. exports increased, disproving the claims of critics who warned that it would stifle trade with other nations.

The Harrison administration followed a more aggressive foreign policy in two other key areas. Secretary of the Navy Benjamin F. Tracy urged Congress to appropriate money for a battle fleet that would not only protect the coastline of the United States but also engage enemies across the oceans. Lawmakers authorized four modern battleships, fewer than what Tracy wanted but nonetheless an expansion of naval power.

The second area of activism in the Harrison years involved greater involvement in Asia. With their eyes on potential markets for produce and crops, business leaders said that the Hawaiian Islands seemed a logical stepping-stone to the Orient. Missionaries had been preaching in the islands since the 1820s; their reports fed American fascination with Hawaii. Trade relations between the United States and Hawaii had grown stronger since the reciprocity treaty, signed in 1875, gave Hawaiian sugar and other products duty-free entry into the United States. In exchange, Hawaii agreed not to grant other countries any concessions that threatened the territorial or economic independence of the island nation. The relationship was further strengthened in 1887 when the treaty was renewed and the United States received the exclusive right to use the superb strategic asset of Pearl Harbor.

Within Hawaii, the white immigrants and the native rulers clashed. The Hawaiian monarch, King Kalakua, had been inclined to accept closer ties between the United States and his nation. He died in 1891, bringing to power his sister, Queen Liliuokalani. She resented the American presence in Hawaii and believed that the white minority should not have dominant power.

Hawaiian politics became more complex after the McKinley Tariff removed the duty-free status of Hawaiian sugar and granted bounties to American cane growers in Louisiana and beet sugar growers in the Rocky Mountain states. The Hawaiian sugar industry slumped and economic conditions on the islands worsened. Calls for annexation arose from Americans in Hawaii and Congress in Washington.

During 1892, the Hawaiian legislature and queen argued over the presence and role of foreigners in the country. As the new year began, the queen dismissed the legislature and put in place a constitution that stripped white settlers of many of the powers they had enjoyed under the previous document. Proponents of annexation launched a revolt and called on the U.S. minister (the official representative of the United States to the islands) and the American navy. With the aid of 150 U.S. Marines, the coup succeeded. The queen capitulated and a provision government was created. The United States agreed to a treaty of annexation with the pro-American and predominantly white rebels on February 14, 1893. It looked as if Hawaii would become a possession of the United States. Then the incoming president, Grover Cleveland, said that the treaty should not be ratified until the new administration took office. The fate of Hawaii remained in limbo as the second Cleveland presidency began.

Despite this temporary pause, the extent of American expansion during the Harrison administration was striking. The navy had grown and its mission had broadened. The ties to Latin American had been extended and the fate of Hawaii seemed to be linked to that of the

© The Granger Collection, New York

When Americans endeavored to bring the Hawaiian Islands under United States control, Queen Liliuokalani led the native Hawaiians in efforts to forestall the end of their independence. Her resistance led the Cleveland administration to block Hawaiian annexation for most of the 1890s.

United States. Harrison and Blaine had launched the nation on a path of greater overseas involvement that would continue through the 1890s. For the moment, however, internal ferment captured the nation's attention as social and political unrest flared in the heartland of the United States.

The Angry Farmers

Of all the groups who found themselves at odds with the direction of American society between 1887 and 1893, the unhappy farmers of the South and West had the greatest impact on the nation and its political system.

The election of Benjamin Harrison in 1888 and Republican control of Congress had allowed the majority party to enact a wide-ranging program of legislative activism. The key measures included the McKinley Tariff, the **Sherman Antitrust Act,** and the Sherman Silver Purchase Act. The tariff law raised rates and the Sherman Act on silver provided for limited government purchases of the white metal. The antitrust act outlawed "combinations in restraint of trade" without providing much means to enforce the new law.

If Republicans expected these accomplishments to please voters, they were soon disillusioned. In the election of 1890, the Democrats capitalized on unhappiness with national Republican policies, as well as a backlash against the Grand Old Party over local issues such as prohibition and laws requiring closing of businesses on the Sabbath. The new McKinley Tariff proved unpopular in the North, and in the South, Democrats used racial issues against their political rivals. The result was a Democratic victory that gave the opposition firm control of the House of Representatives.

The Rise of the Farmers' Alliance

The 1890 election also brought a new force on to the national political scene. Candidates identified with the Farmers' Alliance made impressive gains in the South and West. Alliance candidates won nine seats in the House and elected two members to the U.S. Senate. Their candidates dominated several southern state legislatures and they showed strength as well in such Middle Western states as Kansas, Nebraska, South Dakota, and Minnesota.

The crisis in southern agriculture had been building for decades. As productivity increased between 1865 and 1885, the prices of farm products declined. A bushel of wheat brought almost $1.20 in 1881 but fell to just under $0.70 a bushel in 1889. Cotton was worth almost $0.11 a pound in 1881; by 1890 that figure had fallen to $0.085 per pound.

Farmers had other grievances than low prices. When farm prices declined, western farmers found that the debts they had run up during the 1880s were now more difficult to pay. For southern farmers, whether sharecroppers or tenants, the slide in prices meant that their debts to the "furnish merchant" also mounted up.

Railroads seemed to be villains to western and southern crop growers. High rates cut into the farmers' profits, and there were consistent complaints that the rail lines favored manufacturers and middlemen over agrarians. The railroads wielded this power, said their critics, because they had corrupted the political process.

The system of money and banking also drew scorn. Every dollar in circulation had to have an equal amount of gold bullion behind it to keep the nation's currency on "the gold standard." Gold was stored in banks and at the U.S. Treasury. Since international gold production was static, the amount of money in circulation did not keep up with the growth in the population. The currency became deflated as the value of the dollar rose. Wheat farmers on the plains or cotton farmers in the South had to work harder to maintain the same level of income.

The thoughts of many farmers naturally turned to ways in which the currency might be inflated—that is, ways of putting more dollars into circulation.

The complaints of the farmers were genuine, but workable solutions were another matter. Farm prices were low as a result of the expanding acreage under cultivation. One long-term solution was the consolidation of small farms into larger, more efficient agricultural businesses. Such a process would occur later in the nation's history. But at the end of the nineteenth century, it ran counter to the widely held belief in the importance of small landowners to the health of a democratic society.

The problem of debt was equally complex. Farmers on the plains, for example, had purchased land whose value was expected to increase, and they now faced the ruin of their ventures. Interest rates were not as high as they believed, nor were mortgage companies as tyrannical as agrarian complaints indicated. Nonetheless, the prevailing percept among farmers in the South and West was that they were the victims of a system that took no heed of their needs or interests.

The Farmers' Alliance was formed in Texas to stop horse thieves in Lampasas County. After some early troubles, it emerged as the Texas Farmers' Alliance in 1884. Elsewhere in the South, angry farmers organized into alliances and associations that expressed their grievances. They came up with proposed solutions in a three-stage process.

During the first phase, southern and western farmers looked toward cooperative action. A leader in this effort was Charles Macune, who became president of the Texas Alliance in 1886. He envisioned alliances and cooperative exchanges across the South. These institutions could provide farmers with supplies and equipment at a cost below what local merchants and retailers charged. The farmers would thus gain more control over the marketplace. To spread the creed of the cooperatives, the Alliance sent out "lecturers" who fanned out across the region.

Cooperatives proved easier to organize than to sustain. Marketing crops at a time other than the harvest season required capital because it was necessary to store the crops until prices rose. The farmers lacked the financial resources to make such a scheme work. It also proved difficult to obtain the lower prices through cooperatives. A complex distribution system moved goods across the country, and that process had certain inherent costs no matter who controlled it.

Although economic success eluded the Alliance between 1886 and 1890, its political power grew. The ideology of cooperative action appealed to farm families who often were isolated from one another. The Alliance meetings brought farmers together to hear speeches, enjoy entertainment, and share experiences. The

Alliance thus built on collective emotion among farmers as the 1890s began.

Some members of the Alliance saw African American farmers as potential allies. The Colored Farmers' National Alliance and Cooperative Union was formed in 1886. The interaction between the black Alliance and its white counterpart was uneasy. Whites were usually landowners, even if impoverished ones; blacks tended to be either tenants or farm laborers. In 1891, the Colored Alliance sought to get higher wages for picking cotton. A strike for that purpose, organized by a black leader named Ben Patterson in Lee County, Arkansas, was met with violence. Fifteen of the strikers, including Patterson, were lynched, and the Colored Alliance vanished.

As farm conditions worsened during years of drought and falling crop prices, branches of the Alliance gained members in the Dakotas, Nebraska, and especially Kansas. By 1889, concerted national action seemed a logical next step. Representatives of these various organizations met in St. Louis in December 1889. Out of their deliberations came the **Farmers' Alliance** and Industrial Union. The delegates agreed to leave out the word "white" from the organization's requirements, although state organizations in the South could continue to exclude black members. Three key northern states, Kansas and the two Dakotas, joined the national organization.

Charles Macune offered the most important policy proposal of the conference, the subtreasury plan. Macune recognized that the major problem that confronted cotton and wheat farmers was having to sell their crops at harvest time when supplies were abundant and prices low. To surmount this obstacle, he envisioned a system of government warehouses or subtreasuries where farmers could store their crops until prices went up. To bridge the months between storage and selling, the farmers would receive a certificate of deposit from the warehouse for 80 percent of the crop's existing market value. The charge for this service would be a 1 percent or 2 percent annual interest rate. Farmers would wait, sell their crops for higher prices, repay the loans, and keep the resulting profits.

The subtreasury plan had some weaknesses. If a majority of wheat or cotton farmers waited until prices rose and then sold their crops, the market glut would force prices down again. The certificates that the farmers

Picturing the Past — POLITICS & DIPLOMACY

Populism as Radicalism

Although historians treat the farm protest of the 1880s and 1890s with respect, during the Gilded Age the mainstream press viewed the unhappy agrarians with disdain. In this 1891 cartoon that followed an organizing meeting of the People's party in Cincinnati in May, the movement was depicted as a patchwork of old ideas from the 1870s first advanced by the Knights of Labor and the Greenback party.

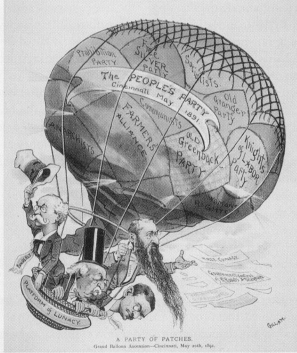

A PARTY OF PATCHES.
Grand Balloon Ascension—Cincinnati, May 20th, 1891.

The participants are also caricatured as ineffectual cranks borne on the winds of discontent. Amused dismissal of Populism would, however, give way to fears for social stability when economic hard times arrived with the Panic of 1893. Such inflationary ideas as free silver, derided in the cartoon, would then be viewed as potentially destructive of the monetary system and the economy. Like so many American protest campaigns, the ideas scorned in this cartoon would in due course be incorporated into how the nation was governed.

DOING HISTORY ONLINE

Populists in Black and White

Using items one and two in this module, explain why the local Colored Farmers' Alliance's resolution would potentially create conflict between blacks and whites in the South.

History Now™   Visit HistoryNOW to access primary sources and exercises related to this topic: http://now.ilrn.com/ayers_etal3e

The People's party used women to recruit new members and thus gave them a greater opportunity to be heard in political life. One of the most successful figures in this process was Annie Diggs of Kansas.

would have received for storing their crops at the subtreasury warehouses would represent another form of paper money that would fluctuate in value. Beyond that, the idea involved a large expansion of government power in an era when suspicion of federal power was still strong. To its agrarian advocates, the subtreasury seemed to be a plausible answer to the harsh conditions they confronted.

During the 1890 election, the protest movement poured its energy into speeches. In Kansas it represented an entirely new party. At a time when women took little direct part in politics, the Alliance allowed female speakers to address audiences. Mary Elizabeth Lease proved one charismatic attraction. Another female attraction was Annie Diggs, who rivaled Lease in her appeal to Kansas voters.

The success of the Alliance in the South and West led their leaders to consider mounting a third-party campaign during the next presidential election. They gathered in Ocala, Florida, in early December 1890 and their platform was known as the Ocala Demands. Their goals included the subtreasury program, abolition of private banks, regulation of transportation facilities, and the free and unlimited coinage of silver into money at a fixed ratio with gold. The issue of a third party was put off until February 1892 to allow the legislatures that had been elected with Alliance support to see what they could accomplish.

As the two major parties, and especially the Democrats, fought back against the Alliance, the idea of a third party gained in appeal. At meeting of the Alliance in February 1892 in St. Louis, the delegates decided to create a third party under the name the People's party or the Populists. They decided to hold their first national convention in Omaha, Nebraska, on July 4, 1892. They even had a candidate, Leonidas L. Polk of North Carolina, who was popular enough to satisfy both northern and southern farmers. Then Polk died a month before the convention. With Polk gone, the Omaha Convention chose James B. Weaver, a longtime third-party politician from Iowa, to be the presidential candidate.

The party's platform took a stern view of the state of the nation. It proclaimed that "We meet in the midst of a nation brought to the verge of moral, political, and material ruin. Corruption dominates the ballot box, the legislature, the Congress, and touches even the ermine of the bench." The specific planks endorsed the subtreasury, other reform proposals, and a new idea that was dominating the dialogue among the Populists—the free coinage of silver.

By 1892, it was evident that the subtreasury plan was going nowhere in Congress. As that proposal faded, the idea that inflation could be promoted by coining silver into money gained support. To expand the currency, raise prices, and reduce the weight of debt on those who owned money, silver was, the Populists argued, the best solution. The nation would base its money on two metals, gold and silver. If silver were coined into money at a ratio of 16 to 1 with gold, there would soon be ample money in circulation.

The country needed controlled inflation. However, the market price of silver stood at closer to 25 to 1, relative to gold. A policy of free coinage would lift the price of the white metal in an artificial way. If that happened, people would hoard gold, silver would lose value, and inflation would accelerate.

The **Populist party** rejected these arguments. They maintained that "money can be created by the government in any desired quantity, out of any substance, with no basis but itself." The idea of crop supports underlying the subtreasury plan and the manipulation of the money supply through the free coinage of silver would become common ideas during the twentieth century. But in 1892 they seemed radical to many Americans.

The Presidential Election of 1892

Republicans and Democrats watched the emergence of Populism with bewilderment and apprehension. They sensed that something important was happening and

Flashpoints | Raising Less Corn and More Hell: Mary Elizabeth Lease

Across Kansas in the autumn of 1890, the farmers were angry. Low wheat prices, a heavy load of debt, and a sense that farmers had forgotten them caused many rural Kansans to look to the Farmers' Alliance for answers. By the hundreds they came to the country crossroads or the county fairgrounds to hear speakers denounce the Republicans and Democrats for their failure to address the plight of the farmer.

As these rallies went on, word spread of a female orator of unusual force and power. In an age when men dominated political life, seeing women on the stage was something fresh. The Alliance had several compelling women speakers; Annie Diggs was one. But the star attraction in 1890 was a tall woman who was a lawyer and a captivating platform attraction. Thirty-seven-year-old Mary Elizabeth Lease had been in politics for several years as a spellbinder on the campaign trail. First as a Republican, then a member of the Union Labor Party, and now an Alliance member, she proclaimed that "Wall Street owns the country. It is no longer a government of the people, for the people, and by the people, but a government of Wall Street, for Wall Street, and by Wall Street." The most famous comment attributed to her (she may not have said it in fact) was her admonition to Kansas farmers to "raise less wheat and corn, and more hell."

The partisan press attacked her in virulent terms. One Republican paper said she was "a miserable

Mary Elizabeth Lease

© The Granger Collection, New York

caricature upon womanhood, hideously ugly in feature and foul of tongue." Yet to her farm audiences, her musical voice and passionate advocacy of her cause enabled her to articulate the anxieties of her audience at the moment when agrarian discontent was bursting onto the national scene.

Lease had only a moment in the national spotlight. In the mid-1890s, she moved to the East and said she was now a Socialist. She then worked for the Republicans in the 1900 presidential campaign and four years later supported Theodore Roosevelt for president. Lease died in 1933, one of the last surviving members of the original group of Populist speakers who galvanized Kansas four decades earlier. Like so many reformers of the late nineteenth century, she found it difficult to sustain the commitments she had made at the start of her public career. In that brief span of time from August to November 1890, she exemplified a protest spirit that shook American politics for the rest of the 1890s.

Questions for Reflection

1. Why was it unusual for a woman to take part in a political campaign as a speaker?

2. What conditions made audiences receptive to Lease's appeal for political action?

3. What was the response of the major parties to the threat that reformers such as Lease posed to their hold on American politics?

wondered how to respond. For the moment, the familiar routines of political life went on. The elections of 1890 had left the Republicans shocked at their losses and aware that President Harrison was not a strong candidate for reelection. Despite a last-minute challenge by James G. Blaine, Harrison was renominated without

much enthusiasm as the best the Republicans could do. His party applauded the protective tariff and prepared for the Democratic onslaught.

The Democrats were confident. Their candidate was Grover Cleveland, who easily won a third nomination from his party. The platform promised lower tariffs and

DOING HISTORY

The Causes of Agrarian Discontent

Populist Party Platform, 1892

"THE CONDITIONS WHICH surround us best justify our cooperation; we meet in the midst of a nation brought to the verge of moral, political, and material ruin. Corruption dominates the ballot box, the Legislatures, the Congress, and touches even the ermine of the bench. The people are demoralized, most of the States have been compelled to isolate the voters at the polling places to prevent universal intimidation and bribery. The newspapers are largely subsidized or muzzled, public opinion silenced, business prostrated, homes covered with mortgages, labor impoverished, and the land concentrated in the hands of capitalists. The urban workmen are denied the right to organize for self-protection, imported pauperized labor beats down their wages, a hireling standing army, unrecognized by our laws, is established to shoot them down, and they are rapidly degenerating into European conditions. The fruits of the toil of millions are boldly stolen to build up colossal fortunes for the few, unprecedented in the history of mankind; and the possessors of these, in turn, despise the Republic and endanger liberty. From the same prolific womb of government injustice we breed two great classes—tramps and millionaires."

C. Wood Davis, "Why the Farmer Is Not Prosperous," *The Forum* (April 1890)

"The working force in the United States is about 23,000,000 persons, of whom 10,000,000 are engaged in agricultural pursuits, employing a capital of $16,000,000,000 invested in farms and their equipment. That the greater part of this host of workers and of this immense capital is unprofitably employed is beyond question; and this state of unthrift has progressed so far as to discourage great numbers of those so unemployed.

This state of affairs is not due to any lack of industry or frugality on the part of the farmer. Nor can it be attributed to crop failures, as is evident from the increasing quantities of products put upon the markets of the world at prices ever growing less. Indeed, our farms are so numerous and productive as to reduce the returns of American agriculture to a point far below a reasonable profit, and to lessen the values of the farms and farm products of Canada, Great Britain, and western Europe."

J. R. Dodge, "Agricultural Depression and Its Causes," U.S. Department of Agriculture Report, March 1890

"During the last ten years more than two million workers in agriculture, armed with improved implements, have been added to the seven million that were making corn and wheat and cotton; and shall they still insist on the same limited range of effort, walk in the same furrows their farmers turned, and seek to live and die in the same overdone and profitless routine? If so agricultural depression will become chronic and intensified to a degree unknown at present. Shall farmers hug the chains of their dependence, limit the range of their industry, refuse to strike out into new paths, and sink into comparative idleness and poverty. There are millions of them too intelligent and enterprising and ambitions to cooperate in any such scheme of self-degradation."

The Populist Platform in 1892 was written by Ignatius Donnelly and consisted of a stinging indictment of the political system. The two other quotations appeared in a popular magazine of the day and a government report from the Department of Agriculture. They reflected eastern attitudes toward the emerging farm discontent that culminated in the emergence of the People's party. The gap in understanding among these perspectives was typical of how American society in the 1890s reacted to the political tensions that Populism represented.

Questions for Reflection

1. How are the Populists reacting to the rise of industrialism and the commercialization of agriculture?

2. How do all three authors respond to the changes that occurred in American life as discussed in Chapters 17 and 18?

3. Despite their differences, are there areas of agreement about the nature of the farm problem at this time?

4. How many of the issues being discussed are still being debated in the United States?

Explore additional primary sources related to this chapter on the Wadsworth American History Resource Center or HistoryNOW websites:

http://history.wadsworth.com/rc/us
http://now.ilrn.com/ayers_etal3e

an end to the government spending they associated with the Republicans. Although he favored the gold standard, Cleveland kept his real views muted so as not to alienate Democrats in the South and West who favored infla-

In 1892, the Republicans tried to use the tariff issue to obtain a second term in the White House for Benjamin Harrison, but he was defeated.

The Homestead strike brought violence between the steelworkers who had left their jobs and the troops sent in to break the walkout. This contemporary illustration depicts the violence that resulted.

tion. In some western states, the Democrats and the Populists struck deals and "fused" their two tickets, with Cleveland getting the electoral vote and the Populists electing state candidates.

On the surface the 1892 campaign was quiet, with the usual round of speeches about the tariff, inflation, and the role of government. The political tradition at the time said that the incumbent president should not make a formal reelection campaign. As a result, Harrison did not make speeches. Cleveland too stayed home. The intense military-style campaigning of the post–Civil War

An Election Wager

By the 1890s, intense political partisanship was receding. As this Joseph Klir painting from 1892 shows, however, male voters still wagered on the outcome of election contests and paid off their bets in a most public way as the loser in this bet pulls the victor through the streets. The banners and American flags attest to the patriotic aura of the proceedings. Election betting survives today in a more electronic

format through casinos and on the Internet. In private transactions, the loser simply hands over the amount of the wager. The painting thus illustrates in its own artistic way the decline in interest in politics from these late nineteenth century rituals to the private, often individual, act of voting and celebrating the outcome that marks the twenty-first century.

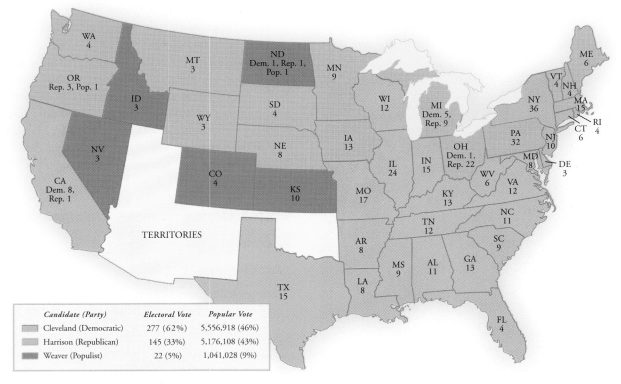

MAP 18.2 **The Election of 1892**

In 1892, the new People's party reached the height of its electoral success in its first national race. James B. Weaver, the Populist candidate, did well in the Plains States and the West, but he did not win enough electoral votes to disturb Grover Cleveland's progress to a second-term victory.

View an animated version of this map or related maps at http://history.wadsworth.com/passages3e

era, with the ranks of marching men parading through the streets, was passing from the scene.

One event revealed the social tensions beneath the surface of politics. For workers at Andrew Carnegie's Homestead steelworks outside Pittsburgh, Pennsylvania, the summer of 1892 was a time of misery and violence. The manager of the plant, Henry Clay Frick, cut wages and refused to negotiate with skilled workers who had unionized their craft. A strike resulted, and violence broke out when detectives hired by management stormed through the town of Homestead to allow strikebreakers to retake the mills. Detectives and workers died in the ensuing battle and state troops came in to restore order. Although the strike was broken, the walkout helped the Democrats in their appeal to labor voters disillusioned with Republicans. The **Homestead strike** seemed to many people to embody the tensions between capital and labor that industrialism had fostered.

The Populists tried to make the same argument about the struggle between agriculture and capital. James B. Weaver drew big crowds, but Democrats in the South pelted him with rotten eggs and tomatoes when he appeared. The Populists had to repel charges that they would promote a return to Reconstruction because they divided white voters. Thomas E. Watson of Georgia emerged as one of the leaders of the Populist cause. Elected to Congress in 1890, he urged black and white farmers in the South to unite against their common enemy.

To repel this challenge, Democrats turned to intimidation and violence. Watson's own reelection campaign failed when the Democrats stuffed the ballot boxes against him. Other Populist candidates were counted out when the Democrats controlled the election process. When the votes in the South had been tallied, the Democrats had carried the region for Cleveland.

On the national level, Cleveland gained a second term by a decisive margin. His plurality over Harrison was almost 400,000 votes, and he won in the electoral tally with 277 votes to 145 for the Republicans. The Democrats gained control of both houses of Congress for the first time since the Civil War. Weaver carried four states and won electoral votes in three additional states for a total of 22 electoral votes. His popular vote total stood at just over 1 million.

For the moment, it appeared as if the Democrats had emerged as the majority party from the long stalemate of 1874–1890. They had captured the mood of discontent that was sweeping the country during the early 1890s. It

The Columbian Exposition of 1892–1893 marked the 400th anniversary of the landing of Christopher Columbus. The "Great White City" in Chicago symbolized the progress of the nation and its technological accomplishments. The outbreak of the Panic of 1893 dulled the luster of the occasion for many Americans.

in American History," Turner stressed that the availability of free land and the presence of the frontier had played a significant part in the development of democracy in the nation. He inquired about what would happen to the nation now that the possibility of free land and a new life in the West was vanishing. Turner's "frontier thesis" became a powerful and controversial explanation of the way the nation had developed.

Conclusion

Like many Americans, Turner was groping to comprehend the changes that had occurred in American life since the Civil War. Industrialism, the rise of the city, and the strains of farm life all contributed to the sense of crisis that gripped the country during the 1890s. With the growth of industrialism, as outlined in Chapter 17, the towns and cities of the country swelled as residents of the rural areas and the new immigrants from Eastern Europe moved to the urban centers. As the center city and the suburbs extended beyond the old walking city of the first half of the century, transportation facilities pushed outward to provide the new population with more mobility. In the city itself, the problems of water, power, and living quarters pressed the local government for solutions. The urban machine and the city boss evolved as one means of addressing these needs.

In the farm belt of the South and West, the spread of farmland and the increased crops that followed meant that prices for farm commodities fell as production soared. With their debt burden growing and money ever harder to obtain, angry farmers turned to political action. The Farmers' Alliance and the People's party gave voice to these sentiments and posed a threat to the two-party system. The inflationary solutions that the Populists proposed frightened middle-class Americans in the early 1890s. They saw private property as under assault. As economic hard times for the nation at large ensued, the farm protest laid the groundwork for more wide-ranging social unrest.

Americans also became more conscious of their place in the world during these years. Overseas expansion seemed one way of addressing the social ills of the nation; it would mean finding new markets in Europe and Asia. A desire to share in the imperial sweep of Europe also motivated proponents of empire. A new Navy and a greater diplomatic role provided the foundation for more expansive initiatives during the second half of the decade.

Despite the progress and sense of optimism that pervaded many parts of society, the country still struggled with the discrimination against minorities that was so rooted in national traditions. Segregation of African Americans in the South took hold. Advocates of this

remained to be seen how Cleveland would carry out his mandate to satisfy the many groups that had deserted the Republicans and appease the restless farmers who had supported Weaver and the Populists.

The American economy was in trouble at the beginning of 1893. Distracting the nation from the gloomy forecasts was the prospect of a large popular spectacle that was planned in Chicago. The World's Columbian Exposition commemorated the arrival of Columbus in "The New World" 400 years earlier. Architect Daniel Burnham and his coworkers created a series of exhibition buildings that became known as "The Great White City." The exhibition summed up the nation's achievements at the end of the nineteenth century.

To commemorate the exposition, the American Historical Association held its annual meeting in Chicago in 1893. There a young historian from the University of Wisconsin, Frederick Jackson Turner, offered a new interpretation of how the United States had changed and the challenges it faced in the immediate future. In his paper, "The Significance of the Frontier

racial policy pressed forward to make it a part of every phase of southern life. For Native Americans, the transition from the 1880s to the 1890s saw the end of the Indian wars that had raged since the Europeans first invaded centuries earlier. As wards of the national government, Native Americans faced economic exploitation and efforts to break down their cultural heritage.

Industrialism, the rise of the city, and the strains of farm life all contributed to the sense of crisis that gripped the country during the 1890s. More a collection of sections than an integrated state, the United States was leaving its agrarian past for the uncertain rewards of a more industrialized, more urbanized, and more international future. Troubling signs of economic difficulties in 1891 and 1892 made citizens wonder if prosperity might disappear and the hard times of the 1870s return. Their fears were realized when the Panic of 1893 changed the direction of American life.

The Chapter in Review

In the years between 1887 and 1893:

- Urban growth accelerated as big cities appeared in the wake of industrialism.
- Poverty and wealth made the city a place of contrasts and social problems.
- Urban machines arose to provide services to residents and opportunity for capitalists.
- Victorian ideas shaped middle-class attitudes as Americans sought certainty in an unstable decade.

- The nation looked outward as overseas expansion became a popular cause.
- Southern and western farmers joined together to battle low prices and the burden of debt through the Populist party.
- The election of 1892 brought Grover Cleveland back to the White House amid growing concerns about the direction of the economy.

Making Connections Across Chapters

LOOKING BACKWARD

The problems that urban and rural Americans faced in the period 1887–1893 grew out of the achievements of industrialism during the preceding decade. This chapter discusses the consequences of rapid economic change and how Americans sought to use existing institutions to respond to these developments.

1. In what ways did the growth of cities test the capacities of local governments?

2. Was the urban machine and city boss a constructive or destructive response to the changes that metropolitan areas experienced?

3. What causes underlay the economic hard times in the South and West for the nation's farmers?

4. Why did inflation seem both necessary and appropriate to those who joined the Farmers' Alliance?

5. What forces produced interest in overseas expansion around 1890? What assumptions about the world did the enthusiasm for empire reflect?

LOOKING AHEAD

Chapter 19 looks at the peak of farm protest during the economic depression of the 1890s. To understand what made the issues of the agrarian sector so explosive will require a good understanding of the roots of the unrest. Consider to what extent this chapter helps anticipate these issues.

1. What assumptions did Americans share about the role of government in this period? How do these premises differ (if they do) from contemporary attitudes?

2. How well equipped was the political sector to deal with the issues the Populists were advocating?

3. What attitudes about farm and city life in this period are still present in modern society?

Recommended Readings

Clanton, O. Gene. *Populism: The Humane Preference in America, 1890–1900* (1991). A sympathetic introduction to the unrest among southern and western farmers.

Clanton, O. Gene. *A Common Humanity: Kansas Populism and the Battle for Justice and Equality, 1854–1903* (2004). An excellent look at how Populism emerged in one of its key states.

Crapol, Edward P. *James G. Blaine: Architect of Empire* (2000). An interpretive biography of one of the moving spirits behind American expansionism.

Cronon, William. *Nature's Metropolis: Chicago and the Great West* (1991). An interesting treatment of how Chicago grew and interacted with the region it dominated.

Duis, Perry R. *Challenging Chicago: Coping with Everyday Life, 1837–1920* (1998). An insightful book about how Americans lived their lives in the industrial cities.

McMath, Robert C. *American Populism: A Social History, 1877–1898* (1993). A thoughtful survey of the forces behind Populism.

Perman, Michael. *Struggle for Mastery: Disfranchisement in the South, 1888–1908* (2001). A thorough synthesis of the way blacks were excluded from politics in the South.

Schneirov, Richard. *Labor and Urban Politics: Class Conflict and the Origins of Modern Liberalism in Chicago, 1864–1894* (1998). Examines the impact of urban industrial growth on politics in a major American city.

Sklar, Kathryn Kish. *Florence Kelley and the Nation's Work: The Rise of Women's Political Culture, 1830–1900* (1995). An excellent biography of an urban reformer in Chicago in the 1890s.

Williams, R. Hal. *Years of Decision: American Politics in the 1890s* (1993). A fine introduction to the decade.

Identifications

Review your understanding of the following key terms, people, events, and dates for this chapter (these terms also appear in the Glossary at the end of the book):

Grover Cleveland
Benjamin Harrison
Jane Addams
Hull House
Ellis Island
political boss
Battle of Wounded Knee
Homer A. Plessy
John L. Sullivan
Edward Bellamy
National American Woman Suffrage Association
Sherman Antitrust Act
Farmers' Alliance
Populist party
Homestead strike

Online Sources Guide

Use this listing to find online documents, images, interactive maps, simulations, and other resources related to this chapter:

American History Resource Center
http://history.wadsworth.com/rc/us

Documents
Dawes Severalty Act of 1887
Frederick Jackson Turner, "The Significance of the Frontier in American History"

Additional Online Readings
Jacob A. Riis, "How the Other Half Lives"

Interactive Maps
Presidential Election Results, 1876–1896

Selected Images
Gardiner Park County, Montana, 1887
Plains Farm
Grover Cleveland

Document Exercises
1889, Andrew Carnegie, "The Gospel of Wealth"

HistoryNOW
http://now.ilrn.com/ayers_etal3e

Primary Source Exercises
Populists in Black and White
Jane Addams, "First Days at Hull House"
Servicing the Urban Poor

19 A Troubled Nation Expands Outward, 1893–1901

Chapter Outline

The belligerent figure of Uncle Sam preparing to fight Spain captures the passions that existed through the era of American imperialism.

During the 1890s, social problems that had been building since the Civil War reached crisis proportions. An economic depression began in 1893. Americans struggled with its effects for four years. With millions out of work and faith in national institutions eroding, the major political parties confronted unhappy voters. The Republicans emerged as the majority party, with the divided Democrats in disarray and the Populists unable to become a viable third party. The election of 1896 brought **William McKinley,** the architect of Republican success, to the White House. He revitalized the presidency after its eclipse since the death of Abraham Lincoln. The events of these years established patterns that affected the early decades of the twentieth century.

As the economy improved at the end of the 1890s, Americans looked outward to an empire in the Caribbean and the Pacific. A war with Spain brought territorial gains and a debate about whether overseas possessions meant fundamental change. World power seemed alluring and troubling at the same time. American institutions and leaders faced the challenge of the new responsibilities. In Europe and Asia, the United States engaged problems that persisted down to the modern era.

The Panic of 1893 and Its Effects

Grover Cleveland began his second term as president on March 4, 1893. In May 1893, the weakened economy collapsed in what became known as the Panic of 1893. Business had expanded during the late 1880s. In 1891 and 1892, investors turned cautious, worried about the soundness of the banking system and the stability of the currency. Banks failed as depositors withdrew their funds and hoarded cash. A decline in export trade further strained the economy. Business activity slowed, workers were laid off, and firms cut back on production. Bad times spread across the country.

By the end of 1893, some 600 banks had failed. Court-appointed receivers ran the 119 bankrupt railroads. Another 15,000 businesses had closed. The stock

Timeline

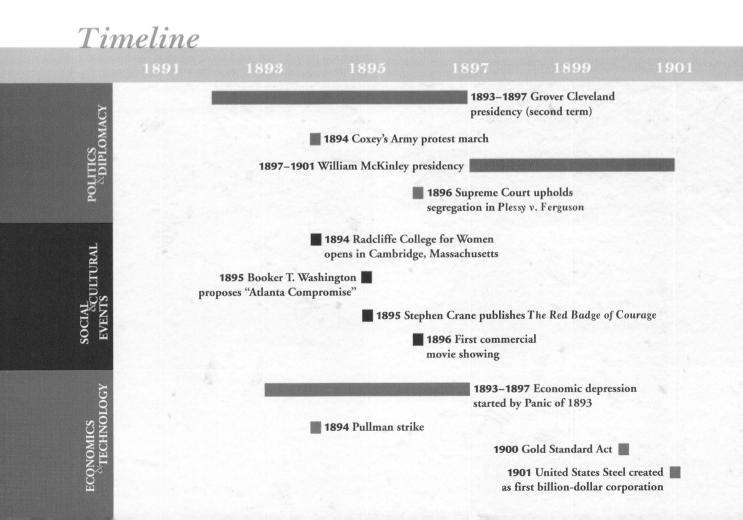

| | 1891 | 1893 | 1895 | 1897 | 1899 | 1901 |

POLITICS & DIPLOMACY

1893–1897 Grover Cleveland presidency (second term)

1894 Coxey's Army protest march

1897–1901 William McKinley presidency

1896 Supreme Court upholds segregation in *Plessy v. Ferguson*

SOCIAL & CULTURAL EVENTS

1894 Radcliffe College for Women opens in Cambridge, Massachusetts

1895 Booker T. Washington proposes "Atlanta Compromise"

1895 Stephen Crane publishes *The Red Badge of Courage*

1896 First commercial movie showing

ECONOMICS & TECHNOLOGY

1893–1897 Economic depression started by Panic of 1893

1894 Pullman strike

1900 Gold Standard Act

1901 United States Steel created as first billion-dollar corporation

market lost hundreds of millions of dollars. Most important, by early January 1894, 2.5 million people were unemployed. The economy was functioning at only three-quarters of its capacity.

The depression fell hardest on the average workers and their families. When their jobs vanished, there were no unemployment insurance payments, no government benefits, no temporary jobs programs to bridge the gap between a living wage and poverty.

States and cities provided some relief. In New York, daily newspapers distributed food, clothing, and fuel to the needy. Charity organizations in Boston, New York, and Chicago coordinated volunteer efforts. Most well-off Americans still believed the federal government should not intervene to alleviate a depression. As a result, people slept in the parks, camped out in railroad stations, and sought food at the soup kitchens that appeared in the big cities. Angry poor people called the soup kitchens "Cleveland Cafés."

To deal with the economic slump, Cleveland proposed a simple solution: repeal the Sherman Silver Purchase Act of 1890. That law had specified that the government buy a fixed amount of silver each month. Cleveland argued that the law produced inflation, undermined business confidence, and caused investors to take money out of the nation's gold reserve at the Treasury Department. If the amount of the reserve fell below $100 million, it would show that the credit of the United States was in danger. In fact, the amount was largely a psychological issue and did not measure the nation's economic condition.

In August 1893, Cleveland called a special session of Congress to repeal the Sherman Act. His own party was split over the issue of money. Northeastern party members believed in the gold standard with religious fervor. In the South and Far West, Democrats contended that the nation needed the free and unlimited coinage of silver into money at the fixed ratio to gold of 16 to 1. By asking his party to repeal the Sherman Act, Cleveland invited Democrats to wage war against each other.

Congress convened for its special session in August 1893. Over the protests of his party and with no tolerance of compromise, Cleveland insisted that Congress repeal the Sherman Act. With the aid of Republican votes, he won the battle. The bill repealing the Sherman Act was signed into law on November 1, 1893.

Having blamed the Sherman Act for the depression, Cleveland waited for a turnaround in the economy. Confidence in the dollar grew and the flow of gold out of the country eased somewhat. But prosperity did not return. As the new year approached, every indicator seemed headed downward. More railroads failed, more businesses closed, and more people were laid off to join the millions who were already unemployed.

In the 1892 campaign, the Democrats had promised to lower tariff rates. Their attempt to keep their word led to more trouble. The Democrats produced a bill to lower tariff rates in the House. With only narrow control in their chamber, Senate Democrats had to write a tariff bill that pleased those hoping to help their own states. In some instances, that meant raising customs rates on key products such as sugar, coal, and iron. The law fell far short of the tariff reform that the Democrats had promised in 1892.

Congress finally passed the Wilson-Gorman Tariff Act in August 1894. It reduced rates on wool, copper, and lumber, and raised duties on many other items. The measure repealed the reciprocal trade provisions of the McKinley Tariff, which had aimed at opening up markets and easing the political costs of protection. To make up for lost revenues, the Wilson-Gorman bill added a modest tax on personal incomes. Disgusted with the outcome, Cleveland let the bill become law without his signature.

The Results of Hard Times

Outside of Washington, as the hard times lingered, some of the unemployed decided to present their grievances to Washington. In the Middle West, those out of work formed "Coxey's Army," uniting behind Jacob S. Coxey, a businessman from Massillon, Ohio. On Easter Sunday 1894, he left for Washington with 300 supporters to petition for a program of road building paid for by $500 million of paper money. Coxey and his son "Legal Tender Coxey" headed the procession, which included more than 40 reporters. Slowly and painfully, the "Commonweal Army of Christ" approached Washington.

Members of Coxey's Army on their way to Washington during the spring of 1894.

Library of Congress, Prints and Photographs Division

Across the nation other armies rode the rails, marched through cities, and demanded jobs from the government. The climax for Coxey and his followers came on May 1, 1894, when they reached Capitol Hill and tried to present their demands to Congress. Police intercepted Coxey, clubbed him, and then arrested him for trespassing and "walking on the grass." The other armies were discouraged and dispersed but the protests undermined the political credibility of the Cleveland administration.

Even more devastating was the major railroad strike that erupted shortly after the Coxey episode ended. **George Pullman,** the developer of the railroad sleeping car, had created a model town outside Chicago where his employees were to reside in apparent comfort and serenity. Employees who lived in Pullman and worked for the Pullman Palace Car Company found that their "model" town was expensive and oppressive. The prices that workers paid for services often ran 10 percent above what was charged in other communities.

When Pullman laid off employees and trimmed wages for others, he did not reduce the rents that his workers paid. As a result, in May 1894 the workers went out on strike. The strikers asked railroad workers across the nation not to handle Pullman's cars to help the walkout. The response from the American Railway Union (ARU) and its president, **Eugene Victor Debs,** was cautious at first. But by late June, the ARU started a sympathetic boycott and decided not to move trains with Pullman cars.

At its height the **Pullman strike** involved 125,000 men representing 20 railroads. The commerce of the nation stalled as freight shipments backed up in stations and train yards. The ARU did not interfere with the mails lest that action arouse the opposition of the federal government. Its economic power could not match that of the railroads' General Managers' Association, which had influence with Cleveland and his attorney general, Richard Olney, himself a former railroad corporation lawyer. On July 2, 1894, the president and the Justice Department obtained a court injunction to bar the strikers from blocking interstate commerce. Federal troops were ordered to Chicago.

Violence erupted as angry mobs, irate at the action of the federal government, destroyed railroad property and equipment. "We have been brought to the ragged edge of anarchy," Olney told the press. The strikers were not to blame for the episode; the rioters were local people. Police and National Guard troops put down the disturbance, but the public gave Cleveland and the federal government the credit. For the moment, the president regained his popularity among conservatives in both parties. His standing with ordinary voters remained low, however.

Debs went to jail for violating the court's injunction, and the U.S. Supreme Court confirmed his sentence in *In re Debs* (1895). By doing so the Court gave businesses a potent way to stifle labor unrest. If a strike began, management could seek an injunction from a friendly federal judge, jail the union leaders, and break the strike. Union power stagnated throughout the rest of the decade.

Politically, the strike divided the Democrats. The governor of Illinois, John P. Altgeld, had protested Cleveland's actions. When the president overruled him, the governor resolved to oppose the administration in 1896. Across the South and West, bitterness against the president became even more intense. Hate mail flooded into the White House, warning him of death if he crossed the Mississippi River. As one observer said, "If this keeps on long, fire and sword will devastate the country."

During the rioting that came with the Pullman strike in 1894 in Chicago, National Guard troops fired at the mob, as depicted in this contemporary drawing from *Harper's Weekly*.

1894: A Significant Election

Approaching the congressional elections of 1894, the Democrats were demoralized and divided. For the Populists, on the other hand, these elections seemed to offer an excellent chance to establish themselves as a credible challenger to the supremacy of the two major parties. The Republicans assailed the Democrats for failing to restore prosperity. Republican speakers urged a return to the policy of tariff protection that they had pursued under Benjamin Harrison. Party leaders, such as William

Table 19.1 Party Strength in Congress, 1886–1900

House of Representatives

CONGRESS AND YEAR ELECTED	REPUBLICANS	DEMOCRATS	OTHER
Fiftieth (1886)	152	169	4
Fifty-first (1888)	166	159	–
Fifty-second (1890)	88	235	9
Fifty-third (1892)	127	218	11
Fifty-fourth (1894)	244	105	7
Fifty-fifth (1896)	204	113	40
Fifty-sixth (1898)	185	163	9
Fifty-seventh (1900)	197	151	9

Senate

CONGRESS AND YEAR ELECTED	REPUBLICANS	DEMOCRATS	OTHER
Fiftieth (1886)	39	37	–
Fifty-first (1888)	39	37	–
Fifty-second (1890)	47	39	–
Fifty-third (1892)	44	38	3
Fifty-fourth (1894)	39	43	6
Fifty-fifth (1896)	47	34	7
Fifty-sixth (1898)	53	26	8
Fifty-seventh (1900)		31	4

Source: *The Statistical History of the United States* (Stamford, CT: Fairfield Publishers, 1965).

McKinley, the governor of Ohio, crisscrossed the Midwest speaking to enthusiastic audiences. Former House Speaker Thomas B. Reed said, "The Democratic mortality will be so great next fall that their dead will be buried in trenches and marked unknown."

Reed's forecast was accurate. The Republicans prevailed in one of the most decisive congressional elections in the nation's history. The Democrats lost 113 seats in the largest transfer of power from one party to another in the annals of the two-party system. The Republicans regained control of the House of Representatives by a margin of 244 to 105. There were 24 states in which no Democrat won a federal office; 6 other states elected only one Democrat. In the Midwest 168 Republicans and only 9 Democrats were elected to Congress.

The stalemated politics of the late nineteenth century had ended in an election that realigned the nation's politics. A Republican electoral majority would dominate American politics until 1929. The decision foreshadowed a Republican victory in the presidential contest in 1896.

The Populists were almost as disappointed as the Democrats with the outcome of the 1894 election. While the total vote for the Populists had increased over 1892, much of that rise occurred in the South where the Democrats then used their control of the electoral machinery to deny victory to Populist candidates. The Populist delegation in Congress went from 11 members to 7. By 1894, the Populists were identified with the free

coinage of silver, which appealed to the debt-burdened South and West. For industrial workers who had to survive on a fixed or declining income, higher prices arising from this inflationary policy seemed less attractive. The Populists told each other that they would do better in 1896, but they assumed that neither the Republicans nor the Democrats would adopt a free-silver position. In fact, the Populists' failure to mount a significant challenge to the major parties during the 1894 election signaled the end of their assault on the two-party system. The party remained a factor in the 1896 election, but its best days were past.

The Pain of Hard Times

The economic impact of the depression of the 1890s was profound and far-reaching. By 1894, the economy operated at 80 percent of capacity. Total output of goods and services was down by some 13 percent. Unemployment ranged between 17 percent and 19 percent of the workforce. As the amount of money in circulation dropped, the nation experienced severe deflation. In the South, for example, cotton prices fell from 8.4 cents per pound in 1892 to 4.6 cents per pound in 1894. Since a figure of 10 cents per pound was necessary to break even, southern cotton farmers faced the prospect of disaster. For people with money, their dollars bought more

In the South agricultural labor continued to be the lot of most African Americans. These people had spent most of their lives in the cotton fields working for low wages and little economic future.

economic need for reorganization. In railroads, for example, major systems such as the Union Pacific were in receivership. The investment banker J. P. Morgan refinanced many of these rail lines and consolidated them to raise profits and increase efficiency. The 32 railroads, capitalized at more than $100 million, controlled nearly 80 percent of the nation's rail mileage. Shippers complained that these railroads gave larger customers unfair advantages in the form of rebates. By the end of the decade, there were increasing pleas from the South and Middle West to revive and strengthen the Interstate Commerce Commission, whose power to oversee railroad rates had been reduced by court decisions.

goods. Among those out of work and without funds, however, lower prices were little comfort when they had no money to pay for the necessities of life.

With their husbands, fathers, and sons laid off, women joined the workforce in greater numbers during the decade. During the 1890s, the total number of women with jobs rose from 3.7 million to just under 5 million. They gained employment in the expanding clerical fields, where they mastered typing and stenography. Traditional occupations such as teaching and nursing also attracted more women. In the factories, Irish-American, French-Canadian, and Italian-American women worked in textile and clothing establishments; or they did piecework for tobacco processors and shoemakers. In commercial food production and laundries the number of women employees also grew. The earnings of these women were necessary for the survival of their families. When the male wage earner brought home only $300 per year, and rents for a tenement dwelling were as much as $200 annually, the contributions of a daughter or wife were vital. However, the wages paid to women were as much as 40 percent below what men earned in industrial jobs.

The depression also brought young children back into the workforce. During the 1880s, the percentage of employed children between the ages of 10 and 15 had fallen from 17 percent to 12 percent. In the next decade, the percentage rose to 18 percent. By 1900, 1,750,000 children were employed. By the end of the century, 30 states had passed child labor laws, but these were often ineffective. Restricting the practice of child labor became an important social cause after 1900.

Reshaping the Economy

In the economy as a whole, the depression brought important changes. As a result of the downturn, the number of bankrupt businesses grew, revealing an obvious

Picturing the Past **SOCIAL & CULTURAL EVENTS**

Child Labor in the 1890s

The spread of industrialism in the late nineteenth century expanded jobs and economic opportunity, but social problems arose as well. Young people found work in factories and small businesses, as this photo of working children exemplifies. The conditions were often primitive and the workweek was very long and demanding. Few protections existed if they hurt themselves on the job, and they might find themselves discharged for small infractions of rules or the whim

of their employer. Efforts to regulate child labor ran up against well-entrenched ideas that work built character in the young, as well as the economic need in large families for extra income. Photographers educated the public about the existence of these conditions in the years 1890 to 1910, and images such as this one helped create the popular awareness behind the political and economic reforms of this period.

In the 1890s, "finance capitalists" like J. P. Morgan challenged the dominance of the "industrial capitalists" of the 1870s and 1880s who had built large enterprises in steel, oil, and railroads. These financiers launched a wave of corporate mergers that began in 1895 and continued for a decade. An average of 300 companies a year were merged with larger firms. Twelve hundred mergers occurred in 1899. Some states, such as New Jersey and Delaware, made it easier for firms to locate holding companies there. In New York a market for industrial stocks enabled bankers to raise capital. In the case of *U.S. v. E. C. Knight* (1895), the Supreme Court ruled that the Sherman Antitrust Act applied only to monopolies of interstate commerce and not to those solely of manufacturing. This decision made it more difficult to enforce the antitrust laws and, as a result, the government took little action against any of the mergers that occurred during the 1890s.

When the economy began to recover in 1897, the public's attention turned to the growth of large businesses and trusts. Consumers believed that it was unfair for a few men or businesses to dominate a single industry or control the price of commodities. There was, said one newspaper editor, "a growing antagonism to the concentration of capital."

The depression of the 1890s aroused fear and apprehension across the country. The accepted values of earlier generations came under scrutiny as people struggled to make sense of their situation. Writers questioned whether the government should simply promote economic expansion and then allow fate to decide who prospered and who did not. For the first time many argued that government should regulate the economy in the interest of social justice. In discussion groups in Wisconsin, at rallies of farmers in Texas, and on the streets of New York and Boston, citizens wondered whether their governments at all levels should do more to promote the general welfare.

A growing number of social thinkers suggested that additional government action was necessary. In 1894, Henry Demarest Lloyd published a book entitled *Wealth Against Commonwealth* that detailed what he believed the Standard Oil Company had done to monopolize the oil industry and corrupt the nation. "Monopoly cannot be content with controlling its own business. . . . Its destiny is rule or ruin, and rule is but a slower ruin." Unimpressed with the idea of merely regulating the large corporations, Lloyd called for public ownership of many transportation and manufacturing firms.

The economic hard times strengthened the resolve of the Social Gospel movement. The church, said Walter Rauschenbusch in 1893, should be the "appointed

DOING HISTORY ONLINE

Eugene Debs Addresses the American Railway Union, and Henry Demarest Lloyd, "Wealth Against Commonwealth," 1894

Where do Debs and Lloyd lay the blame for the state of the nation's economy during the depression?

History ⧖ Now™   Visit HistoryNOW to access primary sources and exercises related to this topic: http://now.ilrn.com/ayers_etal3e

instrument for the further realization of that new society in the world about it." Other young people of the day echoed similar themes. Ray Stannard Baker had reported on Coxey's army for his newspaper. He told his editor that "the national blood is out of order."

The Reform Campaigns

In states such as Illinois and New York, bands of women joined together as consumers to push for better working conditions in factories and fair treatment of employees in department stores. Social workers and charity operatives decided that the plight of the poor was not simply the fault of those in need. Better government and more enlightened policies could uplift the downtrodden. As one settlement worker put it, "I never go into a tenement without longing for a better city government."

Women's participation in the process of change was significant. Julia Lathrop and Florence Kelley worked in Illinois improving state charitable institutions and inspecting factories. Mary Church Terrell led the National Association of Colored Women, founded in 1896, in making the women's clubs in the black community a more effective force for change. **Ida Wells-Barnett** rallied African American women against lynching from her first editorials in 1892 and then joined Terrell in further campaigns against these illegal executions. The suffrage movement and the women's clubs among white, middle-class women and their black counterparts slowly established the basis for additional reforms after 1900.

A leading voice for a new role for women was **Charlotte Perkins Gilman,** whose major work, *Women and Economics,* was published in 1898. Gilman advocated that women seek economic independence. The home, she argued, was a primitive institution that should be transformed through modern industrial practices lest it impede "the blessed currents of progress that lead and lift us all." Housework should be professionalized and homes transformed into domestic factories; women would

Charlotte Perkins Gilman's writings challenged the traditional roles that women occupied in the household. She became an important advocate for a new kind of thinking about how women should function in society.

then be free to pursue their own destinies, which could include social reform. Gilman's work influenced a generation of women reformers as well as future feminists.

The renewed emphasis on reform during the 1890s also affected the long-standing campaign to control the sale and use of alcoholic beverages. In 1895, the Reverend H. H. Russell established the Anti-Saloon League in Oberlin, Ohio. Its organization relied on a network of local Protestant churches throughout the nation. They aimed to regulate saloons as tightly as possible. Unlike previous efforts to pass antiliquor laws, the League focused on a single issue, and it became a model for the kind of lobbying that would characterize reform campaigns during the first two decades of the twentieth century.

The prohibition campaigns in the South brought black women and white women together in a brief alliance to cripple what they both regarded as an important social evil. In some parts of North Carolina, for example, white women organized chapters of the Woman's Christian Temperance Union (WCTU) among black women. When white volunteers did not visit black neighborhoods, black women took over and set up their own organizations. Even as racial barriers rose in the South, black women and white women continued to

work together to curb drinking until the end of the 1890s, when deteriorating race relations made it politically impossible to do so.

To counter the drive for prohibition, brewers and liquor producers created lobbying groups to match the Anti-Saloon League and the persistent militance of the WCTU. Brewing associations appeared in battleground states such as Texas to coordinate strategies in local option elections and to get "wet" voters to the polls. Antiprohibition sentiment flourished among Irish Americans and German Americans in the cities and towns of the Northeast and Midwest. The struggles over liquor often pitted the countryside dwellers against urban residents who wanted liquor to remain available.

Reform in the Cities and States

As the depression revealed social problems and political injustices, efforts at reform were made in the cities. In Detroit, Hazen Pingree had been elected mayor in 1889. During the depression, he decided that city government ought to do more than just stand by while the poor suffered. He constructed his own political machine to pursue social justice through lower utility rates and expanded government services. That brought him into conflict with the streetcar companies and utilities that dominated Detroit politics. In Chicago, a British editor, William T. Stead, visited the city for the Columbian Exposition in 1893. What he saw in the slums led him to write *If Christ Came to Chicago* in 1894. Stead contended that the city needed a spiritual and political revival. He singled out the power of the street railway operator, Charles T. Yerkes, as particularly oppressive because of the high rates and poor service his companies provided. Stead's attack led to the formation of the Chicago Civic Federation, which sought to control gambling, clean up the slums, and limit the power of men like Yerkes. Similar reform groups sprang up in Wisconsin's cities to restrain corporations that provided vital municipal services at an exorbitant cost to taxpayers.

By the mid-1890s, these examples of urban reform sparked the creation of groups to address national urban problems. The National Municipal League came into existence in 1894; in the same year the First National Conference for Good City Government took place. Over the next several years reformers diagnosed the ills of American cities and recommended solutions. Out of these debates came the ideas that would flourish during the Progressive Era a decade later.

As the depression worsened, citizens looked to their state governments for answers and instead found political and social problems that rivaled the plight of the cities. Critics complained of corruption, political machines, and a breakdown of democracy. In Wisconsin a Republican politician, Robert M. La Follette, built a political following by attacking the entrenched organization within his own party. He called for primary elections to choose candidates for office rather than leave the decision to the politicians and their rigged meetings. After his triumphs in the **Spanish-American War, Theodore Roosevelt** was elected governor of New York, where he displayed his vigorous leadership skills in publicizing the activities of large corporations and using state power to conserve natural resources.

The work of reform governors and their supporters in the states led to increased authority for these governments and greater reliance on experts and nonpartisan commissions in making decisions about public policy. Railroad commissions, public utility commissions, and investigative boards to oversee key industries were formed. By the end of the decade, however, observers believed that meaningful reform would come only when the federal government shaped national legislation to curb railroads and trusts engaged in interstate commerce.

Substantive Due Process and Its Critics

Among the most powerful obstacles to reform were judges who upheld business interests. The doctrine of *substantive due process* gave state and federal judges a way to block legislative attempts to regulate economic behavior. According to this doctrine, the due process clause of the Fourteenth Amendment did not apply only to the issue of whether the procedure used to pass a law had been fair. Judges might consider how the substance of the law affected life, liberty, and property. They could then decide whether the law was so inherently unfair that it would be unjust even if the procedures for implementing the statute were unbiased. This approach gave the judiciary the right to decide whether a law regulating business enterprise was fair to the corporation being supervised.

Judges also interpreted federal laws in ways that limited efforts to curb corporate power. The same year (1895) that the Court issued the *E. C. Knight* decision, which constrained the scope of the Sherman Antitrust Act, it also ruled in *Pollock v. Farmers' Loan and Trust Co.* that the income tax provisions of the Wilson-Gorman Tariff were unconstitutional because they were a direct tax that the Constitution prohibited. In labor cases, courts imposed injunctions to bar unions from boycotts and strikes.

A few jurists and lawyers, however, had doubts about this philosophy of favoring corporations. In Massachusetts, Oliver Wendell Holmes, Jr., had published

The Common Law in 1881. Holmes contended that "the life of the law has not been logic; it has been experience." By this he meant that judges should not base their rulings on abstract premises and theories such as freedom of contract, but should consider the rational basis of a law in judging whether it was constitutional or not.

Conservative himself, Holmes was ready to defer to the popular will in legislative matters. If the Constitution did not prohibit a state from building a slaughterhouse or regulating an industry, his response was "God-dammit, let them build it." In Nebraska, Roscoe Pound was evolving a similar reality-based approach to legal thinking that became known as *sociological jurisprudence.* Louis D. Brandeis of Massachusetts was gaining a reputation as the "People's Lawyer" who believed that the legal system should serve small businesses and consumers as well as large corporations.

Pragmatism and Realism

The philosopher William James of Harvard University developed an explanation for what political and legal reformers were trying to do. He called it *pragmatism.* James wanted to show that truth is more than an abstract concept. He believed that truth must demonstrate its value in the real world. "What in short is the truth's cash value in experiential terms?" James asked. To James, pragmatism meant "looking away from first things, principles, 'categories,' supposed necessities; and of looking towards last things, fruits, consequences, facts." James divided the world into tough-minded people, who based their actions on facts and pragmatic truths, and tender-minded people, who were swayed by abstractions. His philosophy emphasized self-reliance and gritty reality. It appealed to a generation of reformers who sought practical solutions to the problems they saw in their communities and the nation as a whole.

Another spokesman for reform was a University of Chicago teacher and philosopher named John Dewey. In his major work, *The School and Society* (1899), Dewey contended that schools should undertake the task of preparing students to live in a complex, industrial world. The public school must do more than transmit academic knowledge for its own sake. As an institution, it should be a means of instilling democratic values and usable skills. Education, Dewey wrote, "is the fundamental method of social progress and reform."

During the 1890s, writers and artists turned to the world around them. They preached the doctrine of realism, and they tried to capture the complexity of a natural world in which science, technology, and capitalism were challenging older values. William Dean Howells, a novelist, examined the impact of capitalism on workers and urban dwellers in New York City in *A Hazard of New Fortunes* (1890). During the depression Howell's novels and essays were sharply critical of the new industrial system. **Stephen Crane** depicted the ways in which the city exploited and destroyed a young woman in *Maggie: A Girl of the Streets* (1893). Crane later wrote a timeless novel about the Civil War, *The Red Badge of Courage*.

Two noteworthy practitioners of literary naturalism were Frank Norris and Theodore Dreiser. Norris wrote about California railroads in *The Octopus* (1901) and about the wheat market in Chicago in *The Pit* (1903). In Norris's Darwinian world, humanity was trapped in the impersonal grip of soulless corporations. In *Sister Carrie* (1900), Dreiser described how a small-town girl went to work in Chicago and was consumed by its temptations. These novels reached a large audience, and their depiction of characters caught in an amoral universe intensified the sentiment for reform.

By the 1890s, then, the currents that would come together as the progressive movement of the 1900–1920 period were forming. Urban reformers, believers in the Social Gospel, politically active women, candidates angry with the established powers in their state's dominant party—all of these groups shared a pervasive discontent with the state of society. The volatile domestic and international events of the 1890s would prepare the ground for a generation of reform.

African Americans and Segregation

In addition to experiencing the economic deprivations affecting the country as a whole during the 1890s, African Americans confronted the ever-tightening grip of segregation in the South. Although blacks had made great strides in building viable communities and economic institutions since Reconstruction, white southerners disliked their advancement. Instead, whites endeavored to return African Americans to a subordinate position. The courts proved unreceptive to the pleas of blacks for equal treatment under the law.

A spokesman for blacks emerged in **Booker T. Washington,** who argued that African Americans should emphasize hard work and personal development rather than rebelling against their condition. Whites applauded Washington's philosophy as the proper course for blacks to take. Meanwhile, race riots and lynchings expressed the bigotry and intolerance that characterized most whites in these years.

Washington believed that African Americans must demonstrate their worthiness for citizenship

---

DOING HISTORY ONLINE

Lynching of Henry Smith, 1893, and "A Summary of Lynchings in 1897"

Historians often are confronted with the challenge of trying to understand actions of people in the past that seem completely alien and incomprehensible to us today. In regard to lynching, how can one explain why seemingly ordinary, moral, upright citizens would take part in or gleefully observe such horrific acts of racial brutality?

History ⊗ Now™   Visit HistoryNOW to access primary sources and exercises related to this topic: http://now.ilrn.com/ayers_etal3e

---

through their own achievements. In 1895, he reached a national audience when he spoke at the Cotton States and International Exposition in Atlanta. His **Atlanta Compromise** told white Americans what they wanted to hear about black citizens. Accordingly, what Washington said made him the leading black figure in the United States for a generation. "In all the things that are purely social, we can be separate as the fingers," Washington proclaimed, "yet one as the hand in all things essential to mutual progress." To his fellow blacks he said, "it is at the bottom of life we must begin" to create an economic base through hard work: "[C]ast down your bucket where you are" and be "patient, law-abiding and unresentful." Any "agitation of questions of social equality" would be "the extremest folly."

Washington's white audience gave him an enthusiastic response, and white philanthropists funded his

© CORBIS

Booker T. Washington was a captivating speaker who preached that African Americans must demonstrate to whites their capacity to achieve progress.

DOING HISTORY

Lynching and the Rights of African Americans in 1898–1900

LYNCHING OF BLACKS in the South persisted throughout the 1890s, and effective federal action to stop this cruel practice did not occur. In 1898, Ida Wells-Barnett was one of a number of white and black politicians who asked President William McKinley to punish those responsible for killing an African-American postmaster, last name Baker, in Lake City, South Carolina. The statement she made, which appears below, laid out her reasons for seeking federal action.

Though he was not responding directly to Wells-Barnett and this case, Senator Benjamin R. Tillman offered a justification for lynching to the U.S. Senate in 1900 that represented the southern rationale for extralegal murders. Their contrasting statements follow.

Ida Wells-Barnett

"For nearly twenty years lynching crimes, which stand side by side with Armenian and Cuban outrages, have been committed and permitted by this Christian nation. Nowhere in the civilized world save the United States of America do men, possessing all civil and political power, go out in bands of 50 and 5,000 to hunt down, shoot, hang or burn to death a single individual, unarmed and absolutely powerless. Statistics show that nearly 10,000 American citizens have been lynched in the past twenty years. To our appeals for justice the stereotyped reply has been that the governor could not interfere in a state matter. Postmaster Baker's case was a federal matter, pure and simply. He died at his post of duty in defense of his country's honor, as truly as did ever a soldier on the field of battle. We refuse to believe this country, so powerful to defend its citizens abroad, is unable to protect its citizens at home."

Benjamin R. Tillman

"We did not disfranchise the negroes until 1895. Then we had a constitutional convention convened which took the matter up calmly, deliberately, and avowedly with the purpose of disfranchising as many of them as we could under the fourteenth and fifteenth amendments. We adopted the educational qualification as the only means left to use, and the negro is as contented and as prosperous and as well protected in South Carolina today as in any State of the Union south of the Potomac. He is not meddling with politics, for he found that the more he meddled with them the worse off he got. As to his 'rights'—I will not discuss them now. We of the South have never recognized the right of the negro to govern white men, and we never will. We have never believed him to be the equal of the white man, and we will not submit to his gratifying his lust on our wives and daughters without lynching them. I would to God the last one of them was in Africa and have none of them had ever been brought to our shores. But I will nut pursue the subject further."

Sources: Wells-Barnett: *Cleveland Gazette,* April 9, 1898, in Herbert Aptheker, ed., *A Documentary History of the Negro People in the United States,* vol. 2 (New York: The Citadel Press, 1970), p. 798. Tillman: U.S. Senate, *Congressional Record,* 56 Cong., 1. Sess. (March 23, 1900): 3223–3224.

Questions for Reflection

1. How did the views of Ida Wells-Barnett and Benjamin R. Tillman differ on the issue of the rights of African Americans? Did they have a contrasting opinion about what it meant to be an American citizen?

2. What role did the states play in the area of civil rights and the future of African Americans for Wells-Barnett and Tillman?

3. What were the dominant motives behind Tillman's justification of lynching? How does Wells-Barnett regard this practice and what arguments, religious and humanitarian, does she raise in attacking it?

4. To what extent did Tillman and his constituents accept the constitutional amendments that resulted from Reconstruction?

Explore additional primary sources related to this chapter on the Wadsworth American History Resource Center or HistoryNOW websites:
http://history.wadsworth.com/rc/us
http://now.ilrn.com/ayers_etal3e

school, the Tuskegee Institute, generously. Behind the scenes, Washington dominated the political lives of blacks and even more secretly he funded court challenges to segregation. In public, however, he came to symbolize an accommodation with the existing racial system.

The Supreme Court put its stamp of approval on segregation as a legal doctrine a year later. Homer A. Plessy's appeal of the Louisiana court's decision upholding segregation of railroad cars had made its way to the Supreme Court. The court heard oral arguments in April 1896 and rendered its judgment five weeks later. By a vote of seven to one in the case of *Plessy v. Ferguson,* the justices upheld the Louisiana law and, by implication, the principle of segregation. Writing for the majority, Justice Henry Billings Brown said that the Fourteenth Amendment "could not have been intended to abolish distinctions based on color, or to enforce social, as distinguished from political equality, or a commingling of the two races upon terms unsatisfactory to either." He rejected the argument that "the enforced separation of the races stamps the colored race with a badge of inferiority." In a dissenting opinion, Justice John Marshall Harlan responded that "Our Constitution is color-blind, and neither knows nor tolerates classes among citizens." This ruling determined the legal situation of African Americans for more than half a century.

As the political rights of blacks diminished, white attacks on them increased. During the North Carolina elections of 1898, race was a key issue that led to a Democratic victory over the Populists, Republicans, and their African American allies. Once whites had won, they turned on the black-dominated local government in Wilmington, North Carolina. Several hundred whites attacked areas where blacks lived in December 1898, killing 11 people and driving residents from their homes. Lynchings in the South continued at a rate of more than 100 per year.

Although black Americans faced daunting obstacles in the 1890s, they made substantial progress toward improved living conditions in ways that showed that they were more than simply the victims of white oppression. They founded colleges in the South, created self-help institutions in black churches, and developed pockets of well-off citizens in cities such as Washington, Boston, Baltimore, and Philadelphia. In the South black women pursued social reform in states with impressive determination. The National Association of Colored Women sought to become, in the words of its president, Mary Church Terrell, "partners in the great firm of progress and reform." African American resistance to segregation shaped the 1890s as much as did the white drive to subjugate blacks in the South and the North.

Foreign Policy Challenges

Amid the political turmoil of the second Cleveland administration, foreign affairs pressed for attention. The nation stood on the verge of becoming a world power, and national leaders debated how to respond to increasing competition with powerful international rivals and the upsurge of nationalism among colonial peoples.

The first pressing issue was Hawaii. Grover Cleveland was not convinced that the revolution that had occurred in 1893 represented the will of the Hawaiian people (see Chapter 18). Holding the treaty of annexation back from the Senate, he dispatched a special commission to investigate conditions. Believing that the native population backed Queen Liliuokalani, he refused to send the treaty to the Senate and asked for restoration of the native government. The revolutionary government declined to yield power, however, and in 1894 the administration granted it diplomatic recognition.

Another foreign policy crisis occurred in 1894 when a dispute arose between Great Britain and Venezuela over the precise boundary line that separated Venezuela and British Guiana. The Cleveland administration concluded that the controversy was also a test of the Monroe Doctrine that barred European influence in the Western Hemisphere. In 1895, the new secretary of state, Richard Olney, sent a diplomatic note to London that asserted that the United States was "practically sovereign on this continent, and its fiat is law upon the subjects to which it confines its interposition." The British responded slowly, and when their answer finally arrived it rejected the arguments of the Cleveland administration. Newspapers talked of a possible war. The president asked Congress for the power to name a commission to decide the boundary dispute and enforce its decision. The British found themselves in a difficult position. In South Africa they were encountering problems that would eventually lead to the Boer War (1899–1902), and they had few European friends when it came to foreign policy. Accordingly they decided to arbitrate their quarrel with Venezuela through a joint Anglo-American-Venezuelan commission to resolve the dispute, and the crisis passed.

The Cuban Crisis

The most dangerous foreign policy issue that confronted Cleveland stemmed from the revolution that Cubans launched against Spanish rule in February 1895. The Wilson-Gorman Tariff had increased import duties on Cuban sugar, damaging the island's economy, which depended on sugar. Rebels took to the battlefield in February 1895 seeking to oust the Spanish. Unable to defeat the rebels in direct combat, the Spanish drove the civilian population into cities and fortified areas. The "reconcentration" camps where these refugees were housed were disease-ridden and overcrowded. The architect of this harsh policy was General Valeriano Weyler, nicknamed "The Butcher" for his cruelty to the captive Cubans.

The American public took a close interest in the Cuban situation. Investments in the island, totaling about $50 million, were threatened by the conflict. Religious denominations saw the brutality and famine of the rebellion as cause for concern and perhaps direct intervention. Sensational newspapers, known as **the yellow press** because one of them carried a popular comic strip about "The Yellow Kid," printed numerous stories about atrocities in Cuba. **William Randolph Hearst,** publisher of the New York *Morning Journal,* and Joseph Pulitzer of the New York *World* were the most sensational practitioners of this kind of journalism. The Cubans also established an office in New York from which their "junta" dispensed propaganda to a receptive audience. Concern about Cuba was a significant element in the nation's foreign policy during the mid-1890s.

President Cleveland tried to enforce the neutrality laws that limited shipments of arms to Cuba. He did not recognize the Cubans as belligerents, and he informed the Spanish that they might count on the good offices of the United States in negotiating an end to the fighting. This position suited Spain, which followed a policy of procrastination to quell the revolt before the United States intervened. By the end of his administration, the president was pressing Spain to make concessions to the Cubans, but he never challenged Spain's right to exercise its sovereignty over the island. Congress prodded the president to take more aggressive action, but he refused. As a result, when the end of the Cleveland administration approached early in 1897, his policy toward Cuba had little support in the United States.

The Battle of the Standards: 1896

The foreign policy problems of the Cleveland administration stemmed in part from the weakened political situation after the 1894 elections. Relations with the Democrats worsened. Preferring to work alone and wary of threats on his life, Cleveland increased the number of guards around the White House and rarely ventured out to meet his fellow citizens.

The reserves of gold were still shrinking, despite the repeal of the Sherman Silver Purchase Act in 1893. To bolster the reserves and bring in gold, the White House sold government bonds. The sale that took place in February 1895 was handled by New York banker J. P. Morgan, who made a nice profit from the transaction. Eventually there were four bond sales, which supplied needed currency for the Treasury but also further alienated Democratic advocates of inflation and free silver. One angry Democratic senator said of the president: "I hate the ground that man walks on."

As the 1896 election approached, the Republicans, after their sweep of the 1894 election, wanted to nominate a candidate who could cash in on their likely victory. The front-runner was William McKinley of Ohio, a veteran of the Civil War, former member of Congress, and governor of Ohio from 1892 to 1896. A popular speaker, he was identified with the protective tariff. With the aid of his close friend Marcus A. Hanna, an industrialist from Ohio, McKinley became the favorite for the Republican nomination. His campaign slogan proclaimed him as "The Advance Agent of Prosperity."

McKinley won on the first ballot at the Republican National Convention in St. Louis in June 1896. The only difficult issue was gold and silver. Eastern Republicans wanted the party to endorse the gold standard. The key plank contained that language, but it also conciliated pro-silver Republicans with a promise to seek wider international use of silver. The Republicans expected to wage a tariff-centered campaign against a nominee saddled with the unpopularity of Cleveland.

Bryan and the Cross of Gold

The Democratic convention, however, took an unexpected turn. After the elections of 1894, the free silver wing of the party dominated the South and West. By 1896, an articulate spokesman for the silver cause would appeal to many Democrats. Among the leading candidates for the nomination, however, none possessed the required excitement and devotion to silver. A young politician from Nebraska named William Jennings Bryan saw himself as the "logic of the situation." During 1895 and early 1896, he urged leaders to think of him as a possible second choice should the convention deadlock. By the time the Democratic National Convention opened in Chicago in July 1896, there was a good deal of latent support for Bryan among the delegates.

Bryan's chance came during the debate over whether the party platform should endorse silver. He arranged to be the final speaker on behalf of free silver. Bryan had a clear, musical voice that could be heard across the convention hall. The speech he gave, entitled the "Cross of Gold," became a classic moment in American political oratory. He asked the delegates whether the party would stand "upon the side of the idle holders of capital, or upon the side of the struggling masses?" His answer was simple. To those who wanted a gold standard, the

The Republican magazines in the East attacked Bryan for his use of religious imagery in his famous "Cross of Gold" speech. In the cartoon, Bryan tramples on the Bible and his followers preach anarchy behind him.

At the age of 36, William Jennings Bryan was a striking and handsome figure during his first race for the presidency in 1896. His musical voice and ardent advocacy of the silver issue gave him a powerful push in the summer until the effects of the Republican campaign turned the tide for William McKinley.

Democrats would say: "You shall not press down upon the brow of labor this crown of thorns, you shall not crucify mankind upon a cross of gold." His audience was enthralled.

The next day the convention nominated Bryan for president on a free silver platform. A wave of support for Bryan swept the country, and the Republicans found their careful plans for the campaign suddenly at risk. Since the Democrats could not raise much in the way of campaign funds, Bryan decided to take his message to the voters. He prepared for an extensive nationwide campaign tour to speak on behalf of the common man, a rural nation, and the older agrarian virtues.

Bryan's nomination left the Populist party in disarray. The Populists had delayed their national convention until after the two major parties had named their candidates, and they now faced a dilemma. If they failed to select Bryan as their candidate, they would be accused of depriving silver of any chance of victory. Yet if they went along with Bryan's nomination, there would be no need for their party. With some reluctance, they ultimately decided to name Bryan as the presidential nominee and picked Thomas E. Watson as their vice presidential choice. The Democrats refused to accept this awkward compromise; all that Watson's selection did was to confuse voters about which Bryan slate of elections they should pick.

Bryan, 36 years old, pursued the presidency with youthful energy. He traveled 18,000 miles and gave more than 600 speeches; his audiences, estimated at a total of 3 million people, turned out to see "The Boy Orator of the Platte River." To counter Bryan, the Republicans raised between $3.5 million and $4 million from fearful corporations. The Democrats charged that the Republicans and their business allies were coercing workers to vote for McKinley. Most industrial workers voted Republican because they feared the inflationary effects of free silver. Mark Hanna, who managed McKinley's campaign, used the party's substantial war chest to distribute several hundred million pamphlets to the voters. Republican speakers took to the campaign trail; party newspapers poured out information about the merits of the tariff and the gold standard.

The key to the Republican campaign was McKinley. He stayed home in Canton, Ohio, and let the voters come to him. As the weeks passed, more than 750,000 people stood in McKinley's yard to hear his speeches about the dangers of free silver. "If the free coinage of silver means a fifty-three cent dollar, then it is not an honest dollar," McKinley said. These addresses appeared in newspapers across the country. By mid-September, the

The Republican candidate also came in for newspaper assault. A Democratic magazine ran a cartoon showing a dispirited Uncle Sam having to accept monopoly power in the nation's capital once McKinley was elected.

tide turned against Bryan, and there were signs that the Republicans would win in November.

The result was the most decisive outcome since the 1872 presidential contest. McKinley had a margin of 600,000 popular votes and won 271 electoral votes to 176 for Bryan. Bryan ran well in the South, the Plains states, and the Far West. McKinley dominated in the Northeast, the mid-Atlantic states, and the Midwest. Despite his appeals to the labor vote, Bryan ran poorly in the cities. Free silver might lead to inflation, an idea that had little appeal to workers on fixed incomes. McKinley's argument that the tariff would restore prosperity also took hold in the more industrialized areas of the country.

The 1896 results confirmed the outcome of the 1894 election. The Republicans had established themselves as the nation's majority party. The South remained solidly Democratic; the industrial North was Republican. The older issue of how much the government ought to promote economic expansion was giving way to the new problem of whether the government should regulate the economy so as to relieve injustices and imbalances in the way that society worked. Bryan and the Populists had

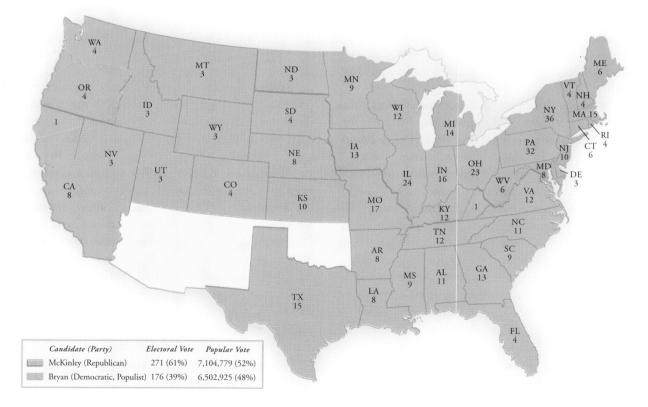

Candidate (Party)	Electoral Vote	Popular Vote
McKinley (Republican)	271 (61%)	7,104,779 (52%)
Bryan (Democratic, Populist)	176 (39%)	6,502,925 (48%)

MAP 19.1 The Election of 1896

The election of 1896 was a climax to the upheavals of the mid-1890s. Note the sectional alignment that divided the nation between the agrarian South and West that supported William Jennings Bryan and the industrialized East and Middle West where William McKinley and the Republicans were strong.

View an animated version of this map or related maps at http://history.wadsworth.com/passages3e

suggested that government should play a larger regulatory role. The voters had chosen instead to accept the economic nationalism of the Republicans as embodied in the tariff and the gold standard.

The War with Spain and Overseas Expansion

When Grover Cleveland departed in March 1897, he left a weakened presidency. McKinley improved relations with the press, which Cleveland had ignored; he traveled extensively to promote his policies; and he used experts and commissions to strengthen the operation of the national government. In domestic policy, McKinley persuaded Congress to enact the Dingley Tariff of 1897, which raised customs rates. He also sought, without success, to convince European nations to agree to wider use of silver through an international agreement. As a result, when the Republicans gained control of both houses of Congress after the 1898 election, the Gold Standard Act of 1900 reaffirmed that gold and only gold was the basis of the nation's currency. Gold discoveries in South Africa and Alaska inflated the currency by making more gold available. Returning prosperity relieved the agricultural tensions of the decade.

Spain and Cuba

McKinley faced a growing crisis in Cuba. He wanted Spain to withdraw from Cuba if its forces could not suppress the rebellion quickly. Any solution must be acceptable to the Cuban rebels. Since they would accept nothing less than the end of Spanish rule, there was little basis for a negotiated settlement. During 1897, however, McKinley tried to persuade Spain to agree to a diplomatic solution. Yet, no Spanish government could stay in power if it agreed to leave Cuba without a fight.

At first it appeared that the president's policy might be working. In the fall of 1897 the Spanish government moved toward granting the Cubans some control over their internal affairs. Foreign policy, however, was to remain in Spanish hands. The practice of moving Cubans into reconcentration camps was abandoned. However, the situation worsened during the early months of 1898 as the rebellion persisted. On January 12, 1898, pro-Spanish elements in Cuba rioted against the autonomy program. To monitor the situation, the White House decided to send a warship to Havana. The battleship U.S.S. *Maine* arrived there on January 25. Spain was pleased that the United States was resuming visits that had earlier been discontinued, but the diplomatic

problem continued. On February 1, Spain insisted that its sovereignty over Cuba must be preserved even if it meant resisting foreign intervention.

On February 9, 1898, newspapers in the United States published a letter written by the Spanish minister to the United States, Enrique Dupuy de Lôme, to a friend; Cuban rebels had intercepted the letter. In it, de Lôme described McKinley as "weak and a bidder for the admiration of the crowd." These insulting remarks led to de Lôme's recall and resignation. The minister's other statements revealed, however, that Spain was playing for time in its negotiations with Washington in hopes that the Americans might change their mind or that pressure from European countries would lead them to do so.

The Sinking of the *Maine*

On February 15, the U.S.S. *Maine* exploded in Havana Harbor; 260 officers and men perished. The cause of the blast, according to modern research, was spontaneous combustion in a coal bunker. In 1898, however, the public believed that Spain had either caused an external explosion or had failed to prevent it. McKinley established a naval board of inquiry to probe the disaster. The deadline for its report was mid-March 1898. While he waited, McKinley made military preparations and explored unsuccessfully the idea of buying Cuba from Spain.

Time was running out for a peaceful solution. On March 17, a Republican senator who had visited Cuba, Redfield Proctor of Vermont, told the Senate that conditions in the country were horrible. The speech swayed the public toward intervention in the war. Two days later, McKinley learned that the naval board had concluded, on the basis of the science of the time and the physical evidence, that an external explosion had caused the destruction of the *Maine*. When the report went to Congress, pressure on the president to intervene in Cuba mounted.

McKinley pushed Spain either to agree to an armistice in the fighting that still raged in Cuba or to permit American mediation that would end in Cuban independence. However, the Spanish were opposed to independence for Cuba directly or through negotiations. Still, McKinley was able to hold off Congress until Spain had another chance to consider its options. When a negative answer arrived from Spain on March 31, 1898, McKinley prepared to put the issue before Congress.

There was one last flurry of diplomatic activity. On April 9, Spain agreed, at the urging of its European friends, to suspend hostilities in Cuba. It was not an

The explosion of the U.S.S. *Maine* on February 15, 1898, produced sensational headlines across the United States and hastened hostilities with Spain.

armistice, which would have meant formal recognition of the Cuban cause. The Spanish military commander in Cuba would determine how long the cessation of the fighting would last. There was no agreement on Cuban independence from Madrid. Thus the Spanish had not yielded on the key demands of the United States.

McKinley sent his message to Congress on April 11. It requested presidential authority to end the fighting in Cuba through armed force if necessary. At the end of his message the president mentioned that Spain had proposed to suspend hostilities, but he gave the idea little significance. Spain's acceptance of a suspension of hostilities did not represent a surrender to the demands of the United States. In fact, the diplomatic impasse between the two countries was unbroken.

Over the following week Congress debated the president's request for authority to intervene. To show that the United States had no selfish motives, the lawmakers adopted an amendment offered by Senator Henry M. Teller, a Colorado Democrat. The Teller Amendment stated that the United States did not intend to control Cuba or annex it. Yet Congress also declined to extend official recognition to the Cuban rebels to preserve freedom of action for the United States. For McKinley, the important result was a resolution authorizing him to act; this was passed on April 19 and the president signed it the following day.

Spain immediately broke diplomatic relations with the United States; it declared war on April 24. Congress replied that a state of war had existed between the United States and Spain since April 21.

The Spanish-American War

The war between the United States and Spain occurred because both sides believed that their cause was just. McKinley had pursued a diplomatic solution until it became clear that Spain would not agree to a negotiated settlement that would end its reign over Cuba. In the end, Spain preferred to lose Cuba on the battlefield rather than at the bargaining table.

The war began with a stunning naval victory. On May 1, 1898, Commodore George Dewey and the Asiatic naval squadron defeated the Spanish navy at Manila Bay in the Philippine Islands. The U.S. unit was in the waters of the Philippines because of war plans that had been developed in 1895 and updated as relations with Spain worsened. The goal was to hit the Spanish hard in the Philippines and thus pressure them to surrender Cuba. The triumph at Manila Bay made Dewey a national hero, but it confronted the president with new opportunities and problems in foreign policy.

To follow up on Dewey's success, the McKinley administration dispatched troops to the Philippines. The president wanted the option of acquiring the islands as a result of the war. He thought that a port in the Philippines might be enough, but he intended to maintain flexibility.

With the Philippines at stake, the Hawaiian Islands gained in strategic value. A treaty of annexation had

Admiral George Dewey, talking with photographer Frances Benjamin Johnson aboard ship, became a national hero for his victory at Manila Bay.

MAP 19.2 The Spanish-American War

The main focus of fighting in the war with Spain in 1898 was the island of Cuba and the Caribbean. This map shows the movement of American and Spanish naval forces toward the decisive battles in the vicinity of Santiago de Cuba as well as the capture of Puerto Rico.

View an animated version of this map or related maps at http://history.wadsworth.com/passages3e

been worked out during 1897, but the pact stalled in Congress. After the war began, the president and congressional leaders turned to a strategy of annexation by means of a legislative resolution that needed only a simple majority from Congress. Through presidential persuasion, the required votes for the resolution were obtained in July 1898, and Hawaii was annexed.

Meanwhile, U.S. policy toward the Philippines and their possible acquisition became a source of tension with Filipino leaders, notably Emilio Aguinaldo, who wanted their islands to be independent. The administration instructed army and navy officers not to have any formal dealings with the Filipinos. The buildup of military strength continued, and the ambitions of the Filipinos were seen as an obstacle to American policy, rather than as a legitimate expression of nationalism.

The main combat of the war took place in Cuba. The U.S. Army numbered 25,000 men, so the nation turned to volunteers. In the first wave of national enthusiasm, there were 1 million volunteers, far more than the army could handle. Eventually about 280,000 men saw active duty. Soldiers complained about shortages of ammunition and supplies and the poor quality of the food rations. The army experimented with canned beef, creating an inedible meal and a postwar controversy over the product.

In the regular army, an important part of the force that fought the Spanish were the four regiments composed of African American soldiers, or the "Smoked Yankees," as the Spanish troops described them. Seasoned fighters against Indians, the black soldiers were ordered to move south and prepare to invade Cuba. On their way through the southern states they encountered scorn, segregation, and threats.

The African American soldiers did not endure such treatment quietly. When they boarded segregated railroad cars, they sat wherever they pleased. If they saw signs that barred their presence, they took down the signs. Violence broke out between white troops and black troops in Florida, and men were killed and wounded in the exchanges of gunfire. Seeing all this, one soldier asked poignantly: "Is America any better than Spain?" Once the black regiments reached Cuba, their military contribution was significant. They earned numerous decorations for bravery and five of them won the Congressional Medal of Honor.

Despite the bravery of the "Smoked Yankees," the Spanish-American War worsened the plight of African Americans. The ideology of imperialism that allowed whites to dominate Cubans and Filipinos also supported racial segregation in the South. McKinley's efforts to reconcile the whites of the North and South brought harmony at the expense of black Americans.

Picturing the Past **SOCIAL & CULTURAL EVENTS**

"Smoked Yankees" and the War with Spain

The Spanish-American War produced a surge of patriotic volunteers and enthusiasm, but the main brunt of the fighting fell to the small regular army that was ready for immediate action in Cuba. As a result, black troops played a significant, if now largely forgotten, role in the successful campaign to oust the Spanish from the Caribbean island.

The picture records some of the black soldiers after a Cuban battle. American society credited white men such as Theodore Roosevelt and his Rough Riders with these victories, and African Americans were deleted from the historical record and their contributions to victory expunged. In the wake of imperialism, the nation became even more segregated. Placing a picture of black soldiers in a textbook is designed to emphasize that the American past is more complicated than the way it is often presented.

© The Granger Collection, New York

In late June, the U.S. Navy found the Spanish fleet in the harbor of Santiago de Cuba, and army detachments went ashore to engage the Spanish forces holding the city. On July 1, the army, commanded by General William R. Shafter, defeated the Spanish defenders at the Battle of San Juan Hill. Theodore Roosevelt and his volunteer regiment of Rough Riders took part in the battle. Roosevelt became a national hero on his way to the presidency, but the Rough Riders might have been defeated had it not been for the timely support they received from their black comrades.

On July 3, the navy destroyed the Spanish fleet when it tried to escape from Santiago Harbor. Negotiations for an armistice began. McKinley insisted that Spain relinquish Cuba and Puerto Rico and that the fate of the Philippines be discussed at the peace conference. Spain did not like these terms, but it had no choice but to accept them, which it did on August 12, 1898.

John Hay, soon to be McKinley's secretary of state, called it "a splendid little war." Victory had been achieved at a low cost in terms of combat deaths, only 281 officers and men. However, malaria, yellow fever, and other diseases killed more than 2,500 others. A public outcry arose after the war about the condition of the army, and McKinley named a commission to investigate the leadership of the War Department and the way the war had been conducted. The commission's report led to reforms such as general staff shake-ups and improved organization that enhanced the future fighting ability of the army. The war also strengthened the power of the presidency because of McKinley's expansive use of his role as commander-in-chief of the armed forces.

Theodore Roosevelt and his Rough Riders captured the popular imagination during the war with Spain.

The peace conference with Spain was held in Paris. McKinley appointed a commission that included several senators who would ultimately vote on any treaty that they negotiated. The president was aware that Germany and Japan had an interest in the Philippines, and he now intended that the United States should retain control of the islands rather than allow them to become the possession of the Germans or Japanese. American officials did not believe that the Filipinos could determine their own destiny; the islands would fall into the hands of a European power. Within the United States, opponents of a policy of expansion, calling themselves anti-imperialists, aroused public sentiment against the administration.

To build support for his foreign policy, McKinley made effective use of the powers of his office. During October, he toured the Midwest. Ordinarily presidents did not take part in congressional election campaigns. However, though billed as a nonpartisan event, McKinley's tour helped Republican candidates in the 1898 congressional contest. It also gave the

President McKinley directed the war with Spain from the White House. The "War Room" kept track of the movement of ships and men.

Enduring Issues Foreign Policy

In the decade of the 1890s, the United States moved on to the world stage as an international power. The Spanish-American War brought new colonial responsibilities in Latin America and Asia and placed the nation in the midst of rivalries among the European powers. Isolation from world affairs was no longer possible, though acceptance of that condition took decades to happen. In the Caribbean and the Pacific, Washington had to deal with instability, the need for naval bases, and the resistance of local populations to an American presence. Foreign policy became a more central concern for policymakers.

These commitments reflected attitudes that had existed since the beginning of the republic in the late eighteenth century. From the outset of its existence, the United States had wanted to remove Europeans from any major role in the destiny of North America and its surroundings. At the same time, the former British colonists sought to expand across the Continent toward the Pacific. That endeavor consumed most of the first half of the nineteenth century and became embroiled in the sectional crisis that precipitated the Civil War. With the exception of the purchase of Alaska in 1868, the nation paused during the era of industrialism to expand internally and build a national market. The security that two oceans provided helped to confirm the teachings of isolationism and keep the United States aloof from foreign quarrels.

During the last quarter of the nineteenth century, however, pressures on behalf of overseas expansion appeared. Religious groups wished to spread the message of Christianity abroad. Business groups and farmers sought new markets for surplus products. Advocates of a stronger navy campaigned for bases from which to extend American power. A desire to join the worldwide rush for colonies and imperial possessions animated other advocates of a greater world role.

The war with Spain brought wider involvement in world affairs. Acquisition of the Philippines meant potential rivalries with Japan and Russia over the markets for American goods in the Orient. As colonial ambitions brought European nations into contention with each other, the United States found itself more aligned with Great Britain and less drawn toward the German Empire. During the presidencies of Theodore Roosevelt and William Howard Taft, the nation balanced with some difficulty the claims of world power with the isolationist tendencies of most citizens.

Under Woodrow Wilson, the United States put aside its historical aloofness from European affairs and became a participant in the First World War as an associated power with the British and French against Germany. After victory was achieved, the United States decided to remain apart from the League of Nations that Woodrow Wilson had done so much to create. An apparent return to isolationism during the 1920s suggested that perhaps the events of the 1890s had not been so decisive after all.

That impression was misleading. The concepts of naval power, overseas bases, and an American presence in the world, along with a desire to promote

president an opportunity to state the case for a more expansive foreign policy. In a typical address he told an Iowa audience that "we do not want to shirk a single responsibility that has been put upon us by the results of the war."

The Philippines were the most divisive issue at the peace conference. On October 25, 1898, the president's commissioners asked him for instructions. On October 28, he responded that he could see "but one plain path of duty, the acceptance of the archipelago." The peace treaty was signed on December 10, 1898. The United States gained the Philippines, Guam, and Puerto Rico. Spain gave up its claims to Cuba and received a payment of $20 million for what it had lost. The United States obtained legal sovereignty over the Philippines but would soon face challenges from the island's inhabitants.

Opponents of imperialism tried to block acceptance of the treaty in the Senate. To win the necessary

two-thirds vote, McKinley employed the power of the presidency in new and creative ways. In December, he went south to woo Democrats. He used patronage to persuade wavering senators and exerted pressure on the state legislatures, which elected senators. Believing that the Democrats would benefit if the issue was settled before the 1900 elections, William Jennings Bryan endorsed the treaty. That action divided the opposition at a key point. The Senate approved the Treaty of Paris on February 6, 1899, by a vote of 57 to 27, one more than the necessary two-thirds.

As the Senate voted, the nation knew that fighting had erupted in the Philippines between U.S. soldiers and the Filipino troops that Aguinaldo commanded. Relations between the two sides had worsened during December 1898 as it became clear that the United States did not intend to leave the islands. Although the president asserted that his nation had "no imperial designs"

democracy and the ideals of the United States, would be powerful forces for the remainder of the twentieth century. The conviction that the United States must save Europe from its follies and protect democratic ideals brought the nation into an alliance with the British and the Russians (as the main military opponent of Nazi Germany) in World War II. The United Nations that came out of the world conflict also carried forward the ideals of Woodrow Wilson and the belief that democratic procedures would lead all nations into a harmonious future.

The Cold War with the Soviet Union from 1945 to 1991 offered another testing ground for the preeminence of American values as a way of organizing the world. The victory that arrived for the United States and its allies seemed to signal that the concepts enshrined in the Constitution and embodied in its political and economic system had world-wide relevance. Some commentators proclaimed the "end of history" and the ascendancy of the American model of society.

The rise of terrorism at the end of the 1990s and the events of September 11, 2001, indicated that not all societies and individuals had accepted the state of American foreign policy dominance. The Bush administration couched the struggle with terrorism as another event in the unfolding saga of American democracy freeing the world from tyranny. The idea of democratizing the Arab community, for example, had Wilsonian overtones that looked back to the original mission of the generation that fought the American Revolution and wrote the Constitution. It was a struggle, argued President George W. Bush, of freedom and democracy against religious fanaticism and backward-looking despotism using terrorist tactics to overthrow civilization.

The United States has always viewed its foreign policy struggles within a moral dimension. Ideas of the national interest, balance of power relations, and even economic necessity (such as the quest for petroleum) have to be reconciled with a sense of a larger American mission in the world. So when Americans fought the war with Spain in 1898 and acquired the Philippines, it was natural that advocates of those policies would invoke moral images to justify their cause. While such motives provided emotional and nationalistic satisfaction to Americans, they did not always sit well with the rest of the world where more cynical judgments about the intentions of the United States resided. As the twenty-first century got underway, it was not clear whether the enduring ideals of American foreign policy, as they had been practiced since 1776, would be a sufficient guide into the new world of religious fundamentalism, terroristic tactics, and a fragile and shaken human civilization.

Questions for Reflection

1. In what ways did the experience of the Spanish-American War and the acquisition of imperial possessions affect the way the United States conducted foreign policy in the twentieth century?

2. Why have Americans thought that in foreign policy our motives and actions are different from those of other nations?

on the Philippines, anti-imperialists and the Filipinos were not convinced. For Aguinaldo and his supporters, it seemed that they had ousted the Spanish only to replace them with another imperial master, the United States.

During 1899, the U.S. Army defeated the Filipinos in conventional battles, and the administration sent out a commission to work out a civil government under U.S. sovereignty. However, the Filipinos turned to guerilla tactics. Their soldiers hit selected targets and then blended back into the population. Faced with this new threat, the U.S. Army responded by killing some Filipino prisoners and torturing others to gain information. The army's purpose was not genocidal, but many soldiers and their officers violated the rules of war and government policy in brutal and inhumane ways. With revelations of these misdeeds, enthusiasm for further imperialistic adventures ebbed.

During the last two years of McKinley's first term, imperialism became a heated issue. An Anti-Imperialist League, created in November 1898, united the opposition against McKinley's foreign policy. Critics of expansionism charged that overseas possessions would damage the nation's democratic institutions. Some people used racist arguments to block the acquisition of lands where nonwhite populations lived. Others evoked moral concern about imperialism. A number of prominent Americans, including steelmaker Andrew Carnegie, House Speaker Thomas B. Reed, and the longtime reformer Carl Schurz, lent their voices to the anti-imperialist campaign.

Advocates of empire adapted the ideas of Social Darwinism and Anglo-Saxon supremacy to justify the acquisition of other countries. Theodore Roosevelt, Henry Cabot Lodge of Massachusetts, and their allies contended that the nation could not escape the world responsibilities that the war with Spain had brought. By 1900, Americans believed that the gains of empire should be retained and protected but not increased. The examination of the nation's goals and purposes contributed to the mood of reform and renewal that emerged at the turn of the century.

Other foreign policy issues emerged from the outcome of the war. The Teller Amendment blocked the annexation of Cuba, but the McKinley administration wanted to ensure that the island did not become a target of European intervention, most notably from Germany. A military government ran Cuba during 1899. As a civil government developed, the United States insisted on guarantees that Cuba would retain political and military ties with the country that had liberated it. The result of this process was the Platt Amendment of March 1901, which barred an independent Cuba from allying itself with another foreign power. The United States had the right to intervene to preserve stability and gained a naval base at Guantanamo in Cuba.

The acquisition of the Philippines heightened interest about the fate of China, where European powers sought to establish economic and political spheres of influence. Worried about the nation's trade with China and concerned to preserve that country's territorial integrity, in September 1899 the administration, through Secretary of State John Hay, issued what became known as the Open Door Notes. The messages asked European countries active in China to preserve trading privileges and other economic rights that gave the United States a chance to compete for markets there. The replies of the powers were noncommittal, but Hay announced in March 1900 that the other nations had accepted the U.S. position in principle. The Open Door Notes became a significant assertion of U.S. interest in China.

When antiforeign sentiment in China, especially against western missionaries, led to the Boxer Rebellion during the summer of 1900, an important test of the Open Door principle occurred. Secret associations known as the "Righteous and Harmonious Fists" (hence Boxers) launched a series of attacks on westerners in China. Europeans who had taken refuge in Peking were rescued by an international force that included 2,500 U.S. soldiers. President McKinley justified sending the troops into a country with which the United States was at peace as a legitimate use of his war power under the Constitution. Secretary Hay reaffirmed the U.S. commitment to the Open Door policy in a diplomatic circular to the powers that he issued on July 3, 1900. McKinley withdrew the troops rapidly after their rescue mission had been completed.

The Spanish-American War and the expansion of American commitments in the Pacific demonstrated the need for a waterway that would link the two oceans and enable the navy to conduct its growing worldwide responsibilities. The McKinley administration laid the groundwork for a canal across Central America when it renegotiated the Clayton-Bulwer Treaty of 1850 with Great Britain. That document prohibited both nations from exercising exclusive control over any future waterway. After extended negotiations with the British a treaty was worked out in the summer of 1901.

The 1900 Election and a New Century

The signs seemed to point to McKinley's reelection. Prosperity had returned, and the conflict in the Philippines was being won. McKinley's vice president, Garret A. Hobart, died in November 1899. Theodore Roosevelt, the popular young governor of New York, became McKinley's running mate. To oppose McKinley, the Democrats again turned to William Jennings Bryan. Bryan made another vigorous campaign. He attacked imperialism as a threat to the nation's institutions, and he accused the Republicans of being the tools of the trusts and the business community. The Democratic candidate also renewed his pleas for a free silver policy. The anti-imperialists did not trust Bryan both for his free silver views and because he had recommended approving the Treaty of Paris in 1899, but they preferred him to McKinley.

Because in that era incumbent presidents did not make speeches, McKinley allowed Theodore Roosevelt to do most of the campaigning. Bryan made so many criticisms that his campaign lacked a clear theme. McKinley increased his margin in the popular vote over what he had achieved four years earlier. The result in the electoral college was 292 for McKinley and 155 for Bryan.

McKinley gained further victories in foreign policy. Congress set up a civilian government for the Philippines when the insurrection had ended, which occurred shortly after the capture of Emilio Aguinaldo in March 1901. On May 27, 1901, the Supreme Court ruled in the *Insular Cases* that the Philippines and Puerto Rico were properly possessions of the United States but that their inhabitants had not become citizens of the country. The decision upheld McKinley's colonial policy and provided legal justification for imperialism.

Meanwhile, the president was turning his attention to two major domestic issues: the growth of big business

Flashpoints | The Death of William McKinley

The president loved to travel. From the time William McKinley was inaugurated on March 4, 1897, he made trips around the nation one of the keynotes of his years in the White House. By 1901, he planned in his second term to break the precedent that barred the chief executive from leaving the borders of the United States during his presidency. So it was natural for McKinley to visit the Pan-American Exposition in Buffalo, New York, in September 1901. He believed that world's fairs were the "timekeepers of progress," and he intended to use the occasion to make a speech for expanded American trade. That oration was well received on September 5, 1901.

The next day McKinley held a public reception in the Temple of Music. In those days, the president was expected, as the first citizen of the United States, to make himself available to greet the people. In mid-afternoon, the people of Buffalo lined up and began to move through the receiving line, shaking hands with McKinley and the members of his traveling party. One man in the procession, however, had come to shoot the president. Leon Czolgosz, an anarchist who saw McKinley as the embodiment of an oppressive government, fired two shots at 4:07 p.m. The president lurched back, mortally wounded. He was rushed to the hospital where he lingered for seven days before he died in the early morning of September 14, 1901.

Vice President Theodore Roosevelt took the oath of office and became the 26th president. He promised to continue McKinley's policies but soon took the nation in what seemed fresh and exciting directions. An act of political murder had changed the course of American history. Because the assassination of the president took place in the first year of the new century, Roosevelt came to be associated with the modern age that was beginning and McKinley represented the passing of the old nineteenth-century way of thinking and behaving. Yet, as the text shows, McKinley had done much to create the modern presidency that Roosevelt expanded and developed. Roosevelt himself carried on the march to world power for the United States that commenced in 1898 when the nation went to war against Spain.

The death of McKinley thus raises the question of whether dramatic events such as an assassination or other human tragedies interrupt the flow of history or are absorbed into the continuum of human activity. Had McKinley lived, for example, would the antitrust policy of Roosevelt have happened anyway, would some political reform have occurred, even in a milder form, and would foreign policy have been essentially the same? The tragedy that befell William McKinley on September 6, 1901, thus provides one of those critical moments when history changed and students of the past can wonder about its significance for the future course of American history.

Questions for Reflection

1. How did McKinley's appearance at Buffalo in September 1901 reflect the changes he had made in the presidency?

2. What differences can be noticed between the presidency in 1901 and the presidency today?

3. From the reading in the text, what difference, if any, did it make that Theodore Roosevelt became president in 1901?

and the issue of high tariffs. By 1901, McKinley was persuaded that some action was necessary to enforce the Sherman Antitrust Act of 1890. He had also modified his earlier support for the protective tariff and now believed that reciprocal trade treaties should be adopted that would lower duties on products entering the United States. Treaties that had been negotiated with such foreign countries as France and Argentina had not yet received Senate action. McKinley intended to prod the Senate to take them up at the next session, which would convene in December 1901. As he had done to secure ratification of the treaty with Spain in 1898, he also planned to travel extensively during 1901 to raise the trade issue with the American people. That decision would bring him to Buffalo, New York, in September 1901 to make a speech about freer trade and reciprocal tariff treaties.

As the new century began, McKinley had revived the power of the presidency after the decades of congressional supremacy that followed the Civil War. He had expanded the size of the president's staff, begun to involve the press in the coverage of White House affairs, and personalized the office through his travels. In many respects, McKinley was the first modern president.

The nation saw the arrival of the twentieth century on December 31, 1900, with a mixture of confidence about what the United States had accomplished and apprehension about what the future held. The depression of the 1890s remained a vivid memory for most citizens, even with the return of prosperity after 1897. The shift in attitudes toward government and its role that had occurred during the hard times led many people to advocate programs of social reform.

With the end of the century in sight, and the experience of the war with Spain still vivid, there was a flurry of public debate about the direction of the nation. A National Social and Political Conference took place in Buffalo, New York, in 1899 that brought together Eugene V. Debs, Henry Demarest Lloyd, Samuel Gompers, and Hazen Pingree, among others. The delegates called for "equality of economic opportunity and political power." Their goals required a more activist government than had been common in the nineteenth century.

In 1900, other future advocates of change appeared. After a long political battle in Wisconsin against the leaders of the Republican party, Robert M. La Follette finally won election as governor. His agenda looked toward changes in the way the state government functioned and more regulation of the state's railroads. Other governors in the Middle West were advancing similar concerns about the power of corporations. The pressure for reform in the states was mounting.

A devastating hurricane in Galveston, Texas, in September 1900 caused significant damage to that Texas city. Political leaders there turned to a new form of government to deal with rebuilding. Commissioners of fire, water, police, and other services replaced the older style of ward leaders. The idea of having officials tied to the workings of city departments rather than representing geographic areas would attract increasing attention after the turn of the new century.

In the academic world, a biting analysis of how Americans used the wealth that they had acquired during the process of industrialization was published. Thorstein Veblen was a professor at the University of Chicago when he wrote *The Theory of the Leisure Class* (1899). In this book he analyzed the ways in which citizens displayed their social status. Although his writings offered more diagnosis than solutions, Veblen was a provocative critic of capitalist institutions and practices at a time when his fellow citizens worried about their impact on national life.

At both ends of the economic spectrum, Americans looked to organizations to address social ills. In 1900, Italian and Jewish immigrants who worked in the clothing business in New York City united to form the International Ladies Garment Workers Union (ILGWU). The membership, predominantly female, used the ILGWU to spread the ideas of unionism to other immigrant workers and to discuss alternatives to the existing system. That would be a hallmark of progressive change. Also in

1900, the more well-to-do business leaders of the day created the National Civic Federation. Made up of representatives from organized labor, the business community, and the public, the NCF sought to promote harmony between labor and capital. The issue of labor relations would become significant in the decade ahead.

Conclusion

A balance sheet on the achievements of the late nineteenth century was a mixed one. Optimists cited the nation's burgeoning productive capacity, the totals of steel produced and railroad tracks laid, and the impressive per capita wealth of U.S. citizens. Most of the population could read, and there were more than 2,000 newspapers available covering a staggering variety of subjects. There was an equally dazzling array of magazines on the newsstands with growing numbers of illustrations of national and world events. Advertisers spent $90 million in 1900 to tempt readers to try their products.

The United States was devoted to education. There were 1,700 libraries in the nation that held more than 5,000 volumes in their collections. Almost 240,000 students attended 977 colleges and universities at the turn of the century, or a little more than 1 percent of Americans between the ages of 15 and 25. Eighty percent of these institutions admitted women to their programs, although men received four times as many degrees as women did. Below the college level, 16 million children went to public schools. The educated, literate workforce that resulted was the envy of competing economies in western Europe.

As the twentieth century began, Americans were eating more massproduced foods. In this advertisement for Postum, a substitute for coffee, two women discuss what the drink can do for their complexion and general health.

On the negative side were the social problems that the nation confronted. An estimated 10 million Americans, or about 13 percent of the population, lived below the poverty line. A visitor to the United States said that half its population was "ill-housed, ill-fed, and ill-clothed." Although the often-anticipated social revolution of the 1890s had not occurred, influential leaders such as Theodore Roosevelt worried about the potential for violence and upheaval if moderate reforms did not take place. In addition, the nation faced the problems of segregation, the future of Native Americans, and the place of immigrants in American society. Americans turned to these questions with an energy that made the twenty years between 1900 and 1920 famous as an age of political reform and government regulation.

The Chapter in Review

In the years between 1893 and 1900:

- The country faced the challenge of a serious economic depression.
- Labor unrest and social dislocation proliferated.
- The Democratic party split into competing factions and lost national power.
- The Populists failed to become a viable third party.
- The Republicans gained a national majority in the 1894 and 1896 elections.
- William McKinley revitalized the presidency.
- Tension with Spain over Cuba led to war in 1898.
- The United States acquired an overseas empire by 1900.

Making Connections Across Chapters

LOOKING BACK

The events that dominated American life in the 1890s stemmed from problems that had been accumulating since the Civil War. This chapter discussed the political and economic systems as they confronted the effects of a major depression and the country's increasing presence on the world stage.

1. What were the options open to the government when an economic collapse occurred?

2. Why did President Grover Cleveland face the political blame for problems with business and finance that he inherited?

3. Why did the Republicans become the big winners in the politics of the 1890s?

4. How did American social commentators react to the Panic of 1893 and its effects on the nation?

5. Should the United States have intervened in Cuba in 1898?

LOOKING AHEAD

In the next chapter, Theodore Roosevelt will take the stage as one of the leaders of the progressive movement of political reform. In what ways does this chapter foreshadow these developments?

1. How did attitudes change during the 1890s about the proper role of government?

2. What problems did imperialism leave to be solved after 1900?

3. How did Americans see themselves and their country as the twentieth century opened?

4. What was the position of the United States in the world in 1900?

Recommended Readings

Campbell, W. Joseph. *Yellow Journalism: Puncturing the Myths, Defining the Legacies* (2001). A skeptical look at the sensational journalism and the war with Spain.

Gilmore, Glenda. *Gender and Jim Crow: Women and the Politics of White Supremacy in North Carolina, 1896–1920* (1996). An excellent study of the ways in which black and white women interacted during the era of segregation.

Hoganson, Kristin L. *Fighting for American Manhood: How Gender Politics Provoked the Spanish-American and Philippine-American Wars* (1998). A provocative new study about the origins of the conflict with Spain.

Offner, John L. *An Unwanted War: The Diplomacy of the United States & Spain Over Cuba, 1895–1898* (1992). Valuable for the interplay of Cubans, Spaniards, and Americans as the war drew near.

Perez, Louis A. *The War of 1898: The United States and Cuba in History and Historiography* (1998). Offers an insightful, sympathetic look at the war from a perspective that takes Cuba into account.

Schlereth, Thomas J. *Victorian America: Transformations in Everyday Life, 1876–1915* (1991). Strong on the social and cultural changes that occurred during the 1890s.

Smith, Joseph. *The Spanish-American War: Conflict in the Caribbean and the Pacific, 1845–1902* (1994). A good one-volume account of the military history of the war.

Traxel, David. *1898: The Birth of the American Century* (1998). An interpretive survey of the war with Spain and its consequences for the nation.

Williams, R. Hal. *Years of Decision: American Politics in the 1890s* (1993). The best narrative account of this important decade.

Zimmerman, Warren. *First Great Triumph: How Five Americans Made Their Country a World Power* (2002). An interesting interpretation of the origins of American imperialism.

Identifications

Review your understanding of the following key terms, people, events, and dates for this chapter (these terms also appear in the Glossary at the end of the book):

Grover Cleveland
William McKinley
George Pullman
Eugene Victor Debs
Pullman strike
Ida Wells-Barnett

Charlotte Perkins Gilman
Spanish-American War
Theodore Roosevelt
Booker T. Washington
Atlanta Compromise
Plessy v. Ferguson
the yellow press
Stephen Crane
William Randolph Hearst

Online Sources Guide

Use this listing to find online documents, images, interactive maps, simulations, and other resources related to this chapter:

American History Resource Center

http://history.wadsworth.com

Documents

Eugene V. Debs, "How I Became a Socialist"
William Jennings Bryan, Views on Imperialism
Two Eyewitness Accounts of the American Naval Attack on the Spanish Fleet in Manila Bay
Walter Rauschenbusch's "Christianity and the Social Crisis"
Theodore Roosevelt's "The Rough Riders"
Plessy v. Fergusson Decision
Booker T. Washington's Atlanta Exposition Address, 1895
Theodore Roosevelt's "The Strenuous Life"

Interactive Maps

Spanish American War in Cuba, 1898

Selected Images

Copper mining town outside Denver, 1897
Indian children at the Carlisle School, 1900
Booker T. Washington at Tuskegee Institute
Advertisement for 1901 phonograph
First Oldsmobile, 1897
William McKinley at home in Canton, Ohio
Mulberry Street in New York City, 1900
Ida Tarbell
Mary Church Terrell, one of the founding members of the NAACP
McKinley/Roosevelt campaign poster, 1900
Battleship *Maine* in Havana Harbor, 1898

Simulation

Early Twentieth Century

Document Exercises

1896 People's Party Platform
1901 Race Riot
1901 Food Poisoning

HistoryNOW

http://now.ilrn.com/ayers_etal3e

Primary Source Exercises

Eugene Debs addresses the American Railway Union, 1894

Henry Demarest Lloyd, Wealth against Commonwealth, 1894

Lynching of Henry Smith, 1893 & A Summary of Lynchings in 1897

20 Theodore Roosevelt and Progressive Reform, 1901–1909

Theodore Roosevelt imparted his energy and enthusiasm to the first decade of the twentieth century. Here he sits astride a horse during one of his frequent trips around the United States. His intense smile became one of the trademarks of his public image.

On September 6, 1901, President William McKinley was shot in Buffalo, New York. A week later he died and Vice President Theodore Roosevelt became president. The eight years that followed have come to be known as part of the Progressive Era. Responding to the social and economic impact of industrialism, Americans endeavored to reshape their nation to curb the power of large businesses, improve conditions for the consumer, and reform the political parties.

The nation confronted new issues. Citizens argued about whether government should regulate the economy and whether the power to do so should be local or national. The political party became a major source of controversy. Its critics contended that intense partisanship had corrupted government and weakened democracy, and that power should be shifted toward the individual voter. Other advocates of change clamored for more voter participation in the electoral system by broadening the ability of citizens to propose laws, choose candidates, and overturn judicial decisions. Thus, during a time of prosperity at home and relative peace abroad, the United States experienced political ferment. The issues that Americans debated at the turn of the twentieth century would dominate the agenda of domestic policy for decades.

The United States at the Start of the Twentieth Century

In 1901, Americans balanced confidence about the future in a new century with worries about the direction in which their society was moving. The population stood at 76 million, up from 63 million 10 years earlier. Immigrants accelerated the population growth.

New arrivals came in at a prodigious rate. There were 488,000 in 1900, 688,000 in 1902, and more than 1.1 million in 1906. Like their late-nineteenth-century predecessors, the majority of these newcomers settled in the nation's growing cities.

Most Americans, however, still lived in rural areas or small towns with fewer than 2,500 residents. Not for another 20 years would the population become more urban than rural. As the cities expanded, tensions between rural and urban areas mounted.

Timeline

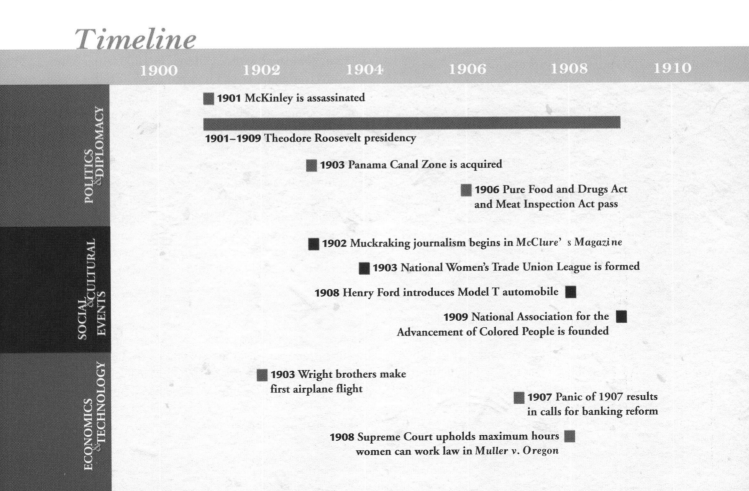

	1900	1902	1904	1906	1908	1910

POLITICS & DIPLOMACY

■ **1901** McKinley is assassinated

1901–1909 Theodore Roosevelt presidency

■ **1903** Panama Canal Zone is acquired

■ **1906** Pure Food and Drugs Act and Meat Inspection Act pass

SOCIAL & CULTURAL EVENTS

■ **1902** Muckraking journalism begins in *McClure's Magazine*

■ **1903** National Women's Trade Union League is formed

1908 Henry Ford introduces Model T automobile ■

1909 National Association for the Advancement of Colored People is founded ■

ECONOMICS & TECHNOLOGY

■ **1903** Wright brothers make first airplane flight

■ **1907** Panic of 1907 results in calls for banking reform

1908 Supreme Court upholds maximum hours women can work law in *Muller v. Oregon* ■

SOCIAL & CULTURAL EVENTS

Immigration in the Progressive Era

Table 20.1 Immigration into the U.S., 1901–1909

1901	487,918
1902	687,743
1903	857,046
1904	812,870
1905	1,026,499
1906	1,100,735
1907	1,285,349
1908	782,870
1909	751,786

Source: *The Statistical History of the United States* (1965), p. 56.

Tables of historical numbers can seem dull and uninformative. In the case of these figures on immigration into the United States during the first decade of the twentieth century, the totals show a dramatic transformation in the population whose effects shaped politics, economics, and culture. The newcomers arrived primarily from southern and eastern Europe, as well as Asia, and soon put their stamp on cities as diverse as New York and San Francisco.

Vibrant immigrant communities arose. The surge produced a backlash in efforts to restrict immigration that ultimately led to cutbacks by the 1920s. But the impact of these new Americans proved lasting in the way people lived and their expectations about the role of government. A more varied, turbulent, and interesting United States came out of the process that these numbers represent.

A Longer Life Span

People lived longer in 1900, a trend that accelerated throughout the century. Life expectancy for white men rose from 47 years in 1901 to almost 54 in 1920. For white women, the increase was from around 51 years in 1901 to almost 55 in 1920. Life expectancy for members of minority groups rose from 34 years in 1901 to just over 45 in 1920.

The population was young in 1900. The median age was 23; it rose to just over 25 by 1920. The death rate for the entire population was 17 per thousand in 1900. It fell to 13 per thousand by 1920. For infants in the Progressive Era, the prospects were less encouraging. In 1915, the first year for which there are accurate numbers, almost 61 deaths were recorded for every 10,000 births. The situation worsened during the next several years, and the infant mortality rate reached more than 68 deaths per 10,000 births in 1921. For nonwhite babies the picture was even worse: there were almost 106 deaths per 10,000 live births in 1915. Some positive changes occurred, however. More and more mothers gave birth in hospitals rather than at home. Improved medical techniques and the antiseptic setting of the hospitals helped reduce the incidence of infant mortality.

Children at Work

The problem of child labor persisted. In 1900, more than 1,750,000 children between the ages of 10 and 15 worked in the labor force. In the South, children worked in cotton mills. Conditions were so bad that reformers called the mills and their communities "the poorest place in the world for training citizens of a democracy." Abolishing child labor was a major goal of reform campaigns after 1900.

Changes in the Family

In families whose children did not have to work, child rearing became more organized and systematic. Kindergartens gained popularity as a way to prepare children for school. There were 5,000 in 1900 and nearly 9,000 twenty years later. The federal government held conferences on child rearing and issued booklets about infant care. Improved methods of contraception led to smaller families. In 1900, the average mother had 3.566 children, compared with 7 children in 1800. Attention shifted to rearing fewer children more successfully.

The status of women also changed after 1900. Some younger women delayed marriage to attend college. Yet, opportunities for women to enter law, medicine, or higher education remained limited. In 1920, fewer than 1.5 percent of all attorneys were women. In 1910, there were only 9,000 women doctors, about 6 percent of all physicians. Restrictive policies on admissions to medical schools and barriers to staff positions at hospitals posed obstacles to women who sought to become doctors. Nursing and social work were more accessible to women, but they still faced condescension from men.

Women at Work

Women in factories, mills, and garment sweatshops also saw little improvement in their condition as the new century began. Their workday was 10 hours long, and six- and seven-day weeks were common. Men received more pay than women; labor unions regarded women as competitors for jobs held by men. Women set up their own unions, such as the **National Women's Trade Union League,** established in 1903. They also formed the backbone of the International Ladies Garment Workers Union (ILGWU), which led strikes in New York City in 1910 and 1911.

Social trends slowly altered the status of women. Their clothes became less confining and cumbersome. The full skirt was still the fashion in 1900, but soon thereafter petticoats and corsets disappeared. Women began to show their ankles and arms in public. Some more daring young women, such as Alice Roosevelt, smoked in public; others used cosmetics openly. In dance halls and restaurants, young people danced the turkey trot and the bunny hug to the rhythms of ragtime.

These changes affected the institution of marriage. Marriage ceremonies used the word "obey" less frequently. Women asked more of their husbands, including companionship and sexual pleasure. Government programs were instituted to encourage family togetherness. In 1914, prodded by advocates of the traditional home (and the florist industry), Congress designated Mother's Day as a national holiday.

Divorce was easier and more common. About four marriages out of every thousand ended in divorce in 1900, but in the ensuing years the divorce rate increased three times faster than the rate of population growth. There were 56,00 divorces in 1900 and 100,000 in 1914. Slowly, attitudes toward broken marriages changed; divorce was less often the occasion for social disgrace.

A Nation of Consumers

In 1900, 76 million people in the United States owned 21 million horses. Some forecasters said that the automobile would replace the horse, but in 1903 only a little more than 11,000 cars were sold. During the next decade, however, Henry Ford of Dearborn, Michigan, created the Model T. Ford's goal was to use mass production techniques to build an automobile that could be sold in large numbers. By 1908, the Model T was ready for distribution, priced at about $850. Sales increased as Ford reduced the car's price. In 1908, 5,986 Model T's were sold; by 1912, the total was 78,611. The mass-produced automobile was a key element in the evolution of the consumer society during the Progressive Era.

Standardized food products also gained popular acceptance. Asa Candler's Coca-Cola became available throughout the country when the parent company licensed bottling plants everywhere. There were 241 bottlers by 1905, 493 by 1910, and 1,095 a decade later. In 1912, Procter & Gamble introduced Crisco, a vegetable shortening, as a way of selling its cottonseed oil. The company used marketing campaigns in popular periodicals,

held "Crisco teas" at which clubwomen could try out their own recipes, and created cooking schools to spread awareness of the new product. By 1915, its advertising proclaimed that "Crisco is rapidly taking the place of butter and lard for cooking." Other famous brands, such as Kellogg's Corn Flakes, Uneeda Biscuit, and Kodak cameras, relied on mass advertising, billboards, and mail flyers to instill popular desire for these new and convenient consumer goods.

Advertising became a central feature of American culture. Newspapers and magazines gave lower rates to advertisers who used entire pages. Billboards appealed to the new motoring public and outraged garden club members when they obscured scenic views. Advertising agencies shaped the content of product information. Men were urged to buy Gillette razors because "You Ought to Shave Every Morning." Toothbrush ads proclaimed that Americans should "keep their teeth and mouths clean." The Kodak camera was an essential part of the Christmas season as "your family historian."

To master these markets, advertisers surveyed potential purchasers. Agencies tracked customers through reports from salespeople, mail surveys, and questionnaires printed in magazines. Coca-Cola, for example, increased its advertising budget annually and in 1913 distributed 5 million metal Coca-Cola signs across the country.

Sears, Roebuck and Company was a leader in consumer marketing. Founded during the economic depression of 1893, the company was the brainchild of Richard Warren Sears, who believed in low prices as a selling technique. Beginning with mail-order watches, Sears expanded to general merchandise that was sold in a catalogue published annually. He cut prices for desirable products such as sewing machines and cream separators and soon produced record sales. Sears spent lavishly on advertising—over $1.5 million in 1902—and promised low prices, guarantees of any products and parts, and the opportunity to order merchandise without prepaying. "Send No Money" was the Sears slogan. Volume sales at low prices built a market for Sears; the company sent out more than 1.5 million catalogues in 1902. For rural Americans the Sears catalogue became their link to the expanding world of consumer products.

In many respects, the United States occupied an enviable position. A British visitor said that the standard of American life had reached a height "hitherto unrealized in a civilized society." National income stood at $17 billion; the average American's annual per capita income of $227 was the highest in the world. Innovations promised further abundance to a prosperous population.

Despite these positive trends, citizens worried about the nation's future. The growth of big business, the spread

© The Granger Collection, New York

The mail-order services of Sears, Roebuck and Company became a familiar part of countless American households as the new century began. In this Consumers Guide, Sears is instructing its customers about comparing the prices of local shopkeepers with the less expensive goods that can be obtained through the mail.

of labor organizations, the corruption in politics, the decline of the individual in a bureaucratic society—all these trends prompted fear that older values and attitudes were under assault. The early twentieth century saw a renewed debate about the purpose and accomplishments of the United States. For white Americans, however, the persistent issue of race and the treatment of minorities did not attract much attention during this period of reform.

Theodore Roosevelt and the Modern Presidency

The president during these dramatic changes in American life was Theodore Roosevelt. At age 42, he was the youngest president. During the war with Spain his volunteer regiment of Rough Riders charged up Kettle Hill in Cuba against the fortified Spanish position. A national hero, he was elected governor of New York in 1898. When he criticized corporate abuses, Republican leaders exiled him to the vice presidency.

The new president pledged to continue McKinley's policies. Yet the youthful and vigorous Roosevelt made news in ways that no previous president had done. He changed the official name of the president's residency to the White House and infused energy into its daily routine. His large family—he had six children—captivated the nation. The president's oldest daughter, Alice Lee, made her debut at the White House, kept a pet snake, and drove around Washington in fast cars. "I can be President of the United States or I can control Alice," Roosevelt told friends who asked him to rein in his daughter, "I cannot possibly do both."

Roosevelt planned to be a strong and forceful president. In time he decided that the president should be the "steward" of the general welfare. As long as the Constitution did not prohibit executive action, the president should stretch the limits of what was possible. Roosevelt built on McKinley's example but he went further, causing the public to see the president as the focus of national authority.

The nation watched him in fascination. Roosevelt reformed college football to make it less violent, pursued simplified spelling of English (*thru* instead of *through*, for example), and waged loud, frequent quarrels with his political enemies. Like a preacher in church, he called the White House his "bully pulpit," using it to give sermons to the country about morality and duty.

The new president wanted to limit the power of big business to avoid pressure for more radical reforms from the Democrats or Socialists. He also believed that the nation had to protect its natural resources. Until he left it in 1912, the Republican party seemed to Roosevelt the best means to implement his goals. As a result, he left the protective tariff alone and cooperated with the conservative Republicans who dominated Congress during his first term. Later on in his presidency when he exerted presidential power with more vigor, his relations with Capitol Hill worsened.

Theodore Roosevelt was the first celebrity president. The spread of newspapers and the emergence of motion pictures made it possible for Americans to follow the nation's leader with greater attention than ever before. Roosevelt dramatized what went on in Washington. By using the power of his office in this way, he strengthened the presidency for future challenges. His first demonstration of his intentions came when he confronted the power of big business.

Roosevelt and Big Business

On February 19, 1902, the Department of Justice announced that it was filing suit under the Sherman Antitrust Act (1890) against the Northern Securities

DOING HISTORY

Theodore Roosevelt and the Regulation of Business

Charles E. Perkins

"I DO NOT believe any question more important to the country than this Rate question was ever before you, because Government rate making means pretty soon Government ownership and the political as well as commercial consequences must to say the least be serious. It is not a Railroad question. Transportation by Rail is either a "business" or it is not. That is the question. It cannot for long be both "business" and "not business"; it must be one or the other. If not business it is politics, and if so decided by the Senate, the man on horseback will soon come to stay. We do not know perhaps what the commercial consequences of Government rate making may be, but we can see, it seems to me, what the political consequences *must* be. Both will undoubtedly be bad enough.

I sometimes wonder if the current which carries us along may not bring us up against practical socialism ending in some kind of a revolution before so very long—not in our day but soon. Or will the common sense of the people get tired of the actors and charlatans who are now in the saddle and return to sound first principles? Does the current of human affairs admit of that?"

Theodore Roosevelt

"A similar extension of the national power to oversee and secure correct behavior in the management of all great corporations engaged in interstate business will in similar fashion render far more stable the present system by doing away with those grave abuses which are not only evil in themselves but are also evil because they furnish an excuse for agitators to inflame well-meaning people against all forms of property and to commit the country to schemes of wild would-be remedy which would work infinitely more harm than the disease itself. The government ought not to conduct the business of the country; but it ought to regulate it so that it shall be conducted in the interest of the public.

Perhaps the best justification of the course which in the National Government we have been pursuing in the past few years, and which we intend steadily and progressively to pursue in the future, is that it is condemned with almost equal rancor by the reactionaries—the Bourbons—on one side, and by the wild apostles of unrest on the other."

During 1905–1906, in the debates over the Hepburn Act to strengthen the power of the Interstate Commerce Commissions, the political process dealt with the issue of government regulation of the economy. On the one side was President Theodore Roosevelt, who believed in the need for such supervision of corporate power. Members of the business community took a different view. One such critic of government intervention in the economy was Charles E. Perkins, president of the Burlington Railroad. Perkins wrote to Senator William Boyd Allison of Iowa to express his dissent from what Roosevelt was proposing to do as far as the rail lines were concerned. In their contrasting views of the priorities of the government and the economy, they reflected a division of opinion over regulation and its effects that has continued down to the present time.

Source: Perkins: Charles E. Perkins to William Boyd Allison, February 23, 1906, William Boyd Allison Papers, Iowa State Department of History and Archives, Des Moines, Iowa. Roosevelt: "Legislative Actions and Judicial Decisions," Address at the Dedication of the New State Capitol Building, Harrisburg, Pennsylvania, October 4, 1906, *The Works of Theodore Roosevelt: American Problems* (20 volumes, New York: Charles Scribner's Sons, 1906), XVI, p. 73.

Questions for Reflection

1. What does Charles E. Perkins mean by "socialism" and how does he think Roosevelt's policies will lead to that result?

2. Why does Perkins believe that more power for the Interstate Commerce Commission will not achieve the results that Roosevelt is seeking?

3. Why does Theodore Roosevelt believe that some degree of government regulation is necessary beyond its immediate economic effect?

4. How would Roosevelt define the public interest and why does he believe that the national government can best represent that interest?

5. In what areas of American life are the issues that Perkins and Roosevelt raise still being debated and decided?

Explore additional primary sources related to this chapter on the Wadsworth American History Resource Center or HistoryNOW websites:

http://history.wadsworth.com/rc/us
http://now.ilrn.com/ayers_etal3e

Company. That firm, created in late 1901, merged major railroads in the Northwest, including the Great Northern, the Northern Pacific, and the Chicago, Burlington, and Quincy Company. The key leaders in assembling this large company were James J. Hill and E. H. Harriman; their financing came from **J. P. Morgan.** The merger sought to reduce destructive competition among warring railroads and make railroad rates more stable. Opposition to the merger came from states across which the company would operate, most notably in Minnesota. Farmers and business operators in the upper Midwest feared that a giant railroad would raise rates and limit their profits. They urged their governors to file suit against the new company in federal court. Many Americans believed that only the federal government could regulate such unbridled corporate power.

The creation of the Northern Securities Company was part of the trend toward larger economic units that had begun during the 1890s. A highly publicized case was the United States Steel Company, which had been formed earlier in 1901. The steel merger symbolized bigness in business in the same way that the railroad combine did. Indeed, the same forces that led to consolidation in railroads promoted a similar result in steel.

At the turn of the century, the Carnegie Steel Company dominated the industry, producing finished steel products at a lower unit cost than its rivals. For J. P. Morgan, the investment banker who had restructured the railroad network in the 1890s, and the steel companies that he represented, Carnegie's power raised the possibility that competing firms might go bankrupt. The logical answer, Morgan concluded, was to buy out Carnegie and create a steel company that could control the entire industry. Morgan sent an aide to see Carnegie. "If Andy wants to sell, I'll buy," said Morgan. "Go and find his price."

Morgan's agent, Charles M. Schwab, found Carnegie on the golf course. Carnegie sent his answer a day later. In a penciled note, he told Morgan that the price was $480 million. Morgan paused and responded: "I accept this price." The merger was made public on March 3, 1901, the day before William McKinley began his second term. Carnegie Steel joined other firms financed by Morgan such as Federal Steel and the National Tube Company. The half-billion dollars that Carnegie

received for his holding was a staggering sum in an era when there was no federal income tax, no capital gains tax, and low inflation. In modern terms, Carnegie probably would have received more than $50 billion.

The Challenge of United States Steel

The new company, United States Steel, was capitalized at $1.4 billion. It had 168,000 employees and controlled 60 percent of the steel industry's productive capacity. Smaller steel companies would have to compete with the vertical integration Carnegie had achieved with the company that Morgan had acquired. Workers in steel now faced a powerful employer that could fix wage levels in any way it chose. The prospect worried outside observers. "We have billion dollar combines," said one editor, "maneuvered by a handful of men who have never been in a plant and think of a factory as just another chip in a gigantic financial poker game."

Theodore Roosevelt worried too. He saw the forces that led to business consolidation as the logical outcome of economic development, but he did not believe that the federal government should stand by. The large corporations, Roosevelt decided, should not be destroyed. Firms that were socially beneficial should be encouraged; those that misbehaved should be regulated. A good firm, in Roosevelt's mind, paid its workers a decent wage, avoided labor strife, did not overcharge the public, and did not corrupt the political process. Bad corporations failed to follow these precepts. At first Roosevelt thought that publicizing the activities of corporations would be enough regulation. He soon concluded that he must establish the power of the federal government to intervene in the economy. The Northern Securities Company was unpopular, so the president acted.

Controlling the Trusts

After the Department of Justice announced its antitrust suit against the Northern Securities Company in February 1902, the stock market fell. J. P. Morgan hurried to Washington to ask the president if additional lawsuits were planned. No, said Roosevelt, "unless we find out . . . [that other companies] have done something wrong." Roosevelt argued that "trusts are creatures of the State, and the State not only has the right to control them, but it is in duty bound to control them wherever the need of such control is shown."

In 1904, the Supreme Court agreed with Roosevelt when the government won its case against the Northern Securities Company. By a 5 to 4 margin the justices ruled that the railroad company violated the Sherman Act. The case reestablished the power of the national government to use the Sherman Act, which had been called into question in the 1895 case of *U.S. v. E. C. Knight.* The American public saw Roosevelt as a "**trustbuster**" who was willing to curb the power of big business. Having established the principle that the government was supreme over any individual corporation, the president used trust-busting sparingly against "bad" trusts and sought to assist "good" trusts with policies that rewarded their positive behavior. A good trust followed enlightened labor policies, courted the consumer, and did not try to drive its competitors out of the market. Bad trusts violated these principles and sought undue economic advantages that thwarted competition.

The Anthracite Coal Strike of 1902 required the intervention of Theodore Roosevelt to settle the dispute between organized labor and the mine owners. He appointed the arbitration commission pictured here in a stereo view.

The Square Deal in the Coal Strike

The nation also applauded when Roosevelt intervened to end a strike in the coal industry during the autumn of 1902. The 140,000 members of the United Mine Workers walked off their jobs in the anthracite (hard coal) fields of Pennsylvania. The miners asked for a pay hike and for the railroads and coal operators to recognize their union. Having lost an earlier strike in 1900, management wanted to break the strike and the union. As the walkout stretched into autumn, fears grew of winter coal shortages. If the voters were cold in November, the Republicans faced political losses in the 1902 congressional elections. Yet neither side in the walkout seemed prepared to yield.

As the crisis worsened, Roosevelt brought both sides to the White House in early October. Throughout a day of talks, Roosevelt urged the workers and owners to settle. The union's president, John Mitchell, agreed to arbitration, but the mine owners refused. Roosevelt responded that he might bring in the army to mine coal. Facing that threat, J. P. Morgan and Elihu Root worked out a deal in which a presidential commission was set up to look into the strike. The panel granted the miners a 10 percent pay increase, but the union was not recognized. Unlike Grover Cleveland during the Pullman strike, Roosevelt wielded presidential power to treat capital and labor on an equal basis. Roosevelt called his approach "the **Square Deal**."

Roosevelt's record limited Republican losses in the congressional elections. The results virtually assured the president's nomination as the Republican candidate in 1904. During the session of Congress that began in December 1902, Roosevelt endorsed the Elkins Act, which would outlaw the rebates railroads gave to favored customers. Roosevelt also called for a law to create a Department of Commerce. One of the agencies of this new department would be a Bureau of Corporations, which would publicize corporate records and indicate which businesses were behaving in the public interest. Roosevelt now had the weapons he sought to distinguish between businesses that he deemed socially good and those that behaved improperly. He attacked the unpopular meat-packing industry, known as the "Beef Trust," and then left business alone until he was safely reelected in 1904.

Race Relations in the Roosevelt Era

While Roosevelt worried about the interaction between business and government, another persistent issue clamored for his attention. On October 16, 1901, Booker T. Washington, the director of the Tuskegee Institute in Alabama and the leading African American in the United States, dined with the president and his family at the White House. The evening meal was social but the purpose of Washington's visit was political. Since he had emerged as a leading advocate for African Americans during the 1890s, Washington had built a political machine among black Republicans in the South. He came to the White House to discuss the new president's nominations for patronage positions in the South. Southerners were not happy to learn that a black man had eaten with the president. A Tennessee newspaper editor called the

Flashpoints   The "Trial" of Henry Simmons

In April 1904, the brutal murder of Lulu Sandberg, a teenage girl, shocked the community of Mason, Texas, a small town outside the state capital of Austin. Suspicion quickly focused on an African American man, Henry Simmons, as the culprit and a manhunt commenced. Simmons eluded capture for two days but then was caught. Housed in the Travis County jail, he was protected by four companies of the state militia prepared to repel any attempt to seize the prisoner from the 1,500 to 2,000 people who gathered to watch the spectacle. Inside the jail, Simmons confessed and told his captors "that he was willing to die by the hand of the law but objected to being chained to a stake and roasted alive."

Over the next several days, the authorities staged a trial in which Simmons appeared in court, his confession was received, and he was sentenced to death, all within a period of three minutes. The next day Simmons was hanged in what a local newspaper called "a record breaker for hangings in this county." In a purported letter to the public, Simmons said, "I do hope that the president and governor will colonize the negro race to themselves; then this won't grow in the negro race. That will be one great thing in this world."

Though this series of events was not a lynching in a technical sense, the haste and casualness of the proceedings attested to the similarity with other examples where black defendants were summarily executed in this period. The editor of the *Austin Statesman* called what

happened "the quiet and orderly execution under the forms and mandate of the law" of a killer. Yet with a mob outside the jail, the use of the military to protect the condemned prisoner, and the likelihood of violent action against Simmons if a court had not found him guilty, the proceedings bore little resemblance to a fair trial even within the terms of the early twentieth century.

So Henry Simmons, guilty though he may have been, faced a terrible choice in 1904. He could be hanged after a brief, mock trial, or he could resist and be dragged from the jail by a mob to be burned at the stake. And this was in a case where a lynching did not occur. When you read about the system of segregation and violence that had established itself in the South, the case of Henry Simmons is a reminder of what it meant, even to a presumably guilty defendant, in human terms.

Questions for Reflection

1. What were the legal rights of an accused African American in the southern states in 1904, based on this case?

2. How did the prospect of lynching form the context within which criminal cases were evaluated and handled?

3. To what extent were there two systems of criminal justice in Texas, one for white defendants and another for their black counterparts?

occasion "the most damnable outrage that has ever been perpetrated by any citizen of the United States."

Roosevelt saw himself as a friend of African Americans, but his conduct indicated how much he shared the prejudices of other whites at this time. Mindful of the need to win the Republican nomination and needing the votes of black delegates to do so, he defended appointing African Americans to post offices and customs houses and resisted efforts to oust them. But Roosevelt did not challenge the system of racial segregation that now permeated the nation.

For the majority of African Americans in the first decade of the twentieth century, bigotry and violence were ever-present facts of life. "Don't monkey with white supremacy," warned a Mississippi newspaper, "it is loaded with determination, gun-powder and dynamite." Eight days after Washington and Roosevelt sat down to dinner, a black man named **"Bill" Morris** was burned at the stake in Balltown, Louisiana. He had allegedly robbed and raped a white woman. Apprehended by a

mob, Morris was "taken back to the scene of his crime." No trial occurred. Instead, "pine knots and pine straw were heaped about him and over this kerosene was poured and the whole set on fire." Between 70 and 80 black citizens of the United States were lynched during each year of Roosevelt's presidency. Lynching had declined from its post–Civil War peak in the 1890s, but it still meant that these horrific events were taking place on the average of every fourth day each year.

Social and economic inequality were the lot of African Americans as well. Conditions had worsened since the passage of segregation laws in the South during the 1880s and 1890s. Nine million southern blacks lived in rural poverty. Black wage workers received much less per day and per hour than their white counterparts in the same trade. Other black men were industrial or agricultural peasants, virtual slaves who received only food and a place to sleep for their labor.

The system of segregation affected every aspect of their existence. "The white man is the boss," said one

SOCIAL & CULTURAL EVENTS

W. E. B. Du Bois and the Struggle for African American Rights

The early twentieth century saw the worst era of racial segregation in the United States as the position of African Americans and other minorities steadily deteriorated North and South.

© Bettmann/CORBIS

A few voices were raised in protest. Of these, the black thinker who had the greatest impact was W. E. B. Du Bois. Pictured here in the conservative clothes and look of middle-class respectability that he favored in this phase of his life, Du Bois waged a vigorous assault on the public ideas of Booker T. Washington and the notion that blacks should accept their subordinate position. Du Bois led the intellectual efforts to repudiate the doctrine that African Americans were inferior to whites in brains and talent. His organizing efforts, especially the Niagara Conference of 1905, laid the basis for what would become the National Association for the Advancement of Colored People. His presence in the text attests to the rich history of African Americans that is too often omitted from popular accounts of the nation's development.

man. "You got to talk to him like he is the boss." Facilities for the races were supposed to be "separate but equal," but this was rarely the case in practice. As a result, the presence of African Americans as a force in southern politics also diminished.

Blacks no longer voted in significant numbers. The white primary, in which only voters with that skin color could participate in the affairs of the Democratic party, meant that African Americans had no real voice in choosing those who would government them. Blacks retained some role in the Republican party because their votes helped to choose the delegates to the national convention. For the most part the bitter comment of one African American politician summed up the situation: "The Negro's status in Southern politics is dark as Hell and smells like cheese."

When he dined with Theodore Roosevelt, Booker T. Washington demonstrated to other African Americans that he could deliver the support of white politicians. Yet to keep the president's friendship and to obtain money from wealthy whites, Washington had to accept the existence of segregation and the racist system it represented. Washington was doing what he had proposed in his speech in Atlanta in 1895 (see Chapter 19). By the time Roosevelt became president, more militant blacks were charging that Washington's methods had failed.

Their leader was **W. E. B. Du Bois,** who had received a doctoral degree from Harvard and taught sociology at Atlanta University, a black institution. After initially supporting Washington's policy, Du Bois decided that blacks had to confront segregation. In *The Souls of Black Folk* (1903), Du Bois criticized Washington's method as having "practically accepted the alleged inferiority of the Negro."

In June 1905, Du Bois led a delegation of 29 blacks to Niagara Falls, New York, where they issued a call for political and social rights. The meeting denied that "the Negro American assents to inferiority, is submissive under oppression and apologetic before insult." The Niagara Conference aroused Booker T. Washington's intense opposition, but it laid the basis for more lasting protests about the worsening situation of African Americans.

Du Bois, Washington, and blacks in general found Roosevelt less sympathetic to their needs in his second term when he was no longer a candidate for the presidency. He made no public statement about a 1906 race riot in Atlanta, Georgia, in which four blacks were killed and many others injured. Later that year, he discharged without a hearing or trial the African American soldiers who were falsely accused of shooting up Brownsville, Texas.

As Roosevelt abandoned them, the plight of African Americans worsened. In August 1908, whites rioted against blacks in Springfield, Illinois; two blacks were lynched. A tide of bigotry swept the nation that neither the president nor the national government did anything to quell. In 1909, prominent white reformers such as Oswald Garrison Villard (grandson of the abolitionist William Lloyd Garrison), Mary White Ovington, and William E. Walling met with W. E. B. Du Bois, Ida Wells-Barnett, and other African Americans to form the **National Association for the Advancement of Colored People (NAACP).** They sought an end to segregation, voting rights for blacks, and equal education for all children. In an era of ethnocentrism and a struggle among the Western powers to subdue colonial peoples, this appeal for racial justice went unheeded.

Roosevelt and Foreign Policy

As part of his efforts to strengthen the presidency and have the United States play a greater role in the world, Theodore Roosevelt wanted to complete the work left over from the Spanish-American War. Because the world was increasingly dangerous, military preparedness was a key goal. "There is a homely adage which runs," the president said, "Speak softly and carry a big stick; you will go far." By 1905, he had added 10 battleships to the navy and improved its gunnery. Although Roosevelt loved to perform on the world stage without having to consult Congress, he always remembered the public's caution about overseas adventures. Except in the Philippines, where the guerilla war sputtered on, during his presidency Roosevelt sent no American forces into armed combat.

He did act vigorously in places where the power of the United States was dominant. In 1902, Germany and Great Britain used their navies to collect debts that Venezuela owed them; Roosevelt sent the U.S. Navy into the region to limit foreign involvement there. Similar problems with the Dominican Republic and its debts two years later led him to pronounce the "**Roosevelt Corollary,**" which he believed was a natural extension of the Monroe Doctrine. In his annual message in 1904, he said that "chronic wrongdoing or impotence" of Latin American nations in paying their debts might lead the United States "to the exercise of an international police power." After 1905, the United States controlled customs revenues and tax services in the Dominican Republic.

Roosevelt also sought better relations with Great Britain. That policy would make it easier to secure a canal across Central America. A possible flashpoint between Washington and London was the boundary between Alaska and Canada. Discoveries of gold in the Yukon region attracted rival miners and speculators and raised the possibility of violence between Canadians and Americans. Roosevelt used an Anglo-American Commission to settle the dispute peacefully in favor of the United States.

The United States had wanted to see a waterway built across Central America for decades, but disease, mud, and the jungle defeated all construction efforts. The most ambitious project collapsed during the 1880s. The New Panama Canal Company, a French firm, left behind some construction work and large financial debts.

During the Spanish-American War, it took the battleship USS *Oregon* two months to go from San Francisco Bay around the tip of South America to join the navy near Cuba. In the Hay-Pauncefote Treaty (1901), Great Britain gave up its rights to participate in a canal project. Congress then decided in 1902 that the best route lay across Panama. Secretary of State John Hay opened talks with Colombia, of which Panama was then a part. In 1903, Hay and a Colombian diplomat concluded the Hay-Herran Convention. They settled on a 6-mile-wide canal zone, running 40 miles from ocean shore to ocean shore (or 51 miles when the shipping distance was taken into full account), under American control, with a 99-year lease. The Colombians would receive a $10 million payment and $250,000 per year in rent. The U.S. Senate ratified the pact.

Colombia was less cooperative. The Colombian Senate believed that the treaty infringed on their country's sovereignty, and the lawmakers wanted more money. Roosevelt was outraged. Within Panama, opponents of Colombian rule, who reflected the mounting spirit of Panamanian nationalism plus a desire to profit from the projected waterway, plotted revolution. Lawyers for the New Panama Canal Company lobbied for American intervention if a rebellion broke out. The uprising occurred in November 1903 amid strong signals that Washington supported the revolution. The presence of American naval vessels discouraged the Colombians from putting down the rebellion. The United States recognized the new Panamanian government, as did other European and Latin American nations.

DOING HISTORY ONLINE

African Americans Boycott Streetcars, 1904

It was not merely coincidence that the railroads and streetcars were the focus of many of the earliest segregation laws and some of the most vocal black protests against Jim Crow ordinances. What are some reasons that can explain this?

History ⓧ Now™　Visit HistoryNOW to access primary sources and exercises related to this topic: http://www.historynow/Ayers

Theodore Roosevelt and the Strong Presidency

One of the key features of politics and government during the twentieth century was the rise of the strong presidency. In the process, presidents became political celebrities. The youthful vigor of Theodore Roosevelt between 1901 and 1909, particularly his keen eye for the limelight, made him the darling of cartoonists in the nation's magazines and newspapers. In this image of the gigantic president striding the isthmus of Panama between the Atlantic and Pacific oceans to build a canal, one gets a sense of how Roosevelt's larger-than-life qualities enhanced the power of his office and fixed public attention on the occupants of the White House. The dropping of the dirt from Roosevelt's shovel on the Colombian capital of Bogotá reflects as well how popular Roosevelt's disdainful treatment of the Colombians was as he made the Canal Zone a reality in 1903–1904.

© The Granger Collection, New York

In November 1903, discussions with the representative of Panama, a Frenchman named Philippe Bunau-Varilla, led to the Hay–Bunau-Varilla Treaty. The new pact created a 10-mile-wide zone across Panama in exchange for the $10 million payment and the $250,000 annual rent. Within the Canal Zone, the United States could act as a sovereign nation, a provision that subsequent Panamanian governments resented. Construction of the canal proceeded slowly until Roosevelt put the U.S. Army in charge. Roosevelt visited Panama himself in 1906, thus becoming the first president to leave the continental United States while in office.

It cost more than $350 million, or the equivalent of several billion dollars in modern funds, to build the Panama Canal. Almost 6,000 workers died of disease and accidents during construction. The official opening took place on August 15, 1914. Theodore Roosevelt regarded the canal as the greatest achievement of his presidency. His infringement on Colombian sovereignty left bitter feelings in Latin America.

The Election of 1904

Roosevelt's domestic and foreign policy triumphs made him the favorite in the 1904 election. The Democrats turned to Alton B. Parker, a very dull, conservative New York state judge. Despite last-minute Democratic charges that big business was behind the Roosevelt campaign, the American people voted for the incumbent. Roosevelt received more than 56 percent of the vote, compared with Parker's 38 percent. The number of Americans who voted, however, was more than 400,000 below the 1900 figure. Turnout also slipped to under 65 percent of the voters in the North, compared with nearly 72 percent four years before. This decline in voter participation from the highs of the late nineteenth century elections would be a hallmark of the century that followed.

On election night, Roosevelt said that the three years he had served represented his first term as president. He would not be a candidate for another term in 1908. By respecting the two-term tradition, he hoped to allay fears that he might remain president for life. Roosevelt thought he then could embark on a campaign of reform without being accused of personal ambition to stay in office.

In his 1904 annual message, read by clerks to the members of Congress at the opening of the legislative session in December, Roosevelt asked Congress to strengthen the power of the **Interstate Commerce Commission** to regulate the railroads. Roosevelt contended that the power of the federal government should be used to make the whole society more just and equitable. He talked of carrying out the Square Deal. With his gift for understanding where public opinion was going, Roosevelt had caught the spirit of change that came to be called the Progressive Movement. In his second term he put the power of the modern presidency behind the new agenda for reform.

Progressive Campaigns to Reform the Nation

Efforts to improve American life acquired national significance in the years just after 1904. Responding to the growth of cities, the problems of industrialism, and fears about the nation's future, some American citizens began calling for political and societal reforms. The movement was called **progressivism.** It sought to expand the power of government and to make politics more just and democratic.

Currents of Reform

Progressivism occurred during a time of prosperity in which Americans saw themselves more as consumers than producers. A sense of well-being allowed middle-class citizens to address the social and economic problems that had emerged during the depression of the 1890s. After the deflation of the late nineteenth century, rising prices aroused popular concern about the high cost of living. Critics of the Republican protective tariff policies charged that customs duties added to inflation. Equally strong were fears of the effects of business consolidation on the smaller companies for which so many people worked. In 1909, 1 percent of firms accounted for 45 percent of manufactured goods.

When Americans focused on the products they bought and used, they listened when investigative reporters said that patent medicines were unsafe. The discovery that meat-packing plants and other food processors tolerated unsafe conditions led to federal regulation in 1906. Pure food and pure drugs were so necessary, reformers argued, that businesses would have to accept more governmental intrusion than ever.

The movement for progressive reform drew upon forces that had been gathering strength for two decades.

As the problems of industrialism and urban growth emerged, a coalition of groups proposed fresh answers. Despite their diversity of goals and approaches, shared assumptions united most people who called themselves progressives.

During the years before World War I in 1914, when Europe was at peace and society seemed to be improving, men and women believed that human nature was basically good and could be made better. The human environment could be reshaped. Government at all levels could promote a better society, and the state had a duty to relieve the ills that were a result of industrial growth.

Two contrasting approaches emerged within progressive reform. One answer for the problems of democracy was more democracy, according to some who styled themselves as progressives. Proposals for a *direct primary* to allow voters to choose the candidates of their political parties became popular. The selection of U.S. senators should be taken away from state legislatures and given to the people. The voters themselves should have the right to vote on public issues in *referenda,* to propose laws in *initiatives,* and to remove or *recall* officials or judges whose decisions offended majority sentiment in a city or state.

Another strand of progressivism focused on producing greater order and efficiency. Government had become corrupt, expensive, and clumsy. Accordingly, efforts were made to improve the structure of cities and states to make them work with more economy and less confusion. The commission form of city government did away with elected aldermen from local wards and replaced them with officials who were chosen in citywide elections and assigned to a specific department such as utilities, transit, or housing. Regulatory agencies like the Federal Trade Commission and the Interstate Commerce Commission, staffed with experts on the industries they supervised, would see that the marketplace operated in an orderly way without partisan influences. A strong distrust of political parties animated this style of reform.

Not all of the progressives advocated changes that would seem appropriate to modern Americans. Some reformers sought programs that emphasized social control of groups and individuals. Prohibition of the use of alcohol, restriction of immigration into the United States, and efforts to shift political power in cities away from the poor and unorganized reflected a desire to compel correct behavior or restrict democracy to native-born white Americans and the "respectable" classes. These coercive aspects of reform became less attractive to later generations.

Despite these failings, progressivism made constructive changes. The regulatory agencies, direct primaries, and other programs did not wipe out all the existing injustices, but they softened the impact of an industrial

DOING HISTORY ONLINE

Tainted Food and Fake Drugs

Which group played a more important role in safeguarding the nation's food and drug supply: progressive reformers or the Congress?

History⧖**Now**™   Visit HistoryNOW to access primary sources and exercises related to this topic: http://now.ilrn.com/ayers_etal3e

social order. The principle that government was responsible for the general welfare of the nation also became well established. Reform did not attack the preeminence of democratic capitalism, but the men and women who joined the crusades for change during the era of Theodore Roosevelt wanted to improve their country, not to revolutionize it.

The Muckrakers

A group of journalists who exposed corruption and weaknesses in American society were important figures in progressive reform. They published their revelations in numerous monthly and weekly magazines. Selling for as little as 10 cents a copy, these magazines, such as *The World's Work*, *The American Magazine*, *Cosmopolitan*, *Everybody's Magazine*, *The American Review of Reviews*, and *Arena*, gained large circulations and advertising revenues. New printing techniques made these periodicals economical and profitable. There were also more than 2,000 daily newspapers that gave reporters expanding opportunities to probe for scandals and scoops.

Samuel S. McClure, publisher of *McClure's Magazine*, helped launch the popular literature of exposure. By 1902, his monthly journal had attracted a wide middle-class audience for its appealing blend of fact and fiction. McClure wanted the magazine to address the major issues of the day. He decided that the rise of big business and trusts provided the "great theme" he sought. He sent one of his star reporters, **Ida Tarbell,** to look into the Standard Oil Company. With Tarbell's articles ready to run in the autumn of 1902, McClure decided to expand on an article that another reporter, Lincoln Steffens, had written about municipal corruption in St. Louis. That essay, "Tweed Days in St. Louis," led to a series on city government in the magazine that was published under the title *The Shame of the Cities* (1904). The January 1903 issue of *McClure's* carried articles by Tarbell and Steffens, along with an essay about the anthracite coal strike by Ray Stannard Baker.

The muckrakers became famous as investigative journalists. Their impact began when *McClure's Magazine* published articles like this issue from November 1902 when Ida Tarbell's article was featured on the cover.

Where McClure had led, other magazines soon followed. One writer called it "government by magazine." Samuel Hopkins Adams exposed fraud in patent medicines; his series contributed to the passage of the Pure Food and Drugs Act in 1906. Ray Stannard Baker wrote about unethical railroad practices; his revelations assisted President Roosevelt in his campaign for regulation. For almost five years, the popular press echoed with disclosures of this nature.

In April 1906, Theodore Roosevelt, unhappy with press attacks on the Republican party and conservative senators, used the label "muckrakers," referring to investigative journalists. He was comparing them to a character in John Bunyan's *Pilgrim's Progress* who spent all his time raking the muck on the floor and therefore could not see heaven above him. The label stuck. **Muckraking** seemed to symbolize a style of reporting that emphasized only the negative. By 1907, popular interest in muckraking waned. While it lasted, however, muckraking gave progressivism much of its momentum. It supported the view of many reformers that once the facts of an evil situation were revealed, the political system would move to correct them.

Women and Progressive Reform

Women were the crucial foot soldiers of progressive reform who made these campaigns successful. Changes in the status of middle-class women gave them more time to devote to progressive causes. The settlement house movement continued to attract young women who were interested in social service. The number of such houses had risen steadily since the 1890s; and by 1905, there were more than 200 of them. Jane Addams of the Hull House in Chicago remained in the forefront of the movement. Other women joined Addams to promote urban-oriented reforms. Florence Kelley guided the National Consumers League. Julia Lathrop supported child labor legislation and in 1912 became the first director of the federal Children's Bureau. In New York, Lillian Wald used the Henry Street Settlement as a base for work to improve conditions for women and children. She also cooperated with the National Association for the Advancement of Colored People to pursue racial justice. Not all settlement house workers were women, but these institutions gave female reformers a supportive environment and a foundation on which to base their role in society.

Women also figured in the conservation movement discussed later in this chapter. In garden clubs and women's improvement clubs, they criticized the spread of billboards, dirty streets, and neglected parks. They called their efforts "municipal housekeeping." Women joined the Audubon Society, the Women's National Rivers and Harbors Congress, and the Sierra Club. They saved species of birds from extinction, fought against dams and destructive logging in the West, and campaigned for more national parks.

The Continuing Fight for Woman Suffrage

The lack of the right to vote frustrated women, and the campaign for woman suffrage became a central concern. Giving women the ballot, said suffrage leaders, would be a "tool with which to build a better nation." Once they could participate in politics, women would promote progressive causes. Carrie Chapman Catt, president of the National American Woman Suffrage Association, said that "the enfranchisement of women will be the crowning glory of democratic government."

To reach that goal, however, the movement had to overcome substantial problems. In Congress, southern Democrats opposed suffrage because it might lead to votes for African Americans. Liquor interests feared that suffrage would help the prohibitionists. Within the suffrage campaign, fund-raising problems and organizational disarray limited the effectiveness of the drive for votes.

By 1910, it was evident that the strategy of pursuing a constitutional amendment at the federal level had stalled. Suffragists turned to the states where they devoted themselves to organizing campaigns that appealed to a majority of male voters. The result was a string of victories in western states such as Washington (1910), California (1911), Oregon (1912), Arizona (1912), Kansas (1912), Montana (1914), and Nevada (1914). While these results were gratifying, advocates of woman suffrage looked to national solutions to produce faster change. They wanted their reform to achieve what had been accomplished elsewhere in the cities and states of the nation.

Reform in the Cities

Progressive reformers made their first important impact in the nation's cities. Two Ohio mayors, Samuel "Golden Rule" Jones of Toledo (1897–1903) and Tom L. Johnson of Cleveland (1901–1909), sought to change the way their cities functioned. A wealthy businessman himself, Johnson lowered streetcar fares and introduced an electric lighting plan to show how rates could be kept low. Jones instituted municipal ownership of the trolley system, provided higher wages for city employees than private industry did, and founded free kindergartens for Toledo's children. Some cities, such as Milwaukee, Syracuse, and Minneapolis, elected Socialist mayors during the Progressive Era. These city executives pushed for the same style of clean, efficient government that their progressive counterparts advocated, and they demonstrated that Socialist politicians could govern responsibly.

More typical of urban reform across the country were efforts to change the structure of city government itself. In September 1900, a devastating hurricane, spawned in the Caribbean, drove into the Gulf of Mexico and fell with all its atmospheric fury on the unsuspecting residents of Galveston, Texas, in their homes, businesses, and gambling dens that the city featured. As they buried their 7,000 dead and surveyed the wreckage of their city, residents were impelled to look at their form of government and implement reforms that had long been brewing in city politics. The changes became known as the commission form of city government, or in its more popular lingo, "The Galveston Idea."

Individual commissioners, elected from the city at large rather than from geographically based wards, conducted the affairs of the police, fire, and utility departments. In that way, the influence of local politics and ward bosses was to be reduced. Refined in Des Moines,

Iowa, in 1908, commission government was in place in 160 cities by 1911. The shift away from ward representation also restricted the power of local interests in a nonpartisan way, according to its advocates. The new approach, however, sometimes reduced the voting impact of minority groups.

Soon, however, the commission form gave way to the "city manager" idea because of the appealing notion that a single, professionally trained executive would be more efficient even than a group of commissioners. Therefore, under this arrangement, the city council named a nonpartisan executive who was trained to administer the city under policies that the council specified. The plan promised efficiency, cost-cutting, and reduced partisan influence. Smaller and medium-sized municipalities began instituting the city manager form around 1908.

Urban reform achieved positive results in many cities. Reduction of political influence and limits on the role of partisanship did produce better government in some instances, if a lack of corruption and efficiency were the only ruling criteria. However, the consequences, even with these transformations, were not always constructive. Middle-class reformers who pursued these changes often did so at the expense of residents of poorer areas of the city who now found it harder to get a hearing from city hall. Stressing the interest of the city as a whole did not always translate into fair treatment for the less advantaged and less powerful. Perhaps on the surface the city ran with more efficiency, but the poor got fewer parks, worse services, and less criminal justice. What "better" government meant always depended on the class, ethnic, or social perspective from which these changes were viewed.

Reform in the States

As urban reformers tried to improve their cities, they often confronted barriers within state government and opposition from state politicians. The constitutions of many states restricted the capacity of a city government to manage its own taxes, regulate its public utilities, or supervise the moral behavior of its citizens. By the beginning of the twentieth century, some cities had obtained "home rule," but frustrated reformers saw state governments as obstacles to change. When progressives looked at their problems on the state level, they detected patterns of corruption and business influence that resembled those they had fought locally. Reformers charged that the political party, tied to business interests, prevented meaningful improvements in state government.

At the state level, progressives favored the initiative and referendum because they limited the power of political parties to shape public policy. Allowing the people

to propose laws or to vote on laws that had been enacted gave less authority to established political figures and institutions. The initiative and referendum first appeared in South Dakota in 1898; other western states adopted them before 1908. By 1915, 21 states had some form of these progressive procedures.

The direct primary spread across most of the nation by 1916; the recall was largely confined to a small number of western states. The primary was popular because it took the power to make nominations out of the hands of party leaders and gave it to the voters. The recall was more controversial. Angry conservatives charged that an election to remove a judge threatened the independence of the judiciary as a whole.

Greater emphasis on the regulatory power of state government accompanied these procedural reforms. Progressives strengthened the authority of existing state railroad commissions and created new commissions to oversee public utilities and insurance companies. These bodies, which would rely on experts in the field, seemed preferable to the whims of partisan lawmaking.

State government attracted popular and effective leaders during the 20 years after 1900. Theodore Roosevelt was a forceful executive for New York during his one term as governor. Also in New York, Charles Evans Hughes became famous for his probe of insurance companies, which gained him the governorship in 1906. Hughes increased the state's role in regulating utilities and railroads. Woodrow Wilson, elected governor of New Jersey in 1910, limited the power of corporations in that state.

The leading symbol of state reform was **Robert M. La Follette,** a Wisconsin Republican. When Republican party leaders opposed him after he was elected as governor in 1900, he launched a crusade against them. During his two terms as governor, from 1901 to 1905, he established the direct primary, regulated Wisconsin's railroads, and levied higher taxes on corporations. He forged a close relationship between the state government and faculty members at the University of Wisconsin who advised him about policy. This reliance on academic experts was called "the Wisconsin Idea."

By 1905, progressivism was moving on to the national stage. The issues that reformers faced in the states and cities now seemed to require action by the federal government. Corporations were interstate in character; only Washington could regulate them effectively. To solve the problems of political parties, the Constitution had to be changed. To create a more moral society, progressives contended, the national government had to grant women the vote, regulate the consumption of alcohol, and limit immigration into the United States.

With growth came problems in defining what it meant to be a progressive and what aims to pursue.

© The Granger Collection, New York

Progressivism drew much of its energy from reformers on the state level. Robert M. La Follette of Wisconsin was one of the most controversial. This cartoon shows what happened to Wisconsin as "Battle Bob" tamed the corporations and created a "model state." La Follette's thick hair made him a favorite of cartoonists.

Where should the balance be struck between the goal of a more democratic society and that of greater efficiency? Efficiency required organization, expertise, and compulsion. Decision making should be left to the experts who knew how to regulate a railroad or a public utility. But that process enabled a well-organized interest group or lobbying campaign to exercise significant influence and sometimes corrupt the system. A major result of progressivism was more opportunities for organized groups to shape public policy.

The changes that sought to make the political process more democratic sometimes had unexpected results. Conservative groups used the initiative and referendum for their own ends. Well-funded pressure groups could employ the ballot to pursue an issue such as lower taxes or to attack an unpopular idea or group. The initiative could also reduce the electorate to deciding such issues as how long the lunch hour of a fire department might last. The direct primary did not mean that good candidates replaced bad candidates. A wealthy but less qualified candidate could circumvent the party and achieve success in the primary.

The direct election of U.S. senators, mandated through the Seventeenth Amendment in 1913, took the power of choice away from the state legislatures and gave it to the

voters in each state. It meant that candidates had to raise larger amounts of money for their campaigns and gave an advantage to wealthy men. Meanwhile, lobbying groups simply found new channels for improper influence. One unexpected consequence of these changes was the declining popular interest in voting that became evident in the 1904 presidential election and in later contests. Political parties, for all their weaknesses, had mobilized voters to come to the ballot box. The progressives never found a replacement for that function of the parties.

During the spring of 1905, however, reform was still fresh. Advocates of change believed that limited and gradual measures could improve society. With Roosevelt in the White House, they had a president who also believed that moderate reform was necessary to avoid radical transformations.

Roosevelt and the Modern Presidency: the Second Term

In the four years after he was elected in his own right, Theodore Roosevelt traveled widely to promote his programs, built up the bureaucratic machinery of the national government, and pushed Congress to consider a wide range of social problems, from child labor to increased taxation of the wealthy. The president attracted bright young men to Washington to join him, and under Roosevelt the nation's capital became the focus of news and controversy.

Roosevelt began his reform campaign with the railroad regulation he had promised in his 1904 annual message. Customers of railroads in the South and West complained that rates were too high. Shippers and politicians maintained that the federal government, not the railroads themselves, should determine whether a rate was fair. To do that, the Interstate Commerce Commission (ICC) should have the power to review railroad rates to ensure that they were reasonable.

Roosevelt agreed. During 1905, he spoke for his program across the South and West. The Department of Justice launched well-publicized probes to find out whether railroads were still giving rebates in violation of the 1903 Elkins Act. Roosevelt dangled the threat of revising the tariff to sway Republican leaders in the House to favor his approach. He shared information about railroad misdeeds with sympathetic reporters. When the rail companies started their own public relations effort, it backfired because the public did not believe the railroad claims.

Still, getting a bill that the White House wanted through Congress was not easy. Matters went smoothly in the House. The Hepburn bill, named after William P. Hepburn of Iowa, initiated to give the ICC greater authority over railroads and their practices, was passed in February 1906 by a vote of 346 to 7. The large House majority was deceptive. Representatives knew that the Senate would make significant changes in their handiwork. Voting against the railroads was a political winner and offered the House members what was in substance a free vote to please their constituents. The Senate was the main obstacle. A long struggle ensued between Roosevelt and the conservative Republican leader, Nelson W. Aldrich of Rhode Island. The issue was whether the courts should have broad power to review the ICC's rulings. If courts had such authority, they could water down the law. The Senate won some victories on the issue, but the Hepburn Act was passed in late June 1906. The ICC now had the power to establish maximum rates and to review the accounts and records of the railroads. Most of all, the Hepburn Act showed what a strong president could do to achieve a major legislative goal when he summoned public opinion to support a popular cause.

The Expansion of Regulation

There was more to Roosevelt's regulatory program besides railroads. Muckrakers had revealed that patent medicines sold over the counter were usually ineffective and sometimes dangerous. Led by Dr. Harvey Wiley of the Department of Agriculture, the government conducted experiments on the purity of food that revealed that toxic chemicals made many food products unsafe. By early 1906, the clamor for reform had led to the introduction of a bill in Congress to restrict the sale of impure or adulterated food and drugs. The measure was passed by the Senate, but stalled in the House of Representatives.

During the winter of 1906, thousands of Americans read *The Jungle,* a novel about the meat-packing industry in Chicago. Written by a young socialist named **Upton Sinclair,** the book depicted shocking conditions in the plants as an argument for government ownership and control of the means of production. The public ignored Sinclair's political message; they were outraged that dirt and filth endangered their meat supply.

President Roosevelt was angered as well. If the government did not take action, he feared that the socialism Sinclair favored might gain followers. The White House supported an amendment to the Agricultural Appropriation Act of 1906 that set up a federal program for meat inspection. The meat-packing industry tried to water down the bill, but the law represented a significant advance in regulatory power.

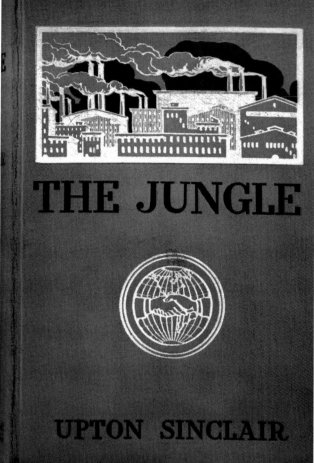

The publication of Upton Sinclair's *The Jungle* in 1906 angered the nation and led Roosevelt to support meat inspection legislation. The cover of the book showed the meat packing plants belching smoke as the slaughter of animals went on inside.

© Bettmann/CORBIS

The controversy over meat inspection cleared the way for House action on the Pure Food and Drugs Act. As a result, that measure was passed on June 30, 1906. A happy president called the three regulatory laws passed during that year's congressional session "a noteworthy advance in the policy of securing Federal supervision and control over corporations."

To achieve that control, Roosevelt placed less emphasis on breaking up large corporations. Instead, he sought to use the Bureau of Corporations to supervise companies that the White House deemed socially responsible. Having decided which businesses and corporate leaders met his standards of morality in the marketplace, he made private agreements with International Harvester and United States Steel. In return for letting the government examine their financial records, these companies would not be subjected to antitrust prosecutions.

Firms that Roosevelt disliked, including Standard Oil, would be disciplined by federal lawsuits. Presidential power, mixed with administrative discretion, would control corporate misdeeds.

Roosevelt and World Politics

Roosevelt matched his activism in domestic policy with equal energy in the conduct of foreign affairs. He carried on secret negotiations without Congress's knowledge, broadened the nation's activities in Asia and Europe, and tried to educate the American people to accept a new role as a world power.

Early in 1904, war broke out between Russia and Japan when the Japanese launched a surprise attack to achieve their territorial objectives on the Asian mainland. The future dominance of such areas as Manchuria was at stake. Roosevelt sympathized with Japan because he regarded the Russians as a threat to the Open Door policy in China. As the Japanese won a series of decisive victories, however, the president concluded that a negotiated settlement would best serve the interests of the United States. He was ready to act as an intermediary when the two parties began negotiations.

Though victorious on the battlefield, Japan was financially exhausted. In April 1905, Tokyo invited Roosevelt to mediate. Roosevelt summoned the combatants to a peace conference to be held at Portsmouth, New Hampshire, in August. The two nations agreed to end the conflict; the Treaty of Portsmouth was signed in September 1905. Meanwhile the Roosevelt administration recognized the supremacy of Japan over its neighbor, Korea. In turn, Japan pledged that it had no aggressive designs on the Philippines. In 1906, Roosevelt received the Nobel Peace Prize for his diplomatic achievement.

In Europe, Roosevelt sought to reduce the growing tension between Germany and the other major powers, France and Great Britain, over Berlin's ambitions to play a larger role on the Continent through its enhanced military and economic power. Roosevelt sympathized with Britain and France, but he wanted to persuade Germany and its leader, Kaiser Wilhelm II, to be reasonable. During 1905, the Germans made a major issue of French dominance of Morocco. The Kaiser wanted a conference to determine Morocco's status. Roosevelt convinced Britain and France to accept a conference rather than go to war over the fate of the North African country. The president expanded the international role of the United States when he sent delegates to the Algeciras Conference. Roosevelt's efforts helped preserve the uneasy European peace for the remainder of the decade while issues loomed again with Japan in the Pacific.

The Gentleman's Agreement

Later in 1906, the lingering problems in Japanese-American relations flared up again. Japan resented the

Roosevelt's diplomatic successes included his successful mediation of the war between Russia and Japan. He summoned delegates from both countries to Portsmouth, New Hampshire. This picture shows the Russians and the Japanese meeting with Roosevelt for what would later be called a "photo opportunity."

Roosevelt's order that the American fleet should sail around the world proved to be a natural inspiration for advertising. This cartoon shows Americans welcoming the vessels back from their cruise.

nativist immigration policies of the United States that discriminated against Japanese newcomers. On the West Coast, the increasing number of Japanese workers and residents intensified nativist and racist sentiments. The San Francisco school board segregated children of Japanese ancestry, and Japan reacted angrily. Washington and Tokyo eventually worked out the "Gentlemen's Agreement" of 1907. The order of the school board was revoked, and Japan agreed to limit the number of immigrants who left that country for the United States. Still, the underlying animosities between the two countries persisted. Roosevelt looked to build up the American navy to act as a deterrent to the Japanese.

To increase funding for the navy from an economy-minded Congress, Roosevelt sent the American navy's "Great White Fleet" on a round-the-world tour from 1907 to 1909. When the vessels stopped in Japan in October 1908, the reception was enthusiastic and friendly. A month later, the two nations negotiated the Root-Takahira Agreement, which called for the Open Door in China, the independence of that country, and preservation of the status quo in the Pacific. For the moment the underlying rivalry between the two countries eased.

When he left office in March 1909, Roosevelt expressed pride that the United States was "at absolute peace" with the rest of the world. His policy in the Caribbean had reaffirmed the supremacy of the United States and made possible the construction of the Panama Canal. In Asia he had done his best with the limited power available to him. Roosevelt's involvement in Europe had been positive, but it had not addressed the interlocking alliance systems that would lead to war in 1914.

Roosevelt's Domestic Policies

As the congressional elections of 1906 approached, the Republican party was still dominant. Some voters were turning away from the Republicans, however, and the Democrats entered the contest with optimism. They had a new asset to help them against the Republicans: organized labor. The American Federation of Labor (AFL) had a membership of nearly 1.7 million by 1904. Its leaders hoped for legislation to limit the power of state and federal courts to block strikes through injunctions. When Republicans in Congress

In the South, women labored in the cotton mills of the region for long hours with low pay. Although the Supreme Court upheld the principle that a state could limit the hours that women worked in *Muller v. Oregon,* the decision had little effect in North Carolina where these women worked in the spinning room of the White Oak Cotton Mill in Greensboro.

One of the leading figures in Roosevelt's administration was his Chief Forester, Gifford Pinchot. He and Roosevelt are shown chatting here during a voyage on the Mississippi River in 1907 with the Inland Waterways Commission.

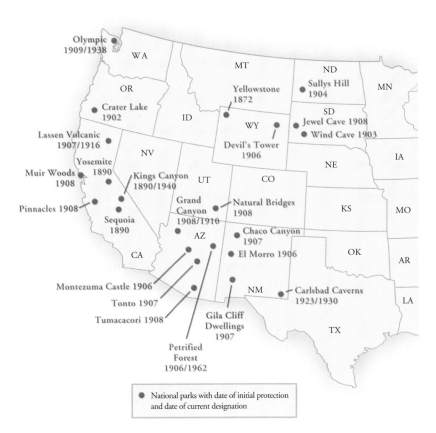

MAP 20.1 **Theodore Roosevelt: National Parks and Monuments**

Thoedore Roosevelt, as a conservationist president, established National Parks and Monuments to preserve the nation's heritage. This map shows what he accomplished in both categories. Several of the National Monuments later became National Parks and thus have the date when Roosevelt established them and the date that their status changed to a park.

rejected such a program, the leader of the union, Samuel Gompers, called for the defeat of Republican candidates who were "hostile or indifferent to the just demands of labor."

In addition to the opposition of the AFL, Roosevelt worried about the growing power of the Socialist party and the most radical wing of the labor movement, the Industrial Workers of the World (IWW). Founded in 1905, the IWW, or as they were nicknamed, "Wobblies," criticized the AFL as timid and called for the overthrow of capitalism. The Socialist party, under the leadership of Eugene V. Debs, also gained strength at the polls. In 1904, Debs won 400,000 votes. Roosevelt believed that his reforms were necessary to stave off more sweeping social change. During the 1906 election campaign, he sent out members of his cabinet to attack the IWW as violent and dangerous.

Despite Roosevelt's efforts, the Republicans lost 26 seats in the elections, but the campaign of the AFL to

unseat Republicans did not do as much damage as Gompers had promised. Nevertheless, the results revealed that the Republicans had significant problems. The protective tariff divided the party. Midwesterners wanted lower duties, whereas Republicans in the East would tolerate no tariff revision. Roosevelt's regulatory policies alienated party conservatives who became angry when Roosevelt regulated railroads, watched over the quality of food products, and attacked large corporations.

Conservatives believed that one branch of the government could withstand the temptations to follow Roosevelt. The judiciary, composed of judges who were usually appointed rather than elected, often ruled in a conservative manner to strike down progressive laws. In the case of *Lochner v. New York* (1905), for example, the Supreme Court overturned a New York law that limited the hours employees could work in a bakery. The Court ruled that the law infringed on the right of the bakers under the Fourteenth Amendment to get the best reward for their labor. Sometimes the justices made an exception and supported progressive laws. For example, in the 1908 case of ***Muller v. Oregon,*** influenced by a brief submitted by Louis D. Brandeis, they upheld an Oregon statute that limited the hours women could work.

In other decisions that same year, however, the Court invalidated the Employers Liabilities Act of 1906 and curbed the power of labor unions in the Danbury Hatters case (*Loewe v. Lawlor*). Roosevelt regarded the courts not as a balance wheel for the political system but an obstacle to needed social change. This division between a popular progressive and the court system would emerge again once Roosevelt had left the White House.

Roosevelt's campaign for the conservation of natural resources also reflected his presidential activism. Using the power of his office, he created refuges for wild birds, preserved the Grand Canyon against intrusion from development, and set aside national parks. During his first term he worked for passage of the Newlands Reclamation Act (1902), which established a system of irrigation reservoirs in the West financed through the sale of public lands. Over the long term, however, the Newlands Act helped large farming corporations more than it did small landowners.

Albert Shaw, A Cartoon History of Roosevelt's Career (1910)

"WILL YOU PLEASE HUSH?"
From the *Herald* (New York)

A cartoon attacks Roosevelt's antibusiness policies as a cause of the Panic of 1907.

Roosevelt worked closely with **Gifford Pinchot** of the United States Forestry Service to formulate conservation policy. Neither man thought that natural resources should be locked up and saved for some indefinite future use. Instead, the national parks, coal lands, oil reserves, water-power sites, and national forests in the West should be managed by trained experts from the federal government to achieve the maximum amount of effective use. For Roosevelt and Pinchot, conservation did not mean that large corporations should be excluded from developing such resources. In fact, corporations might be the best means of exploiting resources in the wisest possible way. Conservationists who were convinced that the wilderness should be preserved rather than developed opposed the Roosevelt-Pinchot policy.

Roosevelt had alerted the American people to a serious national problem. He raised important issues about the future of timber, water, wildlife, and mineral resources. He created national parks, including Mesa Verde and Crater Lake, and established 4 national game preserves, 51 bird reservations, and 150 national forests. He could be proud of the National Monuments Act (1906) that put some important national treasures beyond the reach of development and destruction. He also convened the Governors Conference on Conservation that looked into social issues relating to natural and human resources (1908). The president had alerted the nation to these pressing concerns in an innovative way.

Roosevelt's resource policies required a high degree of control by the federal government and the cooperation

of large corporations. In the West, there was much resentment of programs that Washington had devised without much local support and implemented over the protests of the westerners themselves.

Roosevelt remained popular with the American people during the waning years of his administration. Among conservative Republicans, however, unhappiness with the president mounted. On Capitol Hill, party members in the House and Senate balked at Roosevelt's assertiveness. When problems in the banking industry led to the Panic of 1907, a momentary collapse of the financial system and a brief recession followed. Roosevelt's Republican opponents blamed the economic troubles on his regulatory policies. To stem the danger to banks, Roosevelt agreed to let United States Steel acquire the Tennessee Coal and Iron Company, a decision that came back to affect Roosevelt after his presidency.

The issue of Roosevelt's successor became a central problem for Republicans. Hoping to see his progressive policies carried on, the president decided to support his secretary of war, William Howard Taft, whom he regarded as his natural successor. By early 1907, Roosevelt had become the real campaign manager of Taft's drive to win the Republican nomination.

During early 1908, Roosevelt endorsed more sweeping regulation of corporations, a tax on inheritances of great wealth, and compensation laws for workers. Congressional Republicans reacted coolly to these proposals, and relations between the White House and Capitol Hill worsened throughout 1908.

Meanwhile, Taft advanced toward the Republican nomination at the national convention in June where he won easily on the first ballot. In their platform the Republicans promised to revise the protective tariff at a

---

DOING HISTORY ONLINE

Theodore Roosevelt: Conservationist?

Examine the documents in the modules "Theodore Roosevelt on Conservation, 1901" and "Theodore Roosevelt's African Game Trails, 1910" and consider the following: Was Theodore Roosevelt a conservationist?

History ⧗ Now™   Visit HistoryNOW to access primary sources and exercises related to this topic: http://now.ilrn.com/ayers_eta l3e

In 1908, William Jennings Bryan made his third unsuccessful run for the White House. The "boy orator" of 1896 had less hair and more flesh, but he retained his capacity to enthrall Democratic voters.

special session of Congress shortly after the new president was inaugurated. The public assumed that any change in the tariff would lead to lower rates.

The 1908 Presidential Election

The Democrats nominated William Jennings Bryan for the third time and were optimistic about his chances. After all, Roosevelt was not a candidate and Taft had not been tested at the polls. In the early days of the campaign, Bryan ran well. Then Roosevelt threw his support behind Taft in a series of public statements (incumbent presidents still did not campaign in those days). The Republicans won again: Taft garnered 321 electoral votes to Bryan's 162. The popular vote went solidly for Taft, although Bryan ran much better than Alton B. Parker had in 1904. The election was marked by ticket-splitting: voters cast ballots for Taft for president and Democrats for other offices. The partisan allegiances and loyalties of the late nineteenth century were breaking down.

Roosevelt had picked Taft as his successor because he was convinced that Taft would carry on with his reform policies. Shortly after the election, however, tensions developed between Roosevelt and his political heir over how the pace of reform should be managed. It developed that Taft was more conservative than Roosevelt had perceived. In addition, battles between Roosevelt and Congress flared as inauguration day approached. As Roosevelt prepared to leave office and embark on a hunting trip to Africa, the Republican party remained divided over its future.

WELL BEGUN AND WELL DONE
From the *Evening Mail* (New York)

The transition from Roosevelt to Taft was not as tranquil as this cartoon implies.

Conclusion

Theodore Roosevelt had been an important president. In domestic policy, he had demonstrated how a chief executive could mobilize public opinion behind the policies of the national government. On the world stage, he had involved the nation in European and Asian affairs to preserve international stability.

Not all that Roosevelt did was positive. His handling of race relations was neither consistent nor principled, and he failed to exercise serious leadership on this troubling problem. Sometimes he flirted with excessive power in pursuit of his political enemies. He had also showed little respect for the constraints that the Constitution imposed on his office. Nevertheless, he offered an example of exciting leadership on which other presidents would build.

Theodore Roosevelt had neither caused the progressive movement to emerge nor encouraged all of its campaigns. He had given reform a visible national leader. As a result, progressives would point to numerous successes—railroad regulation, conservation, and pure food and drug legislation. The agenda of change was still incomplete, however. For the new president, the issue was whether to extend reform or to thwart it. Meanwhile, reformers in the states debated issues of cultural and economic policy—prohibition of alcohol, woman suffrage, immigration restriction, and procedural reforms. The Roosevelt years had been exciting, but the climax of progressivism would come during the presidency of William Howard Taft.

The Chapter in Review

During the years when Theodore Roosevelt was president, he:

* launched a program of government regulation
* attacked the trusts
* expanded the role of the United States in the world

At the same time, the progressive movement:

* began with reform in the nation's cities
* expanded to deal with state issues
* became a national force under Roosevelt's leadership
* addressed such social problems as woman suffrage, child labor, and conservation of natural resources
* sought greater democracy and social efficiency

Making Connections Across Chapters

LOOKING BACK

Much of what Theodore Roosevelt tried to do as president built on ideas and attitudes that were advanced during the 1890s and discussed in Chapter 19. In analyzing this chapter, you should be aware of how events such as the Panic of 1893, the election of 1896, and the Spanish-American War influenced the way issues were framed after 1900.

1. How did the experience of the 1890s shape the way Theodore Roosevelt approached the presidency?

2. What obstacles did the Republican party pose to Roosevelt's programs in the White House?

3. Was Roosevelt a progressive or conservative in his approach to government?

4. Why did conservation seem so important during the early twentieth century?

5. In your judgment what made Roosevelt so popular?

LOOKING AHEAD

For all his accomplishments, Roosevelt left some problems for his political successors and the society to solve. In Chapter 21, with William Howard Taft and Woodrow Wilson, you'll see how Roosevelt's mixed legacy shaped how society responded to these very different national leaders.

1. Did Roosevelt strengthen or weaken the Republican party during his presidency?

2. What problems arose because of Roosevelt's love of executive power and presidential discretion?

3. Was accepting big business as an accomplished fact the only way to deal with the problem of large corporations?

4. Was the United States ready to be a world power as Roosevelt envisioned?

Recommended Reading

Cooper, John Milton, Jr. *The Pivotal Decades: The United States, 1900–1920* (1990). Offers a thoughtful and well-informed account of the first two decades of the new century.

Cordery, Stacy. *Theodore Roosevelt: In the Vanguard of the Modern* (2002). A new brief biography of Roosevelt that provides a good look at his historical impact.

Dalton, Kathleen. *Theodore Roosevelt: A Strenuous Life* (2002). A full biography that examines the psychological and family influences on Roosevelt's career.

Diner, Steven J. *A Very Different Age: Americans of the Progressive Era* (1998). An interpretive synthesis that emphasizes social and economic issues.

Gould, Lewis L. *Reform and Regulation: American Politics from Roosevelt to Wilson* (1996). Covers the politics of the era.

Gould, Lewis L. *The Presidency of Theodore Roosevelt* (1991). Reviews the president's achievements in office.

Graham, Sara Hunter. *Woman Suffrage and the New Democracy* (1996). A crisp, thoughtful examination of the evolution of woman suffrage as a progressive movement.

McGerr, Michael. *A Fierce Discontent: The Rise and Fall of the Progressive Movement in America, 1870–1920* (2003). A new interpretation of the reform movement and its results.

Milkis, Sidney M., and Mileur, Jerome M., eds. *Progressivism and the New Democracy* (1999). An interesting collection of essays on the impact of progressive reforms.

Naylor, Natalie, Brinkley, Douglas, and Gable, John, eds. *Theodore Roosevelt: Many-Sided American* (1992). A group of essays on the many aspects of Roosevelt's life.

Tilchin, William. *Theodore Roosevelt and the British Empire* (1997). A good brief introduction to Roosevelt as a world figure.

Identifications

Review your understanding of the following key terms, people, events, and dates for this chapter (these terms also appear in the Glossary at the end of the book):

National Women's Trade Union League
J. P. Morgan
trustbusters
Square Deal
Bill Morris
W. E. B. Du Bois
National Association for the Advancement of Colored People (NAACP)
Roosevelt Corollary
progressivism
Interstate Commerce Commission
Ida Tarbell
Muckraking
Robert M. La Follette
Upton Sinclair
Muller v. Oregon
Gifford Pinchot

Online Sources Guide

Use this listing to find online documents, images, interactive maps, simulations, and other resources related to this chapter:

American History Resource Center

http://history.wadsworth.com/rc/us

Documents

W. E. B. Du Bois's "Thoughts on Booker T. Washington"
Eugene Debs's "How I Became a Socialist"
The Niagara Movement's Declaration of Principles (1905)
Herbert Croly's "The Promise of American Life" (1909)
Belle Linder Israel's "The Way of the Girl" (1909)
Lincoln Steffens's, "Shame of the Cities"

Selected Images

Street in Hazen, Nevada, 1905
Cowboys moving cattle, 1904
Mexican family in Brownsville, Texas, 1908
Faculty Council of Tuskegee Institute, including Booker T. Washington, 1902
Advertisement for a 1901 phonograph
First successful powered Wright brothers flight
Spindletop oilfield, Beaumont, Texas, 1903
"New hub of the universe" cartoon of McKinley as president
Henry Ford
Italian immigrants, 1905
New York City street scene, 1905
Children in tenement district of New York City
Ida Tarbell
Poor people "fishing" for coal, 1902
Construction of Panama Canal, 1907

Simulation

Early Twentieth Century (Choose to be a World War I Doughboy, a Socialist, or an immigrant, and make choices based on the circumstances and opportunities afforded.)

Document Exercises

1901 Race Riot
1901 Food Poisoning
1905 Roosevelt Philippines

HistoryNOW

http://now.ilrn.com/ayers_etal3e

Primary Source Exercises

Theodore Roosevelt in the Presidency
Richmond African Americans Boycott Streetcars, 1904
Tainted Food and Fake Drugs
Theodore Roosevelt on Conservation, 1901, and Theodore Roosevelt's African Game Trails, 1910

Passages 1909 to 1933

Progress seemed everywhere in 1909. Aviators crossed the English Channel for the first time, wireless communication linked ships at sea with their destinations; at home Americans took to the open road in their new Ford automobiles. In such a heady climate of advancing technology and growing economic abundance, writers spoke of an end of war as nations talked out their disputes at the conference table rather than settling them on the battlefield. The path of history seemed well-lit and clear toward a bright future of hope and peace.

Twenty-four years later, in the winter of 1933, the United States lay in the grip of a severe economic depression. Banks had closed, unemployment had soared, and the homeless and destitute roamed the land. Newspapers and magazines ran articles that speculated on whether democracy had failed. To a minority of

Traffic jams like this one attested to the role that automobiles played in transforming American life in the 1920s

The Stock Market Crash of October 1929 ended the ebullient optimism of the 1920s about the future of the American economy and the promise of wealth for millions. The entertainment newspaper *Variety* caught the mood of disillusion that anticipated the Great Depression with its sarcastic headline the day after the averages had tumbled.

Net Production of Electric Energy, by Central Stations, by Class of Ownership: 1907 to 1933

Year	Total Utility and Industrial
1933	102,655
1932	99,359
1931	109,373
1930	114,637
1929	116,747
1928	108,069
1927	101,390
1926	94,222
1925	84,666
1924	75,892
1923	71,399
1922	61,204
1921	53,125
1920	56,559
1917	43,429
1912	24,752
1907	14,121

The rise of Ku Klux Klan reflected the cultural tensions that accompanied the end of the First World War. The hooded order attained nationwide popularity before its own excesses discredited it and its leaders. This illustration shows the union of the cross and the American flag that made the Klan such a potent symbol of intolerance.

Americans, the opposing ideologies of communism and fascism seemed alluring. As the nation faced the prospect of a potential social revolution, its citizens looked back with nostalgia to the early years of the century and wondered what had happened to destroy that optimistic and confident world.

The outbreak of a world war in the summer of 1914 did the most to unhinge the sense of progress that then permeated the United States. If advanced nations could ravage each other on European battlefields, who could any longer believe in the perfectibility of humanity? Americans first tried to stay out of the conflict, but by 1917 they entered the war on the side of France and Great Britain.

In less than 2 years, the experience of World War I accelerated trends toward a more powerful federal government, a more bureaucratic society, and a nation in which large corporations exercised an even greater role. At the same time, the bitter national and ideological conflicts of Europe spilled over into American life. Racial, ethnic, and sectional tensions produced social unrest and group hatreds that raged between 1917 and 1933.

During the war, however, some aspects of prewar reform reached completion. Women gained the vote in 1920 after three generations of struggle. Their ballots did not transform national politics in the years that followed, but their presence in the process ended centuries of a male monopoly of the elective system. The war years also achieved the temperance dream of a national prohibition of alcohol. Despite this reform success, the nation remained divided over its attitude toward liquor, a condition that raised problems for enforcing the new constitutional amendment.

In the aftermath of World War I, Americans rushed forward to embrace the new world of consumer goods and economic affluence. Automobiles, appliances, and installment buying reshaped attitudes about frugality and the future. The spread of mass media and big-time sports brought shared cultural experiences to many Americans. The decade seemed vibrant with the wailing of jazz, the roar of the metropolis, and the excitement of flaming youth.

Not all Americans shared in the prosperity or endorsed the headlong embrace of the modern world. Farmers never experienced the prosperity of the decade, and they encountered economic downturns sooner than did their city counterparts. Rural values remained strong even when transplanted to an urban setting. Some dislocated citizens sought the missing sense of community in an organization such as the Ku Klux Klan, which promised ritual, controversy, and social change in equal measure. Many Americans found that fundamentalist religious denominations spoke to their spiritual needs in ways that the modernist churches did not. Strains between the city and country showed themselves in politics in the 1928 presidential election when the urban, Catholic background of Democrat Al Smith turned many in his party toward the Republican nominee, Herbert Hoover.

Throughout the 1920s, the confidence that the economy would move ever upward sustained people even when they lacked wealth themselves. By the end of the decade, however, the prosperity that consumers had built and corporations relished began to totter. Poor distribution of income, corporate excesses, weaknesses in the banking structure, and mounting problems with international finance led to a stock market crash in 1929 and a Depression that grew steadily worse during the early 1930s.

A generation raised on the prospect of burgeoning prosperity found itself confronted with want, destitution, and despair. Organized charity seemed inadequate to the task of relief, and government at all levels also failed to address the economic problems in effective ways. By the winter of 1932, the nation experienced a tightening spiral of gloom and fear. The sunny days of progressivism and reform were only a grotesque echo of an age that had disappeared. In the American passage, the early 1930s seemed as close as any citizen wished to get to the valley of the shadow.

America and the World: 1909–1933

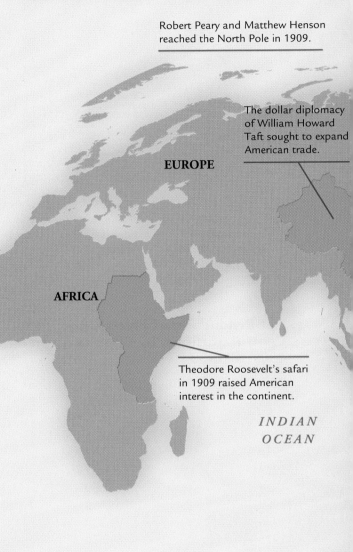

Robert Peary and Matthew Henson reached the North Pole in 1909.

The dollar diplomacy of William Howard Taft sought to expand American trade.

EUROPE

AFRICA

Theodore Roosevelt's safari in 1909 raised American interest in the continent.

INDIAN OCEAN

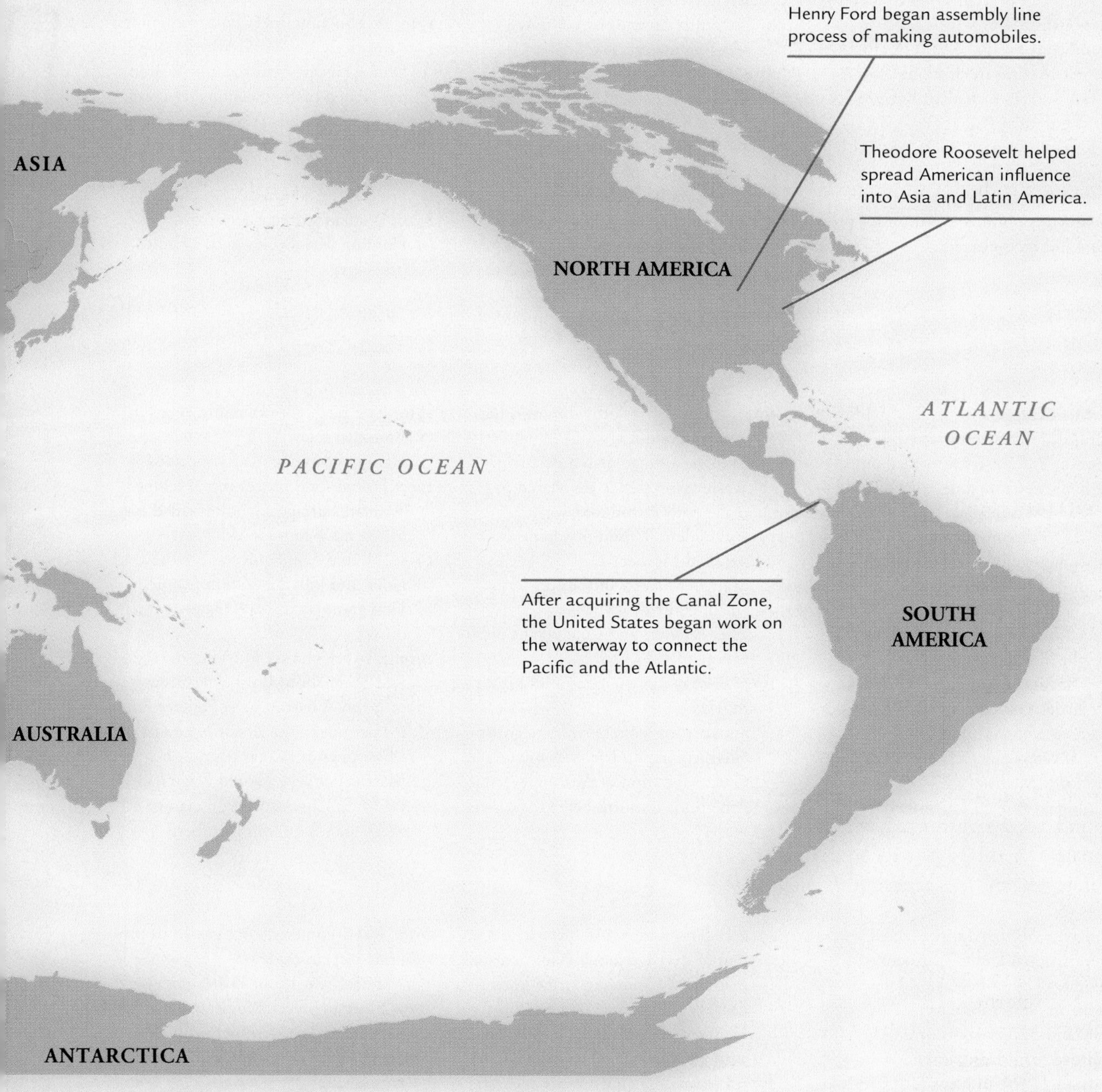

Henry Ford began assembly line process of making automobiles.

Theodore Roosevelt helped spread American influence into Asia and Latin America.

ASIA

NORTH AMERICA

ATLANTIC OCEAN

PACIFIC OCEAN

After acquiring the Canal Zone, the United States began work on the waterway to connect the Pacific and the Atlantic.

SOUTH AMERICA

AUSTRALIA

ANTARCTICA

Chronology

	1909	1913	1917

POLITICS & DIPLOMACY

1909

1909: Ballinger Pinchot controversy over conservation begins
1910: Roosevelt proclaims his New Nationalism
Democrats regain control of House of Representatives in elections
1911: Taft pursues Canadian Reciprocity on tariff but fails
1912: Republican party splits between Roosevelt and Taft
Roosevelt forms Progressive Party
Democrats nominate Wilson for president and he is elected

1913

1913: Wilson address Congress in person, breaking long-time precedent
Underwood Tariff passed
Sixteenth Amendment adopted allowing income tax
1914: Clayton Antitrust law passed
Vera Cruz incident leads to intervention in Mexico
World War begins in Europe
1915: Lusitania sunk
Leo Frank lynched in Georgia
1916: Germany makes Sussex Pledge about submarines
Americans intervene in Mexico to attempt capture of Pancho Villa
Wilson defeats Hughes in presidential election

1917

1917: Zimmerman Telegram released
United States declares war on Germany
1918: Wilson announces Fourteen Points
Armistice ends World War I
Democrats are defeated and Wilson repudiated in congressional elections
1919: Wilson attends Peace Conference, but League of Nations is defeated in Senate
Prohibition adopted
1920: Woman suffrage adopted
Harding defeats Cox and is elected president

SOCIAL & CULTURAL EVENTS

1909

1909: Massachusetts forms first public commission on aging
Motion Picture Trust formed out of early movie companies
1910: Mann White Slave Traffic Act passed to discourage transportation of women across state lines for "immoral purposes"
Jack Johnson defeats James Jeffries ("the Great White Hope") in heavyweight title fight
Boy Scouts of America founded
1911: Harriet Quimby becomes first licensed woman pilot
1912: S.S. Titanic hits iceberg and sinks in North Atlantic
Children's Bureau established
Girl Scouts of America begins

1913

1913: Armory Show provides introduction to modern art
Massive suffrage march occurs in Washington, D.C., on March 3
Brillo pads introduced
1914: President Wilson proclaims first national Mother's Day
Margaret Sanger introduces term "birth control"
New Republic magazine begins publication
1915: Birth of a Nation becomes hit movie
Support for woman suffrage grows
Charlie Chaplin becomes movie star
Great Migration of African Americans to north begins

1917

1916: First birth control clinic opens in Brooklyn, New York
National Woman's Party founded
1917: Frozen food processing developed
Woman suffrage advocates jailed for picketing White House
1918: Influenza epidemic sweeps the globe and kills 21 million people
First granulated soap ("Rinso") introduced
1919: Dial telephones introduced
Red Scare about Bolsheviks occurs
1920: Edith Wharton wins Pulitzer Price for her novel The Age of Innocence
Miss America beauty pageant begins
Marcus Garvey's United Negro Improvement Association claims more than 2 million members

ECONOMICS & TECHNOLOGY

1909

1909: Payne Aldrich Tariff enacted
International Ladies Garment Workers Union begins prolonged strike in New York City
1910: Mann-Elkins Act to strengthen railroad regulation passed
1911: Triangle Fire in New York City produces regulation of sweatshop conditions
1912: Strike occurs in woolen mills, Lawrence, Massachusetts

1913

1913: Federal Reserve Act passed and system of twelve regional banks created
1914: Ludlow, Colorado, strike leads to deaths of 21 people by state militia
Henry Ford introduces $5 day for auto workers
1915: Preparedness movement and war orders revive American economy
1916: Federal Farm Loan Act passed
Adamson Act creates 8 hour day for railroad workers
1917: Production and use of food is regulated through food administration
War Industries Board created

1917

1918: Webb-Pomerene Act passed to promote foreign trade
National War Labor Board established
1919: Economy reverts to peace-time status with little government supervision
Strikes and labor disputes occur nationwide
Inflation becomes problem
1920: Esch-Cummins Act passed to return railroads to private control and broaden powers of Interstate Commerce Commission
Woman's Bureau created in Department of Labor

1921

1921: Harding inaugurated
United States signs separate peace with Germany
1922: Washington Naval Conference
Democrats make gains in congressional elections
1923: Teapot Dome scandal breaks
Harding dies of heart attack
Calvin Coolidge becomes president
1924: Miriam Amanda Ferguson and Nellie Tayloe Ross elected as first woman governors
Democratic convention takes 103 ballots to nominate John W. Davis
Coolidge defeats Davis and third party candidate Robert M. La Follette

1921: Immigration laws set quotas for Eastern Europeans
Shepard-Towner Maternity and Infancy Protection Act passed
1922: Sinclair Lewis, Babbitt, is published
Radio gains in popularity as stations spread
Reader's Digest begins publication
1923: *Time* magazine is launched
Blues singers such as Alberta Hunter and Bessie Smith become popular
1924: Kleenex is introduced
1925: Red Grange becomes national football hero and signs professional contract
Publication of F. Scott Fitzgerald's *The Great Gatsby*
Harlem Renaissance at height in New York City
New Yorker magazine starts

1921: Nation experiences business recession as intense deflation occurs
1922: Fordney-McCumber Tariff Act passed
1923: Supreme Court in *Adkins v. Children's Hospital* invalidates law providing for minimum wage for women in Washington, D.C.
1924: McNary-Haugen Bill to help farmers is introduced

1925

1925: Scopes trial on evolution in Dayton, Tennessee
1926: United States membership in World Court fails
Democrats make gains in congressional elections
1927: President Coolidge says he will not run in 1928
Sacco-Vanzetti executed
1928: Hoover defeats Smith in presidential election
1929: Hoover becomes president
1930: London Naval Conference on disarmament
Democrats erase most of Republican House majority in elections

1926: Publication of Ernest Hemingway's *The Sun Also Rises*
Gertrude Ederle becomes first woman to swim English Channel
1927: Babe Ruth hits sixty home runs
Charles Lindbergh flies across the Atlantic alone
Al Jolson makes talking pictures popular in *The Jazz Singer*
1928: Walt Disney releases his first cartoon, "Plane Crazy"
Eugene O'Neill's play *Strange Interlude* wins Pulitzer Prize
1929: Sales of processed baby food begin
Museum of Modern Art founded in New York City
The first Blue Cross health insurance group starts in Dallas

1925: Florida land boom flourishes
1926: Revenue Act produces substantial tax reduction
Florida land boom collapses
1927: Henry Ford introduces Model A car
1928: Federal Reserve raises interest rates to curb speculation
1929: Stock Market crash occurs in September and October
1930: Great Depression begins
Smoot-Hawley Tariff enacted

1931

1931: Depression deepens
Hoover declares moratorium on war debts
1932: Bonus Marchers dispersed in Washington
Roosevelt defeats Hoover in election
1933: Roosevelt inaugurated president as Depression hits bottom

Amos 'n' Andy radio show becomes nationally popular
1930: Sliced bread introduced commercially
First supermarket opens
1931: Southern Commission on the Study of Lynching formed
Empire State Building, world's tallest, opens in New York City
Al Capone, leading mobster, sentenced to jail for tax evasion
1932: Charles Lindbergh's son kidnapped and found dead
Amelia Earhart makes first solo transatlantic flight by a woman
Radio City Music Hall opens in New York City
1933: Prohibition ends

1931: Hoover administration relief measures address condition of unemployed but do not bring upturn in economy
1932: Reconstruction Finance Corporation created to deal with bank and corporate failures in Depression
Revenue Act cuts government spending
1933: Depression hits bottom as Franklin D. Roosevelt takes office

21 Progressivism at High Tide, 1909–1914

The Triangle Shirtwaist Fire in New York City in 1911, which took dozens of lives, represented the problems that American society faced in the Progressive Era. How far should the nation go to regulate business in the interests of health and safety?

Library of Congress, Prints and Photographs Division

When Theodore Roosevelt left office in March 1909, progressivism entered a phase of partisan upheaval. Under **William Howard Taft** the Republicans split as conservatives and reformers struggled for control. The Democrats moved toward a more active role for the national government and away from state rights. The Socialists mounted a vigorous challenge from the left. For five years it seemed as though the party system might fragment.

Political ferment also revealed the tensions among reformers. Campaigns for woman suffrage, the prohibition of alcohol, restriction of immigration, and social justice created new coalitions that sometimes followed party lines and at other times disrupted them. In the process, progressivism provoked a conservative reaction that limited the possibilities for reform.

The social and economic forces that were creating a consumer society also gathered strength. Henry Ford's low-priced automobile gained greater popularity while other products of industrialism attracted more customers. Women found more opportunities for employment. For minorities, however, these years saw continuing tension and racial strife.

International strains in Europe and revolutions in Latin America and Asia made foreign policy more of a national concern than it had been since the war with Spain in 1898. Still, the outbreak of fighting in Europe during the summer of 1914 came as a shock to the United States. World War I did not resolve the crisis in which progressivism found itself. Instead, it added new complexity to an already turbulent period.

Taft's Conservative Presidency

Soon after William Howard Taft took office on March 4, 1909, Theodore Roosevelt left for his hunting safari in Africa. The hope on Wall Street, ran a joke of the day, was that a lion would do its duty. A celebrity as an ex-president, Roosevelt found that his activities were news, even across the ocean. The issues of regulation, social justice, and corporate power with which he had struggled were also on the agenda for his successor.

Taft came to the White House facing complex problems. Republican conservatives expected him to slow the movement toward reform. Party progressives, on the other hand, wanted the new president to expand Roosevelt's

Timeline

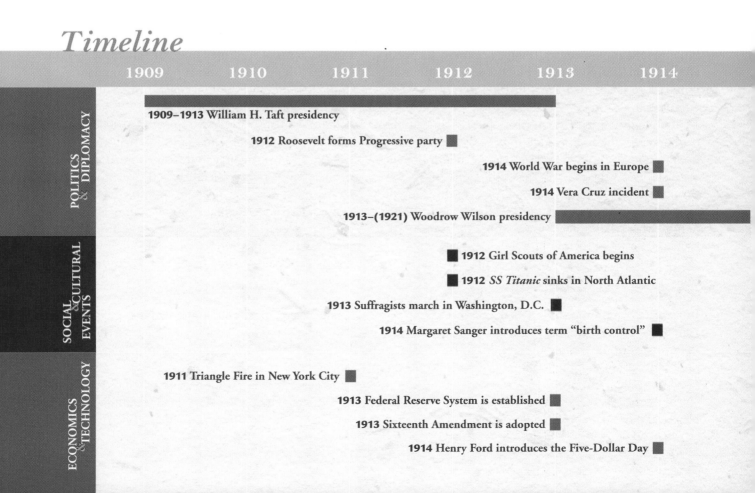

	1909	1910	1911	1912	1913	1914

POLITICS & DIPLOMACY

1909–1913 William H. Taft presidency

1912 Roosevelt forms Progressive party

1914 World War begins in Europe

1914 Vera Cruz incident

1913–(1921) Woodrow Wilson presidency

SOCIAL & CULTURAL EVENTS

1912 Girl Scouts of America begins

1912 *SS Titanic* sinks in North Atlantic

1913 Suffragists march in Washington, D.C.

1914 Margaret Sanger introduces term "birth control"

ECONOMICS & TECHNOLOGY

1911 Triangle Fire in New York City

1913 Federal Reserve System is established

1913 Sixteenth Amendment is adopted

1914 Henry Ford introduces the Five-Dollar Day

President and Mrs. Taft in an automobile in 1909. The new president traveled extensively during his 4 years in office.

legacy. The Republicans had promised in their 1908 platform to revise the tariff but had not specified whether rates would go up or down. The president planned to call a special session of Congress that would revise the tariff downward. Republicans waited to see what Taft would do.

A native of Cincinnati, Ohio, Taft was 51. He had been a lawyer and a federal judge before heading the Philippine Commission in 1900. He proved to be an adept colonial administrator, but Roosevelt summoned him back to the United States in 1904 to serve as secretary of war.

During Roosevelt's presidency, Taft acted as troubleshooter for the administration. When Roosevelt went on vacation, he told reporters that he felt confident because the portly Taft was in Washington "sitting on the lid." Roosevelt looked forward to a continuation of his policies under his successor. But Roosevelt had misjudged where Taft stood on a number of issues, especially the power of the presidency.

Taft was a conservative man who had taken on some of Roosevelt's reform spirit. He did not agree with the expansive view of presidential power that Roosevelt had advanced. Taft believed that the president should act within the strict letter of the law and the constitutional boundaries of his office. Such a philosophy was bound to disappoint Roosevelt and the progressive Republicans.

Taft lacked Roosevelt's sure sense of public relations. He played golf at fashionable country clubs and vacationed

with wealthy men at a time when riches were associated with political corruption. He quarreled with the press and often put off writing speeches until the last minute. The success he had enjoyed as a speaker during the 1908 campaign was soon forgotten as he failed to sway audiences or committed political gaffes. Taft also depended on the advice of his wife, Helen Herron Taft, in political matters, but during the spring of 1909, she had a serious illness that deprived him of her emotional support.

In revising the tariff, Taft confronted the consequences of Roosevelt's postponement of the issue during his two terms. Progressive Republicans favored reductions in customs duties and a move away from protectionism. Conservatives regarded the tariff as the cornerstone of Republicanism and felt that high rates were justified. It would not be easy for Taft to reconcile these contrasting positions.

To maintain Republican unity in Congress, Taft supported the reelection of conservative Joseph G. Cannon as Speaker of the House. If Taft challenged the Speaker, who enjoyed the support of a majority of House Republicans, Cannon could easily stall action on the tariff program.

Once Congress assembled in March 1909, Taft sent it a message asking for a new tariff law that would, as he had said in his inaugural address "permit the reduction of rates in certain schedules and will require the advancement of few, if any." In April, the House passed a tariff bill that lowered rates on sugar, iron, and lumber and placed coal and cattle hides on the free list. The measure was named the Payne bill after its author, Sereno E. Payne, chairman of the Ways and Means Committee.

After it passed the House, the bill then went to the Senate where the Republicans had 61 members, the Democrats 31. The Republican leader, Nelson Aldrich of Rhode Island, was regarded as a virtual dictator of the Senate.

In fact, Aldrich's position was much more vulnerable than it seemed. Among the Senate Republicans, there were 7 to 10 midwesterners, such as Robert La Follette

Table 21.1 Party Strength in Congress, 1894–1918

Senate

CONGRESS	YEAR ELECTED	REPUBLICANS	DEMOCRATS	OTHER
Fifty-fourth	(1894)	43	39	6
Fifty-fifth	(1896)	47	34	7
Fifty-sixth	(1898)	53	26	8
Fifty-seventh	(1900)	55	31	4
Fifty-eighth	(1902)	57	33	—
Fifty-ninth	(1904)	57	33	—
Sixtieth	(1906)	61	31	—
Sixty-first	(1908)	61	31	—
Sixty-second	(1910)	51	41	—
Sixty-third	(1912)	44	51	1
Sixty-fourth	(1914)	40	56	—
Sixty-fifth	(1916)	42	53	—
Sixty-sixth	(1918)	49	47	—

House

CONGRESS	YEAR ELECTED	REPUBLICANS	DEMOCRATS	OTHER
Fifty-fourth	(1894)	244	105	7
Fifty-fifth	(1896)	204	113	40
Fifty-sixth	(1898)	185	163	9
Fifty-seventh	(1900)	197	151	9
Fifty-eighth	(1902)	208	178	—
Fifty-ninth	(1904)	250	136	—
Sixtieth	(1906)	222	164	—
Sixty-first	(1908)	219	172	—
Sixty-second	(1910)	161	228	—
Sixty-third	(1912)	127	291	17
Sixty-fourth	(1914)	196	230	9
Sixty-fifth	(1916)	210	216	6
Sixty-sixth	(1918)	240		

Source: The information in this table is derived from *The Statistical History of the United States* (Stamford, CT: Fairfield Publishers, 1965).

of Wisconsin, Albert J. Beveridge of Indiana, and Jonathan P. Dolliver of Iowa, who wanted to see lower tariffs and limits on Aldrich's power. On the other side of the debate, senators from the East and Far West insisted that goods from their states must be protected against foreign competition. Aldrich did not have a majority of votes for the Payne bill.

Aldrich had the Senate Finance Committee write a bill with 800 amendments, half of which raised rates back toward those of the Dingley Tariff. That move outraged progressive senators among the Republicans. During the summer of 1909, Dolliver, La Follette, and Beveridge attacked Aldrich's bill. They said that the public expected lower tariffs and they denounced attempts to protect it. The Aldrich version finally cleared the Senate in early July by a vote of 45 to 34. Ten Republicans voted against Aldrich.

As a House–Senate conference committee hammered out the final version of the bill, both sides looked to Taft. The president used his leverage to obtain some concessions, such as lower duties on gloves, lumber, and cattle hides, but he failed to obtain reductions on wool, cotton, and industrial products. Convinced that he had gained all he could, Taft signed the Payne-Aldrich Tariff in early August 1909. The battle had split the Republicans because the Payne-Aldrich Tariff had not fulfilled the promises of the 1908 party platform.

Taft endorsed the new tariff during a tour of the Midwest in September. Speaking at Winona, Minnesota, he called the law "the best tariff bill that the Republican party ever passed." Conservatives applauded his remarks while progressives fumed over the outcome of the tariff fight. The president then refused to appoint individuals whom the progressives recommended for federal offices in their states. Republican harmony thus took a beating throughout the autumn of 1909.

The Battle over Conservation

Taft also found himself engaged in a battle that threatened to disrupt his friendship with Theodore Roosevelt. Federal government control of natural resources had been one of Roosevelt's favorite policies. His principal aide had been Chief Forester Gifford Pinchot. Taft disliked Pinchot and doubted whether the policies Roosevelt had pursued were legal. The president and his secretary of the interior, Richard A. Ballinger, pursued conservation policies that conformed to existing laws and allowed less room for presidential initiative. When Ballinger opened lands for development that Pinchot had closed off to settlers and businesses, Pinchot struck back. He accused Ballinger of acting as an agent for J. P. Morgan and a syndicate trying to sell valuable coal lands in Alaska. After looking into the charges, Taft sided with Ballinger.

Pinchot then leaked information about the episode to the press. In early 1910, he went even further, writing a letter of protest to a senator that the lawmaker in turn released to the public. Taft thereupon fired Pinchot for insubordination. In the ensuing controversy, a congressional probe revealed that Taft and Ballinger had not done what Pinchot had charged.

Taft seemed to be attacking a key Roosevelt policy. Roosevelt in Africa received letters from friends saying that Taft was betraying him. The former president responded that perhaps he had made a mistake in picking Taft. Washington buzzed with talk that Roosevelt might run in 1912.

The congressional session in the spring of 1910 compounded Taft's problems. Progressive Republicans joined with Democrats to restrict the power of Speaker Cannon to hold up legislation. Because Taft had supported the Speaker, this move was seen as a rebuke to the White House. Some constructive measures emerged from the session. Railroad legislation broadened the power of the Interstate Commerce Commission over the railroads. The navy was given more money, and progressives enacted a law to encourage private citizens to use federal banks located in post offices. Taft got little credit for these improvements. Progressives charged that he did more to frustrate reform than to push it.

Roosevelt's Return

Meanwhile, Theodore Roosevelt had returned to the United States in June 1910, his ears filled with Taft's

alleged misdeeds. Roosevelt decided that it was up to him to get the Republican party back on the right course. He received a tumultuous welcome when his ship entered New York Harbor. Guns boomed and fireboats shot water into the air. A crowd of 100,000 people cheered him as he rode up the streets. His popularity seemed as strong as ever.

At first, Roosevelt refrained from public quarrels with the president. Meanwhile, the Republicans' internal warfare intensified. Taft used his appointment power once again against the Middle Western progressives in his party; their candidates were not nominated for positions in the federal government. Taft went even further, trying to organize loyal Republicans against reform leaders such as Dolliver, La Follette, and Beveridge. These moves failed, and the president's inability to rally support within his own party emphasized his weakness. Taft knew that his troubles with Roosevelt were growing.

Roosevelt sharpened his quarrel with Taft in a series of speeches during the summer of 1910. He called his program the **New Nationalism.** In a speech at Osawatomie, Kansas, in August, he said that "The New Nationalism regards the executive power as the steward of the public welfare." He wanted the Square Deal of his presidency to be expanded. Roosevelt said the "rules of the game" should be "changed so as to work for a more substantial equality of opportunity and reward for equally good service." He called for an income tax, inheritance taxes on large fortunes, workmen's compensation laws, and legislation to "regulate child labor and work for women." Roosevelt was advocating the modern regulatory state and wanted to achieve it as president.

In the congressional elections of 1910, the Democrats benefited from Republican discord and the desire of the public for a change in parties. The opposition gained control of the House of Representatives when the Republicans lost 58 seats. In the Senate, the Republicans dropped 10 seats. They still had a 10-seat majority, but the progressive Republicans often voted with the Democrats. Republicans suffered their biggest losses in the industrial East where 26 Republican House members were defeated. Stressing inflation and the high cost of living, Democrats won governorships in New York, New Jersey, Ohio, and Indiana. After years of being the opposition party, they looked forward to the presidential election of 1912.

Progressive Victories

Between 1910 and 1913 progressivism intensified, as the movement for social change gathered momentum. The reformers seemed to have public opinion behind them, and conservatives in both parties were on the defensive. The forces of reform pushed forward to achieve their policy goals.

Woman Suffrage

In April 1910, the National American Woman Suffrage Association (NAWSA) presented Congress with a petition that more than 400,000 people had signed. The document sought a constitutional amendment allowing women to vote. Although Congress refused to act, one suffrage worker, surprised by the size of the petition, said that her cause "is actually fashionable now."

Under the leadership of Anna Howard Shaw, NAWSA's membership had grown. In states like Washington (1910), California (1911), and Arizona, Kansas, and Oregon (1912), woman suffrage triumphed. However, referenda to give women the vote failed in Ohio, Wisconsin, and Michigan. Within the movement, younger women, eager for results, urged the older leaders to concentrate on obtaining a constitutional amendment.

Alice Paul led the radical wing of the suffrage movement that aimed to change the Constitution. She had fought for the vote in England and now wanted to apply tactics of picketing and civil disobedience to the United States. Other women joined her, including Lucy Burns and Harriot Stanton Blatch, daughter of Elizabeth Cady Stanton. For a few years, Paul and her allies worked on NAWSA's congressional committee. On March 3, 1913, before **Woodrow Wilson** became president, they staged a well-publicized suffrage parade in Washington. Frustrated at the cautious tactics of NAWSA, Paul and Burns left the organization in early 1914 to form the Congressional Union. The new organization insisted that only a constitutional amendment would win the victory to gain the vote for women.

Significant obstacles to suffrage remained. The liquor industry feared that women who voted would support Prohibition. White southerners worried that if Congress enacted woman suffrage that reform might lead to efforts to safeguard black voting rights across the

© Bettmann/CORBIS

Woman suffrage advocates paraded in Washington on March 3, 1913, before the inauguration of Woodrow Wilson, to jeers and cheers from the crowd.

nation. Men saw their dominance threatened if women took part in politics. To counter these arguments, NAWSA stressed that female voting meant purer and more honest politics. They also played down the argument that women should have equal political rights. Instead, they contended that woman suffrage would offset the votes of immigrants and racial minorities in large cities. Thus, suffragists would be protecting traditional values against "alien" assaults.

Prohibition

Efforts to restrict the use and sale of alcohol also prospered. The Anti-Saloon League had held a dominant

DOING HISTORY ONLINE

Votes for Women, a Practical Necessity, c. 1912

Look at the second and third documents in the module on Woman Suffrage. How have other progressive reform movements influenced the woman suffrage movement?

History ⊗ Now™   Visit HistoryNOW to access primary sources and exercises related to this topic: http://now.ilrn.com/ayers_etal3e

Daddy's in There---

And Our Shoes and Stockings and Clothes and Food Are in There, Too, and They'll Never Come Out.
—*Chicago American.*

WANTED--A FATHER; A LITTLE BOY'S PLEA
JULIA H. JOHNSON

A shy little boy stood peering
Through the door of a bright saloon;
He looked as if food and clothing
Would be thought a most welcome boon.

And one of the men, in passing,
As if tossing a dog a bone,
Asked, "What do you want this evening?"
In a rude and unkindly tone.

"I am wanting"—the boy's lips trembled—
"I am wanting my father, sir,"
And he gazed at the little tables
Where the careless onlookers were.

It was there that he saw his father,
But the man only shook his head.
And the boy, with his thin cheek burning,
Ran away with a look of dread.

Oh, the fathers—the fathers wanted!
How the heart-break, and bitter need,
With the longings, deep and piteous,
For the wandering children plead.

May the children's call arouse them,
May the fathers arise and go
With the young souls waiting for them,
For the little ones need them so!

SERIES G. NO. 23.

The American Issue Publishing Co.
Westerville Ohio

The Anti-Saloon League was one of the primary forces behind the drive for national Prohibition. Its use of cartoons and leaflets made it a precursor of modern issue-oriented campaigning for social causes.

position among prohibitionist organizations since its founding during the 1890s. Older groups, such as the Woman's Christian Temperance Union, played an important role in the crusade, but the Anti-Saloon League used interest group politics that focused on specific, targeted legislative goals. In the case of prohibition, the league sought to limit the power of the liquor industry to sell its product. At first the league sought elections to give voters in a county or state the "local option" to ban the sale of alcohol. By 1906, impatient with the slowness of the local option, the league turned to statewide elections to get the job done more quickly.

Oklahoma adopted **Prohibition** in 1907. By 1914, eight other states had banned the sale of alcohol. Militant prohibitionists (they were called "drys"; anti-prohibitionists were "wets") found the state-by-state

process discouraging. In 1913, prohibitionists in Congress passed the Webb-Kenyon Act, which outlawed the shipment of alcohol into dry states. Skeptical of prohibition as a social cause, President Taft vetoed the bill, but Congress overrode him. The Anti-Saloon League's

Picturing the Past   **SOCIAL & CULTURAL EVENTS**

Chinese Immigration on the West Coast

Immigration into the United States between 1900 and 1914 was not solely a European experience. Despite such obstacles as the Chinese Exclusion Act of 1882, Chinese-Americans found ways to bring young men from their native country to the United States. This picture shows a group of such Chinese newcomers as they went through immigration. They had to demonstrate that they were being brought in as the sons or relatives of American citizens of Chinese origin. Small numbers of Japanese

immigrants also entered the country during these years. Both Asian immigrant groups built prosperous lives and white Americans' resentment of their economic success. Racial tensions persisted and led to friction between the Japanese and American governments during the presidency of Theodore Roosevelt. Sentiment on the West Coast to restrict Asian immigration remained strong into the 1920s and beyond.

next goal was a constitutional amendment to ban the sale of alcohol in the United States.

Restriction of Immigration

The effort to restrict immigration into the United States also accelerated. The flow of newcomers from southern and eastern Europe persisted. There were more than 1 million immigrants in 1910, nearly 2 million in 1913, and over a million more in 1914, before the outbreak of World War I. In addition, revolutionary upheavals in Mexico drove thousands of Hispanic immigrants into the Southwest.

Protestants wanted to keep out Catholic and Jewish newcomers. Labor unions feared that immigrants would become strikebreakers; rural residents saw urban populations growing at their expense. Prejudice against the Chinese and Japanese fed nativist sentiments on the West Coast. Diplomatic friction with Japan followed. By 1913, a bill to impose a literacy test on immigrants passed both houses of Congress. President Taft vetoed the measure and Congress was unable to override.

Progressive reform offered some support to the nativist and racist feelings. Since businesses favored a loose immigration policy, opposition to immigration was portrayed as a way to help workers already in the United States. A feeling that cultures from southern and eastern Europe threatened traditional values led some progressives to endorse restriction.

An incident in Atlanta, Georgia, in 1913, underlined the tensions surrounding immigration restriction. When a young factory worker, Mary Phagan, was murdered, suspicion fell on her superintendent, Leo Frank. A Jew whose parents had come from Russia, Frank was innocent, but he fell victim to anti-Semitism and fear of outsiders. As a "victim worthy to pay for the crime," he was convicted and sentenced to death. After the governor of Georgia commuted his sentence, a mob abducted and lynched him in August 1915. The episode helped to promote the rise of the Ku Klux Klan (a second version of the hooded order appeared in these years), a further testament to the xenophobia and bigotry in the age of reform.

Saving the Children

Americans worried about the future of their children in a changing world where mass entertainment, the lure of the city, and looser attitudes about sex offered new temptations to young people. Three organizations sprang up to address these concerns. In 1910–1911, the Boy Scouts of America, modeled on the British precedent created by Robert Baden-Powell, began training young men in loyalty and service. Boys 12 through 18 enrolled to receive instruction in "the military virtues such as honor, loyalty, obedience, and patriotism."

For young women, there were the Girl Scouts, founded by Juliette Low in 1912, and the Campfire Girls, founded two years earlier. These two groups prepared American girls for future domestic responsibilities. "The homemaker of tomorrow," said one Girl Scout leader, "must be made efficient in her task and happy in it." With the constructive activities that the Girl Scouts, Campfire Girls, and Boy Scouts supplied, delinquency and crime among the young would be reduced, or so their advocates maintained.

The struggle against child labor overshadowed all the other drives to improve the condition of children. In 1910, some 200,000 youngsters below the age of

Library of Congress, Prints and Photographs Division

This cartoon, which appeared on the day of Woodrow Wilson's inauguration, March 4, 1913, illustrates the condescending attitude of the American media toward Mexico and its problems.

DOING HISTORY ONLINE

Night Scene at Indiana Glass Works, 1908
Look at the image in this module and evaluate the following statement: Given the hard work they were doing, the boys in this photograph do not look neglected, ill-treated, or even unhappy to be working.

History ⓍNow™   Visit HistoryNOW to access primary sources and exercises related to this topic: http://now.ilrn.com/ayers_etal3e

12 labored in mills and factories. Attempts to limit child labor in textile firms in the South brought meager results. In 1912, the reformers succeeded in establishing a Children's Bureau within the federal government, but Congress failed to pass any legislation that directly addressed the child labor problem. Proponents of child labor laws hoped to make it an issue for the parties in the 1912 presidential contest.

Despite the many obstacles that progressive reformers faced, there was a sense that the nation was making genuine gains. William Allen White, a Kansas newspaper editor and a friend of many of the leading progressives, recalled that "All over the land in a score of states and more, young men in both parties were taking leadership by attacking things as they were in that day." Women, too, experienced feeling a sense of possibility that infused middle-class reform during the years before World War I.

Labor Protest in a Changing Workplace

Conflict marked the relations between labor and capital. Bitter struggles between workers and employers occurred in the garment unions of New York, among the textile workers of Massachusetts, and in the coal mines of Colorado. American laborers measured their progress in violent and bloody confrontations against harsh conditions in the workplace.

As industrialization spread, factories and businesses grew. In Chicago during these years, Marshall Field's had 5,000 salespeople in its many store departments. The meat-packing firm of Swift and Company employed 23,000 people in its seven plants by 1903. The Amoskeag Company textile mills in Manchester, New Hampshire, dominated the lives of its 17,000 employees with welfare programs and company organizations.

The nature of large corporations changed. Important companies applied scientific research techniques and social science procedures that altered the working experience of Americans. The need to develop new products regularly led such corporations as DuPont and General Electric to emulate the example of German firms. General Electric set up links to universities that allowed scientists and engineers on their faculties to address the needs of the corporations in their research. The ties between business and education helped propel economic growth for the rest of the century.

New Rules for the Workplace

Within the large factories, relationships between employers and workers became more structured and routinized. The informal dominance that the foreman had exercised during the nineteenth century gave way to bureaucratic practices. To control costs and ensure steady production, companies set up procedures for regular reporting on expenditures, centralization of purchasing and maintenance, and measurement of worker productivity.

Out of these innovations came a new way to run the factory and workplace. *Scientific management* was developed by Frederick Winslow Taylor. As a mechanical engineer in the steel industry, Taylor believed that careful study of how each individual task was conducted would lead to efficiency. Once the maximum amount of time to do a specific job was established, workers could be instructed on how to complete the task without any wasted motion. Stopwatches measured the speed of work down to the split second.

As a concept, Taylorism enjoyed great popularity among businesspeople. Although most employers did not adopt all of Taylor's ideas, the principle of managing factories and shops systematically took hold. Since the core of scientific management meant reducing all jobs to a set of simple steps that required little skill, workers resented practices that made them perform repetitive, routine movements all day long. **Henry Ford** claimed that "no man wants to be burdened with the care and responsibility of deciding things." Thus, he believed that workers welcomed freedom from mental strain. In fact, however, employees objected to being "reduced to a scientific formula," said one machinist.

The Limits of Paternalism

While scientific management viewed workers in a detached and bloodless way, some corporations revived paternalism through welfare and incentive programs for their employees. Lunchrooms and toilet areas were cleaned up, recreational facilities established, and plans set up for pensions and profit sharing. National Cash Register of Dayton, Ohio, was a leader in the field, along with H. J. Heinz Company, the Amoskeag Mills, and Remington Typewriter.

Yet the situation for most American workers showed only marginal improvement. Businesses used a variety of techniques to block unions and prevent workers from improving their condition. The National Association of Manufacturers (NAM) pushed for laws to outlaw the union shop (mandating membership in a union to work in the plant) in favor of what was called the "open shop" in which unions were not allowed. Blacklists of pro-union employees were circulated, and new workers often had to sign contracts that barred workers from joining a union. When strikes occurred, employers used nonunion labor (strikers called them "scabs") to end the walkouts. Court injunctions limited the ability of strikers to picket and organize. Violent clashes between workers and police accompanied many strikes.

Unorganized Workers

The working classes in the cities faced the ravages of inflation during these years as prosperity and an increasing supply of gold contributed to a rising price level for consumers. While wages rose, prices accelerated at a faster rate. Many consumer products remained out of reach of the average laborer. These workers faced dangerous conditions in their factories and sweatshops. Many laborers turned to strikes and unions as their best weapons. In New York City and Philadelphia from 1909 to 1911, the International Ladies Garment Workers Union organized workers within the shirtwaist (a woman's blouse or dress with details copied from men's shirts) manufacturing business. Twenty thousand women strikers took their grievances into the streets to demonstrate their solidarity. They managed to wrest some concessions from their employees in the form of union shops and improved working conditions.

Many manufacturers forced their employees to work in deplorable conditions with poor ventilation, dirt and filth, and danger to the lives of those who labored. In March 1911, a fire erupted at the Triangle Shirtwaist Company on New York City's Lower East Side. As the workers fled the flames, they found locked doors to prevent them from taking breaks and no fire escape routes. The conflagration claimed 146 lives. Many women were killed when they jumped to the pavement below. The **Triangle Shirtwaist Fire** spurred reform efforts among politicians in the New York legislature.

Varieties of Labor Protest

Labor unions grew between 1900 and 1914. The American Federation of Labor, led by Samuel Gompers, had several million members. The politics of the AFL had not changed since the end of the nineteenth century. Its craft unions discouraged organization among industrial workers. Women employees received little support from Gompers and his allies.

The Industrial Workers of the World (IWW) appealed to the unskilled masses. Its ultimate goal was still a social revolution that would sweep away industrial capitalism. To the IWW's leadership, including William D. "Big Bill" Haywood and Elizabeth Gurley Flynn, violent strikes seemed the best way to promote industrial warfare.

Strikes in Lawrence and Ludlow

The IWW gained national attention when a strike erupted in the textile mills of Lawrence, Massachusetts, in mid-January 1912. After the textile companies announced substantial wage reductions, the workers walked out. Haywood came to Lawrence to support the strike. The children of strikers were sent to live in other cities, a tactic that publicized the walkout and swayed public opinion to the workers' cause. On March 1, the companies granted them a pay hike. Women strikers were key participants in the victory. As one of their songs put it, they sought "bread and roses," by which they meant a living wage and a life with hope. Despite this local success, the IWW did not build a strong following in the East.

Another controversial strike occurred in Colorado. The United Mine Workers struck against the Colorado Fuel and Iron Company in September 1913. The workers complained about low wages and company camps with brutal guards. John D. Rockefeller, who controlled the coal company, asked the governor to call in the National Guard to maintain order. Confrontations between soldiers and miners ended in the "Ludlow Massacre" of April 20, 1914, in which troops fired on miners in a tent city at Ludlow. Five strikers and one soldier were shot, and two women and eleven children died in the flames that broke out in the tents. Federal inquiries followed, and the workers obtained some concessions. Yet later in 1914 they were forced to end the strike without gaining union recognition.

Changes in the workplace during the progressive period had benefited the employers far more than they had improved the lot of the people who labored in factories and shops. Some social legislation had been enacted to protect the worker from the effects of industrial accidents. The length of the working day had been reduced somewhat. Unlike Great Britain or Germany, however, the United States still did not provide social insurance when a worker became unemployed, pension benefits for old age, or equal bargaining power on the job. The absence of these benefits fed the political passions that surged through the nation during the years that Taft was president. Whether it was in his view of labor relations, his attitude toward progressivism, or his conduct of foreign policy, Taft seemed out of touch with the nation's mood.

Republican Discord and Democratic Opportunity

The Taft administration followed the broad outlines of what Roosevelt and done, but with some new labels for the effort to spread American influence in Asia and

Flashpoints | The Ludlow Massacre, April 20, 1914

Labor unrest and periodic violence between striking workers and their employers often flared during the Progressive Era. One of the most sensational episodes occurred in Ludlow, Colorado, on April 20, 1914, when the Colorado state militia and private strike breakers attacked a tent colony of striking miners at the site of the Colorado Fuel and Iron Company. The coal-mining firm was owned by the Rockefeller family as part of their extensive holdings derived from their original wealth in the oil industry.

The United Mine Workers of America (UMWA) had been seeking for some years to organize the miners who extracted coal in Ludlow. The Colorado Fuel and Iron management sought to preserve what was known as "an open shop" in which the union played no effective role. At Ludlow there were residences, stores, and meeting halls controlled by the company in which any kind of union organizing was forbidden. "The miners get very poor food," said one observer, "and some of the children are dressed in gunny-sacks and their fathers are working every day." Wages were kept as low as possible to maximize the returns to Colorado Fuel and Iron. Recognition of the Mine Workers union would, so management wrote privately, "destroy our profit." In late September 1913, the UMWA called a strike to seek "improved conditions, better wages, and union recognition."

The company evicted the employees from their homes in Ludlow. The strikers then established a tent colony in public areas of the town. By mid-April 1914, the management, with the tacit support of John D. Rockefeller, Jr., decided to deal with the walkout and the miners in their makeshift homes. On Monday, April 20, 1914, a confrontation took place that lasted 14 hours. With the aid of the state militia and private police, the company launched an assault on the miners that left 11 children, 2 women, and 5 militia members dead and the tent colony a charred and smoking ruin. According to the account in the *New York Times*, "the women and children died like trapped rats when the flames swept over them." In the wake of the tragic incident, Rockefeller sought to improve conditions for the workers and restore his public reputation. However, the persons responsible for the incident were not brought to justice and the union did not gain the recognition that it sought for the coal miners at Ludlow. It would be two more decades before American labor law brought a more equitable balance between capital and labor in mines and factories. The Ludlow massacre attested to how painful the process of securing decent working conditions in the United States was before the advent of the New Deal in the 1930s.

Questions for Reflection

1. Why did employers such as the Rockefellers prefer the "open shop" in labor relations?

2. What hazards did the United Mine Workers confront in their organizing efforts at Ludlow?

3. How was Colorado Fuel and Iron able to enlist the state militia on its side?

4. What does this episode say about the level of industrial violence during the Progressive Era?

Latin America. In foreign affairs, William Howard Taft and his secretary of state, Philander C. Knox, adopted the policy of **dollar diplomacy** toward Latin America and Asia. When U.S. corporations traded and invested in underdeveloped areas of the world, peace and stability increased. Instead of military force, the ties of finance and capital would instruct countries in the wise conduct of their affairs. "The borrower is the servant of the lender," said Knox. Military intervention should be a last resort to restore order.

Latin America offered an ideal location for applying the principles of dollar diplomacy. No European countries challenged the supremacy of the United States in that region. In 1909, Taft and Knox induced bankers to loan money to Honduras to prevent British investors from achieving undue influence. In 1911, they compelled the government of Nicaragua to accept another loan from U.S. investors. Unfortunately for Taft, some Nicaraguans regarded the scheme as an intrusion in their affairs, and they rebelled against the government that had made the deal. The Taft administration sent Marines to Nicaragua; the resulting U.S. military presence continued for several decades. A lasting feeling of bitterness marked relations with Latin America.

Taft and Knox also applied dollar diplomacy to China. The government wanted American capitalists to support a railroad in China, first to develop the country and then to offset Japan. Roosevelt had recognized Japanese dominance in the region; Knox challenged it economically. A syndicate of nations would lend China money to purchase existing railroads in Manchuria. The plan collapsed when the British, Russians, and Japanese rejected the idea in early 1910. Instead of promoting stability in China, Knox drove the Japanese and Russians to join forces against American interests. The Knox initiative sparked resentment in Japan, and relations

DOING HISTORY

Theodore Roosevelt and a Third Term: The Clash of Ideas

THE RACE FOR the Republican nomination in 1912 raised the issue of whether Theodore Roosevelt should be seeking a third term in the White House. After declining to run in 1908, Roosevelt contended four years later that there was no chance of his becoming a chief executive for more than one additional term. His critics were not so sure. President William Howard Taft advanced the argument against a third term, to which Roosevelt had to answer. These documents illustrate how the controversy developed.

William Howard Taft

"Mr. Roosevelt would accept a nomination for a third term on what ground? Not because he wishes for himself. He has disclaimed any such desire. He is convinced that the American people think that he is the only one to do the job (as he terms it), and for this he is ready to sacrifice his personal comfort. He does not define exactly what "the job" is which he is to do, but if we may infer from his Columbus platform [in which Roosevelt spoke out for the recall of judicial decisions] it is to bring about a change of the social institutions of this country by legislation and other means which he may be able to secure as president.

We are left to infer, therefore, that "the job," which Mr. Roosevelt is to perform is one that may take a long time, perhaps the rest of his natural life. There is not the slightest reason why, if he secures a third term, and the limitation of the Washington, Jefferson and Jackson tradition is broken down, he should not have as many terms as his natural life will permit. If he is necessary now to the government, why not later?

One who so lightly regards constitutional principles, and especially the independence of the judiciary, one who is so impatient of legal restraints and of due legal procedures, and who has so misunderstood what liberty regulated by laws, could not safely be intrusted with successive presidential terms."

Theodore Roosevelt

"But it was with very real reluctance that I went into politics again. You are quite right in saying that I ought not to have written as I did about another term of the Presidency. But the curious thing is that I thought I had guarded myself explicitly. If I had said that I did not believe in a third consecutive term, it would have been accepted by all my enemies and a large number of my friends as an actual announcement of candidacy after one term had expired and would have had a thoroughly unhealthful effect. What I said was that I was loyal to the substance and not the form of the tradition. Of course, the objection to a third term is merely that a President can perpetuate himself in office. When he is out of office, it is simply preposterous to suppose that the fact that he has been in office is of any consequence, for the whole immense machinery of patronage is in the hands of someone else."

When Theodore Roosevelt became a candidate for the Republican presidential nomination in 1912, the issue arose of whether he was respecting the informal tradition that a chief executive should serve only two elected terms in the White House. In 1904, after his election to a full term, he had announced that he would not be a candidate in 1908 because "the wise custom which limits the President to two terms regards the substance and not the form." Since he would have served almost two full terms, he should then step down. When he decided to seek the presidency once again four years later, he triggered the debate and the kind of criticisms that his rival, William Howard Taft, leveled against him. Roosevelt's idea for popular votes on judicial decisions (known as the recall) also alarmed conservatives. Of course, the deeper issue was whether Americans wanted to see the presidency with the power to perpetuate the incumbent in office. A generation later the Twenty-second Amendment to the Constitution, passed in the wake of Franklin D. Roosevelt's four elections as president, would make permanent the two-term custom.

Sources: Taft is quoted in Henry F. Pringle, *The Life and Times of William Howard Taft* (2 vols., New York: Farra and Rinehart, 1939), II, pp. 780–781; Theodore Roosevelt to John St. Loe Strachey, March 26, 1912, in Elting E. Morison, et al., eds., *The Letters of Theodore Roosevelt* (8 vols., Cambridge: Harvard University Press, 1951–1954), VII, p. 532.

Questions for Reflection

1. What fears did the possibility of a third term for Roosevelt evoke among his political opponents?

2. What merits did Taft's charges have, based on your reading of Roosevelt's political career?

3. How does Roosevelt respond? How convincing is his argument that the key to the issues is whether the person seeking the third term is in or out of office?

4. What does this issue and the way it developed tell you about the characteristics of Roosevelt and Taft as politicians?

Explore additional primary sources related to this chapter on the Wadsworth American History Resource Center or HistoryNOW websites:
http://history.wadsworth.com/rc/us
http://now.ilrn.com/ayers_etal3e

between that country and the United States remained tense. Dollar diplomacy proved to be an ineffective way to achieve world influence.

A foreign policy problem closer to home emerged in 1911. Porfirio Diaz had ruled Mexico for almost 40 years. American investment came because he had maintained apparent calm and stability. In fact, however, his dictatorial rule eventually erupted in a revolution. Francisco I. Madero, the leader of the rebels, came to power hoping to transform the nation. But he aroused the opposition of conservative forces, including the military, large landowners, and the Roman Catholic church. Shortly before Taft's term ended in 1913, Madero was overthrown and murdered. Mexico remained in revolutionary ferment. Nowhere in the world had Taft found the kind of diplomatic success to bolster his credentials as an effective president. Soon he found himself besieged by Theodore Roosevelt.

Following Republican losses in the elections of 1910, Taft and Roosevelt agreed not to attack each other during the first half of 1911. Republican progressives still looked for an alternative to Taft in 1912. To placate the progressives, Taft eased Ballinger out of the cabinet and named two supporters of Roosevelt as secretary of the interior and secretary of war.

Taft's troubles with Congress persisted. He negotiated a trade agreement with Canada based on reciprocal concessions on tariffs. Neither the Democrats nor the progressive Republicans liked Canadian Reciprocity (as the issue was known at the time and is now referred to in textbooks) because it lowered import duties on products that affected their districts. Taft pushed the agreement through Congress in mid-1911, but then Canadian voters rejected the government that had supported it. That left another Taft initiative dead.

Then the president's fragile friendship with Roosevelt collapsed. Unlike Roosevelt, Taft really believed in "busting" the trusts, and his Justice Department attacked large corporations. This distinction between the two Republican presidents over trust policy illustrates the need to resist simple historical stereotypes about who is a reformer and who is not when viewing the past. In October 1911, carrying out Taft's policy views about the wisdom of competition, the Department of Justice filed an antitrust suit against United States Steel. One of the practices that violated the law, according to the indictment, was the company's acquisition of the Tennessee Coal and Iron Company during the Panic of 1907.

Since Roosevelt had approved the merger, the indictment held him up to ridicule. Roosevelt was furious. By the early part of 1912, he decided to challenge Taft for the Republican nomination. "My hat is in the ring, the fight is on, and I am stripped to the buff," he said in February 1912. The prospect of Roosevelt running for a third term as president set off a lively debate about the wisdom of that course and the dangers it might pose for the political system.

The Struggle between Roosevelt and Taft

Throughout the spring of 1912, a bitter battle for the Republican nomination raged. For the first time, a few states held primary elections to choose delegates to the Republican convention. That change gave an obvious advantage to Roosevelt, who enjoyed more popularity than Taft among rank-and-file Republicans. As a result, he attracted a majority of these voters. Taft ran strongly among party regulars (the men who held state and local offices or occupied positions in the Republican organization), who controlled the nominating conventions. As the Republican National Convention opened in Chicago, neither man had a clear majority. Several hundred delegates were contested but the Republican National Committee awarded most of them to Taft. When the national convention upheld what the national committee had done, Roosevelt believed that Taft had stolen from him a prize that was rightfully his.

The Democrats looked forward to victory in 1912 behind Woodrow Wilson. Democratic members of the House of Representatives came to visit the candidate during that summer of optimism, as this stereo view recorded.

Summoning his followers to leave the convention, Roosevelt denounced Taft and promised to fight on. "We stand at Armageddon and we battle for the Lord," he said. For the next two months, Roosevelt prepared to run as a third-party candidate.

The Democratic Opportunity

To exploit the disarray of their opponents, the Democrats needed a credible presidential candidate. One attractive newcomer was the governor of New Jersey, Woodrow Wilson, who had carried that staunchly Republican state by a sizable majority in 1910. Woodrow Wilson was 56 years old in 1912. Born in Virginia, he grew up in the South and shared its racial views. He attended Princeton University in New Jersey, studied law for a time, and then earned a doctorate in history and political science at Johns Hopkins University. He joined the Princeton faculty in 1890, was quickly recognized as an outstanding instructor, and became president of the university in 1902. After initial successes, he ran into resistance from more conservative alumni and faculty when he attacked the exclusive, fraternity-like eating clubs that dominated Princeton's social life. He resigned from the Princeton presidency in 1910. New Jersey Democrats urged Wilson to run for state office and he won the New Jersey governorship in his first try at elective office.

The Wilson Candidacy

Although he was an innovator in his educational ideas, Wilson had been a conservative Democrat for much of his life; political opportunity led him to champion such reform ideas as the direct primary, the initiative, and the referendum. Some Democrats preferred the moderate and less inspiring leadership of the Speaker of the House, James Beauchamp "Champ" Clark of Missouri, who endorsed lower tariffs and not much else. Wilson, Clark, and several other Democratic hopefuls fought for the nomination in primaries and state conventions.

When the national convention met in Baltimore in late June, no candidate was in sight of the two-thirds majority needed for the nomination. As a fresh face, Wilson had strong backing among the delegates as a candidate all Democrats could agree to endorse. He was free from the defeats of the past and offered the prospect of fresh ideas. After 46 ballots, Wilson was nominated and the hopes for victory looked bright in November.

The 1912 Contenders

Once again the Socialist party selected Eugene V. Debs as its candidate. Debs had run in every election since 1900, and his total vote had increased each time. He knew that he would not be elected, but in his mind he was preparing the way for a nation that would in time to turn to socialism. The party also made gains at the state and local levels. Seven hundred thousand voters supported Socialist candidates in 1910, and the following year Socialist mayors or city officials were chosen in 74 cities. Labor unrest seemed to be growing, especially in the Lawrence, Massachusetts, textile strike that broke out in January of 1912. "Comrades," Debs cried, "this is our year."

Socialism gained followers because the party spoke to the grievances of the agricultural and working poor. Disputes within their ranks over whether to pursue reform at the ballot box or through more violent means prevented the party from offering a united front. Moreover, since he had little chance of winning, Debs did not have to frame programs with a view to carrying them out in office.

Those Republicans who supported Roosevelt formed the Progressive party behind his banner and prepared to hold their first national convention. They met in Chicago in August 1912. The atmosphere of the convention mixed the fervor of a revival meeting with the traditional backroom bargaining of other conventions. Delegates sang "Onward Christian Soldiers" as the theme of the meeting and their movement.

To woo the white South, the delegates excluded African Americans from the convention. Roosevelt defended the protective tariff and attacked reciprocity with Canada. The main financial support for the new party came from wealthy newspaper publishers and corporate executives, who liked Roosevelt's belief that

Theodore Roosevelt's new Progressive party assembled in Chicago for its first national convention amid scenes of almost religious fervor about their plans for reform.

big business should be accepted as a fact of economic life and regulated in the way he had discussed during his presidency.

At its core, however, the Progressive party's endorsement of expanded social justice legislation made it more forward-looking than either the Republicans' or the Democrats'. Jane Addams and other social justice reformers joined Roosevelt's crusade for that reason. The party supported woman suffrage, limits on child labor, and a system of "social insurance." The centerpiece of Roosevelt's New Nationalism was the proposal for an "administrative commission" that would "maintain permanent, active supervision over industrial corporations engaged in interstate commerce." Roosevelt continued his policy of distinguishing between "good trusts" that served the public interest and "bad trusts" that harmed society. As a joke of the time went, the difference between a good trust and a bad trust was that when you tickled a bad trust it said "Tee Hee," and when you tickled a good trust it said "TR."

Enacting Roosevelt's program involved a broadening of national authority and an expansion of the bureaucratic machinery of the federal government. The role of the president would also expand to ensure that the public's rights were protected. Roosevelt's position in 1912 looked forward to the regulatory and welfare state that emerged later in the twentieth century. Critics at the time warned that in the wrong hands this increased national power could also threaten individual liberty.

Woodrow Wilson and the New Freedom

At first Woodrow Wilson did not plan to campaign much. As Roosevelt laid out his program, however, the Democratic nominee soon decided that he would have to confront his major rival. Wilson told the voters that only a Democratic president could govern effectively with the Democratic Congress that was certain to be elected. He then offered a program of his own to counter Roosevelt's New Nationalism. He called it the New Freedom.

As Roosevelt began his campaign, Wilson consulted with **Louis D. Brandeis**, a prominent lawyer in Boston and reformist thinker. Brandeis believed that big business was inefficient economically and dangerous to democracy. He told Wilson that the issue Roosevelt was raising could be met with a simple question: shall we have regulated competition or regulated monopoly? Wilson should emphasize the need for greater competition to control monopoly and call for stricter enforcement of the antitrust laws. Rather than relying on trusts and large corporations to act in a socially responsible manner, as Roosevelt contended, the government should create conditions in which competition could flourish.

As for social justice, Wilson said that he supported the goals of eliminating child labor, improving wages for women, and expanding benefits for employees, but he questioned whether the federal government should supply these benefits. In that way he appealed to progressives but also prevented southern Democrats from opposing him as an enemy of state rights (and segregation). Throughout the campaign, Wilson also stressed that the tariff should be reduced to lower prices and to break the link between the government and big business that

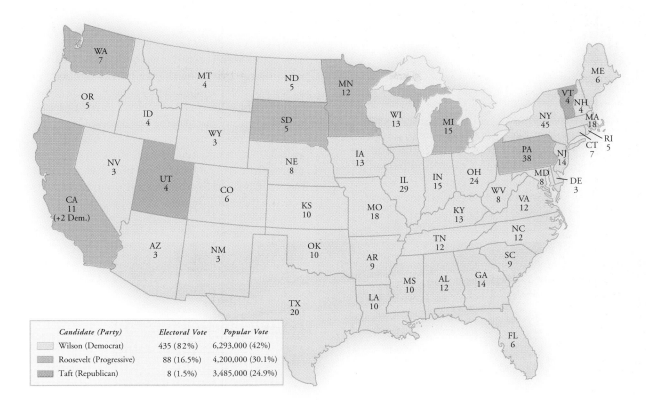

MAP 21.1 The Election of 1912

Because Democrat Woodrow Wilson faced a divided opposition in the presidential election of 1912, the result was a landslide victory in the electoral vote. Theodore Roosevelt's Progressive party ran second, and William Howard Taft's Republicans were a distant third.

Candidate (Party)	Electoral Vote	Popular Vote
Wilson (Democrat)	435 (82%)	6,293,000 (42%)
Roosevelt (Progressive)	88 (16.5%)	4,200,000 (30.1%)
Taft (Republican)	8 (1.5%)	3,485,000 (24.9%)

the Republicans had established. The New Freedom was, like most campaign slogans, broad and vague. It gave Wilson a mandate for action without tying his hands.

The Beginning of Wilson's Presidency

The 1912 election was turbulent down to election day. From the outset of the campaign it was clear that the Democrats had the electoral advantage over the divided Republicans and Progressives. Wilson received 435 electoral votes to 88 for Roosevelt and 8 for Taft. The Democrats swept Congress. They had 51 seats in the Senate to 44 for the Republicans and their margin in the House was 291 to 127. Nevertheless, Wilson was a minority president. He received about 42 percent of the popular vote. Eugene Debs won just over 900,000 popular votes, or 6 percent of the total, and Roosevelt and Taft divided the rest. Voter turnout for the election was lower than it had been in 1908. It was now up to

This cartoon depicts the arrival of Woodrow Wilson in Washington and the departure of former Speaker Joseph G. Cannon as part of the political upheaval of 1912.

Woodrow Wilson Addresses Congress in Person

The spectacle of presidents addressing Congress on national television for State of the Union messages and other important occasions has become a traditional feature of American public life. Yet the modern practice of presidents going to Congress in person to deliver their ideas is less than a century old.

Woodrow Wilson in April 1913 resumed a practice that Thomas Jefferson had abandoned in 1801.

This photograph records the innovation that Wilson was making. While the change provided more visibility to the president and more information to the American people, what Wilson did accelerated the process whereby presidents became celebrities. Over time, as motion pictures and then television covered these events, the presidential address took on more and more of the trappings of show business and became moments staged for the greatest political impact outside the halls of Congress.

Library of Congress, Prints and Photographs Division

Woodrow Wilson to prove that the Democratic party could govern the nation.

In the White House, Woodrow Wilson was a brilliant speaker whose moral rhetoric spoke of lofty ideals. He strengthened the power of the presidency, increased the regulatory role of the national government, and led the nation to play a greater part in international affairs. Even more than Roosevelt, he had the capacity to articulate national values in effective and moving language.

With these strong qualities came important limitations. Before he became president, Wilson had suffered a series of small strokes that increased his natural stubbornness and made him reluctant to accept unwelcome advice. Although he often called for open government and sought what he called "common counsel," he kept his decisions to himself and consulted only a few friends about his policies. His righteousness and

sense of personal virtue caused his political enemies to develop an intense dislike of his methods and tactics. However, when the tide of events ran with Wilson, as they did during his first term, he was a powerful leader.

Tariff Reform

Wilson lost no time in demonstrating his intention to be a strong president. He picked William Jennings Bryan, the leading Democrat in the country, other than Wilson himself, to be Secretary of State in recognition of Bryan's leadership of the party after 1896. In his inaugural address on March 4, 1913, he spoke eloquently of the negative aspects of industrialism. To implement his program, Wilson first asked Congress to take up the issue of the tariff, which symbolized the links between Republicans and big business. He called the lawmakers into a special session in April 1913. To dramatize the problem, he decided to deliver his message to Congress in person. No president had done so since Jefferson had abandoned the practice in 1801, but presidential appearances before Congress became more common once Wilson resumed the technique. The move proved to be an important step in expanding presidential influence both on Capitol Hill and in the nation at large.

In the speech itself, Wilson urged the House and Senate to reduce import duties. The Democratic House responded with a measure to lower tariffs, named after Oscar W. Underwood, the chairman of the Ways and Means Committee. The Underwood bill cut duties on raw wool, sugar, cotton goods, and silks. To compensate for the revenue that would be lost, the new tariff imposed a small tax on annual incomes over $4,000 with rates increasing for those who made more than $20,000 a year. Progressives had secured ratification of the **Sixteenth Amendment** in February 1913, which made the income tax constitutional.

Democrats worried about what would happen when the Underwood bill reached the Senate. They remembered the experience of 1894 and the Wilson-Gorman Tariff, and the Payne-Aldrich Law of 1909, when the Senate changed the House bill in a protectionist way. In fact, the Democrats were relatively unified in 1913, and pressure from large corporations for higher rates had eased. Only smaller businesses, fearing foreign competition, pushed hard for tariff protection. President Wilson added his voice on May 26, when he publicly denounced the "industrious" and "insidious" lobby that was trying to weaken the drive for tariff reform. He said that he would be the people's lobbyist. It was a dramatic gesture, but it was not really necessary. The Democrats stuck together, lowered the duties that the House had set, and passed the bill in August by a vote of 44 to 37. The conference committee's version of the bill passed both houses in October. Wilson signed the Underwood Tariff into law on October 3, 1913. The president and his party had demonstrated that they could provide positive leadership.

The Federal Reserve System

Building on his momentum after success with the tariff, during June 1913 Wilson turned to another important subject. Since the Panic of 1907, there had been a clear need for reform of the nation's banking system. A modern economy could not function efficiently without a central bank with the capacity to control the currency, meet the monetary needs of different sections of the country, and ensure that the money supply was adequate to the demands of the growing economy. The issue became whether private banking interests or the national government should be in charge of the central bank.

Before Wilson was elected, the National Monetary Commission, headed by Nelson Aldrich, had offered the idea of a system of reserve banks that private bankers would supervise. Wilson initially favored this approach until Secretary of State **William Jennings Bryan** and his allies in Congress insisted that the federal government must be supreme over the reserve banks and the currency they would issue. At the urging of Louis Brandeis, Wilson accepted Bryan's ideas.

It took six months to get a banking bill through Congress. Wilson had to appease southern and western Democrats, who wanted two changes in the proposed law. These members sought to expand the credit available to farmers, and they wanted to outlaw the practice known as interlocking directorates, in which banking officials served as directors of banks with which they competed. For reformers, such arrangements symbolized the power of finance capital. The president withstood criticism from the banking community itself, and used patronage and persuasion to win over potential opponents among Democrats in the Senate.

Congress completed its action in mid-December, and Wilson signed the Federal Reserve Act on December 27. This act was one of the most important pieces of economic legislation of the first half of the twentieth century. It established the Federal Reserve Board, whose members the president appointed, and created a structure consisting of 12 reserve banks located in different parts of the country. The Federal Reserve had the power to determine the amount of money in circulation, to expand or contract credit as needed, and to respond to some degree to changes in the business cycle. That proved to be an indispensable weapon for the government in managing the economy in the twentieth century.

Wilson and the Progressive Agenda

Wilson had now gone a good distance toward fulfilling his campaign pledges to reduce the tariff, reform the banking system, and deal with the problem of trusts. Early in 1914, the president asked Congress to consider trusts in a constructive spirit. Some of the legislation passed in that year followed the principles that Wilson had outlined in his campaign. The Clayton Antitrust Act (1914) endeavored to spell out precisely the business practices that restricted competition and then prohibit them.

Enduring Issues Progressive Reform

The political and social movement known as progressivism that appeared at the turn of the twentieth century had effects that have persisted into the modern history of the United States. The underlying assumptions of those who sought change around 1900 was that first the nation needed to have a more democratic political system. Second, and of equal importance, the government had to play a larger and more positive role in regulating the economy for the common good. These goals appealed to many Americans in the two decades after 1900 but the achievement of the ideas fell well short of what the reformers had envisioned. As a result, the legacy of the Progressive Era was a mixed one, and many of the issues that dominated this crucial period are still in dispute 100 years later.

Until the beginning of the twentieth century, the large question dividing American domestic politics was the extent to which the government should promote the growth of the economy. Republicans wanted to use national power to achieve that end; Democrats were more inclined to limit the place of government in the economic realm. As the problems of industrialism became more apparent, some Democrats and Republicans advocated using the power of the state and federal governments to regulate corporations and alleviate social ills. To accomplish those results, however, also required the removal of the restraints on the will of the American people. So cries arose for the direct election of United States senators, the direct primary, the initiative, referendum, and recall, and other devices to

enable the people to influence their government in a positive manner. Newspaper reporters established the tradition of muckraking journalism to expose official wrongdoing.

The emergence of the issue of government regulation and the need for more democratic procedures came together in the progressive movement under presidents Theodore Roosevelt and Woodrow Wilson as well as in states and localities across the country. Between 1900 and 1921, the size of the federal government, its involvement in the economy, and the range of issues that it affected grew in dramatic fashion. While the New Deal of the 1930s would bring an even larger expansion of government, the Progressive Era saw the process commence in earnest.

From the first, however, the campaigns for reform encountered political resistance. Economic and social interests that were affected in an adverse way opposed political change. The Republican party, for example, after tolerating progressivism during the presidency of Theodore Roosevelt, moved away from the idea of government regulation and became the conservative party opposing a stronger national state and supervision of large economic interests. The Democrats did not abandon at once their state rights past, but in the Wilson years they moved leftward toward the commitment to a larger government that would be a hallmark of the New Deal under Franklin D. Roosevelt.

Since these crucial events occurred, the ideological positions of the parties and the fault lines of American

As time passed, however, the president's thinking shifted. He came to favor the creation of a trade commission that would respond to business practices as they evolved, an idea that resembled what Theodore Roosevelt had proposed in 1912. The Federal Trade Commission was established during the fall of 1914. A delighted Wilson said that he had almost completed the program he had promised in his 1912 presidential campaign.

The president's statements left many progressives disappointed. They wanted the Democratic administration to push for social justice legislation. Wilson did not yet believe that Washington should support the demands of progressive interest groups. He also worried about the precedent that might be set by a government that used power to address specific social issues. Such a policy might lead to attacks on racial segregation in the South that Wilson supported. In fact, the Wilson administration expanded racial segregation in the

federal government. The color line, Wilson told a black delegation that came to protest such policies, "may not be intended against anybody, but for the benefit of both."

When supporters of woman suffrage sought Wilson's backing in 1913 and 1914, he turned them down. He also opposed federal aid for rural credits, restrictions on child labor through congressional action, and Prohibition. Court decisions had subjected organized labor to the workings of the antitrust laws, and the unions wanted that policy changed through legislation. Again, Wilson declined to act. Worsening economic conditions during the spring and summer of 1914 reinforced Wilson's belief that his administration should remain conservative on social issues. He tried to reassure businesses that the administration was friendly toward them. These gestures did not appease the Republicans or their business supporters, however. There were indications that the

politics have remained very consistent. Conservatives have challenged the principles of the New Deal and the welfare state. Even a popular program such as Social Security has been a target for conservative criticism and calls for its demolition or transformation into a privatized version. During the 1960s, the Great Society of Lyndon Johnson represented a peak moment for liberalism, with the enactment of Civil Rights legislation, Medicare, and aid to education. The excesses of that period, including the war in Vietnam, undercut support for big government solutions and accelerated the conservative reaction. The coalition that had supported the New Deal and the Great Society fractured over the war, crime in the streets, and the racial issues of African American rights in a manner that eroded confidence in the solutions progressivism had once advanced.

Over the last four decades of the twentieth century, some residual features of progressivism persisted. Efforts at campaign finance reform represented the belief that the political playing field should be as level as possible. In the Watergate crisis, there was a resurgence of the muckraking tradition in journalism that helped to end the presidency of Richard Nixon. Yet by the 1980s, traces of progressivism in American life were harder to find. Many of the institutional achievements of the early twentieth century, such as regulatory agencies, were under attack. The procedural innovations, such as the initiative and referendum, had proven to be tools that the established interests could use to their benefit as much as reformers did.

The United States by 2000 had become a less democratic nation than when the progressives launched their campaigns a century earlier. Special interests had captured many of the political institutions and exploited them for money and power. Society was more stratified and less fair than in 1900. Racial issues, which the progressives had not much addressed, polarized the nation. There was a sense that government and those who controlled it were as out of touch with the real concerns of ordinary Americans as had ever been the case in the country's history.

The progressive movement, for all of its drawbacks, had imparted strong political energies into American history. It raised questions that echoed for decades. That it failed in the end to produce a more just and honest nation attested to the strength of traditional ideas and the resistance to change characteristic of a large and diverse society. Yet, in the event of social upheaval or a prolonged national crisis, many of the underlying ideas of progressive reform could again resonate for Americans unhappy with the existing order.

Questions for Reflection

1. How did progressive reform reflect the American assumption that changing the ways in which government worked would lead to a better and more just society?

2. What have been the most lasting effects of the Progressive Era on American society and culture?

Democrats would have a difficult time at the polls in the 1914 congressional elections.

Social and Cultural Change During the Wilson Years

While politicians worked out Wilson's New Freedom programs during 1913 and 1914, social and cultural transformations accelerated. The Victorian era, with its cultural restraints, seemed to be fading. Americans with a literary or artistic bent turned to the ideas of European thinkers, who emphasized greater freedom for the individual in an uncertain world. Some of these principles came to be defined as modernism. In the days just before World War I, a sense of optimism and possibility filled the air. "Looking back upon it now," wrote Mabel Dodge Luhan, a sponsor of artists and their work, "it

seems as though everywhere, in that year of 1913, barriers went down and people reached each other who had never been in touch before."

Automobiles for a Mass Market

When Wilson went to his inauguration on March 4, 1913, he drove in an automobile. It was the first time a president-elect had traveled to his swearing-in by car. This action symbolized the vast changes that were making the people of the United States more mobile in their daily lives and more eager for the consumer products of an industrial society. In particular, the Henry Ford's innovations in both production and marketing were bringing cars within the reach of the average middle-class American.

If Ford wanted to fulfill his dream of building "a motor car for the great multitude," he had to devise a means of producing cars continually and in even greater

The Model T Ford

The table about Henry Ford's Model T is a revealing look at the impact of the automobile on American society in the years preceding entry into World War I. As Ford introduced assembly line methods into his production facility at Highland Park, Michigan, the output of cars rose steadily. The economies of scale that Ford's engineers achieved allowed them at the same time to bring down the cost to the consumer by more than half ($850 to $360) in an 8-year period. Sales rose as well, enabling Ford to finance his

Table 21.2 Manufacturing and Marketing of Model T Fords, 1908–1916

Calendar Year	Retail Price (Touring Car)	Total Model T Production	Total Model T Sales
1908	$850	n.a.	5,986
1909	950	13,840	12,292
1910	780	20,727	19,293
1911	690	53,488	40,402
1912	600	82,388	78,611
1913	550	189,088	182,809
1914	490	230,788	260,720
1915	440	394,788	355,276
1916	360	585,388	577,036

Source: From *The American System to Mass Production, 1800–1932: The Development of Manufacturing Technology in the United States,* by David Hounshell, p. 224, Table 6.1. © 1985 Johns Hopkins University Press. Reprinted with permission of The Johns Hopkins University Press.

$5-per-day program for workers and to put more capital into his productive capacity.

A careful scrutiny of the table thus discloses some key points about the emergence of a mass economy in the early twentieth century. Ford understood that lower costs for each unit produced greater and more dependable profits for his company. At the same time consumers needed a secure income to afford to buy cars and other products. The information in the table thus offers a snapshot of an economy and society moving away from the industrial system of Andrew Carnegie and John D. Rockefeller, and toward the mass production, consumer-oriented system of the modern United States.

Henry Ford's cheap and efficient car became very popular during the first decade of the new century. This photograph gives a good sense of the simplicity and durability of the Model T.

quantities. He borrowed the concept of the assembly line from the meat-packing industry and his engineers adapted it to carmaking. The Ford plant covered more than 65 acres in Highland Park, Michigan. It featured a large belt, fed by smaller belts, that brought the chassis of the car and its windshields, tanks, batteries, and other parts together in a smoothly functioning operation. At first, it took the work force 93 minutes to turn out a single Model T. By 1920, the cars were coming off the line at the rate of one per minute. In 1914 the Model T cost under $500 and Ford produced more than 260,000 cars.

On January 5, 1914, Ford proclaimed that he would pay his workers $5 for an eight-hour day. At the time the average wage worker in manufacturing made around 20 cents per hour. Ford would be paying three times that to his employees. The announcement was headline news across the country, and Ford became a national hero. He was not a serious economic thinker, but he understood that people needed to earn enough money in wages to be able to afford the cars he was making. He realized that he could make more money by selling large numbers of low-priced vehicles than he could by selling a few expensive cars. Ford thus could be described as an apostle of the emerging mass society.

The Five-Dollar Day program was also designed to head off potential unrest among Ford workers. Absenteeism and high turnover among employees hampered production schedules. In addition, unhappiness among workers might lead to the organization of unions. To offset these trends, the new program aimed at sharing profits in a way that would keep workers at their jobs. In addition, Ford developed a "Sociological Department" to instill in employees the values required for efficient mass production. Workers who were productive and cooperative received higher wages. Those who were not were discharged.

The Growing Use of Electricity

The Five-Dollar Day was an apparent sign of progress. Another was the spreading reliance on electricity. Average annual use of electricity doubled during the 20 years after 1912. New products offered homemakers the chance to ease the dull routines of domestic work. General Electric introduced the Radiant Toaster in 1912, which promised "Crisp, Delicious, Golden-Brown Toast on the Breakfast Table." The Hoover Suction Sweeper would "Sweep With Electricity for 3¢ a Week." Newer stoves and washing machines also came into use. Women could also buy ready-made clothes and spend less time on the sewing that had occupied much of their time a generation earlier.

Other technological developments were still in their early stages. The Wright brothers had made the first powered flight in 1903, and technological progress in flying accelerated during the decade that followed. Harriet Quimby of the United States was the first woman to fly a plane across the English Channel. Meanwhile, the use of wireless telegraphy in marine navigation expanded. The disaster of the *Titanic,* which hit an iceberg in April 1912 and sank with the loss of hundreds of passengers, underlined the need for reliable radio communications for all vessels. Congress enacted a bill mandating the navy to promote radio usage. Within a few years tentative steps would be taken toward broadcasting voices over the airwaves.

Artistic and Social Ferment

Artistic and cultural ferment accompanied the peak years of progressivism. In 1913, the International Exhibit of Modern Art took place at the 69th Regiment Armory in New York City. Quickly dubbed "the Armory Show," it displayed the works of such European painters as Pablo Picasso and Henri Matisse. The modernist paintings, abstract and challenging, offended many critics, who attacked them in vicious terms. Yet the public flocked to see the paintings, and American artists were stimulated and challenged to adopt the new forms of expression. As one critic predicted, "American art will never be the same again."

The period also produced innovative literary figures who would become even more famous during the 1920s. Reporters and novelists clustered in New York's Greenwich Village. Among them were Max Eastman, publisher of *The Masses,* a magazine that assailed conventional values and the established political system; Eugene O'Neill, a playwright; and John Reed, a radical journalist. Outside of New York, Theodore Dreiser was continuing a literary career that included *The Financier* (1912), a novel depicting a ruthless tycoon; Sherwood Anderson was a short story author who criticized middle-class life in the nation's heartland.

Among the influential writers of the day was Walter Lippmann, a Harvard-educated commentator and social critic, who published *A Preface to Politics* (1913) and *Drift and Mastery* (1914). Lippmann sympathized with the New Nationalism of Theodore Roosevelt, and was one of the co-founders, with Herbert Croly, of *The New Republic,* soon a leading journal of political opinion and

George Bellows, "The Cliff Dwellers" 1913. Los Angeles County Museum of Art, Los Angeles.

The American painter George Bellows records the teeming life of New York City in 1913 in his painting that reflects the newer currents of art at the time of the Armory Show and the onset of World War I.

Greater freedom for women in the Progressive Era brought them into places previously reserved for men. These four women are drinking in the bar of a New York hotel.

whose only demand was that its members should "not be orthodox" in their views. In their discussions and in the public meetings they sponsored, they called their doctrine "feminism," which they defined as an attempt on the part of women to be "our whole big human selves."

Heterodoxy represented only a small proportion of American women, but cultural changes occurred even for those who did not call themselves feminists. Women's skirts had become several inches shorter since the beginning of the century when they reached down to the ankle. Bobbed hair became fashionable, and more women smoked openly in public. When movie stars like Mary Pickford became famous, the use of cosmetics spread as women emulated the images of feminine beauty that appeared on screen. The "flapper," with short skirts and bobbed hair, an image associated with the 1920s, actually made her appearance at about this time. The years between 1910 and 1920 saw greater opportunities for women in employment and cultural affairs than would occur in the 1920s.

Americans at Play

The ways in which Americans used their leisure time reflected a trend toward mass entertainment. Boxing was still a major sport. When **Arthur John "Jack" Johnson** became the first African American heavyweight champion in 1908, the white-controlled media clamored for a "white hope" to reclaim the title. Jackson defeated each of his white challengers in the ring, but fled the country when the government accused him of transporting women across state lines for immoral purposes. In 1915, an aging Johnson lost the heavyweight title.

Baseball attained new heights of popularity. The two professional leagues had emerged, and the World Series had become an annual fall ritual to decide the "world's champion." The

cultural commentary. Another important critical voice was H. L. Mencken, editor of *Smart Set,* a New York magazine; he assailed the cultural provincialism of much of American culture.

Women, too, sought to gain greater rights and to share the freedoms that men enjoyed. In 1912, women in Greenwich Village founded a club called Heterodoxy

Jack Johnson, the African American heavy weight champion, shown here on the right in the ring, was so successful that cries arose for a "great white hope" to defeat him.

public avidly absorbed the ample news coverage that baseball received.

Motion Pictures and the Vaudeville Stage

Motion pictures and vaudeville competed for entertainment dollars. In elaborate vaudeville houses, audiences saw such stars as Fanny Brice, Al Jolson, and Sophie Tucker in well-developed routines aimed at the whole family. A circuit of theaters gave performers a reliable market in which to perfect their craft and maintain their popularity. By the time Wilson became president, however, motion pictures challenged the dominance of vaudeville. Movies were evolving from short features into real stories of an hour or more. The places where patrons saw films were upgraded, while the price of admission remained reasonable. An average family of five could see a movie for less than a half a dollar, which put films well within the income of even poorer Americans. Within a decade, the movies emerged as the mass entertainment of the nation. They were lively and up-to-date and conveyed a sense of modern life and spontaneity that made nineteenth-century ideas appear even more dated and obsolete.

New Freedom Diplomacy

Throughout the Progressive Era, domestic political and economic concerns dominated. Newspapers covered international news, and readers could follow the unfolding of European diplomacy if they wished. Isolated from the tensions of world affairs by two vast oceans, Americans allowed their elected leaders to conduct foreign policy as long as the general policies of isolation and noninvolvement with Europe were observed.

Woodrow Wilson and the World

Woodrow Wilson came to the presidency without any experience in foreign policy. In fact, early in 1913 he remarked to a friend that "[it] would be the irony of fate if my administration had to deal chiefly with foreign affairs." Nevertheless, Wilson had definite ideas about how the nation should behave in world affairs. During his first 18 months in the White House, Wilson applied his precepts to diplomatic problems in Asia and Latin America, situations that trained him for the greater trials he would face in World War I.

The president handled most of the business of foreign affairs himself. He appointed William Jennings Bryan as secretary of state, but he never allowed Bryan to have a significant role in shaping policy. Bryan spent some of his time making speeches about public issues and promoting international treaties of conciliation that he thought would end the threat of war. Many countries signed these treaties before the war broke out in 1914; they provided for a "cooling-off" period before countries could begin fighting.

In foreign affairs, Woodrow Wilson believed that the United States should set an example for the world because of the nation's commitment to democracy and capitalism. "Morality and not expediency is the thing that must guide us," he said in 1913.

In Asia, the Wilson administration stepped back from Taft's commitments, instructing American bankers to withdraw from the Chinese railroad consortium that Taft and Knox had sponsored. The United States also recognized the Republic of China, which had come into power following the 1911 revolution that ousted the Manchu dynasty. Wilson and the Democrats put the Philippine Islands on the road toward independence, but their efforts to counter the rise of Japanese influence in Asia proved less successful.

Wilson wanted his policy toward Latin America to be less intrusive and less dominant than Roosevelt's had been. To that end, he worked out a treaty with Colombia that apologized for Roosevelt's actions in helping to foment the Panamanian revolution in 1903–1904. The pact outraged the former president, and the Senate did

One of the more controversial episodes of Wilson's early foreign policy was the intervention in Mexico in 1914. Marines march through the streets of Vera Cruz to carry out the president's pressure on the Mexicans.

not approve the treaty while Wilson was in office. Better relations with Latin America did not, in the president's mind, mean accepting governments that offended his moral values. "I am going to teach the South American Republics to elect good men," he said. That principle led him into the kinds of intervention that he would have preferred to avoid. He kept troops in Nicaragua and extracted further concessions from that country. Other military detachments went to Cuba, Haiti, and the Dominican Republic.

The Mexican Involvement and Its Consequences

In Mexico, Wilson confronted a revolution. The Madero government, which had taken over from Porfirio Díaz in 1911, was ousted just before Wilson was inaugurated in March 1913. The man who toppled Francisco Madero was General **Victoriano Huerta**. Although most European nations quickly recognized Huerta's government, the United States did not. To win recognition from the United States, the Mexicans would have to install a government that relied on law rather than "arbitrary and irregular force."

Wilson instead threw the weight of the United States behind Venustiano Carranza, a rebel against the Huerta government, but his offers of cooperation were not accepted. If Carranza agreed to Wilson's insistence on some U.S. economic and political presence in Mexico, he would have been regarded as pro-American, a fatal weakness to the sensitive Mexican populace.

To block the flow of munitions into Mexico from the United States and Europe, Wilson had sent the navy to patrol the Gulf of Mexico. Sailors from the USS *Dolphin* went ashore at Tampico on April 9 without the necessary permission, and Mexican authorities arrested them. Released quickly and without further incident, they returned to their ship. The admiral on the scene nonetheless demanded that the Mexican authorities apologize and make a 21-gun salute to the American flag. Huerta's government replied that the Mexican flag should be saluted.

The president asked Congress for authority to use force at a time when a German vessel was unloading arms on the Mexican shore. Wilson ordered troops to occupy the port of Vera Cruz. Heavy fighting erupted; more than 100 Mexicans and 19 Americans died. All the warring parties in Mexico denounced the United States. The two countries seemed on the edge of outright war.

Wilson drew back and accepted mediation. The negotiations led to the evacuation of Vera Cruz on November 14. Dependent on outside funds to pay his army, Huerta left office when his money ran out in July 1914. Carranza took power, and Wilson promptly recognized his government. A rebellion against Carranza by one of his generals would lead to further confrontations with the United States during the rest of Wilson's first term.

Revolutionary upheavals in Mexico produced an increase in immigrants from that country into the United States after 1910. A mix of social, political, and economic forces had already produced a rising number of Mexican immigrants after 1900. Although many of those immigrants returned to Mexico after working in the United States for several months, some 35,000 to 75,000 Hispanic immigrants stayed on each year. The dictatorial regime of Porfirio Díaz impelled political dissidents and impoverished peasants to travel north. Once the revolution began in 1911, it drove more Mexicans toward the U.S. border. Throughout these years the spread of irrigation agriculture, railroads, and mining in the Southwest increased the demand for inexpensive labor. The closing off of Japanese immigration after 1907 made Mexican laborers an attractive option for Anglo businesses.

The newcomers from south of the border found work in the sugar beet fields of Colorado; the agricultural valleys of south Texas and southern California, where they picked the lettuce and citrus fruits that grew in irrigated fields; and the towns of Arizona and New Mexico. Other Hispanics labored for daily wages in Los Angeles, El Paso, and San Antonio. They paved streets, built houses, and processed food for the Anglo community. Their wages were low, sometimes less than $1.25 per day.

Major centers of Hispanic life emerged in the southwestern cities. Ethnic communities sponsored mutual aid societies and established Spanish language newspapers to ease the immigrants' adjustment to a new culture. Religious prejudice remained strong, however. When Mexican immigrants settled in San Bernadino, California, one longtime resident warned that he "might use a shotgun on these aliens if necessary." In Texas and California, segregation and poverty limited the opportunities open to Mexican Americans.

The international tension between Mexico and the Wilson administration led to periodic "brown scares" along the border. Anglo residents feared vague conspiracies to reclaim land lost by Mexico during the nineteenth century. Cross-border incursions from Mexico further heightened tensions. By 1915, a violent cultural conflict that claimed hundreds of lives was in progress in south Texas. As a result of these struggles, the Mexican Americans lost much of the land they held in the area. Nevertheless, Hispanics had achieved the basis for a

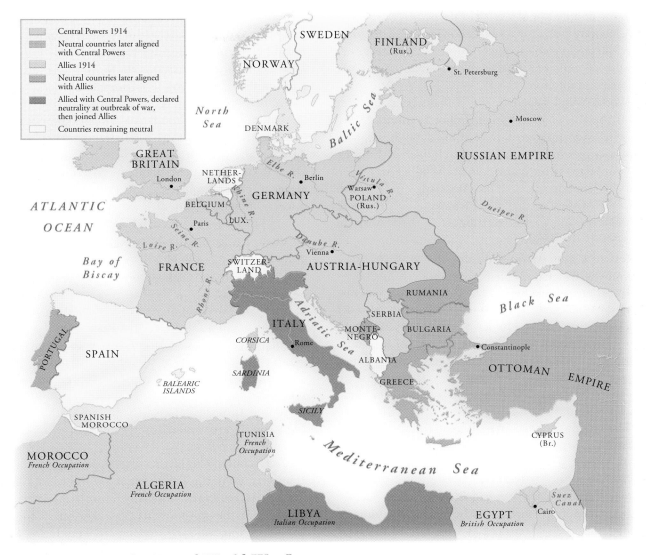

MAP 21.2 Europe on the Eve of World War I

In the summer of 1914, when the First World War erupted, Germany and Austria-Hungary dominated the center of the European land mass. France, Great Britain, and Russia counterbalanced the Central Powers. Once the fighting began, the system of alliances drew most of Europe into the conflict.

greater presence in the United States during the twentieth century.

World War I

By 1914, the major European nations were on edge. If one country found itself at war with another, all the other powers could be drawn into the struggle. On one side stood Germany, in the center of Europe. Its powerful industries and efficient army worried its neighbors, France and Russia. The Germans sought the international respect they believed to be their rightful due. They had built up a large navy that had fueled tensions with Great Britain. Their leader, Kaiser Wilhelm II, had

erratic dreams of world influence that his generals and admirals adapted for their own expansionist purposes. The Germans had treaty links to the sprawling and turbulent nations of Austria-Hungary and the even more ramshackle regime of the Ottoman Turks. Italy had been part of the so-called **Triple Alliance** with Germany and Austria-Hungary, but these ties were frayed by 1914.

Against the Germans stood the French (who coveted territory they had lost in the Franco-Prussian War of 1871), the Russians, and, if the Germans attacked France, the British. The Russian Empire was in decay, with revolutionary sentiments just below the surface. The French feared another defeat at the hands of Germany, and the British worried about German naval strength and Berlin's plans for dominance of western Europe. All the powers had elaborate plans for mobilization in a general crisis. Once these timetables went into effect, the relentless pressure of military events would frustrate efforts at a diplomatic resolution.

World War I began in the Balkans. On June 28, 1914, the Austrian archduke, **Franz Ferdinand,** and his wife were murdered in the town of Sarajevo in Bosnia, a province of the Austro-Hungarian Empire. The Austrians soon learned that the killer had been paid by the Serbians. The Austrians made harsh demands on Serbia that would have left that nation defenseless. The Germans supported their Austrian allies, with the result that the Russians came to the defense of the Serbs. Soon all the European countries were drawn into the conflict.

By early August of 1914, the general war that Europeans had long feared and anticipated was under way. Germany, Austria-Hungary, and Turkey, known as the Central Powers, were fighting against Great Britain, France, and Russia, now called the Allies. Italy remained neutral. Soon the guns of August began a conflagration that lasted four years and consumed the flesh and blood of a generation.

The sudden outbreak of fighting in Europe surprised Americans, even those who were well informed about world events. Although the arms race among the great powers had seemed potentially dangerous, it had been a century since a major war had involved all the major European countries. Surely, the conventional wisdom of the day said, the self-restraint and wisdom of the great nations made a destructive war unlikely. Faith in progress and the betterment of humanity, so much a part of the Progressive Era's creed, made war unthinkable. When the armies marched, Americans were shocked. The world war came at a time of emotional distress for Wilson. His wife, Ellen, died on August 6, 1914. This personal loss devastated the president, who occupied himself in dealing with the war. On the domestic political scene, the Democrats expected serious losses in the congressional elections. The Republicans had won back some of the Progressive voters who had followed Roosevelt in 1912. Until war broke out, it seemed as if politics might be returning to something resembling its normal patterns.

Conclusion

The Republican split between Theodore Roosevelt and William Howard Taft had opened the way for Woodrow Wilson to win the presidency in 1912. That result in turn produced the domestic program that Wilson called the New Freedom. Progressivism thus went through several different phases during the brief period from the New Nationalism of Roosevelt to the governmental activism that Wilson embraced after 1914.

In the process, the contradictions in the reform movement emerged. Should government power be used, as Wilson suggested, to restore competitive balance in the economy without the need for constant regulation? Or, as Roosevelt argued, should the government become bigger to provide consistent supervision of the marketplace? Differences also surfaced over whether society should pursue social justice by doing more for the less fortunate. As these battles were waged, some of the energy and purpose of the reformers ebbed as conservatism made a comeback over such issues as labor's rights and higher taxes.

In the cultural realm, currents of modern thought appeared to question older Victorian values. Women became freer in their relationships with men, artists took a skeptical look at the ills of society, and race relations changed as African Americans moved out of the South. In the years before the World War, optimism about the future of humanity pervaded the United States. Some even talked of an end to war and strife among nations.

The economy took the first steps toward a consumer culture in the 1920s. Henry Ford's Model T car was priced to appeal to many more Americans. In addition, if the spirit of his $5-a-day salary for his employees was followed, customers would also have the money to buy one. Motion pictures became the fastest growing form of popular entertainment, and visionaries spoke of making the new medium of radio available to the masses.

In foreign affairs, the United States sought greater world influence without overseas involvement. The nation remained dominant in Latin America, though the revolution in Mexico underscored how complex the role of foreign policy might become. For all of the problems of Mexico, Haiti, and Nicaragua in this period, the country saw little to worry about from the world at large. Protected by oceans from the tensions of the European countries and the ferment in Asia, the United States could, so the thinking went, follow its own destiny without the mistakes of the old world on the other side of the Atlantic. That comfortable assumption disappeared once the guns of August fired in 1914.

That war produced a lasting change in the course of American history. The nation's isolation from world events ended. Americans had to confront the challenges of a world role. During the seven years that followed, Woodrow Wilson would pursue neutrality, enter the war in 1917, and see his dreams of world peace collapse in 1921. Social and political reform continued for a time and then gave way to conservatism. With all these developments, the impact of progressivism on the direction of American politics remained significant. The issues that had been identified in domestic affairs between 1901 and 1914, particularly the question of the government's role in the economy, endured.

The Chapter in Review

In the years between 1909 and 1914:

- The presidency of William Howard Taft faltered.
- The Republican party split between Taft and Roosevelt.
- The Democrats made a comeback under Woodrow Wilson.

- Wilson's New Freedom was enacted in 1913–1914.
- Consumer culture emerged.
- Movies arose as popular entertainment.
- Progress toward the attainment of woman suffrage was made.
- Cultural ferment led to new trends in art and writing.

Making Connections Across Chapters

LOOKING BACK

The Taft–Roosevelt split that devastated the Republicans had its origins amid the issues discussed in the previous chapter. The basis for the division had been created during the last years of Roosevelt's presidency.

1. Was Theodore Roosevelt as good a politician as he thought he was?

2. How did Roosevelt and Taft differ in their view of what a president should do?

3. How did the New Nationalism represent a culmination of Roosevelt's political philosophy as president?

LOOKING AHEAD

The next chapter considers what happened when progressives encountered the effects of the war raging in Europe beginning in 1914. The outbreak of the conflict called into question the progressive conviction that human beings were basically good. When the United States entered the war in April 1917, some reforms were pushed forward and some progressive issues suffered. The international problems that came out of World War I set the pattern for future disputes in the Middle East and Asia.

1. How did Woodrow Wilson view the United States' role in the world and especially in Latin America?

2. What view of human nature did the reformers have, and why did the outbreak of World War I prove such a shock?

3. How much of a world power was the United States in 1914?

4. Why did Americans believe they could stay out of European quarrels?

5. What kind of presidential leadership did Woodrow Wilson offer to the Democrats?

Recommended Readings

Batchelor, Robert. *The 1900s (American Popular Culture Through History)* (2002). A brisk look at the way Americans lived and entertained themselves at the start of the twentieth century.

Chambers, John Whiteclay II. *The Tyranny of Change: America in the Progressive Era, 1890–1920* (1992). Considers the Taft and Wilson years in the context of reform.

Clements, Kendrick. *The Presidency of Woodrow Wilson* (1992). Provides a crisp, informed examination of Wilson in office.

Gilmore, Glenda E., ed. *Who Were the Progressives?* (2002). A thoughtful collection of essays about how historians have viewed early-twentieth-century reformers.

Margulies, Herbert F. *Reconciliation and Revival: James R. Mann and the House Republicans in the Wilson Era* (1996). Supplies a good guide to the politics of the Taft–Wilson years.

Miller, Char. *Gifford Pinchot and the Making of Modern Environmentalism* (2001). Places one of the leaders of the progressive conservation movement in a broader context.

Rodgers, Daniel T. *Atlantic Crossings: Social Politics in a Progressive Age* (1998). Looks at the international aspects of reform.

Sanders, Elizabeth. *Roots of Reform: Farmers, Workers, and the American State, 1877–1917* (1999). Provides insights into how reform legislation fared in Congress.

Stansell, Christine. *American Moderns: Bohemian New York and the Creation of a New Century* (2000). Discusses how New York City and Greenwich Village affected cultural change.

Unger, Nancy. *Fighting Bob La Follette: The Righteous Reformer* (2000). A biography of the Wisconsin senator who challenged Roosevelt for progressive leadership.

Identifications

Review your understanding of the following key terms, people, events, and dates for this chapter (these terms also appear in the Glossary at the end of the book):

William Howard Taft
New Nationalism
woman suffrage
Henry Ford
Alice Paul
Woodrow Wilson
Prohibition

Triangle Shirtwaist Fire
dollar diplomacy
Louis Brandeis
Sixteenth Amendment
William Jennings Bryan
Jack Johnson
Victoriano Huerta
Triple Alliance
Franz Ferdinand

Online Sources Guide

Use this listing to find online documents, images, interactive maps, simulations, and other resources related to this chapter:

American History Resource Center

http://history.wadsworth.com

Documents

Frederick W. Taylor's "Principles of Scientific Management" (1911)
Jane Addams's "Twenty Years at Hull House" (1911)
Excerpts from Part I of Randolph S. Bourne's "Transnational America" (1916)
Woodrow Wilson's "The New Freedom"
Frederick Lewis Allen's "When America Learned to Dance"

Selected Images

Sharecropper's cabin in North Carolina, 1914
1913 Model T sedan
Immigrants disembarking at Ellis Island, 1911
Suffragist marching, 1912
William Howard Taft on horseback
1912 political cartoon satirizing Roosevelt's Square Deal
Woodrow Wilson, 1912
Construction on Panama Canal, 1910

Simulation

Early Twentieth Century (Choose to be a World War I Doughboy, a Socialist, or an immigrant, and make choices based on the circumstances and opportunities afforded.)

Document Exercises

1913 United States Senators
1914 Jell-O College Girls

HistoryNOW

http://now.ilrn.com/ayers_etal3e

Primary Source Exercises

Votes for Women, a Practical Necessity, c. 1912, and Women and Public Housekeeping, 1913
Night Scene at Indiana Glass Works, 1908
Disfranchisement Debate in the Virginia Legislature, 1902

22 Over There and Over Here: The Impact of World War I, 1914–1921

With the American entry into World War I, the armed forces sought recruits through volunteers and the draft. This poster of a Navy gun crew in action was designed to appeal to the patriotism of potential enlisted men. The government felt impelled to make such arguments because substantial portions of society did not share the fervor for the war.

These Men Have COME ACROSS They Are at the Front NOW JOIN THEM ENLIST in the NAVY

Library of Congress, Prints and Photographs Division

Americans wanted to keep out of the European war. Yet events in the conflict influenced domestic politics, altered the Progressive movement, and changed the fortunes of women, African Americans, and socialists. The nation's traditional values came under repeated attack as the war went on. U.S. entry into the war in April 1917 transformed the country in an even more striking fashion.

The era of progressive reform ended. World War I brought several campaigns for social change, most notably Prohibition and woman suffrage, to national success. Yet by the time these results occurred, the movement for reform had lost momentum. The nation rejected an activist government, expensive programs, and efforts to improve society. When Woodrow Wilson left the White House on March 4, 1921, he gave way to Warren G. Harding, who promised a return to older values and a respite from moral uplift.

Staying Neutral in a World Conflict

President Wilson in August 1914 asked his fellow citizens to "be neutral in fact as well as in name" and "impartial in thought as well as in action." Long an admirer of British literature and the system of government in that country, Wilson himself had more sympathy for the Allies than he had for Germany and its wartime partners. He also believed that some kind of "association of nations" must prevent future world wars. In conducting foreign policy, however, he was as evenhanded toward the two sides as any president could have been.

The War and American Public Opinion

The initial results of Wilson's neutrality decisions came in national politics. Going into the congressional elections

Timeline

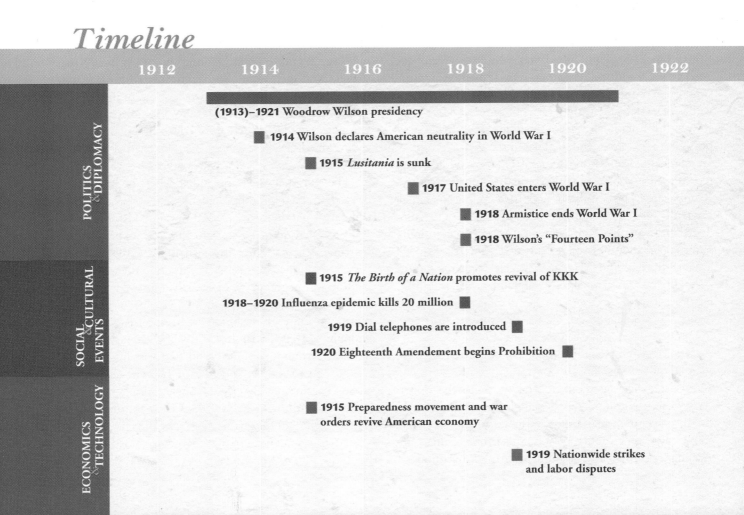

| 1912 | 1914 | 1916 | 1918 | 1920 | 1922 |

POLITICS & DIPLOMACY

(1913)–1921 Woodrow Wilson presidency

1914 Wilson declares American neutrality in World War I

1915 *Lusitania* is sunk

1917 United States enters World War I

1918 Armistice ends World War I

1918 Wilson's "Fourteen Points"

SOCIAL & CULTURAL EVENTS

1915 *The Birth of a Nation* promotes revival of KKK

1918–1920 Influenza epidemic kills 20 million

1919 Dial telephones are introduced

1920 Eighteenth Amendement begins Prohibition

ECONOMICS & TECHNOLOGY

1915 Preparedness movement and war orders revive American economy

1919 Nationwide strikes and labor disputes

of 1914, the Republicans anticipated gains in the House and Senate, but the war issue changed things. In the 1914 elections, the Democratic slogan was "War in the East! Peace in the West! Thank God for Wilson!" The Republicans picked up 63 seats in the House, but the Democrats retained control. In the Senate, the president's party actually added 5 seats.

The issue of peace and war held potential benefits for the president in 1916. The Democrats did well in the Midwest, where support for progressive reforms remained strong. As Wilson looked toward reelection, he decided to form a coalition of southern and western voters united on a platform of peace and reform.

To do so, the president had to pay attention to the interest groups—union workers, farmers, and woman suffrage advocates—that he had rebuffed between 1913 and 1915. If the war stimulated the economy, the combination of peace, prosperity, and reform might give the president a chance at reelection. No one could tell how the European conflict might affect the American economy as the belligerent nations sought to cripple the war-making capacity of their rivals.

The British had inherent advantages in their financial ties with the United States. Economic links with Great Britain were strong, and they intensified as the war progressed. Exports to Britain and France totaled $754 million in 1914; in 1916, they stood at $2.75 billion. Meanwhile, trade with Germany, which had totaled $190 million in 1914, virtually ceased because of the British blockade. The United States could have embargoed all trade with belligerent powers, as many American supporters of Germany recommended, but that strategy would have devastated the U.S. economy.

On the other hand, the Germans also had strong support in the United States. The more than 5 million German Americans, most numerous in the Middle West, represented a sizable bloc of votes that usually favored Republicans. The 3 million–plus Irish Americans hated England and cheered for its enemies. Germany conducted an expensive propaganda campaign consisting of pamphlets and newspaper advertisements. Money directed through the German-dominated brewing industry paid for the campaign. Undercutting their public relations image, however, the Germans also used espionage and sabotage to cripple the British war effort and to hamper American assistance to the Allies.

The British matched German expenditures on propaganda describing the alleged atrocities of their foe. They also relied on their cultural ties with the upper classes and opinion makers in the Northeast to set forth the British case in magazines and newspapers. Over the course of the neutrality period, the British gained an ascendancy in the battle to influence American thinking.

The way the Germans waged the war did the greatest damage to their cause with Americans. In the opening days of the fighting, the German army violated Belgium's neutrality, crossing that nation's borders to invade France. Confronted with a British naval blockade designed to strangle its economy and capacity to wage war, Germany turned to a new weapon, the submarine, early in 1915. In contrast to surface ships, the submarine relied on surprise attacks based on its ability to submerge. Passengers on torpedoed ships were left to drown. Submarines could not provide warnings without risk to themselves, and the Germans resisted pleas that they should do so.

Germany declared that enemy vessels would be sunk on sight, a policy many Americans regarded as a violation of the civilized rules of war. These implicit regulations said that warships should not attack merchant vessels without warning. Neither should they target innocent passengers with their tactics. Despite this aggressive strategy, Germany had only 21 submarines when the fighting began; these new vessels could not win the war by themselves. The use of the submarine, however, put Germany in direct conflict with the United States, the leading neutral country.

The *Lusitania* Crisis

On May 7, 1915, a German submarine fired a torpedo into the British liner ***Lusitania*** off the Irish coast. The huge vessel sank quickly. Among the nearly 1,200 passengers who died were 128 Americans. To most people this event was an audacious atrocity, not an inescapable by-product of modern warfare. Wilson had said that Germany would be held to "strict accountability" for submarine attacks on Americans. He decided, however, that the *Lusitania* was not worth a war.

The president was applauded when he said, three days after the *Lusitania* incident, that "there is such a thing as a man being too proud to fight. There is such a thing as a nation being so right that it does not need to convince others by force that it is right." Allied sympathizers denounced Wilson's words, but the president's readiness to negotiate was generally approved.

Wilson sought an apology and a pledge to limit submarine warfare. His diplomatic response was strong enough, however, that his anti-war Secretary of State William Jennings Bryan, fearful that war might result, resigned in protest in June 1915. He was replaced by Robert Lansing, a pro-Allied diplomat. During the remainder of the summer, the Germans kept the negotiating process going without apologizing or yielding on any point.

Then, in August, the Germans torpedoed a British liner, the *Arabic,* wounding two Americans. Wilson told

The destruction of the *Lusitania* was a shock to Americans who had not expected the war to touch their lives. The banner headlines in the *New York Times* convey something of the sense of amazement and surprise that accompanied the sinking of the passenger liner.

the Germans privately that the United States would break diplomatic relations with them if submarine warfare continued. Still unsure whether the submarine alone could win the war, Berlin offered a conditional pledge not to make unannounced attacks on passenger liners; this defused the situation briefly. In the following year, the Germans sank 37 unarmed liners.

The United States and Its World Role

The neutrality issue forced Americans to consider the nation's future role in a warring world. Many groups wanted the United States to maintain its traditional posture of noninvolvement. German Americans and Irish Americans saw no need to help the British. Progressive reformers regarded war and foreign commitments as the death of reform. In the Midwest and on the Pacific Coast, peace sentiments were widespread.

Led by Theodore Roosevelt, northeastern Republicans supported the allies and called for military "preparedness"

in the event of ultimate American entry into the war. Army and navy officials knew that they would have to expand their forces greatly if they were to play any significant role on the Allied side. In late 1914, Wilson had blocked programs to strengthen the military defense. By the summer of 1915, however, he changed his position and sought a larger army and navy. He promised a navy "second to none" and more troops for the regular army. Many Democrats in the South and West opposed Wilson on the issue of preparedness and the increased spending that it entailed. In early 1916, the president made a speaking tour to arouse popular support for his policy.

As the debate over preparedness intensified, some opinion leaders argued that a world organization should be formed to keep the peace once the fighting stopped. The League to Enforce Peace was created in June 1915, with William Howard Taft as its leader. As 1915 ended, Wilson had not yet thrown his influence behind the idea of a world organization.

Social Change During the Period of Neutrality

During 1915, Americans flocked to theaters to see a new motion picture that vividly depicted sensational events in the nation's past. David Wark Griffith's ***The Birth of a Nation,*** based on an antiblack novel by Thomas Dixon entitled *The Clansman,* portrayed the Reconstruction period in the South as a time when ignorant African Americans terrorized whites and made a travesty of government. An artistic triumph because it used new techniques such as flashbacks and close-ups, the movie twisted history to glamorize the Ku Klux Klan and the white South. Audiences were enthusiastic, box office records were broken, and President Wilson reportedly said: "It is like writing history with lightning." Efforts by African Americans to have the film banned were largely unsuccessful.

This lynching in Waco, Texas, in 1915 became known as the "Waco Horror" for the cruel way the mob killed the victim. Lynching remained an accepted part of race relations in the South.

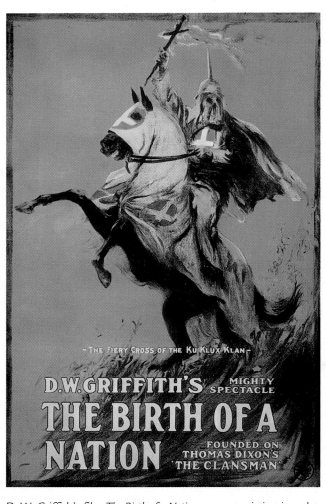

— THE FIERY CROSS OF THE KU KLUX KLAN —

D.W. GRIFFITH'S **MIGHTY SPECTACLE** **THE BIRTH OF A NATION** FOUNDED ON THOMAS DIXON'S 'THE CLANSMAN'

D. W. Griffith's film *The Birth of a Nation* was an artistic triumph with a racist theme. This poster advertising the film depicts the Ku Klux Klan as akin to medieval knights in the garb of chivalry. White audiences ignored the Klan's violent reality for African Americans.

Inspired by the film's portrayal of the Klan, a group of white men burned a cross at Stone Mountain, Georgia, to symbolize their resurgence as a racist order. At first the revived Klan's membership remained under 5,000 nationally, but the social tensions of the postwar era proved a fertile ground for organizing in the South and Midwest.

The political prospects for improved rights for blacks remained as bleak as they had been since the 1890s. The Wilson administration and the Democratic party proved unsympathetic to any efforts to reduce racism. After protests from blacks and a few progressives, the White House retreated from efforts to enforce segregation in the federal government, but that was a minor victory. The Supreme Court did, however, rule in the case of *Guinn v. United States* (1915) that the grandfather clause that Oklahoma used to exempt whites from a literacy test for voting was unconstitutional. That clause exempted from the literacy test whites whose ancestors had been born before a specific date. Oklahoma found other ways to register whites and restrict blacks, but the decision foreshadowed future racial progress toward greater protection of minority rights.

The Great Migration

For African Americans in the South, life was still painful and burdensome. Southern agriculture experienced crippling problems during the first 15 years of the century. Natural disasters hit the region in the form of floods and droughts. The boll weevil, an insect that destroys cotton, undermined the farm economy. Blacks began leaving the South for cities in the North. The **Great Migration** started slowly around 1910 and then accelerated

SOCIAL & CULTURAL EVENTS

The Great Migration of African Americans to the North

The Great Migration of African Americans from the South to northern cities during the second decade of the twentieth century reshaped the nation's cities and, in time, its political, social, and cultural life. This photograph of a black family arriving in Chicago in 1916 reveals in their faces the determination and pain that the journey out of the segregated South demanded. The expressions underscore the rigors of the process, the way in which a few belongings and their best clothes prepared them for the trip, and their apprehension about the uncertain future that they faced in the North.

© Schomburg Center/Art Resource, NY

This photograph comes from the rich collection of images of black life in the Schomburg Center for Research in Black Culture at the New York Public Library. The photographic documentation of African American life in such twentieth century records enables history texts to do better justice to the everyday life of all Americans and the individual families of which they were a part. Thus a simple scene of a family in search of a better life for themselves and their children becomes a symbol of a larger national quest for these values.

DOING HISTORY ONLINE

The Great Migration

Why did so many African Americans migrate from the rural South to the urban North during the war years?

History⟨⟩Now™   Visit HistoryNOW to access primary sources and exercises related to this topic: http://now.ilrn.com/ayers_etal3e

between 1914 and 1920 when more than 600,000 African Americans left the South.

The outbreak of the war played a key role in this process. Immigration from Europe ended. The result was an expanding labor market for unskilled workers in the North. Those who came to the North found a better life but not a paradise. They secured work in the coal mines of West Virginia, the stockyards of Chicago, and the steel mills of Pittsburgh. In Chicago, 60,000 blacks moved to the city between 1916 and 1920, a 148 percent increase in its African American population. Chicago was a natural destination because so many railroads from the South passed through that major transportation hub. Similar percentage increases occurred in Pittsburgh, Cincinnati, and Detroit.

As their population in the North grew, blacks encountered discrimination in housing and public services. Long-standing residents of African American communities in northern cities looked down on the new arrivals. But the southern blacks continued to move north in an historic population shift that reshaped the politics and culture of the nation's largest cities.

The Rise of the Movies

In 1914, a young British comedian began appearing in films for the Keystone company, a filmmaking venture in Los Angeles. Although most of his 35 pictures were very short, one film, *Tillie's Punctured Romance,* ran for 30 minutes. Audiences began asking about the funny actor in the derby hat and little tramp costume. By 1915, the whole nation was talking about Charlie Chaplin and a craze called "Chaplinitis" swept the land. In January 1915, Chaplin signed with Essanay Pictures for the

Table 22.1 Migration of African Americans to Five Northern Cities, 1910–1920

	New York	Chicago	Philadelphia	Baltimore	Detroit
1910	91,709	44,103	84,459	84,749	5,741
1920	152,467	109,458	134,229	108,322	40,838
Percent Rise	66.3	148.2	58.9	27.8	611.3

Source: Robert B. Grant, *The Black Man Comes to the City* (Chicago, 1972).

Washington Evening Star, November, 1915

By 1915, Charlie Chaplin had become one of the most recognizable people in the world. This advertising montage gives a good sense of his varied characters and the popular appeal that he enjoyed.

© Bettmann/CORBIS

Along with Charlie Chaplin, female stars such as Theda Bara, the "It" Girl, helped to make the motion picture industry one of the new cultural developments during the period around World War I.

then-huge sum of $1,250 a week. (An industrial worker made around $600 per *year.*) Within 12 months Chaplin moved on to the Mutual Film Corporation at $10,000 a week. Stardom had come quickly for the 26-year-old actor.

After a shaky start at the beginning of the century, motion pictures had arrived as mass entertainment. There were more than 10,000 nickelodeon theaters by 1912, and up to 20 million Americans went to the movies on a regular basis. Soon movies became longer, and exhibitors began constructing motion picture theaters that could seat up to 5,000 customers.

Although Chaplin was the most famous male performer of his time, he was not the only "star" that the studios created during the era of the silent movie. Executives found that audiences wanted to know about the private lives of the people they saw on the flickering screens. Mary Pickford became "America's Sweetheart" in a series of roles that depicted a demure damsel in acute distress. Douglas Fairbanks used his athletic abil-

ity as the swashbuckling hero of such films as *American Aristocracy* (1916) and *Wild and Woolly* (1917). Theda Bara became the "vamp" in *A Fool There Was* (1915). Advertisements described her as having "the most wickedly beautiful face in the world."

The business of making movies became concentrated in a few large studios that controlled the process of production and distribution. Because of its mild climate, Hollywood, California, emerged as the center of the picture industry. Studios like Vitagraph and Paramount dominated the making and marketing of films.

Most moviegoers lived in cities where the large theaters were located. Immigrants found that they could learn about American life at the movies. Parents worried when their children saw such films as *Women and Wine* or *Man and His Mate*. Reformers clamored for censorship boards to screen films for scenes that showed lustful images or suggested that criminals profited from their crimes.

Shifting Attitudes Toward Sex

Continued challenges to the nation's family and sexual values arose. In 1916, one of every nine marriages ended in the divorce courts. Meanwhile, family size was decreasing. By 1920, two or three children were born to the average mother; in 1860, the average had been five or six.

The most daring women of the decade were the **flappers.** They cut their hair short in the fashionable "bob" and wore shorter skirts than the ankle length fashions earlier in the century. The flapper, wrote social commentator H. L. Mencken in 1915, "has forgotten how to simper; she seldom blushes; it is impossible to shock her." Norms of sexual behavior slowly moved away from the restrictions of the Victorian era. For women born around 1900, the rate of sexual intercourse before marriage was twice as high as it had been for women born a decade earlier. Nevertheless, the overall incidence of premarital sexual behavior remained very low in comparison with the present.

Despite the changes in actual sexual practices, the official attitudes of the nation remained restrictive. Homosexual relationships were outlawed, even though some college-educated women maintained "partnerships" or "Boston marriages." Laws governing the dissemination of information about birth control discouraged the use of contraception. In many states and cities it was a crime to sell condoms or to distribute information about how to avoid pregnancy. A federal statute, the Comstock Law of 1873, barred the making, selling, distribution, or importation of contraceptives, as well as any transmission of birth control information through the mails. The only ground on which abortions were permitted was to save the life of the mother.

Margaret Sanger, a 32-year-old home nurse and radical activist living in Greenwich Village in 1911, saw women suffering from disease and poverty because of the large number of children they bore. Often women had many babies because they lacked knowledge about ways to limit births. In 1914, Sanger coined the term *birth control* and began publishing a periodical called *Woman Rebel.* Women, she wrote, "cannot be on an equal footing with men until they have full and complete control over their reproductive function." Indicted for sending such information through the mails, she went to Europe, consulted with experts on family planning, and returned to the United States determined to arouse support for birth control.

A year later she founded a clinic in a poor neighborhood of Brooklyn that distributed information about contraception to the female residents. The police soon closed the clinic down, and Sanger went to jail. When the case was appealed, a higher court affirmed the right of doctors to prescribe birth control devices. Sanger then organized the Birth Control League to promote her cause. Some feminists regarded birth control as a liberating idea; others saw the availability of contraceptive devices as likely to encourage promiscuity and thus promote male dominance.

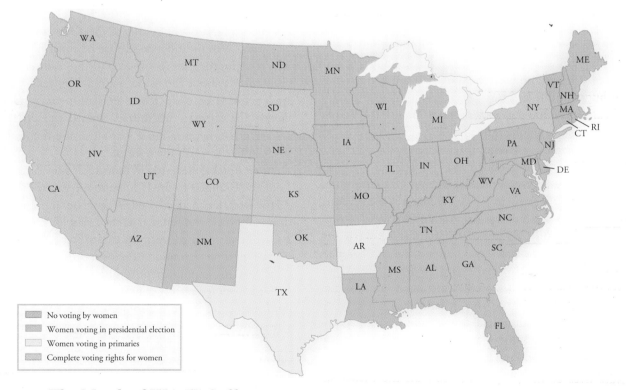

MAP 22.1 The March of Woman Suffrage
This map tracing the progress of woman suffrage gives an excellent sense of the sectional split over the issue with the West and Middle West in favor and the South and East in opposition.

The achievement of woman suffrage was a notable reform of the post–World War I period. The activist supporter of suffrage, Alice Paul, is shown sewing the 36th star on the banner that the National Woman's Party kept to mark the progress of ratifying the Nineteenth Amendment (the amendment to give women the vote). With that addition, the amendment became part of the Constitution in 1920.

Library of Congress, Prints and Photographs Division

The Persistence of Reform

Progressive reform campaigns pressed ahead despite the distractions of the European war. Prohibition capitalized on anti-German sentiment to reduce the political power of the brewing industry. The end of the flow of immigrants from Europe enabled advocates of immigration restriction to gain support for tighter laws. Supporters of woman suffrage also used the war as a way of mobilizing women behind their cause.

Woman suffrage gained strength after 1914 despite serious divisions among the movement's leaders. Alice Paul and the militant Congressional Union pressed for a constitutional amendment to obtain votes for women. Their tactics included demonstrations and a direct challenge to the Democrats as the party in power. In contrast, the National American Woman Suffrage Association (NAWSA), led by Carrie Chapman Catt after 1915, emphasized nonpartisanship and state-by-state organization. Paul and her allies formed the National Woman's party to defeat Wilson and the Democrats. NAWSA, on the other hand, continued its efforts to win the right to vote in individual states, but it now sought a constitutional amendment as well. As the election approached, the momentum for suffrage seemed to be building. Even President Wilson, who had previously opposed the idea, now said that individual states could adopt woman suffrage if they wished.

The drive for Prohibition, the second major cultural reform campaign, also intensified. In 1914, the Anti-Saloon League decided to press for a constitutional amendment to ban the sale of alcohol. At the same time, the efforts to make the states liquor-free went forward, with notable success. In 1913–1914, more than a dozen states adopted Prohibition legislation or held referenda in which the voters adopted Prohibition. Nine more states adopted Prohibition in 1915. Gradually, prohibitionist candidates within the major parties won seats in Congress. The prohibition campaign also gained from the anti-immigrant sentiments that intensified in the nation on the eve of World War I.

Closing the Door for Immigrants

The war in Europe shut off immigration to the United States from the eastern European countries. Belligerent nations needed every person within their borders to sustain the war effort. The reduced flow of newcomers did not stop the campaign to cut down on immigration. Proponents of immigration restriction contended that the eventual peace would open the door to an even greater influx of outsiders. The ethnic tensions that the neutrality debate produced heightened sensitivity about what came to be called "hyphenated Americans." Congress again passed an immigration restriction law with a literacy test in 1915, which President Wilson again vetoed. In the 1916 election, neither major party wanted to alienate ethnic voters.

After 1914, progressive reformers looked to the federal government for help with the agenda of social change. In light of the results of the 1914 congressional elections, Wilson understood that he must move left to win four more years in office. Putting aside his earlier reservations about the use of national power to achieve such reforms as child labor legislation or agricultural credits for farmers, he shifted toward the progressive side. He also became more willing to use the authority of his office to push for reform.

One notable step that Wilson took was to nominate Louis D. Brandeis to the U.S. Supreme Court in January 1916. Brandeis had advised Wilson on the New Freedom, and had won renown as the "People's Lawyer" and a foe of consolidated business enterprise. Since Brandeis was a longtime champion of reform causes and a prominent Jew, his appointment aroused intense, often anti-Semitic, feelings among conservatives. In the end he was confirmed, and Wilson's strong endorsement of him convinced progressives that the president was on their side.

During the months before the election campaign began, Wilson came out for laws to restrict child labor, to promote federal loans to farmers (known as agricultural credits), to provide federal aid for highway construction, and to cover federal employees with workers' compensation laws. When a national railroad strike threatened in August 1916, Wilson compelled Congress to pass

Flashpoints | The Suffrage Picketers

They were outside the White House day after day, a silent rebuke to President Woodrow Wilson and his views on woman suffrage. Beginning in early January 1917, the National Woman's party (NWP), under the direction of Alice Paul, embarked on a campaign to embarrass President Wilson and draw attention to their demands for woman suffrage. Paul believed that only confrontation would move the president to positive action on suffrage that would influence Democrats in Congress to support a constitutional amendment.

The NWP put pickets in front of the White House with banners that read "MR. PRESIDENT, how long must women wait for liberty?" They remained in place as the United States entered World War I. The protestors contrasted the campaign to make the world safe for democracy with the lack of voting rights for women. Wilson tried to ignore the pickets. The other major suffrage group, the National American Woman Suffrage Association (NAWSA), called on the press to remind readers that Paul and her associates did not speak for the entire suffrage cause. They repudiated picketing and stressed the need to work through the political process, even if it moved more slowly than Paul and her associates wanted.

After months of protesting, violence flared in June 1917. A delegation of Russians visited the White House. That country had not yet experienced the Communist revolution and these emissaries were seeking Wilson's support for their new government. The NWP picketers waved banners that stated the United States needed to "liberate its women" before making an alliance with a foreign country. Onlookers tore down the banner and assaulted the protestors. Following this outbreak of violence, the White House cracked down on the NWP with arrests and some jailings.

Meanwhile the NAWSA leadership worked with the press and the Wilson administration to create a news blackout about the treatment of the NWP militants and their continuing demonstrations. The strategy was only partially successful because many papers ran stories about the activities of the NWP pickets. Nonetheless, the episode illustrated how the war spirit impelled some progressive reformers to employ undemocratic means in an attempt to stifle opposition within the suffrage movement. During and after the fighting, Congress did approve the constitutional amendment in one of the last reforms of the progressive era. As the episode of the White House pickets revealed, the success of the campaign came despite some unsavory ways in which the advocates of suffrage in the NAWSA waged their campaign.

Questions for Reflection

1. Why were Woodrow Wilson and the Democrats in Congress reluctant to support woman suffrage?

2. What were the differences in approach about woman suffrage between the National Woman's Party and the National American Woman Suffrage Association?

3. How did the interplay between the two factions of the woman suffrage movement affect the ultimate adoption of this reform?

4. To what extent did wartime passions influence the response to the women who picketed the White House?

---

the Adamson Act, which mandated an 8-hour working day for railroad employees. Labor responded with strong support for Wilson's reelection bid. Meanwhile, the improving economy, driven by orders from the Allies for American products and foodstuffs, helped the Democrats.

Wilson's reelection chances hinged on the uneasy neutrality he had maintained toward the Germans and the British throughout 1916. The Republicans seemed divided between those who wished to do more for the Allies and those who either disliked overseas involvement or wished to help Germany. Wilson would benefit if he could find a middle position that combined defense of American rights with preservation of neutrality.

The president had to deal with several related wartime issues during the first half of 1916. The main problem remained the submarine. By the end of 1915, Wilson had succeeded in obtaining a German apology and indemnity for the Americans who had died on the *Lusitania.* After the sinking of the *Arabic,* the Germans had also pledged not to attack passenger liners without warning. Then the United States suggested an arrangement in which the Germans would limit submarine warfare and the Allies would not arm merchant ships. When this proposal (or *modus vivendi)* collapsed because of British and German opposition, Germany resumed submarine attacks on *armed* shipping, whether it was belligerent or neutral, in February 1916.

On March 24, 1916, a German submarine attacked an unarmed steamer, the *Sussex,* in the English Channel. American passengers on board were injured, and another diplomatic crisis ensued. Wilson sent an ultimatum to Berlin that continued attacks on unarmed merchant vessels without warning would lead to a breaking of diplomatic ties, a prelude to U.S entry into the war. The Germans again faced the question of whether the submarine alone could win the war. At the time, only about 18 of their

52 submarines could be on patrol at any one time. With hopes of a victory on land still glimmering before them, the Germans pledged that they would not conduct attacks on merchant vessels without warning them. The so-called *Sussex* Pledge seemed like a major diplomatic success for Woodrow Wilson because it had staved off a war that most Americans dreaded.

During these same months, Wilson also tried to arrange for a negotiated settlement of the war. In December 1915, he sent his close friend, Colonel Edward M. House, to discuss peace terms with the British, French, and Germans. House's talks led to an agreement with the British foreign minister, Edward Grey, for Anglo-American mediation of the war; if the Germans rebuffed the idea, the United States would enter the war on the side of the Allies. The House-Grey Memorandum, as the agreement was called, never took effect because Wilson watered it down and the British ignored it.

During the first half of 1916, Wilson emerged as a forceful national leader. His speaking tour calling for preparedness swung public opinion behind his program to provide more weapons and personnel for the army and navy. When Congress sought to assert itself through resolutions warning Americans not to travel on the ships of the warring powers, the president pressured Congress to have the resolutions defeated on the grounds that they interfered with his power to conduct foreign policy. In May 1916, the president argued, in a speech to the League to Enforce Peace, that the major nations of the world should find a way to band together to preserve peace.

In the spring of 1916, the issue of Mexico once again grabbed the nation's headlines. The Mexican civil war had continued after the American intervention at Veracruz in 1914. Although Wilson did not like the regime of Venustiano Carranza, he extended diplomatic recognition to it when it became clear that Carranza had emerged as the nation's effective leader.

Then a rebel named Pancho Villa raided towns in New Mexico and Texas in 1916, killing and wounding numerous Americans. The U.S. Army under General John J. Pershing pursued him across the Rio Grande. Heedless of Mexican feelings about this intrusion on their sovereignty, the United States seemed to be headed for a war. Wilson negotiated a diplomatic settlement. Nevertheless, American troops remained in Mexico for two years, placing a continued strain on relations between the two nations.

The 1916 Presidential Election

The Democrats approached the election of 1916 with confidence. The president's program of progressive domestic legislation was moving through Congress; the

Library of Congress, Prints and Photographs Division

Charles Evans Hughes, the Republican presidential candidate in 1916, had an aloof personality, a trait that the Democrats associated with "ice water" in the presidential campaign. This cartoon shows the Republican nominee in a car with his running mate Charles W. Fairbanks, as the vehicle leaks "ice water" while preparing to run against Woodrow Wilson and Thomas Riley Marshall in their faster "Democratic performance car."

international situation appeared to have vindicated Wilson's leadership; and the economy was prosperous because of the war orders that the British and French had placed for munitions, food, and industrial products. The Republicans first had to win back the Progressives, some of whom found Wilson's reform program attractive. Eastern Republicans wanted the United States to intervene on the side of the Allies. In the Midwest, progressive Republicans and German Americans opposed a pro-Allied policy.

Theodore Roosevelt hoped to be the Republican nominee, but his pro-Allied views made him too controversial. The Republicans turned to Supreme Court Justice **Charles Evans Hughes.** He had been a progressive governor of New York, was not scarred with the wounds of 1912, and had said little about foreign policy. A remnant of the Progressive party nominated Roosevelt, but he declined and the party soon disappeared. The Republicans offered assurances that they favored some domestic reforms and carefully straddled the more controversial questions of preparedness, neutrality, and loyalty of ethnic groups such as the German Americans.

For the Democrats, Wilson's nomination was never in question. The excitement occurred over the party's platform and the campaign slogan that arose from it. In that document, the delegates praised Wilson's ability to preserve American neutrality. In his keynote address to the Democratic delegates, a former governor of New York, Martin Glynn, noted that Wilson had maintained neutrality. Each time he referred to this fact the audience exclaimed: "What did we do? What did we do?" and he shouted back: "We didn't go to war! We didn't go to war!" The Democrats had their slogan: "He kept us out of war."

In the campaign that followed, Wilson employed the themes of peace, progressivism, and prosperity in his speeches. Meanwhile, Hughes had difficulty finding a

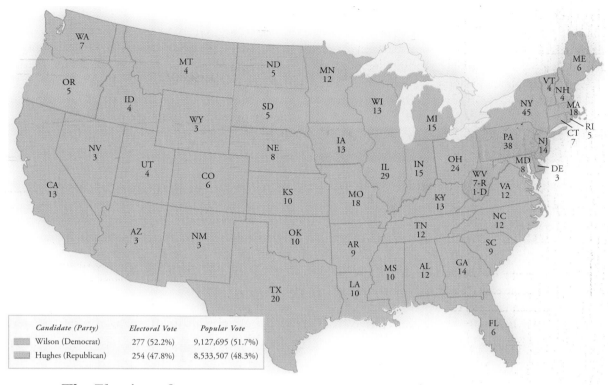

MAP 22.2 The Election of 1916

The election of 1916, fought under the shadow of World War I in Europe, saw Woodrow Wilson campaign on a platform of peace, prosperity, and progressive reform. That was enough to enable the Democratic incumbent to run well in the West and compile a tight victory over Charles Evans Hughes and the Republicans.

way to appeal to Republicans who shared Roosevelt's position and to the German-American voters who wanted the nation to stay out of the conflict. Hughes also proved to be a less effective campaigner than the Republicans had hoped, but he had the benefit of a party that still attracted a majority of voters outside the South. To win, the Democrats assembled a coalition of voters in the South and West, the peace vote, women (who could vote in western and middle western states), and Midwestern farmers who were happy with wartime prosperity. Wilson won one of the closest elections in the nation's history. He gained 277 electoral votes from 30 states, and Hughes won 254 electoral votes from 18 states. The president amassed a little more than 49 percent of the vote, polling 600,000 more popular votes than Hughes did.

Wilson's Attempts to Mediate

The war and its problems had not disappeared during the campaign. Wilson now believed that the time had come to press for a negotiated settlement because both sides regarded the United States with suspicion. Relations with the British had soured during 1916 because of the way the Royal Navy and the British Foreign Office interfered with American shipping in enforcing their blockade against Germany. Meanwhile, the British were becoming more

dependent on American loans and credits to pay for the supplies that they had been buying since 1914. Under the circumstances, the president believed, London might be receptive to an American mediation effort. The president also knew that pressure was rising within the German military for unrestricted use of submarines.

On December 18, 1916, Wilson asked the warring countries to state their terms for a negotiated peace. Both the British and the Germans rejected the president's offer; the solution would have to come on the battlefield. In response, Wilson addressed the U.S. Senate on January 22, 1917, in a speech that called for a "Peace Without Victory." He argued that "only a peace among equals can last," and set out a program that included plans to create a league of nations. The attitude of the warring powers was skeptical. The idea of a league of nations to prevent future wars also aroused opposition in the Senate. Wilson's failure to consult with his political enemies on this matter was an error that would later plague him.

American Intervention in the War

Aware that their military position in the conflict was deteriorating, the German high command decided on January 9, 1917, that only the submarine could win the war before the United States could move troops to

Europe. Unrestricted submarine attacks would be resumed on February 1 to choke off supplies to Great Britain. Wilson learned of the German decision on January 31 and realized that Berlin had not been negotiating in good faith. He broke diplomatic relations on February 4. The

submarine campaign began as scheduled, and American lives were lost. On February 26, the president asked Congress for authority to arm U.S. merchant ships. With peace sentiment still strong on Capitol Hill, the administration faced a tough fight to get the bill passed.

An unexpected revelation about German war aims then happened. British intelligence had intercepted and decoded a secret German diplomatic telegram to its ambassador in Mexico. The **Zimmerman Telegram,** named after the German foreign minister Arthur Zimmerman, dangled the return to Mexico of Arizona, New Mexico, and Texas as bait to entice the Mexicans to enter the war on the German side. Wilson released this diplomatic bombshell to the public on March 1, and the House promptly passed the bill to arm merchant ships. Eleven senators, led by Robert M. La Follette of Wisconsin, filibustered against the bill until Congress adjourned on March 4. In fact, Wilson could arm the ships on his own authority, which he did on March 9.

The Outbreak of Hostilities

The submarine campaign was hurting the Allies badly, and defeat seemed possible. One stumbling block to American support for the Allied cause had always been the presence of Russia on the side of the British and French. Alliance with that autocratic monarchy seemed to mock the notion that the Allies were fighting for democratic values. However, the outbreak of revolution in Russia toppled the regime of Czar Nicholas II and seemed to offer some hope for reform. Meanwhile, the Germans sank three American ships on March 18 with large losses. Wilson decided to call Congress into special session on April 2. On a soft spring evening, the president asked for a declaration of war against Germany. "The world must be made safe for democracy," he told them. "It is a fearful thing to lead this great peaceful people into war, into the most terrible and disastrous of all wars, civilization itself seeming to be in the balance. But the right is more precious than peace." Evoking the language of the sixteenth-century German religious reformer Martin Luther, Wilson said of his nation, "God helping her, she can do no other."

Congress declared war on Germany on April 6, 1917. Although the votes were overwhelming (82 to 7 in the Senate; 373 to 50 in the House), the nation was divided. In large parts of the South and West, peace sentiment was strong because the public felt no need to become involved in European quarrels or to benefit eastern business interests that might profit from the fighting. Opposition to the war remained high among German Americans and Irish Americans. Dedicated reformers and Socialists saw the war as a betrayal of reform ideals.

Picturing the Past **POLITICS & DIPLOMACY**

The Zimmerman Telegram and Code Breaking

The use of codes and ciphers, although traditional in warfare, became more sophisticated and important during the twentieth century as radio and telegraphy developed. One of the most sensational examples of this trend came in the First World War with the revelation of the Zimmerman Telegram. In that document, Germany proposed to Mexico an alliance against the United States in the event of war in 1917. British code-breakers, who had been reading German diplomatic traffic, easily intercepted the message, decoded

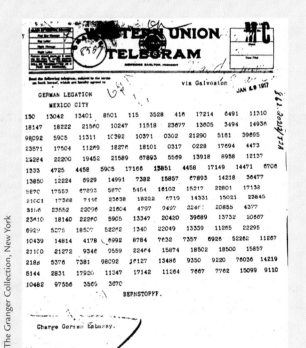

© The Granger Collection, New York

it, and passed it on to Washington. The White House, in turn, used the information to sway reluctant members of Congress to support President Wilson as war with Germany neared. Secret intelligence thus became a publicity tool as well as a military weapon. Published in the newspapers in its encoded and unbroken form, the telegram as pictured here provided a brief but elusive glimpse into a secret world that grew in importance even after the First World War ended.

For Wilson himself, involvement in the war seemed to be the price the nation had to pay to influence the peace settlement. His lofty rhetoric encouraged Americans to believe that a better world could be obtained through the use of military force. In that sense the president paved the way for the later disillusion among Americans that frustrated his ambitious plans for world leadership.

A Nation at War

World War I produced significant changes in the way the United States functioned as a nation. The power of the federal government increased dramatically in response to the need to mobilize the populace for war. Average citizens found that they had to respond to government programs and directives in strange and unfamiliar ways, such as accepting bureaucratic rules for their businesses, listening to government propaganda, and changing their eating habits.

The government assumed that the American contribution to the war would consist of furnishing money and supplies to the Allied cause. It soon became apparent that American soldiers would have to go across the Atlantic and join in the fighting to achieve an Allied victory. Otherwise, a German military success seemed probable. By 1917, the world conflict involved fighting in Africa, Asia, the Middle East, and the focus of the struggle in the beleaguered nation of France.

As of April 1917, the German army still occupied large portions of France that it had seized in 1914. Meanwhile, gigantic battles occurred on the "eastern front" between the Russians on the one hand and the Germans and their Austrian allies on the other. On the "western front," where the Allies and the Germans confronted each other in France, the two sides fought in elaborate trenches from which soldiers fired at each other or mounted attacks against well-fortified positions. Dug-in artillery and machine guns gave the advantage to the defense. The French suffered more than 1,430,000 casualties on the western front in 1915. The Germans tried to break the will of the French at Verdun in 1916; both sides lost more than 300,000 men in the ensuing struggle. The British attacked in northern France in 1916; 60,000 men were killed or wounded in a single day's fighting. Similar carnage occurred when the British renewed their offensive on the Somme River in 1917. After the French went on the attack in 1917 with heavy casualties, their broken armies mutinied against further slaughter by refusing to fight on in hopeless offensives.

The Wilson administration did not want to raise an army through volunteer methods. Experience in Europe had shown that a volunteer system was undependable and did not keep trained individuals at their jobs in key war industries. In May 1917, Congress adopted the Selective Service Act. Men between the ages of 21 and 30 had to register for the draft; local boards were set up to administer the program. By the end of the war 24 million young men had been registered, and about 3 million had been called into the armed forces. Another 340,000 men tried to evade the draft and became "slackers." There were also 65,000 men who claimed exemptions for religious reasons.

To command the American Expeditionary Force (AEF), Wilson selected General John J. Pershing, who had pursued Pancho Villa into Mexico. The nation was ill-prepared for war. The army had no plans for a war with Germany in western Europe, and it did not have the rifles and machine guns necessary for a modern conflict. Its staff structure was loaded with old officers who lacked initiative and experience in commanding large numbers of men.

Training the troops for warfare in Europe was not a simple process, and the indoctrination that the men received often reflected progressive ideals. The government endeavored to maintain the purity of troops with extensive programs to limit excessive drinking and venereal disease. The army also provided an optional opportunity to acquire inexpensive life insurance, which increased popular interest in such programs after the war. The pace of mobilization was slow. It was not until more than a year after the entry into the war that American troops reached France in substantial numbers.

While the army was being raised, the navy faced a more immediate challenge. During April 1917, German submarines sank almost 900,000 tons of Allied shipping. At that rate, half the oceangoing shipping available to the British would disappear by the end of 1917. The British had only enough food for six weeks in reserve.

The American naval commander in Europe, Admiral William S. Sims, turned to convoys to escort vulnerable merchant ships across the Atlantic. American destroyers on escort duty became a key part of the strategy that eventually ended the submarine threat. Troops began to move toward Europe. The Germans did not regard troopships as significant targets because of their belief that American soldiers lacked fighting ability. Two million men were shipped to France before the Armistice was signed and they provided the margin for an Allied victory.

The government raised a third of the money for the war, some $9 billion, through increased taxes. The remainder came from citizens who purchased **Liberty Bonds** from the government. These interest-bearing securities brought in more than $15 billion. Children were taught to save their pennies and nickels for thrift stamps. They learned a rhyme to urge them on:

Hush little thrift stamp,
Don't you cry;
You'll be a war bond
By and by.

Those who were unwilling to contribute were told that failure to buy bonds was unpatriotic and helped the Germans. In some cases, violence was used to coerce the reluctant contributors. That happened in Texas where those who failed to sign up for Liberty Bonds were whipped. The total cost of the war to the United States exceeded $35 billion. The United States loaned more than $11.2 billion to the Allies, most of which was never repaid. Yet Washington had no choice. In June 1917, one British official told his government that "If loan stops, war stops." President Wilson counted on the Allies' financial dependence on the United States as a weapon to use in achieving the goals of his postwar diplomacy.

The Allies also desperately needed food. The British depended on supplies from their empire, which took a long time to reach Europe by ship and were vulnerable to submarine attack. Without American food, sent via convoys under the protection of the U.S. Navy, serious shortages would have impaired Allied ability to wage war. To mobilize the agricultural resources of the United States, Congress passed the Lever Act, which established a Food Administration. Wilson selected Herbert Hoover to head this new agency. A mining engineer from California, Hoover had gained international fame through his work to feed the starving people of Belgium. He threw his abundant energy into persuading Americans to save their food for shipment overseas.

Hoover asked Americans to observe "wheatless days" and "meatless days" because "wheatless days in America make sleepless nights in Germany." Women and children planted "war gardens" to raise more fruits and vegetables. Higher prices induced farmers to expand their production. The wheat crop was 637 million bushels in 1917; a year later it stood at 921 million bushels.

The campaign to conserve food boosted the effort to restrict the sale and use of alcoholic beverages. Scarce grain supplies had to be reserved for soldiers in the field and Allied populations overseas. As a wartime slogan put it, "Shall the many have food or the few have drink?" Prohibitionists argued that drink impaired the fighting ability of the armed forces and those working in defense plants. The connection of the brewing industry with the German Americans also worked in favor of the prohibitionist cause.

Congress passed legislation to restrict the production of liquor, and in December 1917 the lawmakers approved the **Eighteenth Amendment,** which banned the production and sale of alcoholic beverages. All that remained was to ensure ratification of the amendment by the required number of states, a task that the Anti-Saloon League was well equipped to handle.

Managing the Wartime Economy

Coordination of the economy was not limited to the agricultural sector. The president used his power to wage the war to establish the expanded bureaucracy required to manage production of war supplies and oversee their shipment to the Allies. Wilson did not seek to have government take over business. He hoped that a business–government partnership would develop naturally. However, much government encouragement and direction were needed before the business community fully joined the war effort.

The eventual record of mobilization was a mixed one. The United States tried to build ships and planes under the direction of government agencies. Those efforts produced at least one British-designed plane that used American-built engines, and large numbers of merchant ships were constructed in American shipyards. On the other hand, Pershing's men used British and French artillery and equipment. The government had more success with expanding the production of coal, the major source of residential heating and industrial power, through the Fuel Administration. Coal prices were raised to stimulate production, and "daylight savings time" was established to reduce the use of fuel for nonmilitary purposes.

The war challenged the government and the economy in other areas. The nation's railroads became so confused during the first year of the war that immense and costly transportation snarls resulted. The armed forces insisted on immediate passage for railcars with war supplies; tie-ups of rail traffic all over the East Coast resulted. Finally the government took over the railroads in January 1918, placing the secretary of the treasury, William G. McAdoo, in charge of operations. McAdoo raised the wages of railroad workers, dropped inefficient routes, and allowed the lines to raise their rates. The tie-ups soon disappeared.

Even before U.S. entry into the war, the government had made plans for coordinating industrial production. Staffed with "dollar-a-year men" whose salaries were paid by their former companies, the War Industries Board (WIB) was supposed to make sure that the purchasing and allocation of supplies for the armed forces followed rational programs. The WIB fell well short of this standard during 1917 in such industries as munitions, airplane production, and merchant shipping. In March 1918, under pressure from Congress and Republican critics such as Theodore Roosevelt, Wilson placed Bernard Baruch, a Wall Street speculator and contributor to the Democratic party, at the head of the War Industries Board.

Baruch and his aides attacked needless waste in production. They standardized products, established priorities for the shipment of important goods, and set prices to encourage factories to turn out goods quickly. Simply by altering bicycle designs, the WIB saved 2,000 tons of steel for war goods.

Not all industries cooperated willingly. Baruch had to compromise with both the powerful and politically well-connected automobile and steel industries to induce them to abandon peacetime production in favor of handling wartime orders. In the process, the industries made significant profits from their government contracts. As one steel executive put it, "We are all making more money out of this war than the average human being ought to."

On the other hand, the American Federation of Labor and its president, Samuel Gompers, threw their support behind the war effort. In return for the government's agreement to allow unions to participate in economic policy making, Gompers and the AFL promised not to strike or to press for union shops in factories. Between 1917 and 1920, the AFL gained more than 2 million members.

Nonunion workers also benefited from the government's wartime policies. The National War Labor Board, headed by former President William Howard Taft, set standards for wages and hours that were far more generous and enlightened than those private industry had provided. A minimum wage was mandated, as were maximum hours and improved working conditions. In one plant, women saw their wages raised to almost $11 per week. The government also created housing for war workers and began a system of medical care and life insurance for federal employees.

Black Americans in the War

While some blacks wanted no part of the European conflict as a conflict among their white oppressors, most African American leaders agreed with W. E. B. Du Bois that they should "forget about special grievances and close our ranks shoulder to shoulder with our own fellow white citizens." Some 367,000 black soldiers served during the war; 42,000 of them saw combat in France. Most of the African American servicemen, however, were assigned to labor battalions and supply duties. The War Department moved very slowly to commission black officers; at the end of the war there were only 1,200. Several African American units fought bravely. Others were given inadequate training and equipment,

but when they performed poorly in combat the blame was placed on their supposed inferiority. Blacks had little motivation to fight in the first place in a segregated army that represented a segregated nation. Moreover, for some blacks in France, the experience of being in a country without a long tradition of racism made them impatient for greater freedom at home.

African American troops stationed in the United States faced familiar dangers. In August 1917, in Houston, Texas, black soldiers reacted to segregation and abuse by the police with attacks on the police and on white citizens that left 16 whites and 4 soldiers dead. The army indicted 118 soldiers, of whom 110 were convicted by courts-martial. Nineteen black soldiers were hanged.

Racial tensions intensified elsewhere in the nation as whites and blacks confronted each other when northern cities experienced an influx of African Americans. During the summer of 1917, race riots in East St. Louis, Illinois, resulted in the deaths of 40 blacks and 9 whites. Forty-eight lynchings occurred in 1917 and 63 in 1918. Facing discrimination and violence, blacks responded with a heightened sense of outrage. Marches were held to protest the race riots. Banners called upon President Wilson to "Bring Democracy to America Before You Carry It to Europe."

During the war the black migration to northern cities accelerated. As the African American communities in Chicago, New York, Philadelphia, and other northern cities grew, black newspapers began publishing articles about the "**New Negro**" who did not "fear the face of day. The time for cringing is over." The repressive actions of the Wilson administration in such episodes as the Houston riot and the failure to act against lynching fed the new currents of militance among black Americans.

The great achievement of American women during World War I was winning the right of suffrage. The leaders of the National American Woman Suffrage Association decided that identification with the war offered the surest and fastest road to achieving their goal. Carrie Chapman Catt argued that giving women the vote would enable them to offset disloyal elements at home. "Every slacker has a vote," said Catt, a vote that newly enfranchised women could counter. Members of NAWSA appeared at rallies and proclaimed that suffrage should be a "war measure" that would repay women for their contributions to the war. The National Woman's party, on the other hand, picketed the White House to embarrass Wilson for failing to support woman suffrage. The combined impact of these tactics led to the passage of the woman suffrage amendment in the House of Representatives in January 1918. Wilson came out in favor of the amendment just before the congressional elections of that year. The Senate still had to act, but the war

Militant proponents of woman suffrage picketed the White House in 1917–1918 to move President Wilson to support their cause. Their presence embarrassed the president and several of the picketers went to jail for their beliefs.

had made possible the eventual victory of the campaign to give women the vote.

Beyond the success of woman suffrage, however, the war did not go on long enough to produce lasting changes in the condition of American women. Only about 400,000 more women joined the labor force; some 8 million found better-paying jobs as a result of the conflict. More than 20,000 women served in the military. The navy and the marines enlisted 13,000 of them, largely in office jobs. The army employed more than 5,000 as nurses. In industry, women were hired as drivers, farm workers, and secretaries. As soon as the war ended, they were expected to relinquish these jobs to returning servicemen. As a Chicago woman complained, "During the war they called us heroines, but they throw us on the scrapheap now."

Civil Liberties in Wartime

The Wilson administration believed that winning the war required mobilization of public opinion to offset potential opposition to the conflict. As a result, the White House mounted a campaign of laws, agencies, and popular spirit to arouse support for the war and to quell dissent. In doing so, however, Woodrow Wilson

and the men around him abused and restricted the civil liberties of many Americans.

To awaken national enthusiasm, the government created the Committee on Public Information (CPI) on April 13, 1917, and President Wilson named George Creel, a former newspaperman, as its head. Creel called his task "the world's greatest adventure in advertising"; he saw his role as one of fusing Americans into "one white-hot mass . . . with fraternity, devotion, courage, and deathless determination." To spread its message, the CPI used pamphlets, billboards, and motion pictures such as *The American Indian Gets into the War Game.* Seventy-five thousand speakers known as "Four-Minute Men" (because of the length of their talks) spoke to audiences throughout the nation.

The themes of the CPI's appeal were simple, patriotic, and strident. Four-Minute Men asked listeners: "Do you want to take the slightest chance of meeting Prussianism here in America?" The great national goal was unity; the Germans were depraved animals; and the nation was engaged in a crusade to "make the world safe

The Committee on Public Information used "Four-Minute Men" to give brief, pithy speeches in favor of war-bond sales.

for democracy." Wilson's wartime speeches described the United States as "an instrument in the hands of God to see that liberty is made secure for mankind."

The Limits of Dissent

To guard against opposition to the war, the Wilson administration and Congress placed legislative limits on the ability of Americans to criticize the government or the war effort. The Espionage Act of 1917 curbed espionage and sabotage, but made its definitions so sweeping that they embraced even public criticism of the war and its conduct. A person who violated the law could be sentenced to 20 years in prison. The Trading with the Enemy Act, passed in October 1917, authorized the postmaster general to suspend the mailing privileges of foreign-language periodicals and newspapers that he deemed offensive to the government. Postmaster General Albert S. Burleson used that law and the Espionage Act to bar from the mails publications that he considered treasonous or seditious. In 1918, Congress passed the Alien Act, which gave the government broad powers to deport any noncitizen who advocated revolution or anarchism. Most sweeping was the Sedition Act of 1918, which prohibited "uttering, printing, writing, or publishing any disloyal, profane, scurrilous, or abusive language" about either the government or the armed forces.

These laws were vigorously enforced. Burleson pursued critics of the administration relentlessly. The Socialist magazine *The Masses* was barred from the mails for carrying articles claiming that "this is Woodrow Wilson's and Wall Street's War." The Justice Department was equally vigilant. People were sent to prison for saying that "Wilson is a wooden-headed son of a bitch" or remarking that this was "a rich man's war." Eugene V. Debs, the perennial Socialist candidate for president, received a 10-year prison sentence for opposing the draft and the war. The American Protective League, a volunteer organization designed to locate draft evaders, became a vigilante branch of the Justice Department that used wiretapping, illegal searches, and other lawless techniques to find "slackers" and other opponents of the war.

Wartime Hysteria

The zeal of the government to stamp out dissent was matched by private hysteria toward Germans. Sauerkraut became "liberty cabbage," hamburgers reemerged as "Salisbury steak," and some cities gave up pretzels. Speaking the German language in public was banned in half of the states by 1918, and German literary works vanished from libraries. Musicians with German names,

DOING HISTORY ONLINE

The Propaganda War

Study the documents in this module and read the section "A Nation at War" in the textbook. How did America's involvement in the war alter the relationship between the federal government and the people of the nation?

History ⧗ Now™   Visit HistoryNOW to access primary sources and exercises related to this topic: http://now.ilrn.com/ayers_etal3e

such as the violinist Fritz Kreisler, found their careers crippled.

Some German Americans suffered more serious injuries. When they refused to buy war bonds, mobs beat them until they promised to contribute. Editorials warned: "YOUR NEIGHBOR, YOUR MAID, YOUR LAWYER, YOUR WAITER MAY BE A GERMAN SPY." Radicals, too, were the victims of mob violence. Frank Little, an organizer for the Industrial Workers of the World (IWW), was hanged from a railroad trestle in Montana for denouncing the war at a labor rally.

The Political Legacy of Repression

The government had a legitimate reason to be concerned about German espionage, but the repression of civil liberties during the war was excessive. President Wilson did not order cabinet officials to engage in such conduct, but he failed to keep them in check when he learned about what they were doing. The government's campaign against radicals and progressives, key areas of Wilson's coalition in 1916, undermined support for the president in domestic politics. In his eagerness to win the war, Wilson had allowed his government to destroy part of his own political base. He and the Democrats paid for that policy in the 1918 and 1920 election campaigns.

The Road to Victory

During the late winter of 1918, as American troops arrived in France, the Allies faced a dangerous military crisis. In November 1917, the Communist revolution in Russia had taken that nation out of the Allied coalition and enabled the Germans to move troops to the western front. Berlin hoped to achieve victory before the Americans could reinforce the Allies. The German attack

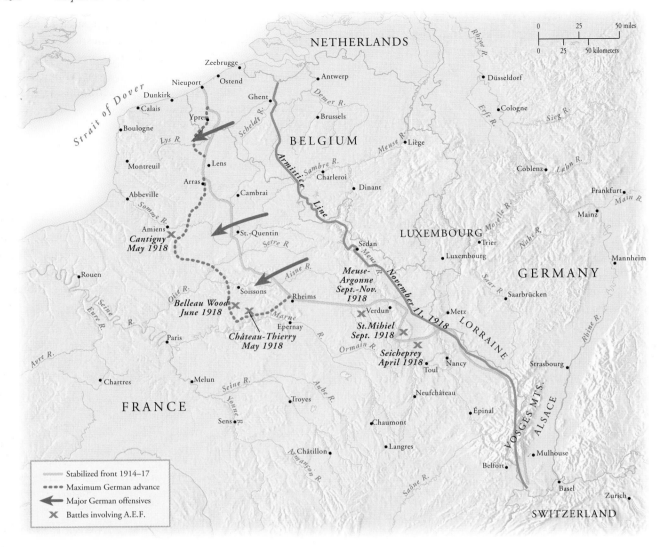

MAP 22.3 American Participation on the Western Front
This map indicates how the American Expeditionary Force helped to repel German offensives in 1918 and then pushed the enemy back toward the German border.

View an animated version of this map or related maps at http://history.wadsworth.com/passages3e

came on March 21, 1918, and made impressive gains until the Allies held. When further attacks were made against the French in April and May, American reinforcements helped stop the assault. At battles near Chateau-Thierry and in Belleau Wood in early June, the men of the AEF endured frightful losses but halted the Germans.

The Germans made one more offensive thrust in mid-July, and the British, French, and Americans repelled it as well. Counterattacks moved the Germans backward, a retreat that continued until the end of the war. In September 1918, the American army went on the offensive at the town of Saint-Mihiel near the southern end of the trenches. At the end of the month, Americans launched another thrust toward the Meuse River and the Argonne Forest. Their casualties were heavy, but the AEF pierced the German defenses to threaten key supply routes of the enemy.

Wilson's Peace Program

Wilson had set out his views on peace in a major address to Congress on January 8, 1918. Using the archives of the Czarist government, the Russian Communists had released secret treaties that the Allies had made before 1917 dividing up Europe and the Middle East once victory was achieved. These documents cast doubt on Allied claims that they were fighting for unselfish reasons. Wilson endeavored to shape the Allied answer and regain the diplomatic initiative.

To present the American cause in a better light, Wilson offered a peace program with 14 specific elements that became known as the **Fourteen Points.** Among the key provisions were freedom of the seas, free trade, and more open diplomacy. Freedom of the seas would prevent a repetition of the submarine threat the United States had faced before entering the war. Wilson believed that secret treaties and balance of power diplomacy had helped bring about the war itself. The president advocated national self-determination for all nations. He meant that the borders of countries should reflect the national origins of the people who lived in a particular area. He also advocated an "association of nations" to keep the peace.

The Fourteen Points would not be easy to achieve. After four years of slaughter, Britain and France wanted to punish Germany and cripple its ability to wage war. They disliked Wilson's criticism of their war aims and his interference with European policies. For the desperate Germans, the Fourteen Points seemed much more appealing than negotiations with London and Paris. In early October a civilian government in Germany asked Wilson to arrange an armistice based on the Fourteen Points. Working through Colonel House, the president negotiated an agreement for an end to the fighting. He also used the threat of a separate settlement with the Germans to induce the British and French to accept the Fourteen Points and attend the peace conference. The fighting ended on November 11, 1918, at 11:00 in the morning.

Woodrow Wilson had achieved a diplomatic triumph with the conclusion of the armistice, but his success proved to be temporary. Even as he prepared to lead the American delegation to Paris, his domestic political base was eroding. During the war, he had proclaimed, "politics is adjourned." In fact, however, partisan battles continued with both Wilson and his enemies using the war for their own political purposes.

The 1918 Elections

Throughout the conflict President Wilson kept the Republicans at arm's length and treated the conflict as a war for Democrats only. He did not bring Republicans into his government at the highest levels, and he attacked Republicans who opposed his policies. Meanwhile, his enemies capitalized on the unhappiness of farmers and workers over the administration's domestic programs. Midwestern farmers, for example, disliked the price controls that had been imposed on wheat. They complained that southerners in Congress had prevented similar price controls from being put on cotton. As a result, wheat farmers saw their profits held down while cotton producers did well. Progressives who had supported Wilson in 1916 recoiled from the administration's repressive tactics toward dissenters. In late October 1918, Wilson tried to stave off the defeat with an appeal to the American people to elect a Democratic Congress. The statement allowed Wilson's enemies to claim that he had been decisively repudiated when the results showed that both the House and the Senate would have Republican majorities. For a president who needed bipartisan support in the Senate for any treaty he might write at the upcoming Peace Conference in Paris, it was a major blunder.

The Paris Peace Conference

In a break with the tradition that presidents did not travel outside the country, Wilson had already decided to attend the Peace Conference. Despite Republican criticism, he believed that he needed to direct the negotiations himself. Moreover, his selection of delegates to accompany him showed his continuing insensitivity to bipartisanship. The five men he chose were his close allies, with only one nominal Republican among them.

Wilson did not send any senators to Paris. Had he done so, he would have had to include Senator **Henry Cabot Lodge** of Massachusetts, the next chairman of the

General John J. Pershing commanded the American Expeditionary Force during World War I. This photograph shows him on horseback at the head of his men during a victory parade in Paris on July 14, 1919.

Foreign Relations Committee. Wilson and Lodge hated each other. Adding to their natural political differences was an element of personality conflict. Lodge believed Wilson was dishonest and tricky; Wilson saw Lodge as a reactionary out to thwart the president's goals for humanity. If Wilson could not take Lodge, he could not invite any other senators. Unwilling to accept advice or share the credit, Wilson also declined to select other prominent Republicans such as William Howard Taft or Elihu Root.

The President in Europe

Europeans greeted Wilson with rapturous applause. When he arrived in Paris, 2 million people cheered him as he rode up the Champs-Elysées. They called him "Wilson *le Juste* (the Just)" and expected him to fulfill their desires for a peaceful world and for revenge against the Germans. To them, the Fourteen Points were a rhetorical device, not a statement of Wilson's real position on issues. Wilson came to believe that he could appeal to the peoples of the world over the heads of their leaders to support his program of international peace.

The other major figures at the conference were David Lloyd George, the prime minister of Great Britain, and Georges Clemenceau, the premier of France. Both men were hard-headed realists who did not share Wilson's idealism. "God gave us the Ten Commandments, and we broke them," said Clemenceau. "Wilson gives us the Fourteen Points. We shall see." Along with the prime minister of Italy, Vittorio Orlando, Wilson, Clemenceau, and Lloyd George made up the "Big Four" who directed the Peace Conference toward a settlement of the issues that the war had raised.

The Shadow of Bolshevism

Four years of war had left the world in disorder, and nations large and small came to Paris to have their fate decided. A striking absentee was the new Soviet Union, the Communist nation that the Russian Bolsheviks had established after their successful revolution. Civil war raged in Russia between the "Reds" of Communism and the "Whites," who wanted to block Bolshevik control of the nation. Meanwhile, the Bolsheviks' authoritarian leader Vladimir Ilyich Lenin and his colleagues wished to extend Communist rule beyond Russia's borders.

In 1919, national leaders worried that the infection of Communism might spread into western Europe, and they had not recognized the government in Moscow. The French and British had tried to strangle the new

regime by providing financial support for its enemies and intervening militarily in some areas of Russia. Helping its allies and trying to undermine Bolshevism, the United States had dispatched small detachments of troops to Siberia and Vladivostok in 1918 and 1919. The American presence in Russia became a long-standing grievance for the Soviet regime that emerged from the Bolshevik victory.

The Terms of Peace

The negotiations about the terms of peace with Germany produced both victories and defeats for Wilson. He had to accept the inclusion in the treaty of a clause that assigned Germany "guilt" for starting the war in 1914. That language proved to be a source of discontent for a resurgent Germany in the 1920s and 1930s. The Germans were also assessed severe financial penalties in the form of reparations that eventually amounted to $33 billion, a provision that further fueled their resentment in the 1930s.

Wilson also achieved partial success in his efforts to establish self-determination in the peace settlement. He accepted Italian desire for control of the city of Fiume on the Adriatic Coast, could not block Japan from territorial gains in China, and was unable to prevent several groups of ethnic and national minorities in eastern Europe from being left under the dominance of other ruling groups, as in the case of Germans in the new nation of Czechoslovakia.

The League of Nations

Wilson's main goal was establishment of the League of Nations. The league consisted of a General Assembly of all member nations; a Council made up of Great Britain, France, Italy, Japan, and the United States, with four other countries that the Assembly selected; and an international court of justice. For Wilson, the "heart of the covenant" of the League of Nations was Article X, which required member nations to preserve each other's independence and take concerted action when any member of the league was attacked.

In February 1919, Wilson returned to the United States for the end of the congressional session. Senator Lodge then circulated a document that 37 senators signed. It stated that the treaty must be amended or they would not vote for it. Such a document, signed by a number of those who agreed with it, went by the term round-robin. This pledge had drawn enough votes to defeat the treaty unless Wilson made changes in the document. The president attacked his critics publicly, further intensifying partisan animosity.

DOING HISTORY

The League of Nations Debate, 1919

Woodrow Wilson

"OUR ISOLATION WAS ended twenty years ago, and now fear of us is ended also, our counsel and association sought after and desired. There can be no question of our ceasing to be a world power. The only question is whether we can refuse the moral leadership that is offered us, whether we shall accept or reject the confidence of the world.

The war and the conference of peace, now sitting in Paris, seem to me to have answered that question. Our participation in the war established our position among the nations, and nothing but our own mistaken action can alter it. It was not an accident or a matter of sudden choice that we are no longer isolated and devoted to a policy which has only our own interest and advantage for its object. It was our duty to go in, if we were, indeed, the champions of liberty and of right.

We answered to the call of duty in a way so spirited, so utterly without thought of what we spent of blood or treasure, so effective, so worthy of the admiration of true men everywhere, so wrought out of the stuff of all that was heroic that the whole world saw, at last, in the flesh, in noble action, a great ideal asserted and vindicated by a nation they had deemed material and now found to be compact of the spiritual forces that must free men of every nation from every unworthy bondage. It is thus that a new role and new responsibility have come to this great nation that we honor and which we would all wish to lift to get higher levels of service and accomplishment."

Senator William E. Borah

"Senators, even in an hour so big with expectancy, we should not close our eyes to the fact that democracy is something more, vastly more, than a mere form of government by which society is restrained into a free and orderly life. It is a moral entity, a spiritual force, as well. And these are things which only and alone in the atmosphere of liberty. The foundation upon which democracy rests is faith in the moral instincts of the people. Its ballot boxes, the franchise, its laws, and constitutions are but the outward manifestations of the deeper and more essential thing—a continuing trust in the moral purposes of the average man and women. When that is lost or forfeited your outward forms, however democratic in terms, are a mockery. Force may find expression through institutions democratic in structure equal with the simple and more direct processes of a single supreme ruler. These distinguishing features of a real republic you can not commingle with the discordant and destructive forces of the Old World and still preserve them. You can not yoke a government whose fundamental maxim is that of liberty to a government whose first law is that of force and hope to preserve the former. These things are in eternal war and must ultimately destroy the other. You may still keep for a time the outward form, you may still delude yourself, as others have done in the past with appearances and symbols, but when you shall have committed this Republic to a scheme of world control based upon force, upon the combined military forced of the four great nations of the world, you will have soon destroyed the atmosphere of freedom, of confidence in the self-governing capacity of the masses, in which along a democracy may thrive. We may become one of the four dictators of the world, but we shall no longer be masted of our own spirit."

In the debate over American membership in the League of Nations, Woodrow Wilson confronted the strong opposition of a group of senators known as the "irreconcilables," led by William E. Borah of Idaho. These two excerpts from speeches given by Wilson and Borah portray the clash of opinions over this heated foreign policy issue. In the end, of course, Borah prevailed and the Treaty of Versailles was not approved. The issues raised in this controversy, however, have echoed in American history ever since.

Source: Woodrow Wilson speech to Congress, *The New York Times,* July 11, 1919; William E. Borah, speech to the Senate, November 10, 1919, *Congressional Record* (November 10, 1919).

Questions for Reflection

1. How does President Wilson view the experience of World War I as far as the United States is concerned? In what ways did participation in the conflict, in his mind, prepare the nation to join the League?

2. How do Borah and Wilson differ over the responsibilities of the United States after the war had been concluded?

3. What does Borah fear will happen if the United States becomes an active participant in European affairs?

4. How do the conceptions of democracy diverge in the speeches of Borah and Wilson?

5. In what ways have the views of Borah and Wilson continued to affect American foreign policy down to the present day?

Explore additional primary sources related to this chapter on the Wadsworth American History Resource Center or HistoryNOW websites:

http://history.wadsworth.com/rc/us
http://now.ilrn.com/ayers_etal3e

Wilson and the Treaty of Versailles

To secure changes in the treaty for the Senate, Wilson had to make concessions to the other nations at the Peace Conference when he returned to Europe. These included the imposition of reparations on Germany, the war guilt clause, and limits on German's ability to rearm. In return, Wilson obtained provisions that protected the Monroe Doctrine from league action, removed domestic issues from the league's proceedings, and allowed any nation to leave the world organization with two years' notice. The final version of the Treaty of Versailles was signed on June 28, 1919, in the Hall of Mirrors at the Palace of Versailles outside Paris. For all of its problems and weaknesses, the treaty was the closest thing to a reasonable settlement that Wilson could have obtained.

The Senate and the League

The Republicans now controlled the Senate 49 to 47, so the president could not win the necessary two-thirds majority without the votes of some of his political opponents. Some Republicans were opposed to the treaty as an infringement upon American sovereignty, no matter what it said. These were the 14 "irreconcilables"; two Democrats were also part of this group. Wilson had to seek help from the 12 "mild reservationists," who wanted only changes in the wording, and the 23 "strong reservationists," who sought to limit the league's power over American actions. The president could count on about 35 of the 47 Democrats in the Senate. Assuming that some of the mild reservationists would support the treaty, the Democrats had to find 20 Republican votes to gain the necessary 64 votes to approve the treaty.

MAP 22.4 **Europe after the Peace Conference, 1920**
The Treaty of Versailles attempted to contain Germany against future aggressive behavior. Note the number of new states created out of the old Russian and Austro-Hungarian empires. Nonetheless, Germany remained a major force in Central Europe.

When Wilson arrived in Europe, he received a hero's welcome. As he embarked in Great Britain and walked in with Lloyd George and King George V, schoolgirls threw flowers in his path.

opinion would turn against the treaty. He had the lengthy treaty read aloud to the Senate. Meanwhile, Wilson insisted that the treaty be approved without changes or "reservations."

Wilson's Tour and Collapse

By September 1919, with the treaty in trouble, Wilson decided to take his case to the American people. Despite audience approval of his speeches, Wilson's health broke under the strain. The circulatory problems that had bothered him for years erupted. He was rushed back to Washington, where he suffered a massive stroke on October 2, 1919. His left side was paralyzed, seriously impairing his ability to govern.

The president's wife and his doctors did not reveal how sick Wilson was. The first lady screened his few visitors and decided what documents her husband would see. People at the time and historians since have argued that she acted as a kind of female president. In fact, Mrs. Wilson did only what her ailing husband allowed her to do. But as for the nation's chief executive, Wilson was only a shell of a president and the government drifted.

In the political battle that ensued, Senator Lodge focused on Article X and the issue of whether Congress should be able to approve any American participation in the league's attempts to prevent international aggression. Lodge also played for time, hoping that public

The most dedicated political opponent of Woodrow Wilson was Senator Henry Cabot Lodge of Massachusetts. He said that he had never expected to hate anyone in politics with the intense dislike that he felt toward Wilson. The feeling was mutual.

THE ACCUSER

March 22, 1920

The fight over the League of Nations aroused intense passions. Cartoonist Rollin Kirby depicted the blood-stained Senate with its sword as having finally killed the treaty and the hopes of humanity in March 1920.

The Influenza Epidemic of 1918

The impact of disease on American history is still understood only in an incomplete way. The influenza epidemic of 1918–1919 was such an event: it shaped the behavior of Americans during the last months of the First World War and into the early period of peacetime. The flu virus, which spread around the world so rapidly, swamped the existing medical facilities and public health apparatus of major cities. Believing that the malady might be spread by mouth, citizens took precautions like the one used by the policeman shown in this photograph directing traffic and selling Liberty Bonds.

National Archives #165-WW-269.c-7

Nothing that was done to halt the pandemic really did much good. In the end, the sickness simply ran its course, leaving millions of people dead worldwide.

Some earlier books about the World War I period barely mentioned it, but in recent years historians have become more sensitive to how sickness and infection operate to influence the course of history. This picture and its appearance in your text is a testament to that change in how historians think about the past. Other examples of similar episodes of illnesses in American history appear elsewhere in the text.

The Defeat of the League

The Senate voted on the treaty on November 19, 1919, with reservations that Lodge had included in the document. Lodge would have required Congress to approve any sanctions imposed by the league on an aggressor. When the Democratic leader in the Senate asked Wilson about possible compromises, he replied that changing Article X "cuts the very heart out of the Treaty." The Senate rejected the treaty with reservations by a vote of 39 to 55. Then the lawmakers voted on the treaty without reservations. It lost, 38 in favor and 53 against. In the end, the decision about a possible compromise with Lodge was Wilson's to make. He told Senate Democrats: "Let Lodge compromise."

From War to Peace

Meanwhile the nation experienced domestic upheaval. Citizens grappled with labor unrest, a Red Scare (fear of Communist or "Red" subversion), a surge in prices following the end of the war, and an influenza epidemic. The postwar period was one of the most difficult that Americans had ever experienced.

The influenza epidemic began with dramatic suddenness at the end of 1918 and spread rapidly through the population. No vaccines existed to combat it; no antibiotics were available to fight the secondary infections that resulted from it. More than 650,000 Americans died of the disease in 1918 and 1919. The number of dead bodies overwhelmed the funeral facilities of many major cities; coffins filled a circus tent in Boston. Children skipping rope made the epidemic part of their song:

> I had a little bird,
> And his name was Enza;
> I opened the window,
> And in flew Enza!

The influenza pandemic receded in 1920, leaving a worldwide total of 20 million people dead. The pandemic had sapped the strength of the Allied armed forces to enforce the peace treaty, had diverted attention from important social problems, and illustrated how vulnerable humanity was to these infectious diseases.

The Waning Spirit of Progressivism

By 1919, the campaigns for Prohibition and woman suffrage were nearing their goals. Enough states had ratified the Eighteenth Amendment (the Prohibition amendment) by January 1919 to make it part of the Constitution. In October 1919, Congress passed the Volstead Act, named after its congressional sponsor, Andrew J. Volstead of Minnesota, to enforce Prohibition. Wilson vetoed the measure as unwarranted after the war had ended, but Congress passed it over his objection. The United States became "dry" on January 15, 1920. Prohibitionists expected widespread compliance and easy enforcement.

After the House passed the Nineteenth Amendment (the woman suffrage amendment) in 1918, it took the Senate another year to approve it. Suffrage advocates then lobbied the states to ratify the amendment. When the Tennessee legislature voted for ratification in August 1920, three-quarters of the states had approved woman suffrage. Women would now "take their appropriate place in political work," said Carrie Chapman Catt.

The Struggles of Labor

After the Armistice, the nation shifted from a wartime economy to peacetime pursuits with dizzying speed. The government declined to manage the changeover from a wartime to a peacetime economy. High inflation developed as prices were freed from wartime controls, and unemployment rose as returning soldiers sought jobs. The government's cost of living index rose nearly 80 percent above prewar levels in 1919 and it went up to 105 percent a year later. Unemployment reached nearly 12 percent by 1921.

Unions struck for higher wages. Seattle shipyard workers walked off their jobs, and the Industrial Workers of the World called for a general strike to support them. When 60,000 laborers took part in the protest, the mayor of Seattle, Ole Hanson, responded with mobilization of police and soldiers that made him, in the eyes of those who agreed with him, "the Saviour of Seattle." Newspapers depicted the strike as a prelude to communist revolution.

The Reaction Against Strikes

The largest industrial strike of the year occurred in the steel industry. The American Federation of Labor tried to organize all steelworkers to end the 7-day week and the 12-hour day. In September, 350,000 steel workers left the mills. The steel manufacturers refused to recognize the union. Strikebreakers were hired from among the ranks of unemployed blacks, Hispanics, and immigrants. The steel companies kept their factories running while they waited for the strike to be broken through police harassment and internal divisions within the unions. Conservatives attacked the radical background of one of the strike organizers, William Z. Foster. Although the strikers remained united for several months, they could not withstand the accumulated financial and political pressure from management. This first effort at a strike by an entire workforce failed in early 1920.

Other strikes of the year included a walkout by coal miners and a strike by police in Boston. Inflation had hit the Boston police hard, and they struck late in 1919. When looting and other criminal acts occurred because of the absence of police, public opinion turned against the striking officers. The governor of Massachusetts, Calvin Coolidge, became a national celebrity when he said: "There is no right to strike against the public safety, by anybody, anywhere, any time." To many middle-class Americans, the social order seemed to be unraveling.

Racial tensions also flared up in the turbulent postwar atmosphere. There were frequent lynchings in the South. In the North, the tide of African American migration produced confrontations with angry whites. Rioting against blacks occurred in Washington, D.C., in June 1919. During the same summer a young black man was stoned and killed when whites found him on a Chicago beach from which African Americans had been excluded. Angry blacks attacked the police who had stood by while the killing occurred. Five days of violence followed in which 38 people, most of them black, were killed and another 500 were injured. Violent episodes roiled two dozen other cities during what one black leader called "the red summer." Racism and antilabor sentiments fed on each other during these months.

Searching for a cause of the social unrest that pervaded the nation, Americans looked to radicalism and communism. The emotions aroused by the government's wartime propaganda fueled the **Red Scare** of 1919–1920. About 70,000 people belonged to one of the two branches of the Communist party. However, the radicals' reliance on violence and terrorism inflamed popular fears. When several mail bombs exploded on May 1, 1919, and dozens of others were found in the mail, press and public called for government action.

Attorney General A. Mitchell Palmer established a division in the Justice Department to hunt for radicals; the division was headed by J. Edgar Hoover, who later became director of the Federal Bureau of Investigation. In November 1919, Palmer launched raids against suspected radicals, and a month later he deported 300 aliens to the Soviet Union. In the process, the legal rights of these suspects were violated, and they were kept in custody, away from their families and attorneys.

Throughout the country civil liberties came under assault. State legislatures investigated alleged subversives. Communist parties were outlawed, antiradical legislation was adopted, and Socialists were expelled from the New York legislature. Suspected members of the IWW and other groups were subjected to vigilante violence and official repression.

The U.S. Supreme Court upheld the constitutionality of most of the laws that restricted civil liberties during the war and the Red Scare. Justice Oliver Wendell Holmes, Jr., devised a means of testing whether the First Amendment had been violated. In *Schenck v. United States* (1919), he asked whether words or utterances posed "a clear and present danger" of interference with the government, the war effort, or civil order. The answer was that they had. The Court also sustained the conviction of Eugene V. Debs for speaking out against the war.

By 1920, however, the Red Scare lost momentum. Palmer forecast a violent uprising on May 1, 1920, and when it did not occur, his credibility suffered. Some government officials, especially in the Department of Labor, opposed Palmer's deportation policies. Other public figures, such as Charles Evans Hughes, denounced New York's efforts against socialist lawmakers. Despite the waning Red Scare hysteria, it was during this period that police in Massachusetts arrested two anarchists and Italian aliens, Nicola Sacco and Bartolomeo Vanzetti, for their alleged complicity in a robbery and murder at a shoe company in South Braintree, Massachusetts. In a case that attracted international attention, the two were convicted and eventually executed (see Chapter 23).

Gradually, the frenzy of Red-hunting abated. During the Wilson administration a dangerous precedent had been set for government interference with individual rights. The bureaucratic machinery was in place for future attempts to compel loyalty and punish dissent.

Harding and "Normalcy"

In early 1920, with Wilson ill and the government leaderless, the Senate once again took up the Treaty of Versailles with reservations in March. On March 19, the treaty received 49 votes in favor and 35 against, 7 short of the number needed to ratify it. Wilson had said that he would not approve the pact with reservations, but the vote showed that a compromise could have been reached. Wilson hoped that the election would be a "solemn referendum" on the treaty, but that did not happen.

The Republicans had expected that Theodore Roosevelt would be their nominee in 1920, but he died on January 6, 1919, of circulatory ailments and heart problems. The Republicans turned to Senator Warren G. Harding of Ohio. A first-term senator, Harding was not a smart man, but the Republicans had had enough of intelligent candidates in Roosevelt, Taft, and Charles Evans Hughes. Harding looked like a president and had made few enemies. He had been engaged in an illicit love affair in his home town of Marion, Ohio, but that information was carefully repressed. To run with him, the convention named Governor Calvin Coolidge of Massachusetts. Harding emphasized a return to older values, which he labeled "normalcy." He called for "not heroics, but healing."

In the 1920 election, Warren G. Harding promised "normalcy." To evoke the spirit of bygone days, he began his campaign from his front porch. Later he took to the campaign trail in a more modern manner. Harding won an overwhelming victory.

Brown Brothers

For the Democrats the nominee was Governor James M. Cox of Ohio, a moderate progressive from the party's antiprohibitionist wing, and his running mate was Franklin D. Roosevelt of New York. The Democratic candidates supported the League of Nations; the Republicans generally dodged the subject until the end of the campaign when Harding advocated rejection of the treaty. The issue did not have much effect. Voters wanted to turn the Democrats out of office because of anger at big government, high taxes, and labor unrest. The electorate rejected progressivism and the use of government to make society more just. They rejected the Democrats in a landslide. Harding received 16 million votes to 9 million for Cox.

Conclusion

The United States was a late entrant into World War I, and that conflict did not produce the revolutionary upheavals that some European nations experienced between 1914 and 1918. Nonetheless, the six years that stretched from the outbreak of the war in August 1914 to the election of Warren G. Harding as president in 1920 brought significant changes. The larger meaning of this chapter lies in the many ways that citizens faced a world in which older values and attitudes now seemed obsolete.

The war cast grave doubt on the progressive faith that human beings were good and could be made even better through democracy and reform. The millions of deaths overseas, among them more than 50,000 American soldiers and sailors, shook the confidence of a generation in the prospect of an ever-improving future for all citizens. With these sobering revelations came also suspicions about the value of bigger government and higher taxes. By 1920, voters longed for a return to prewar certainty or what Harding called "normalcy."

But the changes that jolted society were long lasting. The movement of African Americans from the rural South to the urban north in the Great Migration made race a more national dilemma and shifted politics for both Democrats and Republicans. Woman suffrage marked a major expansion of democracy even if newly enfranchised females did not produce a purer and more enlightened political dialogue. For a time Americans sought to curb the problem of alcohol by an amendment to the Constitution restricting the sale and distribution of such beverages.

In the wake of World War I, the nation briefly contemplated a more active role in the world and then drew back. Woodrow Wilson's League of Nations, building on wartime idealism, seemed less attractive in the harsh light of the postwar disillusionment with attempts to make the world safe for democracy. Though there was no going back to isolation, Americans for a season thought they could let the Old World grapple with the consequences of its mistakes.

Later developments in the twentieth century, including the rise of Nazi Germany and the challenge from the Soviet Union, would make these judgments of the World War I period seem sadly mistaken. How could these men and women not see that in the errors of their great war lay the seeds of another greater conflict a generation later? What this chapter reveals is that in the setting of their time people buffeted by world war and profound social change embraced certainties of their past and pursued reassurance. Not knowing what their descendants would learn, they did their best in an era of upheaval and shock to deal with the world that had changed so much in just six short years.

The Chapter in Review

In the years between 1914 and 1920:

- The nation grappled with how to remain neutral in a world experiencing political upheaval.
- Southern blacks moved to northern cities in what came to be known as the Great Migration.
- The movies emerged as mass entertainment.
- Woodrow Wilson was reelected in 1916.
- The United States entered the World War in April 1917.

- Government power expanded during wartime.
- The American military contributed to the Allied victory.
- The Senate debated and then rejected the League of Nations.
- The country passed through postwar trauma including the Red Scare.
- Warren G. Harding was elected president in 1920.

Making Connections Across Chapters

LOOKING BACK

The problems that reformers encountered after 1914 had their roots in the record of the first years of the twentieth century. Looking back on the era of Theodore Roosevelt, William Howard Taft, and the early years of Woodrow Wilson's presidency, you can see the assumptions about human nature and the role of government that foreshadowed the later problems that weakened the hold of progressivism on the American people.

1. How deeply rooted was the progressive spirit? What groups did it include, and which ones did it leave out?

2. How far did the presidents in this period want to go in changing American society?

3. Why did the First World War have such a devastating effect on progressive assumptions about humanity and the world?

LOOKING AHEAD

In the 1920s, Americans would reject many of the accomplishments of the Progressive Era and repudiate much of what reformers had contributed to government and politics. In the next chapter discover whether these conservative trends went too far. What remained of value in the progressive legacy?

1. Why did the United States adopt Prohibition as an answer to the problems of alcohol?

2. Why did woman suffrage not produce the fundamental changes in American society that its proponents expected?

3. How did Americans feel about their place in the world after the experiences of the First World War and the struggle over the League of Nations?

Recommended Readings

Auchincloss, Louis. *Woodrow Wilson* (2000). A brief, readable life of this important president.

Chambers, John Whiteclay. *The Tyranny of Change: America in the Progressive Era, 1890–1920* (2000). A helpful synthesis of this whole period.

Clements, Kendrick. *The Presidency of Woodrow Wilson* (1992). Offers a thorough guide to the accomplishments of Wilson in office.

Cooper, John Milton. *Breaking the Heart of the World* (2002). An excellent examination of the fight over the League of Nations.

Davis, Donald E., and Trani, Eugene P. *The First Cold War: The Legacy of Woodrow Wilson in U.S.-Soviet Relations* (2002). Considers the impact of Wilson's policies on these two nations.

Graham, Sally Hunter. *Woman Suffrage and the New Democracy* (1996). Describes how women obtained the vote during World War I and afterward.

Levin, Phyllis Lee. *Edith and Woodrow: The Wilson White House* (2001). Looks at the effect of Wilson's illness on his presidency.

Saunders, Ronald M. *In Search of Woodrow Wilson: Beliefs and Behavior* (1998). A very critical account of the president and his record.

Schaffer, Ronald. *America in the Great War: The Rise of the War Welfare State* (1991). An informative text about woman suffrage and race.

Trotter, Joe William, ed. *The Great Migration in Historical Perspective* (1991). An excellent collection of essays about the movement of African Americans to northern cities.

Identifications

Review your understanding of the following key terms, people, events, and dates for this chapter (these terms also appear in the Glossary at the end of the book):

Lusitania
The Birth of a Nation
Great Migration
flappers
Margaret Sanger
Carrie Chapman Catt

Charles Evans Hughes
Zimmerman Telegram
Liberty Bonds
Eighteenth Amendment
New Negro
Fourteen Points
Henry Cabot Lodge
Red Scare

Online Sources Guide

Use this listing to find online documents, images, interactive maps, simulations, and other resources related to this chapter:

American History Resource Center

http://history.wadsworth.com/rc/us

Documents

A Sample of a War Propaganda Pamphlet (WWI)
President Woodrow Wilson's Fourteen Points

Selected Images

Army-Navy college football game, 1916
Immigrant taking oath of citizenship, 1916

W. E. B. Du Bois
Woodrow Wilson at the peak of his power
Lusitania in New York, 1907
General John J. Pershing
American soldier in France
American soldiers firing machine guns in France, 1918
U.S. troops wearing gas masks
Members of the 369th infantry, 1919
Woman welder, World War I
Women aircraft workers, 1919
Navy recruiting poster, 1918
Douglas Fairbanks at a bond rally

Simulation

Early Twentieth Century

Document Exercises

1917 President Wilson's War Message
1919 *Schenck v. United States*

HistoryNOW

http://now.ilrn.com/ayers_etal3e

Primary Source Exercises

Remember! The Flag of Liberty! Support It! 1917
The Propaganda War
The Great Migration

23 The Age of Jazz and Mass Culture, 1921–1927

The Ku Klux Klan was on the march with its message of bigotry in the early 1920s. This pictures shows members of the hooded order as they paraded in Washington, D.C. The tensions that the Klan represented echoed through the entire decade.

© Bettmann/CORBIS

The Aftermath of War

During the 1920s the United States became modern as the automobile and other technological developments reshaped the economy and society. While the country became more urban, cosmopolitan, and uniform, the shared experiences of Americans made the nation more cohesive in that citizens were undergoing similar phenomena within the same context. In that regard, social attitudes toward sex and family life moved away from Victorian restraints. Movies, radio, and big-time sports shaped everyday existence. Young people emerged as a distinct group. Advertising made public relations a significant characteristic of the period.

After a postwar depression, the economy rebounded from 1922 to 1927. The Republican administrations of Warren G. Harding and Calvin Coolidge lowered income taxes and encouraged private enterprise. Issues of culture and morality shaped politics more than did questions of economic reform. Prohibition and the Ku Klux Klan split the Democrats.

In foreign affairs, the decade was officially a time of isolation after the rejection of the League of Nations in 1919–1920. Government policy reinforced perceptions that the United States was aloof from the world. Yet the reality was more complex and subtle. Although involvement in world affairs increased more slowly, the United States maintained a significant stake in the postwar European and Asian economies.

A More Urban Nation

The census of 1920 gave one important indicator of the country's new course. For the first time, the government reported that more Americans lived in towns and cities with 2,500 or more residents than in the countryside. The small-town and rural experience still dominated the lives of most citizens, but the trend toward urban residence was transforming the nation.

More than 10 million Americans lived in cities with a million people or more in 1920; that figure rose to more than 15 million by 1930. Such places as New York, Detroit, and Los Angeles saw large increases in their populations during these years. Some 19 million people left the country for the city over these 10 years. The migration of African Americans from the South to the North continued unabated during this period. The percentage of blacks listed as urban residents rose by nearly 10 percent between 1920 and 1930, compared with a rise of about 5 percent for whites.

Timeline

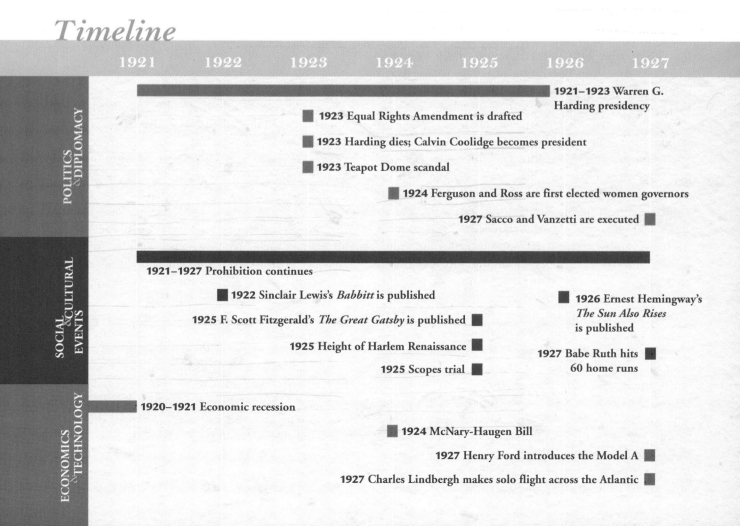

	1921	1922	1923	1924	1925	1926	1927

POLITICS & DIPLOMACY

1921–1923 Warren G. Harding presidency

1923 Equal Rights Amendment is drafted

1923 Harding dies; Calvin Coolidge becomes president

1923 Teapot Dome scandal

1924 Ferguson and Ross are first elected women governors

1927 Sacco and Vanzetti are executed

SOCIAL & CULTURAL EVENTS

1921–1927 Prohibition continues

1922 Sinclair Lewis's *Babbitt* is published

1926 Ernest Hemingway's *The Sun Also Rises* is published

1925 F. Scott Fitzgerald's *The Great Gatsby* is published

1925 Height of Harlem Renaissance

1927 Babe Ruth hits 60 home runs

1925 Scopes trial

ECONOMICS & TECHNOLOGY

1920–1921 Economic recession

1924 McNary-Haugen Bill

1927 Henry Ford introduces the Model A

1927 Charles Lindbergh makes solo flight across the Atlantic

For the young people who flocked to Chicago, New York, and Los Angeles, the city offered a degree of excitement and energy that the sedate farm could not match. Within the concrete canyons and electric avenues, visitors found theaters, dance halls, and vaudeville artists that they could never hope to see in a small town. Many Americans resented the temptations of the city and associated them with foreign influences and assaults on traditional values.

Immigration Restricted

After the war immigration returned to its former pattern. More than 430,000 people sought entry to the United States in 1920, and another 805,000 came in 1921. In response, advocates of immigration restriction renewed their campaign to shut off the flow of entrants from southern and eastern Europe.

Proponents of restriction argued that the immigrants lacked the qualities needed to be successful American citizens. Madison Grant, one of the leading advocates of immigration restriction, said that "these immigrants adopt the language of the [native-born] American, they wear his clothes, they steal his name, and they are beginning to take his women, but they seldom adopt his religion or understand his ideals."

The pressure on Congress grew to block immigration. The American Federation of Labor, which feared the use of aliens as strikebreakers, added its weight to the campaign for immigration restrictions. In 1921, Congress enacted an emergency quota law that limited immigration from Europe to 600,000 people annually. Such countries as Great Britain and Germany were given the highest quotas. Three years later, the lawmakers passed the National Origins Quota Act, which reduced annual legal immigration from Europe to about 150,000 people, gave preference to entrants from northern European countries, and blocked Asian immigrants entirely. The quota of immigrants from each country was determined by the number of residents from these countries counted in the 1890 census.

Despite their racist premises, the new laws did not end immigration during the 1920s. After 1924, the recorded number of immigrants totaled about 300,000 annually until the beginning of the Great Depression. Legal immigrants from Canada and Mexico accounted for much of that total. However, the impact on people who wished to emigrate from southern and eastern Europe was dramatic. For example, 95,000 immigrants had come into the United States from Poland in 1921; for each of the next three years, the annual total of immigrants from that country was only about 28,000.

The longest-running legal case of the 1920s was the controversial murder conviction of Nicola Sacco (right) and Bartolomeo Vanzetti (left). Their appeals of the verdict became a cause that many intellectuals in and out of the United States supported before the two men were executed in 1927.

Since the immigration law did not affect Mexicans, 500,000 newcomers from that country crossed the border during the 1920s and swelled the ranks of Americans of Hispanic ancestry. Mexicans were concentrated in California and Texas.

The Sacco-Vanzetti Case

The widespread tension about immigration played a significant part in the fate of two Italian immigrants whose criminal trial became a major controversy during the decade. In 1920 a murder and robbery took place in South Braintree, Massachusetts. Nicola Sacco and Bartolomeo Vanzetti were arrested for the crime and their trial began in June 1921. Despite allegations that authorities had framed the two men for the crime because of their anarchist beliefs, a jury found them guilty. Numerous appeals for a new trial were made. The case soon became a focus for liberals and intellectuals convinced that **Sacco and Vanzetti** had not received a fair trial because of their foreign origin.

Over the next several years, the attorneys for the convicted defendants filed a series of appeals to overturn the verdict. The lawyers challenged the conduct of the jury, attacked the quality of the evidence against the two men, and questioned the accuracy of the identifications that various witnesses had made. None of this changed the mind of the presiding judge. By October 1924, all motions for a new trial had been denied. The defendants hired a new attorney, and a public campaign for a new trial and their eventual release gained national attention in 1925 and 1926. Within Massachusetts, where animosity against immigrants still raged, the state government did not waver in its belief that Sacco and Vanzetti were guilty.

By 1927, the appeals process had run its course. Despite strong evidence that the two men had not received a fair trial, and substantial indications that they were not guilty, the legal machinery moved them toward the electric chair. The date of the execution was set for July 1927. With a worldwide campaign under way to save Sacco and Vanzetti, pressure intensified on Massachusetts officials to review the case. The governor appointed a special commission to look into the trial. After flawed and biased proceedings, the panel decided to affirm the convictions. Sacco and Vanzetti were executed on August 23. The outcome convinced many radicals of the inherent unfairness of the American legal system. In their minds, more drastic measures would be required to reform American society.

The Ku Klux Klan

The pressures of immigration from abroad and the movement of Americans from the country to the city produced intense social strains. The most sensational and violent of these developments was the reappearance of the Ku Klux Klan. Revitalized after 1915 in the South, the Klan gained followers slowly until the end of World War I. By 1920, the Klan had become a marketing device for clever promoters who used the Klan's brew of racism, anti-Catholicism, and anti-immigrant views to acquire converts. The hooded order spread into northern states as well, with a particularly large presence in Indiana. The Klan claimed that it had 3 million members in the early 1920s. The masks and sheets that members of the order wore provided an anonymity that attracted recruits in the southern countryside and in the cities of the Midwest where formerly rural residents had moved.

A secret ritual added to the mystique of the hooded movement. Members contributed a $10 entrance fee, called a "klecktoken." They read the Kloran and dedicated themselves to "Karacter, Honor, Duty." In time they might rise to become a King Kleagle or a Grand Goblin of the Domain. Members asked each other "Ayak," for "Are you a Klansman?" The proper reply was "Akia," meaning "A Klansman I am."

The Klan's program embraced opposition to Catholics, Jews, blacks, Asians, violators of the Prohibition laws, and anyone else who displeased local Klansmen. In their rallies, marching members carried signs that read "COHABITATION BETWEEN WHITES AND BLACKS MUST STOP." Even more than the Klan of the Reconstruction era, the Klan of the 1920s based its appeal on the desire of many white Americans for a more tranquil and less confusing social order. The Klan's efforts to create such an order initially made it attractive to many citizens who never wore a hood. But the Klan also contained an ugly strain of violence and vigilantism. In many states its members lynched people they disagreed with; tortured blacks, Catholics, and Jews; and made a mockery of law enforcement.

Soon the Klan went into politics. In 1922, its members elected a senator in Texas and became a powerful presence in the legislatures of that state and others in the Southwest. In Indiana, members of the order dominated the police of the state's major cities. The Klan also wielded significant influence in the Rocky Mountain states and the Pacific Northwest.

For the Democrats, the Klan posed a difficult problem. The party was already divided over cultural issues. Southern members favored Prohibition and disliked large cities. In the North, Democrats were ethnically diverse, opposed to Prohibition, and rooted in the new urban lifestyles. The Klan intensified these tensions. Some "dry" Democrats saw the Klan as a legitimate form of political protest. The "wets" in northern cities regarded the Klan as an expression of cultural and regional intolerance.

The Klan's influence peaked around 1923. As the Klan sought greater political power, the two major parties, especially the Democrats, absorbed some of the Klan's appeal and weakened its hold on the public.

The Rise of Black Militance

The resurgence of the Klan came when African Americans were asserting their identity and independence. Black sacrifices during World War I had made blacks impatient and resentful of the indignities of segregation. The recurrence of white-on-black violence, such as the brutal attack on the African American area of Tulsa, Oklahoma, in 1921, underlined the predicament of blacks. A growing spirit of assertiveness and militancy appeared in the art and literature of black intellectuals. A poet named Claude McKay issued his rallying cry in 1922: "If we must die, let it not be like hogs / Hunted and penned in an inglorious spot." Instead, he concluded, "Like men we'll face the murderous, cowardly pack, / Pressed to the wall, dying, but—fighting back."

For the African Americans who crowded into the large northern cities during the Great Migration, the promise of America seemed to be an illusion. They lived in substandard housing, paid higher rents for their apartments than whites did, and could obtain only menial jobs. The Harlem neighborhood of New York City might be "the greatest Negro city in the world," as author James Weldon Johnson called it, but it was also a place where every day blacks saw how white society discriminated against them.

This atmosphere of dissatisfaction greeted **Marcus Garvey,** a young black man who immigrated to the United States in 1916. Garvey preached a doctrine of Pan-Africanism and promised to "organize the 400,000,000 Negroes of the World into a vast organization to plant the banner of freedom in the great continent of Africa." He worked through the Universal Negro Improvement Association (UNIA) to establish societies that were not controlled by imperialist nations. He founded his campaign on international shipping lines and newspapers that would enable blacks to travel to Africa and communicate among themselves. Rallies and conventions in New York and other cities drew up to 25,000 people and raised funds for the UNIA.

Garvey's business ventures failed. The shipping lines collapsed and the investors, mostly African Americans, lost their money. Blacks were divided in their views of the charismatic Garvey. The National Association for the Advancement of Colored People bristled when Garvey attacked its political agenda as too cautious and then met with a Klan leader. His criticisms of labor unions alienated key African American leaders such as A. Phillip Randolph of the Brotherhood of Sleeping Car Porters. Black opponents sent damaging information about Garvey's finances to the Department of Justice and the government indicted him for mail fraud. He was convicted and went to prison in 1925. The important legacy of Garvey and the UNIA was the idea that urban blacks could band together to wield economic and political power.

Dry America: The First Phase

The initial impact of Prohibition on the lives of Americans achieved much of what its proponents had predicted. The national consumption of alcohol declined from about two gallons per capita during the war years annually to around three-fourths of a gallon in 1921 and 1922. Alcohol use rose again during the rest of the decade but remained below pre-war levels. Alcoholism as a medical problem became less prevalent. Many hospitals closed their alcoholism wards because of a lack of patients. Contrary to later legend, Prohibition did affect drinking habits in the United States.

Yet the extent of compliance with Prohibition was spotty. Some people made their own liquor; instructions for doing so were easily obtained. In cities like San Francisco and Boston, centers of "wet" sentiment, the law was never enforced. Several states did not even ratify

The campaign to enforce Prohibition produced some results. Here police pour beer down a sewer.

Library of Congress, Prints and Photographs Division

the Eighteenth Amendment. Others failed to pass state laws to support the federal legislation. Believing that compliance ought to be voluntary, Congress appropriated inadequate funds to the Treasury Department's Prohibition Bureau. There were never enough federal men to cover the nation adequately. Even when agents acted decisively, the rising number of arrests led to huge backlogs in the federal court system.

The upper classes expected the working poor to obey the Prohibition law, but they resisted any change in their own drinking practices. With a ready market for illegal liquor in the major cities, enterprising individuals moved alcohol across the border into the United States. These "rum runners" and "**bootleggers**" brought in shipments of alcohol from Canada and the Caribbean. Their wares were sold at illegal saloons or "speakeasies" where city dwellers congregated in the evenings.

Prohibition did not, however, create organized crime. Nor were the 1920s a decade of rising crime rates. The nation became more aware of crime as a social problem, because of the well-publicized activities of gangsters like **Alphonse "Al" Capone** and Johnny Torrio in Chicago. Prohibition offered individuals already involved in crime another incentive to tap the immense profits to be had from easing the thirst of upper-class Americans. Capone in particular devoted himself to gaining control of gambling, prostitution, and bootlegging in the Chicago area. In New York, other mobsters built up networks of criminal enterprises to provide the same services. These sensational cases undermined faith in the positive effects of Prohibition.

Table 23.1 Estimated Alcohol Consumption in the United States, 1920–1930 (Gallons Per Capita)

Year	Estimated Consumption
1920	n/a
1921	0.54
1922	0.91
1923	1.07
1924	1.05
1925	1.10
1926	1.18
1927	1.12
1928	1.18
1929	1.20
1930	1.06

Source: Derived from table in Joseph R. Gusfield, "Prohibition: The Impact of Political Utopianism," in John Braeman, Robert H. Bremner, and David Brody, eds., *Change and Continuity in Twentieth-Century America: The 1920s* (Columbus, Ohio: Ohio State University Press, 1968), p. 275.

The Klan, immigration restriction, and Prohibition reflected the power of older cultural values.

Harding as President

Because of the scandals associated with his administration, Warren G. Harding is often depicted as the worst president in American history. During his brief term, however, he was very popular. Harding surrounded himself with what he called the "Best Minds," as his selection of Charles Evans Hughes as his secretary of state, banker Andrew Mellon as secretary of the treasury, and Herbert Hoover as secretary of commerce attested. After years in which the presidency had seemed separated from the people, Harding and his wife, Florence, opened up the White House to tourists and greeted visitors from the public with evident pleasure. Throughout the country Harding was a well-regarded president whose speeches appealed to a desire for a calmer, less activist chief executive.

The new administration pressed for a legislative program that combined some constructive reforms with a return to older Republican trade policies. The 1921 Budget and Accounting Act gave the government a more precise sense of how the nation's funds were being spent. It established an executive budget for the president, a General Accounting Office for Congress, and a Bureau of the Budget in the executive branch. The Republicans rebuilt tariff protection in an emergency law of 1921 and then wrote the Fordney-McCumber

Tariff Law a year later. Reflecting the party's suspicion of a powerful national government, Treasury Secretary Mellon pushed for lower income tax rates, particularly for individuals with higher incomes.

The Harding administration stayed aloof from the League of Nations. Since the failure to ratify the Treaty of Versailles left the nation in a technical state of war with Germany, the two countries negotiated a separate peace treaty in 1921. Throughout the 1920s, Washington withheld recognition from the new Soviet Union because of fears that diplomatic relations with the Communist government might spread the bacillus of subversion. American interests turned back toward Latin America. To reduce the nation's military role in the region, the administration withdrew marines from Haiti, the Dominican Republic, and Nicaragua. Trade and investment expanded south of the border.

The Far East claimed a large amount of attention as Japan expanded its power in China. The United States wanted to preserve the Open Door policy and restrain Japanese influence. The White House relied on diplomacy and economic pressure as its main weapons. Both nations were, however, increasing the size of their navies at this time. Congress and the administration called for a conference in which representatives of Great Britain, Japan, and the United States would meet to discuss naval issues and peace in the Far East. The United States and Great Britain arranged for such a meeting in Washington in November 1921.

The Washington Naval Conference began with a dramatic proposal by Secretary of State Hughes to scrap outright 60 battleships of all nations. Limits should also be placed on the number of battleships and aircraft carriers that Japan, the United States, and Britain could build. Out of the conference came the Five Power Treaty, which provided a fixed ratio for warship construction. For every five ships the United States built, the British could also build five, and the Japanese could build three. The Japanese were not happy with the 5-5-3 arrangement, but in return they secured an American pledge not to construct defenses in such U.S. possessions as Guam and the Philippines. For the time, the naval arms race in the Pacific slowed. Though the long-range effects of the Conference were modest, the episode fueled Japanese-American tensions and contributed to the grievances that Tokyo felt regarding how the Western nations treated the rising Oriental power.

The Washington Conference also resulted in two other pacts—the Four Power Treaty and the Nine Power Treaty. The Four Power Treaty ended a long-standing (since 1902) alliance between Great Britain and France, and committed the United States, France, Great Britain, and Japan to respect each country's territorial possessions.

In the Nine Power Treaty, the various nations agreed to avoid interference with China's internal affairs. The Washington Conference ended without the United States having to make commitments that entailed the risk of force or greater international involvement. In diplomacy as in domestic policy, the Harding administration seemed attuned to the desires of the country for a pause·after the turbulence of Theodore Roosevelt and Woodrow Wilson.

The New Economy

The continuing postwar recession dogged the first two years of the Harding administration. Hard times contributed to substantial Republican losses in the 1922 congressional elections. The Democrats gained 74 seats in the House and 6 in the Senate. Yet the long-range news proved beneficial for Republicans. The economy slowly picked up in 1922 and 1923, productive output returned to its 1918 levels, and employment rose. As wages climbed, discontent ebbed, and the Republicans looked forward to the 1924 presidential election with greater optimism.

The improvement in the economy's performance during 1922 began a period of unprecedented prosperity. The gross national product soared almost 40 percent, increasing from nearly $76 billion in 1922 to $97.3 billion in 1927. The per capita income of Americans went up about 30 percent during the same period. Real earnings for wage workers rose more than 20 percent, whereas hours worked declined slightly. The unemployment rate fell from 12 percent of the labor force in 1922 to 4 percent in 1927.

The Car Culture

The number of cars registered in 1920 totaled 8.25 million, while the number of trucks was 1.1 million. By 1927, there were more than 20 million cars on the roads along with more than 3 million trucks and buses. Automobiles needed oil and gasoline to operate, steel for their frames, rubber for their tires, glass for windshields, and service businesses for dealers and drivers. For the traveler on the road, motels offered accommodations, billboards advertised attractions, and roadside restaurants provided food and diversion. The Federal Highways Act of 1921 left road construction to the states, but set national standards for concrete road surfaces and access to roads. The size of the road network grew from 7,000 miles at the end of the war to 50,000 miles in 1927. Gasoline taxes brought in revenues for the states, enabling them to build more roads, which, in

Table 23.2 Automobile Registrations, 1921–1929

Year	Registrations
1921	9,212,158
1922	10,704,076
1923	13,253,019
1924	15,436,102
1925	17,481,001
1926	19,267,967
1927	20,193,333
1928	21,362,240
1929	23,120,897

Source: *The Statistical History of the United States,* New York: Fairfield Press, 1965, p. 462.

turn, fostered the development of suburbs distant from the old city centers. The economic effects of the automobile stimulated many sectors of the economy.

No longer did young women and men have to carry on courtship within sight of parents and chaperones. When fathers urged their daughters not to go out driving with boys, the young women replied: "What on earth do you want me to do? Just sit around all evening?" Cars consumed a large chunk of the working family's income as Americans readily took to the practice of buying their cars on the installment plan.

For many African Americans in the South, owning a car gave them at least some mobility and escape from a segregated life. The enclosed car, initially a prestigious model, soon became standard on the road; by 1927, 83 percent of cars were of this type.

As the decade began, Henry Ford was still the most famous carmaker in the nation. His showplace was the huge factory on the Rouge River near Detroit. Sprawling across 2,000 acres, the Rouge plant employed 75,000 workers to turn out the reliable, familiar Model T car. In 1921, Ford made more than half of the automobiles produced in the United States, turning out a new vehicle every 10 seconds. A car cost less than $300.

The Model T was a popular car but not a very attractive one. The joke was that you could get a Model T in any color, so long as it was black. Ford's failure to develop different car models opened a competitive opportunity to General Motors (GM). Although GM had been in severe financial difficulty in 1920, the DuPont family acquired the firm. They brought in Alfred P. Sloan, Jr., as chief assistant to the president. In 1923, he became president. Sloan set up a system of independent operating divisions that produced models of Chevrolets, Buicks, and other vehicles annually. GM introduced self-starters, fuel gauges, reliable headlights, and other features that consumers liked. The constant flow of new

Automobile Manufacturers competed for car buyers with advertising that stressed the mobility and freedom that these vehicles provided to Americans in the 1920s.

models induced customers to want a fresh vehicle every few years. The General Motors Acceptance Corporation made it easy to acquire a car on the installment plan.

By the middle of the 1920s, Ford's sales fell as those of General Motors rose. Ford dealers switched to General Motors while the used-car market undercut Ford at the other end of the price scale. Henry Ford had revolutionized American transportation before 1920. Now he was losing out because of his resistance to marketing and manufacturing innovation.

During the spring of 1927, Henry Ford ended production of the Model T and turned to the development of a new car. Within months the Model A was ready for consumers. Interest in the product was high; orders for hundreds of thousands were taken before the new model was introduced. Even though it would be months before Ford could meet the customer demand for the automobile, on December 1, 1927, the company unveiled the Model A. Like General Motors, Ford marketed the Model A through a huge advertising campaign. It also created a credit corporation, again modeled on what General Motors had done, to enable buyers to obtain cars on credit. The combined efforts of Ford and Sloan gave the automobile business in the 1920s the structure and style that would dominate until the start of World War II.

Electrical America

Electricity played a comparable part in stimulating the economy during the 1920s. By 1928, electricity drove 70 percent of factory equipment. Two-thirds of the families in towns and cities had electricity in their homes as well, stimulating demand for the electrical appliances that industry was turning out in abundance. Homemakers bought some 15 million electric irons and another 7 million vacuum cleaners. Advertisers appealed to women

with descriptions of the all-electric kitchen "Where Work is Easy!" Sales of consumer appliances were one of the major economic stimulants of the decade. The electric power industry expanded rapidly, as did the firms that made equipment for the power plants.

The diffusion of electricity facilitated the growth of radio. The first station, KDKA in Pittsburgh, went on the air in 1920. There were only four in 1922; a year later, 566 were in operation. In 1923, a New York station, WBAY, began selling time to anyone who would pay for it. Commercial radio caught on quickly. Soon announcers and performers became popular attractions. Listeners wrote to them for advice about love affairs and to praise the human contact that radios provided. In 1923, there were radios in 400,000 households.

Three years later, the Radio Corporation of America (RCA), led by its president David Sarnoff, established the first national network of stations, the National

The spread of mass entertainment through radio made the 1920s the first decade when Americans could experience simultaneously the same programs and stars. Radios became elaborate products as this expensive model, complete with "radiotrons" for $495, reveals.

Broadcasting Company (NBC). Telephone wires carried the broadcast signals to stations scattered across the country. NBC consisted of two networks, the "red" and the "blue." Programming was diverse, and commercial sponsors oversaw the content of such programs as *The Maxwell House Hour* and the *Ipana Troubadours*. Radio was another element in the creation of a mass culture during the decade.

Movies in the Silent Era

Each week, 100 million people went to see movies at one of the 20,000 theaters that showed silent pictures. Some movie houses were plain and functional. Others featured expensive lobbies and plush furniture. Ticket prices were relatively low and stable, usually about 50 cents. As one college student recalled, "You learn plenty about love from the movies." Pictures shaped how young people kissed on dates, what they wore, and what they said. "I cling to my dream world woven about the movies I have seen," said another student.

From their uncertain beginnings at the turn of the century, motion picture studios had developed into large enterprises employing hundreds of people. Studio heads like Adolph Zukor of Paramount Pictures and Louis B. Mayer of Metro-Goldwyn-Mayer (MGM) controlled chains of theaters, to which they allocated the pictures they made on a rigidly controlled basis. To get a popular feature film, theater owners would have to accept the entire yearly production lineup of a major studio.

Motion picture stars were the bedrock of the business. Charlie Chaplin's popularity rose to even greater heights during the early 1920s in such films as *The Gold Rush* (1925). Other box-office attractions included Rudolph Valentino, whose sudden death in 1926 brought thousands of weeping fans, in a line stretching for eight city blocks, to his New York funeral.

To maintain its hold on the popular mind, Hollywood reacted quickly when sex scandals tarnished the industry's image early in the 1920s. The studios recruited Will H. Hays, a prominent Republican, to serve as president of the Motion Pictures Producers and Distributors Association in 1922. Hays tried to persuade moviemakers to inject more moral content into films. Skillful directors such as Cecil B. DeMille circumvented these mild warnings. He argued that the sex scenes in *The Ten Commandments* were based on biblical descriptions.

Later in the decade evidence accumulated that silent films were boring audiences. Filmmakers believed that talking motion pictures were the logical next step. Fearful that they might lose their hold on the public, the major studios agreed that none of them would make talking pictures unless they all did. One of the smaller

John W. Considine, Jr. presents

RUDOLPH VALENTINO

IN

'The Son of the Sheik'

a Sequel to The Sheik'

with **VILMA BANKY**

from the novel by E. M. HULL Adapted to the Screen by FRANCES MARION

A **GEORGE FITZMAURICE** PRODUCTION

· UNITED ARTISTS PICTURE ·

Exotic themes and portraying a sexy hero such as the hero in *The Son of the Sheik* made Rudolph Valentino a box office superstar before his untimely death.

studios, Warner Brothers, was working on a sound picture called **The Jazz Singer.** Its star was Al Jolson, who specialized in rendering popular tunes in blackface. This evocation of a racist past appealed to his listeners nostalgic for a time when white supremacy had been even more dominant than it was in the 1920s. When he ad-libbed his catch phrase, "You Ain't Heard Nothing Yet!" and sang several songs, audiences exploded with applause. Within two years, silent pictures gave way to sound, and Hollywood entered the golden era of the studio system.

Advertising America

Advertisers developed new and effective ways to persuade Americans to acquire the products coming out of the nation's factories and workshops. The advertising business boomed. Before World War I, the total amount spent on advertising stood at about $400 million annually. It soared to $2.6 billion by 1929. Radios brought advertising into the home; billboards attracted the attention of millions of motorists. Advertising, said one of its

WARNER BROS.
Supreme Triumph

AL JOLSON
in
The JAZZ SINGER

Al Jolson in *The Jazz Singer* brought sound to the movies in 1927 and opened a whole new phase of popularity for the cinema. Soon silent pictures had become obsolete as audiences flocked to the new talking movies.

practitioners, "literally creates demand for the things of life that raise the standard of living, elevate the taste, changing luxuries into necessities."

Among the products that advertising promoted was Listerine, which was said to eliminate halitosis, the medical term for bad breath. Other consumers were urged to ingest yeast at least twice a day to fight constipation and skin problems. The ingenious advertising executive Albert Lasker induced Americans to drink orange juice daily at breakfast, broke the taboo against advertising the sanitary napkin Kotex, and described Kleenex as "the handkerchief you can throw away." He also claimed Pepsodent toothpaste would remove "film" from the fortunate user's teeth.

The most celebrated advertising man of the decade was Bruce Barton, who wrote a biography of Jesus Christ in order to demonstrate that advertising went back to biblical times. In *The Man Nobody Knows* (1925), Barton retold the New Testament in terms that Americans of the 1920s could easily grasp. Jesus, wrote Barton, "recognized the basic principle that all good advertising is news." The 12 disciples were a model of an efficient business organization, and Jesus himself was a master salesman. "He was never trite or commonplace; he had no routine." Barton's book became a national

DOING HISTORY ONLINE

Automobile Advertising, 1923
According to the ads in this module, what are some of the ways in which the automobile reshaped Americans' lives?

History ⧖ Now™   Visit HistoryNOW to access primary sources and exercises related to this topic: http://now.ilrn.com/ayers_etal3

best-seller. As long as the economy expanded, advertising prospered and fed the demand of consumers for products they had never known they needed.

Those Left Behind

Not all segments of society shared equally in the return of good times. The postwar depression hit the farm sector with devastating force. Farmers had never benefited from the upturn that marked the cities. For labor also, this was a time of retreat.

Despite the shift toward city living, the United States still relied on farming as a key element in the economy. The 7 million families who lived on farms in 1920 did not generally enjoy the modern conveniences and appliances that had appeared in the cities. In some areas farm life resembled that of the pioneers more than it did the city dwellers. Overproduction of crops drove down prices and led to massive harvests that could not be marketed. In the South, for example, the price of cotton was 40 cents a pound in 1920 but slid to 10 cents a pound in 1921. Wheat stood at $1.82 per bushel in 1920, sagged to $0.926 in 1924, and then recovered to $1.437 in 1925. The postwar recovery of agriculture in Europe meant that overseas markets were smaller as well. The per capita income of most farmers did not rise substantially after 1919, and there was a widening gap between what farmers earned and what city dwellers made.

To improve their lot, farmers sought higher tariff duties on imported products. They also revived the idea of farm cooperatives to market more effectively. Federal legislation to regulate the trading of grain futures and extend more credit to farmers was marginally helpful, but the underlying problem of overproduction continued.

In 1921, a plow manufacturer named George Peek proposed that American farmers ship surplus products overseas and dump them on the world market at whatever price they could obtain. The government would buy farm products at the market price and then sell them abroad. Taxes on the processing of crops would

The Changing Face of Agriculture

American farmers in the 1920s struggled with the problems of abundance. The introduction of mechanized tractors and tillers, like the one depicted here from North Dakota, made it possible for farmers to increase their production far beyond what had been done with horse-drawn equipment. The family watching the new machine from their horse and buggy symbolizes the transition that farmers were experiencing.

As farmers brought their cash crops in through the use of this kind of machinery, they found that success in growing wheat and other staple crops only intensified their economic dilemmas. The price of wheat, for example, plunged during the first half of the decade as a result of national and international overproduction. Small farmers learned that they could not survive in a market that favored larger enterprises with the capital to purchase modern equipment like this plow.

© CORBIS

cover the cost to the government and the taxpayer. The chairs of the House and Senate Agriculture Committees introduced a bill to enact such a program in January 1924. Known as the McNary-Haugen Plan, it gained much support in the Midwest and soon commanded national attention. Critics called it price-fixing at government expense.

Labor in Retreat

After World War I, the Red Scare of 1919–1920 stalled labor's drive to organize coal mining, steel, and other industries that employed thousands of unskilled workers. In the minds of middle-class Americans, labor unions seemed identified with attacks on society itself. The number of unionized laborers dropped from nearly

5 million in 1921 to fewer than 3.5 million 8 years later. The American Federation of Labor (AFL), under its president William Green, presented only weak challenges to employers. It accepted what management called "business unionism," or the nonunion "open shop," which was labeled the "American Plan." Efforts to organize unskilled workers were abandoned.

Government and business threw up numerous obstacles to labor's interests. The U.S. Supreme Court struck down minimum wages for women in Washington, D.C. In the case of *Adkins v. Children's Hospital* the Supreme Court ruled that the law infringed on the right of workers to sell their labor for whatever they could obtain. This "liberty-of-contract" doctrine accordingly barred Congress from passing such a law. In addition to an unsympathetic Supreme Court, unions faced opposition from the White House. When strikes occurred in railroading during 1922, the Harding administration obtained harsh court orders that effectively ended the walkouts.

Businesses used less repressive tactics as well. Some of the bigger and more enlightened firms provided what became known as welfare capitalism. General Electric, International Harvester, and Bethlehem Steel represented companies that sought to appease workers with recreational facilities, benefit plans, and sometimes even profit-sharing opportunities. Estimates indicated that as many as 4 million workers received such rewards. After the middle of the decade, however, these programs stalled as the lack of labor militancy removed the incentive to make concessions to workers. Most workers remained dependent on the goodwill of their employer for whatever job security they possessed. They could not look to the federal government for any positive assistance.

Coolidge cultivated a dour New England demeanor to set himself apart from the excesses of the Harding years. His grim expression hides the playful spirit that liked to inflict practical jokes on his White House staff.

The Harding Scandals

By early 1923, Harding's presidency was mired in rumors of scandal. Attorney General Harry Daugherty was a political ally of the president, but his loose direction of the Justice Department allowed corruption to flourish. Scandals also festered in the Veterans Bureau and the Office of the Alien Property Custodian.

The most serious wrongdoing involved the secretary of the interior, **Albert B. Fall.** Federal oil reserves at Elk Hills, California, and Teapot Dome, Wyoming (where the rocks vaguely resembled a teapot), were leased to private oil companies. Fall received $400,000 in loans from friends in the industry in what many interpreted as payoffs for his leasing decisions. The Teapot Dome scandal emerged after Harding died, but it established his administration's reputation as one of the most corrupt in American history.

A weak president and a poor judge of people, Harding allowed cronies and crooks to infest his administration. By 1923, he knew about the ethical problems in the Veterans Bureau, and he suspected that scandals lurked in the Department of the Interior and the Justice Department. During a tour of the Pacific Northwest in July 1923, the president fell ill. He died in San Francisco on August 2 of heart disease.

Keep Cool with Coolidge

Harding's successor was Calvin Coolidge, the former governor of Massachusetts. Coolidge came to be viewed in Washington as a stereotypical New Englander, a man of few words. In fact, Coolidge was quite talkative in the regular press conferences that he held twice a week. Although he slept 12 hours a day, Coolidge worked hard greeting visitors and addressing the needs of those who told him their problems with the federal government. His wife, Grace, brought glamour and a sense of fun to the White House, offsetting her husband's dour personality.

Coolidge was much more committed to the conservative principles of the Republicans than Harding had been. He proclaimed that "the business of America is business," and he endorsed policies designed to promote corporate enterprise. He extended the tax-cutting policies of Treasury Secretary Mellon. The president also appointed pro-business individuals to head the regulatory agencies and departments that the progressives had established a generation earlier. Meanwhile, he removed the Harding holdovers, such as Harry Daugherty, who might prove politically embarrassing when Coolidge ran for the presidency in 1924.

Coolidge lost little time in gaining control of the Republican party. The president used modern public relations techniques to bolster his image as an embodiment of old-time virtues of morality and frugality. Movie stars came to the White House to endorse the president and, under the leadership of the stylish Grace Coolidge, sing the campaign theme song: "Keep Cool with Coolidge."

The Discordant Democrats

The Democrats hoped that the Teapot Dome scandal and other revelations of wrongdoing in the Harding years would be their ticket back to the White House. When the Teapot Dome scandal could not be linked to anyone in the White House, the issue faded away. Prohibition had split the Democrats between the dry faithful of the South and West, who wanted strict enforcement of the Volstead Act, and the wet residents of the large cities of the North and Midwest, who saw Prohibition as a foolish experiment. The two leading candidates for the Democratic party nomination reflected this regional tension. William G. McAdoo represented the progressive, prohibitionist wing. Governor Alfred E. Smith of New York was a Roman Catholic who opposed Prohibition. The Democratic National Convention left the party with almost no chance of defeating President Coolidge. McAdoo and Smith deadlocked through dozens of ballots. Finally, after 103 ballots, the exhausted delegates compromised and chose a former member of Congress and Wall Street lawyer named John W. Davis.

Senator Robert M. La Follette of Wisconsin, who had been seeking the presidency for many years, became the champion of what remained of the progressive spirit and the anger of the Midwestern farmers. Although he was nominated for president at a convention of the Progressive party, he did not attend the meeting or identify himself with the party. The American Federation of Labor and the railroad unions backed La Follette but with little money or enthusiasm.

The Republicans ignored Davis and concentrated on the alleged radicalism of La Follette and his supporters. The choice, they said, was "Coolidge or Chaos." Coolidge polled more than 15,718,000 votes, more than the combined total of his two rivals. The Republicans retained firm control of both houses of Congress. Yet beneath the surface, electoral trends were moving toward the Democrats. In the northern cities the party's share of the vote grew during the 1920s. If a candidate appeared who could unite the traditionally Democratic South with the ethnic voters of the Northeast, Republican supremacy might be in jeopardy. For the moment, however, Americans seemed less interested in politics than in the art, literature, and music of this turbulent and exciting decade.

A Blossoming in Art and Literature

While politics followed a conservative path during the 1920s, the nation's cultural life experienced a productivity and artistic success that would be unrivaled during the rest of the twentieth century. In music, drama, and

Marcus Garvey led a Back to Africa movement that gained many adherents among African Americans during the 1920s.

literature, the decade brought forth a rare assembly of first-rate talents.

The Harlem Renaissance

In the wake of the Great Migration, African American intellectual life centered in New York City. There, authors and poets lived in the black section known as Harlem. The "Harlem Renaissance" owed much to W. E. B. Du Bois's encouragement of African American writing in *The Crisis,* the journal of the National Association for the Advancement of Colored People (NAACP). In the New York of the early 1920s, the ferment associated with Marcus Garvey, the exciting nightlife, the relative absence of racial bigotry, and the interest of wealthy white patrons enabled a few black writers to pursue literary careers. Their moment of celebrity proved brief, but their impact was significant.

The Harlem Renaissance reached its peak in 1925, when a national magazine ran an article on "Harlem: Mecca of the New Negro." In the same year, **Alain Locke**'s book *The New Negro* was published. Locke argued that African Americans' "more immediate hope" depended on the ability of blacks and whites to evaluate "the Negro in terms of his artistic endowments and cultural contributions, past and prospective." Other major figures in the Renaissance were the poets Langston Hughes

("The Weary Blues"), Countee Cullen ("Do I Marvel"), **Zora Neale Hurston** (the play *Color Struck*), Claude McKay (*Harlem Shadows*), as well as the memoirist and songwriter James Weldon Johnson (*God's Trombones*). Although these writers' artistic merit was undeniable, the Harlem Renaissance did little to alter the segregationist laws and customs that restricted the lives of most African Americans.

The Harlem Renaissance gave an opportunity for numerous black writers and poets to gain a larger audience than would have been possible even 10 years earlier. One of them was the story writer and novelist Zora Neale Hurston, who wrote about the African American masses.

The Sound of Jazz

After World War I, the improvised music that came to be called jazz brought together black musicians and a few white players in Kansas City, Chicago, and New York. At the rent parties where Harlem residents raised money to pay their landlords, in the nightclubs controlled by organized crime, and in the after-hours jam sessions, jazz became a unique American art form.

The major innovators of jazz included trumpeter **Louis Armstrong** and tenor sax player Coleman Hawkins, who took the new music beyond its roots in New Orleans toward a more sophisticated style. Blues artists such as Bessie Smith and Ma Rainey sold "race records" to black and white audiences. Edward Kennedy "Duke" Ellington and Fletcher Henderson led larger orchestras that showed what jazz could accomplish in a more structured setting. The rhythms and sounds of jazz gave the 1920s its enduring title: the Jazz Age.

Writers looked at the postwar world in a critical spirit that grew out of the European ideas and a skepticism about older values. The most popular novelist of the early 1920s was Sinclair Lewis, whose books *Main Street* (1920) and *Babbitt* (1922) examined with unsparing honesty small-town life in the Midwest. His novels *Arrowsmith* (1925) and *Elmer Gantry* (1927) enhanced his reputation, but his artistic powers failed in the 1930s.

Young people devoured the work of the acidic essayist and social critic Henry L. Mencken, who wrote for the

The Cotton Club in Harlem was the nightly center of the social scene of the Harlem Renaissance. The Cotton Club orchestra in 1925 entertained the white patrons who came up from Manhattan to sample the excitement of black music and culture.

F. Scott Fitzgerald and the Jazz Age

This picture of F. Scott Fitzgerald, his wife Zelda, and their daughter in a smart roadster in the 1920s provides an image of domestic harmony that was at odds with the author's real, troubled life. Anxious for the artistic success and acclaim that came with such novels as *The Great Gatsby,* Fitzgerald worked hard at his writing but also drank and partied with equal intensity. He and his wife became celebrities whose lives were the subject of the popular press. Even this picture, posed for the news cameras, was designed to feed the public appetite for personal details of the famous.

The facade soon crumbled. Zelda Fitzgerald succumbed to mental illness, in part because of tensions with her husband over her desire to write fiction too. With the end of the 1920s and the Jazz Age, Scott Fitzgerald's own career hit rough spots and he died in 1940, his fame almost forgotten. In the decades since, his reputation as a keen interpreter of the 1920s has rebounded to the point that his fame is more widespread than when this picture was taken.

© Bettmann/CORBIS

American Mercury. Mencken was a Baltimore newspaperman who had little time for the sacred cows of middle-class culture or, as he called them, the "booboisie." He characterized democracy as "the worship of jackals by jackasses" and said that puritanism was "the haunting fear that somebody, somewhere may be happy." Aimed more at the middle-class audience was *Time,* started in March 1923 by Briton Hadden and Henry Luce. *Time* sought to present the week's news in readable and sprightly prose.

The most influential fiction author of the decade was Ernest Hemingway, whose terse, understated prose spoke of the pain and disillusion that men had suffered during the fighting in World War I. In *The Sun Also Rises* (1925) and *A Farewell to Arms* (1929), Hemingway expressed the anguish of young Americans who had lost faith in the moral customs of their parents.

Another serious novelist of the day was **F. Scott Fitzgerald.** Like Hemingway, he, along with his wife, Zelda, captured attention as the embodiment of the free spirit of the Jazz Age. At the same time, Fitzgerald was a dedicated artist who sought to write a great novel that would ensure his fame. In *The Great Gatsby* (1925), he

came as close to that goal as any author of the time. The book chronicled how the young man Jay Gatsby sought to recapture a lost love among the aristocracy of the Long Island shore. In Gatsby's failure to win his dream, Fitzgerald, like other authors of the Jazz Age, saw the inability of Americans to escape the burdens of their own pasts.

An Age of Artistic Achievement

The list of important authors during the 1920s was long and distinguished. It included such artistic innovators as T. S. Eliot, who lived in Great Britain and whose poems such as "The Waste Land" (1922) influenced a generation of poets on both sides of the Atlantic. Novelists such as John Dos Passos, Sherwood Anderson, Edith Wharton, Willa Cather, and William Faulkner produced a body of work that delved into the lives of aristocratic women (Wharton), prairie pioneers (Cather), the working poor and middle class (Dos Passos), the residents of small towns (Anderson), and the Deep South (Faulkner).

The theater witnessed the emergence of the Broadway musical in the work of Richard Rodgers and Lorenz Hart

(*Garrick Gaieties*), George and Ira Gershwin (*Lady, Be Good*), Jerome Kern and Oscar Hammerstein II (*Showboat*), and Cole Porter (*Paris*). The great age of the American popular song, inspired by the musicals, began in the 1920s and lasted for three decades. Serious drama drew upon the talents of the brooding and pessimistic Eugene O'Neill as well as Elmer Rice and Maxwell Anderson.

In architecture, although the innovative work of Frank Lloyd Wright had given him a reputation for artistic daring before 1920, commercial success eluded him. American architects designed planned, suburban communities modeled on historical models from England or the Southwest. Skyscrapers and city centers such as Rockefeller Center in New York City embodied a building style that emphasized light and air. Amid the prosperity and optimism of the 1920s, it seemed that the possibilities for a lively and vibrant culture were limitless.

© The Granger Collection, New York

The Scopes trial over the teaching of evolution resulted in a notorious legal confrontation between Clarence Darrow (left) and William Jennings Bryan. Many observers saw their duel as a symbol of the urban–rural tensions roiling the nation during the 1920s.

Fundamentalism and Traditional Values

For most Americans, the literary and artistic ferment of the 1920s was part of a broader set of challenges to the older lifestyles with which they had grown up. Residents of small towns and newcomers to the growing cities sought to find reassurance in the older ways that they fondly remembered. The currents of religious and social conservatism remained dominant.

The Fundamentalist Movement

Amid the social ferment that accompanied the rise of the Ku Klux Klan, the tensions over nativism, and the reaction against modern ideas, American Protestantism engaged in a passionate debate over the proper position of Christians toward science, the doctrine of evolution, and liberal ideas. Conservative church leaders in northern Baptist and Presbyterian pulpits spoke of the dangers to faith from a society that had moved away from the Bible and its teachings. In 1920, a minister called the movement "Fundamentalism" because it sought to reaffirm precepts of the Christian creed such as the literal truth of the Bible and the central place of Jesus Christ in saving humanity.

Fundamentalism had a political and social agenda as well as a religious message. On the local and state levels, believers sought to eradicate traces of modern ideas that contradicted biblical teachings. The doctrine of evolution became a special target of fundamentalist wrath. William Jennings Bryan emerged as a leading champion of the crusade. "It is better to trust the Rock of Ages," he said, "than to know the age of rocks." In a dozen state legislatures, lawmakers introduced bills to ban the teaching of evolution in public schools. The Anti-Evolution League hoped to amend the Constitution to bar the teaching of evolution anywhere in the nation. In 1924, Tennessee passed a law that prohibited the spending of public money "to teach any theory that denies the story of the Divine Creation of man as taught in the Bible."

The Scopes Trial

In 1925, a schoolteacher named John T. Scopes taught evolution in Dayton, Tennessee. The local authorities indicted Scopes, and his case came to trial. William Jennings Bryan agreed to help prosecute Scopes, and the American Civil Liberties Union brought in the noted trial lawyer Clarence Darrow for the defense. The proceedings attracted national attention and the trial became a media circus. The judge refused to let Darrow call in scientists to defend evolution.

DOING HISTORY ONLINE

...And Its Discontents

Who or what groups are represented in the second module? What do some of them have in common?

History ⧗ Now™   Visit HistoryNOW to access primary sources and exercises related to this topic: http://now.ilrn.com/ayers_etal3e

Enduring Issues Popular Culture

During the 1920s, the United States witnessed the emergence of the mass media, big-time sports, and the entertainment culture as important trends in the shaping of the national character. The momentum that these developments achieved in this decade continued throughout the remainder of the century to shape American life in distinctive ways. Entertainment values and the demands of celebrity spilled over into government, politics, and the economy. While there were positive features to this trend, the overall impact of the emphasis on show business and its customs raised worrisome questions as well.

The appearance of mass entertainment did not just happen in the decade of the 1920s. For years before the First World War, popular culture had influenced society with songs, shows, and national heroes. The motion picture came into existence at the turn of the twentieth century, and within a decade and a half the star system had evolved. As motion picture production moved to the temperate climate of the West Coast, the beginnings of the major studios could also be discerned. Americans flocked to silent movies, vaudeville, and musical acts during the Progressive Era. Meanwhile, radio was developed and the technological possibilities of that medium were being explored.

After 1920, however, with the rise of commercial radio and the ascendancy of Hollywood studios, mass entertainment became big business. With money to spend in the new consumer society, Americans wanted to hear their favorite radio programs at home and also to go out to the picture show each week. As they did

so, they began to absorb the cultural lessons that the movies and radio taught about gratification, personal satisfaction, and the need for stimulation to make life more fulfilling. Popular art produced some lasting achievements in literature, song, theater, and film, but there were also signs that wider audiences could be reached when producers aimed at the lowest common denominator of taste and appetite.

The Depression of the 1930s slowed these trends to a degree, though in the midst of hard time Americans continued to pursue diversion amid their economic despair. With the onset of World War II and the prosperity that followed victory in 1945, popular culture became more pervasive and influential. The rise of television in the postwar world revealed that a new medium, even more powerful than radio had been, could reshape politics, social mores, and personal decisions. The rise of rock and roll in the 1950s ate away at the older musical and entertainment traditions brought over from vaudeville and the stage. Record producers, movie executives, and burgeoning stars found that simpler entertainment, presented with flair and excitement, could lead to revenues that surpassed all previous results. From long-playing records to video discs, the march of new technologies to package popular culture was inexorable. In the last four decades of the century, the entertainment ethos, driven by the principles of consumption and gratification, dominated the way Americans saw the world. And in many respects that culture permeated the rest of the globe as well.

Darrow summoned Bryan as an expert witness on the Bible. The two men sparred for several days. Bryan defended the literal interpretation of the Bible, but to the reporters covering the trial he seemed to wither under Darrow's cross-examination. Sophisticated Americans regarded Bryan as a joke, but in rural America he remained a hero. The jury found Scopes guilty and assessed him a small fine. Bryan died shortly after the trial. Even though Scopes lost, to many Americans the **Scopes trial** signaled the end of fundamentalism; the political side of the movement did lose momentum during the late 1920s. But during the same period fundamentalism returned to its roots. It concentrated on creating a network of churches, schools, and colleges where its doctrines could be taught to future generations. The forces underlying fundamentalism during the 1920s would remain a potent element in American culture.

Prohibition in Retreat

By the middle of the 1920s, the Prohibition experiment was faltering. Enforcement and compliance waned. The spread of bootlegging and its ties with organized crime meant that state and federal authorities faced an ever-growing challenge in attempting to stop movement of illegal liquor across the Canadian border or from ships that gathered near major U.S. ports. The brewing and liquor interests called for a campaign to repeal the Eighteenth Amendment, and the Association Against the Prohibition Amendment became a strong lobbying force.

Consumption of alcohol rose to more than one gallon annually per capita by 1923 and reached almost one and one-quarter gallons three years later. With the national law on the books, the Anti-Saloon League lost some of its intensity during the 1920s. When the problems

By the start of the twenty-first century, however, the cost of these developments was also becoming more visible. In politics, the reliance on techniques of celebrity and show business to market candidates was a prerequisite for electoral success, especially in presidential elections. The substance of policy, dry, detailed, and complex, could not be conveyed in a sound bite. Soon politicians and their consultants stopped even trying to do so. The press and the media, co-participants within this culture, adopted the concepts of entertainment as well and evaluated candidates as stars rather than as purveyors of ideas. In the world of "spin," what mattered was how a president or a challenger looked and behaved, not what they did in office. When faced with a crisis, the answer was not to address the causes of the problem, but to figure out a political strategy that could be marketed to change the subject.

The prevalence of entertainment values also influenced the way the mass media covered the news. Audience ratings and the sensational stories that attracted viewers drove coverage of events. The plight of a missing young white woman had much more allure for programmers than did issues of social change, the status of minorities, and the complexity of international affairs. The rise of cable television in the 1980s accelerated such trends as broadcasters competed for slivers of the national audience. The truism that television was a barrel with no bottom to it seemed ever more accurate in light of the medium's pursuit of the lurid and the tawdry.

In the world of entertainment, all dilemmas and all intractable issues can be wrapped up before the closing credits run. The real world is less amenable to comforting story arcs and happy endings. Reality would often break in, as happened with the Iraq War after 2003 or Hurricane Katrina in 2005, but the impulse for the media was usually to return to the reassuring and diverting programming that had dominated before the crisis erupted. Pleasing images usually trumped the need to examine pressing problems.

Rich in emotion and diversity, American popular culture since the 1920s has entertained and delighted millions. In its place, it plays an indispensable role in society as part of a common heritage. The problem by the first years of the twenty-first century was that the pervasiveness of entertainment attitudes in other areas of American life worked to move the nation toward a reliance on trivia and away from a confrontation with serious issues. Whether the United States could afford to be the best diverted and entertained society in the history of the world was an unanswered question as the nation dealt with problems of terrorism, environmental pollution, and the effects of global climate change.

Questions for Reflection

1. Is it true to say that celebrity and stardom have become essential components in how Americans define themselves and their place in the world?

2. How useful will popular culture be in helping Americans meet the challenges of the twenty-first century?

associated with drinking declined, its urgency as a social issue receded. The consensus that had brought Prohibition into existence during World War I was crumbling as the 1928 presidential election approached. As yet, however, a majority of Americans opposed outright repeal of Prohibition.

The Youth Culture and Big-Time Sports

During the 1920s, changes in the family gave youth more importance. Women stopped having children at a younger age, and they thus had more time to devote to their own interests. Divorce gained favor as a way of ending unhappy marriages; in 1924, one marriage in seven ended in divorce, a large increase since the turn of the century. The emphasis shifted to making marriages more fulfilling for both partners. Marriage counseling gained in popularity, as did manuals telling men and women how to achieve greater sexual gratification.

As the nature of marriage changed, the role of children in the household was also transformed. Parents were no longer regarded as the unquestioned rulers of the home. One major influence on how American children were raised was the work of the behavioral psychologist John B. Watson. He taught that by manipulating the stimuli that a child experienced, the parents could create the kind of adult they wanted. Children, he said, "are made, not born." He instructed parents to follow a system of reward and punishment to shape the character of their offspring.

The ability of parents to decide what their children should read and think came under attack from the growing pervasiveness of the consumer culture. Young people were bombarded with alluring images of automobiles,

DOING HISTORY

Bryan versus Darrow: The Scopes Trial

THE CULTURAL CLASHES of the 1920s included the sensational trial of John T. Scopes, a Tennessee schoolteacher accused of instructing his students in evolution. That put him in violation of a state law against teaching the subject. His trial on the charges brought great publicity to the small town of Dayton, Tennessee, where the proceedings were held. William Jennings Bryan appeared to assist the prosecution in convicting Scopes of the charges against him. Defending Scopes was the celebrated criminal lawyer Clarence Darrow. The defense called Bryan to the witness stand as an expert in the issues of fundamentalism, the Biblical teachings on creation, and the criticism of evolution that Bryan articulated. The ensuing cross-examination between Bryan and Darrow illustrated the cultural divide of the 1920s and the divergent ways in which these two men, and the cultural views they represented, saw the world.

Darrow: You have given considerable study to the Bible, haven't you, Mr. Bryan?

Bryan: Yes, sir, I have tried to.

Darrow: Then you have made a general study of it?

Bryan: Yes, I have. I have studied the Bible for about fifty years, or sometime more than that, but of course I have studied it more as I have become older than when I was but a boy.

Darrow: You claim that everything in the Bible should be literally interpreted?

Bryan: I believe everything in the Bible should be accepted as it is given there; some of the Bible is given illustratively. For instance: "Ye are the salt of the earth." I would not insist that man was actually salt, or that he had flesh of salt, but it is used in the sense of salt as saving God's people.

Darrow: But when you read that Jonah swallowed the whale—or that the whale swallowed Jonah—excuse me please, how do you literally interpret that?

Bryan: When I read that a big fish swallowed Jonah—it does not say whale . . . That is my recollection of it. A big fish, and I believe it, and I believe in a God who can make a whale and can make a man and make both what He pleases.

Darrow: Now, you say, the big fish swallowed Jonah, and there remained how long—three days—and then he spewed him upon the land. You believe that the big fish was made to swallow Jonah?

Bryan: I am not prepared to say that; the Bible merely says it was done.

Darrow: You don't know whether it was the ordinary run of fish, or made for that purpose?

Bryan: You may guess; you evolutionists guess . . .

Darrow: You are not prepared to say whether that fish was made especially to swallow a man or not?

Bryan: The Bible doesn't say, so I am not prepared to say.

Darrow: But you do believe He made them—that He made such a fish and that it was big enough to swallow Jonah.

Bryan: Yes sir. Let me add. One miracle is just as easy to believe as another.

Darrow: Just as hard?

Bryan: It is hard to believe for you, but easy for me. A miracle is a thing performed beyond what man can perform. When you get within the realm of miracles; and it is just as easy to believe the miracle of Jonah as any other miracle in the Bible.

Darrow: Perfectly easy to believe that Jonah swallowed the whale.

Bryan: If the Bible said so; the Bible doesn't make extreme statements as evolutionists do . . .

This exchange, like the others between Bryan and Darrow, changed few minds in the controversy over evolution. As the contemporary debate over evolution indicates, the differences that existed in the 1920s have persisted down to the present time. In that sense the 1920s were a precursor of debates over social and cultural issues that have not disappeared with the passage of decades.

Source: For the Bryan-Darrow exchange, see Scopes Trial, University of Missouri, Kansas City, School of Law at www.law.umkc.edu/faculty.projects.ftrials/scopes/day7.html.

Questions for Reflection

1. How did Bryan and Darrow differ in their views of the Bible and its relation to science?

2. What assumptions about the world and nature did each man bring to this encounter?

3. How well suited was the Scopes trial for the airing of these questions?

4. How did Bryan and Darrow illustrate some of the contrasting ways in which progressives of the first two decades of the century had respond-

ed to the intellectual and cultural currents of the 1920s?

Explore additional primary sources related to this chapter on the Wadsworth American History Resource Center or HistoryNOW websites:
http://history.wadsworth.com/rc/us
http://now.ilrn.com/ayers_etal3e

makeup, motion pictures, and other attractions. Since children no longer were so important to the wage-earning power of the family, they were given greater freedom to spend their leisure time as they deemed best. A teenager might have four to six evenings a week to spend away from home. Adolescence came to be seen as a distinct phase in the development of young Americans in which they lived within their own subculture and responded to its demands for fun, excitement, and novelty. Dating became a ritualized form of courting behavior carried on at movies, dances, and athletic events, as well as in automobiles.

More young Americans attended high school during the 1920s than ever before, and the percentage of those who went to college increased. The college experience became the model for middle-class white youth across the nation. Freed from parental supervision, college women could smoke in public, go out on dates, and engage in the latest trends in sexual activity, "necking

and petting." Male students with enough income joined fraternities, drank heavily, and devoted endless amounts of time to athletic contests and dates.

The college experience for students from lower-class families, different religious backgrounds, or minority groups was less comfortable. Informal quotas limited the numbers of Jewish students admitted to Yale, Columbia, and Harvard. In the South, African Americans of college age were restricted to predominantly black institutions that struggled with fewer resources and less distinguished faculties. Poorer students at state universities and private colleges worked their way through, often performing the menial tasks that made life pleasant for their affluent colleagues.

Big-Time Sports

During the 1920s, college football grew into a national obsession as money was poured into the construction of stadiums, the coaching staffs, and in many instances, the players themselves. Large stadiums sprang up on the West Coast and in the Midwest. The most famous football player of the era was Harold "Red" Grange of the University of Illinois. When he scored four touchdowns in 12 minutes against the University of Michigan in 1924, his picture appeared on the cover of the new *Time* magazine. After he left college, Grange joined the newly formed National Professional Football League and received $12,000 per game at the start. In contrast, the average worker in 1925 made 65 cents an hour.

Boxing attracted millions of followers. The first popular champion was William Harrison "Jack" Dempsey, who received $1 million for his fight against the Frenchman Georges Carpentier in 1921. To avoid confronting the leading African American contender Henry Willis, Dempsey and his manager agreed to fight James Joseph "Gene" Tunney. Tunney defeated an overconfident Dempsey in 1927 in a bout that featured the "long count." Dempsey knocked Tunney down, but then did not go promptly to a neutral corner. With the referee starting the count late, Tunney was able to get up off the canvas and knock out his rival.

The Scopes Trial was a public relations bonanza for Dayton, Tennessee, as the Clifford K. Berryman cartoon from the Washington *Star* in 1925 illustrates. Although the issue was the teaching of evolution, the trial became caught up in the celebrity culture of the 1920s.

Library of Congress, Prints and Photographs Division

In the heyday of big-time sports, no one was more popular or well known than George Herman "Babe" Ruth of the New York Yankees. His prodigious home runs and gargantuan appetites made him a larger-than-life hero. This photograph shows him hitting one of his home runs.

Baseball: The National Sport

Of all the American sports, baseball symbolized the excitement and passion of the 1920s. The game experienced a wounding scandal in 1919 when it was revealed that members of the Chicago White Sox had conspired to fix the World Series. Although the players were ultimately acquitted of any crime, the "Black Sox" scandal cast a shadow over the game. The owners hired a new commissioner, Kenesaw Mountain Landis, a former federal judge, and gave him sweeping authority over the operations of baseball. Landis barred the "Black Sox" players from the game for life for having cheated and exercised his power vigorously to keep baseball pure.

Baseball underwent even more dramatic changes on the field because of the emergence of a new kind of player in the person of **George Herman "Babe" Ruth.** Ruth was a pitcher for the Boston Red Sox when they sold him to the New York Yankees for $400,000 in 1918. Ruth was the first of the celebrity sluggers; he belted out 54 home runs during the 1920 season. Fans flocked to see him perform. The Yankees decided to construct Yankee Stadium ("the House that Ruth built") to accommodate the customers who wanted to be there when Ruth connected. The Yankees won American League pennants from 1921 to 1923, and in 1923 they won the World Series. Batting averages rose in both leagues, as did attendance records. Professional baseball remained a white man's game, however; talented black players such as Josh Gibson labored in obscurity in the Negro leagues.

The peak of baseball in the 1920s came in 1927 when Babe Ruth hit 60 home runs and the New York Yankees captured the American League pennant and the World Series in four games. Their "Murderers Row" of skilled hitters produced "five o'clock lightning" that resulted in comeback victories in the day games that were organized baseball in that period. When Ruth hit his 60th home run in late September, commentators speculated that his record would stand for decades. The feat summed up the allure of a sports-crazy decade.

New Roles for Women

After the achievement of woman suffrage, most people expected the newly enfranchised voters to produce a genuine change in politics. It soon became apparent that women cast their votes much as men did. The possibility of a cohesive bloc of female voters evaporated. Yet while women did not change politics, they found that their place in society underwent significant transformations.

Flashpoints | Babe Ruth Hits 60 Home Runs, 1927

He was "The Bambino," "The Sultan of Swat," and "The Colossus of Clout." George Herman "Babe" Ruth was the most famous baseball player in the decade when following sports became a national obsession. His tape-measure home runs, his gargantuan appetites on and off the field, and his ability to connect with fans of all ages made him the darling of the media. Big-time sports dominated the consciousness of the average American, and Ruth was the icon along with "Red" Grange in football, Bill Tilden in tennis, and Gertrude Ederle in swimming.

By 1927, the New York Yankees had assembled a "Murderer's Row" of hitters who pounded opposing pitching. In the lineup of Lou Gehrig and Bob Meusel, among others, Ruth stood above the rest as his home run total grew toward the record of 59 that he had set in 1921. Baseball was segregated, and Ruth did not have to face talented black pitchers who labored in relative obscurity in the Negro Leagues (as they were then called). Among his white contemporaries, Ruth was acknowledged as the premier performer of his time. The nation watched as he approached his own record and then tied it late in the 154-game regular season.

On the next to last day of play, September 30, 1927, Ruth hit his 60th home run to break his own record and establish a mark that would last 34 years. Despite Ruth's popularity, the feat did not achieve the same national recognition that would come when Roger Maris broke the Babe's record in 1961. For all people at the time knew, Ruth might do even better in the years to come. That did not happen and Ruth's achievement in

1927 became a standard by which home run hitters were judged for more than three decades.

In time, the 1920s, with their mix of hot jazz, exciting sports events, and bootleg liquor, would seem a time of fun and frivolity before the somber events of the Great Depression. That judgment, despite its exaggerations, had a basic core of truth to it. The feats of an athlete such as Babe Ruth reflected a culture in which fame and celebrity counted for as much and sometimes more than the accomplishments of politicians, diplomats, scientists, and entrepreneurs. Ruth did not create this new world of ballyhoo but he emerged as its most enduring symbol. There is a direct line from Babe Ruth to Mark McGwire and Barry Bonds in baseball and to renowned entertainers such as Michael Jackson and other pop stars. When the Babe hit his 60th on that long ago September afternoon, he helped launch not just a shot into the Yankee Stadium bleachers. He represented a dramatic change in the way Americans thought about sports, fame, and the things that mattered in their lives.

Questions for Reflection

1. What forces in the 1920s made it possible for baseball players such as Ruth to become national heroes?

2. What other events occurred in 1927 that provided a context for Ruth's historic feat?

3. What needs did sports fulfill in the 1920s and in what ways have the role of athletics evolved and changed since that time?

Women in Politics

Following 1923, the more militant wing of the suffragists, identified with Alice Paul and the **National Woman's party,** advocated the Equal Rights Amendment (ERA). The amendment stated that "men and women shall have equal rights throughout the United States and every place subject to its jurisdiction." Other female reformers, such as Florence Kelley and Carrie Chapman Catt, regarded the ERA as a threat to the hard-won legislation that protected women in the workplace on such issues as maximum hours, minimum wage, and safer conditions. These women favored an approach such as the Sheppard-Towner Act of 1921, which supplied federal matching funds to states that created programs in which mothers would be instructed on caring for their babies and safeguarding their own health. Despite the efforts of the National Woman's party and the support of the Republicans, the ERA was not adopted.

Two states, Wyoming and Texas, elected female governors. Nellie Tayloe Ross of Wyoming was chosen to fill out the unexpired term of her husband after he died in office. Miriam Amanda Ferguson of Texas won election in 1924 because her husband, a former governor, had been impeached and barred from holding office in the state. She became his surrogate. Eleven women were elected to the House of Representatives, many of them as political heirs of their husbands. Many more won seats in state legislatures or held local offices. Eleanor Roosevelt, the wife of a rising Democratic politician in New York, built up a network of support for her causes and career among women in her party.

Social causes enlisted women who had started their careers in public life years earlier. Margaret Sanger continued to be a staunch advocate of birth control. She founded the American Birth Control League, which became Planned Parenthood in 1942. Sanger capitalized on a popular interest in "eugenics," a quasi-scientific movement to limit births among "unfit" elements of the population. The racist implications of the theory stirred only modest controversy before the rise of Nazi Germany in the 1930s. Sanger found increased support for birth control among doctors as the 1920s progressed. The greatest effect of the campaign was seen in middle-class women. The poor and minorities turned to older, less reliable methods of avoiding pregnancy and often resorted to abortions when pregnant.

The Flapper and the New Woman

Social feminism confronted a sense that young women were more interested in fun and diversion than in political movements. The "flapper," with her bobbed hair and short skirts, captivated the popular press. Older female reformers noted sadly that their younger counterparts were likely "to be bored" when the subject of feminism came up. In their relations with men, young women of the 1920s practiced a new sexual freedom. Among women born after 1900, the rate of premarital intercourse, while still low by modern standards, was twice as high as it had been among women born a decade earlier.

Women joined the workforce in growing numbers. At the beginning of the decade, 8.3 million women, or about 24 percent of the national workforce, were employed outside the home. Ten years later, the number stood at 10.6 million, or 27 percent. A few occupations accounted for 85 percent of female jobs. One-third of these women worked in clerical positions, 20 percent labored as domestic servants, and another third were employed in factory jobs. Many women with factory jobs worked a full week and continued to spend many hours on household chores as well. The median wage for women usually stood at about 55 percent of what men earned for comparable jobs. At the same time women entered new professions and became celebrities. Amelia Earhart, for example, was the first woman pilot to cross the Atlantic, and emerged as the most famous woman flier of the era.

For the majority of women, however, the barriers to advancement and opportunity remained high. Poor white women in the South often worked at dead-end jobs in textile mills or agricultural processing plants. Black women found it difficult to secure nondomestic jobs either in the North or the South. When African Americans were employed to move supplies or equipment in factories, they did the heavy, menial labor that white workers shunned. In the Southwest, Hispanic women picked crops, shelled pecans, or worked as domestic servants. Labor unions rarely addressed the situation of female workers. When strikes did occur, as in New Jersey and Massachusetts during the middle of the

decade, employers sometimes granted concessions—and then moved their factories to the South where labor was cheaper and unions were weaker.

Career women faced formidable obstacles. When a woman schoolteacher married, many school districts compelled her to resign. College faculties, the medical profession, and the law had more women members but they made it difficult for women to advance in these careers. In government, men received favorable treatment. Although many women worked outside the home out of economic necessity, they were expected to juggle their careers and domestic responsibilities. Women who were "creative" or who had "administrative gifts or business ability," said the feminist Crystal Eastman, and who also had "the normal desire to be mothers, must make up their minds to be sort of supermen."

Coolidge in the White House

The inauguration of President Coolidge on March 4, 1925, was the first to be broadcast over the radio. The administration's policy goals were modest. In 1926, Coolidge asked Congress for a cut in taxes. The lawmakers responded with a measure that lowered the surtax on those people who made more than $100,000 annually, reduced the estate tax to 20 percent, and eliminated the gift tax. Few married couples earned more than the $3,500 exemption and only about 4 million Americans filed tax returns during this period. The changes in the law affected only the most affluent in the society.

The president also supported laws to oversee the expansion of the new airline industry and regulate the growing radio business. On the other hand, Coolidge vetoed a bill to develop the electric power potential of the Tennessee River at Muscle Shoals, Alabama, for public purposes. When Congress twice passed the McNary-Haugen Plan to assist agriculture, Coolidge vetoed it on the grounds that trying to raise crop prices through government intervention was both expensive and wrong.

Coolidge's Foreign Policy

Although the United States remained out of the League of Nations and proclaimed that it would remain aloof from foreign involvements, it was not in fact an isolationist country during the 1920s. The Coolidge administration participated in foreign relations in ways that would have seemed impossible a decade earlier. Its effort to have the United States join the World Court (a part of the League whose official title was the Permanent Court of International Justice) in 1925 and 1926 collapsed when the Senate insisted on major conditions for

American membership, including limits on the court's ability to issue advisory opinions on disputed issues. The government encouraged the expansion of American business around the world, and Washington used corporate executives as ambassadors and in framing monetary policy. Americans applauded U.S. policy in Latin America, Asia, and Europe because it did not involve the use of force or the commitment of soldiers. Sentiment for peace remained strong.

In Latin America, troubled relations with Mexico, especially over control of oil reserves, persisted. The administration sent an emissary, Dwight Morrow, who mediated an agreement to protect American oil companies from further expropriation. Marines were withdrawn from Nicaragua in 1925 but were sent back a year later when civil war erupted again. American efforts to instruct the Nicaraguans in what Washington said were democratic procedures did not produce the desired results by the time the Coolidge presidency ended.

Diplomacy and Finance in the 1920s

After the decision not to join the League of Nations, the U.S. interest in Europe became chiefly financial. American bankers and investors played a large part in providing the reparation payments required of Germany in the Treaty of Versailles. Because of the size of the sums they had to pay, the Germans were unable to meet their obligations without American help. In 1924, the Coolidge administration endorsed a plan that scaled back German reparations and loaned that country money to meet its debts. During the next four years, Germany borrowed almost $1.5 million from the United States. European nations in turn used the money paid to them by the Germans to buy American farm and factory products.

The Coolidge administration continued the policy of nonrecognition of the Soviet Union, but it did not object when business interests, including Henry Ford, made substantial investments there. Americans also sent large amounts of aid and food when the Soviets faced famine during the early 1920s. In China, the U.S. government watched apprehensively as revolution and civil war wracked that nation. Washington extended de facto recognition to the government of the Nationalist leader, Chiang Kai-shek. That stance reflected the general policy of encouraging positive developments overseas without assuming any direct obligations. A symbol of that sentiment came in American support for the idea of outlawing war altogether. When the French foreign minister, Aristide Briand, proposed a mutual security agreement between his country and the United States, the State Department, under Frank B. Kellogg, proposed instead a multilateral agreement to have signatory nations

Picturing the Past   SOCIAL & CULTURAL EVENTS

The Heroic Lindbergh

This picture of Charles A. Lindbergh after his historic flight to Paris captures the fascination that people in the 1920s had with celebrity, science, and the cult of the individual. Although the Atlantic had been crossed in an airplane years earlier, the spectacle of Lindbergh, "the Lone Eagle," braving the elements to fly solo from New York across the ocean enthralled the public in the United States and around the world. While technology made Lindbergh's accomplishment possible, Americans persuaded themselves that the flier was a hero in the

mold of the frontier and the West conquering the dangers of the unknown. Aviation also symbolized the ability of the postwar generation to extend progress in benign ways. In the next decade, the possibility of bombers carrying deadly payloads would reshape how airplanes were seen. But in the heady days of 1927, Charles Lindbergh exemplified how Americans in the 1920s wanted to see themselves—on the cutting edge of change while affirming older, traditional values.

renounce war. Peace groups supported the idea and the Kellogg-Briand Pact was signed in 1928 and ratified a year later. War was not abolished, of course, but Americans in the 1920s thought it was an attainable goal. Meanwhile, they turned their attention to a stunning feat of personal daring and technological expertise.

Lucky Lindy and Retiring Cal

In 1927, two surprising events riveted the attention of Americans. The first came in May when **Charles A. Lindbergh** flew alone across the Atlantic Ocean from

© CORBIS

Charles Lindbergh's solo flight across the Atlantic Ocean in 1927 made him an international hero. Here the youthful Lindbergh stands stiffly in front of his plane, the *Spirit of St. Louis*.

New York to Paris. Lindbergh did not make the first nonstop flight across the ocean. Two British aviators had accomplished that feat eight years earlier, flying from Ireland to Newfoundland in 1919. By 1926, however, a $25,000 prize was offered for the first nonstop flight between New York and Paris, a distance of 3,600 miles. Charles Lindbergh had been an army flier and was working as an airmail pilot for the government when he heard about the contest. He raised money from local leaders in St. Louis and other cities. He called his monoplane the *Spirit of St. Louis*. On May 10, a tired Lindbergh (he had not slept the night before) took off from Roosevelt field in New York on his way to Paris. When he landed in the French capital 36 hours later, he was a worldwide celebrity. He received a ticker tape parade in New York City, medals from foreign nations, and a lifetime in the public eye. To the generation of the 1920s, Lindbergh's feat symbolized the ability of a single person to bend technology to his will and overcome nature. By the summer of 1927, Lindbergh was the most famous person in the United States, eclipsing even President Coolidge.

Calvin Coolidge could easily have sought another term in 1928. The president, however, may have sensed the weaknesses in the economy that would become evident two years later. While vacationing in the Black Hills of South Dakota during the summer of 1927, the president gave reporters a simple statement: "I do not choose to run for President in 1928." This surprise announcement opened up the race for the Republican presidential nomination to other potential contenders such as the secretary of commerce, Herbert Hoover.

As 1927 ended there were some signs that the economy was not as robust as it had been. A slight recession occurred in which wholesale prices fell nearly 4.5 percent. Production slowed, and consumer spending also dropped. Despite these warning signs, the banking system continued to expand credit, and stock market speculation persisted. For the average American there was little concrete evidence that the boom years might be coming to a close. Calvin Coolidge was going out of public life on top with prosperity still a sure thing in the minds of most Americans with money to spend and invest.

Conclusion

The years between World War I and the start of the Great Depression have never lost their reputation for excitement and novelty. Bathtub gin, flappers, syncopation, and gangsters remain part of the national image of that time. Prohibition did encounter serious opposition from the upper classes, and evasion of the law was widespread. On the other hand, liquor control did change drinking habits, so the experiment was not a complete failure.

For women the sense that the 1920s represented a new age of sexual and social liberation was actually rather superficial. Sexual practices did become more flexible, but marriage and family continued to be viewed as the goals toward which most women should aspire. The number of women in the workplace rose, but the percentage of women in the labor force did not change very much. Politics saw an infusion of women into both major parties, but genuine equality remained elusive. The 1920s did not produce anything like the gains in political or social status that had been achieved by women during the previous decade.

In its culture, the United States went through an artistic renaissance. Literature, art, and music explored new channels and brought forth important figures whose influence remained strong through the 1930s and beyond. The works of Hemingway, Fitzgerald, and Mencken, the jazz of Ellington and Armstrong, and the achievements of numerous other artists made the 1920s a high point of American artistic expression.

The 1920s brought important economic changes for many Americans. A consumer culture based on mass appeal tied middle-class society together through common experiences of driving automobiles, listening to radios, and attending films each week. The cultural response was more complex. The Ku Klux Klan, the movement for immigration restriction, and the rise of fundamentalism challenged the newer ways and revealed that the United States was still divided between the values of town and country.

While the potential for social conflict persisted, the economic good times of the decade left few avenues for effective protest and unrest. For a brief period it seemed possible that discord might vanish in a rising tide of economic growth. However, the prosperity of the 1920s did not alter the inequities between rich [and poor?] national belief in a prosperous future v[...] the latent strains within American life [...]

In retrospect, these years would co[...] a time of isolation from the cares and [...] postwar world. The United States was involved overseas with its destiny linked to the economies of Europe and Asia. The American people did not, however, believe that they would have to be militarily committed to the fates of people beyond the two oceans that protected the continent. In the 1930s, that confidence would decrease as dangerous new powers arose to challenge democracy in western Europe and the Pacific. Soon the 1920s would come to be regarded as a time of lost innocence.

The Chapter in Review

During the 1920s, the United States became more modern because of:

- the rise of a consumer society
- the growing popularity of automobiles
- the development of radio and the motion picture industry
- the expanding use of electricity
- greater opportunities for women in the economy

Resisting the trends toward a mass society and culture were:

- the effort to enforce Prohibition
- the rise of the Ku Klux Klan
- the growing tension between secular forces and religious fundamentalism
- continuing discrimination against minorities

Making Connections Across Chapters

LOOKING BACK

The 1920s owed much to the way that the economy made the transition from war to peace between 1918 and 1921. The political effects of the same period prepared the way for Republican dominance throughout the decade. Unhappiness with the League of Nations also shaped American foreign policy.

1. What problems did Warren G. Harding confront when he took office in March 1921?

2. How did the failure of the League of Nations to gain Senate approval affect foreign policy under Harding and Coolidge?

3. What were the roots of the cultural tensions of 1920s that anti-immigration, the Ku Klux Klan, and the revolt against the city reflected?

LOOKING AHEAD

The key elements of the 1920s were economic prosperity, cultural change toward a more urban and cosmopolitan society, and the underlying problems that caused the Great Depression at the end of the decade. As you read, be alert for the ways in which these forces interacted to make the 1920s so important in shaping the rest of the century.

1. Although the 1920s were prosperous, not all sections of American life shared in the bounty. Why was the depressed state of agriculture so important?

2. How solidly based was the consumer culture of the decade in economic terms?

3. How was income distributed and what government tax policies affected that issue under Harding and Coolidge?

4. What accounted for the flowering of the arts and culture during this period? What traces of the 1920s can still be found in mass entertainment now?

Recommended Readings

Brophy, Alfred I., and Kennedy, Randall. *Reconstructing the Dreamland: The Tulsa Race Riot of 1921* (2002). Looks at a case study of racial violence in the decade.

Coben, Stanley. *Rebellion Against Victorianism: The Impetus for Cultural Change in 1920s America* (1991). Discusses how Americans in the 1920s reacted against the ideas and values of an earlier time.

Douglas, Ann. *Terrible Honesty: Mongrel Manhattan in the 1920s* (1995). A cultural history of the decade from the perspective of events in New York City.

Dumenil, Lynn. *The Modern Temper: American Culture and Society in the 1920s* (1995). An excellent analysis of the major trends of the period.

Ferrell, Robert H. *The Strange Deaths of President Harding* (1996). Explodes many of the sensational myths about Harding's career.

Ferrell, Robert H. *The Presidency of Calvin Coolidge* (1998). Provides a good survey of what Coolidge did as president.

Goldberg, David J. *Discontented America: The United States in the 1920s* (1999). Provides a thoughtful narrative about the main currents of this period.

Larson, Edward J. *Summer for the Gods: The Scopes Trial and America's Continuing Debate over Science and Religion* (1997). A prize-winning look at the celebrated trial about evolution.

Leinwand, Gerald. *1927, High Tide of the Twenties* (2001). Considers the year that defined the spirit of the decade.

Parrish, Michael E. *Anxious Decades: America in Prosperity and Depression* (1992). A fascinating treatment of the interwar years.

Identifications

Review your understanding of the following key terms, people, events, and dates for this chapter (these terms also appear in the Glossary at the end of the book):

Sacco and Vanzetti

Marcus Garvey

bootleggers

Alphonse "Al" Capone

The Jazz Singer

Albert B. Fall

Alain Locke

Zora Neale Hurston

Louis Armstrong

F. Scott Fitzgerald

Scopes trial

George Herman "Babe" Ruth

National Woman's party

Charles A. Lindbergh

Online Sources Guide

Use this listing to find online documents, images, interactive maps, simulations, and other resources related to this chapter:

American History Resource Center

http://history.wadsworth.com/rc/us

Documents

La Follette's Progressive Platform, 1924

Transcripts from the Scopes Trial

Lyrics to Classic Blues Songs of the 1920s

Babe Ruth's Children's Story "The Home-Run King"

A contemporary Scholarly Review of the Impact of Movies on Their Viewers

Selected Images

Ford Motor Company showroom, 1925

Children listening to radio, 1923

Advertisement for new hairstyles for women, 1920s

New electrical appliances, 1920s

Coolidge throwing out first baseball, June 1924

Ku Klux Klan parade in Washington, D.C., 1926

Duke Ellington

Langston Hughes

Claude McKay

Mexican American farm workers, 1920s

Simulation

Surviving the Great Depression (Choose to be an African American sharecropper in Alabama, a white farmer in Wisconsin, or a young Italian in New York City and make choices based on the circumstances and opportunities afforded.)

HistoryNOW

http://now.ilrn.com/ayers_etal3e

Primary Source Exercises

Automobile Advertising, 1923
. . . And Its Discontents

24 The Great Depression, 1927–1933

In the wake of the Great Depression, breadlines became a common occurrence in the United States. This one was formed under the Brooklyn Bridge in New York City as desperate people waited for food.

Library of Congress, Prints and Photographs Division

As the end of the 1920s approached, some well-off Americans viewed the future with confidence. Accepting the Republican presidential nomination in 1928, Herbert Hoover proclaimed: "We in America today are nearer to the final triumph over poverty than ever before in the history of any land." Farmers would not have shared Hoover's optimism, nor would African Americans and the poor. Among those who had benefited from the boom of the 1920s, however, the prosperity and abundance enjoyed by the fortunate seemed destined to extend into the immediate future.

Then came the shocks, first of the stock market crash in October 1929, then a severe economic depression that worsened during the early 1930s. The good times of the 1920s were replaced with bread lines, soup kitchens, and the wandering homeless. The administration of President Herbert Hoover took unprecedented actions to relieve the crisis, but nothing seemed to work. Resentment against the president, the economic system, and the wealthy grew. The specter of social revolution arose. Pressures for political change led to the election of **Franklin D. Roosevelt** in 1932.

By 1933, the Great Depression, as it came to be called, affected almost everyone in American society. It worsened the already difficult situation of the nation's farmers. For African Americans, Hispanics, and the poor, it meant even more misery and suffering than they usually faced. A generation of Americans looked to the federal government for answers to the social and economic problems they confronted.

The Stock Market Crash of 1929

When the stock market crashed in October 1929, the incumbent president was Herbert Hoover. Elected in 1928 after a divisive campaign against the Democratic candidate, Governor Alfred E. Smith of New York, Hoover brought to the White House the knowledge gained from a successful career in the mining business and in government as secretary of commerce under Warren G. Harding and Calvin Coolidge. Hoover's intense personal style and love of the limelight led Coolidge to dub him "the Boy Wonder." For the Republicans, he was the natural front-runner in 1928 once Coolidge decided not to run. In the election contest, Hoover had benefited from the suspicion of Smith, a Roman Catholic, that permeated the heavily

Timeline

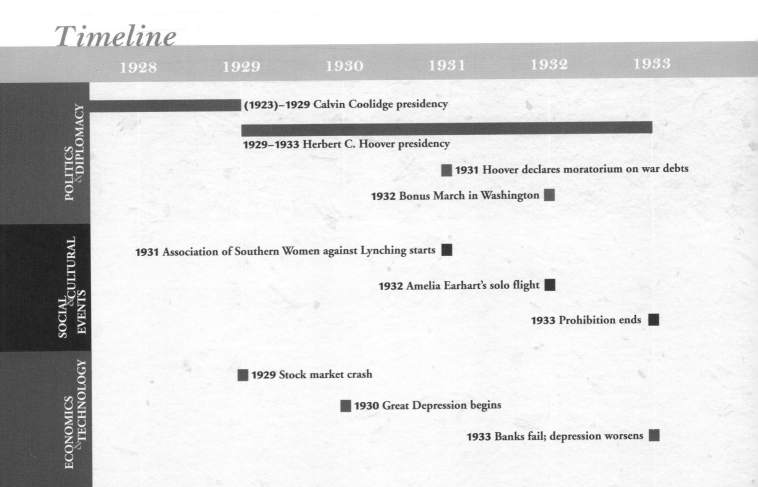

	1928	1929	1930	1931	1932	1933

POLITICS & DIPLOMACY

(1923)–1929 Calvin Coolidge presidency

1929–1933 Herbert C. Hoover presidency

1931 Hoover declares moratorium on war debts

1932 Bonus March in Washington

SOCIAL & CULTURAL EVENTS

1931 Association of Southern Women against Lynching starts

1932 Amelia Earhart's solo flight

1933 Prohibition ends

ECONOMICS & TECHNOLOGY

1929 Stock market crash

1930 Great Depression begins

1933 Banks fail; depression worsens

Flashpoints | The Smith–Hoover Campaign in 1928

It was an unnerving way to run for president. As Alfred E. Smith's campaign train moved through the South in the autumn of 1928, he could look out the window of his car and see the burning crosses that marked his path. The Democrats had nominated the governor of New York, a Roman Catholic, for president of the United States, and the forces of bigotry in the nation had come to life against him. The Republicans and their candidate, Herbert Hoover, denied that they had any part in the attacks against Smith because of his faith or his negative views on the controversial issue of Prohibition. They simply contrasted Hoover's record as a Cabinet officer, his Quaker background, and his support for Prohibition with the positions of his rival. Smith's commitment to the full enforcement of antiliquor laws was equivocal, and the Republicans made the most of his ambivalence on the subject.

In the dark byways of American politics, however, the currents of prejudice against Smith ran deep. Republicans tapped into the suspicion toward Smith in the South and West where Protestant denominations encouraged their members to vote for Hoover. In local campaigns Republican leaders made it clear that they did not mind if religious leaders denounced Smith as a Papist and enemy of Christianity. The Ku Klux Klan and its followers organized the burning of the crosses that Smith witnessed. "The real issue in this campaign," said one Protestant publication, was "PROTESTANT AMERICANISM VERSUS RUM AND ROMANISM."

Smith did not find an effective strategy for dealing with this assault on his character and religion. He made few gestures toward understanding the fears of some moderate Protestants about his Catholic allegiance. It might not have made much difference if he had done so. The nation was prosperous and still Republican in its political character. Hoover would have been a difficult opponent even for a Protestant Democrat. To some degree, Smith's good showing in the major cities, even in defeat, helped Franklin D. Roosevelt and other Democrats win over urban Americans and Catholic voters during the Depression. Nonetheless, the ordeal that Al Smith went through in 1928 attested to the ways in which cultural differences among Americans expressed themselves in the turbulent politics of the decade. It would be another 30 years and more before John F. Kennedy would break the barrier against having a Roman Catholic as president. He learned from the mistakes Smith had made and dealt with the religious issue in a more skillful manner. For Smith, the ordeal was a bitter one that left him disillusioned about the nature of American politics.

Questions for Reflection

1. How did Catholics and Protestants general differ about Prohibition during the 1920s and how did that affect Smith's presidential candidacy?

2. What obstacles did Smith confront in running for president even if his religion had not been an issue?

3. What assets did Herbert Hoover have as a presidential candidate?

4. How might Smith have defused some of the charges against him about his religion?

Protestant South and Middle West. Now the question was whether "the Great Engineer," as Hoover was dubbed, could become a successful president. Much would depend on whether he could keep the economy growing and prosperous.

To the average American, the economic signs during the summer of 1929 seemed encouraging. The prices of stocks traded on the New York Stock Exchange were reaching ever-higher levels. At the beginning of 1928, for example, the industrial index of the *New York Times* was recorded at 245. Within 12 months, it had risen to 331. It soared to 452 by September 1929. Radio Corporation of America stock shot up from $85 a share to $420 a share during 1928. DuPont's stock price went from $310 to $525. A poem appeared in a popular magazine:

Oh, hush thee, my babe, granny's bought some more shares,

Daddy's gone out to play with the bulls and bears,
Mother's buying on tips, and she simply can't lose,
And baby shall have some expensive new shoes!

These giddy investors would be brought up short when the market's rise came to a shuddering halt in the cataclysmic moments of the epic Wall Street downturn that persists in the folklore of capitalism as the Great Crash.

Causes of the Crash

What dire alignment of negative economic forces triggered the calamity of October 1929? The decade of the 1920s had seen a wild investment fever that led all-too-many gullible investors into risky ventures for the allure of quick profits. In the sunshine state of Florida, where dreams of riches blossomed in the humid atmosphere,

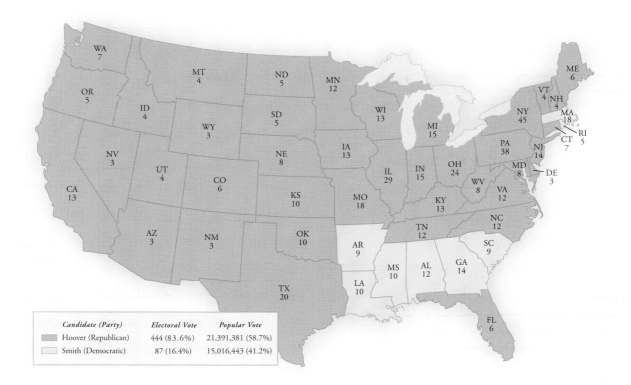

Candidate (Party)	Electoral Vote	Popular Vote
Hoover (Republican)	444 (83.6%)	21,391,381 (58.7%)
Smith (Democratic)	87 (16.4%)	15,016,443 (41.2%)

MAP 24.1 The Election of 1928

In the election of 1928, Herbert Hoover achieved an electoral landslide and cracked the "Solid South" for the first time since Republican successes in Reconstruction. Alfred E. Smith did carry Massachusetts and Rhode Island, whose heavily Roman Catholic populations supported him. Those victories anticipated Democratic gains in the 1930s. View an animated version of this map or related maps at http://history.wadsworth.com/passages3e.

there had been an epic land boom in the middle part of this 10-year span. Asking prices for some of the most favored lots, those near the balmy waters of the subtropical Atlantic Ocean, rose to $15,000 or $20,000 a foot for acreage on the shore. A devastating hurricane in 1926 deflated these dreams. Land prices collapsed. Willing investors then badgered their brokers for other speculative opportunities that would feed the insatiable appetites for quick and profitable returns that dominated the era.

By 1927, the stock market seemed the ideal place to acquire the fast buck that Americans pursued with such ardor in the 1920s. The issuance of Liberty Bonds during World War I had shown citizens the potential upside of stock purchases. Corporations increasingly relied on stock offerings to bring in the cash to finance the growth of their businesses. Stockbrokers hawked their products with hard-sell advertising techniques developed for consumer goods from Kleenex to Fords. Finally, during the go-go years of the Harding and Coolidge presidencies, generous government tax policies allowed the superwealthy to retain money that they then poured into the coffers of brokerage firms in the form of stock purchases. The richest Americans, by legal means,

sometimes paid no income taxes at all. Five hundred families reveled in incomes of more than $1 million in 1929. Awash with funds, these opulent investors saw the stock market as a way to get even richer.

One tempting device for smaller investors was to buy stocks in what was called then, as it is now, "margin" trading. An investor could purchase a stock on credit, putting up only 10 or 15 percent of the actual price. Because Wall Street sentiment believed that stock prices were headed toward even better prices in the future, a person, according to this rosy scenario, could sell the stock at a higher level, pay off the broker, and still pocket a substantial profit. Just as someone might acquire a house or a car on credit, so brokers urged their customers to invest $100 with the prospect of controlling $1,000 or more worth of stock. People borrowed money to buy on margin. In this way, a tiny investment might represent a commitment to buy several thousand dollars worth of stock. Of course, the investor could be required to provide the full price of the stock at any time. But with the market seemingly going up on a permanent basis, that risk seemed a small one.

Abuses of this practice soon followed. Investors with inside knowledge manipulated a stock's price up and

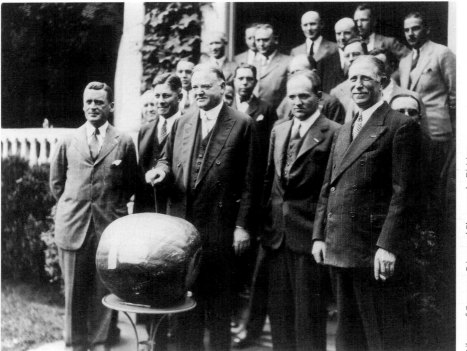

President Herbert Hoover kept up a jaunty public demeanor during the Depression. In this image he accepts a large pumpkin from a delegation that came to the White House for this public occasion. Over time, Hoover's image deteriorated as the Depression worsened.

down in order to fleece the unwary public or, in the phrase of the market, "shear the sheep." A firm called Kolster Radio had no earnings in 1929, but insiders drove the value up to $95 before the value collapsed back to $3 a share. New companies often consisted of nothing more than schemes to issue stock based on the assumption that the market would rise. These firms produced no goods; they were paper empires with no real value, such as Ivar Kreuger's International Match Company. Government regulation of stock issues on both the state and federal levels was very lax, and the stock exchanges themselves had few requirements for revealing the true financial status of these companies. Some of the investment trusts, as they were called, were frauds; those who put money into them lost their entire investment.

Rosy statistics and forecasts made the stock market crash of October 1929 even more of a shock. The problem began in September after stock prices reached their record levels. Stock prices then declined early in the month, regained some strength, and resumed a downward drift. No abrupt collapse had occurred and to many on Wall Street, their confidence unshaken, saw these events as one of the temporary "corrections" that preceded further upward surges. A few people warned of impending problems, but they were dismissed as chronic naysayers who had been wrong before. President Hoover told his financial broker to sell off some of his holdings because "possible hard times are coming." He

did not say that to the public. Most owners of stock simply waited for the rise in prices to begin again.

Then on October 24, 1929, which became known in Wall Street lore as "**Black Thursday**," traders began selling stocks and quickly realized that there were few buyers. Prices collapsed and the total number of shares traded reached 13 million, then an all-time record. Stockholders absorbed, by some estimates, a $9 billion loss in the value of their equities. During the afternoon, a banking syndicate, led by J. P. Morgan, Jr., urged investors to be calm. The syndicate bought stocks, and the market seemed to quiet. Over the weekend, the hope was that normal trading might recover.

The blow fell on October 29. Selling of stocks resumed at an even more intense rate. More than 16 million shares changed hands in a single day. Prestigious stocks such as American Telephone and Telegraph and General Electric recorded declines that wiped out large parts of their equity value. Fistfights occurred on the trading floor and rumors of suicides swept through the exchange. The story went that when one trader checked into a hotel and asked for a room, the clerk inquired: "For sleeping or jumping, sir?" The naive optimism of the 1920s was evaporating as harsh reality came home to Wall Street.

The number of Americans who actually participated in the stock market in 1929 stood at between 1.5 million and 2 million. Most of the corporate dividends in that year went to about 600,000 stockholders whose annual

During the Great Depression, selling apples became one of the ways that poor people eked out an income. This satiric cartoon by Herbert Block (Herblock) from the early 1930s shows a rich man helping out a poor apple seller by buying and eating all the fruit that he can.

incomes were above $5,000. These individuals were betting on the nation's economic future and sought to benefit from a prosperity that appeared to be permanent. The crash of 1929 wiped out many of these investors. Others cut back on their stock holdings and trimmed their personal expenditures.

The stock market collapse revealed serious underlying weaknesses in the economy. The well-to-do citizens who played the market were confident that other investors would buy their stocks at the higher price levels of the precrash period. Because of the way income

---

DOING HISTORY ONLINE

The Crash

Study the documents in this module and the sections in the textbook on "The Stock Market Crash of 1929" and "The Great Depression." What is the connection between the stock market crash and the Depression?

History ⊗ Now™   Visit HistoryNOW to access primary sources and exercises related to this topic: http://now.ilrn.com/ayers_etal3e

---

was distributed in the United States, with the rich getting a far higher share than that of other segments of the population, there were not enough people in the upper brackets for that assumption to be realistic. Once the wealthy investors began to sell their stocks, there were no other potential buyers to keep security prices high. A fall in the market became unavoidable.

The consequences of the stock market's decline were striking. The prices of individual stocks underwent a sustained downward slide. Within a few months such a high-flying issue as General Electric had dropped from $403 a share to $168. Standard Oil shares fell from $83 to $48. One index of stock prices had gone to 469.5 in September and was at 220.1 by November. During the next 12 months, the gross national product went from nearly $88 billion down to $76 billion. The economy was slumping into a prolonged depression.

Brother, Can You Spare a Dime: the Great Depression

Although the stock market crash represented a serious setback for the nation's economic health, the Great Depression of the 1930s that followed the crash arose from causes more deeply rooted than just the decline in stock values that occurred in October 1929. Despite the apparent prosperity of the 1920s, the United States had not dealt with a number of serious structural problems that combined to cause the prolonged economic downturn.

The most pervasive dilemma that the U.S. economy faced had to do with the distribution of income during the 1920s. By 1929, the 5 percent of Americans at the top income level were receiving one-third of the total annual personal income. Those who made up the lowest 40 percent of the population received about one-eighth of the available income. For an economy that depended on the purchase of consumer goods for its expansion, there were not enough people with money to buy the products that industry was turning out. The amount of spendable income that the top 1 percent of the population received rose from 12 percent in 1920 to 19 percent 9 years later. That gain for the wealthy meant that there was less money for the mass of consumers to spend on the products of American factories and businesses than might otherwise have been possible.

Wealth was also concentrated in the hands of those with the highest incomes. More than 21 million families, or 80 percent of the national population, did not have any savings at all. The 2.3 percent of families with incomes above $10,000 a year, on the other hand,

The onset of the Great Depression produced mass unemployment that the nation had not seen for four decades. The downturn hit women as much as men, and these women protested the lack of jobs and asked for public works employment. Like many in their situation struggling to keep up appearances, they wore their best clothes to the demonstration.

possessed two-thirds of the available savings. A consumer society had emerged, but the bulk of the consumers were unable to participate fully in the economic process. Although wealth had been more concentrated earlier in the century, the disparities of the late 1920s had more impact in contributing to the onset of the Depression.

Instead of using the profits that their businesses gained from selling goods during the mid-1920s to invest in new factories or a better-paid workforce, industry leaders had put their gains into the stock market or speculative ventures. Loans to New York stockbrokers, for example, went from $3.5 billion in July 1927 to $8.5 billion in September 1929. By 1927, the market for new cars and new houses began to weaken, indicating that demand for consumer goods was decreasing.

Another chronic weakness of the economy was in agriculture, a sector that never shared in the general prosperity of the 1920s. The problem of overproduction of farm goods had not been addressed successfully, and as prices fell at the beginning of the Depression, the farmers felt the effects most acutely. At the beginning of 1931, cotton stood at 9 to 10 cents per pound; when farmers brought in their crop in the fall, the price had skidded to under 6 cents a pound. Since farmers could not pay off their mortgages, rural banks soon failed. The ripple of banking failures strained a banking system that was already weakened by the effects of the stock market crash. In the countryside, crops rotted because they could not be sold, and farmers talked of strikes and other protests.

The world economy was also fragile as the 1920s came to an end. The settlement of World War I had imposed heavy reparation payments on the defeated Germans. Because the Germans could not pay these sums, they borrowed from investors and banks in the United States. In that way Americans financed the German debt payments to the victorious British and French. Those countries, in turn, could use the funds to pay off their war debts to the United States.

In 1924, the United States had reduced the burden of German war debts, and in 1929, another plan was offered that further cut back on the amount that Germany owed while establishing a payment schedule that extended the length of time for retiring the debt. These concessions alleviated the situation to some degree, but the basic problem persisted. This intricate and interlocking process hinged on the strength of the American economy. The United States, however, created tariff barriers that discouraged European imports and steered American capital toward internal economic development. When the European economies experienced difficulties themselves after 1929, the weakened structure of debts and loans soon collapsed, further damaging the economy of the United States. In fact, President Hoover would later argue that the entire Depression arose from causes beyond the borders of the United States. The debts were important in the overall situation of the world economy, but they were a contributing cause to the Depression in the United States rather than the main element in the crisis.

In 1929–1930, the United States lacked many of the government programs that could have lessened the cumulative effects of a depression. There was no government insurance of bank deposits. Individual banks were vulnerable to sudden demands by depositors to withdraw their money. Many banks had invested in the stock market and thereby placed their assets at risk. Other prominent bankers had embezzled some of the funds under their control to finance their investing. Among banks in general, there was little cooperation when a crisis occurred. To save themselves, the stronger banks called in loans made to smaller banks, thus worsening the condition of weaker banks (see Table 24.1).

Table 24.1 Bank Suspensions, 1927–1933

1927	669
1928	499
1929	659
1930	1352
1931	2284
1932	1458
1933	4004

Source: *Historical Statistics of the United States,* 1985, p. 536.

For an individual employee thrown out of work, there was no unemployment insurance to cushion the effect of a layoff. Old age pensions were also rare. Conventional economic thinking taught that the government should play a minimal role during hard times. Many people believed that the natural forces of the economy must work themselves out without the government intruding into the process. Secretary of the Treasury Andrew Mellon told President Hoover that "a panic was not altogether a bad thing" because "it will purge the rottenness out of the system." Americans who did not have Mellon's wealth and secure income were less persuaded of the therapeutic effects of hard times.

The Depression Takes Hold

The stock market crash did not cause the Depression, and for some months after the disaster on Wall Street it seemed as though the economy might rebound without much assistance from Washington. President Hoover endeavored to strike an encouraging note when he said in late 1929: "the fundamental business of the country is sound." He conferred with leading business figures about measures to maintain public confidence, especially programs to bolster prices and wages. He asked the Federal Reserve System to facilitate business borrowing. For the moment, events seemed to be going Hoover's way. During the first several months of 1930, stock market prices recovered from their 1929 lows.

In 1930, Congress enacted the Smoot-Hawley Tariff, which raised customs duties to high levels. Republicans believed that tariff protection would enable American agriculture and industry to rebound. The bill passed the Senate by a narrow margin, and despite some reservations Hoover signed the measure on June 17, 1930. The Smoot-Hawley law has been blamed for the severity of the worldwide Depression because it made it more difficult for European business to sell goods in the United States. The negative impact of the Smoot-Hawley Tariff has probably been overstated, relative to the other, more severe causes of the Depression. In any case, by the middle of 1930, the effects of the downturn began to be felt in many areas of government activity.

During the 1930s and afterward, many Americans would place the responsibility for the Great Depression on President Hoover and his policies. It was true that, more than any previous chief executive, Hoover endeavored to use the power of his office to address the economic crisis. He favored reduction of taxes, easing of bank credits, and a modest program of public works to provide jobs. Some members of Congress opposed these ideas as too activist; others said that Hoover proposed too little. Meanwhile, the White House issued a series of confident statements to bolster public faith that the economic downturn would be brief. When the stock market turned upward briefly in 1930, for example, the president told the nation: "I am convinced we have passed the worst and with continued effort shall rapidly recover."

But as 1930 continued, it was clear that the Depression was not going away. Bank failures soared from 659 in 1929 to 1,350 a year later. Businesses were closing, investment was declining, and corporate profits were falling off. Industrial production was 26 percent lower at the end of 1930 than it had been 12 months earlier. By October 1930, 4 million people were without jobs (almost 9 percent of the labor force), and the trend worsened as each month passed. Within a year, nearly 16 percent of the labor force was out of work.

To encourage confidence, Hoover exhorted businesses to keep prices up and employees at work. Conferences with industry leaders at the White House were covered extensively in the press. These sessions were designed to show the American people that the Depression was being addressed. The president lacked the power to make corporations retain workers or to prevent price-cutting. Despite any public pledges they might offer to Hoover, corporate executives trimmed payrolls and reduced costs when it seemed necessary. These actions further undercut Hoover's sagging credibility.

Hoover's Programs to Fight the Depression

The president sought to apply his principles of voluntary action to keep the banking system afloat. In October 1931, he persuaded bankers to set up the National Credit Corporation, a private agency that would underwrite banks that had failed and safeguard their depositors. Unfortunately, the management of the banks proved reluctant to acquire the assets of their failed competitors. The experiment was a disaster.

Despite his broadened use of the powers of his office, Herbert Hoover did not view government action as an appropriate way of responding to the Depression. Instead, he believed that the traditional self-reliance and volunteer spirit of the American people provided the most dependable means of ending the economic slump. His policies promoting economic recovery and providing relief for the unemployed stemmed from that fundamental conviction. He asked Americans who had jobs to invest more in their neighbors, to spend something extra to ensure that everyone could work. He set up presidential committees to coordinate volunteer relief efforts for the unemployed. One of those committees

Unemployment During the Great Depression

Table 24.2 Unemployment, 1927–1933

Year	Unemployed	% of Labor Force
1927	1,890,000	4.1
1928	2,080,000	4.4
1929	1,550,000	3.2
1930	4,340,000	8.7
1931	8,020,000	15.9
1932	12,060,000	23.6
1933	12,830,000	24.9

Source: *Historical Statistics of the United States*, 1985, p. 73.

The dimensions of the Great Depression of the 1930s are sometimes hard to grasp in human terms. This table about the rise of unemployment during the late 1920s and into the early 1930s provides the raw totals of people out of work. As the numbers show, the modest unemployment of 1929 rose dramatically by 1930 and then nearly doubled a year later. The increase in the number of people out of work strained the resources of relief agencies, which were then largely private.

Mass unemployment had not been seen for four decades since the hard times of the 1890s. By 1932, the percentage of those unemployed had risen to almost 24 percent, and many other workers saw pay cuts and reductions in the hours that they spent on the job. With no unemployment insurance or organized system of government relief to tide workers over, poverty was the inescapable result. The impact of these stark numbers lingered for more than a decade on the people who found themselves the unexpected victims of this massive and prolonged economic downturn.

was the President's Organization of Unemployment Relief (or POUR). Yet none of these efforts really dealt with the misery that Americans faced every day as the Depression intensified. Hoover seemed more and more out of touch with the nation and its problems.

The programs that Hoover put forward were inadequate for the size of the unemployment situation. By 1931, 8 million people were on the jobless rolls. They overwhelmed the resources of existing charitable agencies that normally provided help to the blind, the deaf, and the physically impaired. Nor were the cities and states capable of providing relief at a time when the Depression reduced their tax revenues and increased the demand for services.

In this situation, the president's informal committees for dealing with unemployment proved ineffective. The POUR program coordinated relief agencies and urged people to help their neighbors. The First Lady, Lou Hoover, long a leader of the Girl Scouts, mobilized its members for the same purpose. These efforts, commendable as they were, did little to deal with the mass unemployment that gripped the country. But when politicians clamored for action by the national government, Hoover remained resolutely opposed.

A symbolic event underscored the president's political ineptitude in dealing with the Depression and its effects. When a drought struck the Midwest in 1930 and 1931, Congress proposed to appropriate $60 million to help the victims of the disaster buy fuel and food. Hoover accepted the idea of allocating money to feed animals, but he rejected the idea of feeding farmers and their families. One member of Congress said that the administration would give food to "jackasses . . . but not starving babies." The president accepted a compromise that spent the money without saying that some of it would be used for food. The spectacle of the president being more solicitous for animals than starving citizens was another testimony to Hoover's inability to empathize with the plight of his fellow Americans.

Everyday Life during the Depression

For most Americans after 1929, there was no single decisive moment when they knew that the economy was in trouble. A husband might find his pay reduced or his hours of work cut back. Soon families were making changes in their lifestyle, postponing purchases, and sending children out to find jobs. When a person lost a job, savings helped tide the family over until another job could be found. As time passed and no jobs appeared, savings ran out and the family home went on the market or the mortgage was foreclosed. The family slipped into the ranks of the unemployed or the poor. In a trend that became a lasting image of the Depression, men selling apples appeared on the street corners in major cities. Beggars and panhandlers became a common sight as well.

For those who were at the bottom of the economy even during boom times, the Depression presented still greater challenges. Blacks had not shared in the relative prosperity of the 1920s. "The Negro was born in depression," said one African American. "It only became official when it hit the white man." In the South, whites seeking work took over the low-paying service jobs that African Americans had traditionally filled. Some black workers in the South encountered violence when whites compelled them to leave their jobs. Elsewhere, white

Distress on the Farm in the Great Depression

This picture of a farm being sold at auction during the Great Depression shows the culmination of the agricultural problems discussed in an earlier Picturing the Past feature in Chapter 23 (page 680) Even with the prosperity of the 1920s, farmers remained trapped in a cycle of overproduction and falling commodity prices. As the bottom dropped out of the economy in the early 1930s and deflation hit all sectors, many farmers found it impossible to pay their debts and make a living. One by one, smaller, less efficient farms went under. As farm bankruptcies spread, scenes like the one in this photograph became commonplace in rural America. The potential for violence from the resentful neighbors became so strong that armed state troopers and National Guardsmen were needed to keep order as the sales went forward. The sense of imminent anger and protest that pervades this picture was a common thread throughout American life during the hard times of the 1930s.

© Bettmann/CORBIS

laborers went on strike, insisting that African American workers be dismissed.

Women were told that they too should relinquish their jobs to men to end the unemployment crisis. Some corporations fired all their married women employees, and school districts in the South dismissed women teachers who married. Because women did the domestic and clerical tasks that men did not care to do even in hard times, the number of women employed did not decline as fast as the number of men. Nevertheless, the Depression retarded the economic progress of women.

For Native Americans, the hard times perpetuated a legacy of neglect that had endured for decades. The Bureau of Indian Affairs (BIA) did not address the many social problems that the people under its jurisdiction confronted. Nearly half the Indians on reservations had no land; the other half subsisted on poor quality land. Poverty pervaded Indian society along with a rate of infant mortality that far exceeded the rate for the white population. Criticism of the BIA mounted, but, despite a rhetorical commitment to reform, the Hoover administration accomplished little to improve Native American life.

On the nation's farms, abundant crops could not find a market, so the produce rotted in the fields. Mortgages were foreclosed, and many former landowners fell into the status of tenant farmers as the Depression went on. In 1929, President Hoover had persuaded Congress to pass an Agricultural Marketing Act that created a Federal Farm Board whose purpose was to stabilize farm prices. When farm surpluses around the world swamped grain markets in 1930, it proved impossible to prevent commodity prices from falling. Talk of strikes and protests

The shantytowns where the homeless and unemployed lived became known as "Hoovervilles." Their presence on the outskirts of the large cities became a common sight as the Depression deepened.

was common among farmers during 1931 and 1932. During the summer of 1932, Milo Reno, an Iowa farmer, created the Farmers' Holiday Association that urged growers to hold their crops off the market until prices rose. The association put its program into verse:

Let's call a farmers' holiday
A holiday let's hold;
We'll eat our ham and wheat and eggs
And let them eat their gold.

In the Southwest, the Hoover administration, faced with growing unemployment in that region, endeavored to reduce the number of people looking for jobs with a program to send Hispanic workers and their families back to Mexico and other Latin American countries. Some 82,000 Mexicans were deported and another half million immigrants crossed the border out of fear that they would be sent back under duress. For Hispanic Americans who stayed in the United States, relief from the government was often hard to find because of a belief that it should be limited to "Americans."

As the Depression deepened, the homeless and unemployed took to the roads and rails, looking for work or better times. Migratory workers moved through the agricultural sections of California, picking figs and grapes for whatever they could earn. Others went from city to city, finding inadequate meals at relief stations, shuffling through a breadline in some cities, stealing or begging for food in others. The homeless lived in shantytowns outside of cities that were dubbed "**Hoovervilles**." Soon derogatory references to the president spread throughout the nation. A pocket turned outward as a sign of distress was

"a Hoover flag." In the Southwest, people killed armadillos and renamed the meat "Depression Pork."

By 1931, a sense of despair and hopelessness pervaded many segments of society. People who had been out of work for a year or two had lost the energy and inner resources to rebound even if a job was available. Others began to question the nation's values and beliefs. Bread riots occurred in several cities; the Communist party forecast that the system was toppling; and the nation's political leaders seemed out of touch with the downward trend of economic events. A popular song caught the nation's angry, restless mood:

Once I built a railroad, made it run
Made it race against time.
Once I built a railroad, now its done
Brother, can you spare a dime?

The Depression did not touch every American in the same way. Despite the economic disruptions, daily life in much of the nation went on as it always had. Families stayed together with the father holding a job, the mother running the home, and their children growing up and attending school. There might be less money to spend, but in these regions poverty had not yet become entrenched. Breadlines and people selling apples happened somewhere else. Nevertheless, the economic uncertainty that gripped so many people contributed to a general sense of unease and doubt that permeated the early 1930s.

Mass Culture during the Depression

Amid the hardships of the Depression, Americans found diversions and amusements in the mass media and popular entertainment that had emerged during the 1920s. Radio's popularity grew despite the hard times. Sales of radio sets in the United States reached $300 million annually by 1933. Consumers said that their radio would be one of the last things they sold to make ends meet. The habit of listening to a favorite program was an integral part of the daily lives of many families.

Radio was becoming more commercial every year. Programming appealed to popular tastes and sought the largest available audience. Listeners preferred daytime dramas such as *One Man's Family* and *Mary Noble, Backstage Wife,* quickly dubbed "soap operas" after the detergent companies that sponsored them. With the increasing emphasis on profits and ratings, commercials became commonplace. Listeners were told

When you're feeling kind blue
And you wonder what to do
Che-e-ew Chiclets, and
Chee-ee-er up!

Freeman Gosden and Charles Correll were the popular radio team of Amos 'n' Andy. They are shown here in blackface for one of the publicity photos for their act.

The four Marx Brothers became one of the popular comedy teams in the movies of the 1930s. Groucho went on to have a career in television after World War II.

The most popular radio program of the Depression years was **Amos 'n' Andy,** which portrayed the lives of two African American men in Harlem as interpreted by two white entertainers, Freeman Gosden and Charles Correll. Performed in heavy dialect, the show captured a huge audience at 7 o'clock each evening. The tales of black life appealed to white stereotypes about African Americans, but they also gained an audience among blacks because the characters' experiences were comparable to those of minority listeners.

With ticket prices very low and audiences hungry for diversion from the trials of daily life, Hollywood presented a wide choice of films between 1929 and 1932. Sound movies had replaced the silent pictures of the 1920s, and escapist entertainment dominated the movie screens across the country. Audiences laughed at the Marx Brothers in *Cocoanuts* (1929) and *Monkey Business* (1931). Musicals found a ready audience, and there was a vogue for gangster films such as *Little Caesar* (1931) with Edward G. Robinson and *The Public Enemy* (1931) with James Cagney. During the early 1930s, Hollywood pressed the limits of tolerance for sexual innuendoes and bawdy themes with stars such as Mae West.

Despite the economic and social limits of the economic downturn, the cultural flowering that had begun during the preceding decade continued. In Kansas City and other midwestern cities, African American musicians were developing a new jazz style that would become known as "swing" when white musicians smoothed its hard edges to make it appealing to their audiences. The hardships of the era evoked artistic creativity and a vibrant popular culture that would dominate the entertainment scene for half a century.

A Darkening World

With the economies of the democratic nations weakened and the structure of international relations tottering, authoritarian forces around the world asserted themselves against the existing order. The democracies and the Hoover administration seemed powerless to alter the trend of events. The course of American foreign policy under Hoover illustrated these concerns.

Herbert Hoover entered the White House with well-formulated ideas about the national role in foreign affairs. Since future wars were unlikely, he believed, it was time to pursue disarmament and let the force of world opinion maintain peace. In Latin America, the president proclaimed "**the good neighbor**" policy. He promised not to repeat previous U.S. interventions in the region, and he withdrew marines from Nicaragua and Haiti. In 1930, the State Department renounced the Roosevelt Corollary of 1904 that had asserted an American right to intervene in nations to the south. Despite outbreaks of revolutions in South America during his term, Hoover kept his word and left Latin American nations alone.

Drawing on his Quaker heritage, Hoover thought that wars were senseless and disarmament imperative. A naval conference in 1927 had brought Great Britain, Japan, and the United States to the diplomatic table. Disagreements about the size of vessels to be covered broke up the meeting. Hoover reassembled the major naval powers in London for a conference on disarmament. The London Treaty of 1930 made only a modest contribution to peace. To reduce military spending, the provisions of the Washington Conference pacts were extended for 5 years. The United States won parity with Britain in all naval vessels, and the Japanese gained the same result for submarines. Japan remained the dominant power in the Pacific, but there was little that the Hoover administration could do to change that reality.

As the U.S. economy deteriorated, the effects spread to Europe and further undermined the power of the democratic nations. With less money to invest, American capitalists could not lend to European governments, especially in Germany. The Smoot-Hawley tariff made it more difficult for Europeans and other importers to sell their products in the United States. International trade stagnated; production in all industrial companies declined. In 1931, Germany and Austria endeavored to set up a customs union to deal with their common problems, but the French objected to the plan and cut off payments to banks in the two countries. In the resulting turmoil, the Creditanstaldt, Austria's central bank, collapsed. The entire structure of international banking stood on the brink of disaster.

Hoover decided that the only answer was a moratorium on the payment of war debts to give the European countries time to regain their financial stability. He declared on June 21, 1931, that the United States would observe an 18-month moratorium on the collection of its foreign debts. The French held back for 2 weeks, putting further strain on German banks. In the end, all the countries involved agreed to Hoover's initiative.

The moratorium was the only possible answer, but it came too late to stop the erosion of the international financial system. A few months later, Great Britain devalued the pound when it could no longer maintain the gold standard. (That meant that the British would no longer buy gold at a fixed price and would allow the value of the pound to fall relative to other currencies.) This step reduced the price of British products and made them more competitive in world markets. However, other nations soon followed this course. Prices began to fall worldwide as production slowed, people took money out of circulation, and economic activity began to halt.

The weakening of the democracies provided an opening for authoritarian powers eager to challenge the existing order. The first test came in the Far East. In September 1931, Japanese troops detonated a weak explosive charge under a Japanese-owned railroad in Manchuria and blamed the episode on the Manchurians. The Japanese military

MAP 24.2 **The Japanese Invasion of Manchuria**

The Japanese invasion of Manchuria extended Japan's power up from Korea to the border of the Soviet Union and also presented them with a base for their ultimate attack on China later in the 1930s. The failure of the Western nations to take effective action against these Japanese actions began a process that would lead in time to the end of the European colonial presence in Asia.

had fabricated the incident as an excuse for attacking Chinese positions in Manchuria. During the weeks that followed, the Japanese army invaded Manchuria and advanced deep into the countryside. The Japanese bombed Chinese cities to deter any opposition to their effort to occupy all of Manchuria.

Frustrated by the power of the Western countries and desperate for raw materials, Japan and its military wanted to establish their nation as the dominant force in Asia and expel the foreign countries that had achieved a political and economic presence in China and the Far East. Anger at the discriminatory racial policies of the United States, Great Britain, and other European powers fed this frustration. Japan was also fearful that a resurgent China might pose a threat to Japanese ambitions and access to crucial materials for Tokyo's economy. Desire for political and economic supremacy in the Pacific completed the Japanese agenda.

A Challenge to the League of Nations

Japan's attack into Manchuria posed a threat to the League of Nations. It also confronted the United States with the problem of what to do about a clear violation of policies and treaties to which Washington was a party, such as the Open Door policy and the Nine-Power Treaty. Yet the American army was no match for Japan's, and the administration had not maintained naval strength at the levels allowed in the various treaties that had been signed during the preceding decade. In addition, Congress would not have been sympathetic to U.S. intervention in a remote foreign quarrel. For the same reason, Washington could not look to European countries. Nor could it endorse an economic boycott against Japan under the sponsorship of the League of Nations. Secretary of State Henry L. Stimson issued statements to China and Japan that proclaimed the unwillingness of the United States to recognize territorial changes in China produced by aggressive actions. This policy of nonrecognition became known as the Stimson Doctrine. The Japanese pressed ahead with their campaign to occupy Manchuria and intimidate China despite the secretary's comments.

The League of Nations criticized the Japanese policy, and Japan responded by withdrawing from the organization early in 1933. The United States and Japan were now embarked on a course that would lead to ever more bitter encounters and ultimately to all-out war.

© CORBIS

Adolf Hitler rose to power with a blend of German nationalism, virulent anti-Semitism, and anger at the outcome of World War I that attracted adoring followers like the ones show in this photograph.

Germany Moves toward the Nazis

In Germany, resentment about the Treaty of Versailles had grown during the Depression. Convinced that they had not lost the war on the battlefield (even though the German Army was on the brink of collapse at the time of the Armistice in 1918), Germans wanted revenge for the restrictions placed on them in the peace settlement. They listened to the anti-Semitic, nationalistic ravings of the National Socialist party under Adolf Hitler. Hitler's message of national power and fanatical hatred of the Jews proved intoxicating to the German people. During 1932, he stood on the brink of obtaining power. Some Americans, insensitive to Hitler's ideology of racial oppression, even admired the policies of Hitler and the Italian dictator Benito Mussolini because they apparently offered decisive action to deal with the economic crisis. The situation of democratic governments,

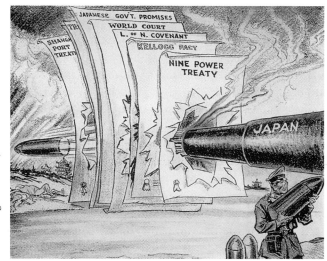

© The Granger Collection, New York

When Japan invaded Manchuria in 1931, it violated a number of international agreements that it had signed. This cartoon provides an American commentary on these actions. The depiction of Japanese militarism would be a running theme in the United States throughout the 1930s and 1940s.

DOING HISTORY ONLINE

Herbert Hoover and the Economy

Read the documents in this module. Why did the Depression so indelibly tarnish Herbert Hoover's reputation?

History ⧖ Now™   Visit HistoryNOW to access primary sources and exercises related to this topic: http://now.ilrn.com/ayers_etal3e

DOING HISTORY

1932: The Clash of Philosophies

IN THE 1932 election, Franklin D. Roosevelt, the Democratic candidate for president, argued that the government must do more to fight the Depression. His position put him at odds with President Herbert Hoover, who contended that Roosevelt's programs meant regimentation and the end of American democracy. The voters elected Roosevelt in November 1932, but the debate that the two men waged has continued to shape politics down to the present time.

Roosevelt articulated his position about government's role in a speech in September 1932 to the Commonwealth Club in San Francisco. In his remarks he mentions the electric utility financier, Samuel Insull, whose corporate empire had collapsed:

"This implication is, briefly, that the responsible heads of finance and industry, instead of acting each for himself, must work together to achieve the common end. They must, where necessary, sacrifice this or that private advantage; and in reciprocal self-denial must seek a general advantage. It is here that formal government—political government, if you choose—comes in.

Whenever in the pursuit of this objective the line wolf, the unethical competitor, the reckless promoter, the Ishmael or Insull whose hand is against every man's, declines to join in achieving an end recognized as being for the public welfare and threatens to drag the industry back to a state of anarchy, the government may properly be asked to apply restraint. Likewise, should the group ever use its collective power contrary to the public welfare, the government must be swift to enter and protect the public interest.

The government should assume the function of economic regulation only as a last resort, to be tried only when private initiative, inspired by high responsibility, with such assistance and balance as government can give, has finally failed. As yet there has been no final failure, because there has been no attempt; and I decline to assume that this nation is unable to meet the situation."

President Hoover, noting that Roosevelt had promised also to use the power of the government to provide more jobs for the unemployed, went on the attack against this program, as well as his opponent's view of government, in a speech in New York in late October 1932. The New York Times covered the event.

"If Mr. Roosevelt undertook to make good his promise to a constituent to support measures for inaugurating self-liquidating projects to provide work for all," Mr. Hoover declared, *it would mean "the total abandonment of every principle on which this government and the American system is founded." Continuing, he said:*

"The stages of this destruction would be first the destruction of government credit, the value of government securities, the destruction of every fiduciary trust in our country, insurance policies and all. It would pull down the employment of those who are still at work by the high taxes and demoralization of credit upon which their employment is dependent. It would mean the pulling and hauling of politics for projects and measures, to favoring of localities, sections and groups. It would mean the growth of a fearful bureaucracy which, once established, could never be dislodged. If it were possible, it would mean one third of the electorate with government jobs earnest to maintain this bureaucracy and to control the political destinies of the country."

The promises and measures advocated by leaders of the Democratic Party and until now not disavowed by Governor Roosevelt, Mr. Hoover said, would mean the "growth of bureaucracy such as we have never seen in our history." They would "break down the savings, the wags, the equality of opportunity among our people," and lead to further centralization of government," he asserted.

Source: *The New York Times,* September 24, 1932 (Roosevelt); *The New York Times,* November 1, 1932 (Hoover).

Questions for Reflection

1. How do Hoover and Roosevelt differ in their views of government power and its impact on the economy?

2. How does Roosevelt propose to use the government to attack the Depression?

3. What does Hoover see as the consequences of policies that would employ the government to create jobs for the unemployed?

4. What contrasts can be made between Roosevelt's view of the business community and what Hoover believes about the same issue?

Explore additional primary sources rel... chapter on the Wadsworth American F... Resource Center or HistoryNOW webs...
http://history.wadsworth.com/rc/...
http://now.ilrn.com/ayers_etal3e...

on the other hand, was perilous as the United States entered the third year of the Depression. Could the United States find the political means to address the massive problems that the Depression had created?

A Political Opportunity for the Democrats

At the beginning of 1932, the Hoover presidency was in dire political trouble. Even his advisors were critical. One official remarked that the president "has a childlike faith in statements," and a political commentator concluded that "there seems to be no class or section where Hoover is strong." Jokes about Hoover circulated across the country. It was said that if you put a flower in his hand it would wilt. Another story had the president asking Secretary of the Treasury Andrew Mellon if he could borrow a nickel (the price of making a telephone call in those days) to call a friend. "Here's a dime," Mellon was supposed to have answered, "call all your friends."

By 1932, the limits of the president's voluntary approach had become evident even to him. During the winter he supported a congressional initiative to establish the Reconstruction Finance Corporation (RFC). Congress authorized this agency to loan up to $2 billion in tax money to save banks, insurance companies, and railroads from financial collapse. The law that set up the RFC repudiated the principle of voluntary action that Hoover had been following since the Depression began. It put the federal government behind the effort to achieve economic recovery and signaled that Washington could no longer take a passive or hands-off role when the economy turned downward.

Republican problems meant opportunity for the Democrats if they could seize the initiative. In their congressional programs, however, the Democrats were not much more creative than their opponents. A deep split persisted within the party over the proper role of government in dealing with the Depression. Many of the

conservatives who had supported **Al Smith** would not look kindly on a candidate who wished to expand government's part in dealing with the Depression.

In the 1930 elections, the Democrats picked up 8 seats in the Senate. The Republicans retained control of the upper house by only a single vote. In the House, the Democratic gain was 49 seats, not enough to give the Democrats a majority, although their total of 216 members put them close. Whether the Democrats could unite behind a coherent program remained an open question in Washington as the presidential election neared.

When Congress reassembled late in 1931, the Democrats had gained several other seats because of the death or retirement of four Republicans. As a result, **John Nance "Cactus Jack" Garner** of Texas became the new Speaker of the House. A crusty conservative with no fresh ideas, Garner's major proposals seemed likely to make the Depression even worse. His answer to the growing budget deficit that the Depression produced was to offer a national sales tax. Such a proposal would have hurt lower-income Americans and, by taking money out of the economy, would also have been deflationary at a time when the economy needed stimulation. Before the bill could pass the House, angry rebels in both parties killed the sales tax idea. The Democrats in Congress seemed as bereft of ideas as the Republicans for fighting the Depression. Increasingly, attention turned to the fight for the Democratic presidential nomination.

The front-runner for the Democratic prize in 1932 was Franklin D. Roosevelt. He came from a wealthy branch of his family that lived on the Hudson River in Hyde Park, New York. After attending the aristocratic Groton School and Harvard University, he had studied law in New York City. In 1910, he won a seat in the New York state senate, and three years later he became assistant secretary of the navy in the Wilson administration. Seven years in Washington had given him a thorough introduction to the politics of that city.

Although Franklin D. Roosevelt was only a distant cousin of Theodore, his wife, Eleanor, was the former

...nt's niece. His connection to a famous name helped ...osevelt secure the Democratic vice presidential nomination in 1920. Although the Democrats lost, the race gave Roosevelt valuable national exposure.

In 1921, Roosevelt was stricken with polio and lost the use of his legs. For the rest of his life he could not walk without crutches and usually used a wheelchair. The public knew of his disability, but the press did not stress his condition. Counted out of politics because of his illness, Roosevelt worked his way back into Democratic affairs during the mid-1920s and in 1928 was elected governor of New York by a narrow margin despite the Hoover landslide. Two years later, he won reelection by a huge majority.

In public, the 50-year-old Roosevelt, his wife, and their five children were the picture of a robust American family. But behind this facade lay personal difficulty. During 1918–1919, the marriage had almost collapsed because of Franklin's affair with another woman. The Roosevelts stayed together, but theirs became a political partnership of convenience. During the 1920s, Eleanor Roosevelt played a greater role in politics herself and gained prominence as an advocate of social reform. In the 1930s her personal drive would help her to transform the role of the first lady.

As for his political views, Roosevelt shared many of the ideas of the mainstream of the Democratic party. He believed in balanced budgets, the gold standard, and capitalism. Yet he also had an instinctive rapport with people in all segments of society, and he relished the exercise of power. His progressive views on the role of government separated him from conservatives in his party, who longed for a return to the pre-Wilsonian traditions of small government, state rights, and minimal government involvement with the economy. Roosevelt trusted no one completely and never confided his deepest thoughts about his political destiny. Many observers judged him to be superficial and shallow.

Roosevelt's campaign got off to a strong start. His manager, James A. Farley, had been wooing potential delegates since 1930, and he had mapped out a strategy to attract both big-city leaders, whose support for the Democrats had been growing, and the Solid South. As a source of ideas for his campaign, Roosevelt turned to the academic community in the Northeast. He recruited several professors from Columbia University in New York to write speeches and formulate concepts for his programs. These scholars were promptly named "the **brain trust**." In his speeches, Roosevelt talked of "the forgotten man at the bottom of the economic pyramid" who was suffering from the effects of the Depression. The answer, Roosevelt said, was "bold, persistent experimentation."

As Roosevelt's campaign gathered strength it became clear from newspaper surveys, crude polls, and the sense that the administration was faltering, that Hoover was going to lose. Other Democrats challenged the frontrunner. Still angry over his 1928 defeat, which he blamed on religious bigotry, and no longer friendly with Roosevelt, Al Smith wanted another chance at the White House. He became a more active candidate as the weeks passed, and his strength in the Northeast made him a serious rival to Roosevelt. Roosevelt was clearly the choice of a majority of the Democrats, but party rules mandated that a nominee receive two-thirds of the votes of the convention delegates. If Garner and Smith teamed up against him and their delegates stood firm, Roosevelt could not win.

The Democratic National Convention opened in Chicago on June 20, 1932. The Roosevelt forces faced many difficulties during the days that followed. But when it came to the actual balloting, his opponents could not rally around anyone else. In the end, Speaker Garner decided to release his delegates to Roosevelt; his reward would be the vice presidential nomination, which he said was "not worth a pitcher of warm piss." At the same time, the California delegation swung its support to Roosevelt on the fourth ballot.

A New Deal

In a dramatic break with the political tradition that barred candidates from appearing at a convention to accept a nomination, Roosevelt boarded a plane and flew to Chicago through stormy weather. There he delivered his speech in which he used a phrase that would become the trademark of his presidency: "I pledge you, I pledge myself to a new deal for the American people." The candidate seemed poised and self-assured, and he radiated optimism. The convention band played the new Democratic theme: "Happy Days Are Here Again." Meanwhile, the gloomy Republicans nominated Hoover and braced for defeat. As the politicians prepared for battle, the economy remained on a downward path.

The Economy in Distress

To deal with the growing budget deficit, Congress imposed new taxes in the Revenue Act of 1932. The sales tax idea had been dropped, but other levies on corporations, estates, and incomes made this the greatest peacetime increase in taxes in the nation's history. At a time when the economy needed fiscal stimulus, the tax measure drew funds out of the hands of consumers.

Raising taxes in an election year added to Hoover's growing unpopularity.

The weakening of the Hoover administration and the increasing power of the Democrats led to an important change in labor policy during 1932. For many years employers had used friendly federal judges and the power of injunctions to cripple the ability of labor unions to win strikes. The Norris-LaGuardia Act of 1932, by contrast, extended to workers "full freedom of association" in unions and labor representation, restricted the use of injunctions, and barred reliance on "yellow-dog" contracts, which prevented workers from joining unions.

As the Depression worsened during its third year, the plight of unemployed Americans deteriorated well beyond the ability of cities and states to provide aid. Congress became restive as the Reconstruction Finance Corporation extended loans to large corporations and the White House resisted legislation to help the needy and distressed. Bills were introduced to provide direct assistance to the unemployed, but a coalition of Republicans and southern Democrats blocked their passage. As news spread about how much money businesses had received from the RFC, pressure intensified for Congress to do something. The result was the Emergency Relief and Construction Act of 1932, which required states to attest that they could not raise any money themselves before federal funds were allocated to them. The law limited the kinds of construction projects that could be funded, but it represented at least a symbolic step toward a greater federal role in meeting the needs of desperate Americans in the midst of an economic crisis.

The Bonus March

During the summer of 1932, other desperate citizens sought immediate relief from the government in the form of cash. After World War I, Congress had promised war veterans cash bonuses in the form of paid-up life insurance to be disbursed in 1945. During the Hoover presidency, the needs of veterans as a group had been generously funded, and on the whole they had suffered less from the Depression than had some other groups. As the Depression worsened, however, the veterans clamored for early access to their "bonus" money. Hoover vetoed a proposal to allow veterans to borrow against the value of their bonuses in 1931. During the spring of 1932, Congress decided not to authorize early payment of the bonuses.

To make their presence felt, thousands of veterans organized the Bonus Expeditionary Force, or the **Bonus Army,** which came to Washington during the

The economic hard times of the Depression forced many Americans to live in shantytowns that became known as Hoovervilles. These children exemplify the resentment that built toward Hoover as his presidency went on.

summer of 1932 to listen to Congress debate the bonus proposal. They camped out in tar paper dwellings and tents on the banks of the Anacostia River; some slept in government buildings. The authorities in Washington generally cooperated with the veterans and did what they could to provide them with food and shelter during their stay. Hoover ignored them. When it became clear that Congress was not going to help the Bonus Marchers and would adjourn in mid-July 1932, the Hoover administration urged the Bonus Army to leave Washington and even allocated $100,000 to pay for the cost of sending the men home. Some of the marchers took advantage of this offer and left Washington. Others stayed on, hoping for a change in government policy.

Some officials in the Hoover administration wanted a confrontation with the marchers in order to bolster the president's reputation as a champion of law and order. On July 28, the secretary of war ordered the police to remove marchers from government buildings. When the police moved in, the veterans resisted and fighting occurred. A police pistol went off; other officers began shooting; and soon two Bonus Marchers lay dead. The president ordered the federal troops in Washington, commanded by General Douglas MacArthur, to restore order. The general took his men, armed with tanks and machine guns, across the Anacostia River into the main camp of the Bonus Army. The veterans fled in terror as the soldiers approached. Tear gas canisters were hurled, tents were burned, and the crowd dispersed in a panic. Motion picture cameras caught MacArthur in full military regalia directing the attack, and moviegoers across the nation saw newsreels of American soldiers ousting the Bonus Army from its camp.

The Hoover administration laid the blame for the incident on the influence of Communists inside the veterans' camp. There were a few Communists among the veterans, but they had little influence on the protest. Law enforcement agencies found no evidence of an organized conspiracy among the marchers, and public opinion favored the veterans. "If the Army must be called out to make war on unarmed citizens," said a newspaper editor, "this is no longer America."

The 1932 Election

The economic devastation produced by the Great Depression offered groups outside the two-party system a promising chance to win votes for more radical solutions to the nation's problems. The Communists, for example, organized Unemployed Councils to stage protests against high rents and evictions of tenants. Socialists and other left-wing groups cooperated with the

The case of the African American men accused in the Scottsboro trial became another controversial episode in racial injustice in the early 1930s. Guarded by state troopers, the defendants in the case consult with their attorney.

Communists in protest marches and petitions for relief. Efforts to organize sharecroppers and tenant farmers in the South also went forward under the sponsorship of the Communists during these years. The Communists wooed African American support when they defended the "**Scottsboro boys**," a group of young black men who had been unjustly accused of raping two white women in Alabama in 1931. In 1932, some prominent intellectuals endorsed the Communist presidential campaign or supported the Socialist candidate, Norman Thomas.

For the majority of Americans who were still aligned with the two-party system, however, the only real choice lay between Roosevelt and Hoover. Many of Roosevelt's advisors told him that he did not have to campaign to win the race. Roosevelt saw the matter differently. If he ran a passive, traditional campaign, he would not persuade the voters who were looking for a change. A front-porch campaign would also have fed rumors that he could not withstand the physical rigors of the presidency. So Roosevelt crisscrossed the country, making speeches that assailed the Republican leadership and attacked Hoover's record.

Roosevelt's Campaign

Roosevelt wanted to occupy the political middle ground, and as a result his campaign speeches took a variety of contradictory positions. At times he seemed to be calling for a more activist federal government that would adapt "existing economic organizations to the service of the people." On other occasions he attacked Hoover's budget deficits and wasteful government spending. Most of Roosevelt's appeal came down to hope, confidence, and the promise of political change.

The incumbent president knew he was going to lose, but he campaigned doggedly. Hoover told the voters that the nation faced a choice between "two philosophies of government," with freedom and individual initiative the philosophy of the Republicans and socialism and regimentation the aim of the Democrats. Roosevelt countered that the country needed new ideas to get out of the Depression. He left it unclear just what those new ideas would be. Abandoned by many of his fellow Republicans and unpopular with the voters, Hoover staggered through his lifeless campaign.

Hoover Defeated

On election day, the Democratic candidate won overwhelmingly in the popular vote and scored a 472-to-59 triumph in the electoral college. His party

ECONOMICS & TECHNOLOGY

A Bank Fails

One of the most unsettling aspects of the Great Depression was the increasing numbers of bank failures. Since there was no national system to insure bank deposits, those who had money in a financial institution were vulnerable when a bank failed or a "run" occurred as depositors sought to get out whatever money they could. With no federal authority to help banks in trouble, the collapse of one major bank could trigger a ripple effect of failures that could paralyze commerce in an entire region or state. This picture shows an anxious crowd milling about outside a bank in New York City that until this crisis had paid 4 percent interest on "thrift accounts." The sense of fear that is evident in the body language of passersby peering into the bank conveys the worry that more and more Americans felt about their financial security as the Depression continued its downward course in the early 1930s.

© Bettmann/CORBIS

secured almost 57 percent of the popular vote and made significant gains in Congress: 90 seats in the House and 13 in the Senate. The election proved a major disappointment to both the Socialists and the Communists. Norman Thomas, running on the Socialist ticket, received fewer than a million votes. William Z. Foster, the Communist candidate, gained just over 100,000 ballots. Americans were still faithful to the two-party system even in this moment of severe economic difficulty.

By 1932, politicians realized that the 4-month period between the time that a president was elected and the inauguration was too long for a modern industrialized nation. A quicker transition to the incoming administration was imperative. A constitutional amendment moving the date of the inauguration to January 20 was under consideration, but the **Twentieth Amendment** would not go into effect until 1937. Meanwhile, the country faced a worsening economic crisis.

During these 4 months, the Depression reached its lowest point. One-quarter of the workforce could not find jobs and the relief system had broken down. The gross national product, which had stood at more than $103 billion in 1929, had slid to $58 billion by 1932. Wheat sold for 30 cents a bushel compared with the $3 a bushel it had brought in 1920. Farmers threatened more action to stop foreclosures of delinquent mortgages in their states. In December, hunger marchers came to Washington to ask for government aid. The growing

The terrible events of 1932 left many American families impoverished. These migrants in New Mexico, shown in August 1936, had left Iowa in 1932 after their father became sick and could not work. Their plight is representative of those Americans on whom the Depression fell with crushing force in the mid-1930s.

numbers of failing banks presented a dire threat: 1,453 banks shut their doors in 1932, and political leaders feared that the nation's entire financial structure could be threatened.

Neither Hoover nor Roosevelt was able to deal with these growing problems. The defeated president believed that the cause of the Depression lay beyond the nation's borders. Wary of making commitments before taking office, Roosevelt dodged Hoover's efforts to obtain his backing. Hoover became convinced that Roosevelt cared little for the welfare of the country, whereas Roosevelt saw his defeated rival as a sore loser who was trying to win through subterfuge what he had lost at the polls.

Roosevelt devoted most of his energy to forming a cabinet and getting ready to take over the presidency. The president-elect also survived an assassination attempt 2 weeks before the inauguration. At a speaking engagement in Miami during a break from a fishing trip, Roosevelt was talking with the mayor of Chicago, Anton Cermak, when a would-be assassin fired five shots at Roosevelt. None hit him, but one wounded Cermak, who died shortly afterward.

Meanwhile, a crisis of confidence in banks gripped the country. Alarm about the banking system had been spreading since October 1932. During that month the governor of Nevada proclaimed a 12-day bank "holiday" to end depositor runs on banks. The news spurred depositors in other states to remove funds from their local banks. In Michigan, two banks in Detroit seemed about to fail by mid-February. Hoover tried to persuade business leaders, including Henry Ford, to place deposits in the troubled banks. Ford was willing, but others were not. The governor of Michigan intervened and declared a bank holiday on February 14. Depositors in other states, fearing that their deposits would be frozen, tried to withdraw their money from local banks. Governors in nine other states were forced to announce bank holidays.

Hoover pressed the incoming president for immediate joint action. Roosevelt was still reluctant to tie his own hands before he took office. The days passed as February ended with no agreement on either side to do anything about the banking crisis. The two men held one last awkward business meeting on March 3 but came to no positive result.

As the transition of power neared, general apprehension increased. By the morning of March 4, banks in New York City, the nation's financial capital, were shutting their doors. A weary Hoover concluded in a moment of personal despair: "We are at the end of our string." Shortly before eleven o'clock, the outgoing president joined Franklin Roosevelt in a waiting limousine and the two men drove off toward the Capitol. Roosevelt waved to well-wishers in the crowd as Hoover sat in silence. A nation mired in the worst depression in its history waited to hear what the new president would say.

Conclusion

The economic slump of the early 1930s was one of the most significant events in American history. It called into question faith in the brighter future that the nation promised to all. The Depression also changed the way Americans viewed the federal government. Although they retained their suspicion of intrusive national power, they expected that Washington would prevent future depressions and relieve the effects of the one that was occurring. Radical solutions that involved dismantling capitalism or redistributing income on a large scale gained relatively few adherents.

Simulation

Surviving the Great Depression (In this simulation you can choose to be an African American sharecropper in Alabama, a white farmer in Wisconsin, or a young Italian in New York City and make choices based on the circumstances and opportunities afforded.)

Document Exercises

Roosevelt's First Inaugural Address, 1933

HistoryNOW

http://now.ilrn.com/ayers_etal3e

Primary Source Exercises

The Crash

Herbert Hoover and the Economy

Passages 1933 to 1960

Americans who grew up in the Depression, served their country during World War II, and ushered in the enormous prosperity of the 1950s and beyond, have been celebrated in recent books and movies as "the greatest generation." There are good reasons for such praise. In no other period except the Civil War and Reconstruction was America as severely tested, its direction as radically changed. The 1930s saw the worst economic catastrophe in modern history. Banks collapsed, farms failed, factories closed, bread lines formed in the cities. Yet what truly defined the nation in this decade was its passionate response to misfortune—the way Americans mixed protest, innovation, and reform. Dramatic changes occurred. The Great Depression not only increased the social responsibilities of government, it also opened the political process to millions of "forgotten Americans," who exercised power by joining labor unions, switching political parties, and migrating to places where they could vote and be represented. In contrast to the violent ideological struggles that gripped much of Europe in the 1930s, the United States witnessed a remarkable expansion of the democratic principles it held so dear.

Although the Great Depression would linger until World War II, the federal government provided Americans with food and employment, optimism and hope. Furthermore, the vast public works projects of that era—the roads, dams, bridges, tunnels, schools, hospitals, post offices, airports, parks, and playgrounds—created a physical infrastructure that tied the nation together while it spurred its future success. World War II brought on new challenges and opportunities. Battling on two fronts, the nation resolutely mobilized a superb U.S. fighting force and a masterful homefront effort in which almost everyone took part. The war provided better employment for minorities and for women, although discrimination in wages and skilled jobs remained. So, too, did segregation in the armed forces—a hypocrisy that did not end till 1948. Nevertheless, Americans stood shoulder-to-shoulder against the villainy of fascism, Pearl Harbor, and Nazi genocide.

The enormous prosperity following World War II quickly pushed fears of economic depression aside. What remained in place, however, were the structural reforms that made banks safer, capitalism stronger, and people more secure. Postwar Americans strongly supported an active government role in domestic and foreign affairs. There was little opposition to expanding the social security system, increasing the defense budget, or providing hefty benefits to veterans of the war. Soldiers came home and picked up their lives. The marriage rate soared, a baby boom followed, and young families rushed to the suburbs. Peacetime consumption replaced wartime production as the key to national prosperity, with the sale of new homes, automobiles, and appliances reaching record heights.

The prosperity and good feelings generated by World War II, however, were not equally shared. Employment opportunities for women fell dramatically after the veterans returned. Racial prejudice

The New Deal forged a legacy of magnificent public works structures, including the Grand Coulee Dam, the 100-mile causeway linking Florida to Key West, the Triborough Bridge in New York City, and the Golden Gate Bridge in San Francisco.

The landing craft—or LST—became a symbol of American fighting power during World War II. Thousands were produced to carry troops, vehicles, and equipment ashore in the Pacific, North Africa, Anzio, and Normany.

remained a national disgrace. The South still required segregation by law, while other regions discriminated more subtly in housing, education, and jobs. Furthermore, growing fears about Soviet expansion and domestic communism dissolved the political unity, or bipartisanship, that had marked American foreign policy throughout the war. The resulting Red Scare, fueled by opportunistic politicians like Senator Joseph R. McCarthy, challenged America's most cherished ideals.

Still, the nation prospered and grew. The 1950s saw the spread of a powerful civil rights movement and the demise of Senator McCarthy. Breakthroughs in medicine and technology ended the nightmare of polio, fueled the space race, and brought the miracle of television into almost every American home. The economic boom continued, raising living standards and national confidence to even greater heights. As 1960 approached, the nation appeared content and comfortable—thanks in large part to "the greatest generation," now approaching middle age.

Following the former Soviet Union's spectacular launch of *Sputnik I*, the United States created the National Aeronautics and Space Administration (NASA) in 1958 to manage civilian space operations. Among its first tasks was the selection and training of astronauts (pictured) for Project Mercury, the human spaceflight program.

America and the World: 1933–1960

The Normandy invasion of 1944, known as Operation OVERLORD, was instrumental in the collapse and surrender of German forces in World War II.

The Nazi invasion of Poland in 1939 plunged Europe into World War II.

The North Korean invasion of South Korea in 1950 led to a 3-year conflict that involved the United States and Communist China.

ASIA

EUROPE

AFRICA

In August 1945, the United States dropped two atomic bombs on the Japanese cities of Hiroshima and Nagasaki, hastening the Japanese surrender that ended World War II.

INDIAN OCEAN

AUSTRAL

ANTARCTICA

The Montgomery Bus Boycott of 1955 energized the struggle against racial segregation in the American South.

NORTH AMERICA

The Japanese attack on Pearl Harbor in 1941 brought the United States into World War II.

ATLANTIC OCEAN

The "Dust Bowl" distaster of the 1930s drove millions of Great Plains residents from their land.

PACIFIC OCEAN

SOUTH AMERICA

Chronology

	1932	**1940**	**1946**
POLITICS & DIPLOMACY	**1932:** Franklin Roosevelt elected president **1933:** Adolph Hitler becomes chancellor of Germany U.S. recognizes the Soviet Union **1935:** Congress passes Social Security **1936:** Spanish Civil War **1937:** Court-packing plan defeated **1939:** Nazi forces invade Poland	**1940:** Roosevelt wins unprecedented third term **1941:** Japanese bomb Pearl Harbor **1942:** Incarceration of Japanese-Americans **1943:** German army crushed at Stalingrad **1944:** Normandy Invasion **1945:** Germany surrenders Atomic bombs dropped on Hiroshima and Nagasaki Japan surrenders	**1946:** Cold War emerges **1947:** Truman Doctrine and Marshall Plan implemented **1948:** Alger Hiss indicted for perjury **1949:** Communists triumph in China
SOCIAL & CULTURAL EVENTS	**1932:** Bonus Army march **1933:** Prohibition ends **1935:** Congress of Industrial Organizations formed **1936:** Jesse Owens dominates the Berlin Olympics **1939:** John Steinbeck publishes *The Grapes of Wrath* Marian Anderson sings at Lincoln Memorial	**1941:** A. Philip Randolph threatens March on Washington **1943:** Race riot in Detroit **1944:** GI Bill passed **1945:** 12.5 million Americans in uniform	**1946:** Dr. Spock publishes *Common Sense Book of Baby and Child Care* **1947:** Jackie Robinson breaks baseball's color line **1948:** *Kinsey Report* **1949:** Sears, Roebuck catalogue advertises television set
ECONOMICS & TECHNOLOGY	**1932:** Unemployment reaches 25 percent Thousands of banks close **1933:** Tennessee Valley Authority created **1937:** Severe recession	**1941:** Manhattan Project begins **1945:** United States produces more than half the world's manufactured goods	**1946:** Reconversion **1949:** Soviet Union tests atomic bomb

1950

1956

1958

1950: Senator Joseph McCarthy raises
Communist issue
Korean War begins
1952: Dwight Eisenhower elected
president
1953: Cease-fire in Korea
Stalin dies
1954: U.S. Senate censures Joseph
McCarthy
Brown v. Board of Education

1956: Hungarian Revolution
Suez crisis
1957: Federal troops sent to Little Rock

1959: Cuban Revolution

1951: Alan Freed hosts rock 'n' roll radio
show
1955: Montgomery bus boycott

1956: Elvis Presley appears on
Ed Sullivan Show
1957: Jack Kerouac publishes *On the
Road*

1959: TV quiz show scandals

1954: IBM markets business computer
1955: Salk polio vaccine

1956: Federal Highway Act
1957: *Sputnik* launched

1958: U.S. manned space program begins

25 The New Deal, 1933–1939

This *New Yorker* cartoon, sketched well before the inauguration, accurately predicted feelings of both men—the glum Hoover and the exuberant Roosevelt—as they rode down Pennsylvania Avenue together on March 4, 1933.

On March 4, 1933, Franklin Roosevelt took the presidential oath of office in a steady, chilling rain. "Only a foolish optimist can deny the dark realities of the moment," he told the huge crowd and the millions who listened on radio. Roosevelt's voice radiated confidence and concern. "This nation asks for action, and action now," he declared. Comparing the Depression to an all-out war of survival, he vowed to ask Congress for the "broad executive power . . . that would be given to me if we were in fact invaded by a foreign foe."

Roosevelt offered few specifics in his inaugural address. His objective was to convince a dispirited people to have faith in him and in themselves. Standing erect in his cumbersome leg braces, Roosevelt stressed four major themes: sacrifice, discipline, compassion, and hope. "The only thing we have to fear," he assured the nation, "is fear itself."

Rock Bottom

This fear was understandable. The winter of 1932–1933—the political interregnum between Hoover's defeat and Roosevelt's inauguration—was a time of intense suffering and despair. Unemployment reached a staggering 25 percent. Banks were failing everywhere. Food prices had collapsed, forcing farmers from their land. Roosevelt understood how deeply the Depression had shaken the country and sapped its confidence. "I have [seen] the faces of thousands of Americans," he confided to a friend. "They have the frightened look of children. . . . They are saying, 'We are caught in some thing we don't understand; perhaps this fellow can help us out.'"

Taking Charge

Roosevelt's words reflected both his compassion for common people and his detachment from their lives. He would become a father figure to them in perilous times—bold and caring, yet distant and elusive. He would be their protector, their steward, but not their social peer.

No peacetime president ever faced a tougher challenge, or a greater opportunity. Respected commentators were predicting the end of capitalism if the Depression hung on much longer. At the very least, Americans were desperate for change. And that meant almost any initiative designed to revive the economy, feed the hungry, and put people back to work.

Timeline

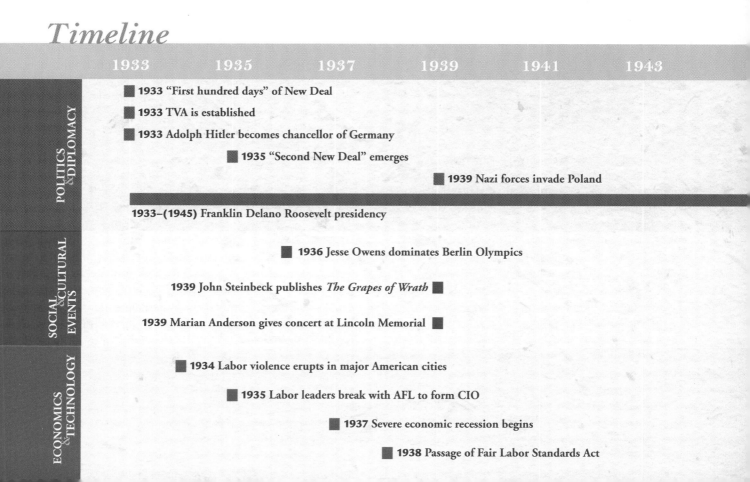

	1933	1935	1937	1939	1941	1943

POLITICS & DIPLOMACY

- 1933 "First hundred days" of New Deal
- 1933 TVA is established
- 1933 Adolph Hitler becomes chancellor of Germany
- 1935 "Second New Deal" emerges
- 1939 Nazi forces invade Poland

1933–(1945) Franklin Delano Roosevelt presidency

SOCIAL & CULTURAL EVENTS

- 1936 Jesse Owens dominates Berlin Olympics
- 1939 John Steinbeck publishes *The Grapes of Wrath*
- 1939 Marian Anderson gives concert at Lincoln Memorial

ECONOMICS & TECHNOLOGY

- 1934 Labor violence erupts in major American cities
- 1935 Labor leaders break with AFL to form CIO
- 1937 Severe economic recession begins
- 1938 Passage of Fair Labor Standards Act

FDR and Polio

Franklin Roosevelt contracted infantile paralysis, later known as polio, in 1921, at the age of 39. The disease permanently paralyzed him from the waist down. Though Americans, of course, were aware of his disability, it did not seem a part of the Roosevelt they knew. As president, FDR had an unspoken agreement with the press not to be photographed in a wheelchair or in a helpless position. The Secret Service prepared for his appearances by constructing wooden ramps and putting handgrips on the podium. When Roosevelt fell—as he did at the 1936 Democratic National Convention—the press did not report it.

© Bettmann/CORBIS

The photograph here typifies what Americans saw: FDR on his feet, leaning on a cane while grasping the arm of an aide. As biographer Hugh Gallagher, himself a polio victim, has written: "Among the thousands of political cartoons and caricatures of FDR, not one shows the man physically impaired. In fact, many of them have him as a man of action—running, jumping, doing things." Some have criticized Roosevelt for hiding his disability and not doing enough to alter the popular image of the handicapped. But the president believed that concerns about his health and stamina would detract from his ability to lead the nation in perilous times.

Roosevelt possessed neither a comprehensive plan to end the Depression, nor a rigid set of economic beliefs. What he did have was the willingness to experiment, to act decisively, and to use the government as a powerful weapon in the struggle for economic recovery. "Take a method and try it," he liked to say. "If it fails admit it frankly and try another."

Roosevelt surrounded himself with men and women of talent, accomplishment, and wide-ranging progressive views. His closest advisors included Republicans and Democrats, agricultural theorists and urban planners, college professors and political pros. In addition, the **New Deal** attracted thousands of young people to Washington, drawn by the opportunity to do something meaningful—and perhaps historic—with their lives.

The Bank Crisis

More than 5,000 banks had failed in the United States between 1930 and 1932, wiping out countless savings accounts and stalling the nation's credit. Panicked depositors, unable to tell a good bank from a bad one, lost faith in them all. An avalanche of withdrawals resulted. By the time Roosevelt took office, 19 states had declared "bank holidays" (or closings) to head off a full-scale collapse.

On March 6, 1933, the president called Congress back into special session and proclaimed a national "bank holiday." Three days later, his emergency banking proposal was enacted in a matter of hours. The new law provided for the federal inspection of all banks. Those with liquid assets would be allowed to reopen with a license from the Treasury Department; the others would be reorganized, if possible, or closed for good.

On March 12, Roosevelt addressed the nation in the first of his "fireside chats." About half of America's homes had radios in 1933, and the president's audience that Sunday evening was estimated at 60 million people. "I want to talk for a few minutes about banking," he began, assuring everyone that the system was now safe. The listeners believed him. In the following days, as the stronger banks reopened, deposits greatly exceeded withdrawals. By the end of March, almost $1 billion had been returned from mattresses to bank vaults. The crisis was over.

Roosevelt's handling of the bank emergency revealed his essential pragmatism. In the midst of such turmoil, he could easily have taken a more radical approach—by nationalizing the banks, for example, or by instituting much tighter controls. Instead, he demonstrated that his primary mission would be to preserve capitalism, not to replace it. And that meant *reforming* its institutions with substantial federal aid.

The president also showed himself to be a master of communication. His ability to reach people in the radio age, to win their confidence, was perhaps his greatest gift. He would use it often in the coming years, as the nation faced the twin crises of economic hardship and global war.

Extending Relief

The special session of Congress lasted from March 9 to June 16, 1933, a period known as "the first hundred days." In that time, more than a dozen major bills proposed by the White House were enacted. With both the House and the Senate now under firm Democratic control, Roosevelt had little trouble getting his legislation passed. As the banking crisis ended, he moved quickly to help those too desperate to help themselves.

The problem was daunting. By conservative estimates, more than 30 million Americans were now living in family units with no income at all.

The Hoover administration had refused to consider federal payments to the jobless. As a result, state and local governments had been forced to ration what little relief they could muster. In 1932, the average weekly payment to an "out-of-work" family in New York City was $2.39. In Detroit, the figure dropped to 15 cents a day before the money ran out. Some cities were forced to limit relief to families with three or more children; others offered free food and fuel.

Roosevelt believed that relief efforts should be a local responsibility. He, too, worried about the cost of funding such efforts, and about the consequences of giving people money that they hadn't actually earned. Yet there seemed to be no alternative. It was essential, said one of Roosevelt's advisors, to pursue "long-run" economic growth. The problem, he added, is that "people don't eat in the long run—they eat every day."

On March 21, the White House sent two major relief proposals to Capitol Hill. The first one created the **Civilian Conservation Corps (CCC).** Based on a program that Roosevelt had implemented as governor of New York, the CCC combined the president's enthusiasm for nature with his belief in national service for the young. It provided government conservation jobs to "city boys," age 17 to 24, in isolated camps run by the U.S. Army. The pay was $30 a month, with $22 going directly to the worker's family.

The CCC was both popular and successful. It eased unemployment a bit, lowered crime rates in the cities, and kept countless families off relief. It also helped to protect and restore the nation's environment, while teaching young men about the discipline of hard work.

One of the New Deal's most popular programs was the Civilian Conservation Corps, which took unemployed young men from the cities and put them to work on conservation projects in the country.

More than half a million recruits cleaned beaches, built wildlife shelters, fought forest fires, and stocked rivers and streams.

Roosevelt's second relief measure was the Federal Emergency Relief Administration (FERA), which had a budget of $500 million to assist individual states in their efforts to help the unemployed. Hoping to spend the money as quickly and humanely as possible, Roosevelt chose **Harry Hopkins,** a former social worker who had directed New York's relief effort, to run the FERA. With boundless energy and an ego to match, Hopkins personified the New Deal's activist, freewheeling style. He became Roosevelt's closest advisor.

Most of the funding went to the jobless in the form of free food or a simple "dole." This troubled Hopkins, who understood both the need for such relief and the damage it could do. Real work "preserves a man's morale," he insisted. Knowing that Roosevelt felt the same way, he convinced the president to approve a federal work relief program for the unemployed.

With Hopkins in charge, the **Civil Works Administration (CWA)** hired more than 4 million people in a matter of months. Its aim was to create jobs and restore self-respect by handing out pay envelopes instead of relief checks. In reality, CWA workers sometimes performed worthless tasks, known as "boondoggles," such as raking leaves in huge circles or lugging shovelsful of dirt to faraway piles.

But this was only part of the story. The CWA spent much of its $1 billion budget on projects of lasting value. Its workers built more than 400 airports and 200,000 miles of roads. They ran nursery schools and

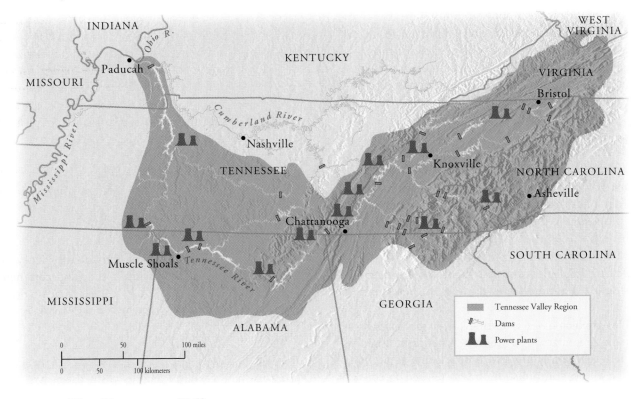

MAP 25.1 The Tennessee Valley

The Tennessee Valley Authority, acclaimed as the most visionary model of government planning in the New Deal era, brought electric power, flood control, and employment to one of the nation's most impoverished regions.

taught more than a million adults to read and write. They immunized children, served hot school lunches, and took garbage off the streets. Yet Roosevelt ended the CWA experiment after only 4 months, citing its spiraling costs. He expected federal job programs to be short-term experiments, nothing more. Otherwise, he warned, they will "become a habit with the country."

Conservation, Regional Planning, and Public Power

In the spring of 1933, FDR appeared to be governing the nation by himself. His proposals were so sweeping, and so easily enacted, that Congress seemed to have no independent function of its own. Never before had the White House taken such initiative on domestic legislation; never before had it been so successful.

At Roosevelt's behest, Congress created the Securities and Exchange Commission (SEC) to oversee the stock and bond markets. It established the Federal Deposit Insurance Corporation (FDIC) to insure bank deposits up to $5,000. It provided funds to refinance one-fifth of the nation's home and farm mortgages. And it effectively ended Prohibition by permitting the sale of beer and wine with an alcoholic content of 3.2 percent. (The Eighteenth Amendment would be repealed on December 5, 1933.)

Some of Roosevelt's early proposals had very personal roots. The Civilian Conservation Corps was one example; the **Tennessee Valley Authority (TVA),** created in May 1933, was another. Like many progressives, Roosevelt had a deep interest in the related issues of conservation, regional planning, and public power. Believing that poverty could be eradicated through the careful development of natural resources, he turned the Tennessee Valley into a laboratory for his most cherished ideas.

Covering seven states and 40,000 square miles, the Tennessee Valley was America's poorest region. Most of its 4 million people—mainly small farmers and share-croppers—lived in isolated communities, without electricity, medical care, proper schooling, or paved roads. The TVA transformed this region in fundamental ways. Within a decade, 16 huge dams and hydroelectric plants were in operation along the Tennessee River, providing flood control, cheap, abundant power, and thousands of jobs. Per capita income rose dramatically. Electric power gave local residents what millions of other Americans already took for granted: radios and refrigerators, plumbing, lights in houses and barns.

TVA was widely viewed as one of the New Deal's greatest achievements. Yet its critics included many residents of the Tennessee Valley, whose complaints reflected the changing face of reform. To their thinking, TVA displaced thousands of people, attracted low-wage factory jobs, and caused serious environmental damage. At best, they argued, it brought a measure of comfort and prosperity to a badly depressed region. At worst, it allowed distant bureaucrats to decide how local people should live.

Economic Recovery

With the bank crisis over and federal relief flowing to those most desperately in need, the Roosevelt administration turned to the long-term issue of providing a structure for the nation's economic recovery. In agriculture, which accounted for one-quarter of all American jobs, the problems were severe. Most farmers had been slumping badly since the 1920s. The introduction of tractors and high-grade fertilizer had made them more productive than ever. Yet their share of the world market had declined because of high tariff walls and tough foreign competition.

If overproduction plagued American agriculture in this era, the problem facing American industry was quite the reverse. So many factories had closed their doors during the Depression that too little was being produced. The resulting unemployment caused a drop in purchasing power, which forced even more factories to shut down. Something had to be done to break this vicious cycle.

Trouble on the Land

The Roosevelt administration turned first to the agricultural problems. Farmers in 1932 were earning less than one-third of their meager 1929 incomes. As food prices collapsed, there was talk of open rebellion in the heartland. Farmers blocked roads, clashed with police, and threatened to lynch any official who foreclosed a family farm. Roosevelt was sympathetic. He believed that low farm income was a leading cause of the Depression, and he needed the support of rural legislators to get his New Deal programs adopted. The proposal he sent Congress, therefore, incorporated the ideas of the nation's major farm interest groups. Passed in May 1933, the **Agricultural Adjustment Act** confronted the problems of overproduction and mounting surpluses that had conspired to erode farm income over the years. The act also created the Agricultural Adjustment Administration (AAA) to oversee this process.

The AAA had one clear goal in mind: to raise farm prices by encouraging farmers to produce less. The idea was no longer to win back world markets, but rather to limit domestic output in order to achieve "parity," or fair price levels, within the United States. The act compensated farmers who voluntarily removed acreage from production. And it funded these payments through a tax on farm processors—such as flour millers, meatpackers, and cotton gin operators.

Problems quickly arose. Because spring planting was already underway, the AAA encouraged farmers to plow under a large portion of their crops. Producing less food while millions were going hungry was difficult for people to understand. But destroying food seemed particularly senseless and cruel. Secretary of Agriculture Henry A. Wallace described the process as "a shocking commentary on our civilization." Yet there seemed to be no other way to fix an economic system awash in idle workers and empty factories, hungry people and abundant food.

Within a year, more than 3 million farmers had signed individual contracts with the AAA. The early results were encouraging. Cotton, wheat, and corn production fell significantly as farmers cultivated fewer acres and cashed their government checks. Farm income shot up almost 60 percent between 1932 and 1935—the result of rising food prices, generous mortgage assistance, and federal loans to those who stored their surpluses in government warehouses.

Nature played a role as well. During the 1930s, the American farm belt experienced record highs in temperature and record lows in rainfall. The Great Plains were hardest hit. Terrifying dust storms swept through Kansas, Nebraska, Colorado, Oklahoma, Texas, and the Dakotas like a black blizzard, packing gale force winds and stripping nutrients from the soil. Cornfields were turned into sand dunes and livestock were buried in their tracks. "This is the ultimate darkness," a Kansas woman wrote in her diary. "So must come the end of the world."

The "**Dust Bowl**" disaster triggered one of the largest internal migrations in the nation's history. More than 3 million people abandoned their Dust Bowl farms in the 1930s, with Oklahoma, Kansas, and South Dakota losing huge chunks of population. By one account, "The people did not stop to shut the door—they just walked out, leaving behind them the wreckage of their labors: an ugly little shack with broken windows covered by cardboard, a sagging ridgepole, a barren, dusty yard, the windmill creaking in the wind."

Many set out for California, where the "fortunate" among them found work picking fruit, boxing vegetables, and baling hay. Living in hellish squatter camps,

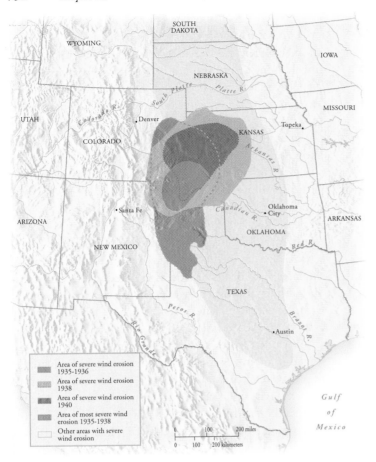

MAP 25.2 **The Dust Bowl**

The immense dust storms that blew through the high plains in the 1930s covered nearly 100 millions acres in the hardest hit states of Texas, Oklahoma, Kansas, Colorado, and New Mexico. Though some historians blame local farmers for causing this environmental catastrophe by wearing out the land in search of quick profits, others see the Dust Bowl as the unfortunate result of a prolonged drought. Either way, the dust storms caused terrible economic hardship and a mass migration from the high plains, with tens of thousands of displaced farmers heading west to California.

enduring disease and discrimination ("Negroes and Okies Upstairs," read a local theater sign), they moved from field to orchard in the San Joaquin and Imperial Valleys, earning pitiful wages and "going on relief."

Tenants and Landowners

The AAA helped countless farm families and ignored countless others. The large farmers got the biggest subsidies. Yet the system barely touched those at the bottom of the pile: the tenants and sharecroppers who comprised almost one-half of the nation's white farm families and three-quarters of the black farm families. Most of them lived in desperate poverty, working the cotton fields of the rural South. Under AAA regulations, these tenants were supposed to get a fair share of the acreage reduction payments. But this rarely occurred. Few landlords obeyed the rules, and some evicted their tenants in order to take even more land out of production.

In response, tenants and sharecroppers formed their own organization, the Southern Tenant Farmers' Union (STFU), to fight for their rights. "The landlord is always betwixt us, beatin' us and starvin' us," complained a black sharecropper from Arkansas. "There ain't but one way for us to get him where he can't help himself and that's for us to get together and stay together."

This would not be easy. Despite the strong support of Norman Thomas and his Socialist party, the STFU could not match the power and resources of its opponents. Tenants who joined the union were evicted from their shacks, blacklisted by employers, and denied credit at banks and stores. Union organizers were beaten and jailed.

President Roosevelt did not intervene. He understood the racial implications of this struggle—most tenants were black; the landlords were white. He did not want to jeopardize the AAA by offending powerful southern interests in Congress. "I know the South . . . ," he told Thomas, "and we've got to be patient." In the meantime, Roosevelt created the Resettlement Administration, with modest funding, to assist evicted tenants and migrant farm workers. Headed by Rexford Tugwell, an outspoken civil rights advocate, the RA became a kind of "mini-AAA" for the rural poor—the New Deal's most class-conscious agency.

Conditions were no better in the Southwest and Far West, where destitute Mexican farm workers struggled to survive. Many had been brought north by American ranchers and growers seeking cheap labor in better times. Now, as the demand for workers decreased, and job competition with poor whites (including the Dust Bowl refugees) intensified, their desperation grew. Since most of these farm workers were not U.S. citizens, local governments often denied them relief. Between 1930 and 1935, moreover, the federal government deported at least 200,000 Mexicans, some of whom were longtime residents of Texas, Arizona, and California; a larger number returned to Mexico on their own. Those who stayed behind toiled for starvation wages in the fields. Like the Tenant Farmer's Union in Arkansas, their attempts to unionize were crushed by local vigilantes and police. In 1936, John Steinbeck reported on a

© Bettmann/CORBIS

Texas Dust Bowl refugees on the long road to California.

The NIRA created two more federal agencies: the Public Works Administration (PWA) and the National Recovery Administration (NRA). The former, with a budget of $3.3 billion, was supposed to "prime the economic pump" by providing jobs for the unemployed and new orders for the factories that produced steel, glass, rubber, cement, and heavy equipment. What made the PWA so appealing was its emphasis on private employment. Workers were to be hired and paid by individual contractors, not by the federal government.

Roosevelt selected Secretary of the Interior Harold Ickes, a veteran progressive, to run the PWA. It proved to be a controversial choice. Known for his prickly, tightfisted ways, Ickes scrutinized almost every construction contract himself, sometimes line by line. He wanted PWA projects to be free of graft, and he insisted that each one add something useful to a community's well-being. In the end, the PWA would spend only $2.8 billion of its budget.

Still, Ickes's legacy was immense. Under his leadership, the PWA constructed schools, hospitals, post offices, and sewage systems. It built the Golden Gate Bridge in San Francisco and the Triborough Bridge in New York City, the Grand Coulee Dam in Washington State, and the Boulder Dam in Colorado. No one brought more honest efficiency to government than Harold Ickes, and no one got more value for the dollar.

The key to Roosevelt's recovery program, however, was the NRA. Under the flamboyant leadership of General Hugh S. Johnson, the NRA encouraged representatives of business and labor to create codes of "fair practice" designed to stabilize the economy through planning and cooperation. Johnson's agency promised something to everyone, though not in equal amounts. Business leaders, who dominated the code-writing process, got the biggest gift of all: the suspension of antitrust laws that had dogged them for years.

In return for such generosity, these leaders agreed to significant labor reforms. Each NRA code featured a maximum hour and minimum wage provision (usually 40 hours and $12 per week). Child labor was forbidden, and yellow-dog contracts were banned. Most important, Section 7A of the NIRA guaranteed labor unions the right to organize and bargain collectively.

General Johnson barnstormed the country by airplane, giving speeches and lining up support. His tactics were the same ones he had used to mobilize Americans in the bond drives and mass rallies of World War I. With a patriotic symbol (the blue eagle) and a catchy slogan

strike of Mexican lettuce workers near his home in Salinas, California. "The attitude of the employer," he wrote, "is one of hatred and suspicion, his method is the threat of the deputies' guns. The workers are herded about like animals. Every possible method is used to make them feel inferior and insecure."

The AAA revolutionized American agriculture. Never before had the federal government been as deeply involved in the affairs of the American farmer; never before had it encouraged its citizens to produce fewer goods, not more. Though key elements of the AAA would be struck down by the Supreme Court in *United States v. Butler* (1936), the concept of federal farm subsidies continues to dominate America's agricultural policy to the present day.

Centralized Economic Planning

The Roosevelt administration had an equally ambitious plan to revive the economy, reopen idle factories, and put people back to work. On June 13, 1933, Congress passed the **National Industrial Recovery Act (NIRA)** amidst a flood of optimistic projections. Modeled on both the voluntary trade associations of the 1920s and the industrial mobilization during World War I, the NIRA was designed as a vehicle for centralized economic planning. Roosevelt himself viewed it as the primary weapon in his crusade against the Depression. The act, he boasted, "is the most important and far reaching legislation ever enacted by the American Congress."

Child Labor in the 1930s

Few employment issues have proved as contentious and enduring as child labor. From colonial times forward, children worked on farms and in family businesses, often alongside parents and siblings. With the coming of industrialization, children labored in coal mines, canneries, sweatshops, and factories (like the spindle boys pictured here in a Georgia cotton mill), working long hours for pitifully low wages.

By 1900, the abolition of child labor had become a powerful force in American politics, supported by progressive reformers, but opposed by many business groups. In 1918, the U.S. Supreme Court, in *Hammer v. Daggenhart,* struck down the first national child labor law. In the 1920s, a proposed constitutional amendment to end this shameful practice also fell short. But the movement gained fresh support during the Great Depression, as adult unemployment rose dramatically and new technologies decreased the need for unskilled factory labor. In 1938, with FDR's blessing, Congress passed the Fair Labor Standards Act, which largely ended child labor in the United States. Three years later, a more liberal Supreme Court unanimously upheld this law. Today, child labor is again on the rise, especially among illegal aliens and school dropouts. The issue is far from resolved.

© Bettmann/CORBIS

("We Do Our Part"), Johnson organized the biggest public spectacles of the Depression era. In the summer of 1933, more than 250,000 New Yorkers paraded down Fifth Avenue singing:

> Join the good old N.R.A., Boys, and we will end this awful strife.
> Join it with the spirit that will give the Eagle life.
> Join in folks, then push and pull, many millions strong.
> While we go marching to Prosperity.

Johnson signed up the big industries—coal, steel, oil, autos, shipbuilding, chemicals, and clothing—before going after the others. By the end of 1933, the NRA had 746 different agreements in place. There was a code for the mop handle makers, another for the dog food industry, and even one for the burlesque houses that determined the number of strippers in each show.

Before long, however, the NRA was in trouble. Small businessmen complained that the codes encouraged monopolies and drowned them in paperwork. Labor leaders charged that employers ignored the wage and hour provisions, while cracking down on union activity. And consumers blamed the NRA for raising prices at a time when their purchasing power was extremely low.

All of this was true. Because the codes were voluntary, they carried no legal weight. (Johnson naively assumed that the power of public opinion would keep potential violators in line.) The large companies obeyed them when it was in their interest to do so and ignored them when it wasn't. As a result, the codes became a device for fixing prices, stifling competition, and limiting production. This may have guaranteed a profit for some companies, but it was the wrong remedy for solving an economic crisis in which the revival of consumer spending was a key to recovery.

In 1934, General Johnson suffered a nervous breakdown, leading Roosevelt to replace him with a five-member executive board. The president seemed relieved when the Supreme Court, in *Schechter Poultry Company v. United States* (1935), struck down the NRA on the grounds that Congress had delegated too much legislative authority to the executive branch. "It has been an awful headache," Roosevelt confided to an aide. "I think perhaps NRA has done all it can do."

New Deal Diplomacy

Foreign affairs were not high on President Roosevelt's agenda. His riveting inaugural address had devoted one sentence to the entire subject. "In the field of world policy," he declared, "I would dedicate this nation to the policy of the good neighbor"—a theme already sounded by outgoing president Herbert Hoover. The United States was in turmoil, struggling through the worst economic crisis in its history. "I favored as a practical policy," said Roosevelt, "the putting of first things first."

The Soviet Question

FDR was no isolationist. He believed deeply in the concepts of international cooperation and global security, as Americans would shortly discover. One of his first diplomatic moves, in November 1933, was to extend formal recognition to the Soviet Union. The move was criticized by groups as varied as the American Legion and the American Federation of Labor, which viewed the Soviet Union as a godless, totalitarian society bent on exporting "communist revolution" throughout the world. But Roosevelt believed that the United States could no longer afford to ignore the world's largest nation.

The move did not pay quick dividends to either side. Trade with the Soviet Union remained low, partly because Soviet dictator Joseph Stalin was determined to make his nation self-sufficient. The Russians also ignored their promise not to spread "communist propaganda" in the United States, and then refused to pay their $150 million war debt to Washington. Yet for all of these problems, a major hurdle was cleared. Relations between the United States and the Soviet Union would slowly improve in the 1930s and early 1940s, as ominous world events drew them closer together. For FDR, recognition of Stalin's regime seemed less a threat than an opportunity.

The Good Neighbor

The Roosevelt administration showed a growing interest in Latin America, where U.S. companies had billions of dollars invested in the production of foodstuffs like coffee and sugar, and raw materials such as copper and oil. Along with efforts to increase trade in this region, the United States extended the Good Neighbor Policy by affirming at the 1933 Pan-American Conference in Uruguay that no nation "has the right to intervene in the internal or external affairs of another." Shortly thereafter, the Roosevelt administration recalled several hundred U.S. Marines stationed in Haiti and signed a treaty with Panama recognizing the responsibility of both nations to operate and defend the Panama Canal.

There were exceptions, however. In Cuba, a nation of vital economic and strategic importance to the United States, intervention was a way of life. In 1934, the State Department used its considerable leverage to help bring an "acceptable" government to power in Havana, more sympathetic to North American business interests. With a friendly new regime in place, led by Sergeant Fulgencio Batista, the United States agreed to renounce direct intervention under the Platt Amendment in return for permission to keep its huge naval base at Guantánamo Bay.

The Good Neighbor Policy faced its sternest test even closer to home. In 1934, President Lázaro Cárdenas of Mexico began a national recovery program much like FDR's New Deal. Pledging "Mexico for the Mexicans," Cárdenas attempted to nationalize the agricultural and mining properties of all foreign corporations, as required by the Mexican Constitution of 1917. Though Cárdenas promised "fair compensation" for these holdings, American and British companies demanded more than the Mexicans were willing to pay. (American oil interests wanted $262 million; the Cárdenas government offered $10 million.) Over the objections of many businessmen, the Roosevelt administration convinced Mexico to pay $40 million in compensation for foreign-owned lands it had seized, and another $29 million for the oil fields.

Roosevelt's caution was understandable. The president realized that better relations with Latin America required a new approach. "Give them a share," he urged in private. "They think they are just as good as we are, and many of them are." Roosevelt's policy was also tied to larger world events. With fascism rising in Europe and in Asia, the need for inter-American cooperation was essential.

Critics: Right and Left

By 1934, the Depression seemed to be easing. Though enormous problems remained, there was less talk about the dangers of starvation, violent upheaval, or complete economic collapse. The New Deal had injected a dose of hope and confidence into the body politic. Yet as things got better, people inevitably wanted more. The spirit of unity, the shared sense of hardship and struggle, began to dissolve.

The American Liberty League and the 1934 Election

The first rumblings came from the political right. In the summer of 1934, a group of conservative business leaders formed the American Liberty League to combat the alleged "radicalism" of the New Deal. They believed that Roosevelt was leading the country down "a foreign path" by attacking free enterprise, favoring workers over employers, and increasing the power of the federal government. "There can be only one capital," said a Liberty League spokesman, "Washington or Moscow."

The league generously supported Roosevelt's political opponents in the 1934 congressional elections. But the results served only to reinforce the president's enormous popularity, or so it appeared. Instead of losing ground—the normal pattern for the majority party in midterm elections—the Democrats picked up nine seats in the Senate and nine in the House. Few pundits could recall a more lopsided election, and some questioned the future of the Republican party. As publisher William Allen White put it, Roosevelt had been "all but crowned by the people."

In reality, the election results were a mixed blessing for the Democrats. Most Americans approved of the New Deal. Their main criticism was that it had not gone far—or fast—enough to end the Depression.

In Minnesota, for example, Governor Floyd Olsen was reelected on an independent "Farmer-Labor" ticket that advocated the state ownership of utilities and railroads.

In neighboring Wisconsin, the sons of "Fighting Bob" LaFollette formed a new Progressive party that endorsed the idea of a welfare state. And in California, Upton Sinclair, author of *The Jungle,* ran for governor on a program called EPIC (End Poverty in California), which promised to hand over idle factories and farmland to the poor and unemployed. Sinclair received almost 900,000 votes in a bitter, losing effort—a sign of things to come.

"Every Man a King"

The most serious challenge to Roosevelt's leadership was offered by Louisiana's **Huey P. Long.** Known as the "Kingfish," after a strutting, smooth-talking character on the popular radio program *Amos 'n' Andy,* Long combined a gift for showmanship with ruthless ambition. On the campaign trail, he wore a white linen suit, orchid shirt, pink necktie, straw hat, and two-toned shoes. A superb orator and a master storyteller, he understood the value of the spoken word in a state

© Bettmann/CORBIS

Senator Huey P. Long combined showmanship with ruthless ambition to become Franklin Roosevelt's most influential critic and political rival. Claiming the New Deal did not do enough to help poor people, Long proposed a radical program to redistribute wealth that attracted millions of followers.

where few people owned radios, read newspapers, or traveled far from home.

As governor of Louisiana, Long pushed his unique brand of southern populism. By revising the tax codes to make corporations and wealthy citizens pay more, he was able to construct new hospitals, bring paved roads and bridges to rural areas, and give free textbooks to the poor. At the same time, he built a political machine of almost totalitarian proportions. When Long vacated the governor's chair to enter the U.S. Senate in 1932, he controlled the legislature, the courts, and the civil service system of Louisiana.

"I came to the United States Senate," Long wrote, "to spread the wealth of the land among all of the people." As a Democrat, he campaigned hard for Roosevelt in 1932 and supported much of the early New Deal. But as time passed, he grew restless with the slow pace of reform. In 1934, Long proposed his own agenda for economic recovery. Once in place, he promised, it would "make every man a king."

Under Long's plan, no one would be allowed to earn more than $1.8 million per year or to keep a personal fortune in excess of $5 million. After confiscating this surplus, the government would provide each family with a house, a car, a radio, and an annual income of at least $2,500. Veterans would get their bonus, the elderly would receive pensions, and deserving students could attend college free of charge.

Most economists were appalled. They knew that there weren't nearly enough millionaires around to finance Long's proposal. According to one study, the government would have had to confiscate all yearly incomes above $3,000—not $1.8 million—to provide each family with $2,500. Long didn't much care about the arithmetic. "You don't have to understand it," he told his followers. "Just shut your damned eyes and believe it. That's all."

By 1935, Long's "Share Our Wealth Society" claimed 8 million members nationwide. It lured in people by promising them what the New Deal could not possibly deliver. At local meetings across the nation, his followers sang:

> Every man a king, every man a king
> For you can be a millionaire
> But there's something belongs to others
> There's enough for all to share.

The Radio Priest and the Pension Doctor

Long did not lack for competitors. In Royal Oak, Michigan, a working-class suburb of Detroit, Father Charles Edward Coughlin was busy leading a protest

Known as the "Radio Priest," Father Charles E. Coughlin, pictured here, became one of the New Deal's most important and controversial critics, eventually opposing President Franklin Roosevelt's reelection in 1936.

movement of his own. As the pastor of a small Catholic church called the Shrine of the Little Flower, Coughlin became a towering figure in the 1930s by mixing prayer with politics in a way that touched millions—and frightened millions more.

Coughlin could be heard every Sunday on 17 CBS radio outlets nationwide. An early Roosevelt supporter, he compared the New Deal to "Christ's Deal," assuring listeners that "Gabriel is over the White House, not Lucifer." Like Senator Long, Coughlin deplored the fact that too much wealth was concentrated in too few hands. Unlike Long, however, he blamed this evil on a tight money supply, manipulated by international bankers in London and New York.

Coughlin believed that "free silver"—the old Populist nostrum—would solve this problem and bring prosperity to all. His attacks on British bankers won him strong support in the Irish-Catholic community, and his call for monetary reform appealed to debt-ridden farmers and merchants in America's small towns. Before long, Coughlin's radio show, *Golden Hour of the Little Flower,* had more listeners (an estimated 40 million) than *Amos 'n' Andy* and *Gracie Allen.* He needed 150 clerks and 4 personal secretaries to handle the thousands of letters and donations that poured into his office. Some of this money was used to construct a new church of granite and marble, seven stories high, bathed in floodlights, with a huge Christ figure on top.

By 1934, the "Radio Priest" was souring on the New Deal. Angered by Roosevelt's disinterest in his "silver solution," he formed the National Union for Social Justice to challenge the president's leadership. "I glory in the fact that I am a simple Catholic priest,"

Coughlin declared, "endeavoring to inject Christianity into the fabric of an economic system woven upon the loom of the greedy."

A third protest movement, led by Francis E. Townsend, a retired physician living in California, offered yet another solution to the ills of the 1930s. Townsend had no desire to punish the rich, alter the money supply, or challenge the capitalist order. What disturbed him was the sight of elderly men and women sifting through garbage cans for food. In 1934, Townsend proposed a measure to revive the economy by meeting the specific needs of older Americans. It guaranteed a pension of $200 per month to those over 60 who promised to stay out of the job market and to spend the $200 by month's end. The pensions would be funded by a 2 percent sales tax on all "business transactions."

According to Townsend, his plan would create jobs for the young, increase the country's purchasing power, and provide security for the elderly. What he didn't say was that his plan, known as Old Age Revolving Pensions Limited, was impossibly expensive. By most estimates, Townsend needed a sales tax approaching 70 percent in order to properly fund his proposal. When asked about this at a congressional hearing, the doctor replied: "I'm not in the least interested in the cost of the plan."

Neither were his followers. By 1935, more than 10 million Americans had signed petitions supporting Townsend's idea, and public opinion polls showed strong support for a government-sponsored pension plan. Townsend had unleashed a powerful new interest group, the elderly, and American politics would never be the same.

"second New Deal." He requested—and received—$4.8 billion in work relief for the unemployed, the largest single appropriation in the nation's history. After allocating generous shares to his favorite projects, such as the CCC, Roosevelt established yet another agency, the Works Progress Administration (WPA), with Hopkins in charge, to create "jobs, jobs, jobs!"

In that task, it was very successful. At its height in 1936, the WPA employed 25 percent of the nation's entire workforce. Many of these jobs, however, were low-paying and temporary so as to avoid competition with private enterprise. Concentrating on small construction projects, the WPA built schools and playgrounds, repaired countless bridges and landing fields, and improved 650,000 miles of roads. Its National Youth Administration, inspired by **Eleanor Roosevelt,** provided part-time work to several million high school and college students.

Social Security

The president's "must" list included a social welfare plan that challenged the cherished concepts of voluntarism and individual responsibility. At the urging of Labor Secretary Frances Perkins, the nation's first woman cabinet member, Roosevelt proposed legislation (passed as the Social Security Act of 1935) to create a national pension fund, an unemployment insurance system, and public assistance programs for dependent mothers and children, the physically disabled, and those in chronic need. The pension was financed by a payroll tax to begin in 1937. Benefits were purposely

The Second New Deal

The American Liberty League, the victories of Floyd Olsen and the La Follette brothers, the rumblings of Long, Coughlin, and Townsend—all raised nagging problems for Franklin Roosevelt and the New Deal. Though national income in 1935 was a full 25 percent above the 1933 level, millions were still living on handouts, without much hope of a permanent job. Inside the White House, Roosevelt's key advisors were nudging him further to the left. "Boys—this is our hour," said the opportunistic Harry Hopkins. "We've got to get everything we want—a works program, social security, wages and hours, everything—now or never."

Jobs, Jobs, Jobs

In the spring of 1935, Roosevelt presented Congress with a "must" list of reforms, the so-called

Secretary of Labor Frances Perkins, the first woman to hold a cabinet position, was instrumental in the formulation and passage of the Social Security Act.

The New Deal and the Arts

Among the most controversial parts of FDR's New Deal was "Federal One," an experiment to provide government funding for the arts. Established under the huge Works Progress Administration, Federal One aimed to employ out-of-work professionals to help bring "culture" to the masses. Its Federal Theater Project performed everything from Shakespeare to puppet shows for audiences that rarely, if ever, had seen a live production. Its Federal Arts Project produced museum exhibits, murals for public buildings (like the one pictured here in San Francisco's Coit Tower), and painting classes for the poor. Playwright Arthur Miller worked for Federal One, as did Actor Burt Lancaster, artist Jackson Pollock, and writers Saul Bellow and Richard Wright. Though some criticized these projects as wasteful and politically slanted to the New Deal (note the clean, well-fed, contented workers in the mural), they remained popular with the American public. Asked about the artwork, FDR said: "Some of it is good, some of it not so good, but all of it is native, human, eager and alive—all of it painted by their own kind in their own country."

WPA Mural; Coit Tower, San Francisco

modest—about $20 to $30 per month—because Roosevelt did not intend "Social Security" to be the *main* source of personal retirement income, as it has become for many people today.

The Social Security Act had numerous defects. It excluded millions of vulnerable wage earners, such as domestics, farm workers, and the self-employed, from the pension fund. It taxed all participants at a fixed rate, forcing those with the lowest incomes to pay a far greater share of their wages into the system. Over time, the Social Security fund emerged as the country's most important and expensive domestic program.

"Class Warfare"

Roosevelt had never been a strong supporter of organized labor. He wanted to help workers through his own social programs, rather than having them organize unions to help themselves. He felt uneasy about the tactics of labor leaders such as **John L. Lewis,** head of the United Mine Workers, who had tripled his membership (from 150,000 to almost 500,000) with an aggressive organizing campaign that declared, "The president wants you to join a union!" Roosevelt worried that labor's militant new spirit would accelerate the violent confrontations of 1934, when pitched battles erupted between striking workers and police on the streets of Minneapolis, San Francisco, and Detroit.

In the wake of these disturbances, Senator Robert Wagner of New York authored a bill to protect the rights of workers to organize and bargain collectively. His legislation filled a dramatic void, because the Supreme Court had just declared parts of the NIRA—including Section 7A regarding labor union rights—to be unconstitutional. Passed in 1935, the National Labor Relations Act prohibited employers from engaging in a wide

Unemployment 1925–1945

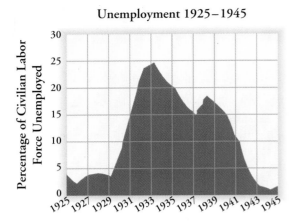

CHART 25.1 Unemployment, 1925–1945
This chart shows the two great peaks of unemployment—the first in 1933, as FDR took office; the second (and smaller one) during the recession of 1938, when federal spending was reduced. The chart also shows the enormous impact of World War II in bringing unemployment—and the Great Depression itself—to an end.

range of "unfair labor practices," such as spying on their workers. The law also created the National Labor Relations Board (NLRB) to supervise union elections and determine the appropriate bargaining agents.

The Wagner Act revealed deep divisions within the union movement. At the American Federation of Labor's annual convention in 1935, John L. Lewis pleaded with fellow leaders to begin serious membership drives in the steel mills, automobile plants, and rubber factories. Lewis wanted these mass production workers to be organized by industry rather than by craft. Only then, he argued, could the power of big business be successfully confronted.

Most AFL leaders were unmoved. As representatives of skilled craftsworkers, such as masons and carpenters, they had little interest in organizing industrial unions composed largely of African Americans and ethnic groups from eastern and southern Europe. Indeed, after Lewis finished his emotional plea to the AFL convention, Carpenters' President "Big Bill" Hutcheson called him a "bastard." Lewis floored Hutcheson with a solid right to the jaw and stormed out of the convention.

In November 1935, Lewis formed the Committee for Industrial Organization (CIO) to charter new unions in the mass production industries. He was joined by a handful of AFL leaders from the needle trades, including Sidney Hillman of the Amalgamated Clothing Workers and David Dubinsky of the International Ladies' Garment Workers. Although the AFL suspended these men and their unions for "fomenting insurrection," Lewis never looked back. His attention had turned to the CIO's organizing drives in the auto and steel industries. Labor's "civil war" had begun.

The Fascist Challenge

As the 1936 presidential election approached, Americans watched events in Europe with growing apprehension. From the Soviet Union came stories about a regime that was brutalizing its people in an attempt to "collectivize" the society and stamp out internal dissent. In Germany and Italy, powerful dictators emerged, preaching race hatred and vowing to expand their nation's borders. For millions of Americans, the scene was frighteningly familiar—a replay of events that had led Europe, and eventually the United States, into the bloodiest war of all time.

Hitler and Mussolini

Adolf Hitler became the German chancellor in January 1933, a few months before FDR was sworn in as president. Born in Austria in 1889, Hitler had moved to Bavaria as a young man and fought in the German army during World War I. Wounded and jobless, he helped form the National Socialist (Nazi) party, one of the many extremist groups that thrived in the economic chaos of war-battered Germany. In 1923, Hitler was arrested in Munich for staging an unsuccessful coup against the Weimar government. From his prison cell, he wrote *Mein Kampf* ("My Struggle"), a rambling account of his racial theories, plans for Germany, and hatred of Jews.

As the Weimar government collapsed in the Depression, the Nazis gained strength. Millions welcomed their promise to create jobs, restore German glory, and avenge the "humiliation" of Versailles. Nazi representation in the *Reichstag* (parliament) rose from 12 in 1928 to 230 by 1932. A year later, Hitler became chancellor of Germany. The results were alarming. Constitutional

Flashpoints | The 1936 Berlin Olympics

At the first modern Olympic Games in Athens, Greece, in 1896, the athletes had competed as individuals, not as members of a team. But that changed quickly, as the outcome of these Games, held every four years in a different country, became a matter of intense national pride. At the 1908 Olympics in London, U.S. shot-putter Ralph Rose refused to lower the American flag as he passed the royal box, angering the British but making him an instant hero in the United States. Returning home that year, the U.S. athletes were given a huge ticker-tape parade in New York City.

The 1916 Olympics, scheduled for Berlin, were cancelled by the outbreak of World War I. Four years later, the Games were held in Antwerp to commemorate Belgium's terrible suffering in that conflict. The impact of politics on the Olympics became even more obvious when the defeated Central Powers were banned from competition until 1928. Shortly thereafter, the International Olympic Committee chose Berlin to host the 1936 Games in a gesture of reconciliation. But when Adolph Hitler and the Nazis came to power in 1933, tremendous pressure arose to move the Olympics elsewhere. Though opinion polls in the United States showed about half the pubic favoring a boycott, the American Olympic Committee decided to participate.

Perhaps no sporting event has ever matched the Berlin Olympics for drama and controversy. Hitler spent more than $25 million, an enormous sum in this era of economic depression, to construct 150 venues, including a 100,000-seat stadium.

A special radio hookup broadcast the events to 41 nations. Electronic devices were installed to time the athletes and to judge "photo finishes." Filmmaker Leni Riefenstahl produced a lavish documentary that revolutionized the staging of sporting events and introduced the Olympic torch.

Above all, however, it was the American track-and-field athletes who captured center stage. After personally honoring the early winners, Hitler left the stadium rather than shake hands with Cornelius Johnson, one of 11 African Americans on the U.S. team, who had just set a world record in the high jump. In the following days, Jesse Owens, an African American from Ohio State University, won four gold medals, further mocking the Nazi boasts of "Aryan supremacy."

But trouble arose in American circles when word spread that two Jewish American sprinters, Marty Glickman and Sam Stoller, had been pulled from the 400-meter relay team at the last minute so as not to further embarrass the Nazi hosts. Though U.S. officials denied it, Jesse Owens, among many others, insisted the story was true. Anti-Semitism, it appeared, had denied two American runners the chance to compete.

Three years later, the world was once again at war. The Olympic Games would not be held again until 1948.

At the controversial Berlin Olympics of 1936, American track and field athlete Jesse Owens won four gold medals, turning him into a national hero and a symbol of resistance to Nazi racism.

© Bettmann/CORBIS

Questions for Reflection

1. What was the state of the world in 1936 that made the Berlin Olympics so symbolic to so many nations?

2. Why does athletic competition, in particular, bring out such deep nationalistic feelings? What other examples, besides the Berlin Olympics, were contested with such intensity?

rights were suspended and competing political parties were banned. Nazi supporters held mass book-burning rallies, drove Jews from universities, boycotted their businesses, and attacked them in the streets. "Hitler is a madman," President Roosevelt told a French diplomat.

Under the Nazis, the state increased its control over industry, while leaving it in private hands. This allowed Hitler to begin a massive rearmament program, which produced badly needed jobs. By 1934, German factories were producing tanks and military aircraft. A year later,

DOING HISTORY

The Battle Over Neutrality

NO FOREIGN POLICY issue proved more divisive than the ongoing debate over American neutrality, which began with the rise of Nazi and fascist aggression in Europe and Africa in the mid 1930s and continued until the Japanese attack on Pearl Harbor in December 1941. The first Neutrality Acts, passed overwhelmingly by Congress in 1935 and 1936, had reflected the American public's understandable fear of being pulled into another world war. Though President Roosevelt had signed these Neutrality Acts, he did not believe that they allowed him the leeway he needed to support the nations that were threatened by German, Italian, and Japanese aggression. In his famous Quarantine Speech of October 5, 1937, Roosevelt spoke out for the first time about the dangers posed by strict neutrality—dangers not only to the current victims of aggression, he warned, but to Americans as well.

"The political situation in the world, which of late has been growing progressively worse, is such as to cause grave concerns and anxiety to all peoples and nations who wish to live in peace and amity with their neighbors . . .

Innocent people, innocent nations, are being cruelly sacrificed to a greed for power and supremacy which is devoid of all senses of justice and humane consideration . . .

If [these] things come to pass in other parts of the world, let no one imagine that America will escape, that America may expect mercy, that this Western Hemisphere will not be attacked and that it will continue tranquilly and peacefully to carry on the ethics and arts of civilization."

Among the president's strongest critics was Colonel Charles A. Lindbergh, the first aviator to have flown a plane nonstop from the United States to Europe. A true national hero, and a dedicated isolationist, Lindbergh was a leading spokesman for the America First Committee, which opposed all attempts to intervene in the European war. In various speeches, Lindbergh praised the German military, brushed off reports of Nazi atrocities, and claimed that American Jews were responsible for pushing the nation toward war. In this particular speech, he warned Americans that support for England against the Nazis would drag the United States into a conflict it couldn't win.

"I know I will be severely criticized by the interventionists in America when I say we should not enter a war unless we have a reasonable chance of winning . . . And I know that the United States is not prepared to wage war in Europe successfully at this time . . .

In time of war, truth is always replaced by propaganda. I do not believe we should be too quick to criticize the actions of a belligerent nation. There is always the question whether we, ourselves, would do better under similar circumstances. But we in America have a right to think of the welfare of America first . . .

There is no better way to give comfort to any enemy than to divide the people of a nation over the issue of foreign war. There is no shorter road to defeat than by entering a war with inadequate preparation . . .

The United States is better situated from a military standpoint than any other nation in the world. Even in our present condition . . . no foreign power is in a position to invade us today. If we concentrate on our own defenses and build the strength that this nation should maintain, no foreign army will ever attempt to land on American shores."

Source: "Addresses and Messages of Franklin D. Roosevelt," Senate Document No. 188, 77th Congress, 2d Session, pp. 21–24; Charles A. Lindbergh, "We Cannot Win This War for England," *Vital Speeches*, May 1, 1941, pp. 424–426.

Questions for Reflection

1. What are the key arguments and issues represented by President Roosevelt and Colonel Lindbergh?

2. Why is the mobilization of public opinion so important to both sides?

3. Were the arguments put forth by Roosevelt and Lindbergh unique to American intervention in World War II, or do they continue to have relevance today?

Explore additional primary sources related to this chapter on the Wadsworth American History Resource Center or HistoryNOW websites:

http://history.wadsworth.com/rc/us

http://now.ilrn.com/ayers_etal3e

Hitler proposed a 500,000-man army and instituted the draft. In 1936, Nazi forces marched into the Rhineland—a clear violation of the Versailles treaty—and reoccupied it without firing a shot. "Today Germany," the Nazis chanted, "tomorrow the world."

Hitler had modeled himself, to some degree, after Italian dictator Benito Mussolini, the father of fascism in modern Europe. Born in 1883, Mussolini had served in the Italian army during World War I. Playing upon the social unrest and economic turmoil of the postwar era, he seized national power in 1922 and proclaimed *Fascismo.* As the supreme leader, or *Duce,* he preached national unity and state management (though not ownership) of Italy's industrial base. Like Hitler, he destroyed labor unions, censored the press, abolished all political parties but his own, and relied on a secret police force to maintain order and silence his critics.

In 1935, Italian forces invaded Ethiopia from their neighboring colonies of Eritrea and Somaliland. For Mussolini, the attack was a way of restoring Italy's ancient glory. The fighting in Ethopia was brutal and one-sided, pitting Italian tanks and machine guns against local defenders armed with little more than spears and bows and arrows. At the League of Nations, Ethiopian Emperor Haile Selassie pleaded for support. The league responded by branding Italy the aggressor, but sent no military help. After annexing Ethiopia in 1936, Mussolini signed a pact of friendship with Hitler, known as the Rome-Berlin Axis.

The Neutrality Acts

Americans did not want to become involved in European squabbles, as they had in the past. They were determined that history must not repeat itself—that American blood must not be shed again on foreign soil. There was only one way to avoid another war, most people believed, and that was to remain truly neutral in world affairs.

Although this sentiment had deep historical roots, running all the way back to George Washington, the key to understanding America's anxiety in the early 1930s was the legacy of World War I—the belief that U.S. participation had been a mistake, that America had been lured into the conflict, against its vital interests, by a conspiracy of evil men. In 1934, the U.S. Senate set up a committee, chaired by isolationist Gerald P. Nye of North Dakota, to investigate the reasons for America's involvement in World War I. The Nye committee highlighted a series of well-known facts: large banks and corporations had made huge profits during World War I by giving loans and selling arms to the various combatants. It followed, therefore, that the United States had been led into this conflict by greedy bankers and businessmen determined to protect their investments. The press dubbed them "merchants of death."

This was a simplistic explanation, to be sure. It ignored the rather tangled reality of American intervention—from submarine warfare to the Zimmermann Telegram, from President Wilson's rigid morality to the defense of neutral rights. Yet the Nye committee findings enjoyed wide popular support in a nation determined to avoid another war.

The isolationist impulse was particularly strong in the Great Plains and Upper Midwest, where populist suspicions of Wall Street and international bankers went back a long way. It attracted many Americans of German descent, who remembered their brutal treatment during World War I; of Irish descent, who opposed aid to Great Britain in any form; and of Italian descent, who viewed Mussolini as a hero in these years. Isolationism—in some cases combined with pacifism—also appealed to ministers, peace groups, and college students.

Congress responded to this public mood with legislation designed to avoid the "entanglements" that had led to American participation in World War I. The first Neutrality Act, passed after the Ethiopian invasion of 1935, empowered the president to determine when a state of war existed anywhere in the world. In that event, the president would declare an embargo on all combatants. American arms shipments would cease, and American citizens would be warned against traveling on the vessels of belligerents. In February 1936, Congress passed a second Neutrality Act, prohibiting American banks from extending loans or credits to any nation at war.

President Roosevelt did not like these bills. He believed that absolute neutrality favored powerful aggressor nations by forcing the United States to treat all sides equally. Yet FDR signed them into law for political reasons. The Neutrality Acts had wide popular support. He knew that a veto would give strong ammunition to the Republicans in the coming presidential campaign.

Mandate From the People

As the 1936 election approached, FDR had reason for concern. Although personal income and industrial production had risen dramatically since he took office in 1933, neither had reached the pre-Depression levels of 1929. Millions of Americans were still unemployed, labor violence was spreading, and the federal deficit continued to climb. In addition, more than 80 percent of the nation's newspapers and most of the business community remained loyal to the Republican party, meaning that Roosevelt's major presidential opponent could count on strong editorial and financial support.

The 1936 Election

In June, the Republicans gathered in Cleveland to nominate their presidential ticket. Herbert Hoover, anxious for another crack at Roosevelt, received a thunderous ovation. But the convention delegates, seeking a winner, not a martyr, chose Kansas Governor Alfred M. Landon to head the Republican ticket, and Frank Knox, a Chicago publisher, to be the vice presidential nominee.

Landon, a political moderate, promised "fewer radio talks, fewer experiments, and a lot more common sense." His problem was that he radiated little of the compassion and confidence that made Roosevelt so popular with the masses. Worse, Landon's bland pronouncements were overshadowed by the broadsides of more conservative Republican leaders, who denounced the New Deal as a radical plot to subvert free enterprise and individual rights.

Roosevelt also faced presidential challenges from the left. Both the Communists and the Socialists ran spirited campaigns in 1936, demanding more federal aid for the poor. But Roosevelt's most serious concern—a political merger involving Coughlin, Townsend, and Long—was effectively eliminated in September 1935, when an assassin's bullet killed the Louisiana senator in Baton Rouge. To replace the charismatic Long, these dissident forces nominated William "Liberty Bill" Lemke, an obscure North Dakota congressman, to be their presidential candidate on the new Union party ticket.

Roosevelt's political strategy differed markedly from 1932. In that campaign, he had stressed the common hopes and needs that bound people together; in 1936, he emphasized the class differences that separated those who supported the New Deal from those who opposed it. Time and again, Roosevelt portrayed the election as a contest between common people and privileged people, between compassion and greed. In his final campaign speech at New York's Madison Square Garden, he declared that the "forces of selfishness" had "met their match" in the Roosevelt administration. "They are unanimous in their hatred of me," the president thundered, "*and I welcome their hatred.*"

On November 3, FDR crushed Landon and Lemke in the most one-sided election since 1820. The final totals showed Roosevelt with 27,752,869 popular votes, Landon with 16,674,665, and Lemke with 882,479. (The Socialist and Communist party candidates polled fewer than 300,000 votes between them.) Roosevelt won every state except Maine and Vermont, and the Democratic party added to its huge majorities in both houses of Congress. A few days after the election, Father Coughlin announced his retirement from the radio.

African Americans and the New Deal

Roosevelt's landslide victory signaled a dramatic shift in American politics. A new majority coalition had emerged. In the farm belt, Roosevelt won over long-time Republicans with federal subsidies and price supports. In the cities, he attracted workers grateful for welfare benefits and WPA jobs. And he appealed to ethnic minorities by filling so many White House positions, cabinet posts, and federal judgeships with Catholics and Jews.

Adding to the president's strength was the support he received from the CIO. Describing Roosevelt as "the worker's best friend," the CIO campaigned tirelessly for him in key industrial states, and the effort paid off. FDR captured the working-class vote in 1936 by a margin of four to one.

The most striking political change, however, occurred within the nation's African American community. The steady migration of blacks to northern cities, where they could vote, increased their political power. Historically, most blacks supported the Republican party, an allegiance that dated back to Abraham Lincoln and the Civil War. In 1932, Herbert Hoover won an overwhelming share of their votes.

Although few blacks voted in the South during the 1930s, their growing numbers in northern cities like Chicago and New York increased their political influence within the New Deal coalition.

With the New Deal, a massive switch took place. In large part, African Americans became Democrats because the Roosevelt administration provided jobs and welfare benefits to all Americans, regardless of race. This federal assistance was especially welcome in black communities, where poverty and discrimination had long been facts of life. "The Negro was born in depression," a black leader recalled. "It only became official when it hit the white man."

By 1933, black unemployment had reached 50 percent. Fortunately, the two New Deal administrators most responsible for creating jobs were sympathetic to minority needs. At the PWA, Harold Ickes insisted that blacks receive equal pay and minimum quotas on all construction projects. Though local officials often ignored these rules, the PWA provided thousands of jobs for African Americans, while building black schools and hospitals throughout the segregated South. At the WPA, Harry Hopkins set the same standards with somewhat better results. Blacks received a generous share of WPA work in northern cities—a testimony to both their joblessness and political clout. "Let Jesus Lead You and Roosevelt Feed You" became a rallying cry in African American churches during the election of 1936.

Many blacks viewed the New Deal as a progressive social force. They welcomed an administration that showed some interest in their struggle. And they particularly admired the efforts of First Lady Eleanor Roosevelt, who served as the White House conscience on matters pertaining to minority rights.

Eleanor Roosevelt had a passion for public service and a deep commitment to the poor. Her interest in civil rights had been fueled, in large measure, by her friendship with prominent African Americans such as **Mary McLeod Bethune,** founder of Bethune-Cookman College in Florida. Born in a sharecropper's shack, the fifteenth child of former slaves, Bethune had acquainted the first lady with the special problems facing African Americans—from the scandal of lynching to the crisis in public education. In 1936, Eleanor Roosevelt recommended Bethune to head the National Youth Administration's Office of Negro Affairs.

As the New Deal's highest-ranking black appointee, Bethune presided over the administration's "black cabinet," which advised the White House on minority issues. Working together with Eleanor Roosevelt and other civil rights advocates, she helped to encourage— and monitor—the New Deal's racial progress. Much of it was symbolic. In an age of rigid segregation, Eleanor Roosevelt visited black colleges, spoke at black

Marian Anderson entertained a crowd of 75,000 at the Lincoln Memorial on Easter Sunday, 1939, after the Daughters of the American Revolution refused to allow her to perform at Washington's Constitution Hall.

© Bettmann/CORBIS

conferences, and socialized with black women. (She raised eyebrows by inviting Bethune to tea at the White House.) When the Daughters of the American Revolution refused to allow **Marian Anderson,** a gifted black contralto, to perform at Washington's Constitution Hall, Eleanor Roosevelt resigned from the organization. A few months later, Harold Ickes arranged for Anderson to sing at the Lincoln Memorial on Easter Sunday, 1939. An integrated audience of 75,000 gathered to hear her.

Yet the good work of Eleanor Roosevelt and others could not mask larger New Deal failures in the field of civil rights. Throughout his presidency, for example, Franklin Roosevelt never attempted to challenge southern racial customs. He made no effort to break down segregation barriers or to enable blacks to vote. And he remained on the sidelines as federal antilynching bills were narrowly defeated in Congress. Without his leadership, not a single piece of civil rights legislation was enacted in the New Deal years.

Roosevelt argued that he could not support civil rights legislation without alienating southern Democrats who controlled the most important committees in Congress. "They will block every bill I [need] to keep America from collapsing," Roosevelt said. "I just can't take that risk."

The president's position did not prevent blacks from supporting him in 1936. Roosevelt received 76 percent of their votes—the same total that Herbert Hoover had won four years before. On balance, African Americans viewed the New Deal as a clear improvement over the Republican past. "My friends, go turn Lincoln's picture to the wall," a black editor wrote in 1935. "That debt has been paid in full."

Popular Culture in the Depression

The economic struggles of the 1930s shaped not only the politics of American life, but the culture as well. Hard times encouraged federal participation in the arts and triggered a leftward tilt among many intellectuals and writers. A flurry of "proletarian literature" emerged in the early Depression years, emphasizing the "class struggle" through stories about heroic workers resisting the exploitation of evil employers. Several important black writers—including Ralph Ellison, Richard Wright, and Langston Hughes—identified with the Communist party because it appeared to actively support civil rights. For most intellectuals, however, the fascination with communism was fleeting. As free thinkers, they could not adjust to the party's rigid conformity or its blind support of the Soviet dictator Joseph Stalin.

The Depression era also witnessed the spread of a popular culture born in the preceding decades. Photojournalism came of age in the 1930s with the publication of magazines such as *Life* and *Look,* and the vivid imagery of government-sponsored photographers like Walker Evans and Dorothea Lange. In the comics trade, "Superman" (1938) demonstrated that Americans were anxious to get beyond the tame characters from the newspaper strips. He was quickly followed by comic books featuring "Batman" and "Captain Marvel." In popular music, the "swing era" brought the jazz of African American artists to a much broader public. In radio and in movies, the changes were most dramatic and profound.

The Big Screen

By the 1930s, the motion picture was the leading form of popular culture in the United States. Most Americans attended at least one movie a week; many followed the lives of their favorite stars in gossip columns and fan magazines. Theater owners attracted customers by offering inducements such as the "double feature," which dramatically increased the number of films produced during this decade. In the larger cities, movie theaters were transformed into fantasy palaces, with thick carpets, winding staircases, ushers in tuxedoes, and the twinkling lights of chandeliers. For millions, the theater became a temporary escape from the bleak realities of the Depression.

Hollywood mirrored the changing attitudes of the 1930s. It was no accident that the most popular movie of 1932, the year America hit rock bottom, was Mervyn LeRoy's *I Am a Fugitive From a Chain Gang,* the story of a decent man, unjustly convicted of a crime, who escapes from a brutal southern penal farm. In the final scene, the hero meets his former girlfriend, who asks him how he survives. From the shadows of a dark alley—representing the Depression itself—he whispers: "I steal."

Other early films from this decade, such as *Little Caesar* (1930) and *Public Enemy* (1931), focused on big city mobsters who ruthlessly shot their way to the top. Although these "bad guys" were either killed or brought to justice on screen, the public's fascination with criminal activity reached a peak in these years with the romanticizing of bank robbers (and cold-blooded murderers) like John Dillinger, Bonnie Parker and Clyde Barrow, Baby Face Nelson, and Ma Barker. All died in shoot-outs with local police or the FBI.

The evolving optimism of the 1930s—the promise of better times—was apparent in Hollywood films. The 1930s saw Fred Astaire whirling Ginger Rogers across the nightclub dance floor; Mickey Rooney courting Judy Garland in the blissfully innocent "Andy Hardy" movies; and Walt Disney raising the animated cartoon to an art form in his feature film *Snow White and the Seven Dwarfs* (1937). Wildly popular in this decade (and beyond) were the Marx brothers—Groucho, Harpo, and Chico—whose classic comedies demolished upper-class snobbery, foolish tradition, and much of the English language.

More significant were the moral dramas of director Frank Capra, including *Mr. Deeds Goes to Town* (1936), starring Gary Cooper, and *Mr. Smith Goes to Washington* (1939), with Jimmy Stewart. Both the movies and the leading men represented the inherent virtues of heartland America, with its strong sense of decency and cooperation. Common people could be fooled by greedy bankers and selfish politicians, but not for long. Life got better when "good folks" followed their instincts.

The most memorable films of this era, *Gone with the Wind* and ***The Grapes of Wrath,*** showcased Hollywood's ability to transform best-selling fiction into successful movies, seen by millions who had read the novels of Margaret Mitchell, John Steinbeck, and others—and millions more who had not. Both films related the epic struggle of families in crisis, trying desperately to survive. *The Grapes of Wrath,* set in the Depression, depicts the awful conditions faced by the Dust Bowl farmers who migrated to California. True to the 1930s, it is a story of marginal people confronting economic injustice—people who stick together and refuse to give up. The hero, Tom Joad, promises his Ma that "wherever they's a fight so hungry people can eat, I'll be there. Wherever they's a cop beatin' up a guy, I'll be there." Ma Joad is a source of strength and common sense. "They ain't gonna wipe us out," she insists. "Why, we're the people—we go on."

The Radio Age

Like the movie boom, the rapid growth of radio in the Depression encouraged the spread of popular culture. Politicians and public figures such as President Roosevelt and Father Coughlin used radio to great effect. So, too, did companies seeking to mass market their products. Organized along commercial lines in the 1920s, radio continued firmly down that path in the 1930s, with two giant firms—the National Broadcasting Company (NBC) and the Columbia Broadcasting System (CBS)—dominating the nation's airwaves.

In an odd way, the economic turmoil of the 1930s aided radio by weakening other forms of entertainment. As vaudeville failed and the infant recording industry struggled, popular performers, including Al Jolson and Jack Benny, continued their careers on the radio. For morning and afternoon fare, the networks relied on domestic dramas such as *Ma Perkins* and *Helen Trent,* which appealed to women working in the home. Often sponsored by soap and beauty companies, these programs, known as "soap operas," doled out the story line in daily 15-minute installments. In the evenings, as entire families gathered around the radio, the entertainment broadened to include quiz shows, talent contests, and adventure programs like *Inner Sanctum* and *The Green Hornet.* Surveys showed that the average American in the 1930s listened to more than 4 hours of radio each day.

Radio carried sporting events, political conventions, and the news. Millions followed the 1936 Berlin Olympics, where Jesse Owens, the African American track star, embarrassed Adolf Hitler by winning four gold medals. Two years later, the heavyweight title fight from Yankee Stadium between Joe Louis, the black champion, and Max Schmeling, the German challenger, was broadcast throughout the world. When Louis knocked out Schmeling in the first round, Americans celebrated in the streets.

Perhaps nothing better demonstrated the power of radio than the infamous "War of the Worlds" episode. On Halloween evening, 1938, actor Orson Welles, star of CBS's *Mercury Theater,* did a powerful reading of the H. G. Wells novel, presenting it as a simulated newscast in which violent aliens from Mars land in the New Jersey town of Grovers Mills. "I can see the thing's body," sobbed a "roving reporter" at the scene. "It's large as a bear and it glistens like wet leather. That face . . . the black eyes and saliva dripping from its rimless lips." Although Welles repeatedly interrupted the program to explain what he was doing, a national panic ensued. Thousands fled their homes, believing that the Martians had wiped out the New Jersey State Police and were advancing toward New York City. Traffic came to a halt in parts of the Northeast; bus and train stations were jammed; churches overflowed with weeping families. A few commentators blamed the hysteria on world events; the rising tide of fascism in Europe made people uneasy. Everybody else blamed Welles for misusing—or at least misjudging—the power of radio. Newspaper headlines screamed: "Radio War Terrorizes U.S." and "Panic Grips Nation As Radio Announces 'Mars Attacks World.'" When the furor died down, President Roosevelt invited Welles to the White House. "You know, Orson," he joked, "you and I are the two best actors in America."

Orson Welles, arms upraised, caused a national panic during his radio dramatization of "War of the Worlds" in 1938.

The Second Term

In his second inaugural address, FDR emphasized the New Deal's unfinished business. "I see one-third of a nation ill-housed, ill-clad, ill-nourished," he declared. The president was optimistic. The election had provided him with a stunning popular mandate and with huge Democratic majorities on Capitol Hill. To Roosevelt's thinking, only one roadblock lay in his path: the Supreme Court.

A confrontation seemed inevitable. The Supreme Court was dominated by elderly, conservative justices, appointed in the Harding–Coolidge years, who despised the New Deal and worked zealously to subvert its legislation. In Roosevelt's first term, the Court had struck down the NRA, the AAA, and a series of social welfare laws. In the coming months, it would be reviewing—and likely overturning—the National Labor Relations Act and the Social Security Act, two of the New Deal's most precious accomplishments.

Roosevelt struck first. In February 1937, without consulting Congress, he unveiled sweeping legislation to reorganize the federal court system. Under his plan, 50 new judgeships would be created by adding one judge for each sitting justice over the age of 70 who refused to retire. The Supreme Court would get a maximum of 6 new members, raising its total to 15.

The plan was legal. The Constitution sets no limits on the size of the Supreme Court; indeed, the number of justices, determined by Congress, had fluctuated between 6 and 10 in the previous century. Roosevelt assumed that his overwhelming reelection in 1936 had given him the green light to crush all opposition to the New Deal, regardless of the source.

He was badly mistaken. His plan met quick and furious opposition. Many Americans, including Louis D. Brandeis, the Supreme Court's oldest and most liberal justice, were offended by Roosevelt's jab at the elderly. Others worried that his "Court-packing" plan would undermine judicial independence and threaten the balance of power among the three branches of government. As the opposition grew stronger, aides urged Roosevelt to withdraw the bill.

In the spring of 1937, the Supreme Court changed course. By votes of five to four, with one moderate justice switching sides, it upheld both the Wagner Act and the Social Security Act. Then, one by one, the old conservatives decided to retire. This allowed Roosevelt—the only president in American history to make no Supreme Court appointments during his first 4-year term—to fill five vacancies in the next 3 years. The justices he chose—including Hugo Black, Felix Frankfurter,

and William O. Douglas—would steer a more liberal course for decades to come.

Nevertheless, the Court battle wounded Roosevelt in significant ways. By refusing to withdraw his legislation, he subjected fellow Democrats to a bitter Senate debate—and to eventual defeat. The Court-packing incident also emboldened Roosevelt's opponents by proving that the president could be beaten. "The New Deal," wrote one observer, "would never be the same."

Union Struggles

Away from Washington, new battles raged in the automobile plants of Michigan, the textile mills of North Carolina, and the coal fields of Kentucky as industrial workers demanded union recognition under the banner of the CIO. In perhaps the most spectacular episode, autoworkers at a General Motors plant in Flint, Michigan, went on strike *inside* the factory, refusing to leave. Their spontaneous technique, known as the "sit-down," spread quickly to other sites. Though Roosevelt privately criticized these strikers for violating property rights, he declined to send in troops. In February 1937, GM recognized the CIO's United Automobile Workers (UAW) as the bargaining agent for its employees. Chrysler came to terms a few months later.

The victory at GM forced other employers into line. Firestone signed a contract with the CIO's Rubber Workers, General Electric and RCA with the Electrical Workers. Even U.S. Steel, an old enemy of organized labor, agreed to generous terms with the Steelworkers—union recognition, a 40-hour week, and a 10 percent wage increase.

Autoworkers celebrate the end of their "sit-down" strike at a General Motors plant in Flint, Michigan, in 1937.

There were some holdouts, however. Henry Ford hired an army of thugs to rough up union organizers and disrupt strikers on the picket lines. Republic Steel of Chicago stockpiled more weapons than did the city police department. "I won't have a contract with an irresponsible, racket-eering, violent communistic body like the CIO," fumed Republic President Tom C. Girdler.

The worst violence occurred outside Republic's South Chicago mill on Memorial Day 1937. There heavily armed police battled rock-throwing strikers on the picket line. Before it ended, 10 workers had been killed by gunfire, and dozens more had been injured. In the following months, Ford and Republic Steel came to terms. Under pressure from the National Labor Relations Board, they gradually accepted industrial unionism as a legitimate force in American life. With a membership approaching 3 million, the CIO had come a long way since its break with the conservative, craft-oriented American Federation of Labor a few years before.

Hitler Youth in Germany rounding up books to be burned, including the works of Thomas Mann and Albert Einstein. As Joseph Goebbels, the Nazi propaganda minister, declared: "These flames not only illuminate the final end of an old era; they also light up the new."

Losing Ground

The Court battle and the sit-down strikes slowed down the political momentum that followed FDR's reelection landslide in 1936. Further problems loomed in Europe, where fascism continued to gain strength, and in the United States, where a serious recession in 1937 eroded public confidence in the New Deal. For President Roosevelt, the road ahead appeared even more menacing than before.

Fascist Advances

Late in 1936, civil war broke out in Spain. A group of military officers, led by General Francisco Franco, attempted to overthrow the recently elected government. Because Franco represented the *Falangist,* or fascist elements in Spain, he received military aid from Hitler and Mussolini. On the other side, Joseph Stalin aided the government (or "loyalist") forces, which contained a large socialist and communist contingent. The war itself was brutal, with extreme cruelty on both sides. Before it ended, more than 600,000 people were killed.

The Spanish civil war triggered strong emotions in the United States. Some Americans praised Franco as a bastion against communism and a strong supporter of the Catholic Church. Others condemned him as a fascist thug, determined to overthrow a popularly elected government by force. Several thousand Americans went to Spain as part of the Abraham Lincoln Brigade, organized

by the Communist party, to fight on the Loyalist side. As Ernest Hemingway said of Franco, "There is only one way to quell a bully and that is to thrash him."

Most Americans disagreed. In 1937, Congress passed a third neutrality bill that extended the arms embargo to include *civil wars* like the one raging in Spain. The bill also prohibited Americans from traveling on belligerent vessels, even at their own risk. However, it did permit nations at war to purchase "non-military" goods if they paid cash (no loans) and carried them away on their own ships. President Roosevelt quickly signed the bill into law.

The Rising Nazi Menace

In central Europe, meanwhile, Hitler marched boldly toward war. Vowing to unite all German-speaking people, he moved on Austria in 1938, adding 6 million "Germans" to the Third Reich. Then he demanded the Sudetenland, a region in western Czechoslovakia where 3 million ethnic Germans lived. The Czechs possessed both a well-trained army and a defense treaty with France. As central Europe's only remaining democracy, Czechoslovakia looked to the French and British for support against the Nazi threat.

That support never came. Neither France nor England wanted a showdown with Germany. France had lost half of its male population between the ages of 20 and 32 during World War I. In Britain, Oxford students adopted a resolution in the 1930s declaring that they would not take up arms for their country under any

In 1939, more than a thousand Jews fleeing from Germany aboard the ocean liner *St. Louis* were refused entry into the United States at the port of Miami and forced to return to Europe—and certain death.

sentiment, and hard times kept the "golden door" tightly shut. Most Americans did not want "foreigners" competing with them for jobs and resources in the midst of the Depression.

The result was disastrous. At a time when many Jews had the ability to flee Hitler, there was almost no place for them to go. Between 1935 and 1941, the United States took in an average of 8,500 Jews per year—a number far below the annual German quota of 30,000 set by the National Origins Act of 1924. (Among those allowed to enter were "high profile" Jewish refugees such as Albert Einstein and composer Kurt Weill.) Furthermore, President Roosevelt refused to take additional steps against Hitler because he feared a political backlash. Thus, he did not make a strong diplomatic protest or attempt to lessen trade with the Nazi regime.

circumstances. Antiwar feeling was so strong that a kind of diplomatic paralysis set in. The result was the Munich debacle of 1938.

At Munich, Prime Minister Neville Chamberlain of England and Premier Edouard Daladier of France agreed to Hitler's demand for the Sudetenland. In return the German leader promised not to take any more territory. Daladier then pressured the Czechs to accept this dismal bargain, while Chamberlain congratulated everyone— Hitler included—for bringing "peace in our time."

The news from inside Germany was even worse. Early in 1938, the Nazis torched Munich's Great Synagogue and began the initial deportation of Jews to the infamous concentration camp at Buchenwald. On the evening of November 9—known as *Kristallnacht,* the "night of broken glass"—Nazi mobs burned synagogues, looted stores, and attacked Jews in cities throughout Germany. Dozens were murdered, hundreds were beaten and raped. In addition, the Nazis passed new laws to confiscate Jewish property, bar Jews from meaningful employment, and deprive them of ordinary liberties such as attending school and driving a car.

When word of these events reached the United States, President Roosevelt was furious. "I myself could scarcely believe that such things could occur in a twentieth century civilization," he told reporters. Roosevelt immediately called a conference of 32 nations to discuss plans for accepting desperate Jewish refugees from Germany, Austria, and Czechoslovakia. But no country, with the exception of small and densely populated Holland, showed a willingness to help. In the United States, a combination of anti-Semitism, isolationist

An End to Reform

Until 1937, the American economy had been making steady, if uneven, progress. National income and production finally reached 1929 levels, stock prices were climbing, profits were up. Roosevelt now hoped to slow down government spending as the business picture improved. He wanted to balance the federal budget and cut the mounting national debt.

The president knew that national recovery had been fueled by the New Deal's farm subsidies, relief programs, and public works. He was familiar with the writings of British economist John Maynard Keynes, who advocated a policy of deficit spending in hard times to spur economic growth. Yet Roosevelt had never been fully comfortable with government's expanding role. He feared that the growing national debt would generate inflation, and he worried about the effect of federal welfare programs upon the recipients' initiative and self-respect.

In 1937, Roosevelt slashed funding for both the PWA and WPA, cutting almost 2 million jobs. At the same time, the new Social Security payroll tax took effect, removing billions of dollars of purchasing power from the economy. The result was recession—the most serious economic plunge of the Roosevelt years. As unemployment rose and production plummeted, the nation slipped back toward the nightmare of 1933, with breadlines and soup kitchens dotting the landscape.

In October, Roosevelt called Congress into special session. Within weeks, a $5 billion expenditure was approved for federal relief and public works. The economy responded, showing the impact of government spending once again. But the recession further weakened Roosevelt's image as a forceful leader in perilous times.

© Bettmann/CORBIS

Table 25.1 Key New Deal Programs and Legislation

1933	Emergency Banking Act
	Civilian Conservation Corps
	Agricultural Adjustment Act
	Tennessee Valley Authority
	Glass-Steagall Banking Act (creates Federal Deposit Insurance Corporation)
	Federal Emergency Relief Act
	National Industrial Recovery Act
	Civil Works Administration
1934	Securities and Exchange Act
1935	National Labor Relations Act
	Social Security Act
	Emergency Relief Appropriation Act (creates Works Progress Administration)
	Revenue Act ("Wealth Tax")
	Rural Electrification Administration
	National Youth Administration
1936	Soil Conservation Act
1937	National Housing Act
1938	Fair Labor Standards Act

By 1938, the New Deal had clearly lost momentum. Harry Hopkins blamed it on 6 grinding years of Depression and reform, claiming the public was "bored with the poor, the unemployed, the insecure." Facing a more combative Congress—Republicans and conservative Democrats made significant gains in the 1938 elections—Roosevelt decided to "tread water" for a while. Among his few legislative achievements that year was passage of the Fair Labor Standards Act, which abolished child labor in most industries, and provided a minimum hourly wage (40 cents) and a maximum workweek (40 hours) to be phased in over time. Like Social Security, the act did not cover those who needed it most, such as farm workers and domestics. Yet almost a million Americans had their wages raised immediately by this law, and countless millions had their work hours shortened as well.

Conclusion

In responding to the enormous challenges of the Great Depression, Franklin Roosevelt's New Deal altered politics and society in fundamental ways. For the first time, the federal government provided massive assistance to the poor and the unemployed. It stabilized the banking system, protected farmers with price supports, guaranteed the rights of organized labor, and created a national pension plan. The New Deal also produced a more class-oriented Democratic party, appealing to industrial workers, hard-pressed farmers, and urban minorities. Avoiding the political extremes that plagued other nations in the Depression era, Roosevelt steered a middle course between laissez-faire and Socialism—a course that combined free enterprise and democracy with national planning and social reform.

During the New Deal years, the size and scope of the federal government increased dramatically. Facing a catastrophic depression, FDR used the presidential office, as never before in U.S. history, to extend needed relief, stimulate job growth, and regulate the economy. He became the first president to regularly fashion his own legislative agenda for Congress to consider, tilting the future balance of political power strongly in favor of the executive branch. At times Roosevelt badly overreached himself, as in his failed attempt to "pack" the Supreme Court in 1937. On the whole, though, he proved a remarkably popular and resourceful figure, using his ebullient personality, his courageous struggle with polio, and his understanding of the media, especially radio, to form a powerful bond with the people.

What the New Deal did best was to restore a sense of hope and purpose to a demoralized nation. Yet its overriding goal in these years—the promise of full economic recovery—remained elusive at best. Fearful of mounting budget deficits and ever-growing relief rolls, President Roosevelt never committed himself to the level of consistent federal spending urged by economists like John Maynard Keynes. When the New Deal ended in 1939, more than 8 million Americans were still unemployed. It would take a world war, and the full mobilization that followed, to put them permanently back to work.

The Chapter In Review

In the years between 1933 and 1939:

- The United States hit rock bottom economically as banks collapsed and millions lost their jobs.
- Congress enacted emergency legislation to provide needed relief during the "first hundred days."
- The nation slowly recovered, leading to Roosevelt's landslide reelection in 1936.
- The New Deal laid the foundation for a welfare state with programs such as social security and unemployment insurance.

- Unions won recognition following successful strikes against employers in the automobile, steel, and other industries.
- Drought and dust storms caused great ecological damage in parts of Kansas, Nebraska, Oklahoma, Texas, and Colorado.

- Fascist aggression and Japanese militarism led to a bitter national debate regarding America's role in the world.

Making Connections Across Chapters

LOOKING BACK

Chapter 25 considers the impact of the Great Depression on the social, economic, and political structure of the United States. Among the key issues considered is the new relationship between the federal government and the average citizen.

1. What were the most pressing problems facing the Roosevelt administration when it came to power, and how did it address them?

2. Who were President Roosevelt's major critics, and how did they propose to deal with the Great Depression?

3. What impact did the Great Depression have on the realignment of the major political parties?

4. How did the American people view international relations in the 1930s, and what factors were responsible for the perceptions of America's role in the world?

LOOKING AHEAD

Chapter 26 examines the impact of World War II on American society. Following the Japanese attack on Pearl Harbor, isolationist sentiment would end, the nation would mobilize its defenses, and 15 million men and women would serve in the armed forces against the Axis powers of Germany, Italy, and Japan.

1. What impact would the coming of World War II have on the economic problems facing Americans in the 1930?

2. What would happen to the powerful isolationist movement of this era?

3. Given the darkening world situation, would President Roosevelt decide to break with political precedent and run for a third presidential term?

Recommended Readings

Brinkley, Alan. *Voices of Protest: Huey Long, Father Coughlin, and the Great Depression* (1982). A revealing account of Depression era dissidents.

Cohen, Lizabeth. *Making a New Deal: Industrial Workers in Chicago* (1990). Examines working-class protest and culture during the Depression.

Cooke, Blanche Wiesen. *Eleanor Roosevelt* (1992). Follows the life of the nation's most active first lady.

Fraser, Steve, and Gerstle, Gary, eds. *The Rise of the New Deal Order* (1989). Contains a series of original essays about the New Deal's impact on American life.

Goodman, James. *Stories of Scottsboro* (1994). Vividly recreates the most important civil rights trial of the 1930s.

Leuchtenburg, William. *The Supreme Court Reborn: The Constitutional Revolution in the Age of Roosevelt* (1995). Studies the conflicts and changes that altered the Supreme Court in the 1930s and beyond.

McElvaine, Robert S. *The Great Depression* (1984). An excellent survey of American life and politics during the New Deal era.

Terkel, Studs. *Hard Times* (1970). Views the Depression through the oral histories of those who lived through it.

Ware, Susan. *Holding Their Own: American Women in the 1930s* (1982). Explores the role of women in America's worst economic crisis.

Worster, Donald. *Dust Bowl: The Southern Plains in the 1930s* (1979). Examines the causes and the impact of this ecological disaster.

Identifications

Review your understanding of the following key terms, people, events, and dates for this chapter (these terms also appear in the Glossary at the end of the book):

New Deal
Civilian Conservation Corps (CCC)
Harry Hopkins
Civil Works Administration (CWA)
Tennessee Valley Authority (TVA)
Agricultural Adjustment Act

Dust Bowl
National Industrial Recovery Act (NIRA)
Huey P. Long
John L. Lewis
Eleanor Roosevelt
Mary McLeod Bethune
Marian Anderson
The Grapes of Wrath

Online Sources Guide

Use this listing to find online documents, images, interactive maps, simulations, and other resources related to this chapter:

American History Resource Center

http://history.wadsworth.com/rc/us

Documents

Frances Perkins's *People at Work* (1934)
Excerpt from the Supreme Court decision in *Schechter Poultry Corp. v. United States* (1935)
Dorothy Day's account of the 1937 violence at Republic Steel Mills

Selected Images

Depositors gathering outside a bank, April 1933
Eleanor Roosevelt, 1933
A&P Grocery Store advertisement, 1933
National Recovery Administration Eagle poster
President Roosevelt visits a Civilian Conservation Corps camp in 1933
Working a farm near Tupelo, Miss., 1936
Dust storm, Elkhart, Kan., 1937
Tennessee Valley Authority dam

1934 cartoon depicting FDR and the growth of the New Deal agencies
The Great Depression hits African American tenant farmers, 1939

Simulation

Surviving the Great Depression (In this simulation you can choose to be an African American sharecropper in Alabama, a white farmer in Wisconsin, or a young Italian in New York City and make choices based on the circumstances and opportunities afforded.)

Document Exercises

1936–1943 posters from the WPA

HistoryNOW

http://now.ilrn.com/ayers_etal3e

Primary Source Exercises

Letters from the "Forgotten Man" to Mrs. Roosevelt, 1934
John L. Lewis on the NRA, 1934
National Labor Relations Act, 1935

26 The Second World War, 1940–1945

...*we here highly resolve that these dead shall not have died in vain*...

REMEMBER DEC. 7th!

Prime Minister Neville Chamberlain's "peace in our time" lasted fewer than 6 months. In March 1939, the Germans marched into central Czechoslovakia. To the south, Franco's forces won a final victory in the Spanish civil war, and Mussolini's army annexed neighboring Albania. Throughout the summer months, Nazi threats multiplied. "So long as Germans in Poland suffer grievously, so long as they are imprisoned away from the Fatherland," warned Hitler, "Europe can have no peace."

President Roosevelt declared neutrality, reflecting the clear sentiment of the American people. At the same time, he worked to mobilize the nation's defense effort and to shape public opinion steadily against the Axis powers. If possible, Roosevelt hoped to aid Great Britain and the Allies through "all measures short of war." If need be, however, he vowed to use military force to prevent a Nazi victory in Europe.

War in Europe

In August 1939, Hitler and Stalin stunned the world by signing a nonaggression pact. Both dictators were buying time for an inevitable showdown between their armed forces. And both had designs on Polish territory, which they secretly divided in their agreement. On September 1, German ground troops and armored divisions stormed into Poland from the west, backed by their powerful air force *(Luftwaffe)*. Two weeks later, Soviet troops attacked from the east, reclaiming the territory that Russia had lost to Poland after World War I. In the following months, Stalin moved against the Baltic states, subduing Estonia, Latvia, and Lithuania.

Blitzkrieg

Hitler's *Blitzkrieg* (lightning strike) into Poland shattered the lingering illusions of Munich. Having pledged themselves to guarantee Poland's borders, England and France reluctantly declared war on Germany. The British sent a small, ill-equipped army to defend western Europe against further Nazi aggression. The French reinforced their "impregnable" Maginot Line facing Germany, and the Nazis fortified their Siegfried Line in the Rhineland facing France. An eerie calm settled over Europe, as all sides prepared for battle.

Timeline

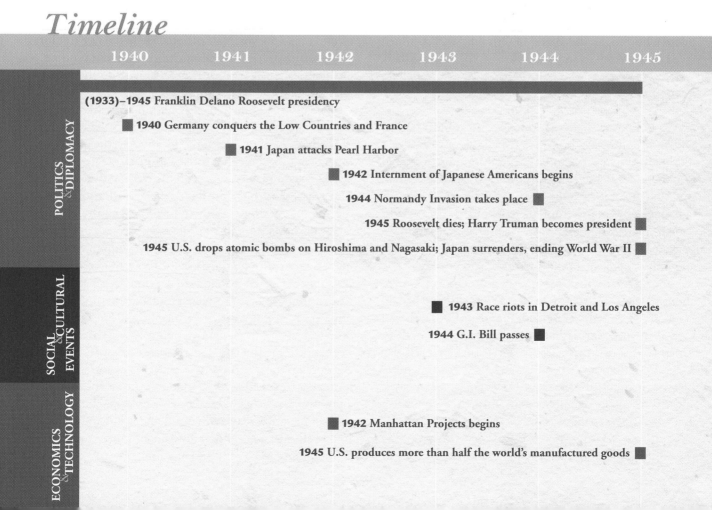

	1940	1941	1942	1943	1944	1945

POLITICS & DIPLOMACY

(1933)–1945 Franklin Delano Roosevelt presidency

1940 Germany conquers the Low Countries and France

1941 Japan attacks Pearl Harbor

1942 Internment of Japanese Americans begins

1944 Normandy Invasion takes place

1945 Roosevelt dies; Harry Truman becomes president

1945 U.S. drops atomic bombs on Hiroshima and Nagasaki; Japan surrenders, ending World War II

SOCIAL & CULTURAL EVENTS

1943 Race riots in Detroit and Los Angeles

1944 G.I. Bill passes

ECONOMICS & TECHNOLOGY

1942 Manhattan Projects begins

1945 U.S. produces more than half the world's manufactured goods

That 6-month calm, known as the "phony war," ended in April 1940 when the Nazis overran Denmark and Norway. In May, they invaded Belgium, Holland, Luxembourg—and France itself. From the skies, the Luftwaffe strafed fleeing civilians and flattened cities such as Rotterdam. On the ground, German troops and armor swept through the Ardennes Forest, skirting the Maginot Line. The huge French army collapsed in disarray. Within weeks, German units had reached the French coastline, trapping the British army at Dunkirk, with its back to the sea. In early June, a flotilla of small ships from England—tugs, pleasure craft, and naval vessels—ferried 330,000 soldiers to safety. It was both a defeat and a deliverance for the British forces, who had been badly mauled but rescued from disaster.

In mid-June, as Paris fell to the advancing Nazi army, Mussolini attacked France from the south. Following the French surrender on June 22, the German Luftwaffe attacked England in force. Hitler's plan was to gain control of the skies in preparation for a full-scale invasion of the British Isles. Day and night, German planes dropped their bombs on London, Coventry, and other cities in a murderous attempt to break civilian morale. Day and night, the British Royal Air Force rose up to meet the Luftwaffe, with devastating effect. By early fall, Nazi air losses forced Hitler to abandon his invasion plans. "Never in the field of human conflict," said England's new Prime Minister **Winston Churchill** of the brave pilots who fought the Battle of Britain, "was so much owed by so many to so few."

A Third Term for FDR

Events in Europe shattered America's isolationist façade. Unlike Woodrow Wilson in 1914, President Roosevelt did not ask the people to be "neutral in thought as well as in action." If England fell to the Nazis, he believed, the United States would become an isolated fortress, vulnerable to attack from the air and the sea. Most Americans felt the same way. A national poll found 83 percent hoping for a British victory, 16 percent neutral, and only 1 percent supporting the Nazis.

The German Blitzkrieg increased American concerns about defense. In August 1940, as the Battle of Britain raged in the skies over England, President Roosevelt and Congress worked to fashion the first peacetime draft in American history, the Selective Service Act, as well as a $10.5 billion appropriation for defense. With factories now open round-the-clock to build tanks, war planes, and naval vessels, unemployment virtually disappeared. The Great Depression was over.

Building a strong defense was one thing, aiding the Allies quite another. As Michigan Senator Arthur Vandenberg, a leading isolationist, put it: "I do not believe that we can become an arsenal for one belligerent without becoming a target for another." Vandenberg used World War I as his example, charging that America's support for the Allied war effort had led to its participation in the war itself. With a presidential election on the horizon, FDR would have to answer this charge.

Until the last moment, however, there was no assurance that Roosevelt would even run. The loss of New Deal momentum and the Court-packing disaster pointed to his political retirement. Furthermore, no American president had ever served a third term—a taboo that reflected the public's deep suspicion of entrenched federal power.

By 1940, the picture had changed. The idea of tested presidential leadership took on added appeal. Roosevelt expected to run again. Hoping to defuse the third-term issue, he allowed himself to be "drafted" by the Democratic National Convention in Chicago, thus appearing reluctant but dutiful in the public's mind. "The salvation of the nation rests in one man, because of his experience and great humanitarian thinking," declared Mayor Edward J. Kelly of the host city. Roosevelt selected the enigmatic Henry Wallace to be his vice presidential running mate.

The Republicans, meeting in Philadelphia, nominated **Wendell Willkie** of Indiana for president and Senator Charles McNary of Oregon for vice president. As a Wall Street lawyer and the head of a large utilities corporation, Willkie held two positions almost guaranteed to make the voters suspicious. He had never run for public office or held an appointive government position. His political ascent was due, in large part, to the public relations skills of his advisors.

The 1940 campaign was dominated by foreign affairs. Though Willkie shared Roosevelt's views about the dangers of Nazi aggression, he attacked the president for moving too quickly on the European stage. Among Willkie's complaints was a controversial decision by FDR to supply England with "overage" destroyers. In the summer of 1940, Churchill had begged the United States for naval support to protect British sea lanes from Nazi submarine attacks. In September, without consulting Congress, the president sent 50 old but serviceable warships to England in return for long-term leases to British military bases in Newfoundland, Bermuda, and other parts of the Western Hemisphere. The agreement outraged isolationists, who viewed it as a clear violation of American neutrality. Willkie charged that FDR's foreign policy meant "more wooden crosses for sons and brothers and sweethearts," forcing the president to make a promise that he would not be able to keep. "I have said this before, but I shall say it again and again and again," Roosevelt told a cheering crowd in Boston. "Your boys are not going to be sent into any foreign wars."

Movie continued

- Us was forbid to sell weapons
- Cash and carry bases. to sell weapons
- Thought about cash and carry they would be taking sides. they didn't want to take England's side and not oppose the axis.
- Lend and lease policy was given
- Atlantic Charter assurance of freedom and without fear.
- December 7, 1941 Hawaii
  PEARL HARBOR
- The U.S. was attacked by Japan.
- After the U.S. was attacked decided to go to War.
- Saturation Bombing a new way by air force power
- June 6 1944 D-Day
- FDR wins a fourth term and a new secretary
- April 12, 194   F. D. Roosevelt died.
- War was a safeguard for democracy

July Seventeen

July 17, 200

FDR MOVIE

- 1936-1939
Germany became
the arm giant
of Europe, were
restoring their
army
- Unic Pact British
settled a peace
treaty w/ Germany
- When peace was
broken U.S was
in trouble, they
wanted to continue
being neutral wanted
to keep themselves out of war.

- Pased 15 new laws
in 100 days in
office
- Social Security for
elderly, disabled, and
people without any
jobs.
- Year of dictator
"Hitler"
Baseball was better
than the battle
field

OutLine

Lansing-Ishi   Clark Memo
Wash. Naval Conf.   Good Neighbor Pol.
Stimson   Cardonas
Kellogg-Briand   "quaratine"
Moore   Hitler
Hughes   "Cash + Carry"
Neutrality Act   American First
Calles   White
Morrow   WilliKie

Lend Lease   WPD
Robin Moor   OPA
Churchill   Price Stabilization
Atlantic Charter   Eisenhower
Reuben James   Rommel
Tripartite (Axis)   Mussolini
Vichy   Normandy
Hull   Bulge
Bataan   Eden
Coregidor   Molotov
                             Ching Kai-Shek

Stalin
Tito
Macarthur
Kamikaze
Hiroshima
Nazasaki

Picturing the Past   **POLITICS & DIPLOMACY**

Breaking Tradition: A Presidential Third Term

Franklin Roosevelt's decision to seek a third term in 1940 broke a long-standing precedent. Note the political poster here, which uses the authoritative, nonpartisan image of Uncle Sam to make this point. At that time, the Constitution set no limits on the number of terms a president could serve. In the nation's formative years, Presidents George Washington, Thomas Jefferson, and James Madison had all retired after two full terms in office, setting an informal standard for the future. Though former President Ulysses S. Grant had unsuccessfully sought the Republican nomination for a third term in 1880, and former President Theodore Roosevelt was

defeated in his quest for a third term on the Progressive party ticket in 1912, no *sitting* president had campaigned for a third term until FDR. Given the state of world affairs in 1940, the third term issue generated little interest; Americans were far more focused on the coming of war. When Roosevelt ran for a fourth term in 1944, Republicans raised the issue obliquely, describing the president and his advisors as "tired old men." In 1947, however, a Republican-led Congress passed an amendment that limited presidents to two terms. The Twenty-Second Amendment was ratified, with little public rancor or discussion, in 1951.

Franklin D. Roosevelt Library

Roosevelt defeated Willkie with ease—27 million votes to 22 million, 449 electoral votes to 82. He carried all of America's major cities, piling up impressive totals among blacks, Jews, ethnic minorities, and union members. New York Mayor Fiorello LaGuardia put it well: "Americans prefer Roosevelt with his known faults to Willkie with his unknown virtues." Still, the margin of FDR's popular victory made this the closest presidential election since 1916.

The End of Neutrality

Shortly after the election, Roosevelt learned that England could no longer afford the supplies it needed to fight the Nazi war machine. He responded by asking Congress for the authority to sell or lease "defense material" to any nation he judged "vital to the defense of the United States." Roosevelt compared his "**Lend-Lease**" proposal to the simple act of lending a garden

hose to a neighbor whose house was on fire. In Europe, he said, the British desperately needed tanks, guns, and planes to extinguish the raging inferno of Nazism. Only one nation had the ability to supply them. "We must be the great arsenal of democracy," Roosevelt declared.

Lend-Lease

Lend-Lease set off a furious national debate. In 1940, FDR's opponents organized the America First Committee to keep the nation "neutral" by defeating Lend-Lease. Supported by Henry Ford, Charles Lindbergh, and Robert E. Wood, chairman of Sears, Roebuck, it appealed to the isolationist notion that America should be prepared to defend its own territory, leaving Europe's wars to the Europeans. At times, however, the committee's message became muddled and conspiratorial, as when Lindbergh described American Jews as the "principal war agitators" behind Lend-Lease.

By 1941, Roosevelt gained the upper hand. Public opinion moved sharply against isolationism as Hitler became a more ominous threat. Polls showed a clear majority of Americans willing to risk war with Germany in order to help the British survive. In March, a $7 billion Lend-Lease bill sailed through Congress, assisted by powerful lobbying groups such as the Committee to Defend America by Aiding the Allies.

In June 1941, Hitler shattered the recent Nazi-Soviet Pact by invading Russia with more than 2 million troops. Roosevelt responded by offering Stalin immediate Lend-Lease support. The idea of aiding a Communist dictator was hard for Americans to accept. But Roosevelt stood firm, believing that wars made strange bedfellows and that Hitler must be stopped at all costs. At his insistence, the Soviets received $12 billion in aid over the next 4 years.

With Lend-Lease in place, Roosevelt abandoned all pretense of neutrality. To ensure that American goods reached England, he instructed the navy to protect merchant shipping in the North Atlantic sea lanes. In August 1941, Roosevelt and Churchill met aboard the USS *Augusta*, off the Newfoundland coast, to discuss their mutual aims and principles. The result was a communiqué known as the Atlantic Charter, which called for freedom of the seas, freedom from want and fear, and self-determination for all people in the postwar world.

At this meeting, Roosevelt secretly promised Churchill that the United States would try "to force an 'incident' that could lead to war" with Germany. In the fall of 1941, as Nazi submarines sank one Britain-bound freighter after another, the president armed America's merchant fleet and authorized U.S. destroyers to hunt these U-boats under a policy known as "active defense." In October, a German submarine sank a U.S. destroyer off Iceland, with the loss of 100 American lives. In his ballad to the men who died, Woody Guthrie asked: "What were their names, tell me, what were their names? Did you have a friend on the good *Reuben James?*"

War would come shortly, but not where Roosevelt expected.

The Road to Pearl Harbor

As Hitler swept relentlessly though Europe, another power was stirring halfway around the globe. Like Germany and Italy, Japan had become a militarist state controlled by leaders with expansionist ideas. In the 1930s, the Japanese had invaded China, routing its army, terror-bombing cities, and brutalizing civilians in the infamous "rape of Nanking." The United States barely protested. With his focus on the Nazis, Roosevelt sought to avoid a crisis with Japan, even after its planes bombed an American gunboat, the *Panay*, on the Yangtze River in 1937, killing 3 sailors and injuring 43 more.

In 1938, the Japanese unveiled their plan for empire, known as the "Greater East Asia Co-Prosperity Sphere." Viewing themselves as superior to their neighbors, they aimed to rule their region by annexing European colonies in Southeast Asia and the Western Pacific. Control of French Indochina, the Dutch East Indies, and British Malaya would provide the food and raw materials to make Japan self-sufficient and secure. Only one obstacle stood in the way—the United States.

Japan purchased the bulk of its steel, oil, heavy equipment, and machine parts from U.S. suppliers. To help prevent further Japanese expansion, the Roosevelt administration placed an embargo on certain strategic goods to Japan and moved the Pacific Fleet from San Diego to **Pearl Harbor.** The Japanese responded by negotiating a defense treaty (the so-called Tripartite Pact) with Germany and Italy. Relations steadily declined. Hitler's Blitzkrieg left defeated France and Holland unable to defend their Asian colonies. When Japan moved against Indochina in April 1941, Roosevelt retaliated by freezing all Japanese assets in the United States and blocking shipments of scrap iron and aviation fuel to Japan. In September, Japanese leaders requested a meeting with Roosevelt to end the deepening crisis. The president agreed—but with certain conditions. Before he would sit down with them, he said, the Japanese must withdraw from both China and Indochina.

The Japanese refused. Though talks were held at a lower level, both sides prepared for war. Military analysts expected Japan to move southwest, toward the Dutch East Indies and British Malaya, in search of needed rubber and oil. Instead, on November 26, 1941, a huge Japanese naval fleet, led by Admiral Chuichi Nagumo, left the Kurile Islands, just north of mainland Japan, and headed due east into rough Pacific waters. The armada included 6 aircraft carriers with 400 warplanes, 2 battleships, 2 cruisers, 9 destroyers, and dozens of support vessels. Traveling at 13 knots, under complete radio silence, the fleet was destined for Pearl Harbor, Hawaii, 5,000 miles away.

On Sunday morning, December 7, 1941, Admiral Nagumo's fleet reached its takeoff point, 220 miles north of Pearl Harbor. At 7:40 A.M., the first wave of Japanese warplanes appeared. The wing commander radioed back the words, "Tora (tiger), Tora, Tora," meaning that surprise had been complete. The battleship *Arizona* suffered a direct hit and went up in flames. More than 1,200 of her crew were killed. The *Oklahoma* capsized after taking 3 torpedoes, trapping 400 men below deck. A second Japanese assault at 9 o'clock completed the carnage. All told, 18 warships had been sunk

The Japanese attack on Pearl Harbor—December 7, 1941—destroyed 18 warships, killed 2,400 Americans, and plunged the nation into World War II.

or were badly damaged, 300 planes had been lost, and 2,400 Americans had died.

It could have been worse. The aircraft carriers *Lexington* and *Enterprise* were away from Pearl Harbor on maneuvers. And Japanese commanders made a strategic error by not launching a third air attack against the oil depots, machine shops, and repair facilities. As a result, most of the damaged warships were back in action within 2 years.

Why was Pearl Harbor so woefully unprepared? By the fall of 1941, the United States had broken the Japanese diplomatic code, known as MAGIC. American planners knew that war was coming. On November 27, Army Chief of Staff George C. Marshall sent a warning to all American military outposts in the Pacific. "Negotiations with Japan appear to be terminated to all practical purposes," it said. "Japanese future action unpredictable, but hostile action possible at any moment."

Yet Pearl Harbor was not viewed as the likely point of attack. It was thousands of miles from Japan and supposedly well defended. The very idea of a Japanese fleet sailing so far without detection seemed utterly fantastic. At Pearl Harbor, the commanders most feared sabotage from the large Japanese population living in Hawaii. Though some Americans believed that Roosevelt secretly encouraged the Japanese attack in order to bring the United States into World War II, the truth is more mundane. The debacle at Pearl Harbor was caused by negligence and errors in judgment, not by a backroom conspiracy at the White House.

On December 8, Congress declared war against Japan. Only Montana's Representative Jeanette Rankin dissented. (A longtime peace activist, she also had voted against President Wilson's war message in 1917.) On December 11, Germany and Italy honored the Tripartite Pact by declaring war on the United States. Almost instantly, Americans closed ranks. The foreign policy battles were over. As Roosevelt's former enemy Senator Burton Wheeler put it, "The only thing to do now is lick the hell out of them."

Early Defeats

The attack on Pearl Harbor began one of the bleakest years in American military history. In the North Atlantic, allied shipping losses reached almost a million tons per month. On the Eastern front, Nazi forces approached the outskirts of Moscow, where Soviet resistance was fierce. In Egypt, German General Erwin Rommel's elite Afrika Korps threatened the Suez Canal.

The news from Asia was grimmer still. Following Pearl Harbor, Japan moved quickly against American possessions in the Pacific, overrunning Guam, Wake Island, and eventually the Philippines. On December 10, 1941, the Japanese attacked the British fleet off Malaya, sinking the battleship *Prince of Wales* and the cruiser *Repulse.* In the following weeks, Burma, Hong Kong, Singapore, Malaya, and the Dutch East Indies fell like dominoes to Japanese invaders. Japan now had the resources—the oil, tin, rubber, and foodstuffs—to match its appetite for empire.

The Bataan Death March, following the surrender of U.S. troops in the Philippines, further fueled America's boiling hatred of Japan.

Enduring Issues The Military Draft in World War II—and Beyond

Conscription—defined as "compulsory service in the armed forces"—has long been controversial. Though the U.S. Constitution grants Congress the power "to raise and support armies," it does not say how this should be done. During the Revolutionary War, the Continental Congress rejected General George

The nation experienced fewer problems with the draft during World War II than at any other time, but the issue of military conscription remains controversial to this day.

Washington's request to have the central government institute a draft, favoring instead an army comprised of paid volunteers. During the War of 1812, Congress turned down a similar draft request from President James Madison. Indeed, the first wartime draft did not come into being until the 1860s, when both sides in the Civil War, North and South, raised a small percentage of their armies through conscription. The draft proved extremely unpopular, however, because it allowed draftees to avoid military service either by paying a fee ($300 in the North, $500 in the South), or by hiring a "substitute" to take their place. Antidraft activity flared in many cities, including New York, where poor immigrants, furious at the inequities of conscription, rioted for days until federal troops were brought in to restore order.

The modern draft was instituted during World War I. A Selective Service System was put in place, with a national headquarters and several thousand local "draft boards" spread throughout the country. Though deferments were provided on the basis of occupation, family need, and personal health, one could no longer avoid conscription by paying a fee or hiring a substitute. In 1917 and 1918, the military drafted almost 3 million men from a pool of 24 million registrants. For the first time in the country's history, a majority of the U.S. armed forces came from the ranks of draftees, not volunteers.

For Americans, the most galling defeat occurred in the Philippines, where 100,000 U.S. and Filipino troops surrendered to the Japanese after a bloody 6-month struggle. The military campaign had actually been lost on December 8, 1941, when the Japanese successfully bombed Clark Field, destroying 100 planes based there to defend the islands. (The failure to prepare for such an attack 1 day after Pearl Harbor was scandalous.) Lacking air cover, the defenders retreated to the jungles of the **Bataan Peninsula,** just north of Manila. As food ran out, they ate snakes, monkeys, cavalry horses, plants, and grass. Their songs were of hopelessness and despair.

> We're the battling bastards of Bataan;
> No Mama, no papa, no Uncle Sam.
> No aunts, no uncles, no cousins, no nieces;
> No pills, no planes, no artillery pieces.
> . . . And Nobody gives a damn!

In March 1942, President Roosevelt ordered the commanding officer, **General Douglas MacArthur,** to slip out of the Philippines, leaving his troops behind. The trapped defenders made their stand at Corregidor,

a fortresslike island in Manila Bay. After 2 months of constant bombardment, General Jonathan Wainwright surrendered to the Japanese. His diseased and starving men were brutalized by their captors on the infamous Bataan Death March—an event that further fueled America's boiling hatred of Japan.

Despite these disasters, the nation remained united and confident of victory. The road ahead would be long, the challenges immense. As *Time* magazine reminded its readers, "At the end of six months of war, the U.S. has: Not yet taken a single inch of enemy territory. Not yet beaten the enemy in a single major battle . . . Not yet opened an offensive campaign. The war, in short, has still to be fought."

The Homefront

The United States had begun to mobilize for World War II before the attack on Pearl Harbor. The draft was already in place, and defense plants were hiring new workers in the mad scramble to keep England, then the

The system was far from perfect, however. Some Americans showed their opposition to the war by openly opposing conscription; others easily evaded the draft. By most estimates, 10 percent of the nation's eligible males failed to register with their local boards during World War I, and 10 percent of those who were drafted did not report for duty.

In 1940, following the Nazi invasion of Western Europe, and the fall of France, Congress enacted the first peacetime draft in American history. When war came a year later, the draft was extended for the length of the conflict. Brought together by the attack on Pearl Harbor, and determined to beat back Nazi and Japanese aggression, the American people were far more unified than they had been during World War I. Six million men volunteered for military service between 1942 and 1945 and another 10 million were drafted. Deferments were severely limited, draft evasion relatively rare. The Selective Service System permitted those who opposed war on religious grounds to register as conscientious objectors, a status that permitted them to fulfill their obligation by doing nonmilitary tasks in the Army Medical Corps or by working in civilian hospitals or on selected public works projects. The small number who refused to cooperate in any manner, especially Jehovah's Witnesses, were sometimes arrested and sent to federal prison.

Following World War II, the Selective Service System remained in place. Those who were drafted, a number that rose and fell with the level of international tension, were expected to give 21 months of military service. Not surprisingly, draft resistance escalated during the 1960s, as protests against the increasingly unpopular Vietnam War gained momentum. Hundreds of thousands of young men evaded conscription, some moving to Canada; an even larger number, mostly from the middle-class, received student deferments. Unlike in World War II, where the military burden was equally shared, the draft calls in the 1960s fell hardest on those from working-class families.

Though Selective Service remains in place today, with men aged 18 to 25 required to register, the military has long since moved to an all-volunteer army. Whether the draft will ever return is an open question, subject to the power of public opinion and to the needs of the nation's armed forces.

Questions for Reflection

1. Why has the draft remained so controversial throughout our history? What made it different in World War II?

2. Can you imagine a situation in which the draft will be restored?

Soviet Union, and now America, fully supplied. Furthermore, the positive feelings about this conflict—a "good fight" against Nazi and Japanese aggression—eased many of the problems associated with a democratic nation going to war. Few men refused to register for military service, unlike World War I, and millions rushed to enlist. On the home front, Americans vowed to outproduce their enemies and to sacrifice for the "boys" at the front. "Our great strength," said a defense worker from San Diego, "is that we're all in this together."

War Production

FDR named Donald Nelson of Sears, Roebuck to run the newly created War Production Board (WPB). Nelson's main job was to oversee the transformation of American factories—to get companies such as Ford and General Motors to make tanks and warplanes instead of automobiles. To accomplish this, the federal government offered generous incentives. Antitrust laws were suspended so military orders could be filled quickly without competitive bidding. Companies were given low-interest loans to retool, and "cost-plus" contracts that guaranteed them a profit. Not surprisingly, the industrial giants made out best. As the war progressed, America's top 100 companies increased their percentage of the nation's total production from 30 to 70 percent. Ford, for example, began construction of a huge new factory in 1941, named Willow Run, to build B-24 Liberator bombers. In the next 4 years, it turned out 8,685 airplanes—one every 63 minutes. When questioned about these enormous profits and market shares, Secretary of War Henry Stimson replied that "in a capitalist country, you have to let business make money out of the process or business won't work."

Between 1940 and 1945, the nation's gross national product doubled, and the federal budget reached $95 billion, a tenfold increase. In the first half of 1942, the government placed more than $100 billion in war orders, requesting more goods than American factories had ever produced in a single year. The list included 60,000 planes, 45,000 tanks, 20,000 antiaircraft guns, and 8 million tons of merchant shipping. The orders for

American fighter planes roll off the assembly line during World War II.

1943 were even larger. By war's end, military spending exceeded $300 billion.

Roosevelt hoped to finance this effort without dramatically raising the national debt. That meant taxation over borrowing, a policy Congress strongly opposed. The result was a compromise that combined both of these elements. The Revenue Act of 1942 added millions of new taxpayers to the federal rolls and dramatically raised the rates paid by Americans in higher income brackets. Along with increases in corporate and inheritance rates, taxation provided about 45 percent of the war's total cost—less than Roosevelt wanted, but far more than the comparable figures for World War I or the Civil War.

Borrowing accounted for the rest. The national debt reached $260 billion in 1945, six times higher than that in 1941. The government relied on banks and brokerage houses for loans, but common people did their share. "There are millions who ask, 'What can we do to help?'" said Treasury Secretary Henry Morgenthau in 1942. "Right now, other than going into the Army and Navy or working in a munitions plant, there isn't anything to do. . . . The reason I want a [war bond campaign] is to give people an opportunity to do something."

Morgenthau sold bonds in inventive ways. Hollywood stars organized "victory tours" through 300 communities. Hedy Lamarr promised to kiss anyone who bought a $25,000 bond. Carol Lombard died in a plane crash on her way home from a bond rally. Factory workers participated in payroll savings plans by putting a percentage of their earnings into government bonds. The Girl Scouts and Boy Scouts raised $8 billion in bond pledges.

By 1942, the problem was no longer finding enough work for the people, it was finding enough people for the work to be done. Factories stayed open around the clock, providing new opportunities to underemployed groups such as women, blacks, and the elderly. Seventeen million new jobs were created during World War II. Wages and salaries more than doubled, due in large part to the overtime that people put in. Per capita income rose from $373 in 1940 to just over $1,000 by 1945. As a result, the United States experienced a rare but significant redistribution of wealth, with the bottom half of the nation's wage earners gaining a larger share of the pie.

Making Do

Though Americans took home larger paychecks than ever before, they found less and less to spend them on. In 1942, Congress created the Office of Price Administration (OPA) to ration vital goods, preach self-sacrifice to the public, and control the inflation caused by too much money chasing too few goods. Gas, tires, sugar, coffee, meat, butter, alcohol—all became scarce. Most car owners were issued coupon books limiting them to 3 gallons of gasoline per week. Pleasure driving virtually ended, causing thousands of restaurants and drive-in businesses to close. As manufacturers cut back on cloth and wool, women's skirts got shorter, two-piece swimsuits (midriff exposed) became the rage, and men's suits no longer had cuffs. Metal buttons, rubber girdles, and leather shoes simply disappeared.

Changes on the home front could be seen through "the prism of baseball," the national game. Many wanted major league baseball suspended during the war, but Roosevelt disagreed, claiming that it united Americans and built up their morale. The 1941 season had been one of the best ever, with Ted Williams batting over 400 and Joe DiMaggio's 56-game hitting streak. The next year was very different, indeed. Night games were banned because of air-raid "blackouts." Spring training took place in the northern cities, rather than in Florida, to cut back on travel and save fuel. Ballparks held blood drives and bond drives, and soldiers in uniform were admitted free of charge. In 1942, Detroit Tigers slugger Hank Greenberg became the first major leaguer to be drafted into the armed forces. By 1943, most of the stars were gone, replaced by men who were too old or physically unfit for duty, such as Pete Gray, a one-armed outfielder for the St. Louis Browns. In response to public concerns, FBI Director J. Edgar Hoover declared that his agents had investigated the new major leaguers and found no draft-dodgers among them. But recruiting ball players became so difficult that the St. Louis Cardinals placed an advertisement in the *Sporting News:* "We have positions open on our AA, B, and D minor league clubs," it said. "If you believe you can qualify for one of these good baseball jobs, tell us about yourself."

Opportunity and Discrimination

In many respects, World War II produced a social revolution in the United States. The severe labor shortage caused an enormous migration of people from rural areas to cities, from South to North, and especially to the West Coast, where so many war industries were located. With defense factories booming and 15 million people in the armed forces, Americans were forced to reexamine long-held stereotypes about women and minorities in the workplace and on the battlefield. The war provided enormous possibilities for advancement and for change. It also unleashed prejudices that led to the mass detention of American citizens, and others, on largely racial grounds.

Women and the War Effort

The war brought new responsibilities and opportunities for American women. During the Depression, for example, women were expected to step aside in the job market to make way for unemployed men. A national poll in 1936 showed an overwhelming percentage of both sexes agreeing that wives with employed husbands should not work. Furthermore, the majority of employed women held poorly paid jobs as clerks and "salesgirls," or as low-end industrial workers in textile and clothing factories.

The war brought instant changes. More than 6 million women took defense jobs, half of whom had not been previously employed. They worked as welders and electricians, on assembly lines and in munitions plants. More than three-quarters of these women were married, and most were over 35—a truly remarkable change. Some had husbands in the armed forces. (The standard monthly allotment for a serviceman's family was $50.) Young mothers were not expected to work, although a sizable number did. Because the government and private industry provided little childcare assistance, absenteeism and job turnover among younger women were extremely high.

The symbol of America's new working woman was "**Rosie the Riveter,**" memorialized by Norman Rockwell in *The Saturday Evening Post* with her overalls, her work

The labor shortages of World War II created new employment opportunities for women, most of whom were married and over 35. More than 6 million women worked in defense industries across the country, including shipyards, munitions plants, and aircraft factories.

tools, and her foot planted on a copy of *Mein Kampf,* helping to grind fascism to dust.

> All the day long whether rain or shine—
> She's a part of the assembly line—
> She's making history working for victory—
> Rosie the Riveter.

Rosie was trim and beautiful, signifying that a woman could do a man's job—temporarily—without losing her feminine charm. Advertisers played heavily on this theme. A hand-cream company praised the "flower-like skin of today's American Girl, energetically at work six days a week in a big war plant." A cosmetics ad went even further: "Our lipstick can't win the war, but it symbolizes one of the reasons why we are fighting . . . the precious right of women to be feminine and lovely."

Although this work paid very well, wage discrimination was rampant in the defense industries, where women earned far less than did men in the same jobs. Employers and labor unions rationalized such inequities by noting that men had seniority, put in more overtime, and did the really "skilled" work. In 1945, female factory workers averaged $32 per week, compared with $55 for men.

Women also were told that their work would end with the war's completion, when defense spending dropped and the veterans came home to reclaim their old jobs. Many women welcomed a return to domesticity after 4 years of struggle, sacrifice, and separation from a husband overseas. But a survey of female defense workers in 1944 showed that most of them—particularly married, middle-aged women—hoped to continue in their present jobs.

This was not to be. Though more women than ever remained in the labor force following World War II, the bulk of them were pushed back into lower-paying "feminized" work. Still, a foundation had been laid. As a riveter from Los Angeles recalled, "Yeah, going to work during the war made me grow up and realize I could do things. . . . It was quite a change."

The "Double V" Campaign

For millions of American blacks, the war against racist Germany and Japan could not be separated from the ongoing struggle to achieve equal rights. The *Pittsburgh Courier,* an influential African American newspaper, demanded a "Double V" campaign from the Negro community—"victory over our enemies at home and victory over our enemies on the battlefields abroad." To the cynical suggestion that minorities secretly wished for an American defeat, black heavyweight champion Joe Louis responded: "America's got lots of problems, but Hitler won't fix them."

One obvious problem was the small number of blacks employed in high-paying factory jobs. "The Negro will be considered only as janitors," stated North American Aviation, one of the nation's leading military contractors. "Regardless of their training as aircraft workers, we will not employ them." In 1941, A. Philip Randolph, president of the Brotherhood of Sleeping Car Porters, an all-Negro labor union, proposed a "March on Washington" to protest job discrimination in the defense industries and segregation of the armed forces. "We loyal Americans," he said, "demand the right to work and fight for our country." Fearing the negative publicity, President Roosevelt convinced the organizers to call off their march in return for an Executive Order (8802) declaring that "there shall be no discrimination in the employment of workers because of race, creed, or national origin." To facilitate the order, Roosevelt appointed a Fair Employment Practices Committee (FEPC) to "investigate complaints" and "redress grievances." With a tiny budget and no enforcement powers, the FEPC held public hearings, preached equality in the workplace—and was largely ignored.

Still, the desperate need for labor provided new opportunities for minorities. More than a million blacks migrated to the North and West during World War II, taking factory jobs in New York and California, Michigan and Illinois. Most were attracted by the higher wages and the chance to escape stifling oppression; many came from the Deep South, where the invention

of the mechanical cotton-picker forced them from the land. The percentage of African Americans in the war industries reached 7.5 percent by 1944—less than their share of the population but a vast improvement over 1941. The work itself was often menial, such as cleaning

Picturing the Past **SOCIAL & CULTURAL EVENTS**

African American Nurses in World War II

Thousands of African American women enlisted in the armed forces during World War II. Some joined the newly created Women's Army Corps, taking non-combatant positions as clerks, cooks, and drivers. Others (pictured here) served in the Army and Navy Nurse Corps, helping to evacuate casualties and staffing hospitals throughout the United States, Europe, and the Pacific theater. As with African American men, African American women were forced to serve in racially segregated units. Indeed, despite a

shortage of nurses, the Surgeon General issued a directive limiting the service of black nurses to "hospitals or wards devoted exclusively to the treatment of Negro soldiers." As one African American newspaper complained: "There are hundreds of young colored nurses. They are eager to serve in the Army, the Navy, the Marine Corps . . . and [possess] skills acquired through long apprenticeship in recognized hospitals. Given equal opportunity for training, the Negro nurse has no superior in any national or racial group in the world." By 1945, as the demands of war increased, African American nurses often treated wounded soldiers regardless of race.

factory bathrooms and sweeping the floors. Black workers had little access to the skilled, high-paying jobs, because powerful craft unions like the Machinists and the Carpenters remained lily-white. But thousands of African Americans took semiskilled positions on the assembly line, which meant higher wages than ever before.

For black working women, the changes were more dramatic. On the eve of World War II, about 70 percent of them labored as servants in private homes. By war's end, that figure had fallen below 50 percent, as 400,000 black females left domestic work for the defense plants. "The war made me live better, it really did," recalled an aircraft worker who moved from rural Texas to Los Angeles. "My sister always said that Hitler was the one that got us out of the white folks' kitchen."

Where racial barriers were crossed, however, violence often followed. In Mobile, Alabama, the promotion of 11 black welders led white shipyard workers to go on a rampage through the African American community, severely beating dozens of residents. In Philadelphia, white transit workers walked off their jobs to protest the elevation of 8 blacks to the rank of motorman. Their stoppage brought the city to a halt, effectively closing the vital Philadelphia Navy Yard. Moving quickly, federal officials sent 8,000 fully armed soldiers to run the buses and streetcars, and threatened to fire the strikers and draft them into the armed forces. The walkout collapsed 2 days later.

The worst racial violence flared in Detroit, the nation's leading war production center. With good jobs available on the assembly lines of Chrysler, General Motors, and Ford, Detroit's areawide labor force grew from 400,000 in 1940 to almost 900,000 by 1943. With the war effort receiving the government's full attention, little thought was given to building new homes, schools, and hospitals. Indeed, state spending for health and education actually declined in Michigan during World War II. Those who arrived in Detroit, mainly poor, rural people of both races, found themselves competing for living space and social services with Detroit's established blue-collar labor force—and with each other. One half of Detroit's wartime black population lived in miserable, substandard housing, often one family to a room, with no indoor toilets or running water. Bulging public schools went to half-day sessions. Infant mortality rates skyrocketed, and tuberculosis reached epidemic proportions.

In 1942, an angry mob in Detroit kept several black families from moving into a public housing project in a white neighborhood. The following year, a fight between whites and blacks at a municipal park sparked a race riot involving huge mobs with guns, knives, and clubs. Detroit's poorly trained police force, weakened by the departure of its best men to the armed forces, did little to stop the carnage. By the time federal troops established calm in the city, 35 people were dead, and more than 700 were wounded. The police shot 17 "looters" during the riot, all of whom were black.

Mob violence on the West Coast involved other victims. In California, a hate campaign led by local politicians and the press blamed Mexican Americans for an alleged rise in drugs, crime, and gang warfare. In June 1943, white sailors from surrounding naval bases roamed the Mexican districts of Los Angeles, Long Beach, Pasadena, and other cities looking for "zooters"—young Mexican Americans in ducktail haircuts wearing long jackets with wide pleated pants, pegged at the cuff. Cheered on by white crowds, the sailors became a vigilante mob—stripping the young men of their "zoot suits," cutting their hair, and beating them senseless. "Throughout the night the Mexican communities were in the wildest possible turmoil," wrote a Los Angeles reporter. "Scores of mothers were trying to locate their youngsters and several hundred Mexicans milled around the police substations and the Central jail trying to get word of the missing members of their families."

The zoot-suit violence had other roots as well. Unlike the Depression era, when jobs were scarce and Mexicans were deported in large numbers, the United

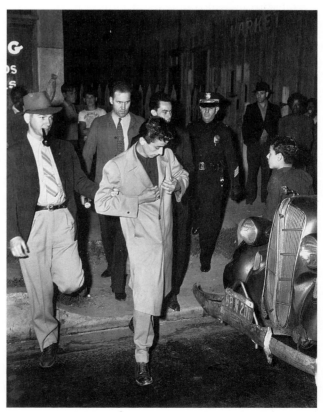

Police in Los Angeles take a young man to jail during the 1943 "zoot-suit" riots in which hundreds were injured and arrested.

States now needed all the labor it could get. In 1942, the American and Mexican governments agreed to a so-called "bracero" (contract labor) program in which several hundred thousand Mexicans were brought to the United States to plant and harvest crops. In addition, the shortage of factory labor during World War II led to an influx of Hispanic workers in the shipyards and defense plants of Southern California. In cities like Los Angeles, where African American and Hispanic workers arrived at a rate of 10,000 per month, crowding and competition bred resentment and fear.

To many residents of Southern California, the "zooters" came to represent the Hispanic community as a whole. Rumors flew that Mexican Americans were hindering the war effort by evading the draft. In fact, the reverse was true. Mexican Americans served in numbers far greater than their percentage of the general population—350,000 out of 1.4 million—and 17 were awarded the Congressional Medal of Honor.

African Americans were rigidly segregated in the armed forces during World War II. One of the most celebrated black units was the 99th Air Force Fighter squadron, known as the Tuskegee Airmen.

Mexican Americans were integrated in the armed forces during World War II; African Americans were not. All branches except the tiny Coast Guard practiced race discrimination as a matter of course. The marines did not take blacks until 1943, when 20,000 were recruited to unload supplies and munitions during the amphibious Pacific landings—an extremely hazardous duty that subjected them to withering artillery and sniper fire from dug-in Japanese defenders. The navy segregated blacks by occupation, with most working as food handlers, stevedores, and "mess-boys." In July 1944, a huge explosion at an ammunition depot in Port Chicago, California, killed 250 black sailors from a segregated work unit. When 50 survivors refused an order to return to work, claiming they had been singled out for these dangerous jobs on account of race, they were court-martialed, convicted of mutiny, and sentenced to prison. Following an intense publicity campaign in the Negro press, the black sailors were returned to duty.

More than 500,000 African Americans served in the army, which placed them in segregated divisions, commanded by white officers. Because most training facilities were located in the Deep South, where the weather was mild and construction costs were low, black recruits faced hostile surroundings. Racial clashes at military posts were regularly reported in the Negro press, as were the murders of black soldiers by white mobs in Arkansas, Georgia, Mississippi, and Texas.

Only one black army division saw significant combat—the 92nd Infantry in Italy. When questioned about this, Secretary of War Henry Stimson claimed

that "Negroes have been unable to master efficiently the techniques of modern weapons." The truth, however, was that racial prejudice dominated the military chain of command. When given the opportunity, black units performed superbly. The 99th Air Force Fighter squadron, known as the Tuskegee Airmen, earned two Distinguished Unit Citations and shot down a dozen Nazi planes during the Anzio invasion of 1943. Escorting American bombers over Germany in 1944 and 1945, pilots of the 99th compiled a perfect record. Not a single bomber under their protection was lost to enemy fire.

Such treatment fueled anger, protest, and pride. The Negro press became more assertive in the drive for equal rights. America's leading black organization, the National Association for the Advancement of Colored People (NAACP), increased its wartime membership from 70,000 to 500,000. In 1942, young activists, black and white, formed the Congress of Racial Equality to challenge segregated restaurants in Washington and Baltimore, chanting, "We die together. Let's eat together." A powerful civil rights movement was slowly taking shape.

Internment of Japanese Americans

President Roosevelt was determined to avoid a recurrence of the federal repression and vigilante activity that had marred the home front during World War I. Yet the years between 1942 and 1945 witnessed the most glaring denial of civil liberties in American history. The victims included people of Japanese ancestry—citizen and

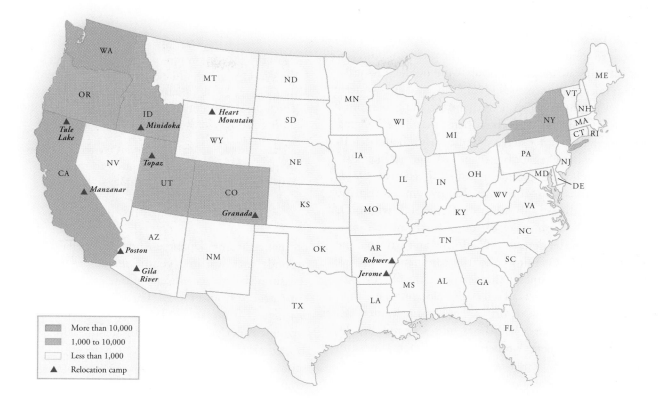

MAP 26.1 Japanese American Relocation

The 120,000 Japanese Americans removed from the West Coast during World War II were sent to internment camps in six states, run by the newly established War Relocation Authority. The relocation order did not affect the small number of Japanese Americans living elsewhere in the United States or the large Japanese population living in Hawaii.

noncitizen alike—living mainly on the West Coast of the United States.

On December 8, 1941, Roosevelt issued a standard executive order requiring enemy aliens to register with local police. Before long, however, the president lifted the enemy alien designation for Italians and Germans in the United States, but not for the Japanese. The attack on Pearl Harbor, the Bataan Death March, the fall of Hong Kong and Singapore, Wake Island and the Philippines—all sent shock waves across the United States. Though J. Edgar Hoover saw no evidence of a Japanese "threat" to American security, the public thought otherwise. *Time* magazine published an article after Pearl Harbor entitled "How to Tell Your Friends from the Japs," which included such tips as "Japanese—except for wrestlers—are seldom fat" and "Japanese are likely to be stockier and broader-hipped than Chinese." More ominous were the words of Henry McLemore, a columnist for the *San Francisco Examiner.* "I am for the immediate removal of every Japanese on the West Coast to a point in the interior," he wrote. "Herd 'em up, pack 'em off, and give 'em the inside room in the badlands. . . . Personally, I hate the Japanese. And that goes for all of them."

More than 90 percent of the 125,000 Japanese Americans lived in California, Oregon, and Washington. (Two-thirds were citizens, or **Nisei,** born in the United States; the rest were noncitizens, or Issei, born in Japan and ineligible for naturalization under the Immigration Laws of 1882 and 1924.) Few in number, politically powerless, and less well assimilated than European ethnic groups, the Japanese in America made perfect targets. Military leaders raised the dangers of allowing them to live so close to aircraft plants and naval bases. Patriotic groups linked them to the atrocities committed by the Japanese armed forces 8,000 miles away. Local farmers and fishermen resented the economic success of these hardworking people. All wanted their removal from the West Coast.

President Roosevelt capitulated. In February 1942, he issued **Executive Order 9066,** giving Secretary of War Stimson the authority to designate military zones inside the United States "from which any or all persons may be excluded." A few days later, the army interpreted that order to include the entire West Coast and all people of Japanese extraction. "A Jap's a Jap," said General John DeWitt, head of the West Coast Defense

Command. "It makes no difference whether he is an American citizen or not."

Roosevelt preferred a "voluntary" removal and resettlement to rural parts of the West. The problem, however, was that the Japanese Americans were unlikely to leave their homes and businesses voluntarily, and the western states were unwilling to take them. As the governor of Idaho said, "If you send them here, they'll be hanging from every tree in the state. Why not send them back to Japan? They live like rats, breed like rats, and act like rats."

In March, the president issued Executive Order 9102, establishing the War Relocation Authority. Milton Eisenhower—brother of **General Dwight D. Eisenhower**—became its director. Internment camps were set up in the deserts of California and Arizona, the mountains of Wyoming, and the scrublands of Utah and Colorado. Japanese Americans on the West Coast were given a few weeks to sell their belongings, get their affairs in order, and report to "processing centers" at converted racetracks, ballparks, and fairgrounds. By June, 120,000 men, women, and children—most of them American citizens—reached the internment camps.

Conditions there were harsh but not brutal. Families lived together in spartan army barracks with little privacy and poor sanitation. Most worked as farm laborers. "All of Manzanar was a stockade, actually—a prison," wrote a young Japanese American woman of her California camp. "We were in jail. There was barbed wire all around, there were great big watch towers in the corners, and there were spotlights turned on during the night."

The Supreme Court did not intervene. In *Hirabayashi v. United States* (1943) it upheld a curfew

DOING HISTORY ONLINE

Civil Liberties in Wartime

Read the section on Internment and refer back to the World War I module on The Propaganda War (in Chapter 22). Evaluate the following statement: The federal government restricted civil liberties more during World War II than during World War I.

History ⓧ Now™   Visit HistoryNOW to access primary sources and exercises related to this topic: http://now.ilrn.com/ayers_etal3e

ordinance against Japanese Americans in Seattle on the grounds that wartime conditions sometimes justified measures that "place citizens of one ancestry in a different category from others." The Court also ruled (*Korematsu v. United States,* 1944) that the evacuation of Japanese Americans was appropriate, but added (*Endo v. United States,* 1944) that the War Relocation Authority should attempt to separate "loyal" internees from "disloyal" ones, and set the loyal free.

It took almost 40 years for a measure of justice to prevail. In 1981, a congressional panel concluded that the internment program had resulted from a combination of race prejudice, war hysteria, and the failure of political leadership. It had nothing to do with "military necessity," as its supporters had claimed. In 1988, Congress awarded each survivor of the internment camps $20,000 in "reparations" for the terrible wrong that had been done.

Executive Order 9066 provided for the removal of 120,000 people of Japanese ancestry from the West Coast of the United States to isolated internment camps like this one in Manzanar, California.

The Grand Alliance

Most Americans saw Japan as the primary villain of World War II. Opinion polls showed the public overwhelmingly in favor of concentrating the war effort in the Pacific against a "barbaric" and "treacherous" foe. Yet President Roosevelt and his military advisors felt otherwise. To their thinking, American power should be directed against the stronger enemy—Germany. Roosevelt viewed the Nazis as the real threat to world peace, and Europe as the key battleground.

North Africa, Stalingrad, and the Second Front

America's two major allies had conflicting strategies, interests, and concerns. The British did not believe in confronting Hitler with immediate, massive force. They remembered their staggering losses to the Germans during World War I, and they had felt the power of the Nazis at Dunkirk and in the London air raids. The British, moreover, had a far-flung empire to defend. Their strategy was to strike at "the soft underbelly" of the Axis in North Africa and the Mediterranean, rather than to confront Hitler directly in France.

The Russians strongly disagreed. Already facing a huge Nazi force deep inside their territory, they wanted the United States and Britain to open a "second front" in western Europe so as to relieve German pressure on them in the east. That meant a major Allied invasion of France. As one American diplomat said of Soviet Foreign Minister V. M. Molotov, "He knows only four words of English—'yes,' 'no' and 'second front.'"

Though America's top military advisors leaned toward the Russian strategy, President Roosevelt favored the British approach. At present, he realized, the United States was unprepared for a full-scale invasion of Europe. But a smaller operation against Nazi forces in North Africa, as the British proposed, had the benefit of getting the United States into the war quickly on the proper scale.

To make this possible, the United States had to gain control of the ocean. In the first 3 months of 1942, German submarines sank almost 1 million tons of Allied shipping. The so-called "wolf-packs" were so close to American shores that bathers on the New Jersey and Virginia coasts watched in horror as merchant ships were torpedoed. By 1943, however, technological advances in antisubmarine warfare turned the tide. The use of sonar and powerful depth charges made German U-boats more vulnerable underwater, and the development of long-range attack planes and sophisticated radar allowed American aircraft to spot and destroy them as they surfaced to recharge their batteries. The toll was enormous. More than 900 of the 1,162 German submarines commissioned during World War II were sunk or captured.

In November 1942, American troops under the command of General Dwight D. Eisenhower invaded the French North African colonies of Morocco and Algeria in an operation code-named TORCH. At virtually the same moment, British forces badly mauled General Rommel's army at El Alamein in Egypt, ending Nazi hopes of taking the Suez Canal. Though Hitler rushed reinforcements to North Africa, the Allies prevailed, capturing 250,000 German and Italian troops and taking enemy-held territory for the first time in the war.

In North Africa, the Allies fought and defeated 12 Nazi divisions. In the Soviet Union, the Russians were fighting 200 German divisions along an enormous 2,000-mile front. The pivotal battle occurred at Stalingrad, a vital transportation hub on the Volga River, in the bitter winter of 1942–1943. As the Germans advanced, Stalin ordered his namesake city held at all costs. The fighting was block-to-block, house-to-house, and finally hand-to-hand. Hitler would not let his forces retreat, even after they ran out of fuel and food. Surrounded by Russian forces, overwhelmed by starvation, exposure, and suicide, the German commander surrendered on February 2, 1943.

Stalingrad marked the turning point of the European war. The myth of German invincibility was over. The Russians were advancing steadily in the east, aided by a stream of tanks, planes, food, and clothing from the United States under Lend-Lease. Now Stalin expected an Allied thrust from the west—the long-promised second front.

Churchill had other ideas. At a meeting with Roosevelt in Casablanca, he convinced the president to put off a cross-channel invasion in favor of an assault on Axis troops across the Mediterranean in Italy. Roosevelt attempted to pacify Stalin by promising to open a second front the following year and to accept nothing less than Germany's unconditional surrender. But the Soviets, having sacrificed more troops at Stalingrad than the United States would lose in the entire war, were suspicious and displeased.

The Italian campaign began in the summer of 1943. Sicily fell in a month, and Mussolini along with it. Overthrown by antifascist Italians, the Duce fled to Nazi lines in the north. The new Italian government then declared war on Germany and was recognized as a "cobelligerent" by England and the United States. The battle for Italy was intense. A young American soldier, badly injured in the campaign, wrote to his wife: "So many buddies gone and so many wounded! . . . We walked straight into death, not one man flinched or tried to save himself. I am proud to say, darling, that I was one of those brave lost children. We were only children after all. The dead boys were cuddled up, the wounded cried for dead friends. All children, after all."

The Italian campaign dragged on for almost 2 years, draining troops and resources for the planned invasion of France. (In April 1945, antifascists captured Mussolini, killed him, and strung him up by his heels.) Suspicions between Stalin and his wartime allies deepened as Roosevelt and Churchill set the terms of Italy's surrender without consulting the Soviet leader. In addition, postponement of the second front gave Stalin the opportunity to gobble up much of central Europe as his troops pushed toward Germany from the east.

The three Allied leaders met together for the first time in November 1943 at the Tehran Conference in Iran. Roosevelt and Churchill promised to launch their

Flashpoints | The Correspondent and the War

During World War II, newspaper and magazine circulation rose dramatically in the United States, as people hungered for battlefield news. Unlike today, the press was content to write favorably about the war effort, seeing this is as a patriotic duty to help boost the nation's morale. Criticism was rare; stories about poor leadership or cowardice were discouraged, as were

Ernie Pyle, the nation's favorite war correspondent, was celebrated for capturing the hopes and fears of the common soldier.

photos of dead or badly wounded GIs. For millions of Americans, however, one man seemed to go beyond this sanitized reporting to bring home a truer picture of the war. His name was Ernie Pyle.

Born in Dana, Indiana, in 1900, Pyle had studied journalism at Indiana University before leaving to become a small town reporter and then a columnist for the Scripps-Howard newspaper chain. In 1940, he was sent to England to report on the nightly German bombings of London, popularly known as the Blitz. From there, he covered the U.S. military campaigns in

North Africa, Italy, and France. His columns from the battlefield, which earned him a Pulitzer Prize in 1944, appeared in hundreds of newspapers across the United States.

What made Pyle so popular was his focus on the common soldier. Living among them, experiencing the same primitive conditions, he brought the war back to America in starkly human terms. "I love the infantry," he wrote in one column, "because they are the underdogs." He went on to describe the daily fire fights, deadly sniper fire, and ear-splitting artillery duels that had turned innocent young men "from Broadway and Main Street" into grizzled veterans who appeared to have been "doing this forever, and nothing else." Soldiers grew up quickly, he wrote, and the lucky ones survived.

In 1945, Pyle moved on to the Pacific theater to cover the final push against Japan. Overwhelmed by the death and destruction he had witnessed in Europe, he wrote General Dwight D. Eisenhower that the war, for him, had become "a flat, black depression without highlights . . . an exhaustion of the spirit." He spoke of the sacrifices made by soldiers on all sides, adding: "I hope we can rejoice in victory—but humbly."

He didn't live to see it. On April 18, 1945, while covering the bloody Okinawa campaign, Pyle was killed by Japanese machine gun fire on the island of Ie Shima.

His death, at age 44, was mourned by a nation that had come to depend on his unique brand of reporting—his ability to describe the horrors of modern warfare in a way that made each soldier count. The job of war correspondent would never be the same.

Questions for Reflection

1. Ernie Pyle has been called the father of modern war reporting. How did he help to change the job of a battlefield correspondent?

2. There is, and will always be, a tension between the media and the government over the proper way to cover a war. What are the different views and objectives of these two sides?

3. What, to your thinking, should be the proper role of a war correspondent?

AP/Wide World Photos

cross-channel invasion the following spring. The future of Poland, the partition of Germany, and need for a United Nations were also discussed. In public, at least, Allied unity was restored. "We are going to get along fine with Stalin and the Russian people," Roosevelt declared.

The Normandy Invasion

By 1944, the Allies were in complete control of the skies over western Europe, and in command of the seas. Their amphibious landings in North Africa and Italy had provided valuable experience for the job that lay ahead. In April and May, General Eisenhower assembled his huge invasion force in England—3 million men, 2.5 million tons of supplies, thousands of planes, landing craft, and escort vessels. Meanwhile, Allied aircraft pounded the Atlantic Wall, a line of German fortifications stretching hundreds of miles along the coast of France and the Low Countries.

Despite meticulous preparation, Eisenhower faced enormous risks. The Nazis had 55 divisions in France. To keep them dispersed and guessing, Allied intelligence spread false information about the planned invasion sites. The deceptions worked. Hitler and his generals put their strongest defense at Pas de Calais, the English Channel's narrowest point.

The massive D-Day invasion—**Operation OVERLORD**—began on the morning of June 6, 1944. Eisenhower's biggest worry was the weather. A channel storm had postponed one attempt, and another storm was predicted. Before the men left, he told them: "You are about to embark upon the Great Crusade, toward which we have striven these many months. The eyes of the world are upon you."

The invasion succeeded. With overwhelming air cover, Allied forces assaulted Normandy and dropped paratroopers behind enemy lines. The heaviest fighting took place at Omaha Beach, where U.S. Rangers scaled sheer cliffs under withering fire to silence Nazi gunners. By nightfall, 150,000 men were ashore.

Others quickly followed. Within 2 months, more than a million Allied troops were in France—liberating Paris in August, reaching the German border by September. With the Soviets pressing from the east, a Nazi surrender seemed only weeks away. But the Germans counterattacked in December 1944, taking British and American forces by surprise. The Battle of the Bulge was Hitler's last gasp—a failed attempt to crack Allied morale. U.S. troops took heavy casualties but stood firm. Germany lost 100,000 men and the will to fight on. Hitler committed suicide in his Berlin bunker on April 30, 1945, with Russian soldiers a few miles away. Germany surrendered a week later. The Thousand-Year Reich had lasted a dozen murderous years.

Facing the Holocaust

In the spring of 1945, Allied troops liberated the Nazi concentration camps in Poland and Germany. Ghastly pictures of starving survivors and rotting corpses flashed around the world, recording the almost inconceivable horror in which 6 million European Jews and 4 million others (including Poles, Gypsies, homosexuals, and political dissidents) were exterminated during World War II.

To American leaders, these photos of the Holocaust produced shock but hardly surprise. Evidence of the death camps had reached the United States in 1942, yet the government paid scant attention to the consequences. The State Department, well known for its anti-Semitism in that era, made it virtually impossible for refugees

© Bettmann/CORBIS

On June 6, 1944, Allied troops stormed the beaches of Normandy in the massive D-Day invasion. By nightfall, more than 150,000 troops were ashore, and others quickly followed, beginning the long-awaited "second front" that sealed Hitler's fate.

MAP 26.2 The War in Europe

The U.S. military effort against German and Italian forces in World War II began in North Africa, moved to Italy, and culminated in the D-Day invasion of France in 1944. With the aid of England and other nations, the Allied forces reached Germany from the west in 1945. Meanwhile, following a tenacious defense of their homeland, Russian troops pushed deep into Germany from the east, destroying the bulk of Nazi fighting forces and playing a key role in the German surrender.

DOING HISTORY

Bombing the Death Camps

ONE OF THE most controversial aspects of the Allied war effort in Europe involved the failure of American and British warplanes to bomb the rail lines leading to the Nazi death camp at Auschwitz, Poland, where tens of thousands of European Jews were being murdered in gas chambers. When British Prime Minister Winston Churchill urged such bombings in 1944 to prevent "probably the greatest and most horrible crime ever committed in the whole history of the world," he was told by his air force commanders that only the United States had the resources to get the job done.

To this day, it is unclear whether President Roosevelt seriously considered the possibility of bombing Auschwitz and its surrounding rail lines. For years Assistant Secretary of War John J. McCloy insisted that the president had not been briefed on this matter because military planners were convinced that such bombings would divert crucial resources from the larger war effort. But shortly before his death in 1989, McCloy claimed that he did speak to Roosevelt about this matter, and that the president had opposed bombing Auschwitz on grounds that it would kill innocent Jewish victims without doing any real harm to their German oppressors.

In November 1944, John H. Pehle, director of the War Refugee Board, wrote to McCloy urging the immediate bombing of Auschwitz and other death camps.

"I send you herewith copies of two eye-witness descriptions of the notorious . . . extermination camps. . . . No report of Nazi atrocities received by the Board has quite caught the gruesome brutality of what is taking place in these camps of horror as have these sober, factual accounts of conditions at Auschwitz and Birkenau. I earnestly hope you will read these reports.

The destruction of large numbers of people apparently is not a simple process. The Germans have been forced to devote considerable technical ingenuity and administrative know-how in order to carry out murder on a mass production basis. . . . If [these] elaborate murder installations . . . were destroyed, it seems clear that the Germans could not reconstruct them for some time. . . .

I am convinced that the point has now been reached where such military action is justifiable if it is deemed feasible by competent military authorities."

McCloy responded to Pehle 10 days later:

"The Operations Staff of the War Department has given careful consideration to your suggestion that the bombing of these camps be undertaken. In consideration of this proposal the following points were brought out:

Positive destruction of the camps would necessitate precision bombing . . . by low flying or dive bombing aircraft, preferably the latter.

The target is beyond the maximum range of [such aircraft] located in United Kingdom, France or Italy.

Use of heavy bombardment from United Kingdom bases would necessitate a hazardous round trip flight unescorted of approximately 2000 miles over enemy territory.

. . . The positive solution to this problem is the earliest possible victory over Germany, to which end we should exert our entire means."

Despite McCloy's claims, there is little doubt that the U.S. Air Force, sending hundreds of bombers over German cities and military targets in 1944, could have easily spared the planes required to destroy Auschwitz and the surrounding rail lines. Whether innocent lives would have been saved by these missions will never be known. What is certain, however, is that McCloy was well aware of the horrors that were occurring in these death camps and of the increasingly desperate pleas for help.

Source: John H. Pehle to John J. McCloy, November 8, 1944; McCloy to Pehle, November 18, 1944, War Refugee Board Records, Franklin D. Roosevelt Library, cited in Richard D. Polenberg, *The Era of Franklin D. Roosevelt, 1933–1945*, pp. 222–223.

Questions for Reflection

1. What is the key argument put forth in favor of, and in opposition to, the bombing of the Nazi death camps?

2. What information should have been provided to President Roosevelt in order for him to have made an informed decision about these bombings?

3. Even if no lives had been saved, was it important for the Allies to have destroyed these death camps as a way of expressing their horror at the genocide that was unfolding?

Explore additional primary sources related to this chapter on the Wadsworth American History Resource Center or HistoryNOW websites:

http://history.wadsworth.com/rc/us
http://now.ilrn.com/ayers_etal3e

fleeing the Nazis to enter the United States. An applicant for a wartime visa had to provide the names of two American sponsors before submitting six copies of a form that measured 4 feet in length. As a result, only 10 percent of America's immigration quotas were met during World War II, leaving almost 200,000 slots unfilled.

President Roosevelt did not seriously intervene. Consumed by the responsibilities of leading his nation in a global war, he insisted that the best way to aid the victims of Nazism was to defeat Hitler's armies as quickly as possible. His only acknowledgment of the impending disaster came in 1944, when he created the War Refugee Board, which helped finance the activities of Raoul Wallenberg, the courageous Swedish diplomat who prevented thousands of Hungarian Jews from being deported to the death camps. Had it been formed earlier, and supported more firmly by the White House, the War Refugee Board might have played a major role in the saving of innocent lives.

The United States had other options as well. Its bombers could have attacked the rail lines leading to the death camps, as well as the gas chambers and crematoria that lay inside. The War Department avoided these targets, claiming they were too dangerous and too far away. This clearly was not true. In 1944, Allied bombers flew hundreds of missions within a 35-mile radius of Auschwitz.

When liberation came to the concentration camps, the vast majority of prisoners were dead. One survivor at Dachau recalled the very moment the American troops arrived. "We were free. We broke into weeping, kissed the tank. A Negro soldier gave us a tin of meat, bread, and chocolate. We sat down on the ground and ate up all the food together. The Negro watched us, tears in his eyes."

The question of whether Allied bombers should have destroyed the rail lines leading to the Nazi death camps has been a matter of great controversy ever since.

The Pacific War

Shortly after the attack on Pearl Harbor, Admiral Isoroku Yamamoto, Japan's leading naval strategist, issued a stern private warning. "In the first six months to a year of war against the U.S. and England," he said, "I will run wild and I will show you an uninterrupted succession of victories: I must tell you that, should the war be prolonged for two or three years, I have no confidence in our ultimate victory." Yamamoto understood America's overwhelming advantage in population and productivity. What he doubted was the will of its people to fight—and win—a long, bloody struggle.

Turning the Tide

The Japanese hoped to create an impregnable defense line in the Pacific. Their strategy included new conquests, such as Australia, and a naval thrust against the U.S. carrier fleet. Yet two key engagements in the spring of 1942 shattered Yamamoto's illusion about American will power and naval strength. On May 7, a task force led by two American carriers—the *Lexington* and *Yorktown*—held its own against a larger Japanese force at the Battle of the Coral Sea, just north of Australia. Though the "Lady Lex" was sunk, heavy Japanese losses saved Australia from invasion or certain blockade.

A month later, the two sides clashed again. Admiral Yamamoto brought a huge fleet to **Midway Island,** 1,000 miles west of Hawaii, to flush out and destroy the American carrier fleet. But the U.S. Navy, having broken the Japanese military code, was well aware of his intentions. In a 3-day battle, brilliantly commanded by Rear Admiral Raymond A. Spruance, the Americans sank four Japanese carriers (losing the *Yorktown*) and shot down 320 planes. Japan would never fully recover from this beating.

Closing in on Japan

After Midway, the United States followed a two-pronged plan of attack. Admiral Chester Nimitz was to move west from Hawaii toward Formosa, while General Douglas MacArthur was to come north from Australia toward the Philippines, with their forces combining for an eventual assault on Japan. The Pacific theater would see no massed land battles like Stalingrad or the Bulge. The fighting would be sporadic but brutal, involving air attacks, naval duels, and amphibious landings by U.S. Marines on selected Japanese-held islands. It would be "a war without mercy," with bitter racial hatreds on both sides.

The first American offensive occurred at Guadalcanal, a small tropical island in the Solomons, off New Guinea,

Picturing the Past

POLITICS & DIPLOMACY

The War in the Pacific

America's war against Japan was fought differently than the war against Germany. In the Pacific, the United States did the great bulk of the Allied fighting; in Europe, that burden was shared by others, including Great Britain, and most important, the Soviet Union. As shown on the map, the war against Japan was waged largely at sea and from the air; though American marines met fierce resistance in clearing Guadalcanal, Saipan, Iwo Jima, Okinawa, and other Japanese-held strongholds, there were no massed land battles to match the Soviet defeat of German forces at Stalingrad or the Allied counterattack at the Bulge.

In Europe, armor and artillery were essential to the Allied victory; in the Pacific, it was aircraft carriers and submarines. By war's end, the United States had lost 128 combatant vessels to Japanese warships and aircraft, but only 29 to German fire. The Japanese surrender in 1945 ended the largest naval war in history.

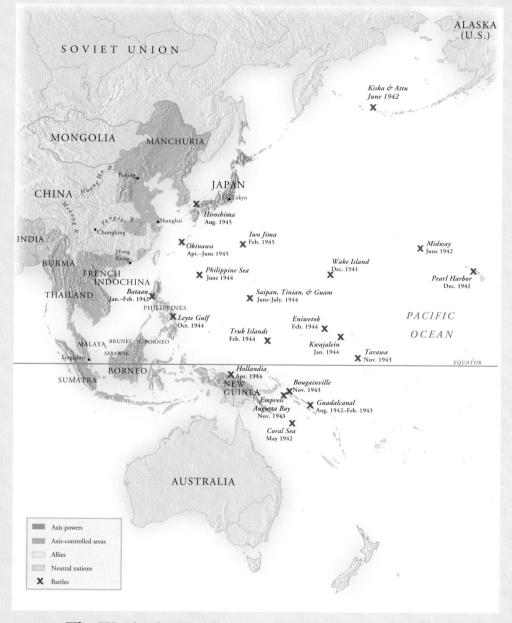

MAP 26.3 **The War in the Pacific**

in August 1942. Guadalcanal had strategic importance as both a supply depot and a base from which to assault the Japanese air and naval complex at Rabaul. For 6 months, American marines waged a desperate campaign in swamps and jungles, battling intense heat, malaria, dysentery, infection, and leeches, as well as the Japanese. When the island was finally secured in February 1943, General MacArthur began a "leapfrog" campaign across New Guinea to the Philippines, attacking some islands while bypassing others. By 1944, Manila was in his sights.

In the central Pacific, Admiral Nimitz was moving west, ever closer to Japan. In November 1943, the marines assaulted Tarawa, a tiny strip of beach in the Gilbert Islands, incurring 3,000 casualties in a successful three-day assault. Next came the Marshall Islands; the Marianas—Guam, Tinian, and Saipan—followed. Control of the Marianas, only 1,200 miles from Tokyo, placed major Japanese cities within range of America's new B-29 bombers. The battle for Saipan raged through June and July of 1944. The Japanese defenders fought, quite literally, to the last man. Worse, thousands of Japanese civilians on the island committed suicide—a preview, some believed, of what lay ahead in Japan.

The end seemed near. In October 1944, MacArthur returned to the Philippines in triumph, while an American naval force destroyed four Japanese carriers at the Battle of Leyte Gulf, outside Manila. To the north, American troops took the island of Iwo Jima in brutal combat, and then attacked Okinawa, less than 400 miles from Japan. Admiral Nimitz assembled a huge force for the invasion—180,000 troops, most of his carriers, and 18 battleships. The Japanese had an army of 110,000 on Okinawa, the final barrier to the homeland itself.

The battle took 3 months, from April through June of 1945. Waves of Japanese kamikaze (suicide) planes attacked the Allied fleet, inflicting terrible damage.

Table 26.1 Second World War Casualties

Country	Battle Deaths	Wounded
Canada	32,714	53,145
France	201,568	400,000
Germany	3,250,000	7,250,000
Italy	149,496	66,716
U.S.S.R.	6,115,000	14,012,000
Australia	26,976	180,864
Japan	1,270,000	140,000
New Zealand	11,625	17,000
United Kingdom	357,116	369,267
United States	291,557	670,846

Source: *Information Please Almanac* (Boston: Houghton Mifflin Co., 1988).

American troops suffered a casualty rate of 35 percent, the highest of the war. Seven thousand were killed on land, 5,000 at sea, and 40,000 were wounded. The Japanese lost 1,500 kamikazes and virtually all of their soldiers. These appalling losses would be a factor in America's decision to use atomic weapons against Japan.

A Change in Leadership

In November 1944, the American people reelected Franklin Roosevelt to an unprecedented fourth presidential term. Roosevelt defeated Republican Thomas Dewey, the moderate 42-year-old governor of New York. The president's handling of the war was not an issue in the campaign. Dewey hammered away at problems on the home front, such as food shortages, gas rationing, squalid housing for war workers, and government "red tape." Roosevelt campaigned as the war leader, urging voters "not to change horses in midstream." To bolster his chances, Democratic party leaders removed the increasingly unpopular Vice President Henry Wallace from the ticket and replaced him with Senator **Harry S Truman** of Missouri.

The Yalta Accords

When Truman visited the White House to plan campaign strategy with Roosevelt, he was appalled by the president's feeble condition. In February 1945, with Germany near collapse, an exhausted FDR met with Churchill and Stalin at Yalta, in southern Russia, to lay the groundwork for peace and order in the postwar world. On several issues, agreement came easily. The Russians promised to enter the Pacific war after Germany's defeat in return for territorial concessions in the Far East. The three leaders also blessed the formation of a new international body, known as the United Nations.

But agreement on the larger issues proved elusive. The Soviet Union had suffered staggering losses at

German hands. At least 20 million Russians were dead or wounded; thousands of towns, factories, and collective farms had been destroyed. From Stalin's perspective, the Soviets deserved more than simple gratitude for their role in defeating the great bulk of Hitler's army. They needed the means to rebuild their nation and to protect it from further attacks.

Stalin hoped to ensure Soviet security through the permanent partition of Germany. And he demanded huge reparations from the Germans—at least $20 billion—with Russia getting half. Furthermore, Stalin had no intention of removing Soviet troops from the lands they now controlled in eastern Europe. In both world wars, Germany had marched directly through Poland to devastate the Russian heartland. Stalin would not let this happen again.

Roosevelt and Churchill had other ideas. Both men viewed a healthy, "de-Nazified" Germany as essential to the reconstruction of postwar Europe, and both feared the expansion of Soviet power into the vacuum created by Hitler's defeat. The British also claimed a moral stake in Poland, having declared war on Germany in 1939 to help defend the Poles from the Nazi assault. To desert them now—to permit a victorious Stalin to replace a defeated Hitler—smacked of the very appeasement that had doomed Allied policy a decade before. Few believed that the Polish people would pick Stalin or communism if given a free choice.

The Yalta Accords created a legacy of mistrust. The parties agreed to split Germany into four "zones of occupation"—American, Russian, British, and French. Berlin, deep inside the Soviet zone, also was divided among the Allies. Yet the vital issue of reparations was postponed, as were plans for Germany's eventual reunification. At Roosevelt's urging, Stalin accepted a "Declaration for a Liberated Europe" that promised "free and unfettered elections" in Poland and elsewhere at some unspecified date. But these words did not mean the same thing in Moscow as in the West. An American advisor accurately described the agreement as "so elastic that [Stalin] can stretch it all the way from Yalta to Washington without ever technically breaking it."

In the weeks following Yalta, Roosevelt's optimism about Soviet–American relations seemed to fade. Pledges of free elections in Europe were ignored. The Yalta Accords did not prevent Stalin from ordering the murder of political dissidents in Romania and Bulgaria and the arrest of anticommunist leaders in Poland. His ruthlessness seemed to highlight the unpleasant truth that America had little or no influence in the nations now occupied by Soviet troops. "We can't do business with Stalin," FDR complained privately. "He has broken every one of the promises he made at Yalta."

Truman in Charge

On April 12, 1945—less than 2 months into his fourth term—FDR died of a massive stroke at his vacation retreat in Warm Springs, Georgia. The nation was shocked. Roosevelt had been president for 12 years, leading the people through the Great Depression and World War II. "He was the one American who knew, or seemed to know, where the world was going," wrote *Life* magazine. "The plans were all in his head."

The new president was largely unknown. Born on a Missouri farm in 1884, Harry Truman had served as an artillery officer in World War I before jumping into local politics in Kansas City. Elected to public office in the 1920s with the aid of Tom Pendergast, a crooked Democratic boss, Truman walked a fine line between efficient service to his constituents and partisan loyalty to a corrupt political machine. Fair and honest himself, Truman went about the business of building better roads and improving public services while ignoring the squalor of those who put him in office.

Working for the Pendergast machine sensitized Truman to the needs of different people, fueled his belief in a welfare state, and got him elected to the U.S. Senate in 1934. On the other hand, the label of "machine politician" would plague him for years. It was hard to earn respect as a legislator when the newspapers kept referring to him as "the senator from Pendergast."

Truman did not inspire immediate confidence in his ability to fill Roosevelt's giant shoes. Small in stature, with thick glasses and a high-pitched midwestern twang, he seemed thoroughly ordinary to all but those who knew him best. As vice president, he was largely excluded from the major discussions relating to foreign policy and the war. After taking the presidential oath of office, Truman turned to reporters and said, "Boys, if you ever pray, pray for me now."

As expected, Truman received conflicting advice. A number of FDR's confidantes, including Henry Wallace and Eleanor Roosevelt, urged him to keep the wartime alliance alive by accommodating Russia's economic needs and security demands. But others, such as Averell Harriman, U.S. ambassador to the Soviet Union, prodded Truman to demand Russia's strict compliance with the Yalta Accords. The new president did not want a confrontation with Stalin. He still hoped for Soviet help in ending the Pacific war and building a lasting peace. Yet the more Truman learned about events in Poland and eastern Europe, the angrier he became. Ten days after taking office, he confronted Soviet Foreign Minister V. M. Molotov at the White House, claiming that Russia had ignored the Yalta Accords, and warning him that economic aid to Russia would never get through

Winston Churchill, Harry Truman, and Joseph Stalin clasp hands at the Potsdam Conference in July 1945. The good feeling did not last long, as Churchill's ruling party was defeated at the polls in England, and relations between the United States and the Soviet Union moved swiftly downhill.

Congress so long as this attitude persisted. When Truman finished, Molotov told him that "I've never been talked to like that in my life." "Carry out your agreements," Truman shot back, "and you won't get talked to like that."

In July 1945, Truman left the United States aboard the USS *Augusta* for his first face-to-face meeting with Stalin and Churchill at Potsdam, near Berlin. The three leaders agreed on a number of important issues, including the terms of peace for defeated Germany and public trials for Nazi war criminals. "I can deal with Stalin," Truman wrote in his diary. "He is honest—but smart as hell."

His optimism didn't last long. The conference was halted for several days by the stunning defeat of Winston Churchill's Conservative party in the British parliamentary elections. Churchill returned to England, replaced by the new Labour prime minister, Clement Attlee. When the talks resumed, Stalin brushed aside Truman's concerns about Poland and eastern Europe, and Truman rebuffed Stalin's attempt to claim reparations from the western zones of occupation in Germany. The conference ended on a chilly note. There seemed little doubt that Russia would remain in the lands it now controlled, and that Germany would remain divided for some time to come.

The Atomic Bomb

One of Truman's first decisions concerned the use of atomic weapons. As the United States took control of the island chains east of Japan in 1944, a ferocious

bombing campaign of the Japanese home islands took place. In March 1945, 300 American B-29s led by Major General Curtis LeMay firebombed Tokyo, killing 100,000 people, leaving 1 million homeless, and destroying much of the city. These raids were particularly devastating because Japan had few planes left to defend its densely populated areas. In the following months, conventional (nonatomic) bombings pounded half of Japan's 66 major cities.

Shortly after taking office, President Truman was told about the atomic bomb by Secretary of War Stimson, who called it "the most terrible weapon ever known in human history." The decision to build this bomb had been made by President Roosevelt in response to reports from refugee scientists, such as Italy's Enrico Fermi and Germany's Albert Einstein, that the Nazis were already at work on one. The American effort, known as the Manhattan Project, included top-secret facilities in Hanford, Washington; Oak Ridge, Tennessee; and Los Alamos, New Mexico, to design and construct this bomb, and produce the fissionable material for an atomic explosion.

At President Truman's direction, an Interim Committee was formed to advise him about the bomb. Chaired by Henry Stimson, the committee recommended the use of atomic weapons against Japan, without warning, as soon as they became available. Another group, the Target Committee, chose four major cities—Hiroshima, Kokura, Niigata, and Nagasaki—based on their strategic importance, and the fact that each of them, unlike Tokyo, was untouched by war. On July 16, 1945, the atomic bomb was successfully tested near Alamogordo, New Mexico. The explosion, equivalent to 15,000 tons of dynamite, was visible 200 miles away. Truman learned of the test while attending the Allied Summit meeting in Potsdam. He immediately issued a public ultimatum to the Japanese, calling on them to surrender unconditionally or face "prompt and utter destruction."

A number of top scientists on the Manhattan Project objected. Having urged one president to build the atomic bomb to counter Germany, they now found themselves begging another president not to use it against Japan. These scientists were joined by several ranking civilian and military officials, who argued that Japan was close to surrender, that the naval blockade was going well, and that use of the bomb would trigger a dangerous arms race with the Russians.

But Truman held firm, believing that the bomb would save American and Japanese lives by ending the

© AFP/Getty Images

On August 6, 1945, a B-29 named after the mother of Colonel Paul W. Tibbets, and piloted by him (center), dropped an atomic bomb on the Japanese city of Hiroshima, killing at least 100,000 people. Since that time, a debate has raged over the atomic bombings of Hiroshima and Nagasaki—in particular, their role in ending the war.

© Bettmann/CORBIS

Japanese representatives signed the formal declaration of surrender aboard the battleship *Missouri* on September 2, 1945.

war quickly. On the morning of August 6, 1945, a B-29 named **Enola Gay** dropped an atomic bomb over Hiroshima, incinerating the industrial city and killing at least 100,000 people. (Thousands more would die of radiation effects, a problem poorly understood by scientists at that time.) Three days later, a B-29 named *Bock's Car* dropped a second atomic bomb on Nagasaki, with

much the same effect. On August 14, the Japanese asked for peace.

Though Americans overwhelmingly supported these bombings, the decision remains controversial to this day. Some believe that Truman dropped the bomb to scare the Russians in Europe and to keep them out of the Asian war. Others think the decision was based on racism and revenge. Still others argue that the United States should have provided a "demonstration" of the bomb's power for the Japanese or made it clear to them that the terms of "unconditional surrender" did not mean that the emperor would have to be removed. For all the controversy, however, one inescapable fact remains: Japanese leaders could not bring themselves to surrender until two atomic bombs had been dropped.

World War II formally ended on September 2, 1945, when the Japanese signed the document of surrender aboard the battleship *Missouri* in Tokyo Bay. More than 25 million soldiers and civilians died in the struggle. Speaking from the deck of the *Missouri* that day, General MacArthur issued a warning for the new atomic age. "We have had our last chance," he said. "If we do not devise some greater and more equitable system, Armageddon will be at our door."

Conclusion

In many ways, World War II was to Americans of the mid-twentieth century what the Civil War had been to Americans of the mid-nineteenth century: a watershed event, defining the course of history for generations to come. When the war erupted in Europe in 1939, there seemed little chance that the United States would become involved. Bitter memories of World War I and its aftermath still prevailed. More concerned by the lingering effects of the Great Depression than by the growing menace posed by Germany, Italy, and Japan, the American people seemed relieved by President Roosevelt's campaign pledge in 1940 that "your boys are not going to be sent into any foreign war."

When war did come with the Japanese bombing of Pearl Harbor, the nation quickly came together. The United States had been attacked and virtually everyone understood the evil of the enemies the country now faced. The war shattered the illusion that Americans could remain separate from the world's problems. In leading the Grand Alliance against Axis aggression, the United States took on the full responsibilities of a global power. In doing so, it served notice that America's influence on world affairs would be substantial in the postwar era, whether in containing the spread of communism, constructing a nuclear arsenal, spending billions in foreign aid, or rebuilding the battered economies of Western Europe and Japan. The days of isolationism were gone for good.

World War II had an equally profound impact on domestic affairs. It ended the Great Depression, created full employment, and increased mean family income an astonishing 25 percent. It demonstrated the ability of an ethnically diverse nation to unite in a just cause, though racial segregation remained in place and basic civil liberties, in the case of Japanese Americans, were tragically denied. And it opened new opportunities for women and minorities in the workplace, although full economic and political equality in the United States remained a dream unfulfilled. In 1945 Americans looked to the future with cautious optimism—proud of their accomplishments and yearning for better times.

The Chapter in Review

In the years between 1940 and 1945:

- Roosevelt won an unprecedented third term in 1940 by vowing to keep the country out of war.
- The Japanese attack on Pearl Harbor plunged the nation into World War II.
- Heavy war production brought the Great Depression to an end.
- Married women joined the labor force in record numbers, taking jobs normally reserved for men.
- Allied forces in the North Atlantic Theater stormed the beaches of France in 1944, following heavy fighting in North Africa and in Italy.

- Roosevelt, Stalin, and Churchill met at Yalta in 1945 to map strategy for the postwar world.
- Vice President Harry S Truman became president following the death of FDR in April 1945.
- Germany surrendered a month later, following the suicide of Adolph Hitler and the Allied assault on Berlin.
- Japan surrendered in August 1945, following the dropping of two atomic bombs.

Making Connections Across Chapters

LOOKING BACK

Chapter 26 examines both the way in which the United States fought World War II and the great changes that occurred in domestic and international affairs.

1. How did America mobilize for war? What changes took place on the home front that aided the war production?

2. How lasting and substantial were the gains made by women and minorities during the war?

3. How well did the Grand Alliance work, what strategies were employed to keep it together, and what problems arose regarding the interests of the different parties?

LOOKING AHEAD

Chapter 27 looks at American society following World War II, tracing the impact of the war on foreign and domestic affairs, from the Cold War to the baby boom to the growth of suburbia.

1. What decisions were made, or avoided, during World War II that had a direct impact on the diplomatic problems facing the United States and the Soviet Union in the coming years?

2. How difficult would it be for America's 15 million veterans to readjust to civilian life following the war?

3. Would the tremendous wartime prosperity in the United States be maintained once the conflict was over?

Recommended Readings

Birdwell, Michael. *Celluloid Soldiers* (1999). Carefully examines Hollywood's war effort against the Nazis.

Dower, John. *War Without Mercy: Race and Power in the Pacific War* (1986). Explores the racial attitudes of the United States and Japan in the brutal Asian conflict.

Hartmann, Susan. *The Homefront and Beyond: American Women in the 1940s* (1982). Documents the extraordinary impact of World War II on women at home and in the workplace.

Jeffries, John. *Wartime America* (1996). Concentrates on the home front during World War II.

Kennett, Lee. *G.I.: The American Soldier in World War II* (1997). Describes the day-to-day order of life of the average American soldier in the training camps, in combat, and in victory.

O'Neill, William. *A Democracy at War: America's Fight at Home and Abroad in World War II* (1993). Examines both the military front and the home front in lively detail.

Robinson, Gregg. *By Order of the President: FDR and the Internment of Japanese Americans* (2001). Offers a sobering account of Roosevelt's personal role in the internment process.

Tuttle, William. *Daddy's Gone to War* (1993). Recreates these years in generational terms through the eyes of America's wartime children.

Walker, J. Samuel. *Prompt and Utter Destruction: Truman and the Use of Atomic Bombs Against Japan* (1997). Offers a balanced account of the factors leading to the president's fateful decision.

Wyman, David S. *The Abandonment of the Jews* (1984). Examines the failure of American policy-makers, the press, and the larger public to provide a sanctuary for victims of the Holocaust.

Identifications

Review your understanding of the following key terms, people, events, and dates for this chapter (these terms also appear in the Glossary at the end of the book):

Winston Churchill
Wendell Willkie
Lend-Lease
Pearl Harbor
Bataan Peninsula
General Douglas MacArthur

Rosie the Riveter
Nisei
Executive Order 9066
General Dwight D. Eisenhower
Operation OVERLORD
Midway Island
Harry S Truman
Enola Gay

Online Sources Guide

Use this listing to find online documents, images, interactive maps, simulations, and other resources related to this chapter:

American History Resource Center

http://history.wadsworth.com/rc/us

Documents

"The Atlantic Charter" (1941)
Lindbergh address to the America First Committee (1941)
Roosevelt's "War Message" to Congress (December 8, 1941)
Gar Alperovitz, "Why We Dropped the Bomb" (1945)
A. Philip Randolph's call to fight racial discrimination

Selected Images

Explosion of the USS *Shaw* during attack on Pearl Harbor
General Dwight Eisenhower meets with paratroopers before D-Day
American troops on D-Day
Nazi death camp at Dachau
American troops wading ashore at Butaritari, November 1943
Flag raising on Iwo Jima
Navajo Signal Corp

Simulation

World War II (In this historical simulation you can choose to be a GI, a woman, or a Japanese American, and make choices based on the circumstances and opportunities afforded.)

HistoryNOW

http://now.ilrn.com/ayers_etal3e

Primary Source Exercises

Civil Liberties in Wartime
The End of the Pacific War

27 Postwar America, 1946–1952

American soldiers return home at the end of World War II.

© Bettmann/CORBIS

enry R. Luce was a man of grand visions and powerful views. One rival dubbed him "Lord of the Press" because his publishing empire included *Time, Life,* and *Fortune,* among other mass circulation magazines. In February 1941, Luce composed an editorial prodding the American people to accept their new role as citizens of "the strongest and most vital nation in the world." The time had come, he insisted, to exert "the full measure of our influence, for such purposes as we see fit" in the dawning "American Century."

The belief in America's destiny was as old as the country itself. Yet the challenges of World War II had turned this rhetoric into reality by placing the United States at the very center of the international stage. Old empires lay in ruins; an atomic era had begun. Only the United States seemed to possess the combination of military strength, economic resources, and political stability to rebuild a world battered by war. What worried Luce and others was the failure of American resolve. As columnist Dorothy Thompson put it, the United States "must lead now or take a back seat in history."

Reconversion

The United States faced two major problems following World War II. The first one concerned relations with the Soviet Union. Would the two nations be able to maintain the Grand Alliance, or would their obvious differences about the shape and direction of postwar Europe degenerate into conflict, and possibly war? The second problem related to the domestic economy. Many Americans feared that the Great Depression might return after World War II, as defense spending dropped and factory jobs disappeared. In the months following Japan's surrender, the federal government cancelled more than $30 billion in military contracts, forcing 800,000 layoffs in the aircraft industry alone. Could the United States handle the difficult reconversion from a wartime to a peacetime economy? Or would it slip back into the dark days of joblessness, poverty, and despair?

The Veterans Return

President Truman's first job was to bring the soldiers home. Twelve million Americans were still in uniform in

Timeline

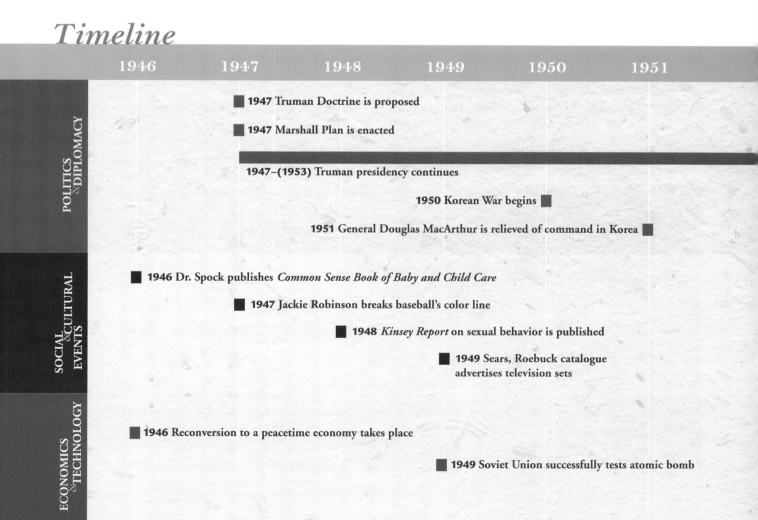

1946 1947 1948 1949 1950 1951

POLITICS & DIPLOMACY

1947 Truman Doctrine is proposed

1947 Marshall Plan is enacted

1947–(1953) Truman presidency continues

1950 Korean War begins

1951 General Douglas MacArthur is relieved of command in Korea

SOCIAL & CULTURAL EVENTS

1946 Dr. Spock publishes *Common Sense Book of Baby and Child Care*

1947 Jackie Robinson breaks baseball's color line

1948 *Kinsey Report* on sexual behavior is published

1949 Sears, Roebuck catalogue advertises television sets

ECONOMICS & TECHNOLOGY

1946 Reconversion to a peacetime economy takes place

1949 Soviet Union successfully tests atomic bomb

1945, most of them young men, ages 18 to 34, who had experienced the dual hardships of economic depression and war. Their dream was to return home quickly and get on with their lives. Throughout Europe and the Pacific, GIs grumbled about the slow pace of demobilization, while their loved ones barraged Congress and the White House with angry mail. One soldier put his feelings in a poem:

> Please Mr. Truman, won't you send us home?
> We have captured Napoli and liberated Rome.
> We have licked the master race.
> Now there's lots of shipping space.
> So, won't you send us home.

This pressure brought results. Within a year, the number of men and women in the armed forces had dropped to 3 million, despite the growing Soviet threat.

For many GIs, however, these were anxious, difficult times. The divorce rate shot up dramatically in 1945, reflecting the tensions of readjustment to civilian life. A major housing shortage, brought on by the virtual absence of home-building during World War II, made things even worse. Washington, D.C., reported 25,000 homeless veterans, Chicago more than 100,000. North Dakota veterans took to living in converted grain bins. One serviceman complained: "You fight a damn war and you finally come home and everybody slaps you on the back and tells you what a wonderful job you did . . . but when it comes to really doing something, then nobody's home."

In fact, however, assistance for returning veterans had received careful attention from the wartime Congress, which passed the popular Servicemen's Readjustment Act in 1944. Known as the GI Bill, it provided almost $20 billion for various programs in the decade following World War II. The social and economic effects of this legislation were enormous. The GI Bill fueled a nationwide construction boom by providing long-term, low-interest mortgages to veterans, plus a $2,000 bonus toward the purchase of a new home. Furthermore, it allowed former soldiers to fulfill the dream of a college degree, thereby expanding the system of higher education as never before. In 1947, for example, more than half of the 30,000 students at the University of Minnesota were veterans of World War II. Older, more serious, and determined to make up for lost time, they formed the nucleus of America's expanding white-collar workforce in the prosperous years ahead.

Lurching toward Prosperity

The fear of another economic depression in the United States did not last long. The increase in federal spending for veterans helped to offset the decrease in defense spending. And a surge of consumer demand held out the promise of prosperity based on peace. For the past 5 years, Americans had worked overtime in offices and factories, banking their paychecks, buying savings bonds, and dreaming of the day when cars, appliances, prime beef, and nylon stockings would reappear in the nation's stores and showrooms. Between Pearl Harbor and the Japanese surrender, the public had accumulated an astonishing $140 billion in savings and liquid securities, while the average weekly wage had almost doubled, from $24.20 to $44.30. "I'm tired of ration books and empty shelves," said one factory worker. "I'm ready to spend."

But factories could not change from fighter planes to automobiles overnight. Reconversion took time. With the demand for consumer goods far outpacing the supply, President Truman hoped to keep inflation in line by extending wartime price controls. His plan met strong opposition from the business community, which lobbied hard to "strike the shackles from American free enterprise." In June 1946, controls were lifted and prices shot up. The cost of meat doubled in 2 weeks, leading the *New York Daily News* to quip:

> PRICES SOAR, BUYERS SORE
> STEERS JUMP OVER THE MOON

Not surprisingly, the labor movement took a militant stance. Since higher prices meant a drop in real wages, the United Automobile Workers (UAW) demanded an average pay hike of 33 cents an hour from General Motors in 1946, from $1.12 to $1.45. When the corporation offered a 10-cent hourly raise, the union struck for 113 days, eventually settling for 18 cents. Shortly thereafter, the

Veterans register for college. The GI Bill of 1944 expanded and democratized higher education as never before.

© Bettmann/CORBIS

UAW and the auto companies agreed to a cost-of-living adjustment (COLA) clause in future contracts.

The country was soon plagued by a wave of strikes. In 1946 alone, 5 million workers were involved in 4,630 work stoppages totaling 120 million days of lost labor. When two railroad brotherhoods threatened a national strike designed to shut down the country's rail service, President Truman signed an executive order seizing the railroads. "If you think I'm going to sit here and let you tie up this whole country," he told union leaders, "you're crazy as hell." A few weeks later, the United Mine Workers (UMW) went on strike, forcing power stations and factories to close for lack of fuel.

In response, President Truman went on the radio to demand that the miners return to work at once. They did, coaxed along by a federal court injunction that led to $3.5 million in damages against the UMW. For Truman, these victories came at a heavy cost. Not only did he offend large parts of the labor movement, he also appeared incapable of governing a nation wracked by consumer shortages, labor strife, soaring inflation, and an approaching cold war.

In November 1946, the Democratic party suffered a crushing defeat at the polls. Campaigning against the ills of reconversion ("Had Enough?") and the president's alleged incompetence ("To Err Is Truman"), the Republicans gained control of the Senate and the House for the first time since 1928. When the Truman family returned to Washington from a campaign trip on election eve, no one showed up to greet them. The train station was deserted. "Don't worry about me," the president told his daughter, Margaret. "I know how things will turn out and they'll be all right."

An advertisement for the "dream kitchen." A surge of consumer spending after World War II quickly erased fears that America would slip back into economic depression.

Affluence and Anxiety

The pain and sacrifice of the Great Depression and World War II led most Americans to yearn for both emotional security and material success. As expected, the family grew in importance, providing a sense of comfort and stability to people after years of separation and loss. Along with the focus on families came a changing middle-class culture, based on suburban living, a **baby boom,** an emphasis on more traditional sex roles, and an explosion of consumer goods. In the coming years, the nation's unprecedented prosperity would be measured by the increased size and abundant possessions of its thriving middle class.

The Postwar American Family

One of the songs made popular by returning American veterans was titled "I've Got to Make Up for Lost Time." Beginning in 1946, the United States experienced a surge

in marriage and birth rates, following record lows in the Depression decade. The young adults (ages 18 to 30) of this era became the most "marrying" generation in American history, with 97 percent of the women and 94 percent of the men taking marriage vows. By 1950, the age of marriage for American women had dropped below 20, another record, while the percentage of divorces, initially high among returning veterans, reached an all-time low.

The baby boom was equally dramatic. The number of children per family in the United States jumped from 2.6 in 1940 to 3.2 by decade's end. Birthrates doubled for a third child, and tripled for a fourth, as the American population grew by 20 million in the 1940s. At a time when access to birth control information was rapidly increasing, U.S. population growth rivaled not England's, but rather India's.

These spiraling marriage and birth rates went hand in hand with a shift back to more traditional sex roles following World War II. Actress Ann Sothern exemplified the reordering of domestic priorities when she advised women, shortly before Japan's surrender, to begin "planning our house—our perfect house" and to think about

Marriage and birth rates rose dramatically in the postwar years, following record lows in the Depression era.

A trip to the suburban supermarket in postwar America.

the nursery. "I know a lot of men are dreaming of coming back not only to those girls who waved goodbye to them," she added. "They are dreaming of coming back to the mothers of their children and the least we can do as women is to try to live up to some of these expectations." Indeed, one of the most popular wartime advertisements showed a mother in overalls about to leave for the factory. She is at the door when her little daughter asks: "Mother, when will you stay home again?" And she responds: "Some jubilant day, mother will stay home again doing the job she likes—making a home for you and daddy when he gets back."

Quite naturally, this emphasis on family life strengthened long-held prejudices against married women holding full-time jobs outside the home. As a result, the gains made in female employment during World War II largely disappeared. Returning veterans reclaimed millions of factory jobs held by women and minorities. The female labor force dropped from a wartime high of 19 million in 1945 to less than 17 million by 1947. On the Ford and General Motors assembly lines, the percentage of women plummeted from 25 to 6 percent. Though many women gladly returned to their former domestic lives, the vast majority, according to postwar surveys, hoped to keep their jobs. "I'd stay if they wanted me to," said a female aircraft worker, "but without taking a man's place from him."

The social pressures on women were enormous. A host of "experts," including psychiatrists, psychologists, and pediatricians, asserted that women belonged in the home for their own good as well as the good of society— that women *needed* to be housewives and mothers in order to be fulfilled. In their 1947 best-seller, *Modern Women: The Lost Sex,* Marynia Farnham and Ferdinand Lundberg noted that "all mature childless women are emotionally disturbed," and that "the pursuit of a career is essentially masculine." Furthermore, these experts claimed that returning veterans needed special love and attention after so many years away from home.

The concept of "mothering" as central to the postwar family was further popularized by Dr. Benjamin Spock, whose *Common Sense Book of Baby and Child Care* (1946) became the standard reference for parents of the "baby boom" generation. While most reviewers noted Spock's relaxed, more permissive attitude toward child rearing, another message came through as well. Women must be the primary caregivers, Spock insisted. It was their role to shape the infant into a normal, happy adult. For Spock and countless others, a man's success was measured by his performance in the outside world, a woman's success by her skills in raising well-adjusted children. As feminist author Betty Friedan recalled, "Oh, how Dr. Spock could make me feel guilty!"

Dr. Kinsey and the Sexual Revolution

In 1948, Dr. Alfred Kinsey, a professor at Indiana University, became a national celebrity with the publication of his 804-page study, *Sexual Behavior in the Human Male*. The photo of Kinsey here, with his crew cut and bow tie, conveys the conservative, old-fashioned image he liked to portray. In truth, his personal habits were anything but conventional. Kinsey had experienced many different sexual relationships throughout his life.

His scientific research, based on thousands of detailed interviews, showed that American men were more sexually active—and less bound by traditional codes of morality—than had previously been imagined.

His book became a best-seller, followed in 1953 by a sequel, *Sexual Behavior in the Human Female*, which drew similar conclusions about American women. Kinsey hoped that his work would lead to greater tolerance for a wide range of sexual behavior, including homosexuality. He was mistaken. Though opinion polls showed most Americans in agreement with his findings, angry critics, led by church leaders and politicians, condemned Kinsey for undermining the nation's moral standards. In response, his main benefactor, the Rockefeller Foundation, withdrew its financial support, undermining future projects. Kinsey died shortly thereafter, in 1956, at the age of 62.

© Bettmann/CORBIS

The emphasis on traditional sex roles also affected female education. World War II had opened up new opportunities for women in science, engineering, and medicine. For the first time in history, women constituted a majority of the nation's college graduates. But the return of male veterans, combined with the educational benefits provided them by the GI Bill, reversed these temporary gains. Although the number of college women increased after World War II, the percentage of females in the college population declined dramatically. At Cornell University, for example, women comprised 50 percent of the wartime classes, but only 20 percent of the postwar classes. More significantly, the percentage of college women who actually graduated fell from 40 percent during World War II to 25 percent by 1950.

The steepest declines occurred in professional education. Engineering colleges, which doubled their enrollments to more than 200,000 by 1946, accepted fewer than 1,300 women, with more than half of these schools accepting no women at all. Female enrollments in medical schools dropped from a high of 15 percent during World War II to 5 percent by 1950. A study of medical students in this era showed deep prejudice among the men and self-limiting attitudes among the women. The majority of men, believing they made better doctors, thought that women should face tougher admission standards. The majority of women, insisting that marriage was more important than a career, claimed they would cut back their hours, or even stop working, to meet their family obligations. On campuses across the

The vast majority of working women in the postwar era were employed in low-paying, often part-time jobs, as clerks, secretaries, waitresses, domestics, and telephone operators.

nation, educators struggled to find the proper curriculum for female students. The ideal, said one college president, was to enable women "to foster the intellectual and emotional life of her family and community"—to fill the American home with proper moral values, a love of culture, and an appreciation of good wine and gourmet cooking.

Before long, the postwar American woman became the nation's primary consumer. Between 1946 and 1950, Americans purchased 21 million automobiles, 20 million refrigerators, 5.5 million electric stoves, and more than 2 million dishwashers. This consumer explosion resulted from a combination of factors: the baby boom, the huge savings accumulated during World War II, the availability of credit, and the effectiveness of mass advertising in creating consumer demand. The average American now had access to department store charge accounts and easy payment plans with almost no money down. "Buy Now, Pay Later," urged General Motors, and most people obliged. In 1950, as consumer debt surpassed $100 billion, the Diner's Club introduced America's first credit card. The Depression age virtues of thrift and savings seemed as remote as the Depression itself.

Ironically, this new consumer society led millions of women back into the labor force. By 1950, more women were working outside the home than ever before. The difference, however, was that postwar American women returned to low-paying, often part-time employment in "feminine" jobs such as clerks, salespeople, secretaries, waitresses, telephone operators, and domestics. Working to supplement the family income, to help finance the automobile, the kitchen appliances, the summer vacation, the children's college tuition, American women earned but 53 percent of the wages of American men in 1950—a drop of 10 percent since the heady years of "Rosie the Riveter" during World War II.

Suburbia

No possession was more prized by the postwar American family than the suburban home. In 1944, fewer than 120,000 new houses were built in the United States, a figure that rose to 900,000 by 1946, and 1.7 million by 1950. More than 80 percent of these new houses were built in suburban areas surrounding established cities. While prosperity and population growth produced the need for more housing, the rush to suburbia was accelerated by a flood of federal mortgage money and a revolution in the building of affordable, single-family homes.

The GI Bill provided the cash to bolster demand. With mortgage money now available, the housing shortage quickly disappeared. Leading the way were builders like William Levitt, who purchased several thousand acres of farmland in Hempstead, New York, 25 miles east of Manhattan, for the mass production of private homes. Levitt modeled his operation after Henry Ford's automobile assembly plants. His building materials were produced and precut in Levitt factories, delivered by Levitt trucks, and assembled by Levitt work crews, each performing a single task such as framing, pouring concrete, or painting window shutters. In good weather, Levitt workers put up 180 houses a week. The typical dwelling—a solid, two-bedroom Cape Cod, with a kitchen–dining room, living room with fireplace, single bath, and expansion attic—sold for $7,900. When completed, **Levittown,** Long Island, contained 17,000 houses, plus dozens of parks, ballfields, swimming pools, churches, and shopping areas for the 82,000 residents. Levitt followed his Long Island venture with similar towns in Pennsylvania and New Jersey.

City dwellers were attracted by Levittown's good schools, safe streets, and open space. The idea of owning one's home, moreover, was a central part of the American dream. And these suburban neighborhoods, filled with young families, provided a sense of shared experience and community that large cities sometimes lacked.

What stood out to others, however, was the "sameness" of Levittown—a place where people lived in similar houses, accumulated similar possessions, and

The GI Bill helped fuel the boom in suburban housing after World War II.

© Bettmann/CORBIS

conformed to similar rules. Levitt salesmen restricted their communities to white applicants, who then signed pledges saying they would not resell their homes to blacks. As late as the 1960s, the percentage of African Americans living in the three Levittown developments was well below 1 percent, a figure that represented most suburban areas nationwide. Furthermore, Levittown appeared to reinforce the traditional family roles of postwar America, with mothers caring for their children while fathers commuted long distances to work.

The Soviet Threat

Relations between the United States and the Soviet Union were moving swiftly downhill. The failure to find common ground on a host of vital issues—from "free elections" in Poland to the German payment of reparations—raised anger and suspicion on both sides. Soviet leaders now viewed the United States as largely indifferent to the security needs of the Russian people, and American leaders increasingly portrayed the Soviet Union as a belligerent force in the world, bent more on expanding its empire than on defending its territory. The Grand Alliance was over; the Cold War had begun.

DOING HISTORY ONLINE

The Six Thousand Houses That Levitt Built, 1948

Read the article in this module along with the section on Suburbia in the textbook. Imagine that you are a newly married World War II veteran or someone married to a soldier just returned from the war in 1947. Would you want to live in Levittown? Why or why not?

History ⧗ Now™   Visit HistoryNOW to access primary sources and exercises related to this topic: http://now.ilrn.com/ayers_etal3e

---

Containment

Within hours of Germany's surrender, President Truman had signed an executive order ending Lend-Lease aid to the Allies. Though Truman reversed himself under a storm of criticism, Congress abolished Lend-Lease following Japan's surrender in August 1945. A few months later, the United States gave England a low-interest $3.75 billion loan, and ignored a similar request from the Russians.

Stalin angrily viewed these moves as a sign of American indifference to the suffering of his people. In February 1946, the Soviet leader delivered a major address predicting the collapse of capitalism and the dawn of a communist world. The following month, with Truman at his side, former Prime Minister Churchill told an audience at Westminster College in Missouri that Russia had drawn an "iron curtain" across Europe. The West must unite against Soviet expansion, Churchill said, adding that "God had willed" the atomic bomb to Britain and America so as to ensure their ultimate triumph over this totalitarian foe.

A more compelling rebuttal to Stalin's speech came from a 42-year-old foreign service officer stationed at the U.S. Embassy in Moscow. In an 8,000-word telegram, George F. Kennan laid out the doctrine of "containment" that would influence American foreign policy for the next 20 years. According to Kennan, Russia was an implacable foe, determined to expand its empire and to undermine Western democratic values. America must be patient, Kennan believed. It must define its vital interests and then be prepared to defend them through "the adroit and vigilant application of counterforce at a series of constantly shifting geographical and political points."

Kennan's "long telegram" arrived in Washington at the perfect time. Poland and Eastern Europe were now lost causes; there seemed little that the United States could do to change their dismal fate. The present objective, Truman believed, was to block communist expansion into new areas vulnerable to Soviet influence and control. "Unless Russia is faced with an iron fist and strong language another war is in the making," he predicted. "I am tired of babying the Soviets."

The Truman Doctrine and the Marshall Plan

The new trouble spot appeared to be the Mediterranean, where Russia was demanding territorial concessions from Iran and Turkey, and where communist-led guerrillas were battling the Greek government in a bloody civil war. Early in 1947, Great Britain, the traditional

Flashpoints | The Rosenberg Case

It was called the "spy trial of the century." In the summer of 1950, Julius and Ethel Rosenberg, a married couple with two small children, were arrested and charged with conspiracy to commit espionage—in this case, the passing of atomic secrets to the Soviet Union. Their trial, which began the following year, riveted worldwide attention on the federal courthouse in Manhattan's Foley Square. Following several weeks of testimony, the jury found the couple and two accomplices guilty as charged, but only the Rosenbergs were sentenced to death. "I consider your crime worse than murder," the judge declared. "I believe your conduct has already caused . . . the Communist aggression in Korea . . . and altered the course of history to the disadvantage of your country."

Julius and Ethel Rosenberg lived and breathed the Communist cause. Describing himself as a "soldier of Stalin," Julius wanted to help the Russians modernize their military. In the summer of 1942, as an engineer for the U.S. Army Signal Corps, he had stolen classified material and passed it to Soviet intelligence agents. But his biggest prize came purely by chance, when Ethel's brother, a machinist named David Greenglass, was drafted in 1944 and sent to Los Alamos, New Mexico, site of the top-secret Manhattan Project. Once there, at the urging of Julius Rosenberg, Greenglass provided highly sensitive information about the detonation of the atomic bomb.

There is little doubt today about the guilt of Julius Rosenberg. The trial testimony of David Greenglass in 1951 was later corroborated by the release of classified files from intelligence agencies in both the former Soviet Union and the United States—all of which showed Julius Rosenberg to be an active and important Russian spy. The evidence against Ethel Rosenberg, however, is much less convincing. Although she almost certainly knew (and perhaps approved of) her husband's role in espionage, she did not appear to play a role in it. Indeed, the government seemed to put her on trial to pressure her husband into confessing, which he, and she, refused to do. The Rosenbergs died in the electric chair at New York's Sing Sing Prison on June 19, 1953, protesting their innocence to the end.

Were a fair trial and a just sentence really possible in the prevailing atmosphere of Cold War anger and fear? This question is still bitterly debated. The crimes of Julius Rosenberg were very real indeed. But the execution of a husband and wife, leaving two children orphaned, remains an ominous reminder of a deeply troubled time.

Questions for Reflection

1. What forces were at work in the late 1940s and early 1950s that served to heighten the fear of Communist subversion in the United States?

2. How did the fear of Communist subversion become a major political issue in this era?

3. Why does the case of Julius and Ethel Rosenberg continue to generate so much controversy to this day?

---

power in that area, informed the United States that it could no longer provide military and economic assistance to Greece and Turkey. Exhausted by World War II, England urged the United States to maintain that aid in order to prevent further Soviet expansion.

At a White House meeting 6 days later, **General George C. Marshall,** the new secretary of state, presented the case for American aid to congressional leaders from both parties. When Marshall's soft-spoken approach failed to rally the meeting, his assistant Dean Acheson took over. In sweeping terms, Acheson portrayed the future of Greece and Turkey as a test case of American resolve against Soviet aggression. If Greece fell to the communists, Acheson warned, other nations would follow "like apples in a barrel infected by one rotten one." When he finished, Republican Senator Arthur Vandenberg of Michigan summed up the feeling in the room. "Mr. President," he said, turning to Harry Truman, "if you will say that to Congress and the country, I will support you and I believe most members will do the same."

On March 12, 1947, the president offered his **Truman Doctrine** before a joint session of Congress and a national radio audience. In the present crisis, he began, "every nation must choose between alternative ways of life." One way guaranteed "individual liberty" and "political freedom," the other promoted "terror" and "oppression." In a world of good and evil, Truman declared, it "must be the policy of the United States to support free peoples who are resisting attempted subjugation by armed minorities or by outside pressures."

Some critics noted that the regimes in Greece and Turkey were a far cry from the democratic ideals that the president lauded in his speech. Others worried that the Truman Doctrine would lead the United States into an expensive, open-ended crusade against left-wing forces around the globe. Yet most Americans supported Truman's position, and Congress allocated $400 million in military aid for Greece and Turkey.

On June 5, 1947, at the Harvard University commencement, Secretary of State Marshall unveiled a far more ambitious proposal known as the European Recovery Plan (ERP), or the **Marshall Plan.** The danger seemed clear: without massive economic aid, European governments might collapse, leaving chaos in their wake. "Our policy is not directed against any country or doctrine," Marshall said, "but against hunger, poverty, desperation, and fear."

Several weeks later, 17 European nations, including the Soviet Union, met in Paris to assess their common needs. But the Russians walked out after a few sessions, forcing nations like Poland and Hungary to leave as well. The Soviets balked at the idea of divulging critical information about their economy to outsiders. And they surely feared that massive American aid would tie them and the nations they now controlled to a capitalist orbit that might undermine the communist system.

Truman was not sorry to see them leave. He had been forced to invite all European nations to participate in order to avoid the appearance of worsening the Cold War. Yet he realized that Congress would not look favorably upon the prospect of spending billions of dollars to reconstruct a nation that seemed so brutal to its neighbors and so threatening to the United States. With the Russians and their satellites out of the picture, the remaining European nations prepared an agenda for economic recovery that came to $27 billion, a huge sum. After 6 months of bitter debate, Congress reduced that figure by about one-half. The largest expenditures went to England, Germany, and France.

The Marshall Plan proved a tremendous success on both sides of the Atlantic. By creating jobs and raising living standards, it restored economic confidence throughout Western Europe and curbed the influence of local Communist parties in Italy and France. Furthermore, the Marshall Plan increased American trade and investment in Europe, opening vast new markets for U.S. goods. As President Truman noted, "peace, freedom, and world trade are indivisible."

The rising prosperity in Western Europe was matched by growing repression in the East. Stalin moved first on Hungary, staging a rigged election backed by Russian troops. Opponents of the new Communist regime were silenced and imprisoned. Next came Czechoslovakia, where the Soviets toppled a coalition government led by Jan Masaryk, a statesman with many admirers in the West. A few days later, Masaryk either jumped or was pushed to his death from an office window in Prague. Against this ominous background, President Truman proposed legislation to streamline the nation's military and diplomatic services. Passed as the National Security Act of 1947, it unified the armed forces under a single Department of Defense, created the National Security Council

The Marshall Plan at work in West Berlin. Billions of dollars in American aid helped rebuild much of war-ravaged Europe.

(NSC) to provide foreign policy information to the president, and established the Central Intelligence Agency (CIA) to coordinate intelligence gathering abroad. By 1948, the Cold War was in full swing.

Liberalism in Retreat

In foreign affairs, President Truman could count on strong bipartisan support. Republican legislators had joined with Democrats to endorse early Cold War initiatives like the Truman Doctrine and the Marshall Plan. But the president had no such luck on domestic issues. For one thing, the widening rift with Russia produced a growing concern about the influence of communists and their "sympathizers" inside the federal government. For another, the president's attempt to extend the liberal agenda through ambitious social and economic legislation—known as the "Fair Deal"—met with stiff resistance in Congress after 1946. As one Republican leader put it: "We have to break with the corrupting idea that we can legislate prosperity, legislate equality, legislate opportunity."

The Cold War at Home

The **Iron Curtain** that descended on Europe had a tremendous psychological impact on the United States. Americans were fearful of communism and frustrated by the turn of global events. The defeat of fascism had not made the world a safer place. One form of totalitarianism had been replaced by another. The result was an erosion of public tolerance for left-wing activity, spurred on by prominent government officials like Attorney General Tom Clark, who warned that communists were "everywhere" in the United States—"in factories, offices, butcher shops, on street corners, in private businesses, and each carries with him the germs of death for society."

In fact, the American Communist party was far weaker in 1947 than it had been a decade before, and its numbers were dwindling by the day. Yet that did not stop President Truman from establishing a Federal Loyalty–Security Program for the first time in American history. Truman acted, in large part, to keep congressional conservatives from fashioning an even tougher loyalty program. The one he put in place called for extensive background checks of all civilian workers in the federal bureaucracy. The criteria for disloyalty included everything from espionage to "sympathetic association" with groups deemed "subversive" by the attorney general. The Loyalty–Security Program provided minimal safeguards for the accused. Even worse, it frightened the country by conceding the possibility that a serious problem existed.

The congressional assault on domestic subversion was led by the **House Un-American Activities Committee (HUAC).** Formed in the 1930s to investigate Nazi propaganda in the United States, HUAC had been revived after World War II as a watchdog against communist propaganda. Among its more visible members was a young congressman from southern California named Richard M. Nixon. In 1947, HUAC launched a spectacular investigation of the motion picture industry, alleging that "flagrant communist propaganda films" had been produced during World War II on the specific orders of President Roosevelt. The committee subpoenaed a number of pro-communist writers and directors, who angrily refused to answer questions about their political beliefs and associations. Known as the "Hollywood Ten," these individuals were cited for contempt, sent to jail, and "blacklisted" from working in the entertainment industry, a practice that became increasingly common in the late 1940s and 1950s. HUAC also heard from a host of "friendly" Hollywood witnesses, including movie stars Gary Cooper, Ronald Reagan, and the dapper Adolphe Menjou, who declared: "I am a witch-hunter if the witches are communists. I am a Red-baiter. I would like to see them all back in Russia."

The following year brought HUAC even more publicity. A witness named Whittaker Chambers, then a senior editor for *Time* magazine, claimed to have once been part of a "communist cell" in Washington that included **Alger Hiss,** a former government official who had advised President Roosevelt in foreign affairs. Hiss denied Chambers's allegations in testimony before HUAC a few days later. When Chambers repeated the charge on a national radio broadcast, Hiss sued him for libel.

Chambers struck back hard, producing dozens of classified State Department documents from the 1930s that, he claimed, had been stolen by Hiss and passed on to the Russians. Suddenly the ground had shifted to espionage, a more serious charge. The evidence—known as the "Pumpkin Papers" because Chambers had briefly hidden it in a pumpkin patch on his Maryland farm—included five rolls of microfilm and summaries of confidential reports written by Hiss in longhand or typed on a Woodstock typewriter he once owned. In December 1948, a federal grand jury indicted Hiss for perjuring himself before HUAC. (The 10-year statute of limitations on espionage had just run out.) The first trial ended in a hung jury; the second one sent Hiss to jail.

The guilty verdict sent shock waves through the nation. Not only did it bolster Republican charges about the threat of communists in government, it also served to undermine the liberal-internationalist philosophy that had guided the Democratic party since 1933. If Alger Hiss was a traitor, some wondered, how many just like him were still loose in the Truman administration, working secretly to help the Soviet Union win the Cold War? This question would come to dominate American politics over the next several years.

Alger Hiss is sworn in at a hearing of the House Un-American Activities Committee in 1948. Accused by Whittaker Chambers of being part of a Soviet espionage ring, Hiss went to federal prison in 1950 after a jury convicted him of perjury.

The Domestic Agenda

The Republican landslide of 1946 appeared to signal the decline of American liberalism. In the following months, the Republican Congress brushed aside President Truman's proposals for national health insurance and federal aid to education, and passed major legislation, known as the Taft-Hartley Act, to curb the power of organized labor. Taft-Hartley generated strong public support, given the crippling strikes of the previous year. Republican leaders viewed the union movement as both an ally of the Democratic party and a threat to the employer's authority in the workplace. In 1947, organized labor was at the height of its influence, with 15 million members nationwide. More than 35 percent of all nonagricultural workers belonged to a union, the highest total ever reached in the United States.

To counter the threats of powerful unions like the United Mine Workers, Taft-Hartley gave the president authority to impose an 80-day "cooling-off" period to prevent strikes that threatened the national interest. More important, the bill outlawed the closed shop, a device that forced workers to join a union at the time they were hired, and it encouraged the states to pass "right to work" laws that made union organizing more difficult. Though Truman strongly opposed Taft-Hartley, the Republican Congress easily overrode his veto.

Truman also confronted the issue of racial discrimination, long ignored in the White House and on Capitol Hill, by forming a special task force on civil rights. Its final report included a series of bold recommendations, such as the desegregation of the armed forces and the creation of a special division within the Justice Department devoted solely to civil rights. Truman endorsed these recommendations, although his personal feelings about them were mixed. As a political leader, he had to balance the interests of two distinct Democratic party voting blocs: southern whites and northern blacks. As an individual, he believed that all citizens deserved political rights and equal opportunity, yet he felt uncomfortable with the notion of *social* equality for African Americans, as did most white people of that era. Addressing the NAACP's national convention in 1947—the first American president to do so—Truman spoke out strongly against prejudice and hate. "The only limit to a [person's] achievement," he declared, "should be his ability, his industry, and his character."

Breaking the Color Line

Truman's statement seemed particularly appropriate in 1947. On April 15, Major League baseball broke its long-standing "color line" in an opening day game at Brooklyn's Ebbets Field. "History was made here Tuesday afternoon," reported the *Pittsburgh Courier*, an African American newspaper, "when smiling Jackie Robinson trotted out on the green-swept diamond with the rest of his Dodger teammates."

Baseball had been all-white for generations. Blacks played in the so-called Negro Leagues. Poorly paid, they often barnstormed from town to town, taking on local teams in exhibitions that combined great baseball with crowd-pleasing entertainment. The top players—pitcher Leroy "Satchel" Paige, catcher Josh Gibson, infielder George "Cool Papa" Bell—were as good, if not better, than the top Major League stars. Hall of Fame pitcher Walter Johnson claimed that Gibson "can do everything. He hits the ball a mile. He catches so easy he might as well be in a rocking chair. Throws like a rifle. Too bad this Gibson is a colored fellow."

The vast majority of Major League owners opposed integration. Branch Rickey of the Brooklyn Dodgers was an exception. Mixing deep religious values with shrewd business sense, Rickey insisted that integration was good for America, for baseball, and for the Dodgers. "The Negroes will make us winners for years to come," he said, "and for that I will happily bear being called a bleeding heart and a do-gooder and all that humanitarian rot."

To break the color line, Rickey selected Jack Roosevelt Robinson, 27, a man of tremendous talent and pride. The son of sharecroppers and the grandson of slaves, Robinson moved from rural Georgia to Pasadena, California, where his athletic skills earned him a scholarship to UCLA. A letterman in four different sports—baseball, football, basketball, and track—he also won tournaments in tennis and golf. Drafted into the army during World War II, Robinson fought bigotry at every turn. As a second lieutenant in a segregated tank unit, he was court-martialed for insubordination, and acquitted, after refusing to move to the rear of an army bus. Honorably discharged in 1944, he joined the Kansas City Monarchs, a Negro League team, as a shortstop at $400 a month. On a road trip to Oklahoma, teammate Buck O'Neill recalled, Robinson personally broke the color line at a local filling station by demanding to use the rest room. When the attendant refused, Robinson told him: "Take the hose out of the tank. If we can't go to the rest room, we won't get gas here." Startled, the attendant replied: "Well, you boys can go to the rest room, but don't stay long."

Rickey met secretly with Robinson in the fall of 1945. Talent was not an issue. Robinson was hitting .385 for the Monarchs and stealing bases by the bunch. What most concerned Rickey was Robinson's temper. How would he react to racial slurs, to pitches thrown at his head, to runners sliding into him spikes first? For 3 hours, Rickey grilled Robinson about the need for absolute self-control. "Do you want a ballplayer who's

AP/Wide World Photos

Jackie Robinson, who broke Major League baseball's color line in 1947, led the Brooklyn Dodgers to six pennants and a World Series victory in his brilliant career.

afraid to fight back?" Robinson asked. "I want a ballplayer with enough guts *not* to fight back," Rickey answered. "You will symbolize a crucial cause. One incident, just one incident, can set it back twenty years." "Mr. Rickey," Robinson replied, "if you want to take this gamble, I will promise you there will be no incident."

Robinson kept his word, enduring segregated hotels, racial insults, even death threats against his family. His pioneering effort caught the public's fancy, and huge crowds followed him everywhere. Chicago, Cincinnati, Philadelphia, Pittsburgh, St. Louis—all set attendance records when Robinson appeared, with black fans leading the way. As one writer put it, "Jackie's nimble/ Jackie's quick. Jackie's making the turnstiles click." By season's end, Robinson had led the Dodgers to the National League pennant and won "Rookie of the Year."

The struggle was far from over. It would be another decade before all Major League teams accepted integration. Yet the efforts begun by Branch Rickey and **Jackie**

DOING HISTORY ONLINE

Jackie Robinson and the Negro Leagues, 1948

Read the documents in this module. How does the document on The Decline of the Negro Leagues, 1948 relate to the others in this unit?

History⊠Now™   Visit HistoryNOW to access primary sources and exercises related to this topic: http://now.ilrn.com/ayers_etal3e

Robinson helped change the face of America by democratizing its "National Game." Looking back on the events of 1947, sportswriter Jimmy Cannon recalled a side of Robinson that captured both his courage and his pain. He was, said Cannon, "the loneliest man I have ever seen in sports."

Man of the People

As the 1948 presidential election approached, Harry Truman seemed a beaten man. His relations with Congress were stormy and unproductive, especially in domestic affairs. The press, remembering the elegant and fatherly FDR, portrayed Truman as too small for the job. Likely supporters deserted him in droves. In December 1947, a band of left-wing Democrats formed the Progressive Citizens of America, with an eye toward the coming election. Their leader was Henry Wallace, the former vice president and secretary of commerce, who had been fired by Truman for criticizing the administration's firm stance toward the Soviet Union. Wallace opposed both the Truman Doctrine and the Marshall Plan. Though he had no hope of winning the presidential election in 1948, his Progressive party seemed likely to split the Democratic vote.

Some urged Truman not to run. A number of Democratic leaders suggested other presidential candidates, including General Dwight D. Eisenhower. *The New Republic,* a favorite of liberals, ran the front cover headline: "HARRY TRUMAN SHOULD QUIT." The Democrats convened in Philadelphia, where the heat was oppressive and tempers grew short. When word reached the convention that Eisenhower was unavailable, "Boss" Frank Hague of Jersey City threw down his cigar. "Truman," he mumbled. "Harry Truman, oh my God!"

Left with no alternative, the delegates nominated Truman for president and Alben Barkley, the popular but aging Senate majority leader from Kentucky, for vice president. Barkley had strong ties to the South. Yet even he could not prevent the convention from dividing along sectional lines when northern liberals, led by Mayor Hubert Humphrey of Minneapolis, demanded the endorsement of Truman's civil rights initiatives. "The time has arrived," said Humphrey, "for the Democratic party to get out of the shadow of states' rights, and walk forthrightly into the bright sunshine of human rights."

The passage of a strong civil rights plank led many southern Democrats to walk out of the convention. Two days later, waving Confederate flags and denouncing Harry Truman, they formed the States' Rights (Dixiecrat) party at a gathering in Birmingham, Alabama. The Dixiecrats chose governors Strom Thurmond of South

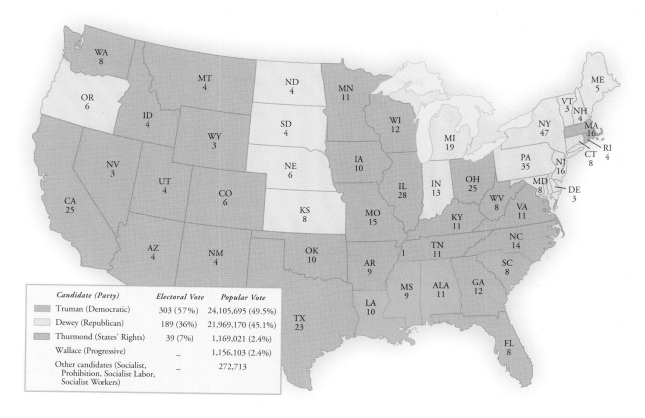

MAP 27.1 The Election of 1948

The presidential election of 1948 is considered one of the greatest upsets in American political history. Because there were four significant candidates, two running on third-party tickets, the victor, President Truman, captured a majority of the electoral votes without actually winning a majority of the popular vote.

Carolina and Fielding Wright of Mississippi to be their presidential and vice presidential candidates. Their platform demanded "complete segregation of the races."

Divided into three camps, the Democratic party appeared hopelessly overmatched. Not only did President Truman face Henry Wallace on his left and Strom Thurmond on his right, but the national Republican ticket of New York Governor Thomas E. Dewey for president and California Governor Earl Warren for vice president was the strongest in years. Truman's campaign strategy was to portray himself as a common people's president, protecting the voters and their hard-earned New Deal benefits from a heartless Republican assault. To highlight these differences, he called a special session of Congress to demand passage of an eight-point program that included civil rights, public housing, federal aid to education, a higher minimum wage, and storage facilities for farmers. When the Republican Congress refused to act, calling Truman's move a "publicity stunt," the president lambasted the Republicans as selfish politicians, interested only in the rich.

Truman also used his presidential power in significant ways. He showed support for the new state of Israel by offering it political recognition and economic assistance. He issued his promised executive order desegregating the armed forces. And he forcefully confronted Stalin in a showdown over Germany and Berlin.

In June 1948, Russian troops blockaded West Berlin to protest the merging of the French, British, and American occupation zones into the unified nation of West Germany. The city lay deep inside Soviet-controlled territory. With all roads and rail lines through East Germany now closed to allied traffic, its future seemed bleak. Truman ruled out force to break the blockade because American troops were greatly outnumbered. Instead, he and his advisors decided to supply West Berlin from the air. In the coming months, Western pilots made close to 300,000 flights into the city, delivering food, fuel, and medical supplies. By the time the Russians called off their blockade, Berlin, the former Nazi capital, had become the symbol of resistance to communist oppression.

Truman could see his fortunes rising as the 1948 campaign progressed. Crisscrossing the nation by train, he drew huge, friendly crowds at each whistle stop. To shouts of "Give 'em hell, Harry!" he ripped into the

After Soviet troops blockaded the roads and rail lines leading into West Berlin in 1948, American and British pilots led a massive effort to keep the isolated city supplied from the air.

"do-nothing" Republican Congress and their "plans" to dismantle Franklin Roosevelt's work. "The Republican politicians don't like the New Deal. They want to get rid of it," Truman repeated. "This is a crusade of the people against the special interests, and if you back me up we're going to win."

The experts didn't think so. Opinion polls showed Dewey with a substantial lead. On election eve, the staunchly Republican Chicago *Tribune* carried the now-famous mistaken headline: "Dewey Defeats Truman."

A beaming Harry Truman holds up the mistaken *Chicago Daily Tribune* headline following his upset victory over Republican candidate Thomas Dewey in the 1948 presidential election.

In fact, Truman won the closest presidential contest since 1916, collecting 24.1 million votes to Dewey's 22 million, and 303 electoral votes to Dewey's 189. Strom Thurmond captured 1.1 million votes and four southern states under the Dixiecrat banner, and Henry Wallace won no states and barely a million votes. Ironically, the three-way Democratic split appeared to help Truman by allowing him to speak out forcefully against Soviet expansion and to aggressively court African American voters in the pivotal northern industrial states. In the end, the people chose Truman's frank, common appeal over Dewey's stiff, evasive demeanor. The New Deal coalition had held for another election.

Trouble in Asia

Truman had little time to savor his victory. In the summer of 1949, an American spy plane returned from a flight over the Soviet Union with photographs revealing strong traces of radioactive material. The conclusion was obvious: Russia had exploded an atomic device. Combined with alarming new developments in Asia, the loss of America's atomic monopoly served to heighten global tensions in the coming months while dramatically increasing the fear of communism at home.

The Fall of China

President Truman broke the news in a one-sentence statement to the press: "We have evidence an atomic explosion occurred in the USSR." Domestic reaction was severe. Ever since Hiroshima, Americans had been taught to depend on nuclear superiority in the Cold War and to believe that Russia, a supposedly backward nation, could not possibly develop an atomic bomb before the mid-1950s, if ever. That could mean only one thing: espionage. The Soviets, it appeared, had stolen the biggest secret of all.

The news from China was equally grim. Following World War II, Chiang Kai-shek and his Nationalist (Kuomintang) forces had renewed their offensive against the communist forces of Mao Tse-tung. Chiang counted heavily on American support. He believed that his fight against communism, his powerful friends in Congress, and his image as China's savior would force the Truman administration to back him at all costs.

Chiang was mistaken. The president and his advisors were far less interested in Asia than they were in Western Europe. They were not about to be trapped into an open-ended commitment in the Far East. From 1946 to 1949, the United States gave Chiang's government about $2 billion in military aid—enough, it was hoped, to satisfy Chiang's American friends without seriously affecting the more important buildup in Europe.

As civil war raged in China, Chiang's forces met defeat after defeat. Much of the American weaponry was discarded by fleeing Nationalist troops; it would end up in communist hands. In August 1949, the State Department issued a 1,054-page "White Paper on China," conceding that the world's largest country was about to fall to the communists. "The unfortunate but inescapable fact," said Dean Acheson, the new secretary of state, "is that the ominous result of the civil war in China was beyond [our] control." Though Acheson was correct, his White Paper sounded more like an excuse than an explanation. Americans were angered and bewildered by Chiang's demise. How well did "containment" really work, many wondered, when more than 600 million people were "lost" to communism?

Determined to prevent further communist expansion elsewhere, the United States joined with 11 West European nations to create the North Atlantic Treaty Organization (NATO) in 1949. The treaty was extremely significant; in promising to support fellow NATO members in the event of Soviet attack, it formally ended America's long tradition of avoiding entangling alliances abroad. A year later, Secretary of State Acheson and Paul Nitze, his deputy, produced a secret document known as National Security Council Paper 68, which advocated the use of military force to stop communist aggression throughout the world. According to NSC 68, the United States should act in concert with other nations wherever possible, but alone if need be. The document called for an unprecedented peacetime increase in military spending—from $13 billion to $50 billion per year—and for the construction of a huge new "thermonuclear device," the hydrogen bomb. Though Truman never showed this document to Congress, it became, in Acheson's words, "the fundamental paper" governing America's defense policy in the coming years.

War in Korea

On June 25, 1950, troops from Communist North Korea invaded anti-Communist South Korea with infantry, armor, and artillery in a massive land assault. Korea had been arbitrarily divided by Russian and American troops at the end of World War II. In 1948, an election to unify Korea had been cancelled when the Soviets refused to allow U.N. observers north of the dividing line at the 38th parallel. A stalemate thus developed, with Kim Il Sung, the pro-Communist dictator of North Korea, and Syngman Rhee, the anti-Communist dictator of South Korea, making daily threats to "liberate" each other's land.

The North Korean attack put great pressure on President Truman. His administration had treated the Rhee government with indifference, removing American combat troops from Korea in 1949 and implying that Korea itself was not vital to the free world's security. Yet here was a classic case of aggression, Truman believed. To ignore it was to encourage it elsewhere—and to turn away from NSC 68.

There were political considerations, too. If the president did nothing, he would only reinforce the Republican charge that his administration was "soft" on communism. Thus, Truman moved quickly, proposing a U.N. resolution that offered "such assistance to South Korea as may be necessary to repel armed attack." (The Russians, boycotting the Security Council to protest the U.N.'s refusal to seat Communist China, were unable to cast a paralyzing veto.) A week later, without consulting Congress, Truman dispatched ground troops to South Korea.

Public opinion seemed favorable. Letters and telegrams of support poured into the White House, and the news from the front kept improving. After 2 months of backward movement, U.N. troops under the command of General Douglas MacArthur took the offensive. In September 1950, MacArthur outflanked the enemy with a brilliant amphibious landing at Inchon, on South Korea's west coast. By October, U.N. troops had crossed the 38th parallel in pursuit of the routed

General Douglas MacArthur and President Harry Truman meet to discuss Korean War strategy at Wake Island shortly before Communist China entered the conflict.

© Bettmann/CORBIS

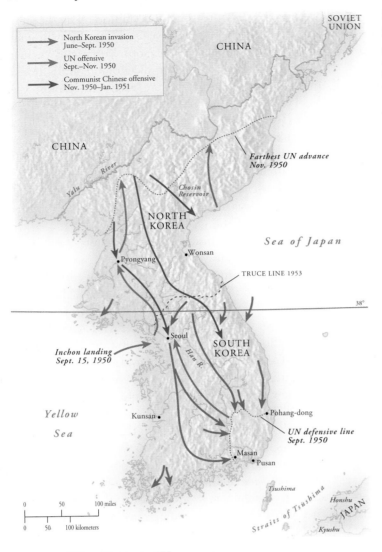

MAP 27.2 The Korean War

This map shows the main offensive thrusts: the North Korean attack into South Korea in June 1950; the Inchon Landing of September 15, 1950; the U.N. offensive in the fall of 1950; and the Communist Chinese counteroffensive beginning in November of 1950. The war ended in stalemate, with the final truce line almost identical to the previous division of Korea into North and South at the 38th parallel.

North Korean army. As the public listened in amazement, MacArthur spoke of having his men "home before Christmas."

There were ominous signs, however. First, by sending troops into North Korea, President Truman and the United Nations had gone beyond their original mandate to defend South Korea from outside aggression. Second, General MacArthur appeared oblivious to the possibility that Communist China might enter the war. As U.N. forces drove north, they captured scores of Chinese Communist troops near the Yalu River that divided North Korea and Manchuria. On November 5, the Chinese attacked—300,000 strong—pushing MacArthur's startled army back toward the 38th parallel. In the

following weeks, American army and marine units fought their way through mountain blizzards and a wall of Chinese infantry to form a defense line just south of the 38th parallel. Although disaster had been averted, the nation was shocked by what *Time* magazine described as "the worst military setback the United States has ever suffered."

By March 1951, the Communist offensive had stalled. U.N. forces pushed ahead to the 38th parallel, where the two sides faced each other in a bloody standoff. Not surprisingly, General MacArthur called for an escalation of the war. Killing Chinese soldiers was not enough, he argued, for replacements could always be found. MacArthur recommended a naval blockade of China's coast, massive bombing of its factories and power plants, and an invasion of the Chinese mainland by the forces of Chiang Kai-shek.

This plea for an expanded war was understandable. MacArthur, like most Americans, believed in the concept of total victory. His message, quite simply, was that the lands surrendered to the Communists by weak-kneed civilians like Truman and Acheson could be recaptured through the full exercise of American military power.

The president saw things differently. Any attempt to widen the war, he realized, would alarm other U.N. participants and perhaps bring Russia into the conflict. The Soviets might send troops to the Asian front or put pressure on Western Europe. Furthermore, Russia's involvement raised the threat of nuclear attack. As General Omar Bradley noted, MacArthur's strategy was the very opposite of the one proposed by President Truman and the Joint Chiefs of Staff. "So long as we regard the Soviet Union as the main antagonist and Western Europe as the main prize," he said, "it would involve us in the wrong war, at the wrong place, at the wrong time, and with the wrong enemy."

Despite repeated warnings from the president, MacArthur refused to keep his views to himself. The final blowup came in April 1951, when Republicans in Congress released a letter that MacArthur had sent them from the battlefield that criticized Truman's refusal to meet force "with maximum counterforce," and ended with the oft-quoted phrase: "There is no substitute for victory." Furious at such insubordination, the president relieved MacArthur of his command.

MacArthur returned to the United States a genuine folk hero, a man who symbolized old military values in a world complicated by the horrors of nuclear war. Cities across the nation burned President Truman in effigy. Letters to the White House ran 21 to 1 against

MacArthur's firing. On Capitol Hill, angry representatives placed some of the telegrams they received into the *Congressional Record:* "Impeach the Imbecile" and "We Wish to Protest the Latest Outrage by the Pig in the White House." Harry Truman's old standard—"If you can't stand the heat, stay out of the kitchen"—had never been more strenuously tested.

McCarthyism and the Election of 1952

On a bleak February evening in 1950, a little-known politician delivered a speech about "communist subversion" in the federal government to a Republican women's club in Wheeling, West Virginia. The topic was a common one, and large portions of the speech had been lifted word for word from a recent address by Congressman Richard Nixon. Only one explosive sentence had been added. "I have here in my hand," Senator **Joseph R. McCarthy** of Wisconsin told his audience, "a list of 205 Communists that were made known to the secretary of state and who are still working and shaping the policy of the State Department." The message was clear: America, the strongest nation on earth, was losing the Cold War to the evil forces of communism because the U.S. government was filled with "dupes" and "traitors" like Alger Hiss who *wanted* the communists to win.

The Rise of Joe McCarthy

Wisconsin's junior senator was an erratic politician, known for his reckless ambition and raucous behavior. He held no list in his hand that night in Wheeling. He knew nothing about communists in government or anywhere else. But the newspapers printed his charges, and the public was aroused. McCarthy had struck a nerve in the country, rubbed raw by Soviet aggression in Europe, the Communist victory in China, the Alger Hiss case, and the news of the Russian atomic bomb. As Americans searched for explanations, McCarthy provided the simplest answer of all. The real enemy was not in Moscow, he thundered, but rather in Washington, D.C.

McCarthy's charges of treason in high places made him an instant celebrity. His face adorned the covers of *Newsweek* and *Time*. The *Washington Post* cartoonist Herblock coined a new word to describe his reckless behavior: "McCarthyism." But prominent Republicans, sensing the political benefits of the "communist issue," rallied to his side. Senator Robert Taft of Ohio, known as "Mr. Republican," privately dismissed McCarthy's charges as "nonsense." Yet he told McCarthy to keep punching—"if one case doesn't work, try another."

The Blacklist

As the Cold War heated up in the late 1940s, a number of powerful sources in and out of government charged that Communists and their sympathizers were polluting the nation's entertainment industry—radio, television, and movies—with subversive propaganda.

Fearful of an angry public reaction, industry leaders agreed to check the political backgrounds of their employees. This, in turn, led to the blacklisting of

dozens of entertainers, who were denied work for allegedly supporting the Communist cause. The most influential blacklist of this era, *Red Channels* (pictured), demonstrates the "guilt by association" technique often used by Red-hunters of this era, who made accusations against people based on their connection, however fleeting, with groups deemed "communist" or "un-American." Compiled by three former FBI agents, *Red Channels* included the names of conductor Leonard Bernstein, composer Aaron Copeland, actress Lena Horne, and more than 100 others. Much of the information was erroneous. In the late 1950s, a Texas broadcaster named John Henry Faulk exposed the sordid nature of *Red Channels* by successfully suing its publisher for libel. The final blow came in 1960, when a major Hollywood studio hired the blacklisted writer Dalton Trumbo to do the screenplay for the hit movie *Spartacus* under his own name. "The blacklist was a time of evil," Trumbo observed. "None of us—right, left, center—emerged from that long nightmare without sin."

DOING HISTORY

Senator Smith Confronts Senator McCarthy

ON FEBRUARY 9, 1950, an obscure Republican senator from Wisconsin named Joseph R. McCarthy gave one of the most famous—and inflammatory—speeches in modern American political history. In it, he charged that the Truman administration was riddled with traitors who had helped to deliver much of the world to the Communist enemy. The speech turned McCarthy into a national celebrity, seen by millions as a truthful patriot, and by millions as a dangerous fraud.

"The reason why we find ourselves in a position of impotency is not because [the] enemy has sent men to invade our shores . . . but rather because of those . . . who have had all the benefits that the wealthiest nation on earth has to offer—the finest homes, the finest college education, and the finest jobs in government we can give.

Margaret Chase Smith of Maine, the Senate's only woman, became the first Republican to speak out against Senator Joseph McCarthy's controversial crusade against domestic subversion.

This is glaringly true in the State Department. There the bright young men who were born with silver spoons in their mouths are the ones who have been the worst. . . . While I cannot take the time to name [them], I have in my hand 205 cases of individuals who would appear to be either card carrying members or certainly loyal to the Communist Party, but who nevertheless are still helping to shape our foreign policy.

One thing to remember in discussing the Communists in our government is that we are not dealing with spies who get thirty pieces of silver to steal the blueprints of a new weapon. We are dealing with a far more sinister type of activity because it permits the enemy to guide and shape our policy."

His speech caused a furor in the U.S. Senate, which began an immediate investigation of his charges. For months afterward, McCarthy's Republican colleagues either supported McCarthy or remained silent. But on June 1, 1950, Senator Margaret Chase Smith of Maine, the Senate's lone woman, spoke out against McCarthy without actually mentioning him by name. She called her speech a "Declaration of Conscience."

"I speak as a Republican. I speak as a woman. I speak as a United States Senator. I speak as an American.

The United States Senate has long enjoyed worldwide respect as the greatest deliberative body in the world. But recently that deliberative character has too often been debased to the level of a forum of hate and character assassination sheltered by the shield of congressional immunity. . . .

I think it is high time for the United States Senate and its members to do some soul-searching—for us to weigh our consciences—on the manner in which we are performing our duty to the people of America—on the manner in which we are using or abusing our individual powers and privileges. . . .

Those of us who shout the loudest about Americanism in making character assassinations are all to frequently those who, by our own words and acts, ignore some of the basic principles of Americanism:
The right to criticize;
The right to hold unpopular beliefs;
The right to protest;
The right of independent thought. . . .

The American people are sick and tired of being afraid to speak their minds lest they be politically smeared as 'Communists' or 'Fascists' by their opponents. Freedom of speech is not what it used to be in America. It has been so abused by some that it is not exercised by others."

Source: Congressional Record, February 12, 1950; June 1, 1950.

Questions for Reflection

1. What recent events were responsible for Senator McCarthy's rise from obscurity?

2. What made McCarthy's charges seem believable to so many Americans?

3. Why would Senator Smith call her speech a "Declaration of Conscience?" What point was she trying to make?

Explore additional primary sources related to this chapter on the Wadsworth American History Resource Center or HistoryNOW websites:

http://history.wadsworth.com/rc/us
http://now.ilrn.com/ayers_etal3e

President Truman viewed McCarthy as a shameless publicity hound who would say anything to make headlines. He was right about the senator yet helpless to stop him. The fear of communism kept growing, aided by the outbreak of war in Korea. Air raid drills, including simulated bombings of American cities, became the order of the day. In school practice drills, students were taught to dive under their desks and shield their eyes against atomic blasts. In New York City, school officials distributed metal "dog tags." "If a bomb gets me in the street," a first-grader explained, "people will know what my name is." In Washington, a typical real estate ad read: "Small farm—out beyond the atomic blasts." Mayor Mike DiSalle of Toledo, Ohio, tried to calm worried residents by joking that he would build large neon signs directing communist pilots to Cleveland and Detroit.

McCarthy's attacks grew bolder. As the 1952 presidential campaign approached, he called George C. Marshall a traitor, mocked Dean Acheson as the "Red Dean of fashion," and described President Truman as a drunkard, adding, "the son-of-a-bitch ought to be impeached." Yet party colleagues continued to encourage McCarthy, viewing him as the man who could turn public anxiety and distrust into Republican votes.

"I Like Ike"

By 1952, Harry Truman's public approval rating had dropped to 23 percent—the lowest ever recorded by an American president. *The New Republic* called Truman "a spent force politically" and urged him to withdraw from the coming presidential campaign. In March, Truman did just that. "I shall not be a candidate for reelection," he declared.

Truman did not sulk on the sidelines, however. As the leader of his party, he wanted the Democratic nominee to defend the New Deal–Fair Deal philosophy with the same energy and enthusiasm that he himself had shown in 1948. The most impressive candidate, Governor Adlai Stevenson of Illinois, had earned a reputation as a liberal

reformer. Eloquent and witty, he appealed both to party regulars and to the liberal intelligentsia, much like FDR had. Stevenson had his handicaps, including a recent divorce and a past friendship with Alger Hiss. The Democrats nominated him for president on the third convention ballot. Senator John Sparkman of Alabama, a Fair Dealer and a segregationist, was given the vice presidential nod.

The battle for the Republican presidential nomination was in many ways a battle for control of the Republican party. The moderate wing, represented by Governor Thomas Dewey of New York and Senator Henry Cabot Lodge, Jr., of Massachusetts, was committed to internationalism and to many New Deal reforms. The conservative wing, led by Senator Robert Taft of Ohio, was suspicious of the New Deal and wary of America's expanding global commitments, especially the defense and reconstruction of Europe. Beyond these views was a yearning for the past, for the pre-Depression days when government was smaller, cheaper, and less intrusive.

Senator Taft, the son of former President and Chief Justice William Howard Taft, had earned the respect of his colleagues and the plaudits of Washington reporters, who voted him "best senator" in 1949. On many domestic issues, such as public housing, Taft was more flexible than his conservative supporters. Yet he, too,

DOING HISTORY ONLINE

Undercover in the Communist Party, 1951

Read the article in this module along with the section on McCarthyism in the textbook. Why did the Communist party target the steel industry, as Mary Markward said it did in her congressional testimony?

History ⊠ Now™   Visit HistoryNOW to access primary sources and exercises related to this topic: http://now.ilrn.com/ayers_etal3e

Civil Defense in the Atomic World

Though Americans had practiced civil defense during World War II, the movement gained new momentum following reports that the Soviet Union had successfully tested an atomic bomb. In 1951, at the height of the Korean War, President Truman created the Federal Civil Defense Administration, which used most of its budget to educate the public about the best ways to survive a nuclear attack. The list ranged from the building of private bomb shelters to the scheduling of air raid drills in which city dwellers were herded into designated areas—mainly basements and subway tunnels—where food, water, and medical supplies

© Bettmann/CORBIS

were stockpiled. The photograph here shows one of the civil defense drills, with students ducking under their desks and shielding their eyes from an atomic blast. Later in the 1950s, with the development of the more powerful hydrogen bomb, the Eisenhower administration promoted a different version of civil defense relying on the mass evacuation of populated areas. The policy, said one critic, had changed from "Duck and Cover" to "Run Like Hell." Never popular with most Americans, who viewed such measures as a futile response to the threat of nuclear annihilation, civil defense all but disappeared with the signing of the Limited Nuclear Test Ban Treaty in 1963.

feared that a powerful commitment to Western Europe could lead the United States into another world war.

Only one man stood between Taft and the Republican nomination. But he was a very powerful opponent. In 1948, the leaders of both major political parties had begged him, unsuccessfully, to enter their presidential primaries. "I don't believe a man should try to pass his historical peak," said General Dwight D. Eisenhower. "I think I pretty well hit mine when I accepted the German surrender in 1945."

Yet his moderate Republican supporters, believing that Eisenhower alone could defeat Taft for the presidential nomination, convinced the general that people wanted him, the country needed him, duty called once again.

Eisenhower, 61, was raised in Abilene, Kansas, a prairie town west of Topeka. He attended schools with no lights or plumbing and earned his diploma while working the night shift in a dairy. In 1911, the young man—nicknamed Ike—won an appointment to the U.S. Military Academy at West Point. After graduating near the middle of his class, Eisenhower married Mamie Dowd, the daughter of a Denver businessman, and began his swift climb through the ranks. In the 1930s, he served as chief aide to General Douglas MacArthur, recalling: "Oh, yes, I studied dramatics under him for seven years." In 1941, he moved to the War Department and helped plan the D-Day invasion of France. His work was so outstanding that President Roosevelt named him Commanding General, European Theater of Operations—a promotion that jumped him over hundreds of officers with greater seniority.

It turned out to be one of the best decisions of World War II. Eisenhower commanded history's most successful coalition force—American, British, French, Polish, and Canadian troops—with courage, diplomacy, and skill. He was brilliant at handling people and reconciling the most diverse points of view. In the following years, Eisenhower served as Army Chief of Staff, president of Columbia University, and commander of NATO forces.

The Republican convention nominated Eisenhower on the first ballot. Most delegates did not believe he would make a better president than Taft, simply a better candidate. Eisenhower defused the bitter feelings of conservatives by selecting Richard Nixon to be his running mate and by accepting a party platform that accused the Democrats of lining their pockets, shielding traitors in high places, and bungling the Korean War. As the campaign began, Republican leaders summed up their strategy with a simple formula: K1, C2—Korea, Communism, and Corruption.

On the campaign trail, General Eisenhower talked about leadership and morality, while Senator Nixon attacked from below. Traveling by train on the "Look Ahead Neighbor Special," Eisenhower visited more than 200 cities and towns. At every stop, he introduced Mamie, praised America, bemoaned the "mess in Washington," and promised to clean it up. Then the whistle sounded and the train pulled away to the chants of "I Like Ike."

On September 28, 1952, the *New York Post,* a pro-Democratic newspaper, broke the biggest story of the campaign: "Secret Rich Men's Fund Keeps Nixon in Style Far Beyond His Salary." The Nixon fund of $18,000, donated by a group of California supporters, had never been a secret; it had been used for routine political

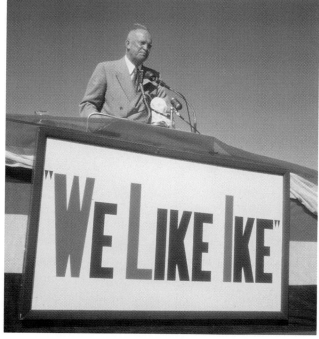

America liked Ike—who won a smashing victory at the polls in 1952, ending 20 years of Democratic party rule.

expenses; and it was similar to those of other politicians. Nixon responded by blaming the "Reds" for his troubles. "The communists, the left-wingers, have been fighting me with every smear," he declared. "They did it yesterday. They tried to say I had taken the money."

The campaign ground to a halt. Aboard the Eisenhower train, anxious advisors suggested that Nixon resign from the ticket. How could the general campaign against Democratic party corruption, they wondered, when his own running mate stood accused of taking secret gifts? On September 23, Nixon went on national television to explain his side of the story. To an audience estimated at 55 million, he spoke about his boyhood, his family, his war record, his finances, and his admiration for General Eisenhower. He explained how the fund worked, asked the American people to support him, and then described the one gift he would never return. It was, said Nixon, "a little cocker spaniel dog and our little girl named it Checkers. And you know the kids love that dog and I just want to say that we're going to keep it."

The reaction was volcanic. More than 2 million phone calls and telegrams poured into Republican offices across the country. They were followed by millions of letters, running 300 to 1 in Nixon's favor. Eisenhower had no choice but to keep his running mate on the ticket. The "Checkers Speech" saved Nixon's career.

It also demonstrated the emerging power of television in national affairs. In the campaign's final weeks, the Republican party ran dozens of 20-second TV spots for Eisenhower, who used the ads to soothe voter anxiety about his views on popular New Deal welfare programs. "Social security, housing, workmen's compensation, unemployment insurance—these are things that must be kept above politics and campaigns," he said. "They are rights, not issues." The general also vowed that if elected, he would visit Korea "to help serve the American people in the cause of peace."

Stevenson tried to ridicule the announcement. "If elected," he replied, "I shall go to the White House." But few Americans were amused. On November 4, Eisenhower overwhelmed Stevenson—33.9 million votes to 27.3 million, and 442 electoral votes to 89. Eisenhower became the first Republican in decades to crack the solid South, winning four states and coming close in several others. He did well in cities, where ethnic voters, concerned about the rise of communism in Europe, deserted the Democrats in droves. Nearly 25 percent of Eisenhower's total came from men and women who had supported Harry Truman in 1948.

Some observers spoke of a new Republican era, but this was not the case. Almost everywhere, Eisenhower ran well ahead of his ticket. Although the Republicans managed to gain a slim majority in Congress, they did so by riding the general's coattails to victory.

Conclusion

Even before World War II ended, American planners, confident of victory, could sense the troubles that lay ahead. They saw big problems looming in foreign affairs, from the threat of Soviet expansion to the reconstruction of Western Europe. And they worried about the impact of peace on the nation's wartime economic boom. What would happen when defense spending dropped and factory jobs disappeared? Was it possible that the United States might slip back into the nightmare of the 1930s, when millions were hungry and unemployed?

The economic worries proved groundless. The war had created a near full-employment economy, leaving Americans with a great pile of disposable income—and a powerful urge to spend. Congress, meanwhile, passed the Servicemen's Readjustment Act (or GI Bill), designed to help returning soldiers as well as to bolster the economy by encouraging veterans to go to college and buy a new home. The economy took off, fueled by a baby boom, a rush to suburbia, and an explosion of consumer goods. The postwar years were the most prosperous in U.S. history.

Things did not go as smoothly in foreign affairs. The reconstruction of Japan and Western Europe proved remarkably successful. At the same time, however, relations with the Soviet Union began a downward spiral, as the two remaining superpowers entered into a Cold War punctuated by military threats and a growing arms race. One foreign policy crisis followed another: the Iron

Curtain descending over Eastern Europe, the Berlin Blockade, the fall of mainland China to communism, and the North Korean invasion of South Korea. By 1950 the threat of international communism seemed as ominous to the American people as the threat of Nazism had been a decade before.

Life in the postwar United States was marked by a combination of affluence and anxiety. Following two decades of depression and war, most Americans were finally enjoying the benefits of economic security, material comfort, and stable family lives. They wanted a leader who would steer a moderate course in domestic and foreign affairs; a leader who would heal old wounds and moderate angry passions without turning back the clock; a leader who would end the present conflict in Korea without widening it or compromising the nation's honor. In 1952, Dwight D. Eisenhower seemed to be the one.

The Chapter in Review

In the years between 1946 and 1952:

- The United States moved from a wartime to a peacetime economy.
- Returning veterans received generous education and housing benefits under the GI Bill.
- A tremendous surge in marriage and birth rates spurred a rush to suburbia.
- Soviet–American relations deteriorated as an Iron Curtain descended over Eastern Europe.
- A symbolic step toward racial justice occurred with the integration of Major League Baseball in 1947.

- The Alger Hiss case heightened fears of Soviet espionage in the United States.
- Harry Truman's surprise reelection in 1948 kept the New Deal coalition intact.
- The Korean War raised fears of a widening conflict with Communist China and a nuclear confrontation with the Soviet Union.
- Dwight Eisenhower's victory in 1952 ended two decades of Democratic control of the executive branch.

Making Connections Across Chapters

LOOKING BACK

Chapter 27 looks at the United States in the post–World War II years, following one of the defining moments in its history. Key points include the baby boom, the growth of suburbia, and the beginning of the Cold War.

1. What accounted for the worsening of relations between the Soviet Union and the United States?

2. Why did the wartime prosperity continue, and greatly increase, following World War II? What factors accounted for this?

3. Why did Harry Truman defeat Thomas Dewey for the presidency in 1948? Why did so many pundits think Dewey would win?

4. What impact did the case of Alger Hiss have on the rise of Senator Joseph R. McCarthy? What else was responsible for the popular support that McCarthy received?

LOOKING AHEAD

Chapter 28 examines the United States in the 1950s, a time of continued economic prosperity and material comfort, on the one hand, and a time of enduring Cold War tensions and momentous racial stirrings, on the other.

1. What were the major problems Dwight Eisenhower would face in assuming the presidency?

2. Was it possible that a new administration in Washington would be better able to deal with international problems than the old one, especially problems relating to the Cold War?

3. Would the prosperity of the early postwar era last into the future, and would it expand to include the poorest groups in society?

Recommended Readings

Ackerman, Marsha. *Cool Comfort* (2002). Well describes how air-conditioning changed the way middle-class Americans lived and worked in this new age of affluence.

Bennett, Michael. *When Dreams Came True* (1996). Studies the impact of the GI Bill on the making of modern America.

Boyer, Paul. *By the Bomb's Early Light* (1985). Considers the impact of atomic weaponry on American society in the early Cold War years.

Grossman, Andrew. *Neither Dead Nor Red* (2001). Focuses on the often bizarre plans of American officials to fight and survive a nuclear war.

Hamby, Alonso. *Man of the People* (1995). Examines the personal life and political career of President Harry Truman.

Jackson, Kenneth. *Crabgrass Frontier* (1985). Analyzes the suburbanization of America, especially after World War II.

Jones, James. *Alfred Kinsey: A Public/Private Life* (1997). The biography of the nation's leading sex researcher and his impact on American culture.

Spock, Dr. Benjamin. *Common Sense Book of Baby and Child Care* (1946). Had a lasting impact on child rearing and gender roles in the United States.

Tanenhaus, Sam. *Whittaker Chambers* (1997). Tells the absorbing story of the man who helped ignite the nation's anti-Communist crusade in the late 1940s.

Tygiel, Jules. *Baseball's Great Experiment* (1983). A fine account of Jackie Robinson and the integration of Major League Baseball.

Identifications

Review your understanding of the following key terms, people, events, and dates for this chapter (these terms also appear in the Glossary at the end of the book):

baby boom
Levittown
Iron Curtain
General George C. Marshall

Truman Doctrine
Marshall Plan
House Un-American Activities Committee (HUAC)
Alger Hiss
Jackie Robinson
Joseph R. McCarthy

Online Sources Guide

Use this listing to find online documents, images, interactive maps, simulations, and other resources related to this chapter:

American History Resource Center

http://history.wadsworth.com/rc/us

Documents

George Orwell, newspaper column on negotiations in the United Nations (1946)
George F. Kennan, "Long Telegram"
Excerpts from NSC-68
The Truman Doctrine
Lillian Hellman defies HUAC
Joseph McCarthy, speech warning of Communist threat
Excerpts from Harry Truman's "Message to Congress," September 6, 1946

Selected Images

Harry Truman addressing Congress after Roosevelt's death
Mushroom cloud from atomic bomb covering Bikini Atoll

Medics remove a wounded soldier during the Korean War
American troops guarding demilitarized zone between North and South Korea
Jackie Robinson

Simulations

The Cold War (In this historical simulation you can choose to be an African American or a suburbanite and make choices based on the circumstances and opportunities afforded.)

Document Exercises

1946 Winston Churchill's "Iron Curtain" Speech

HistoryNOW

http://now.ilrn.com/ayers_etal3e

Primary Source Exercises

The Six Thousand Houses That Levitt Built, 1948
Jackie Robinson and the Negro Leagues, 1948
Undercover in the Communist Party, 1951

28 The Eisenhower Years, 1953–1960

An American street scene at mid-twentieth century, with a mother, a father, and children in the new suburbia.

The United States at the middle of the twentieth century was far different from the nation we live in today. The **Cold War** was at its height, U.S. soldiers were dying in Korea, and communism seemed a formidable foe. The American population of 153 million contained a small and declining number of foreign born, the result of strict immigration quotas installed in the 1920s. Most blacks still lived in the South, where racial segregation was the law. Blue-collar workers outnumbered white-collar workers, and labor unions, led by charismatic figures like John L. Lewis and Walter Reuther, were at the height of their power. Major League baseball had only 16 teams, none west of St. Louis. There were no supermarkets or shopping malls, no motel chains or ballpoint pens. Television was just beginning, rock music still a few years away. More than half of the nation's farm dwellings had no electricity. It cost three cents to mail a letter and a nickel to buy a Coke.

Marriage rates were at an all-time high, and divorce rates kept declining. In 1954, *McCall's* magazine used the term "togetherness" to describe American family life, with shared activities such as Little League, car rides, and backyard barbecues. Though more women worked outside the home in 1950 than in 1944, the height of

World War II, they did so mainly to supplement the family income, not to seek full-time careers. In the growing cult of motherhood, fulfillment meant meeting the needs of others. Feminism was described in psychology books as a "deep illness," entirely out of place.

America at mid-twentieth century saw an acceleration of postwar trends. As 40 million people moved to the suburbs, the large cities declined in population, political power, and quality of life. Racial lines remained rigid, with census data showing the suburbs to be more affluent than the cities they surrounded—and 98 percent white. Automobile sales skyrocketed, creating whole new industries to service the American traveler. Inventions poured forth, from the computer to the polio vaccine. And a new president was elected to guide the country through these anxious, demanding times.

A New Direction

Dwight Eisenhower entered the White House in 1953 on a wave of good feeling. His lack of political experience appeared to be an asset after the turmoil of the Truman years. Americans trusted Eisenhower's judgment

Timeline

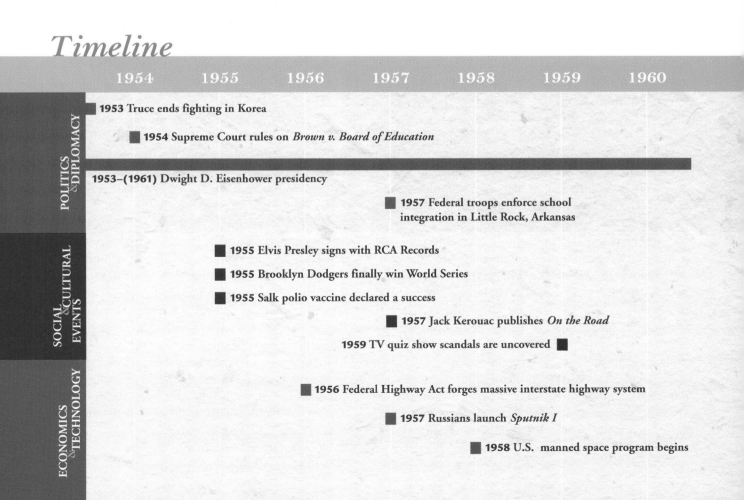

	1954	1955	1956	1957	1958	1959	1960

POLITICS & DIPLOMACY

1953 Truce ends fighting in Korea

1954 Supreme Court rules on *Brown v. Board of Education*

1953–(1961) Dwight D. Eisenhower presidency

1957 Federal troops enforce school integration in Little Rock, Arkansas

SOCIAL & CULTURAL EVENTS

1955 Elvis Presley signs with RCA Records

1955 Brooklyn Dodgers finally win World Series

1955 Salk polio vaccine declared a success

1957 Jack Kerouac publishes *On the Road*

1959 TV quiz show scandals are uncovered

ECONOMICS & TECHNOLOGY

1956 Federal Highway Act forges massive interstate highway system

1957 Russians launch *Sputnik I*

1958 U.S. manned space program begins

Urban, Suburban, and Rural Americans 1940–1960

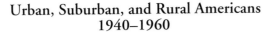

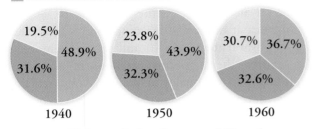

■ Central-city dwellers

□ Suburban dwellers

■ Rural and small-town dwellers

CHART 28.1 Urban, Suburban, and Rural Americans, 1940–1960

These charts point to a number of important changes. First is the steady loss of population in small-town America. Second is the stagnation of the inner cities, reflecting both a loss of population in the older northern and midwestern cities and a growth in the sun belt cities of the South and West. Third is the surge of population in the suburbs, which continues to this day.

and admired his character. They believed that his enormous skills as a military leader would serve him equally well as president of the United States.

Modern Republicanism

Yet few Americans knew where Eisenhower stood on important domestic or international issues. His presidential campaign in 1952 had been intentionally vague. On the political spectrum, he stood somewhere between the Fair Deal Democrats of Harry Truman and the conservative Republicans of Robert Taft. The new president described himself as a moderate, using the term "modern Republicanism" to define his political approach.

Eisenhower filled his cabinet with prominent business leaders. For secretary of defense, he chose Charles E. ("Engine Charlie") Wilson, former president of General Motors, who proclaimed at his confirmation hearing that "what was good for our country was good for General Motors, and vice versa." For secretary of the treasury, Eisenhower selected George Humphrey, a fiscal conservative. "We have to cut one-third out of the budget and you can't do that just by eliminating waste," Humphrey declared. "This means, whenever necessary, using a meat axe."

Eisenhower avoided such rhetoric. He had no intention of dismantling popular New Deal programs such as Social Security or unemployment insurance, and he supported a significant hike in the minimum hourly wage, from 75 cents to a dollar. Yet wherever possible, he

worked to balance the budget, trim government expenditures, and stimulate private enterprise. "I'm conservative when it comes to money," Eisenhower claimed, but "liberal when it comes to human beings."

In his first year as president, federal spending and federal income taxes were both cut by 10 percent. Eisenhower also opposed expansion of such popular but expensive federal programs as price supports for farmers and cheap public power from government dams and electric plants. In perhaps his most controversial early move, the president strongly supported passage of the Tidelands Oil Act, which transferred coastal oil land worth at least $40 billion from the federal government to the states. Critics, fearing the exploitation of these vital reserves by a few giant corporations, described "Tidelands" as the "most unjustified giveaway program" of the modern era.

A Truce in Korea

One member of Eisenhower's cabinet, Secretary of State John Foster Dulles, stood above the rest. The son of a minister and grandson of a former secretary of state, Dulles trained from his earliest days to serve God and country. Most observers found him arrogant, stubborn, and sour. Yet Eisenhower respected his secretary as a tough, knowledgeable advisor who willingly took the heat for actions the president himself had formulated. "I know what they say about Foster—dull, duller, Dulles—and all that," Eisenhower told a friend. "But the [critics] love to hit him rather than me."

The president's first priority in foreign affairs was to end the Korean conflict. Though willing to accept the same terms that Truman had proposed—two Koreas, North and South, divided at the 38th parallel—Eisenhower demanded a prompt resolution. To speed this process, Dulles apparently warned the Communist Chinese (through diplomatic channels in India) that the United States would not rule out the use of atomic weapons if the Korean stalemate dragged on.

The impact of this "nuclear threat" is difficult to gauge. The Chinese Communists probably viewed Eisenhower, a military leader, as a more dangerous foe than Harry Truman. Yet huge Communist battlefield losses, coupled with the sudden death of Joseph Stalin, helped spur the peace process. In July 1953, a truce was signed that stopped the fighting without formally ending the war. More than 50,000 Americans were killed and 103,000 were wounded in Korea. The Pentagon estimated that 2.4 million civilians died or were seriously injured in the 3 years of terrible fighting, along with 850,000 troops from South Korea, 520,000 from North Korea, and 950,000 from Communist China.

The Cold War at Home and Abroad

When Republicans took control of Congress and the White House in 1953, the "communist issue" gained center stage. On Capitol Hill, 185 of the 221 House Republicans applied for duty on the House Un-American Activities Committee, where Chairman Harold Velde of Illinois vowed to hunt down communists like "rats." At the White House, President Eisenhower promised both a crackdown on "subversives" in government and a "New Look" in military affairs, designed to streamline American forces for the continuing struggle against "worldwide communist aggression."

The Hunt for "Subversives"

Shortly after taking office, President Eisenhower issued an executive order that extended the scope of the Federal Loyalty Security Program. A few months later, he announced that 1,456 federal workers had been fired as "security risks," including "alcoholics," "homosexuals," and "political subversives." The most controversial security case involved J. Robert Oppenheimer, the distinguished physicist who directed the Manhattan Project during World War II. Oppenheimer's prewar association with left-wing radicals was widely known. He had been checked and rechecked by the FBI, cleared and recleared by the Atomic Energy Commission until 1953, when the Eisenhower administration suspended his top security clearance. Many believed that Oppenheimer's troubles resulted from his public opposition to the building of the hydrogen bomb—a charge the administration vigorously denied.

In Congress, the Red-hunting fervor was even more intense. The Senate assault was led by Joseph McCarthy, newly appointed chairman of the Committee on Government Operations and its powerful Subcommittee on Investigations. Filling key staff positions with ex-FBI agents and former prosecutors like Roy M. Cohn, an abrasive young attorney from New York, McCarthy looked for "communist influence" in the State Department and other government agencies. His hearings didn't uncover any communists. They did, however, ruin numerous careers, undermine worker morale, and make the United States look fearful in the eyes of the world. Not surprisingly, Republican criticism of McCarthy began to build. After all, he was now attacking a federal bureaucracy controlled by his own party.

Many expected Eisenhower to put the senator in his place. But the new president was slow to respond, believing that a brawl with McCarthy would divide Republicans into warring camps and seriously demean

Culver Pictures

Picturing the Past — POLITICS & DIPLOMACY

Searching for "Reds" in Government

The search for communists in government became one of the key political issues of the early Cold War era. This cartoon gives the impression that communists were rampant in the federal bureaucracy in the 1950s and that Uncle Sam was adept at the tough but vital job of weeding them out. Was this perception correct? Recent evidence—gleaned from newly opened Soviet security archives and a supersecret American

code-breaking project known as Venona—suggests that communist espionage in government was indeed a serious problem during the late 1930s and World War II and that among those Americans who spied for the Soviet Union was Alger Hiss (pages 793–794). The new evidence, however, does not support the sensational charges of Senator Joseph R. McCarthy and others that hundreds of communists were still at work in the federal government in the 1950s. Indeed, it appears that such penetration declined dramatically after World War II, due, in large part, to the defections of key communist espionage agents in the United States. In 1953—the time of this cartoon—the Eisenhower administration announced that 1,456 federal employees had been fired under the Federal Loyalty Program. It turned out, however, that the vast majority were released for offenses such as alcoholism, malingering, and "sexual misconduct." Almost none was dismissed for reasons pertaining to disloyalty.

Senator Joseph McCarthy, America's premier Red-hunter, lectured army counsel Joseph Welch (hand on head) about the Communist party during the celebrated Army–McCarthy hearings in 1954.

the presidential office. Time and again, he told his aides: "I just will not—I *refuse* to get into the gutter with that guy."

Eisenhower changed his mind after McCarthy's subcommittee, spearheaded by Roy Cohn, began to investigate charges that a "communist spy ring" was operating at Fort Monmouth, New Jersey, home of the Army Signal Corps. Army officials responded that Cohn was harassing the service in order to win preferential treatment for a close friend and part-time McCarthy staffer named G. David Schine, who had recently been drafted into the army. Early in 1954, the Senate agreed to investigate these conflicting allegations. Furious at the attacks upon his beloved army, Eisenhower convinced Republican Senate leaders to televise the hearings. The president wanted the American people to see McCarthy in action, and it proved to be a very shrewd move. For 36 days, the nation watched the senator's frightening outbursts and crude personal attacks. The highlight of the hearings came on June 9, 1954, when army counsel Joseph Welch sternly rebuked McCarthy for his menacing behavior, asking: "Have you no sense of decency, sir? Have you left *no sense of decency?*" The spectators burst into applause.

A few months later, the Senate censured McCarthy for bringing that body "into dishonor and disrepute." The vote was 67 to 22, with only conservative Republicans opposed. Many believed that McCarthy's censure was linked to the easing of Cold War tensions at home. The Korean War was over, Stalin was dead, and the radical right was in disarray. For McCarthy, things came apart at a wicked rate of speed. Reporters and colleagues ignored him, and his influence disappeared. Unable to get his message across, McCarthy spent his final days drinking in private and railing against those who had deserted his cause. He died of acute alcoholism in 1957, virtually alone, at the age of 48.

Brinksmanship and Covert Action

Like Truman before him, President Eisenhower supported the containment of communism through military, economic, and diplomatic means. What most worried him were the spiraling costs. "If we let defense spending run wild," he said, "we get inflation . . . then controls . . . then a garrison state . . . and *then* we've lost the very values we were trying to defend." Eisenhower called his solution the "New Look." It was fruitless to match the communists "man for man, gun for gun," he reasoned. The Korean stalemate showed the folly of that approach. In place of conventional forces, the United States must emphasize "the deterrent of massive retaliatory power." This meant using America's edge in nuclear weapons and long-range bombers to best advantage.

The New Look allowed Eisenhower to cut defense spending by 20 percent between 1953 and 1955. The number of men and women in uniform went down each year, and the production of atomic warheads dramatically increased. Secretary of State Dulles viewed the New Look as a way to intimidate potential enemies with the implied threat of atomic attack. He called this "brinksmanship," claiming that "the ability to get to the verge without getting into the war is the necessary art."

Critics, however, saw brinksmanship as a dangerous game. Intimidation meant little, they warned, if the United States did not intend to back up its words. Was Eisenhower willing to consider atomic weapons as a viable option in every international crisis? If not, he undermined America's credibility; if so, he risked nuclear destruction. To increase his flexibility in foreign affairs, the president needed other options as well.

In 1953, Eisenhower appointed Allen Dulles, younger brother of the secretary of state, to head the Central Intelligence Agency (CIA). Dulles emphasized "covert action" over intelligence gathering—a change the president fully endorsed. Most of the CIA's new work was cloaked in secrecy, and much of it was illegal. Covert action became one of Eisenhower's favorite foreign policy tools.

Iran was a case in point. In 1953, the new government of Mohammed Mossadegh nationalized the British-controlled oil fields and deposed the pro-Western Shah of Iran. The United States, believing Mossadegh's government to be pro-communist, feared for its oil supplies in the Middle East. President Eisenhower thus approved a CIA operation that toppled Mossadegh and returned the young Shah to power. A few months later,

Iran agreed to split its oil production among three Western nations, with American companies getting 40 percent, British companies 40 percent, and Dutch companies 20 percent. The grateful Shah told the CIA: "I owe my throne to God, my people, my army, and to you."

In 1954, the CIA struck again, forcing the overthrow of Guatemala's democratically elected president, Jacobo Arbenz. Guatemala was one of the world's poorest nations. Its largest employer and landholder, the American-owned United Fruit Company, controlled much of the Guatemalan economy. After taking office, Arbenz supported a strike of banana workers on United Fruit plantations, who were seeking wages of $1.50 a day. Far more provocative, however, was a new law, known as Decree 900, which expropriated millions of acres of private property for the use of landless peasant families. Under this law, the Arbenz government offered United Fruit $1.2 million for 234,000 acres of its land—a figure based on the absurdly low tax assessments given United Fruit in the past.

The company had powerful allies in the United States. Numerous government officials, including both Dulles brothers, were linked to United Fruit through their previous corporate positions. Defending the company's interests came naturally to them, and the idea of expropriating American property smacked of "communist thinking." If Arbenz succeeded, they reasoned, the notion could spread across Latin America like wildfire.

Eisenhower moved quickly, authorizing the overthrow of Arbenz by Guatemalan exiles trained at CIA bases in Honduras and Nicaragua. The small invasion force, backed by CIA pilots, tore through Arbenz's poorly equipped army. The American press, meanwhile, accepted the Eisenhower–Dulles account that Guatemalan liberators had ousted a dangerous, pro-communist regime with minimal American help. In the following months, the new government of General Carlos Castillo Armas established a military dictatorship, executed hundreds of Arbenz supporters, and returned the expropriated lands to United Fruit.

Events in Indochina (or Vietnam) did not turn out as well for the American interests. Following World War II, nationalist forces in that French colony, led by **Ho Chi Minh,** a popular Marxist leader, began an armed struggle for independence. The United States, viewing Ho (incorrectly) as a puppet of Moscow, supported French attempts to crush the Vietnamese resistance, known as the Vietminh. By 1953, American military aid to France in the Indochina conflict totaled nearly $3 billion.

It failed to turn the tide. The Vietminh grew stronger. In 1954, Ho's forces surrounded 12,000 elite French troops at an isolated garrison called Dien Bien Phu. Facing sure defeat, the French appealed to the United States for help. When Secretary of State Dulles, Vice President Nixon, and several U.S. military officials suggested tactical nuclear weapons, Eisenhower was appalled. "You boys must be crazy," he said. "We can't use those awful things against Asians for the second time in ten years. My God!"

Eisenhower also refused to send American ground troops to Indochina. And he rejected the use of conventional air strikes to save Dien Bien Phu unless the British took part—but Churchill sternly said no. On May 7, 1954, the battered garrison surrendered, effectively ending French rule in Vietnam.

At peace talks in Geneva, Switzerland, the two sides agreed to a cease-fire and a temporary partition of Vietnam at the 17th parallel, with French troops moving south of that line and Vietminh forces moving north. Free elections were scheduled for 1956, at which time the French were to fully withdraw. The United States refused to recognize the Geneva Accords. Eisenhower and Dulles were not about to acquiesce to a unified Vietnam under the leadership of Ho Chi Minh, the certain winner in the proposed election of 1956. The U.S. plan, therefore, was to prevent that election, while creating a permanent anti-communist government in South Vietnam supported by American economic and military aid.

To Eisenhower, the survival of South Vietnam became the key to containing communism in Asia. He described the so-called "**domino theory**" at a press conference about Indochina in 1954. "You have a row of dominoes set up," he began. "You knock over the first one, and what will happen to the last one is a certainty that it will go over quickly. So the possible consequences of the loss [of Vietnam] are just incalculable to the free world."

The Civil Rights Movement

The 1950s witnessed enormous gains in the struggle for minority rights. In federal courts and in cities throughout the South, African Americans struggled to eradicate the system of racial segregation that denied them dignity, opportunity, and equal protection under the law. Though the Eisenhower administration proved far less sympathetic to the cause of civil rights than the Truman administration had been, the movement for racial justice took on a power and a spirit that would transform the nation in the coming years.

Brown v. Board of Education

In September 1953, Chief Justice Fred Vinson died of a heart attack, requiring President Eisenhower to make his

Flashpoints | The Murder of Emmett Till

The photographs were gruesome. In August 1955, the brutally beaten and decomposed corpse of a 14-year-old African-American male from Chicago was found floating in the Tallahatchie River, deep in the Mississippi Delta, with a heavy fan attached to the neck. The teenager had been visiting relatives that summer when

The brutal murder of black teenager Emmett Till in Mississippi in 1955 shocked the nation's conscience and helped energize the growing civil rights movement.

he entered a grocery store in the tiny hamlet of Money, Mississippi, and encountered the clerk, a young white woman named Carolyn Bryant. What happened next—whether he squeezed the white woman's hand,

grabbed her waist, asked her for a date, wolf-whistled at her, or did none or all of these things—will never be known. Witnesses offered markedly different versions of what they claimed to have seen. But as word of the incident filtered though the community, it was clear that a serious racial line had been crossed by this unsuspecting "Chicago boy," and that a heavy price would be paid.

The teenager's name was Emmett Till. His body was sent back to Chicago, where his mother demanded that the pine casket be kept open so "the world can see what they did to my boy." Thousands passed through the funeral home to pay their respects. In Mississippi, meanwhile, Carolyn Bryant's husband and his half-brother were arrested, charged, and put on trial for murder. The high point came when Till's uncle, Moses Wright, a 64-year-old sharecropper, courageously pointed out the two whites as the men who had come to his shack and taken Emmett away. Nevertheless, 12 white jurors found the defendants not guilty after deliberating for just over an hour. It would have gone even quicker, said one, if they hadn't stopped to drink Coca-Cola.

The verdict caused outrage in most parts of the country—more so because the defendants, knowing they could not be retried for the same crime, quickly admitted to the murder. For many young blacks in the South, the Till case became the spark that ignited their interest in civil rights. As John Lewis, a leader of the Freedom Rides of the1960s and a future U.S. congressman, recalled: "I was fifteen, black, on the edge of my own manhood just like him. He could have been me. *That* could have been me, beaten, tortured, dead at the bottom of a river."

In 2004, the federal government reopened the Till case amid charges that more than a dozen people may have been involved in the abduction and murder, and that several are still alive. For a 14-year-old boy from Chicago, there may be justice after all.

Questions for Reflection

1. What are some other civil rights landmarks from this era, and how did they combine to fuel the protests for equal rights in the South?

2. Do you think the fact that Emmett Till came from the North had an impact on the amount of press coverage given to his murder and the subsequent trial?

3. Do you believe it is important to reopen the Till case 50 years after his murder?

AP/Wide World Photos

first appointment to the U.S. Supreme Court. Eisenhower offered the position to California Governor Earl Warren, who won prompt Senate approval. Warren had been the Republican party's vice presidential nominee in 1948. Far more liberal than Eisenhower on social issues, he would sometimes anger the president in the coming years, but rarely lose his respect.

The major issue facing the Supreme Court in 1953 was civil rights. For more than a decade, a group of talented African American attorneys had been filing legal challenges to segregated public facilities in the South, hoping to erode the "separate but equal" doctrine of *Plessy v. Ferguson.* Led by Thurgood Marshall and William Hastie of the NAACP's Legal Defense Fund, these attorneys targeted specific areas, such as professional education (law, medicine, teaching), to establish precedents for the larger fight.

This strategy worked well. In 1950, the Supreme Court stretched the *Plessy* doctrine to its limits in two lawsuits brought by the NAACP. In *Sweatt v. Painter,* the Court ruled that Texas authorities must admit a black applicant to the all-white state law school in Austin because they had failed to provide African Americans with a comparable facility, thereby violating the equal protection clause of the Fourteenth Amendment. And in *McLaurin v. Oklahoma,* the Court struck down a scheme that segregated a black student *within* that state's graduate

school of education, forcing him to sit alone in the library and the lecture halls in a section marked "Reserved for Coloreds." "State-imposed restrictions which produce such inequalities," the Court noted, "cannot be sustained."

With these victories, the NAACP took on the larger challenge of racial segregation in the nation's public schools. Unlike *Sweatt* and *McLaurin,* which involved a small number of adult students, the new cases touched millions of children, white and black, in 21 states and the District of Columbia. By 1953, five separate lawsuits had reached the Supreme Court, including *Brown v. Board of Education of Topeka.*

The case involved a Kansas law that permitted cities to segregate their public schools. With NAACP support, the Reverend Oliver Brown sued the Topeka school board, arguing that his 8-year-old daughter should not be forced to attend a Negro school a mile from her home when there was a white public school only three blocks away. The Supreme Court was badly divided. Several justices supported the *Plessy* doctrine; others argued that it fostered racial inequality. Believing racial segregation to be both unconstitutional and morally wrong, Chief Justice Warren insisted that the Supreme Court speak in a powerful, united voice against this evil. Anything less, he reasoned, would encourage massive resistance in the South.

On May 17, 1954, the Supreme Court overturned *Plessy v. Ferguson* in a stunning 9–0 decision, written by

Attorneys representing the NAACP's Legal Defense Fund, led by Thurgood Marshall (center), celebrate *Brown v. Board of Education* on the steps of the Supreme Court, May 17, 1954.

© Bettmann/CORBIS

Jim Crow was a way of life in the South, where theaters, restaurants, trains, buses, blood banks, hospitals, drinking fountains, waiting rooms, and cemeteries were all segregated by law.

© Bern Keating/Black Star

DOING HISTORY

The Long Reach of *Brown*

ONE OF THE great spurs to the civil rights movement following World War II was the unanimous U.S. Supreme Court opinion in Brown v. Board of Education, *written by Chief Justice Earl Warren, which overturned the "separate but equal" doctrine set down 58 years before in* Plessy v. Ferguson. *Racial segregation in the nation's public schools was unconstitutional, the Warren Court ruled, and "any language . . . contrary to this finding is rejected." The opinion stated:*

"Today, education is perhaps the most important function of state and local governments . . . It is required in the performance of our most basic public responsibilities, even service in the armed forces. It is the very foundation of good citizenship . . . In these days, it is doubtful that any child may reasonably be expected to succeed in life if he is denied the opportunity of an education . . . .

We come then to the question presented: Does segregation of children in public schools, solely on the basis of race . . . deprive the children of the minority group of equal educational opportunities? We believe that it does . . . .

Segregation of white and colored children in public schools has a detrimental effect upon the colored children. The impact is greater when it has the sanction of the law; for the policy of separating the races is usually interpreted as denoting the inferiority of the negro group. A sense of inferiority affects the motivation of a child to learn. Segregation with the sanction of law, therefore, has a tendency to [retard] the educational and mental development of Negro children and to deprive them of some of the benefits they would receive in a racial[ly] integrated school system. . . .

We conclude that in the field of public education the doctrine of 'separate but equal' has no place. Separate educational facilities are inherently unequal . . . ."

The Brown *decision caused a furor in much of the South. Many whites vowed to resist it, including Alabama Governor George C. Wallace, who promised to "stand in the schoolhouse door" rather than permit two black students to enter the then all-white University of Alabama. Like other white Southern officials, Wallace phrased his objections to* Brown *in constitutional terms—as a judicial threat to local self-government and the will of the people. He said:*

"The unwelcomed, unwanted, unwarranted and force-induced intrusion upon the campus of the University of Alabama today . . . offers a frightful example of oppression . . . by officers of the Federal Government. . . . Only the Congress makes the law of the United States [and] there has been no legislative action by Congress justifying this intrusion.

When the Constitution of the United States was enacted, a Government was formed upon the premise that people, as individuals, are endowed with the rights of life, liberty, and property, and with the right of local self-government. . . . There can be no submission to the theory that the Central Government is anything but a servant of the people. We are God-fearing people—not Government-fearing people. We practice today the free heritage bequeathed to us by the founding fathers.

I stand here today, as Governor of this sovereign state, and refuse to willingly submit to illegal usurpation of power by the Central Government. I claim today for all the people of the state of Alabama those rights reserved to them under the Constitution of the United States. Among those powers so reserved and claimed is the right of state authority in the operation of public schools, colleges, and universities."

Source: Brown v. Board of Education, *349 U.S. 294, 1954;* New York Times, *June 12, 1963.*

Questions for Reflection

What sort of arguments were used in the *Brown* opinion regarding race and education that went beyond the more traditional interpretations of the Fourteenth Amendment's "equal protection" clause?

1. Why do you think the Supreme Court waited a full year before issuing guidelines for the implementation of the *Brown* decision?

2. Can you think of other instances in which public officials have accused the federal government, and especially the judicial branch, of exercising too much power while restricting local self-government?

Explore additional primary sources related to this chapter on the Wadsworth American History Resource Center or HistoryNOW websites:

http://history.wadsworth.com/rc/us
http://now.ilrn.com/ayers_etal3e

Warren himself. Relying on the studies of social scientists such as Kenneth Clark, the chief justice claimed that racial segregation had a "detrimental effect" on black children by making them feel inferior to whites. "In the field of public education the doctrine of 'separate but equal' has no place," he stated. "Separate educational facilities are inherently unequal."

The Supreme Court put off its implementation guidelines (known as *Brown II*) for a full year, hoping to let passions cool in the South. *Brown II* required local school boards to draw up desegregation plans with the approval of a federal district judge. But there were no timetables, and the wording was intentionally vague. Integration should proceed, it said, "with all deliberate speed."

White southern reaction was intense. "You are not required to obey any court which passes out such a ruling," Senator James O. Eastland of Mississippi told his constituents. "In fact, you are obligated to defy it." Violence flared across the South. "In one school district after another," wrote an observer, "segregationists staged the same drama: forcing young blacks to enter a school by passing rock-throwing white mobs and white pickets shouting 'Nigger,' 'Nigger,' 'Nigger.'" The Ku Klux Klan came alive in the 1950s, and new groups like the White Citizens' Council were formed to defend segregation and the "Southern way of life." In the summer of 1955, a black Chicago teenager named Emmett Till, visiting relatives in Mississippi, was murdered for allegedly flirting with a white woman at a country store. Two suspects—the woman's husband and his half-brother—were acquitted by an all-white jury in just over an hour. "If we hadn't stopped to drink pop," a juror noted, "it wouldn't have taken so long."

Many Americans looked to the White House for guidance about civil rights. But Eisenhower had little to say about the issue, partly because he personally opposed the "forced integration" of the races. When asked at a press conference if he had any advice for the South on how to handle the *Brown* decision, Eisenhower replied: "Not in the slightest. The Supreme Court has spoken and I am sworn to uphold the constitutional processes in this country; and I will obey."

The Montgomery Bus Boycott

The battle over public school integration was but one of many such struggles in the South during this era. Some were fought by attorneys in federal courtrooms; others involved ordinary men and women determined to challenge the indignities of racial segregation and second-class treatment in their daily lives. "Nothing is quite as humiliating, so murderously angering," said one African American, "as to know that because you are black you may have to walk a half mile farther than whites to urinate; that because you are black you have to receive your food through a window in the back of a restaurant or sit in a garbage-littered yard."

The black people of Montgomery, Alabama, had experienced such treatment for years. Known as "the cradle of the Confederacy," Montgomery enforced segregation and racial etiquette in meticulous detail. Blacks always tipped their hats to whites, always stood in the presence of whites unless told to sit, and always addressed whites with a title of respect. ("Boss," "Sir," and "Ma'am" were most common.) Restrooms, drinking fountains, blood banks, movie theaters, cemeteries—all were separated by race. It was illegal for whites and blacks to play checkers together on public property or to share a taxi cab. On the local buses, blacks paid their fares in the front, got off the vehicle, and entered the "colored section" through the rear door. They also had to relinquish their seats to white passengers when the front section filled up.

On December 1, 1955, a simple yet revolutionary act of resistance occurred on a crowded Montgomery bus. **Rosa Parks,** a 42-year-old black seamstress and member of the local NAACP, refused to give up her seat to a white. The bus driver called the police. "They got on the bus," Parks recalled, "and one of them asked me why I didn't stand up. I asked him, 'Why do you push us around?' He said, '. . . I don't know, but the law is the law and you're under arrest.'"

News of Parks's defiance electrified the black community. Within days a boycott of Montgomery's bus system was begun, organized by local clergymen and the Women's Political Council, the black alternative to the all-white League of Women Voters. Calling themselves the Montgomery Improvement Association (MIA), they

---

DOING HISTORY ONLINE

The Right of Interposition, 1955

Read the articles in this module and consider the following questions:

   If a state were to base its response to the *Brown* decision on the doctrine of interposition, what actions could it potentially take?

   How could the federal government respond to a state that used interposition as the basis for its opposition to the Supreme Court's decision?

History ⧖ Now™   Visit HistoryNOW to access primary sources and exercises related to this topic: http://now.ilrn.com/ayers_etal3e

© Bettmann/CORBIS

Rosa Parks rides a nearly empty but integrated Montgomery bus following the successful boycott she triggered in 1955.

chose a young minister named **Martin Luther King, Jr.,** to lead the struggle for open seating in public transportation, a small but highly symbolic step.

King, 26, was a newcomer to Montgomery. He was selected, in part, because his youth and vocation made him less vulnerable to economic and political pressure from whites. The son of a well-known Atlanta pastor, King earned his college degree at Morehouse and his doctorate at Boston University's School of Theology before heading south with his new wife, Coretta Scott King, to serve as pastor of Montgomery's Dexter Avenue Baptist Church in 1954. Dr. King was familiar with the works of Gandhi and Thoreau. He viewed mass action and nonviolent resistance as essential weapons in the war against racial injustice.

King rallied the black community with the eloquent passion of his words. "There comes a time when people get tired," he told a packed rally after Rosa Parks's arrest. "We are here this evening to say to those who have mistreated us so long that we are tired—tired of being segregated and humiliated, tired of being kicked about by the brutal feet of oppression. We have no alternative but to protest."

King's reputation soared. He kept the movement together despite police harassment and the firebombing of his home. Blacks in Montgomery formed car pools to get people to their destinations. The churches raised money for fuel, and black-owned garages did repair work free of charge. Many people rode bicycles or simply walked for miles. The boycott nearly bankrupted the city bus system and badly hurt the white merchants

downtown. Mother Pollard, bent with age, inspired the movement with her simple remark: "My feets is tired, but my soul is rested."

In November 1956, the federal courts struck down the Alabama law requiring racial segregation in public transportation. A month later, blacks sat in the front of the Montgomery buses without incident. The boycott, lasting 381 days, demonstrated both the power of collective action and the possibility of social change. In 1957, Dr. King joined with other black ministers to form the Southern Christian Leadership Conference (SCLC), an organization devoted to racial justice through peaceful means. "Noncooperation with evil," King declared, "is as much a moral obligation as is cooperation with good."

The Age of Television

In the 1950s, social commentators analyzed a host of new issues in American life. Some worried about the struggle between individuals and organizations, the apparent quest for security over adventure, the monotony of modern work. A few focused on the supposed emptiness of suburban living, the growing cult of domesticity among women, the changing standards of success. Yet what struck virtually all critics and commentators in the 1950s was the impact of television on American life—an impact that altered politics, news gathering, consumer tastes, and popular culture in truly revolutionary ways.

The Magic Box

When World War II ended, there were 17,000 TV sets in the United States. The late 1940s saw major changes in television technology, such as the use of coaxial cable and the introduction of color. In 1949, a TV set appeared for the first time in the Sears, Roebuck catalogue—$149.95 "with indoor antenna." A year later, Americans were buying 20,000 television sets a day. The two most popular shows of that era were Milton Berle's *Texaco Star Theater* and Ed Sullivan's *Toast of the Town*. Berle, a physical comedian, seemed perfect for a visual medium like TV. His fast-paced humor relied on sight gags instead of verbal banter. The press called him "Mr. Television."

Sullivan, a former gossip columnist, was awkward and unsmiling on camera. What made him unique was his ability to provide fresh entertainment to Americans of all tastes and ages. Sullivan's Sunday night variety show, mixing opera with acrobats, ran for 23 years on CBS. His guests included Elvis Presley, Dean Martin and Jerry Lewis, pianist Van Cliburn, dancer Rudolf Nureyev,

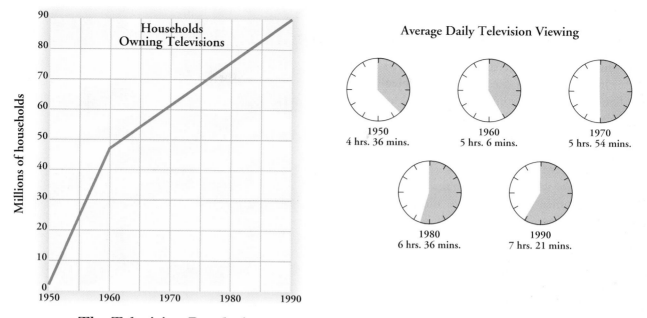

CHART 28.2 The Television Revolution, 1950–1990

As television became commonplace in the 1950s, TV viewing altered the nature of American politics and culture. Average daily television viewing has increased in each decade, with Americans now spending almost half their waking hours with their sets turned on.

Source: Statistical Abstracts of the United States

singer Lena Horne, and the Beatles. "Ed Sullivan will last," said pianist Oscar Levant, "as long as other people have talent."

Television's potential was impossible to ignore. In 1951, an obscure Tennessee politician named Estes Kefauver became a national figure by holding televised hearings into organized crime. Senator Kefauver grilled prominent mobsters like New York's Frank Costello as 25 million viewers watched in amazement. The TV cameras perfectly captured Costello's discomfort by focusing for several minutes on his jittery, sweat-soaked hands.

Nixon's "Checkers speech" and the Army–McCarthy hearings further highlighted the impact of television in the political arena. Above all, however, TV possessed the power to sell. In 1950, local stations, desperate for programming, aired a series of old "Hopalong Cassidy" movies starring an obscure cowboy-actor named William Boyd. Within months, "Hopalong Cassidy" clothing and six-guns were in frantic demand, grossing $30 million before the craze died out. Walt Disney struck gold with his three-part series on Davy Crockett, which aired nationally in 1954. Millions of children wore coonskin caps to school. There were Davy Crockett shirts and blankets, toothbrushes and lunch boxes. One department store chain sold 20,000 surplus pup tents in less than a week by printing "Davy Crockett" on the flap.

By 1954, three national networks were firmly in place. As the major radio powers, ABC, CBS, and NBC held a decided advantage over potential competitors in technology and talent. Indeed, these networks filled their early airtime by moving popular radio programs like *Jack Benny, Burns & Allen,* and *Amos 'n' Andy* over to TV. The faster television grew, the more its schedule expanded. Important advertisers signed on, sponsoring entire programs such as *Kraft Television Theater* and *Motorola Playhouse.* This, in turn, provided work for hundreds of performers at a time when the motion picture industry was losing ground to television. New York City, the early center of TV production, became a magnet for young actors and writers like Paul Newman, Sidney Poitier, Joanne Woodward, Rod Serling, Neil Simon, and Mel Brooks.

Some critics called this era the "golden age" of television. They pointed to the high quality of plays and dramas, the original comedy of Sid Caesar and Jackie Gleason, and the powerful documentaries of Edward R. Murrow on *See It Now.* Yet by 1955, this "golden age" was largely over. The networks abandoned most live broadcasts in favor of filmed episodes, with Hollywood quickly replacing Manhattan as television's capital. Popular new shows like *Dragnet* and *I Love Lucy* showed the advantages of film over live TV. Production was less demanding. Errors could be corrected, scenes could be shot at different locations, and episodes could be shown more than once, creating additional revenues.

Many television shows of the 1950s reflected both the yearnings and stereotypes of American society.

Popular comedies such as *Father Knows Best, Ozzie and Harriet,* and *Leave It to Beaver* portrayed the charmed lives (and minor problems) of middle-class white families in the suburbs. Mother was a housewife. Dad held a pressure-free white-collar job. The kids were well-adjusted and witty. Money was never a problem. No one stayed angry for long. "You know, Mom," said Beaver Cleaver, "when we're in a mess, you kind of make things seem not so messy." "Well," June Cleaver replied, "isn't that sort of what mothers are for?"

Married women in TV "sitcoms" did not work outside the home. Their husbands would not permit it. This rule even applied to childless couples like Ralph and Alice Kramden of *The Honeymooners,* one of television's rare programs about urban, working-class people. Furthermore, single women in sitcoms rarely took their jobs seriously. Like Eve Arden in *Our Miss Brooks* and Ann Sothern in *Private Secretary,* they spent most of their time hunting for a husband.

Though racial minorities almost never appeared in these sitcoms, they did play major—if stereotypical—roles in two or three popular shows of the 1950s. There was "Beulah," the big-hearted domestic in a white suburban household, and "Rochester," the wisecracking butler on the *Jack Benny Show.* Above all, there was *Amos 'n' Andy,* an adaptation of the popular radio show created by two white men, Freeman Gosden and Charles Correll, that featured an all-black cast. The NAACP angrily denounced *Amos 'n' Andy* for portraying blacks as "clowns" and "crooks," but others praised the performers for transforming racist stereotypes into "authentic black humor."

The Quiz Show Scandals

No event raised more concerns about the control and direction of commercial television in the 1950s than the quiz show scandals. Quiz shows were a throwback to the radio era; they appeared early on television but did not generate much interest until Revlon cosmetics produced a "big money" version called *The $64,000 Question,* which aired on CBS in June 1955.

The rules were simple. After choosing a topic, such as science or baseball, the contestant fielded questions that began at $64 and doubled with each correct answer. At the $16,000 plateau, the contestant entered a glass "isolation booth." The tension was enormous, since a wrong answer wiped out all previous winnings. The show drew the highest ratings in TV history—a whopping 85 percent audience share—when contestants went for the $64,000 question.

Contestants Charles Van Doren and Vivian Nearing battle it out on the rigged quiz show *Twenty-One.*

The show caused a windfall for Revlon. The company's products flew off the shelves. Annual sales rose from $34 million to $86 million, and Revlon stock jumped from $12 to $20 a share.

Before long, the airwaves were flooded with imitations. In 1956, *The $64,000 Question* lost its top rating to NBC's *Twenty-One,* which pitted two competitors in a trivia contest structured like the blackjack card game. The stakes grew ever larger. Charles Van Doren, a handsome English instructor at Columbia University, won $129,000 on *Twenty-One* and became an instant national hero.

His good fortune did not last long. A grand jury investigation revealed that numerous quiz show contestants had been given the questions in advance. It turned out that both *The $64,000 Question* and *Twenty-One* were rigged, with players coached about every detail of their performance. The contestants blamed the producers, who then implicated the sponsors. Van Doren admitted the painful truth after first protesting his innocence. "I was involved, deeply involved, in a deception," he said, adding, "I would give almost anything to reverse the course of my life."

The public was outraged. President Eisenhower condemned the "selfishness" and "greed" of the perpetrators. Yet there was nothing illegal about these shows. Indeed, some sponsors defended them as a form of *entertainment,* akin to professional wrestling or a ghostwritten book. As public anger mounted, however, Congress passed legislation to prevent the rigging of TV quiz shows, and the networks promised to regulate themselves. *The $64,000 Question, Twenty-One,* and other big money game shows quickly left the air.

The quality of television did not appear to improve. New programs became clones of each other—bland sitcoms or violent westerns and crime dramas. Advertising now consumed 20 percent of television airtime, with more money spent making commercials than producing the shows themselves. "The feeling of high purpose that lit the industry when it was young," wrote the *New York Times*, "is long gone." Yet television's power kept expanding. One study in the 1950s estimated that an American youngster spent 11,000 hours in the classroom through high school and 15,000 hours in front of the TV. Another concluded that adults spent more time watching television than working for pay. There were complaints that television tended to isolate people and to shorten their attention spans. Nobody needed to concentrate for more than a half hour—and not very hard at that.

As television expanded, other media outlets declined. Mass circulation magazines such as *Look* and *Collier's* folded in the 1950s, and newspaper readership went way down. Movie attendance dropped and radio lost listeners, forcing both industries to experiment in order to survive. Hollywood tried Cinemascope, Technicolor, 3-D glasses, drive-in movies, and big budget spectacles like *The Ten Commandments* and *Ben Hur*. Radio moved from soap operas and big band music to "hip" disc jockeys spinning rock 'n' roll. Nevertheless, television was now king. People watched the same programs in Boston and San Diego, in rural hamlets and in cities, in rich areas and in poor. America's popular culture, consumer needs, and general information—all came increasingly from TV.

Youth Culture

In the 1950s, a distinctive "teenage culture" emerged, rooted in the enormous prosperity and population growth that followed World War II. America's young people were far removed from the grim events of the previous two decades. Raised in relative affluence, surrounded by messages that undermined traditional values of thrift and self-denial, these new teenagers were perceived as a special group with a unique subculture. They rarely worked, yet their pockets were full. By 1956, the nation's "teenage market" topped $9 billion a year. The typical adolescent spent as much on entertainment as had the average family in 1941.

A New Kind of Music

Nothing defined these 13 million teenagers more clearly than the music they shared. In the 1940s, popular music was dominated by the "big bands" of Glenn Miller and Tommy Dorsey, the Broadway show tunes of Rodgers and Hammerstein, and the mellow voices of Bing Crosby, Frank Sinatra, and the Andrews Sisters. These artists appealed to a broad white audience of all ages. Other forms of popular music—blue-grass, country, rhythm-and-blues—were limited by region and race.

But not for long. The huge migration of rural blacks and whites to industrial centers during World War II profoundly altered popular culture. The sounds of "race" music, "hillbilly" music, and gospel became readily available to mainstream America for the first time. Record sales tripled during the 1950s, aided by technological advances like the transistor radio and the 45 rpm vinyl disc (or "single"). The main consumers were young people who acquired new tastes by flipping the radio dial.

In 1951, a Cleveland, Ohio, record dealer noticed that white teenagers at his store were "going crazy" over the songs of black rhythm-and-blues artists like Ivory Joe Hunter and Lloyd Price. He told a local disc jockey named **Alan Freed,** who decided to play these records on the air. Freed's new program, *The Moondog Party,* took Cleveland by storm. Soon Freed was hosting live shows at the local arena to overflow crowds. Pounding his fists to the rhythm, chanting "go man, go," Freed became the self-proclaimed father of rock 'n' roll.

"I'll never forget the first time I heard his show," a writer recalled. "I couldn't believe sounds like that were coming out of the radio." Freed understood the defiant, sensual nature of rock 'n' roll, the way it separated the young from everyone else. It was their music, played by their heroes, set to their special beat. Indeed, rock's first national hit, "Rock Around the Clock," by Bill Haley and the Comets, became the theme song for *Blackboard Jungle,* a movie about rebellious high school students set to the throbbing rhythms of rock 'n' roll.

The Rise of Elvis

Haley's success was fleeting. He didn't generate the intense excitement or sexual spark that teenagers craved. As Haley faded, a 21-year-old truck driver from Memphis exploded onto the popular music scene. His name was Elvis Presley; the year was 1955.

Born in rural Mississippi, Presley was surrounded by the sounds of country music, gospel, and blues. As a teenager in Memphis, he listened to WDIA—"the Mother Station of Negroes"—and frequented the legendary blues clubs along Beale Street. The music moved him deeply, providing both spiritual force and physical release.

Memphis was also home to Sun Records, a label with strong southern roots. Owned by Sam Phillips, Sun recorded white country singers like Johnny Cash and

Combining the sounds of black music and white music with enormous sexual charisma, Elvis Presley became the most successful recording star in history.

© Bettmann/CORBIS

black bluesmen such as B. B. King. What Phillips most wanted, however, was an artist who combined these two sounds instinctively, without appearing artificial or forced. "If I could find a white man who had the Negro sound and the Negro feel," Phillips said, "I could make a million dollars."

Presley was that man. Signing with Sun Records in 1954, he took the region by storm. The press described his unique style as "a cross between be-bop and country," and "a new hillbilly blues beat." It wasn't just the sound. Tall and handsome, with long sideburns and slicked-back hair, Presley was a riveting performer, combining little boy shyness with enormous sexual charisma. A fellow artist described young Presley on tour:

> This cat came out in red pants and a green coat and a pink shirt and socks, and he had this sneer on his face. And he stood behind the mike for five minutes, I'll bet, before he made a move. Then he hit his guitar a lick, and he broke two strings. I'd been playing ten years, and I hadn't broken a *total* of two strings. So there he was, these two strings dangling, and he hadn't done anything yet, and these high school girls were screaming and fainting and running up to the stage, and then he started to move his hips real slow like he had a thing for his guitar.

When Presley became too big to handle, Sun Records sold his contract to RCA for $35,000, a sizable amount at that time. Before long, he was a national sensation. His early hits topped the charts in popular music, country, and rhythm-and-blues—the first time that had ever occurred. In less than a year, Elvis recorded 8 number-one

songs and 6 of RCA's all-time top 25 records. When he appeared on *Ed Sullivan,* the cameras carefully shot him from the waist up. The ratings were extraordinary. "I want to say to Elvis and the country," Sullivan told his audience, "that this is a real decent, fine boy."

Young Elvis was modest and polite. He didn't smoke or drink or use drugs. He was so devoted to his parents that friends laughingly described him as a mama's boy. Yet his exaggerated sexuality on stage made him the target of those who believed that rock 'n' roll was a vulgar and dangerous assault on America's youth. "Popular music," wrote one television critic, "has reached its lowest depths in the grunt and groin antics of Mr. Presley."

Such criticism served only to enhance Presley's stature in the teenage world. And his success led the major record companies to experiment more aggressively with black rhythm-and-blues. At that time, white "cover artists" still were used to record toned-down versions of "race" music for white teenage audiences. In 1954, Big Joe Turner's legendary "Shake, Rattle, and Roll" did not make the popular charts, but Bill Haley's cover version became a number-one hit. Turner began:

> Well you wear low dresses
> The sun comes shinin' through
> I can't believe my eyes
> That all of this belongs to you.

Haley sang:

> You wear those dresses
> Your hair done up so nice
> You look so warm
> But your heart is cold as ice.

In 1956, rock music reached a milestone when **Little Richard**'s sensual recordings of "Long Tall Sally" and "Rip It Up" outsold the "sanitized" versions of Pat Boone, America's leading white cover artist.

There was more to rock 'n' roll, of course, than Elvis Presley and rhythm-and-blues. Teenagers adored the sweet sounds of the Everly Brothers, the lush harmony of the Platters, and the clean-cut innocence of Ricky Nelson. Furthermore, jazz and folksinging retained a healthy following, as did popular artists like Sinatra, Perry Como, and Nat "King" Cole. Nevertheless, the music that defined this era for most Americans, but for teenagers in particular, was hard-edged rock 'n' roll. It was the car radio blasting Presley's "Hound Dog," Chuck Berry's "Maybellene," and Little Richard's "Tutti Frutti" on a carefree Saturday night. *A wop bop a lu bop a lop bam boom!*

The Beat Generation

Whatever else might be said about Elvis Presley and other rock heroes, they loved the system that made them millionaires. Elvis spent lavishly. His first royalties were used to purchase three new homes and matching Cadillacs for his parents, though his mother didn't drive. Material rewards were the standard by which Presley, and countless others, measured their success.

The Beat movement was different. Composed of young writers and poets based mainly in San Francisco and New York, it blossomed in the mid-1950s as a reaction against mainstream standards and beliefs. The word "beat" described a feeling of emotional and physical exhaustion. The Beats despised politics, consumerism, and technology. They viewed American culture as meaningless, conformist, banal. Their leading poet, Allen Ginsberg, provided a bitter portrait of generational despair in *Howl* (1955).

The Beats linked happiness and creativity with absolute freedom. Their model was Dean Moriarty, the hero of Jack Kerouac's *On the Road,* an autobiographical novel about the cross-country adventures of Kerouac and his friends finding adventure and renewal (not to mention sex and drugs) beyond the confines of middle-class life. *On the Road* became both a national best-seller and a cult book on America's college campuses. In a sense, Kerouac and Presley had something important in common: both appealed to young people who seemed dissatisfied with the apparent blandness of American culture.

Crises and Celebration

In September 1955, President Eisenhower suffered a heart attack while vacationing in Colorado. The news raised obvious questions about his present and future course. At 65, Eisenhower was one of the oldest presidents in American history. How quickly would he recover, if at all? Who would guide the nation in his absence?

Eisenhower spent the next 4 months recovering in the hospital and at his Gettysburg farm. Fortunately, the fall of 1955 was a time of political tranquility, with Congress out of session, no bills to sign or veto, and no crises looming on the international scene. The president stayed in close contact with his advisors as he slowly regained his health. Returning to the White House early in 1956, he announced his plan to seek reelection. The public was vastly relieved. As columnist James Reston noted, Eisenhower was more than a president; he was "a national phenomenon, like baseball."

Conquering Polio

The president's full recovery was not the only positive "health news" of 1955. On a far larger front, a medical research team led by Dr. Jonas Salk, a virologist at the University of Pittsburgh, announced the successful testing of a vaccine to combat poliomyelitis, the most frightening public health problem of the postwar era. More than 50,000 polio cases were reported in 1954, mostly of children who took sick during the summer months. The disease produced flulike symptoms in most cases, but a more virulent form, which entered the central nervous system, led to paralysis and sometimes death. The cause of polio was uncertain; the virus seemed to be excreted in fecal matter and then passed through hand-to-hand contact. Not surprisingly, the epidemic produced a national panic. Cities closed swimming pools and beaches; families cancelled vacations, boiled their dishes, and avoided indoor crowds. Children were warned against jumping in puddles, drinking from water fountains, and making new friends.

The March of Dimes became America's favorite charity, raising millions to find a cure for polio and to finance the care of patients through therapy, leg braces, and iron

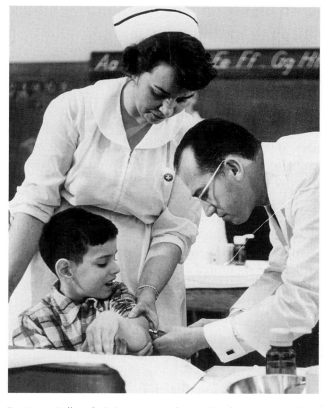

AP/Wide World Photos

Dr. Jonas Salk, administering a polio vaccine he developed in 1954, helped eradicate a disease that terrorized Americans in the postwar era.

Enduring Issues   The "Golden Age" of Medicine

By the start of the twentieth century, most Americans had come to accept the so-called "germ theory of disease." They understood that they shared their communities, their homes, even their bodies with an invisible, often dangerous, world of microorganisms. They knew from bitter experience that what you *don't* see can make you very sick.

Research in this era was moving at a dramatic pace. No problem now seemed beyond the scope of the laboratory. A series of remarkable breakthroughs occurred, beginning with German scientist Paul Ehrlich's 1910 discovery that an arsenic compound could wipe out syphilis, a highly contagious sexual disease. By 1920, the mass vaccination of American children with a successful antitoxin had all but ended the scourge of diphtheria, a deadly bacterial infection. The 1930s saw the coming of sulfa-based drugs as well as the discovery of the electron microscope, which allowed scientists to see the tiny microbes known as viruses and to study their impact on the structure of individual cells.

In 1941, two British scientists, Howard Florey and Ernst Boris Chain, refined Alexander's Fleming's previous discovery of penicillin by purifying the compound and then encouraging drug companies in the United

© Bettmann/CORBIS

States and Great Britain to mass-produce it for public use. Penicillin became the first true antibiotic, capable of destroying a wide range of bacteria without also poisoning the human body. Hailed as "the most glamorous drug ever invented," it treated everything from deadly pneumonia to the common sore throat, saving millions of lives.

lungs. Determined to provide immediate protection against the disease, Dr. Salk began testing a "dead" polio virus vaccine on schoolchildren in 1954. (His critics, led by Dr. Alfred Sabin, insisted that only a "live" polio vaccine would trigger the immunities needed to provide a lasting solution.) Aided by the March of Dimes and an army of volunteers, Salk tested the vaccine—and a placebo—on several million youngsters nationwide. "It was the largest peacetime mobilization of its kind," wrote one observer, "one in which the mothers of America rose up to save, in many cases, their own children."

The testing proved extremely successful. The federal government approved the polio vaccine in 1955, touching off emotional public celebrations. "People observed moments of silence, rang bells, honked horns, blew factory whistles, drank toasts, hugged children, attended church." Although the government did not provide the funds to vaccinate all school-age children immediately—in part because the American Medical Association objected to this "socialist" proposal—public opinion soon forced a more compassionate approach. In 1960, fewer than a thousand new polio cases were reported in the United States.

Interstate Highways

The nation's confidence soared even higher with passage of the Federal Highway Act of 1956, which authorized $25 billion in new taxes on cars, trucks, and gasoline for the construction of 40,000 miles of interstate roads over the next 10 years. The huge highway network, linking all cities with more than 50,000 people, allowed a driver to travel the continent uninterrupted, save stops for food and gas. Eisenhower viewed this project as both a convenience to motorists and a boost to the economy. The president also linked good highways to Cold War events, warning that cities must be evacuated quickly in the event of nuclear war.

The Highway Act spurred enormous economic growth. Improved roads meant higher oil revenues, soaring car sales, more business for truckers, and greater mobility for travelers. The so-called "highway trade" took off. Ray Krock opened his first McDonald's in 1955 in Des Plaines, Illinois, a suburb of Chicago. In Memphis, meanwhile, Kemmons Wilson unveiled the first Holiday Inn, featuring a restaurant, a swimming pool, and clean, air-conditioned rooms with free TV. Before long McDonald's golden arches and Holiday Inn's green neon

Though nothing could quite match the record of penicillin, there were other successes as well. In 1943, biologists at Rutgers University, led by Selman Waksman, produced a soil-based antibiotic known as streptomycin that proved successful in controlling tuberculosis, one of history's deadliest infections. By the 1950s, antibiotic remedies were being pursued at universities and commercial laboratories around the world. The U.S. government also became involved in these years, with dramatic funding increases for the National Institutes of Health (NIH). Between 1955 and 1960, the NIH budget swelled from $81 million to $400 million, much of it going to control the spread of infectious disease.

The most obvious effect of these medical advances was that people in many parts of the world were now living longer, healthier lives. In the United States, for example, the average life expectancy climbed from 49 years in 1900 to 68 years by 1950, the largest jump ever recorded. There were several reasons for this, including better diet, purer food and water, and stricter personal hygiene. But the most important factor, experts agreed, was the dramatic progress made in medical research. In 1900, infectious disease had been the leading cause of death in the United States; by

1950, this was no longer true. Americans now worried more about heart disease and cancer than they did about tuberculosis and pneumonia. The future had never looked brighter. Medical science seemed within sight of a most unlikely goal: a world free of deadly infectious disease. "Will such a world exist?" a prominent scientist asked in the 1950s. "We believe so."

It turned out to be a wildly optimistic prediction. The coming years would see the horrifying outbreaks of previously unknown infectious agents, such as HIV, Ebola virus, and avian influenza. Indeed, the ever-changing social and ecological conditions of our increasingly interconnected world have raised the possibility of even deadlier global pandemics, involving millions of people on different continents. Infectious disease has proved a remarkably adaptable foe. For medical researchers, the battle goes on.

Questions for Reflection

1. Why were researchers so optimistic about their ability to control and even wipe infectious disease from the face of the earth?

2. What conditions in the world today have raised the possibility of new pandemics reaching all parts of the globe?

---

lettering were among the most recognizable logos in America.

Opposing the Highway Act of 1956 was akin to opposing prosperity, progress, and national defense. A few social critics like Lewis Mumford expressed concern about the deterioration of urban centers, the stink of auto pollution, and the future of interstate rail service, but they were drowned out by the optimistic majority. As the prestigious *Architectural Forum* noted, America's new highway system was "the greatest man-made physical enterprise of all time with the exception of war."

Hungary and Suez

In the fall of 1956, at the height of the presidential campaign, foreign affairs took center stage. From central Europe came a dangerous challenge to the Eisenhower–Dulles rhetoric about liberating nations from communist oppression. From the Middle East came a crisis that pitted the United States against its most loyal allies— Israel, England, and France.

Following Stalin's death in 1953, Russian leaders called for "peaceful coexistence" between the Communist

bloc and "differing political and social systems." In 1956, Soviet Premier **Nikita Khrushchev** stunned the Twentieth Communist Party Congress in Moscow by denouncing Stalin's brutality and hinting at a relaxation of the Soviet grip on central and eastern Europe.

The reaction was predictable. Protests flared throughout the Soviet bloc, demanding an end to Russian rule. In Warsaw, angry crowds sacked the Communist party headquarters, and in Budapest street battles escalated into full-scale civil war.

The Hungarian revolt put Eisenhower on the spot. In 1952, his campaign rhetoric had blasted the Democrats for being "soft" on communism. From 1953 forward, his administration had vowed to "roll back" the communist wave, not simply to contain it. Now the time had come to put words into action by supporting the anti-communist freedom fighters in Hungary. Yet Eisenhower refused to send American troops, or even to airlift supplies to the resisters, for fear of starting an all-out war with the Soviet Union. In October 1956, Russian tanks and troops stormed into Budapest to crush the revolt.

At the very moment of the Hungarian revolt, another crisis erupted in the Middle East, a region of

Picturing the Past   **ECONOMICS & TECHNOLOGY**

America's Dream Car

The decade following World War II marked the height of America's love affair with the automobile. Each year's sales proved better than the last; in 1955 alone, more than 7 million cars rolled off the nation's assembly lines. This dramatic growth was not shared equally, however. As the 1950s progressed, the "Big Three" automakers—General Motors, Ford, and Chrysler—took over the market as the poorly funded "independents" disappeared: Kaiser and Willys in 1955, Nash and Hudson in 1957, Packard in 1958. As this advertisement demonstrates, the American automobile of the postwar era became ever more powerful and luxurious, representing not just a means

of transportation, but a status symbol as well. Indeed, General Motors produced five different cars with five distinct images: Chevrolet for "hoi polloi," Pontiac for "the poor but proud," Oldsmobile for "the comfortable but discreet," Buick for "the striving," and Cadillac (pictured here) for "the rich." Yet even the cheaper models came with a V-8 engine, automatic transmission, air-conditioning, tail fins, miles of chrome, and whitewall tires. Around 1957, a series of small, economical European imports, led by the Volkswagen "beetle," arrived to compete with America's overdesigned, gas-guzzling behemoths. The battle was on.

Happy Resolution for a Happy New Year!

Cadillac

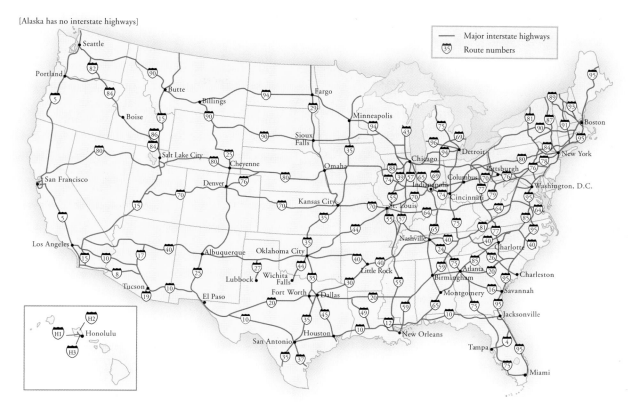

[Alaska has no interstate highways]

— Major interstate highways
35 Route numbers

MAP 28.1 The National Highway System

The ability to drive almost anywhere in the continental United States on a superhighway transformed the nation's economy as well as its culture. Private transportation overwhelmed public transportation. Workers commuted longer distances between their homes and their jobs, spending more time on the road. Whole new industries arose to service the business traveler and vacationer, who no longer had to drive through the center of small towns or large cities to reach their destination.

growing interest and concern to the United States. Though American policy supported the new State of Israel, it also recognized the strategic importance and economic power of Israel's Arab neighbors. In 1952, a young Egyptian military officer named Gamal Abdel Nasser had dramatically altered Middle Eastern politics by overthrowing the corrupt regime of King Farouk. As an Arab nationalist, Nasser steered a middle course between the Cold War powers, hoping to play off one side against the other. To the Egyptian people, he promised both the destruction of Israel and an end to British control of the Suez Canal.

The United States tried to woo Nasser with economic aid. It even agreed to finance his pet project, the Aswan Dam, a huge hydroelectric plant on the Nile River. But trouble arose in 1956 when Secretary Dulles withdrew the Aswan offer to protest Egypt's recognition of Communist China. Unable to punish the United States directly, Nasser did the next best thing by seizing the Suez Canal.

The move could not be ignored. In 1955, Nasser had blockaded the Gulf of Aqaba, Israel's sole outlet to the Red Sea. Now he controlled the waterway that linked western Europe to its oil supply in the Middle East. On October 29, 1956, Israeli armor poured into the Sinai, routing Egyptian forces. Two days later, French and British paratroopers landed near Alexandria and easily retook the Suez Canal.

Eisenhower immediately condemned this invasion. At the very least, he believed, the attack undermined Western interests in the Middle East by forcing Egypt and other Arab states closer to the Soviet bloc. Fearing the worst, Eisenhower placed U.S. armed forces on full alert. If the Russians "start something," he warned, "we may have to hit 'em—and, if necessary, with *everything* in the bucket."

It never came to that. Privately, the White House pressured England, France, and Israel to withdraw. Publicly, the United States supported a U.N. resolution that denounced the invasion and called for negotiations regarding the canal. On November 6, a cease-fire was signed, ending the crisis but not the ill will.

Events in Hungary and Suez came in the midst of Eisenhower's 1956 reelection campaign. Expecting an easy victory, the president worried most about picking the proper running mate, a critical choice given his advanced age and questionable health. Eisenhower did

Protesters in Budapest stand on a captured Soviet tank during the Hungarian uprising of 1956.

spreading, with some white southerners interpreting Eisenhower's virtual silence on the issue as a sign that he supported their resistance to integrated schools. In 1956, more than 100 congressmen from the former Confederate states issued a "Southern Manifesto" that vowed to resist court-ordered integration "by all lawful means." A year later, in Little Rock, Arkansas, Governor **Orval Faubus** triggered the inevitable confrontation between national authority and "states' rights" by defying a federal court order to integrate the all-white Central High School. First the Arkansas National Guard, and then a crowd of angry whites, turned away the nine black students.

As televised scenes of mob violence in Little Rock flashed around the world, President Eisenhower finally, but firmly, took command. Vowing to use "the full power of the United States . . . to carry out the orders of the federal court," he nationalized the Arkansas Guard and dispatched 1,000 fully equipped army paratroopers to surround the high school and escort the black students to their classes. The soldiers remained for months, though peace was quickly restored. Ironically, Dwight Eisenhower became the first president since Reconstruction to protect the civil rights of African Americans through the use of military force.

not believe that Vice President Nixon was the best person to lead the nation in a crisis. "I've watched Dick a long time and he just hasn't grown," Ike told an aide. "So I just haven't honestly been able to believe that he is presidential timber."

In a private meeting, Eisenhower urged Nixon to trade in his vice presidential hat for a cabinet post. Yet when Nixon resisted, the president backed down, fearing a backlash within Republican ranks. In November 1956, Eisenhower and Nixon trounced the Democratic slate of Adlai Stevenson and Senator Estes Kefauver by almost 10 million votes, a margin of victory even wider than in 1952. Nevertheless, the Democrats easily retained their majorities in both houses of Congress, demonstrating that Eisenhower, who accepted New Deal reforms as a permanent part of American life, remained far more popular than the political party he led.

Sputnik and Its Aftermath

On October 4, 1957, the Soviet Union launched *Sputnik I* (or "traveling companion"), the first artificial satellite, weighing less than 200 pounds. The admiral in

A Second Term

Eisenhower returned to office on an optimistic note. Events in Hungary and the Middle East faded momentarily from view. *Time* magazine even praised the president for his moderation "in time of crisis and threat of World War III." The economy was strong; unemployment was low. The nation seemed confident, prosperous, and secure.

Confrontation at Little Rock

These good feelings did not last long. Throughout the South, opposition to the *Brown* decision was

President Eisenhower nationalized the Arkansas Guard and dispatched army paratroopers to escort black students to Little Rock's Central High School in the fall of 1957. Although reluctant to act, Eisenhower became the first president since Reconstruction to use military force to protect the constitutional rights of African Americans.

charge of America's satellite program dismissed *Sputnik I* as "a hunk of iron almost anybody could launch." But 1 month later, the Russians orbited *Sputnik II,* a 1,100-pound capsule with a small dog inside.

The news provoked anger and dismay. Americans had always taken for granted their technological superiority. Even the Soviet atomic bomb was seen as an aberration, most likely built from stolen U.S. blueprints. But *Sputnik* was different; it shook the nation's confidence and wounded its pride. The feeling grew that America had become complacent in its affluence, and that danger lay ahead. "The time has clearly come," said an alarmed senator, "to be less concerned with the depth of the pile of the new broadloom or the height of the tail fin of the new car and to be more prepared to shed blood, sweat, and tears."

The nation's educational system came under withering fire. Critics emerged from every corner, bemoaning the sorry state of America's schools. In an issue devoted to the "Crisis in Education," *Life* magazine followed a 16-year-old Russian student and his American counterpart through a typical high school day. Alexi took difficult courses in science and math. He spoke fluent English, played chess and the piano, exercised vigorously, and studied 4 hours after class. Stephen, meanwhile, spent his day lounging through basic geometry and learning how to type. The students around him read magazines like *Modern Romance* in their English class. No one seemed to study. The end result, warned the *Life* editors, was a generation of young Americans ill-equipped "to cope with the technicalities of the Space Age."

The launching of *Sputnik* in October 1957 raised serious doubts about America's military and technological superiority in the Cold War era.

The embarrassments continued. In December 1957, millions watched on television as the U.S. Navy's much-publicized Vanguard rocket caught fire on takeoff and crashed to the ground. (The newspapers dubbed it "*Flopnik*" and "*Kaputnik.*") A month later, the army launched a 10-pound satellite named *Explorer I* aboard its new Jupiter rocket. Determined to calm public fears, President Eisenhower insisted that the United States was well ahead of the Soviet Union in nuclear research and delivery systems. But the people thought otherwise, especially after the Russians orbited a third satellite weighing almost 3,000 pounds.

In fact, however, Eisenhower was correct. His own information, not available to the public, made two vital points. First, the Russians *needed* more powerful missiles because the warheads they carried were heavier and cruder, owing to inferior technology. Second, the Soviets did not have enough intercontinental ballistic missiles (ICBMs) to counter America's huge lead in manned nuclear bombers. Put simply, the United States was in no real danger of being outgunned.

Eisenhower got this information from the CIA's U-2 spy planes, which crossed the Soviet Union at 70,000 feet. The U-2 flights were both secret and illegal, a clear violation of Russian air space. But the cameras on board, capable of picking up license plate numbers in the Kremlin's parking lot, provided American intelligence with a detailed picture of the Soviet war machine. Of course, the president could not speak candidly about Russian military power without also admitting the existence of these U-2 flights.

This was an awful dilemma. Critics now demanded expensive crash programs for weapons research, missile construction, and community "fallout" shelters to protect against nuclear attack. Eisenhower vigorously opposed these programs, claiming that they undermined economic prosperity and threatened the "very values we are trying to defend." Using his exalted stature as general and war hero, he battled hard—and successfully—to keep military budgets stable during these years. Defense spending increased from $38 billion in 1957 to $41 billion in 1960, a tiny jump after inflation.

Still, the impact of *Sputnik* did not quickly disappear. For the first time, Americans started to view their educational system in terms of national security. This meant greater emphasis on science, mathematics, and foreign language study. In 1958, Congress passed the National Defense Education Act, which funded high school programs in these fields and college scholarships for deserving students. That same year, Eisenhower reluctantly endorsed the creation of the National Aeronautical and Space Agency (NASA), in response to overwhelming public pressure.

The Kitchen Debate

This famous photograph of Soviet Premier Nikita Khrushchev and Vice President Richard Nixon squaring off in their impromptu "Kitchen Debate" in Moscow in 1959 demonstrates that the Cold War had a cultural component that went beyond military confrontation. Standing nose-to-nose in a "model" American kitchen, the two leaders argued about the merits of Western consumer culture. Khrushchev saw America's love affair with "gadgetry" as a sure sign of capitalist laziness and decay.

Looking grumpily at the array of gleaming appliances, he asked: "Don't you have a machine that puts food in your mouth and pushes it down?" But Nixon, known as a militant anti-communist, won praise for responding to Khrushchev that it was "better to compete in the relative merits of washing machines than in the strength of rockets." The Cold War would continue for years, but for the moment, the battlefield seemed a far different place.

© Elliot Erwitt/Magnum Photos

End of an Era

In November 1958, the Democrats won a smashing victory in the off-year elections, increasing their majorities in the House (282–153) and the Senate (62–34) to the largest level since 1936. *Sputnik* was partly responsible for this landslide, but so, too, was an economic recession in 1957 that lingered for the next 2 years. Determined to avoid the inflationary risks of increased federal spending, Eisenhower did little to counter a steady rise in unemployment and a sharp (if temporary) decline in the annual rate of economic growth.

There were optimistic signs, however. In the summer of 1959, Vice President Nixon visited Moscow at Khrushchev's invitation to open a trade show featuring consumer products from Russia and the United States. Several weeks later, Khrushchev accepted President Eisenhower's invitation to visit the United States. Khrushchev toured an Iowa farm and an IBM plant near San Francisco. At a Hollywood studio, he watched the filming of *Can-Can* and then, offended by the skimpy costumes, launched into a diatribe against capitalist "pornography." When his trip to Disneyland was canceled for security reasons, Khrushchev was furious. "What's wrong?" he yelled. "Do you have rocket launching pads there? Or have gangsters taken hold of the place?"

The trip ended on a hopeful note with a visit to the presidential retreat at Camp David, where Khrushchev and Eisenhower spent 2 days in leisurely conversation. They announced that Eisenhower would visit the Soviet Union in 1960 following a summit meeting of world leaders in Paris. The main issues, they agreed, were nuclear disarmament and the future of Berlin.

The summit meeting was a disaster. As he left for Paris in May 1960, Eisenhower learned that a U-2 spy plane was missing. A few days later, Khrushchev revealed that an American aircraft had been shot down deep inside the Soviet Union. Assuming that the pilot was dead, Eisenhower falsely described the U-2 as a weather research plane that had veered off course during a routine flight over Turkey. But Khrushchev then produced the pilot, **Francis Gary Powers,** frightened but very much alive.

At the summit, Eisenhower took full responsibility for the incident but refused to apologize. Indeed, he justified the U-2 flights by insisting that Soviet espionage inside the United States was rampant and that U-2 photographs were essential to America's defense, given the closed nature of Russian society. In response, Khrushchev turned the summit into a tirade against Western "banditry," adding that Eisenhower was no longer welcome on Soviet soil.

The failure at Paris deeply wounded the president. In his "farewell address" to the people, he warned that years of Cold War tensions were sapping America's strength and concentrating too much power in the hands of "a military-industrial complex." Speaking boldly, at times sadly, he urged the people to be on guard against militarism and greed, and to reject a "live for today" mentality. At risk, the president concluded, was "the loss of our political and spiritual heritage."

The Election of 1960

Who would lead the United States into the next decade? Unlike the predictable Eisenhower landslides of 1952 and 1956, the election of 1960 generated drama from the start. Both major candidates were tough, hard-driving campaigners. Both were born in the twentieth century—a political first—and both entered Congress in 1946 after serving as junior naval officers during World War II. But the similarities ended there.

Richard Nixon, the 47-year-old vice president, grew up in modest circumstances. His Quaker parents ran a small grocery store in Whittier, California, near Los Angeles, where Nixon worked as a boy. Neighbors and classmates recalled him as serious and socially ill at ease. After graduating from Whittier College and Duke Law School, he married Patricia Ryan in 1940 and obtained his naval commission the following year.

Nixon's political rise was dramatic. As a new Republican congressman, he played a major role in the Alger Hiss case and then won a U.S. Senate seat in 1950 after accusing his Democratic opponent of being "soft on communism." As vice president from 1953 to 1960, Nixon emerged as the Republican party's most aggressive defender.

John Kennedy took a different path to power. Born to wealth and privilege, he grew up in Boston, attended the finest private schools, and graduated from Harvard. His self-made millionaire father, Joseph P. Kennedy, served as ambassador to England under Franklin Roosevelt.

Preaching competition and excellence, Joseph Kennedy expected his oldest son, Joe Jr., to become the first Catholic president of the United States. When Joe Jr. died in combat during World War II, the torch was passed to John Kennedy, the next oldest son. In 1943, John barely escaped death himself after his PT boat was rammed by a Japanese warship in the South Pacific. Elected to Congress in 1946, and to the Senate in 1952, Kennedy did not excel as a legislator. In constant pain from his war wounds, he underwent delicate spinal surgery and then was diagnosed with Addison's disease, an adrenal malfunction that required daily doses of cortisone. While recuperating, Kennedy won the Pulitzer Prize for *Profiles in Courage,* an intriguing book, written almost entirely by his staff, about politicians who took brave but unpopular positions on the great issues of their time.

In 1956, Kennedy ran a close second to Estes Kefauver for the Democratic party's vice presidential nomination. "You know, if we work like hell the next four years," Kennedy told an aide, "we will pick up all the marbles." Healthy once again, he traveled the country with his glamorous wife, Jacqueline, to line up presidential support. The crowds they drew were so large and adoring that reporters used the word *charisma* to describe the growing Kennedy mystique.

The Republican convention nominated Richard Nixon on the first ballot. As expected, Nixon chose a moderate easterner, Henry Cabot Lodge, Jr., of Massachusetts, to be his vice presidential running mate. The Democratic convention was more dramatic. Also winning

Nixon and Kennedy revolutionized political campaigning with the first televised presidential debates in American history.

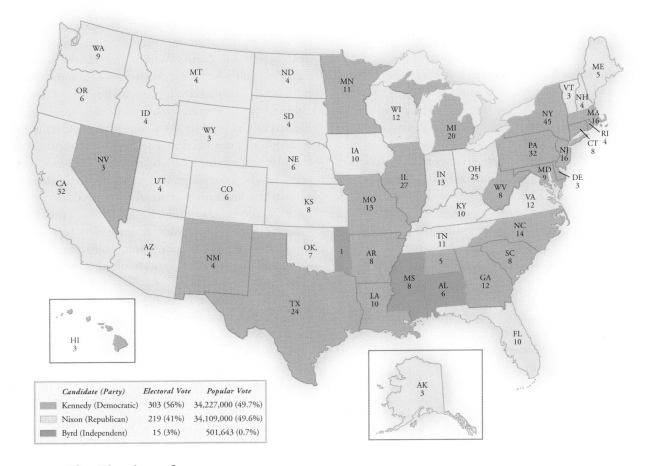

MAP 28.2 The Election of 1960

In winning one of the closest presidential contests in American history, John F. Kennedy barely kept the Democratic New Deal coalition together. Several key factors were at work in this election, including the impact of the first televised presidential debates, the Catholic issue, and the suspicion of voter fraud in the key states of Texas and Illinois.

View an animated version of this map or related maps at http://history.wadsworth.com/passages3e.

a first ballot victory, Kennedy surprised almost everyone by selecting Senator Lyndon Johnson, a longtime rival, for the vice presidential slot. As a Texan with liberal instincts, Johnson was expected to help Kennedy in the South without hurting him in the North. "The world is changing," Kennedy proclaimed in his acceptance speech. "We stand today on the edge of a New Frontier."

The two candidates were evenly matched. Nixon campaigned on the 8-year Eisenhower record, reminding Americans that their nation was prosperous and at peace. Kennedy attacked that record without criticizing the popular Eisenhower by name. Portraying the United States as stagnant in a changing world, he promised new leadership "to get the country moving once again."

Kennedy had two main hurdles to overcome: religion and inexperience. No Roman Catholic had ever been elected president, a fact underscored by the crushing defeat of Al Smith in 1928. Religion became an open issue in the 1960 campaign after a group of Protestant

ministers issued a statement questioning Kennedy's fitness to govern on the grounds that Roman Catholicism was "both a church and a temporal state." Kennedy confronted this issue in a powerful speech to a Baptist audience in Texas. Vowing to uphold the constitutional separation of church and state, he added: "If this election is decided on the basis that 40,000,000 Americans lost their chance of being president on the day they were baptized, then it is the whole nation that will be the loser in the eyes of history."

Kennedy's other hurdle—inexperience—was removed in a series of televised debates with Nixon that marked the beginning of modern presidential campaigns. The first debate had the greatest impact, as more than 80 million Americans watched on television or listened on radio. Though both candidates spoke well, the difference lay in cosmetics and style. The handsome, well-groomed Kennedy radiated confidence and charm. Nixon, by contrast, seemed awkward and pale. The hot

TV lights made him sweat profusely, smudging his makeup. Those who heard the debate on radio scored it a draw. Those who saw it on television thought Kennedy the clear victor.

Kennedy won the election with 303 electoral votes to Nixon's 219. Yet the popular vote was the closest since 1888, with Kennedy getting 34,227,000 (49.7 percent) and Nixon 34,109,000 (49.6 percent). A swing of several thousand votes in Texas and Illinois, where suspicions of ballot fraud were rampant, would have given the election to Nixon. Kennedy did well among traditional Democrats (minorities, urban dwellers, the working class), and swept the Catholic vote, yet polls showed his religion costing him dearly in rural Protestant areas. Kennedy suspected that television won him the White House, and he may have been correct. The four debates, and a flood of prime-time advertisements, appeared to influence voters as never before.

Conclusion

Americans often look back nostalgically to the 1950s. These years were far more tranquil than the war-torn 1940s or the Depression-scarred 1930s. The Korean War ended in 1953 and the Cold War thawed a bit with the death of Joseph Stalin, Russia's brutal dictator. There would be other foreign policy crises in the 1950s, in Suez and Hungary, in Guatemala and Lebanon, but U.S. soldiers would not be dying in faraway lands. The ugliness of McCarthyism would recede as well with the

Senate's condemnation of Joseph McCarthy in 1954. The Roosevelt–Truman years had come to a close, yet the New Deal legacy remained largely undisturbed. Dwight Eisenhower accepted the idea that government must provide a safety net for its citizens. And he, too, pledged to contain Communist expansion around the globe.

The 1950s saw an explosion of mass culture, from the coming of commercial television to the birth of rock and roll. A national highway system was constructed, spurring the boom in automobiles and connecting the nation as never before. The widespread use of wonder drugs, such as penicillin and a successful polio vaccine, gave hope for a future in which laboratory science would make life healthier for humankind.

The 1950s also witnessed *Brown v. Board of Education*, perhaps the most significant Supreme Court decision of the post–Civil War era. The African-American communities of Montgomery and Little Rock helped awaken America to the longstanding injustice of racial segregation, and new leaders emerged with innovative strategies to carry on the fight.

As the 1950s ended, however, nagging questions remained. Would prosperity and racial justice ever reach into the far corners of the land? Would the civil rights movement retain its momentum and nonviolent stance? Would the nation's expanding Cold War military commitments drain its economic strength—and moral authority? Would the lure of materialism and consumerism undermine precious national values? These questions would dominate the American agenda in the tumultuous years ahead.

The Chapter in Review

In the years between 1953 and 1960:

- The 1953 truce in Korea eased Cold War tensions and ended an increasingly unpopular war.
- The civil rights movement gained dramatic momentum with *Brown v. Board of Education*, the Montgomery bus boycott, and the school integration crisis in Little Rock.
- The condemnation of Senator McCarthy cooled passions surrounding the volatile issue of domestic subversion.

- A distinct youth culture emerged, fueled by the postwar baby boom.
- The launching of *Sputnik* in 1957 raised concerns that the United States was falling behind the Soviet Union in the critical fields of science and technology.
- Senator John F. Kennedy was elected president in 1960 by a razor-thin margin, returning the White House to Democratic control.

Making Connections Across Chapters

LOOKING BACK

Chapter 28 examines the promise and prosperity of the United States in the 1950s—a time of great medical and technological advances, the growth of commercial television, an exploding youth culture, and great legal advances and burgeoning movements in the struggle for equal rights.

1. What ideological principles and personal qualities defined the Eisenhower presidency? Why did this presidency seem to fit the national mood so well?

2. How did the spread of commercial television both define and reflect the cultural values of post–World War II America?

3. Why did the Soviet launching of *Sputnik* have such a profound effect on U.S. society? Why did it cause so much national soul-searching and self-reflection?

4. How did the combination of legal victories and local protests combine to fuel the civil rights movement of the 1950s?

LOOKING AHEAD

Chapter 29 considers the turbulent times that followed the relative tranquility of the 1950s, showing the connections between these periods and following the political and cultural events that so badly divided the nation.

1. Did the narrow election victory of John F. Kennedy in the 1960 presidential election send a signal that Americans wanted a change of political course? If so, what sort of change did they have in mind?

2. Would it be possible to build on the major civil rights victories of the 1950s and fulfill the promises of Reconstruction almost a century before—the promises of voting rights, economic opportunity, and equal protection under the law?

3. Would the Cold War with the Soviet Union continue to dominate international relations, and would it expand into other regions of the world?

Recommended Readings

Biskind, Peter. *Seeing Is Believing: How Hollywood Taught Us to Stop Worrying and Love the Fifties* (1983). Examines the way moviemaking shaped popular culture.

Dudziak, Mary. *Cold War, Civil Rights* (2000). Examines the impact of America's civil rights movement on the international scene.

Guralnick, Peter. *Last Train to Memphis: The Rise of Elvis Presley* (1994). Traces the early years of rock 'n' roll's most popular artist and the reasons for his extraordinary success.

Gilbert, James. *A Cycle of Outrage* (1986). Looks at the nation's reaction to juvenile delinquency in the 1950s.

Halberstam, David. *The Fifties* (1993). Offers an encyclopedic account of this decade, from McCarthyism to McDonalds.

Kahn, Roger. *The Boys of Summer* (1971). Recalls the glory days of Major League baseball in a simpler time.

Lewis, Tom. *Divided Highways* (1997). Shows how the building of the interstate highway system transformed American life.

Marling, Karal Ann. *As Seen on TV* (1994). Looks at the rise of visual culture in a new age of leisure.

May, Elaine. *Homeward Bound: American Families in the Cold War Era* (1988). Ties the anxieties associated with anti-communism and the atomic bomb to the national quest for security and stability in the American home.

Oshinsky, David M. *A Conspiracy So Immense: The World of Joe McCarthy* (1983). Explores the life of America's great Red-hunter and the era that bears his name.

Identifications

Review your understanding of the following key terms, people, events, and dates for this chapter (these terms also appear in the Glossary at the end of the book):

Cold War
Ho Chi Minh
domino theory
Brown v. Board of Education
Rosa Parks

Montgomery bus boycott
Martin Luther King, Jr.
Alan Freed
Little Richard
Nikita Khrushchev
Orval Faubus
Sputnik I
Francis Gary Powers

Online Sources Guide

Use this listing to find online documents, images, interactive maps, simulations, and other resources related to this chapter:

American History Resource Center

http://history.wadsworth.com/rc/us

Documents

John Foster Dulles, "Massive Retaliation" speech
John Clellon Holmes, "This is the Beat Generation"
Eisenhower's response to the Little Rock Crisis (1957)
John Kenneth Galbraith, *The Affluent Society* (1958)
Brown v. Board of Education
Martin Luther King, Jr., statement on ending the Montgomery bus boycott

Selected Images

Dwight Eisenhower
women's fashions, 1954
Elvis Presley
Protest against segregation of schools
North Carolina school refusing to admit African Americans, 1956
Martin Luther King, Jr.

Simulations

The Cold War (In this historical simulation you can choose to be an African American or a suburbanite and make choices based on the circumstances and opportunities afforded.)

Document Exercises

1954 Censure of Senator Joseph McCarthy

HistoryNOW

http://now.ilrn.com/ayers_etal3e

Primary Source Exercises

Affluence and Anxiety
The Right of Interposition, 1955

Passages 1960 to 2005

W ho could have predicted the turmoil and tragedy of the 1960s? The previous decade, after all, gave scant warning that trouble lay ahead. Filled with momentous milestones, such as the National Highway Act and *Brown v. Board of Education,* the 1950s seemed to reflect the optimism and stability of a confident nation—a place of widely shared values and little public complaint. All was well in prosperous postwar America, or so it appeared.

The tumult of the 1960s came suddenly, without letup or relief. It began with the jailings and beatings of civil rights workers in the South, which turned many activists against the philosophy of nonviolence. The civil rights movement, in turn, spawned a women's movement, and then a student movement, which further challenged the status quo. Meanwhile, the escalating Vietnam War eroded the credibility of American officials and divided the nation in dangerous ways. Against the backdrop of

The arrival of the Beatles in New York City in 1964, known as the "British Invasion," would help revolutionize popular styles as well as rock music throughout the world.

increasing bloodshed in Southeast Asia, the United States endured a horrifying cycle of homegrown violence in the 1960s, including inner-city riots, militant campus upheavals, and the assassination of prominent public figures like President John F. Kennedy, his brother Robert, and the Reverend Martin Luther King, Jr.

The 1970s brought little relief. An American president resigned from office for the first time in the nation's history. The North Vietnamese communists took over South Vietnam. Americans faced gas shortages, high unemployment, and staggering inflation. They watched with anger and embarrassment as their embassy in Iran was attacked and 52 Americans were held hostage for more than a year.

Republican Ronald Reagan won the 1980 presidential election by promising to reverse the nation's apparent decline. Mixing personal charm and optimism with the darker politics of resentment, he attracted mainstream voters by vowing to strengthen family values, reward hard work, and increase respect for America around the world. At the same time, he reinforced the notion among white working-class voters (known as "Reagan Democrats") that the party of Franklin Roosevelt had deserted their

interests—that the real enemies of working people were no longer big business and the very rich, but rather big government and the very poor. During the 1980s, the Reagan administration's policies regarding taxes, wages, unions, banking, and antitrust produced one of the most dramatic redistributions of wealth in American history, with the top 1 percent seeing its yearly income rise by 75 percent, and the rest of the nation experiencing almost no gain at all. Nevertheless, Reagan remained a popular president, a politician who articulated the fears and dreams of Americans with extraordinary skill.

Through all the tumult of these decades, one certainty remained—the specter of international communism, centered in Moscow. Although the fear of domestic subversion stirred up by Senator Joseph McCarthy had largely subsided by 1960, the anxieties generated by Soviet power and influence remained solidly in place. During the 1960s, the United States and Russia tangled over Berlin and Cuba, where the placement of offensive missiles, 90 miles from the Florida coast, led to the most dangerous confrontation of the entire Cold War. In Vietnam, meanwhile, American officials defended the growing involvement as a test of will against Soviet-inspired aggression. The larger

The fall of the Berlin Wall symbolized the end of the Cold War.

goals, they insisted, were to halt the spread of world communism and to maintain American credibility around the globe.

The 1970s brought an apparent thaw in U.S.–Soviet relations. The two sides signed a momentous agreement limiting nuclear weapons known as SALT I. President Nixon also visited the Soviet Union as well as Communist China, raising hopes for serious dialogue, or détente. It didn't happen. As Nixon freely admitted, his visit to China was intended, in large part, to drive a wedge between the Russians and the Chinese, the world's two leading communist powers. Furthermore, the very idea of negotiating with the Soviet Union over issues such as human rights and arms control offended hard-line anticommunists who believed that American military power must largely determine the outcome of the Cold War. In the 1980 presidential campaign, Ronald Reagan promised a much tougher stand against communism in the future.

The Reagan administration dramatically increased the nation's defense budget. It also funded military campaigns against leftist rebels and Marxist governments in Africa, Asia, and Latin America. In one instance, it funneled money from a secret arms deal with Iran to illegally finance a right-wing guerilla army in Nicaragua. President Reagan made no apologies for this activity. The Soviets had created an "Evil Empire," he declared, and it had to be destroyed.

In fact, that empire was already in trouble. Assuming power in 1985, Soviet Premier Mikhail Gorbachev well understood the problems his nation faced. Believing that communism must become more democratic and market-oriented in order to survive, he encouraged the policies known as *glasnost* (openness) and *perestroika* (restructure). In trying to save communism, however, Gorbachev set in motion the very forces that would bring it down. A wave of protest swept through Eastern Europe, demanding more freedom and closer contacts with the West. Unlike Hungary in 1956 and Czechoslovakia in 1968, the Soviet Union did not rush in troops to restore order. On a trip to West Berlin in 1987, President

DESMOND BOYLAN/Reuters/Landov

The U.S.-led invasion of Iraq in 2003 toppled the brutal dictatorship of Saddam Hussein, but left a bloody insurgency in its wake.

Reagan encouraged the protesters by demanding: "Mr. Gorbachev, tear down this wall." In 1989, the communist governments in Eastern Europe fell like dominoes—Hungary, Poland, Czechoslovakia, East Germany, Romania. It was one of those rare instances, noted *Time* magazine, "when the tectonic plates of history shift beneath men's feet, and nothing after is quite the same."

In 1991, the Soviet Union collapsed, and Russians began the painful transition to democratic politics and a free market economy. For the United States, meanwhile, a new set of challenges emerged. As the world's only remaining "superpower," it now faced a post–Cold War era marred by ethnic violence in the Balkans, tribal warfare in Africa, military aggression in the Middle East, nuclear proliferation in India and Pakistan, and continuing human rights violations from Latin America to China. In addition, a booming world birthrate and the specter of global warming raised serious environmental concerns, and the rapid spread of technology and information linked people together in truly remarkable ways. During the 1990s, the president who faced these issues, Bill Clinton, saw the economy achieve unprecedented levels of prosperity, and the lingering problem of the budget deficits eased dramatically. Yet good times at home did not mean political calm. The Republicans regained control of the House of Representatives in 1994 for the first time in four decades and a second term for Clinton seemed doubtful. Yet he won again in 1996, only to face impeachment charges arising from a sex scandal in 1998. Despite his acquittal in 1999, his presidency ended under a cloud. His vice president, Al Gore, lost a close election to Republican George W. Bush in 2000. On September 11, 2001, terrorist attacks

© MARC SEROTA/Reuters/CORBIS

The devastation caused by Hurricane Katrina in 2005 in flooded New Orleans and the neighboring Gulf Coast region raised troubling questions about the ability of government at all levels—federal, state, and local—to deal quickly and effectively with a large-scale emergency.

on the United States stunned the American people and plunged the nation into war at home and in faraway Afghanistan. As the early years of the millennium unfolded the menace of terrorism tested the country's institutions and the courage of its people.

By 2003 the United States had invaded Iraq and toppled the regime of Saddam Hussein. But a continuing insurgency against the American presence kept Iraq in turmoil. At home, George W. Bush won reelection but found his second term beset with troubles from hurricanes in the Gulf of Mexico in August and September 2005 and an increasingly polarized electorate. The first decade of the millennium was thus filled with the challenge of terrorism, fears of global warming, and social divisions that tested the country's institutions and the courage of its people.

America and the World: 1960–2005

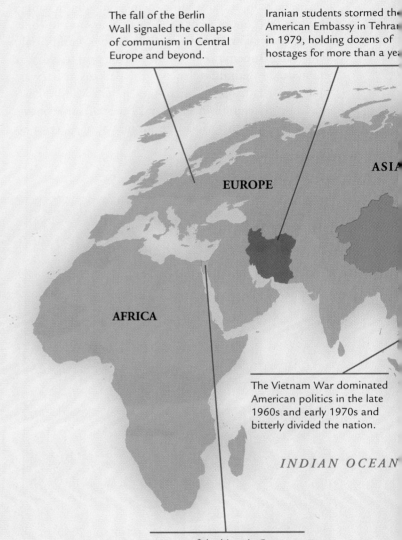

The fall of the Berlin Wall signaled the collapse of communism in Central Europe and beyond.

Iranian students stormed the American Embassy in Tehran in 1979, holding dozens of hostages for more than a year

EUROPE

ASIA

AFRICA

The Vietnam War dominated American politics in the late 1960s and early 1970s and bitterly divided the nation.

INDIAN OCEAN

As part of the historic Camp David Accords, Egypt agreed to recognize the State of Israel, while Israel pledged to return the captured Sinai Peninsula to Egypt.

President Richard Nixon's dramatic visit to Communist China in 1972 opened the way for cultural and diplomatic exchange between the two former enemies.

NORTH AMERICA

ATLANTIC OCEAN

The devastating attacks on the World Trade Center in Manhattan and the Pentagon in Washington, D.C. on September 11, 2001, brought the menace of foreign terrorism to American soil.

PACIFIC OCEAN

The attempt by the Soviet Union to deploy offensive missiles in Fidel Castro's Cuba in 1962 led to the most dangerous confrontation of the Cold War.

SOUTH AMERICA

AUSTRALIA

ANTARCTICA

Chronology

1960	1972	1983

POLITICS & DIPLOMACY

1960: John Kennedy elected president
1961: Berlin Wall erected
1962: Cuban missile crisis
1963: President Kennedy assassinated
1964: President Johnson elected by record margin
Landmark Civil Rights Act passed
1965: U.S. troop levels exceed 100,000 in Vietnam
Malcolm X assassinated
1967: Antiwar protests multiply
1968: Tet offensive
Martin Luther King, Jr., assassinated in Memphis
Robert Kennedy assassinated in Los Angeles
Richard Nixon elected president
1970: U.S. troops invade Cambodia

1972: President Nixon visits mainland China
Watergate burglary
1973: Vice President Agnew resigns
1974: President Nixon resigns
1975: South Vietnam falls
1976: Jimmy Carter elected president
1977: Panama Canal treaties
1978: Camp David Accords
1979: Hostage crisis in Iran
1980: Ronald Reagan elected president
1981: Reagan survives assassination attempt
Sandra Day O'Connor becomes first woman appointed to Supreme Court
1982: Democrats gain seats in congressional elections

1983: Strategic Defense Initiative (SDI) proposed
Invasion of Grenada
1984: Geraldine Ferraro becomes first woman to be nominated for vice president by major party
Reagan wins sweeping reelection
1985: Mikhail Gorbachev becomes leader of Soviet Union
1986: Democrats regain control of Senate
Iran-Contra scandal begins
1987: Nomination of Robert Bork to Supreme Court defeated
1989: George H. W. Bush wins presidential election over Michael Dukakis on "no new taxes" pledge
Berlin Wall torn down
1990: Iraq invades Kuwait
Bush abandons "no new taxes" pledge

SOCIAL & CULTURAL EVENTS

1961: Freedom Rides
1962: Students for a Democratic Society formed
1963: Betty Friedan publishes *The Feminine Mystique*
1964: Beatles tour the United States
1965: Race riot in Watts
1966: National Organization for Women formed
1967: Haight-Ashbury "summer of love"
1968: Cesar Chavez leads California grape strike
Antiwar protests disrupt Democratic National Convention

1969: Woodstock music festival
1970: College protesters killed at Kent State and Jackson State
1973: Abortion legalized
1974: Antibusing protests in Boston
1981: AIDS epidemic begins in United States
1982: Vietnam War Memorial dedicated in Washington
David Letterman show premieres on NBC late night

1983: Sally Ride first American woman in space
1984: Summer Olympics in Los Angeles
1985: Rock Hudson dies of AIDS
1986: *Challenger* space shuttle explodes
1987: Scandals engulf televangelist ministry of Jim and Tammy Faye Bakker
1988: Antidepressant drug Prozac introduced
1989: Actresses Bette Davis and Lucille Ball die
Oil tanker *Exxon Valdez* goes aground in Alaska causing environmental damage

ECONOMICS & TECHNOLOGY

1960: Oral contraceptive marketed
1962: John Glenn orbits the earth aboard *Friendship 7*
1969: Apollo moon landing

1973: Arab oil embargo triggers energy crisis
1979: Nuclear accident at Three Mile Island
1981: Reagan tax cut package adopted
Air traffic controllers strike
1982: Recession ends
Budget deficit exceeds $100 billion for first time

1983: Social Security reforms adopted
1984: Macintosh computer introduced
1985: President Reagan signs Gramm-Rudman-Hollings Act to reduce government spending
1986: Tax Reform Act passed
1987: Stock market closes about 2,000 on Dow Jones, but loses 508 points on a single day in October
1988: United States, Canada arrive at free trade agreement
President George H. W. Bush approves $300 billion plan to bail out savings and loan industry

1991

1991: Persian Gulf War brings Iraq's
ouster from Kuwait
Clarence Thomas–Anita Hill controversy erupts
1992: Bill Clinton defeats George H. W.
Bush and Ross Perot in presidential
race
1993: Branch Davidians besieged in
Waco, Texas, which results in fiery
confrontation
Clinton's deficit-reduction plan
passes Congress by a single
Democratic vote in Senate
1994: Republicans regain control of
House of Representatives for first
time in 40 years
1995: Bombing in Oklahoma City kills
more than 160 people; fears about
militias aroused
Republicans force government
shutdown

1990: Hubble space telescope launched
1991: Basketball star Magic Johnson
reveals that he is HIV positive (AIDS
virus)
1992: Vice President Dan Quayle attacks
single mother premise of sitcom
Murphy Brown
1993: Author Toni Morrison wins Nobel
Prize for literature
1994: O. J. Simpson murder trial grips
nation
Death of Jacqueline Kennedy Onassis
1995: Simpson's acquittal sparks national
furor

1990: American dependence on foreign
oil reaches historic high
1991: Economy enters recession that will
last until late 1992
1992: Unemployment reaches 7.8 percent,
the highest since 1983
1993: United States and Europe agree on
new terms for General Agreement on
Tariffs and Trade (GATT)
Clinton administration proposes
national health care plan
North American Free Trade Agreement
(NAFTA) approved in Congress

1996

1995: (*continued*) Settlement of Bosnian
conflict reached at Dayton, Ohio
1996: Clinton and Bob Dole wage presidential contest
Clinton reelected to second term
1997: Balanced budget agreement
reached
1998: Clinton sex scandals break
President Clinton impeached by
House of Representatives in
December
1999: Clinton acquitted by Senate
NATO launches air war against
Serbia over treatment of Albanians in
Kosovo
School massacre in Littleton, Colorado, sets off debate about violence
and gun control
Air war against Serbia ends
successfully

1996: Jazz singer Ella Fitzgerald dies
Virginia Military Institute admits
women
1997: Movie *Titanic* sets all-time box
office record for receipts
Princess Diana killed
Spice Girls group has top pop album
Spice
1998: Singer Frank Sinatra dies
Slugger Mark McGwire hits 70 home
runs for all-time record
1999: Death of baseball star Joe
DiMaggio

1994: Clinton health care plan dies in
Congress
1995: Budget battle in Congress produces closing of federal government
in December
1996: Congress passes sweeping welfare
reform bill

2000

2000: Disputed election results in
Florida end in Supreme Court ruling
that George W. Bush is president
Hillary Rodham Clinton elected to
the U.S. Senate
2001: Terrorist attack occurs on
September 11
War in Afghanistan
2002: Republicans regain control of
Senate and dominate all branches of
government
2003: United States invades Iraq and
topples regime of Saddam Hussein
2004: United States faces persistent
insurgent resistance in Iraq
George W. Bush reelected president
over Democrat John Kerry
2005: Chief Justice William Rehnquist dies
John Roberts confirmed as his
replacement
Iraqi resistance continues

Michael Jordan (basketball) and
Wayne Gretzky (hockey) retire from
professional sports
*Star Wars, Episode I, The Phantom
Menace* opens to long lines and critical panning
2001: Michael Jordan returns to basketball
2002: Former President Jimmy Carter
receives Nobel Peace Prize
2003: Columbia space shuttle explodes,
killing all seven astronauts
Fred Rogers dies
2005: Hurricane Katrina devastates
New Orleans and Gulf Coast

2001 Congress passes Bush's tax cut
1997: Unemployment rate in May falls
to 4.8 percent, the lowest since 1973
Budget surplus reported and future
surpluses are projected
1998: Dow Jones average closes above
9,000 in April
1999: Dow Jones hovers around 11,000
in May
United States has strongest economy
in world as twentieth century draws
to a close, but stability of world
financial system is still a concern

29

The Turbulent Years, 1960–1968

President Kennedy delivered a stirring inaugural address on a cloudless, bitter-cold afternoon in January 1961.

George Silk/Time Life Pictures/Getty Images

The 1960s opened on an ambivalent note. The gross national product reached $500 billion for the first time, yet talk of economic recession was in the air. The darkest days of McCarthyism were over, yet the fear of communism remained. The development of new products and technologies bred optimism, yet the spread of new weapons caused alarm.

Hints of protest and trouble had begun to appear. In Greensboro, North Carolina, four black college students sat down at a Woolworth lunch counter and were denied service, but refused to leave. Word of their defiance triggered "sit-in" protests across the South, with demonstrators bravely confronting Jim Crow. Half a world away, supporters of North Vietnam's Communist ruler Ho Chi Minh announced the formation of a National Liberation Front to overthrow the anti-Communist government of President Ngo Dinh Diem in South Vietnam. President Diem did not seem concerned. With U.S. support, he boasted, his forces would quickly subdue these "Viet Cong"

(or Vietnamese Communists) and bring peace to his land.

Early Tests

The 1960 election was a landmark event in American political history. At age 43, John Kennedy became the first Catholic president, the youngest candidate to win a presidential election, and the first president to be born in the twentieth century. His inauguration on January 20, 1961, seemed to herald a new era of idealism, commitment, and change. Kennedy declared that the "torch has been passed to a new generation of Americans," adding: "Ask not what your country can do for you; ask what you can do for your country."

Idealism and Caution

The new administration appeared to mirror these words. Young people converged on Washington with a fervor

Timeline

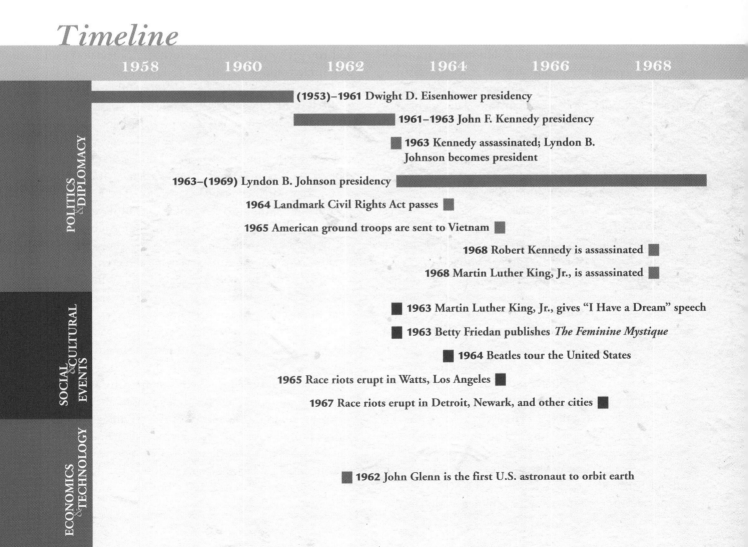

| | 1958 | 1960 | 1962 | 1964 | 1966 | 1968 |

POLITICS & DIPLOMACY

(1953)–1961 Dwight D. Eisenhower presidency

1961–1963 John F. Kennedy presidency

1963 Kennedy assassinated; Lyndon B. Johnson becomes president

1963–(1969) Lyndon B. Johnson presidency

1964 Landmark Civil Rights Act passes

1965 American ground troops are sent to Vietnam

1968 Robert Kennedy is assassinated

1968 Martin Luther King, Jr., is assassinated

SOCIAL & CULTURAL EVENTS

1963 Martin Luther King, Jr., gives "I Have a Dream" speech

1963 Betty Friedan publishes *The Feminine Mystique*

1964 Beatles tour the United States

1965 Race riots erupt in Watts, Los Angeles

1967 Race riots erupt in Detroit, Newark, and other cities

ECONOMICS & TECHNOLOGY

1962 John Glenn is the first U.S. astronaut to orbit earth

reminiscent of the early New Deal years. Public service became a badge of honor. Kennedy's White House staff included 15 Rhodes scholars and numerous Ivy League professors. The new secretary of state, Dean Rusk, came from the Rockefeller Foundation; the new defense secretary, Robert McNamara, left the presidency of the Ford Motor Company to help "streamline" the nation's armed forces. Kennedy chose his younger brother Robert to become attorney general. Under Jacqueline Kennedy's direction, the White House became a center for the arts. Cellist Pablo Casals performed at the Executive Mansion, as did the American Shakespeare Festival Theatre.

Despite the lofty rhetoric and the fanfare, Kennedy took a measured approach to his early presidential duties, particularly in domestic affairs. For one thing, he lacked the huge popular mandate given to previous first-term presidents such as Franklin Roosevelt in 1932 and Dwight Eisenhower in 1952. For another, he worried about his relations with a Congress in which conservative Republicans and southern Democrats held the balance of power.

Several of Kennedy's early initiatives were in the New Deal tradition. He worked successfully to increase Social Security benefits and to raise the minimum wage from $1 to $1.25. Yet the Congress easily blocked his efforts to provide health insurance for the aged and to create a cabinet-level Department of Urban Affairs. Worse still was the defeat of Kennedy's $2.3 billion education bill for school construction and higher teachers' salaries, which raised nagging questions about the federal role in education. Would funds be given to racially segregated public schools or to private religious schools? At first, Kennedy opposed parochial school assistance, fearing a political backlash. Amid the confusion, the education bill died in committee.

In other areas, the new administration achieved success. By executive order, Kennedy launched the Peace Corps in March 1961, an idea modeled partly on Franklin Roosevelt's Civilian Conservation Corps. Directed by the president's brother-in-law R. Sargent Shriver, the Peace Corps sent thousands of American volunteers to underdeveloped nations to provide educational and technical assistance. With a tiny budget, it became one of Kennedy's great triumphs, showcasing American idealism and know-how throughout the world. Within 3 years, almost 10,000 volunteers were at work in 46 countries, teaching school, staffing hospitals, and planting new crops.

Even more popular, though far more expensive, was the space program. Unlike Eisenhower, who opposed a costly "race to the moon with Russia," the new president viewed an American victory in this contest as essential to national prestige. Setting the goal of a manned moon landing "before this decade is out," Kennedy convinced a skeptical Congress to allocate billions of dollars for

space research and rocketry, an astronauts training program, and a mission control center in Houston.

The "space race" captivated the world. In April 1961, Soviet Cosmonaut Yuri Gagarin orbited the globe in less than 2 hours. A month later, Commander Alan Shepard rocketed 300 miles from Cape Canaveral in a suborbital flight, and in February 1962, Lieutenant Colonel **John Glenn** orbited the earth three times aboard *Friendship 7* before touching down in the Caribbean. Glenn became a national hero, with ticker tape parades and a televised address before a joint session of Congress.

The Bay of Pigs

Kennedy inherited his first crisis from the previous administration. As president-elect, he was told of a secret plan, personally approved by Eisenhower, to overthrow the new Marxist government of **Fidel Castro** in Cuba. The plan called for several hundred anti-Castro exiles, trained and equipped by the CIA, to invade Cuba and trigger an anti-communist revolution.

Kennedy endorsed the plan for several reasons. He believed that Castro set a dangerous example by aligning Cuba with the Soviet Union and by expropriating the property of American corporations. Kennedy had promised to "get tough" with Castro during the 1960 campaign. He could not easily back down now.

On April, 17, 1961, a brigade of 1,500 waded ashore at the **Bay of Pigs,** on Cuba's southern coast. Nothing went as planned. The landing site had sharp coral reefs and swampy terrain, making it hard to unload supplies and move out from the beaches. Local workers quickly spotted the invaders, and news of their arrival sparked no popular uprising against Castro.

Kennedy refused to lend vital air and naval support to the brigade in a futile attempt to hide America's role in this disaster. More than 100 invaders were killed, and 1,200 were captured. After reviewing the events with his advisors, Kennedy took a walk on the White House lawn. It was "the first time in my life," a friend recalled, "that I ever saw tears come to his eyes."

The Bay of Pigs fiasco left a troubled legacy. On the one hand, it angered other Latin American governments and drove Castro even closer to the Russian embrace. On the other, it fueled Kennedy's interest in covert operations and his desire to control them more directly. After removing longtime CIA Director Allen Dulles, the president approved a top-secret program, code-named Operation Mongoose, to topple the Cuban government and assassinate its leaders. Its plans included the destruction of Cuba's vital sugar crop, and a box of exploding cigars for Castro.

Most important was the public reaction. Rather than hurting Kennedy, the incident marked him as a man of action, willing to take chances in the war against communism. Opinion polls gave him higher ratings after the Bay of Pigs than at any other point in his presidency. "It's just like Eisenhower," he quipped. "The worse I do the more popular I get."

The Berlin Wall

In June 1961, Kennedy met with Soviet leader Nikita Khrushchev in Vienna. Khrushchev tried to bully the new president, threatening to give East Germany full control over road and rail access to West Berlin, in violation of previous guarantees. Berlin was both a danger and an embarrassment to Khrushchev. The prosperous western sector stood as a model of democratic capitalism behind the Iron Curtain. Each day, more than a thousand refugees from the communist side poured into West Berlin. At this rate, East Germany would lose most of its skilled workers to the West.

Kennedy was not intimidated. Calling West Berlin "the great testing place of courage and will," he declared that NATO forces would defend the city at all costs. To emphasize this point, the president tripled draft calls, mobilized reserve units, and requested $3 billion in additional defense appropriations, which Congress quickly granted. The crisis ended in August 1961. As the world watched in amazement, workers in East Berlin constructed a wall of barbed wire and concrete around the western edge of their city, sealing off East Berlin, and eventually all of East Germany, from the noncommunist world. In a tactical sense, Khrushchev achieved his objective of stopping the East German exodus to the West. In a larger sense, however, the wall became an admission of failure—a monument to oppression and to freedom denied.

The Freedom Riders

Kennedy's first domestic crisis occurred in the field of civil rights. An integrationist at heart, the president wanted change to come slowly, without the mass protests and violent incidents that had made headlines around the world. He worried, too, that White House support for *immediate* desegregation would cost him the good will of powerful southerners in Congress.

Yet, as Kennedy discovered, the real momentum for civil rights came from below. In 1961, the Congress of Racial Equality (CORE) announced plans to test a recent Supreme Court decision, *Boynton v. Virginia,* which prohibited racial segregation in bus terminals, train stations, and airports engaged in interstate transportation. CORE's objective, said its national director, was "to provoke the southern authorities into arresting us and thereby prod the Justice Department into enforcing the law of the land."

In May 1961, 13 "**freedom riders**"—7 blacks and 6 whites—left Washington on a Greyhound bus bound for New Orleans. Most were veterans of the sit-ins. At each stop, they ignored the "white" and "colored" signs that hung by the toilets, lunch counters, and waiting rooms in defiance of federal law. Trouble erupted in Anniston, Alabama, when their bus was firebombed by a white mob. As the passengers struggled outside, they were beaten with fists and clubs. One rider suffered permanent brain damage from repeated blows to the head.

When the violence continued in Montgomery and Birmingham, Alabama, Attorney General **Robert Kennedy** urged CORE to end the freedom rides, claiming that they embarrassed President Kennedy on the eve of his summit with Premier Khrushchev. "Doesn't the attorney general know," a black Alabaman responded, "that we've been embarrassed all our lives?"

As new freedom riders arrived to replace the wounded, the Kennedy administration sent in federal marshals to protect them. It had no choice, given the violent scenes that flashed around the world. In September 1961, the federal government banned interstate carriers from using any terminal that segregated the races. After months of bloody struggle, the freedom riders prevailed.

The New Economics

Despite his increasing focus on civil rights, President Kennedy considered the economy to be his number-one domestic concern. Economic growth in the Eisenhower years had been steady but increasingly slow. Though real wages for an average family rose a remarkable 20 percent in the 1950s, a series of recessions toward the end of Eisenhower's second term prompted both a drop in factory production and a rise in unemployment. By the time Kennedy took office, more Americans were out of work than at any time since the end of World War II.

In 1962, Kennedy unveiled an economic program that differed sharply from the spending model of the New Deal and Fair Deal. Instead, he proposed a major tax cut for consumers and businesses, designed to stimulate purchasing power and encourage new investment. For Kennedy, the goal of full employment required sizable budget deficits in the short run as tax revenues declined. What worried him was the specter of inflation as the economy heated up.

To prevent this, Kennedy lobbied business and labor leaders to respect the wage–price guidelines his administration recommended to keep inflation in check. The Teamsters, Auto Workers, and Steel Workers all agreed to modest wage hikes in 1962 with the understanding

Table 29.1 Persons Below Poverty Level: 1959–1969

| YEAR | Number Below Poverty Level (in millions) | | | Percent Below Poverty Level | | |
	TOTAL	WHITE	BLACK AND OTHER RACES	TOTAL	WHITE	BLACK AND OTHER RACES
1969	24.3	16.7	7.6	12%	10%	31%
1968	25.4	17.4	8.0	13	10	33
1967	27.8	19.0	8.8	14	11	37
1966	28.5	19.3	9.2	15	11	40
1965	33.2	22.5	10.7	17	13	47
1964	36.1	25.0	11.1	19	15	50
1963	36.4	25.2	11.2	19	15	51
1962	38.6	26.7	12.0	21	16	56
1961	39.6	27.9	11.7	22	17	56
1960	39.9	28.3	11.5	22	18	56
1959	39.5	28.5	11.0	22	18	56

Note: The poverty threshold for a nonfarm family of four was $3,743 in 1969 and $2,973 in 1959.

Source: Congressional Quarterly, *Civil Rights: A Progress Report*, 1971, p. 46.

that their employers would not raise prices. Two weeks later, U.S. Steel, the nation's third largest corporation, announced a whopping price increase of $6 a ton, leading other steel companies to do the same.

Calling the move an "irresponsible defiance of the public interest," Kennedy used his influence to roll back the price increase. Within days, the Justice Department threatened to investigate antitrust violations in the steel industry, and the Defense Department announced that it might not purchase steel from the "price-gouging" offenders.

Under enormous pressure, the steel companies gave in. The president had won a major victory in his battle against inflation, although his rough tactics aroused deep anger in the business community. Nevertheless, the economy prospered in the early 1960s, achieving low unemployment, stable prices, and steady growth.

Social and Political Challenges

Before long, President Kennedy's political caution began to ease. A year of trial and error led him to take more confident stands in certain areas, such as U.S.–Soviet relations and the push for civil rights. As events unfolded in 1962, the president faced challenges in familiar places—the Deep South and the waters off Cuba. This time, the stakes were much higher.

The Battle for Ole Miss

In the fall of 1962, a federal court ordered the admission of James Meredith, a black air force veteran, to the all-white University of Mississippi, known as Ole Miss. Governor Ross Barnett led the opposition. A virulent racist, who claimed that "God made the Negro different to punish him," Barnett had kept a previous black applicant from entering Ole Miss by having him committed to a mental hospital. Now Barnett invoked the doctrine of interposition—a throwback to antebellum times—by warning that Mississippi would ignore all federal rulings in order to keep segregation in place.

Kennedy responded to Barnett's challenge by dispatching several hundred federal marshals to Ole Miss. They were met by a well-armed mob, more than 2,000 strong. In the riot that followed, 2 people were killed and hundreds were injured, including 28 marshals hit by gunfire. Like Eisenhower during the Little Rock crisis, Kennedy rushed in troops and federalized the State Guard. With 23,000 soldiers on campus—five times the student population—Meredith registered for classes under army bayonets. The battle at Ole Miss was over; the larger struggle for Mississippi lay ahead.

The Missiles of October

In October 1962, the world faced the most dangerous confrontation of the entire Cold War. It began with rumors, confirmed by **U-2** spy plane photos, that the Russians were deploying Intermediate-Range Ballistic Missiles (IRBMs) in Cuba. Speed was essential, for the missiles would become operational in less than a month. Kennedy convened an executive committee (known as ex-Comm) to provide a suitable response.

Castro's need for security was understandable. In addition to Operation Mongoose, the Kennedy

Picturing the Past ECONOMICS & TECHNOLOGY

Poverty in America

In an era of increased abundance and consumerism, it was easy to forget that our country's great wealth and prosperity were not shared by all. This painful truth became the subject of a pathbreaking book, *The Other America,* by socialist author Michael Harrington, in 1962. Harrington estimated that more than 40 million people—almost one-quarter of the nation's population—lived in an "economic underworld" of joblessness, marginal wages, hunger, and despair. He emphasized that poverty could be found in every corner of the nation—among whites and blacks, natives and immigrants, rural folk and city dwellers. The picture here is from Appalachia, one of the region's highlighted in Harrington's book. It demonstrates the author's point that poverty is "a culture, an institution, a way of life" passed from one generation to the next. The powerful response to Harrington's book led to a vast array of social programs popularly known, in the words of President Lyndon Johnson, as the War on Poverty.

© Joffre Clark/Black Star

administration had imposed an economic embargo on Cuba and engineered its expulsion from the Organization of American States. At Castro's urging, the Soviet Union sent thousands of military advisors to Cuba, as well as defensive missiles to shoot down invading planes. Yet the deployment of *offensive* weapons, capable of reaching Chicago or Washington with nuclear warheads, was an alarming escalation designed to tip the balance of terror in Moscow's favor.

Some ex-Comm members recommended immediate air strikes to take out the missile bases. Others, including Robert Kennedy, proposed a naval blockade of Cuba. The president carefully studied both options before choosing the latter. A blockade shifted the burden of responsibility to Khrushchev while allowing both sides to seek a solution short of war.

On October 22, 1962, Kennedy revealed the existence of the missiles in a nationally televised address. After describing the naval blockade, he demanded that Russia remove the IRBMs already in place. Any missile fired from Cuba, he warned, would be regarded "as an attack by the Soviet Union on the United States," requiring a "full retaliatory response." American forces went on full alert. A U-2 plane over Cuba was shot down, and its pilot killed. The entire world watched anxiously as Russian vessels in the Caribbean inched closer to American warships enforcing the blockade.

On October 26, Kennedy received an emotional note from Khrushchev suggesting a settlement: Russia would remove its missiles if the United States pledged never to invade Cuba. Before the president could respond, however, a second note arrived demanding that

MEDIUM RANGE BALLISTIC MISSILE BASE IN CUBA
SAN CRISTOBAL

LAUNCH POSITION

MISSILE-READY TENTS

MISSILE ERECTORS

LATE OCTOBER

© Bettmann/CORBIS

U-2 photos, such as this one, of missile bases being constructed in Cuba led to the most dangerous confrontation of the Cold War.

the United States also remove its Jupiter missiles along the Soviet border in Turkey. This new demand did not pose a security problem, because the Jupiter missiles were obsolete and about to be scrapped. Yet the president could not remove them without appearing to buckle under Soviet pressure.

Robert Kennedy provided the solution. Respond to the first note, he said, and ignore the second one. On October 27, the president vowed not to invade Cuba if the IRBMs were dismantled. In private, meanwhile, Robert Kennedy assured Soviet Ambassador Anatoly Dobrynin that the Jupiter missiles would be removed from Turkey in the near future. Kennedy also gave Dobrynin a deadline. If the Cuban missiles were not dismantled within 48 hours, the United States would destroy them.

On October 28, Khrushchev accepted the deal. The Soviet premier had badly miscalculated the stern American reaction to the placement of offensive missiles in Cuba, though his restraint in the crisis helped to assure a peaceful solution. Khrushchev soon left office in disgrace, and Kennedy's reputation soared. For 2 weeks in October, the world had seemed headed for nuclear war.

That fact alone seemed to sober both sides. In July 1963, a direct telephone link, known as the "hotline," was established between the White House and the Kremlin. In August, the United States and Russia joined with 90 other nations to sign the "Treaty Banning Nuclear Weapons Tests in the Atmosphere, in Outer Space, and Under Water." The treaty did not prevent underground

testing or provide for on-site inspection, and several emerging atomic powers, such as France and China, refused to take part. Yet a first step had been taken to cleanse the environment of radioactivity—a symbolic step on the road to a safer world.

Trouble in Vietnam

President Kennedy came away from the missile crisis with greater confidence in his ability to manage foreign problems. His primary goal, in military terms, was to replace the Eisenhower–Dulles doctrine of "massive retaliation" with a "flexible response" policy that would maximize his options in any foreign crisis. The plan called for a buildup in nuclear missiles, conventional ground troops, and Special Forces such as the "Green Berets." Not surprisingly, the defense budget rose rapidly in the Kennedy years, with Congress approving virtually all of the president's military spending requests. Under JFK, the armed forces added 10 Polaris submarines, 200,000 ground troops, and 400 Minutemen missiles, giving the United States a sizable advantage over Russia in nuclear weapons.

When Kennedy entered the White House, American aid to South Vietnam topped $1 billion, and several hundred American military advisors were in the field. Like Eisenhower, Kennedy hoped to formalize Vietnam's temporary partition at the 17th parallel by turning the South Vietnamese regime of Ngo Dingh Diem into a military and economic power capable of defending itself against attacks from Ho Chi Minh's Communist government in the North.

Kennedy welcomed the challenge. Under the doctrine of "flexible response," U.S. Special Forces were dispatched to train South Vietnam's army, along with CIA personnel to direct covert operations and economic experts to supervise the aid programs intended to stabilize Diem's regime. Among the worst problems, it turned out, was Diem himself. Educated in the United States, a Catholic in a largely Buddhist land, Diem had little in common with the people he ruled. The South Vietnam he envisioned did not include the vital measures, such as land reform and religious toleration, that were needed to keep him in power.

In 1963, protests erupted in Saigon and other South Vietnamese cities over Diem's autocratic rule. The Buddhists held mass demonstrations against religious oppression, with several monks setting fire to themselves. As the protests escalated, army units attacked Buddhist temples and arrested their priests, sparking even greater protests from the Buddhist majority. Isolated in his presidential palace, Diem seemed oblivious to the crisis.

AP/Wide World Photos

Quang Duc, a Buddhist monk in Saigon, burned himself to death in June 1963 to protest the crackdown on Buddhists by South Vietnamese President Ngo Dinh Diem. The Buddhist protests helped bring down the Diem government later that year.

That fall, Diem was overthrown in a military coup engineered by South Vietnam's top generals. American officials knew about the coup, but did nothing to stop it. To their surprise, however, the generals murdered Diem and his brother, Ngo Dinh Nhu, after taking them prisoner on the palace grounds.

By that time, 16,000 American "advisors" were stationed in South Vietnam. For Kennedy and his advisors, the struggle had become a test of will against "communist aggression." Yet the president also worried that the use of American troops created a dangerous momentum of its own. "It's like taking a drink," he said. "The effect wears off and you have to take another."

The year 1962 also witnessed the publication of two pathbreaking books about the underside of modern society: Michael Harrington's *The Other America* and Rachel Carson's *Silent Spring*. Carson, a marine biologist, exposed the contamination of wildlife, water supplies, and farmland by pesticides such as DDT. Her book helped revive America's naturalist movement. In 1963, two more seminal works appeared: Betty Friedan's *The Feminine Mystique*, which spurred the struggle for women's rights, and James Baldwin's *The Fire Next Time*, which warned of the growing racial divide. "To be a Negro in this country and to be relatively conscious," wrote Baldwin, "is to be in a rage all the time."

From Birmingham to Washington

By 1963, racial injustice in America was a central issue. Birmingham, Alabama, became the new battleground, as a coalition of civil rights groups, led by Martin Luther King's Southern Christian Leadership Conference, attempted to break down the walls of discrimination in a city where African Americans had few economic opportunities or political rights. Birmingham was so rigidly segregated that a book featuring black rabbits and white rabbits eating together was removed from city libraries, and a campaign was underway to banish "Negro music" from "white" radio stations.

Dr. King hoped to integrate Birmingham with a series of nonviolent protests code-named "Project C," for confrontation. Using the local black churches as

The Rights Revolution: Early Steps

In the early 1960s, the fires of social and political protest slowly came alive, fanned by the civil rights movement and the New Frontier's vision of idealism and change. In 1962, as James Meredith challenged the once impenetrable wall of segregation at Ole Miss, a 35-year-old Mexican American named **Cesar Chavez** moved to Delano, California, with his wife and eight children. A naval veteran of World War II, Chavez toiled in the plum orchards and strawberry fields of central California before turning to community organizing. With unshakable conviction, he aimed to better the lives of impoverished migrant farm laborers by uniting them under a single banner—the black Aztec eagle of the fledgling United Farm Workers of America.

AP/Wide World Photos

Led by Eugene ("Bull") Connor, Birmingham police used attack dogs and high-pressure fire hoses to disperse civil rights demonstrators.

meetinghouses, he recruited hundreds of followers with his revivalist appeals.

The demonstrations challenged segregation on many fronts. There were sit-ins at lunch counters, kneel-ins at white churches, and voter registration marches to city hall. Boycotts were organized to protest the all-white hiring practices of downtown department stores. Birmingham authorities cracked down hard. Led by Commissioner Eugene ("Bull") Connor, city police dispersed the protesters—many of them schoolchildren— with attack dogs and high-pressure fire hoses.

Dr. King was among the hundreds arrested for violating local court orders against marching and picketing. From his jail cell, he defended the morality of civil disobedience, noting that "segregation statutes are unjust because segregation distorts the soul." President Kennedy offered firm support. After dispatching federal troops to Birmingham, he assisted in an agreement that integrated the city's lunch counters and department stores. At that very moment, however, Governor George C. Wallace— proclaiming "Segregation Now! Segregation Tomorrow! Segregation Forever"—vowed to block the admission of two black students to the University of Alabama by "standing in the schoolhouse door." When federal marshals arrived, Wallace dramatically stepped aside.

The president's decisive action in Alabama signaled a major change. Viewing civil rights for the first time as a *moral* issue, Kennedy delivered a moving appeal for justice on national television. "One hundred years have passed since President Lincoln freed the slaves," he said, "yet their heirs, their grandsons, are not fully free. . . . And this nation, for all its hope and all its boasts, will not be fully free until all its citizens are free." Later that evening, civil rights activist Medgar Evers was assassinated outside his Jackson, Mississippi, home by a member of the Ku Klux Klan.

In June 1963, Kennedy sent Congress one of the most sweeping civil rights bills of the twentieth century. The bill, which prohibited discrimination in employment, federally assisted programs, and public accommodations such as restaurants and hotels, caused a furor on Capitol Hill. Southern legislators accused the president of "race-mixing," and others, including Senator Barry Goldwater of Arizona, criticized him for abusing the "property rights" of business owners. As the bill's momentum stalled, a number of civil rights groups led by A. Philip Randolph, longtime president of the Brotherhood of Sleeping Car Porters, announced a "March on Washington for Jobs and Freedom."

On August 28, 1963, more than 200,000 people gathered at the Lincoln Memorial in the largest civil rights demonstration ever held on American soil. They listened to the spirituals of Mahalia Jackson, locked

From the steps of the Lincoln Memorial, Martin Luther King, Jr., delivered his eloquent "I Have a Dream" address to a gathering of 200,000 people who had come to Washington to push for passage of a landmark civil rights bill in August 1963.

arms in solidarity as Joan Baez sang "We Shall Overcome," the anthem of the civil rights struggle, and rose in thunderous applause to the final words of Martin Luther King's now legendary address, "I Have a Dream."

Feminist Stirrings

The civil rights movement always possessed a strong female strain. From Rosa Parks in Montgomery to **Fannie Lou Hamer** of the Mississippi Freedom Democratic party, women played a prominent role in the struggle for black equality. By 1963, the spirit of these protests created a sense of determination that sparked other movements, such as women's rights.

The revival of feminism in the 1960s seemed long overdue. More than four decades after winning the vote, American women played a minor role in government affairs. In 1963, there were no women governors, cabinet officers, or Supreme Court justices. The U.S. Senate contained one female member, Margaret Chase Smith of Maine. Women comprised 51 percent of the population, but only 3 percent of state legislators nationwide.

Discrimination also pervaded the workplace. Though more women were working outside the home in the early 1960s than ever before, they were increasingly concentrated in low-paying service and clerical jobs, despite their rising level of education. Fewer than 4 percent of the nation's lawyers, and 1 percent of the top business executives, were female. As a result, full-time working women earned about 60 percent of the income of men.

These inequities were highlighted in 1963 by the final report of the Presidential Commission on the Status of Women. Led by Eleanor Roosevelt (who died in 1962) and Esther Peterson, an assistant secretary of labor, the commission detailed a wide range of problems, including job discrimination, unequal wages, lack of child care, and legal restrictions that prevented women, in some states, from sitting on juries or making wills. In direct response, President Kennedy issued an executive order banning sex discrimination in federal employment. A few months later, Congress passed the Equal Pay Act of 1963, requiring employers to provide equal wages to men and women who did the same work.

Even more important in terms of the emerging women's movement was the publication of *The Feminine Mystique.* In the opening chapters, **Betty Friedan** described "the problem that has no name," the emptiness felt by middle-class women who sacrificed their dreams and careers to become the "happy homemakers" of suburban America. Blaming educators, advertisers, social scientists, and government officials for creating a climate in which femininity and domesticity went hand in hand, Friedan concluded that "we can no longer ignore that voice in women that says: 'I want something more than my husband and my children and my home.'"

The Feminine Mystique became an instant best-seller because it voiced the unspoken feelings of so many women. Their unhappiness was not caused by individual neuroses, Friedan argued, but rather by a set of cultural values that oppressed women while pretending to improve their lives. The message, she added, was that women must grasp their common problems in order to solve them.

Tragedy and Transition

By the fall of 1963, the fast pace and rapid changes of the new decade were leaving their mark. A growing economy, an emerging rights revolution, an expanding war in Southeast Asia, a frantic race to the moon—each would serve to reshape the fabric of American life in the years ahead. First, however, tragedy intervened.

Dallas

In late November 1963, John and Jacqueline Kennedy traveled to Texas on a political fence-mending tour. The 1964 presidential race was approaching, and Texas, which had narrowly supported the Kennedy–Johnson ticket three years before, could not be taken for granted.

Moving through the streets of Dallas, President Kennedy's limousine headed toward Dealy Plaza—and tragedy—on November 22, 1963.

After greeting friendly crowds in Fort Worth, the Kennedys took a motorcade through Dallas, with the bubble-top of their limousine removed on a warm and cloudless day. Along the route, people waved from office buildings and cheered from the sidewalks. As the procession reached Dealy Plaza, shots rang out from the window of a nearby book depository. President Kennedy grabbed his throat and slumped to the seat. Texas Governor John Connally was wounded in the back, wrist, and leg. The motorcade raced to Parkland Hospital, where the president was pronounced dead.

Within hours, the Dallas police arrested a 24-year-old suspect named **Lee Harvey Oswald.** Two days later, Oswald was shot and killed in the basement of Dallas police headquarters by Jack Ruby, a local nightclub owner with a shady past. These shocking events led many Americans to conclude that Oswald was innocent or that he did not act alone. Dozens of theories surfaced about the Kennedy assassination, blaming leftists and rightists, Fidel Castro and the Mafia, the Ku Klux Klan and the CIA. The most logical theory, that a deranged man had committed a senseless act of violence, did not seem compelling enough to explain the death of a president so young and full of life.

Few events in the nation's history produced so much bewilderment and grief. Charming and handsome, a war hero with a glamorous wife, Kennedy seemed the ideal president for the electronic political age. The media likened his administration to Camelot, a magical place that symbolized courage, chivalry, and hope. His tragic death added the further dimension of promise unfulfilled.

The reality was rather different, of course. Kennedy's 1,037 days in office were marked by failures as well as successes, and his leadership was more decisive in foreign policy than it was in domestic affairs. Since his death, moreover, evidence of his extramarital affairs and other personal shortcomings have raised legitimate questions about his character and morality. Still, the president's final months were his most productive by far. The Test Ban Treaty offered hope for a safer world, and a new civil rights bill had been sent to Capitol Hill. There is also the suggestion—disputed by some—that Kennedy was rethinking his position on Vietnam. "If I tried to pull out completely now," he told Senator Mike Mansfield, "we would have another Joe McCarthy red scare on our hands, but I can do it after I'm reelected."

The trip to Dallas shattered those hopes and plans.

LBJ

Within hours of the assassination, Lyndon Johnson took the presidential oath of office aboard *Air Force One,* with his wife, Lady Bird, and Jacqueline Kennedy standing at his side. As the nation mourned its fallen leader, President Johnson vowed to continue the programs and policies of the Kennedy administration. "All I have," he told a special session of Congress, "I would gladly have given not to be standing here today."

Lyndon Baines Johnson—known as LBJ—bore little resemblance to the president he replaced. Born in the Texas hill country in 1908, Johnson came from a different region, a lower social class, and an older political generation. After graduating from a public college, he worked in the Washington office of a Texas congressman before returning home to become state director of the National Youth Administration, a New Deal agency that provided work-study funds for needy students. Under Johnson's leadership, the Texas NYA became a model for the nation, providing employment for blacks and whites in the construction of neighborhood playgrounds and roadside parks. The experience turned him into an avid New Dealer, with confidence in the government's ability to help people in need. Johnson described Franklin Roosevelt, his mentor and role model, as "like a daddy to me."

In the following years, Johnson won a seat in Congress, served as a naval officer during World War II, and

Lyndon Johnson provided a smooth transition by promising to continue the programs and policies of President Kennedy. Yet retaining Kennedy's key advisors served to limit Johnson's options, particularly in foreign affairs.

became a U.S. senator in 1949. (His margin of victory, a mere 87 votes, earned him the nickname "Landslide Lyndon.") Elected Senate majority leader by his Democratic colleagues in the 1950s, Johnson worked efficiently with the Eisenhower White House to craft important legislation on defense spending, highway construction, and civil rights.

LBJ lacked the good looks and regal charm of John Kennedy. He seemed crude and plodding by comparison, with his heavy drawl, cowboy boots, and earthy language. Yet few people in Washington knew more about the political process—how things really got done. Johnson recognized the true pockets of power. He knew when to flatter, when to bully, and when to bargain. Incredibly ambitious and hardworking—he survived a near-fatal heart attack in 1955—Johnson entered the White House with three decades of political experience under his belt.

Tax Cuts and Civil Rights

The new president moved quickly to restore public confidence through a smooth transition of power. To calm mounting suspicion of conspiracy, he appointed a seven-member commission, headed by Chief Justice Earl Warren, to investigate the Kennedy assassination and issue a report. To provide stability in the executive branch, he convinced Secretary of State Dean Rusk, Secretary of Defense Robert McNamara, chief economic advisor Walter Heller, and other key officials to remain at their jobs. Where Kennedy had proclaimed "Let us begin," Johnson added "Let us *continue!*"

One of his first acts as president was to work for the tax cut that Heller and Kennedy had supported. To please fiscal conservatives in Congress, Johnson agreed to slash the federal budget. He believed that lower taxes would spur economic growth and lower unemployment, thereby increasing federal revenues down the road. In February 1964, Johnson signed a measure that cut taxes by $10 billion over the next 2 years.

The economy responded. With more money available for investment and consumption, the gross national product shot up 7 percent in 1964 and 8 percent the following year, and unemployment fell below 5 percent for the first time since World War II. Furthermore, the economic boom generated even greater federal revenues—just as Johnson had predicted.

Within weeks after taking office, the president met with Martin Luther King, Jr., and other black leaders to assure them of his commitment to civil rights. This was essential, for Johnson's public record was mixed. As a young senator, he had opposed virtually all of President Truman's civil rights initiatives. Yet as majority leader, he had helped pass legislation giving the Justice Department more authority to enforce school integration and protect black voting rights. In his heart, Johnson considered segregation to be an immoral system that retarded an entire region's advancement. "He felt about the race question much as I did," a Texas friend recalled, "namely that it obsessed the South and diverted it from attending to its economic and educational problems."

The civil rights bill had strong public backing outside the South. In February, the House of Representatives easily approved it by a vote of 290 to 130, but the bill hit a wall in the Senate, where southern opponents used the filibuster to prevent its passage. The bill's success depended on a vote for cloture, ending debate, which required the agreement of two-thirds of the Senate. Working together, Senators Hubert Humphrey (D-Minnesota) and Everett Dirksen (R-Illinois) gathered bipartisan support. The Senate voted for cloture on June 10, 1964 (ending a 75-day filibuster), and passed the bill the following afternoon. Described by the *New York Times* as "the most far-reaching civil rights [legislation] since Reconstruction days," it withheld federal funds from segregated public programs, created an Equal Employment Opportunity Commission, and outlawed discrimination in public accommodations, such as theaters, restaurants, and hotels. Furthermore, a last-minute lobbying effort by Senator Margaret Chase Smith and other women's rights supporters added another category—"sex"—to the clause in Title VII that prohibited employment discrimination based on race, creed, or national origin. What seemed like a minor addition became a powerful asset to working women in the future.

President Johnson signed the bill into law on July 2, 1964. Though compliance came slowly, the Civil Rights Act marked a vital turning point in the struggle for equal rights. Quoting Victor Hugo, Senator Dirksen declared that "no army can withstand the strength of an idea whose time has come."

Landslide in 1964

LBJ entered the 1964 presidential campaign on a tidal wave of popularity and good will. His early months in office were blunder-free. The nation prospered, Vietnam appeared as a distant blip on the screen, and the only war on Johnson's public agenda was the one against poverty, which he promised to wage—and win—after his expected victory at the polls.

The summer of 1964, however, offered signs of the trouble to come. In Mississippi, an attempt to register black voters by local activists and northern college students met violent resistance from white mobs. On June 21, three volunteers—James Chaney, Andrew Goodman, and Michael Schwerner—disappeared after inspecting the ruins of a firebombed black church. Because Goodman and Schwerner were northern whites, the incident made the front pages of newspapers across the country. Five weeks later, FBI agents found three bodies buried in an earthen dam. The civil rights workers had been murdered by local Klansmen and police, seven of whom were eventually convicted and sent to jail.

Racial tensions that summer were not confined to the South. In July, a confrontation between residents and police officers in Harlem led to several nights of arson and looting. The trouble was followed by disturbances in the black neighborhoods of Philadelphia, Pennsylvania; Paterson, New Jersey; and Rochester, New York. At the Democratic National Convention in Atlantic City, moreover, the race issue took center stage. Although the nomination of President Johnson and Senator

Humphrey, his running mate, went smoothly, a floor fight erupted over the seating of two rival Mississippi delegations—one composed of state party segregationists, the other representing the biracial Mississippi Freedom Democratic party (MFDP).

Led by Fannie Lou Hamer, the twentieth child of illiterate sharecroppers, the MFDP spoke for the disenfranchised black majority in Mississippi. "I was beaten till I was exhausted," Hamer told the national convention. "All of this on account we wanted to register, to become first class citizens. If the Freedom Democratic party is not seated now, I question America."

Johnson hoped to compromise. Acting through Senator Humphrey, he offered the Freedom party two voting delegates and the promise of a fully integrated Mississippi delegation at future national conventions. The compromise pleased no one. Mrs. Hamer rejected it as a "token" gesture, and several white Mississippi delegates left Atlantic City in a huff.

Picturing the Past **POLITICS & DIPLOMACY**

A New Era in Political Advertising

By 1964, the use of television for political advertising was on the rise. But negative TV spots, so common in election campaigns today, were still relatively rare. All that changed, however, with an ad (shown here) produced for the Democrats by Doyle Dane Bernbach, one of America's largest advertising firms, which portrayed Republican presidential candidate Barry Goldwater as a dangerous extremist who could easily plunge the world into nuclear war. By following the individual frames, one can see a little girl innocently pulling the petals from a daisy. As she reaches the number

nine, an adult voice begins a reverse countdown for the launching of an atomic device. At zero, the girl's face is engulfed by a huge mushroom cloud. The ominous voice-over appears under the final three frames. Ironically, the notorious "Daisy Ad" aired only once on television; the Democrats pulled it after the Republicans filed a formal complaint with the Fair Campaign Practices Committee. But news programs showed the ad over and over again, sending the message into millions of American homes.

"Ten, nine, eight, seven . . .

six, five, four, three . . .

two, one . . .

These are the stakes. To make a world in which all of God's children can live . . .

or to go into the dark. We must either love each other or we must die . . .

The stakes are too high for you to stay home."

At the Republican National Convention in San Francisco, the simmering feud between moderates and conservatives boiled over, with delegates shouting down opponents with catcalls and boos. After bitter debate, the convention chose Senator Barry Goldwater of Arizona for the presidential nomination, and Representative William Miller of New York for the vice presidential spot. In a defiant acceptance speech, Goldwater promised a "spiritual awakening" for America, adding: "Extremism in the defense of liberty is no vice. Moderation in the pursuit of justice is no virtue."

Goldwater opposed "big government" in domestic affairs, but supported large military budgets to deter "Communist aggression." His Senate record included votes against social security increases, the Nuclear Test Ban Treaty of 1963, and the Civil Rights Act of 1964. In contrast to Goldwater, President Johnson came across as the candidate of all Americans, with promises galore. "We're in favor of a lot of things and we're against mighty few," he said.

Even in foreign affairs, his least favorite subject, Johnson appeared confident and controlled. In August 1964, two U.S. Navy destroyers, the *Maddox* and *C. Turner Joy,* engaged several North Vietnamese torpedo boats in the Gulf of Tonkin. The truth about this incident—Did a battle really occur? Who fired first? What were American warships doing in these waters?—was overshadowed by Johnson's dramatic response. First he ordered U.S. planes to bomb military targets deep inside North Vietnam. Then he requested—and received—a congressional resolution authorizing the president to "take all necessary measures" to repel "further aggression."

The **Gulf of Tonkin Resolution** gave Johnson the authority he would need to escalate the Vietnam War. During the 1964 campaign, however, he assured voters that nothing could be further from his mind. "We don't want American boys to do the fighting for Asian boys," he declared. "We don't want to get tied down in a land war in Asia."

The election was never in doubt. Johnson projected optimism and energy, while Goldwater appeared defensive and out-of-touch. The president won 61 percent of the popular vote (43 million to 27 million) and 44 of the 50 states (486 electoral votes to Goldwater's 52). In addition, his lopsided margin of victory allowed the Democrats to increase their substantial majorities in both houses of Congress.

For Republicans, however, the news was not all bad. The election returns showed that a new coalition was forming in their ranks, with the party gaining strength among middle-class white voters in the South and Southwest. Furthermore, Goldwater attracted thousands of young recruits who were determined to reshape the Republican party along more conservative lines. For these legions, 1964 was a beginning rather than an end.

The Great Society

President Johnson viewed his landslide victory as a mandate for change. Anxious to leave his mark on history, he spoke of creating "a great society" for Americans in which the "quality of our goals" exceeded the "quantity of our goods," a society in which poverty, ignorance, and discrimination no longer existed, and the spirit of "true community" prevailed.

Declaring War on Poverty

The centerpiece of Johnson's expansive vision was his "War on Poverty," a concept that President Kennedy and his aides had explored shortly before his death. To maintain continuity, Johnson named R. Sargent Shriver, Kennedy's brother-in-law, to coordinate the numerous programs created by the Economic Opportunity Act of 1964, including the Job Corps, the Neighborhood Youth Corps, and Volunteers in Service to America (VISTA), a domestic service program modeled on the Peace Corps. Though Congress allocated $3 billion for these programs in 1965 and 1966, this figure would decline as the Vietnam War expanded.

The most controversial aspect of the "War on Poverty" was its emphasis on "community action," which encouraged neighborhood groups to play an active role in federally funded projects. Some initiatives, such as food stamps and Head Start, a preschool enrichment program, proved very successful. Others were cited for waste and fraud. Of greatest lasting impact, it appeared, was the increase of minority participation in local affairs.

Poverty did decline dramatically in this era—the result of an expanding economy as well as federal programs aimed directly at the poor. In 1960, more than 40 million Americans (20 percent of the population) lived beneath the poverty line; by 1970, that figure had dropped to 24 million (12 percent). For all of its problems, the much maligned and seriously underfunded War on Poverty achieved a fair measure of success.

Health Care and Immigration Reform

The Great Society included a mixture of original programs and borrowed ideas. A kind of infectious optimism gripped Washington, much like the early days of the New Deal. Nothing seemed politically impossible with Lyndon Johnson in charge.

Health care was a good example. When Johnson took office in 1963, a majority of older Americans were without health insurance, one-fifth of the nation's poor had never visited a doctor, and the infant mortality rate showed no signs of declining, despite the introduction of lifesaving vaccines. Johnson believed that medical care for the poor and the elderly was an essential part of the Great Society. Yet the idea of federal involvement raised fundamental questions about the role of government in a free enterprise system. The American Medical Association (AMA) and private insurers strongly opposed such intervention, calling it "socialized medicine."

After months of intense lobbying, Congress passed the landmark legislation, known as Medicare and Medicaid, that Johnson requested. Medicare provided federal assistance to the elderly for hospital expenses and doctors' fees, and Medicaid extended medical coverage to welfare recipients through matching grants to the states. Both programs grew rapidly, reaching 40 million Americans by 1970. Though supporters pointed with pride to statistics showing both an increase in life expectancy and a drop in infant mortality, critics noted the exploding federal costs, the gaps in coverage, and the inferior quality of health care to the poor. Few government programs proved more controversial and expensive to maintain than Medicare and Medicaid, and none would prove more difficult to reform.

The Great Society also included a new immigration law, passed in 1965. Though vitally important to the nation's future, it went largely unnoticed at the time. In one bold sweep, the Immigration Act removed the "national origins" quotas, as well as the ban on Asians, which dated back to 1924. Although it set a ceiling of about 300,000 immigrants per year, the law permitted the family members of American citizens (both naturalized and native-born) to enter the United States without limit.

The impact was dramatic. Prior to 1965, Europe accounted for 90 percent of the new arrivals to the United States; after 1965, only 10 percent. By the mid-1970s, a majority of legal immigrants came from seven Asian and Latin American countries: Korea, Taiwan, India, the Philippines, Cuba, the Dominican Republic, and Mexico.

The Expanding War

Lyndon Johnson inherited a rich agenda from the Kennedy White House, including the War on Poverty and the push for civil rights. But nothing proved as important, or damaging, to his presidency as the conflict in Vietnam. When Johnson assumed office, there were fewer than 20,000 American "advisors" in that divided country, training the soldiers and bureaucrats of anti-Communist South Vietnam. Within 3 years, that number had risen to almost 500,000, with no end in sight. Vietnam quickly became Johnson's war, and, ultimately, his nightmare.

Point of No Return

Vietnam was part of a larger "containment" effort that had guided American foreign affairs since the end of World War II. Like Presidents Truman, Eisenhower, and Kennedy, LBJ based his commitment to Vietnam on a series of powerful assumptions, such as saving "democracy" in Asia, halting the spread of communism, and maintaining America's credibility around the globe. It hardly mattered that South Vietnam was neither a democracy nor the victim of an international communist plot. What did matter was the need for strength and staying power in a world crisis—the belief that a defeat for the United States anywhere would undermine its standing everywhere.

Johnson understood the political stakes. "I am not going to lose Vietnam," he said. "I am not going to be the president who saw [it] go the way China went." His plan was to pressure the communist enemy in a measured fashion that would neither alarm the American public nor divert resources from his cherished domestic programs. The Gulf of Tonkin Resolution gave him the authority to move forward. The Viet Cong attack at Pleiku provided the motive.

Pleiku, a market town in the central highlands of South Vietnam, was home to a military airstrip guarded by American Special Forces. In February 1965, a Viet Cong mortar barrage killed 8 Americans and wounded more than 100. Several days later, U.S. warplanes began the massive bombing of North Vietnam. Known first as Operation Rolling Thunder, the air strikes hit targets checked personally by President Johnson, who boasted that "they can't even bomb an outhouse without my approval." The problem, however, was that air power had little impact on North Vietnam's ability to wage war. The bombings killed thousands, flattened factories and power plants, and ravaged the economy; yet the flow of communist troops and supplies into South Vietnam never stopped.

In March 1965, two marine batallions arrived at the huge new U.S. Air Force base in Da Nang, raising the American troop total in South Vietnam above 100,000. By December, troop levels reached 184,000 and rose each month thereafter. Draft calls zoomed from 100,000 in 1964 to 340,000 by 1966, leading millions of young men to seek student deferments or to join the National Guard in the hope of avoiding combat in Vietnam.

By 1965, at least half of South Vietnam was controlled by Viet Cong or North Vietnamese troops. The new South Vietnamese government of General Nguyen Van Thieu appeared more stable than previous ones, but its army was no match for the well-disciplined communist soldiers. As Johnson saw it, American forces would defend South Vietnam until its people were ready to defend themselves. "We will not be defeated," the president vowed. "We will not withdraw."

American strategy in Vietnam had both a military and political objective: to wear down the enemy with superior firepower, and to "win the hearts and minds" of the South Vietnamese people. Neither proved successful. North Vietnam, a nation of 19 million, continued to field a large army despite enormous casualties, while the Viet Cong provided able support. Fighting on native soil, these soldiers waged relentless, often brutal war against a "foreign aggressor" and its "puppets" inside South Vietnam. Between 1965 and 1966, U.S. combat deaths rose tenfold, from 636 to 6,664.

Americans fought bravely, and morale at this point remained high. Yet the very nature of the war alienated these soldiers from the people they had come to defend. It would have been trying, under the best of circumstances, to distinguish between innocent civilians and Viet Cong. Unfamiliar with the language and culture of Vietnam, Americans increasingly viewed everyone as the enemy. Each village appeared as "a dark room full of deadly spiders," a soldier recalled.

American planners tried numerous strategies to isolate the Viet Cong and deprive them of their sanctuaries. Most included the movement of peasant populations from their ancestral lands to "strategic hamlets" or to cities unprepared for the arrival of thousands of homeless refugees. Between 1960 and 1970, the percentage of South Vietnamese living in urban areas jumped from 20 to 43 percent. In these bulging cities, jobs were scarce, prostitution flourished, and families split apart.

Those who remained in the countryside faced terror from all sides. There were North Vietnamese mortar attacks, Viet Cong assassination squads, and American assaults from the ground and the air. U.S. planes and helicopters defoliated the fields and forests with chemical sprays, and pounded suspected enemy strongholds with bombs and napalm (jellied gasoline). In one of the most telling remarks of the war, an American officer explained his mission bluntly: "We had to destroy this town in order to save it."

Early Protests

Even as President Johnson escalated the war in 1965, he expected the Great Society to move freely ahead. A "rich nation can afford to make progress at home while meeting its obligations abroad," he declared. The United States could have both guns and butter; there was no need to choose.

For a time, his domestic agenda remained impressive. Fueled by the immense economic prosperity of 1965 and 1966, the Great Society added an Education Act that extended federal aid to public and private schools, and a Model Cities Act that provided funds to upgrade housing, health services, crime prevention, and parks. In addition, LBJ reaffirmed his commitment to civil rights by appointing the first African American Supreme Court justice, Thurgood Marshall, and the first African American cabinet member, Robert Weaver, to head the new Department of Housing and Urban Development (HUD).

The momentum didn't last. The decision to escalate in Vietnam divided the nation and sapped the president's strength. The first rumblings of antiwar protest came from the college campuses, where a new group, calling itself **Students for a Democratic Society (SDS),** was gaining ground. Formed in Port Huron, Michigan, in 1962, SDS issued a "Declaration of Principles" that denounced "racism" and "militarism," among other evils, and promised a new politics based on socialist ideals. Limited at first to "elite" colleges and major state universities, such as Harvard, Berkeley, and Wisconsin, the organization expanded in direct proportion to the war itself.

The early student leaders called their movement the "New Left." Some of them, known as "Red-diaper babies," were the children of "Old Left" radicals from the 1930s and 1940s. Others came from the burgeoning civil rights movement. Impatient and idealistic, they identified with the "revolutionary" movements of the emerging Third World. To their eyes, Fidel Castro and Ho Chi Minh were positive forces in history, representing a fundamental shift in power from the privileged elites to the struggling masses. Not surprisingly, Vietnam became the New Left's defining issue—a symbol of popular resistance to America's "imperialist" designs.

Early in 1965, antiwar students and faculty at the University of Michigan held the nation's first "teach-in" to discuss the consequences of escalation in Vietnam. The idea spread rapidly from campus to campus—with the University of Maine's teach-in attracting 300 people, and Berkeley's drawing more than 12,000. On Easter Sunday, a crowd of 30,000 attended the first major antiwar rally in Washington, sponsored by SDS. The speakers, including radical journalist I. F. Stone and folk singer Joan Baez, linked the Vietnam demonstrations to other issues that were percolating within the larger society, such as civil rights, women's rights, and the role of universities in fostering protest and dissent.

DOING HISTORY

Visions of the "Multiversity"

THE STUDENT MOVEMENTS of the 1960s had many sources. At the University of California at Berkeley, for example, what began as a protest against campus restrictions on certain types of political activity soon expanded to a full-blown attack on the growing power exerted by corporations and government agencies over American higher education. In 1963, University of California President Clark Kerr coined the term "multiversity" to describe the massive, impersonal institutions that had replaced the smaller, student-friendly colleges of the past. Kerr saw this as progress. Above all, he believed, universities must provide the basic research needed to drive modern societies forward. He wrote:

> "The basic reality, for the university, is the widespread recognition that new knowledge is the most important factor in economic and social growth. We are just now perceiving that the university's invisible product, knowledge, may be the most powerful single element in our culture, affecting the rise and fall of professions and even of social classes, of regions and even of nations. . . .
>
> This reality is reshaping the very nature and quality of the university. Old concepts of faculty-student relations, of research, of faculty-administration roles are being changed at a rate without parallel. . . . Thus the university has come to have a new centrality for all of us, as much as for those who never see the ivied halls as for those who pass through them or reside there."

Kerr's view offended many students of this era, who found their college experience to be increasingly regimented and dull. Among these students was Mario Savio, a philosophy major who led the growing protests at Berkeley. Addressing 800 students during a campus sit-in, he said:

> "The University [of Clark Kerr] is well structured, well-tooled, to turn out people with all the sharp edges worn off, the well-rounded person. The University is well-equipped to produce that sort of person, and this means that the best among the people who enter must for four years wander aimlessly much of the time questioning why they are on campus at all, doubting whether there is any point in what they are doing, and looking toward a very bleak existence afterward in a game in which all of the rules have been made up, which one cannot really amend.
>
> It is a bleak scene. . . . America is becoming ever more the Utopia of sterilized, automated contentment. The 'futures' and 'careers' for which American students now prepare are for the most part intellectual and moral wastelands. This chrome-plated consumers paradise would have us grow up to be well-behaved children. But an important minority of men and women coming to the front today have shown that they will die rather than be standardized, replaceable and irrelevant."

Source: Clark Kerr, *The Uses of the University,* 1963, Foreword; *Humanity,* December, 1964.

Questions for Reflection

1. What were the other sources of the student movement in this era? What else drove the student protests of the 1960s?

2. How much of a generational struggle is evident in Mario Savio's comments?

3. Does his description ring true to young people today?

4. Has Clark Kerr's vision of the "multiversity," driven by research, come to pass?

5. Did he correctly predict the future of higher education in the United States?

Explore additional primary sources related to this chapter on the Wadsworth American History Resource Center or HistoryNOW websites:

http://history.wadsworth.com
http://now.ilrn.com/ayers_etal3e.

© Bettmann/CORBIS

Mario Savio, pictured here, led the Free Speech movement at the University of California at Berkeley in 1964 that spurred similar campus protests throughout the nation.

The Rights Revolution: Center Stage

The national mood of unity and reconciliation that followed President Kennedy's assassination in November 1963 did not last much beyond the landslide election of 1964. The war in Vietnam created divisions that grew wider by the year. Americans became more skeptical of their leaders and less likely to believe official explanations of events. Even a master consensus-builder like Lyndon Johnson faced an overwhelming task.

Voting Rights

Following passage of the landmark Civil Rights Act of 1964, the struggle for racial justice moved to the next battleground: voting rights in the Deep South. The campaign was already under way in places like Selma, Alabama, where local activists, facing intense white resistance, asked Martin Luther King, Jr., and his Southern Christian Leadership Conference for support.

The Selma demonstrations began early in 1965. Local blacks marched daily to the courthouse, where Sheriff Jim Clark—wearing a huge button with the single word NEVER—used force to turn them away. Thousands were arrested, beaten with clubs, and shocked with cattle prods for attempting to register with the local election board. In March, Dr. King decided to lead a protest march from Selma to Montgomery, the state capital, 50 miles away. "We are not asking, we are demanding the ballot," he declared.

On March 9—known as Bloody Sunday—a contingent of Sheriff Clark's deputies and Alabama state police attacked the marchers, sending 17 to the hospital. Hundreds of civil rights leaders, entertainers, politicians, and clergy rushed to Selma to lend their support, but the violence continued. James Reeb, a Unitarian minister from Boston, was beaten to death by a gang of whites, and Viola Luizzo, a civil rights activist from Michigan, was shot and killed by the Klan.

On March 15, President Johnson made a special trip to Capitol Hill to urge passage of a new voting rights bill. In the most eloquent speech of his career, Johnson said:

> What happened in Selma is part of a larger movement which reaches into every section and state of America. It is the effort of Negroes to secure for themselves the full blessing of American life.
>
> Their cause must be our cause, too. Because it is not just Negroes, but really it is all of us who must overcome the crippling legacy of bigotry and injustice.
>
> And we shall overcome.

The Watts Explosion

Five days later, on August 11, a riot erupted in Watts, a black section of Los Angeles, triggering the worst urban violence since World War II. The disturbance began with the arrest of a black motorist by a white highway patrolman. A crowd gathered, police reinforcements arrived, and several arrests were made. As word of the incident spread, several thousand people—mostly young

---

Picturing the Past | POLITICS & DIPLOMACY

Black Voter Registration

Black voter registration in the South was one of the great accomplishments of the civil rights movement. Spurred by the Selma demonstrations, President Johnson signed the Voting Rights Act on August 6, 1965, which abolished discriminatory practices such as the literacy test, and authorized federal examiners to register voters, instead of relying on the individual states. As this table demonstrates, the act profoundly altered the political landscape of the South.

Within months of its passage, more than 2 million black Southerners were registered to vote. Most supported the Democratic party of Presidents John F. Kennedy and Lyndon Johnson, which had endorsed the cause of civil rights. At the same time, however, white southerners deserted the Democrats and moved overwhelmingly into the Republican party. In the 1968 presidential election (see Map 29.2, page 870), Democratic candidate Hubert Humphrey would win only one southern state, beginning a trend of Republican dominance in the South that has lasted, with few notable exceptions, to the present time.

Table 29.2 Black Voter Registration

State	1960	1966	Percent Increase
Alabama	66,000	250,000	278.8
Arkansas	73,000	115,000	57.5
Florida	183,000	303,000	65.6
Georgia	180,000	300,000	66.7
Louisiana	159,000	243,000	52.8
Mississippi	22,000	175,000	695.4
North Carolina	210,000	282,000	34.3
South Carolina	58,000	191,000	229.3
Tennessee	185,000	225,000	21.6
Texas	227,000	400,000	76.2
Virginia	100,000	205,000	105.0

Source: U.S. Bureau of the Census, *Statistical Abstract of the United States: 1982–83* (103d edition) Washington, D.C., 1982.

Flashpoints | *Miranda v. Arizona* (1966)

"You have the right to remain silent. You have the right to the presence of an attorney. If you cannot afford one, an attorney will be appointed. Any statement that you make may be used against you in a court of law." Almost everyone is familiar with these words, thanks to the extraordinary reach of television dramas such as "NYPD Blue" and "Law and Order." But far fewer people know about the case of *Miranda v. Arizona*, which brought these words into the public arena.

Ernesto Miranda, young, uneducated, with a criminal record, was convicted of kidnapping and rape after confessing to police following 2 hours of questioning.

He then appealed on grounds that he had not been given the chance to speak with an attorney—thereby violating his Fifth Amendment right against self-incrimination. Though the Arizona State Supreme Court affirmed Miranda's conviction, the U.S. Supreme Court, led by Chief Justice Earl Warren, overturned it on a narrow 5-4 vote. For Warren, the case was about equal justice: a poor defendant deserved the same protection as a wealthy one. But others on the Court saw *Miranda* as a disastrous ruling for the future of law enforcement. It was, wrote Justice John M. Harlan, a "dangerous experiment" in an era of already rising crime.

Harlan wasn't alone. Perhaps no ruling of the Warren Court proved as controversial as *Miranda*.

Police chiefs across the nation warned that it would put dangerous criminals back on the street. Campaigning for president in 1968, Richard Nixon vowed to reverse the Warren Court's "folly" by appointing only tough law-and-order judges to the federal bench. Over the years, however, these emotions have cooled, and most Americans, polls show, have come to accept the "Miranda warning" as a way to protect the rights of defendants while also professionalizing the work of the police.

For his part, Ernesto Miranda continued his life of crime. In 1976, following several more arrests, he was killed by two illegal aliens during a poker game. One was never found; the other, upon capture, was read his "Miranda warning" in both English and Spanish: "You have the right to remain silent. You have the right to the presence of an attorney . . ." The man chose not to speak.

Questions for Reflection

1. What made the Miranda case so controversial? What sort of practices was it designed to protect against?

2. Can you think of modern-day examples that test the delicate balance between the rights of individual suspects and the protection of society?

---

men—rampaged down Crenshaw Boulevard, looting stores, burning buildings, and overturning cars. The violence flared each evening for a week. It took 14,000 National Guardsmen to restore order. At least 34 people were killed, 1,000 injured, and 4,000 arrested, with property damage estimated at $200 million.

DOING HISTORY ONLINE

The Voting Rights Act, 1965

Read the document in this module. Lyndon Johnson was the strongest advocate of civil rights to occupy the White House in the twentieth century. Why, then, did the northern ghettos suffer through four years of summer race riots, when angry and disaffected African Americans took to the streets to dramatize their demands for change?

History ⧗ Now™   Visit HistoryNOW to access primary sources and exercises related to this topic: http://now.ilrn.com/ayers_etal3e

News of the **Watts riot** shocked President Johnson. "We simply hadn't seen the warnings," recalled Attorney General Ramsey Clark. "We had looked at [civil rights] as basically a southern problem, but . . . in fact the problems of the urban ghettos exceeded any that we were dealing with in the South."

Times had changed. By 1965, almost half of America's black population lived outside the South, mostly in large cities, and Watts epitomized the conditions of day-to-day urban life. Good housing was scarce. As black neighborhoods became overcrowded, residents wishing to move elsewhere were trapped by racial discrimination. Inferior schools hampered upward mobility. Two out of three adults in Watts lacked a high school education, and one in eight was illiterate. Watts had the highest unemployment rate, and lowest income level, of any Los Angeles neighborhood except Skid Row. Two hundred of 205 policemen assigned to Watts were white. Crime was rampant, public services poor. "The sewers stank in the summer, there was not enough water to flush toilets, not enough pressure to fight fires," said one Watts resident. "The social fabric just couldn't stand the strain."

The Watts riot of 1965 began a cycle of urban destruction that engulfed dozens of cities in the coming years.

Some rioters targeted white businesses in Watts for arson and looting. The Los Angeles police, suspecting a radical plot, stormed the Black Muslim Temple and arrested 59 people. Local residents knew better. The riot was a spontaneous event, not a planned act of destruction. In the next 3 years, hundreds of northern black neighborhoods would explode. The worst riots, in Newark and Detroit, would begin, as Watts did, with an incident between local blacks and white police.

Most African Americans deplored the riots and took no part. Yet a competing vision, far different from the one preached by Dr. King, was gathering strength in the black community. As he walked the streets of Watts after the riot, King met a group of youths shouting, "We won!" He asked how anyone could claim victory in the face of such violence and destruction. "We won," a young man answered, "because we made them pay attention to us."

Black Power

By the mid-1960s, Dr. King's leadership in the civil rights movement was increasingly under attack. Younger African Americans, in particular, seemed reluctant to follow his course. At a 1966 rally in Mississippi, a recent Howard University graduate named Stokely Carmichael brought this issue to a head. Just released from jail for leading a peaceful civil rights protest, Carmichael vented his anger as a clearly uncomfortable Dr. King sat behind

him on the stage. "This is the twenty-seventh time I've been arrested," Carmichael shouted, "and I ain't going to jail no more. The only way we gonna stop them white men from whuppin' us is to take over. What we gonna start saying now is '**Black Power**.'" The crowd took up the chant: "Black Power! Black Power! Black Power!"

Black Power became a symbol of African American unity in the mid-1960s, stressing group strength, independent action, and racial pride. In local communities, black activists lobbied school boards to add African American history and culture to the curriculum. On college campuses, black students pressed administrators to speed up minority recruitment, establish Black Studies programs, and provide separate living quarters—a demand that alarmed integrationists, black and white. In the political arena, Carl Stokes of Cleveland and Richard Hatcher of Gary, Indiana, became the first African American mayors of northern cities by combining hard work with racial solidarity. Across the nation, black men and women donned African clothing, took on African names, and wore their hair unstraightened in an "Afro" style. "Black is Beautiful" became a powerful slogan in this era, as did "Say it loud, I'm black and I'm proud" by soul singer James Brown.

To militants like Stokely Carmichael, Black Power meant a political separation of the races. His position reflected a generational split between "old" civil rights groups such as the NAACP, which viewed racial integration as the key to black advancement, and "new" movement groups like Carmichael's Student Nonviolent Coordinating Committee (SNCC), which began to exclude whites. "Black people," said Carmichael, "must be seen in positions of power doing and articulating for themselves."

The separatist impulse had deep roots in the African American community. Its renewed strength in the 1960s was due, in large part, to a black nationalist movement that appealed to young people in the bleakest neighborhoods of urban America, far removed from civil rights and the Great Society. "There is a different type of Negro emerging from the 18- to 25-year-old bracket," said a black leader in Watts. "They identify with Malcolm X's philosophy."

Malcolm X was the most popular and controversial Black Muslim leader of the 1960s. Born Malcolm Little, he joined the Nation of Islam while serving a prison term for robbery and adopted the "X" to replace "the white slave-master name which had been imposed upon my paternal forebears by some blue-eyed devil." The Nation of Islam was a black nationalist group, organized

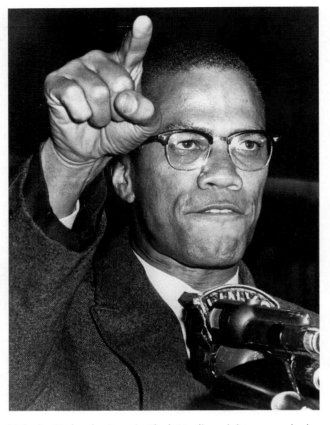

Malcolm X, the charismatic Black Muslim minister, preached a doctrine of black nationalism, self-help, and racial separation that held wide appeal for thousands of African Americans. He was assassinated by a rival Muslim group in 1965.

in Detroit in 1931, which preached a doctrine of self-help, moral discipline, and complete separation of the races. Its code of behavior, based on the rejection of racist stereotypes, stressed neatness, abstinence, and a firm division of male and female roles. Black Muslims were forbidden to smoke, drink alcohol, eat pork or cornbread, or have sex outside of marriage. "Wake up, clean up, and stand up," their motto declared.

Created by Elijah Poole, who renamed himself Elijah Muhammad, the Black Muslims were strongest in the urban ghettos, where their membership reached upwards of 100,000, with a far larger mass of sympathizers. Assigned by Elijah Muhammad to a temple in Harlem, Malcolm X became a charismatic figure to young black men, in particular, with his bold statements about the impact of white injustice on black behavior and self-esteem. "The worst crime the white man has committed," he said, "is to teach us to hate ourselves."

Malcolm also preached self-defense, saying that blacks must protect themselves "by any means necessary" and that "killing is a two-way street." Such rhetoric made it easy to label the entire Black Muslim movement as extremist, and to construe its message as one of violence and hate.

Malcolm created a public furor by describing the assassination of President Kennedy as an instance of "the chickens come home to roost." Expelled from the Nation of Islam by Elijah Muhammad, he traveled to Mecca on a spiritual pilgrimage and discovered, to his surprise, the insignificance of color in Islamic thought. This led him to form a rival Muslim group, the Organization of Afro-American Unity, which emphasized black nationalism in a manner that did not demonize whites. Assassinated in 1965 by followers of Elijah Muhammad, Malcolm became a martyr to millions of African Americans, some praising his militant call for self-defense, others stressing his message of self-discipline and self-respect.

Occasionally Black Power became a vehicle of rage and racial revenge. SNCC Chairman H. Rap Brown, for example, urged a crowd in Cambridge, Maryland, to "burn this town down," adding: "Don't love the white man to death, shoot him to death." And some went beyond rhetoric by forming terrorist groups like the Black Panthers to take their grievances to the streets.

Founded in 1966 by an Oakland, California, ex-convict named Huey Newton, the Panthers provided a violent alternative to other black movements of this era. Portraying themselves as defenders of "oppressed" people against a "racist-capitalist police state," the Panthers demanded the release of all blacks from prison and the payment of "slave reparations" by whites.

Adept at self-promotion, the Panthers won modest support in black neighborhoods through their community work. With perhaps 5,000 members nationwide, most in the San Francisco Bay area, they ran food banks, health clinics, and preschool programs in rundown city neighborhoods. At the same time, however, Newton and his aides routinely engaged in extortion, drug dealing, and other criminal acts. Heavily armed, wearing black clothing and dark sunglasses, the Panthers became a feared enemy—and primary target—of law enforcement, including the FBI. At least 28 members and 11 policemen were killed in shoot-outs and ambushes between these forces.

"Sisterhood Is Powerful"

The rights revolution of the 1960s included demands for sexual, as well as racial, equality. Both the Equal Pay Act of 1963 and the Civil Rights Act of 1964 were important steps in the battle against gender discrimination, yet progress had been slow. In the fall of 1966, a band of activists formed the National Organization for Women (NOW) to speed the pace of change.

At NOW's first convention, the 300 delegates elected Betty Friedan president and issued a statement endorsing "the world-wide revolution for human rights

Betty Friedan (right) attends the second NOW convention in 1967. At her side is Dr. Kathryn Clarenbach, who chaired the convention.

taking place within and beyond our national borders." Never radical, NOW pursued its major goals—passage of an equal rights amendment and sexual equality in the workplace—through political means. Its leaders took pains to portray NOW as an organization *for* women, not of women, which welcomed male support.

NOW grew slowly. Its membership in 1970 totaled 15,000—mostly white, middle-aged, and middle-class. Yet NOW's impact on the emerging women's movement was enormous, both in what it represented and what it seemed to lack. For many younger women, raised in the affluence of suburban America, the resurgence of feminism went beyond the fight for political and economic equality. What attracted them was the call for female solidarity—the power of sisterhood—in the larger struggle for sexual liberation.

Some of these women were veterans of the civil rights movement. Others worked for SDS and were active in the antiwar protests on college campuses. Although deeply committed to these causes, they discovered that sexism—the assumption of male superiority—also existed in organizations devoted to justice and equal rights. Thus, women found themselves thankful for the skills and self-confidence they had developed, yet resentful of their expected roles as cooks, secretaries, and sexual objects. When asked what positions women filled in his organization, Stokely Carmichael brought roars of male laughter by noting: "The position of women in SNCC is prone."

Committed to equal rights, adept at organizing, and determined to confront sexism on all fronts, these "new feminists" developed strategies and communities of their own. As women's liberation emerged in the mid-1960s, feminist study groups appeared, along with feminist

newspapers, health clinics, and bookstores. The more radical elements, viewing men as the enemy, opposed heterosexual relationships, denounced marriage as "legal whoredom," and regarded the nuclear family as a form of female slavery. While rejecting such notions, liberal feminists also struggled with the dilemma of how to achieve greater power and fulfillment in a male-dominated culture.

The new feminism met immediate resistance—and not only from men. Surveys of American women in the 1960s showed both a growing sensitivity to issues of sex discrimination and a strong distaste for "women's lib." Most housewives expressed pride in their values and experiences and resented the "elitism" of the feminist movement—the implication that outside employment was more fulfilling than housework or that women degraded themselves by trying to appear attractive to men. As the country artist Tammy Wynette sang: "Don't Liberate Me, Love Me." A long and difficult struggle lay ahead.

The Counterculture

The emerging radicalism of America's youth in the 1960s had both a cultural and political base. Bound together with civil rights, women's rights, and the antiwar protests was a diffuse new movement, known as the counterculture, which challenged traditional values. To many young people, the counterculture symbolized personal liberation and generational strength—a break with the humdrum, hollow world of adults.

In 1965, a San Francisco journalist used the term "hippie" to describe a new breed of rebel—passionate, spontaneous, and free. Like the Bohemians of the early 1900s and the Beats of the 1950s, the hippies defined themselves as opponents of the dominant culture, with its emphasis on competition, consumerism, and conformity. By rejecting such "empty values," they tapped into a seam of youthful alienation so brilliantly portrayed in Mike Nichols's *The Graduate* and Paul Simon and Art Garfunkel's "Sounds of Silence." Unlike the "uptight" nine-to-five crowd, the hippies wore their hair long, dressed in jeans and sandals, and sought a "higher consciousness" through experimentation and uninhibited living.

The counterculture offered numerous attractions. Many young people embraced the chance to try out new arrangements and ideas. A few joined communes, explored ancient religions, studied astrology, or turned to the occult. Far more pervasive was the sexual freedom, the vital new music, and the illegal drug use that marked these turbulent times.

Thousands of young people migrated to the Haight-Ashbury section of San Francisco in 1967 for a "summer of love." Having no means of support, many turned to drug dealing, panhandling, and prostitution.

The counterculture did not begin the sexual revolution of the 1960s. That process was already under way, fueled by the introduction of oral contraceptives in 1960, the emergence of a women's rights movement, and a series of Supreme Court decisions that widened public access to "sexually explicit" material. The counterculture played a different but equally important role by challenging conventional morality at every turn.

The results were dramatic. When the Beatles took America by storm in 1964, their chart-busting songs included "I Want to Hold Your Hand," "She Loves You," and "Please, Please Me." Marijuana use, a federal crime since 1937, was rare in middle-class society, and lysergic acid diethylamide (LSD) was largely unknown. By 1967, however, the Beatles were imagining "Lucy in the Sky with Diamonds" (LSD) and wailing, "Why Don't We Do It in the Road!"

The counterculture spread inward through America from the east and west coasts. In Cambridge, Massachusetts, a Harvard researcher named Timothy Leary became the nation's first psychedelic guru by promoting LSD as the pathway to heightened consciousness and sexual pleasure. In San Francisco, author Ken Kesey (*One Flew over the Cuckoo's Nest*) and his Merry Pranksters staged a series of public LSD parties, known as Acid Tests, that drew thousands of participants in 1966. Wearing wild costumes, with painted faces, the revelers danced to the sounds of Jerry Garcia and his Grateful Dead.

To much of the public, San Francisco became synonymous with the counterculture. Acid rock flourished in local clubs like the Fillmore West, where Jimi Hendrix ("Purple Haze"), Steppenwolf ("Magic Carpet Ride"), and the Jefferson Airplane ("White Rabbit") celebrated drug tripping in their songs. In 1967, more than 75,000 young people migrated to San Francisco's Haight-

Ashbury district to partake in a much publicized "summer of love." The majority of arrivals, studies showed, were runaways and school dropouts with no means of support. By summer's end, Haight-Ashbury was awash in drug overdoses, venereal disease, panhandling, and prostitution.

At first the national media embraced the counterculture as a "hip" challenge to the blandness of middle-class suburban life. Magazines as diverse as *Time* and *Playboy* doted on every aspect of the hippie existence, and the Levi-Strauss corporation used acid rockers to promote its new line of jeans. Hollywood celebrated the counterculture with films such as *Easy Rider,* about two footloose drug dealers on a motorcycle tour of self-discovery, and *I Love You, Alice B. Toklas,* in which a dull lawyer becomes a fun-loving hippie after accidentally taking hashish. The smash hit of the 1968 Broadway season was the rock musical *Hair,* depicting a draft evader's journey through the pleasure-filled Age of Aquarius.

Yet most young people of the 1960s experienced neither the nightmare of Haight-Ashbury nor the dream world of *Hair.* Millions of them remained on the margins of the counterculture, admiring its styles and sounds while rejecting its revolutionary mantra. And millions more entered adulthood without the slightest sign of protest or alienation. Indeed, some commentators spoke of a serious *intra*generational split in this era, pitting young people who accepted, or aspired to, America's middle-class promise against more radical young people who did not.

A Divided Nation

As 1968 began, **General William Westmoreland,** commander of U.S. forces in Southeast Asia, offered an optimistic assessment of the Vietnam War. In his view, American and South Vietnamese (ARVN) troops were gaining strength and confidence as the fighting progressed. Their new vitality, he insisted, stood in direct contrast to the enemy's sagging morale.

The Tet Offensive

Four days later, 70,000 Communist troops assaulted American and ARVN positions throughout South Vietnam. Their lightning offensive, begun on the lunar New Year holiday of Tet, took Westmoreland by surprise. In Saigon, Viet Cong units reached the American Embassy before being driven back. After capturing Hue, one of South Vietnam's oldest cities, Communist soldiers murdered thousands of civilians and dumped their bodies into a mass grave.

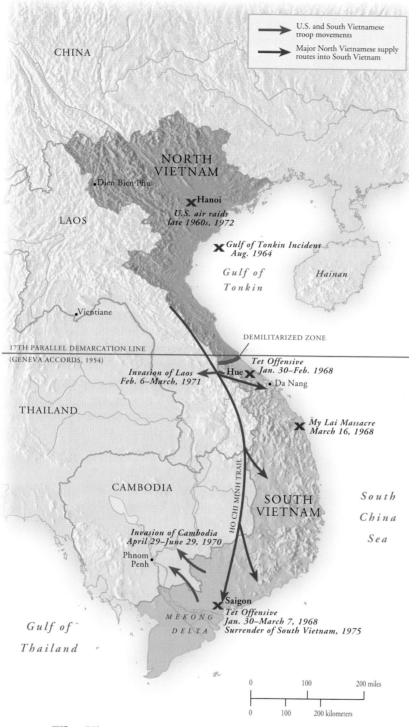

U.S. and South Vietnamese troop movements

Major North Vietnamese supply routes into South Vietnam

CHINA

NORTH VIETNAM

•Dien Bien Phu

✕ Hanoi
U.S. air raids late 1960s, 1972

LAOS

✕ *Gulf of Tonkin Incident Aug. 1964*

Gulf of Tonkin

Hainan

•Vientiane

17TH PARALLEL DEMARCATION LINE
(GENEVA ACCORDS, 1954)

DEMILITARIZED ZONE

Invasion of Laos Feb. 6–March, 1971   Hue ✕ *Tet Offensive Jan. 30–Feb. 1968*

•Da Nang

THAILAND

✕ *My Lai Massacre March 16, 1968*

HO CHI MINH TRAIL

CAMBODIA

SOUTH VIETNAM

South China Sea

Invasion of Cambodia April 29–June 29, 1970

Phnom Penh

✕ Saigon
Tet Offensive Jan. 30–March 7, 1968
Surrender of South Vietnam, 1975

Gulf of Thailand

MEKONG DELTA

0   100   200 miles
0   100   200 kilometers

MAP 29.1 The Vietnam War

The map charts the evolution of American military involvement from the Gulf of Tonkin incident in August 1964 to the surrender of South Vietnam in April 1975. In 1970 and 1971, U.S. and South Vietnamese troops briefly expanded the land war into Cambodia and Laos, stirring further antiwar sentiment inside the United States.

troops and 150 American marines. Viet Cong losses were so severe that the brunt of the ground fighting after Tet would have to be shouldered by North Vietnamese troops.

In psychological terms, however, the Tet offensive marked a turning point in the war. The sheer size of the Communist attacks, their ability to strike so many targets in force, made a mockery of Westmoreland's optimistic claims. Reporting from Saigon after the Tet offensive, Walter Cronkite, America's most popular television journalist, claimed that a military victory was nowhere in sight. At best, Cronkite predicted, "the bloody experience of Vietnam is to end in a stalemate."

A stalemate was exactly what Americans feared most. The Tet offensive accelerated Johnson's political decline. His approval rating dropped from 48 to 36 percent, with most Americans expressing skepticism about official claims of military progress in Vietnam. Columnist Art Buchwald compared LBJ to General Custer at the Little Big Horn, and the prestigious *Wall Street Journal* warned that "the whole war effort is likely doomed."

The President Steps Aside

As Lyndon Johnson pondered his political future, the memory of Harry S Truman was fresh in his mind. In 1952, Truman decided not to seek reelection after losing the New Hampshire Democratic presidential primary to Senator Estes Kefauver of Tennessee. The main issue then was the stalemate in Korea. In 1968, LBJ faced a spirited challenge in New Hampshire from Senator Eugene McCarthy of Minnesota. The main issue now was the stalemate in Vietnam.

McCarthy's presidential campaign reflected the deep divisions within Democratic party ranks. The "peace faction," led by younger activists like Allard Lowenstein, hoped to "dump Johnson" by mobilizing antiwar sentiment against him in key primary states. Hundreds of college students arrived in New Hampshire to work for the McCarthy campaign. Long hair and beards were taboo; well-scrubbed volunteers in sports coats and dresses ("be clean for Gene")

As a military operation, the **Tet offensive** clearly failed. Using their overwhelming firepower, American and ARVN forces inflicted frightful casualties on the enemy. In the 3-week battle to recapture Hue, more than 5,000 Communist soldiers were killed, along with 400 ARVN

Although U.S. troops inflicted heavy casualties on the Viet Cong and the North Vietnamese during the Tet offensive of 1968, the intensity of the fighting shocked the American public and increased public criticism of the war.

A Violent Spring

Early in April, Martin Luther King, Jr., traveled to Memphis to support a strike of city garbage workers for better wages and conditions. His social vision was ever expanding, as he challenged Americans to confront the "interrelated" evils of racism, militarism, and poverty. In 1968, Dr. King's projects included a "Poor People's March on Washington" and a "moral crusade" to end the war in Vietnam.

On the evening of April 3, King delivered a passionate sermon at a Memphis church. Demanding justice for the poor and the powerless, he seemed to sense the danger he was in. "I've been to the mountaintop," he cried. "I may not get there with you, but I want you to know that we as a people will get to the promised land." The following night, King was shot by James Earl Ray, a white racist, as he stood on the balcony of the Lorraine Motel. He died instantly, at the age of 39.

News of Dr. King's death touched off riots in African American communities from Boston to San Francisco. At the White House, President Johnson proclaimed a day of national mourning for Dr. King against a backdrop of

ran phone banks, stuffed envelopes, and canvassed house to house. "These college kids are fabulous," one Democratic leader remarked. "They knock at the door and come in politely, and actually want to talk to grown-ups, and people are delighted."

The New Hampshire results sent shock waves through the political system. McCarthy came within a whisker of defeating President Johnson, who received less than 50 percent of the Democratic primary vote. Polls showed McCarthy winning the support of "hawks" who demanded victory in Vietnam, as well as "doves" who wanted to pull out at once. For Johnson, the results amounted to a vote of "no confidence" on his handling of the war.

Four days later, Robert Kennedy entered the presidential race. As the former attorney general and a current U.S. senator from New York, he was both a critic of the Vietnam War and a champion of minority causes, especially in the field of civil rights. Millions saw "Bobby" as the keeper of Camelot, the heir to his fallen brother's legacy.

On March 31, President Johnson announced his political retirement in a stunning televised address: "I shall not seek, and I will not accept, the nomination of my party for another term as your President." A few weeks later, Vice President Hubert Humphrey entered the presidential race as the "regular" Democratic candidate, endorsed by Johnson himself. Humphrey's strategy was to line up delegates for the presidential nomination without contesting Kennedy or McCarthy in the volatile state primaries, where his chances of winning were slim.

Robert Kennedy's presidential campaign in 1968 both energized and split the Democratic party, leading, in part, to Lyndon Johnson's decision to announce his political retirement. Kennedy was assassinated after winning the vital California primary in June 1968.

© Bettmann/CORBIS

United Farm Workers leader Cesar Chavez led a series of strikes and boycotts to win better wages and working conditions for union members. Behind him is the symbol of the organization, the black Aztec eagle.

a Mass of thanksgiving. Despite enormous media coverage, and a national boycott of table grapes, the strike dragged on.

In June 1968, Kennedy took a major step toward the Democratic presidential nomination by defeating Eugene McCarthy in the delegate-rich California primary. That night, after greeting supporters at a Los Angeles hotel, Kennedy was shot and killed by a deranged Arab nationalist named Sirhan Sirhan. The nation went numb. Who could have imagined the horror of four national leaders—John F. Kennedy, Malcolm X, Martin Luther King, Jr., and Robert F. Kennedy—all dead at the hands of assassins? "My dreams were smashed," a young man recalled. "I shared with a lot of other people these feelings of loss and despair and grim, grim days ahead."

wailing police sirens and billowing smoke. Forty-five people died in these national riots, including 24 in Washington, D.C.

Among the presidential candidates, Robert Kennedy seemed closest to the message of Dr. King. Centering his campaign on the connection between domestic unrest and the Vietnam War, Kennedy visited migrant labor camps, Indian reservations, and inner-city neighborhoods to highlight the problems of disadvantaged Americans and the work to be done. He also supported the labor strike of Cesar Chavez and his National Farm Workers against the grape growers in central California.

The two had met when Kennedy chaired a Senate investigation into the squalid living and working conditions of migratory labor. Both men were close to 40, both were devout Catholics, and both admired the nonviolence of King and Gandhi in the struggle for justice and social change. As Kennedy campaigned in California, the grape strike was entering its third year. To protest the stalemate, and the growing violence on both sides, Chavez began a fast that continued for 21 days. He ended it, in poor health, by breaking bread with Senator Kennedy at

The Chicago Convention

Throughout the spring of 1968, a coalition of antiwar groups prepared for a massive peace demonstration at the Democratic National Convention in Chicago. Originally expecting 500,000 people, the organizers dramatically lowered their estimates following the withdrawal of President Johnson in March and the murder of Senator Kennedy in June. Furthermore, Mayor Richard Daley made it clear that protesters were not welcome in his city, no matter how well they behaved. Fearing serious bloodshed at the Democratic convention, Senator McCarthy urged young demonstrators to stay away.

There was reason for concern. The continued military buildup in Vietnam had created a violent cycle of protest and response at home. That spring, thousands of young men burned their draft cards in public; some were beaten by angry crowds. Demonstrators tried to block troop trains and army induction centers, leading to bloody clashes with police. At Columbia University, students from SDS took over several buildings and trashed them to protest "war-related" research on campus. Hundreds were arrested, a general strike followed, and the university closed down for the semester.

Chicago resembled a war zone in August 1968, with 6,000 army troops, 5,000 National Guardsmen, and hundreds of Chicago riot police patrolling the streets. Denied permits to rally in public places, the protesters—perhaps 4,000 strong—gathered in a park opposite the Hilton Hotel, where many Democratic party leaders were staying. Conflict was inevitable. Radical speakers from SDS and the Black Panthers harangued the crowd with calls for "guerrilla warfare." Abbie Hoffman and Jerry Rubin, founders of the Youth International ("Yippie") party, held workshops on LSD production and then chose a pig as their candidate with the slogan:

DOING HISTORY ONLINE

Martin Luther King and Economic Justice, 1966

Read the document in this module. Why did Martin Luther King turn his attention to issues other than civil rights in the late 1960s?

History ⧖ Now™   Visit HistoryNOW to access primary sources and exercises related to this topic: http://now.ilrn.com/ayers_etal3e

"They nominated a president and he eats the people. We nominate a president and the people eat him."

On the evening of August 28, the demonstrators tried to march to the convention arena. As millions watched on

Chicago police wade into a crowd of protesters during the Democratic National Convention in 1968.

television, the police moved in with clubs and mace, while National Guardsmen fired tear gas at the crowd. Hundreds were badly beaten, including reporters and bystanders, in what investigators later described as a "police riot." Even so, the blame did not rest entirely with one side. "We were not just innocent people who were victimized," Abbie Hoffman admitted. "We came to plan a confrontation."

News of the street violence shocked the Democratic convention. From the podium, Senator Abraham Ribicoff of Connecticut condemned "the Gestapo tactics on the streets of Chicago." His remark set off booing, cursing, and wild applause. Television cameras caught a furious Mayor Daley hurling ethnic insults at Ribicoff and telling the "lousy mother_____" to "go home."

The shaken delegates chose Hubert Humphrey and Senator Edmund Muskie of Maine to be their presidential and vice presidential nominees. A staunch liberal, with strong ties to organized labor and the civil rights movement, Humphrey exemplified the New Deal Democratic tradition of

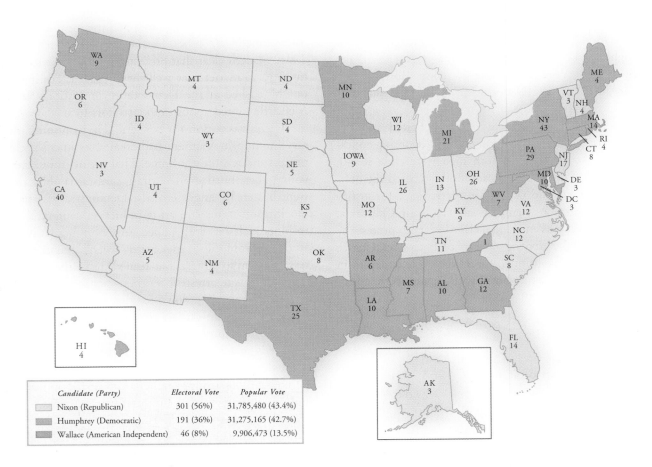

Candidate (Party)	Electoral Vote	Popular Vote
Nixon (Republican)	301 (56%)	31,785,480 (43.4%)
Humphrey (Democratic)	191 (36%)	31,275,165 (42.7%)
Wallace (American Independent)	46 (8%)	9,906,473 (13.5%)

MAP 29.2 The Election of 1968

In a bitterly fought three-way contest for the presidency, held against the backdrop of a nation badly split by the Vietnam War, Richard Nixon won with a razor-thin victory with only 43 percent of the popular vote.

View an animated version of this map or related maps at http://history.wadsworth.com/passages3e.

Richard Nixon and family celebrate his long-awaited presidential victory in November 1968.

and the court-ordered busing of schoolchildren to achieve racial integration were vital concerns. In blunt, sometimes explosive language, Wallace lashed out at "liberal judges," "welfare cheats," and "pot-smoking freaks in their beards and sandals."

Early opinion polls showed Nixon far ahead of Humphrey, with Wallace running a strong third. Yet the gap closed considerably in the campaign's final weeks when President Johnson ordered a temporary bombing halt in North Vietnam, and millions of Democratic voters, fearful of a Nixon presidency, returned to the party fold. On election day, Nixon won 43.4 percent of the votes and 301 electoral votes, to 42.7 percent and 191 for Humphrey, and 13.5 percent and 46 for Wallace.

Roosevelt, Truman, Kennedy, and LBJ. His great weakness in 1968 was his loyal (if reluctant) support for Johnson's handling of the war. To many Americans, Humphrey endorsed the very policies that had divided the nation and left the Democratic party in disarray.

Nixon's the One

Meeting in Miami, the Republicans faced a much simpler task. The Goldwater defeat of 1964 opened the door for candidates with broader political appeal, such as **Richard Nixon.** Having lost a bruising election for president in 1960 and another for governor of California in 1962, Nixon kept his fortunes alive by marketing himself as both a devoted Republican and an experienced public figure. After choosing him on the first ballot in 1968, the delegates selected Governor Spiro T. Agnew of Maryland to be his vice presidential running mate.

Nixon campaigned as the spokesman for America's "silent majority"—the people who worked hard, paid their taxes, went to church, obeyed the law, and respected the flag. In a nation grown weary of urban riots and campus demonstrations, he vowed to make "law and order" his number one domestic priority, and to bring "peace with honor" to Vietnam.

For the first time since 1948, the presidential campaign attracted a serious third-party candidate, Governor George Wallace of Alabama. An ardent segregationist, Wallace showed surprising strength in white working-class areas of the North and West, where issues such as rising crime rates, draft deferments for college students,

Conclusion

Few decades in American history provided more drama and tragedy than the 1960s. What began with such hope and promise soon gave way to deep suspicion and despair, as Americans reeled from one crisis to another.

Most Americans welcomed the vibrancy of President Kennedy as they had welcomed the steadiness of President Eisenhower 8 years before. They applauded Kennedy's call for young people to get involved in public service, as well as his tough stance against international communism, especially during the Cuban missile crisis of 1962. In truth, Kennedy's record in domestic affairs was relatively thin. Lacking a large electoral mandate and facing stiff congressional opposition, Kennedy moved cautiously in civil rights and federal spending for social programs. His assassination in 1963 left a deeply grieving nation to ponder the legacy of a leader who died so young—and with so much left undone.

Using the memory of this fallen president, and retaining most of his key advisors, Lyndon Johnson pressed forward in both domestic and foreign affairs. He crafted legislation that produced landmark advances in civil rights and the "war on poverty," while continuing the escalation of America's military commitment to an independent, anti-Communist South Vietnam. As Johnson soon discovered, however, the war in Vietnam undermined his domestic programs and created deep skepticism about the truth of his claims that the war was being won—or was worth the cost. The shocks of 1968, beginning with Johnson's decision not to seek reelection, continuing with the assassinations of Dr. Martin Luther King, Jr. and Robert F. Kennedy, and culminating in the riotous Democratic National Convention in Chicago, left Americans reeling and alarmed.

© Bettmann/CORBIS

To a large degree, Richard Nixon rode the political whirlwind that swept America in 1968. His margin of victory against Hubert Humphrey was nearly as narrow as his margin of defeat against John Kennedy in 1960. Yet the combined total for Nixon and Wallace in 1968—almost 57 percent—signaled a major swing to the right. The radical protests of the 1960s had fueled an inevitable backlash against the liberal party in power. The Great Society lay in ruins. The Nixon years had begun.

The Chapter in Review

In the years between 1960 and 1968:

- The Cuban missile crisis was settled peacefully in 1962, ending the most serious nuclear confrontation of the Cold War.
- The war in Vietnam entered public consciousness in 1963, as the number of American military advisors increased and the government of South Vietnam was overthrown in a military coup.
- President Kennedy's assassination in Dallas threw the nation into mourning and brought Lyndon Johnson to the Oval Office.
- Following a landslide victory in 1964, Johnson unveiled plans to create a "great society" modeled after the social programs begun during the New Deal.
- The expanding war in Vietnam pushed Johnson's ambitious domestic agenda to the side.
- Johnson decided not to seek reelection amidst growing antiwar protests and racial violence in America's cities.
- The assassinations of Dr. King and Senator Kennedy combined with violent events during the National Democratic Convention to stun the nation in 1968.
- Richard Nixon was elected president, vowing to end the war in Vietnam while restoring "law and order" at home.

Making Connections Across Chapters

LOOKING BACK

Chapter 29 examines the impact of the rights revolution, the Vietnam War, and the cultural struggles in the United States during the 1960s, one of the most challenging and bitterly divisive periods in recent history.

1. What accounts for the enduring popularity of President John F. Kennedy? Was it his policies, his vision, or were other factors at work as well?

2. In what ways did the assumptions of U.S. leaders regarding Communist expansion remain fixed in the 1960s, and in what ways did they change? Was Lyndon Johnson a prisoner to assumptions that went back to the early days of the Cold War?

3. What impact did the movement for racial equality have on other so-called rights movements in the 1960s? In what ways did the civil rights struggle itself change in this decade?

LOOKING AHEAD

Chapter 30 considers the consequences of the tumultuous events of the 1960s. The nation would wrestle with President Nixon's strategy to withdraw U.S. troops from Vietnam and, in an amazing turn of events, watch the president become embroiled in the greatest political scandal in U.S. history.

1. Would a nation as bitterly divided as the United States begin to heal its wounds with a new president at the helm, a president who vowed "to bring the American people together"?

2. Would the "rights revolution" of the 1960s continue to gain momentum in the coming years, and how would its impact be felt in the courts and in the political arena?

3. Was it possible to rekindle interest in the core programs of the Great Society, or would Americans move away from the ideas and proposals that had defined domestic liberalism since the New Deal Era?

Recommended Readings

Baughman, James. *The Republic of Mass Culture* (1992). Assesses the media's enormous impact on modern American culture.

Brennan, Mary. *Turning Right in the Sixties* (1995). Analyzes the impact of Goldwater conservatism on a changing Republican party.

Farber, David. *Age of Great Dreams* (1994). Provides an excellent synthesis of the political and cultural changes of the 1960s.

Friedan, Betty. *The Feminine Mystique* (1963). A pathbreaking account of the domestic restrictions placed on women following World War II by those who shape American culture.

Harrington, Michael. *The Other America* (1962). Riveted national attention on the issue of poverty, leading to major government programs and reforms.

Horne, Gerald. *Fire This Time* (1995). Offers an interesting analysis of the Watts riot and the rise of black nationalism.

Karnow, Stanley. *Vietnam* (1983). Remains the best one-volume survey of American involvement in our nation's longest war.

Munoz, Carlos, Jr. *Youth, Identity, Power* (rev. ed. 2000). Carefully examines the origins of the Chicano movement.

McDougall, Walter. *". . . The Heavens and the Earth": A Political History of the Space Age* (1985). Captures both the policy making and the drama behind the race to the moon.

Miller, James. *Democracy in the Streets: From Port Huron to the Siege of Chicago* (1987). A thorough history of the student movement that revolutionized American culture and politics in the 1960s.

Identifications

Review your understanding of the following key terms, people, events, and dates for this chapter (these terms also appear in the Glossary at the end of the book):

John Glenn
Fidel Castro
Bay of Pigs
freedom riders
U-2
Robert Kennedy
Cesar Chavez
Betty Friedan

Fannie Lou Hamer
Lee Harvey Oswald
Lyndon Baines Johnson
Gulf of Tonkin Resolution
Students for a Democratic Society (SDS)
Watts riot
Black Power
Malcolm X
General William Westmoreland
Tet offensive
Richard Nixon

Online Sources Guide

Use this listing to find online documents, images, interactive maps, simulations, and other resources related to this chapter:

American History Resource Center

http://history.wadsworth.com/rc/us

Documents

"The Port Huron Statement" of the Students for a Democratic Society (1962)
Betty Friedan, *The Feminine Mystique*
"Old Voices, New Voices: Mainland Puerto Rican Perspectives and Experiences"
Lyndon B. Johnson, "Great Society" speech
Excerpts from the Civil Rights Act of 1964
Martin Luther King, Jr., "Beyond Vietnam"

Selected Images

The arrest of civil rights protesters, 1965
Civil rights march, Alabama, 1965

Chinook helicopter
B-52 bomber taking off from Marianas Islands
American soldiers on a search and destroy mission, 1967
U.S. marshals keeping antiwar protesters away from the Pentagon, 1967

Document Exercises

1963 Kennedy's Address on Cuban Missile Crisis
1964 Free Speech Movement

HistoryNOW

http://now.ilrn.com/ayers_etal3e

Primary Source Exercises

Martin Luther King and Economic Justice, 1966
The Voting Rights Act, 1965

30 Crisis of Confidence, 1969–1980

Chapter Outline

"One giant leap for mankind." Neil Armstrong sets foot on the moon's surface, July 20, 1969.

© Bettmann/CORBIS

Richard Nixon had been in politics for most of his adult life. As a congressman, a senator, and a vice president, he thrived on controversy and kept moving ahead. Bitter defeats in the presidential election of 1960 and the California gubernatorial race of 1962 did not diminish his ambition or ruin his dreams. On the morning after his presidential victory in 1968, Nixon addressed a nation battered by racial turmoil, urban violence, generational conflict, political assassinations, and continuing war. Vowing to unite the country and to restore confidence in its institutions, he recalled a campaign stop he had made in the little town of Deshler, Ohio. Near the back of the crowd a teenager held up a sign reading "Bring Us Together." That message, he assured his listeners, "will be the great objective of this administration . . . to bring the American people together." The tragic presidency of Richard Nixon was under way.

America United and Divided

The new era began with optimistic signals and improbable events. For a time, the dark days of 1968 were pushed aside by the miracles of 1969. In January, the New York

Jets, led by "Broadway" Joe Namath, the nation's most celebrated bachelor, won the football Super Bowl by crushing the heavily favored Baltimore Colts. In October, the New York Mets, once regarded as the worst team in Major League baseball history, defeated the Baltimore Orioles in a World Series that left millions of Americans screaming, "Ya gotta believe!" Sandwiched between these events were two enormous spectacles, each affecting the nation in a very different way.

The Miracles of 1969

In the summer of 1969, NASA fulfilled John F. Kennedy's bold promise to land a man on the moon "before this decade is out." The lunar mission culminated 8 years of extraordinary progress and awful failure, including the 1967 *Apollo 1* disaster in which three astronauts died on the launch pad when their capsule exploded in flames. On July 16, astronauts Neil Armstrong, Edwin "Buzz" Aldrin, and Michael Collins began their 286,000-mile lunar mission—*Apollo 11*—from Cape Kennedy aboard the command vessel *Columbia*. As they neared their destination, Armstrong and Aldrin entered the *Eagle*, a fragile moon module, for the final descent. On July 20, before a

Timeline

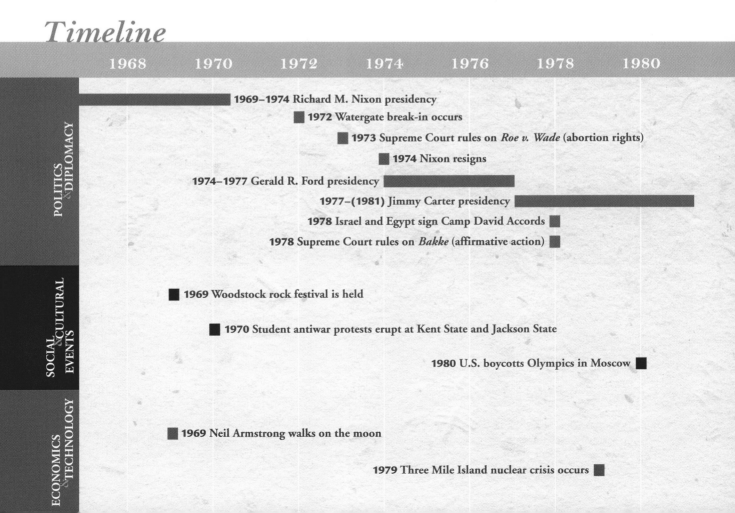

	1968	1970	1972	1974	1976	1978	1980

POLITICS & DIPLOMACY

1969–1974 Richard M. Nixon presidency
1972 Watergate break-in occurs
1973 Supreme Court rules on *Roe v. Wade* (abortion rights)
1974 Nixon resigns
1974–1977 Gerald R. Ford presidency
1977–(1981) Jimmy Carter presidency
1978 Israel and Egypt sign Camp David Accords
1978 Supreme Court rules on *Bakke* (affirmative action)

SOCIAL & CULTURAL EVENTS

1969 Woodstock rock festival is held
1970 Student antiwar protests erupt at Kent State and Jackson State
1980 U.S. boycotts Olympics in Moscow

ECONOMICS & TECHNOLOGY

1969 Neil Armstrong walks on the moon
1979 Three Mile Island nuclear crisis occurs

"That's one small step for man, one giant leap for mankind."

Armstrong and Aldrin spent 21 hours on the moon. A television camera beamed back pictures of the men gathering samples, measuring temperature (234 degrees Fahrenheit in sunlight, 279 below zero in darkness), and planting a small American flag. What struck viewers was the sight of two spacesuited figures leaping from place to place in the light gravity against a background of perfect desolation. As they rocketed back to Earth, the astronauts provided breathtaking pictures of the world from 175,000 miles away. "No matter where you travel," Armstrong joked, "it's nice to get home."

Other moon missions followed, including the dramatic rescue of *Apollo 13* in 1970. Americans marveled at the skill and bravery of these astronauts without fully understanding the scientific value of their missions. By studying lunar rocks and photographs, geologists learned that the earth and the moon were formed at the same time—about 4.6 billion years ago—and that both had been pounded for millions of years by a hail of comets, asteroids, and meteorites that helped reshape their outer crust. The moon missions spurred the growth of computer technology and led to numerous product advancements, from fireproof clothing to better navigation systems for jetliners.

A month after the moon landing, national attention shifted to an earthly extravaganza, the **Woodstock Music and Art Fair,** on a 600-acre dairy farm in the Catskill Mountains northwest of New York City. Billed as an "Aquarian Exposition," Woodstock fused rock music, hard drugs, free love, and antiwar protest into 3 days of mud-splattered revelry. Expecting a crowd of perhaps 100,000—a ridiculously low estimate for a pageant

that included Janis Joplin, Jimi Hendrix, Joan Baez, The Grateful Dead, and Jefferson Airplane, among others— the organizers were overwhelmed by the response. More than 400,000 people showed up, knocking down the fences and ticket windows, creating mammoth traffic jams, gobbling up the available food and water, pitching tents in the fields, bathing nude in cattle ponds, and sharing marijuana and LSD.

Some news reports breathlessly portrayed the event as a cultural watershed. One magazine called Woodstock "an art form and social structure unique to our time." Another saw it as "the model of how good we will all feel after the revolution." In truth, however, the long weekend at Max Yasgur's farm was far less than that. The vast majority at Woodstock were middle-class students and workers, not cultural dropouts or political revolutionaries. "They would always keep something of Woodstock in their hearts," wrote one perceptive observer, "but that would be while they were making it in the system, not overthrowing it."

What survived Woodstock were the new attitudes of young people toward self-fulfillment, personal expression, political activism, and, in some cases, dangerous excess. These things did not die out in the 1970s, though they took rather different forms. The mellow portrait of Woodstock soon gave way to the ugly spectacle of Altamont, near San Francisco, where a rock concert featuring the Rolling Stones turned into a bloodbath, with one man beaten to death. In 1970, drug and alcohol addiction claimed the lives of Janis Joplin and Jimi Hendrix. For many young people, the age of innocence was over.

Vietnamization

In order to bring America together, Richard Nixon realized, he had to end its military involvement in Vietnam.

During his inaugural parade on January 20, 1969, Nixon heard the chants of antiwar protesters as his limousine made its way from the Capitol to the White House. The next morning he was handed the weekly American casualty figures from Vietnam: 85 killed, 1,237 wounded—a chilling reminder, he wrote, of the war's "tragic cost."

Within weeks, Nixon unveiled a plan, known as **Vietnamization,** to end America's participation in the war. It called for the gradual replacement of U.S. troops by well-trained and supplied South Vietnamese soldiers—a process that included the deployment of American air power and the intensification of peace efforts aimed at getting American and North Vietnamese troops out of South Vietnam. From Nixon's perspective, Vietnamization represented the best solution to a dreadful dilemma. He refused to abandon Vietnam. "I will not," he

© Bettmann/CORBIS

More than 400,000 revelers enjoyed the sounds of Jimi Hendrix, Joan Baez, Jefferson Airplane, and others at the Woodstock festival north of New York City in the summer of 1969.

repeated, "be the first President of the United States to lose a war." Yet he could not continue a conflict that cost 14,600 American lives and $30 billion in 1968 alone.

Vietnamization did not work well on the battlefield, as time would show. But it did have the advantage of substituting Asian casualties for American ones, which made it popular in the United States. In June 1969, President Nixon announced that 25,000 American combat troops were being withdrawn from Vietnam—the first stage of a pull-out to be completed by late 1972. At the same time, the U.S. Air Force stepped up its missions over North and South Vietnam, and Cambodia as well.

Confrontation at Home

Despite Vietnamization and troop withdrawals, the antiwar movement retained considerable force. On November 15, 1969—"Mobilization Day"—hundreds of thousands of people attended rallies in New York, Boston, San Francisco, Washington, and other cities to demand the immediate removal of all American troops from Vietnam. Some considered the war immoral; others viewed it as a lost cause that was ripping the

nation apart. To show his contempt for the protests, President Nixon made a point of listing his schedule that afternoon, which included several hours of watching the Washington Redskins on television.

In March 1970, the White House announced the withdrawal of 150,000 more combat troops over the coming year. The nation's leading antiwar group, the Vietnam Moratorium Committee, responded by closing its national office. But a month later, in a startling development, the president told the nation that American troops had just invaded Cambodia to disrupt enemy supply lines that ran through that country along the so-called Ho Chi Minh Trail. The very success of Vietnamization depended on the elimination of these North Vietnamese sanctuaries, he declared, adding: "We are a strong people and we shall not be defeated in Vietnam."

Nixon misjudged the public reaction. The idea of expanding the war under any circumstances brought protesters back into the streets. At **Kent State University** in Ohio, several thousand students rampaged through the business district and clashed with local police. That evening, Kent State's ROTC building went up in flames, leading the governor to send in the National Guard. The

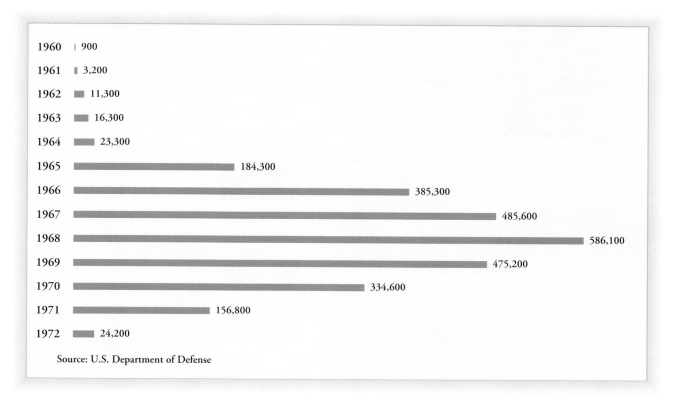

1960	900
1961	3,200
1962	11,300
1963	16,300
1964	23,300
1965	184,300
1966	385,300
1967	485,600
1968	586,100
1969	475,200
1970	334,600
1971	156,800
1972	24,200

Source: U.S. Department of Defense

CHART 30.1 U.S. Troop Levels in Vietnam, 1960–1972
American troop levels increased dramatically in 1965, following the Gulf of Tonkin incident and the Viet Cong attack on U.S. Marines at Pleiku. As the chart shows, troop levels began to decrease significantly in 1969, as newly elected President Richard Nixon began his policy of Vietnamization.
Source: U.S. Department of Defense

Picturing the Past   SOCIAL & CULTURAL EVENTS

Tragedy at Jackson State

In May 1970, news of the American incursion into Cambodia led to massive protests on college campuses. Six students died in separate incidents at Kent State in Ohio and Jackson State in Mississippi. The incidents, though very different, were lumped together in the press as disturbances against the war. In fact, the troubles at Jackson State were racially motivated. Jackson, the capital of Mississippi, was rigidly segregated, and students at the all-black college had clashed repeatedly with the all-white police

© Bettmann/CORBIS

force and highway patrol. On the night of May 14, following a series of rock-throwing episodes, the police fired more than 150 rounds into a dormitory, killing two students and wounding a dozen more. This chilling photo shows the violent police reaction. In comparison to Kent State, the Jackson State incident got little publicity, leading some to conclude that the death of black students was less important to mainstream America than the death of whites.

troops were ordered to prevent students from gathering in large blocs—an ironic twist, since a noontime rally was planned to protest the guard's presence. On May 4, the guardsmen confronted 500 students at the rally, where rocks and bottles were thrown from a distance and tear gas was lobbed in return. Suddenly, without warning, a group of guardsmen fired their rifles at the crowd, killing four and wounding nine others.

Word of the shootings touched off campus protests nationwide. ROTC buildings were attacked, and governors in 16 more states called out the National Guard. Many colleges simply shut down for the semester, canceling final exams and mailing diplomas to the graduates. Surveys showed a clear majority of Americans approving of the National Guard's response at Kent State and supporting forceful measures against those who challenged government authority through unlawful, or even disrespectful, behavior. Many blue-collar workers fumed at the sight of draft-deferred, middle-class students protesting the war from the safety of a college campus while their own sons and brothers were slogging through the jungles of Vietnam. That rage turned to violence in New York City, when several hundred construction workers charged into an antiwar rally and severely beat the demonstrators and onlookers with hammers, pipes, and fists. A week later, President Nixon invited the leader of New York's construction workers' union to the White House, where the two men exchanged gifts and compliments. Nixon described his "honorary hard hat" as a symbol of "patriotism to our beloved country."

The violence continued in fits and spurts. Left-wing radicals bombed the headquarters of Mobil Oil, IBM, and other pillars of the "imperialist war machine." At the University of Wisconsin, the late-night bombing of a science center that housed a military research laboratory left one graduate student dead. In New York City, three radicals accidentally blew themselves to bits while mixing explosives. And in Chicago, a splinter group of the dormant Students for a Democratic Society attempted to "trash" the downtown business district in a final assault upon the "ruling class." Three hundred looters and window-smashers were arrested.

My Lai and the Pentagon Papers

The news from Vietnam was equally grim. Reports surfaced about a massacre of civilians by U.S. troops at the village of My Lai, a suspected Viet Cong stronghold, in 1968. Encountering no resistance, an infantry unit led by Lieutenant William Calley methodically executed the villagers and dumped their bodies into a mass grave. A number of the women were raped; at least 200 people, many of them children, were murdered. Evidence of these atrocities was ignored by field commanders until a soldier not connected with the incident sent letters to the Pentagon and the press.

Most Americans considered My Lai an aberration. Yet the public reaction to Lieutenant Calley's court-martial verdict (guilty) and sentence (life imprisonment) in 1971 raised the very issues that had divided Americans since the war began. Some believed that government policy in

Vietnam made such tragedies inevitable. Others insisted that Calley acted out of frustration after seeing so many of his fellow soldiers killed. Still others blamed a society—as one GI put it—that "forced these kids to die in a foreign land for a cause it refused to defend at home." Congress and the White House were flooded with letters opposing the conviction. "Free Calley" signs appeared on car bumpers, in store windows, even in churches. Following numerous appeals and a personal case review by President Nixon, Calley was paroled in 1974.

The My Lai incident raised nagging questions about the fitness of American troops as the war dragged on. By all accounts, U.S. soldiers had fought superbly under trying circumstances until 1969. But the process of Vietnamization, the stepped-up troop withdrawals, the rising antiwar protests—all served to isolate those who remained in Vietnam. Drug use increased dangerously, with many soldiers turning from marijuana to heroin. Racial tensions flared, as did violent attacks on officers, known as "fraggings," in which disgruntled soldiers used hand grenades as weapons. Some men ignored direct orders to fight. They were reluctant to risk their lives for a cause that appeared all but lost.

Within weeks of Calley's court-martial, another crisis erupted with publication of the Pentagon Papers, a secret report of the decision-making process that led to American involvement in Vietnam. Commissioned in 1967, and containing numerous classified documents within its 7,000 pages, the report was made public by Daniel Ellsberg, a former intelligence officer who had turned against the war. Ellsberg gave a copy to the *New York Times,* which printed the first installment on June 13, 1971.

The report focused mainly on the Kennedy–Johnson years. From a political standpoint, President Nixon welcomed the embarrassment it caused his Democratic opponents. "This is about their administrations," he told his aides. "Let them argue about it." Yet Nixon soon viewed Ellsberg's behavior as a threat to his own presidency as well. He feared that continued leaks of classified material might reveal damaging information about current policies, such as the secret bombing of Cambodia. As a result, the White House sought a court injunction to halt further publication of the Pentagon Papers on grounds that national security was at stake. The Supreme Court rejected this argument, however, ruling six to three that suppression violated First Amendment guarantees.

Nixon did not give up the fight. Obsessed by the Ellsberg incident, he authorized the creation of a special White House unit, known as the "Plumbers," to "stop security leaks and investigate other sensitive matters." In a tape-recorded conversation on September 18, 1971, Nixon demanded that "the roughest, toughest people

[get] to work on this." A few weeks later, the Plumbers carried out their first assignment, burglarizing the office of Ellsberg's psychiatrist in an attempt to gather embarrassing information. Nixon's top domestic advisor, John Ehrlichman, casually informed the president that other "little operations" were planned. "We've got some dirty tricks underway," he said. "It may pay off."

Activism, Rights, and Reform

Political and social activism did not end with the 1960s, as the environmental movement and the antiwar protests clearly showed. While the angry, media-centered radicalism of groups like SDS and the Black Panthers largely disappeared, the movements for women's rights and minority rights remained very much alive, bringing progress and backlash in their wake.

Expanding Women's Rights

On August 26, 1970, feminist leaders organized a nationwide rally to mark the fiftieth anniversary of the Nineteenth Amendment, which had given women the right to vote. Thousands showed up with signs ranging from "Sisterhood is Powerful" to "Don't Cook Dinner—Starve a Rat Today." The speeches focused on equality for women in education and employment, the need for reproductive freedom, and passage of the **Equal Rights Amendment (ERA),** an idea first proposed in 1923.

The revived women's movement was already making strides. In 1969, feminist protests forced a number of the nation's best colleges, including Yale and Princeton, to end their all-male admissions policy, and the military academies soon followed suit. Between 1970 and 1974, the number of women attending law school and medical school more than doubled. During the 1970s as a whole, female graduates from the nation's law schools rose from 5 to 30 percent of each class; and at medical schools from 8 to 23 percent. Yet the number of women elected to public office or promoted to high management positions lagged far behind, and the wages of full-time working women remained well below those of men.

The women's movement had many voices and a wide range of ideas. Nothing better illustrated this diversity than the outpouring of books and magazines that provided an alternative to older publications such as *Good Housekeeping* and *Ladies' Home Journal,* which focused on motherhood, domesticity, and consumerism as the primary female roles. Handbooks like *Our Bodies, Ourselves* (1971) and *The New Woman's Survival Catalogue* (1972) sold millions of copies by combining a new feminist ideology, based on professional achievement and

DOING HISTORY

Women Debate the Equal Rights Amendment

AS THE WOMEN'S rights movement gained momentum in the 1970s, new emphasis was placed on passage of the Equal Rights Amendment to the U.S. Constitution, which required both Congressional approval and ratification by three-quarters of the states. The debate over the ERA often focused on the role of married women, especially regarding their family responsibilities. In 1970, during hearings before the Senate Judiciary Committee, feminist leader Gloria Steinem addressed the "sex-based myths" that pervaded American society, such as "women are biologically inferior to men," "women are already treated equally in this society," and "women hold great economic power." She then turned to the issue of child-rearing.

"Another myth [is] that children must have full-time mothers. American mothers spend more time with their homes and children than those of any other society we know about. . . . The truth is that most American children seem to be suffering from too much mother and too little father. Part of the program of Women's Liberation is a return of fathers to their children. If laws permit women equal work and pay opportunities, men will then be relieved of their role as sole breadwinner. Fewer ulcers, fewer hours of meaningless work, equal responsibility for his own children: these are a few of the reasons that Women's Liberation is Men's Liberation too. As for the psychic health of the children, studies show that the quality of time spent by parents is more important than the quantity. The most damaged children were not those whose mothers worked, but those whose mothers preferred to work but stayed home out of the role-playing desire to be a 'good mother.'"

Among the ERA's staunchest critics was Phyllis Schlafly, an attorney and a mother, who based her opposition to the Amendment on the innate differences that separated men from women. To ignore these differences, she warned, would turn the traditional male-female relationship of cooperation into one of endless conflict. Men and women would become "adversaries" rather than "partners."

"The woman's liberationist . . . is imprisoned by her own negative view of herself and of her place in the world around her. . . . The Positive Woman looks upon her femaleness and her fertility as part of her purpose, her potential, and her power. She rejoices that she has a capability for creativity that men can never have. . . .

The Positive Woman recognizes the fact that, when it comes to sex, women are simply not the equal of men. The sexual drive of men is much stronger than that of women. This is how the human race is designed in order that it might perpetuate itself. The other side of the coin is that it is easier for women to control their sexual appetites. A Positive Woman cannot defeat a man in a wrestling or boxing match, but she can motivate him, inspire him, encourage him, teach him, restrain him, reward him, and have power over him that he can never achieve over her with all his muscle. How or whether a Positive Woman uses her power is determined solely by the way she alone defines her goals and develops her skills.

The differences between men and women are also emotional and psychological. Without woman's innate maternal instinct, the human race would have died out centuries ago. . . . This is not to say that every woman must have a baby in order to be fulfilled. But it is to say that fulfillment for most women involves expressing their natural maternal urge by loving and caring for someone."

Source: Testimony before Senate Judiciary Committee, May 6, 1970; Schlafly, *The Positive Woman,* 1977, pp. 10–18.

Questions for Reflection

1. How do Gloria Steinem and Phyllis Schlafly differ in their views of the biological destiny of the sexes?

2. Why do you think the ERA failed to become part of the Constitution?

3. Have the issues raised by the ERA faded into history, or are they still relevant today?

Explore additional primary sources related to this chapter on the Wadsworth American History Resource Center or HistoryNOW websites:

http://history.wadsworth.com
http://now.ilrn.com/ayers_etal3e

Picturing the Past SOCIAL & CULTURAL EVENTS

The Struggle For The Equal Rights Amendment

Few issues proved more divisive in the 1970s than the Equal Rights Amendment.

Written by feminist Alice Paul (see Chapter 21) a half century earlier, it declared that "equality of rights under the law shall not be denied or abridged . . . on account of sex." In 1972, following a powerful new lobbying effort by women's groups, Congress passed the ERA and sent it to the states for ratification. But a powerful countermovement arose, led by a conservative activist named Phyllis Schlafly, who condemned the ERA as "a total assault on the family" and an insult to God's plan for the sexes. The map clearly shows the regional and cultural divisions over the ERA, with much of the opposition coming from rural and/or southern states. Only 30 of the needed 38 states voted in the end for ratification, and the amendment died.

MAP 30.1 **The Struggle for the Equal Rights Amendment**

personal freedom, with medical and psychological strategies for good health. A flood of best-sellers emerged— Kate Millett's *Sexual Politics* (1969), Shulamith Firestone's *The Dialectic of Sex* (1970), and Germaine Greer's *The Female Eunuch* (1970) among them— contending that women could never experience fulfillment within the traditional confines of marriage and family life. In 1972, three scholarly journals devoted to women's studies appeared, as did the Berkshire Conference on the History of Women. That same year marked the publication of *Ms.,* the first feminist magazine to attract a mass circulation. A sampling of its articles showed how dramatically times had changed: "Raising Kids Without Sex Roles," "Women Tell the Truth About Their Abortions," and "Do Feminists Do It Better?"

Minority Power

The political and cultural upheavals of the 1960s had produced a "rights consciousness" that spread from group to group, and movement to movement, as the decade progressed. For many such groups, 1969 was a pivotal year, marking their emergence on the national scene. That summer, for example, a routine police assault against homosexuals at the Stonewall Inn in Manhattan's Greenwich Village produced a most

AP/Wide World Photos

"Women's March for Equality" moves down New York's Fifth Avenue.

DOING HISTORY ONLINE

Rejecting Gender-Free Equality, 1977

Read the excerpt in this module. How could feminists rebut Phyllis Schlafly's arguments against the Equal Rights Amendment?

History⏳Now™ Visit HistoryNOW to access primary sources and exercises related to this topic: http://now.ilrn.com/ayers_etal3e

which had grown from 3 million in 1960 to more than 9 million a decade later. The increase, consisting mainly of Cuban Americans and Puerto Ricans on the nation's East Coast, and Mexican Americans throughout the West, provided unique opportunities for change.

On September 16, 1969, Mexican American students across the Southwest boycotted classes to celebrate ethnic pride (or "Chicanismo") on Mexico's Independence Day, while a group at Cal-Berkeley, shouting "Brown Power," staged a sit-in to demand a program in Chicano Studies. (Within a few years, more than 50 universities would have such a program.) Furthermore, political leverage by Hispanic groups spurred Congress to improve conditions for migrant farm workers, many of whom were Mexican American, and to provide federal funding for bilingual education, a much-debated concept that soon included the right of non-English-speaking students to schooling in their native language. Mexican Americans were also elected to the U.S. House of Representatives in Texas and California, to the U.S. Senate in New Mexico, and to the governorships of Arizona and New Mexico.

In the fall of 1969, several dozen Native Americans took over Alcatraz Island, an unoccupied former federal penitentiary in San Francisco Bay, to publicize the claims and grievances of a younger, more militant generation. "It has no running water; it has inadequate sanitation facilities; there is no industry; there are no health

uncommon response. For the first time the patrons fought back, triggering several days of rioting and protest against the harassment of homosexuals. The "Stonewall Riot" led to the formation of the Gay Liberation Front, which, in turn, began the movement to encourage group solidarity within the homosexual community and to confront openly the prejudice that gay men and women had suffered, in fearful silence, for so many years. "We reject society's attempt to impose sexual roles and definitions of our nature," announced the Gay Liberation Front. "We are stepping outside these roles and simplistic myths. We are going to be who we are."

In 1969, Mexican American activists in Texas formed **La Raza Unida,** a political party devoted to furthering "Chicano" causes and candidates through the ballot. This new party, which spread to several southwestern states, reflected the growing demand for political power and cultural self-determination within the Hispanic community,

© Bettmann/CORBIS

Sparked by Manhattan's Stonewall Riot of 1969, in which homosexuals confronted police harassment with force, organizations like the Gay Liberation Front emerged to encourage group solidarity in the struggle for equal rights.

Mexican American activists formed La Raza Unida in 1969 to further "Chicano" causes. This poster advertises a benefit for striking grape workers in California.

care facilities," said one protest leader, comparing the rocky island to a typical Indian reservation. The group spent 19 months on Alcatraz, symbolically offering to buy it for "$24 in glass beads and red cloth."

The protest signaled a change in the American Indian community. By any measure, Native Americans were the most deprived single group in the United States, with an unemployment rate 10 times higher, and a life expectancy 20 years lower, than the national average. In the late 1960s, a new group known as American Indian Movement (AIM), inspired by the black freedom struggles, began to preach a philosophy of "Red Power" that rejected the "assimilationist" policies of their elders. In 1972, AIM supported a march on Washington—named the Trail of Broken Treaties—that ended with a group of protesters barricading themselves inside the Bureau of Indian Affairs and wrecking much of the building. A year later, AIM militants seized the South Dakota village of Wounded Knee on the Pine Ridge Sioux Reservation, site of an infamous massacre by federal troops in 1890, to highlight both the squalid conditions there and the

"broken promises" that stripped Native Americans of their independence and their land. Two Indians were killed in the 71-day standoff with federal agents.

This pressure took political and legislative forms as well. In 1970, the federal government returned 48,000 acres of sacred land to the Taos Pueblo of New Mexico, beginning a cautious policy of negotiation that grew significantly in the coming years. In addition, the Nixon administration targeted minority aid programs for Native Americans living in urban areas, and Congress added funding through the Indian Education Act of 1972. Nevertheless, the alarming rates of suicide, alcoholism, and illiteracy among Native American children continued throughout the 1970s and beyond—a clear warning of how much remained to be done.

Black Capitalism and Civil Rights

Richard Nixon took office at a crucial juncture in the campaign for civil rights. The epic struggles of the 1950s and early 1960s had formally abolished *de jure* (legal) segregation in public schools and public accommodations—a remarkable achievement—yet serious problems remained. The vast majority of southern children still attended all-white or all-black schools in defiance of *Brown v. Board of Education,* and the situation was little better in the North and West, where *de facto* segregation in housing and employment kept most neighborhood schools rigidly segregated by race. Furthermore, although the percentage of "middle-class" African Americans increased substantially in the 1960s, the rate of black unemployment remained twice the national average, and male joblessness in urban areas sometimes reached 40 percent. This meant a deepening economic split within the African American community, with almost half the black families enjoying middle-class status, and an equal percentage living below the poverty line in run-down, unsafe, segregated neighborhoods where jobs were scarce and single women, increasingly, raised children on their own.

Civil rights did not rank high on Nixon's domestic agenda. Because most blacks voted Democratic—Hubert Humphrey got 95 percent of their votes in 1968—the president owed them no political debt. On the contrary, he hoped to create a "new Republican majority" by winning over white working-class Democrats, north and south, who feared that minorities were getting too much attention from the federal government. Choosing his words carefully, Nixon described racial integration as a process that demanded a slow but steady pace. "There are those who want instant integration and those who want segregation forever," he said. "I believe that we need to have a middle course between those two extremes."

Nixon's boldest civil rights initiatives related to business and employment. In 1969, he created the Office of Minority Business Enterprise, noting that "people who own their own homes and property do not burn their neighborhoods." Over the next 3 years, the federal government tripled its assistance to minority enterprises through grants and low-interest loans. More controversial was the administration's proposal to bring black workers into the high-wage, "lily-white" construction industry. Known as the Philadelphia Plan, it required the construction unions—carpenters, masons, electricians, and the like—to set up "goals" and "timetables" for hiring black apprentices on government-sponsored projects. Some civil rights leaders praised the Philadelphia Plan as a major step toward economic equality; others condemned it as a cynical ploy to woo black voters away from the Democratic party. Everyone agreed, however, that the plan went far beyond the intent of the 1964 Civil Rights Act, which simply banned job discrimination on the basis of race, religion, sex, or national origin.

On the emotional issue of public school integration, the president took a more cautious approach. Hoping to win white political converts in the South, he supported the efforts of Mississippi officials in 1969 to postpone court-ordered school integration, while firmly opposing efforts to deny federal funding to segregated schools. When told that Justice Department officials were planning to speed up school integration, the president warned them to "knock off this crap," adding: "Do what the law allows you and not one bit more." As a result, the battle shifted back to the courts, especially the U.S. Supreme Court, where major changes were now under way.

The Burger Court

In 1969, Chief Justice Earl Warren stepped down from the bench. The 77-year-old Warren had submitted his resignation in 1968, expecting President Johnson to choose a suitably liberal replacement. But problems arose when Johnson nominated his close friend Associate Supreme Court Justice Abe Fortas to become the new chief justice. Senate conservatives, charging "cronyism," organized a filibuster to deny Fortas the post; then a brewing scandal over his finances forced Fortas to resign from the Court. This gave incoming President Nixon the luxury of appointing two Supreme Court justices at once.

The first choice went smoothly. The Senate quickly confirmed Judge Warren E. Burger, a moderate northern Republican, to replace Warren as chief justice. But Nixon's other nominee, Judge Clement Haynsworth, a conservative from South Carolina, ran into trouble when Senate liberals raised questions about his antagonism toward civil rights and organized labor. Fifteen Republicans joined forty Democrats to reject Haynsworth—a rare event for the Senate, which had not defeated a Supreme Court nominee since the days of Herbert Hoover.

Stung by the vote, President Nixon nominated another southerner, Judge G. Harrold Carswell, whose general qualifications and civil rights record were far inferior to Haynsworth's. The Senate rejected him as well. Nixon angrily blamed "hypocritical" northern liberals for the defeats of Haynsworth and Carswell, claiming that "the real reasons for their rejection [were] their legal philosophies . . . and the fact that they were born in the South." A few weeks later, the Senate unanimously confirmed Nixon's third choice, Judge Harry Blackmun of Minnesota. Ironically, the president got to make two more Supreme Court nominations the following year when Justices Hugo Black and John Marshall Harlan retired. His selections—William Rehnquist, a prominent Arizona conservative, and Lewis Powell, a distinguished Virginia attorney—were easily confirmed.

The Burger Court proved more independent than most people, including Nixon, had expected. Among other decisions, it upheld publication of the Pentagon Papers; struck down "capricious" state laws imposing the death penalty for rape and murder, thereby halting capital punishment for almost two decades (*Furman v. Georgia,* 1972); and ruled against President Nixon's claims of executive privilege in the **Watergate** scandals. In addition, the Burger Court held that state laws prohibiting abortion were unconstitutional because they violated a woman's "right to privacy" under the Fourteenth Amendment (***Roe v. Wade,*** 1973). Justice Blackmun's majority opinion permitted a state to outlaw abortion in the final 3 months of pregnancy, noting, however, that the life and health of the mother must be considered at all times. The following year, almost 1 million legal abortions were performed in the United States.

The Burger Court also confronted segregation in the public schools. Its unanimous ruling in *Swann v. Charlotte–Mecklenburg Board of Education* (1971) served notice that controversial methods like "forced" busing could be used as legal remedies to achieve racial balance. Though millions of youngsters rode buses to school each day, the idea of transporting children to different neighborhoods in the name of racial integration fueled parental anger and fear. Opinion polls showed that whites overwhelmingly opposed forced busing, and that African Americans, by a smaller margin, also disapproved. For many black parents, busing simply obscured the problems of neglect and underfunding that had plagued their school districts for years.

Violence sometimes followed. In Boston, a court-ordered plan in 1974 to bus white schoolchildren to Roxbury, a poor black neighborhood, and black children to South Boston, a poor white neighborhood, led to mob action reminiscent of Little Rock, Arkansas, in 1957. Buses were stoned, black students were beaten, and federal marshals rushed in to protect them. Ironically, the schools in both neighborhoods were in awful condition, unlike the wealthy suburban Boston schools, which were not included in the desegregation plan. All too often, forced busing became a class issue, involving poorer people of all races.

New Directions at Home and Abroad

Like John F. Kennedy, President Nixon cared more about foreign policy than about domestic affairs. "I've always thought the [United States] could run itself without a president," Nixon mused. "All you need is a competent Cabinet to run the country at home." As a moderate Republican in the Eisenhower mold, Nixon endorsed the basic outlines of the modern welfare state, which included social security, unemployment insurance, a minimum wage, the right to unionize, and health care for the elderly. Yet Nixon also understood—and exploited—the public's growing concern that the Great Society era had tilted too far in favor of poor people and minority groups. Convinced that Americans were fed up with wasteful government programs and angry street demonstrations, he tried to find, in his words, a domestic "middle ground."

Rethinking Welfare

President Nixon moved cautiously on the domestic front. His immediate goals were to implement a revenue-sharing plan that sent more tax dollars back to the states and localities, and to simplify the welfare system, making it more efficient and less expensive. Revenue sharing, designed to limit the power of the national government, was a modest success. Congress passed legislation transferring $30 billion in federal revenue over five years— less than Nixon wanted, but more than state and local governments had received in the past. Welfare reform proved a much harder sell. Here the president looked to domestic advisor Daniel P. Moynihan, a social scientist whose controversial writings on poverty and family breakup in the African American community reflected a shifting emphasis from equal rights, which focused on constitutional guarantees, to equal opportunity, which stressed socioeconomic gains. Everyone agreed that the current welfare system—Aid to Families with Dependent Children (AFDC)—was seriously flawed. Its programs lacked accountability, and the payments varied widely from state to state. At Moynihan's urging,

President Nixon offered an alternative to AFDC, known as the Family Assistance Plan (FAP).

The new plan proposed a national standard for welfare designed to reduce the number of recipients—and bureaucrats—over time. Instead of providing a host of costly welfare services, the government would guarantee a minimum annual income to the poor, beginning at $1,600 for a family of four, with additional funding for food stamps. The individual states were expected to subsidize this income, and able-bodied parents (excepting mothers of preschool children) were required to seek employment or job training. Not surprisingly, FAP ran into withering criticism from all sides. Liberals complained that $1,600 was unreasonably low; conservatives opposed the very concept of a guaranteed annual income. The National Welfare Rights Organization resisted the work requirement for women with school-age children; community leaders and social workers worried about the elimination of vital services (and perhaps their own jobs).

To his credit, Nixon did not trim needed programs as his own plan went down to defeat. On the contrary, he supported Democratic-sponsored measures in Congress to increase food stamp expenditures, ensure better medical care for low-income families, and provide automatic cost-of-living adjustments (COLAs) for social security recipients to help them keep up with inflation. Although Nixon did not care to publicize this achievement, he became the first president since Franklin Roosevelt to propose a federal budget with more spending for social services than for national defense.

Protecting the Environment

On April 22, 1970, millions of Americans gathered in schools, churches, and parks to celebrate Earth Day, an event sponsored by environmental groups like the Sierra Club to educate people about the ecological problems afflicting the modern world. Begun a few years earlier, following the appearance of Rachel Carson's *Silent Spring*, the environmental movement gained strength after a series of well-publicized disasters, such as the chemical fire that ignited Cleveland's Cuyahoga River, the giant oil spill that fouled the beaches of Santa Barbara, and the "death" of Lake Erie by farm runoff and factory waste. The dire predictions of scientists about population growth, poisoned food and water, endangered species, and air pollution added fuel to the cause. As biologist Barry Commoner noted in his best-selling 1971 book, *The Closing Circle,* "our present course, if continued, will destroy the capability of the environment to support a reasonably civilized human society."

At first, President Nixon showed little interest in environmental problems. Indeed, his administration accidentally marked Earth Day by approving a project that raised serious ecological concerns, the 800-mile Alaskan oil pipeline. Yet Nixon soon considered environmentalism to be a powerful force—one that cut across class, racial, and political lines. Unlike many other issues, it gave the appearance of uniting Americans against a common foe.

Moving quickly, his administration banned the use of DDT in the United States, though not its sale to foreign countries; and stopped production of chemical and biological weapons, though not the plant defoliants or napalm used in Vietnam. More significantly, the White House supported a bipartisan congressional effort to establish the Environmental Protection Agency (EPA) and to pass the Clean Air Act of 1970 and the Endangered Species Act of 1973.

These were notable achievements. The Clean Air Act set strict national guidelines for the reduction of automobile and factory emissions, with fines and jail sentences for polluters. The Endangered Species Act protected rare plants and animals from extinction. The list included hundreds of categories above the microscopic level, from the spotted owl to the snail-darter, with the lone exemption being "pest insects." Congress also passed the Water Pollution Control Act over Nixon's veto in 1972. The law, mandating $25 billion for the cleanup of America's neglected lakes and rivers, was too costly for the president, though it proved effective in bringing polluted waters back to life. The EPA, meanwhile, monitored the progress of these laws and required environmental "impact studies" for all future federal projects.

Though Americans readily agreed about the need for clean air, pure water, and protecting wildlife, the cost of doing these things did not fall equally on everyone's shoulders. Auto manufacturers warned that the expense of meeting the new emission standards would result in higher car prices and the layoff of production workers. Loggers in the Northwest angrily accused the EPA of being more interested in protecting a few forest birds than in allowing human beings to earn a living and feed their families. A common bumper sticker in Oregon read: "If You're Hungry And Out Of Work, Eat An Environmentalist." In response to pressure from labor unions and businesses about lost jobs, rising costs, and endless paperwork, the EPA modified some of its goals and deadlines for compliance with these new laws. Could strategies be devised to protect jobs and the environment simultaneously? Could American corporations effectively compete with foreign companies that did not face such restrictions? Should the United States abandon atomic power, offshore oil drilling, and other potential threats to the environment at a time when the demand for energy was rapidly increasing? Protecting the environment raised serious questions for the future.

DOING HISTORY ONLINE

Endangered Species Act, 1973

Read the document in this module. What possible reasons were there for Richard Nixon, a Republican, to decide to sign the Endangered Species Act, a piece of legislation promoted by liberals and environmental groups that typically were allied with the Democratic party?

History ⧖ Now™   Visit HistoryNOW to access primary sources and exercises related to this topic: http://now.ilrn.com/ayers_etal3e

---

A New World Order

Richard Nixon loved the challenge of foreign affairs. The secrecy, intrigue, and deal making fascinated him in ways that domestic matters never could. Determined to control foreign policy even more rigidly than previous presidents, Nixon bypassed the State Department in favor of the National Security Council, based in the White House itself. To direct the NSC, he chose **Henry Kissinger,** a German refugee and Harvard political scientist. In Kissinger, the president found the perfect match for his "realistic" view of foreign affairs in which hard assessments of the national interest took precedence over moral and ideological concerns.

Both men agreed that America's bipolar approach, based on the "containment" of Soviet Communism, no longer made sense. They wanted a more flexible policy that recognized not only the limits of American influence, but also the growing strength of Western Europe, Communist China, and Japan. They believed that the United States could no longer afford to play the world's police in every skirmish, or to finance an arms race that grew more dangerous—and expensive—with each passing year. The Nixon–Kissinger approach meant talking with old enemies, finding common ground through negotiation, and encouraging a more widespread balance of world power.

This innovative thinking, however, did not extend to all parts of the globe. The president still viewed Fidel Castro as a mortal enemy, and openly encouraged the CIA to undermine the democratically elected, left-wing government of Chilean President Salvadore Allende, who was overthrown and apparently murdered by right-wing military forces in 1973. "I don't see why we have to allow a country to go Marxist just because its people are irresponsible," Henry Kissinger argued. In Latin America, at least, the New World Order appeared strikingly similar to the old one.

The China Opening

In one sense, Richard Nixon seemed an odd choice to strip away years of rigid Cold War thinking in foreign affairs. He was, after all, a rough-and-tumble anti-Communist known for his bitter attacks on State Department officials during the McCarthy years. Yet that is what made his new initiatives all the more remarkable. Nixon's skill in foreign affairs lay in his ability to seize opportunities in a rapidly changing world. One of his first moves was to take advantage of the widening rift between Communist China and the Soviet Union.

The United States at this time did not even recognize Communist China. Since 1949, American policy considered the anti-Communist regime on Taiwan the legitimate government of mainland China. There were some who believed that only a politician with Nixon's Red-hunting credentials would dare to change this policy after so many years. No one could seriously accuse this president—as he had accused so many others—of being "soft on communism."

Nixon wanted a new relationship with China for several reasons. The trade possibilities were enormous. Better relations also increased the chances of a peace settlement in Vietnam, while strengthening America's bargaining position with the Soviet Union, which feared any alliance between Washington and Beijing. Most of all, Nixon realized that China must now be recognized as a legitimate world power. The United States could no longer afford to ignore this reality.

Nixon worked behind the scenes, knowing that Americans considered China the "most dangerous" nation on earth. The first public breakthrough came in 1971, when an American table tennis team was invited to China for an exhibition tour. This "Ping-Pong diplomacy" led both nations to ease trade and travel restrictions. Meanwhile, Henry Kissinger secretly visited Beijing to plan a summit meeting between Chinese and American leaders. President Nixon hinted at his future plans in a remarkable magazine interview. "If there is anything I want to do before I die," he said, "it is to go to China."

Nixon arrived there on February 22, 1972—the first American president ever to set foot on Chinese soil. For the next 8 days, the world watched in amazement as he walked along the Great Wall and strolled through the Forbidden City. "The Chinese Army band played 'America the Beautiful' and 'Home on the Range,'" wrote the *New York Times.* "President Nixon quoted Chairman Mao Zedong approvingly, used his chopsticks skillfully, and clinked glasses with every Chinese official in sight."

The trip ended with a joint statement, known as the Shanghai Communiqué, that promised closer relations between the two countries in trade, travel, and cultural exchange. Each nation agreed to open a legation (not an embassy) in the other's capital city, beginning the process of diplomatic recognition that would take 7 more years to complete. The most important issues, such as human rights and nuclear proliferation, were tactfully ignored. And the most controversial issue—the future of Taiwan—demonstrated the deep rift that still existed. Communist China asserted its claim to the island, demanding that American troops on Taiwan be removed. The United States called for a "peaceful solution" to the "Taiwan question" and promised to reduce its forces as "tensions" in the region declined. Still, the historic significance of Nixon's visit overshadowed the problems that lay ahead. "We have been here a week," he declared. "This was the week that changed the world."

Détente

Three months later, the president traveled to Moscow for a summit meeting with Soviet leader Leonid Brezhnev. A master of timing in foreign affairs, Nixon believed that his successful trip to China, coupled with a faltering Russian economy, would make the Soviets more likely to strike a serious deal with the United States. The key issues were arms control and increased trade. Both sides possessed huge atomic arsenals that cost billions of dollars and increased the chances of catastrophic war. The Russians desperately needed grain, heavy equipment, and technical assistance; American farmers and manufacturers saw new markets for their goods.

The Moscow Summit further enhanced the Nixon–Kissinger record in foreign affairs. On May 22, 1972, the United States and the Soviet Union signed a Strategic Arms Limitation Treaty (SALT) that limited the number of long-range offensive missiles (ICBMs), and an ABM agreement that froze the production of antiballistic missiles for the next 5 years. No one believed that the arms race was now over; both sides would continue to build long-range nuclear bombers and to develop the Multiple Independent Re-entry Vehicles (MIRVs), which permitted several warheads to be fired from a single missile. Yet these initial treaties, committing the superpowers to the principle of arms reduction, represented a stunning breakthrough in Soviet–American relations.

The economic agreements were less successful. Though U.S.–Soviet trade more than tripled over the next 3 years, the greatest increase came in a single wheat deal with American farmers and grain dealers that caused a temporary shortage in the United States. Not surprisingly, American consumers fumed at the idea of shipping low-priced wheat to a foreign country while bread prices rose dramatically at home.

Nevertheless, the Moscow Summit provided a solid foundation for **détente,** with both sides pledging to reduce world tensions and to coexist peacefully. As President Nixon left Moscow, he noted the differences between the Soviet leaders he faced in 1959, when he was vice president, and the ones who endorsed détente. The current leaders, he wrote, "do not have as much of an inferiority complex as was the case in Khrushchev's period. They do not have to brag about everything in Russia being better than anything anywhere else. But they still crave to be respected as equals, and on this point I think we made a good impression."

Four More Years?

After a full term in office, Richard Nixon could look back on a record of notable achievement. Relations with Cold War opponents like the Soviet Union and Communist China had dramatically improved as détente replaced confrontation. Although the Vietnam War continued, the steady withdrawal of American troops meant fewer casualties and an end to the draft. Even the economy looked better, with unemployment and inflation presently under control.

The Landslide of 1972

Nixon's Democratic challengers faced an uphill battle. From the political right, Governor **George Wallace** of Alabama continued the presidential odyssey he began in 1968, when he captured five southern states as a third-party candidate. Campaigning this time as a Democrat, Wallace won wide support among white working-class voters for his opposition to forced busing and his attacks on "welfare cheats." After winning the Democratic presidential primary in Florida, and running a close second in Wisconsin, Wallace was shot and paralyzed by a would-be assassin, ending his presidential quest.

A few weeks later, on June 17, 1972, five men were arrested while burglarizing the Democratic National Headquarters at the Watergate complex in Washington, D.C. Four of them were Cubans who had worked previously for the CIA; they were led by James W. McCord, the security director for Richard Nixon's Committee to Re-Elect the President, known as CREEP. Supervising from a nearby hotel, and later arrested, were two presidential aides—Gordon Liddy and E. Howard Hunt—who belonged to the newly created "Plumbers" unit. Responding to the break-in, Nixon assured the public that no one "presently employed" in his administration was involved "in this very bizarre incident," adding: "What really hurts is if you try to cover it up."

At the Republican National Convention in Miami, the delegates enthusiastically renominated the Nixon–

Agnew team. The Democratic race, however, proved far more contentious. The candidates included Hubert Humphrey, the 1968 presidential nominee; Senator **George McGovern** of South Dakota, the favorite of younger, more liberal Democrats; and Representative Shirley Chisholm of New York, the first African American to seek the presidential nomination of a major political party.

The Democratic National Convention, meeting in Miami Beach, reflected the party reforms that followed the bloody "siege of Chicago" in 1968. The changes were dramatic, with the percentage of female delegates increasing from 13 to 38 percent, blacks from 5 to 15 percent, and those under 30 years old from 3 to 23 percent. Moreover, these new delegates embraced the causes of numerous "out groups" in society, such as homosexuals, migrant workers, prisoners, and the urban poor. Deeply committed to the "rights revolution" of the 1960s, they proposed a major redistribution of political power and cultural authority in the United States.

The delegates chose George McGovern for president and Senator Thomas Eagleton of Missouri for vice president. But the campaign faced trouble from the start. Reporters learned that Senator Eagleton had been hospitalized in the past for mental depression and fatigue, twice undergoing electroshock therapy. At first, McGovern stood by his running mate, offering him "1,000 percent" support. As criticism mounted, however, McGovern replaced Eagleton with former Peace Corps Director Sargent Shriver, who accepted the position after six others turned it down. Appearing weak and opportunistic, McGovern dropped further in the polls.

Far more damaging was the lack of unity within Democratic ranks. Many of McGovern's key positions, such as amnesty for draft resisters, liberalization of marijuana laws, and greater welfare benefits for the poor, offended moderate and working-class Democrats who believed their party had moved too far to the left. On election day, Nixon overwhelmed McGovern, carrying every state but Massachusetts and winning 61 percent of the popular vote.

Yet Nixon's landslide victory was more limited than it appeared. Ticket splitting flourished in 1972, with the Democratic party easily retaining control of Congress. Thus, legions of Democratic voters rejected McGovern's message without deserting the party itself. Furthermore, the percentage of eligible voters who cast ballots in presidential elections continued to fall, from 62 percent in 1964, to 61 percent in 1968, to 56 percent in 1972. This suggested a growing alienation from the political process—and a hint of the protest to come.

Exit from Vietnam

Richard Nixon's impressive reelection victory seemed a sure sign that passions were cooling and better times lay ahead. The president's first task was to end the Vietnam conflict on honorable terms and secure the release of American prisoners of war. But the key to any settlement, Nixon understood, was the future security of South Vietnam. What would happen after U.S. troops left that country? Would the American sacrifice be in vain?

In the spring of 1972, North Vietnam had mounted a major offensive in the South, gambling that Nixon's concern about the coming presidential election would prevent the United States from responding. The offensive failed miserably, however, when Nixon ordered massive bombing raids against North Vietnam. That fall, secret negotiations between Henry Kissinger and North Vietnam's Le Duc To produced a temporary cease-fire. The United States agreed to withdraw its remaining troops from Vietnam in return for the release of its POWs. President Thieu would continue to govern South Vietnam, and North Vietnamese troops were allowed to remain there until a final settlement was reached. A week before the 1972 presidential election, Kissinger declared that "peace is at hand."

The claim was premature. President Thieu opposed the cease-fire, demanding the removal of North Vietnamese troops from South Vietnam, and the North Vietnamese seemed intent on adding even more soldiers for a final assault. Following his reelection, President Nixon tried to force a settlement through a fierce air assault against North Vietnam. "These bastards," he said, "have never been bombed like they're going to be bombed this time." In late December 1972, American B-52s filled the skies over Hanoi and Haiphong, dropping more tonnage than all American planes had dropped in the previous 2 years. The damage done to North Vietnam was staggering: harbors, factories, railway lines, storage facilities, and sometimes adjoining neighborhoods, were destroyed. Moreover, where only one B-52 had been lost in combat throughout the entire war, 15 were shot down in these so-called "Christmas bombings." North Vietnam's Communist allies did not strongly protest, even when a Soviet ship was damaged in Haiphong Harbor. Interested above all in continuing the process of détente with America, the Russians signaled North Vietnam to return to the bargaining table and make the best deal. On January 27, 1973, the United States and North Vietnam signed an agreement quite similar to the one that had fallen apart a few months before. President Nixon got Thieu's reluctant support by vowing to "respond in full force" if North Vietnam renewed the fighting in the South. The United States, he proclaimed, had achieved "peace with honor" at last.

What Nixon got, in reality, was an American exit from Vietnam that left the vulnerable Thieu government at the mercy of its Communist opponents. Despite his pledge, the United States could only respond to future treaty violations with air power; sending troops back into combat was now unthinkable. The agreement ended American involvement without guaranteeing South Vietnam's long-term survival.

The American public expressed relief at the settlement, but little jubilation. The war had divided the country, raised suspicions about government to dangerous levels, and drained billions of dollars from vital domestic programs. More than 50,000 U.S. soldiers were killed in Vietnam and 300,000 were wounded. At least 1 million Asians died, and more would perish in the coming years. As the *New York Times* noted, "There is no dancing in the streets, no honking of horns, no champagne."

Public attention soon shifted to the return of 587 American POWs. Many had spent up to 7 years in North Vietnamese jails, and some had been tortured. "We are honored to have the opportunity to serve our country under difficult circumstances," said their senior officer as his plane touched down on American soil. That very day, former President Lyndon Johnson died in his sleep. "His tragedy—and ours," Senator Edmund Muskie stated, "was the war."

Watergate and the Abuse of Power

As 1973 began, Richard Nixon's public approval rating stood at a remarkable 68 percent. With Vietnam behind him, the president appeared ready to launch a successful second term. Yet all that ended in April, when the Watergate burglars pleaded guilty to minor charges of theft and wiretapping in order to avoid a public trial. Suspecting a cover-up, federal judge John Sirica convinced the lead burglar, James McCord, to admit that high-ranking White House officials were involved in planning the break-in. This startling confession, combined with the investigative stories of *Washington Post* reporters Bob Woodward and Carl Bernstein, turned the Watergate affair into front-page news.

During the spring of 1973, President Nixon reluctantly appointed Harvard Law School professor Archibald Cox as an independent prosecutor in the Watergate case. The Senate formed a special investigating committee chaired by 73-year-old Sam Ervin of North Carolina, who modestly described himself as "a simple country lawyer." Under Ervin's careful direction, the committee heard sworn testimony from present and former Nixon aides about a "seamless web" of criminal activity designed to undermine the president's critics and political opponents. In meticulous detail, John Dean, the former

Enduring Issues   Watergate: The Biggest Presidential Scandal of All

When Richard Nixon resigned his presidency in August 1974, there was more relief than celebration. The country had been spared a lacerating impeachment process. A new president, widely hailed for his honesty, had been sworn into office without violence or disorder.

From *Herblock: A Cartoonist's Life* (Times Books 1998). Reprinted with Permission.

"The long national nightmare is over," Gerald R. Ford assured the public. "Our constitution works."

Ford was hardly exaggerating. What began as a break-in at the Democratic National Headquarters at the Watergate complex in Washington, D.C., quickly escalated into a dangerous constitutional crisis, with the Nixon White House pitted against a special prosecutor and a disillusioned Congress that was united to impeach the president—and then remove him from office. There had been presidential scandals before in our history—many related to charges of influence-peddling and financial corruption by White House aides or cabinet officials—but none that directly involved the President of the United States in criminal activity. The Watergate scandal would eventually send more than 30 members of the Nixon administration to federal prison, including the president's chief of staff, H. R. Haldeman; his chief counsel, John Dean; and his closest confidant, former Attorney General John N. Mitchell. Indeed, had Richard Nixon not resigned his office and been given a blanket pardon, there is a possibility that he would have been put on trial, found guilty of obstructing justice, and sent to jail.

Americans were riveted by the drama of Watergate. The televised hearings, held throughout the summer of 1973, were filled with stunning plot turns and priceless characters. There was Tony Ulasewicz, the tough-talking former New York City policeman, who worked as a "bagman" for the Nixon campaign; John J. Sirica, the no-nonsense federal judge who got the Watergate burglars to confess; Alexander Butterfield, the befuddled White House aide who innocently dropped the

Former White House counsel John Dean documented President Nixon's role in the Watergate cover-up during his testimony before the Ervin committee in 1973.

© Fred Ward/Black Star

White House counsel, implicated Nixon himself in a plan to ensure the silence of the imprisoned burglars by paying them "hush money."

Nixon, however, denied any involvement in Watergate. On national television, he took "responsibility" but no blame for the scandal, explaining that he had been too busy running the nation to bother with the day-to-day workings of his reelection campaign. Many Americans—and most Republican leaders—took Nixon at his word. As House minority leader Gerald R. Ford of Michigan declared, "I have the greatest confidence in the president and am absolutely positive he had nothing to do with this mess."

In July, White House aide Alexander Butterfield stunned the Ervin committee by revealing that Nixon had secretly recorded his Oval Office conversations since 1971. Sensing that the true

bombshell that President Nixon had secretly installed a taping system in the Oval Office; Barbara Jordan, the young African-American congresswoman from Texas, whose eloquence regarding the Constitution, and Nixon's abuse of it, appeared to restore the public's confidence in politics; and Howard Baker, the ranking Senate Republican on the Watergate Committee, who framed the key question of the hearings: "What did the president know, and when did he know it?"

Whether President Nixon actually knew about the Watergate burglary in advance is still in dispute. What is clear, however, is that Nixon took a leading role in the criminal conspiracy to cover up the break-in because he knew that an independent investigation would expose a wide range of other illegal activity coordinated from inside the White House, such as spying on those who had criticized the Nixon administration, and funding a massive campaign of "dirty tricks" to sabotage the various Democratic presidential candidates in 1972.

It is true, of course, that the surveillance of critics and political opponents did not begin with Richard Nixon. The so-called "Imperial Presidency" that arose in the middle of the twentieth century, combined with the growing power of investigative agencies like the FBI and the CIA, created an atmosphere that encouraged widespread lawbreaking in the name of national security. Still, the Nixon administration's secret war against its critics, real and imagined, was of a scope that seemed almost unimaginable when finally exposed. And much of the blame could be placed directly at the feet of Richard Nixon—a man whose fear of normal

opposition, and cynicism about the political process, had long marked his career.

Many analysts see a silver lining in the cloud of Watergate. They agree with Gerald Ford that the system of checks and balances put in place by the Founding Fathers had done its job well. Law-breaking at the highest levels was exposed and punished. A president resigned his office to avoid impeachment, and the government moved forward without a hitch, showing both the wisdom of the Constitution and the power of our laws. But others are less certain, noting that had it not been for the tenacity of two young reporters named Bob Woodward and Carl Bernstein, the intuition of a federal judge named John Sirica, and the innocent response of a White House staffer named Alexander Butterfield, the scandal known as Watergate may never have been exposed.

Someone else had helped as well. For more than 30 years, Woodward and Bernstein had shielded the identity of their most crucial source in the Watergate story, promising to reveal his name only after his death. But in June 2005, a 91-year-old former FBI official named W. Mark Felt stepped forward to claim credit for his role. "I'm the guy they used to call 'Deep Throat,'" he declared. Woodward and Bernstein quickly admitted it was true. The biggest remaining mystery of Watergate had finally been put to rest.

Questions for Reflection

1. Why has Watergate been singled out as the most dangerous presidential scandal in our history?

2. What are the lessons of Watergate for future generations of Americans?

---

story of presidential involvement in the Watergate scandal could now be uncovered, Judge Sirica, Special Prosecutor Cox, and Chairman Ervin all demanded to hear the relevant tapes. But Nixon refused to release them, citing executive privilege and the separation of powers. When Cox persisted, Nixon ordered Attorney General Elliot Richardson to fire him. Richardson and his top deputy refused, leading to their swift removal. These dramatic developments, known as the "Saturday Night Massacre," produced angry calls for Nixon's impeachment.

There was trouble for the vice president as well. In 1973, a Baltimore grand jury looked into allegations that Spiro Agnew, as governor of Maryland, had accepted illegal payoffs from building contractors. After first denying these charges, the vice president resigned his office and pleaded *nolo contendere* (no contest) to one count of income tax evasion. He received 3 years' probation plus a $10,000 fine.

Under the Twenty-fifth Amendment, adopted in 1967, the president is obligated to nominate a vice president "who shall take the office upon confirmation by a majority vote of both houses of Congress." To bolster his declining fortunes, Nixon chose the well-respected **Gerald Ford,** who was quickly confirmed. But the president ran into more trouble when the Internal Revenue Service (IRS) disclosed that he owed $500,000 in back taxes from 1970 and 1971; Nixon had paid less than $1,000 in each of these years. Responding emotionally, Nixon told a press conference that "I am not a crook."

By this point, however, public confidence in Nixon had disappeared. The testimony of John Dean, the Saturday Night Massacre, the resignation of Spiro Agnew, the embarrassing IRS disclosures—all cast doubt on the president's morality and fitness to lead. A Gallup poll taken in November 1973 showed Nixon's public approval had dropped to 27 percent. In desperation, the

Facing certain impeachment and removal from office, President Nixon resigned on August 9, 1974.

president released transcripts of several Watergate-related conversations (but not the tapes themselves), claiming that they cleared him of wrongdoing. Many thought otherwise. The transcripts contained ethnic and racial slurs, vulgar language (with "expletives deleted"), and strong hints of presidential involvement in a cover-up.

Nixon's refusal to release the tapes reached a climax in July 1974, when the House Judiciary Committee debated charges of presidential impeachment before a national television audience. Led by Chairman Peter Rodino of New Jersey and the eloquent Barbara Jordan of Texas, the committee approved three charges—obstruction of justice, abuse of power, and contempt of Congress—at the very moment that a unanimous Supreme Court ordered Nixon to comply with Judge Sirica's subpoena for the Watergate tapes. On August 5, the president released the material that sealed his fate. Although they provided no evidence that Nixon knew about the Watergate burglary in advance, the tapes showed him playing an active role in the attempt to cover up White House involvement in the crime.

Faced with certain impeachment and removal, Richard Nixon became the first president to resign from office. In a tearful farewell to his staff on August 9, he preached the very advice that he, himself, was incapable of following. "Never get discouraged. Never be petty," he said. "Always remember. . . . Those who hate you don't win unless you hate them. And then you destroy yourself."

OPEC and the Oil Embargo

In the midst of the Watergate scandal, a serious crisis erupted over the nation's energy needs. On October 6,

1973—the Jewish high holiday of Yom Kippur—Egypt and Syria attacked Israel from two sides. After some hesitation, the United States backed Israel, a longtime ally, by airlifting vital military supplies. American aid proved essential in helping Israel repel the attack, and the Organization of Petroleum Exporting Countries (OPEC), led by Saudi Arabia and other Arab nations, responded by halting oil shipments to the United States, Western Europe, and Japan.

The oil embargo created an immediate panic, though the problem had been building for years. As the U.S. economy flourished after World War II, its energy consumption soared. Americans, barely 6 percent of the world's population in 1974, used more than 30 percent of the world's energy. Furthermore, as the expense of exploring and drilling for domestic oil increased, the United States turned to foreign suppliers, especially in the Middle East. Between 1968 and 1973, America's consumption of imported oil tripled from 12 to 36 percent.

This reliance on foreign sources left the United States extremely vulnerable to the OPEC embargo. No nation was more dependent on fossil fuels, and no nation had been more wasteful. As the cold weather set in, President Nixon warned that "we are heading toward the most acute shortage of energy since World War II." In response, the government reduced highway speed limits to 55 miles per hour, lowered thermostats in office buildings to 68 degrees, approved daylight savings time in winter, eased environmental restrictions on coal mining, and pushed the development of nuclear power. Across the nation, stores and factories closed early, families dimmed their Christmas lighting, and northern colleges canceled their midwinter semesters. Long lines formed at the gas stations, which were closed on Sundays to conserve precious fuel.

The oil embargo ended in April 1974, but the impact lingered on. Energy costs rose dramatically, even as supplies returned to normal, because OPEC tripled its price. A gallon of gas in the United States rose from 30 cents (before the embargo) to 75 cents and more. Consumers faced soaring inflation, and manufacturers confronted higher production costs. Some regions, such as the automobile- and steel-producing Midwest, were particularly hard hit; other areas, like the energy-producing Sunbelt, gained in population and political influence.

Above all, the energy crisis shook the foundations of the American dream. For three decades, a booming economy had produced a standard of living unparalleled in terms of material comfort, home ownership, and access to higher education. American culture thrived on the assumption of upward mobility—that the nation's

The OPEC oil embargo of 1973–1974 left Americans high and dry at the gas pumps.

children would do better than their parents had done. After 1973, that assumption was in peril.

Prosperity could no longer be taken for granted. Following the oil embargo, average weekly earnings in the United States (adjusted for inflation) stopped growing for the first time in 30 years. So, too, did worker productivity. The increased cost of energy, combined with spiraling federal deficits and aggressive foreign competition in manufacturing and technology, made the American economy more vulnerable than before. Some experts predicted a new age in which limits and sacrifice replaced abundance and expansion.

Gerald Ford in the White House

Vice President Gerald Ford, a former football star at the University of Michigan who had served honorably for two decades in the U.S. House of Representatives, seemed like the ideal figure to restore public confidence in the presidency. As a Republican party loyalist, he had

opposed most of Lyndon Johnson's Great Society legislation, while strongly supporting the war in Vietnam. Yet even Ford's political opponents praised his decency, his integrity, his humble, straightforward ways. After the charisma of John Kennedy, the explosive energy of Lyndon Johnson, and the divisive appeals of Richard Nixon, Americans were ready, it appeared, for a leader with common values and an ordinary touch. As the new president joked, "I'm a Ford, not a Lincoln."

The Watergate Legacy

Gerald Ford entered the White House at a pivotal time. Although not an activist by nature, he inherited a situation in which the legislative branch of government, emboldened by the disasters of Watergate and Vietnam, appeared anxious to restore its former authority by cutting the executive branch down to size. In 1973, for example, Congress passed the War Powers Act that required the president to notify Congress within 48 hours about the foreign deployment of American

President Ford entered the White House after Watergate with the vow to "put Watergate behind us." His pardon of President Nixon, however, opened old wounds.

combat troops. If Congress did not formally endorse that action within 60 days, the troops would be withdrawn. In addition, Congress passed the Freedom of Information Act, which gave the American people unprecedented access to classified government material.

The Senate also held a series of spectacular hearings into the abuses, and criminal activity, of executive intelligence agencies such as the FBI and the CIA. The public learned that FBI agents had routinely harassed, blackmailed, and wiretapped prominent Americans such as Martin Luther King, Jr., and CIA operatives had engaged in illegal drug experiments, money laundering, and bungled assassinations of world leaders like Fidel Castro. These revelations led President Ford to create a monitoring device known as the Intelligence Oversight Board. But Congress, with fresh memories of the Watergate cover-up, formed a permanent watchdog committee to investigate such behavior on its own.

Ford, too, fell victim to the Watergate morass. During his vice presidential confirmation hearing in 1973, he had gone on record against a possible presidential pardon for Richard Nixon. "I do not think the public would stand for it," he declared. Yet in September 1974, President Ford reversed his earlier position by granting Nixon a "full, free, and absolute pardon" for all crimes he "may have committed" during his term in office. Ford based his decision on a number of factors, including the impact of a criminal trial on Nixon's health. Above all, however, Ford hoped that a presidential pardon would finally put the "national nightmare" of Watergate to rest.

In fact, the opposite occurred. By appearing to place one man above the law, the pardon raised serious doubts about Gerald Ford's most cherished asset: his spotless character. Within days, the new president's public approval rating dropped from 72 to 49 percent. What bothered many Americans was the fact that Ford had granted the pardon without demanding contrition in return. Richard Nixon barely apologized for Watergate. He never admitted his crimes. For Gerald Ford, the pardon was an act of mercy, but others wanted justice as well.

The new president also tried to heal the internal wounds of the Vietnam War. Within days of taking office, he offered "conditional amnesty" to the 350,000 Americans of draft age who had refused service in the armed forces by leaving the country. Under Ford's plan, a draft resister might be permitted to reenter the United States in return for alternative service in a hospital or a charitable institution. Not surprisingly, the program met stiff resistance. Many who left the country believed they had performed an act of conscience, whereas veterans' groups viewed them as military deserters who should serve their time in jail. As a result, only 20,000 people took part in the program.

The Fall of South Vietnam

In October 1974, at a secret conclave outside Hanoi, the leaders of Communist North Vietnam prepared their final plans for the conquest of South Vietnam. Their main concern was the United States. Would it respond "in full force" to Communist violations of the 1973 peace accords? The North Vietnamese did not think so. "Having already withdrawn from the South," they reasoned, "the United States could hardly jump back in."

Their assessment was correct. The North Vietnamese launched a massive assault in March 1975, overwhelming South Vietnamese forces near the Demilitarized Zone (DMZ). The Viet Cong, still suffering from the frightful losses inflicted during the Tet offensive of 1968, played a minor role in the fighting. As North Vietnamese troops advanced, a mixture of chaos and panic gripped South Vietnam, with thousands of soldiers deserting their units and masses of civilians clogging the highways in desperate flight. Ignoring a plea from President Ford, Congress refused to extend emergency aid to South Vietnam. On April 23, Ford acknowledged the obvious. The Vietnam War, he said, "is finished as far as America is concerned."

Saigon fell to the Communists on April 29. The televised images of Americans desperately boarding the last helicopters from the embassy grounds seemed a painful yet fitting conclusion to our nation's longest war. "What we need now in this country," said a solemn Henry Kissinger, "is to put Vietnam behind us and to concentrate on problems of the future."

This was easier said than done. The humiliating collapse of South Vietnam raised serious questions about the soundness of America's foreign policy and the limits of its military power. Furthermore, for those most deeply affected—the veterans of Vietnam—the collapse raised personal questions about the meaning of their sacrifice to the nation and to themselves. With the exception of the POWs, these veterans received no public tributes, no outpouring of thanks. Congress passed no special "GI Bill" to pay for their college tuition, to help them find employment, or to finance their new homes. Some Americans condemned the veterans for serving in an "immoral war"; others blamed them for participating in the nation's first military defeat. "The left hated us for killing," said one dejected veteran, "and the right hated us for not killing enough."

The vast majority of Vietnam veterans expressed pride in their military service and a willingness to fight there again. Most of them adjusted well to civilian life, although a sizable minority (one out of six, according to the Veterans Administration) suffered from posttraumatic stress disorder, substance abuse, and sometimes both. In addition, some veterans claimed that their exposure to

As South Vietnam fell to the Communists on April 29, 1975, people scrambled to board the final helicopters on the roof of the American embassy in Saigon.

Agent Orange, a toxic herbicide used to defoliate the jungles of Vietnam, had produced high rates of cancer, lung disease, and even birth defects in their children. After more than a decade of controversy, Congress passed legislation that extended benefits to Vietnam veterans with medical conditions linked to Agent Orange.

Public sentiment softened over time. Opinion polls by the late 1970s showed that most Americans considered the Vietnam veteran to be both a dutiful soldier and the victim of a tragic war. In 1982, the Vietnam Veterans Memorial, a dramatic wall of black granite with the names of 58,000 Americans who died or are missing in that war, was unveiled on the Mall in Washington, D.C. Attracting large, respectful crowds, the memorial affords recognition for the sacrifices of all who served in Vietnam.

Stumbling toward Defeat

The pardon of Richard Nixon and the fall of South Vietnam served to erode much of the goodwill that had accompanied Gerald Ford's early days in office. The president also faced a bleak economic picture, darkened by spiraling energy costs, in which unemployment and inflation reached their highest levels in years. "The state of the union," Ford admitted in 1975, "is not good."

The president and the Congress disagreed about the best medicine for the economic slump. The Republican Ford, believing that a balanced federal budget was the key to cutting inflation, proposed sizable cuts in government programs and a voluntary citizen's campaign to curb rising prices, which he called "Whip Inflation Now" (WIN).

The Democratic Congress called for increased federal spending to spur the economy and to lower unemployment by creating new jobs. Although Ford vetoed more than 60 bills during his brief tenure in office, Congress overrode the president to increase social security benefits, fund public works projects, and raise the minimum wage.

In foreign affairs, Ford tried to maintain the policy of détente begun by Nixon and Kissinger, who remained as secretary of state. But unlike Nixon, the new president worried conservatives with his alleged weaknesses as a negotiator. Of particular concern was the Helsinki Accord of 1975, which pledged the United States and the Soviet Union, among other nations, to recognize the Cold War boundaries dividing Eastern and Western Europe and to respect human rights within their borders. Many Americans were dismayed by the formal acceptance of Soviet domination over nations such as Poland and East Germany; many more were skeptical about any Russian promise regarding human rights. "I am against this agreement," said former Governor Ronald Reagan of California, "and I think all Americans should be against it."

Even Ford's occasional successes left controversy in their wake. In 1975, for example, communists in Cambodia seized the American merchant ship *Mayaguez* in international waters off the Cambodian coast. The president responded with a daring rescue mission in which 41 U.S. Marines were killed and 49 were wounded, although it turned out that the Cambodians had already released the *Mayaguez* and its crew. Though Ford received some criticism for not consulting Congress before sending troops into action, most Americans, recalling the *Pueblo* incident and the fall of South Vietnam, applauded his decisive action. "It was wonderful," declared Senator Barry Goldwater. "It shows we've still got balls in this country."

The Election of 1976

Gerald Ford dreamed of winning the White House in his own right. Yet unlike previous incumbents, who normally breezed through the presidential nominating process, Ford faced a serious challenge in 1976 from Ronald Reagan and the Republican right. Reagan's polished presence and outspoken conservatism played well against

Flashpoints | "Live, From New York . . ."

It premiered on October 11, 1975, at 11:30 p.m., from NBC studio 8-H in New York City. A cast of barely known young performers, calling themselves "The Not Ready for Prime Time Players," starred in a 90-minute comedy-variety show called *Saturday Night Live*. For NBC, it seemed a gamble worth taking. The network already dominated late-night programming with the highly rated *Tonight Show*, starring Johnny Carson. What it wanted was a way to extend this control into the weekend by appealing to a powerful "demographic" not normally known for spending Saturday nights in front of a TV set: 18- to 34-year-olds.

Using a guest host and a different musical act each week, the show revolved around a series of skits, heavy on satire, from comedians and writers with a brilliant flair for mimicry and character invention. The original group included John Belushi, whose manic energy produced the immortal Samurai chef; Gilda Radner, who hilariously portrayed the self-important newshound Barbara Wawa and the flaky advice guru Roseanne Roseannadana ("It's always something"); Chevy Chase, whose weekly imitation of a bumbling Gerald Ford was said by political analysts to have influenced the 1976 presidential election; and Dan Akroyd, whose perfectly pitched, endlessly annoying portrayal Jimmy Carter did for the new president what Chevy Chase had done for the old.

SNL soon became a magnet for talent. As the original cast members departed, others aptly filled the void. The list of those who launched their careers at Studio 8-H reads like a who's who of modern comedy: Bill Murray, Eddie Murphy, Julia Louis Dreyfus, Billy Crystal, Martin Short, Daman Wayans, Joan Cusack, Phil Hartman, Dana Carvey, Adam Sandler, and Chris Rock.

If there was something new and refreshing about *SNL*, there also were powerful links to the past. One of the things that had distinguished the "golden age of television" in the 1950s was that most of the shows were done live, before enthusiastic audiences, with all of the challenges that such a medium entailed. Many observers saw *SNL* as a throwback to that era, most resembling *Your Show of Shows*, a 90-minute comedy-variety format starring Sid Caesar that had aired Saturday nights on NBC. The pressure of grinding out so much material had forced the performers to improvise and think on their feet. And it had led, as well, to a relatively swift burn-out of the cast, requiring constant transfusions of new talent. As a result, *Your Show of Shows* had spawned the likes of Mel Brooks, Carl Reiner, playwright Neil Simon, Woody Allen, and Larry Gelbart, the creator of *MASH*.

The great difference, however, is that *SNL* has lasted for 30 years. Its cast has turned over many times, its ratings have fluctuated wildly, and its comedy has ranged from brilliant to dismal. Yet it remains, by all accounts, among the most important and innovative shows in the history of television.

Questions for Reflection

1. Why has *Saturday Night Live* succeeded so well, and for so long, while other comedy-variety shows have failed?

2. In your view, does the political and social satire of the *SNL* skits have an effect upon those who watch it? If so, in what ways?

3. What other television shows in the last 30 years have had a significant impact on the viewing public?

Ford's reserved manner and middle-of-the-road approach. With great fanfare, Reagan portrayed Ford as a weak president, unable to tame a Democratic Congress or to confront the Russians at Helsinki. In his sharpest attack, Reagan blasted Ford for opening negotiations aimed at reducing American control of the Panama Canal. "We built it, we paid for it, it's ours," Reagan thundered, "and we should tell [Panama] that we are going to keep it."

Though Reagan battled Ford to a draw in the state primaries, the president won a narrow victory at the Republican National Convention in Kansas City by agreeing to support a party platform sympathetic to the Reagan forces. The platform condemned both the Helsinki agreement and the Panama Canal negotiations, and endorsed constitutional amendments to legalize school prayer and prohibit abortions. For vice president,

the Republican delegates selected Senator Bob Dole of Kansas, a tough campaigner with conservative views.

Because Ford appeared so vulnerable in 1976, the Democratic race for president attracted a very large field. Among the candidates was a little known former governor of Georgia named James Earl ("Jimmy") Carter, Jr. Few observers took him seriously at the start, and the voters asked, "Jimmy who?" When Carter told his mother that he intended to run for president, she replied, "president of what?" Yet Carter ran an effective, well-financed campaign, portraying himself as a political outsider, untainted by the arrogance and corruption of Washington.

Carter struck the right pose for the post-Watergate era. A deeply religious man, who promised voters, "I will never lie to you," he combined the virtues of small town America with the skills of the modern corporate world.

Born in Plains, Georgia, in 1924, Carter attended local schools, graduated with distinction from the U.S. Naval Academy, and spent 7 years as a naval officer working on nuclear submarines. Following the death of his father in 1953, Carter returned to Plains to run the family's farm supply and peanut business. As the company prospered, he turned to politics, winning a state senate seat in 1962 and the Georgia governorship 8 years later. Known as a "new South" politician, Carter supported progressive causes and reached out to black constituents through his concern for civil rights.

Meeting in New York City, the Democratic National Convention chose Carter for president and Senator Walter Mondale of Minnesota for vice president. Carter ran a safe campaign that fall, avoiding controversial issues while claiming that America was no longer "strong" or "respected" in the world. The media, meanwhile, caught Ford in a series of bumbling accidents—banging his head on a car door, tripping on the steps of an airplane, falling down on the ski slopes, whacking spectators on the golf course with his tee shots—that made him look clownish and inept. Before long, the comedian Chevy Chase was beginning almost every episode of *Saturday Night Live* by taking a terrible tumble in the role of Gerald Ford. And the president only made things worse for himself with a series of embarrassing verbal blunders, such as his insistence during the televised debate with Carter that "there [was] no Soviet domination of Eastern Europe." By election day, many Americans viewed Ford as a decent man, doing his best in a job that appeared to overwhelm him.

Still, the race was very close. Carter won 40.8 million votes, Ford 39.1 million. The electoral count was 297 to 240. Carter swept the entire South (except for Virginia) and the key industrial states of Ohio, Pennsylvania, and New York. Ford did well in the West, carrying every state but Texas. Polls showed Carter with large majorities among both minority voters and working-class whites who had rejected McGovern in 1972. In this election, at least, the New Deal coalition held firm.

Jimmy Carter became the first president from the Deep South in more than a century, signifying that region's increased strength—and acceptance—in the national arena. Furthermore, his election witnessed the growing importance of state primaries in the nominating process as well as the influence of the new Fair Campaign Practices Act of 1974. The law provided federal funds to the major candidates ($22 million each in this election); it also established limits on personal contributions and a stricter accounting of how funds were disbursed. The result, as the 1976 election amply displayed, was a longer, more expensive presidential campaign season, with television advertising playing an ever larger role.

The Ford–Carter election continued the downward trend in voter turnout, from 55.7 percent in 1972 to 54.4 percent in 1976. Polls showed a growing sense of apathy and disillusionment among the American people, a loss of connection with politics as a positive force in their lives. As one bumper sticker put it, "Don't Vote. It Only Encourages Them!"

The Carter Years

The new Democratic administration began with promise and hope. President-elect Carter took the oath of office as Jimmy (not James Earl) Carter before leading the inaugural parade on foot down Pennsylvania Avenue dressed in a simple business suit. Determined to be a "people's president," Carter surrounded himself with populist symbolism—giving fireside chats in a sweater and blue jeans, attending town meetings from New Hampshire to New Mexico, and staying overnight in the homes of ordinary Americans. "We must have a new spirit," he declared. "We must once again have full faith in our country—and in one another."

As the "people's president," Jimmy Carter led his inaugural parade on foot down Pennsylvania Avenue in 1977.

Civil Rights in a New Era

As governor of Georgia, Jimmy Carter had opened the doors of government to minorities. As president, he did much the same thing. Women, African Americans, and Hispanics were appointed to federal positions in record numbers as judges, ambassadors, and White House aides. Women, for example, filled three of Carter's cabinet-level positions and numerous other policy-making roles. In addition, Carter's wife, Rosalyn, greatly expanded the role of first lady by serving as a key advisor to the president and representing him on diplomatic missions.

Though Carter strongly supported civil rights and gave special attention to the plight of minorities in the inner cities, the momentum for racial change in the 1970s had shifted from the executive branch to the federal courts. During Carter's term, the issue of affirmative action took center stage in *University of California Regents v. Bakke* (1978). Allan Bakke, a 38-year-old white man, was denied admission to the University of California medical school at Davis. He sued on the grounds that his test scores exceeded those of several black applicants who were admitted under a policy that reserved 16 of 100 spots for minorities in each entering class. The policy amounted to "reverse discrimination," Bakke charged, and thus violated his right to equal protection under the law. The case raised a fundamental conflict between the government's obligation to treat all citizens equally regardless of race, and its responsibility to help the long-suffering victims of racial discrimination enter the mainstream of American society. In a five-to-four ruling, the Supreme Court struck down the medical school's quota policy as a violation of Bakke's constitutional rights. But it held that universities might consider race as a factor in admission "to remedy disadvantages cast on minorities by past racial prejudice."

The *Bakke* decision began a passionate debate over affirmative action that continues to this day. Opponents considered it to be a racially divisive policy as well as a dangerous step away from the American tradition of individual rights. Why penalize innocent whites, they argued, for the sins of their ancestors? But supporters of affirmative action viewed it as the surest way to remedy discrimination, past and present. "In order to get beyond racism, we must take race into account," wrote Justice Thurgood Marshall. "There is no other way."

Human Rights and Global Realities

President Carter knew little about foreign affairs. His political career had been spent entirely on state and local concerns. Yet Carter viewed his inexperience as an asset, freeing him from worn-out thinking and stale ideas. He believed that a fresh approach to foreign affairs would move America beyond the "big power" rivalries of the Cold War era. What America needed, he thought, was a foreign policy that stressed democracy and human rights—in short, the idealism of the United States.

Carter chose a diverse foreign policy team. His U.N. ambassador, Andrew Young, was a black civil rights leader who emphasized better U.S. relations with the developing world, especially in Africa. His secretary of state, Cyrus Vance, was an experienced diplomat who worked tirelessly to keep détente alive. And his national security advisor, Zbigniew Brzezinski, was a Columbia University professor, born in Poland, who proposed a tough front against the Soviet Union, which he blamed for most of the world's ills. Their conflicting advice sometimes left the president confused.

Yet Carter scored some impressive foreign policy successes. Emphasizing human rights in Latin America, he withdrew American support for Chile, cut off aid to the repressive Somoza regime in Nicaragua, and encouraged the governments of Brazil and Argentina in their halting steps toward democracy. Carter also presented the Senate with a treaty that relinquished American control over the Panama Canal by the year 2000, and a second one that detailed American rights in the Canal Zone thereafter. Both treaties provoked fierce national debate; both passed the Senate by a single vote.

Carter's greatest triumph occurred in the Middle East. In 1977, Egyptian President Anwar Sadat stunned the Arab world by visiting Israel to explore peace negotiations with Prime Minister Menachem Begin. Their discussions were cordial but fruitless, for neither man seemed willing to take the risks that peace demanded. When the talks broke down, President Carter invited Sadat and Begin to his presidential retreat at Camp David in Maryland. For 2 full weeks in September 1978, Carter shuttled between the cabins of the two Middle Eastern leaders, patiently working out the details of a "peace process" between Egypt and Israel that other nations might later join.

The **Camp David Accords** led to a historic treaty the following year. Egypt agreed to recognize the state of Israel, which previously had been unthinkable for an Arab nation, and Israel pledged to return the captured Sinai Peninsula to Egypt. The treaty did not consider other vital issues, such as the fate of displaced Palestinians and the future of Israeli-held Arab territory in Gaza and the West Bank. Yet few could deny the enormity of what had transpired, or the pivotal role played by President Carter in bringing it about.

Economic Blues

Early success in foreign affairs, however, could not mask Carter's problems with the troubled economy. During the 1976 presidential campaign, candidate Carter had focused on high inflation (6 percent) and unemployment (8 percent) that gripped the United States.

Anwar Sadat (left) and Menachem Begin shake hands at Camp David, Maryland, as Jimmy Carter, who brought the men together, smiles in the background.

Combining these figures into a "misery index" of 14, he had promised the American people immediate relief.

Carter's program to stimulate the economy depended on a mixture of tax cuts, public works, and employment programs—a kind of "pump priming" reminiscent of Franklin Roosevelt's New Deal. The Democratic-controlled Congress responded sympathetically by funding large public works projects, reducing taxes by $30 billion, and raising the minimum wage from $2.30 to $3.35 over a 5-year span. The good news was that unemployment dropped to 6 percent by 1978; the bad news was that inflation rose to 10 percent—and kept climbing.

Carter changed his approach. Creating jobs took a backseat to the problem of runaway inflation. Unlike Richard Nixon, who fought this problem by implementing wage and price controls, Carter tried to attack inflation by tightening the money supply (through higher interest rates) and by controlling the federal deficit. This meant reduced government spending, a turnabout that alienated the Democratic Congress. Moreover, Carter's new policies appeared to increase unemployment without curbing inflation—the worst of both worlds. Before long, the "misery index" stood at 21.

This was not all Carter's fault, of course. The decline of American productivity, the growth of foreign competition, and the surging cost of imported oil had plagued the nation for some time. In 1977, Carter offered a substantive plan for the energy crisis, which he described as "the moral equivalent of war." (Critics called it "meow.") The plan arrived on the heels of the worst winter in modern American history, a season of blizzards, record low temperatures, and Arctic winds. Based mainly on conservation—or reduced energy use—it ran into immediate opposition from oil companies, gas producers, the auto industry, and others who advocated the increased

production of fossil fuels and the deregulation of prices. "This country didn't conserve its way to greatness," a Texas oil man complained. "It produced its way to greatness."

The National Energy Act, passed in November 1978, did little to reduce America's energy consumption or its reliance on foreign oil. Carter's original plans to stimulate conservation efforts were overshadowed by incentives to increase domestic energy production through tax breaks for exploration, an emphasis on alternative sources (solar, nuclear, coal), and the deregulation of natural gas. The law did not address, much less solve, the nation's fundamental energy problems—as Americans would soon discover.

The Persian Gulf

In January 1979, a chain of events unfolded that shook the nation's confidence and shattered Jimmy Carter's presidency. The year began with the overthrow of America's dependable ally, Shah Riza Pahlavi of Iran; it ended with the United States appearing helpless and dispirited in the face of mounting challenges at home and abroad.

On a visit to Iran in 1977, President Carter had described it as "an island of stability in one of the most troubled areas in the world." Iran was vital to American interests, both as an oil supplier and a bastion against Soviet influence in the Middle East. Thousands of American workers and their families lived in Iran, and thousands of Iranian students attended college in the United States. Ironically, President Carter's concern for human rights did not extend to Iran, where the army and secret police used widespread torture and repression to keep the shah and his ruling elite in power. Against all evidence, Carter even congratulated the shah for "the admiration and love your people give to you."

The Iranian Revolution was led by Ayatollah Ruhollah Khomeini, an exiled cleric, and his devoted followers. Their aim was not to set up a democracy, but rather to form a fundamentalist Islamic state. When demonstrations paralyzed Iran, the shah fled his country, leaving the religious fundamentalists in control. One of Khomeini's first moves was to end oil shipments to "the Great Satan" America, thus allowing other OPEC countries to raise their prices even more. In the United States, long gas lines reappeared and the price reached an incredible $1 per gallon.

With Americans reeling from months of bad news, President Carter went on national television to speak partly about the energy crisis, but mostly about a "crisis of confidence" that struck "at the very heart and soul and spirit of our national will." His address was

In 1979, student militants stormed the American embassy in Iran and took dozens of U.S. citizens hostage. Unable to negotiate their release, President Carter approved a secret rescue mission that ended in disaster.

remarkably candid. Rather than assuring anxious Americans that they had nothing to fear, or trying to rally them with ringing phrases about honor and duty, the president spoke of a nation in trouble, struggling with the values of its cherished past. In place of "hard work, strong families, and close-knit communities," he said, too many Americans "now worship self-indulgence and consumption. Human identity is no longer defined by what one does but by what one owns."

Having passionately diagnosed the illness, Carter provided no cure. The "crisis of confidence" deepened. In October, the deposed shah of Iran, suffering from cancer, was allowed to enter the United States for medical treatment. This decision, which Carter viewed as a simple humanitarian gesture, produced an explosive backlash in Iran. On November 4, militant students stormed the American embassy in Tehran, taking dozens of American hostages and parading them in blindfolds for the entire world to see. The militants demanded that the United States turn over the shah for trial in Iran. Otherwise, the Americans would remain as captives—and perhaps be tried, and executed, as spies.

Carter had almost no leverage with these militants, who were supported by Khomeini himself. His attempts to settle the crisis through the United Nations were ignored by Iran. His orders to embargo Iranian oil and suspend arms sales were empty gestures, because other nations refused to do the same. The remaining options—freezing Iran's assets in American banks or threatening to deport Iranian students from the United States—did nothing to change the fate of the hostages in Tehran.

For a time, the American people rallied behind their president. Carter's approval rating jumped from 30 to 61 percent in the first month of the crisis. Yet Carter

grasped what many others did not: there was no easy solution to the hostage standoff. "It would not be possible, or even advisable," he warned, "to set a deadline about when, or if, I would take certain acts in the future." As the nation waited, public patience grew thin.

The year ended with yet another nasty surprise. In December, Russian soldiers invaded neighboring Afghanistan to quell a revolt led by Muslim fundamentalists against the faltering pro-Soviet regime. The invasion ultimately backfired; fanatical resistance from Afghan fighters turned the country into a graveyard for Russian troops. Determined to act boldly in light of the continuing Iran hostage crisis, Carter cut off grain shipments to the Soviet Union and cancelled America's participation at the upcoming Summer Olympic Games in Moscow—a boycott that many nations chose to ignore. More significantly, he announced a "Carter Doctrine" for the Persian Gulf, warning that "outside aggression" would "be repelled by any means necessary, including military force." For the first time since Vietnam, young men were ordered to register for the draft. In addition, Carter requested a major increase in defense spending, with $50 billion set aside for new weapons systems such as the multiple-warhead MX missile, which moved from place to place on secret railroad cars to prevent the enemy from tracking it. By 1980, the Cold War was heating up again. Afghanistan and its aftermath had dealt a serious blow to détente.

Death in the Desert

As President Carter and the American people staggered through the repeated shocks of 1979, one issue dominated the national agenda: the fate of the hostages in Iran. The crisis took on symbolic importance as an example of America's declining power in the world—its inability to defend its citizens, its vital interests, its national honor. The television networks flashed nightly pictures of the hostages on humiliating public display in Tehran while frenzied crowds shouted "Death to Carter" and "Down with the United States." In Washington, meanwhile, the president met regularly with the families of the hostages and worked tirelessly to find a diplomatic solution. But this seemed all but impossible, because the Iranians, demanding both the shah and an American apology for supporting him, were not interested in a quick settlement. Reluctantly, Carter ordered a secret mission to free the hostages by force.

The result was disastrous. In April 1980, American commandos reached the Iranian desert, where two of their helicopters were disabled by mechanical problems. Another

| Picturing the Past | ECONOMICS & TECHNOLOGY |

Three Mile Island

By the mid-1960s, nuclear power had emerged as a viable alternative to fossil fuels—a cheaper, cleaner, and virtually inexhaustible energy source for the future. As the number of commercial nuclear power plants increased, so, too, did their size. Among the largest was Three Mile Island (pictured) in the Susquehanna River near Harrisburg, Pennsylvania. Though a growing environmental movement in the 1970s had raised safety concerns regarding these huge facilities, and Hollywood had recently produced a box office smash, *The China Syndrome,* about a nuclear power plant disaster, the

© Bettmann/CORBIS

dangers still seemed remote. Then, in March 1979, a mechanical failure at Three Mile Island threatened to blanket the surrounding countryside with radioactive fallout, and thousands fled their homes. Though engineers were successful in stabilizing the damaged reactor, the looming white stacks of Three Mile Island came to symbolize the tremendous risks associated with nuclear power. There are just over 100 nuclear power plants in the United States today; almost all were constructed before the awful scare at Three Mile Island.

hit a U.S. cargo plane, killing eight members of the rescue mission. The commandos departed without ever getting close to the hostages in Tehran. To make matters worse, the Iranians proudly displayed the burned corpses for television crews. Most Americans blamed the president for the debacle. What little remained of Jimmy Carter's credibility disappeared that fateful day in the Iranian desert.

DOING HISTORY ONLINE

American Hostages in Iran, 1979

Read the accounts in this module. John Limbert and Bill Belk tell different stories about being taken hostage at the American embassy in Iran. Why do their accounts differ so much?

History ⧖ Now™   Visit HistoryNOW to access primary sources and exercises related to this topic: http://now.ilrn.com/ayers_etal3e

Conclusion

The United States in 1980 was an uneasy land. The social upheavals of the 1960s and 1970s had fostered anxiety as well as progress. The movement for civil rights, so certain in the era of bus boycotts, lunch counter sit-ins, and voting rights marches, was now deeply divided over issues such as forced busing and affirmative action. So, too, the struggle for women's rights generated fierce controversy over abortion, sex roles, workplace equality, and the ERA. On the economic front, Americans faced a world of new troubles—a world of stagnant incomes, rising unemployment, mounting trade deficits, and skyrocketing inflation. No longer were young people

AP/Wide World Photos

By 1980, many Americans looked for someone to rescue the nation and restore its damaged prestige.

guaranteed the prospect of moving a rung or two above their parents on the ladder of success. For millions, the American dream was now on hold.

Above all, the nation appeared momentarily to lose confidence in its leaders and its goals. Watergate, OPEC, the fall of South Vietnam, the near disaster at Three Mile Island, the Iran hostage crisis, the bungled rescue attempt—all seemed to reflect a loss of national purpose, authority, and prestige. As the 1980 election approached, many Americans looked back into the past with a deep sense of nostalgia, hoping for someone to rescue the country and restore the American dream.

The Chapter in Review

In the years between 1969 and 1980:

- The spectacular moon landing in 1969 gave a weary and divided nation a welcome reason to celebrate.

- As the U.S. military gradually transferred the burden of fighting the Vietnam War to the South Vietnamese, American troop levels dropped substantially, slowing the antiwar protests that had divided the nation for more than five years.

- The rights revolution took on even greater momentum, as movements for women's rights and minority rights expanded dramatically in universities, in the workplace, and in the courts.

- Following a string of remarkable successes, including a path-breaking visit to Communist China and a lopsided reelection victory, President Nixon became the first president to resign his office following revelations of his involvement in the Watergate scandal.

- The collapse of South Vietnam in 1975 ended one of the longest, most divisive chapters in American military history and raised troubling questions about the soundness of U.S. foreign policy in the Cold War era.

- Following decades of unprecedented growth, the American economy entered a period of uncertainty and decline, marked by lower productivity, soaring energy prices, higher interest rates, and runaway inflation.

- The Iran hostage crisis marked a new direction in U.S. relations with the Islamic world.

Making Connections Across Chapters

LOOKING BACK

Chapter 30 examines the political, economic, and psychological impact of the Watergate scandal, the OPEC oil embargo, the fall of South Vietnam, and other crises on the American people and their vision of the future.

1. What impact did the "rights revolution" of the 1960s have on political events in the 1970s? What role did the federal courts play in this process?

2. What were the defining features of the Watergate affair? Why is it considered to be the most significant, and potentially dangerous, political scandal in U.S. history?

3. Though Americans most remember the Iran hostage crisis, the United States achieved some notable successes in foreign policy during the 1970s. What were these successes, and how were they achieved?

LOOKING AHEAD

Chapter 31 looks at the so-called Reagan Revolution, the attempt by a new president, with a different political philosophy, to restore national confidence and redirect the nation along more conservative lines.

1. How would President Reagan deal with the economic problems facing Americans in this era?

2. How would he differ from previous presidents in his dealings with the Soviet Union and in his personal view of international communism and the Cold War?

3. Was it possible to narrow the social and cultural divisions that had plagued the United States in the 1960s and 1970s, or would they continue to widen over time?

Recommended Readings

Carroll, Peter. *It Seemed Like Nothing Happened: America in the 1970s* (1982). A critical overview of American life in the new age of limits.

Chavez, Lydia. *The Color Bind* (1998). Analyzes the political battle surrounding affirmative action in California.

Hull, N. E. H., and Peter Hoffer. *Roe v. Wade* (2001). Provides an excellent analysis of the abortion rights controversy in American history.

Isaacson, Walter. *Kissinger* (1992). A comprehensive biography of the man who helped shape America's foreign policy in the 1970s and beyond.

Kutler, Stanley. *Abuse of Power: The New Nixon Tapes* (1997). The story of a president's demise told through the secret tapes that brought him down.

Lukas, J. Anthony. *Common Ground: A Turbulent Decade in the Lives of Three American Families* (1986). Examines the busing crisis in Boston from several perspectives.

Rudenstine, David. *The Day the Presses Stopped: A History of the Pentagon Papers Case* (1996). Looks at the legal and political issues surrounding the decade's most heralded First Amendment crisis.

Schoenwald, Jonathan. *A Time for Choosing* (2001). Describes the rise of modern conservatism leading to Ronald Reagan's election.

Shilts, Randy. *And the Band Played On* (1987). A superb account of the spreading AIDS epidemic in the homosexual community.

Wandersee, Winifred. *On the Move: American Women in the 1970s* (1988). Highlights the political struggle of women in this decade and the changes that occurred.

Identifications

Review your understanding of the following key terms, people, events, and dates for this chapter (these terms also appear in the Glossary at the end of the book):

Woodstock Music and Art Fair
Vietnamization
Kent State University
Equal Rights Amendment (ERA)
La Raza Unida
Watergate

Roe v. Wade
Henry Kissinger
détente
George Wallace
George McGovern
Gerald Ford
Jimmy Carter
Camp David Accords

Online Sources Guide

Use this listing to find online documents, images, interactive maps, simulations, and other resources related to this chapter:

American History Resource Center

http://history.wadsworth.com/rc/us

Documents

An Account of the Tet Offensive from the Defense Department's Pentagon Papers (1971)
Paris Peace Accord (1973)
A Denunciation of Antiwar Protestors by Vice President Spiro Agnew
Roe v. Wade
Jessie Lopez de la Cruz, "Women and Unions"
A Teacher's Diary of the Desegregation of South Boston High School
Jimmy Carter, 1980 State of the Union speech

Selected Images

Richard Nixon answering media questions during Watergate
Spiro T. Agnew
Gerald Ford taking oath of office
Liftoff of Apollo 11, July 1969
Cesar Chavez
Gerald Ford
Jimmy Carter

HistoryNOW

http://now.ilrn.com/ayers_etal3e

Primary Source Exercises

Endangered Species Act, 1973
American Hostages in Iran, 1979
Rejecting Gender-Free Equality, 1977

31 The Reagan–Bush Years, 1981–1992

Ronald Reagan captured the nation's attention with his friendly manner, rugged looks, and cowboy demeanor. His policies of building up defense and cutting taxes were controversial in the 1980s. His admirers see him as the architect of American victory in the Cold War.

The presidency of **Ronald Reagan** defined the decade of the 1980s. His election in 1980 brought to office the most conservative president since Herbert Hoover, and his efforts to redirect the nation toward a smaller and less activist government aroused bitter controversy. After two decades of what some have called "failed presidencies," Reagan's ability to serve for two consecutive presidential terms contributed to a mood of renewed optimism that endured until he left office.

The actual achievements of Reagan and his successor George H. W. Bush remain in dispute. During these two administrations, the Cold War ended, the Berlin Wall toppled, and the Soviet Union collapsed. Reagan's partisans gave him the credit for ending the threat of what he had called "the evil empire." Yet victory in the Cold War did not result in any reduction of foreign policy threats and a safer world for the United States.

While the economy boomed during the 1980s, the federal government's budget deficit increased. Rich Americans became richer, and the gulf between the affluent and the poor widened. Under the pressures of global economic change, American businesses became more efficient and less unwieldy. The price, however, was a loss of jobs in many key industries as American workers faced the trauma of what was described at that time as "downsizing." By the end of the 1980s, despite the prosperity of the Reagan era, apprehension about the economic future of the average American grew. For all the ebullience and optimism of the Reagan–Bush period, critical social questions remained unanswered.

The Reagan Revolution

When Ronald Wilson Reagan took the oath as president of the United States on January 20, 1981, he was the oldest man to assume the nation's highest office. Born in Illinois in 1911, he had been an actor and television personality. Disillusioned with the political liberalism of his youth, he became a Republican and ran for governor of California in 1966, promising to reduce spending and provide a leaner government.

Timeline

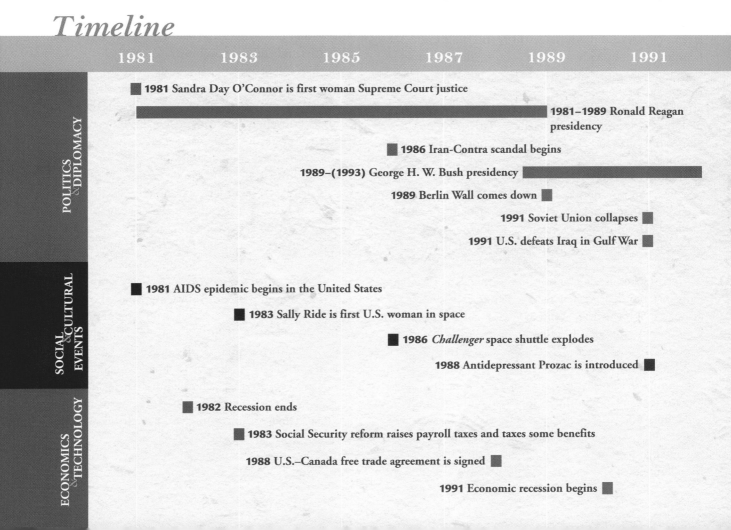

	1981	1983	1985	1987	1989	1991

POLITICS & DIPLOMACY

- 1981 Sandra Day O'Connor is first woman Supreme Court justice
- 1981–1989 Ronald Reagan presidency
- 1986 Iran-Contra scandal begins
- 1989–(1993) George H. W. Bush presidency
- 1989 Berlin Wall comes down
- 1991 Soviet Union collapses
- 1991 U.S. defeats Iraq in Gulf War

SOCIAL & CULTURAL EVENTS

- 1981 AIDS epidemic begins in the United States
- 1983 Sally Ride is first U.S. woman in space
- 1986 *Challenger* space shuttle explodes
- 1988 Antidepressant Prozac is introduced

ECONOMICS & TECHNOLOGY

- 1982 Recession ends
- 1983 Social Security reform raises payroll taxes and taxes some benefits
- 1988 U.S.–Canada free trade agreement is signed
- 1991 Economic recession begins

It proved more difficult for Reagan to enact his conservative agenda than he had anticipated. He had promised reduced spending and smaller government, but taxes rose and the California government bureaucracy grew. Nevertheless, his blend of conservative rhetoric and a sunny disposition made him a favorite among conservatives in the 1970s. He lost a race for the Republican presidential nomination to Gerald Ford in 1976 but became the party's nominee 4 years later with George H. W. Bush as his running mate.

The problems of the Jimmy Carter administration gave Reagan his opportunity. He became the embodiment of the new national sentiment for lower taxes, restraints on government spending, and concern about inflation. At the same time, he promised increased spending on national defense and a stronger U.S. role overseas to meet the threat of communism.

The Election of 1980

The 1980 presidential election campaign took place in the shadow of an ongoing crisis involving 52 American hostages who had been seized in Iran during that country's revolution against the shah. Initially the plight of the hostages helped Jimmy Carter fend off the challenge of Senator Edward M. Kennedy of Massachusetts for the Democratic presidential nomination. A failed military attempt to rescue the hostages in April 1980 undercut Carter's standing with the voters and made his nomination a hollow prize. Still, most Democrats believed that the president could defeat Reagan. The White House attached little significance to the third-party candidacy of John Anderson, a Republican member of Congress, who ran as a moderate alternative to both major party nominees.

During the campaign, Reagan assailed Carter's record on the economy and national defense. The president fired back that Reagan was a dangerous and unreliable political extremist. The election came down to a televised debate between the two men in late October 1980.

Polls indicated that the race was a dead heat. When Carter attacked Reagan's position on Medicare, the challenger responded with a wry remark: "There you go again," making Carter seem petulant and carping. In winding up the debate, Reagan asked the American people "Are you better off?" than 4 years earlier.

Reagan and the Republicans won the election by a substantial margin in the popular vote: 44 million ballots for Reagan to 35 million for Carter and 5.7 million for John Anderson. In the electoral college, Reagan garnered 489 votes and Carter 49. The Republicans regained control of the Senate, picking up 12 seats from the Democrats.

Reagan in Office

Reagan set out his goals in a single sentence: "We must balance the budget, reduce tax rates, and restore our defenses." The incoming president believed that it would be possible to achieve all of these objectives at the same time. Reagan brought striking political gifts to the White House. His long career in Hollywood had given him a skill in conveying his views that won him the title of "**The Great Communicator.**" When delivering a prepared speech with a teleprompter to guide him, Reagan could read a text with practiced artistry. His use of humor, especially when he stressed his own foibles, was deft; it reinforced his rapport with his fellow citizens. He exuded a degree of optimism about his country, sincerity about his positions, and confidence in the rightness of his views that made him a masterful politician during his first 6 years as president.

Yet Reagan had significant weaknesses, too. He knew very little about the actual operation of the federal government and displayed scant curiosity about such matters. He read very few of the documents that crossed his desk and watched movies when he should have been reading position papers. As a friend put it, "He lived life on the surface where the small waves are, not deep down where the heavy currents tug." Reagan believed that there were few hard choices in governance, and he did not inform the nation of the serious alternatives that had to be faced in reducing the deficits and curbing government spending.

The president was not a simple man. Many commentators said that Reagan played the role of president better than any incumbent since Franklin D. Roosevelt because of his previous experience in show business. After the glow of the performance faded, there remained the question of whether the president had done more than walk through his job.

Part of the success that Reagan achieved during his first term came about because of the effective staff that managed his daily activities. His chief of staff was James Baker, a Texas politician who had not been close to the Reagans before the election. Joining him were Michael Deaver, who directed media activities, and Edwin Meese—a longtime friend from California who tended to policy issues. These men "packaged" the president in settings that capitalized on his warm relationship with the American people. The gritty details of government went on out of the public's view. The approach worked well, partly because these aides allowed Reagan to deal with the large issues that interested him instead of the mundane details of governing, for which he had little aptitude or serious interest.

Another important player in the Reagan presidency was his wife Nancy. Criticized for her opulent lifestyle

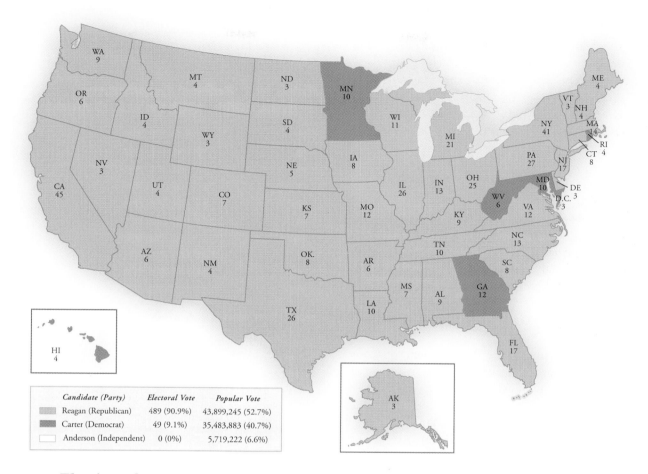

MAP 31.1 Election of 1980

This election map reveals the repudiation of Jimmy Carter and his administration in 1980 and the swing to the right that put Ronald Reagan in the White House. Carter's economic record and the foreign policy problems of the late 1970s left him without an effective national political base.

during her early days as first lady, she won over the Washington media with a deft blend of self-deprecating humor and commitment to a "Just Say No" campaign against drugs. Behind the scenes she managed the president's schedule with the help of an astrologer. She also fretted about Reagan's place in history and urged the president privately to promote some degree of détente with the Soviet Union over nuclear weapons.

As Reagan started his administration, the Republicans controlled the White House and the Senate, where they commanded a 53 to 46 majority. Democrats remained the majority in the House of Representatives, 242 to 190. In 1980, the inflation rate was over 12 percent, the unemployment rate was above 7 percent, and the prime interest rate had gone to almost 20 percent. The national debt had reached $908 billion. In Reagan's view, the responsibility for these ominous figures lay with the federal government. As he told Congress on February 18, 1981, "The most important cause of our economic problems has been the government itself."

To remedy the situation, the administration embraced a program that combined traditional Republican suspicion of government spending with an aggressive reduction in federal income taxes. The term "supply-side economics" became shorthand for what this program promised to do. The government should lower income and corporate tax rates to give private business and individual taxpayers more money to spend. The predicted surge in productive economic activity would result in an increase in tax revenues, which would prevent large budget deficits.

Carrying Out the Reagan Agenda

In his first year Reagan implemented his policy agenda as promised. The release of U.S. hostages in Iran on January 20, 1981, removed that troublesome issue from the public sphere. When Reagan was shot on March 30, 1981, the would-be assassin's bullet came closer to ending his life than the public knew. The president's

AP/Wide World Photos

The assassination attempt against Ronald Reagan on March 30, 1981, wounded the president more seriously than was revealed at the time. His optimism and high spirits in the face of his wound added to public confidence. This picture shows an unidentified Secret Service agent yelling instructions after shots were fired.

courage and good humor in this moment of crisis increased his popularity and added to the reservoir of goodwill that he commanded.

A second event that raised Reagan even higher in the polls was his handling of a strike by the Professional Air Traffic Controllers Organization (PATCO). As government employees, the controllers could not legally strike, and the president fired them when they refused to heed a back-to-work order. The message for the nation was that the White House would be tough on organized labor.

During the first half of 1981, a coalition of Republicans and "boll weevil Democrats" (southern and western conservatives) pushed through legislation that trimmed tax rates by 25 percent over 3 years. In tandem with the tax measure, the administration sought budget cuts for a number of discretionary social programs (ones where payments to recipients were not mandated in law) to advance the president's goal of a balanced budget by 1984. Although the budget act, passed in the House on June 25, 1981, promised future reductions in spending, during its first year it provided only $16 billion in immediate cuts. That was $200 billion less than would have been required to achieve a real step toward a balanced budget.

Two major policy commitments limited what the Reagan administration could accomplish. The president declined to make cuts in what he termed "the social safety net": Social Security, Medicare, veterans' benefits, Head Start, and school lunch programs. All of these spending policies had vocal and powerful supporters. The practical result was that almost half of the federal budget was placed beyond the reach of congressional budget-cutting efforts.

Picturing the Past — ECONOMICS & TECHNOLOGY

Federal Government Deficits

Table 31.1 Federal Government Deficits, 1980–1989 (in U.S. Dollars)

Year	Deficit
1980	73,808,000,000
1981	78,936,000,000
1982	127,940,000,000
1983	207,764,000,000
1984	185,324,000,000
1985	212,260,000,000
1986	221,140,000,000
1987	149,661,000,000
1988	155,151,000,000
1989	153,319,000,000

Source: *World Almanac*, 1995, p. 108.

One of the hotly disputed issues of the 1980s was the burgeoning federal budget deficit. Under Ronald Reagan, as this table shows, the annual deficit rose to as high as $221 billion in 1986 and stayed around $150 billion annually for the last six years of the Reagan presidency. Balanced budgets became an illusory goal. Republicans asserted that lower tax rates would produce more revenues, which did occur. At the same time, however, the White House and Congress engaged in more spending on defense and entitlement programs such as Medicare and Social Security with governmental red ink being the result.

Interest on the federal debt became one of the major expenditures of the government. Both parties seemed quite willing to pass these debts on to future generations rather than confront the electorate with the unpleasant choices of higher taxes or lower spending. This simple table thus raises questions about the sense of responsibility in 1980s politics and the larger social health of the United States in that period.

The other priority of the Reagan administration was a sharp increase in defense spending. Reagan believed that the nation's military establishment had been neglected during Carter's presidency. In 1979, however, the Democratic Congress and the administration had begun a long-range program to build up American military power, and the Reagan White House expanded on that initiative. During the Ford–Carter years, defense budgets had been less than $200 billion annually. Under Reagan, the Pentagon budget rose to nearly $300 billion per year by 1985.

The outcome of modest cuts in social programs and entitlements, sharp hikes in defense spending, and a reduction in tax rates was a growth in the government deficit to $128 billion by 1982. The ballooning federal deficits continued throughout the Reagan era, producing a surge in the national debt. The goal of a balanced budget in 1984 vanished quickly, never to return while Reagan was in the White House. A dramatic change had occurred in the government's fiscal situation, with serious consequences for the future. The huge deficits drove economic policy for the decade that followed and future generations were left with a massive debt to fund and pay off.

Deregulation

In his inaugural address, President Reagan proclaimed: "In this present crisis, government *is* not the solution to our problem; government *is* the problem." As part of his response to a large, intrusive government, Reagan advocated an extensive program of deregulation to lessen regulation of the private sector.

The Reagan administration pursued a new course in environmental policy. Secretary of the Interior James G. Watt, a conservative who disliked all restrictions on public lands in the West, sought to open new areas for oil drilling, cut back on the acquisition of land for national parks, and put in place other bureaucrats eager to reduce the amount of environmental regulation that the government conducted. Appointees in the Environmental Protection Agency (EPA) came under fire for having used regulations for political and personal gain.

The most spectacular and disastrous example of deregulation occurred in 1982, when Congress and the White House agreed to lift restrictions from the savings and loan industry. During a time of high inflation and rising interest rates, savings and loan institutions had difficulty earning a profit because of the low rates of interest they were allowed by law to pay on their deposits. In 1980, Congress increased federal insurance coverage to $100,000 per account and allowed savings and loan companies to offer even higher interest rates. These measures did not, however, increase the profits on the money that the thrift institutions loaned. Partly in response to lobbying by the industry and the large campaign contributions that lawmakers received, Congress decided to deregulate these companies and allow them to invest in higher-risk assets, including commercial real estate, fine art, and, in some instances, speculative or fraudulent ventures.

At the same time that lending practices were relaxed, the Reagan administration cut back on the number of banking and regulatory examiners. With federal deposit insurance guaranteeing that they would be bailed out, savings and loan operators plunged into ventures that were risky and often illegal. At first, there seemed to be few problems, but by 1983 and 1984 troubling signs of weakness appeared in the banking and savings and loan

DOING HISTORY ONLINE

Reaganomics

Read the section on "The Reagan Revolution" in the textbook and consider the documents in this module to answer the following question: Why were some conservatives not concerned about the large deficits that resulted from Reagan's economic policies?

History ⧖ Now™   Visit HistoryNOW to access primary sources and exercises related to this topic: http://now.ilrn.com/ayers_etal3e

businesses in the form of bad loans, poorly financed individual companies, and corrupt operators who were looting their firms.

By the early 1980s, Social Security, the most popular New Deal program, had reached a funding crisis. During the 1970s, Congress and the Nixon administration had established a system of cost-of-living adjustments (COLAs) that raised benefits for Social Security recipients as the rate of inflation rose (known as indexing). Indexing of benefits caused the cost of Social Security to soar as the population aged and more people received Social Security checks. But efforts to trim COLAs seemed futile because of the political fact that tinkering with Social Security benefits guaranteed electoral defeat for anyone who tried it.

President Reagan learned that lesson in the spring of 1981 when the administration proposed a cut in benefits for early retirees (those who would begin receiving benefits at age 62). When the initiative was announced, gleeful Democrats assailed it and Republicans in Congress deserted Reagan. Social Security did not come up again until December 1981, when the president appointed a bipartisan panel to deal with long-range funding of the retirement program. The result, announced after the 1982 elections, was a compromise that raised payroll taxes to pay for Social Security, taxed some of the benefits of people over 65 who had high incomes, and put off providing for the long-term viability of the system. For the moment, the Social Security system seemed to be on solid ground once again.

Reagan and Foreign Policy

In foreign affairs, the new administration came into office with what seemed to be a clear, simple agenda about the relationship of the United States to its principal adversary. In 1983, Reagan called the Soviet Union "an evil empire" and said that the Cold War was a

Flashpoints | The Marines in Lebanon

One of the aspects of history that makes it relevant to modern concerns is the way that events in the past, once believed to be settled, turn out to have had consequences that were not apparent at the time. One such case involves the bombing of the U.S. Marine barracks in Lebanon in October 1983 in which 231 Americans died. When it happened, it seemed a cautionary lesson about the dangers of the United States becoming involved in the Middle East and the ability of the administration of President Ronald Reagan to withdraw from a commitment that had become a political liability. In the wake of the terrorist attacks of September 11, 2001, however, it became clear that the response of the White House to the loss of American life had convinced militant Arab terrorists that the United States would not defend itself against the threat of violence.

The marines went into Lebanon first as a peacekeeping force in August 1982 between the Israelis and the Palestine Liberation Organization (PLO). After a few weeks, they were withdrawn. Then a fresh wave of violence that led to the Israeli occupation of Beirut, Lebanon, brought the return of the marines. Lebanese Arabs saw the military force of the United States being used on behalf of Israel. That perception led in turn to a terrorist attack on October 23, 1983, when a truck loaded with explosives was detonated outside the marine barracks. The result was the deaths of the 231 marines and the conclusion in the Reagan administration that the United States must pull its forces out of Lebanon. The withdrawal was done smoothly without further loss of life, and commentators applauded the ability of the Reagan administration to minimize the political fallout and preserve the president's credibility. The marine disaster soon faded from memory when the United States attacked the island of Grenada.

Two decades later, when the nation was under the threat of further terrorist attacks, analysts found that groups opposed to the United States had concluded from the withdrawal of the marines that the Reagan administration would not stand firm in the Middle East. Given the political environment in 1983, there would have been no popular support in America for more aggressive action after the bombing of the marines. Still, the episode demonstrated how deep were the roots of Arab discontent with American policy and the tangled process by which these grievances erupted in further violence decades after an event that few in the United States even remembered.

Questions for Reflection

1. How does American public opinion affect the way that the government carries out foreign policy?

2. Where did the Middle East fit into the priorities of the Reagan administration?

3. What limits existed on the ability of the United States government to conduct military operations in a country such as Lebanon?

4. How has the passage of time and subsequent events changed the way the bombing of the marine barracks can be viewed?

---

struggle between "right and wrong and good and evil." In dealing with the Soviets, then, the president insisted arms agreements be based on the principle of "trust but verify." He was convinced that the United States could outspend the Soviet Union in an arms race. Faced with an aging and incompetent Soviet leadership between 1981 and 1985, the White House avoided any summit meetings during that period. As a result, Soviet–American relations experienced a distinct chill during Reagan's first term.

This stern language did not rule out flexibility in some areas. Early in the new administration the president lifted the grain embargo that President Carter had established when the Soviet Union invaded Afghanistan in 1980. It was an action that pleased American wheat farmers. Reagan also reiterated his view that a nuclear war could not be won and should never be fought. Although the new White House team did not like the SALT II Treaty that Carter had negotiated, it largely observed the pact's provisions. Increased tensions between East and West overshadowed these gestures of restraint.

One area where the rivalry between the two superpowers flared was Central America. The Reagan administration believed that the victory of the Sandinistas in Nicaragua in 1979 represented a serious threat to U.S. interests in the region, especially in neighboring El Salvador. By late 1981, the United States was underwriting a rebellion against the Sandinista regime led by a faction called the "**Contras.**" Although President Reagan likened the anti-Sandinistas to the patriots of the American Revolution, in 1982 the Democratic House of Representatives adopted an amendment that sought to block funds from being used to oust the Sandinistas. In Latin America, suspicion about U.S. policy increased during 1982.

Reagan and his administration paid a political price for the policies of the first 2 years. A severe recession

One of the most hotly debated foreign policy issues of the 1980s had to do with the Reagan administration's support for the rebels against the Sandinista government in Nicaragua. The "Contras," as they were known, are shown here training in a remote area of their country.

continued until almost the end of 1982. Although Reagan argued that the recession would soon end, the Republicans suffered a setback at the polls in the congressional elections. The Democrats gained 27 seats in the House but the Republicans maintained their dominance in the Senate. Nevertheless, President Reagan again urged his fellow Republicans to "stay the course."

Shortly after the election the economy picked up steam, stimulated by the Reagan tax cuts. The inflation rate declined and unemployment receded. As the recovery gained strength, so did Reagan and his party. Adding to the president's popularity was the U.S. invasion of the Caribbean island of Grenada in October 1983. Fearing that radicals close to Fidel Castro and Cuba were about to turn Grenada into a Soviet base (an unlikely outcome), the administration launched a powerful invasion force that secured control of the island after a brief struggle. The episode was a public relations success and further enhanced Reagan's image as a decisive leader.

In fact, the foreign policy scene was more complex than the victory in Grenada indicated. The war in Nicaragua was not going well for the Contras, and El Salvador was experiencing atrocities from right-wing death squads that murdered their opponents and left-wing insurgents sympathetic to Nicaragua. In 1984, Congress adopted a second, more restrictive, amendment to prevent the government from aiding the Contras.

In the Middle East Reagan's hopes of producing a lasting peace between Israel and its neighbors were also frustrated. The administration did not stop Israel from invading Lebanon in June 1982, and U.S. Marines were sent into the region as part of a multinational peace-keeping force. American involvement in Lebanon's

turbulent politics led to the death of 239 marines when a terrorist bomb blew up a barracks in 1983. The marines were withdrawn, and terrorists concluded that the United States would not stand firm in a crisis. The long-term consequences of that perception proved dangerous for the nation and future administrations.

In March 1983, the most significant defense policy initiative of the first Reagan term came when the president announced what he called the **Strategic Defense Initiative (SDI).** Reagan envisioned a system of weapons, based in space, that would intercept and shoot down Soviet missiles before they could reach the United States. Influenced by memories of science fiction serials in which he had starred as a young man, as well as by advocates of an antimissile system, Reagan wanted "a defensive screen that could intercept those missiles when they came out of their silos."

An appealing vision on the drawing board or in animated versions for television, SDI confronted immense technical problems that made it unlikely that it could be deployed for years. Critics promptly dubbed it "Star Wars" after the hit movie and questioned its technical rationale. For Reagan, the program represented an answer to the problem of relying on nuclear deterrence to stave off war between the superpowers. He pressed forward with SDI over the objections of his political opponents and the displeasure of the Soviet Union, whose leaders knew that their faltering economy could never duplicate SDI if the Americans ever achieved it. Twenty years after Reagan first proposed the program, its operational status remains in doubt and its effectiveness in question.

Social Tensions of the 1980s

The possibility of nuclear war was only one of the threats to the American people that contributed to the societal tensions of the decade. New medical challenges loomed for Americans, and they confronted as well sweeping changes in technology that would transform lives. Computers and the Internet would begin to reshape communications. Meanwhile, the rise of the religious right would reveal tensions about fundamental beliefs that would ripple through American history for decades. But first came the specter of AIDS.

The Challenge of AIDS

In the early Reagan years Americans learned of a new and deadly disease. Scientists called it AIDS (for acquired immune deficiency syndrome). The source of the virus was in Africa, and it first appeared in the United States in 1981. The virus ravaged the immune system of its victims, and there was no known cure. Most of those infected were doomed to an inevitable and painful death. By the end of Ronald Reagan's first term, the number of confirmed AIDS deaths had reached 3,700 in the United States.

The major process by which the virus spread within the population was through the exchange of bodily fluids. Mothers who were infected passed the condition on to their children; infected blood was transferred during transfusions. The most vulnerable groups were drug addicts, bisexuals, and homosexuals. During the first half of the decade, the spread of AIDS and fears about the fatal prognosis for those who had the disease seemed to be confined to the homosexual community. Later, largely through the sharing of needles for drug injection and unsafe sexual practices, AIDS began spreading more rapidly among heterosexuals, especially in low-income communities.

In October 1985, the public's perception of the AIDS threat intensified when movie star Rock Hudson died of the disease. More than 6,700 other Americans succumbed to AIDS in 1985, and the death toll shot up to 15,504 annually within 2 years. The Reagan administration approached the AIDS issue from a conservative point of view. The White House resisted attempts to distribute condoms to those at high risk for AIDS. Few initiatives to stop the spread of the disease came from the Reagan presidency.

The sudden emergence of the AIDS epidemic was only one of the rash of new social and cultural developments that occurred during the early 1980s. The nation experienced the initial stages of a revolution in communications and culture that left American society dramatically altered by the time Reagan left office in 1989. The elements of this revolution included the development of the personal computer and the ability of individuals to use the new technology to improve their lives. At the same time the spread of cable television and the emergence of alternatives to then major television networks allowed news and entertainment to be shared with ever-increasing speed.

Table 31.2 New AIDS Cases in the United States, 1988–1993

1988	30,648
1989	33,576
1990	41,642
1991	43,660
1992	45,883
1993	102,780

Source: *World Almanac*, 1997, p. 975.

The personal computer appeared in the 1980s and spread into every corner of American life in the decades that followed.

The Personal Computer

In 1981, International Business Machines (IBM) announced that it would market a computer for home use. Recognizing the potential impact of such a product, two young computer software writers proposed to develop the operating system for the new machine. Bill Gates and Paul Allen of Microsoft adapted an existing software program and transformed it into DOS (disk operating system), which ran the hardware created by IBM. Important changes followed throughout the decade, including the Lotus 1-2-3 spreadsheet program in 1982, Microsoft Windows in 1983, and the Apple Macintosh Computer in 1984. After January 1983, sales of personal computers rose from 20,000 annually to more than half a million per year.

The computer revolution gathered momentum over the course of the 1980s. People found that they could publish books from their desktops, trace financial accounts, make travel reservations, and play a wide assortment of computer games. Growing out of the Advanced Research Projects Agency of the Pentagon was a network of computers founded in 1969. As computer users and researchers exchanged messages over this and other networks in the late 1970s and early 1980s, the National Science Foundation promoted what became known as the Internet as an overall network bulletin board. Usenet groups and e-mail became more common as the 1980s progressed.

In 1981, a new network appeared on cable television. Music Television (MTV) presented round-the-clock videos of rock performers aimed at a teenage audience. At about the same time, Ted Turner launched the Cable News Network (CNN) and a related programming service, Headline News, which presented the news in half-hour segments 24 hours a day. As cable television expanded during the 1980s, the dominance of the three major television networks (ABC, CBS, and NBC) gave way to a dizzying array of programming that offered viewers such all-sports channels as Entertainment Sports Programming Network (ESPN), all country music channels such as Country Music Television (CMT), and several services showing first-run movies.

The American Family in the 1980s

The American people responded to new and troubling changes in the family and its place in society during Reagan's presidency. In 1981, the number of divorces stood at nearly 1.2 million annually, the highest rate ever. At the same time, the number of births to unmarried women rose dramatically during the 1970s. With these developments came a marked increase in the number of single-parent families, which rose from 3.8 million in 1970 to 10.5 million by 1992. The impact of this trend was especially evident among African Americans: by the end of the 1980s, more than 60 percent of all African American families were single-parent families.

The erosion of the traditional family translated into economic hardship for many children of single-parent homes. In 1983, the Bureau of the Census reported that 13 million children under age 6 were growing up in poverty. Much of the government's spending on efforts to alleviate poverty was directed at the elderly, so by the end of the 1980s, they received from the federal government 11 times the amount spent to address the needs of children.

One major area of concern for families was the state of the public schools. A series of high-profile national studies suggested that American education was "a disaster area." Students did not receive instruction in the skills needed if they were to succeed in a complex and competitive world. Parents complained that their children had to do little homework, were graded too easily, and often graduated without marketable skills. Conservatives blamed this state of affairs on the National Education Association (NEA), the teachers union, and government policies that "threw money" at schools. Liberals countered that government must spend even more to address the problems of the public schools. By 1983, another national survey, titled *A Nation at Risk,* said that the country faced dire consequences if public education did not undergo sweeping reform.

As families felt the effects of these economic and social changes, Americans responded with contradictory approaches. On the one hand, sexual mores became more tolerant. On the other, efforts to recapture "traditional family values" animated many groups on the conservative end of the political spectrum. The boundaries that had governed the depiction of sexual behavior in the movies and on television relaxed in significant ways during the 1980s. On prime-time television, viewers could hear language and see sexual intimacy depicted in a fashion that would have been unthinkable a few years earlier. Materials that previous generations would have considered pornographic now seemed to be readily available, even to children and teenagers.

The Religious Right

A major force in pressing for older cultural values and a return to the precepts of an earlier time was the political power and votes of evangelical Christians. One manifestation of the clout was the **Moral Majority,** an organization founded by the Reverend Jerry Falwell of Virginia in 1979. Falwell tapped into the expanding base of evangelicals in denominations such as the Southern Baptist Convention. The Moral Majority assailed abortion, homosexuality, rock music, and drugs.

Throughout the 1980s, evangelical Christianity permeated American politics. On cable television, viewers tuned in to Pat Robertson's *700 Club* on the Christian Broadcasting Network that Robertson had founded. Other ministers such as Jim Bakker with his *PTL (Praise the Lord)* program and the fiery evangelist Jimmy Swaggart commanded sizable audiences. Though both Bakker and Swaggart eventually ran afoul of the law for fraud (Bakker) and sexual misadventures (Swaggart), their message resonated in many areas of the nation. Ronald Reagan never implemented the evangelical agenda, but he gave them a sympathetic hearing that enhanced their influence on American public life.

The volatile issue of abortion helped fuel the rise of the Christian Right. Following the Supreme Court decision in *Roe v. Wade* (1973), the number of abortions in the United States stood at 1.5 million per year. Foes of abortion, most notably in the Roman Catholic Church and among evangelical Protestants, asserted that the unborn baby was a human being from the moment of conception and entitled to all the rights of a living person. To reduce the number of abortions and to overturn the *Roe* decision, the "right to life" forces, as they called themselves, pressured lawmakers to cut back on the right of abortion and to enact restrictive laws. The Hyde amendment, adopted in Congress in 1976, banned the use of Medicaid funds to pay for abortions for women on welfare.

The antiabortion forces, impatient with legislative action, believed that more direct tactics were warranted. They conducted picketing and boycotts of abortion clinics in the 1980s and arranged for massive public demonstrations. Operation Rescue tried to prevent patients from entering abortion clinics. Other protestors turned to bombing of buildings that housed clinics and assassination of doctors. The Republican party became largely antiabortion in its policies and programs. The Democrats were equally committed to what was called "a woman's right to choose" or a "pro-choice" position.

The 1984 Presidential Election

At the beginning of 1984, Reagan's popularity rating stood at 55 percent, and the electoral map seemed to favor the Republicans. The Democratic base in the South was disappearing as former members of that party defected to the Grand Old Party. The president had made substantial gains among what were known as "Reagan Democrats," people who shared the president's social conservatism and who disliked the pro–civil rights stances of the Democrats. Reagan's only apparent vulnerability was his age. At 73, he was sometimes detached and vague, and he clearly lacked stamina. Unless something happened to emphasize his age, Reagan was the favorite to win another term.

Democrats experienced staggering problems in finding a plausible candidate to run against the incumbent president. In the initial stages the front-runner seemed to be former Vice President **Walter Mondale** of Minnesota. Mondale had strong ties to the traditional elements of the Democratic party—labor, women, and environmentalists. He was not a good public speaker and lacked a vibrant personality, yet it was widely expected that he would win the nomination.

Faced with a popular incumbent and a likely defeat, Democratic presidential candidate Walter Mondale took a chance and named Geraldine Ferraro, a New York congresswoman, as his vice presidential candidate. The gesture put Ferraro into history as the first woman chosen by a major political party for its national ticket, but it did not help Mondale avoid a decisive defeat at the hands of Ronald Reagan.

Two challengers emerged to stop Mondale's bid for the nomination. The first was the Reverend **Jesse Jackson,** a veteran of the civil rights movement, who combined powerful oratory with espousal of causes that spoke to the left wing of the party. He became the first credible African American candidate to seek the nomination of a major party, but he proved unable to reach beyond black voters in the primaries. The other Democratic hopeful was Senator Gary Hart of Colorado, who styled himself a "new Democrat," which meant that he did not endorse the use of government power to regulate society to the extent that Mondale did. Although Hart won a surprise victory in the New Hampshire primary, Mondale countered with effective television ads and won a majority of the convention delegates before the Democrats gathered in San Francisco in July.

Mondale's chances of winning the election against Reagan were slim at best. Under those circumstances, the choice of the vice presidential nominee became largely symbolic. Mondale came under intense pressure to select a woman as his running mate, and in the week before the convention opened he agreed to the selection of Representative Geraldine Ferraro of New York. An intelligent, thoughtful politician, Ferraro did little for the Mondale campaign where it needed help the most, in the South and West.

The Republicans had all the best of the 1984 campaign. President Reagan's popularity crested during the celebrations of the fortieth anniversary of the D-Day invasions in June, and his appearance at the 1984 Olympic Games in Los Angeles identified him with an event in which American athletes dominated the competition. In a time of patriotic enthusiasm, Reagan seemed more in tune with the optimism and confidence of the moment.

Mondale versus Reagan

The only stumble for Reagan came in the first of two televised debates. He showed his age and lack of a clear grasp of many issues. The consensus was that Mondale had won a clear victory over the president. Two weeks later, after much Republican soul-searching, however, Reagan rebounded. When a questioner asked him about his age, the president replied that he would not allow age to be an issue. "I am not going to exploit, for political purposes, my opponent's youth and inexperience," he said.

Reagan won by a landslide. He carried 49 of the 50 states; Mondale narrowly won his home state and swept the District of Columbia. The president collected 59 percent of the popular vote. The Republicans retained control of the Senate; the Democrats lost seats in the House but maintained their dominance of that chamber.

DOING HISTORY

Debating Ronald Reagan's Legacy

WHEN RONALD REAGAN died in June 2004, one of the authors of this text, Lewis L. Gould, discussed how history might judge the former president. He examined how the reputations of other presidents, from Warren G. Harding to John F. Kennedy, had changed over time and suggested that Reagan would be subjected to the same process of reevaluation and reappraisal The article that appeared in the Washington Post *carried the author's e-mail address for reader's responses. An excerpt from the article and what some e-mail correspondents, pro and con, said about the article follow. They illustrate how contentious Ronald Reagan's legacy remains. First, a passage from the article and then the selected responses along with some questions for you to ponder about how history evaluates presidents.*

"The stakes are high for Reagan's reputation because enough time has passed for a generation of younger Americans to have grown up with only a vague sense of what made him so controversial in his day. For those approaching 30 who were in their mid-teens or younger when Reagan gave way to George H. W. Bush in January 1989, the 'Great Communicator' is a historical figure speedily receding into the past. Those who will be entering college this year were born in 1986, as Reagan's second term was winding down. Making the episode of the Reagan years come alive for that new cadre of undergraduates will not be easy. Nothing is quite so dead for young people as the stake disputes of a vanished era, even one that was, in human terms, not so long ago. What was PATCO anyway, or Gramm-Latta, or Iran-Contra?"

Responses:

"Ronald Reagan's legacy has already been imprinted in world history. Perhaps you should listen again to Margaret Thatcher's parting words. Or recall his landslide 49 out of 50 state reelection victory. Or listen to President Reagan's acceptance of blame for sending the Marines to Beirut and for the Iran Contra mistake."

"Why has so little been mentioned of Reagan's domestic legacy, which left not only the poor poorer, but many middle class families like my own, worse off. To say nothing of

the failed 'trickle-down' policy. Why has he repetitively been described as much more popular than he was?"

"I guess when it comes to you Liberals/Progressives/Commies, no matter what President Reagan did it will never be enough or good or meet your approval. So 'we the people' have decided that President Reagan will go down in history as the second best president of the 20th century. There, I have said it. 'We the People' do not care what you elitists or commie journalists have to say. All that had to be said and done was said done by President Reagan. It is all in the history books now and no matter how you idiots try to re-write the history of Reagan, will be of no avail. Eat your hearts out."

"Reagan's ability to convince the public that 'government is the problem,' playing on the public's anger and fatigue after assassinations, Civil Rights struggles, Vietnam and Watergate, led to the dismantling of hard-won government protections and social programs—not least our public education—that we will never recover. He and his spiritual heirs have led this Cadillac of a country right into a swamp."

Source: Lewis L. Gould, "History in the Remaking," *Washington Post,* June 13, 2004.

Questions for Reflection

1. What accounts for the polarized view of Reagan's accomplishments and his potential historical legacy?

2. What elements in Reagan's political style attracted such devoted followers and repelled others?

3. What effect does the passage of time and the shift in events have on a president's reputation?

4. Where do you think, based on your reading of this chapter and documents that appear in this essay, that Ronald Reagan's historical reputation now stands? How is it likely to change in the future?

Explore additional primary sources related to this chapter on the Wadsworth American History Resource Center or HistoryNOW websites:
http://history.wadsworth.com/rc/us
http://now.ilrn.com/ayers_etal3e

Reagan's Second Term

Changes in the president's staff marked the transition from one administration to the other. The team that had initially guided Reagan's fortunes broke up. The White House chief of staff, James Baker, agreed to exchange jobs with the secretary of the treasury, Donald Regan. The president accepted the swap without much thought, a friendly gesture that had serious consequences. Regan lacked political skill and did not know how to showcase the president's better qualities to his advantage.

Tax Reform and Deficits

Despite Reagan's pledge to balance the federal budget by 1984, the combinations of tax cuts and increased spending on both defense and discretionary programs widened the budget deficit. Federal receipts reached $666 billion by 1984, but outlays stood at almost $852 billion, with a resulting deficit of $186 billion.

The administration did not have a strategy to trim the deficit, but the Senate devised a plan for doing so. Created by a new Republican senator, Phil Gramm of Texas, the measure required that federal spending programs be reduced by specified amounts or face across-the-board percentage reductions. Sponsored by Senators Warren Rudman of New Hampshire, one of Gramm's Republican colleagues, and Senator Ernest F. "Fritz" Hollings, a South Carolina Democrat, the scheme quickly became known as "Gramm-Rudman-Hollings." It promised to produce lower deficits without requiring lawmakers to choose among tough options. Congress embraced it enthusiastically, especially because the tough cuts in government spending would not be mandated until after the 1986 elections.

The 1986 Tax Reform Battle

The administration did achieve one major domestic policy success, which the president embraced eagerly, even though he was not its primary sponsor. In 1986, Congress made significant reforms in the nation's tax laws.

After passing the House in late 1985, the tax bill faced uncertain prospects in the Senate. By April 1986, the Senate Finance Committee seemed likely to kill the bill or load it with special preferences. At that point, lawmakers devised a bill with a much lower top rate for all taxpayers and an end to many time-honored deductions. The proposed law was quickly approved by the Finance Committee, and sailed through the Senate by a vote of 97 to 3 in June 1986. After a difficult passage through a Senate–House conference committee, the tax reform law was approved and signed in September 1986.

The Age of the Yuppie

The economic boom of the mid-1980s fostered an atmosphere of moneymaking and social acquisitiveness. Wall Street traders like Michael Milken and Ivan Boesky promoted lucrative corporate mergers through high-risk securities known as "junk bonds." Top executives received staggering annual salaries. The head of Walt Disney, for example, earned the then unprecedented sum of $40 million annually in 1987. Wall Street experienced a "merger mania" in which corporations acquired competitors through hostile takeovers.

The youth culture reflected the spirit of materialism that permeated the 1980s. Tennis star Andre Agassi appeared in ads asserting "image is everything." In the centers of technological change on the East and West Coasts, the press proclaimed the emergence of the "young urban professionals," dubbed "yuppies" by the media. These individuals had cosmetic surgery to retain a young look, took expensive vacations, and purchased costly sports equipment. Self-indulgence seemed to be a hallmark of young people.

Yet a sobering moment in the frenetic decade came on January 28, 1986, when the space shuttle *Challenger* exploded. All seven crew members perished in the disaster. The event happened live before a shocked audience that watched the spacecraft lift off normally and then explode a few seconds later into a mass of wreckage.

An official investigation followed while the shuttle fleet was grounded. Its proceedings revealed that the space program had grown overconfident about its procedures. Slipshod technology had contributed to the tragedy, but the incident did not undermine the public's faith in scientific progress and material abundance. By the end of the 1980s, the shuttle program had resumed its regular series of flights.

Toward Better Relations with the Soviet Union

Soviet–American relations entered a new phase when **Mikhail Gorbachev** came to power in Moscow. Aware of the weaknesses in his society and its economy, Gorbachev pursued a more conciliatory policy toward the West while trying to implement a restructuring of Soviet society that came to be known as *perestroika* (broadly defined as "restructuring"). He announced reductions in the deployment of Soviet missiles and said that the Soviet Union wanted to be part of Europe, not an opposing ideology. He and Reagan agreed to hold a summit conference in Geneva in November 1985. Although not much was achieved at the meeting, the two leaders discovered that they liked each other. The two world leaders met again at Reykjavik, Iceland, in October 1986. There they attempted to outdo each other in calling for reductions in the number of nuclear weapons, with the president even offering to rid the world of all such weapons. Again there were no substantive results, but the experience indicated that a genuine arms agreement might be possible. Both the president and Nancy Reagan hoped to crown Reagan's second term with an arms control treaty that would establish his historical reputation as a peacemaker.

The Iran-Contra Affair

In November 1986 the American public first learned that the United States had sold arms to the Islamic regime in Iran that had sponsored terrorist activities for most of the 1980s against the United States. Within a month the revelation came that money obtained from the arms sales had been used to support the Nicaraguan Contras in violation of congressional amendments barring the practice. The Reagan administration had deceived Congress, broken the law, and lied to the American people.

In 1985, members of the National Security Council (NSC) became convinced that the release of American hostages held in Lebanon could be secured if the United States sold arms to Iran. National Security Advisor Robert McFarlane believed that alleged "moderates" in Iran (those presumed to be more sympathetic to the West) would use their political influence to free hostages if American weapons were forthcoming. The evidence that such moderation existed in Iran was largely fanciful. The Iranians could use weapons in their bitter war with Iraq, which had been going on since 1982. Since disclosure of this new policy would have outraged Americans and provoked congressional investigations, the president's approval of arm sales was kept secret.

The actual shipment of weapons to Iran was carried out by Israel, with the United States replacing the transferred munitions. Unfortunately, the Iranians accepted the antitank and antiaircraft missiles but released only three hostages. The Iranian government had deceived the United States.

In the course of the arms deals, however, the transactions generated profits. A member of the NSC staff, Marine Colonel **Oliver North,** had what he later called a "neat idea." He proposed that profits from the sale of weapons to Iran be used to support the Contras in Nicaragua. Although North maintained that his actions did not break the law, they were in clear violation of congressional directives barring the provision of aid to the Contras. Moreover, the use of funds without legislative approval was against the law. In addition, a privately financed, unaccountable, and clandestine foreign policy operation was well outside constitutional limits.

News of the scandal leaked out in October 1986 when the Sandinistas shot down one of the planes taking weapons to the Contras. A captured crew member revealed the Central Intelligence Agency's links

---

Picturing the Past — SOCIAL & CULTURAL EVENTS

The *Challenger* Disaster

In the 1980s, cable television brought live events into American homes on a 24-hour basis. Reality sometimes meant instant tragedy as happened with the explosion of the *Challenger* space shuttle on January 28, 1986, before a shocked audience at the scene and millions of television viewers. The immediate realization that the seven crew members had died was written on the faces of family members and other onlookers. Subsequent revelations about technological and management failures added to the gravity of

the incident. At the time young people told interviewers that the explosion would long remain the defining moment of their lives. As years passed, however, and other calamities occurred, the *Challenger* incident receded in the popular consciousness until another shuttle accident destroyed *Columbia* in February 2003. Even that terrible event did not rekindle more than transitory memories of the *Challenger* calamity 17 years earlier. Judgments about historical significance shift with the passage of time.

The Iran-Contra scandal produced a congressional investigation at which the star witness was Marine Colonel Oliver North. His appearance in his winter uniform in midsummer (with all of his ribbons) and his aggressive tactics toward his questioners made him a national hero to conservatives.

to the operation. Early in November news of the arms-for-hostages deal surfaced in the Middle East. The reports did not affect the congressional elections in which the Democrats regained control of the Senate for the first time in six years and retained their majority in the House as well.

For several weeks the Reagan White House tried to mislead Congress and the public about what had taken place. On November 13, 1986, the president told the American people: "We did not—repeat, did not—trade weapons or anything else for hostages, nor will we." He maintained this position even though it conflicted with the known facts.

Attorney General Edwin Meese conducted a slow, ineffective probe of what had happened. In late November conclusive proof of the diversion of money to the Contras came out. The president fired Oliver North and accepted the resignation of John Poindexter, McFarlane's successor as national security advisor and one of the central figures in the clandestine operation, which the press was now calling the **Iran-Contra scandal.**

Three separate probes of the scandal began in early 1987. Reagan appointed the Tower Commission, named after its chair, former Senator John Tower of Texas, to look into the White House's role in the scheme. The House and Senate created a joint committee to examine the policy and its execution. The lawmakers soon decided to grant immunity to many of the involved individuals in exchange for their testimony.

That decision hampered the task of the special counsel, Lawrence Walsh, who was named to consider whether specific laws had been violated.

Although everyone concerned professed a desire to get to the bottom of the scandal, there was little inclination, even among Democrats, to see Ronald Reagan impeached for his role in it. His second term had only a year and a half to run, and many Washington insiders questioned whether it would be good for the country to have another president driven from office in disgrace.

The Tower Commission, for its part, chastised the president for an inept "management style" that allowed his subordinates to lead him into the scandal. On March 4, 1987, Reagan said that he accepted the commission's findings and reiterated that he had not intended to trade arms for hostages. His poll ratings rose and once again the public responded to his leadership.

For others involved in the scandal, the hearings brought a surge of notoriety that made North a subject of national debate and discredited the other Reagan aides involved. When North testified before the House–Senate Committee during the summer of 1987 in his winter marine uniform that provided for the best display of his medals and battle ribbons, he proved a compelling presence on television. He exaggerated his closeness to Reagan and made some inaccurate or misleading statements. But his skill before the cameras deflected some of the blame from Reagan.

North and the other participants were indicted by Lawrence Walsh and convicted for some of their misdeeds, including perjury, mishandling government moneys, and other crimes. Because Congress had granted them immunity, however, higher courts overturned their convictions on the ground that the trials had been influenced by what had been heard in the congressional proceedings.

Whatever the legalities of the Iran-Contra affair, it demonstrated the weaknesses of Reagan's handling of foreign policy. Reagan had failed to ask hard questions about the arms-for-hostages proposals, and he had allowed erratic subordinates like North to mishandle the nation's foreign policy. The outcome discredited the American stance on terrorism and indicated that Reagan's command of his own government was weak and uncertain.

Remaking the Supreme Court: The Nomination of Robert Bork

One of the Reagan administration's major goals was to make the federal judiciary more conservative. The White House succeeded in doing so in the lower courts because, during 8 years in office, Reagan nominated more than half the members of the federal judiciary.

© Wally McNamee/CORBIS

Sandra Day O'Connor, the first woman to serve on the U.S. Supreme Court, became an influential member among the justices in her tenure on the bench.

AP/Wide World Photos

A search for Soviet–American understanding was a notable feature of Ronald Reagan's second term. His friendship with the Soviet leader Mikhail Gorbachev resulted in a marked lessening of the Cold War tensions as the decade of the 1980s ended.

In July 1981, Reagan named the first woman to be appointed to the Court, **Sandra Day O'Connor** of Arizona. The president did not have another opportunity to appoint a justice until Chief Justice Warren Burger resigned in 1986. Reagan elevated Justice William Rehnquist to replace Burger and named Antonin Scalia, a federal appeals court judge, to take the seat that Rehnquist vacated. Scalia was the first Italian American appointed to the court, and his intellectual brilliance appealed to conservatives.

In June 1987, after the Democrats had regained control of the Senate, Justice Lewis Powell resigned and President Reagan named Robert Bork, another federal appeals court jurist, to replace him. During a long career as a legal writer before becoming a judge, Bork had taken many controversial stands on divisive issues. He had opposed the decision in *Roe v. Wade* (1973) that established a woman's right to have an abortion, and he had questioned other decisions in the areas of privacy and civil rights. The nomination galvanized Democrats in the Senate, the civil rights movement, and women's groups in a campaign to defeat Bork.

The judge's admirers claimed that his enemies had distorted his record, but his foes were able to depict Bork as a conservative ideologue outside the mainstream of American judicial thinking. Bork's performance before the Senate Judiciary Committee failed to counteract the negative public opinion that his opposition had generated. In October 1987, Bork was defeated when 58 senators voted against him. Anthony Kennedy was nominated and confirmed to the Court early in 1988. Although he was a conservative, Kennedy sometimes voted in ways that were too liberal for conservatives and they came to regard him as an example of what happened when true conservatives were not placed on the Supreme Court.

Reagan and Gorbachev: The Road to Understanding

The Iran-Contra affair produced changes in Reagan's administration that prepared the way for genuine foreign policy achievements. Former Senator Howard Baker became Reagan's chief of staff, Frank Carlucci was named secretary of defense, and Lieutenant General **Colin Powell** served as the national security advisor.

These more pragmatic operators encouraged Reagan to seek further negotiations with the Soviets. By late 1987, negotiators for the two sides had agreed to remove from Europe intermediate range missiles with nuclear warheads. Gorbachev came to Washington in December 1987 for the formal signing of the pact. Seven months later, Reagan went to Moscow to meet Gorbachev in an atmosphere of hope and reconciliation. Tensions between the two countries eased as the Soviets pulled out of Afghanistan and indicated that they no longer intended to stir up international problems. The improvement in the superpower rivalry helped Reagan regain some of his popularity with the American people as his administration neared its end.

The 1988 Presidential Election

With Ronald Reagan ineligible to seek a third term, the Republican party had to pick a successor to carry its banner against the Democrats. Vice President George Bush soon emerged as the front-runner.

George H. W. Bush came from an aristocratic New England background but had moved to Texas after combat service in the navy during World War II. Elected to the House of Representatives in 1966, he stayed for two terms and made a losing bid for the Senate in 1970. Service in the Ford administration as envoy to China and director of the Central Intelligence Agency added to his impressive roster of government posts. He ran against Reagan for the Republican nomination in 1980 and became the vice presidential choice despite doubts among conservatives about his allegiance to their cause. In the race for the nomination, Bush's superior organization and strength in the South enabled him to defeat Senator Robert Dole of Kansas.

At the Republican convention in New Orleans, Bush made two important decisions. For his running mate, he selected Senator J. Danforth Quayle of Indiana. Handsome and young, Quayle was generally regarded as a lightweight by his Senate colleagues, but he provided a contrast to Bush's age and experience. Quayle's candidacy got off to a shaky start when it was revealed that he had entered the Indiana National Guard at a time when enlistment there precluded active service in the Vietnam War.

Bush's other major decision involved the issue of deficits and taxes. In his acceptance speech, he predicted that Democrats in Congress would pressure him to raise taxes. He promised to reject all such proposals. "Read my lips," would be his answer to Democrats, "No new taxes!" Repeated and emphasized throughout the campaign, this pledge became identified with Bush as a solemn promise to the electorate.

The Democratic Choice

As for the Democrats, with Reagan no longer a candidate, they believed that they now had a chance to retake the White House. The prospective front-runner for the nomination was Senator Gary Hart, but his candidacy collapsed amid charges of sexual misbehavior. Jesse Jackson ran again, but his strength remained concentrated among black voters. Out of the field of other candidates, Massachusetts Governor Michael Dukakis emerged as the best-financed and best-organized contender. He defeated Jackson in a series of primaries in the spring and came to the Democratic convention with the nomination locked up.

Dukakis emphasized his family's Greek immigrant background and stressed his success in stimulating the Massachusetts economy during the 1980s. Democrats paid less attention to his tepid personality and lackluster abilities as a campaigner. At the convention, he selected Senator Lloyd M. Bentsen of Texas as his running mate. When the Democratic convention ended, Dukakis had a strong lead in the public opinion polls.

The campaign that followed was a nasty one. The Republicans raised questions about Dukakis that undermined his lead. The most penetrating of these issues had to do with prison furloughs that Massachusetts law granted to jailed criminals. In one case, a black convict named William Horton had been released on furlough, then fled Massachusetts and committed a rape in another state. The Republicans and their surrogates used the "Willie" Horton case in powerful television commercials to demonstrate Dukakis's ineptitude as governor, but the racial dimensions of the incident were also evident. Bush won the election with a solid margin in the electoral vote, though the Democrats retained control of Congress.

The Reagan Legacy

Even before Ronald Reagan left office on January 20, 1989, the debate about the impact of his presidency was under way. His partisans proclaimed the "Reagan Revolution" had transformed American attitudes toward government. They also assigned him a major role in winning the Cold War. Critics pointed to the huge federal budget deficits and growing national debt that persisted throughout the 1980s, blamed Reagan for policies that had widened the gap between rich and poor, and pointed out that he had failed to address serious urban problems.

Both Reagan's admirers and his enemies overstated his influence on American history. By the early twenty-first century, the nation still seemed to want a smaller government in theory and more government services in practice. Reagan had halted the expansion of the welfare state, but

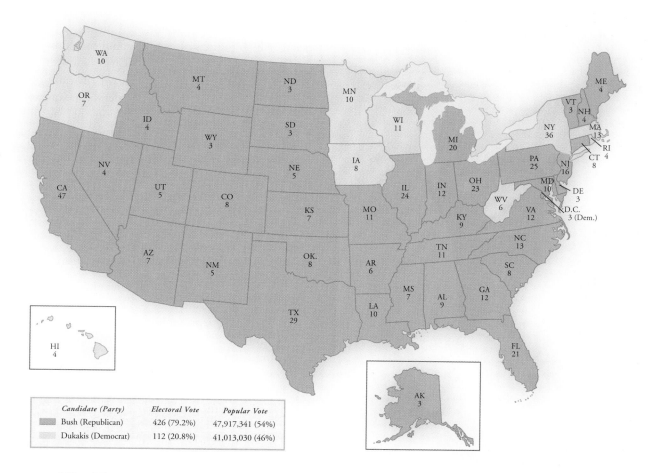

MAP 31.2 The Election of 1988

In the 1988 presidential election, George H. W. Bush built on the legacy of Ronald Reagan to forge a decisive victory over Democrat Michael Dukakis.

Candidate (Party)	Electoral Vote	Popular Vote
Bush (Republican)	426 (79.2%)	47,917,341 (54%)
Dukakis (Democrat)	112 (20.8%)	41,013,030 (46%)

that would probably have occurred in any event by the 1980s. Reagan certainly deserved some credit for the decline of the Soviet Union, though that nation's internal difficulties were more significant than the actions of the United States at the end of the Cold War. Reagan's most enduring legacy was the federal budget deficit. Although Congress appropriated the money, he set national priorities, and his spending for defense went well beyond affordable levels. Reagan proved that big spenders could come in conservative as well as liberal models.

The Bush Succession

George H. W. Bush came into office pledging to carry on Reagan's policies, but promising to do so in a more humane and judicious manner. He spoke of a "kinder, gentler" nation and government that would carry out conservative programs with less harshness than had marked the Reagan years. He urged Americans to engage in charitable endeavors that would become "a thousand points of light" to inspire others to good works. Bush had no grand vision of what his administration should accomplish in the domestic arena.

Foreign affairs interested the new president much more than did shaping policy on health care, the environment, or social policy. Attuned to diplomacy because of his service as director of the CIA and ambassador to China, he prized the personal contacts he had made around the world and used them to good effect at moments of crisis. He had an effective foreign policy team. His secretary of state, James A. Baker, was a close friend and an adroit power broker; the national security advisor, Brent Scowcroft, and the chair of the Joint Chiefs of Staff, General Colin Powell, executed the president's policies with skill and efficiency. The collapse of communism in 1989–1990, the challenge of Iraqi expansionism in the Middle East, and the shaping of a new role for the United States gave the Bush administration's foreign policy makers much to do.

George H. W. Bush won the Republican nomination and the presidential election in 1988 on his promise to continue the legacy of Ronald Reagan and on his pledge of "no new taxes."

© Bettmann/CORBIS

The first half of the Bush administration went very well. The president relished the art of governing and he approached his job by engaging in a frenzy of activity. His press conferences demonstrated his command of information in a way that Reagan never displayed. The public became used to seeing Bush jogging, entertaining numerous visitors to the White House, and rushing around the country from one event to another.

As time passed, however, questions arose about the purpose behind all this frenetic exertion. Bush spoke of the need to set larger goals for his presidency. He called it, in the abrupt shorthand that he often employed, "the vision thing." The phrase came into general use in discussions of whether Bush wanted to accomplish anything as president or simply wished to occupy the nation's highest office.

Bush's Domestic Policy

The president and his chief of staff, John Sununu, had no intention of breaking new ground in domestic

affairs. They wanted to accomplish whatever they could without violating the campaign pledge of "no new taxes." Much to the dismay of Republican conservatives, Bush went along with Democratic legislation such as the Clean Air Act and the Americans with Disabilities Act, which involved a growth in the federal bureaucracy and expanded regulations. Any legislation that he did not like, such as an increase in the minimum wage, he vetoed. During the first 3 years of his presidency, Congress failed to override any of Bush's 28 vetoes.

Bush's relations with Congress were not always successful. At the beginning of his administration he named former Senator John Tower to be secretary of defense. After a bitter struggle focusing on Tower's problems with alcoholism and other personal indiscretions, the Senate rejected their former colleague. To replace Tower, Bush picked Representative Richard Cheney.

On some domestic issues, Bush favored exhortation over government programs. He promised to be the "education president" but left most of the responsibility for changes in the system to the states and localities. The "war on drugs" was renewed, with emphasis on stopping the inflow of narcotics to the United States rather than reducing the demand for them among the population. An overall decline in drug use enabled the administration to claim victory for its strategy.

By 1989, however, the Bush administration had to deal with another major domestic issue. The deregulated savings and loan industry had a major collapse that left the taxpayers with a $500 billion cost to bail out depositors for the failed institutions. Congress established the Resolution Trust Corporation to sell off the assets of the failed banks and savings and loans and to obtain as much money as possible from their sale.

The Continuing AIDS Crisis

Both funding for research on AIDS and public awareness of the disease increased during the Bush years. Congress created the National Commission on AIDS in 1989, and federal government funds for treatment and research rose to over $2 billion by 1992. Still, the number of new cases continued to increase, reaching 45,603 in 1992 and 83,814 a year later. Total deaths from AIDS in the United States reached 198,000. However, opinions regarding what to do about the epidemic remained polarized. AIDS activists wanted more money for research and greater cultural tolerance for those afflicted with the disease. Conservatives like Senator Jesse Helms of North Carolina contended that most AIDS victims were homosexuals who had brought their condition upon themselves through their own behavior. After some initial sympathy toward AIDS patients, the

Bush administration's attitude toward AIDS patients cooled under conservative pressure as the 1992 election approached.

Foreign Policy Successes, 1989–1990

At the end of 1988, Gorbachev had told the United Nations that the nations of Eastern Europe were free to determine their own destiny without Soviet interference. During 1989, the old order in Eastern Europe crumbled. Poland held free elections; Hungary allowed its borders to open; and East Germany eased the barriers to travel to West Germany. By the end of 1989, the Cold War seemed to be over with the United States the clear winner. In Nicaragua, voters ousted the unpopular Sandinista government in 1990.

The Bush administration handled these developments carefully. Mindful of the nuclear weapons in the hands of the Soviet military, the president avoided gloating over the success of the West. The trend in favor of the United States continued into 1990 as Gorbachev, in February, renounced the Communist party's monopoly over political power. The White House faced hard choices about which leader to support as rivals to Gorbachev emerged during 1990, particularly the new president of the Russian Republic, Boris Yeltsin.

One country where the administration's foreign policy encountered difficulty was China. Student protests during the spring of 1989 led to a brutal crackdown on demonstrators in Beijing's **Tiananmen Square.** The spectacle of students being killed and wounded, as well as the repressive policies of the Chinese government, produced an outcry in the United States. However, Bush believed that it was important to maintain good relations with the Chinese leaders, so the administration's response to the events of June 1989 was muted and cautious.

Closer to home, however, the Bush administration took more decisive action toward Panama's strongman ruler, Manuel Noriega. Corrupt and deeply involved in the international narcotics trade, Noriega had been on the U.S. payroll for many years as an informant on drug matters. In 1989, his dictatorial regime refused to adhere to the results of national elections. The White House sent additional troops to Panama and called for an uprising against Noriega. For his part, Noriega declared a state of war on American military personnel and ordered that their families be captured and tortured.

In late December, the United States launched an invasion that quickly overcame the Panamanian army. Noriega eluded capture for a few embarrassing days until he sought refuge in a Vatican embassy. In early 1990, he surrendered to the Americans and in 1992 was tried and

The mass protests in China in the spring of 1989 were part of the events that shook communism during the end of the Cold War. On May 27, 1989, student leader Wang Den addressed a huge crowd in Tiananmen Square in Beijing. A week later Chinese troops crushed the uprising.

AP/Wide World Photos

convicted of drug trafficking in a federal court in Florida. The episode raised Bush's standings in the polls.

By the spring of 1990, President Bush's pledge of "no new taxes" had become ingrained in the minds of the American people. Conservative Republicans expected him to adhere to the commitment in spite of the desire of the Democratic majorities in Congress to raise taxes as a means of dealing with the budget deficit. In 1989, the president worked out a strategy with Congress that provided for budget savings. Bush also wanted to lower the tax rate on capital gains, but that legislation became stalled in the Senate. With the budget deficit growing, however, the Democrats did not see how spending cuts alone could reduce it. Having suffered setbacks in the 1988 elections, the Democrats were not going to propose tax increases unless President Bush agreed to them. Meanwhile, the Gramm-Rudman-Hollings law provided for substantial reductions in spending by the fall of 1990 if the president and Congress did not reach a viable budget agreement.

By early 1990, there were signs that the economy had begun to slow down. The gross domestic product had grown slowly in 1989; there had been a slight loss in manufacturing jobs; and producer prices had risen. With a weakening economy, a budget stalemate posed dangers for both parties, and neither side really wanted to face the implications of the cuts that Gramm-Rudman-Hollings contemplated.

Negotiations between the president and congressional Democrats continued until, on June 26, 1990, Bush announced that dealing with the deficit problem might have to include "tax revenue increases." Republicans reacted with fury. Although the reversal of "no new taxes" may have made economic and political sense to those close to Bush, the president had squandered much of the trust that the American people had placed in him in 1988. Despite the foreign policy victories that lay ahead, he never fully regained it over the rest of his administration.

Iraq and Kuwait

Foreign policy events soon overshadowed the political fallout from the broken tax pledge. On August 2, 1990, the Iraqi army of Saddam Hussein invaded the oil-rich kingdom of Kuwait and seized it within a few days. Suddenly the oil supplies of the United States and the industrialized world faced a new and ominous threat from the Iraqi dictator. Bush's response and the war that followed restored his popularity temporarily and seemed at the time to make his reelection a certainty.

During the 1980s, Iran and Iraq had fought a brutal and costly war that had drained the human and material resources of both countries. The United States had not taken sides in the conflict, hoping that the two countries, both of which were hostile toward the United States, would exhaust each other. Once the war ended, however, the Bush administration had pursued a conciliatory policy, allowing Iraq to purchase heavy machinery and paying little attention to its efforts to build a nuclear bomb and acquire weapons of mass destruction. During the spring of 1990, the American ambassador in Baghdad had informed Hussein that the United States took "no position" on Iraq's dispute with Kuwait. In fact, the Iraqis regarded Kuwait as part of their nation.

When Iraqi military units rolled into Kuwait, Bush decided that the takeover must be resisted. "Iraq will not be permitted to annex Kuwait," he told Congress. Heavy economic sanctions were put into effect. More important, in Operation Desert Shield the United States deployed American troops in Saudi Arabia to deter Hussein from attacking that country. Behind the scenes, the administration had already decided that if necessary it would use military force to oust the Iraqis from Kuwait.

For the remainder of 1990, the Bush administration moved military forces into Saudi Arabia. The end of the Cold War meant that the United States had the support of the Soviet Union in isolating Iraq from the rest of the world and therefore had much greater freedom of action than would have been the case even 2 years earlier. Bush displayed impressive diplomatic skill in assembling and holding together an international coalition to oppose Iraq.

The Budget Battle

On the domestic side, the budget issue remained unsettled until the president and the Democratic leadership worked out a deficit reduction plan in September 1990. Republicans in the House of Representatives lobbied against the plan, which was defeated a few days later. Intense negotiations between the White House and Capitol Hill produced a deficit reduction agreement at the end of October that involved both tax increases and spending cuts. Angry Republicans charged that Bush had capitulated to the opposition. The Republicans went into the fall elections in a divided and unhappy mood. Their losses were modest—eight seats in the House and one in the Senate—but the conservative faithful continued to smolder with anger against Bush. The president informed conservatives that the White House had fulfilled its legislative agenda for the presidency.

War in the Persian Gulf

After the elections, Bush stepped up the pressure on Saddam Hussein to leave Kuwait. The United Nations Security Council agreed to the use of armed force against Iraq if Kuwait had not been freed by January 15, 1991. As the diplomatic options faded, Congress insisted on a vote over whether American troops should go into combat in the Middle East. The result, on January 12, 1991, was a victory for the president, although the margin in the Senate was only five votes. Five days later, Operation Desert Storm began.

The military outcome was never in doubt. In a devastating series of strikes, the allied coalition bombed the Iraqi army into submission. The most that Hussein could do in retaliation was to send Scud missiles against Israel in hopes of fracturing the coalition. The Iraqi ruler also set Kuwaiti oil wells on fire and dumped oil into the Persian Gulf. None of these actions, however, posed a serious threat to the buildup of the allied armies. Yet the use of air power alone did not compel Hussein to leave Kuwait.

The second phase of Desert Storm began on February 24, 1991, with a huge assault of American and allied troops against the weakened Iraqi defenders. A series of encircling maneuvers ousted the Iraqis from Kuwait

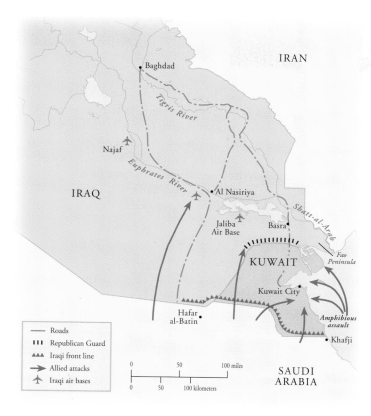

MAP 31.3 The War in the Persian Gulf

This map reveals the strategy of the allies in 1991 against the Iraqi army. The long arrow to the west represents the sweep around the enemy's flanks to encircle the Iraqi army and destroy it. After 100 hours of combat, the Bush administration stopped the fighting, and the main remaining elements of the enemy escaped to reimpose Saddam Hussein's power on Iraq after the allied forces departed.

View an animated version of this map or related maps at http://history.wadsworth.com/passages3e.

with huge losses in troops and equipment. Estimates of the number of Iraqi soldiers killed ranged as high as 100,000. American deaths totaled 148, including 11 women. Within 100 hours, the ground phase of the war ended in a complete victory on the battlefield for the anti-Iraq forces. President Bush decided not to press for Hussein's removal from power, a decision that was later criticized, and key units of the Iraqi army were left intact to fight again against their own people. The Bush administration warned that an effort to oust Hussein would have fractured the coalition and raised the prospect of a protracted war against an Iraqi resistance.

Victory in the Gulf War sent Bush's popularity soaring to record levels; he received approval ratings of nearly 90 percent in some polls. The nation basked in the glow of military success, which seemed to end the sense of self-doubt that had persisted since the Vietnam War. The chairman of the Joint Chiefs of Staff, General Colin Powell, became a nationally respected military figure and a possible vice presidential or presidential candidate. Bush's own reelection seemed assured. Major figures in the Democratic party decided not to challenge Bush in 1992.

Yet the political dividends from Bush's military triumph did not last long. Hussein bounced back from his defeat to reassert his power in Iraq and, despite United Nations inspections, rebuilt his nation's economy. Whether he had also reconstructed his war-making capacity became a matter of heated debate in foreign policy circles.

Other international problems troubled the White House during 1991. In Russia, Gorbachev faced a coup designed to bring hardliners back into power. A rival of Gorbachev, Boris Yeltsin, led demonstrations against the plotters in Moscow and their coup, which then failed. Thereupon the Soviet Union collapsed and its component nations broke apart. Yeltsin consolidated his power with promises of economic reform and put himself in a position to succeed Gorbachev. With the demise of the Soviet Union, the major threat of the Cold War had ended, but the instability in Eastern Europe posed new threats to world peace.

The decisive victory in the Gulf War of 1991 restored American self-confidence about military matters but left the problem of Iraq unsolved during the decade and a half that followed.

Victory in the Gulf War

The war in the Persian Gulf produced striking images of victory such as this one of Iraqi prisoners captured by the First Marine Division on February 26, 1991. President George H. W. Bush and others proclaimed that the coalition triumph had erased "the Vietnam Syndrome" from American life. The 100-hour war played well on television, and Bush's popularity soared for a time. The failure to end the rule of Saddam Hussein, however, meant that the apparent military success was incomplete. In the dozen years that followed, Hussein reemerged as a threat and by 2003 the second war in the Persian Gulf occurred. A picture that seemed to mark an American victory when it was taken thus became a testament to a continuing problem with terrorism and nations such as Iraq that resisted the will of the international community.

AP/Wide World Photos

One area of turmoil was Yugoslavia, where the Communist government had long suppressed historic rivalries among Serbs, Croats, Bosnians, and other nationalities. Tensions between Christians and Muslims added to the dangerous potential of the situation. Civil war broke out in 1991 as Serbs battled Croats, Slovenes, and Bosnians. The Bush administration recognized Bosnia as an independent nation and thus became involved in a Balkan struggle whose problems spilled over into the next presidency.

The Battle over the Clarence Thomas Nomination

Like Ronald Reagan, George H. W. Bush wanted to continue the conservative trend that the Supreme Court had been following since the 1970s. That goal seemed even more important in light of the Court's ruling in *Webster v. Reproductive Health Services* (1989), whereby the justices decided in a 5–4 ruling that states could set limits on the ability to obtain an abortion. Any change in the Court could affect that volatile controversy. When the liberal justice William Brennan retired in 1990, the president named David Souter of New Hampshire to succeed him. Confirmation by the Senate came easily because no one was quite sure where Souter stood on abortion.

The next nomination, in 1991, led to one of the most sensational confirmation struggles in the nation's history. When Justice Thurgood Marshall retired, many wondered whether Bush would name an African American to succeed him. The president selected **Clarence Thomas,** a Reagan appointee to the federal bench who had long opposed such programs as affirmative action.

Thomas's qualifications for the Supreme Court were modest, but he seemed to be on the way to easy confirmation until it was revealed that a black law professor at the University of Oklahoma, **Anita Hill,** had accused Thomas of sexual harassment when she had worked for him at the Equal Employment Opportunity Commission during the early 1980s. Her charges led to dramatic hearings in which Hill laid out her allegations and

Thomas denied them. A national television audience watched the hearings in fascination. In the end, the Senate voted 52 to 48 to confirm Thomas, who proved to be an intense advocate of conservative positions. The controversy played a major role in alerting the public to the prevalence of sexual harassment in the workplace.

A Sense of Unease

When the controversy over the Thomas nomination ended, many observers believed that George H. W. Bush could expect easy reelection in 1992. No strong Democratic candidates had emerged to challenge him. Bush had the support of most Republicans, although there were rumblings of opposition among conservatives. It seemed probable, however, that Bush would be renominated and would then defeat whomever the Democrats put up against him. After 12 years of Bush and Reagan, the Republican coalition seemed in solid control of the nation's politics and its policy agenda.

When the Republicans made such optimistic assumptions, they failed to notice that the American people were anxious and fearful as the 1990s began. Major corporations had cut their payrolls to reduce costs in what became known as "downsizing." Large firms like IBM, Procter & Gamble, and Chrysler Corporation trimmed their payrolls dramatically. IBM reduced its workforce by 100,000. Other businesses moved production facilities overseas in search of lower labor costs. The economy created millions of jobs, but many of them were low-paying service jobs. Multinational corporations became a focus of voter anger, as did the specter of immigrants taking jobs away from native-born Americans.

In 1990, the press began commenting on "Generation X," the generation of Americans under age 25, which accounted for some 75 million people. Following on the heels of the baby boomers of the 1960s and 1970s, Generation Xers were derided as a "generation of self-centered know-nothings" in search of personal gratification and quick riches. The offspring of broken

marriages and single-parent homes, they had raised themselves while their parents were at work, spent endless time before television sets and computer games, and were sexually active at ever younger ages.

As 1992 began, there was a growing sense that the nation faced serious choices. One law student in North Carolina said, "For the first time I feel that a group of Americans is going to have to deal with the idea that they're not going to live as well as their parents." That fear of diminished possibility and reduced opportunity would seem odd later in the 1990s, but it was a genuine concern in the popular mind as the 1992 election approached.

Conclusion

The Reagan–Bush years began with a national mood of apprehension and fear about the future. Twelve years of Republican rule saw the end of communism, the victory in the Gulf War, and the return of economic prosperity. Yet somehow, for all the rhetoric of "Morning in America" under Reagan and "a New World Order" under Bush, the reality did not add up to the sunny prospects that the triumph over communism was supposed to bring. The nation looked for the new choices and new opportunities that a presidential election could provide.

DOING HISTORY ONLINE

The New World Order

Based on the documents in this module, write a thesis paragraph that articulates the principles that guided American foreign policy during the George H. W. Bush presidency.

History Now™   Visit HistoryNOW to access primary sources and exercises related to this topic: http://now.ilrn.com/ayers_etal3e

---

The Chapter in Review
During the years between 1981 and 1992:

- The United States incurred large budget deficits.
- The nation embarked on a program to build up national defense.
- Computers became an integral part of the economy and communication system.
- There was increasing political polarization over issues such as abortion.

- The Cold War drew to a close with a total victory for the United States and its allies.
- The Middle East emerged as an even more crucial foreign policy challenge during the first Iraq war.
- The United States moved to the right during the presidencies of Ronald Reagan and George H. W. Bush.

Making Connections Across Chapters

LOOKING BACK

Chapter 31 examines the impact of the Ronald Reagan and George H. W. Bush administrations in the context of the 1980s and early 1990s. A key point in the chapter is the nation's rightward shift in political terms and the consequences of that change for foreign policy and domestic priorities

1. What problems confronted the new Reagan administration in 1981 as a result of the events of the Carter administration?

2. What was the international position in economic, political, and military terms relative to the Soviet Union in the early 1980s?

3. In what ways did Ronald Reagan change the role of the president? Which of his achievements have proved the most enduring and also the most controversial?

4. What were the most significant cultural and economic changes Americans experienced during the 1980s and early 1990s?

5. Was the first Iraq war as much of a victory as it was portrayed at the time?

LOOKING AHEAD

The concluding chapter of the book considers the administrations of Bill Clinton and George W. Bush. The problem of terrorism, which was barely on the national agenda as this chapter comes to an end, will arise as a central concern of domestic and foreign policy as we assess the current situation in the United States.

1. What problems did the first Bush administration leave on the national agenda for the Clinton presidency?

2. What economic choices did the people of the United States have to make in the mid-1990s as a result of the actions taken between 1981 and 1993?

3. Why were policymakers, the media, and the people generally slow to grasp the dangers of terrorism?

4. How did the legacy of Ronald Reagan affect the politics of the 1990s?

5. Has the second Iraq war made the United States more or less safe?

Recommended Reading

Cannon, Lou. *President Reagan: The Role of a Lifetime* (1991). A biography of the president by a reporter who covered his entire career.

Draper, Theodore. *A Very Thin Line: The Iran-Contra Affair* (1991). A thorough review of the scandal and its effects.

Fitzgerald, Frances. *Way Out There in the Blue: Reagan, Star Wars, and the End of the Cold War* (2000). A critical look at the Strategic Defense Initiative

Greene, John Robert. *The Presidency of George Bush* (2000). Covers the George H. W. Bush presidency thoroughly.

Johnson, Haynes. *Sleepwalking Through History: America in the Reagan Years* (1991). Supplies the perspective of a Washington reporter on the 1980s.

Johnson, Haynes. *Divided We Fall: Gambling with History in the Nineties* (1994). Covers the Reagan–Bush transition and carries the story down to the outset of the Clinton presidency.

Mervin, David. *George Bush and the Guardianship Presidency* (1998). Provides the perspective of a British scholar on the George H. W. Bush administration.

Parmet, Herbert. *George Bush: The Life of a Lone Star Yankee* (1997). The best biography of the forty-first president.

Pemberton, William E. *Exit with Honor: The Life and Presidency of Ronald Reagan* (1997). A sound one-volume study of the man and his impact on the nation.

Sloan, John W. *The Reagan Effect: Economics and Presidential Leadership* (2000). Looks at the president's handling of the economy.

Identifications

Review your understanding of the following key terms, people, events, and dates for this chapter (these terms also appear in the Glossary at the end of the book):

Ronald Reagan
Moral Majority

The Great Communicator
Contras
Strategic Defense Initiative (SDI)
Walter Mondale
Jesse Jackson

The 1992 presidential contest interrupted the pattern of Republican electoral victories that had, with the exception of Jimmy Carter in 1976, dominated American politics since 1968. William Jefferson ("Bill") Clinton of Arkansas defeated incumbent George H. W. Bush and billionaire independent candidate Ross Perot in a campaign that involved Americans in campaigning and voting in greater numbers than had occurred in many years.

Clinton's victory began a turbulent decade. The new president stumbled during his first year in office. Popular discontent with his performance helped the Republicans regain control of both houses of Congress in 1994 for the first time in four decades. Then, defying predictions that he was finished, Clinton rebounded to win a second term in 1996 and became the first Democrat since Franklin D. Roosevelt in 1936 to be reelected to a second term. Personal scandals led to his impeachment, trial, and acquittal. The Republicans won the disputed 2000 election behind George W. Bush. Then, in a sudden turn of events, the terrorist attacks of September 11, 2001, confronted the nation with new dangers that led in 2003 to a war in Iraq. By 2005, after 4 years of battling terrorism, the United States had not yet found a strategy that united Americans to deal with the demands of the twenty-first century.

An Angry Nation: 1992

The onset of the 1992 presidential election found Americans fretful and anxious. The economy had slipped into a recession by mid-1991 with unemployment rising, consumer confidence waning, and corporations laying off large numbers of employees. Americans again feared that downsizing and restructuring meant that their jobs were disappearing overseas.

Outside Washington, unhappiness intensified about how officials in Congress and the White House conducted themselves. Speaker of the House of Representatives James Wright (D-Texas) had resigned under an ethical cloud in 1989 because he had accepted money

Timeline

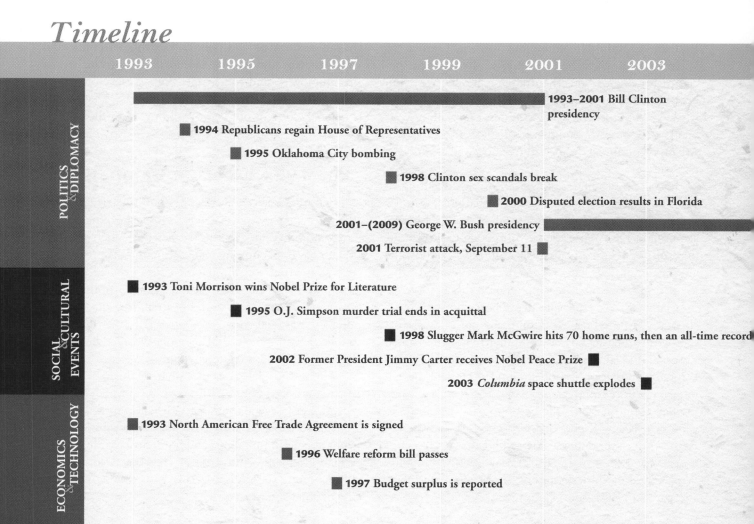

	1993	1995	1997	1999	2001	2003

POLITICS & DIPLOMACY

1993–2001 Bill Clinton presidency

1994 Republicans regain House of Representatives

1995 Oklahoma City bombing

1998 Clinton sex scandals break

2000 Disputed election results in Florida

2001–(2009) George W. Bush presidency

2001 Terrorist attack, September 11

SOCIAL & CULTURAL EVENTS

1993 Toni Morrison wins Nobel Prize for Literature

1995 O.J. Simpson murder trial ends in acquittal

1998 Slugger Mark McGwire hits 70 home runs, then an all-time record

2002 Former President Jimmy Carter receives Nobel Peace Prize

2003 *Columbia* space shuttle explodes

ECONOMICS & TECHNOLOGY

1993 North American Free Trade Agreement is signed

1996 Welfare reform bill passes

1997 Budget surplus is reported

from lobbyists and special interest groups. Other lawmakers of both parties had abused the procedures of the House bank to write checks for which there were not sufficient funds in their accounts. The House post office had been handled in a corrupt way as well. Campaign finance reform stalled as members continued to accept large contributions from corporations, labor unions, and special interest groups with a stake in the outcome of legislation. Voter anger surged during 1991.

The outcome of the Gulf War seemed at the time to assure the reelection of President George H. W. Bush. But then his poll numbers, which had already slipped from the lofty postwar levels, began to drop further. Conservatives in his own party assaulted his political leadership. The president seemed to many Americans to have little awareness of their problems and hopes. Nonetheless, Bush stood off a challenge from within the Grand Old Party and secured a renomination. His Democratic opponent was the governor of Arkansas, **William Jefferson "Bill" Clinton.**

From the outset, Clinton aroused conflicting passions among Democrats and the voters in general. He was a young, attractive southern governor who campaigned as a "New Democrat" with a strong civil rights record. He had supported education and economic growth in Arkansas. On the negative side, however, critics charged that he had cheated on his wife Hillary Rodham Clinton with numerous women. During the Vietnam War, which he had opposed, he received special treatment to avoid the draft but never gave a full explanation about how he had behaved. There were also whispers about his business dealings, especially investments in a land development called **Whitewater.** An Arkansas columnist dubbed him "Slick Willie," and the tag stuck.

Racial rioting in Los Angeles during the spring of 1992 underscored the tense nature of national attitudes as the presidential election approached. Sparked by the acquittal of Los Angeles police officers on trial for beating **Rodney King,** a black suspect in their custody, the violence indicated that passions over race festered while the nation's political leadership ignored these problems.

Many citizens, especially Republicans, looked for an alternative to the Bush–Clinton matchup. The national spotlight turned to a Texas computer billionaire named Ross Perot. Plainspoken and tough-talking, the feisty Perot argued that professional politicians lacked the will to deal with the country's problems. Faced with a losing football team, he said, "the best approach would be to get a new coach, a new quarterback, start with basics, clean it up." Announcing his candidacy on talk show host Larry King's national call-in television program, Perot stirred enthusiasm among citizens looking for an alternative to Bush and Clinton.

AP/Wide World Photos

For a season, Ross Perot brought fresh energy and new ideas into American politics. He captivated hordes of reporters when his campaign was still a novelty and his personality seemed attractive.

During the spring of 1992, Perot benefited from a grassroots movement that put his name on the ballot in all of the states. He soon led Bush and Clinton in the polls. Without specifying just what he would do, he promised to grapple with the budget deficit and clean up Washington. As the media investigated his previous record in business and politics, evidence of erratic and silly behavior surfaced. He monitored the private lives of his employees, and some called him "Inspector Perot." His poll numbers sank. Just before the Democratic National Convention, Perot withdrew from the race.

The 1992 Election Campaign

Bill Clinton received an electoral boost when Perot left the race, and the Arkansas governor swept to the Democratic nomination. He selected Senator Albert Gore of Tennessee as his running mate. Although the presence of two southerners on the national ticket defied political wisdom, the Democratic team seemed youthful and energetic. A bus tour of the heartland of the country after the national convention attracted much favorable publicity. Clinton's lead in the polls widened before the Republicans held their convention in August.

The GOP delegates nominated Bush and Vice President Quayle amid an atmosphere in which the conservative social agenda dominated. In a fiery speech, Patrick Buchanan declared a cultural war to reclaim America from liberals, immigrants, and homosexuals. He assailed Hillary Rodham Clinton as well. The spectacle added to Bill Clinton's support, especially with women voters in the nation's suburbs.

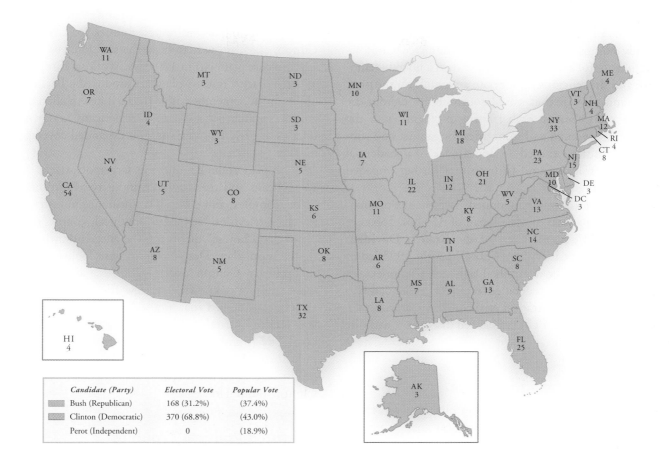

MAP 32.1 The Election of 1992

This map shows the ability of Bill Clinton to capitalize on the discontent with George Bush and the Republicans to carve out a landslide electoral victory. Because Clinton received only 43 percent of the vote, however, Republicans soon questioned his legitimacy as president.

Candidate (Party)	Electoral Vote	Popular Vote
Bush (Republican)	168 (31.2%)	(37.4%)
Clinton (Democratic)	370 (68.8%)	(43.0%)
Perot (Independent)	0	(18.9%)

In October 1992, Ross Perot changed his mind and reentered the presidential race, choosing Admiral James Stockdale, a Vietnam prisoner of war, as his vice presidential choice. The three candidates then debated the issues before large national television audiences. The election engaged voter interest to an extent that had not been seen in several decades. Perot did not regain the levels of support that he had enjoyed in the spring, yet he retained a large and enthusiastic following. Bush closed the gap somewhat during the final weeks of the campaign, but the Perot candidacy split the Republican base in many states. The result was a Clinton-Gore victory. Clinton received 44,908,254 popular votes and 370 electoral ballots to Bush's 39,102,343 votes and 168 electoral votes. Perot made the best popular showing of any third-party candidate in American history with 19,741,065 votes. However, he won no electoral votes. The Democrats continued their control of Congress, but the Republicans gained 1 Senate seat and picked up 14 members in the House.

A notable feature of the 1992 election was the number of women candidates who won seats in the U.S. Senate. In the aftermath of the Clarence Thomas and Anita Hill controversy, Democratic women candidates won Senate seats in California (Barbara Boxer and Dianne Feinstein), Illinois (Carol Moseley Braun), and Washington (Patti Murray). The results, said pundits, made it "The Year of the Woman" in national politics. The Democrats seemed to dominate the national scene, but their political ascendancy would soon evaporate.

The Clinton Presidency

Clinton's presidency faltered even before he took office. As one of his first announced priorities, the president-elect indicated that he intended to lift the long-standing ban against declared homosexuals serving in the armed forces. After much debate within the military, the

Clinton administration adopted a "Don't Ask, Don't Tell" approach in which gay personnel would not be asked about their sexual orientation and should not be openly homosexual. This stance contradicted Clinton's election appeal as a moderate rather than a liberal Democrat, and the religious right began an assault on the president and his wife that would continue throughout the next 4 years. Several embarrassing problems with the selection of women and minorities for cabinet and sub-cabinet positions caused an appearance of presidential disarray to form around Clinton that further impeded his ability to govern.

After Clinton was inaugurated, an armed confrontation between agents of the Bureau of Alcohol, Tobacco, and Firearms and members of the **Branch Davidian** religious sect outside Waco, Texas, in April 1993 led to the fiery deaths of many of the Davidians. Opponents of gun control and the federal government contended that the Clinton administration envisioned dictatorial rule. That fear on the far right further fed discontent with the new president.

Clinton's Domestic Agenda

During his first 2 years, Bill Clinton achieved several domestic objectives at a high political cost. With the barest of voting margins in both the House and Senate, he secured adoption of an economic package that combined tax increases and spending cuts to lower the deficit for 1993 to $255 billion and for 1994 to $203 billion. Republicans depicted the president as returning to a traditional Democratic strategy of raising taxes, and they predicted economic calamity ahead. Clinton responded that the burden of higher levies fell only on the most wealthy Americans. Although the economy remained strong and the nation was prosperous throughout 1993 and 1994, the Republicans won the political argument against the Democratic tax legislation.

Clinton pursued the cause of freer world trade when he advocated passage of the North American Free Trade Agreement (NAFTA), which cleared Congress in late 1993. The trade agreement split the Democrats, and approval came with the help of Republican votes. In late 1994, the White House also secured congressional endorsement of the General Agreement on Tariffs and Trade (GATT) in a lame-duck session of the Democratic Congress. Again, Republican votes were central to this administration victory.

Reforming Health Care

The major goal of the new administration was reform of the nation's system of health care. Nearly 40 million citizens did not have health insurance, and the costs of medical care were rising at an alarming rate. In a dramatic expansion of the responsibilities for first ladies, Clinton asked his wife to head the task force to prepare a health care plan within 100 days. Working throughout 1993, Hillary Clinton's planners produced a health care blueprint in September. It envisioned health alliances to emphasize managed care, asked Americans to pay more to consult private physicians, and expanded coverage to include all citizens.

The plan soon became the target of attacks from Republicans and the insurance industry as too bureaucratic, complex, and costly. The insurance industry used effective television ads of a mythical couple named "Harry and Louise" discussing the alleged drawbacks of the Clinton plan. Despite the intense lobbying efforts that Hillary Clinton expended, the "Clinton Health Plan," as it was known, had few friends in Congress. Republicans denied that any serious health care reform was needed and refused to present alternatives of their own. The drumbeat of opposition from the insurance industry took its toll on public opinion. By 1994 the health care issue had become a major liability for the Clinton White House.

Clinton's Political Troubles

Despite his domestic accomplishments, President Clinton's popular approval ratings remained low, often below 50 percent of the electorate. From the political right, the president and his wife stirred dislike that bordered on outright hatred. Republicans charged that the Clintons were socialists bent on entrenching homosexuals, bureaucrats, and atheists in power in Washington. When an aide to the president, Vincent Foster, committed suicide during the summer of 1993, right-wing talk show hosts circulated wild and unfounded rumors that Foster had been murdered at the instructions of the president and his wife.

More serious were the charges of financial impropriety and ethical lapses that dogged the Clintons from their years in Arkansas. Investments that they had made in an Arkansas real estate venture on the Whitewater River became entangled with the failed savings and loan firm run by business associates of the Clintons, James and Susan McDougal. Federal regulators grew interested in these transactions, and in 1993 press reports disclosed that the Clintons could be named as potential witnesses and even targets of an investigation. Accusations soon surfaced that an effort at a cover-up had been mounted from the White House. The all-purpose label for these and other related scandals was "Whitewater." As subsequent investigations revealed, the allegations against the

Clintons about their finances had little basis in fact but the impression of corruption provided a useful weapon to their enemies.

The charges against the Clintons led to the appointment of an independent counsel, or special prosecutor, in 1994. The first counsel was a Republican named Robert Fiske. When he concluded that Vincent Foster's death was a suicide, angry conservatives had him replaced with another counsel, **Kenneth Starr,** a former federal judge and solicitor general during the Bush administration. Starr was more conservative than Fiske and his allies expected him to find wrongdoing on the part of both the president and the first lady.

Personally embarrassing to President Clinton were allegations that he had sexually harassed an Arkansas state employee named Paula Corbin Jones in 1991. Jones filed a civil rights lawsuit in the spring of 1994 in which she claimed that then Governor Clinton had made unwanted sexual advances in a hotel room, including exposing himself to her. The president's lawyers attempted to have the suit delayed until after the end of his administration on the grounds that such litigation disrupted his ability to carry out his official duties.

Clinton and the World

Bill Clinton came into office with his mind concentrated on domestic issues, and, as a result, his foreign policy got off to a rocky start. He faced a complex set of circumstances in the world in early 1993. The United States was heavily involved in a number of places around the globe—Haiti, Bosnia, and Somalia—but the previous administration had not linked these commitments to any kind of coherent structure other than George H. W. Bush's vague references after the Gulf War to a "New World Order."

As a result, Clinton's first year produced a number of foreign policy problems and disasters that created an image of the president as out of his depth on the world stage. In October 1993, 18 American servicemen died in a raid in Somalia that included television footage of crowds dragging the body of an American pilot through the streets. The White House also suffered a setback in Haiti after a peacekeeping force was repulsed by angry inhabitants of the island threatening violence.

The main foreign policy problem of these initial months was in Bosnia where Clinton had been so critical of the Bush administration and its policies during the 1992 campaign. In office, the proper course of action seemed less clear. With United Nations peacekeeping troops, predominantly British and French, on the ground, the military options for Clinton were limited because the first targets of retaliation from the Serbs would be the allied troops. Working through the United

In a troubled first year in office, a handshake between two Middle Eastern enemies, Rabin and Arafat, at the White House represented one of the foreign policy successes for the Clinton administration.

Nations also proved frustrating for the White House. Tensions rose between Washington and its allies throughout 1993 over the proper course of action in the Balkans.

In less publicized ways, the administration had some accomplishments on the world stage. It succeeded in obtaining the withdrawal of Russian troops from the Baltic Republic of Estonia in 1994. Clinton also helped to broker peace negotiations among Ireland, Great Britain, and the Irish Republican Army's political arm Sinn Fein ("Ourselves Alone"). In the Middle East, State Department negotiators facilitated talks between Yasir Arafat of the Palestine Liberation Organization and Prime Minister Yitzhak Rabin of Israel that led to a celebrated handshake on the White House lawn. The United States also intervened in Haiti in 1994 and produced the ouster of the military rulers as a prelude to more democratic government.

The perception that Clinton was weak in foreign policy exacerbated his political troubles at home. During his first 2 years in office, Clinton's popularity ratings fell, his hold on the country remained weak, and there was speculation that he would be another one-term president. On the right, the determination to oust Clinton in 1996 gathered momentum.

The Republican Revolution: 1994

By 1994 the cumulative effect of the charges against the president and a Republican resurgence from the setback of 1992 transformed the political scene as the congressional elections approached. Several elements fed the Republican offensive. In the House of Representatives,

The Republican Revolution of 1994

The Republican takeover of Congress in 1994 was orchestrated by Newt Gingrich of Georgia, pictured here with his fellow GOP House candidates on September 27, 1994. The use of striking visuals such as the blue background for the "Contract with America" slogan and the American flags that the candidates wave attest to the influence of television on how political campaigns are marketed. The provisions of the "Contract" had also been poll-tested with focus groups to ensure the maximum electoral popularity.

This photograph shows how American politics in the 1990s had become a series of visually alluring, highly staged productions designed to address substantive issues but to evoke a desired response from viewers. The Republicans in 1994 proved far more adept at turning the techniques of show business and Hollywood to their advantage than did their Democratic rivals.

AP/ Wide World Photos

the Republicans chose as their next leader their ideological champion, Representative Newton ("Newt") Gingrich of Georgia. An adroit political tactician, the burly, rumpled Gingrich used the television coverage of Congress that began in the late 1970s (called C-SPAN) to broadcast his ideas to a national constituency. His militancy contributed to a partisan intensity in the House, and he saw his greatest initial triumph when he forced Speaker Jim Wright from office for financial misconduct in 1989. Gingrich continued his abrasive tactics into the early 1990s, and conservative members in the House rallied to his banner.

To dramatize their appeal, Gingrich and the Republicans offered "A **Contract with America**" as their election platform. Composed of proposals tested in focus groups for their popularity with the voters, the Contract promised action on such items as a balanced budget amendment, term limits for Congress members, and making legislators obey the regulations they applied to society. All of these measures and others would be acted on within the first 100 days of a Republican victory. As the elections began, the Republicans found their poll numbers rising, the Democrats in retreat, and the prospect of regaining control of Congress a real possibility for the first time in four decades.

The Democrats and President Clinton stumbled throughout the autumn of 1994. The failure to achieve reform of the health care system and a general weariness with big government underlined the apparent futility of the incumbents. Efforts to scare the voters about the prospect of a Republican takeover fell flat. On election night, the Republicans swept to victory. They had 235 seats in the House to 197 for the Democrats, and they controlled the Senate by a margin of 53 to 47. **Newt Gingrich** became Speaker of the House and Robert Dole was the Senate majority leader. The elections immediately prompted predictions that President Clinton's prospects for regaining the White House in 1996 were bleak.

Race, Ethnicity, and Culture Wars in the 1990s

While Washington watched the 1994 elections with great intensity, Americans spent more time that autumn transfixed by what promised to be the last "Trial of the Century." In mid-June 1994, Nicole Brown Simpson, the estranged ex-wife of professional football star and Heisman Trophy winner Orenthal James "O. J." Simpson, was brutally murdered at her home. Nearby lay the corpse of Ronald Goldman, an acquaintance and restaurant employee. Police suspicions soon focused on O. J. Simpson, whose Ford Bronco had blood that could be traced to the crime scene and who had apparently left physical evidence of his presence there.

Although Simpson's playing career in the National Football League had ended some years earlier, he remained a national celebrity because of appearances in movies and television advertising. It soon became evident that the nation was polarized about Simpson's guilt or innocence. Most white Americans believed that the strong evidence pointed to Simpson as the killer. Many black Americans talked of a police conspiracy to frame the former football star and associated his prosecution with earlier examples of racial injustice.

These opinions solidified during the protracted trial that began during the fall of 1994 and stretched on into much of 1995. Televised daily and covered in excruciating detail, the trial played out as a racially charged drama that dominated talk shows, tabloids, and popular opinion in what became a national obsession. As the months of testimony and controversy went on into 1995, commentators argued that the proceedings offered the nation a chance to examine serious issues of race and class. That opportunity was missed. Instead, the Simpson trial became one of the first indicators of how cable television could fixate on events that boosted audience ratings while leaving more pressing social questions unexplored. Over the next decade, cable television would refine the lessons learned from the Simpson case into techniques that diverted its audiences from hard issues of war and peace and thus ill-served the nation.

The Simpson case ended in an acquittal for the defendant in a result that further split public opinion. Black audiences cheered the verdict as it was announced. Whites watching on television expressed dismay. The national debate intensified as commentators divided along racial lines about the significance of Simpson's acquittal.

In October 1995, another racial event underscored the persistence of these divisions. The Nation of Islam and its controversial leader, **Louis Farrakhan,** organized "a holy day of atonement and reconciliation" for black men. The event became known as the "**Million Man March**" that would bring that number of black males to Washington, D.C. Whether Farrakhan met his goal was in dispute. Because of his espousal of anti-Semitic sentiments and his expressed dislike for white Americans, Farrakhan's event did not have the moral resonance of Martin Luther King's March on Washington in 1963.

The Immigration Backlash

Adding to these social tensions was the issue of immigration, both illegal and legal. Voters in California adopted Proposition 187 in 1994, a ballot initiative that barred illegal immigrants from receiving state benefits in education and health. Immigration into the United States had grown dramatically during the 1980s. By the early 1990s legal immigrants, most of whom were Hispanics and Asians, totaled almost 600,000 per year. Estimates of the number of illegal immigrants to settle in the United States ranged from 300,000 to half a million. The Immigration and Naturalization Service (INS) forecast that there might be as many as 13 million immigrants coming to the United States during the 1990s. That would be the largest amount in all of American history.

Debate about the value and cost of this wave of immigrants roiled American politics during the first half of the 1990s. Critics of immigration charged that "the racial and ethnic balance of America is being radically altered through public policy." Studies demonstrated that immigrants, both legal and illegal, contributed more to society in taxes and productivity than they consumed from government services, but the mere increased presence of Hispanics and Asians, the so-called "browning of America," produced political conflict, especially in California. In 1994, the rising discontent about immigration in California led to a landslide election victory for Proposition 187. After its adoption, court challenges delayed its implementation, but by 1996 the governor ordered many of its provisions into effect. On the national level Congress debated immigration restrictions as it decided what to do about reform of the welfare system. The crosscurrents over immigration persisted over the next 10 years with politicians pressed to take action. So volatile was the issue that little constructive could be done either to stem the flow of illegal immigrants or to assimilate the people who came to the United States seeking a better life.

The Culture Wars

The Simpson trial, the Million Man March, and the debate about immigration took place in the context of an ongoing national debate. The issue was what the United States should do about racial injustice and the presence

Hispanics Enter Politics

The shifting nature of the population in the United States began a slow but important change in the nation's politics in the 1990s as ethnic diversity became more pronounced. One of the most important groups in this process was Americans of Hispanic origin. In the states of the Southwest and the Far West, Hispanics made their presence felt at the polls, both as candidates and as voters. This picture, taken in California during the 1990s, offers visual evidence of the rising importance of Hispanic candidates in that state. A decade later, both major parties were competing vigorously for the expanding vote that Hispanics represented. In the initial phase the Democrats had an advantage over their Republican rivals. These election signs also attest to the ways in which the American political system accommodated to the tide of immigration that occurred in the 1990s. More than just advertisements for individual candidates, election posters and signs can, if watched carefully, measure subtle changes in the way Americans conduct their political activities.

© John Ledgard/The Economist

of diverse minority groups within the existing culture. These arguments soon broadened out into discussions about multiculturalism, gay rights, and religious values.

A problem that grew out of the racial divide in the country was the policy of affirmative action in industry, higher education, and government. The stated purpose of these initiatives was to provide minorities with greater opportunities for advancement. The Supreme Court had ruled in the late 1970s that race could be employed in university admissions when the goal was to achieve diversity in the student body. Then the justices scaled back on that commitment in a number of cases involving policies such as minority set-aside programs or congressional districts drawn to produce heavily minority-populated districts.

Unhappiness with affirmative action as a policy led some states, such as California with Proposition 209, to pass a referendum that abolished programs to assist minorities. In the *Hopwood v. Texas* case (1996), a federal circuit court overturned the affirmative action plan of the University of Texas Law School, noting that any effort by the university to promote affirmative action was unconstitutional. Texas adopted a plan to admit the top 10 percent of graduating high school students,

irrespective of their race or ethnicity, to its state universities. But the problem of affirmative action and its consequences remained unsolved during the first decade of the twenty-first century.

These tensions affected the academic world in the debate about the concept of multiculturalism. In the 1980s, academic institutions sought to open up the study of history and literature to a wider range of cultural and social experiences among groups not previously included in the American past. Addressing gender, class, and racial concerns, multiculturalism sought to draw attention to such issues as the role of black soldiers in the Civil War, Japanese Americans in World War II internment camps, and women in the American Revolution, to pick among many examples.

By early 1890s, however, multiculturalism had come under attack from enemies on the right. Conservatives accused its proponents of enforcing what was called **"political correctness."** The critics of multiculturalism said that the academic left was using the movement to balkanize society into warring ethnic groups, was limiting free speech on campus, and was repudiating the whole tradition of Western culture. While some of the criticisms of multiculturalism did identify areas of exaggeration and overstatements, the attackers overdramatized isolated incidents and inflated small errors into larger trends. By the end of the 1990s, passions about multiculturalism had cooled, but tensions in other areas of society remained volatile, especially over an issue such as gay rights.

The efforts of gays and lesbians to attain political and social equality within the United States were met with a strong counteroffensive from conservatives who regarded homosexuals as a threat to the nation's values. In the 1990s, homosexuals contended that they should have the right to marry (in what were called "same sex" marriages) just as heterosexuals did. Identifying their campaign with the civil rights movement of the 1960s, gay groups wanted attacks on those who were openly homosexual to be classified as "hate crimes."

Conservative groups assailed homosexuality as a sin or a disease. Christian groups ran elaborate advertising campaigns to persuade homosexuals to abandon their lifestyle and seek religious redemption. Periodic acts of violence directed against gays spurred calls for federal legislation to prevent such actions. Passions surrounding the issue intensified during the first decade of the twenty-first century as efforts to ban same sex marriages included a proposed constitutional amendment to outlaw such unions. From their enhanced political power after the elections of 1994, Republicans found such "wedge" issues as homosexuality an important contribution to their rise to greater dominance in American politics.

The Republicans in Power

The new Republican majorities in Congress went to work in January 1995 with great energy to implement their "Contract with America." Laboring long hours at the start, they enacted a measure to make the regulations they imposed on Americans apply to Capitol Hill as well. The Republicans also pushed for a balanced budget amendment to the Constitution. Meanwhile, President Clinton accepted some of the Republican ideas in his State of the Union message and praised his own record on the economy.

The pace of the "Republican Revolution" remained hectic into the spring of 1995. Although the balanced budget amendment failed by a single vote in the Senate, Congress did pass a law to restrict itself from making the states enforce regulations without supplying the necessary funds to do so. Clinton approved the "unfunded mandates" measure on March 22, 1995. The Republicans failed, however, to pass a constitutional amendment imposing term limits on members of Congress. By April, Republicans proclaimed that they had enacted most of the contract within the 100 days they had set for themselves.

Tragedy in Oklahoma City

Then an act of political terrorism shifted the political landscape. On April 19, 1995, an explosion ripped through the Alfred P. Murrah Federal Building in Oklahoma City, killing 168 people inside. Two suspects, Timothy McVeigh and Terry Nichols, were quickly arrested and identified as having links with an extremist "militia" movement that sought the violent overthrow of the government of the United States. The public learned that small groups of militia met secretly in the countryside to practice guerrilla warfare tactics against the day when the ZOG (Zionist Occupation Government) in Washington would precipitate the final confrontation on behalf of the United Nations and the "New World Order." The glare of publicity revealed that the militia movement, though violent and dangerous, commanded only a small cadre of followers.

The aftermath of the bombing enabled President Clinton to regain a position of trust and confidence with the American people. He went out to Oklahoma City in the wake of the tragedy and participated in the ceremony of national mourning for the victims. Clinton's speech on that occasion struck a resonant note of national healing and identified the president with the broad political center of the country. The two suspects, McVeigh and Nichols, were both tried and convicted for their roles in the bombing.

The Republicans Falter

Republican overreaching also contributed to the president's rebound in the polls during the remainder of 1995. As the Republicans in Congress attacked environmental legislation and sought to remove government regulations on business, the White House assailed them for endangering the gains that the nation had made in clean air and clean water. Clinton threatened to veto legislation that cut back on environmental spending and money for education. He cast his first veto as president in June 1995 when he turned down a Republican spending measure that would have trimmed more than a billion dollars from education funding.

Troubles dogged Clinton during 1995, especially the long-running Whitewater saga, which saw congressional committees probe the scandal in detail. Despite the best efforts of Republican lawmakers, the inquiry did not turn up evidence that would incriminate the president or his wife in wrongdoing. The special prosecutor, Kenneth Starr, continued his investigations with indictments and convictions of several Arkansas political and business figures, but that effort also yielded nothing to embarrass the Clintons directly.

With the perception after the 1994 elections that Clinton would be a one-term president, the Republicans had an abundance of potential challengers for their nomination in 1996. The most formidable candidate would be General Colin Powell, whose service as chairman of the Joint Chiefs of Staff in the Gulf War had made him a national military hero associated with military success. As the first African American to be a serious contender for the Republican prize, Powell would be an asset to the party's ticket if he would agree to run as vice president. Throughout most of 1995, Powell hinted that he was a Republican and thinking about running for president.

Beyond Powell, the Republican field for 1996 included Senator Robert Dole, who began as the presumed front-runner. Because the party generally selected the leading candidate in the polls, Dole was likely to be nominated unless he stumbled badly. At 72, Dole had to overcome the age problem, his reputation as a strident partisan, and a perception that he would be the easiest target for a resurgent Clinton.

Clinton Resurgent: Bosnia

The big political winner in the second half of 1995 continued to be President Clinton. Against all the critics who charged that his policy in Bosnia would lead to an American involvement and a military disaster, the president succeeded by the end of the year in producing a cease-fire in the conflict. The price was the presence of American ground troops in the Balkans, but even that risky commitment did not lead to the disaster that so many had anticipated. The opportunity for a cease-fire emerged out of a complex series of events during the summer and fall of 1995. In July, a Serb offensive imperiled several cities that were regarded as "safe havens" for refugees from the fighting. Helped by arms that had come in from Muslim countries, Croatian and Bosnian forces launched an offensive against the Serbs. At the end of August, Clinton authorized air strikes against the Bosnian Serbs. Within a week, a tentative peace agreement was declared, and a month later a cease-fire was reached. The United States then brokered peace negotiations in Dayton, Ohio, which produced a settlement. American troops were dispatched to help enforce the peace agreement.

Clinton Wins a Second Term

Despite the intervention in the Balkans, the main focus of American politics remained on the running battle between President Clinton and the Republicans in Congress. As the budget negotiations produced no result toward the end of 1995, some of the more militant members of the GOP majority in the House called for a concerted effort to shut down the government as a way of pressuring the White House to agree to their position. Assuming that Clinton lacked the resolve to withstand a closing of the government, these Republicans foresaw a humiliating cave-in from a president they distrusted and hated.

The Republican strategy backfired. Two government shutdowns occurred, a brief one in November and a second that lasted for 21 days from mid-December 1995 into early January 1996. Rather than blaming the president for the deadlock, as the Republicans had anticipated, the public put the responsibility on the Republicans for the government closures that affected tourists in Washington and at popular national parks. In early 1996, the Republicans realized that the protracted shutdown was hurting their cause. They reached a deal with the White House to end the crisis. By January 6, the government had resumed normal operations.

While President Clinton had the upper hand in the national political arena, the long-running Whitewater saga took an ugly turn for Hillary Rodham Clinton in the early days of January. Billing records from Hillary Clinton's former law firm in Arkansas, sought by the special prosecutor in 1994, turned up in the White House. Kenneth Starr, the Whitewater prosecutor, subpoenaed Mrs. Clinton to testify before his Washington grand jury. Her appearance marked the first time that a first lady had testified in a criminal proceeding while her husband was in office. She spent 4 hours before the grand jury panel, but no results followed from her testimony. In fact, all of the probes into the Clinton's financial affairs resulted in no actions against the couple. That aspect of the president's personal conduct proved a dry hole for the Republicans.

As the 1996 election approached, Robert Dole solidified his position at the head of the Republican party. A decorated World War II veteran and a gifted lawmaker, Dole had run in 1988 against George H. W. Bush for the GOP prize but had lost badly. An indifferent speaker at best, Dole campaigned in a frenetic but often unfocused manner. He was not a good organizer, and friends worried about his ability to sustain a national presidential campaign.

Dole faced a number of challengers to his candidacy as 1996 began, but he won the key South Carolina primary on March 2. Successive victories brought the Kansas senator within sight of the nomination by April 1996. The early victory left the Dole campaign broke and unable to counter Clinton's advertising until after the Republican National Convention in late summer when

half of the decade. In 1996, 18 million people, or about 9 percent of the population, accessed the Internet on a regular basis. A year later the figure stood at 30 million adults. By 1998, 20 percent of all American households had Internet access, and the growth continued unabated into the twenty-first century. With more than 96 million computers in use in 1995, or 364.7 per 1,000 Americans, the United States led the world in its share of Internet usage.

Dominating the new field were such corporations as America Online, which provided connections for 30 percent of all Internet users in the country in 1996. Other businesses sought consumers on the Web through specific Web pages or by purchasing advertising space on popular websites. Some new firms, such as the discount bookseller Amazon.com, saw their common stock soar in value in 1998 because of the potential growth of their markets. Popular movies such as *You've Got Mail* (1998) and the rise of news outlets on the Web that included "Salon," "Slate," and the "Drudge Report" (named after its host, conservative Matt Drudge) underscored how the Internet had permeated American life. Investments in Internet stocks helped fuel the economic boom of the late 1990s.

So important had computers and the Internet become by 1998 that the prospect of a computer breakdown in the year 2000 emerged as a major social problem. Y2K, as it was known, stemmed from the inability of older computers to read the year 2000 correctly and remain functioning. Finding and fixing embedded computer codes cost business and government hundreds of billions of dollars in 1998 and 1999. Some Americans hoarded food and weapons in preparation for what they forecast as a breakdown of civilization on January 1, 2000. In any case the fate of the nation's economy was now tied to the operation. When the date came, nothing bad occurred, but the Y2K episode revealed the degree to which humanity had become interdependent.

© Bettmann/CORBIS

Senator Robert Dole of Kansas attained his long-held dream of winning the Republican presidential nomination in 1996, but he could not unseat a popular incumbent. This picture, taken at a rally in New Hampshire while he is being introduced, fails to show the war wounds to his right hand and the pencil that he always gripped.

Dole received federal matching funds as the official Republican nominee. To jump-start his lagging candidacy, Dole tried a sensational gesture and resigned his Senate seat in June to campaign as a man without office or Washington power. He remained behind in the polls.

The Rise of the Internet

While politicians and commentators focused on the 1996 presidential contests, another force was affecting the economy and American culture. The powerful growth of the Internet and the World Wide Web in the 1990s transformed the way Americans got their news and communicated with each other. The development of browsers that could read the Hyper Text Markup Language (HTML) facilitated this process during the first

---

DOING HISTORY ONLINE

Windows 95 Is Unveiled to the Public

Read the article in this module and speculate on why Microsoft has become the dominant software provider in the world.

History ⧖ Now™   Visit HistoryNOW to access primary sources and exercises related to this topic: http://now.ilrn.com/ayers_etal3e

Welfare and Other Reforms in Congress

With the election approaching and polls showing their standing with the public in jeopardy, the Republican majority on Capitol Hill saw cooperation with the White House as a political necessity. As a result, the president and Congress found common ground on reform of the nation's welfare system in the summer of 1996. A compromise measure came out of Congress at the end of July. The bill produced sweeping changes in caring for the poor. In place of the long-standing Aid for Dependent Children (AFDC) program, lawmakers established a system of block grants to the individual states. The federal responsibility to provide for the poverty-stricken, adopted during the New Deal and expanded in succeeding decades, ended. The measure also specified that legal immigrants into the United States would not be eligible for benefits during their first 5 years of residence. The legislation fulfilled Clinton's 1992 campaign promise to "end welfare as we know it," but it left many Democrats unhappy with the current direction of their party.

The waning days of the Congress saw other accomplishments that gave the president issues on which to run and allowed the Republican Congress to rebut the charges that it was unable to act constructively. In August, lawmakers enacted a raise in the minimum wage in two steps to $5.15 per hour. It was the first hike since 1991 and came after intense Republican opposition. Responding to the continuing public unhappiness with immigration problems, Congress included in its spending legislation funds for new personnel for the Immigration and Naturalization Service, the hiring of additional Border Patrol agents, and more severe penalties for bringing in illegal aliens. Republicans failed to get language that would have barred public education to the children of illegal immigrants. The achievements of Congress undercut Dole's argument that Clinton was not an effective leader.

Mindful of their public relations disaster in Houston in 1992, the Republicans sought to reassure voters that they were an acceptable and inclusive alternative to the Democrats. Their problem remained, however, one of making Senator Dole an exciting and charismatic figure who could compete with Clinton, an adroit and skilled campaigner. Dole launched his preconvention offensive with the promise of a 15 percent tax cut over a 3-year period. Reflecting the sentiment within the party for what was known as a "flat tax," an income tax at a low rate for all citizens, he advocated a "fairer, flatter tax." To Democratic charges that his proposal would "blow a hole in the deficit," Dole responded by saying that he would propose prudent spending cuts to find the $548 billion needed to offset his tax reductions. For Dole,

long a champion of a balanced budget, the tax cut proposal represented an eleventh-hour conversion to the supply-side ideology of the Reagan wing of his party. The second daring maneuver came when Dole announced that he had asked former Congressman Jack Kemp of New York to be his running mate. A favorite of the conservatives, Kemp had long endorsed tax cuts and was popular among African American voters. In many respects, the choice was an odd one. Kemp brought little electoral strength to the ticket. The Republicans had no hopes of carrying New York State, for example. Kemp was also an indifferent campaigner, but at the convention his selection lifted the spirits of the Republican delegates who saw Dole trailing badly in the polls to the incumbent president.

Midway between the conventions of the major parties came the meeting of the **Reform party** that Ross Perot had established as the vehicle for his second presidential candidacy. Perot won the nomination easily. Yet he had not captured the public's imagination as had happened in 1992. Perot's hope was to elbow his way into the presidential debates against Clinton and Dole, but, despite efforts to use the federal courts to gain access, Perot had to watch from the sidelines.

With a commanding lead in the public opinion polls, President Clinton enjoyed a harmonious convention when the Democrats met in Chicago in late August. The platform stressed centrist themes and spoke of a "New Democratic party." Clinton and Vice President Gore were renominated, and the president promised four more years of prosperity and moderate reform in what he called his last election campaign.

During September 1996, the campaign unfolded as though Clinton and the Democrats were certain winners. Despite some fluctuations, the lead over Dole in the polls remained strong. The two presidential debates did not attract the attention that had characterized the 1992 debates, and Dole failed to crack Clinton's armor with attacks on his character and administration scandals. By the middle of October, optimistic Democrats predicted a landslide for the president and a good chance that the party might recapture the House and Senate from the Republicans.

Then newspaper reports appeared about improprieties and possible crimes in the fund-raising for the Democratic party and the Clinton campaign. Money had flowed into the president's campaign war chest from Asian sources, and possible links to Communist China and Indonesian businesses emerged. Every day as the campaign wound down, new revelations of questionable campaign contributors and dubious funding sources followed. The lead for the Democratic congressional candidates eroded and even some slippage occurred for President Clinton.

Rather than a triumphal march, the waning days of the 1996 election saw Clinton and his party staggering toward the finish line under a severe cloud of scandal.

A Mixed Result

Clinton's lead wavered a little as the election neared, largely because of the barrage of press coverage of the campaign finance issue. Although most news organizations predicted a double-digit presidential win, that did not happen. Nor did Clinton achieve the majority of the popular vote that he sought to overcome the Republican taunt that he was a minority president. The result over Dole was never really in doubt on election night, but the triumph was more limited than had seemed possible when the campaign started.

The Democratic ticket won 379 electoral votes and 49 percent of the popular vote to 41 percent (159 electoral votes) for Dole and Kemp. Ross Perot and the Reform party lagged with 8 percent of the popular vote and no electoral votes. Clinton's electoral coalition included California (to which he had devoted attention all during his first term), New York, Illinois, Michigan, and Ohio. The president also carried two staunchly Republican states—Florida and Arizona.

Although Dole had lost badly, the Republicans gained some consolation out of the election results. Despite a heavy assault from organized labor and Democratic congressional candidates, the Republicans retained control of both houses of Congress. In the House the Republicans had a diminished majority of only 10 seats. The Republicans picked up 2 Senate seats for a 55 to 45 margin over the Democrats. Because they needed 60 votes to block a Democratic filibuster, the Republicans would have to compromise with their opponents to get any legislation passed. The stage was set for another scenario of divided government to which the nation had become accustomed since the late 1960s.

A New Cabinet

For his second term, President Clinton assembled a new cabinet. To succeed the outgoing secretary of state, Warren Christopher, the president selected the ambassador to the United Nations, Madeleine Albright. She became the first woman to serve as secretary of state, and she soon emerged as one of the most effective and popular members of the government. Her ability to work with the chairman of the Senate Foreign Relations Committee, Jesse Helms of North Carolina, smoothed the way for diplomatic initiatives in early 1997 on such issues as reforming the United Nations and the Bosnian policy.

The major architect of Clinton's foreign policy in his second term was Secretary of State Madeleine Albright, shown in a 1997 visit to American troops in the Balkans.

AP/Wide World Photos

In a gesture of bipartisanship, Clinton named former Maine Republican Senator William Cohen as his secretary of defense. Long interested in defense issues, Cohen was a moderate who could build coalitions with his former colleagues in the Senate while enjoying good relations with Democrats as well. More inclined to end the Bosnian commitment than Madeleine Albright, Cohen was a cautious voice in the Pentagon. Few crises, however, disturbed his early months in office.

For his second term, President Clinton avoided large initiatives that might put him at odds with the Republican Congress. During the winter of 1997, he worked out a budget agreement that promised a balance within a few years. The American economy proved so robust through the summer of 1997 that the deficit fell rapidly and forecasters projected that a budget surplus might emerge by the end of the year. The stock market soared throughout this period, reaching above 8,000 on the Dow Jones Industrial Average in July.

Clinton's goals for a second term seemed indistinct and modest well into 1997. Carrying forward the strategy of his reelection victory, he identified himself with small, incremental ideas such as a V-chip to enable parents to control the television programming that their children watched, a voluntary television ratings system, and greater computer training for schoolchildren.

An Ambitious Foreign Policy

For a president who had come into office promoting domestic issues, Clinton seemed to relish the international stage during his fifth year in office. He pushed hard for the North Atlantic Treaty Organization to add members from former Communist states in Eastern Europe and saw his vision fulfilled when Poland, Hungary, and the Czech Republic were added to the alliance. To overcome Russian opposition to expansion of NATO, the United States and its allies told Moscow in May 1997 that neither nuclear weapons nor large numbers of combat forces would be placed on the soil of the new member states. That publicly placated the Russians.

In other areas of foreign policy, the world's trouble spots remained volatile. The situation in Bosnia, though improved since the Dayton agreement, still pitted Serbs, Croats, and Bosnians against each other despite the uneasy peace that American troops in NATO helped maintain. As for the Middle East, tensions between Palestinians and Israelis worsened amid sporadic terrorist violence. The Clinton administration pressed both sides for more movement to implement peace, but progress was elusive. Throughout the world there were rumblings about Islamic terrorism, but that seemed to most Americans, in and out of government, an improbable threat.

Each month brought new products to introduce consumers to the wonders of the digital age. Here a salesman in an electronics store demonstrates the high definition television that was forecast to replace older television sets by the year 2000.

An Economic Boom

Throughout 1997, the American economy roared into high gear. Unemployment fell to 4.8 percent and inflation no longer seemed a problem. With jobs plentiful and prices stable, a sense of economic optimism pervaded the nation and kept Clinton's job approval ratings around the 60 percent mark.

Adding to the euphoria was the apparent end of the budget deficit problem that had shaped politics for so many years. Surging tax revenues meant that red ink started to disappear. The 1997 budget deficit was only $25 billion, the lowest since 1974, and 1998 promised the unheard of—a budget surplus. As a result of these trends, Congress and the president worked out a balanced budget agreement in May that was signed into law on August 5. Clinton proclaimed: "The sun is rising on America again." Politicians could suddenly believe they could look forward to budget surpluses for years to come. This success relied on using the money in the Social Security Trust Fund to offset other spending, but elected officials played down this budgetary sleight-of-hand in their public comments. Few realized at the time that many of the revenue statements of the corporations in the "New Economy" were fraudulent. Major examples of this practice were the energy giant Enron and the communications company WorldCom, both of which were largely crooked schemes by the late 1990s.

Clinton Embattled

The political result of these favorable economic events was a good year for President Clinton that left him popular and Democrats optimistic about regaining control of the House in 1998. The major setback of the year came when the Supreme Court ruled 9–0 on May 27, 1997, in *Clinton v. Jones* that the sexual harassment lawsuit against the president could go forward while he was in office. Other problems dogged Clinton. Congressional probes on the 1996 campaign scandal indicated that the president and Vice President Al Gore had played a larger role in raising money than they had earlier admitted. Kenneth Starr's Whitewater investigation moved along without major indictments but still posed a potential threat to the White House.

The Monica Lewinsky Scandal

Then, in mid-January 1998, a stunned nation learned that a former White House intern named **Monica Lewinsky** had been involved in a sexual relationship with President Clinton during her employment. Once

President Clinton's admission of his sexual intimacy with Monica Lewinsky proved abundant source material for cartoonists. Jules Feiffer in the *New York Times* offers one interpretation of the president's misbehavior.

© Jules Feiffer

On August 17, 1998, Clinton acknowledged "inappropriate" conduct with Lewinsky when he testified before Starr's Washington grand jury from the White House. That night he told the nation the same thing in a four-and-a-half-minute speech that was widely regarded as a low point of his presidency.

A few weeks later Starr sent a report to the House of Representatives alleging that there were grounds for impeaching Clinton for lying under oath, obstruction of justice, abuse of power, and other offenses. The House Judiciary Committee recommended that an impeachment inquiry commence, and the House voted to authorize a probe after the 1998 elections.

The Monica Lewinsky scandal and its fallout left Clinton a wounded president. He retained the ability to achieve foreign policy successes such as a deal he brokered between Israelis and Palestinians in October 1998. With Clinton's resiliency as a politician, a rebound during his last 2 years was possible. But his tactics and conduct in handling the Lewinsky matter had cost him dearly in terms of his political capital with the American people by the end of 1998.

The 1998 Elections

The Republicans entered the 1998 election season with high ambitions to build on their majorities in the House and Senate. In the Senate, they hoped to reach a total of 60 Republicans, which would enable them to end Democratic filibusters. After Clinton's speech on August 17, it seemed as if a Republican rout was in the offing. Alienated Democrats were predicted to stay home and energized Republicans would flock to the polls to rebuke Clinton. With the Monica Lewinsky scandal working for them, the Republicans had only to run out the clock for a big victory.

Instead, the Republicans overplayed their hand. Their moves to impeach Clinton awakened the Democrats and

the news broke, Clinton asserted that he had not had sex with Lewinsky. For 7 months he reiterated that version of events. Meanwhile, Kenneth Starr investigated whether Clinton had lied under oath in the Paula Jones case when he said he had not had sex with Lewinsky, whether he had obstructed justice, and whether he had asked others to lie on his behalf. This sordid spectacle absorbed vast amounts of television news coverage throughout 1998.

Clinton's strategy of delay worked in the short run. His poll numbers remained high, and Starr's popularity sagged. In the end, however, abundant evidence emerged that Clinton and Lewinsky had been physically intimate.

produced a backlash. By the time the Republicans figured out what was going on, it was too late. On November 3, 1998, the Democrats in the House actually gained 5 seats, not enough to regain control, but an amazing feat in the sixth year of a two-term presidency. Republican control of the House narrowed to 223–211, a very thin majority. In the Senate, the two parties battled to a draw, with the Republicans holding the same 55–45 edge that existed when election day dawned. Two significant Republican victories came in Florida and Texas, where the two sons of George H. W. Bush, Jeb Bush in Florida and **George W. Bush** in Texas, were elected governor. For George W. Bush, his reelection made him the prospective front-runner for the Republican presidential nomination in 2000.

Clinton Impeached and Acquitted

Despite the results of the congressional elections, Republican leaders in Congress pressed ahead with the impeachment of President Clinton. In December the House Judiciary Committee, on a nearly party-line breakdown, sent four articles of impeachment to the full House. That body adopted two articles of impeachment charging President Clinton with perjury in his grand jury testimony in August 1998, and with obstruction of justice in his relationship with Monica Lewinsky, members of his staff, and other individuals. The Senate opened its trial in mid-January. By the end of the month, it became evident that the 45 Democrats would not vote for conviction and a two-thirds majority to convict and remove the president did not exist.

President Clinton's popularity with the public remained high, and his State of the Union address on January 19, 1999, drove his poll ratings still higher. He was acquitted on both counts when the Senate voted on February 12, 1999. On the perjury count, the total was 45 Republican senators voting to convict the president and all 45 Democrats as well as 10 Republicans voting for acquittal. On the second article involving obstruction of justice, the Senate split evenly with 50 Republican votes for conviction and 45 Democrats and 5 Republicans voting for acquittal. William Jefferson Clinton remained in office, a wounded chief executive with 2 years left on his second term.

The impeachment episode reflected the intense emotions that Clinton had provoked

during his time in the White House. To the Republicans and Americans on the right, he was an illegitimate president who had committed crimes in office that warranted his removal. To the remainder of the country, some 65 percent according to most polls, he was a president who, while probably guilty of the offenses with which he was charged, was performing well in office and should not be removed.

During the weeks following the end of the impeachment trial, pundits forecast that Clinton's poll ratings would drop once the crisis was over. That did not happen as the economy remained prosperous and the Dow Jones Industrial Average hovered around 10,000. In late March 1999, NATO began airstrikes against the Serbian government to stop "ethnic cleansing" of the Albanians near the city of Kosovo. Despite the warning of Clinton's critics, the air campaign ended in success for the NATO forces.

The much feared Y2K crisis proved to be largely a nonevent, though the government did report having foiled several terrorist plots set for January 2000. Once the date had passed without major incident amid

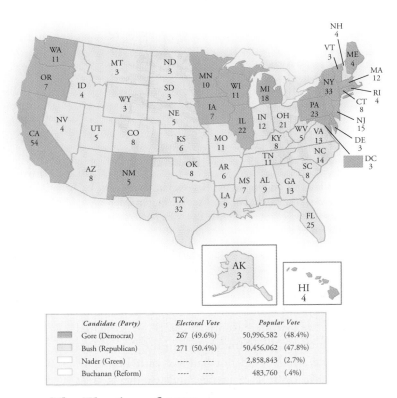

Candidate (Party)	Electoral Vote	Popular Vote
Gore (Democrat)	267 (49.6%)	50,996,582 (48.4%)
Bush (Republican)	271 (50.4%)	50,456,062 (47.8%)
Nader (Green)	---- ----	2,858,843 (2.7%)
Buchanan (Reform)	---- ----	483,760 (.4%)

MAP 32.2 The Election of 2000

The map of the 2000 election reflects the closeness of the electoral vote. Note the extent to which the voters were distributed into a pro-Gore coalition on the coasts and a pro-Bush coalition in the interior of the nation, with some key exceptions in the Middle West and Far West. A comparison with the presidential election of 1896 (see page 564) gives an interesting sense of how partisan alignments changed during the twentieth century.

worldwide celebrations of the calendar change, Americans turned to the onset of the presidential election season.

The 2000 Presidential Campaign: Bush versus Gore

The Republican front-runner was Governor George W. Bush of Texas, the son of the former president. Elected in 1994 and reelected in 1998, the Texan announced for president in mid-1999 and soon amassed a campaign treasury that ultimately reached more than $100 million. Bush promised that he would be "a compassionate conservative" who would "change the tone" in Washington after the partisan discord of the Clinton era. He advocated a $1.6 trillion tax cut and promised to reform the educational system.

Bush lost the New Hampshire primary to Senator John McCain of Arizona, but then won a number of primaries to lock up the delegates needed to control the national convention in Philadelphia. With Richard "Dick" Cheney as his running mate, Bush had a double-digit lead over his Democratic opponent, Vice President Al Gore.

Gore had easily won his party's nomination but had problems separating himself from the scandals of the Clinton years. He also faced a hostile press corps that focused on every lapse to paint Gore as indecisive and opportunistic. Gore emerged from the Democratic convention behind Bush but closed the gap during September 2000. The election hinged on the three presidential debates.

Although neither candidate did well, Bush exceeded the low expectations that media pundits set for him. Gore was better on substance but was labeled arrogant

and condescending. As a result, the race remained tight down to the election. As the votes were counted, the Republicans retained control of the House of Representatives, and the Senate split evenly with 50 Democrats and 50 Republicans. Gore led in the presidential popular vote, but the electoral vote produced a dead heat. It became clear that the state of Florida would determine the result because its 25 electoral votes would push either of the two candidates past the 271 electoral votes needed. State officials put Florida in the Bush column by fewer than 600 ballots after going over the official returns that came in during the week after the election. Gore's forces noted irregularities and flawed ballots in several Democratic counties and sought a recount in those areas.

The Bush camp insisted that the result favoring its man should be final, and charges of fraud, manipulation, and political pressure flashed back and forth throughout November. Finally, the case of *Bush v. Gore* reached the U.S. Supreme Court in mid-December. On the key issue of whether a recount should occur, the Court ruled 5–4 in favor of Bush in a decision that many commentators dubbed both hasty and partisan. Gore accepted the outcome as final and conceded the election.

Terrorism and the Bush Presidency

In office, Bush governed as a conservative who opposed abortion, rolled back environmental regulations, and pursued foreign policy initiatives that placed less reliance on working with the nation's overseas allies. Congress enacted Bush's large tax cut, but the president saw control of the Senate slip out of Republican hands when Senator James Jeffords of Vermont left the GOP to become an independent. The economy was slowing and the stock market experienced substantial losses. Corporations such as Enron and WorldCom led a wave of corporate failures based on corrupt accounting.

September 11, 2001, and After

One issue, international terrorism, had not been of central concern to most Americans during the 1990s. A bombing of the World Trade Center in New York City in 1993 had not shaken the nation out of its indifference to the threat. Other attacks on American embassies in Africa in 1998 and a similar assault on the destroyer USS *Cole* in Yemen in October 2000 had not brought the issue home. The name of the leader of one terrorist group—Osama bin Laden—was largely unknown to the

The three televised debates between George W. Bush and Albert Gore proved unusually important in deciding the outcome of the 2000 presidential election.

© Reuters/CORBIS

DOING HISTORY

Colin Powell and Weapons of Mass Destruction, February 5, 2003

IN THE RUN-UP to the invasion of Iraq in March 2003, one of the decisive moments was the speech that Secretary of State Colin Powell delivered to the Security Council of the United Nations on February 5. Using information supplied to him by George Tenet, director of the Central Intelligence Agency, Powell made the case that Saddam Hussein had weapons of mass destruction and was engaged in the systematic violation of the sanctions of the United Nations. Powell put his personal prestige behind the speech and it had a significant impact on press opinion in the United States and around the world. One of the key points of the address was the charge that Iraq possessed the capability to use biological weapons from mobile laboratories. As the secretary said in his remarks:

"One of the most worrisome things that emerges from the thick intelligence file we have on Iraqi weapons is the existence of mobile production facilities used to make biological agents. Let me take you inside the intelligence file and share with you what we know from eye witness accounts. We have first hand descriptions of biological weapons factories on wheels and on rails.

The trucks and train cars are easily moved and are designed to evade detection by inspectors. In a matter of months they can produce a quantity of biological poison equal to the amount that Iraq claimed to have produced in the years prior to the Gulf War. Although Iraq's mobile production program began in the mid-1990s, U.N. inspectors at time had only vague hints of such programs. Confirmation came later, in the year 2000.

The source was an eye witness, an Iraqi chemical engineer who supervised one of these factories and actually was present during biological agent production runs. He was also at the site when an accident occurred in 1998. Twelve technicians died from exposure to biological agents."

Powell then added that the defector was "currently hiding in another country with the certain knowledge that Saddam Hussein will kill him if he finds him."

Source: "U.S. Secretary of State Colin Powell Addresses the U.N. Security Council," February 5, 2003, at www.whitehouse.gov/news/releases/2003/02/20030205-1.html.

In August 2005, CNN did an analysis about the Powell speech and the assertion that "Saddam had bioweapons mounted on trucks that would be almost impossible to find." The program then went on to say:

"In fact, Secretary Powell was not told that one of the sources he was given as a source of this information had indeed been flagged by the Defense Intelligence Agency as 'a liar, a fabricator,' according to David Kay, the chief weapons inspector for the CIA in Iraq. That source, an Iraqi defector who had never been debriefed by the CIA, was known in the intelligence community as 'Curveball.'"

The program then quoted Powell's chief of staff, Colonel Lawrence Wilkerson, about the secretary's reaction to this news when he learned it from CIA director George Tenet:

"George actually did call the Secretary, and said 'I'm really sorry to have to tell you. We don't believe there were any mobile labs for making biological weapons.' This was the third or fourth telephone call. And I think it's fair to say the Secretary and Mr. Tenet at that point, ceased being close. I mean, you can be sincere and you can be honest and you can believe what you're telling the Secretary, but three or four times on substantive issues like that? It's difficult to maintain any warm feelings."

Source: "Former aide: Powell WMD speech 'lowest point in my life.'" CNN.com, August 19, 2005.

Questions for Reflection

1. How important were the allegations about the existence of weapons of mass destruction in Iraq in shaping American public opinion behind the war against the regime of Saddam Hussein?

2. What pressures existed on the Central Intelligence Agency to find evidence of weapons of mass destruction?

3. How did the revelations about the absence of these weapons in Iraq influence attitudes toward the war in 2004–2005?

Explore additional primary sources related to this chapter on the Wadsworth American History Resource Center or HistoryNOW websites:

http://history.wadsworth.com

http://now.ilrn.com/ayers_etal3e

Flashpoints | Cindy Sheehan and the Iraq War, 2005

By the summer of 2005, the war in Iraq had become a polarizing, contentious issue in the United States. More than 2 years after the invasion that toppled the regime of Saddam Hussein, the American military was fighting a persistent, effective insurgency in Iraq that had killed more than 1,800 U.S. troops and wounded thousands of others. As the war dragged on without a clear end in sight, protests at home intensified. The poll numbers for President George W. Bush sank and support for the war eroded as well. Republicans and Democrats continued to endorse the American presence in Iraq and to resist calls for a withdrawal timetable to reduce the nation's presence in that Middle Eastern country.

As President Bush vacationed during August 2005 at his residence in Crawford, Texas, a single antiwar protester became the focus of media attention. Cindy Sheehan of Vacaville, California, came to Crawford to see President Bush. Her son, Casey Sheehan, had been killed in combat in Iraq in 2004. She had had a brief visit with Bush after her son's death that left her unsatisfied with the president's reaction to her family's sacrifice. Now she wanted to ask what was "the noble cause" in Iraq for which her son had lost his life. The president would not see her, and so Sheehan camped out on a road near the president's place throughout the month of August. The mass media found her lonely vigil compelling television, especially during the relatively quiet month of August when other news was scarce.

Seeing Sheehan as a political enemy, the White House and its conservative allies mounted an attack on her credibility and antiwar political views that verged

Cindy Sheehan, whose son Casey died in combat in the Iraq war, became an antiwar critic of President Bush and took her protest to the president's ranch in Crawford, Texas, in August 2005.

© Jeff Mitchell/Reuters/CORBIS

into personal invective. One pundit argued that the dead Casey Sheehan would have opposed what his mother was doing on his behalf. Sheehan attracted followers herself and "Camp Casey" swelled in size. Counterprotesters came to harass Sheehan herself and demonstrate on behalf of the president and his policies. After first ignoring Sheehan, President Bush began arguing that the sacrifice of the soldiers in Iraq required carrying the war on to a successful conclusion. By the end of August 2005, Sheehan was preparing for a nationwide bus tour to keep the pressure on the president. The hurricane disasters took attention away from Sheehan as August ended, but she intended to persist in her campaign. The rights and wrongs of Sheehan's protest or Bush's policies would not be evident for years, but the episode of the grieving mother outside the president's vacation residence symbolized the many ways in which the Iraq war had revealed serious fault lines in American society.

Questions for Reflection

1. What had happened during the first 2 years of the Iraq war to erode support for President Bush and his policies?

2. What strains did the war place on the American military and their families?

3. In what ways did the presence of the mass media shape the actions of those in favor or against Sheehan's protest?

4. How difficult is it for democratic nations to fight unpopular wars?

average citizen, even though bin Laden, a fundamentalist Muslim of Saudi Arabian origin, sought the violent end of American influence in the Middle East from his base in Afghanistan. Even a frightening report from a prestigious commission in February 2001 warning of a likely terrorist attack on American soil did little to disturb the lack of alertness that pervaded the government and the mass media. President Bush received a briefing on August 6, 2001, that bin Laden was planning an attack somewhere inside the United States.

Ground Zero After the Attack of September 11, 2001

The terrorist attack of September 11, 2001, left many enduring images of the pain that Americans felt when the World Trade Center towers were hit and then collapsed. The area where the debris from the two buildings came down was quickly named Ground Zero as crews worked tirelessly to remove the rubble and look for the remains of the dead. The devastation of the site itself, within the buildings of Lower Manhattan, confirmed the impact of this calamitous event. Yet plans for reconstruction of the area and work to remove the effects of the terrorist assault began almost at once as society rebounded. This concluding image for the Picturing the Past section thus speaks to the continuity of American history and the resilience of the American people in moments of trial and danger. In time this picture, like all the others that have been discussed in this phase of the textbook, will slip into the past and become an artifact of a vanished era. For the moment, with the pain of September 11 still fresh, it reveals the dangers and hope that the country faces as the twenty-first century begins.

© Pool/Don EMMERT/AFP/Getty Images

On the morning of **September 11, 2001,** two hijacked jetliners slammed into the twin towers of the World Trade Center in New York City. Both buildings collapsed into flames and rubble, and almost 3,000 people died. A third airliner crashed into the Pentagon leaving another 200 people dead. A fourth plane fell to the ground in rural Pennsylvania after the passengers attacked the hijackers. All air traffic was grounded for several days, consumer spending slumped, and the weakened economy slipped into recession.

This devastating attack on American soil, which was quickly linked to bin Laden and his terrorist network, Al Qaeda, rattled the nation's morale as it became clear that the terrorists sought nothing less than the destruction of the United States itself. President Bush promised "**war on terrorism**" and launched air strikes and ground troops into Afghanistan to fight its Taliban regime that harbored bin Laden. Soon the Taliban government had

been toppled and Al Qaeda disrupted, but American forces remained in Afghanistan into 2005 as the Taliban resisted the presence of outside troops.

The Bush administration targeted Saddam Hussein and his government in Iraq as the other focus of the antiterrorist effort. The White House argued that Iraq was linked to Al Qaeda, but the evidence for such a connection was thin. Convinced that the invasion of Iraq was necessary, the Bush administration issued warnings that weapons of mass destruction could be used against the United States. This policy led Washington, in the words of a British official, to see that intelligence was "fixed" (or manipulated) around the policy of invading Iraq.

Preparations for war accelerated during 2002 while the White House sought diplomatic support for efforts to curb Hussein and the weapons of mass destruction he possessed. By the autumn of 2002, a United Nations resolution calling on Hussein to admit inspectors had

The American invasion of Iraq in 2003 ended the regime of Saddam Hussein, but the interaction between American troops and the average Iraqi contributed to the resentment at an occupation that fueled the insurgency against the presence of the United States.

Colin Powell's speech to the United Nations on February 5, 2003, was national news, and New Yorkers followed what he said on the giant screen in Times Square in Manhattan.

been passed. Hussein said that his government would agree to the resolution, but his previous flouting of the inspections process made the United States suspicious. The administration moved toward war as 2002 ended. The director of the Central Intelligence Agency, George Tenet, responded to a question from President Bush about where weapons of mass destruction existed in Iraq by saying it was "a slam dunk" that they were present.

The terrorist threat validated George W. Bush as a national leader, and his popularity rose. In the congressional elections of 2002 the Republicans, using a strong organization and ample campaign contributions, rode Bush's campaigning and the public confidence in his leadership to victory. Security issues affected the voters more than did the faltering economy and the Democratic emphasis on domestic problems. The GOP regained control of the Senate and widened its majority in the House. As 2003 began, the president and his party seemed poised to enact their conservative agenda.

Meanwhile, preparations for war with Iraq intensified. Secretary of State Colin Powell argued the case for war in a speech to the United Nations in February 2003. Powell's calm, direct presentation convinced many skeptics that Iraq and Saddam Hussein did indeed possess destructive weapons. Only after the war began did it become apparent that Powell's speech was based on faulty, misleading, and fabricated evidence.

Dissatisfied with the work of the United Nations weapons inspectors, the United States had failed to obtain a second United Nations resolution authorizing force. The strong opposition of the international community to an American invasion of Iraq, combined with diplomatic setbacks by the Bush White House, left Washington frustrated. The Bush administration, along with its only major ally, Great Britain, decided that an attack on Saddam Hussein's brutal regime could not be delayed. Expectations were for a swift resolution of the fighting on the order of what had occurred during the ground war in the Gulf in 1991. Vice President Cheney said that "significant elements" of Hussein's military force were "likely to step aside" once war began. In this mood of confidence about victory, President Bush told the military "let's go" on March 19, 2003, and the war commenced.

Once launched, the powerful offensive of the American coalition swept through Iraq in a dramatic 3-week campaign that left the United States in military control of the nation. Saddam Hussein was either dead or in hiding, the major officials of Iraq were captured, and the symbols of Hussein's rule had been destroyed. On May 1, 2003, President Bush declared the major combat phase of the war at an end.

© Rick Wilking/Reuters/CORBIS

George Bush and John Kerry held three presidential debates in the fall of 2004. Kerry won the debates; Bush triumphed in the election.

© Robert Galbraith/Reuters/CORBIS

The devastation of Hurricane Katrina in late August and early September 2005 left many residents of New Orleans, Louisiana, begging for help from potential rescuers.

Convinced that they would win an easy victory, the Bush administration had not made plans for the occupation of Iraq. Soon they faced an insurgent movement that resisted the American presence through car bombs, improvised explosive devices that blew up under the lightly armored U.S. vehicles, and guerrilla attacks. By September 2005, almost 1,900 American troops had been killed and thousands more wounded. No weapons of mass destruction were found and inspectors concluded that Hussein had abandoned these efforts after his 1991 defeat. Political efforts to provide a new government for Iraq continued well into 2005.

Angry Democrats looked for a winning presidential candidate in 2004 without success. The election pitted Senator John F. Kerry of Massachusetts against President Bush in a bitterly contested race. Bush won a majority of the popular vote and secured 286 electoral votes to 252 for Kerry. The Republicans picked up seats in both the House and the Senate, and spoke of a mandate for their conservative philosophy during the 4 years to come.

Bush's second term, however, got off to a rocky start. An intense effort from Bush to change Social Security toward private accounts encountered Democratic resistance and popular discontent. The war in Iraq, with no end in sight and persistent American casualties each month, became a political liability for the president. His poll ratings slipped in the summer of 2005 to their lowest levels for his time in office.

In August 2005, Hurricane Katrina hit the Gulf Coast, devastating large portions of Alabama, Mississippi, and Louisiana. New Orleans became flooded, and estimates of the loss of life reached into the tens of thousands, although those numbers were eventually revised downward. Although there had been ample warnings of the dangers to the city of a Category 4 hurricane and forecasts of where Katrina would hit as landfall approached, the city, state, and federal governments performed badly in the crisis. The actions of the federal government represented the greatest shortfall in actual results. President Bush had named inept cronies to head the Department of Homeland Security and the Federal Emergency Management Agency, and those two arms of the national government were late, slow, and inefficient in meeting the challenges of the crisis. A terrible disaster worsened because of the shoddy reaction of Washington and the Bush administration.

The result called into question whether the United States could respond to a terrorist attack where there would be no warning in advance. Bush's standing as a national leader also sagged when he failed to cut short his vacation to deal with the crisis and seemed out of touch when he visited the stricken area. By September 2005, the people of the United States wondered whether they really were any safer than they had been when terrorism struck on September 11, 2001.

Conclusion

As the twenty-first century began in January 2001, the United States seemed to be an optimistic and confident society with a strong economy, declining crime rates, and a powerful international position. By the end of the year, the future seemed darker. The terrorist threat posed the likelihood of a long, expensive conflict that might change the openness of American society into a more disciplined and less free nation. Whether the people of the United States fully grasped the danger that they faced remained in doubt.

Beyond the immediate menace of terrorism lay other concerns. The issue of race amid an increasingly diverse population was still unresolved, with the potential to disrupt the social fabric. The exploitation of the environment threatened the degradation of the natural world and the resources on which prosperity depended. Within national politics, there were signs that the public's commitment to democratic values could be fraying. The United States had made a significant historical journey from the time when Europeans first appeared on the North American continent down to the age of the Internet. But the future course of the American Passage was an unfolding story in which the optimism of the nation's history would be a precious asset in the dangerous times that lay ahead for the people of the United States.

The Chapter in Review

In the years following Bill Clinton's election as president in 1992:

- Political turmoil culminated in Republican control of Congress after 1994.
- Racial, ethnic, and cultural tensions continued unabated.
- The rise of the Internet and a growing reliance on computers changed the way people do business and communicate.

- Bill Clinton was impeached and acquitted.
- George W. Bush was elected president in 2000.
- The attacks of September 11, 2001, brought the threat of domestic and foreign terrorism to the forefront of Americans' consciousness.
- A prolonged war in Iraq dragged on.

Making Connections Across Chapters

LOOKING BACK

The 1990s and early 2000s have become contested terrain in the polarized politics of the modern United States. The two most recent presidents, Bill Clinton and George W. Bush, aroused intense feelings for and against them. The emphasis on personality and character that dominated politics also diverted attention from the serious problems that the nation faced as the threat of terrorism and environmental disasters arose.

1. Where does Bill Clinton fit within the recent history of the Democratic party?

2. Why did terrorism not receive more attention during the 1990s?

3. How did the conservatism of George W. Bush resemble or differ from previous conservative presidencies?

4. What are the political strengths and weaknesses of American government in the early twentieth century?

LOOKING AHEAD

This is the last chapter of the book and so these questions are not for further reading. Think about these issues as you ponder the sweep of American history and what could occur during your lifetime as the national passage moves on.

1. What will it take to win the war on terrorism? What should the United States do to resolve the conflict while at the same time preserving its democratic heritage?

2. How different will American society be in 25 years because of the developments in the 1990s and early twenty-first century?

3. Should optimism or pessimism be the dominant theme in evaluating the future of the United States in light of the history you have just finished reading?

Recommended Readings

Benjamin, Daniel, and Steven Simon. *The Age of Sacred Terror* (2002). An excellent look at the roots of terrorism and the American response during the 1990s.

Berman, William C. *From the Center to the Edge: The Politics & Policies of the Clinton Presidency* (2001). A brief, analytic survey of Clinton's record in office.

Clinton, Bill. *My Life* (2004). The former president's memoir of his career and administration.

Conason, Joe, and Gene Lyons. *The Hunting of the President* (2000). Looks at the anti-Clinton campaign and its development.

Diamond, Larry. *Squandered Victory: The American Occupation and the Bungled Effort to Bring Democracy to Iraq* (2005). An examination of the American attempt to make Iraq a democratic nation.

Drew, Elizabeth. *Showdown: The Struggle Between the Gingrich Congress and the Clinton White House* (1996). Drew's account of the internal politics of the Clinton White House in the struggle with Newt Gingrich and the Republicans.

Halberstam, David. *War in a Time of Peace: Bush, Clinton, and the Generals* (2001). Examines the nation's involvement in the Balkans.

Minutaglio, Bill. *First Son: George W. Bush and the Bush Family Dynasty* (1999). Offers biographical background on the future president.

Toobin, Jeffrey. *Too Close to Call* (2001). Considers the events of the disputed presidential election of 2000 in Florida.

Walker, Martin. *The President We Deserve* (1996). A perceptive look at Clinton from a British perspective.

Woodward, Bob. *Bush's War* (2002). Provides an inside look at the early phase of the struggle against terrorism.

Identifications

Review your understanding of the following key terms, people, events, and dates for this chapter (these terms also appear in the Glossary at the end of the book):

William Jefferson "Bill" Clinton
Whitewater
Rodney King
Branch Davidians
Kenneth Starr
Newt Gingrich
Contract with America
Oklahoma City bombing
Louis Farrakhan
Million Man March
political correctness
Monica Lewinsky
Reform party
George W. Bush
September 11, 2001
war on terrorism

Online Sources Guide

Use this listing to find online documents, images, interactive maps, simulations, and other resources related to this chapter:

American History Resource Center

http://history.wadsworth.com/rc/us

Documents

An Account of the Lives of Undocumented Immigrants in Texas (1994)

An Argument in Favor of Immigration Restriction
A Report on the Advantages of Immigration (1997)
Clinton's speech at the Democratic Convention (1996)
Excerpts from the Starr Report

Selected Images

Bill Clinton
Hillary Clinton

Document Exercises

1995 Feminist.com
1996 Green Party of the United States
1999 The Impeachment Trial of President Clinton

HistoryNOW

http://now.ilrn.com/ayers_etal3e

Primary Source Exercises

Windows 95 Is Unveiled to the Public
Impeachment

Appendix

The Declaration of Independence
The Unanimous Declaration of the Thirteen United States of America

When in the Course of human events it becomes necessary for one people to dissolve the political bands which have connected them with another, and to assume among the Powers of the earth, the separate and equal station to which the Laws of Nature and of Nature's God entitle them, a decent respect to the opinions of mankind requires that they should declare the causes which impel them to the separation.

We hold these truths to be self-evident, that all men are created equal, that they are endowed by their Creator with certain unalienable Rights, that among these are Life, Liberty and the pursuit of Happiness. That to secure these rights, Governments are instituted among Men, deriving their just Powers from the consent of the governed. That whenever any Form of Government becomes destructive of these ends, it is the Right of the People to alter or to abolish it, and to institute new Government, laying its foundation on such principles and organizing its Powers in such form, as to them shall seem most likely to effect their Safety and Happiness. Prudence, indeed, will dictate that Governments long established should not be changed for light and transient causes; and accordingly all experience hath shewn, that mankind are more disposed to suffer, while evils are sufferable, than to right themselves by abolishing the forms to which they are accustomed. But when a long train of abuses and usurpations, pursuing invariably the same Object evinces a design to reduce them under absolute Despotism, it is their right, it is their duty, to throw off such Government, and to provide new Guards for their future security. Such has been the patient sufferance of these Colonies; and such is now the necessity which constrains them to alter their former Systems of Government. The history of the present King of Great Britain is a history of repeated injuries and usurpations, all having in direct object the establishment of an absolute Tyranny over these States. To prove this, let Facts be submitted to a candid world.

He has refused his Assent to Laws, the most wholesome and necessary for the public good.

He has forbidden his Governors to pass Laws of immediate and pressing importance, unless suspended in their operation till his Assent should be obtained; and when so suspended, he has utterly neglected to attend to them.

He has refused to pass other Laws for the accommodation of large districts of people, unless those people would relinquish the right of Representation in the Legislature, a right inestimable to them and formidable to tyrants only.

He has called together legislative bodies at places unusual, uncomfortable, and distant from the depository of their Public Records, for the sole Purpose of fatiguing them into compliance with his measures.

He has dissolved Representative Houses repeatedly, for opposing with manly firmness his invasions on the rights of the People.

He has refused for a long time, after such dissolutions, to cause others to be elected; whereby the Legislative Powers, incapable of Annihilation, have returned to the People at large for their exercise; the State remaining in the mean time exposed to all the dangers of invasion from without, and convulsions within.

He has endeavoured to prevent the Population of these States; for that purpose obstructing the Laws for Naturalization of Foreigners; refusing to pass others to encourage their migrations hither, and raising the conditions of new Appropriations of Lands.

He has obstructed the Administration of Justice, by refusing his Assent to Laws for establishing Judiciary Powers.

He has made Judges dependent on his Will alone, for the tenure of their offices, and the amount and payment of their salaries.

He has erected a multitude of New Offices, and sent hither swarms of Officers to harass our People, and eat out their substance.

He has kept among us, in times of peace, Standing Armies without the Consent of our legislatures.

He has affected to render the Military independent of and superior to the Civil Power.

He has combined with others to subject us to a jurisdiction foreign to our constitution, and unacknowledged by our laws; giving his Assent to their Acts of pretended Legislation:

Text is reprinted from the facsimile of the engrossed copy in the National Archives. The original spelling, capitalization, and punctuation have been retained. Paragraphing has been added.

For Quartering large bodies of armed troops among us:

For protecting them, by a mock Trial, from Punishment for any Murders which they should commit on the Inhabitants of these States:

For cutting off our Trade with all parts of the world:

For imposing Taxes on us without our Consent:

For depriving us in many cases, of the benefits of Trial by Jury:

For transporting us beyond Seas to be tried for pretended offences:

For abolishing the free System of English Laws in a neighbouring Province, establishing therein an Arbitrary government, and enlarging its Boundaries so as to render it at once an example and fit instrument for introducing the same absolute rule into these Colonies:

For taking away our Charters, abolishing our most valuable Laws, and altering fundamentally the Forms of our Governments:

For suspending our own Legislatures, and declaring themselves invested with Power to legislate for us in all cases whatsoever.

He has abdicated Government here, by declaring us out of his Protection, and waging War against us.

He has plundered our seas, ravaged our Coasts, burnt our towns, and destroyed the lives of our people.

He is at this time transporting large Armies of foreign Mercenaries to compleat the works of death, desolation and tyranny, already begun with circumstances of Cruelty and perfidy scarcely paralleled in the most barbarous ages, and totally unworthy the Head of a civilized nation.

He has constrained our fellow Citizens taken Captive on the high Seas to bear Arms against their Country, to become the executioners of their friends and Brethren, or to fall themselves by their Hands.

He has excited domestic insurrections amongst us, and has endeavoured to bring on the inhabitants of our frontiers, the merciless Indian Savages, whose known rule of warfare, is an undistinguished destruction of all ages, sexes and conditions.

In every stage of these Oppressions We have Petitioned for Redress in the most humble terms: Our repeated Petitions have been answered only by repeated injury. A Prince, whose character is thus marked by every act which may define a Tyrant, is unfit to be the ruler of a free People.

Nor have We been wanting in attentions to our British brethren. We have warned them from time to time of attempts by their legislature to extend an unwarrantable jurisdiction over us. We have reminded them of the circumstances of our emigration and settlement here. We have appealed to their native justice and magnanimity, and we have conjured them by the ties of our common kindred to disavow thee usurpations, which, would inevitably interrupt our connections and correspondence. They too have been deaf to the voice of justice and of consanguinity. We must, therefore, acquiesce in the necessity, which denounces our Separation, and hold them, as we hold the rest of mankind, Enemies in War, in Peace Friends.

We, therefore, the Representatives of the United States of America, in General Congress, Assembled, appealing to the Supreme Judge of the world for the rectitude of our intentions, do, in the Name, and by Authority of the good People of these Colonies, solemnly publish and declare, That these United Colonies are, and of Right ought to be Free and Independent States; that they are Absolved from all Allegiance to the British Crown, and that all political connection between them and the State of Great Britain, is and ought to be totally dissolved; and that, as Free and Independent States, they have full Power to levy War, conclude Peace, contract Alliances, establish Commerce, and to do all other Acts and Things which Independent States may of right do. And for the support of this Declaration, with a firm reliance on the protection of divine Providence, we mutually pledge to each other our Lives, our Fortunes and our sacred Honor.

The Constitution of the United States of America

We the People of the United States, in Order to form a more perfect Union, establish Justice, insure domestic Tranquility, provide for the common defence, promote the general Welfare, and secure the Blessings of Liberty to ourselves and our Posterity, do ordain and establish this Constitution for the United States of America.

Article I.

Section 1. All legislative Powers herein granted shall be vested in a Congress of the United States, which shall consist of a Senate and House of Representatives.

Section 2. The House of Representatives shall be composed of Members chosen every second Year by the People of the several States, and the Electors in each State shall have the Qualifications requisite for Electors of the most numerous Branch of the State Legislature.

No Person shall be a Representative who shall not have attained to the Age of twenty five Years, and been seven Years a Citizen of the United States, and who shall not, when elected, be an Inhabitant of that State in which he shall be chosen.

Representatives and direct Taxes[1] shall be apportioned among the several States which may be included within this Union, according to their respective Numbers, which shall be determined by adding to the whole Number of free Persons, including those bound to Service for a Term of Years, and excluding Indians not taxed, three fifths of all other Persons.[2] The actual Enumeration shall be made within three Years after the first Meeting of the Congress of the United States, and within every subsequent Term of ten Years, in such Manner as they shall by Law direct. The Number of Representatives shall not exceed one for every thirty Thousand, but each State shall have at Least one Representative; and until such enumeration shall be made, the State of New Hampshire shall be entitled to chuse three; Massachusetts eight; Rhode Island and Providence Plantations one; Connecticut five; New York six; New Jersey four; Pennsylvania eight; Delaware one; Maryland six; Virginia ten; North Carolina five; South Carolina five; and Georgia three.

When vacancies happen in the Representation from any State, the Executive Authority thereof shall issue Writs of Election to fill such Vacancies.

The House of Representatives shall chuse their Speaker and other Officers; and shall have the sole Power of Impeachment.

Section 3. The Senate of the United States shall be composed of two Senators from each State, chosen by the Legislature thereof, for six Years; and each Senator shall have one Vote.[3]

Immediately after they shall be assembled in Consequence of the first Election, they shall be divided as equally as may be into three Classes. The Seats of the Senators of the first Class shall be vacated at the Expiration of the second Year, of the second Class at the Expiration of the fourth Year, and of the third Class at the Expiration of the sixth Year, so that one third may be chosen every second Year; and if Vacancies happen by Resignation, or otherwise, during the Recess of the Legislature of any State, the Executive thereof may make temporary Appointments until the next Meeting of the Legislature, which shall then fill such Vacancies.[4]

No Person shall be a Senator who shall not have attained to the Age of thirty Years, and been nine Years a Citizen of the United States, and who shall not, when elected, be an Inhabitant of that State for which he shall be chosen.

The Vice President of the United States shall be President of the Senate, but shall have no Vote, unless they be equally divided.

The Senate shall chuse their other Officers, and also a President pro tempore, in the Absence of the Vice President, or when he shall exercise the Office of President of the United States.

The Senate shall have the sole Power to try all Impeachments. When sitting for that Purpose, they shall be on Oath or Affirmation. When the President of the United States is tried, the Chief Justice shall preside: And no Person shall be convicted without the Concurrence of two thirds of the Members present.

Judgment in Cases of Impeachment shall not extend further than to removal from Office, and disqualification to hold and enjoy any Office of honor, Trust or Profit under the United States: but the Party convicted shall nevertheless be liable and subject to Indictment, Trial, Judgment and Punishment, according to Law.

Section 4. The Times, Places and Manner of holding Elections for Senators and Representatives, shall be

---

Text is from the engrossed copy in the National Archives. Original spelling, capitalization, and punctuation have been retained.
[1] Modified by the Sixteenth Amendment.
[2] Replaced by the Fourteenth Amendment.

---

[3] Superseded by the Seventeenth Amendment.
[4] Modified by the Seventeenth Amendment.

prescribed in each State by the Legislature thereof, but the Congress may at any time by Law make or alter such Regulation, except as to the Places of chusing Senators.

The Congress shall assemble at least once in every Year, and such Meeting shall be on the first Monday in December, unless they shall by Law appoint a different Day.[5]

Section 5. Each House shall be the Judge of the Elections, Returns and Qualifications of its own Members, and a Majority of each shall constitute a Quorum to do Business; but a smaller Number may adjourn from day to day, and may be authorized to compel the Attendance of absent Members, in such Manner, and under such Penalties as each House may provide.

Each House may determine the Rules of its Proceedings, punish its Members for disorderly Behaviour, and, with the Concurrence of two thirds, expel a Member.

Each House shall keep a Journal of its Proceedings, and from time to time publish the same, excepting such Parts as may in their Judgment require Secrecy; and the Yeas and Nays of the Members of either House on any question shall, at the Desire of one fifth of those Present, be entered on the Journal.

Neither House, during the Session of Congress, shall, without the Consent of the other, adjourn for more than three days, nor to any other Place than that in which the two Houses shall be sitting.

Section 6. The Senators and Representatives shall receive a Compensation for their Services, to be ascertained by Law, and paid out of the Treasury of the United States. They shall in all Cases, except Treason, Felony and Breach of the Peace, be privileged from Arrest during their Attendance at the Session of their respective Houses, and in going to and returning from the same; and for any Speech or Debate in either House, they shall not be questioned in any other Place.

No Senator or Representative shall, during the Time for which he was elected, be appointed to any civil Office under the Authority of the United States, which shall have been created, or the Emoluments whereof shall have been encreased during such time; and no Person holding any Office under the United States, shall be a Member of either House during his Continuance in Office.

Section 7. All Bills for raising Revenue shall originate in the House of Representatives; but the Senate may propose or concur with Amendments as on other Bills.

Every Bill which shall have passed the House of Representatives and the Senate shall, before it become a Law, be presented to the President of the United States; If he approve he shall sign it, but if not he shall return it, with his Objections to that House in which it shall have originated, who shall enter the Objections at large on their Journal, and proceed to reconsider it. If after such Reconsideration two thirds of that House shall agree to pass the Bill, it shall be sent, together with the Objections, to the other House, by which it shall likewise be reconsidered, and if approved by two thirds of that House, it shall become a Law. But in all such Cases the Votes of both Houses shall be determined by yeas and Nays, and the Names of the Persons voting for and against the Bill shall be entered on the Journal of each House respectively. If any Bill shall not be returned by the President within ten Days (Sundays excepted) after it shall have been presented to him, the Same shall be a Law, in like Manner as if he had signed it, unless the Congress by their Adjournment prevent its Return, in which Case it shall not be a Law.

Every Order, Resolution, or Vote to which the Concurrence of the Senate and House of Representatives may be necessary (except on a question of Adjournment) shall be presented to the President of the United States; and before the Same shall take Effect, shall be approved by him, or being disapproved by him shall be repassed by two thirds of the Senate and House of Representatives, according to the Rules and Limitations prescribed in the Case of a Bill.

Section 8. The Congress shall have power To lay and collect Taxes, Duties, Imposts and Excises, to pay the Debts and provide for the common Defence and general Welfare of the United States; but all Duties, Imposts and Excises shall be uniform throughout the United States;

To borrow Money on the credit of the United States;

To regulate Commerce with foreign Nations, and among the several States, and with the Indian Tribes;

To establish an uniform Rule of Naturalization, and uniform Laws on the subject of Bankruptcies throughout the United States;

To coin Money, regulate the Value thereof, and of foreign Coin, and fix the Standard of Weights and Measures;

To provide for the Punishment of counterfeiting the Securities and current Coin of the United States;

To establish Post Offices and post Roads;

To promote the Progress of Science and useful Arts, by securing for limited Times to Authors and Inventors the exclusive Right to their respective Writings and Discoveries;

To constitute Tribunals inferior to the supreme Court;

To define and punish Piracies and Felonies committed on the high Seas, and Offences against the Law of Nations;

---

[5]Superseded by the Twentieth Amendment.

To declare War, grant Letters of Marque and Reprisal, and make Rules concerning Captures on Land and Water;

To raise and support Armies, but no Appropriation of Money to that Use shall be for a longer Term than two Years;

To provide and maintain a Navy;

To make Rules for the Government and Regulation of the land and naval Forces;

To provide for calling forth the Militia to execute the Laws of the Union, suppress Insurrections and repel Invasions;

To provide for organizing, arming, and disciplining, the Militia, and for governing such Part of them as may be employed in the Service of the United States, reserving to the States respectively, the Appointment of the Officers, and the Authority of training the Militia according to the discipline prescribed by Congress;

To exercise exclusive Legislation in all Cases whatsoever, over such District (not exceeding ten Miles square) as may, by Cession of particular States, and the Acceptance of Congress, become the Seat of the Government of the United States, and to exercise like Authority over all Places purchased by the Consent of the Legislature of the State in which the Same shall be, for the Erection of Forts, Magazines, Arsenals, dock-Yards, and other needful Buildings;—And

To make all Laws which shall be necessary and proper for carrying into Execution the foregoing Powers, and all other Powers vested by this Constitution in the Government of the United States, or in any Department or Officer thereof.

Section 9. The Migration or Importation of such Persons as any of the States now existing shall think proper to admit, shall not be prohibited by the Congress prior to the Year one thousand eight hundred and eight, but a Tax or duty may be imposed on such Importation, not exceeding ten dollars for each Person.

The Privilege of the Writ of Habeas Corpus shall not be suspended, unless when in Cases of Rebellion or Invasion the public Safety may require it.

No Bill of Attainder or ex post facto Law shall be passed.

No Capitation, or other direct, Tax shall be laid, unless in Proportion to the Census or Enumeration herein before directed to be taken.

No Tax or Duty shall be laid on Articles exported from any State.

No Preference shall be given by any Regulation of Commerce or Revenue to the Ports of one State over those of another: nor shall Vessels bound to, or from, one State, be obliged to enter, clear, or pay Duties in another.

No Money shall be drawn from the Treasury, but in Consequence of Appropriations made by Law, and a regular Statement and Account of the Receipts and Expenditures of all public Money shall be published from time to time.

No Title of Nobility shall be granted by the United States: And no Person holding any Office of Profit or Trust under them, shall, without the Consent of the Congress, accept of any present, Emolument, Office, or Title, of any kind whatever, from any King, Prince, or foreign State.

Section 10. No State shall enter into any Treaty, Alliance, or Confederation; grant Letters of Marque and Reprisal; coin Money; emit Bills of Credit; make any Thing but gold and silver Coin a Tender in Payment of Debts; pass any Bill of Attainder, ex post facto Law, or Law impairing the Obligation of Contracts, or grant any Title of Nobility.

No State shall, without the Consent of the Congress, lay any Imposts or Duties on Imports or Exports, except what may be absolutely necessary for executing its inspection Laws: and the net Produce of all Duties and Imposts, laid by any State on Imports or Exports, shall be for the Use of the Treasury of the United States; and all such Laws shall be subject to the Revision and Controul of the Congress.

No State shall, without the Consent of Congress, lay any Duty of Tonnage, keep Troops, or Ships of War in time of Peace, enter into any Agreement or Compact with another State, or with a foreign Power, or engage in War, unless actually invaded, or in such imminent Danger as will not admit of delay.

Article II.

Section 1. The executive Power shall be vested in a President of the United States of America. He shall hold his Office during the Term of four Years, and, together with the Vice President, chosen for the same Term, be elected, as follows:

Each State shall appoint, in such Manner as the Legislature thereof may direct, a Number of Electors, equal to the whole Number of Senators and Representatives to which the State may be entitled in the Congress: but no Senator or Representative, or Person holding an Office of Trust or Profit under the United States, shall be appointed an Elector.

The Electors shall meet in their respective States, and vote by Ballot for two Persons, of whom one at least shall not be an Inhabitant of the same State with themselves. And they shall make a List of all the Persons voted for, and of the Number of Votes for each; which List they shall sign and certify, and transmit sealed to the

Seat of the Government of the United States, directed to the President of the Senate. The President of the Senate shall, in the Presence of the Senate and House of Representatives, open all the Certificates, and the Votes shall then be counted. The Person having the greatest Number of Votes shall be the President, if such Number be a Majority of the whole Number of Electors appointed; and if there be more than one who have such Majority, and have an equal Number of Votes, then the House of Representatives shall immediately chuse by Ballot one of them for President; and if no Person have a Majority, then from the five highest on the List the said House shall in like Manner chuse the President. But in chusing the President, the Votes shall be taken by States, the Representation from each State having one Vote; A quorum for this Purpose shall consist of a Member or Members from two thirds of the States, and a Majority of all the States shall be necessary to a Choice. In every Case, after the Choice of the President, the Person having the greatest Number of Votes of the Electors shall be the Vice President. But if there should remain two or more who have equal Votes, the Senate shall chuse from them by Ballot the Vice President.[6]

The Congress may determine the Time of chusing the Electors, and the Day on which they shall give their Votes; which Day shall be the same throughout the United States.

No Person except a natural born Citizen, or a Citizen of the United States, at the time of the Adoption of this Constitution, shall be eligible to the Office of President, neither shall any Person be eligible to that Office who shall not have attained to the Age of thirty five Years, and been fourteen Years a Resident within the United States.

In Case of the Removal of the President from Office, or of his Death, Resignation, or Inability to discharge the Powers and Duties of the said Office, the Same shall devolve onthe Vice President, and the Congress may by Law provide for the Case of Removal, Death, Resignation or Inability, both of the President and Vice President, declaring what Officer shall then act as President, and such Officer shall act accordingly, until the Disability be removed, or a President shall be elected.[7]

The President shall, at stated Times, receive for his Services, a Compensation, which shall neither be encreased nor diminished during the Period for which he shall have been elected, and he shall not receive within that Period any other Emolument from the United States, or any of them.

Before he enter on the Execution of his Office, he shall take the following Oath or Affirmation:—"I do solemnly swear (or affirm) that I will faithfully execute the Office of President of the United States, and will to the best of my Ability, preserve, protect and defend the Constitution of the United States."

Section 2. The President shall be Commander in Chief of the Army and Navy of the United States, and of the Militia of the several States, when called into the actual Service of the United States; he may require the Opinion, in writing, of the principal Officer in each of the executive Departments, upon any Subject relating to the Duties of their respective Offices, and he shall have Power to grant Reprieves and Pardons for Offences against the United States, except in Cases of Impeachment.

He shall have Power, by and with the Advice and Consent of the Senate, to make Treaties, provided two thirds of the Senators present concur; and he shall nominate, and by and with the Advice and Consent of the Senate, shall appoint Ambassadors, other public Ministers and Consuls, Judges of the supreme Court, and all other Officers of the United States, whose Appointments are not herein otherwise provided for, and which shall be established by Law; but the Congress may by Law vest the Appointment of such inferior Officers, as they think proper, in the President alone, in the Courts of Law, or in the Heads of Departments.

The President shall have Power to fill up all Vacancies that may happen during the Recess of the Senate, by granting Commissions which shall expire at the End of their next Session.

Section 3. He shall from time to time give the Congress Information of the State of the Union, and recommend to their Consideration such Measures as he shall judge necessary and expedient; he may, on extraordinary Occasions, convene both Houses, or either of them, and in Case of Disagreement between them, with Respect to the Time of Adjournment, he may adjourn them to such Time as he shall think proper; he shall receive Ambassadors and other public Ministers; he shall take Care that the Laws be faithfully executed, and shall Commission all the Officers of the United States.

Section 4. The President, Vice President and all civil Officers of the United States, shall be removed from Office on Impeachment for, and Conviction of, Treason, Bribery, or other high Crimes and Misdemeanors.

Article III.

Section 1. The judicial Power of the United States, shall be vested in one supreme Court, and in such inferior Courts as the Congress may from time to time ordain

---

[6] Superseded by the Twelfth Amendment.
[7] Modified by the Twenty-fifth Amendment.

and establish. The Judges, both of the supreme and inferior Courts, shall hold their Offices during good Behaviour, and shall, at stated Times, receive for their Services, a Compensation, which shall not be diminished during their Continuance in Office.

Section 2. The judicial Power shall extend to all Cases, in Law and Equity, arising under this Constitution, the Laws of the United States, and Treaties made, or which shall be made, under their Authority;—to all Cases affecting Ambassadors, other public Ministers and Consuls;—to all Cases of admiralty and maritime Jurisdiction;—to Controversies to which the United States shall be a Party;—to Controversies between two or more States;—between a State and Citizens of another State;[8]—between Citizens of different States,—between Citizens of the same State claiming Lands under Grants of different States, and between a State, or the Citizens thereof, and foreign States, Citizens or Subjects.

In all Cases affecting Ambassadors, other public Ministers and Consuls, and those in which a State shall be Party, the supreme Court shall have original Jurisdiction. In all the other Cases before mentioned, the supreme Court shall have appellate Jurisdiction, both as to Law and Fact, with such Exceptions, and under such Regulations as the Congress shall make.

The Trial of all Crimes, except in Cases of Impeachment, shall be by Jury; and such Trial shall be held in the State where the said Crimes shall have been committed; but when not committed within any State, the Trial shall be at such Place or Places as the Congress may by Law have directed.

Section 3. Treason against the United States, shall consist only in levying War against them, or in adhering to their Enemies, giving them Aid and Comfort. No Person shall be convicted of Treason unless on the Testimony of two Witnesses to the same overt Act, or on Confession in open Court.

The Congress shall have Power to declare the Punishment of Treason, but no Attainder of Treason shall work Corruption of Blood, or Forfeiture except during the Life of the Person attainted.

Article IV.

Section 1. Full Faith and Credit shall be given in each State to the public Acts, Records, and judicial Proceedings of every other State. And the Congress may by general Laws prescribe the Manner in which such Acts, Records and Proceedings shall be proved, and the Effect thereof.

Section 2. The Citizens of each State shall be entitled to all Privileges and Immunities of Citizens in the several States.

A Person charged in any State with Treason, Felony, or other Crime, who shall flee from Justice, and be found in another State, shall on Demand of the executive Authority of the State from which he fled, be delivered up, to be removed to the State having Jurisdiction of the Crime.

No Person held to Service or Labour in one State, under the Laws thereof, escaping into another, shall, in Consequence of any Law or Regulation therein, be discharged from such Service or Labour, but shall be delivered up on Claim of the Party to whom such Service or Labour may be due.

Section 3. New States may be admitted by the Congress into this Union; but no new State shall be formed or erected within the Jurisdiction of any other State, nor any State be formed by the Junction of two or more States, or Parts of States, without the Consent of the Legislatures of the States concerned as well as of the Congress.

The Congress shall have Power to dispose of and make all needful Rules and Regulations respecting the Territory or other Property belonging to the United States; and nothing in this Constitution shall be so construed as to Prejudice any Claims of the United States, or of any particular State.

Section 4. The United States shall guarantee to every State in this Union a Republican Form of Government, and shall protect each of them against Invasion; and on Application of the Legislature, or of the Executive (when the Legislature cannot be convened) against domestic Violence.

Article V.

The Congress, whenever two thirds of both Houses shall deem it necessary, shall propose Amendments to this Constitution, or, on the Application of the Legislatures of two thirds of the several States, shall call a Convention for proposing Amendments, which, in either Case, shall be valid to all Intents and Purposes, as Part of this Constitution, when ratified by the Legislatures of three fourths of the several States, or by Conventions in three fourths thereof, as the one or the other Mode of Ratification may be proposed by the Congress; Provided that no Amendment which may be made prior to the Year One thousand eight hundred and eight shall in any Manner affect the first and fourth Clauses in the Ninth Section of the first Article; and that no State, without its Consent, shall be deprived of its equal Suffrage in the Senate.

[8]Modified by the Eleventh Amendment.

Article VI.

All Debts contracted and Engagements entered into, before the Adoption of this Constitution, shall be as valid against the United States under this Constitution, as under the Confederation.

This Constitution, and the Laws of the United States which shall be made in Pursuance thereof; and all Treaties made, or which shall be made, under the Authority of the United States, shall be the supreme Law of the Land; and the Judges in every State shall be bound thereby, any Thing in the Constitution or Laws of any State to the Contrary notwithstanding.

The Senators and Representatives before mentioned, and the Members of the several State Legislatures, and all executive and judicial Officers, both of the United States and of the several States, shall be bound by Oath or Affirmation, to support this Constitution; but no religious Test shall ever be required as a Qualification to any Office or public Trust under the United States.

Article VII.

The Ratification of the Conventions of nine States, shall be sufficient for the Establishment of this Constitution between the States so ratifying the Same.

Done in Convention by the Unanimous Consent of the States present the Seventeenth Day of September in the Year of our Lord one thousand seven hundred and Eighty seven and of the Independence of the United States of America the Twelfth. In witness whereof We have hereunto subscribed our Names,

Articles in Addition to, and Amendment of, the Constitution of the United States of America, Proposed by Congress, and Ratified by the Legislatures of the Several States, Pursuant to the Fifth Article of the Original Constitution.

Amendment I[9]

Congress shall make no law respecting an establishment of religion, or prohibiting the free exercise there-of; or abridging the freedom of speech, or of the press; or the right of the people peaceably to assemble, and to petition the Government for a redress of grievances.

Amendment II

A well regulated Militia, being necessary to the security of a free State, the right of the people to keep and bear Arms shall not be infringed.

---

[9]The first ten amendments were passed by Congress September 25, 1789. They were ratified by three-fourths of the states December 15, 1791.

Amendment III

No Soldier shall, in time of peace, be quartered in any house, without the consent of the Owner, nor in time of war, but in a manner to be prescribed by law.

Amendment IV

The right of the people to be secure in their persons, houses, papers, and effects, against unreasonable searches and seizures, shall not be violated, and no Warrants shall issue, but upon probable cause, supported by Oath or affirmation, and particularly describing the place to be searched, and the persons or things to be seized.

Amendment V

No person shall be held to answer for a capital or otherwise infamous crime, unless on a presentment or indictment of a Grand Jury, except in cases arising in the land or naval forces, or in the Militia, when in actual service in time of War or public danger; nor shall any person be subject for the same offence to be twice put in jeopardy of life or limb; nor shall be compelled in any criminal case to be a witness against himself, nor be deprived of life, liberty, or property, without due process of law; nor shall private property be taken for public use, without just compensation.

Amendment VI

In all criminal prosecutions, the accused shall enjoy the right to a speedy and public trial, by an impartial jury of the State and district wherein the crime shall have been committed, which district shall have been previously ascertained by law, and to be informed of the nature and cause of the accusation; to be confronted with the witnesses against him; to have compulsory process for obtaining witnesses in his favor, and to have the Assistance of Counsel for his defence.

Amendment VII

In suits at common law, where the value in controversy shall exceed twenty dollars, the right of trial by jury shall be preserved, and no fact tried by a jury, shall be otherwise reexamined in any Court of the United States, than according to the rules of the common law.

Amendment VIII

Excessive bail shall not be required, nor excessive fines imposed, nor cruel and unusual punishments inflicted.

Amendment IX

The enumeration in the Constitution, of certain rights, shall not be construed to deny or disparage others retained by the people.

Amendment X

The powers not delegated to the United States by the Constitution; nor prohibited by it to the States, are reserved to the States respectively, or to the people.

Amendment XI[10]

The Judicial power of the United States shall not be construed to extend to any suit in law or equity, commenced or prosecuted against one of the United States by Citizens of another State, or by Citizens or Subjects of any Foreign State.

Amendment XII[11]

The Electors shall meet in their respective States and vote by ballot for President and Vice-President, one of whom, at least, shall not be an inhabitant of the same State with themselves; they shall name in their ballots the person voted for as President, and in distinct ballots the person voted for as Vice-President, and they shall make distinct lists of all persons voted for as President, and of all persons voted for as Vice-President, and of the number of votes for each, which lists they shall sign and certify, and transmit sealed to the seat of the government of the United States, directed to the President of the Senate;—The President of the Senate shall, in the presence of the Senate and House of Representatives, open all the certificates and the votes shall then be counted;—The person having the greatest number of votes for President, shall be the President, if such number be a majority of the whole number of Electors appointed; and if no person have such majority, then from the persons having the highest numbers not exceeding three on the list of those voted for as President, the House of Representatives shall choose immediately, by ballot, the President. But in choosing the President, the votes shall be taken by states, the representation from each state having one vote; a quorum for this purpose shall consist of a member or members from two-thirds of the states, and a majority of all the states shall be necessary to a choice. And if the House of Representatives shall not choose a President whenever the right of choice shall

devolve upon them, before the fourth day of March next following, then the Vice-President shall act as President, as in the case of the death or other constitutional disability of the President.—The person having the greatest number of votes as Vice-President, shall be the Vice-President, if such number be a majority of the whole number of Electors appointed, and if no person have a majority, then from the two highest numbers on the list, the Senate shall choose the Vice-President; a quorum for the purpose shall consist of two-thirds of the whole number of Senators, and a majority of the whole number shall be necessary to a choice. But no person constitutionally ineligible to the office of President shall be eligible to that of Vice-President of the United States.

Amendment XIII[12]

Section 1. Neither slavery nor involuntary servitude, except as a punishment for crime whereof the party shall have been duly convicted, shall exist within the United States, or any place subject to their jurisdiction.

Section 2. Congress shall have power to enforce this article by appropriate legislation.

Amendment XIV[13]

Section 1. All persons born or naturalized in the United States, and subject to the jurisdiction thereof, are citizens of the United States and of the State wherein they reside. No State shall make or enforce any law which shall abridge the privileges or immunities of citizens of the United States; nor shall any State deprive any person of life, liberty, or property, without due process of law; nor deny to any person within its jurisdiction the equal protection of the laws.

Section 2. Representatives shall be apportioned among the several States according to their respective numbers, counting the whole number of persons in each State, excluding Indians not taxed. But when the right to vote at any election for the choice of electors for President and Vice-President of the United States, Representatives in Congress, the Executive and Judicial officers of a State, or the members of the Legislature thereof, is denied to any of the male inhabitants of such State, being twenty-one years of age, and citizens of the United States, or in any way abridged, except for participation in rebellion, or other crime, the basis of representation therein shall be reduced in the proportion which the number of such

---

[10]Passed March 4, 1794. Ratified January 23, 1795.
[11]Passed December 9, 1803. Ratified June 15, 1804.

[12]Passed January 31, 1865. Ratified December 6, 1865.
[13]Passed June 13, 1866. Ratified July 9, 1868.

male citizens shall bear to the whole number of male citizens twenty-one years of age in such State.

Section 3. No person shall be a Senator or Representative in Congress, or elector of President and Vice-President, or hold any office, civil or military, under the United States, or under any State, who, having previously taken an oath, as a member of Congress, or as an officer of the United States, or as a member of any State legislature, or as an executive or judicial officer of any State, to support the Constitution of the United States, shall have engaged in insurrection or rebellion against the same, or given aid or comfort to the enemies thereof. But Congress may by a vote of two-thirds of each House, remove such disability.

Section 4. The validity of the public debt of the United States, authorized by law, including debts incurred for payment of pensions and bounties for services in suppressing insurrection or rebellion, shall not be questioned. But neither the United States nor any State shall assume or pay any debt or obligation incurred in aid of insurrection or rebellion against the United States, or any claim for the loss or emancipation of any slave; but all such debts, obligations, and claims shall be held illegal and void.

Section 5. The Congress shall have the power to enforce, by appropriate legislation, the provisions of this article.

Amendment XV[14]

Section 1. The right of citizens of the United States to vote shall not be denied or abridged by the United States or by any State on account of race, color, or previous conditions of servitude—

Section 2. The Congress shall have power to enforce this article by appropriate legislation.

Amendment XVI

The Congress shall have power to lay and collect taxes on incomes, from whatever source derived, without apportionment among the several States, and without regard to any census or enumeration.

Amendment XVII[15]

The Senate of the United States shall be composed of two Senators from each State, elected by the people thereof, for six years; and each Senator shall have one vote. The electors in each State shall have the qualifications requisite for electors of the most numerous branch of the State legislatures.

When vacancies happen in the representation of any State in the Senate, the executive authority of such State shall issue writs of election to fill such vacancies: *Provided,* That the legislature of any State may empower the executive thereof to make temporary appointments until the people fill the vacancies by election as the legislature may direct.

This amendment shall not be so construed as to affect the election or term of any Senator chosen before it becomes valid as part of the Constitution.

Amendment XVIII[16]

Section 1. After one year from the ratification of this article the manufacture, sale, or transportation of intoxicating liquors within, the importation thereof into, or the exportation thereof from the United States and all territory subject to the jurisdiction thereof for beverage purposes is hereby prohibited.

Section 2. The Congress and the several States shall have concurrent power to enforce this article by appropriate legislation.

Section 3. This article shall be inoperative unless it shall have been ratified as an amendment to the Constitution by the legislatures of the several States, as provided in the Constitution, within seven years from the date of the submission hereof to the States by the Congress.

Amendment XIX[17]

The right of citizens of the United States to vote shall not be denied or abridged by the United States or by any State on account of sex.

Congress shall have power to enforce this article by appropriate legislation.

Amendment XX[18]

Section 1. The terms of the President and Vice-President shall end at noon on the 20th day of January, and the terms of Senators and Representatives at noon on the 3d day of January, of the years in which such terms would have ended if this article had not been ratified; and the terms of their successors shall then begin.

---

[14]Passed February 26, 1869. Ratified February 2, 1870.
[15]Passed May 13, 1912. Ratified April 8, 1913.

[16]Passed December 18, 1917. Ratified January 16, 1919.
[17]Passed June 4, 1919. Ratified August 18, 1920.
[18]Passed March 2, 1932. Ratified January 23, 1933.

Section 2. The Congress shall assemble at least once in every year, and such meeting shall begin at noon on the 3d day of January, unless they shall by law appoint a different day.

Section 3. If, at the time fixed for the beginning of the term of the President, the President elect shall have died, the Vice-President elect shall become President. If a President shall not have been chosen before the time fixed for the beginning of his term, or if the President elect shall have failed to qualify, then the Vice-President elect shall act as President until a President shall have qualified; and the Congress may by law provide for the case wherein neither a President elect nor a Vice-President elect shall have qualified, declaring who shall then act as President, or the manner in which one who is to act shall be selected, and such person shall act accordingly until a President or Vice-President shall have qualified.

Section 4. The Congress may by law provide for the case of the death of any of the persons from whom the House of Representatives may choose a President whenever the right of choice shall have devolved upon them, and for the case of the death of any of the persons from whom the Senate may choose a Vice-President whenever the right of choice shall have devolved upon them.

Section 5. Sections 1 and 2 shall take effect on the 15th day of October following the ratification of this article.

Section 6. This article shall be inoperative unless it shall have been ratified as an amendment to the Constitution by the legislatures of three-fourths of the several States within seven years from the date of its submission.

Amendment XXI[19]

Section 1. The eighteenth article of amendment to the Constitution of the United States is hereby repealed.

Section 2. The transportation or importation into any State, Territory, or possession of the United States for delivery or use therein of intoxicating liquors, in violation of the laws thereof, is hereby prohibited.

Section 3. This article shall be inoperative unless it shall have been ratified as an amendment to the Constitution by conventions in the several States, as provided in the Constitution, within seven years from the date of the submission hereof to the States by the Congress.

Amendment XXII[20]

No person shall be elected to the office of the President more than twice, and no person who has held the office of President, or acted as President, for more than two years of a term to which some other person was elected President shall be elected to the office of the President more than once.

But this Article shall not apply to any person holding the office of President when this Article was proposed by the Congress, and shall not prevent any person who may be holding the office of President, or acting as President, during the term within which this Article becomes operative from holding the office of President or acting as President during the remainder of such term.

Amendment XXIII[21]

Section 1. The District constituting the seat of Government of the United States shall appoint in such manner as the Congress may direct:

A number of electors of President and Vice President equal to the whole number of Senators and Representatives in Congress to which the District would be entitled if it were a State, but in no event more than the least populous State; they shall be in addition to those appointed by the States, but they shall be considered, for the purposes of the election of President and Vice President, to be electors appointed by the State; and they shall meet in the District and perform such duties as provided by the twelfth article of amendment.

Section 2. The Congress shall have power to enforce this article by appropriate legislation.

Amendment XXIV[22]

Section 1. The right of citizens of the United States to vote in any primary or other election for President or Vice President, or for Senator or Representative in Congress, shall not be denied or abridged by the United States or any State by reason of failure to pay any poll tax or other tax.

Section 2. The Congress shall have power to enforce this article by appropriate legislation.

Amendment XXV[23]

Section 1. In case of the removal of the President from office or of his death or resignation, the Vice President shall become President.

---

[19] Passed February 20, 1933. Ratified December 5, 1933.
[20] Passed March 12, 1947. Ratified March 1, 1951.
[21] Passed June 16, 1960. Ratified April 3, 1961.
[22] Passed August 27, 1962. Ratified January 23, 1964.
[23] Passed July 6, 1965. Ratified February 11, 1967.

Section 2. Whenever there is a vacancy in the office of the Vice President, the President shall nominate a Vice President who shall take office upon confirmation by a majority vote of both Houses of Congress.

Section 3. Whenever the President transmits to the President pro tempore of the Senate and the Speaker of the House of Representatives his written declaration that he is unable to discharge the powers and duties of his office, and until he transmits them a written declaration to the contrary, such powers and duties shall be discharged by the Vice President as Acting President.

Section 4. Whenever the Vice President and a majority of either the principal officers of the executive department or of such other body as Congress may by law provide, transmit to the President pro tempore of the Senate and the Speaker of the House of Representatives their written declaration that the President is unable to discharge the powers and duties of his office, the Vice President shall immediately assume the powers and duties of the office of Acting President

Thereafter, when the President transmits to the President pro tempore of the Senate and the Speaker of the House of Representatives his written declaration that no inability exists, he shall resume the powers and duties of his office unless the Vice President and a majority of either the principal officers of the executive department or of such other body as Congress may by law provide, transmit within four days to the President pro tempore of the Senate and the Speaker of the House of Representatives their written declaration that the President is unable to discharge the powers and duties of his office. Thereupon Congress shall decide the issue, assembling within forty-eight hours for that purpose if not in session. If the Congress, within twenty-one days after receipt of the latter written declaration, or, if Congress is not in session, within twenty-one days after Congress is required to assemble, determines by two-thirds vote of both Houses that the President is unable to discharge the powers and duties of his office, the Vice-President shall continue to discharge the same as Acting President; otherwise, the President shall resume the powers and duties of his office.

Amendment XXVI[24]

Section 1. The right of citizens of the United States, who are eighteen years of age or older, to vote shall not be denied or abridged by the United States or by any State on account of age.

Section 2. The Congress shall have power to enforce this article by appropriate legislation.

Amendment XXVII[25]

No law, varying the compensation for the service of the Senators and Representatives, shall take effect, until an election of Representatives shall have intervened.

---

[24] Passed March 23, 1971. Ratified July 5, 1971.
[25] Passed September 25, 1789. Ratified May 7, 1992.

Glossary

abolitionism The movement that emerged in the 1830s in the United States dedicated to the immediate end of slavery.

Abraham Lincoln The sixteenth president (1861–1865), he led the United States throughout the Civil War.

African American soldiers Finally allowed to enlist in May 1863, African American soldiers accounted for more than one hundred eighty thousand troops and played a major role in the Union victory.

Agricultural Adjustment Act Created under Roosevelt's New Deal program to help farmers, its purpose was to reduce production of staple crops, thereby raising farm prices and encouraging more diversified farming.

Al Smith A vigorous reformer as governor of New York, he became the first Roman Catholic to win the nomination of a major party for president of the United States.

Alain Locke An African American poet and an important member of the Harlem Renaissance.

Alan Freed The self-proclaimed father of rock 'n' roll, he was the first DJ to play black rhythm and blues artists on the radio.

Albert B. Fall The secretary of the interior involved in the Teapot Dome scandal.

Alexander Graham Bell His invention of the telephone at the end of the nineteenth century changed the nature of life in the United States.

Alexander Hamilton The first U.S. secretary of the treasury (1789–1795), he established the national bank and public credit system. In 1804 Hamilton was mortally wounded in a duel with his political rival Aaron Burr.

Alger Hiss A U.S. public official accused of espionage at the height of the Cold War, he was convicted of perjury in 1950 in a controversial case.

Alice Paul A main figure in the radical wing of the woman's suffrage movement in the early twentieth century.

Alphonse "Al" Capone A gangster devoted to gaining control of gambling, prostitution, and bootlegging in the Chicago area.

Amistad A slave ship on which forty-nine Africans rebelled in 1839 off the coast of Cuba. The ship sailed to Long Island Sound where Spanish authorities demanded they be turned over for punishment. A group of American abolitionists, led by former President John Quincy Adams, fought for and won their freedom in 1841. The thirty-five who survived returned to Africa.

Amos 'n' Andy The most popular radio program of the Depression years, it portrayed the lives of two African American men in Harlem as interpreted by two white entertainers, Freeman Gosden and Charles Correll.

Anaconda Plan Term given to the strategy employed by the North during the Civil War in which the Confederacy would be slowly strangled by a blockade.

Andrew Carnegie A major business leader in the evolution of the steel industry.

Andrew Jackson The seventh president of the United States (1829–1837) who, as a general in the War of 1812, defeated the Red Sticks at Horseshoe Bend (1814) and the British at New Orleans (1815). As president he denied the right of individual states to nullify federal laws and increased presidential powers.

Andrew Johnson The seventeenth president of the United States (1865–1869); he succeeded the assassinated Abraham Lincoln.

Anita Hill She brought charges of sexual misconduct against Clarence Thomas and herself became a very polarizing figure as a result.

Anne Hutchinson English-born American colonist and religious leader who was banished from Boston (1637) for her religious beliefs, which included an emphasis on an individual's direct communication with God.

annexation To append or attach, especially to a larger or more significant thing.

Antietam The battle near Sharpsburg, Maryland, in September 1862 in which the Union Army stopped the Confederacy's drive into the North. With twenty-five thousand casualties, it was the bloodiest single-day battle of the Civil War.

anti-imperialists A league created during the last two years of McKinley's first term to unite the opposition against McKinley's foreign policy.

Antonio López de Santa Anna Leader of Mexico at the time of the battle at the Alamo. Taken prisoner when attacked at San Jacinto, he signed treaties removing Mexican troops from Texas, granting Texas its independence, and recognizing the Rio Grande as the boundary.

Appomattox The small Virginia village that served as the site of surrender of Confederate forces under Robert E. Lee to Ulysses S. Grant on April 9, 1865, generally recognized as bringing the Civil War to an end.

Articles of Confederation The compact first adopted by the original thirteen states of the United States in 1781 that remained the supreme law until 1789.

Atlanta Compromise A program for African American acceptance of white supremacy put forth by Booker T. Washington.

Atlantic slave trade In the 1440s Portugal initiated the trans-Atlantic trade that lasted four centuries. During that time, other European nations participated in a commerce that took more than ten million people from Africa.

Aztec Inhabitants of the Valley of Mexico who founded their capital, Tenochtitlán, in the early fourteenth century. Prior to the arrival of the Spanish, the Aztecs built a large empire in which they dominated many neighboring peoples. Their civilization included engineering, mathematics, art, and music.

baby boom A sudden increase in births in the years after World War II.

Bank of the United States The first bank was established in 1791 as part of the system proposed by Alexander Hamilton to launch the new government on a sound economic basis.

Bataan Peninsula U.S. and Philippine World War II troops surrendered this peninsula in western Luzon, Philippines, to the Japanese in April 1942 after an extended siege; U.S. forces recaptured the peninsula in February 1945.

Battle of Wounded Knee The last major chapter in the Indian wars, it was fought on the Pine Ridge Reservation in South Dakota.

Bay of Pigs Fifteen hundred Cuban exiles, supported by the CIA, landed here on April 17, 1961, in an unsuccessful attempt to overthrow the new Communist government of Fidel Castro.

Benjamin Franklin An American public official, writer, scientist, and printer. He proposed a plan for union at the Albany Congress (1754) and played a major part in the American Revolution. Franklin helped secure French support for the colonists, negotiated the Treaty of Paris (1783), and helped draft the Constitution (1787). His numerous scientific and practical innovations include the lightning rod, bifocal spectacles, and a stove.

Benjamin Harrison The twenty-third president of the United States, he lost the popular vote but gained a majority of the electoral college votes in the 1888 election.

Betty Friedan A feminist who wrote *The Feminist Mystique* in 1963 and founded the National Organization for Women in 1966.

bicameral legislature A legislature with two houses or chambers.

Bill Morris A black man burned at the stake in Balltown, Louisiana, for allegedly robbing and raping a white woman; no trial was held.

Bill of Rights The first ten amendments to the Constitution. These contain basic protection of the rights of individuals from abuses by the federal government, including freedom of speech, press, religion, and assembly.

Black Power Movement that developed in the mid-1960s calling for renewed racial pride in their African American heritage. They believed that to seek full integration into the existing white order would be to capitulate to the institutions of racism.

Black Thursday October 29, 1929, the day the spectacular New York stock market crash began.

Bleeding Kansas Nickname given to the Kansas Territory in the wake of a number of clashes between proslavery and antislavery supporters.

Bonus Army Thousands of veterans, determined to collect promised cash bonuses early, came to Washington during the summer of 1932 to listen to Congress debate the bonus proposal.

Booker T. Washington A spokesman for blacks in the 1890s who argued that African Americans should emphasize hard work and personal development rather than rebelling against their conditions.

bootleggers Enterprising individuals who moved alcohol across the border into the United States from Canada and the Caribbean during Prohibition. Their wares were sold at illegal saloons or "speakeasies" where city dwellers congregated in the evenings.

border ruffians Missouri settlers who crossed into Kansas to lend support for proslavery issues (1855).

Boss Politics An urban "political machine" that relied for its existence on the votes of the large inner-city population. The flow of money through the machine was often based on corruption.

Boston Massacre (1770) A pre-Revolutionary incident growing out of the resentment against the British troops sent to Boston to maintain order and to enforce the Townshend Act.

Boston Tea Party In 1773 Bostonians protested the Tea Act, which retained the Townshend duty on tea and granted a monopoly on tea sales in the colonies to the East India Company, by dumping chests of tea into Boston Harbor.

brain trust A group of prominent academics recruited as a source of ideas for the Roosevelt campaign to write speeches.

Branch Davidians A religious sect involved in a siege by government agents in Waco, Texas, in April 1993 that ended in deadly violence.

Brown v. Board of Education The unanimous Supreme Court decision ruling that segregated facilities in public education were "inherently unequal" and violated the Fourteenth Amendment's guarantee of equal protection under the law. This decision overruled the longstanding "separate but equal" doctrine of *Plessy v. Ferguson*.

Camp David Accords The historic treaty between Egypt and Israel, brokered by President Carter at Camp David in 1978, that returned the Sinai Peninsula to Egypt in return for Egypt's recognition of the State of Israel.

Carrie Chapman Catt A leader in the woman's suffrage campaign.

Cesar Chavez A labor organizer who founded the National Farm Workers Association in 1962.

Charles A. Lindbergh His solo flight across the Atlantic Ocean in 1927 made him an international hero.

Charles Evans Hughes A Supreme Court justice, he was the Republican candidate for president in the 1916 election. He had been a progressive governor of New York and said little about foreign policy.

Charles Grandison Finney An American evangelist, theologian, and educator (1792–1875). Licensed to the Presbyterian ministry in 1824, he had phenomenal success as a revivalist in the eastern states, converting many who became noted abolitionists.

Charles Sumner U.S. senator from Massachusetts (1851–1874), he was a noted orator with an uncompromising opposition to slavery.

Charlotte Perkins Gilman An ardent advocate of feminism.

Christopher Columbus An Italian mariner who sailed for Spain in 1492 in search of a western route to Asia. He located San Salvador in the West Indies, opening the Americas to European exploration and colonization.

Civil Works Administration (CWA) The agency tasked with creating jobs and restoring self-respect by handing out pay envelopes instead of relief checks. In reality, workers sometimes performed worthless tasks, known as "boondoggles," but much of the $1 billion budget was spent on projects of lasting value including airports and roads.

Civilian Conservation Corps (CCC) One of the New Deal's most popular programs, it took unemployed young men from the cities and put them to work on conservation projects in the country.

Clarence Thomas A Supreme Court justice appointed by President George H. W. Bush in 1991 whose confirmation became controversial due to allegations of sexual misconduct made against him.

Cold War War or rivalry conducted by all means available except open military action. Diplomatic relations are not commonly broken.

Colin Powell He served as chairman of the Joint Chiefs of Staff from 1989 to 1996 and was influential in planning U.S. strategy during the Persian Gulf War.

Common Sense Published by Thomas Paine in January 1776, *Common Sense* convinced the American public of the need for independence.

Confederacy The Confederate States of America.

Constitutional Convention Fifty-five delegates met in Philadelphia in May 1787 to reform the U.S. government. They chose to draft a new constitution rather than revise the Articles of Confederation.

contrabands Term used by the Union for the black people who made their way to the Union ranks. This term usually applies to goods prohibited by law or treaty from being imported or exported.

Contract with America The Republican election platform of the 1990s, promising action on such items as a balanced budget amendment, term limits for Congress members, and making legislators obey the regulations they applied to society.

Contras A Nicaraguan military force trained and financed by the United States that opposed the socialist Nicaraguan government led by the Sandinista party.

Copperheads A term used by some Republicans to describe Peace Democrats. It implied that they were traitors to the Union. Peace Democrats thought that the war was a failure and should be abandoned.

Crazy Horse Native American Sioux leader who defeated George Custer in battle.

daguerreotypes An early photographic process with the image made on a light-sensitive, silver-coated metallic plate.

Dawes Act This act distributed land to the Indians so that it could be sold to whites.

Dayton Peace Accords A peace settlement involving Bosnia in 1995 that was worked out in Dayton, Ohio; it did not prove to be a permanent solution for the problems in the Balkans.

Declaration of Independence The document, drafted primarily by Thomas Jefferson, that declared the independence of the thirteen mainland colonies from Great Britain and enumerated their reasons for separating.

Denmark Vesey American insurrectionist. A freed slave in South Carolina, he was implicated in the planning of a large uprising of slaves and was hanged. The event led to more stringent slave codes in many southern states.

détente An easing of tensions among countries, which usually leads to increased economic, diplomatic, and other types of contacts between former rivals.

dollar diplomacy A phrase used to describe Secretary of State Philander C. Knox's foreign policy under President Taft, which focused on expanding American investments abroad, especially in Latin America and China.

Dominion of New England In an effort to centralize the colonies and create consistent laws and political structures, James II combined Massachusetts, New Hampshire, Maine, Plymouth, Rhode Island, Connecticut, New York, and New Jersey under the Dominion of New England.

domino theory A theory that if one nation comes under Communist control, neighboring nations will soon follow.

Dorothea Dix An American philanthropist, reformer, and educator who took charge of nurses for the U.S. in the Civil War.

***Dred Scott* case** An enslaved man sued for his freedom in 1847, leading to a crucial Supreme Court decision in 1857 in which the Court ruled that African Americans held no rights as citizens and that the Missouri Compromise of 1820 was unconstitutional. The decision was widely denounced in the North and strengthened the new Republican party.

Dust Bowl The name given to areas of the prairie states that suffered ecological devastation in the 1930s and then again to a lesser extent in the mid-1950s.

Edmond Genêt French ambassador who enlisted American mercenaries to assist the French against the British. Genêt's move threatened relations between the United States and Britain.

Edward Bellamy The author of *Looking Backward* (1888), a major protest novel.

Eleanor Roosevelt A diplomat, writer, and First Lady of the United States (1933–1945) as the wife of President Franklin D. Roosevelt. A delegate to the United Nations (1945–1953 and 1961–1962), she was an outspoken advocate for human rights. Her written works include *This I Remember* (1949).

election of 1840 The election between Democrat Martin Van Buren and the Whig party's William Henry Harrison, won by Harrison.

electoral college The group that elects the president. Each state received as many electors as it had congressmen and senators combined.

Eli Whitney American inventor and manufacturer whose invention of the cotton gin (1793) revolutionized the cotton industry. He also established the first factory to assemble muskets with interchangeable parts.

Elizabeth Cady Stanton American feminist and social reformer who helped organize the first woman's rights convention, held in Seneca Falls, New York (1848), for which she wrote a Declaration of Sentiments calling for the reform of discriminatory practices that perpetuated sexual inequality.

Elizabeth I Queen of England (1558–1603) who succeeded the Catholic Mary I and reestablished Protestantism in England. Her reign was marked by several plots to overthrow her, the execution of Mary Queen of Scots (1587), the defeat of the Spanish Armada (1588), and domestic prosperity and literary achievement.

Ellis Island An immigration station opened in 1892 where new arrivals were passed through a medical examination and were questioned about their economic prospects.

emancipation The ending of slavery, initiated in the Emancipation Proclamation of 1863 but not accomplished in many places until the Confederate surrender in 1865.

Enlightenment A philosophical movement of the eighteenth century that emphasized the use of reason to scrutinize previously accepted doctrines and traditions and that brought about many humanitarian reforms.

Enola Gay The B-29 bomber, named after the mother of pilot Colonel Paul W. Tibbets, that dropped the first atomic bomb on the Japanese city of Hiroshima on August 6, 1945, killing more than one hundred thousand people.

Equal Rights Amendment (ERA) Congress overwhelmingly passed the Equal Rights Amendment in 1972, but by the mid-1970s conservative groups had managed to stall its confirmation by the states.

Era of Good Feelings Period in U.S. history (1817–1823) when, the Federalist party having declined, there was little open party feeling.

Erie Canal The first major American canal, stretching two hundred fifty miles from Lake Erie across the state of New York to Albany, where boats then traveled down the Hudson River to New York City. Begun in 1818, it was completed in 1825.

Eugene Debs Leader of the American Railway Union, which struck in sympathy with the workers at the Pullman Palace Car Company. This labor dispute experience helped persuade Debs to become a leader of the Socialist party.

Executive Order 9066 Issued by President Roosevelt on February 19, 1942, it designated certain parts of the country as sensitive military areas from which "any or all persons may be excluded," which led to the forced evacuation of more than one hundred twenty thousand people of Japanese ancestry from the West Coast of the United States.

F. Scott Fitzgerald A serious novelist of the day and author of *The Great Gatsby* who, along with his wife Zelda, captured attention as the embodiment of the free spirit of the Jazz Age.

Fannie Lou Hamer Daughter of illiterate Mississippi sharecroppers, she helped lead the civil rights struggle in Mississippi, focusing on voting rights for African Americans and representation in the national Democratic party.

Fidel Castro Cuban revolutionary leader who overthrew the corrupt regime of dictator Fulgencio Batista in 1959 and soon after established a Communist state. Prime minister of Cuba from 1959 to 1976, he has been president of the government and First Secretary of the Communist party in Cuba since 1976.

fire-eaters Southerners who were enthusiastic supporters of southern rights and later of secession.

flappers Young, single, middle-class women who wore their hair and dresses short, rolled their stockings down, used cosmetics, and smoked in public. Signaling a desire for independence and equality, flappers were self-reliant, outspoken, and had a new appreciation for the pleasures of life.

Fort Sumter The fort in the harbor of Charleston, South Carolina, that was fired on by the Confederacy on April 12, 1861, triggering the Civil War.

forty-niners Mostly men lured to California by the gold rush of 1849.

Fourteen Points Wilson's peace program, which included freedom of the seas, free trade, and more open diplomacy.

Francis Drake English naval hero and explorer who was the first Englishman to circumnavigate the world (1577–1580) and was vice admiral of the fleet that destroyed the Spanish Armada (1588).

Francis Gary Powers Pilot of a U.S. U-2 high altitude reconnaissance aircraft shot down over the Soviet Union on May 1, 1960.

Franklin D. Roosevelt The thirty-second president of the United States, he assumed the presidency at the depth of the Great Depression and helped the American people regain faith in themselves. He brought hope with his inaugural address in which he promised prompt, vigorous action and asserted that "the only thing we have to fear is fear itself."

Franz Ferdinand An Austrian archduke murdered along with his wife in Sarajevo, Bosnia. Austria's response to the dual murder led to the beginnings of World War I.

Frederick Douglass American abolitionist and journalist who escaped from slavery (1838) and became an influential lecturer in the North and abroad. He wrote *Narrative of the Life of Frederick Douglass* (1845) and cofounded and edited the *North Star* (1847–1860), an abolitionist newspaper.

free blacks The name often given to the hundreds of thousands of unenslaved African Americans who lived in the American South, especially in the Upper South states of Maryland and Virginia and in all the major cities of the region, during the days of slavery.

Freedmen's Bureau A federal agency created in 1865 to supervise newly freed people. It oversaw relations between whites and blacks in the South, issued food rations, and supervised labor contracts.

freedom riders Interracial groups who rode buses in the South so that a series of federal court decisions declaring segregation on buses and in waiting rooms unconstitutional would not be ignored by white officials.

Free-Soil party A U.S. political party formed in 1848 to oppose the extension of slavery into the territories; merged with the Liberty party in 1848.

French and Indian War The name often used for the Seven Years' War in North America. The conflict began in 1754 in the Ohio Valley between British colonists and the French and their Indian allies.

Fugitive Slave Act The federal act of 1850 providing for the return between states of escaped black slaves.

General Douglas MacArthur He served as chief of staff (1930–1935) and commanded the Allied forces in the South Pacific during World War II. Initially losing the Philippines to the Japanese in 1942, he regained the islands and accepted the surrender of Japan in 1945. He commanded the UN forces in Korea (1950–1951) until a conflict in strategies led to his dismissal by President Truman.

General Dwight D. Eisenhower The thirty-fourth president of the United States and supreme commander of the Allied Expeditionary Force during World War II. He launched the invasion of Normandy

(June 6, 1944) and oversaw the final defeat of Germany in 1945.

General George C. Marshall A soldier, diplomat, and politician who, as U.S. secretary of state (1947–1949), organized the European Recovery Plan, often called the Marshall Plan, for which he received the 1953 Nobel Peace Prize.

General William Westmoreland General who was the senior commander of U.S. troops in Vietnam from 1964 through 1968.

George Armstrong Custer Colonel famous for his battle at Little Big Horn against the Sioux Indians.

George B. McClellan Major General of the United States Army who led forces in Virginia in 1861 and 1862. He was widely blamed for not taking advantage of his numerical superiority to defeat the Confederates around Richmond. McClellan ran against Abraham Lincoln for president in 1864 on the Democratic ticket.

George Dewey On May 1, 1898, he inflicted a decisive defeat on the Spanish Navy at Manila Bay in the Philippine Islands.

George H. W. Bush The forty-first president of the United States, he was in office when the Soviet Union collapsed.

George Herman "Babe" Ruth This Boston Red Sox pitcher was sold to the New York Yankees in 1918 for $400,000. He belted out fifty-four home runs during the 1920 season, and fans flocked to see him play.

George McGovern A U.S. senator from South Dakota, he opposed the Vietnam War and was defeated as the 1972 Democratic candidate for president.

George Pullman Developer of the railroad sleeping car and creator of a model town outside Chicago where his employees were to live.

George Rogers Clark American military leader and frontiersman who led raids on British troops and Native Americans in the West during the Revolutionary War.

George W. Bush The forty-third president of the United States.

George Wallace A three-time governor of Alabama, he first came to national attention as an outspoken segregationist. Wallace ran unsuccessfully for the presidency in 1968 and 1972.

George Washington Commander-in-chief of the Continental Army during the American Revolution, presiding officer at the Constitutional Convention, and the first president of the United States (1789–1797).

Gerald Ford The thirty-eighth president of the United States, he was appointed vice president on the resignation of Spiro Agnew and became president when Richard Nixon resigned over the Watergate scandal. As president, Ford granted a full pardon to Nixon in 1974.

Geronimo An Apache leader who resisted white incursions until his capture in 1886.

Gettysburg Address A brief speech given by President Lincoln at the dedication of the Gettysburg Cemetery in November 1863 that declared that the Civil War was dedicated to freedom.

Gifford Pinchot He worked closely with Roosevelt to formulate a conservation policy that involved managing natural resources, not locking them up for indefinite future use.

Glorious Revolution The English Revolution of 1688–1689 against the authoritarian policies and Catholicism of James II. James was forced into exile, and his daughter Mary and her husband William of Orange took the throne. The revolution secured the dominance of Parliament over royal power.

good neighbor policy A new Latin American policy wherein Hoover withdrew the Marines from Nicaragua and Haiti, and in 1930 the State Department renounced the Roosevelt Corollary of 1904.

Granville T. Woods A black inventor who devised the "third rail" to convey electric power to streetcars.

Great Awakening An immense religious revival that swept across the Protestant world.

great compromise A plan proposed by a delegation from Connecticut that established a bicameral Congress with a House of Representatives, based on a state's population, and the Senate, in which each state would be represented equally.

Great Migration A massive movement of blacks leaving the South for cities in the North that began slowly in 1910 and accelerated between 1914 and 1920. During this time, more than six hundred thousand African Americans left the South.

Grimké sisters The first female abolitionist speakers; they were prominent figures in the antislavery movement of the late 1830s.

Grover Cleveland The twenty-second and twenty-fourth president of the United States, he was the first Democrat elected to the presidency after the Civil War.

Gulf of Tonkin Resolution Following reports of a confrontation with North Vietnamese in the Tonkin Gulf in 1964, President Johnson requested, and received, congressional authority to "take all necessary measures" to repel "further aggression" in Vietnam, giving the president formal authority to escalate the war.

Half-Way Covenant The Puritan practice whereby parents who had been baptized but had not yet experienced conversion could bring their children before the church and have them baptized.

Harpers Ferry A Virginia town that was the site of John Brown's raid in 1859, a failed attempt to lead a slave insurrection. It ignited public opinion in both the North and the South.

Harriet Beecher Stowe Author of *Uncle Tom's Cabin* (1852), the most important abolitionist novel.

Harriet Tubman An escaped slave who returned to the South and led hundreds of enslaved people to freedom in the North. Active throughout the 1850s, Tubman became famous as the most active member of the Underground Railroad.

Harry Hopkins Roosevelt's choice to run the Federal Emergency Relief Administration. He eventually became Roosevelt's closest advisor.

Harry S Truman The thirty-third president of the United States, he took office following the death of Franklin D. Roosevelt. Reelected in 1948 in a stunning political upset, Truman's controversial and historic decisions included the use of atomic weapons against Japan, desegregation of the U.S. military, and dismissal of General MacArthur as commander of U.S. forces during the Korean War.

Hartford Convention A gathering of Federalists in 1814 that called for significant amendments to the Constitution and attempted to damage the Republican party. The Treaty of Ghent and Andrew Jackson's victory at New Orleans annulled any recommendation of the convention.

Haymarket Affair On May 4, 1886, workmen in Chicago gathered to protest police conduct during a strike at a factory of the McCormick Company.

Henry Cabot Lodge A Massachusetts senator best remembered for spearheading Senate blockage of American membership in the League of Nations on the ground that its covenant threatened American sovereignty.

Henry Clay American politician who pushed the Missouri Compromise through the U.S. House of Representatives (1820) in an effort to reconcile free and slave states.

Henry Ford An automaker who developed the assembly line and low-priced automobiles.

Henry Kissinger A German-born American diplomat, he was national security advisor and U.S. secretary of state under Presidents Nixon and Ford. He shared the 1973 Nobel Peace Prize for helping to negotiate the Vietnam ceasefire.

Herman Melville Author of *Moby Dick* (1851), often considered to be the greatest American novel of the nineteenth century.

Hernán Cortés Spanish explorer who conquered the Aztecs initially in 1519, retreated when they rebelled, then defeated them again, aided by a smallpox epidemic, in 1521.

Ho Chi Minh Vietnamese leader and first president of North Vietnam. His army was victorious in the French Indochina War, and he later led North Vietnam's struggle to defeat the U.S.-supported government of South Vietnam. He died before the reunification of Vietnam.

Homer A. Plessey In a test of an 1890 law specifying that blacks must ride in separate railroad cars, this one-eighth-black man boarded a train and sat in the car reserved for whites. When the conductor instructed him to move, he refused and was arrested.

Homestead strike A labor uprising of workers at a steel plant in Homestead, Pennsylvania, in 1892 that was put down by military force.

Hoovervilles Makeshift "villages" usually at the edge of a city with "homes" made of cardboard, scrap metal, or whatever was cheap and available and named for President Hoover who was despised by the poor for his apparent refusal to help them.

Horace Greeley Grant's opponent in the 1872 election. Seen as a political oddball in the eyes of many Americans, the sixty-one-year-old editor favored the protective tariff and was indifferent to civil service reform. He was also passionate about ideas such as vegetarianism and the use of human manure in farming.

horizontal integration A procedure wherein a company takes over competitors to achieve control within an industry.

House Un-American Activities Committee (HUAC) Formed in the 1930s as a watchdog against Nazi propaganda, HUAC was revived after World War II as a watchdog against Communist propaganda.

Huey P. Long A Populist but dictatorial governor of Louisiana (1928–1932), he instituted major public works legislation, and as a U.S. senator (1932–1935), he proposed a national "Share-the-Wealth" program.

Hull House Founded in 1889 by Jane Addams and Ellen Gates Starr as a settlement home in a Chicago neighborhood to help solve the troubling problems of American city life.

Ida Tarbell A preeminent female crusading journalist.

Ida Wells Barnett An African American leader of an antilynching campaign.

impeachment The act of charging a public official with misconduct in office.

Indian Removal Act Passed in 1830, this act set aside land in the Oklahoma Territory for American Indians to be removed from the eastern United States. Over the next eight years, tens of thousands of Choctaw, Chickasaw, and Cherokee people were transported from their homes on what the Cherokees called the "Trail of Tears."

Interstate Commerce Act Passed by Congress in 1887, this act set up an Interstate Commerce Commission (ICC), which could investigate complaints of railroad misconduct or file suit against the companies.

Interstate Commerce Commission Passage of the Hepburn Act in 1906 gave this commission the power to establish maximum rates and to review the accounts and records of the railroads.

Iran-Contra scandal A major scandal of the second Reagan term that involved shipping arms to Iran and diverting money from the sale of these weapons to the Contra rebels in Nicaragua.

Iron Curtain The military, political, and ideological barrier established between the Soviet bloc and Western Europe from 1945 to 1990.

J. P. Morgan He purchased Carnegie Steel Company in 1901 for $480 million from Andrew Carnegie, creating United States Steel, which controlled 60 percent of the steel industry's productive capacity.

Jack Johnson The first African American heavyweight boxing champion, taking the title in 1908.

Jackie Robinson The first African American player in the Major Leagues in the twentieth century, he was a second baseman for the Brooklyn Dodgers, had a lifetime batting average of .311, and was inducted into the Baseball Hall of Fame in 1962.

James Buchanan The fifteenth president of the United States (1857–1861). He tried to maintain a balance between proslavery and antislavery factions, but his views angered radicals in both the North and South.

James Madison The fourth president of the United States (1809–1817). A member of the Continental Congress (1780–1783) and the Constitutional Convention (1787), he strongly supported ratification of the Constitution and was a contributor to *The Federalist Papers* (1787–1788), which argued the effectiveness of the proposed constitution.

James Monroe The fifth president of the United States (1817–1825), whose administration was marked by the acquisition of Florida (1819), the Missouri Compromise (1820) in which Missouri was declared a slave state, and the profession of the Monroe Doctrine (1823), declaring U.S. opposition to European interference in the Americas.

James Oglethorpe Along with John Viscount Percival, Oglethorpe sought a charter to colonize Georgia, the last of the British mainland colonies. Upon royal approval, he founded the colony with the intention of establishing a society of small farmers, without slavery or hard liquor.

James Wolfe British general in Canada. He defeated the French at Quebec (1759) but was mortally wounded in the battle.

Jamestown The first permanent English settlement in America (1607), it was located on the James River in Virginia.

Jane Addams Pioneer of settlement houses in Chicago and a major reform leader.

Jay Treaty Concluded in 1794 between the United States and Great Britain to settle difficulties arising mainly out of violations of the Treaty of Paris of 1783 and to regulate commerce and navigation.

Jefferson Davis United States senator, secretary of war and then president of the Confederacy (1861–1865). He was captured by Union soldiers in 1865 and imprisoned for two years. Although he was indicted for treason (1866), he was never prosecuted.

Jesse Jackson A Baptist minister and civil rights leader, he directed national antidiscrimination efforts in the mid-1960s and 1970s. His concern for the oppressed and his dramatic oratory attracted a large grass-roots constituency.

Jimmy Carter The thirty-ninth president of the United States, his successes in office, including the Camp David Accords, were overshadowed by domestic worries and an international crisis involving the taking of

American hostages at the U.S. Embassy in Iran. He was defeated by Ronald Reagan in the 1980 presidential election.

John Adams The first vice president (1789–1797) and second president (1797–1801) of the United States. He was a major figure during the American Revolution: he helped draft the Declaration of Independence and served on the commission to negotiate the Treaty of Paris (1783).

John Brown American abolitionist who, in 1859 with twenty-one followers, captured the U.S. arsenal at Harpers Ferry as part of an effort to liberate southern slaves. His group was defeated, and Brown was hanged after a trial in which he won sympathy as an abolitionist martyr.

John C. Calhoun Vice president of the United States (1825–1832) under John Quincy Adams and Andrew Jackson. In his political philosophy he maintained that the states had the right to nullify federal legislation that they deemed unconstitutional.

John Calvin French-born Swiss Protestant theologian who broke with the Roman Catholic Church (1533) and set forth the tenets of his theology, the Reformed tradition including Puritans, Huguenots, Presbyterians, and Dutch Reformed, in *Institutes of the Christian Religion* (1536).

John D. Rockefeller Key figure in the development of the oil industry and the growth of large corporations.

John F. Kennedy The thirty-fifth president of the United States, he was the first Catholic to win the White House and the first president born in the twentieth century. He was assassinated in 1963 during a trip to Dallas, Texas.

John Glenn On February 20, 1962, aboard the *Friendship 7,* he was the first American to orbit the earth, and in 1998 he was the oldest person to participate in a space flight mission as a crew member of the space shuttle *Discovery.* From 1974 to 1998 he served as U.S. Senator from Ohio.

John Jay American diplomat and jurist who served in the Continental Congress and helped negotiate the Treaty of Paris (1783). He was the first chief justice of the U.S. Supreme Court (1789–1795) and negotiated the agreement with Great Britain that became known as the Jay Treaty (1794–1795).

John L. Lewis A labor leader who was president of the United Mine Workers of America (1920–1960) and the Congress of Industrial Organizations (1935–1940).

John L. Sullivan A famous Irish American boxing champion of the late nineteenth century.

John Locke An English philosopher and author of *An Essay Concerning Human Understanding* (1690), which challenged the notion of innate knowledge, and *Two Treatises on Civil Government* (1690), which discussed the social contract.

John Marshall American jurist and politician who served as the chief justice of the U.S.

Supreme Court (1801–1835) and helped establish the practice of judicial review.

John Nance "Cactus Jack" Garner Speaker of the House in 1931 whose answer to the growing budget deficit was to offer a national sales tax. He ran against Roosevelt for the Democratic nomination for president but released his delegates and was in turn rewarded with the vice presidential nomination.

John Pemberton An Atlanta druggist who in 1886 developed a syrup from an extract of the cola nut that he mixed with carbonated water and called "Coca Cola."

John Smith English colonist, explorer, and writer whose maps and accounts of his explorations in Virginia and New England were invaluable to later explorers and colonists.

John Wilkes Booth An actor and southern sympathizer who assassinated Abraham Lincoln on April 14, 1865.

Joseph McCarthy A U.S. senator from Wisconsin (1947–1957), he presided over the permanent subcommittee on investigations and held public hearings in which he accused Army officials, members of the media, and public figures of being Communists. These charges were never proved, and he was censured by the Senate in 1954.

Joseph Smith An American religious leader who founded the Church of Jesus Christ of Latter-Day Saints (1830) and led his congregation westward from New York State to western Illinois, where he was murdered by an anti-Mormon mob.

Juan de Oñate Spanish explorer and conquistador who claimed New Mexico for Spain in 1598 and served as its governor until he was removed on charges of cruelty in 1607.

Kansas-Nebraska Act Written by Stephen A. Douglas, the act declared that people of new territories could decide for themselves whether or not their states would permit slaves and slaveholders.

Kenneth Starr Special prosecutor appointed to investigate the Whitewater affair. He expanded his investigation into other matters and eventually sent a report to the House of Representatives alleging that there were grounds for impeaching Clinton for lying under oath, obstruction of justice, abuse of power, and other offenses.

Kent State University National Guardsmen were sent to this Ohio campus to restore order following a series of tumultuous anti-war protests in May 1970. They fired into a crowd of students, killing four and wounding nine others.

Knights of Labor A labor organization that combined fraternal ritual, the language of Christianity, and a belief in the social equality of all citizens.

Know-Nothings The popular name for the American party, an anti-immigration party of the mid-1850s, derived from their response to any question about their activities: "I know nothing."

La Raza Unida Formed in 1969 by Mexican American activists, it reflected the growing demand for political and cultural recognition of "Chicano" causes, especially in the Southwest.

Lee Harvey Oswald Alleged assassin of President John F. Kennedy, he was shot two days later while under arrest.

Lend-Lease Passed in 1941, this act forged the way for the United States to transfer military supplies to the Allies, primarily Great Britain and the Soviet Union.

Levittown An unincorporated community of 53,286 people in southeast New York on western Long Island, which was founded in 1947 as a low-cost housing development for World War II veterans.

Lewis and Clark expedition From 1804 to 1806 Meriwether Lewis and William Clark led the Corps of Discovery from St. Louis to the Pacific coast and back. They informed Native Americans that the United States had acquired the territory from France and recorded geographic and scientific data.

Liberal Republicans Organization formed in 1872 by Republicans discontented with the political corruption and the policies of President Grant's first administration.

Liberty Bonds Thirty-year government bonds sold to individuals with an annual interest rate of 3.5 percent. They were offered in five issues between 1917 and 1920, and their purchase was equated with patriotic duty.

Liberty party A U.S. political party formed in 1839 to oppose the practice of slavery; it merged with the Free-Soil party in 1848.

Lincoln-Douglas debates Seven debates between Stephen A. Douglas and Abraham Lincoln for the Illinois senatorial race of 1858.

Little Richard An American rock 'n' roll singer noted for his flamboyant style, he influenced many artists including Elvis Presley and the Beatles.

Louis Armstrong A trumpeter and a major innovator of jazz.

Louis Brandeis A prominent Boston lawyer and reformist thinker who was a consultant to Wilson during his campaign for election in 1912.

Louis Farrakhan Leader of the Nation of Islam who became controversial for his intense criticism of whites and their policies toward blacks.

Louisiana Purchase The acquisition in 1803 of the Louisiana Territory west of the Mississippi River and New Orleans by the United States from France for $15 million.

Lusitania A British liner hit by a German torpedo in May of 1915. Among the nearly twelve hundred passengers who died were 128 Americans.

Lyndon Baines Johnson The thirty-sixth president of the United States, he took over following President Kennedy's assassination in 1963 and was elected in a landslide the following year. He piloted a number of important initiatives through Congress,

including the Civil Rights Act of 1964 and the Voting Rights Act of 1965.

Malcolm X A popular Black Muslim leader who advocated nationalism, self-defense, and racial separation. He split with the Black Muslim movement and formed the Organization of Afro-American Unity, which attracted thousands of young, urban blacks with its message of socialism and self-help. He was assassinated by a Black Muslim at a New York rally in 1965.

manifest destiny The belief that the United States was destined to grow from the Atlantic to the Pacific and from the Arctic to the tropics. Providence supposedly intended for Americans to have this area for a great experiment in liberty.

Marbury v. Madison The first decision by the Supreme Court to declare unconstitutional and void an act passed by Congress that the Court considered in violation of the Constitution. The decision established the doctrine of judicial review, which recognizes the authority of courts to declare statutes unconstitutional.

Marcus Garvey A Jamaican immigrant who promised to "organize the 400 million Negroes of the World into a vast organization to plant the banner of freedom in the great continent of Africa."

Margaret Sanger Living in Greenwich Village, New York, she saw women suffering from disease and poverty because of the large number of children they bore. In 1914 she coined the term "birth control" and began publishing a periodical called *Woman Rebel.*

Marian Anderson An opera singer and human rights advocate, she performed on the steps of the Lincoln Memorial before a crowd of seventy-five thousand after being denied the use of Constitution Hall by the Daughters of the American Revolution. She helped focus national attention on the racial prejudice faced by African Americans in all facets of national life.

Marshall Plan Also known as the European Recovery Plan, this 1947 U.S. plan costing about $13 billion was credited with restoring economic confidence throughout Western Europe, raising living standards, curbing the influence of local Communist parties, and increasing U.S. trade and investment on the Continent.

Martin Luther German theologian and leader of the Reformation. His opposition to the wealth and corruption of the papacy and his belief that salvation would be granted on the basis of faith alone rather than by works caused his excommunication from the Catholic Church (1521). Luther confirmed the Augsburg Confession in 1530, effectively establishing the Lutheran Church.

Martin Luther King Jr. An African American cleric whose eloquence and commitment to nonviolent tactics formed the foundation of the civil rights movement of the 1950s and 1960s. He led the 1963 march on Washington at which he delivered his now famous "I Have a Dream" speech. He was awarded the Nobel Peace Prize in 1964 and was assassinated four years later in Memphis, Tennessee.

Martin Van Buren The eighth president of the United States (1837–1841). A powerful Democrat from New York, he served in the U.S. Senate (1821–1828), as secretary of state (1829–1831), and as vice president (1833–1837) under Andrew Jackson before being elected president in 1836. He unsuccessfully sought reelection in 1840 and 1848.

Mary McLeod Bethune An educator who sought improved racial relations and educational opportunities for black Americans, she was part of the U.S. delegation to the first United Nations meeting (1945).

Massachusetts Bay colony Founded in 1630 by non-Separatist Puritans with the intention of creating a society in New England that would serve as a model for reforming the Anglican Church.

Maya Inhabitants of the Yucatan Peninsula whose civilization was at its height from AD 300 to 900. Their civilization included a unique system of writing, mathematics, architecture and sculpture, and astronomy.

Mayflower Compact When the *Mayflower* reached land at Cape Cod and the colonists decided to settle there, they lacked the legal basis to establish a government. Thus the adult males of the colony signed a mutual agreement for ordering their society later referred to as the Mayflower Compact.

Metacom Wampanoag leader who waged King Philip's War (1675–1676) with New England colonists who had encroached on Native American territory.

middle passage The transport of slaves across the Atlantic from Africa to North America.

midnight appointments Federal judicial officials appointed to office in the closing period of a presidential administration. The Republicans accused Adams of staying awake until midnight in order to sign the commissions for Federalist officeholders.

Midway Island A naval battle in World War II in which land and carrier-based U.S. planes decisively defeated a Japanese fleet on its way to invade Midway Island.

Mikhail Gorbachev General secretary of the Soviet Communist party in the mid-1980s and president of the USSR from 1989 to 1991, he ushered in an era of unprecedented *glasnost* (openness) and *perestroika* (restructuring) and won the Nobel Peace Prize in 1990.

Millard Fillmore The thirteenth president of the United States (1850–1853), who succeeded to office after the death of Zachary Taylor. He struggled to keep the nation unified but lost the support of his Whig party.

Million Man March A protest march in October 1995 in Washington, D.C., that was organized by Louis Farrakhan to draw attention to black grievances.

Missouri Compromise Measure passed by the U.S. Congress in 1820–1821 to end the first of a series of crises concerning the extension of slavery.

Monica Lewinsky An unpaid intern and later a paid staffer who had an affair with President Clinton in the White House.

Monroe Doctrine Authored by James Monroe, the doctrine declared U.S. opposition to European interference in the Americas.

Montgomery bus boycott Begun in December 1955 as a result of an act of protest by Rosa Parks against the segregated transportation facilities and humiliating treatment facing African Americans in the capital city of Alabama, the boycott soon became an international event.

Moral Majority A political action group founded in 1979 and composed of conservative, fundamentalist Christians. Led by evangelist Rev. Jerry Falwell, the group played a significant role in the 1980 elections through its strong support of conservative candidates.

muckraking The name given to investigative reporters in the early 1900s.

Muller v. Oregon Case in which the Supreme Court upheld limits on working hours for women.

Nat Turner American slave leader who organized about seventy followers and led a rebellion in Virginia, during which approximately fifty whites were killed (1831). He was then captured and executed.

Nathaniel Bacon American colonist who led Bacon's Rebellion (1676), in which a group of landless freemen attacked neighboring Indians and burned Jamestown in an attempt to gain land and greater participation in the government of Virginia.

Nathaniel Hawthorne Author of several important novels including *The Scarlet Letter* (1850) and *The House of Seven Gables* (1851).

National American Woman Suffrage Association This association was formed in 1890 through the efforts of Lucy Stone Blackwell, and its first president was Elizabeth Cady Stanton.

National Association for the Advancement of Colored People (NAACP) An organization that fights against racial injustice.

National Farmers' Alliance This group led to the emergence of the Populist party.

National Industrial Recovery Act (NIRA) Enacted on June 16, 1933, this emergency measure was designed to encourage industrial recovery and help combat widespread unemployment.

National Woman's party Created by Alice Paul, this organization pushed for the Equal Rights Amendment during the 1920s.

National Women's Trade Union League A feminist labor organization.

New Deal The name given to the many domestic programs and reforms instituted by President Franklin D. Roosevelt and his administration in response to the Great Depression of the 1930s.

New Jersey Plan Written by William Paterson, the New Jersey Plan proposed a one-house (unicameral) Congress in which states had equal representation.

New Nationalism Roosevelt's far-reaching program that called for a strong federal government to stabilize the economy, protect the weak, and restore social harmony.

New Negro African Americans after World War I who wanted their rights.

Newt Gingrich A congressman from Georgia first elected in 1978, he served as Speaker of the House from 1994 until he resigned from Congress in 1999.

Ngo Dinh Diem A Vietnamese political leader who became president of South Vietnam in 1954. He was assassinated in a military coup d'état.

Nikita Khrushchev A Soviet politician and Stalin loyalist in the 1930s, he was appointed first secretary of the Communist party in 1953. As Soviet premier, he denounced Stalin, thwarted the Hungarian Revolution of 1956, and improved his country's image abroad. He was deposed in 1964 for failing to establish missiles in Cuba or improve the Soviet economy.

Nisei A person born in the United States of parents who emigrated from Japan.

Northwest Ordinance Adopted by the Congress in 1787 to establish stricter control over the government of the Northwest territories ceded to the United States by the states. The ordinance was the most significant achievement of Congress under the Articles of Confederation.

Oklahoma City bombing Militant right-wing U.S. terrorists bombed the Alfred P. Murrah Federal Building in Oklahoma City in April 1995, causing the deaths of 168 people.

Oliver Evans American inventor who developed the first application of steam power in an industrial setting. He also developed a method of automating flour mills that a generation later was standard in U.S. mills.

Oliver North A member of the NSC staff and a Marine colonel, he was a central figure in the Iran-Contra scandal.

omnibus bill Grouping a number of items together in an attempt to get them passed; often used to enact controversial legislation.

Opechancanough Brother of Powhatan. In the 1620s Opechancanough organized a military offensive against English settlers.

Operation OVERLORD The name given to the Allied invasion of the European continent through Normandy.

Orval Faubus Governor of Arkansas in 1957 who triggered a confrontation between national authority and states' rights by defying a federal court order to integrate the all-white Central High School.

P. G. T. Beauregard American Confederate general known for his flamboyant personal style and dashing, but not always successful, strategic campaigns. He ordered the bombardment of Fort Sumter in April 1861.

panic of 1837 A financial crisis that began a major depression that lasted six years.

Paxton Boys To gain greater protection from Indian attacks in western Pennsylvania, the "Paxton Boys" of Lancaster County murdered a number of Christian Indians at Conestoga, then marched on Philadelphia.

Pearl Harbor The site of a U.S. naval base on the southern coast of Oahu, Hawaii, which the Japanese attacked on Sunday, December 7, 1941; the United States entered World War II the following day.

Peggy Eaton Wife of John Eaton and the central figure in a controversy that would divide President Jackson's cabinet into pro- and anti-Eaton factions.

Platt Amendment This amendment barred an independent Cuba from allying itself with another foreign power and gave the United States the right to intervene to preserve stability.

Plessy v. Ferguson The 1896 Supreme Court case that approved racial segregation.

Plymouth colony A colony established by the English Pilgrims, or Separatists, in 1620. The Separatists were Puritans who abandoned hope that the Anglican Church could be reformed. Plymouth became part of Massachusetts in 1691.

political correctness Of, relating to, or supporting broad social, political, and educational change, especially to redress historical injustices in matters such as race, class, gender, and sexual orientation.

popular sovereignty The concept that settlers of each territory would decide for themselves whether to allow slavery.

Populist party Also known as the People's party, they held their first national convention on July 4, 1892. The party platform took a stern view of the state of the nation, with planks endorsing the subtreasury, free coinage of silver, and other reform proposals.

Powhatan An Algonquian leader who founded the Powhatan confederacy and maintained peaceful relations with English colonists after the marriage of his daughter Pocahontas to John Rolfe (1614).

praying towns Established by John Eliot, praying towns were villages in which the Indians were supposed to adopt English customs and learn the fundamentals of Puritan religion.

predestination A theory that states that God has decreed who will be saved and who will be damned.

Prince Henry of Portugal Henry "the Navigator" (1394–1460) established a school for navigators and geographers. He sought to increase the power of Portugal by promoting exploration of trade routes to the East by way of Africa.

Proclamation of 1763 In an attempt to keep white settlers out of the Ohio Valley, the Proclamation of 1763 drew a line along the crest of the Appalachian Mountains from Maine to Georgia and required all colonists to move east of the line.

Prohibition An effort to ban the sale of alcohol; it was achieved in 1919.

Protestant Reformation The religious rebellion against the Roman Catholic Church that began in 1517 when Martin Luther posted his ninety-five theses on a church door in Wittenberg, Germany.

Pullman strike Strike by railway workers that led to nationwide unrest in 1894.

Puritanism The strain of English Calvinism that demanded purification of the Anglican Church, including elimination of rituals, vestments, statues, and bishops.

Ralph Waldo Emerson An American writer, philosopher, and central figure of American transcendentalism. His poems, orations, and especially his essays, such as *Nature* (1836), are regarded as landmarks in the development of American thought and literary expression.

Red Scare A label attached to the fear of many Americans that a radical movement existed within the United States that was determined to establish a Communist government here.

Reform party A political party founded by Ross Perot in 1995 as an alternative to the Democratic and Republican parties.

republican motherhood The idea of Dr. Benjamin Rush that nurturing incorruptible future leaders, or "republican motherhood," was women's principal responsibility under the new government.

Richard Nixon The thirty-seventh president of the United States. Known early in his career as a hard-line anti-Communist, he was the first U.S. president to visit Communist China. He also worked skillfully to ease tensions with the Soviet Union. He became the first president to resign from office, due to his involvement in the Watergate scandal.

Roanoke Island England's first attempt to establish a colony in North America was at Roanoke Island in 1585.

robber barons Railroad industry leaders such as Cornelius Vanderbilt and Jay Gould who became renowned for their ruthless methods against competitors.

Robert E. Lee American general who led the Army of Northern Virginia in the American Civil War.

Robert Kennedy He served as attorney general during the presidency of his brother John F. Kennedy. Elected to the Senate in 1964, he was assassinated in Los Angeles while campaigning for the presidency.

Robert La Follette Progressive governor and senator from Wisconsin.

Robert Morris American Revolutionary politician and financier. A signer of the Declaration of Independence, he raised money for the Continental Army, attended the Constitutional Convention (1787), and was financially ruined by land speculation.

Rodney King The victim of a violent beating by Los Angeles police that was caught on videotape and became the central event of the 1992 riots.

Roe v. Wade Decided by the Supreme Court in 1973, this case along with *Doe v. Bolton* legalized abortion in the first trimester.

Roger B. Taney American jurist who served as the chief justice of the U.S. Supreme Court (1836–1864). In the *Dred Scott* decision (1857) he ruled that slaves and their descendants had no rights as citizens.

Roger Williams English cleric in America who was expelled from Massachusetts for his criticism of Puritan policies. He founded Providence Plantation (1636), a community based on religious freedom, and obtained a charter for Rhode Island in 1644.

Ronald Reagan The fortieth president of the United States, he represented the ascendancy of conservatism during the 1980s.

Roosevelt Corollary Roosevelt's extension of the Monroe Doctrine to Latin American states and the right to supervise their behavior.

Rosa Parks Her refusal to give up her seat on a bus to a white man in Montgomery, Alabama, resulted in a citywide boycott of the bus company and stirred the civil rights movement across the nation.

Rosie the Riveter A symbol of the new breed of working women during World War II.

Ross Perot A businessman, he first came to national attention during the Iran hostage crisis when he funded an operation that rescued two of his employees from an Iranian prison. In 1992 he emerged as an independent candidate for president, expressing serious concern over the national debt.

royal fifth A tax on silver and gold of which one-fifth of its value went to the king of Spain.

Rutherford B. Hayes Nineteenth president of the United States, he was beneficiary of the most fiercely disputed election in American history.

Sacagawea Shoshone guide and interpreter who accompanied the Lewis and Clark expedition (1805–1806).

Sacco and Vanzetti Two immigrants tried for murder in Massachusetts in the 1920s whose trial attracted worldwide attention because of allegations that the men had been unjustly convicted.

Salem witch trials The prosecution in 1691 and 1692 of almost two hundred people in Salem, Massachusetts, and its environs on charges of practicing witchcraft. Twenty people were put to death before Governor William Phips halted the trials.

Samuel F. B. Morse American painter and inventor. He refined and patented the telegraph and developed the telegraphic code that bears his name.

Samuel J. Tilden Governor of New York selected to run as the Democratic candidate in the 1876 presidential election. He narrowly lost what has been considered the most controversial election in American history.

Samuel Slater British-born textile pioneer in America. He oversaw construction of the nation's first successful water-powered cotton mill (1790–1793).

Sandra Day O'Connor Appointed during the presidency of Ronald Reagan, she was the first woman justice on the Supreme Court.

Scopes trial Local authorities indicted this Dayton, Tennessee, schoolteacher for teaching evolution in one of his classes. The jury found him guilty and assessed a small fine.

Scottsboro boys A group of black youths accused of raping a white woman in Alabama who became a source of controversy and the focus of civil rights activism in the early 1930s.

Second Bank of the United States Created to prevent inflation and deflation of the American economy. Many prominent figures believed the Second Bank of the United States had too much power, one of whom was President Jackson, who vetoed the bank's attempt to recharter.

Second Great Awakening A series of Protestant religious revivals that began in 1797 and lasted into the 1830s.

Seminoles A Native American people made up of various primarily Creek groups who moved into northern Florida during the eighteenth and nineteenth centuries, later inhabiting the Everglades region as well.

Seneca Falls Convention The first major gathering of woman's rights advocates was held in Seneca Falls, New York, in 1848.

September 11, 2001 On this date al Qaeda terrorists carried out a plan by Osama bin Laden that destroyed the World Trade Center towers and damaged the Pentagon in Washington, D.C.

Seven Years' War The world conflict (1754–1763) fought in Europe, India, and North America between Great Britain, Hanover, and Prussia on one side and France, Austria, Spain, and other nations on the other side.

sharecropping Working land in return for a share of the crops produced instead of paying cash rent. A shortage of currency in the South made this a frequent form of land tenure, and African Americans endured it because it eliminated the labor gangs of the slavery period.

Shays's Rebellion The revolt by western Massachusetts farmers in 1786–1787 named after one of the leaders, Daniel Shays. Their demands included a more responsive state government, paper money, and tender laws that would enable them to settle debts and pay taxes with goods rather than with specie.

Sherman Antitrust Act This legislation was passed in 1890 to curb the growth of large monopolistic corporations.

Sieur de La Salle French explorer in North America who claimed Louisiana for France (1682).

Sir Edmund Andros English colonial administrator in America whose attempt to unify the New England colonies under his governorship (1686–1689) was met by revolt.

Sitting Bull Ally of Crazy Horse in the Custer battle.

Sixteenth Amendment Ratified in 1913, this amendment made an income tax constitutional.

Smoked Yankees The term used by Spanish troops to denote African American soldiers who fought in the war with Spain.

Social Darwinism A philosophy that allegedly showed how closely the social history of humans resembled Darwin's principle of "survival of the fittest." According to this theory, human social history could be understood as a struggle among races, with the strongest and the fittest invariably triumphing.

Sojourner Truth A former slave who became an advocate for abolitionism and for woman's rights.

Spanish-American War The conflict that brought the United States a world empire.

Special Field Order 15 Issued by William T. Sherman in January of 1865, this order reserved land in coastal South Carolina, Georgia, and Florida for former slaves. Those who settled on the land would receive forty-acre plots.

spoils system A system by which the victorious political party rewarded its supporters with government jobs.

Sputnik I Launched by the Soviet Union in October 1957, it was the first artificial space satellite. News of its success provoked both anger and anxiety among the American people who had always taken their country's technological superiority for granted.

Squanto A Patuxet Indian who helped the English colonists in Plymouth develop agricultural techniques and served as an interpreter between the colonists and the Wampanoags.

Square Deal Roosevelt's approach to treating capital and labor on an equal basis.

Stamp Act In 1765 the British Parliament passed a law requiring colonists to purchase a stamp for official documents and published papers, including wills, newspapers, and pamphlets.

Stephen A. Douglas American politician who served as U.S. representative (1843–1847) and senator (1847–1861) from Illinois. He proposed legislation that allowed individual territories to determine whether they would allow slavery (1854), and in the senatorial campaign of 1858 he engaged Abraham Lincoln in a famous series of debates.

Stephen Crane Author of *The Red Badge of Courage.*

stock market crash of 1929 The collapse of stock prices that ended the speculative boom of the 1920s and is associated with the onset of the Great Depression.

Stono Uprising A revolt of enslaved Africans against their owners near the Stono River in South Carolina.

Strategic Defense Initiative (SDI) A research and development program of the U.S. government tasked with developing a space-based system to defend the nation from attack by strategic ballistic missiles.

Students for a Democratic Society (SDS) Formed in Port Huron, Michigan, in 1962, this group became one of the leading New Left antiwar organizations of the 1960s, exemplifying both the idealism and the excesses of radical student groups in the Vietnam era.

suffrage The right to vote that was extended to African American males after the Civil War.

Susan B. Anthony Advocate of woman's suffrage and leader in the woman's rights movement along with Elizabeth Cady Stanton.

Tecumseh Shawnee leader who attempted to establish a confederacy to unify Native Americans against white encroachment. He sided with the British in the War of 1812 and was killed in the Battle of the Thames.

temperance Reducing the influence and the effect of alcoholic beverages in American life.

temperance movement The act of abstaining from partaking of alcoholic beverages.

Tennessee Valley Authority (TVA) Created in 1933 during the New Deal's first hundred days, it was a massive experiment in regional planning that focused on providing electricity, flood control, and soil conservation to one of the nation's poorest regions, covering seven states in the Tennessee Valley.

Tet offensive A major military operation by the North Vietnamese and Viet Cong in 1968. Though beaten back, there were tremendous casualties, and the enormity of the offensive served to undermine President Johnson's claim that steady progress was being made in Vietnam.

The Birth of a Nation A twisted movie portrayal of the Reconstruction period in the South that depicted African Americans as ignorant and that glamorized the Ku Klux Klan.

The Book of Mormon The holy book of the Church of Jesus Christ of Latter-Day Saints, or the Mormons.

The Federalist Papers James Madison, Alexander Hamilton, and John Jay wrote a series of eighty-five essays in support of the Constitution. First published in newspapers, they appeared in book form as *The Federalist* in the spring of 1788.

The Grapes of Wrath Written by John Steinbeck and published in 1939, this novel depicts the struggle of ordinary Americans in the Great Depression, following the plight of the Joad family as it migrated west from Oklahoma to California.

The Great Communicator A nickname given to Ronald Reagan for his skill in conveying his views.

The Jazz Singer One of the first motion pictures with sound, it starred Al Jolson who specialized in blackface renditions of popular tunes.

theocracy A government ruled by or subject to religious authority.

Theodore Roosevelt The twenty-sixth president of the United States, the youngest president in the nation's history. He brought new excitement and power to the presidency as he vigorously led Congress and the American people toward progressive reforms and a strong foreign policy.

Thirteenth Amendment Passed in 1865, this constitutional amendment abolished slavery.

Thomas Alva Edison The inventor of the phonograph, electric lights, and countless other products.

Thomas J. "Stonewall" Jackson American Confederate general who commanded troops at both battles of Bull Run (1861 and 1862) and directed the Shenandoah Valley campaign (1862). He was accidentally killed by his own troops at Chancellorsville (1863).

Thomas Jefferson The third president of the United States (1801–1809). A member of the second Continental Congress, he drafted the Declaration of Independence (1776). His presidency was marked by the purchase of the Louisiana Territory from France (1803) and the Embargo of 1807.

Thomas Paine Author of *Common Sense* (1776) and other pamphlets, Paine was a recent immigrant from England.

Tiananmen Square Adjacent to the Forbidden City in Beijing, China, this large public square was the site of many festivals, rallies, and demonstrations. During a student demonstration there in 1989, Chinese troops fired on the demonstrators, killing an estimated two thousand or more.

Tories The term referred to the followers of James II and became the name of a major political party in England. Americans who remained loyal to the British during the Revolution were called Tories.

Trail of Tears After determined efforts to move the Cherokee, the tribe was deported from Georgia to what is now Oklahoma; thousands died on the march known as the Trail of Tears.

transcendentalists Members of an intellectual and social movement of the 1830s and 1940s that emphasized the active role the mind plays in constructing what we think of as reality. A loose grouping of intellectuals in Massachusetts sought to "transcend" the limits of thought in conventional America, whether religious or philosophical.

Treaty of Paris Signed on September 3, 1783, the Treaty of Paris established the independence of the United States from Great Britain. It set specific land boundaries and called for the evacuation of British troops.

Treaty of Tordesillas The Treaty of Tordesillas (1494) located the Line of Demarcation 370 leagues (about 1,000 miles) west of the Azores and expanded the principle of "spheres of influence."

Treaty of Utrecht Ending Queen Anne's War between Great Britain and France, the Treaty of Utrecht ceded control of Nova Scotia, Newfoundland, and the Hudson Bay territory to the English.

Triangle Shirtwaist Fire A tragic fire at the Triangle Shirtwaist Company in which dozens of female workers perished.

Triple Alliance An alliance between Italy, Germany, and Austria-Hungary whose ties were frayed in 1914.

Truman Doctrine Reflecting a tougher approach to the Soviet Union following World War II, President Truman went before Congress in 1947 to request $400 million in military aid for Greece and Turkey, claiming the appropriation was vital to the containment of Communism and to the future of freedom everywhere.

trustbusters Term applied to Theodore Roosevelt's efforts to enforce the Sherman Act.

Tweed Ring The most celebrated example of political corruption in the Reconstruction Era, led by William Magear Tweed, Jr.

Twentieth Amendment This amendment moved the presidential inauguration date from four months after the election to January 20.

U-2 A U.S. spy plane. One piloted by Francis Gary Powers was shot down over the Soviet Union in 1960, which led to the angry breakup of a Summit meeting in Paris between President Eisenhower and Soviet Premier Nikita Khrushchev.

Ulysses S. Grant The eighteenth president of the United States; commander of the Union Army in the American Civil War.

Uncle Tom's Cabin Novel by author Harriet Beecher Stowe that helped change white attitudes toward African Americans.

Upton Sinclair A writer whose novel *The Jungle* exposed abuses in the meat-packing industry.

vertical integration A procedure wherein a company gains control of all phases of production.

viceroy A man who is the governor of a country, province, or colony, ruling as the representative of a sovereign.

Vicksburg Mississippi battle site under siege by Grant's army for six weeks. Before falling it became the symbol of Confederate doggedness and Union frustration.

Victoriano Huerta The Mexican general who presented a problem for President Wilson.

Vietnamization A policy whereby the South Vietnamese were to assume more of the military burdens of the war. This transfer of responsibility was expected to eventually allow the United States to withdraw.

Virginia Company In 1606 King James I chartered the Virginia Company; one group was centered in London and founded Jamestown, a second group from Plymouth in western England founded the Plymouth colony.

Virginia Plan Written by James Madison, the Virginia Plan proposed a powerful central government dominated by a National Legislature of two houses (bicameral). It also favored a system of greater representation based on a state's population.

W. E. B. Du Bois Initially a supporter of Booker T. Washington's education policy, he later criticized Washington's methods as having "practically accepted the alleged inferiority of the Negro."

Walt Whitman A visionary poet who wrote *Leaves of Grass* (1855), inventing a new American idiom.

Walter Mondale Vice president of the United States under Jimmy Carter, he earlier served as a U.S. senator from Minnesota and was the unsuccessful 1984 Democratic nominee for president.

war on terrorism In response to the September 11 attacks, President George W. Bush declared war on the terrorists and sent U.S. troops to invade first Afghanistan and later Iraq.

Watergate The Democratic National Headquarters at the Watergate complex in Washington, D.C., was burglarized in 1972, which led to criminal convictions for several top government officials and forced President Nixon to resign from office in 1974.

Watts riots Among the most violent urban disturbances in U.S. history, it erupted in an African American neighborhood in Los Angeles following the arrest of a black motorist. By the time it ended, five days later, forty-one people were dead, hundreds were injured, property damage topped $200 million, and National Guardsmen had to be called in to restore order.

Wendell Wilkie A Wall Street lawyer who ran against Franklin D. Roosevelt in his bid for a third consecutive term, which Roosevelt won.

Whiskey Rebellion In the early 1790s western Pennsylvania farmers resisted the whiskey tax: they held protest meetings, tarred and feathered collaborators, and destroyed property. In 1794 the Washington administration sent thirteen thousand troops to restore order, but the revolt was over by the time they arrived.

Whitewater The popular name for a failed Arkansas real estate venture by the Whitewater Development Corporation in which then Governor Bill Clinton and his wife, Hillary, were partners.

William Henry Harrison While governor of the Indiana Territory, he attacked and burned Prophetstown in 1811. The ninth president of the United States (1841), he died of pneumonia after one month in office.

William Howard Taft The twenty-seventh president of the United States, who split with Theodore Roosevelt once in office.

William Jefferson "Bill" Clinton The forty-second president of the United States.

William Jennings Bryan Named secretary of state by Wilson, he pursued world peace through arbitration treaties.

William Lloyd Garrison American abolitionist leader who founded and published *The Liberator* (1831–1865), an antislavery journal.

William McKinley The twenty-fifth president of the United States, he won by the largest majority of popular votes since 1872.

William Penn An English Quaker leader who obtained a charter for Pennsylvania from Charles II in exchange for a debt owed to Penn's father. Penn intended to establish a model society based on religious freedom and peaceful relations with Native Americans, in addition to benefiting financially from the sale of the land.

William Pitt A British political leader and orator who directed his country's military effort during the Seven Years' War.

William Randolph Hearst The most celebrated publisher of the yellow press.

William T. Sherman Union general under Ulysses S. Grant who took Atlanta and led the "March to the Sea."

William Walker A proslavery Tennesseean who pushed for expansion of the American territory into Cuba or Central America, places where slavery could flourish.

Winston Churchill A British politician and writer, as prime minister (1940–1945 and 1951–1955) he led Great Britain through World War II. He published several books, including *The Second World War* (1948–1953), and won the 1953 Nobel Prize for literature.

woman suffrage Women achieved the right to vote in 1919–1920 after an intense struggle in Congress.

Woodrow Wilson The twenty-eighth president of the United States, he was an advocate for the New Freedom and the League of Nations.

Woodstock Art and Music Fair A fusion of rock music, hard drugs, free love, and an antiwar protest drawing four hundred thousand people in the summer of 1969.

writs of assistance General search warrants; a writ of assistance authorized customs officials to search for smuggled goods.

XYZ Affair Name given to the episode in which the French government (the Directory) demanded, through three agents known to the American public as X, Y, and Z, that the U.S. government pay a bribe and apologize for criticizing France.

yellow press (yellow journalism) A type of journalism that stressed lurid and sensational news to boost circulation.

Zachary Taylor The twelfth president (died in his first year in office in 1850), he became famous as a general in the war with Mexico. As Whig president, he tried to avoid entanglements of both party and region.

Zimmermann Telegram A secret German diplomatic telegram to the German ambassador in Mexico that was intercepted and decoded by the British. It dangled the return to Mexico of Arizona, New Mexico, and Texas as bait to entice the Mexicans to enter the war on the side of Germany.

Zora Neale Hurston An African American novelist who embodied the creative and artistic aspirations of the Harlem Renaissance in the 1920s.

Photo Credits

Chapter 1
2T, Colonial Williamsburg Foundation; 2B, © The Granger Collection, New York; 3T, Duke University Special Collections; 3B, © Atwater Kent Museum of Philadelphia, Courtesy of Historical Society of Pennsylvania Collection, Atwater Kent Museum of Philadelphia/Bridgeman Art Library; 8, © Craig Aurness/ CORBIS; 10, ASM specimen A-26556, Santa Cruz on puff plate form Snaketown, Arizona. State Museum, University of Arizona. Helgatweis, photographer; 11, Courtesy, National Museum of the American Indian, Smithsonian Institution, #P18523; 13, Depiction of Cahokia Mounds AD 1150 by William R. Ieminger. Courtesy of Cahokia Mounds Historic Site; 14L, © The Granger Collection, New York; 14R, © British Museum, London, UK/Bridgeman Art Library; 17, National Maritime Museum; 18, © The Granger Collection, New York; 19, © The Granger Collection, New York; 20, © The New York Public Library/Art Resource, NY; 21, Library of Congress, Prints and Photographs Division; 22, Courtesy of the John Carter Brown Library at Brown University; 25, © ARPL/HIP/The Image Works; 29, ©Biblioteca Medicea-Laurenziana, Florence, Italy/Bridgeman Art Library; 31, Courtesy of The John Carter Brown Library at Brown University; 33, By kind permission of His Grace the Duke of Bedford and the Trustees of the Bedford Estates, © His Grace the Duke of Bedford and the Trustees of the Bedford Estates

Chapter 2
36, © Bettmann/CORBIS; 38, ©Kevin Fleming/CORBIS; 39, © Jerry Jacka; 42, © The Granger Collection, New York; 43L, © The Granger Collection, New York; 43R, © The Granger Collection, New York; 44, Colonial Williamsburg Foundation; 46L, © The Trustees of The British Museum; 46R, Library of Congress, Prints and Photographs Division; 47, North Wind Picture Archives; 51, Museum of The City of New York; 53, Plymouth Plantation, Inc. photographer, Gary Andrashko; 54L, Courtesy of the Massachusetts Historical Society; 54R, © The Granger Collection, New York; 56, Worcester Art Museum, Worcester, MA, Gift of Mr. & Mrs. Albert W. Rice, 1963.134; 57, © The Granger Collection, New York; 58, North Wind Picture Archives; 59, Courtesy Enoch Pratt Free Library, Baltimore; 62, © The New York Public Library/Art Resource, NY

Chapter 3
66, © The Granger Collection, New York; 68L, The Structure of Praise by Arthur Mazmarian © 1970 by Beacon Press. Reprinted by permission of Beacon Press, Boston; 68R, The Structure of Praise by Arthur Mazmarian © 1970 by Beacon Press. Reprinted by permission of Beacon Press, Boston; 69, Courtesy of Special Collections, University Research Library, University of California at Los Angeles; 70TL, © Brooklyn Museum of Art, New York, USA, Bequest of Mrs Wiliam Sterling Peters, by exchange/Bridgeman Art Library; 70BL, © Ashmolean Museum, University of Oxford, UK/Bridgeman Art Library; 70R, © South West Museum, Los Angeles, CA/Bridgeman Art Library; 72, Courtesy of Historic St. Mary's City; 75, Historical Society of Pennsylvania; 76, The Historical Society of Pennsylvania; 77, By courtesy of the National Portrait Gallery, London; 79, Courtesy, Peabody Essex Museum, Salem, Mass;. 88L, © The New York Public Library/Art Resource, NY; 88R, Colonial Williamsburg Foundation; 89, Courtesy, American Antiquarian Society; 91, North Wind Picture Archives

Chapter 4
96, © The Philadelphia Museum of Art/Art Resource, NY. Philadelphia Museum of Art: Mr. and Mrs. Wharton Sinkler Collection (58-132-1); 99T, Courtesy, American Antiquarian Society; 99B, Courtesy, American Antiquarian Society; 100, © Private Collection, Paul Freeman/ Bridgeman Art Library; 102, © The Granger Collection, New York; 103, © The Granger Collection, New York; 105, Courtesy, Winterthur Museum; 111, From Indians in Pennsylvania by Paul A.W. Wallace, published by the Pennsylvania Historical and Museum Commission.; 112, By permission of Yale University Press; 116, The Historical Society of Pennsylvania; 117, © Private Collection/Phillips, Fine Art Auctioneers, New York, USA/Bridgeman Art Library; 118, © CORBIS; 120, Maryland Historical Society; 121, Maryland Historical Society; 122, The Library Company of Philadelphia; 123, Colonial Williamsburg Foundation; 126T, Courtesy, American Antiquarian Society; 126B, Courtesy of the U.S. Naval Academy Museum; 127TL, The Metropolitan Museum of Art, Rogers Fund, 1942 (42.95.16) Photograph © 1989 The Metropolitan Museum of Art; 127TR, By Permission of the Yale University Press

Chapter 5
132, Courtesy, American Antiquarian Society 136, Library of Congress, Prints and Photographs Division; 140, The Library Company of Philadelphia; 141, Courtesy of the Rhode Island Historical Society, Neg. #RHi (x4)1; 142, © The Granger Collection, New York; 144, Samuel Adams, John Singleton Copley, American, 1738–1815, about 1772 Oil on canvas, 125.73 × 100.33 cm (49 1/2 × 39 1/2 in.), Photograph © 2006 Museum of Fine Arts, Boston. Deposited by the City of Boston.; 145, © BRIAN SNYDER/Reuters/CORBIS; 146, Collection of the New York Historical Society; 147, Independence National Historical Park; 148, © The Granger Collection, New York; 149, Anne S. K. Brown Military Collection, Brown University Library; 151, © Bettmann/CORBIS; 152, Library of Congress, Prints and Photographs Division; 154, © The Granger Collection, New York; 156, Courtesy, American Antiquarian Society; 157, New York State Historical Association, Cooperstown; 159, © The Granger Collection, New York

Chapter 6
164, © Bettmann/CORBIS; 167, © The Granger Collection, New York; 168L, Colonial Williamsburg Foundation; 168R, Courtesy of the Rhode Island Historical Society, #RHi X5 32 Mas.1900.6.1; 169, Courtesy, Winterthur Museum; 170, Abby Aldrich Rockefeller Folk Art Center, Williamsburg; 171, © Hulton Archive/Getty Images; 172, The Library Company of Philadelphia; 173, Abby Aldritch Rockefeller Folk Art Center, Williamsburg; 177, © The Granger Collection, New York; 178, Courtesy of the Museum of American Art at the Pennsylvania Academy of Fine Arts, Philadelphia. Bequest of Richard Ashhurst; 181, © The Granger Collection, New York; 184, © The Granger Collection, New York; 185B, © Bettmann/CORBIS; 185T, © The Granger Collection, New York; 186, © The Granger Collection, New York; 187, Independence National Historical Park; 189, Eastern National Park & Monument Association; 190, © The Granger Collection, New York

Chapter 7
196, © The Granger Collection, New York; 198, © The Granger Collection, New York; 201, © Bettmann/CORBIS; 202, Independence National Historical Park; 203B, © The Granger Collection, New York; 203T, © The Granger Collection, New York; 204, © The Granger Collection, New York; 205, Smithsonian Institution; 206L, Library of Congress, Prints and Photographs Division; 206R, © The New York Public Library/Art Resource, NY; 208, National Archives; 210T, © The Granger Collection, New York; 210B, Courtesy of the Bancroft Library, University of California, Berkeley; 211, Courtesy, Museo Naval de Madrid and Robin Imglis; 214, Independence National Historical Park; 215, © Huntington Library/Superstock

Chapter 8
222, © The Granger Collection, New York; 224B, The Library Company of Philadelphia; 224T, Collection of the New York Historical

Society; **225,** Moorland-Spingarn Research Center, Howard University; **227,** North Wind Picture Archives; **228,** © Smithsonian American Art Museum, Washington, DC/Art Resource, NY; **229,** Library of Congress, Prints and Photographs Division; **230,** Historical Society of Pennsylvania (Bb 882 B756 44); **232,** From the Collections of the New Jersey Historical Society, Newark, New Jersey; **233,** © The Granger Collection, New York; **235,** The Architect of the Capitol; **236,** © The Granger Collection, New York; **239,** By permission of Houghton Library, Harvard University; **244,** Smithsonian Institution, Bureau of American Ethnology; **246,** Fenimore Art Museum, Cooperstown, NY; **247,** © The Granger Collection, New York; **248,** Anne S.K. Brown Military Collection, Brown University Library; **253T,** © New York Public Library/Art Resource, NY; **253B,** © The Granger Collection, New York

Chapter 9
258, © The Granger Collection, New York; **260,** © The Granger Collection, New York; **264,** © The Granger Collection, New York; **265,** © The Granger Collection, New York; **266,** © Bettmann/CORBIS; **267,** © The Granger Collection, New York; **268,** Abby Aldrich Rockefeller Folk Art Center, Williamsburg, VA; **270,** George Henry Durrie, *Winter in the Country,* c. 1858,Oil on canvas, 45.7 × 61.1 cm (18 × 24 1/16 in.), Collection of Mr. and Mrs. Paul Mellon, © Board of Trustees, National Gallery of Art, Washington, DC. 1994.59.1; **272,** © The Granger Collection, New York; **273,** © The Granger Collection, New York; **278,** Courtesy of the Tennessee State Library and Archives; **279,** Library of Congress, Prints and Photographs Division; **280,** © Bettmann/CORBIS; **282,** Cincinnati Museum Center–Cincinnati Historical Society

Chapter 10
286, © National Portrait Gallery, Smithsonian Institution/Art Resource, NY; **288,** © The Granger Collection, New York; **289,** © Bettmann/CORBIS; **290,** © The Granger Collection, New York; **292,** © Bettmann/CORBIS; **293,** © The Granger Collection, New York; **295,** © New York Public Library/Art Resource, NY; **296,** © The Granger Collection, New York; **298,** © Smithsonian American Art Museum, Washington, DC/Art Resource, NY; **301,** Woolaroc Museum, Bartlesville, Oklahoma; **302L,** © The Granger Collection, New York; **302R,** © The Granger Collection, New York; **303,** Old Dartmouth Historical Society–New Bedford Whaling Museum, Gift of William F. Havemeyer (187); **305,** © Bettmann/CORBIS; **306,** *Catharine Wheeler Hardy and Her Daughter,* Jeremiah Pearson Hardy, American, 1800–1887, about 1845, Oil on canvas, 74.29 × 91.76 cm (29 1/4 × 36 1/8 in.) M. and M. Karolik Collection. Photograph © 2006 Museum of Fine Arts, Boston; **307T,** © The Granger Collection, New York; **307B,** © The Granger Collection, New York; **308,** Library of Congress, Prints and Photographs Division

Chapter 11
312, 1945.4.1, Inness, George, *The Lackawanna Valley,* Gift of Mrs. Huttleston Rogers, Image © 2005 Board of Trustees, National Gallery of Art, Washington, c.1865; **314,** Museum of the City of New York; **315,** *The First Railroad Train on the Mohawk and Hudson Road,* Edward Lamson Henry (1841–1919) 1892–93, Oil on canvas, Albany Institute of History & Art, Gift of the Friends of the Institute through Catherine Gansevoort (Mrs. Abraham) Lansing, x1940.600.57, Photograph by Joseph Levy; **319,** Library of Congress, Prints and Photographs Division; **320,** The Historic New Orleans Collection, Accension #1975.931&2; **321,** Library of Congress, Prints and Photographs Division; **322,** Courtesy of Special Collections, University of Miami Libraries; **324,** Library of Congress, Prints and Photographs Division; **325T,** Courtesy of the American Tract Society, Garland, TX; **325B,** North Wind Picture Archives; **326,** Oberlin College Archives, Oberlin, Ohio; **328,** © The Granger Collection, New York; **329,** Library of Congress, Prints and Photographs Division; **330,** © The Granger Collection, New York; **331,** © The Granger Collection, New York; **332L,** © The Newark Museum/Art Resource, NY; **332TR,** Courtesy of the Edgar Allan Poe Museum, Richmond, VA; **332BR,** © The Granger Collection, New York; **333,** Library of Congress, Prints and Photographs Division; **338,** Courtesy of the Massachusetts Historical Society

Chapter 12
342, © Peabody Essex Museum, Salem, Massachusetts, USA/Bridgeman Art Library; **344,** Exeter, N.H. Volunteers leaving for the Mexican War. Possibly after E. Punderson, daguerreotype, 1/4 plate, ca. 1846, P1979.33/ Amon Carter Museum, Fort Worth, Texas; **346,** Library of Congress, Prints and Photographs Division; **350,** © The Granger Collection, New York; **351T,** Courtesy of California History Section, California State Library, Sacramento, California; **351B,** © The Granger Collection, New York; **352,** Mormon Panorama Eighteen/Crossing the Mississippi on the Ice, by C.C.A. Christensen © Courtesy Museum of Art, Brigham Young University. All rights reserved; **353,** © The Granger Collection, New York; **356L,** © The Granger Collection, New York; **356R,** The J. Paul Getty Museum, Los Angeles; **357,** Women's Rights National Historical Park, Courtesy of Seneca Falls Historical Society; **360L,** © The Granger Collection, New York; **360R,** © The Granger Collection, New York; **361L,** © Bettmann/CORBIS; **361R,** © The Granger Collection, New York; **363,** © CORBIS; **364,** © Bettmann/CORBIS; **365L,** © The Granger Collection, New York; **365R,** © Bettmann/CORBIS; **366,** Library of Congress, Prints and Photographs Division; **367,** Library of Congress, Prints and Photographs Division; **369,** © CORBIS; **373,** Winslow Homer's "Sunday Morning in Virginia" 1877 Cincinnati Art Museum, John M. Emerey Funds. Acc. 1924.247

Chapter 13
378, © The Granger Collection, New York; **382,** Courtesy of the Daughters of the Republic of Texas Library; **384T,** The Kansas State Historical Society, Topeka, Kansas; **384B,** © The Granger Collection, New York; **385,** Courtesy of the Massachusetts Historical Society; **386R,** Library of Congress, Prints and Photographs Division; **386L,** © The Granger Collection, New York; **388,** © The Granger Collection, New York; **390,** © CORBIS; **393,** © Bettmann/CORBIS; **394,** Library of Congress, Prints and Photographs Division; **396,** © Bettmann/CORBIS; **397L,** Library of Congress, Prints and Photographs Division; **397B,** © The Granger Collection, New York; **398,** © The Granger Collection, New York; **399,** PR-065-791-7, Collection of the New-York Historical Society

Chapter 14
402, © The Granger Collection, New York; **406,** North Wind Picture Archives; **408L,** Library of Congress, Prints and Photographs Division; **408L,** public domain no credit needed; **409L,** The Museum of the Confederacy, Richmond, Virginia. Copy photography by Katherine Wetzel; **409R,** © The Granger Collection, New York; **410T,** Courtesy Sidney King; **410M,** Courtesy of the National Park Service, Kennesau Mountain National Park. Photo, Harpers Peng Conservation Center; **410B,** Courtesy of the Carl Vinson Institute of Government–The University of Virginia. Photo by Ed Jackson; **412T,** © CORBIS; **412B,** © The Granger Collection, New York; **414,** © Geoffrey Clements/CORBIS; **415,** Williamson Art Gallery & Museum, Birkenhead, England; **416,** © The Granger Collection, New York; **418B,** Benjamin Adworth Richardson, Merrimac in Dry Dock Being Converted into The Iron Battery Virginia, ca.1907, Oil on canvas, 9 × 12 inches, Gift of the Brothers Anson T. and Philip T. McCook. Chrysler Museum of Art, Norfolk, VA (54.5.2); **418T,** Museum of the City of New York, The Harry T. Peters Collection. 57-300-21; **420,** PR-065-808-7, Collection of The New-York Historical Society; **421,** The Western Reserve Historical Society, Cleveland, Ohio; **422,** Chicago Historical Society, P&S-1932.0027; **423,** The Western Reserve Historical Society, Cleveland, Ohio; **425,** New Hampshire Historical Society; **426,** Courtesy of The Library of Virginia; **427,** National Park Services, Antietam National Battlefield; **428,** © Stock Montage, Inc.

Chapter 15
432, © Bettmann/CORBIS; **434,** The Library of Virginia; **435,** Chicago Historical Society, ICHi-22049; **436,** © Kean Collection/Hulton Archive/Getty Images; **437,** © The Stock Montage, Inc.; **441,** © The Granger Collection, New York; **442,** Library of Congress Prints and Photographs Division; **443,** © The Stock Montage, Inc.; **446,** © Bettmann/CORBIS; **449T,** Neg. no. 42793, Collection of The New-York Historical Society;

449B, Library of Congress, Prints and Photographs Division; **453R,** Library of Congress, Prints and Photographs Division; **453L,** © CORBIS; **454,** © Bettmann/CORBIS; **455T,** North Wind Picture Archives; **455B,** © The Granger Collection, New York; **458R,** © CORBIS; **458L,** © CORBIS; **459,** North Wind Picture Archives; **460T,** Library of Congress, Prints and Photographs Division; **460B,** © The Granger Collection, New York; **461,** © The Granger Collection, New York; **462,** Library of Congress, Prints and Photographs Division

Chapter 16
466, © Stock Montage, Inc.; **468,** © CORBIS SYGMA; **469,** Library of Congress, Prints and Photographs Division; **472,** © The Granger Collection, New York; **473,** California History Section, California State Library; **474,** Library of Congress, Prints and Photographs Division; **476,** Kansas State Historical Society; **477L,** © The Granger Collection, New York; **477R,** © Bettmann/CORBIS; **479,** Library of Congress, Prints and Photographs Division; **480,** © The Granger Collection, New York; **482,** Library of Congress, Prints and Photographs Division; **483,** Library of Congress, Prints and Photographs Division; **484,** Library of Congress, Prints and Photographs Division; **487T,** Library of Congress, Prints and Photographs Division; **487B,** Library of Congress, Prints and Photographs Division; **492L,** Library of Congress, Prints and Photographs Division; **492R,** S.S. *Pennland,* Steerage Deck, 1893. Museum of the City of New York. The Byron Collection. 93.1.118432; **493,** © Bettmann/CORBIS

Chapter 17
498, © Rykoff Collection/CORBIS; **503,** Courtesy of the Rockefeller Archive Center; **504,** © Bettmann/CORBIS; **505,** Library of Congress, Prints and Photographs Division; **508,** © The Granger Collection, New York; **509,** Library of Congress, Prints and Photographs Division; **511,** © The Granger Collection, New York; **513,** Library of Congress, Prints and Photographs Division; **515,** Kansas State Historical Society; **516,** © CORBIS; **519,** © Bettmann/CORBIS; **522,** Library of Congress, Prints and Photographs Division

Chapter 18
526, © The Granger Collection, New York; **529,** © The Granger Collection, New York; **530,** © The Granger Collection, New York; **531,** © CORBIS; **532,** Library of Congress, Prints and Photographs Division; **533T,** Library of Congress, Prints and Photographs Division; **533B,** © The Granger Collection, New York; **535,** © The Granger Collection, New York; **536,** © George Barker/Henry Guttmann/Getty Images; **539,** © The Granger Collection, New York; **541,** © The Granger Collection, New York; **542,** The Kansas State Historical Society; **543,** © The Granger Collection, New York; **545T,** © David J. & Janice L. Frent Collection/CORBIS; **545BL,** © Bettmann/CORBIS; **545BR,** Chicago Historical Society, #CHI-03590; **547,** Chicago Historical Society

Chapter 19
550, © The Granger Collection, New York; **552,** Library of Congress, Prints and Photographs Division; **553,** Library of Congress, Prints and Photographs Division; **555T,** Library of Congress, Prints and Photographs Division; **555B,** © CORBIS; **557,** Library of Congress, Prints and Photographs Division; **559,** © CORBIS; **563L,** © The Granger Collection, New York; **563R,** Library of Congress, Prints and Photographs Division; **564,** © The Granger Collection, New York; **566T,** © The Granger Collection, New York; **566B,** Library of Congress, Prints and Photographs Division; **568,** © The Granger Collection, New York; **569T,** Library of Congress, Prints and Photographs Division; **569B,** Library of Congress, Prints and Photographs Division; **574,** Culver Pictures

Chapter 20
578, © The Granger Collection, New York; **582,** © The Granger Collection, New York; **585,** © Bettmann/CORBIS; **587,** © Bettmann/CORBIS; **589,** © The Granger Collection, New York; **591,** © The Granger Collection, New York; **594,** © The Granger Collection, New

York; **595,** © Bettmann/CORBIS; **596L,** Library of Congress, Prints and Photographs Division; **596R,** Library of Congress, Prints and Photographs Division; **597L,** Library of Congress, Prints and Photographs Division; **597R,** Library of Congress, Prints and Photographs Division; **599,** Albert Shaw, A Cartoon History of Roosevelt's Career (1910); **600T,** © The Granger Collection, New York; **600B,** By Homer Davenport. From the Evening Mail (New York); **604,** © Hulton Archive/Getty Images; **605L,** © The Granger Collection, New York; **605R,** © Bettmann/CORBIS

Chapter 21
610, Victor Joseph Gatto, Triangle Fire (March 25.1911) 1944-1945. Museum of the City of New York. 54.75; **612,** Library of Congress, Prints and Photographs Division; **615,** © Bettmann/CORBIS; **616L,** Library of Congress, Prints and Photographs Division; **616R,** © The Granger Collection, New York; **617,** Library of Congress, Prints and Photographs Division; **623,** Library of Congress, Prints and Photographs Division; **624,** Library of Congress, Prints and Photographs Division; **625,** Library of Congress, Prints and Photographs Division; **626,** Library of Congress, Prints and Photographs Division; **630,** From the Collections of The Henry Ford, ID:30.1781.1/T.9470; **631,** George Bellows, "The Cliff Dwellers" 1913. Los Angeles County Museum of Art, Los Angeles; **632T,** © Bettmann/CORBIS; **632B,** © Bettmann/CORBIS; **633,** Library of Congress, Prints and Photographs Division

Chapter 22
640, Library of Congress, Prints and Photographs Division; **643,** © The Granger Collection, New York; **644B,** © The Granger Collection, New York; **644T,** Library of Congress, Prints and Photographs Division; **645,** © Schomburg Center/Art Resource, NY; **646L,** Washington Evening Star, November, 1915; **646R,** © Bettmann/CORBIS; **648,** Library of Congress, Prints and Photographs Division; **650,** Library of Congress, Prints and Photographs Division; **652,** © The Granger Collection, New York; **656T,** © Bettmann/CORBIS; **656B,** Library of Congress, Prints and Photographs Division; **659,** Library of Congress, Prints and Photographs Division; **663T,** U.S. Signal Corps. PhotoNo. 111-SC-62979 in the National Archives; **663BL,** © Bettmann/CORBIS; **663BR,** © Bettmann/CORBIS; **664,** National Archives #165-WW-269.c-7; **666,** Brown Brothers

Chapter 23
670, © Bettmann/CORBIS; **672,** © Bettmann/CORBIS; **674,** Library of Congress, Prints and Photographs Division; **677T,** Library of Congress, Prints and Photographs Division; **677B,** No credit needed; **678,** © The Granger Collection, New York; **679,** Library of Congress, Prints and Photographs Division; **680,** © CORBIS; **681,** © Bettmann/CORBIS; **682,** © Underwood & Underwood/CORBIS; **683T,** © The Granger Collection, New York; **683B,** © Frank Driggs Collection/Getty Images; **684,** © Bettmann/CORBIS; **685,** © The Granger Collection, New York; **689,** Library of Congress, Prints and Photographs Division; **690,** © Bettmann/CORBIS; **693,** © The Granger Collection, New York; **694,** © CORBIS

Chapter 24
698, Library of Congress, Prints and Photographs Division; **701,** Library of Congress, Prints and Photographs Division; **703,** Library of Congress, Prints and Photographs Division; **704,** © Bettmann/CORBIS; **707,** © Bettmann/CORBIS; **708,** © Bettmann/CORBIS; **709T,** © Bettmann/CORBIS; **709B,** © Bettmann/CORBIS; **711B,** © The Granger Collection, New York; **711T,** © CORBIS; **715,** © CORBIS; **716,** © The Granger Collection, New York; **717,** © Bettmann/CORBIS; **718,** Library of Congress, Prints and Photographs Division; **722,** © Bettmann/CORBIS; **723T,** U.S. Coast Guard Photo no. 26-WA-6J-14 in the National Archives; **723B,** © Bettmann/CORBIS

Chapter 25
728, © The Granger Collection, New York; **730,** © Bettmann/CORBIS; **731,** © Bettmann/CORBIS; **735,** © Bettmann/CORBIS; **736,** © Bettmann/CORBIS; **738,** © Bettmann/CORBIS; **739,** © Bettmann/

Index

GREENLAND
(Den.)

RUSSIA   ALASKA
                (U.S.)

CANADA

UNITED
STATES

ATLANTIC

OCEAN

BAHAMAS

MEXICO   CUBA   DOMINICAN REP.
        HAWAII   Puerto Rico (U.S.)
        (U.S.)   JAMAICA HAITI   ST. KITTS
                        BELIZE   VIRGIN ISLANDS   ANTIGUA
                                                DOMINICA
        GUATEMALA HONDURAS   ST. LUCIA BARBADOS
        EL SALVADOR NICARAGUA ST. VINCENT   GRENADA   GUI
                                            TRINIDAD & TOBAGO
PACIFIC   COSTA RICA   GUYANA
                        PANAMA   VENEZUELA   SURINAME
                                                FR. GUIANA
                        COLOMBIA

                        ECUADOR

OCEAN   PERU   BRAZIL

        NAURU   KIRIBATI
SOLOMON   TUVALU   TOKELAU
ISLANDS   WEST.
        VANUATU FIJI SAMOA AM.   BOLIVIA
                              SAMOA   PARAGUAY
                COOK
                IS.
        NEW   TONGA NIUE (N.Z.) FRENCH
CALEDONIA   (N.Z.)   POLYNESIA
(Fr.)
                                PITCAIRN
                                (U.K.)
                                            URUGUAY

NEW
ZEALAND

                                            FALKLAND IS.
                                            (U.K.)